Alphabetical Listings of Readings in Transnational Management, 3/e

TRANSNATIONAL MANAGEMENT

McGraw-Hill Advanced Topics in Global Management

United Kingdom
(The *INSÉAD* Global Management Series)

Dutta/Manzoni
Process Re-Engineering, Organizational Change and Performance Improvement

El Kahal
Business in Europe

Goddard and Demirag
Financial Management for International Business

Hayes et al.
Principles of Auditing: An International Perspective

Lasserre and Schütte
Strategy and Management in Asia Pacific

Walter and Smith
Global Capital Markets and Banking

Canada

Beamish/Woodcock
Strategic Management: Text, Readings and Cases, 5/e

McShane
Canadian Organizational Behaviour

Australia

Clark
Human Resource Management

Deery
Industrial Relations: A Contemporary Analysis

Hughes
Management Skills Series
- **Managing Information**
- **Managing Operations – Customer Service**
- **Managing Operations – Productivity**
- **Managing Operations – Innovations**
- **Managing Operations – Change**
- **Managing Effective Working Relationships**
- **Managing and Developing Teams**
- **Managing and Organising Work for Goal Achievement**
- **Managing Performance and Goal Achievement**
- **Managing Grievances and Disputes**
- **Managing People – Workplace Practice**
- **Managing People – Recruitment, Selection and Induction**
- **Managing Group Problem Solving and Decision Making**
- **Managing People – Training and Development**

McKenna
New Management

Meredith
Managing Finance

Page
Applied Business & Management Research

Travaglione
Human Resource Strategies

United States

Ball/McCulloch
International Business – The Challenge of Global Competition, 7/e

Bartlett, Ghoshal
Transnational Management: Text, Cases, and Readings in Cross-Border Management, 3/e

Beamish, Morrison, Rosenzweig, Inkpen
International Management, Text, and Cases, 4/e

de la Torre, Doz, Devinney
Managing the Global Corporation, 2/e

Hill
Global Business Today, 1/e

Hill
International Business – Competing in the Global Marketplace, 3/e

Hodgetts and Luthans
International Management, 4/e

TRANSNATIONAL MANAGEMENT

Text, Cases, and Readings in Cross-Border Management

THIRD EDITION

Christopher A. Bartlett
Harvard Business School

Sumantra Ghoshal
London Business School

Boston   Burr Ridge, IL   Dubuque, IA   Madison, WI   New York   San Francisco
St. Louis   Bangkok   Bogotá   Caracas   Lisbon   London   Madrid   Mexico City
Milan   New Delhi   Seoul   Singapore   Sydney   Taipei   Toronto

McGraw-Hill Higher Education

A Division of The **McGraw-Hill** *Companies*

2 3 4 5 6 7 8 9 0 DOC/DOC 9 0 9 8 7 6 5 4 3 2 1

ISBN 0-256-24781-1

Vice president/Editor in chief: *Michael W. Junior*
Publisher: *Craig S. Beytien*
Senior sponsoring editor: *Jennifer Roche*
Editorial assistant: *Tracy Jensen*
Marketing coordinator: *Christine Witt*
Project manager: *Christina Thornton-Villagomez*
Production supervisor: *Rose Hepburn*
Designer: *Kiera Cunningham*
Supplement coordinator: *Carol A. Bielski*
Compositor: *Interactive Composition Corporation*
Typeface: *10/12 Times Roman*
Printer: *R. R. Donnelley & Sons, Inc.*

Library of Congress Cataloging-in-Publication Data

Bartlett, Christopher A. (date)
    Transnational management : text, cases, and readings in cross-border management / Christopher A. Bartlett, Sumantra Ghoshal.
      p. cm. (McGraw-Hill advanced topics in global management)
    ISBN 0-256-24781-1
    Includes bibliographical references and index.
    1. International business enterprises—Management. I. Ghoshal, Sumantra.
II. Title.
HD62.4.B365   2000
658'.049 dc—21   99-34641

http://www.mhhe.com

Preface

To many, the attraction of the field of international business management lies in its constant change—the new global strategic imperatives, the new transnational organizational demands. But some old international hands insist that beyond all the hype, the basic tasks of cross-border management remain much as they have always been—understanding one's host country environment, being sensitive to cross-cultural differences, and being able to manage operations separated by the barriers of distance, language, time, and culture.

In a sense, both views are right, and we are reminded of this as we deal with the diverse set of pressures and tensions we must resolve every time we make revisions for a new edition of *Transnational Management*. In this third edition, more than half of the cases and readings are new, a reflection of the vibrancy of the field and a response to those pushing for new materials. But the classic favorites remain, a recognition of the timeless nature of cross-border management issues. Based on the publisher's survey of material usage and fit, as reported by faculty adopters, we have sought to manage this balance between retaining the most widely used cases and articles that continue to work effectively for them, while adding new material that captures the emerging management issues that will keep their courses fresh and their students challenged. The scorecard for this edition reads as follows:

- Seventeen new cases join twelve enduring favorites
- Eight new articles are lined up along ten retained classics
- One new text chapter on cross-border innovation and learning is integrated into our overarching research-based conceptual framework.

Overall, our objective for the third edition of *Transnational Management* remains as it has been from the start: to allow teachers of international management and strategy courses to present leading-edge issues in a rich and holistic fashion that is attuned to the realities of today's complex competitive business environment. Rather than the traditional approach of compartmentalizing the world into neat functional boxes where "international" becomes a weak qualifying adjective, this framework allows the cases and readings to present issues in the way managers receive them—in complex packages in which marketing choices are shaped by development and manufacturing resources, where strategic challenges are linked to operational realities, and where organizational capabilities are bound up with managerial competencies. It is a set of challenges that makes our field unique and exciting, and one that continually stretches us as teachers, researchers, and authors.

Once again, this book is the output of many people's efforts and insights. First, we must thank our faculty colleagues at hundreds of institutions around the world who have adopted this book, and particularly the subset of those who have provided us with feedback and suggestions for its improvement. Specifically, we would like to recognize the 40 faculty who responded to the detailed survey of the structure and content of the second edition. Your comments and proposals became the basis for the restructuring of this volume.

Next, we owe an enormous debt of gratitude to the researchers and authors who contributed new cases and/or articles to this edition. New cases were provided by HBS Professors Linda Hill (Rudi Gassner), Ashish Nanda (Walt Disney), Debora Spar (White Nights, Gerber, and Toys "R" Us) and Michael Yoshino (Star TV). Similarly, new articles incorporate the interesting and important recent research of Ikujiro Nonaka, David Garvin, Tony Gross, Richard Pascal and Anthony Athos, Chan Kim and Renee Mauborgne, Jim Collins and Jerry Porras, and Susan Schneider. To all of them we offer our sincere thanks.

We must also acknowledge the coordination task undertaken by our respective administrative assistants who worked over many months to coordinate the flow of manuscript documents back and forth between London and Boston. To Meg Wozny and Sharon Wilson we give our heartfelt thanks for helping us through the long and arduous revision process. As always, you were there to bail us out and to provide subtle reminders about our frequently missed deadlines. To Jennifer Roche, our new editor at Irwin/McGraw Hill, we thank you for your patience and tolerance through this long process and look forward to a long and productive working relationship. And finally to Craig Beytien, our previous sponsoring editor and now publisher of Irwin/McGraw Hill, we owe the greatest vote of thanks. Always encouraging, but always firmly pushing us to deliver on a manuscript, Craig has been our supportive friend throughout the whole process, and to him we offer our sincere thanks.

Despite the best efforts of all the contributors, however, we must accept responsibility for the shortcomings of the book that remain. Our only hope is that they are outweighed by the value that you find in these pages and the exciting challenges that they represent in the constantly changing field of transnational management.

Christopher A. Bartlett
Sumantra Ghoshal
May 1999

Contents

Chapter 1

Cross-Border Management: Motivations and Mentalities

This book focuses on the management challenges associated with developing strategies and managing the operations of companies whose activities stretch across national boundaries. Clearly, operating in an international rather than a domestic arena presents the manager with many new opportunities. Having worldwide operations not only gives a company access to new markets and specialized resources, it also opens up new sources of information and knowledge to stimulate future product development and broadens the options of strategic moves and countermoves the company might make in competing with its domestic and international rivals. However, with all these new opportunities come the challenges of managing strategy, organization, and operations that are innately more complex, diverse, and uncertain.

In this introductory chapter, we provide a conceptual baseline and a historical backdrop for the more detailed discussions of these management opportunities and challenges that run through the text, cases, and readings in the rest of the book. Our starting point is to focus on the dominant vehicle of internationalization, the multinational corporation (MNC), and briefly review its role and influence in the global economy.[1] Next, we examine the motivations that led such companies to expand abroad and describe how these motivations have evolved over time. We are then ready to review some of the typical attitudes and mentalities that shape the actions of managers in MNCs and suggest how these attitudes and mentalities evolve as their offshore operations progress from the state of initial

---

[1]Such companies are referred to variously—and often interchangeably—as *multinational, international, and global corporations.* In later chapters, we want to give each of those terms specific different meanings, but will adopt the widely used MNC abbreviation in the broader, more general sense in referring to all companies whose operations extend across national boundaries.

investments to a fully integrated worldwide network of affiliates. In the concluding section of the chapter, we highlight some of the differences between managing an MNC and a purely domestic firm and describe the particular management perspective that influences the structure and content of this book.

THE MNC: DEFINITION, SCOPE, AND INFLUENCE

An economic historian could trace the origins of international business back to the seafaring traders who were central to the ancient civilizations built by the Greeks and Egyptians. Through the centuries, international flow of products continued, and in medieval Venice the merchant traders had developed much of the sophistication of modern-day Japanese trading companies.

An important chapter in this history was written by the great British and Dutch trading companies that flourished in the 17th and 18th centuries, establishing outposts from Hudson's Bay to the East Indies. By the 19th century, the newly emerged capitalists in industrialized Europe began investing in the less-developed areas of the world (including the United States), but particularly within the vast empires held by Britain, France, Holland, and Germany.

Definition

In terms of the working definition we use, few if any of these entities through history could be called true MNCs. Most of the traders would be excluded by our first qualification, which requires that an MNC have *substantial direct investment* in foreign countries, not just an export business. And most of the companies with international operations in the 19th century would be excluded by our second criterion, which requires that they be engaged in the *active management* of these offshore assets rather than simply holding them in a passive financial portfolio.

Thus, while companies that source their raw materials offshore, license their technologies abroad, export their products into foreign markets, or even hold minority equity positions in overseas ventures without any management involvement may regard themselves as "international," by our definition they are not true MNCs unless they have substantial direct investment in foreign countries *and* actively manage those operations and regard those operations as integral parts of the company both strategically and organizationally.

Scope

Under our definition, the MNC is a very recent phenomenon, dating back to less than a century. In fact, a vast majority have been developed only in the post–World War II years. However, their motivations for international expansion and the nature of their offshore activities have evolved significantly over this relatively short period, and we explore some of these changes later in this chapter.

Among the more important recent trends have been the emergence of service MNCs and a shift from traditional ownership patterns between the parent company and its worldwide operations to a new and varied set of financial, legal, and contractual relationships with different foreign affiliates. Our definition of MNCs can incorporate these new developments, as long as we recognize that foreign "investment" need not be restricted to production facilities alone and that "active management" does not require direct control but only substantive influence over the activities of foreign units that can often be exercised without full or even majority ownership.

It is interesting, in this context, to observe how the United Nations has changed its definition of the MNC over the last two decades.[2] In 1973, it defined such an enterprise as one "which controls assets, factories, mines, sales offices, and the like in two or more countries." By 1984, it had changed the definition to

> an enterprise (a) comprising entities in two or more countries, regardless of the legal form and fields of activity of those entities, (b) which operates under a system of decision making permitting coherent policies and a common strategy through one or more decision-making centers, (c) in which the entities are so linked, by ownership or otherwise, that one or more of them may be able to exercise a significant influence over the activities of the others, and, in particular, to share knowledge, resources, and responsibilities with others.

In essence, the changing definition highlights the importance of strategic and organizational integration and, thereby, *management integration* of operations located in different countries as the key differentiating characteristic of an MNC. The resources committed to those units can just as well take the form of skilled people or research equipment as plant and machinery or computer hardware. What really differentiates the MNC is that it creates an internal organization to carry out key cross-border tasks and transactions internally rather than depending on trade through the open markets. With this understanding, our definition of MNCs includes American Express, Andersen Consulting, and Fuji Bank just as well as IBM, Unilever, and Hitachi.

MNC Influence in the Global Economy

Most frequent international business travelers have had an experience like the following. She arrives on her British Airways flight, rents a Toyota at Hertz, and drives to the downtown Hilton hotel. In her room, she flips on the Sony TV, and absent-mindedly gazes out at the neon signs flashing "Coca-Cola," "Canon," and "BMW." The latest episode of "Friends" is flickering on the screen when room service

---

[2]The generic term for companies operating across national borders in most UN studies is the *transnational corporation* (TNC). Because we will use that term very specifically, we will continue to define the general form of organizations with international operations as MNCs.

delivers dinner along with the bottle of Perrier she ordered. All of a sudden, a feeling of disorientation engulfs her. Is she in Sydney, Singapore, Stockholm, or Seattle? Her surroundings and points of reference over the past few hours have provided few clues.

Such experiences, more than any data, provide the best indication of the enormous influence of MNCs in the global economy. As the cases and articles in this book will show, few sectors of the economy and few firms—not even those that are purely domestic in their operations—are free from this pervasive influence. Collectively, MNCs account for over 40 percent of the world's manufacturing output and almost a quarter of world trade. About 85 percent of the world's automobiles, 70 percent of computers, 35 percent of toothpaste, and 65 percent of soft drinks are produced and marketed by MNCs.

While not all MNCs are large, most large companies in the world are MNCs. In fact, about 450 companies with annual revenues in excess of $1 billion account for over 80 percent of the total investment made by all companies outside their home countries. A different perspective on their size and potential impact is provided by Table 1–1, which compares the annual gross national products (GNPs) of selected countries with the annual revenues of several large MNCs. One must be careful, however, in basing conclusions on this table. A country's GNP is not directly comparable with a company's revenues. Besides, only a handful of companies are as large as those shown in the table and, increasingly, small companies are becoming important players internationally. Nevertheless, most of the world's attention tends to focus on these large MNCs, which have the greatest influence on the global economy, employ a high percentage of business graduates, and pose the most complex strategic and organizational challenges for their managers. For the same reasons, they will provide the focus for much of our attention in this book.

TABLE 1–1   Comparison of Country GNPs and Company Revenues: 1996

Company	Annual Revenue ($ billions)	Country	Annual GNP ($ billions)
General Motors	168	Denmark	168
Ford	146	Hong Kong	153
Mitsui	144	Norway	151
Mitsubishi	140	South Africa	132
Ituchu	135	Poland	124
Royal Dutch Shell	128	Greece	120
Marubeni	124	Finland	119
Exxon	119	Portugal	100
Sumitomo	119	Singapore	93
Toyota	108	Israel	90

Source: World Development Report published by the United Nations and *Fortune*'s list of the 500 largest companies in the world.

THE MOTIVATIONS: PUSHES AND PULLS TO INTERNATIONALIZE

What motivates companies to expand their operations internationally? While occasionally the motives may be entirely idiosyncratic, such as the desire of the CEO to spend time in Mexico or in Europe, an extensive body of research suggests some more-systematic patterns.

Traditional Motivations

Among the earliest motivations that drove companies to invest abroad was the need to *secure key supplies,* especially minerals, energy, and scarce raw material resources. Aluminum producers needed to ensure their supply of bauxite, tire companies went abroad to develop rubber plantations, and oil companies wanted to open up new fields in Canada, the Middle East, and Venezuela. By the early part of this century, Standard Oil, Alcoa, Goodyear, Anaconda Copper, and International Nickel were among the largest of the emerging MNCs.

Another strong trigger of internationalization could be described as the *market-seeking* behavior. This motivation was particularly strong in companies that had some intrinsic advantage, typically related to their technology or their brand recognition, that gave them some competitive advantage in offshore markets. Although their initial attitudes were often opportunistic, many companies eventually realized that these additional sales allowed them to exploit economies of scale and scope, thereby providing a source of competitive advantage over their domestic rivals. This was a particularly strong motive for some of the European multinationals whose small home markets were insufficient to support the volume-intensive manufacturing processes that were sweeping through industries from food and tobacco to chemicals and automobiles. Companies like Nestlé, Bayer, and Ford expanded internationally primarily in search of new markets.

Another traditional and important trigger of internationalization was the desire to *access low-cost factors* of production. Particularly as tariff barriers declined in the 1960s, many U.S. and European companies for whom labor represented a major cost found that their products were at a competitive disadvantage compared to imports. In response, a number of companies in clothing, electronics, household appliances, watchmaking, and other such industries established offshore sourcing locations for producing components or even complete product lines. Soon it became clear that labor was not the only productive factor that could be sourced more economically overseas. For example, the availability of lower-cost capital (perhaps through a government investment subsidy) also became a strong force for internationalization.

These three motives (or two, if we ignore the historical differences and combine securing supplies and accessing low-cost factors into a single resource-seeking motive) were the main traditional driving forces behind the overseas expansion of a vast majority of MNCs. The ways in which these motives interacted to push companies—particularly those from the United States—to become MNCs are captured in the well-known product cycle theory developed by Professor Raymond Vernon.[3]

This theory suggests that the starting point for the internationalization process is typically an innovation that a company creates in its home country. Because large, economically advanced, and technologically sophisticated countries like the United States historically provided the most incentives and the greatest opportunities for developing new products or ideas, most of these innovations tend to be created by companies located in these countries.

Consider the case of a typical U.S. company that has developed an innovative new product. In the first phase of exploiting the development, the company will build production facilities in its home market not only because this is where its main customer base is located, but also because of the need to maintain close linkages between research and production in this phase of the development cycle. In this early stage, some demand may also be created in other developed countries—in European countries, for example—where consumer needs and market development are similar to the United States. These requirements normally would be met out of home production, thereby generating exports for the United States.

As the product matures and production processes become standardized, the company enters a new stage. By this time, demand in the European countries may have become quite sizable and export sales, from being a marginal side benefit, are now an important part of the revenues from the new business. Furthermore, competitors will probably begin to see the growing demand for the new product as a potential opportunity to establish themselves in markets served by exports. To prevent or counteract such competition and also to meet the foreign demand more effectively, the innovating company typically sets up production facilities in the importing countries, thereby making the transition from being an exporter to becoming a true MNC.

Finally, in the third stage, the product becomes highly standardized and many competitors enter the business. Competition now focuses on price and, therefore, on cost. This activates the resource-seeking motive, and the company moves production to low-wage developing countries, both to meet local demand that has by now sprung up in these countries, and also to meet the demands of its customers in the developed markets at a lower cost. In this final phase, the developing countries may become net exporters of the product while the developed countries become net importers.

The record of international expansion of companies in the post–World War II era is quite consistent with the pattern suggested by the product cycle theory. For example, between 1950 and 1980, U.S. firms' direct foreign investment (DFI) increased from $11.8 billion to $200 billion. In the 1950s, much of this investment focused on the neighboring countries in Latin America and Canada. By the early 1960s, attention had shifted to Europe and the EEC's share of U.S. firms' DFI

---

[3]Raymond Vernon, "International Investment and International Trade in the Product Cycle," *Quarterly Journal of Economics,* May 1966, pp. 190–207.

increased from 16 percent in 1957 to 32 percent by 1966. Finally, in the 1970s, attention shifted to developing countries, whose share of U.S. firms' DFI grew from 18 percent in 1974 to 25 percent in 1980.

Although the product cycle theory provided a useful way to describe much of the internationalization of the postwar decades, by the 1980s its explanatory power was beginning to wane as Professor Vernon was quick to point out. As the international business environment became increasingly complex and sophisticated, companies developed a much richer rationale for their worldwide operations.

Emerging Motivations

An examination of the decisions that triggered early international expansion of most MNCs reveals that few did so with any clearly defined global objectives or well-developed international strategy. Internationalization was typically a gradual and an incremental process, most often linked to the company's basic home market strategic objectives. Some were trying to secure critical raw material supplies, for example, while others were seeking new markets or lower-cost sources in order to protect or improve competitive position at home.

However, once they had established international sales and production operations, the perceptions and strategic motivations of most of these companies gradually changed. Initially, the typical attitude was that the foreign operations were strategic and organizational appendages to the domestic business, and should be managed opportunistically. Gradually, however, as managers recognized some of the important advantages of operating internationally, they began to think about their strategy in a more integrated worldwide sense. In this process, the forces that originally triggered their expansion overseas often became secondary to a new set of motivations that underlay their emerging global strategies.

In many cases, these new motivations were driven by a set of economic, technological, and social developments that made internationalization essential for a company to survive in particular businesses. For example, successive rounds of technological change brought about by the adoption of integrated circuits, auto-insertion machines, printed circuit boards, and computerized assembly and testing raised the efficient scale for production of color television sets from about half a million sets a year to over 3 million sets. As a result, companies that had historically focused only on their domestic markets had to either become international or go out of business since few countries were large enough to support production at such scale by individual companies.

Escalating R&D costs and shortening product life cycles were also internationalizing forces. For example, the advent of digital technology raised the costs of developing a public telephone switching system to about a billion dollars. At the same time, because of accelerating technological developments, telecommunications companies had increasingly shorter time periods to sell a particular product before it was made obsolete by new technology. The combination of these two factors made it impossible for such companies to remain in business unless they had access to worldwide markets to amortize past R&D expenses and fund ongoing research.

In essence, those forces of *increasing scale economies, ballooning R&D investments,* and *shortening product life cycles* transformed many industries into global rather than national structures and made worldwide scope of activities not a matter of choice but indeed an essential prerequisite for companies to survive in those businesses. In the next chapter, we discuss these globalizing forces and examine their implications in much greater detail.

Although it was less frequently the original motivating trigger that induced companies to invest abroad, an important secondary effect that often became a critical factor in a company's international strategy was its global *scanning and learning* capability.[4] A company drawn offshore to secure supplies of raw materials was more likely to become aware of alternative low-cost production sources around the globe; a company tempted abroad by market opportunities was often exposed to new technologies or market needs that stimulated innovative product development. The very nature of an MNC's worldwide presence gave it a huge informational advantage that could result in locating more-efficient sources or more-advanced or appropriate product and process technologies. Thus, a company whose international strategy was triggered by a technological or marketing advantage could enhance that advantage through the scanning and learning potential inherent in its worldwide network of operations.

Another benefit that soon became evident was that being a multinational rather than a national company brought important advantages of *competitive positioning.* Certainly, the most controversial of the many global competitive strategic actions taken by MNCs in recent years have been those based on cross-subsidization of markets. For example, a Korean TV producer could challenge a national company in the United States by subsidizing its U.S. losses with funds from its profitable Asian or South American operations. If the U.S. company depended entirely on its home market, its competitive response could only be to defend its position—typically by seeking government intervention or by matching or offsetting the competitive price reductions. Recognition of these competitive implications of multicountry operations led some companies to change the criteria for their international investment decisions so as to reflect not only market attractiveness or factor cost-efficiency choices, but also to reflect the leverage such investments provided over competitors.[5]

Although for purposes of analysis—and also to reflect some sense of historical development—the motives behind the expansion of MNCs have been reduced to a few distinct categories, it should be clear that companies were rarely driven by

---

[4]This motivation was highlighted by Raymond Vernon in "Gone Are the Cash Cows of Yesteryear," *Harvard Business Review,* November–December 1980, pp. 150–55.

[5]These competitive aspects of global operations, the focus of our discussions in Chapter 3, have been highlighted in a number of articles by authors such as Michael Porter, Bruce Kogut, C. K. Prahalad, Gary Hamel, John Stopford, and George Yip; see readings and references in Chapter 3.

a single motivating force. Indeed, as managers became more knowledgeable and sophisticated about the newly discovered international environment, the diverse and often vague motivations became recognized as more-concrete potential benefits of operating as worldwide companies. The more-adaptable companies soon learned how to capitalize on all of the potential advantages available from their international operations—ensuring critical supplies, entering new markets, tapping low-cost factors of production, leveraging their global information access, and capitalizing on the competitive advantage of their multiple market positions—and began to use these strengths to play a new strategic game that we will describe in later chapters as *global chess.*

Beyond Motivation: The Prerequisites for Internationalization

Motivation alone, however, is not enough for a company to become a multinational. Before it can build and manage an effective integrated network of worldwide operations, the MNC must also develop certain strategic and organizational assets.

In each national market, a foreign company suffers from some disadvantages vis-à-vis local competitors, at least initially. Being more familiar with the national culture, industry structure, government requirements, and other aspects of doing business in that country, domestic companies have a huge natural advantage. Their existing relationships with relevant customers, suppliers, regulators, and so on provide additional advantages that the foreign company must either match or counteract with some unique strategic capability.

Most often, this countervailing strategic advantage is found in the MNC's superior knowledge or skills that typically take the form of advanced technological expertise or specific marketing competencies. At other times, scale economies in R&D, production, or some other part of the value chain become the main source of the MNC's advantage over the domestic firm. It is important to note, however, that the MNC cannot expect to succeed in the international environment unless it has some such distinct competency so as to overcome the liability of its foreignness.[6]

But even such knowledge- or scale-based strategic advantages are, by themselves, insufficient to justify the internationalization of operations. A company can, after all, sell or license its technology to foreign producers, franchise its brand name internationally, or sell its products abroad through general trading companies or local distributors, without having to set up its own offshore operations. This was the approach explicitly adopted by General Sarnoff who decided that RCA should aggressively license its extensive television and other patents to

---

[6]The need for such strategic advantages for a company to become an MNC is highlighted in what is referred to as the *market imperfections theory of MNCs.* For a comprehensive review of this theory, see Richard E. Caves, *Multinational Enterprise and Economic Analysis* (Cambridge, England: Cambridge University Press, 1982).

European or Japanese companies rather than setting up its own international operations. He argued that the safe return from license fees were preferable to the uncertainties and complexities of multinational management.

The other precondition for a company to become an MNC, therefore, is that it must have the organizational capability to leverage its strategic assets more effectively through its own subsidiaries than through contractual relations with outside parties. If superior knowledge is the main source of an MNC's competitive advantage, for example, it must have an organizational system that allows better returns from extending and exploiting its knowledge through direct foreign operations than the return it could get by selling or licensing that knowledge.[7]

To summarize, three conditions must be met for the existence of an MNC. First, some foreign countries must offer certain location-specific advantages so as to provide requisite *motivation* for the company to invest there. Second, the company must have some *strategic competencies* to counteract the disadvantages of its relative unfamiliarity with foreign markets. Third, it must also have some *organizational capabilities* so as to get better returns from leveraging its strategic strengths internally rather than through external market mechanisms such as contracts or licenses.[8] Understanding these preconditions is important not only because they explain why MNCs exist but also, as we show in Chapter 3, because they help define the strategic options for competing in worldwide businesses.

THE EVOLVING MENTALITY: INTERNATIONAL TO TRANSNATIONAL

Even from this brief description of the changing motivations for internationalization, it should be clear that there has been a gradual evolution in the strategic role that foreign operations played in emerging MNCs. We categorize this evolutionary pattern into four stages that may be visualized as the way in which management thinking has developed over time as changes have occurred in both the international business environment and in the MNC as a unique corporate form.

Although such classification is necessarily overgeneralized and undoubtedly somewhat arbitrary, it allows us to achieve two objectives. First, it highlights the fact that for most MNCs the objectives that initially induced management to go overseas usually evolve into a very different set of motivations over time, thereby progressively changing management attitudes and actions. Second, such a classification allows us to develop a specific language system that we use throughout

---

[7] This issue of organization capability is the focus of what has come to be known as the *internalization theory of MNCs*. See Alan N. Rugman, "A New Theory of the Multinational Enterprise: Internationalization versus Internalization," *Columbia Journal of World Business,* Spring 1982, pp. 54–61. For a more detailed exposition, see Peter J. Buckley and Mark Casson, *The Future of the Multinational Enterprise* (London: Macmillan, 1976).

[8] These three conditions are highlighted in John Dunning's eclectic theory. See John H. Dunning, *International Production and the Multinational Enterprise* (Winchester, Mass.: Allen & Unwin, 1981).

the book, to describe the very different strategic approaches adopted by various MNCs.[9]

International Mentality

In the earliest stages of internationalization, many MNC managers tend to think of the company's overseas operations as some kind of distant outposts whose main role is to support the domestic parent company in different ways such as contributing incremental sales of the domestic product lines, or supplying raw materials or components to the domestic manufacturing operations. This is what we label as the *international* strategic mentality.

The *international* terminology derives directly from the international product cycle theory that reflects many of the assumptions implicit in this approach. Products are developed for the domestic market, and only subsequently sold abroad; technology and other knowledge are transferred from the parent company to the overseas operators; and offshore manufacturing is seen as a means to protect the company's home market.

Companies with this mentality regard themselves fundamentally as a domestic company with some foreign appendages. Managers assigned to overseas operations are often the domestic misfits who happen to know a foreign language or who have previously lived abroad. Decisions related to the foreign operations tend to be made in an opportunistic or ad hoc manner.

Multinational Mentality

The exposure of the organization to foreign environments and the growing importance of sales and profits from these sources gradually convince managers that the international activities can provide opportunities of more than marginal significance. Increasingly, they also realize that to leverage those opportunities, they have to do more than ship out old equipment, technology, or product lines that had been developed for the home market. Local competitors in the foreign markets and the host governments often accelerate the learning of companies that retain an unresponsive international mentality for too long.

A *multinational* strategic mentality develops as managers begin to recognize and emphasize the differences among national markets and operating environments. Companies with this mentality adopt a more flexible approach to their international operations by modifying their products, strategies, and even management practices country by country. As they develop national companies that are increasingly

---

[9]It should be noted that the terms *international, multinational, global, and transnational* have been used very differently—and sometimes interchangeably—by various writers. We want to give each term *specific* and *different* meaning, and ask that you put aside your previous usage of the terms—at least for the duration of our exposition.

sensitive and responsive to their local environments, these companies develop a strategic approach that is literally multinational: Their worldwide strategy is built on the foundation of the multiple, nationally responsive strategies of the company's worldwide subsidiaries.

In companies operating with such a multinational mentality, managers of foreign operations tend to be highly independent entrepreneurs, often nationals of the host country. Using their local market knowledge and the parent company's willingness to invest in these growing opportunities, these entrepreneurial country managers are often able to build up significant local growth and considerable independence from headquarters.

Global Mentality

While the multinational mentality typically results in very responsive marketing approaches in the different national markets, it also gives rise to an inefficient manufacturing infrastructure within the company. Plants are often built more to provide local marketing advantages or to improve political relations than to maximize production efficiency. Similarly, the proliferation of products designed to meet local needs also contributes to a general loss of efficiency in design, production, logistics, distribution, and other functional tasks.

In an operating environment of improving transportation and communication facilities and falling trade barriers, some companies adopted a very different strategic approach in their international operations. These companies, many of them of Japanese origin, think in terms of creating products for a world market and manufacturing them on global scale in a few highly efficient plants, often at the corporate center.

We define this as a classic *global* strategic mentality because it views the world as its unit of analysis. The underlying assumption is that national tastes and preferences are more similar than different, or that they can be made similar by providing customers with standardized products with adequate cost and quality advantages over those national varieties that they have been used to. Managers with this global strategic approach subscribe to Professor Theodore Levitt's argument that the future belongs to those companies that make and sell "the same thing, the same way, everywhere."[10]

This strategic approach requires considerably more central coordination and control than the others and is typically associated with an organization structure in which various product or business managers have worldwide responsibility. In such companies, research and development and manufacturing activities are typically managed from the headquarters, and most strategic decisions are also taken at the center.

---

[10]See Theodore Levitt, "The Globalization of Markets," *Harvard Business Review*, May–June 1983, pp. 92–102, reproduced in the readings section of the next chapter.

Transnational Mentality

Throughout the 1970s and 80s, many of these global companies seemed invincible. In a rapidly globalizing environment, they chalked up overwhelming victories, not only over local companies, but over international and multinational competitors as well. Their very success, however, created and strengthened a set of countervailing forces of localization.

To many host governments, for example, these global companies appeared to be a more powerful and thus more threatening version of the earlier unresponsive companies with their unsophisticated international strategic mentality. Particularly in an era when many countries faced crushing interest burdens on their foreign debt and mounting trade deficits, the global company's focus on home-country exports and centralized control caused concern. In response, many host governments increased both the restrictions and the demands they placed on global companies, requiring them to invest, transfer technology, meet local content requirements, and so forth.

Customers also contributed to this strengthening of the localizing forces by rejecting homogenized global products and reasserting their national preferences—albeit without relaxing their expectation of the high-quality levels and low costs that global products had offered. Finally, the increasing volatility in the international economic and political environments, especially the rapid changes in currency exchange rates, also undermined the efficiency of such a centralized global approach.

As a result of these developments, many worldwide companies recognized that the demands to be responsive to local market and political needs and the pressures to develop global-scale competitive efficiency were simultaneous, if sometimes conflicting. Under these conditions, the either/or attitude reflected in both the multinational and the global strategic mentalities were increasingly inappropriate. The emerging requirement was for companies to become more responsive to local needs while retaining their global efficiency—an emerging approach to worldwide management that we call the *transnational* strategic mentality.

In such companies, key activities and resources are neither centralized in the parent company, nor decentralized so that each subsidiary can carry out its own tasks on a local-for-local basis. Instead, the resources and activities are dispersed but specialized, so as to achieve efficiency and flexibility at the same time. Furthermore, these dispersed resources are integrated into an interdependent network of worldwide operations.

In contrast to the global model, the transnational mentality recognizes the importance of flexible and responsive country-level operations—hence the return of *national* into the terminology. And compared to the multinational approach, it provides for linking and coordinating those operations to retain competitive effectiveness and economic efficiency—as indicated by the prefix *trans.* The resulting need for intensive organizationwide coordination and shared decision making implies that this is a much more sophisticated and subtle approach to MNC management. In future chapters, we will explore its strategic, organizational, and managerial implications.

It should be clear, however, that there is no inevitability in either the direction or the end point of this evolving strategic mentality in worldwide companies. Depending on the industry, the individual company's strategic position, the host countries' diverse needs, and a variety of other factors, a company might reasonably operate with any one of these strategic mentalities. More likely, bearing in mind that this is an arbitrary classification, most companies will probably exhibit some attributes of each of these different strategic approaches.[11]

MANAGING ACROSS BORDERS: THE STRATEGIC AND ADMINISTRATIVE CHALLENGES

The study of MNCs is a relatively new field, with much still to be learned. Historically, at least in the United States, management studies have tended to focus on domestic companies and the study of multinational management has been considered as a narrow and special area of interest engaging a handful of managers, students, and management academics. In Europe and Japan, in contrast, while management research and education received less attention in general, there has been relatively greater sensitivity to the international dimension. To a large extent, this difference in orientation reflects the size and sophistication of the U.S. market that allowed U.S. managers to treat foreign markets as incremental or tangential to their huge domestic opportunities. While this preoccupation with the domestic market sometimes led to problems with offshore operations, U.S. companies' preeminent position in the world of business seemed to protect the ethnocentric focus of their managers.

This situation changed significantly during the 1970s and particularly the 1980s. In an increasingly interdependent and interconnected world economy, *international business has now become the general case.* Most industries of any significance are now worldwide in their scope, and no company—no matter how large its home market base—is immune from the effects of the international environment. But, since most of our management theories and concepts are explicitly or implicitly grounded in the context of a domestic company, it is necessary to identify some of the distinguishing and differentiating attributes of an MNC.

Distinguishing Characteristics of the MNC

The most fundamental distinction between a domestic company and an MNC derives from the social, political, and economic context in which each exists. The former operates in a single national environment where social and cultural norms, government regulations, customer tastes and preferences, and the social and

---

[11]Professor Howard Perlmutter was perhaps the first to highlight the different strategic mentalities. See his article, "The Tortuous Evolution of the Multinational Corporation," *Columbia Journal of World Business,* January–February 1969, pp. 9–18, reproduced in the readings section of this chapter.

economic structures of a business tend to be fairly consistent. While differences do exist among different parts of the same country for most, if not all, of these factors, they are nowhere near as diverse and conflicting as the pattern of demands and pressures the MNC faces in its multiple host countries.

The one feature that categorically distinguishes these intercountry differences from the intracountry ones, however, is that of *sovereignty*.[12] Unlike the local or regional bodies within countries, for most issues, the nation-state represents the ultimate rule-making authority against whom no appeal is feasible. Consequently, the MNC faces an additional and unique element of risk: the political risk of operating in countries with different political philosophies, legal systems, and social attitudes toward private property, corporate responsibility, and free enterprise.

A second major difference relates to competitive strategy. The purely domestic company can respond to competitive challenges only within the context of its single market; the MNC can, and often must, play a much more complex competitive game. Global-scale or low-cost sourcing may be necessary to achieve competitive position, implying the need for complex logistical coordination. Furthermore, competitive interactions can take place on an international battlefield, and effective global competitive strategy might require that the response to an attack in one country be directed to a different country—perhaps the competitor's home market. These are options and complexities a purely domestic company does not face.

Third, a purely domestic company can measure its performance in a single comparable unit—the local currency. The MNC is required to measure results with a flexible measuring stick as the value of currencies fluctuate against each other. In addition, it is exposed to the economic risks associated with shifts in both nominal and real exchange rates.

Finally, the purely domestic company must manage an organizational structure and management systems that reflect its product and functional variety; the MNC organization is intrinsically more complex since it must provide for management control over its product, functional, *and* geographic diversity. Furthermore, the resolution of this three-way tension must be accomplished in an organization that is divided by barriers of distance and time, and impeded by differences in language and culture.

The Management Challenge

Historically, the study of international business focused on the environmental forces, structures, and institutions that provided the context within which MNC managers had to operate. In such a macro approach, countries or industries rather than companies were the primary units of analysis. Reflecting the environment of

---

[12]This difference is elaborated in J. N. Behrman and R. E. Gross, *International Business and Governments: Issues and Institutions* (Columbia: University of South Carolina Press, 1990). See also J. J. Boddewyn, "Political Aspects of MNE Theory," *Journal of International Business Studies,* 19, no. 3 (1988), pp. 341–63.

its time, this traditional approach directed most attention to trade flows and the capital flows that defined the foreign investment patterns.

During the late 1960s and early 1970s, a new perspective on the study of international management began to emerge. In contrast to much of the previous work, the focus of this body of research was on the multinational enterprise and management behavior, rather than on global economic forces and international institutions. With the firm as the primary unit of analysis and management decisions as the key variables, these studies both highlighted and provided new insights on the management challenges associated with international operations. This company- and management-level perspective will provide the main focus of this book.

That is not to suggest that we will ignore the important and legitimate perspectives, interests, and influences of other key actors in the international operating environment. In fact, the next chapter will focus on the sociocultural, political, and economic contexts within which the MNC has to function. However, we will be interested in the effects of these diverse forces from the perspective of the company, and will be primarily concerned with understanding how these forces shape the strategic, organizational, and operational tasks of MNC managers. Subsequent chapters will explore how companies can and do respond to these complex environmental challenges of worldwide management.

Case 1–1   *Ingvar Kamprad and IKEA*

With a 1988 turnover of $14\frac{1}{2}$ billion Swedish Kronor (US \$1 $\approx$ SKr 6 in 1988) and 75 outlets in 19 countries, IKEA had become the world's largest home furnishings retailer. As the company approached the 1990s, however, its managers faced a number of major challenges. Changes in demographics were causing some to question IKEA's historical product line policy. Others wondered if the company had not bitten off too much by attempting major new market entries simultaneously in two European countries (U.K. and Italy), the United States, and several Eastern Bloc countries. Finally, there was widespread concern about the future of the company without its founder, strategic architect, and cultural guru, Ingvar Kamprad.

IKEA Background and History

In 1989, furniture retailing worldwide was still largely a fragmented national industry in which small manufacturers and distributors catered to the demands of their local markets. Consumer preferences varied by region, and there were few retailers whose operations extended beyond a single country. IKEA, however, had repeatedly bucked market trends and industry norms. Over three and a half decades it had built a highly profitable worldwide network of furniture stores. (See Exhibit 1.)

Company Origins

IKEA is an acronym for the initials of the founder, Ingvar Kamprad, his farm Elmtaryd, and his county,

This case was prepared by Professor Christopher A. Bartlett and Research Associate Ashish Nanda.

Copyright © 1990 by the President and Fellows of Harvard College. Harvard Business School case 390-132.

EXHIBIT 1   IKEA Growth and Performance Indicators*

Year	Turnover (m SKr)	Outlets	Countries	Co-workers	Catalogs (000s)
1954	3	1	1	15	285
1964	79	2	2	250	1,200
1974	616	10	5	1,500	13,000
1984	6,770	66	17	8,300	40,000
1988	14,500	83	20	13,400	44,000

Year	1979–1980	1980–1981	1981–1982	1982–1983	1983–1984	1984–1985	1985–1986	1986–1987	1987–1988
Turnover (billion SKr)	3.6	4.1	4.8	6.0	6.8	8.2	10.7	12.6	14.5
Estimated PAT (million SKr)	250	280	300	420	500	500	630	930	1,100
Total surface area (000 square meters)	425	458	483	533	606	825	907	953	973
Number of visitors (millions)	25	30	34	36	38	44	53	60	65

Region	Percentage of Sales (1988)	Region	Percentage of Purchases (1988)
West Germany	29.7%	Scandinavia	50%
Scandinavia	27.5	East Europe	20
Rest of Europe	28.5	Rest of Europe	22
Rest of the world	14.3	Rest of the world	8

*IKEA was a closely held private company. Accounting data were not made public. The company's capitalized market value was estimated conservatively at SKr 10 billion in 1987. Profits are best estimates from available information.

Sources: 1. Company documents.
             2. *Affärsvárlden,* December 8, 1987.

Agunnaryd, in Småland, South Sweden. In 1943, at the age of 17, Kamprad began his entrepreneurial career by selling fish, Christmas magazines, and seeds. Within a few years he had established a mail-order business featuring products as diverse as ball-point pens and furniture. It was in furniture, however, that he saw the greatest opportunity.

Even as the pent-up wartime demand found expression in the post-war boom, the traditional Swedish practice of handing down custom-made furniture through generations was giving way to young householders looking for new, yet inexpensive, furniture. But while demand was growing, inter-association supply contracts and agreements between Swedish manufacturers and retailers kept prices high while foreclosing entry. As a result, between 1935 and 1946 furniture prices rose 41% faster than prices of other household goods. Kamprad felt that this situation represented both a social problem and a business opportunity. He commented:

> A disproportionately large part of all resources is used to satisfy a small part of the population. . . . IKEA's aim is to change this situation. We shall offer a wide range of home furnishing items of good design and function at prices so low that the majority of people can afford to buy them. . . . We have great ambitions.

When Kamprad's upstart company started participating in the annual furniture trade fair in Stockholm, traditional retailers complained that IKEA was selling imitations. In 1951, when the company

---

EXHIBIT 2   IKEA and the Swedish Furniture Industry, 1961

Personnel Occupied with	*Personnel Functions in Swedish Furniture Stores in 1961*		
	IKEA	*Furniture Stores*	*Furniture Sections of Department Stores*
Selling	29%	42%	65%
Clerical	44	13	6
Warehouse	17	11	16
Transportation	5	13	5
Workshop	5	21	8

Measure	*Productivity of Swedish Furniture Retailers in 1961*		
	IKEA	*Large Store**	*Average Store*
Annual turnover in 1,000 SKr/employee	202	114	93
Annual turnover in SKr/square meter	1,453	1,076	704
Rent as percent of annual turnover	0.6%	3.0%	3.4%
Annual stockturn	3.2	2.9	2.3

*Annual turnover SKr 1 million or more.

Source: R. Marteson, *Innovations in Multinational Retailing: IKEA in Swedish, Swiss, German, and Austrian Markets,* Doctoral Dissertation, (University of Gothenburg: Gothenburg, Sweden, 1981).

---

was explicitly forbidden from selling directly to customers at the fairs, it responded by only taking orders. In 1952, such order-taking was banned at the fair, so Kamprad told employees to take down the names of potential customers and contact them after the fair. Subsequently, IKEA was forbidden from showing prices on its furniture. Finally, the retail cartel members pressured the manufacturers cartel not to sell to IKEA. Kamprad responded by buying from a few independent Swedish furniture makers and by establishing new sources in Poland. To his delight, he found that his costs actually fell and he could charge even lower prices. "[IKEA] resembles the monsters of old times," fumed one retailer in a letter to the cartel. "If we cut one of its heads, it soon grows another."

In 1953, Kamprad converted a disused factory in Älmhult into a warehouse-showroom. Company sales grew from SKr 3 million in 1953 to SKr 6 million in 1955. By 1961, IKEA's turnover was over SKr 40 million—80 times larger than the turnover of an average furniture store. (See Exhibit 2.) Of a total SKr 16.8 million furniture mail-order business in Sweden, IKEA had SKr 16 million.

In 1965, Kamprad opened a second outlet in Stockholm. Sensitive to the impact of the automobile on shopping habits, he gave priority to creating ample parking space rather than the focus, as was traditional, on downtown location. His new store, built on the outskirts of the city, was the largest in Europe at the time. Several of IKEA's basic practices were developed in this period: the self-service concept facilitated by the wide distribution of informative catalogs and the use of explanatory tickets on display merchandise, the knockdown kits that allowed stocks of all displayed items to be kept in store warehouses in flat pack boxes, and the development of suburban stores with large parking lots that brought the cash-and-carry concept to furniture retailing. Each of these practices resulted in economies that reinforced IKEA's position as the industry's low-price leader.

Between 1965 and 1973, IKEA opened seven new stores in Scandinavia, capturing a 15% share of the Swedish market. Rather than appeal to the older, more affluent consumers who had been the prime target of those offering the traditional, more expensive lines of furniture, Kamprad focused on younger buyers, who were often looking to furnish their first apartments. (See Exhibit 3 for customer data.) However, by the early 1970s, growth in the Swedish furniture market was stagnating. Kamprad felt it was time for IKEA to expand internationally.

Entry into Continental Europe

"It is our duty to expand," Kamprad said, dismissing those who insisted that furniture retailing was a strictly local business. "He ignored the economic downturn caused by the 1973 oil shock," remarked an executive, "and oddly, it worked in our favor. Our overhead costs were low, and the customers really appreciated our value-for-money approach." Because the German-speaking countries constituted the largest market for furniture in Europe, they became his priority, with Switzerland being the first target.

As in other European countries, Swiss furniture retailing was highly fragmented, with 67% of all firms employing three people or less. Most were in expensive, downtown locations. IKEA opened a large store in the suburbs of Zurich, in a canton which had about 20% of the country's consumer purchasing power. Ignoring the fact that furniture in Switzerland was of traditional design, very sturdy construction, and made from dark woods, the new store offered IKEA's line of simple contemporary designs in knockdown kits. Besides, rather than conform to the local service-intensive sales norms, the IKEA stores introduced self-service and cash-and-carry concepts. By distributing half a million catalogs and backing them with humorous, off-beat advertising (see Exhibit 4), the new store attracted 650,000 visitors in its first year.

In 1974, IKEA opened near Munich. Not only was West Germany Europe's largest and best organized furniture market (estimated at DM 12 billion in 1973), but it was also the largest furniture producer and exporter. German retailers were set up as elaborate furniture showrooms and they had adopted the role of order takers for manufacturers, holding little inventory of their own. As a result, consumers typically had to wait weeks for delivery, and manufacturers often faced sharp swings in demand as styles changed or the economy slowed. Again IKEA promoted itself as "those impossible Swedes with strange ideas." Promising inexpensive prices, immediate delivery, and the quality image of the Swedish Furniture Institute's Möbelfakta seal, the company attracted 37,000 people to the store during its first three days.

German retailers responded vigorously. Their trade association complained that the Möbelfakta requirements of the Swedish Furniture Institute were "considerably below the minimum requirements for quality furniture in West Germany and neighboring countries." Following legal proceedings against IKEA for deceiving customers with the Möbelfakta seals, the German court put constraints on how IKEA could use the seals. Other retailers initiated legal action challenging the truthfulness of IKEA's aggressive advertising. Again, the courts supported the German retailers and curtailed IKEA's activities.

Nonetheless, business boomed, with IKEA opening 10 new stores in West Germany over the next five years. By the late 1970s, it had built a 50% share in the cash-and-carry segment of the West German market. Retailers who had earlier fought IKEA's entry began to acknowledge the potential of this new retailing concept, and imitators began to mushroom. IKEA continued opening stores in Europe and franchising others outside Europe into the 1980s. (Exhibit 5 details IKEA's worldwide expansion.)

IKEA's Culture, Strategy, and Organization

As IKEA's spectacular growth and expansion continued, its unique management philosophy and

EXHIBIT 3   IKEA Customer Profile and Buyer Behavior

Profile of IKEA Customers (Stockholm, 1975)

Age	Percent	Children	Percent	Status	Percent	Income (000 SKr)	Percent	Education (years)	Percent	Home	Percent
0–25	47%	0	55%	Married	65%	0–2	6%	0–6	24%	House	25%
25–35	32	1	22	Single	35	2–4	31	7–11	63	Apartment	63
35–45	14	2	16			4–6	25	12+	38	Condominium	12
45+	7	3	7			6+	38				

Buyer Behavior at IKEA (1975)

Primary Determinants of Purchase	Percent
Design	14%
Price	44
Quality	3
Large assortment	16
Catalog	11
Recommendations	1
Guarantees	0
Others	11
Total	100%

Importance of Criteria for Store-Choice	High	Low	No Response
Design	69%	5%	26%
Price	54	11	35
Quality	90	0	10
Distance	19	66	15

Consumer Attitude to IKEA	Positive	Negative	Neither
Design	51%	10%	39%
Price	73	4	23
Quality	27	29	44
Distance	56	29	15

Purchase Decisions Were Based On	Percent
Prior visits to the store	37%
Visits to other stores	72
Information from catalog	78

Source: R. Marteson, *Innovations in Multinational Retailing: IKEA in Swedish, Swiss, German, and Austrian Markets,* Doctoral Dissertation, (University of Gothenburg: Gothenburg, Sweden, 1981).

EXHIBIT 4 Introductory Promotion Campaigns of IKEA in Continental Europe

Advertising Themes for IKEA Store Opening: Switzerland, 1973 (six letters from Herr Bunzli)

Number	Theme	Abstract from the Advertisement
1	The new sales concept	Jokes about Swiss unwillingness to transport and assemble furniture, even for lower prices.
2	No delivery by IKEA	"That is a stupid thing."
3	Assembly of knocked-down furniture	"You can't do that to us Swiss."
4	The wood used for furniture	"No teak . . . we are not Swedes."
5	The Swiss needing furniture as status symbol	"Swedes go home."
6	Swiss quality	"Quality can come only from Switzerland."

Advertising Themes for IKEA Store Opening: Munich, 1974

Number	Theme
1	Young people have more taste than money.
2	We achieve the impossible.
3	On October 17, we'll open Munich's furniture highway.
4	At long last, the impossible furniture store will open on October 17.
5	Trees off the ground we take, and furniture for you we make.

Promotion Campaigns: West Germany, 1974–1979

Number	Campaign	Theme
1	The day of the singles	Single visitors could get their socks washed at IKEA.
2	The day of the baker	Crispy bread straight from the oven to all store visitors.
3	The day of the barber	Free manicure and haircut to store visitors.
4	The day of the breakfast	All visitors were offered free breakfasts.
5	IKEA birthday	Free gifts to visitors.
6	Rent a Christmas tree	Customers could rent a Christmas tree for 10 deutsche marks, refundable after Christmas if the tree was returned.
7	Day of the sleeper	Offered 300 people the opportunity to test the new IKEA mattresses overnight in its store, and buy them the next morning for 10 deutsche marks.

organizational approach developed and changed. At the core was the founder, Ingvar Kamprad.

Ingvar Kamprad

Ingvar Kamprad seemed driven by a vision larger than IKEA. "To create a better everyday life for the majority of people," he said, "once and for all, we have decided to side with the many. We know that in the future we may make a valuable contribution to the democratization process at home and abroad." One of his executives said of him, "He focuses on the human aspect. What motivates Ingvar is not profit alone but improving the quality of life of the people."

Throughout IKEA, Kamprad was revered as a visionary: "He consistently turned problems into opportunities and showed us how it is not dangerous to be different," said one executive. But

EXHIBIT 5   IKEA Retail Outlets Worldwide

Austria		Area in Square Meters*
1977(81)	Vienna	23,500
1981	Wels	11,700
1989	Graz†	14,900

Belgium		Area in Square Meters*
1984	Ternat (Brussels)	15,100
	Nossegem (Brussels)	11,100
1985	Wilrijk (Antwerp)	14,200
	Hognoul (Liège)	12,900

Canada		Area in Square Meters*
1976(83)	Vancouver	14,700
1977(87)	Toronto	20,000
1978(85)	Edmonton	10,400
1979	Calgary	5,700
	Ottawa	6,600
1992	Quebec	9,600
1982(86)	Montreal	15,400

Denmark		Area in Square Meters*
1969(75)	Tåanstrup (Copenhagen)	39,500
1980	Århus	9,700
1982	Aalborg	6,700
1985	Odense	1,400

France		Area in Square Meters*
1981	First establishment no longer in use	
1982(87)	Lyon	18,900
1983	Evry (south of Paris)	24,000
1985	Vitrolles (Marseilles)	15,700
1986	Paris-Nord	24,800
1988	Lomme† (Lille)	15,100

Italy		Area in Square Meters*
1989	Fulvio Testi† (Milano)	11,900

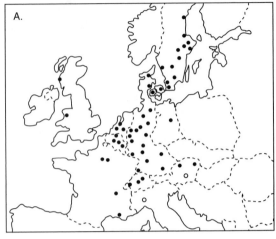

A.

The Netherlands		Area in Square Meters*
1979	Sliedrecht (Rotterdam)	16,600
1982(85)	Amsterdam	19,600
1983	Duiven	10,800

Norway		Area in Square Meters*
1963(75)	Slependen (Oslo)	19,600
1984	Bergen	10,500
1988	Forus† (Stavanger)	14,000

Sweden		Area in Square Meters*
1958	Älmhult	18,400
1965	Stockholm	44,000
1966	Sundsvall	11,800
1967(77)	Malmö	19,900
1972	Gothenburg	24,700
1977	Linköping	16,000
1981(87)	Jönköping	3,500
	Gävle	6,700
1982(88)	Helsingborg	11,600
1982	Örebro	2,300
1982(86)	Uppsala	13,000
1984	Västerås	10,900

(continued)

EXHIBIT 5 *(concluded)*

Switzerland		Area in Square Meters*
1973(79)	Spreitenbach (Zürich)	25,500
1979	Aubonne (Lausanne)	17,500
1986	Emmen (Lucerne)	3,000

United Kingdom		Area in Square Meters*
1987	Warrington	17,100
1988	Brent Park† (London)	23,300

U.S.A.		Area in Square Meters*
1985	Philadelphia	15,000
1986	Woodbridge (Washington)	14,500
1988	Baltimore†	19,700
1989	Pittsburgh†	19,900

West Germany		Area in Square Meters*
1974(86)	Eching	24,800
1975(78)	Godorf (Cologne)	16,100
1975	Dorsten	17,600
1976	Grossburgwedel (Hanover)	14,300
	Stuhr (Bremen)	12,900
1977	Kaltenkirchen (Hamburg)	8,000
1977(85)	Wallau (Frankfurt)	23,800

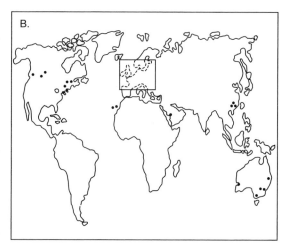

B.

West Germany (cont.)		Area in Square Meters*
1978	Kamen (Dortmund)	14,200
	Stuttgart	4,300
1979	Berlin	17,700
	Kaarst (Düsseldorf)	14,200
1980	Kassel	4,200
1981	Poppenreuth (Fürth/Nuremberg)	19,100
	Schwalbach-Bous (Saarbrücken)	6,200
	Frieburg	6,100
	Walldorf	18,300
1983	Löhne-Gohfeld	6,200
1989	Schnelsen† (Hamburg)	22,800

Figures in brackets refer to the date of rebuilding.
*Includes adjacent warehouses.
†Will be inaugurated after August 31, 1988. Not included in total figures.

Kamprad also paid extraordinary attention to the details of his business, and could operate simultaneously on multiple levels. "In a group of 600 items, he will ask about a particular product, know its price, its cost and its source, and he will expect you to know it, too. He checks everything and wants to do everything he can. He does not seem to believe in delegation. He is constantly bypassing formal structures to talk directly with front-line managers, particularly the designers and the purchasing group."

Kamprad's interest in front-line operations also extended to IKEA's staff. Whenever he visited a store he tried to meet and shake hands with every employee, offering a few words of praise, encouragement or advice as he did so. The simple—some said spartan—values of his native Småland had stayed with Kamprad, and he still rose early, worked hard, lived simply, and took a common-sense approach to management. One executive's account of Kamprad's recent visit to a newly opened store in Hamburg captured much of the founder's management style:

> During his rounds of the new store, he made points that covered 19 pages of notes. They ranged from comments about the basic design (he felt the building had far too many angles which added to construction costs) to the size of the price tags and the placement of posters in the store.
>
> He invited the employees to stay after work—and almost all did—so he could thank them for their efforts, since most had transferred from a distant store site. The dinner was typical IKEA style—the employees went first to the buffet, the managers went next, and Ingvar Kamprad was among the last when only the remnants were left. After dinner, Ingvar shook hands and talked with all 150 present, finally leaving the store well past midnight. That experience will keep the motivation high for weeks. Each employee will go back home and tell his family and his friends that Ingvar shook hands with him.
>
> When the store manager arrived at 6:30 the next morning, he found that Ingvar had been in the store for over an hour. Although he was staying in a modest hotel, he remarked that it was probably priced 5 DM too high. That story will probably circulate through the company as many others do—like the one about Ingvar driving around town late at night checking hotel prices, till he found one economical enough. It's all part of the aura and the legend that surrounds him.

IKEA's Management Philosophy and Practices

In many ways, IKEA developed as an extension of Kamprad and his view of life. "The true IKEA spirit," he remarked, "is founded on our enthusiasm, on our constant will to renew, on our cost consciousness, on our willingness to assume responsibility and to help, on our humbleness before the task, and on the simplicity in our behavior." Over the years a very distinct organization culture and management style had emerged.

The company operated very informally. It was reflected in the neat but casual dress of the employees (jeans and sweaters were the norm), in the relaxed office atmosphere with practically everyone sitting in an open-plan office landscape, and in the familiar and personal way the employees addressed each other—with the personal "du" rather than the more formal "sie" in Germany, and in France, with "tu" rather than "vous." Kamprad noted, "A better everyday life means getting away from status and conventions—being freer and more at ease as human beings." But a senior executive had another view: "This environment actually puts pressure on management to perform. There is no security available behind status or closed doors."

The IKEA management process also stressed simplicity and attention to detail. "Complicated rules paralyze!" said Ingvar Kamprad. An oft-repeated IKEA saying was "Retail is detail." Store managers and corporate staff alike were expected to fully understand the operations of IKEA's stores. The company organized "antibureaucrat weeks" that required all managers to work in store showrooms and warehouses for at least a week every year. The work pace was such that executives joked that IKEA believed in "management by running around."

Cost consciousness was another strong part of the management culture. "Waste of resources," said Kamprad, "is a mortal sin at IKEA. Expensive solutions are often signs of mediocrity, and an idea without a price tag is never acceptable." Although cost consciousness extended into all aspects of the operation, travel and entertainment expenses were particularly sensitive. The head-office travel department had circulated a pamphlet titled "Travelling for IKEA," which contained tips on qualifying for the most inexpensive air fares, and listed economical, simple "IKEA hotels." "We do not set any price on time," remarked an executive, recalling that he had once phoned Kamprad to get approval to fly first class. He explained that economy class was full, and that he had an urgent appointment to keep. "There is no first class in IKEA," Kamprad had replied, refusing his request. "Perhaps you should go by car." The executive completed the 350-mile trip by taxi.

The search for creative solutions was highly prized within IKEA. Kamprad had written, "Only while sleeping one makes no mistakes. The fear of making mistakes is the root of bureaucracy and the enemy of all evolution." Though planning for the future was encouraged, overanalysis was not. "Exaggerated planning can be fatal!" Kamprad advised his executives. "Let simplicity and common sense characterize your planning."

Kamprad had created company legends out of stories where creative common sense experiments had changed the way the company did business. On opening day of the original Stockholm store, for example, the warehouse could not cope with the rush of customers. The store manager suggested that they be allowed to go into the warehouse to pick up their purchases. The result was so successful that future warehouses were designed to allow self-selection by customers, resulting in cost savings and faster service.

Because it had such a strong and unique culture, IKEA preferred not to recruit those who had already been immersed in another cultural stream. Nor was higher education necessary or even advantageous in IKEA. "The Stockholm-raised, highly educated, status-oriented individuals often find it difficult to adjust to the culture of the company," remarked one executive. "Younger, more open recruits not only keep costs low, but they also absorb and amplify the enthusiasm of the company. We can develop them quickly by delegating responsibilities early, rotating them frequently, and offering rapid promotions to the high performers. The average age of a store manager is only 34." An executive listed the characteristics of the successful new applicants to IKEA:

"They are people who accept our values and are willing to act on our ideas. They tend to be straightforward rather than flashy, and not too status-conscious. They must be hardworking and comfortable dealing with everyone from the customer

to the owner to the cashier. But perhaps the most important quality for an Ikean is *ödmjukhet*—a Swedish word that implies humility, modesty, and respect for one's fellow man. It may be hard to translate, but we know it when we see it. It's reflected in things like personal simplicity and self-criticism."

The people and the values resulted in a unique work environment of which Kamprad was genuinely proud. "We take care of each other and inspire each other. One cannot help feeling sorry for those who cannot or will not join us," he said.

In 1976, Kamprad felt the need to commit to paper the values that had developed in IKEA during the previous decade. His thesis, *Testament of a Furniture Dealer,* became an important means for spreading the IKEA philosophy during a period of rapid international expansion. (Extracts are given in Exhibit 6.) With the help of this document, the organization strove to retain much of its unique culture, even as it spread into different countries. The big ideas contained in Kamprad's thesis were spread through training and "mouth to ear" transfer. Specially trained "IKEA ambassadors" were assigned to key positions in all units to spread the company's philosophy and values by educating their subordinates and by acting as role models. By 1989, about 300 such cultural agents had been trained in a special week-long seminar which covered not only the company's history and culture (presented personally by Kamprad), but also detailed training on how to spread the message.

The Adapting IKEA Strategy

At the heart of the IKEA strategy was its product range. Ingvar Kamprad called it "our identity" and set up clear and detailed guidelines on profile, quality, and price. While leaving considerable flexibility for fringe products, he decreed that IKEA should stand for essential products for the home—simple, durable, and well designed—priced to be accessible to the majority of the people.

IKEA had over 20,000 product offerings, of which 12,000 formed the core of simple, functional items common across IKEA stores worldwide. Of

EXHIBIT 6   Extracts from the 11-Page Document, *Testament of a Furniture Dealer*

What is good for our customers is also good for us in the long run. . . . We know we can have an important effect on practically all markets. We know that we may make a valuable contribution to the democratization process at home and abroad. . . . That is why it is our duty to expand.

The following section describes our product range and price philosophy, which is the backbone of our work. Furthermore, we describe rules and methods which will continue to make IKEA a unique company.

1. *The Product Range—Our Identity*

   Range: To cover the total home area, indoors as well as outdoors, with loose as well as fixed home furnishings. This range shall always be limited.
   Profile: Our basic range shall be . . . simple and straightforward . . . durable and easy to live with . . . (and) shall express design, color, and joy. In Scandinavia [it] should be regarded as typically IKEA and outside Scandinavia as typically Swedish.
   Quality: Throw-away products is not IKEA. But quality should never be an end in itself. It should always be adapted to the consumer's interests in the long run.
   Changes: Our basic policy to serve the majority of people can never be changed.

2. *The IKEA Spirit—A Strong and Living Reality*

   The true IKEA spirit is still founded on our enthusiasm, on our constant will to renew, on our cost consciousness, on our willingness to assume responsibility and help, on our humbleness before the task, and on the simplicity in our behavior. . . . The IKEA spirit is still here, but it has to be taken care of and developed with time. **Development, however, is not always equal to progress.** It depends upon you, as a leader and a responsible person, to make development progressive.

3. *Profit Gives Us Resources*

   Profit is a wonderful word! Let us rely on ourselves when it comes to creating resources. The aim for accumulating our resources is **to obtain the best results in the long run.**

4. *To Reach Good Results with Small Means*

   Expensive solutions . . . are often a sign of mediocrity. We have no interest in a solution until we know what it costs.

5. *Simplicity Is a Virtue*

   Bureaucracy complicates and paralyzes! Exaggerated planning can be fatal. . . . Simplicity in our behavior gives us strength.

6. *The Different Way*

   By daring to be different, we find new ways . . . I hope we never have two stores completely alike (because) a healthy appetite for experimenting will lead us forward.

7. *Concentration of Energy—Important to Our Success*

   The general who splits up his forces inevitably fails. . . . We too have to concentrate. We cannot do everything everywhere, at the same time.

8. *To Assume Responsibility—A Privilege*

   To assume responsibility has nothing to do with education, economy, or position. In our IKEA family we want to keep the human being in the center, and to support each other. . . . To make mistakes is the privilege of the active person.

9. *Most Things Still Remain to Be Done—A Glorious Future*

   Happiness is not to reach one's goal but to be on the way. Experience is the drag on all evolution. . . . Humbleness, will, and strengths are your secret weapons. . . . Time is your most important asset. What we want, we can and will do. Together. A glorious future!

these, the 2,000–3,000 items displayed in the catalog received special attention since the catalog was the centerpiece of the company's product promotion policy. Indeed, management saw it as the principal means of educating consumers to the IKEA product line and concept. By 1988, the annual distribution of 44 million catalogs in 12 languages and 27 editions accounted for half the company's marketing budget.

In order to maintain its low-price reputation and allow catalog prices to be guaranteed for a year, management promoted an organization-wide obsession with cost control. The importance of production flexibility and responsiveness led to the following activities:

- **Finding low-priced materials:** IKEA designers and buyers were always looking for less expensive, good quality alternative materials, and, in the early 1960s, led the trend to replace traditional teak with less costly oak materials. In the 1970s, IKEA helped win a broader acceptance of inexpensive pinewood furniture.
- **Matching products to capabilities:** "We don't buy products, we buy production capacities," remarked a purchase executive. In an effort to maximize production from available capacity, IKEA constantly searched for unconventional suppliers. For example, it had offered contracts for table manufacture to a ski supplier, and cushion covers to a shirt manufacturer with excess capacity. "If the suppliers have capacity, we ask them to produce first, and then we worry about selling the output. It is by ensuring our suppliers' delivery schedule security and by filling their available manufacturing capacity that we maintain our unique price levels."
- **Developing long-term relations with suppliers:** IKEA supported its suppliers both technically and financially even to the point of designing their factories, buying their machines, and setting up their operations. In order to meet cost objectives and maintain long-term supplier relationships, designers worked two to three years ahead of current products. By ensuring a high,

steady volume of orders, IKEA encouraged the suppliers to invest and drive down manufacturing costs. In furniture alone, IKEA purchased from about 1,500 suppliers in more than 40 countries. Purchases were consolidated in 12 central warehouses, which maintained high inventories not only because of commitments to suppliers, but also to meet the company's 90% to 95% service level objective on catalog items.

The most visible aspect of IKEA's strategy was its highly successful retail operations. The distinctive stores with their constant innovations had changed the face of furniture retailing in Europe. As IKEA expanded, a tremendous internal competitiveness developed among the stores. "The newly setup stores would look at the previously developed stores and try their hardest to improve on them," recalled an executive. "One would set up a green plant department, so the next would create a clock section." It was by this process that some of the unique distinguishing characteristics of the typical IKEA store emerged: supervised play areas for children, which featured a large "pool" filled with red styrofoam balls; in-store cafes that served inexpensive exotic meals, such as Swedish meatballs; and fully equipped nursery and baby-changing facilities.

Although this interstore competition resulted in numerous innovative new ideas, it also led to a certain amount of unnecessary differentiation and wheel reinvention. So much so that by the mid-1980s, some senior managers began proposing greater coordination and standardization of the diverse operations and multiple approaches. They argued that not only would such standardization project a clearer IKEA image, but it could also result in considerable savings. An executive recalled:

Hans Ax was the major champion of the "IKEA concept." He felt that we were spending too much on diverse development projects instead of taking the best ideas, standardizing our approach, and applying it to all the stores. As a result of this effort, a uniform concept has emerged. Guidelines have developed ranging from the basic color of the IKEA signs to the size of plants sold in our garden shops.

An important part of the IKEA concept was the development of standard in-store display areas. In every store there were five or six areas called studios which displayed some of the best-selling products. Under the IKEA concept, the locations of the studios within the retail store and their display settings were standardized, down to the last centimeter of layout design.

The concept also specified store architecture more precisely, defining the classic IKEA traffic flow that took customers through the store in a four-leafed clover pattern to maximize their exposure to the product line. It prescribed standard in-store facilities including baby-changing rooms, a supervised play area for children, information centers, and cafes. "We have become a little like McDonald's in our insistence that all the stores conform on these points," said one headquarters executive. "We want to create a unique ambience that makes IKEA not just a furniture store, but a family outing destination that can compete with the entertainment park and the zoo for family time."

The Evolving Organization

When IKEA started internationalizing, Kamprad organized its non-Scandinavian business into an Expansion Group and an Operations Group. (See Exhibit 7.) The former was responsible for initial planning for new market entry. First, a construction team was sent in to set up the new facility. Then, two months before the opening, a "build-up" team from the first-year group would take charge, training the staff, establishing operations, and managing the opening. After about a year, they would hand over to the Operations Group.

This organization allowed rapid growth, and also propelled many of IKEA's top managers to positions of responsibility. Recalled an IKEA executive:

> The pioneering spirit of a core group allowed our international expansion to succeed. With no guidelines except Ingvar's thesis and a general objective, young entrepreneurs would buy land, build and set up a store, and quickly move on to the next store. The pace was breathtaking. You could be hired on Monday and sent out on Thursday on a key mission. The company had unbelievable confidence in its people, but this

experience created today's leaders in IKEA—Anders Moberg, Thomas Blomquist, and many others.

Responsibilities shifted frequently and careers progressed rapidly. Most senior executives were in their thirties. Anders Moberg, now IKEA's CEO at 38, had started his career in store administration, moving to work in build-up groups before being appointed store manager in Austria and in Switzerland. He then led the IKEA entry into France as country manager.

In the early 1980s, with a well-established international organization, IKEA retail was reorganized into four geographical regions, headed by regional managers. However, the purchasing, distribution, and design functions continued to be centrally controlled and were staffed by specialists who rarely migrated to other functions. Most purchasers, for example, came from Småland, Kamprad's home region whose inhabitants were renowned for their thriftiness. They rarely had a college education, and their job rotation and career growth were slower and more specialized than the retailers'.

IKEA's senior management remained predominantly Scandinavian. "There is an efficiency in having a homogeneous group," reasoned a Swedish manager of a foreign operation. "They instinctively follow the Scandinavian management philosophy of simple, people-oriented, nonhierarchic operations." Although there was no overt discrimination, some non-Swedes felt it was important to speak Swedish and understand the Smålandish psyche to be a member of the inner management circle since the dominant company ethic was viewed internally as systematized Smålandish common sense. Indeed, IKEA's president, Anders Moberg, had been publicly quoted as saying, "I would advise any foreign employee who really wants to advance in this company to learn Swedish. They will then get a completely different feeling for our culture, our mood, our values. All in all, we encourage all our foreign personnel to have as much contact with Sweden as possible, for instance, by going to Sweden for their holidays."

Over the years, the legal ownership structure of the IKEA group had been shaped by several influences. Above all, Kamprad wanted to ensure that

EXHIBIT 7   Organization of the IKEA Group during the 1970s and the Early 1980s

Organization of the IKEA Group during the Early 1970s

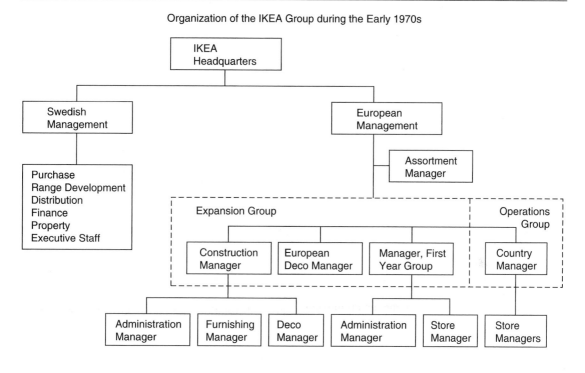

Organization of the IKEA Group during the Early 1980s

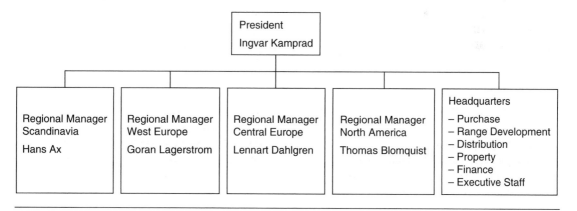

the business would live on after him and would not be broken up in some kind of inheritance dispute. He and his family controlled a company whose income derived from franchise fees and royalties paid by IKEA stores. Operating profits were transferred to a charitable foundation Kamprad had set up in the Netherlands to escape stringent Swedish taxes and foreign exchange regulations. (See Exhibit 8.) Kamprad himself had moved to Lausanne, Switzerland, partly to escape the high Swedish taxes.

EXHIBIT 8   Ownership Structure of the IKEA Group

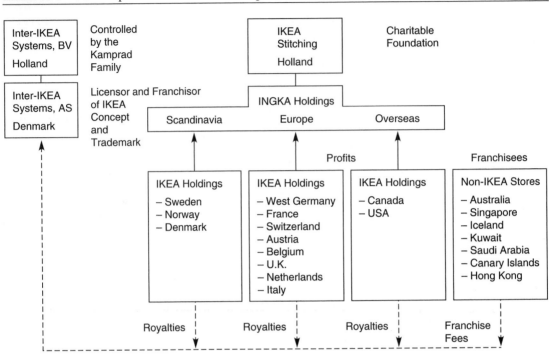

New Directions and Future Issues

By the late 1980s, Kamprad and his management team were working on some bold new strategies to take IKEA into the next decade. Along with the new directions, however, came some questions about how long the company could maintain its remarkable record of growth and expansion.

New Horizons

In 1979, Kamprad had bought a faltering IKEA franchise in Canada, and turned it into a lucrative business within three years. Thereafter, management had been eyeing the United States, the largest furniture market in the world (estimated at $15 billion in 1985). The decision process leading to entry into the United States was in classic IKEA style, as Björn Bayley, head of the Canadian operations at the time, recalled:

> The U.S. market had enormous potential. There are 18 million people in New York alone—more than

the population of Scandinavia. Once it became known within IKEA that we were planning to open stores in the United States, three or four managers staked out a claim to head the U.S. operations. But Ingvar was not ready to decide and, for several months, confusion reigned. Finally, he called me from a railway station in Stuttgart. He had decided to run the new U.S. stores as part of the Canadian operation. He wanted us to open two stores on the East Coast with as little hoopla as possible, and, once these were successful, follow with further expansion.

As usual, it didn't take long for imitators to appear. Indeed, a California-based retailer calling itself Stör began emulating IKEA's concepts so exactly—from product designs to ball-filled children's play areas—that the company launched legal proceedings against them. To preserve its image and to preempt imitators, management decided to accelerate its national expansion plans. By 1989, stores had been opened in Philadelphia, Washington,

Baltimore and Pittsburgh, and six more openings were scheduled by 1992.

In 1987, IKEA entered the U.K., a market estimated at £5 billion, and home of the only other large multinational furniture retailer—the more upscale Habitat. A successful entry in Warrington (in the northwest) was followed by the opening of the country's largest home furnishing store close to London. Plans for another 10 stores in the U.K. were announced.

In 1989, IKEA opened its first store in Italy—one of Europe's largest furniture markets. Again its initial reception was excellent. For the first three days of operation, there were one-hour-long queues outside the store. As soon as it could obtain the necessary permits, the company hoped to expand south from its base in Milan.

IKEA had also taken the first steps in its plans to build a major presence in Russia and East Europe. Not surprisingly, the unconventional idea was hatched by Ingvar Kamprad in the mid-1980s. Recalled an IKEA executive, "Our entire East European strategy was mapped out by Ingvar on a small paper napkin. Just about every aspect of the entry strategy was laid out on this small piece of paper—we call it his Picasso—and for the past few years we have just built on and expanded that original vision."

The bold plans called for new skills and involved different risks. To source from 15 factories in Russia and many others in East Europe would require an investment in excess of SKr 500 million. The limited ability to transfer hard currency from East Europe forced the company to plan for extensive countertrade deals so that dividends and capital repayment could be replaced by furniture exports to the West. Some felt that it was too early to risk heavy resource dependence on the Eastern Bloc countries, given their low reliability of service and poor quality image. Others were concerned that recent economic and political reforms in many of these countries could easily suffer major reversals. However, in face of Kamprad's persistence, IKEA was proceeding with this major thrust.

The site of its first East Europe outlet was in Budapest, where the company took a 50% share

in a joint venture with a Hungarian retail chain. Soon after, it entered an agreement to open a store in Leningrad. In 1988, IKEA Poland decided to build a $25 million warehouse and retail center near Warsaw. As part of that plan, IKEA would buy furniture and establish a joint-venture woodworking factory in Poland. Outlets were also planned in Yugoslavia. An office in Vienna coordinated the administration of these various East European activities.

New Organization and Leadership

In 1986, Ingvar Kamprad appointed 35-year-old Anders Moberg as president. At the same time, IKEA operations were reorganized on functional lines (see Exhibit 9). At the top of the group was the four-person supervisory board, which reviewed the group's general direction. Under the supervisory board was the executive board, which was responsible for the day-to-day operations of the group. Except for Björn Bayley, all executive board members were based in IKEA's 50-person headquarters in Humlebaek, Denmark. Of the group's four basic functions, product range, purchasing, and distribution service reported directly to Moberg in his operating capacity as head of wholesale. Ingvar Kamprad also continued his deep involvement with the purchase and product range functions and often spent time discussing the intricacies of purchasing or design with managers five or more levels below him.

The leadership shift had an impact on the company's management style. Remarked one executive, "With over 13,000 employees worldwide, some have begun to push for a more formalized approach. Anders is more committed to systematization, and he delegates much more than Ingvar." In 1988 Moberg introduced a formal budgeting and planning process. Business plans from the various country operations and product groups were integrated and modified at the executive board level. A corporate plan with three years' horizon was developed and sent back to the country units and the product groups to ensure their actions were in conformity with the plan.

EXHIBIT 9   Organization Structure of IKEA after 1986

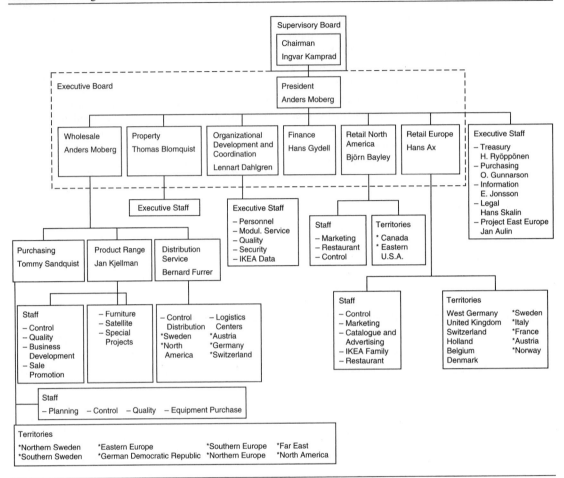

Blanket cost consciousness at all levels was giving way to cost-benefit studies. Instead of seeking out the least expensive sites, the company was now more willing to locate new stores at A-class sites, where justified. Furthermore, while earlier stores had been built for the midweek crowds, newer store capacity was being matched with weekend crowds. Although many applauded the changes as overdue, some felt they were not coming fast enough:

> There is a time bomb ticking inside IKEA's growing profitability that makes employees less willing to sacrifice and more anxious to share the rewards.

There is often a conflict between cost consciousness and efficiency. It's hard to keep the old spirit of frugality when the business is doing so well.

Future Directions and Concerns

Overall, IKEA hoped to reach a turnover of SKr 19 billion by 1990 and perhaps three times that amount by the year 2000, principally through rapid geographical expansion. But there was some cause for concern. Said one executive, "We are currently making annual risk capital investment of about SKr 500 million, which translates to opening four to six new stores every year. But our expansion plans are much more ambitious. In the United States alone, our rollout plan calls for two to three new stores every year, accelerating to five or six a year by the mid-1990s. I just hope we are not overextending ourselves."

Over the next few years, the median age and income level in most developed countries was expected to rise, while IKEA's target market segment of young, low- to middle-income families would be shrinking. A senior executive reflected:

We have to expand into other segments like office furniture and more traditional designs for the older, richer people. In our advertising also, we have started playing down the image of the "crazy Swedes," replacing it with a superior quality image. In entering the United States, for example, we have tried to project a sober image right from the begining. But we cannot risk making our profile too diffuse, or distorting the IKEA image.

Perhaps the biggest concern was whether the rapid growth and increasing geographic spread of IKEA would make it difficult to retain the company's cultural values. With over 13,000 employees worldwide and 1,000 new recruits being added annually, many newcomers had only a vague sense of the IKEA way. Björn Bayley, head of North American operations, commented:

The only constraint to our growth is people. At the top levels, our commitment to Ingvar's thesis still exists. But these days the pioneers are having to learn how to fill in forms. IKEA is adding about 10% to its workforce every year, in addition to normal personnel turnover, which can be as high as 20% in some departments. Inculcating the IKEA way into such a rapidly growing community is itself a tremendous challenge.

Another barrier we now face is the difference in attitudes between America and Scandinavia. Because of the low job security here, American employees are always looking for guidance—despite their higher education and need to achieve. The IKEA way requires openness and a willingness to take responsibility. We want people to stand up and disagree with authority if they have confidence in their beliefs. Despite inten-

sive training programs it has been hard making the IKEA way their way of life here in the United States.

Even Kamprad conceded:

Before, it was more concrete, the will to help each other, the art of managing with small means—being cost conscious almost to the point of stinginess, the humbleness, the irresistible enthusiasm and the wonderful community through thick and thin. Certainly it is more difficult now when the individual is gradually being wiped out in the gray gloominess of collective agreements.

The importance of a homogeneous management group in maintaining this common cultural bond was also being debated within the company. "When we open in a new country, we need the top management to be culture bearers for IKEA," remarked an executive, "so they are Scandinavian." Of the 65 senior executives in IKEA, 60 were Swedish or Danish, and almost all the non-Scandinavians were concentrated in distribution services. Furthermore, most of the senior executives came from the retail side of business. Some in the company felt such similarity of background was no longer in IKEA's best interest, as reflected by the comments of one company executive:

Sometimes, I think there is too much ideology bordering on religion. You sell your soul to IKEA when you start internalizing the culture. Ingvar is obsessed with his own ideas, and there is an element of fanaticism and intolerance towards people who think differently. I, for one, react negatively to the stingy mentality that sometimes shows through our cost-consciousness, or when Ingvar says that we can reach self-fulfillment only through our jobs—we work hard, but there is no reason that our jobs should necessarily dominate our lives.

Concerns were also being raised about how far IKEA could or should push its common concept across all stores even as it rapidly expanded internationally. As one executive put it:

Our common concept should leave sufficient room for creativity and freedom at the individual store level. Very often, market orientation and IKEA concept orientation clash. The U.S. market wants shelves with space for TV sets while European shelves are designed only for books. Should we adapt our line, or continue to sell bookshelves in the United States? The Scandinavian-designed bed and mattress is fundamentally different from the standard approach that is the norm in continental Europe. Should we continue to push the Scandinavian sleeping preferences on the rest of Europe?

But it's more than an issue of product design—it extends to how much we should adapt our organization and culture. Humility may be a virtue in Europe, for example, but should we impose it on our U.S. organization? Or is the attitude of "success breeds success" more appropriate there? Should our business drive our culture, or should our culture drive our business?

Perhaps the deepest concern was one that was often unspoken. How well would IKEA survive Ingvar Kamprad's eventual departure from the company? To this concern, Ingvar Kamprad responded, "The IKEA ideology is not the work of one man but the sum of many impulses from all the IKEA leadership. Its supporting framework is massive." But others were less sanguine. One manager summed up the concerns of many: "Ingvar is a patriarch. His dominating personality has been the life breath of the company, and you have to question how we will survive when he is gone."

Case 1–2   *Lincoln Electric: Venturing Abroad*

Returning late to his half-finished lunch of rice and stir-fried vegetables, Michael Gillespie, president for the Asia region of the Lincoln Electric Company, reviewed his plans to expand the company's production base in his area. Although this venerable U.S.-based manufacturer of welding machinery and consumables had sold products throughout Asia for decades, these had been produced at plants in Australia, the United States, and Europe. Anthony Massaro, Lincoln's new CEO and—like Gillespie—a newcomer to the company, had encouraged the Asia president to develop plans to open welding consumables factories in several Asian countries. Such facilities would enable Lincoln to take advantage of low labor costs and avoid trade barriers.

Specifically, Gillespie now turned his attention to plans for Indonesia. He faced several sets of choices. The first concerned whether to build a factory in Indonesia at all, given the particular political and economic conditions in that country, the nature of the market for welding products, and the competitive situation. If he decided this in the affirmative, he would need to choose whether to enter the market through a wholly-owned factory or a joint venture. Finally, Gillespie wondered whether the planned operation should adopt Lincoln Electric's famous incentive system, credited with rapid, steady increases in productivity in the company's flagship plant in Cleveland, Ohio. Although no immediate deadline loomed for these decisions, he would be asked to discuss his plans at the September 1996 meeting between Massaro and the presidents of Lincoln's five worldwide regions, scheduled for the following Monday in Cleveland.

Lincoln in the United States[1]

Founded by John C. Lincoln in 1895 in Cleveland to manufacture electric motors and generators, Lincoln Electric introduced its first machine for arc

This case was prepared by Research Associate Jamie O'Connell under the supervision of Professor Christopher A. Bartlett.

Copyright © 1998 by the President and Fellows of Harvard College. Harvard Business School case 398-095.

[1]This section draws on The Lincoln Electirc Company (HBS No. 376-028) by Professor Norman Berg.

welding in 1911. The company eventually became the world leader in sales of welding equipment and supplies (such as welding electrodes). (Exhibit 1 gives more detail on welding technology and Lincoln's products.) James F. Lincoln, John's younger brother, joined in 1907 and complemented his older brother's flair for technical innovation with a proficiency in management and administration. The company remained closely held by the family and employees until 1995, when a new share issue put 40% of its equity into the hands of the general public. These new shares acquired voting rights in the year 2005.

Founding Philosophy

James F. Lincoln's independent ideas about human motivation formed the basis of Lincoln Electric's management methods and incentive compensation system. At the foundation of his philosophy was an unbounded faith in the individual and a belief in the equality of management and workers. He also believed that everyone could develop to his or her fullest potential through a system of proper incentives designated to encourage both competition and teamwork. In 1951 he wrote in his company-published monograph, *Incentive Management:*

> There will always be greater growth of man under continued proper incentive. The profit that will result from such efficiency will be enormous . . . How, then, should the enormous extra profit resulting from incentive management be split? . . . If the worker does not get a proper share, he does not desire to develop himself or his skill . . . If the customer does not have part of the savings in lower prices, he will not buy the increased output . . . Management and ownership must get a part of the savings in larger savings and perhaps larger dividends . . . All those involved must be satisfied that they are properly recognized or they will not cooperate—and cooperation is essential to any and all successful application of incentives.

Incentive System

James F. Lincoln implemented his philosophy of "incentive management" through an unusual structure of compensation and benefits. He wrote, "There never will be enthusiasm for greater efficiency if the resulting profits are not properly distributed. If we

continue to give it to the average stockholder, the worker will not cooperate." The system had four key components: wages for most factory jobs based solely on piecework output; a year-end bonus that could equal or exceed an individual's regular pay; guaranteed employment; and limited benefits.

Piecework. Nearly all production workers—about half of Lincoln's total U.S. workforce—received no base salary but were paid on the basis of the number of pieces they produced. A Time Study Department established piecework prices that stayed constant until production methods were changed. The prices enabled an employee working at what was judged to be a "normal" rate to earn, each hour, the average wage for manufacturing workers in the Cleveland area. (Rates were adjusted annually for local wage inflation.) Each worker also had to ensure his or her own quality, however, repairing any defects identified by quality control inspectors before being paid for the piece in question. But there was no limit on how much could be earned by those who worked faster or harder than the normal rate.

Annual bonus. Since 1934 Lincoln had paid each worker a bonus at the end of each year based on his or her contribution to the company's total performance. The U.S. *Employee's Handbook* explained, "The bonus is not a gift and it does not happen automatically. The bonus is paid at the discretion of the Board of Directors of the Company. It is a sharing of the results of efficient operation and is based upon the contribution of each person to the overall success of the Company for that year." Until the 1980s, the annual bonus averaged nearly as much as the total wages of those eligible: the average worker in an average year received a bonus that almost doubled his or her base pay. In the 1980s and 1990s higher base wages and competitive pressures reduced bonuses to 50% to 60% of base pay.

Nearly all Lincoln employees were eligible for a bonus, including office workers and managers whose regular compensation was not based on piecework. Each individual's share of the bonus pool was determined by a semiannual "merit rating"

EXHIBIT 1   Arc Welding

Arc welding is a group of joining processes that utilize an electric current produced by a transformer or motor generator (electric or engine powered) to fuse various metals. The temperature at the arc is approximately 10,000 Fahrenheit.

The welding circuit consists of a welding machine, ground clamp, and electrode holder. The electrode carries electricity to the metal being welded and the heat from the arc causes the base metals to join together. The electrode may or may not act as a filler metal during the process; however, nearly 60% of all arc welding that is done in the United States utilizes a covered electrode that acts as a very-high-quality filler metal.

The Lincoln Electric Company manufactured a wide variety of covered electrodes, submerged arc welding wires and fluxes, and a unique self-shielded, flux-cored electrode called Innershield. The company also manufactured welding machines, wire feeders, and other supplies that were needed for arc welding.

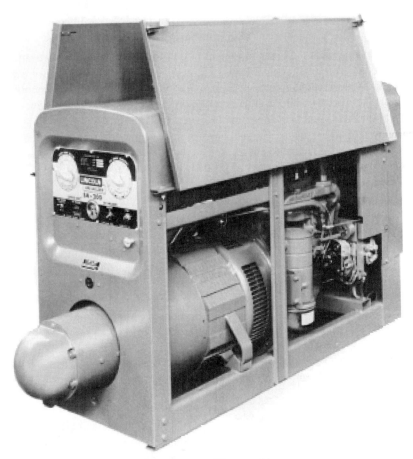

Lincoln arc welding machine

that measured his or her performance compared to those of others in the same department or work group. The rating depended on four factors: output, ideas and cooperation, dependability, and quality. (Exhibit 2 explains these factors in further detail.) Each department received a pool of points for each factor that would allow employees in each department to average 25 points on each factor. Supervisors then allocated the points among individuals according to their relative performance. Merit ratings varied widely, with some workers receiving total ratings as low as 50 and some as high as 150. Each individual's share of the bonus pool was determined entirely by the ratio of his or her points to the total awarded.

The combination of piecework and the annual bonus enabled Lincoln's best employees to earn much more than their counterparts at other manufacturing companies. In 1995 the highest paid production worker at Lincoln's U.S. operations received $131,000 in base pay and bonus, while the average employee received $51,911 in pay and bonus—82.8% above the Cleveland average for manufacturing workers.

Guaranteed employment.   James F. Lincoln saw guaranteed employment as an essential part of his system, writing: "Higher efficiency means fewer man-hours to do a job. If the worker loses his job more quickly, he will oppose higher efficiency." He

---

EXHIBIT 2   Criteria for Merit Rating for Annual Bonus (U.S. plants)

The section of Lincoln Electric's *Employee Handbook* concerning the annual bonus described the four criteria on which supervisors rated employees. (Employees received a rating card for each criterion.)

1.   Dependability

This card rates how well your supervisors have been able to depend upon you to do those things that have been expected of you without supervision. It also rates your ability to supervise yourself, including your work safety, performance, orderliness and care of equipment, and effective use of your skills.

2.   Quality

This card rates the quality of the work you do. It also reflects your success in eliminating errors and in reducing scrap and waste.

3.   Output

This card rates how much productive work which conforms to Lincoln standards you actually complete. It reflects your willingness to maintain high standards of effort and efficiency. It also takes into account your attendance record. Your rating score on "Output" is affected by absence from your job. A deduction of four-tenths of one point from your "Output" rating will be made for each day of absence other than [jury duty, military service, injury on the job, bereavement, vacation, and attendance at company events, but not sickness]. For any one incident of absence a deduction will be made for no more than four days, or a maximum of 1.6 points. If absences are habitual or excessive, regardless of the reasons, other action, including further reduction in merit rating and/or termination, will be considered. The output card will show the number of incidences of absence, total countable days missed in the rating period and the total point deduction.

4.   Ideas and cooperation

This card rates your cooperation, ideas and initiative. New ideas and methods are important to the Company in its continuing effort to reduce costs, increase output, improve quality, improve safety and enhance our relationship with our customers. This card credits you for your ideas and initiative as well as your acceptance of change. It also rates your cooperation including how well you work with others as a team. Factors considered include your attitude toward supervision, co-workers and the Company; your efforts to share your expert knowledge with others; and your cooperation in installing new methods smoothly.

also believed that the costs of recruiting and training the highly motivated, creative workers who thrived in his system would outweigh any savings achieved by cutting the payroll during downturns. In 1958 he introduced the Guaranteed Continuous Employment Plan, which assured employment for at least 75% of the standard 40-hour week to every full-time employee who had been with the company at least three years.[2]

James F. Lincoln's successors agreed broadly with these views. When orders dropped, the company took advantage of falling materials prices to produce for inventory. If demand still did not pick up, management could cut hours to 30 per week and redeploy workers to maintenance and other tasks. During the deep recession of 1982, for example, production workers were retrained and sent out as salespeople, selling $10 million worth of a new product in their first year alone. Such techniques had enabled Lincoln to avoid laying off a single employee in the United States, even one with less than three years' experience, since 1948.

Limited benefits.   James F. Lincoln's radical individualism also led him to minimize company-paid benefits under the rationale that fewer benefits enhanced profits and, thereby bonuses and worker compensation. While Lincoln employees received paid vacation, they had no paid holidays off, even Christmas. (They could, however, stay home on recognized holidays without their merit rating suffering.) Taking a day off for sickness also meant giving up a day's pay. The company did not oppose benefits as such—it provided employees with access to a group health insurance policy if they paid the full premium—but it preferred to pay employees with higher cash wages and bonuses, rather than fixed benefits, to give them maximum choice.

---

[2]Although there was very high turnover in the first three years of employment—and particularly in the first 12 months—overall, Lincoln's turnover rate had historically been less than 1% compared to 4–5% for all manufacturing companies.

Management Style and Culture

James Lincoln strove to erase hierarchical distinctions, and management's approachable style combined with the system of rational incentives to build a spirit of cooperation between management and employees. The mutual respect was reinforced by the workers' recognition that management worked as hard as they did, often putting in 60- to 70-hour weeks. Through its constant monitoring of the incentives and other work systems, Lincoln managers strove to build a sense of trust with the workforce. There were no reserved parking places in the company parking lot and executives ate in the same institutional cafeteria as janitors.

Open communication was regarded as essential, and management from the CEO down historically had spent hours of each work day on the shop floor. Furthermore, executives followed James Lincoln's "open-door" policy toward all employees, encouraging them to bring suggestions for improvement and complaints straight to the executive offices, which were located adjacent to the Cleveland plant. Since 1914, an Advisory Board of elected employee representatives had met twice a month with Lincoln's top executives. It provided a forum in which employees could bring issues to top management's attention, question company policies, and make suggestions for their improvement. Advisory Board representatives also communicated management's perspectives to their fellow employees, and minutes of all meetings were posted on bulletin boards throughout the plant and discussed among employees.

The culture that resulted from Lincoln's incentive program and unusual management style seemed to encourage individual employees to produce and innovate. For example, over the years, Lincoln's engineers and operators had collaborated to modify most equipment to run at two to three times its original rate, and had even developed some proprietary machinery. Lester Hillier, a welder with 17 years' experience at Lincoln, was a good example. In 1994 he told *The New York Times*, "I don't work for Lincoln Electric—I work for myself. I'm an entrepreneur." Hillier had put forward some 50 suggestions for cost reductions during the first half of 1994, about 30 of which management had accepted. Chief Financial Officer H. Jay Elliott gave his view of the atmosphere:

> If I go down to the cafeteria, the guy in grubby clothes sitting next to me is just as proud of his job as the chairman in a suit—who's sitting next to him! I think this is the best thing that piecework, the bonus system, guaranteed employment, and many employees' participation in our stock purchase plan have created: a sense of ownershp of the company from top to bottom.

Performance

Since 1911 Lincoln Electric executives and employees had attributed much of the company's financial health to its innovative management style and, particularly, its incentive system. The company grew quickly, even as giants such as Westinghouse and General Electric entered the U.S. welding market. Although Lincoln maintained a significant cost advantage over its competitors, during World War II, a patriotic James Lincoln offered to share the company's proprietary methods and equipment designs in order to boost industry productivity. Although its competitors' costs were close to Lincoln's in the immediate post-war period, company data showed Lincoln's productivity per worker was increasing at twice the rate of benchmark manufacturing companies.

Eventually, Lincoln's competitors began to wither in the face of the company's high productivity growth, and by the 1980s the large companies had withdrawn from the market entirely. When Lincoln acquired British Oxygen's U.S. welding company, Airco, management was able to confirm that they had again outdistanced the competitors. In a similar facility, Lincoln was achieving three times the output with half the people. George Willis, Lincoln's CEO in the late 1980s and early 1990s, summarized the company's competitiveness this way: "We're not a marketing company, we're not an R&D company, and we're not a service company. We're a manufacturing company, and I believe that we are the best manufacturing company in the world."

By 1995, Lincoln Electric estimated that it held 36% of the $1.5 billion U.S. market for welding equipment and supplies, making it the leading competitor in an otherwise fragmented industry. "It's a simple strategy," explained one manufacturing manager. "We strive for high productivity based on employee effort, continuous improvement in production processes, and seven-day-a-week utilization of equipment. By passing on cost savings to our customers, we generate very high demand that allows you to send everything you make straight out the door."

Early Ventures Abroad

Canada

Lincoln started exporting from Cleveland early on, and in 1916 established a sales organization for electric motors in Toronto, Canada. In 1925, it opened a manufacturing plant there and produced the full line of Lincoln products, almost solely for the Canadian market, until the early 1990s. At that time, the advent of the North American Free Trade Agreement (NAFTA) led the U.S. and Toronto plants to specialize in different product lines.

The operation quickly adopted most of the U.S. incentive system, including an annual bonus starting in 1940 and piecework beginning in 1946. Like the U.S. company, Lincoln Canada did not pay piecework employees for sick leave. Holidays were paid, however, as required by Canadian law, and a guarantee of employment was never introduced. A senior executive who had spent most of his career with the subsidiary believed that piecework and the bonus had played a key role in motivating employees to high productivity. Executives' open-door policy and the worker Advisory Council ensured communication among the subsidiary's 200 employees. These workers, like the U.S. ones, resisted unionization, turning it down in a vote in the 1970s.

Australia

Lincoln continued gradually to expand its international manufacturing presence. In 1940, William

Miskoe, a disciple of James Lincoln, moved from the United States to Australia to manage a plant Lincoln had opened in 1938. He introduced piecework for most production jobs and an annual bonus that usually amounted to between 25% and 35% of pre-bonus compensation. Although a commitment was never formalized, employees considered their jobs to be secure, and management cut employees' hours during several recessions to avoid layoffs. Australia was one of the most highly unionized societies in the world, but Lincoln workers rebuffed organizing attempts on several occasions. A senior Lincoln Australia executive believed that Miskoe's introduction of the incentive system when the operation had fewer than 100 employees had facilitated its initial acceptance; later hires embraced the system because their factory-floor colleagues liked it.

High Australian tariffs led Lincoln Australia to diversify into a nearly complete range of welding equipment and consumables. The company eventually began exporting to Asian countries, developing relationships with distributors and building the Lincoln brand name.

France

In 1955, Lincoln responded to a request from the French government for U.S. manufacturing investment under the Marshall Plan and opened a factory that made welding consumables, and later, equipment. It sold its products throughout western Europe, along with ones made by Lincoln in the United States, through one of Lincoln's U.S. distributors that also had rights to sell into Europe.

Expatriates from Cleveland helped implement the incentive system—including piecework, merit ratings, and a bonus that averaged 10% to 15% of pre-bonus compensation—in the late 1950s. A formal guaranteed employment policy was in effect from then until its repeal in the early 1970s. (Vacation, holiday, and sick pay were either mandated by law or by industry norms to which Lincoln adhered, varying the U.S. model.) Although Lincoln France had not studied its workers' productivity, its executives believed that it had created a much greater enthusiasm for the work and commitment to the

company than existed at other French companies. "There is no question in my mind that the incentive system is a major source of Lincoln France's success. I am deeply convinced that it is essential to our competitiveness," one remarked. From its founding through the late 1980s, the subsidiary had just one unprofitable year, after the oil crisis of the early 1970s, and paid a bonus every year except that one.

Despite this international growth, the Cleveland factory accounted for approximately 85% of worldwide production and monopolized new product development through the late 1980s. The three foreign factories manufactured on a small scale for local and regional markets and relied on U.S. plants for a number of key parts. Corporate executives, based in Cleveland, paid them little attention, content with their healthy, if modest, financial contribution.

International Expansion, 1988–1994

Upon James Lincoln's death in 1965, William Irrgang became the first nonfamily member to lead the company. Under Chairman Irrgang, however, Lincoln launched no new international ventures. Having fled Nazi Germany in the 1930s for the United States, Irrgang had a deep mistrust of all governments but that of his adopted country. This led him to turn down several oversees expansion proposals over the years, many from his President, George Willis.

Following Irrgang's death in 1986, Willis became CEO and finally had the freedom to expand the company's international manufacturing presence aggressively. He believed that a slowdown in U.S. market growth, as manufacturing's share of the country's economy continued to decline, would force Lincoln to find most future growth abroad. In the mid-1980s the importance of regional trade blocs, such as the European Community and the Andean Pact appeared to be increasing. The new chairman felt that his company needed manufacturing facilities inside each major bloc to ensure that external trade barriers did not render it uncompetitive with local producers. The European Community's (EC's) planned elimination of internal tariffs in 1992 was a source of particular interest.

Believing that the opportunity for immediate market presence made acquisitions more attractive than new "greenfield" factories, between 1988 and 1992 Willis acquired plants in nine countries. Finding no appropriate acquisition candidates, he also built new ones in Japan and Venezuela. In anticipation of European market integration in 1992, prices of many target acquisitions had been bid up to record level. As a result, Lincoln incurred long-term debt for the first time in its history. (Exhibit 3 lists the locations of Lincoln factories as of 1986 and 1992.)

Managing the New Subsidiaries

After years of domestic focus under Irrgang's leadership, Lincoln's corporate headquarters contained no managers with substantial international experience. As a result, Willis retained the existing managers of most of the acquired companies to take advantage of their local knowledge, but directed them to implement Lincoln's incentive and manufacturing systems. To help them, he sent out U.S. managers who knew the system in Cleveland, and also linked overseas supervisors and foremen with mentors among their U.S. counterparts. Beyond this, however, corporate headquarters largely left the new subsidiaries to manage on their own.

Most of Lincoln's acquisitions were unionized, and at each relations between management and labor historically had been less cordial than at Lincoln. Corporate executives felt that this would change with time. William Miskoe, the former Lincoln Australia chief, who had become corporate

---

EXHIBIT 3   Locations of Lincoln Electric Manufacturing Facilities, 1986 and 1992

	1986	1992
North America	United States	United States
	Canada	Canada
Asia and Australia	Australia	Australia
		Japan*
Europe	France	France
		Germany*
		Ireland
		Italy
		Netherlands
		Norway
		Spain
		United Kingdom
Latin America		Brazil*
		Mexico
		Venezuela*

*Plants in these countries were closed in 1993 and 1994.

senior vice president for international sales, told a reporter for *Cleveland Enterprise:*

> [Workers in the acquisitions] have to learn to trust management, which is not something they are accustomed to doing. That means we have to be completely honest and not pull any punches. We give them the facts, and let them make their own decisions.

Resistance from many quarters hindered the implementation of key elements of the incentive system, however. Many of the European managers and workers were philosophically opposed to piecework and seemed to value vacation time more highly than extra income from bonuses. Regulations presented additional obstacles: in Brazil any bonus paid for two consecutive years became a legal entitlement and in Germany piecework was illegal.

Financial Trouble

In 1991, while internal reworking was still in progress, the new subsidiaries' sales were hit hard by a severe recession in Europe and Japan. By 1992, nearly all of the newly acquired plants, plus France, were operating in the red. Nevertheless, corporate executives, still focused primarily on Cleveland, paid little attention. They remained optimistic that modified versions of the incentive system would eventually help most plants abroad achieve rapid productivity growth similar to Cleveland's. Mexico had successfully implemented the system already and Willis told an interviewer that he expected the European operations to have some form of it in place within two years. Fred Stueber, the firm's outside counsel and later its senior vice president and general counsel, recalled, "In 1992, Lincoln was in denial about the severity of the financial problems. They didn't realize their full scale until 1993."

When the 1992 results were reported in early 1993, the situation was plain: the new plants, especially those in Europe, were dragging the whole corporation down, and Lincoln Electric had lost money for the first time in its history. Despite strong performance in the United States, 1993 saw another loss.

(Exhibit 4 shows net sales and profits for Lincoln's operations by geography.) Recalled Stueber, "The company was almost in a death spiral: it had shareholders' equity approaching $300 million, and had lost over $80 million in two years. It was hemorrhaging so severely in Europe that prospects were scary." $217 million in long-term debt made the 1993 financial statements terrifying reading for Lincoln's historically cautious board of directors. (Exhibit 5 shows Lincoln's income statements and Exhibit 6 its balance sheets from 1987 through 1995.)

A New Broom . . .

In 1992, company president Don Hastings was named CEO, in the middle of what he later called "the nightmare years." His first move was to assemble an International Strategic Liaison Team to analyze the foreign operations and set attainable goals and performance guidelines for which local management would be held accountable. Despite its efforts, the team, comprised entirely of Cleveland-based managers, was unable to stanch the losses.

Recognizing that Lincoln lacked the expertise needed to handle the crisis, Hastings decided to look outside for executives with international experience. In April 1993, he hired Tony Massaro, former worldwide group president at Westinghouse Electric, as a consultant and brought him on permanently in August as director of international operations. Jay Elliott, former international vice president for finance at Goodyear Tire and Rubber Corporation, joined Lincoln in August as international chief financial officer to work closely with Massaro. The two were the first senior executives Lincoln had ever hired from outside the company. Hastings also added four heavyweight outsiders to the board of directors, including Edward E. Hood, Jr., former vice chairman of General Electric and Paul E. Lego, former chairman of Westinghouse.

Massaro's first priority was to conduct an intensive examination of Lincoln's new overseas subsidiaries. With Elliott's help, he quickly identified several causes of the subsidiaries' poor financial performance. First, they recognized that because most attention had been focused on the quality of

EXHIBIT 4 Lincoln Electric Financial Growth by Geography (figures in U.S.$000s)

	1987	1988	1989	1990	1991	1992	1993	1994	1995
*Net Sales to unaffiliated customers**									
United States	$363,857	$442,605	$474,060	$500,992	$461,876	$487,145	$543,458	$641,607	$ 711,940
Europe	29,454	52,401	135,923	215,378	288,251	275,520	211,268	156,803	201,672
Other	57,029	89,639	98,576	94,788	93,560	90,342	91,273	108,194	118,786
Corporate total	450,340	584,645	708,559	811,158	843,687	853,007	845,999	906,604	1,032,398
Income before taxes and extraordinary items[†]									
United States	49,874	55,910	53,039	28,205	30,806	24,860	42,570	71,650	87,044
Europe	1,480	3,099	4,423	2,057	(14,377)	(52,828)	(68,865)	3,945	11,350
Other	1,321	1,960	(555)	(6,780)	(2,949)	(7,183)	(22,903)	5,520	10,246
Eliminations	(2,781)	(5,102)	(8,369)	6,878	20,931	721	2,248	(947)	(605)
Corporate total	49,894	55,867	48,538	30,360	34,411	(34,430)	(46,950)	80,168	108,035

* For 1987–1991 net sales includes interest and other income of between 1.2% and 2.5% of corporate total.
† For 1987–1991 includes income from interest and other income. For 1992–1994 does not include income from interest and other income. 1995 income figures are for operating profit equal to net sale minus cost of goods sold; sales, general and administrative expenses; and foreign exchange loss.

Source: Lincoln Electric SEC filings

EXHIBIT 5 Lincoln Electric Company Consolidated Income Statements, 1987–1995 (U.S.$ millions)

	1987	1988	1989	1990	1991	1992	1993	1994	1995
Net sales	443.2	570.2	692.8	796.7	833.9	853.0	846.0	906.6	1,032.4
Interest income	5.9	12.3	12.7	11.4	6.0	3.1	1.6	1.4	1.7
Other income	1.2	2.2	3.1	3.1	3.8	4.4	2.9	3.1	2.2
	450.3	584.6	708.6	811.2	843.7	860.5	850.5	811.1	1,036.3
Costs and expenses									
Cost of goods sold	279.4	361.0	441.3	510.5	521.8	553.1	532.8	556.3	634.6
Selling, general and administrative expenses and freight out	72.6	100.7	149.1	190.6	214.1	298.3	276.8	258.0	287.9
Restructuring charges (income)	0	0	0	0	0	23.9	70.1	(2.7)	0
Year-end incentive cash bonus	41.1	50.4	51.8	53.7	45.0	*	*	*	*
Payroll taxes paid by company on bonus	2.1	2.4	3.1	3.5	3.1	*	*	*	*
Hospital and medical expense	5.2	6.7	7.0	7.6	8.3	*	*	*	*
Foreign exchange loss	0	7.7	7.6	3.8	1.2	0.9	0.2	3.7	1.9
Interest expense				11.1	15.7	18.7	17.6	15.7	12.3
	400.4	528.8	660.0	780.8	809.3	894.9	897.5	831.0	936.7
Income before income taxes and extraordinary items	49.9	55.9	48.5	30.4	34.4	(34.4)	(47.0)	80.2	99.6
Provision for income taxes	22.3	21.5	21.0	19.3	20.0	11.4	(6.4)	32.2	38.1
Extraordinary items	0	0	0	0	0	0	2.5†	0	0
Net income	27.6	34.4	27.6	11.1	14.4	(45.8)	(38.1)	48.0	61.5

* Incentive bonus, all payroll taxes, and medical expenses included in selling, general and administrative expenses after 1992.
† Effect of change in method of accounting for income taxes.

Source: Lincoln Electric Company Annual Reports and 10-K filings.

EXHIBIT 6 Lincoln Electric Company Consolidated Balance Sheets, 1987–1995 (U.S.$ millions)

	1987	1988	1989	1990	1991	1992	1993	1994	1995
Assets									
Cash and equivalents	61.0	23.9	19.5	15.5	20.3	20.6	20.4	10.4	10.1
Net receivables	61.7	90.9	100.8	127.3	118.0	111.3	110.5	126.0	140.8
Inventories	74.7	116.3	120.5	164.4	206.3	171.3	143.7	155.3	182.9
Other current assets	9.1	12.0	14.4	14.5	17.5	18.0	51.1	21.7	23.3
Total current assets	206.4	243.1	255.1	321.7	362.1	321.2	325.7	313.4	357.1
Gross property, plant and equipment	195.7	274.8	328.2	387.7	422.9	435.2	406.7	444.5	490.6
Accumulated depreciation	121.2	148.6	170.2	193.1	213.3	226.8	237.0	260.3	285.0
Net property, plant, and equipment	74.5	126.3	158.0	194.7	209.6	208.4	169.7	184.2	205.6
Investments at equity	0.3	0.0	0.0	0.0	0.0	0.0	0.0	0.0	0.0
Intangibles, including goodwill	0.0	10.6	26.8	38.0	41.2	50.3	40.1	41.9	40.7
Other assets	13.4	23.2	15.8	17.9	27.4	23.4	24.1	17.3	14.4
Total assets	294.7	403.2	455.8	572.2	640.3	603.3	559.5	556.9	617.8
Liabilities									
Current debt, including notes payable and long-term debt due within one year	6.6	39.2	41.6	40.6	50.7	27.1	33.4	18.1	29.8
Accounts payable	23.4	36.8	40.0	44.3	46.6	44.2	43.5	54.8	53.9
Other current liabilities	32.7	38.1	41.0	52.5	61.4	77.2	99.0	71.2	85.0
Total current liabilities	62.7	114.2	122.6	137.3	158.6	148.5	175.9	144.1	168.6
Long-term debt	0.0	17.5	30.2	109.2	155.5	221.5	216.9	194.8	93.6
Deferred taxes	7.0	10.1	9.8	7.4	7.9	8.5	6.1	6.6	7.1
Minority interest	11.9	31.4	42.6	47.4	41.7	16.8	7.9	6.8	5.5
Other liabilities	8.4	5.1	6.8	16.7	12.4	9.2	9.2	10.3	13.0
Total liabilities	90.0	178.4	211.9	317.9	376.1	404.6	416.0	362.7	287.8
Total stockholders' equity	204.7	224.8	243.8	254.3	264.1	198.7	143.5	194.1	329.9
Total liabilities and equity	294.7	403.2	455.8	572.2	640.3	603.3	559.5	556.9	617.8

Source: Standard & Poor's Compustat PC Plus

the acquisition target's manufacturing facilities, several of the newly acquired European companies had small market shares and weak sales organizations.

Another problem was that fragmented production had kept costs high. Instead of concentrating manufacturing of each product in one factory to take advantage of the EC's elimination of intra-European tariffs in 1992, each European factory had continued to manufacture a nearly full line of welding products. In the resulting Balkanized organization, many plants suffered from overcapacity and competed with each other. Ray Bender, a Cleveland veteran, appointed director of manufacturing for Europe, had realized upon arrival that rather than increase production—the classic Cleveland approach—he had to squeeze costs. "Managers ran operations like national fiefdoms," Elliott noted, "and Lincoln lacked the confidence to bring them to heel. Headquarters let the subsidiaries do their own thing and never said 'no.'"

In Venezuela and Brazil, Massaro and Elliott found different problems. There, the company had replaced inherited managers with former Lincoln distributors who were enthusiastic about Lincoln's manufacturing and incentive systems but who had no manufacturing experience. Cleveland had given them little assistance, leaving them to succeed or fail on their own. "The Lincoln culture was so focused on individualism that corporate took a 'sink or swim' attitude with the subsidiaries," commented Elliott.

The new executives' analysis concluded that Lincoln's lack of international experience had led management to believe that the new acquisitions and the greenfield in Japan would accept its unusual incentive systems and management style easily. Massaro remarked, "Part of the problem was that they tried to do things the Lincoln way everywhere, rather than adjust to local conditions." With the benefit of hindsight, Hastings agreed:

> We found that operating an international business calls for a lot more than just technological skill. And to be candid, in many cases we didn't truly understand the cultures of those countries where we

expanded. For example, we had an incentive program that was based on the belief that everybody in the world would be willing to work a little harder to enhance their lives and their families and their incomes. It was an erroneous assumption.[3]

. . . Sweeps Clean

With firm support from Hastings and the board of directors, Massaro and Elliott set about restructuring international operations to achieve profitability. Massaro explained,

> The cleanup had two main stages. Some subsidiaries could not be saved and we had to shut these down. After that, we rationalized the product lines of the remaining plants in Europe and improved the sales force to increase volume.

The plants in Germany, Japan, Venezuela, and Brazil were judged too troubled to keep. In Germany, for example, sales costs were out of control, yet labor laws limited Lincoln's flexibility to respond. Massaro noted that the plant's militant union, IG Metall, was especially resistant to proposed changes, and the company ended up closing the subsidiary in 1994 at the cost of 464 jobs. Elsewhere in Europe, approximately 200 administrative and other nonproduction workers lost their jobs, leaving European operations' overhead costs 20% below their 1993 level. Plant closings in Brazil, Venezuela, and Japan the same year eliminated another 120 positions.

The process of rationalizing production within Europe proved contentious. In the hope of preventing their production being moved elsewhere, subsidiary managers argued incessantly about whose costs were lower. When incompatible accounting systems made comparison impossible at first, Massaro developed an approach to solving the problem, as Elliott explained:

> Tony did not follow the historical Lincoln practice of imposing a solution from on-high. Instead, he created

---

[3]Quoted in Richard M. Hodgetts, "A conversation with Donald F. Hastings of The Lincoln Electric Company," *Organizational Dynamics,* January 1997.

a European management team, comprised of the general manager of each European subsidiary, plus himself, me, Ray Bender, and Cleveland's former head of internal audit. We were collectively responsible for gathering comparable data, then analyzing them to determine which plants would close and how production would be shifted around.

A variety of other efforts boosted volume and, through it, profitability. For example, Massaro replaced several managers deemed unable to handle the changes, and hired new European sales and marketing staff who had experience in international business. He negotiated long-term supply agreements with key customers and arranged for some products being manufactured in the United States for export to Europe to be transferred to European plants. These moves increased volume and utilization and cut tariff costs. Increasing reliance on local materials also reduced tariff bills. Finally, at Massaro's behest, Lincoln's engineering department developed new products that met European customers' needs better than the U.S. designs the company had been offering.

Significantly, Massaro and Elliott also gave up trying to implement the full Lincoln incentive system in the acquired plants. After the restructuring, most plants stopped focusing on incentive-based compensation systems. Employees in most locations received bonuses based on their factory's results, but these comprised relatively small percentages of total compensation. However, a new bonus program was created for approximately 40 top European managers. Based on pan-European results, it was designed to encourage their cooperation in the service of the corporation as a whole. "Previously, they had no incentive to do anything but maximize their local profitability. The new system ensures that they aren't penalized for contributing to other Lincoln subsidiaries' production and efficiency," Massaro explained.

Following the restructuring, the overseas subsidiaries rebounded. In 1994 European operations made a profit as the continent emerged from recession and their profits grew through 1995 and 1996. The plant in Mexico followed a similar trajectory, while Canada boomed following the NAFTA-related rationalization.

A New Approach, 1996

In March 1996, Massaro was named President and Chief Operating Officer of The Lincoln Electric Company, and in November succeeded Hastings as CEO. The first outsider among the company's six CEOs and the only one with substantial international experience, Massaro looked to expand Lincoln's presence abroad. Two years earlier, foreign customers had accounted for 36% of the company's sales, but with the international operations in crisis, the newcomer had questioned whether the figure could reach 50% by the turn of the millennium.

Massaro's approach differed dramatically from that of George Willis, the CEO who had overseen the rapid international expansion of the late 1980s and early 1990s. The new CEO judged that the mature North American and European markets would grow only half as fast as those in less-developed countries. Therefore, in 1995, Lincoln had begun extending its sales and distribution networks in Latin America and Asia, and Massaro's next priority was to build manufacturing capacity in the developing markets.

As part of the new strategy, the new CEO also planned to oversee the international ventures more actively. In preparation for further expansion, he created a new structure for the company's international operations, naming a president for each of five regions: North America (including the United States and Canada), Europe, Russia/Africa/Middle East, Latin America, and Asia (including Australia). With vice-presidential rank in the corporate structure, these presidents supervised sales staff in their territories, advised Massaro on whether Lincoln needed to create manufacturing capacity in their regions, and developed plans for new factories. The five met as a group with the CEO every two months to discuss global strategy. Their compensation reflected Massaro's desire for interregional cooperation. A sophisticated bonus system motivated each to develop profitable production operations and maximize sales within his or her territory, but made it most personally rewarding to source goods from the Lincoln factory that could provide them most profitably, even if it was located in another territory.

Finally, Massaro was more flexible than his predecessors about how Lincoln workers abroad would be compensated. He believed that Lincoln's incentive system was an important source of competitive advantage in the United States, but was not convinced that it made sense everywhere. He gave his international managers full freedom to employ only the elements of the system that they judged appropriate for their countries' particular cultural and economic contexts, saying, "If the incentive system makes sense in a particular plant, we'll use it, but we'll also feel free to operate more traditionally or to pick and choose to create an appropriate mixture."

Lincoln Electric—Asia

As of mid-1996, plans to expand Lincoln's international presence in manufacturing had proceeded farthest in the Asia region. Gillespie, a 13-year veteran of ESAB, a Swedish manufacturer of welding products, had already spent six years in Asia when he was recruited in 1995 by Massaro, then Lincoln's director of international operations.

Strategy

As president of Lincoln Asia, Gillespie had developed an integrated sales and manufacturing strategy that would build on the company's existing relationships with distributors and customers. While continuing to source equipment from Australia and elsewhere, Gillespie planned to build factories in Asian countries to manufacture consumables for their local markets. (Trade barriers and the cost of transport made consumables more difficult to import profitably than equipment.) He estimated that each factory would take two to three years to break even.

The strategy was that Lincoln consumables would build brand awareness and loyalty, generating new sales of imported Lincoln equipment. It targeted the construction and manufacturing industries, which

were large consumers of welding products and accounted for much of Asian economies' rapid growth. Ray Bender—former head of manufacturing for Europe who now had been appointed to the same post for Asia—summarized the situation:

> Local production of basic consumables will build our market share and thereby enable us to pull higher-end consumables and equipment from other Lincoln factories. In this way, the local production, on which we will earn a modest but reasonable return, will boost higher-margin activities outside Indonesia and increase Lincoln's global return on equity.

Indonesia

Country and market. Indonesia was one of Gillespie's first targets for a new factory. The country's market for welding products was large, but unsophisticated. Most customers used hand-held stick welders rather than the semiautomatic or fully automatic machines more common in developed countries. About 50,000 tons (50 million kilos) per year of stick welding consumables were sold each year in Indonesia, representing a market about one-fourth the size of those of more developed countries, such as South Korea. To date, Lincoln had been confined to the equipment and automatic consumables segments, while its participation in the stick consumables market was negligible. (Exhibit 7 shows approximate market shares in each segment for Lincoln and key competitors.)

The bulk of the stick consumables market was served by two multinationals that had local factories and well-developed distribution networks—although some reports of distributor problems had been circulating. Several local firms had significant market shares, but their products were of lower quality. Tariffs of approximately 30% and shipping costs of approximately 7% of factory cost made it impossible for Lincoln to compete in the low-margin stick consumables segment without a local manufacturing base.

Lincoln's reputation as a high-quality producer was well established, and Gillespie believed that customers would switch to Lincoln stick

EXHIBIT 7   Indonesian Welding Market Segments, 1996

	Automatic Welding Process		Semiautomatic Welding Process		Stick Welding Process	
	Equipment	Consumables	Equipment	Consumables	Equipment	Consumables
Size (per year, in metric tons)	NA	1,500	NA	5,000	NA	50,000
Annual growth rate	NA	12%	NA	12%	NA	9%
Market shares (%)						
Lincoln Electric*	55%	50%	15%	0%	30%	1%
International company #1	0	5	0	40	0	45
International company #2	30	25	30	20	35	15
Indonesian companies	0	0	0	0	0	35
Imports by other companies	15	20	55	40	35	4

NA = Not available
*Imported from plants outside Indonesia.
Notes: All Lincoln products were imported. The two major international and the local competitors manufactured stick consumables locally, but imported nearly all of their semiautomatic and automatic consumables and stick equipment, and all of their semiautomatic and automatic equipment.

Source: Lincoln Electric estimates

consumables if these were offered at a competitive price. He envisioned a factory that could produce about 7,500 tons of electrodes per year at full capacity. Although only one shift's worth of production workers would be hired initially, others would be added as sales grew, and the plan anticipated using a full three shifts within about three years.

In addition to welding market, Gillespie had to consider broader political and economic risks in deciding whether to enter Indonesia. Political power in the country was concentrated in the hands of President Suharto, a former general who had seized power in a 1965 coup. In the months of civil strife and violence after the coup, up to one million Indonesians had been killed. By 1996, the 76-year-old Suharto's health was deteriorating, but he had designated no successor and continued to repress political opposition. During riots in July, government opponents had burned 10 buildings, including two state-run banks, and some analysts feared that a bloody succession struggle might follow the president's eventual death.

Indonesia's economy was growing rapidly but presented significant challenges to foreign investors. Suharto's relatives controlled large portions of it through personal conglomerates. *Business International* consistently cited the government as one of the world's most corrupt, and officials at all levels routinely demanded "gratuities" to process imported goods, grant licenses, and perform other functions. Local companies dominated the import, export, and distribution businesses, partly for these reasons but also because local customers seemed to prefer dealing with their own countrymen.

Another major concern was the economy's stability. Some observers had expressed concern that financial troubles or economic bottlenecks—mismatches in capacity between interlocking sectors of the economy—could cause the overheated economy to stumble. A slump could cause the currency to drop, reducing demand for Lincoln's imports and the dollar value of profits from the local factory.

Economic and political risks were serious, but Indonesia's regulatory environment had been improving. While distribution companies had to be joint ventures with local partners, 100% foreign ownership of manufacturing ventures was now permitted. Furthermore, the government imposed no restrictions on repatriation of profits and the rupiah was freely convertible. As a result, foreign direct investment in the country was booming, having risen 13.3% in the first quarter of 1996. (Exhibit 8 provides economic and social data on Indonesia.)

Entry strategies. If Gillespie decided to enter Indonesia, he could choose from a variety of methods. While 100% ownership of a manufacturing venture would give Lincoln full control and the right to all its profits, a joint venture would provide access to a partner's local expertise and relationships with key people in business and government. Gillespie knew that such contacts could be important during the process of constructing the factory as well as for operations and distribution. His marketing manager described a good local partner as "essential" to provide the company with local knowledge and contacts.

The most obvious possible joint venture partners were Lincoln's two local distributors: Tira Austenite (Tira) and Suryiasurana Hidupjaya (SSHJ). The two were very different. The Indonesian-owned Tira had a network of 14 offices throughout the country and sold a full range of hardware products, including welding equipment and supplies. It had been distributing Lincoln products in Indonesia

---

EXHIBIT 8   Indonesia: Economic and Social Characteristics

GDP, 1995	US$ 186 billion*
Population, 1995	196,600,000
GDP per capita, 1995	US$ 945*
Real GDP growth, average per year, 1991–1995	7.3%
Consumer price inflation, average per year, 1991–1995	9.0%
Exchange rate, September 1, 1996	U.S.$1 = 2,342 rupiah
Rupiah, average annual depreciation, 1991–1995	3.5%
Construction industry growth, 1996	12.4%
Manufacturing industry growth, 1996	11.0%
Prevailing monthly pay for full-time production workers in manufacturing as of September 1996 (Lincoln estimate)	250,000 rupiah
Legal minimum monthly pay for full-time workers (September 1996)	170,000 rupiah
Adult literacy (est.)	84%
Unemployment, official figures, 1994	3%
Underemployment, unofficial estimates, 1994	40%

*Converted at market exchange rate.

Sources: The Economist Intelligence Unit, *EIU Country Profile;* The Economist Intelligence Unit, *EIU Country Report;* The Economist Intelligence Unit, *Business Asia;* Central Intelligence Agency *The World Factbook 1996.*

since 1991, and while it had good access to medium-sized and large customers in a variety of industries, its sales force tended to sell from Tira's vast catalog of products it had sold for decades, servicing their existing clients' established needs. The company's high-level relationships with government officials enabled it to circumvent the bureaucratic obstacles that routinely presented themselves to businesses in Indonesia. However, having to hold inventories of many different products, Tira seemed to be spread thin financially, and management felt it probably would not be able to invest much equity in a joint venture.

SSHJ was a subsidiary of Sin Soon Huat, a Singaporean-Chinese family firm that had distributed Lincoln products in Singapore for nearly 20 years. Its operations in Vietnam, Burma, and China also sold Lincoln products. Founded in 1994 after Lincoln gave Sin Soon Huat permission to distribute its products in Indonesia, SSHJ had only two offices in the country. However, the Lincoln sales staff found the new distributor had adopted a more professional sales style than Tira. SSHJ salespeople visited potential customers and demonstrated the technical advantages and cost savings that Lincoln products could bring them, persuading them to switch from their current brands. SSHJ sold few products other than Lincoln welding equipment and supplies, and its managers from Singapore had years of experience with these. Finally, although it lacked Tira's extensive government contacts, SSHJ's financial strength made it attractive as a joint venture partner. On previous occasions, the parent, Sin Soon Huat, had taken a loss to help Lincoln enter new markets. Because the Lincoln franchise brought the distributor prestige, Gillespie believed that SSHJ would be willing to put up some of the cost of building the new factory and help cover early operating losses.

Gillespie recognized that he could invite one, or both companies to become joint venture partners. Or he could set up a wholly owned manufacturing company and continue to employ them as distributors, although such a move might reduce their commitment to Lincoln. The decision was a difficult one since Gillespie already found it challenging to modulate relationships between two distributors and keep their competition energizing rather than destructive.

Compensation. Beyond these strategic questions, Gillespie also pondered the issue of compensation and incentives, ever-important at Lincoln. If he did build a factory, should he pay production workers prevailing wages or introduce some form of incentive system? The only legal requirement was that the company pay the legal minimum wage of 170,000 rupiah per month. At an exchange rate of 2,342 rupiah per U.S. dollar, this represented the lowest wage rate in the Lincoln factory system. However, the prevailing rate at large manufacturing companies was 250,000 rupiah per month, plus an annual bonus equal to two months' salary. At a minimum, Gillespie felt he would have to match this rate, but his inclination was to go further.

Echoing James Lincoln's individualist philosophy, he stated, "I believe strongly in rewarding people for the quality and quantity of their work." Reflecting this belief, Gillespie felt that another option was to make the annual bonus merit-based and link it directly to factory performance, an approach that would require workers to put part of their compensation at risk. He envisioned a scheme based on the Cleveland model, but simplified for the less-educated Indonesian workforce. His thought was to offer a merit-based bonus that could reach 30% of the worker's base pay in good years, but which could disappear if the plant were not profitable.

In discussions with Ray Bender, who had joined Lincoln Asia as head of manufacturing, a third option emerged. On the basis of his experience in Cleveland and in Europe, Bender felt that most factory workers did not connect bonuses to their daily work practices. "People think about bonuses twice a year when they get their merit rating," he said. In his view, the real power of the Lincoln incentive system came from piecework. He was convinced that if selected and trained properly, workers in most countries would embrace such a compensation system, because it would provide them the opportunity to earn substantially more money through individual effort. From the company's perspective, he argued that once the workers became familiar with the system, their higher productivity would yield 20% to 40% more output from the same equipment. (Exhibit 9 summarizes the impact of such an increase on gross margins.)

Although his experience with Indonesian labor practice was limited, Gillespie knew of no factory in that country that was using piecework. However, he believed it would not be illegal as long as workers earned the prescribed minimum monthly wage. As a relative newcomer to Lincoln, he was less committed to the approach than veterans like Bender were, and his initial reaction was skeptical. "My experience with Indonesian workers is that they are more effectively managed with traditional management methods," he said. "I'm not sure that

the systems that work in Cleveland would be effective there."

Finally, in considering the options, Gillespie realized that ethical and public relations considerations added another wrinkle to these calculations. A number of western multinationals had come under fire for paying employees in developing countries prevailing wages that seemed low to observers in their home countries. Indonesian manufacturing workers generally lived in poor conditions and some supported large families. Gillespie expected that most Lincoln workers in Indonesia would earn more through piecework than under a wage system, but some could earn less. Even a merit-based bonus scheme could put the earnings of the lowest-ranked workers below what they might have earned with a traditional two-month guaranteed bonus. Should these factors affect the compensation system he designed?

As Gillespie discarded his empty styrofoam plate and returned to a stack of reports, he wondered what plans he would report the next week to his colleagues and Tony Massaro.

EXHIBIT 9   Cost Structure for One Kilogram of Stick Welding Electrodes Manufactured and Sold in Indonesia

Scenario	Plant Running Three Shifts, Normal Labor Productivity	Piecework Boosts Labor Productivity by 20%	Piecework Boosts Labor Productivity by 40%
Price	$1.35	$1.35	$1.35
Costs			
Materials	0.70	0.70	0.70
Share of fixed costs (including SG&A, depreciation)	0.20	0.17	0.14
Variable cost (including energy, lubricants)	0.08	0.08	0.08
Direct labor	0.02	0.02	0.02
Profit	0.35	0.38	0.41
Gross margin	25.9%	28.1%	30.4%

Notes: Figures are U.S. dollars. Figures do not represent a single kind of stick welding electrode, but rather a composite of high- and low-margin electrodes, weighted according to their approximate share of the Indonesian market.

Source: Lincoln Electric estimates (disguised).

Case 1–3   *Jollibee Foods Corporation: International Expansion*

Protected by his office air conditioner from Manila's humid August air, in mid-1997, Manolo P. ("Noli") Tingzon pondered an analysis of the youth market in San Francisco. As the new head of Jollibee's International Division, he wondered if a Philippine hamburger chain could appeal to mainstream American consumers or whether the chain's planned U.S. operations should continue to focus on recent immigrants and Philippine expatriates. On the other side of the Pacific, possible store opening in the Kowloon district of Hong Kong raised other issues for Tingzon. While Jollibee was established in the region, local managers were urging the company to adjust its menu, change its operations, and refocus its marketing to draw ethnic Chinese customers. Finally, he wondered whether entering the nearly virgin territory of Papua New Guinea would position Jollibee to dominate an emerging fast food market—or simply stretch his recently-slimmed division's resources too far.

With only a few weeks of experience in his new company, Noli Tingzon knew that he would have to weigh these decisions carefully. Not only would they shape the direction of Jollibee's future internalization strategy, they would also help him establish his own authority and credibility within the organization.

Company History

Started in 1975 as an ice cream parlor owned and run by the Chinese-Filipino Tan family, Jollibee had diversified into sandwiches after company President Tony Tan Caktiong (better known as TTC) realized that events triggered by the 1977 oil

This case was prepared by Professor Christopher A. Bartlett and Research Associate Jamie O'Connell.

crisis would double the price of ice cream. The Tans' hamburger, made to a home-style Philippine recipe developed by Tony's chef father, quickly became a customer favorite. A year later, with five stores in metropolitan Manila, the family incorporated as Jollibee Foods Corporation.

The company's name came from TTC's vision of employees working happily and efficiently, like bees in a hive. Reflecting a pervasive courtesy in the company, everyone addressed each other by first names prefaced by the honorific "Sir" or "Ma'am," whether addressing a superior or subordinate. Friendliness pervaded the organization and became one of the "Five Fs" that summed up Jollibee's philosophy. The others were flavorful food, a fun atmosphere, flexibility in catering to customer needs, and a focus on families (children flocked to the company's bee mascot whenever it appeared in public). The company's value proposition offered all of these to customers at an affordable price.

Jollibee expanded quickly throughout the Philippines, financing all growth internally until 1993. (Exhibit 1 shows growth in sales and outlets.) Tan family members occupied several key positions, particularly in operations management, but brought in professional managers to supplement their expertise. "The heads of marketing and finance have always been outsiders," TTC noted. (Exhibit 2 shows a 1997 organization chart.) Many franchisees were also members or friends of the Tan family. In 1993, Jollibee went public and in an initial public offering raised 216 million pesos (approximately U.S. $8 million). The Tan family, however, retained the majority ownership and clearly controlled Jollibee. Although the acquisition of Greenwich Pizza Corporation in 1994 and the formation of a joint venture with Deli France in 1995 diversified the company's fast food offerings, in 1996 the chain of Jollibee stores still generated about 85% of the parent company's revenues.

EXHIBIT 1 Jollibee Philippines Growth, 1975–1997

Year	Total Sales (millions of pesos)	Total Stores at End of Year	Company-Owned Stores	Franchises
1975	NA	2	2	0
1980	NA	7	4	3
1985	174	28	10	18
1990	1,229	65	12	54
1991	1,744	99	21	80
1992	2,644	112	25	89
1993	3,386	124	30	96
1994	4,044	148	44	106
1995	5,118	166	55	113
1996	6,588	205	84	124
1997	7,778	223	96	134

NA = Not available

(Exhibits 3 and 4 contain Jollibee's consolidated financial statements from 1992 through 1996.)

McDonald's: Going Burger to Burger

The company's first serious challenge arose in 1981, when McDonald's entered the Philippines. Although Jollibee already had 11 stores, many saw McDonald's as a juggernaut and urged TTC to concentrate on building a strong second-place position in the market. Many in the Tan family, however, felt more ambitious. TTC called a special meeting of his senior management to discuss the future. They concluded that although McDonald's had more money and highly developed operating systems, Jollibee had one major asset: Philippine consumers preferred Jollibee's taste. Operating by consensus, the group decided to compete directly with McDonald's for leadership in the Philippine fast food market. "Maybe at that time we were very young, but we felt we could do anything," TTC recalled. "We felt no fear."

McDonald's moved briskly at first, opening six restaurants within two years and spending large sums on advertising. Per-store sales quickly surpassed Jollibee's and by 1983, McDonald's had grabbed a 27% share of the fast food market, within striking range of Jollibee's 32%. The impressive performance of the Big Mac, McDonald's largest and best-known sandwich, led Jollibee to respond with a large hamburger of its own, called the Champ. Jollibee executives bet that the Champ's one wide hamburger patty, rather than the Big Mac's smaller two, would appeal more to Filipinos' large appetites. Market research indicated that Filipinos also preferred Jollibee burgers' spicy taste to McDonald's Western recipe, so the Champ's promotions focused on its taste, as well as its size.

But the Champ's intended knockout punch was eclipsed by larger events. In August 1983, political opposition leader Benigno Aquino returned from exile and was assassinated as he stepped off his plane in Manila. The economic and political crisis that followed led most foreign investors, including McDonald's, to slow their investment in the Philippines. But Jollibee pressed ahead, employing nationalistic advertising to capitalize on a wave of patriotism. By 1984, the appeal of McDonald's foreign brand and its advantage in per-store sales were fading.

In 1986, dictator Ferdinand Marcos fled the Philippines in the face of mass demonstrations of "people power" led by Aquino's widow, Corazon. After she took office as president, optimism returned to the country, encouraging foreign companies to

EXHIBIT 2   Jollibee Corporation Organization Chart, 1997 (members of Tan family shaded)

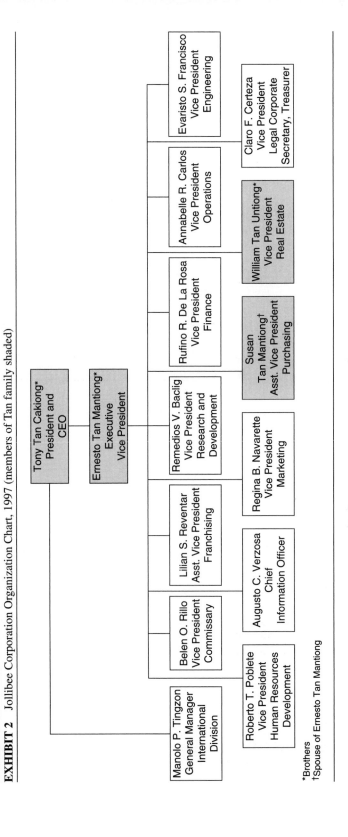

*Brothers
†Spouse of Ernesto Tan Mantiong

EXHIBIT 3   Jollibee Foods Corporation Consolidated Balance Sheets (in Philippine pesos)

	Years Ended December 31,				
	1996	*1995*	*1994*	*1993*	*1992*
Assets					
Current assets					
Cash and cash equivalents	480,822,919	355,577,847	474,480,298	327,298,749	116,716,643
Accounts receivable:					
Trade	579,089,680	206,045,303	135,663,597	107,680,327	86,885,668
Advances and others	105,836,646	70,731,546	66,224,534	35,838,295	15,091,648
Inventories	323,019,198	201,239,667	183,154,582	135,263,988	116,828,086
Prepaid expenses and					
other current assets	223,689,221	132,077,935	88,995,824	41,462,780	66,028,987
Total current assets	1,712,448,664	965,672,298	948,518,835	647,544,139	401,551,032
Investments and advances	283,758,590	274,878,713	132,277,028	67,000,362	60,780,936
Property and equipment	2,177,944,193	1,181,184,783	753,876,765	568,904,831	478,857,474
Refundable deposits and					
other assets—net	363,648,234	224,052,247	91,575,543	92,035,464	72,310,079
Total assets	4,537,799,681	2,645,788,041	1,926,248,171	1,375,484,796	1,013,499,521
Liabilities and Stockholders' Equity					
Current liabilities:					
Bank loans	771,690,724	—	—	—	—
Accounts payable and					
accrued expenses	1,274,801,219	715,474,384	497,238,433	323,029,967	297,029,436
Income tax payable	58,803,916	28,103,867	17,205,603	23,206,109	19,851,315
Notes payable	—	—	—	—	133,000,000
Current portion of					
long-term debt	6,707,027	7,524,098	—	—	22,034,635
Dividends payable	16,810,812	—	—	—	—
Total current liabilities	2,128,813,698	751,102,349	514,444,036	346,236,076	471,915,386
Long-term debt	28,936,769	33,725,902	—	—	21,127,827
Minority interest	45,204,131	1,479,723	1,331,529	—	—
Stockholders' equity					
Capital stock—par value	880,781,250	704,625,000	563,315,000	372,000,000	66,000,000
Additional paid-in capital	190,503,244	190,503,244	190,503,244	190,503,244	—
Retained earnings	1,263,560,589	964,351,823	656,654,362	466,745,476	454,456,308
Total stockholders' equity	2,334,845,083	1,859,480,067	1,410,472,606	1,029,248,720	520,456,308
Total liabilities	4,537,799,681	2,645,788,041	1,926,248,171	1,375,484,796	1,013,499,521
Average exchange rate					
during year: pesos per U.S.$	26.22	25.71	26.42	27.12	25.51

EXHIBIT 4   Jollibee Foods Corporation Consolidated Statements of Income and Retained Earnings
(in Philippine pesos)

	Years Ended December 31,				
	1996	*1995*	*1994*	*1993*	*1992*
	Income				
Sales	6,393,092,135	4,403,272,755	3,277,383,084	2,446,866,690	2,074,153,386
Royalties and franchise fees	511,510,191	448,200,271	328,824,566	255,325,825	221,884,104
	6,904,602,326	4,851,473,026	3,606,207,650	2,702,192,515	2,296,037,490
	Cost and Expenses				
Cost of sales	4,180,809,230	2,858,056,701	2,133,240,206	1,663,600,632	1,469,449,458
Operating expenses	1,943,536,384	1,403,151,840	1,013,999,640	674,288,268	545,749,275
Operating income	780,256,712	590,264,485	458,967,804	364,303,615	280,838,757
Interest and other income—net	44,670,811	102,134,296	83,342,805	32,716,223	(13,599,219)
Minority share in net earnings of a subsidiary	—	—	499,770	—	—
Provision for income tax	219,900,353	168,589,520	138,001,953	104,230,670	66,172,056
Income before minority interest and cumulative efffect of accounting change	605,027,170	523,809,261	403,808,886	292,789,168	201,067,482
Minority interest	2,829,654	137,694	—	—	—
Cumulative effect of accounting change		13,733,644			
Net income	602,197,516	537,405,211	403,808,886	292,789,168	201,067,482
Earnings per share	0.68	0.61	0.81	0.59	0.58
Average exchange rate (pesos per $U.S.)	26.22	25.71	26.42	27.12	25.51

reinvest. As the local McDonald's franchisee once again moved to expand, however, its management found that Jollibee now had 31 stores and was clearly the dominant presence in the market. The situation forced McDonald's to settle for "a distant second," in a long-time manager's words.

Industry Background

In the 1960s, fast food industry pioneers, such as Ray Kroc of McDonald's and Colonel Sanders of Kentucky Fried Chicken, had developed a value proposition that became the standard for the industry in the United States and abroad. Major fast food

outlets in the United States, which provided a model for the rest of the world, aimed to serve time-constrained customers by providing good-quality food in a clean dining environment and at a low price.

Managing a Store

At the store level, profitability in the fast food business depended on high customer traffic and tight operations management. Opening an outlet required large investments in equipment and store fittings, and keeping it open imposed high fixed costs for rent, utilities, and labor. This meant attracting large numbers of customers ("traffic") and, when possible, increasing the size of the average order (or "ticket"). The need for high volume put a premium on convenience and made store location critical. In choosing a site, attention had to be paid not only to the potential of a city or neighborhood but also to the traffic patterns and competition on particular streets or even blocks.

Yet even an excellent location could not make a store viable in the absence of good operations management, the critical ingredient in reducing waste and increasing staff productivity. Good store managers were the key to motivating and controlling crew members, the lowest-ranking staff of a fast food restaurant, responsible for taking orders, preparing food, and keeping the restaurant clean. Efficient use of their time—preparing raw materials and ingredients in advance, for example—not only enabled faster service, but could also reduce the number of crew members needed.

Managing a Chain

The high capital investment required to open new stores led to the growth of franchising which enabled chains to stake out new territory by rapidly acquiring market share and building brand recognition in an area. Such expansion created the critical mass needed to achieve economies of scale in both advertising and purchasing.

Fast food executives generally believed that consistency and reliability throughout a chain was a key driver of success in the business. Customers patronized chains because they knew, after eating at one restaurant in a chain, what they could expect at any other restaurant. This required standardization of the menu, raw material quality, and food preparation. Particularly among the U.S. chains that dominated the industry, there also was agreement that uniformity of image also differentiated the chain from competitors: beyond selling hamburger or chicken, they believed they were selling an image of American pop culture. For these reasons, as Jollibee began to expand, major international fast food chains were pushing their international subsidiaries to maintain or impose internationally standardized menus, recipes, advertising themes, and store designs.

Moving Offshore: 1986–1997

Jollibee's success in the Philippines brought opportunities in other Asian countries. Foreign businesspeople, some of them friends of the Tan family, heard about the chain's success against McDonald's and began approaching TTC for franchise rights in their countries. While most of his family and other executives were caught up in the thriving Philippine business, TTC was curious to see how Jollibee would fare abroad.

Early Forays

Singapore. Jollibee's first venture abroad began in 1985, when a friend of a Philippine franchisee persuaded TTC to let him open and manage Jollibee stores in Singapore. The franchise was owned by a partnership consisting of Jollibee, the local manager, and five Philippine-Chinese investors, each with a one-seventh stake. Soon after the first store opened, however, relations between Jollibee and the local manager began to deteriorate. When corporate inspectors visited to check quality, cleanliness, and efficiency in operations, the franchisee would not let them into his offices to verify the local records. In 1986, Jollibee revoked the franchise agreement and shut down the Singapore store. "When we were closing down the store, we found that all the local company funds were gone, but some suppliers had not been paid," said TTC. "We had no hard evidence that something was wrong, but we had lost each other's trust."

Taiwan. Soon after the closure in Singapore, Jollibee formed a partnership with a Tan family friend in Taiwan. Although sales boomed immediately after opening, low pedestrian traffic by the site eventually led to disappointing revenues. Over time, conflict arose over day-to-day management issues between the Jollibee operations staff assigned to maintain local oversight and the Taiwanese partner. "Because the business is basically operations, we felt we had to back our experienced Jollibee operations guy, but the partner was saying, 'I'm your partner, I've put in equity. Who do you trust?'" When the property market in Taiwan took off and store rent increased dramatically, Jollibee decided to dissolve the partnership and pulled out of Taiwan in 1988.

Brunei. Meanwhile, a joint venture opened in August 1987 in the small sultanate of Brunei, located on the northern side of the island of Borneo, was prospering. (Exhibit 5 shows the locations of Jollibee International stores as of mid-1997.) TTC had responded to a proposal from the CEO of Shoemart, one of the Philippines' largest department stores, that Jollibee form a joint-venture with a Shoemart partner in Brunei. By the end of 1993, with four successful stores in Brunei, TTC identified a key difference in the Brunei entry strategy: "In Singapore and Taiwan, the local partners ran the operation, while we provided just technical support. In Brunei, the local investor was a silent partner. We sent managers from the Philippines and the local partner supported us."

Indonesia. An opportunity to enter southeast Asia's largest market came through a friend of William Tan, TTC's brother, and the company's VP for Real Estate. in 1989, Jollibee opened its first store, in Jakarta. Initially, the operation struggled, facing competition from street vendors and cheap local fast food chains. When conflict between the local partners and the manager they had hired paralyzed the operation, in late 1994, Jollibee dissolved the partnership and sold the operation to a new franchisee. Nevertheless, the company viewed the market as promising.

Early Lessons
TTC summed up the lessons Jollibee had learned from its first international ventures:

> McDonald's succeeded everywhere they went because they were very good at selecting the right partners. . . . One of the challenges we are still facing internationally is how to get the right partner. We

don't have the name that McDonald's does; they can get 100 candidates and choose the best—we don't have that choice.

> Another key factor in this business is location. If you're an unknown brand entering a new country or city, you have trouble getting access to prime locations. McDonald's name gets it the best sites. People were telling us not to go international until we had solved these two issues: location and partner.

Building an Organization
In 1993, TTC decided that Jollibee's international operations required greater structure and more resources. Because most of his management team was more interested in the fast-growing domestic side of the business, in January 1994, he decided to hire an experienced outsider as Vice President for International Operations. He selected Tony Kitchner, a native of Australia, who had spent 14 years in Pizza Hut's Asia-Pacific regional office in Hong Kong. Reporting directly to TTC, Kitchner asked for the resources and autonomy to create an International Division.

Kitchner felt that his new division needed to be separate from Jollibee's Philippine side, with a different identify and capabilities. He agreed with TTC that attracting partners with good connections in their markets should be a priority, but worried that Jollibee's simple image and basic management approach would hamper these efforts. To project an image of a world-class company, he remodeled his division's offices on the seventh floor of Jollibee's Manila headquarters and instituted the company's first dress code, requiring his managers to wear ties. As one manager explained, "We had to look and act like a multinational not like a local chain. You can't have someone in a short-sleeved open-neck shirt asking a wealthy businessman to invest millions."

Within weeks of his arrival, Kitchner began recruiting experienced internationalists from inside and outside Jollibee. To his inherited three-person staff, he added seven more professionals, three from outside Jollibee—in marketing, finance, and quality control and product development—and four

EXHIBIT 5 Locations of Jollibee International Division Stores, Mid-1997 (countries in which Jollibee had a presence are shaded; cities with Jollibee outlets are underlined)

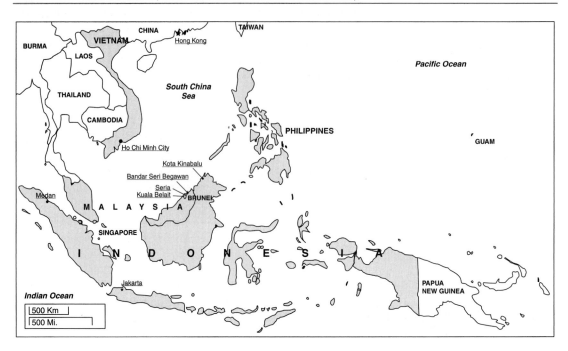

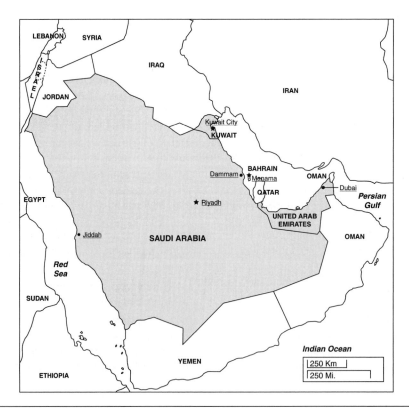

from Jollibee's Philippine side—two in operations, one for training, and one in human resources. The addition of two secretaries rounded out his staff. He claimed that greater internal recruiting had been constrained by two factors—management resistance to having their staff "poached," and by a general lack of interest in joining this upstart division.

Strategic Thrust

While endeavoring to improve the performance of existing stores in Indonesia and Brunei, Kitchner decided to increase the pace of international expansion, a strategy that won TTC's full support. Kitchner's choice of markets rested on two main themes that he had formulated during a planning session in the fall of 1994—"targeting expats" and "planting the flag."

The Division's new chief saw the hundreds of thousands of expatriate Filipinos working in the Middle East, Hong Kong, Guam, and other Asian territories as a latent market for Jollibee. But he saw them as a good initial base of support, not a permanent niche, and aimed eventually to expand Jollibee's appeal to local people and become a full-fledged competitor in each market.

Looking for a new market to test this concept, he focused on the concentrations of Filipino guest-workers in the Middle East. After opening stores in Dubai, Kuwait, and Dammam, however, he found that this market was limited on the lower end by restrictions on poorer workers' freedom of movement, and on the upper end by wealthier expatriates' preference for hotel dining, where they could consume alcohol.

The other strategic criterion for choosing markets rested on Kitchner's belief in first-mover advantages in the fast food industry. Jay Visco, International's Marketing manager, explained:

> We saw that in Brunei, where we were the pioneers in fast food, we were able to set the pace and standards. Now, we have six stores there, while McDonald's has only one and KFC has three. . . . That was a key learning: even if your foreign counterparts come in later, you already have set the pace and are at the top of the heap.

The International Division therefore began to "plant the Jollibee flag" in countries where competitors had little or no presence. The prevailing belief was that the number of stores in a market significantly influenced brand awareness which in turn, strongly impacted sales. The problem with this approach was its circularity: only after achieving critical mass of sales could the local operations support the advertising and promotion needed to build brand awareness; yet advertising was a key tool in building critical mass. The other challenge was that rapid expansion led to resource constraints—especially in International Division staff time.

Due to Jollibee's success in the Philippines and the Tan family's network of acquaintances, Kitchner found he could choose from the many franchising inquiries from businesspeople in various countries. Selection was based on fit with the division's two strategic themes, and, between November 1994 and April 1997, the company opened 19 new stores in 8 new national markets. (See Exhibit 6.)[1]

Operational Management

Market entry. Once Jollibee had decided to enter a new market, Tony Kitchner negotiated the franchise agreement, sometimes with an investment by the parent company, to create a partnership with the franchisee. At that point he handed responsibility for the opening to one of the division's Franchise Services Managers (FSM). About a month before the opening, the FSM hired a project manager, typically a native of the new market who normally would go on to manage the first store. The FSM and project manager made most of the important decisions themselves during this process, with the franchisees' level of involvement varying from country to country. In addition, the FSM coordinated inputs by the International Division's functional specialists and outside vendors, such as architects and construction contractors.

---

[1]Not all planned openings were successful. For example, a plan to open a store in Rumania ("our gateway to Europe," according to one manager) was abandoned due to growing political instability and civil strife.

EXHIBIT 6 Jollibee International Store Openings (new market entries are italicized)

Location	Date Opened	
Bandar Seri Begawan, *Brunei*	August 1987	
Bandar Seri Begawan, Brunei (second store)	June 1989	
Seria, Brunei	August 1992	
Jakarta, *Indonesia*	August 1992	
Jakarta, Indonesia (second store)	March 1993	
Bandar Seri Begawan, Brunei (third store)	November 1993	International Division created
Kuala Belait, Brunei	November 1994	
Dubai, *United Arab Emirates*	April 1995	
Kuwait City, *Kuwait*	December 1995	
Dammam, *Saudi Arabia*	December 1995	
Guam	December 1995	
Jiddah, Saudi Arabia	January 1996	
Bahrain	January 1996	
Kota Kinabalu, *Malaysia*	February 1996	
Dubai (second store)	June 1996	
Riyadh, Saudi Arabia	July 1996	
Kuwait City, Kuwait (second store)	August 1996	
Kuwait City, Kuwait (third store)	August 1996	
Jiddah, Saudi Arabia (second store)	August 1996	
Hong Kong	September 1996	
Bandar Seri Begawan, Brunei (fourth store)	October 1996	
Ho Chi Minh City, *Vietnam*	October 1996	
Medan, Indonesia	December 1996	
Hong Kong (second store)	December 1996	
Dammam, Saudi Arabia	April 1997	
Hong Kong (third store)	June 1997	
Jakarta, Indonesia (third store)	July 1997	
Jakarta, Indonesia (fourth store)	September 1997	

The key first step of selecting and securing the site of the first store was one responsibility in which franchisee was deeply involved, often with advice from International Division staff, who visited the country several times to direct market research. (Sometimes the franchisee had been chosen partly for access to particularly good sites.) Once the franchisee had negotiated the lease or purchase, the project manager began recruiting local store managers.

Jollibee engaged local architects to plan the store. The kitchen followed a standard Jollibee design that ensured proper production flow, but the counter and dining areas could vary according to the demands of the space and the preferences of the franchisee. The FSM reviewed and approved the local architects' plans, paying special attention to seating capacity, electrical requirements, and aspects of design, such as signage and color scheme, that related to brand integrity.

During the planning phase, the project manager worked with International Division finance staff on the budget for raw materials, labor, and other major items in the operation's cost structure. He or she also identified local suppliers, and—once International Division quality assurance staff had accredited their standards—negotiated prices. (Some raw materials and paper goods were sourced centrally and distributed to franchisees throughout Asia.)

Once architectural and engineering plans were approved, construction began. As it often did in other offshore activities, the International Division staff had to develop skills very different from those of their Jollibee colleagues working in the Philippines. For example, high rents in Hong Kong forced them to learn how to manage highly compacted construction schedules: construction there could take one-third to one-half the time required for similar work in the Philippines. During construction, the project manager also worked on sourcing minor equipment from the local area and obtaining permission to import major items, such as stoves.

For each new market, the International Division staff prepared marketing plans for the opening and first year's operation. They included positioning and communications strategies and were based on their advance consumer surveys, aggregate market data, and analysis of major competitors. The Division also trained the local marketing manager and the local store manager and assistant managers who typically spent three months in Philippine stores. (Where appropriate local managers had not been found, the store managers were sometimes drawn from Jollibee's Philippine operations.) Just before opening, the project manager hired crew members, and International Division trainers from Manila instructed them for two weeks on cooking, serving customers, and maintaining the store. (Exhibit 7 shows the organization of a typical Jollibee franchise.)

Oversight and continuing support. After a store opened, the FSM remained its key contact with Jollibee, monitoring financial and operational performance and working to support and develop the store manager. For approximately two months

EXHIBIT 7   Organization of Typical Jollibee International Franchise

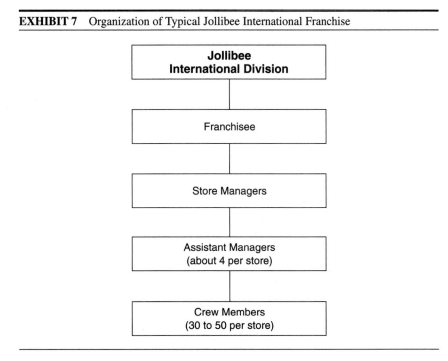

after opening, FSMs required stores in their jurisdictions to fax them every day their figures for sales by product, customer traffic, and average ticket. As operations stabilized and the store manager started to see patterns to sales and operational needs, FSMs allowed stores to report the same data weekly and provide a monthly summary.

FSMs used this information not only to project and track royalty income for corporate purpose, but also to identify ways they could support the local franchisee. When the data suggested problems, the FSM would contact the store manager, highlight the issue, and ask for an appropriate plan of action. For example, if FSM Gina Buan saw a decline in sales for two consecutive weeks, she demanded specific plans within 24 hours of her call. If managers could not come up with solutions themselves, she would coach them to help them generate answers. "My aim," she remarked with a smile, "is to turn them into clones of me—or at least teach them my expertise."

In addition to the required sales reports, many stores reported voluntarily on their costs, because they found FSM's analysis so helpful. This openness fit with TTC's view of franchise relations. "We get data from franchisees more to help us provide consulting assistance than for control," he said. If a store required more specialized support, the FSM might arrange for Division staff assistance, or might suggest that store management attend one of the courses that the Division offered. Ernesto Tan, TTC's brother and Jollibee's Executive Vice President, explained that although Jollibee's royalty was a percentage of franchisees' sales, and local operations were focused more on profits, their interests were similar: "We want sales to grow, so that our royalty grows. But this will not happen if stores are not profitable, because franchisees will not push to expand."

TTC acknowledged that International Division was concerned with control, as well as support: "We try to keep close control of day-to-day operations, especially quality." Unannounced on-site inspections every quarter were Jollibee's primary tool. Over two days, the FSM evaluated every aspect of operations in detail, including product quality and preparation (taste, temperature, freshness, availability, and appearances), cleanliness, restaurant appearance, service speed, and friendliness. The manual for intensive checks was several inches thick. All international staff had been trained in Jollibee's quality standards and conducted less detailed "quick checks" whenever they traveled. Based on a 15-page questionnaire, a quick check took roughly two hours to complete and covered all of the areas that intensive ones did, although with less rigor and detail. Each store received an average of two quick checks per quarter.

In addition to their own typically rich industry experiences—Gina Buan, for example, had managed stores, districts, and countries for Jollibee and another chain—FSMs could draw on the expertise of International Division functional staff. While they tried to shift responsibility to the franchisee, the staff groups often bore much of the responsibility long after startup. For example, the marketing staff tried to limit their role to developing general international marketing strategy, creating initial marketing plans for new openings, and responding to franchisee request to review new store plans. However, often they were drawn into the planning of more routine campaigns for particular stores, work they felt should be handled by the franchisee and store managers.

International vs. domestic practice. As operations grew, Kitchner and his staff discovered that international expansion was not quite as simple as the metaphor of "planting flags" might suggest. It sometimes felt more like struggling up an unconquered, hostile mountain. After numerous market entry battles, the international team decided that a number of elements of Jollibee's Philippine business model needed to be modified overseas. For example, the company's experience in Indonesia led Visco to criticize the transplantation of Jollibee's "mass-based positioning":

> When Jollibee arrived in Indonesia, they assumed that the market would be similar to the Philippines. But the Indonesian masses are not willing to spend as

much on fast food as the Philippine working and lower-middle class consumers, and there were lots of cheap alternatives available. We decided to target a more up-market clientele. We learned that we needed to reposition ourselves abroad.

Kitchner and Visco also felt that Jollibee needed to present itself as "world class," not "local." In particular, they disliked the Philippine store design,—a "trellis" theme combined garden motifs with a mural depicting some aspect of the store's environment, such as a school located nearby— which had been transferred unchanged as Jollibee exported internationally. Working with an outside architect, a five-person panel from the International Division developed three new store decors, with better lighting and higher quality furniture. After Kitchner got TTC's approval, the Division remodeled the Indonesian stores and used the designs for all subsequent openings.

International also redesigned the Jollibee logo. While retaining the bee mascot, it changed the red background to orange and added the slogan, "great burgers, great chicken." Visco pointed out that the orange background differentiated the chain's logo from those of other major brands, such as KFC, Coca-Cola, and Marlboro, which all had red-and-white logos. The slogan was added to link the Jollibee name and logo with its products in people's minds. Visco also noted that, unlike Wendy's Old Fashioned Hamburgers, Kentucky Fried Chicken, and Pizza Hut, Jollibee did not incorporate its product in its name and market tests had found that consumers outside the Philippines guessed the logo signified a toy chain or candy store.

Kitchner and his staff made numerous other changes to Jollibee's Philippine model to address operational issues. For example, marketing created a library of promotional photographs of each food product that could be assembled, in-house, into collages illustrating new promotions (e.g., a discounted price for buying a burger, fries, and soda). In the Philippines, each promotion required a separate, expensive photo shoot; the photo library gave the International Division flexibility in designing promotions, without the Philippine side's scale

economies. And purchasing changed from styrofoam to paper packaging to appeal to foreign consumers' greater environmental consciousness.

Customizing for local tastes. While such changes provoked grumbling from many in the large domestic business who saw the upstart international group as newcomers fiddling with proven concepts, nothing triggered more controversy than the experiments with menu items. Arguing that the "flexibility" aspect of Jollibee's "Five Fs" corporate creed stood for a willingness to accommodate differences in customer tastes, managers in the International Division believed that menus should be adjusted to local preferences.

The practice had started in 1992 when a manager was dispatched from the Philippines to respond to the Indonesian franchisee's request to create a fast food version of the local favorite *nasi lema,* a mixture of rice and coconut milk. Building on this precedent, Kitchner's team created an international menu item they called the Jollimeal. This was typically a rice-based meal with a topping that could vary by country—in Hong Kong, for example, the rice was covered with hot and sour chicken, while in Vietnam it was chicken curry. Although it accounted for only 5% of international sales, Kitchner saw Jollimeal as an important way to "localize" the Jollibee image.

But the International Division expanded beyond the Jollimeal concept. In Dubai, in response to the local franchisee's request to create a salad for the menu, product development manager Gil Salvosa spent a night chopping vegetables in his hotel room to create a standard recipe. That same trip, he acquired a recipe for chicken masala from the franchisee's Indian cook, later adapting it to fast food production methods for the Dubai store. The International Division also added idiosyncratic items to menus, such as dried fish, a Malaysian favorite. Since other menu items were seldom removed, these additions generally increased the size of menus abroad.

While adding those new items, Kitchner committed to protecting Jollibee's "core" products,—its specially-flavored hamburgers, fried chicken, and spaghetti—but adapted them to local tastes where necessary. In Guam, for example, to accommodate extra-large local appetites, division staff added a fried egg and two strips of bacon to the Champ's standard large beef patty. And franchisees in the Middle East asked the Division's R&D staff to come up with a spicier version of Jollibee's fried chicken. Although Kentucky Fried Chicken (KFC) was captivating customers with their spicy recipe, R&D staff on the Philippine side objected strenuously. As a compromise, International developed a spicy sauce that customers could add to the standard Jollibee chicken.

Overall, the International Division's modification of menus and products caused considerable tension with the Philippine side of Jollibee. Yet even the most hard-line proponents of product standardization understood that some changes were necessary in certain markets. So while there was no controversy about reformulating hamburgers for Muslim countries to eliminate traces of pork, adding new products or changing existing ones led to major arguments. As a result, International received little cooperation from the larger Philippine research and development staff and customization remained a source of disagreement and friction.

Strained International–Domestic Relations

As the International Division expanded, its relations with the Philippine-based operations seemed to deteriorate. Tensions over menu modifications reflected more serious problems that had surfaced soon after Kitchner began building his international group. Philippine staff saw International as newcomers who, despite their lack of experience in Jollibee, "discarded practices built over 16 years." On the other side, International Division staff reported that they found the Philippine organization bureaucratic and slow-moving. They felt stymied by requirements to follow certain procedures and go through proper channels to obtain assistance.

The two parts of Jollibee continued to operate largely independently, but strained relations gradually eroded any sense of cooperation and reduced

already limited exchanges to a minimum. Some International Division staff felt that the Philippine side, which controlled most of Jollibee's resources, should do more to help their efforts to improve and adapt existing products and practices. Visco recalled that when he wanted assistance designing new packaging, the Philippine marketing manager took the attitude that international could operate separately. Similarly, Salvosa wanted more cooperation on product development from Philippine R&D, but was frustrated by the lengthy discussions and approvals that seemed to be required.

However the domestic side viewed things differently. Executive Vice President Ernesto Tan, who was in charge of Jollibee in the Philippines, recalled:

> The strains came from several things. When International tried to recruit people from the Philippine side, they talked to them directly, without consulting with their superiors. There also was some jealousy on a personal level because the people recruited were immediately promoted to the next level, with better pay and benefits.
>
> The international people also seemed to have a superiority complex. They wanted to do everything differently, so that if their stores did well, they could take all the credit. At one point, they proposed running a store in the Philippines as a training facility, but we thought they also wanted to show us that they could do it better than us. We saw them as lavish spenders while we paid very close attention to costs. Our people were saying, "We are earning the money, and they are spending it!" There was essentially no communication to work out these problems. So we spoke to TTC, because Kitchner reported to him.

Matters grew worse throughout 1996. One of the first signs of serious trouble came during a project to redesign the Jollibee logo, which TTC initiated in mid-1995. Triggered by International's modification of the old logo, the redesign project committee had representatives from across the company. Having overseen International's redesign, Kitchner was included. During the committee's deliberations, some domestic managers felt that the International vice-president's strong opinions were obstructive and early in 1996 Kitchner stopped attending the meetings.

During the time, TTC was growing increasingly concerned with the performance of the International Division. Around November 1996, he decided that he could no longer support Kitchner's strategy of rapid expansion due to the continuing financial problems it was creating. Many of the International stores were not profitable, and despite the fact that even unprofitable stores generated franchise fees calculated as a percentage of sales, TTC was uncomfortable:

> Kitchner wanted to put up lots of stores, maximizing revenue for Jollibee. Initially, I had supported this approach, thinking we could learn from an experienced outsider, but I came to believe that was not viable in the long term. We preferred to go slower, making sure that each store was profitable so that it would generate money for the franchisee, as well as for us. In general, we believe that whoever we do business with—suppliers and especially franchisees—should make money. This creates a good, long-term relationship.

In February 1997, Kitchner left Jollibee to return to Australia. A restructuring supervised directly by TTC shrank the International Division's staff from 32 to 14, merging the finance, MIS and human resources functions with their bigger Philippine counterparts. (Exhibits 8 and 9 compare organization charts before and after the restructuring.) Jay Visco became interim head of the remaining International Division staff while TTC searched for a new Division leader.

A New International Era: 1997

In the wake of Kitchner's departure, TTC consulted intensively with Jollibee's suppliers and other contacts in fast food in the Philippines regarding a replacement. The name that kept recurring was Manolo P. ("Noli") Tingzon, one of the industry's most experienced managers. Although based in the Philippines his entire career, Tingzon had spent much of this time helping foreign chains cracks the

Philippine market. In 1981 he joined McDonald's as a management trainee and spent the next 10 years in frustrating combat with Jollibee. After a brief experience with a food packaging company, in 1994 he took on the challenge to launch Texas Chicken, another U.S. fast food chain, in its Philippines entry. When TTC contacted him in late 1996, he was intrigued by the opportunity offered by his old nemesis and joined the company in July 1997 as general manager, International Division.

A Fresh Look at Strategy

Upon his arrival, Tingzon reviewed International's current and historical performance. (See Exhibit 10 for current performance data.) He concluded that because of the scale economies of fast food franchising, an "acceptable" return on investment in international operations would require 60 Jollibee restaurants abroad with annual sales of U.S. $800,000 each, the approximate store level sales at McDonald's smaller Asian outlets. Feeling that Jollibee's international expansion had sometimes been driven less by business considerations than by a pride in developing overseas operations, Tingzon thought that a fresh examination of existing international strategies might reveal opportunities for improvement. As he consulted colleagues at Jollibee, however, he heard differing opinions.

Many of his own staff felt that the rapid expansion of the "planting-the-flag" approach had served Jollibee well and should be continued. Visco argued that establishing a presence in each market before other competitors conferred important first-mover advantages in setting customer expectations, building brand, and gaining share. He and others felt that Jollibee's success in the Philippines and Brunei illustrated this point especially well. Because heavyweight competitors were expanding rapidly in east Asia, they urged continued aggressive expansion.

Others, particularly on Jollibee's domestic side, felt the flag-planting strategy was ill-conceived, leading the company into what they saw as rash market choices such as the Middle East, where outlets continued to have difficulty attracting expatriate or local customers. For example, Ernesto Tan

EXHIBIT 8   International Division Organization Chart, Late 1996 (pre-restructuring)

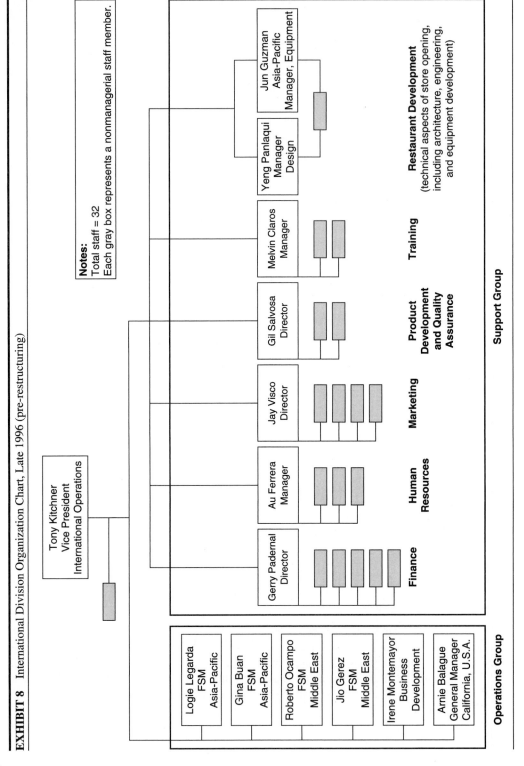

EXHIBIT 9 International Division Organization Chart, March 1997 (post-restructuring)

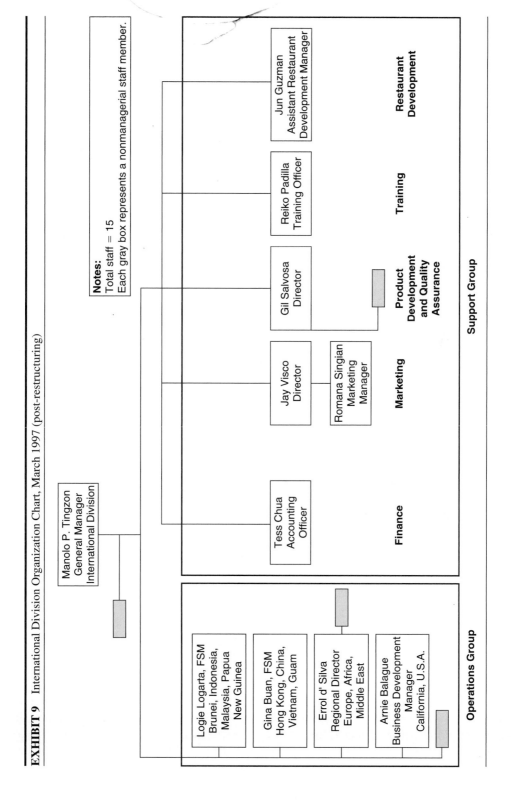

Manolo P. Tingzon
General Manager
International Division

Notes:
Total staff = 15
Each gray box represents a nonmanagerial staff member.

Tess Chua
Accounting
Officer

Finance

Jay Visco
Director

Romana Singian
Marketing
Manager

Marketing

Gil Salvosa
Director

**Product
Development
and Quality
Assurance**

Reiko Padilla
Training Officer

Training

Jun Guzman
Assistant Restaurant
Development Manager

**Restaurant
Development**

Support Group

Logie Logarta, FSM
Brunei, Indonesia,
Malaysia, Papua
New Guinea

Gina Buan, FSM
Hong Kong, China,
Vietnam, Guam

Errol d' Silva
Regional Director
Europe, Africa,
Middle East

Arnie Balague
Business Development
Manager
California, U.S.A.

Operations Group

69

EXHIBIT 10   International Store Sales by Country: 1996 (in U.S. dollars at contemporary exchange rates)

	1996	
	Sales	*Number of Stores*
Bahrain	262,361	1
Brunei	2,439,538	6
Guam	1,771,202	1
Hong Kong	1,142,240	2
Indonesia	854,259	3
Kuwait	864,531	3
Malaysia	391,328	1
Saudi Arabia	976,748	4
United Arab Emirates	487,438	2
Vietnam	112,578	1
Total	U.S.$ 9,302,223	24

advised Tingzon to "focus on building share in a few countries while making sure each store does well." He urged Tingzon to focus on existing Jollibee markets that had either high profit potential, such as Hong Kong, or relatively mild competition, such as Malaysia and Indonesia.

With respect to focusing on Filipino expatriates as an initial customer base in new markets, Tingzon appreciated that this approach had eased Jollibee's entry into Guam and Hong Kong, but wondered whether it might trap the chain. "Might we risk boxing ourselves into a Filipino niche that prevents us from growing enough to support operations in each country?" he asked. Depending on who he talked to, he was urged to favor one of two choices: Approach new markets by first targeting expatriates, through site choices and marketing, and then expand its target to the whole market. Or target locals immediately rather than risk being pigeonholed as a Philippine chain.

Tingzon also had concerns about the internal tensions customization had caused. Philippine managers explained their concern that customization could erode the coherence of Jollibee's brand, make quality control more difficult, and reduce economies of scale in raw materials sourcing and marketing. However, he also recognized the legiti-

macy of his international staff's arguments and local franchisees urging for the need to respond to local cultural difference and taste preferences.

Strategy in Action: Three Decisions

Although he eventually wanted to resolve these strategic and organizational questions at the level of policy, Tingzon faced three immediate growth opportunities that he knew would shape the emergence of the future strategy.

Papua New Guinea: Raising the standard.   In early 1996, at the recommendation of Quality Assurance Manager Gil Salvosa, a local New Guinea entrepreneur in the poultry business approached Tony Kitchner about a Jollibee franchise. He described a country of five million people served by only one poorly managed, three-store fast food chain, that had recently broken ties with its Australian chicken restaurant franchise. "Port Moresby does not have a single decent place to eat," he told Tingzon. He believed Jollibee could raise the quality of service and food enough to take much of the Australian chain's market share while discouraging further entrants.

Although the original plan had been to open just one store in the foreseeable future—in the capital,

Port Moresby—Tingzon was certain that the franchisee could only cover the costs of developing the market if he put in three or four stores over the next three years. But he was uncertain whether Papua New Guinea could support the 20 stores that he was viewing as the target for critical market mass. (For comparison, in the Philippines, approximately 1,200 fast food outlets competed for the business of 75 million people. GNP per capita in both countries was almost identical at U.S.$2,500.)

When Tingzon explained his concerns, the would-be franchisee's response was that he would negotiate with a major petroleum retailer to open stores in five of their service stations around the country. Furthermore, he emphasized that he was willing to build more stores if necessary and would put up all the capital so that Jollibee would risk no equity in the venture.

Hong Kong: Expanding the base. Also on Tingzon's plate was a proposal to expand to a fourth store in Hong Kong. The franchise, owned by Jollibee in partnership with local businessmen, opened its first store in September 1996 to instant, overwhelming success. Located near a major transit hub in the Central district and in a mall full of stores selling Philippine products, it became a gathering place for Filipino expatriates. However, appealing to the locals had proven more difficult. While volume was high on weekends, when Filipino domestic workers came to Central to socialize, it fell off during the week, when business was primarily from local office workers.

One problem was that, despite strenuous efforts, Jollibee had been unable to hire many local Chinese as crew members. According to one manager, Chinese customers who did not speak English well were worried that their orders might not be understood by the predominantly Philippine and Nepalese counter staff and that they would be embarrassed. Another problem was that in a city dominated by McDonald's, Jollibee's brand recognition among locals was weak. Although two more Jollibee stores in Central had attracted many Filipinos,

they were less well located than the first store, and generated sales of only about one-third of the first outlet. Working with sub-franchisee Henry Shih, who owned the second store, a Jollibee project officer was trying to help launch a thematic advertising campaign, but due to the Hong Kong operation's small size, the franchise could not inject sufficient funds.

Shih also blamed rigidity over menu offerings for Jollibee's difficulties appealing to Chinese customers. In early 1997, his Chinese managers had suggested serving tea the Hong Kong way—using tea dust (powdered tea leaves) rather than tea bags and adding evaporated milk. "Tommy King (the joint venture's managing director) said he liked using tea bags, and Manila said they would look into it," Shih recalled. More than six months later, he had still not received a go-ahead. His proposals to develop a less-fatty chicken recipe had met more direct resistance. "The Chinese say that if you eat lots of deep-fried food you become hot inside and will develop skin problems and other ailments." He felt the International Division had been receptive, but believed that the domestic side had pressured them to reject any experimentation with this "core" menu item.

Meanwhile, staffing problems were worsening. The four locally recruited Chinese managers clashed with the five Filipinos imported from King's Philippine stores, with the Chinese calling the Filipinos' discipline lax and their style arrogant, while the Filipinos saw the Chinese managers as uncommitted. By August 1977, all of the Chinese managers had resigned, leaving Jollibee with only Filipinos in store-level management positions. Shih was afraid this would further undermine Jollibee's ability to hire local crews, as Chinese preferred to work for Chinese.

Partly due to staff turnover, store managers were focused on dealing with day-to-day operations issues such as uneven product quality and had little time to design even short-term marketing strategies. King's focus on his Philippine stores slowed decision-making. And while Buan, the FSM, had visited Hong Kong more often than any other markets she supervised (including for an extraordinary month-long stay), she had been unable to resolve the management problems. In June, King appointed Shih General Manager to oversee the entire Hong Kong venture.

In this context, Shih and King proposed to open a fourth store. The site in the Kowloon district was one of the busiest in Hong Kong, located at one of just two intersections of the subway and the rail line that was the only public transport from the New Territories, where much of the city's workforce resided. However, the area saw many fewer Filipinos than Central and the store would have to depend on locals. Acknowledging that the fourth store would test Jollibee's ability to appeal to Hong Kong people, Shih argued that the menu would have to be customized more radically. However, Tingzon wondered whether expansion was even viable at this time, given the Hong Kong venture's managerial capacity. Even if he were to approve the store, he wondered if he should support the menu variations that might complicate quality control. On the other hand, expansion into such a busy site might enhance Jollibee's visibility and brand recognition among locals, helping increase business even without changing the menu. It was another tough call.

California: Supporting the settlers.   Soon after signing his contract, Tingzon had learned of a plan to open one Jollibee store per quarter in California starting in the first quarter of 1998. Supporting TTC's long-held belief that Jollibee could win enormous prestige and publicity by gaining a foothold in the birthplace of fast food, Kitchner had drawn up plans with a group of Manila-based businessmen as 40% partners in the venture. Once the company stores were established, they hoped to franchise in California and beyond in 1999.

Much of the confidence for this bold expansion plan came from Jollibee's success in Guam, a territory of the U.S. Although they initially targeted Filipinos, management discovered that their menu appealed to other groups of Americans based there. They also found they could adapt the labor-intensive

Philippine operating methods by developing different equipment and cooking processes more in keeping with a high labor cost environment. In the words of one International Division veteran, "In Guam, we learned how to do business in the United States. After succeeding there, we felt we were ready for the mainland."

The plan called for the first wave of stores to be located in the San Francisco and Los Angeles areas, in communities with large Filipino populations but relatively low concentrations of fast food competitors. (California had one of the highest concentrations of Filipino expatriates in the world.) The menu would be transplanted from the Philippines without changes. After initially targeting Filipinos, the plan was to branch out to appeal to other Asian Americans and, eventually, Hispanic Americans. On the basis of this solid foundation, the hope was that Jollibee would then expand to the all-American consumers.

Like the expansion strategies in PNG and Hong Kong, this project had momentum behind it, not least of which was TTC's public support. Yet Tingzon realized that he would be the one held accountable for its final success and wanted to bring an objective outsider's perspective to this plans. Could Jollibee hope to succeed in the world's most competitive fast food market? Could they provide the necessary support and control to operations located 12 hours by plane and nine time zones away? And was the Filipino-to-Asian-to-Hispanic-to-mainstream entry strategy viable or did it risk boxing them into an economically unviable niche?

Looking Forward

Noli Tingzon had only been in his job a few weeks, but already a few things were clear. First, he saw his predecessor's ambition to become one of the top 10 global food service brands by the year 2000 as a pipe dream—particularly when viewed in the light of Kitchner's plans to open 1,000 Jollibee stores abroad before the turn of the century. But that did not mean the new International Division president was not bold or ambitious. "It took McDonald's 20 years for its international division to count for more than 50% of total sales," he said. "I'll be happy if I can do it in 10."

The big question was how to grow to account for half Jollibee's sales. The decisions he made on the three entry options before him would have a significant impact on the strategic direction his international division took and on the organizational capabilities it needed to get there.

Reading 1–1

THE TORTUOUS EVOLUTION OF THE MULTINATIONAL CORPORATION

Howard V. Perlmutter

Four senior executives of the world's largest firms with extensive holdings outside the home country speak:

Company A: "We are a multinational firm. We distribute our products in about 100 countries. We manufacture in over 17 countries and do research and development in three countries. We look at all new investment projects—both domestic and overseas—using exactly the same criteria."

Company B: "We are a multinational firm. Only 1% of the personnel in our affiliate companies are non-nationals. Most of these are U.S. executives on temporary assignments. In all major markets, the affiliate's managing director is of the local nationality."

Company C: "We are a multinational firm. Our product division executives have worldwide profit responsibility. As our organizational chart shows,

Trained as an engineer and a psychologist, Howard V. Perlmutter spent eight years at M.I.T.'s Center for International Studies and five years at the Institut pour l'Etude des Methodes de Direction de l'Enterprise (IMEDE) in Lausanne, Switzerland. His main interests are in the theory and practice of institution building, particularly the international corporation. He has recently been appointed Director for Research and Development of Worldwide Institutions in association with the Management Science Center at the University of Pennsylvania, as well as a member of the faculty at the Wharton School.

the United States is just one region on a par with Europe, Latin America, Africa, etc., in each product division."

Company D (non-American): "We are a multinational firm. We have at least 18 nationalities represented at our headquarters. Most senior executives speak at least two languages. About 30% of our staff at headquarters are foreigners."

While a claim to multinationality based on their years of experience and the significant proportion of sales generated overseas is justified in each of these four companies, a more penetrating analysis changes the image.

The executive from Company A tells us that most of the key posts in Company A's subsidiaries are held by home-country nationals. Whenever replacements for these men are sought, it is the practice, if not the policy, to "look next to you at the head office" and "pick someone (usually a home-country national) you know and trust."

The executive from Company B does not hide the fact that there are very few non-Americans in the key posts at headquarters. The few who are there are "so Americanized" that their foreign nationality literally has no meaning. His explanation for this paucity of non-Americans seems reasonable enough: "You can't find good foreigners who are willing to live in the United States, where our headquarters is located. American executives are more mobile. In addition, Americans have the drive and initiative we like. In fact, the European nationals would prefer to report to an American rather than to some other European."

The executive from Company C goes on to explain that the worldwide product division concept is rather difficult to implement. The senior executives in charge of these divisions have little overseas experience. They have been promoted from domestic posts and tend to view foreign consumer needs "as really basically the same as ours." Also, product division executives tend to focus on the domestic market because the domestic market is larger and generates more revenue than the fragmented European markets. The rewards are for global performance, but the strategy is to focus on domestic. His colleagues say "one pays attention to what one understands—and our senior executives simply do not understand what happens overseas and really do not trust foreign executives in key positions here or overseas."

The executive from the European Company D begins by explaining that since the voting shareholders must by law come from the home country, the home country's interest must be given careful consideration. In the final analysis he insists: "We are proud of our nationality; we shouldn't be ashamed of it." He cites examples of the previous reluctance of headquarters to use home-country ideas overseas, to their detriment, especially in their U.S. subsidiary. "Our country produces good executives, who tend to stay with us a long time. It is harder to keep executives from the United States."

A Rose by Any Other Name . . .

Why quibble about how multinational a firm is? To these executives, apparently being multinational is prestigious. They know that multinational firms tend to be regarded as more progressive, dynamic, geared to the future than provincial companies which avoid foreign frontiers and their attendant risks and opportunities.

It is natural that these senior executives would want to justify the multinationality of their enterprise, even if they use different yardsticks: ownership criteria, organizational structure, nationality of senior executives, percent of investment overseas, etc.

Two hypotheses seem to be forming in the minds of executives from international firms that make the extent of their firm's multinationality of real interest. The first hypothesis is that the degree of multinationality of an enterprise is positively related to the firm's long-term viability. The "multinational" category makes sense for executives if it means a quality of decision making which leads to survival, growth and profitability in our evolving world economy.

The second hypothesis stems from the proposition that the multinational corporation is a new kind of institution—a new type of industrial social architecture particularly suitable for the latter third of the twentieth century. This type of institution could make a valuable contribution to world order and conceivably exercise a constructive impact on the nation-state. Some executives want to understand how to create an institution whose presence is considered legitimate and valuable in each nation-state. They want to prove that the greater the degree of multinationality of a firm, the greater its total constructive impact will be on host and home nation-states as well as other institutions. Since multinational firms may produce a significant proportion of the world's GNP, both hypotheses justify a more precise analysis of the varieties and degrees of multinationality.[1] However, the confirming evidence is limited.

State of Mind

Part of the difficulty in defining the degree of multinationality comes from the variety of parameters along which a firm doing business overseas can be

---

[1]H. V. Perlmutter, "Super-Giant Firms in the Future," *Wharton Quarterly,* Winter 1968.

described. The examples from the four companies argue that (1) no single criterion of multinationality such as ownership or the number of nationals overseas is sufficient, and that (2) external and quantifiable measures such as the percentage of investment overseas or the distribution of equity by nationality are useful but not enough. The more one penetrates into the living reality of an international firm, the more one finds it is necessary to give serious weight to the way executives think about doing business around the world. The orientation toward "foreign people, ideas, resources," in headquarters and subsidiaries, and in host and home environments, becomes crucial in estimating the multinationality of a firm. To be sure, such external indices as the proportion of nationals in different countries holding equity and the number of foreign nationals who have reached top positions, including president, are good indices of multinationality. But one can still behave with a home-country orientation despite foreign shareholders, and one can have a few home-country nationals overseas but still pick those local executives who are home-country oriented or who are provincial and chauvinistic. The attitudes men hold are clearly more relevant than their passports.

Three primary attitudes among international executives toward building a multinational enterprise are identifiable. These attitudes can be inferred from the assumptions upon which key product, functional and geographical decisions were made.

These states of mind or attitudes may be described as ethnocentric (or home-country oriented), polycentric (or host-country oriented) and geocentric (or world-oriented).[2] While they never appear in pure form, they are clearly distinguishable. There is some degree of ethnocentricity, polycentricity or geocentricity in all firms, but management's analysis does not usually correlate with public pronouncements about the firm's multinationality.

----

[2]H. V. Perlmutter, "Three Conceptions of a World Enterprise," *Revue Economique et Sociale,* May 1965.

Home-Country Attitudes

The ethnocentric attitude can be found in companies of any nationality with extensive overseas holdings. The attitude, revealed in executive actions and experienced by foreign subsidiary managers, is: "We, the home nationals of X company, are superior to, more trustworthy and more reliable than any foreigners in headquarters or subsidiaries. We will be willing to build facilities in your country if you acknowledge our inherent superiority and accept our methods and conditions for doing the job."

Of course, such attitudes are never so crudely expressed, but they often determine how a certain type of "multinational" firm is designed. Table 1 illustrates how ethnocentric attitudes are expressed in determining the managerial process at home and overseas. For example, the ethnocentric executive is more apt to say: "Let us manufacture the simple products overseas. Those foreign nationals are not yet ready or reliable. We should manufacture the complex products in our country and keep the secrets among our trusted home-country nationals."

In a firm where ethnocentric attitudes prevailed, the performance criteria for men and products are "home-made." "We have found that a salesman should make 12 calls per day in Hoboken, New Jersey (the headquarters location), and therefore we apply these criteria everywhere in the world. The salesman in Brazzaville is naturally lazy, unmotivated. He shows little drive because he makes only two calls per day (despite the Congolese salesman's explanation that it takes time to reach customers by boat)."

Ethnocentric attitudes are revealed in the communication process where "advice," "counsel," and directives flow from headquarters to the subsidiary in a steady stream, bearing this message: "This works at home; therefore, it must work in your country."

Executives in both headquarters and affiliates express the national identity of the firm by associating the company with the nationality of the headquarters: this is "a Swedish company," "a Swiss

TABLE 1   Three Types of Headquarters Orientation toward Subsidiaries in an International Enterprise

Organization Design	Ethnocentric	Polycentric	Geocentric
Complexity of organization	Complex in home country, simple in subsidiaries	Varied and independent	Increasingly complex and interdependent
Authority; decision making	High in headquarters	Relatively low in headquarters	Aim for a collaborative approach between headquarters and subsidiaries
Evaluation and control	Home standards applied for persons and performance	Determined locally	Find standards which are universal and local
Rewards and punishments; incentives	High in headquarters, low in subsidiaries	Wide variation; can be high or low rewards for subsidiary performance	International and local executives rewarded for reaching local and worldwide objectives
Communication; information flow	High volume to subsidiaries; orders, commands, advice	Little to and from headquarters. Little between subsidiaries	Both ways and between subsidiaries. Heads of subsidiaries part of management team
Identification	Nationality of owner	Nationality of host country	Truly international company but identifying with national interests
Perpetuation (recruiting, staffing, development)	Recruit and develop people of home country for key positions everywhere in the world	Develop people of local nationality for key positions in their own country	Develop best men everywhere in the world for key positions everywhere in the world

company," "an American company," depending on the location of headquarters. "You have to accept the fact that the only way to reach a senior post in our firm," an English executive in a U.S. firm said, "is to take out an American passport."

Crucial to the ethnocentric concept is the current policy that men of the home nationality are recruited and trained for key positions everywhere in the world. Foreigners feel like "second-class" citizens.

There is no international firm today whose executives will say that ethnocentrism is absent in their company. In the firms whose multinational investment began a decade ago, one is more likely to hear, "We are still in a transitional stage from our ethnocentric era. The traces are still around! But we are making progress."

Host-Country Orientation

Polycentric firms are those which, by experience or by the inclination of a top executive (usually one of the founders), begin with the assumption that host-country cultures are different and that foreigners are difficult to understand. Local people know what is best for them, and the part of the firm which is located in the host country should be as "local in identity" as possible. The senior executives at headquarters believe that their multinational enterprise can be held together by good financial controls. A polycentric firm, literally, is a loosely connected group with quasi-independent subsidiaries as centers—more akin to a confederation.

European multinational firms tend to follow this pattern, using a top local executive who is strong and trustworthy, of the "right" family and who has an intimate understanding of the workings of the host government. This policy seems to have worked until the advent of the Common Market.

Executives in the headquarters of such a company are apt to say: "Let the Romans do it their way. We really don't understand what is going on there, but we have to have confidence in them. As long as they earn a profit, we want to remain in the background." They assume that since people are different in each country, standards for performance, incentives and training methods must be different. Local environmental factors are given greater weight (see Table 1).

Many executives mistakenly equate polycentrism with multinationalism. This is evidenced in the legalistic definition of a multinational enterprise as a cluster of corporations of diverse nationality joined together by ties of common ownership. It is no accident that many senior executives in headquarters take pride in the absence of non-nationals in their subsidiaries, especially people from the head office. The implication is clearly that each subsidiary is a distinct national entity, since it is incorporated in a different sovereign state. Lonely senior executives in the subsidiaries of polycentric companies complain that: "The home office never tells us anything."

Polycentrism is not the ultimate form of multinationalism. It is a landmark on a highway. Polycentrism is encouraged by local marketing managers

who contend that: "Headquarters will never understand us, our people, our consumer needs, our laws, our distribution, etc. . . ."

Headquarters takes pride in the fact that few outsiders know that the firm is foreign-owned. "We want to be a good local company. How many Americans know that Shell and Lever Brothers are foreign-owned?"

But the polycentric personnel policy is also revealed in the fact that no local manager can seriously aspire to a senior position at headquarters. "You know the French are so provincial; it is better to keep them in France. Uproot them and you are in trouble," a senior executive says to justify the paucity of non-Americans at headquarters.

One consequence (and perhaps cause) of polycentrism is a virulent ethnocentrism among the country managers.

A World-Oriented Concept

The third attitude which is beginning to emerge at an accelerating rate is geocentrism. Senior executives with this orientation do not equate superiority with nationality. Within legal and political limits, they seek the best men, regardless of nationality, to solve the company's problems anywhere in the world. The senior executives attempt to build an organization in which the subsidiary is not only a good citizen of the host nation but is a leading exporter from this nation in the international community and contributes such benefits as (1) an increasing supply of hard currency, (2) new skills and (3) a knowledge of advanced technology. Geocentrism is summed up in a Unilever board chairman's statement of objectives: "We want to Unileverize our Indians and Indianize our Unileverans."

The ultimate goal of geocentrism is a worldwide approach in both headquarters and subsidiaries. The firm's subsidiaries are thus neither satellites nor independent city states, but parts of a whole whose focus is on worldwide objectives as well as local objectives, each part making its unique contribution with its unique competence. Geocentrism is expressed by function, product and geography. The question asked in headquarters and the subsidiaries is: "Where in the world shall we raise money, build our plant, conduct R&D, get and launch new ideas to serve our present and future customers?"

This conception of geocentrism involves a collaborative effort between subsidiaries and headquarters to establish universal standards and permissible local variations, to make key allocational decisions on new products, new plants, new laboratories. The international management team includes the affiliate heads.

Subsidiary managers must ask: "Where in the world can I get the help to serve my customers best in this country?" "Where in the world can I export products developed in this country—products which meet worldwide standards as opposed to purely local standards?"

Geocentrism, furthermore, requires a reward system for subsidiary managers which motivates them to work for worldwide objectives, not just to defend country objectives. In firms where geocentrism prevails, it is not uncommon to hear a subsidiary manager say, "While I am paid to defend our interests in this country and to get the best resources for this affiliate, I must still ask myself the question 'Where in the world (instead of where in my country) should we build this plant?'" This approach is still rare today.

In contrast to the ethnocentric and polycentric patterns, communication is encouraged among subsidiaries in geocentric-oriented firms. "It is your duty to help us solve problems anywhere in the world," one chief executive continually reminds the heads of his company's affiliates. (See Table 1.)

The geocentric firm identifies with local company needs. "We aim not to be just a good local company but the best local company in terms of the quality of management and the worldwide (not local) standards we establish in domestic and export production." "If we were only as good as local companies, we would deserve to be nationalized."

The geocentric personnel policy is based on the belief that we should bring in the best man in the world regardless of his nationality. His passport should not be the criterion for promotion.

The EPG Profile

Executives can draw their firm's profile in ethnocentric (E), polycentric (P) and geocentric (G) dimensions. They are called EPG profiles. The degree of ethnocentrism, polycentrism and geocentrism by product, function and geography can be established. Typically R&D often turns out to be more geocentric (truth is universal, perhaps) and less ethnocentric than finance. Financial managers are likely to see their decisions as ethnocentric. The marketing function is more polycentric, particularly in the advanced economies and in the larger affiliate markets.

The tendency toward ethnocentrism in relations with subsidiaries in the developing countries is marked. Polycentric attitudes develop in consumer goods divisions, and ethnocentrism appears to be greater in industrial product divisions. The agreement is almost unanimous in both U.S.- and European-based international firms that their companies are at various stages on a route toward geocentrism but none has reached this state of affairs. Their executives would agree, however, that:

1. A description of their firms as multinational obscures more than it illuminates the state of affairs;
2. The EPG mix, once defined, is a more precise way to describe the point they have reached;
3. The present profile is not static but a landmark along a difficult road to genuine geocentrism;
4. There are forces both to change and to maintain the present attitudinal "mix," some of which are under their control.

Forces Toward and Against

What are the forces that determine the EPG mix of a firm? "You must think of the struggle toward functioning as a worldwide firm as just a beginning—a few steps forward and a step backward," a chief executive puts it. "It is a painful process, and every firm is different."

Executives of some of the world's largest multinational firms have been able to identify a series of external and internal factors that contribute to or hinder the growth of geocentric attitudes and decisions. Table 2 summarizes the factors most frequently mentioned by over 500 executives from at least 17 countries and 20 firms.

From the external environmental side, the growing world markets, the increase in availability of managerial and technological know-how in different countries, global competition and international customers' advances in telecommunications, regional political and economic communities are positive factors, as is the host country's desire to increase its balance-of-payments surplus through the location of export-oriented subsidiaries of international firms within its borders.

In different firms, senior executives see in various degrees these positive factors toward geocentrism: top management's increasing desire to use human and material resources optimally, the observed lowering of morale after decades of ethnocentric practices, the evidence of waste and duplication under polycentric thinking, the increased awareness and respect for good men of other than the home nationality, and, most importantly, top management's own commitment to building a geocentric firm as evidenced in policies, practices and procedures.

The obstacles toward geocentrism from the environment stem largely from the rising political and economic nationalism in the world today, the suspicions of political leaders of the aims and increasing power of the multinational firm. On the internal side, the obstacles cited most frequently in U.S.-based multinational firms were management's inexperience in overseas markets, mutual distrust between home-country people and foreign executives, the resistance to participation by foreigners in the power structure at headquarters, the increasing difficulty of getting good men overseas to move, nationalistic tendencies in staff, and linguistic and other communication difficulties of a cultural nature.

Any given firm is seen as moving toward geocentrism at a rate determined by its capacities to build on the positive internal factors over which it has control and to change the negative internal factors which are controllable. In some firms the geocentric goal is openly discussed among executives of different nationalities and from different subsidiaries as well as headquarters. There is a consequent improvement in the climate of trust and acceptance of each other's views.

Programs are instituted to assure greater experience in foreign markets, task forces of executives are upgraded, and international careers for executives of all nationalities are being designed.

But the seriousness of the obstacles cannot be underestimated. A world of rising nationalism is hardly a precondition for geocentrism; and overcoming distrust of foreigners even within one's own firm is not accomplished in a short span of time. The route to pervasive geocentric thinking is long and tortuous.

Costs, Risks, Payoffs

What conclusions will executives from multinational firms draw from the balance sheet of advantages and disadvantages of maintaining one's present state of ethnocentrism, polycentrism or geocentrism? Not too surprisingly, the costs and risks of ethnocentrism are seen to out-balance the payoffs in the long run. The costs of ethnocentrism are ineffective planning because of a lack of good feedback, the departure of the best men in the subsidiaries, fewer innovations, and an inability to build a high calibre local organization. The risks are political and social repercussions and a less flexible response to local changes.

The payoffs of ethnocentrism are real enough in the short term, they say. Organization is simpler. There is a higher rate of communication of know-how from headquarters to new markets. There is more control over appointments to senior posts in subsidiaries.

Polycentrism's costs are waste due to duplication, to decisions to make products for local use but

TABLE 2   International Executives' View of Forces and Obstacles toward Geocentrism in Their Firms

Forces toward Geocentrism		Obstacles toward Geocentrism	
Environmental	*Intra-Organizational*	*Environmental*	*Intra-Organizational*
1. Technological and managerial know-how increasing in availability in different countries	1. Desire to use human versus material resources optimally	1. Economic nationalism in host and home countries	1. Management inexperience in overseas markets
2. International customers	2. Observed lowering of morale in affiliates of an ethnocentric company	2. Political nationalism in host and home countries	2. Nation-centered reward and punishment structure
3. Local customers' demand for best product at fair price	3. Evidence of waste and duplication in polycentrism	3. Military secrecy associated with research in home country	3. Mutual distrust between home-country people and foreign executives
4. Host country's desire to increase balance of payments	4. Increasing awareness and respect for good people of other than home nationality	4. Distrust of big international firms by host-country political leaders	4. Resistance to letting foreigners into the power structure
5. Growing world markets	5. Risk diversification in having a worldwide production and distribution system	5. Lack of international monetary system	5. Anticipated costs and risks of geocentrism
6. Global competition among international firms for scarce human and material resources	6. Need for recruitment of good people on a worldwide basis	6. Growing differences between the rich and poor countries	6. Nationalistic tendencies in staff
7. Major advances in integration of international transport and telecommunications	7. Need for worldwide information system	7. Host-country belief that home countries get disproportionate benefits of international firms' profits	7. Increasing immobility of staff
8. Regional supranational economic and political communities	8. Worldwide appeal products	8. Home-country political leaders' attempts to control firm's policy	8. Linguistic problems and different cultural backgrounds
	9. Senior management's long-term commitment to geocentrism as related to survival and growth		9. Centralization tendencies in headquarters

which could be universal, and to inefficient use of home-country experience. The risks include an excessive regard for local traditions and local growth at the expense of global growth. The main advantages are an intense exploitation of local markets, better sales since local management is often better informed, more local initiative for new products, more host-government support, and good local managers with high morale.

Geocentrism's costs are largely related to communication and travel expenses, educational costs at all levels, time spent in decision making because consensus seeking among more people is required, and an international headquarters bureaucracy. Risks include those due to too wide a distribution of power, personnel problems and those of reentry of international executives. The payoffs are a more powerful total company throughout, a better quality of products and service, worldwide utilization of best resources, improvement of local company management, a greater sense of commitment to worldwide objectives, and last, but not least, more profit.

Jacques Maisonrouge, the French-born president of IBM World Trade, understands the geocentric concept and its benefits. He wrote recently:

"The first step to a geocentric organization is when a corporation, faced with the choice of whether to grow and expand or decline, realizes the need to mobilize its resources on a world scale. It will sooner or later have to face the issue that the home country does not have a monopoly of either men or ideas. . . .

"I strongly believe that the future belongs to geocentric companies. . . . What is of fundamental importance is the attitude of the company's top management. If it is dedicated to 'geocentrism,' good international management will be possible. If not, the best men of different nations will soon understand that they do not belong to the 'race des seigneurs' and will leave the business."[3]

_____

[3]Jacques Maisonrouge, "The Education of International Managers," *Quarterly Journal of AIESEC International,* Feburary 1967.

Geocentrism is not inevitable in any given firm. Some companies have experienced a "regression" to ethnocentrism after trying a long period of polycentrism, of letting subsidiaries do it "their way." The local directors built little empires and did not train successors from their own country. Headquarters had to send home-country nationals to take over. A period of home-country thinking took over.

There appears to be evidence of a need for evolutionary movement from ethnocentrism to polycentrism to geocentrism. The polycentric stage is likened to an adolescent protest period during which subsidiary managers gain their confidence as equals by fighting headquarters and proving "their manhood," after a long period of being under headquarters' ethnocentric thumb.

"It is hard to move from a period of headquarters domination to a worldwide management team quickly. A period of letting affiliates make mistakes may be necessary," said one executive.

Window Dressing

In the rush toward appearing geocentric, many U.S. firms have found it necessary to emphasize progress by appointing one or two non-nationals to senior posts—even on occasion to headquarters. The foreigner is often effectively counteracted by the number of nationals around him, and his influence is really small. Tokenism does have some positive effects, but it does not mean geocentrism has arrived.

Window dressing is also a temptation. Here an attempt is made to demonstrate influence by appointing a number of incompetent "foreigners" to key positions. The results are not impressive for either the individuals or the company.

Too often what is called "the multinational view" is really a screen for ethnocentrism. Foreign affiliate managers must, in order to succeed, take on the traits and behavior of the ruling nationality. In short, in a U.S.-owned firm the foreigner must "Americanize"—not only in attitude but in dress and speech—in order to be accepted.

Tokenism and window dressing are transitional episodes where aspirations toward multinationalism outstrip present attitudes and resources. The fault does not lie only with the enterprise. The human demands of ethnocentrism are great.

A Geocentric Man—?

The geocentric enterprise depends on having an adequate supply of men who are geocentrically oriented. It would be a mistake to underestimate the human stresses which a geocentric career creates. Moving where the company needs an executive involves major adjustments for families, wives and children. The sacrifices are often great and, for some families, outweigh the rewards forthcoming—at least in personal terms. Many executives find it difficult to learn new languages and overcome their cultural superiority complexes, national pride and discomfort with foreigners. Furthermore, international careers can be hazardous when ethnocentrism prevails at headquarters. "It is easy to get lost in the world of the subsidiaries and to be 'out of sight, out of mind' when promotions come up at headquarters," as one executive expressed it following a visit to headquarters after five years overseas. To his disappointment, he knew few senior executives. And fewer knew him!

The economic rewards, the challenge of new countries, the personal and professional development that comes from working in a variety of countries and cultures are surely incentives, but companies have not solved by any means the human costs of international mobility to executives and their families.

A firm's multinationality may be judged by the pervasiveness with which executives think geocentrically—by function, marketing, finance, production, R&D, etc., by product division and by country. The takeoff to geocentrism may begin with executives in one function, say marketing, seeking to find a truly worldwide product line. Only when this worldwide attitude extends throughout the firm, in headquarters and subsidiaries, can executives feel that it is becoming genuinely geocentric.

But no single yardstick, such as the number of foreign nationals in key positions, is sufficient to establish a firm's multinationality. The multinational firm's route to geocentrism is still long because political and economic nationalism is on the rise, and, more importantly, since within the firm ethnocentrism and polycentrism are not easy to overcome. Building trust between persons of different nationality is a central obstacle. Indeed, if we are to judge men, as Paul Weiss put it, "by the kind of world they are trying to build," the senior executives engaged in building the geocentric enterprise could well be the most important social architects of the last third of the twentieth century. For the institution they are trying to erect promises a greater universal sharing of wealth and a consequent control of the explosive centrifugal tendencies of our evolving world community.

The geocentric enterprise offers an institutional and supranational framework which could conceivably make war less likely, on the assumption that bombing customers, suppliers and employees is in nobody's interest. The difficulty of the task is thus matched by its worthwhileness. A clearer image of the features of genuine geocentricity is thus indispensable both as a guideline and as an inviting prospect.

Reading 1–2

MANAGING IN A BORDERLESS WORLD

Kenichi Ohmae

Most managers are nearsighted. Even though today's competitive landscape often stretches to a global horizon, they see best what they know best: the customers geographically closest to home. These managers may have factories or laboratories in a dozen countries. They may have joint ventures in a dozen more. They may source materials and sell in markets all over the world. But when push comes to shove, their field of vision is dominated by home-country customers and the organizational units that serve them. Everyone—and everything—else is simply part of "the rest of the world."

This nearsightedness is not intentional. No responsible manager purposefully devises or implements an astigmatic strategy. But by the same token, too few managers consciously try to set plans and build organizations as if they saw all key customers equidistant from the corporate center. Whatever the trade figures show, home markets are usually in focus; overseas markets are not.

Effective global operations require a genuine equidistance of perspective. But even with the best will in the world, managers find that kind of vision hard to develop—and harder to maintain. Not long ago, the CEO of a major Japanese capital-goods producer canceled several important meetings to attend the funeral of one of his company's local dealers. When I asked him if he would have done the same for a Belgian dealer, one who did a larger volume of business each year than his late counterpart in Japan, the unequivocal answer was no. Perhaps headquarters would have had the relevant European manager send a letter of condolence. No more than that. In Japan, however, tradition dictated the CEO's presence. But Japanese tradition isn't everything, I reminded him. After all, he was the head of a global, not just a Japanese organization. By violating the principle of equidistance, his attendance underscored distinctions among dealers. He was sending the wrong signals and reinforcing the wrong values. Poor vision has consequences.

It may be unfamiliar and awkward, but the primary rule of equidistance is to see—and to think—global first. Honda, for example, has manufacturing divisions in Japan, North America, and Europe—all three legs of the Triad—but its managers do not think or act as if the company were divided between Japanese and overseas operations. Indeed, the very word *overseas* has no place in Honda's vocabulary because the corporation sees itself as equidistant from all its key customers. At Casio, the top managers gather information directly from each of their primary markets and then sit down together once a month to lay out revised plans for global product development.

There is no single best way to avoid or overcome nearsightedness. An equidistant perspective can take many forms. However managers do it, however they get there, building a value system that emphasizes seeing and thinking globally is the bottom-line price of admission to today's borderless economy.

A Geography without Borders

On a political map, the boundaries between countries are as clear as ever. But on a competitive map, a map showing the real flows of financial and industrial activity, those boundaries have largely disappeared. What has eaten them away is the persistent, ever speedier flow of information—information that governments previously monopolized, cooking it up as they saw fit and redistributing in forms of their own devising. Their monopoly of knowledge about things happening around the world enabled them to fool, mislead, or control the people because only the governments possessed real facts in anything like real time.

Today, of course, people everywhere are more and more able to get the information they want directly from all corners of the world. They can see for themselves what the tastes and preferences are in other countries, the styles of clothing now in fashion, the sports, the lifestyles. In Japan, for example, our leaders can no longer keep the people in substandard housing because we now know—directly—how people elsewhere live. We now travel abroad. In fact, ten million Japanese travel abroad annually these days. Or we can sit in our living rooms at home, watch CNN, and know instantaneously what is happening in the United States. During 1988, nearly 90% of all Japanese honeymooners went abroad. This kind of fact is hard to ignore. The government now seriously recognizes that it has built plants and offices but has failed to meet the needs of its young people for relaxation and recreation. So, for the first time in 2,000 years, our people are revolting against their government and telling it what it must do for them. This would have been unthinkable when only a small, official elite controlled access to all information.

In the past, there were gross inefficiencies—some purposeful, some not—in the flow of information around the world. New technologies are eliminating those inefficiencies, and, with them, the opportunity for a kind of top-down information arbitrage—that is, the ability of a government to benefit itself or powerful special interests at the expense of its people by following policies that would never win their support if they had unfettered access to all relevant information. A government could, for example, protect weak industries for fear of provoking social unrest over unemployment. That is less easy to do now, for more of its people have become cosmopolitan and have their own sources of information. They know what such a policy would cost them.

In Korea, students demonstrate in front of the American embassy because the government allows the United States to export cigarettes to Korea and thus threaten local farmers. That's what happens when per capita GNP runs in the neighborhood of $5,000 a year and governments can still control the flow of information and mislead their people. When GNP gets up to around $10,000 a year, religion becomes a declining industry. So does government.

At $26,000 a year, where Japan is now, things are really different. People want to buy the best and the cheapest products—no matter where in the world they are produced. People become genuinely global consumers. We import beef and oranges from the United States, and everyone thinks it's great. Ten years ago, however, our students would have been the ones throwing stones at the American embassy. Our leaders used to tell us American and Australian beef was too lean and too tough to chew. But we've been there and tasted it and know for ourselves that it is cheap and good.

Through this flow of information, we've become global citizens, and so must the companies that want to sell us things. Black-and-white television sets extensively penetrated households in the United States nearly a dozen years before they reached comparable numbers of viewers in Europe and Japan. With color television, the time lag fell to about five or six years for Japan and a few more for Europe. With videocassette recorders, the difference was only three or four years—but this time, Europe and Japan led the way; the United States, with its focus on cable TV, followed. With the compact disc, household penetration rates evened up after only one year. Now, with MTV available by satellite across Europe, there is no lag at all. New music, styles, and fashion reach all European youngsters almost at the same time they are reaching their counterparts in America. We all share the same information.

More than that, we are all coming to share it in a common language. Ten years ago when I would speak in English to students at Bocconi, an Italian university, most of them would listen to me through a translator. Last year, they listened to me directly in English and asked me questions in English. (They even laughed when they should at what I said, although my jokes have not improved.) This is a momentous change. The preparation for 1992 has taken place in language much sooner than it has in politics. We can all talk to each other now, understand each other, and governments cannot stop us. "Global citizenship" is no longer just a nice phrase in the lexicon of rosy futurologists. It is every bit as real and concrete as measurable changes in GNP or trade flows. It is actually coming to pass.

The same is true for corporations. In the pharmaceutical industry, for example, the critical activities of drug discovery, screening, and testing are now virtually the same among the best companies everywhere in the world. Scientists can move from one laboratory to another and start working the next day with few hesitations or problems. They will find equipment with which they are familiar, equipment they have used before, equipment that comes from the same manufacturers.

The drug companies are not alone in this. Most people, for example, believed that it would be a very long time before Korean companies could produce state-of-the-art semiconductor chips—things like 256K NMOS DRAMs. Not so. They caught up with the rest of the Triad in only a few short years. In Japan, not that long ago, a common joke among the chip-making fraternity had to do with the "Friday Express." The Japanese engineers working for different companies on Kyūshū, Japan's southwestern "Silicon Island" only 100 km or so away from Korea, would catch a late flight to Korea on Friday evenings. During the weekend, they would work privately for Korean semiconductor companies.

This was illegal, of course, and violated the engineers' employment agreements in Japan. Nonetheless, so many took the flight that they had a tacit gentleman's agreement not to greet or openly recognize each other on the plane. Their trip would have made no sense, however, if semiconductor-related machines, methods, software, and workstations had not already become quite similar throughout the developed world.

Walk into a capital-goods factory anywhere in the developed world, and you will find the same welding machines, the same robots, the same machine tools. When information flows with relative freedom, the old geographic barriers become irrelevant. Global needs lead to global products. For managers, this universal flow of information puts a high premium on learning how to build the strategies and the organizations capable of meeting the requirements of a borderless world.

What Is a Universal Product?

Imagine that you are the CEO of a major automobile company reviewing your product plans for the years ahead. Your market data tell you that you will have to develop four dozen different models if you want to design separate cars for each distinct segment of the Triad market. But you don't have enough world-class engineers to design so many models. You don't have enough managerial talent or enough money. No one does. Worse, there is no single "global" car that will solve your problems for you. America, Europe, and Japan are quite different markets with quite different mixes of needs and preferences. Worse still, as head of a worldwide company, you cannot write off any of these Triad markets. You simply have to be in each of them—and with first-rate successful products. What do you do?

If you are the CEO of Nissan, you first look at the Triad region by region and identify each market's dominant requirements. In the United Kingdom, for example, tax policies make it essential that you develop a car suitable for corporate fleet sales. In the United States, you need a sporty "Z" model as well as a four-wheel-drive family vehicle. Each of these categories is what Nissan's president, Yutaka Kume, calls a "lead country" model—a product carefully tailored to the dominant and distinct needs of individual national markets. Once you have your short list of "lead-country" models in hand, you can ask your top managers in other parts of the Triad whether minor changes can make any of them suitable for local sales. But you start with the lead-country models.

"With this kind of thinking," says Mr. Kume, "we have been able to halve the number of basic models needed to cover the global markets and, at the same time, to cover 80% of our sales with cars designed for specific national markets. Not to miss the remaining 20%, however, we also provided each country manager with a range of additional model types that could be adapted to the needs of local segments. This approach," Mr. Kume reports, "allowed us to focus our resources on each of our largest core markets and, at the same time, provide a pool of supplemental designs that could be adapted to local preferences. We told our engineers to 'be American,' 'be European,' or 'be Japanese.' If the Japanese happened to like something we tailored for the American market, so much the better. Low-cost, incremental sales never hurt. Our main challenge, however, was to avoid the trap of pleasing no one well by trying to please everyone halfway."

Imagine, instead, if Nissan had taken its core team of engineers and designers in Japan and asked them to design only global cars, cars that would sell all over the world. Their only possible response would have been to add up all the various national preferences and divide by the number of countries. They would have had to optimize across markets by a kind of rough averaging. But when it comes to questions of taste and, especially, aesthetic preference, consumers do not like averages. They like what they like, not some mathematical compromise. Kume is emphatic about this particular point. "Our success in the U.S. with Maxima, 240 SX, and Pathfinder—all designed for the American market—shows our approach to be right."

In high school physics, I remember learning about a phenomenon called diminishing primaries. If you mix together the primary colors of red, blue, and yellow, what you get is black. If Europe says its consumers want a product in green, let them have it. If Japan says red, let them have red. No one wants the average. No one wants the colors all mixed together. Of course it makes sense to take advantage of, say, any technological commonalities in creating the paint. But local managers close to local customers have to be able to pick the color.

When it comes to product strategy, managing in a borderless world doesn't mean managing by averages. It doesn't mean that all tastes run together into one amorphous mass of universal appeal. And it doesn't mean that the appeal of operating globally removes the obligation to localize products. The lure of a universal product is a false allure. The truth is a bit more subtle.

Although the needs and tastes of the Triad markets vary considerably, there may well be market segments of different sizes in each part of the Triad that share many of the same preferences. In the hair-care market, for instance, Japanese companies know a lot more about certain kinds of black hair, which is hard and thick, than about blond or brown hair, which is often soft and thin. As a result, they have been able to capture a few segments of the U.S. market in, say, shampoos. That makes a nice addition to their sales, of course. But it does not position them to make inroads into the mainstream segments of that market.

Back to the automobile example: there is a small but identifiable group of Japanese consumers who want a "Z" model car like the one much in demand in the United States. Fair enough. During the peak season, Nissan sells about 5,000 "Z" cars a month in the United States and only 500 in Japan. Those 500 cars make a nice addition, of course, generating additional revenue and expanding the perceived richness of a local dealer's portfolio. But they are not—and cannot be—the mainstay of such portfolios.

There is no universal "montage" car—a rear axle from Japan, a braking system from Italy, a drive train from the United States—that will quicken pulses on all continents. Remember the way the tabloids used to cover major beauty contests? They would create a composite picture using the best features from all of the most beautiful entrants—this one's nose, that one's mouth, the other one's forehead. Ironically, the portrait that emerged was never very appealing. It always seemed odd, a bit off, lacking in distinctive character. But there will always be beauty judges—and car buyers—in, say, Europe, who, though more used to continental standards, find a special attractiveness in the features of a Japanese or a Latin American. Again, so much the better.

For some kinds of products, however, the kind of globalization that Ted Levitt talks about makes excellent sense. One of the most obvious is, oddly enough, battery-powered products like cameras, watches, and pocket calculators. These are all part of the "Japan game"—that is, they come from industries dominated by Japanese electronics companies. What makes these products successful across the Triad? Popular prices, for one thing, based on aggressive cost reduction and global economies of scale. Also important, however, is the fact that many general design choices reflect an in-depth understanding of the preferences of leading consumer segments in key markets throughout the Triad. Rigid model changes during the past decade have helped educate consumers about the "fashion" aspects of these products and have led them to base their buying decisions in large measure on such fashion-related criteria.

With other products, the same electronics companies use quite different approaches. Those that make stereophonic equipment, for example, offer products based on aesthetics and product concepts that vary by region. Europeans tend to want physically small, high-performance equipment that can be hidden in a closet; Americans prefer large speakers that rise from the floor of living rooms and dens like the structural columns of ancient temples. Companies that have been globally successful in white goods like kitchen appliances focus on close interaction with individual users; those that have

prospered with equipment that requires installation (air conditioners, say, or elevators) focus on interactions with designers, engineers, and trade unions. To repeat: approaches to global products vary.

Another important cluster of these global products is made up of fashion-oriented, premium-priced branded goods. Gucci bags are sold around the world, unchanged from one place to another. They are marketed in virtually the same way. They appeal to an upper bracket market segment that shares a consistent set of tastes and preferences. By definition, not everyone in the United States or Europe or Japan belongs to that segment. But for those who do, the growing commonality of their tastes qualifies them as members of a genuinely cross-Triad, global segment. There is even such a segment for top-of-the-line automobiles like the Rolls-Royce and the Mercedes-Benz. You can—in fact, should—design such cars for select buyers around the globe. But you cannot do that with Nissans or Toyotas or Hondas. Truly universal products are few and far between.

Insiderization

Some may argue that my definition of universal products is unnecessarily narrow, that many such products exist that do not fit neatly into top-bracket segments: Coca-Cola, Levi's, things like that. On closer examination, however, these turn out to be very different sorts of things. Think about Coca-Cola for a moment. Before it got established in each of its markets, the company had to build up a fairly complete local infrastructure and do the groundwork to establish local demand.

Access to markets was by no means assured from day one; consumer preference was not assured from day one. In Japan, the long-established preference was for carbonated lemon drinks known as saida. Unlike Gucci bags, consumer demand did not "pull" Coke into these markets; the company had to establish the infrastructure to "push" it. Today, because the company has done its homework and done it well, Coke is a universally desired brand. But it got there by a different route: local replication of an entire business system in every important market over a long period of time.

For Gucci-like products, the ready flow of information around the world stimulates consistent primary demand in top-bracket segments. For relatively undifferentiated, commodity-like products, demand expands only when corporate muscle pushes hard. If Coke is to establish a preference, it has to build it, piece by piece.

Perhaps the best way to distinguish these two kinds of global products is to think of yourself browsing in a duty-free shop. Here you are in something of an oasis. National barriers to entry do not apply. Products from all over the world lie available to you on the shelves. What do you reach for? Do you think about climbing on board your jetliner with a newly purchased six-pack of Coke? Hardly. But what about a Gucci bag? Yes, of course. In a sense, duty-free shops are the precursor to what life will be like in a genuinely borderless environment. Customer pull, shaped by images and information from around the world, determine your product choices. You want the designer handbag or the sneakers by Reebok, which are made in Korea and sold at three times the price of equivalent no-brand sneakers. And there are others like you in every corner of the Triad.

At bottom, the choice to buy Gucci or Reebok is a choice about fashion. And the information that shapes fashion-driven choices is different in kind from the information that shapes choices about commodity products. When you walk into the 7-Elevens of the world and look for a bottle of cola, the one you pick depends on its location on the shelf, its price, or perhaps the special in-store promotion going on at the moment. In other words, your preference is shaped by the effects of the cola company's complete business system in that country.

Now, to be sure, the quality of that business system will depend to some extent on the company's ability to leverage skills developed elsewhere or to exploit synergies with other parts of its operations—marketing competence, for example, or economies of scale in the production of concen-trates. Even so, your choice as a consumer rests on the power with which all such functional strengths have been brought to bear in your particular local market—that is, on the company's ability to become a full-fledged insider in that local market.

With fashion-based items, where the price is relatively high and the purchase frequency low, insiderization does not matter all that much. With commodity items, however, where the price is low and the frequency of purchase high, the insiderization of functional skills is all-important. There is simply no way to be successful around the world with this latter category of products without replicating your business system in each key market.

Coke has 70% of the Japanese market for soft drinks. The reason is that Coke took the time and made the investments to build up a full range of local functional strengths, particularly in its route sales force and franchised vending machines. It is, after all, the Coke van or truck that replaces empty bottles with new ones, not the trucks of independent wholesalers or distributors. When Coke first moved into Japan, it did not understand the complex, many-layered distribution system for such products. So it used the capital of local bottlers to re-create the kind of sales force it has used so well in the United States. This represented a heavy, front-end, fixed investment, but it has paid off handsomely. Coke redefined the domestic game in Japan—and it did so, not from a distance, but with a deliberate "insiderization" of functional strengths. Once this sales force is in place, for example, once the company has become a full-fledged insider, it can move not only soft drinks but also fruit juice, sport drinks, vitamin drinks, and canned coffee through the same sales network. It can sell pretty much whatever it wants to. For Coke's competitors, foreign and domestic, the millions of dollars they are spending on advertising are like little droplets of water sprinkled over a desert. Nothing is going to bloom—at least, not if that is all they do. Not if they fail to build up their own distinctive "insider" strengths.

When global success rests on market-by-market functional strength, you have to play a series of domestic games against well-defined competitors. If the market requires a first-class sales force, you simply have to have one. If competition turns on dealer support programs, that's where you have to excel. Some occasions *do* exist when doing more better is the right, the necessary, course to follow. Still, there are usually opportunities to redefine these domestic games to your own advantage. Companies that fail to establish a strong insider position tend to mix up the strategies followed by the Cokes and the Guccis. The managers of many leading branded-goods companies are often loud in their complaints about how the Japanese market is closed to their products. Or, more mysteriously, about the inexplicable refusal of Japanese consumers to buy their products when they are obviously better than those of any competitor anywhere in the world. Instead of making the effort to understand Japanese distribution and Japanese consumers, they assume that something is wrong with the Japanese market. Instead of spending time in their plants and offices or on the ground in Japan, they spend time in Washington.

Not everyone, of course. There are plenty of branded-goods companies that *are* very well represented on the Japanese retailing scene—Coke, to be sure, but also Nestlé, Schick, Wella, Vicks, Scott, Del Monte, Kraft, Campbell, Unilever (its Timotei shampoo is number one in Japan), Twinings, Kellogg, Borden, Ragú, Oscar Mayer, Hershey, and a host of others. These have all become household names in Japan. They have all become insiders.

For industrial products companies, becoming an insider often poses a different set of challenges. Because these products are chosen largely on the basis of their performance characteristics, if they cut costs or boost productivity, they stand a fair chance of being accepted anywhere in the world. Even so, however, these machines do not operate in a vacuum. Their success may have to wait until the companies that make them have developed a full range of insider functions—engineering, sales, installation, finance, service, and so on. So, as these factors become more critical, it often makes sense for the

companies to link up with local operations that already have these functions in place.

Financial services have their own special characteristics. Product globalization already takes place at the institutional investor level but much less so at the retail level. Still, many retail products now originate overseas, and the money collected from them is often invested across national borders. Indeed, foreign exchange, stock markets, and other trading facilities have already made money a legitimately global product.

In all these categories, then, as distinct from premium fashion-driven products like Gucci bags, insiderization in key markets is the route to global success. Yes, some top-of-the-line tastes and preferences have become common across the Triad. In many other cases, however, creating a global product means building the capability to understand and respond to customer needs and business system requirements in each critical market.

The Headquarters Mentality

By all reasonable measures, Coke's experience in Japan has been a happy one. More often than not, however, the path it took to insiderization—replicating a home-country business system in a new national market—creates many more problems than it solves. Managers back at headquarters, who have had experience with only one way to succeed, are commonly inclined to force that model on each new opportunity that arises. Of course, sometimes it will work. Sometimes it will be exactly the right answer. But chances are that the home-country reflex, the impulse to generalize globally from a sample of one, will lead efforts astray.

In the pharmaceutical industry, for example, Coke's approach would not work. Foreign entrants simply have to find ways to adapt to the Japanese distribution system. Local doctors will not accept or respond favorably to an American-style sales force. When the doctor asks a local detail man to take a moment and photocopy some articles for him, he has to be willing to run the errands. No ifs, ands, or buts.

One common problem with insiderization, then, is a misplaced home-country reflex. Another, perhaps more subtle, problem is what happens back at headquarters after initial operations in another market really start paying off. When this happens, in most companies everyone at home starts to pay close attention. Without really understanding why things have turned out as well as they have, managers at headquarters take an increasing interest in what is going on in Japan or wherever it happens to be.

Functionaries of all stripes itch to intervene. Corporate heavyweights decide they had better get into the act, monitor key decisions, ask for timely reports, take extensive tours of local activities. Every power-that-be wants a say in what has become a critical portion of the overall company's operations. When minor difficulties arise, no one is willing to let local managers continue to handle things themselves. Corporate jets fill the skies with impatient satraps eager to set things right.

We know perfectly well where all this is likely to lead. A cosmetics company, with a once enviable position in Japan, went through a series of management shake-ups at home. As a result, the Japanese operation, which had grown progressively more important, was no longer able to enjoy the rough autonomy that made its success possible. Several times, eager U.S. hands reached in to change the head of activities in Japan, and crisp memos and phone calls kept up a steady barrage of challenges to the unlucky soul who happened to be in the hot seat at the moment. Relations became antagonistic, profits fell, the intervention grew worse, and the whole thing just fell apart. Overeager and overanxious managers back at headquarters did not have the patience to learn what really worked in the Japanese market. By trying to supervise things in the regular "corporate" fashion, they destroyed a very profitable business.

This is an all-too-familiar pattern. With dizzying regularity, the local top manager changes from a Japanese national to a foreigner, to a Japanese, to a foreigner. Impatient, headquarters keeps fitfully searching for a never-never ideal "person on the spot." Persistence and perseverance are the keys to long-term survival and success. Everyone knows it. But headquarters is just not able to wait for a few years until local managers—of whatever nationality—build up the needed rapport with vendors, employees, distributors, and customers. And if, by a miracle, they do, then headquarters is likely to see them as having become too "Japanized" to represent their interests abroad. They are no longer "one of us." If they do not, then obviously they have failed to win local acceptance.

This headquarters mentality is not just a problem of bad attitude or misguided enthusiasm. Too bad, because these would be relatively easy to fix. Instead, it rests on—and is reinforced by—a company's entrenched systems, structures, and behaviors. Dividend payout ratios, for example, vary from country to country. But most global companies find it hard to accept low or no payout from investment in Japan, medium returns from Germany, and larger returns from the United States. The usual wish is to get comparable levels of return from all activities, and internal benchmarks of performance reflect that wish. This is trouble waiting to happen. Looking for 15% ROI a year from new commitments in Japan is going to sour a company on Japan very quickly. The companies that have done the best there—the Coca-Colas and the IBMs—were willing to adjust their conventional expectations and settle in for the long term.

Or, for example, when top managers rely heavily on financial statements, they can easily lose sight of the value of operating globally—because these statements usually mask the performance of activities outside the home country. Accounting and reporting systems that are parent-company dominated—and remember, genuinely consolidated statements are still the exception, not the rule—merely confirm the lukewarm commitment of many managers to global competition. They may talk a lot about doing business globally, but it is just lip service. It sounds nice, and it may convince the business press to write glowing stories, but when things get tough, most of the talk turns out to be only talk.

Take a closer look at what actually happens. If a divisionalized Japanese company like Matsushita or Toshiba wants to build a plant to make widgets in Tennessee, the home-country division manager responsible for widgets often finds himself in a tough position. No doubt, the CEO will tell him to get that Tennessee facility up and running as soon as possible. But the division manager knows that, when the plant does come on-stream, his own operations are going to look worse on paper. At a minimum, his division is not going to get credit for American sales that he used to make by export from Japan. Those are now going to come out of Tennessee. The CEO tells him to collaborate, to help out, but he is afraid that the better the job he does, the worse it will be for him—and with good reason!

This is crazy. Why not change company systems? Have the Tennessee plant report directly to him, and consolidate all widget-making activities at the divisional level. Easier said than done. Most companies use accounting systems that consolidate at the corporate, not the divisional, level. That's traditional corporate practice. And every staff person since the time of Homer comes fully equipped with a thousand reasons not to make exceptions to time-honored institutional procedures. As a result, the division manager is going to drag his feet. The moment Tennessee comes on-line, he sees his numbers go down, he has to lay off people, and he has to worry about excess capacity. Who is going to remember his fine efforts in getting Tennessee started up? More to the point, who is going to care—when his Japanese numbers look so bad?

If you want to operate globally, you have to think and act globally, and that means challenging entrenched systems that work against collaborative efforts. Say our widget maker has a change of heart and goes to a division-level consolidation of accounts. This helps, but the problems are just beginning. The American managers of a sister division that uses these widgets look at the Tennessee plant as just another vendor, perhaps even a troublesome one because it is new and not entirely reliable. Their inclination is to treat the new plant as a

problem, ignore it if possible, and to continue to buy from Japan where quality is high and delivery guaranteed. They are not going to do anything to help the new plant come on-stream or to plan for long-term capital investment. They are not going to supply technical assistance or design help or anything. All it represents is fairly unattractive marginal capacity.

If we solve this problem by having the plant head report to the division manager, then we are back where we started. If we do nothing, then this new plant is just going to struggle along. Clearly, what we need is to move toward a system of double counting of credits—so that both the American manager *and* the division head in Japan have strong reasons to make the new facility work. But this runs afoul of our entrenched systems, and they are very hard to change. If our commitment to acting globally is not terribly strong, we are not going to be inclined to make the painful efforts needed to make it work.

Under normal circumstances, these kinds of entrepreneurial decisions are hard enough to reach anyway. It is no surprise that many of the most globally successful Japanese companies—Honda, Sony, Matsushita, Canon, and the like—have been led by a strong owner-founder for at least a decade. They can override bureaucratic inertia; they can tear down institutional barriers. In practice, the managerial decision to tackle wrenching organizational and systems changes is made even more difficult by the way in which problems become visible. Usually, a global systems problem first comes into view in the form of explicitly local symptoms. Rarely do global problems show up where the real underlying causes are.

Troubled CEOs may say that their Japanese operations are not doing well, that the money being spent on advertising is just not paying off as expected. They will not say that their problems are really back at headquarters with its superficial understanding of what it takes to market effectively in Japan. They will not say that it lies in the design of their financial reporting systems. They will not say that it is part and parcel of their own reluctance to make long-term, front-end capital investments in new markets. They will not say that it lies in their failure to do well the central job of any headquarters operation: the development of good people at the local level. Or at least they are not likely to. They will diagnose the problems as local problems and try to fix them.

Thinking Global

Top managers are always slow to point the finger of responsibility at headquarters or at themselves. When global faults have local symptoms, they will be slower still. When taking corrective action means a full, zero-based review of all systems, skills, and structures, their speed will decrease even further. And when their commitment to acting globally is itself far from complete, it is a wonder there is any motion at all. Headquarters mentality is the prime expression of managerial nearsightedness, the sworn enemy of a genuinely equidistant perspective on global markets.

In the early days of global business, experts like Raymond Vernon of the Harvard Business School proposed, in effect, a United Nations model of globalization. Companies with aspirations to diversify and expand throughout the Triad were to do so by cloning the parent company in each new country of operation. If successful, they would create a mini-U.N. of clonelike subsidiaries repatriating profits to the parent company, which remained the dominant force at the center. We know that successful companies enter fewer countries but penetrate each of them more deeply. That is why this model gave way by the early 1980s to a competitor-focused approach to globalization. By this logic, if we were a European producer of medical electronics equipment, we had to take on General Electric in the United States so that it would not come over here and attack us on our home ground. Today, however, the pressure for globalization is driven not so much by diversification or competition as by the needs and preferences of customers. Their needs have globalized, and the fixed costs of meeting them have soared. That is why we must globalize.

Managing effectively in this new borderless environment does not mean building pyramids of cash flow by focusing on the discovery of new places to invest. Nor does it mean tracking your competitors to their lair and preemptively undercutting them in their own home market. Nor does it mean blindly trying to replicate home-country business systems in new colonial territories. Instead, it means paying central attention to delivering value to customers—and to developing an equidistant view of who they are and what they want. Before everything else comes the need to see your customers clearly. They—and only they—can provide legitimate reasons for thinking global.

Chapter 2

Responding to Conflicting Demands: The Environmental Challenge

The past 25 years have brought changes in the international business environment that have revolutionized the task facing MNC managers. Important shifts in political, social, economic, and technological forces have combined to create management challenges in the 1990s that are not only fundamentally different from those facing MNCs in the early 1960s, but are even at variance with accepted practice in the 1980s.

In an environment where the nature of these various forces of change is not always clearly understood, it is little wonder that their strategic and organizational implications are even more widely disputed. Nowhere was this more clearly illustrated than in the firestorm of debate and discussion triggered by Professor Theodore Levitt's *Harvard Business Review* article on "The Globalization of Markets." In his usual lively and provocative style, Levitt presented an interesting and insightful analysis of some of the forces of change that were reshaping markets around the world. In his view, technological, social, and economic trends were combining to create a unified world marketplace that was driving companies to develop globally standard products that enabled them to capture global economies. He was an articulate, if somewhat extreme, analyst of the globalizing forces that have recently captured the attention of so many managers—particularly those in major Western economies.

His critics, however, claimed that Levitt presented only one side of the story. They suggested that, like many managers, he had become so focused on the forces for globalization that he was blind to their limitations and to the countervailing forces that were also emerging.

The ensuing debate helped better define the diverse, changeable, and often contradictory forces that were reshaping so many industries in the 1970s and 1980s. In this chapter, we summarize a few of the most powerful of these environmental forces and suggest how they have collectively led to a new and complex set of challenges for managers of multinational companies.

THE ECONOMIC FORCES FOR GLOBAL COORDINATION

The phenomenon of globalization of certain industries described by Levitt was not a sudden or discontinuous development. It was simply the latest round of change brought about by a set of economic, technological, and competitive factors that, a hundred years earlier, had transformed the structures of many industries from regional to national scope. Economies of scale, economies of scope, and national differences in the availability and cost of productive resources were the three principal economic forces that had driven this process of structural transformation of businesses of which globalization was perhaps the last and final stage.[1]

Economies of Scale

The Industrial Revolution created pressure for much larger plants that could capture the benefits of the economies of scale offered by the new technologies it had spawned. Cheap and abundant energy, combined with good transportation networks, provided the incentives to restructure capital-intensive industries. For the first time, companies combined intermediate processes into single plants and developed large-batch or continuous-process technologies to achieve the lowest possible per unit cost through volume production.

However, per unit costs in plants using the new technologies also rose much more rapidly if volumes fell below the minimum efficient level (usually around 80 to 90 percent of rated capacity) than in labor-intensive industries. Costs and profits were determined by plant utilization, or throughput, rather than by absolute capacity levels. In many industries, like fine chemicals, automobiles, and oil refining, production at scale economy volumes exceeded the sales levels individual companies could achieve in all but the largest nations, forcing them to become international or perish. Even in businesses where the largest companies retain a large enough share of their domestic markets to achieve scale economies without exports, companies in the next rung were often forced to seek markets outside their home countries if they were to remain competitive.

---

[1]For a more detailed analysis of these environmental forces, read Alfred D. Chandler. Jr., "The Evolution of the Modern Global Corporation," in *Competition in Global Industries,* ed. Michael Porter (Boston: Harvard Business School Press, 1986) pp. 405–48. For those interested in an even more detailed exposition, Chandler's book. *Scale and Scope* (Cambridge, Mass.: Harvard University Press, 1990), will prove to be compelling reading.

Economies of Scope

Less-capital-intensive industries were usually less affected by scale economies. They often could expand by simply adding workers and machines or building new plants, without radical changes in their production methods. Many of these, however, were transformed by opportunities for economies of scope that came with the advent of worldwide communication and transportation networks providing cheap, reliable links throughout and between nations.

One classic example of how such economies could be exploited internationally was provided by trading companies handling consumer goods. By handling the products of many companies, they achieved a greater volume and lower per unit cost than any narrow-line manufacturer could in the marketing and distribution of its products. By handling a number of related products through a single set of facilities, they captured the economies that accrued to a broader scope of operations.

In other industries, like industrial goods manufacturing, there were opportunities for both economies of scope and of scale. At first, commercial intermediaries benefited from offering a range of similar products to customers in dispersed markets. Later, as higher production volumes created the need to sell standardized products to a wider range of markets, economies of scale grew large enough that producers began preferring to establish their own marketing and sales network. The need to provide installation support, service and repair, and consumer credit was also a driving force behind the creation of these networks, which emerged first at the national level and then particularly in the post–World War II era, expanded into the international level. Such expensive infrastructure was often uneconomical to maintain for a narrow product line but could be supported as the range of products broadened. Consumer electronics service networks or automobile dealerships provide good examples of the kind of investment that requires scope economies to support it abroad.

Factor Costs

With changes in technology and markets came the requirement for access to new resources at the lowest possible cost. Often there were no home-country sources of supply for companies wishing to expand into new industry segments. European oil companies, for example, explored the Middle East because they had limited domestic sources, and U.S. companies preferred to import the "sweet crude" that was more easily refined into light compounds like kerosene. Others went overseas in search of bauxite from which to produce aluminum, rubber to produce tires for a growing automobile industry, and tea to be consumed by an expanding middle class.

Less-capital-intensive industries like textiles, apparel, and shoes turned to international markets as a source of cheap labor. The increased costs of transportation and logistics management were more than paid for by much lower production costs. However, many companies found that, once educated, the cheap labor rapidly became expensive. Indeed, the typical life cycle of a country as a source of cheap labor for an industry is now only about five years. This forced companies to chase cheap labor from Southern Europe, to Central America, to the Far East, and now to Eastern Europe.

Other industries became worldwide in scope as companies established overseas operations to take advantage of cheap energy, lower costs of capital, reduced regulation, and other differences in total production cost. Other forces like shifting exchange rates and rapid changes in process technology also made it difficult to operate strategies based solely on domestic market positions.

The Expanding Spiral of Globalization

Particularly in the decade of the 1970s, these forces began to globalize the structure and competitive characteristics of a variety of industries. In some, the change was driven by a major technological innovation that forced a fundamental realignment of industry economics. Companies that could develop and manufacture products on a global basis not only could take advantage of the available scale economies, but could also accelerate the convergence of consumer preferences and needs worldwide. The impact of transistors and integrated circuits on the design and production of radios, television, tape recorders, and other such products represents a classic example. The introduction of quartz technology provided the watchmaking industry with an equally compelling opportunity to be transformed into a scale-intensive global industry.

However, in many other industries, such strong external forces of change were not present. Nonetheless, observing the substantial competitive advantages achieved by those who had been able to capture global economies, managers in a wide variety of businesses began to look for ways in which they might be able to achieve similar successes. They turned their attention to rationalizing their product lines, standardizing parts design, and specializing their manufacturing operations. Through such internal restructuring, a second wave of globalization was triggered by companies in industries as diverse as automobiles, office equipment, industrial bearings, construction equipment, and machine tools that have been able to gain competitive advantage by capturing global scale economies.

More recently, even some companies in classically local rather than global businesses, have begun to examine the opportunities for capturing economies beyond their national borders. Rather than responding to differences in consumer tastes and market structures that have historically endured across European countries, many of the large branded packaged goods companies are transforming traditionally national businesses like soap and detergent manufacturing. By standardizing product formulations, rationalizing pack sizes, and printing multilingual labels, they have been able to restructure and specialize their nationally dominated plant configurations and achieve substantial scale economies, gaining significant advantage over purely local competitors.

In market terms also, the spread of global forces expanded from businesses in which the global standardization of products was relatively easy (calculators and cameras, for example) to others in which consumers' preferences and habits were only slowly converging (automobiles and appliances, for instance). Again, major external discontinuities greatly facilitated the change process as in the case of the oil shocks of the 1970s, which triggered a worldwide demand for smaller, more fuel-efficient cars.

Even in markets where national tastes or behaviors varied widely, however, globalizing forces could be activated if one or more competitors in a business chose to activate and influence changes in consumer preferences. Food tastes and eating habits were long thought to be the most culture-bound of all consumer behaviors. Yet, as companies like McDonald's, Coca-Cola, and Kellogg have shown, in Eastern and Western countries alike, even these culturally linked preferences can be changed.

Global Competitors as Change Agents

As the forces driving companies to coordinate their worldwide operations spread from industries where such changes were triggered by some external structural discontinuity to others where managers had to create the opportunity themselves, there emerged a new globalization force that spread rapidly across a large number of businesses. It was a competitive strategy that some called *global chess* and that could only be played by companies that managed their worldwide operations as interdependent units implementing a coordinated global strategy. Unlike the traditional multinational strategic approach that was based on an assumption that each national market was unique and independent of others, these global competitive games assumed that a company's competitive position in all markets was linked by financial and strategic interdependence. Regardless of consumer tastes or manufacturing scale economies, it was suggested that the corporation with worldwide operations had a great advantage over the national company in that it could use funds generated in one market to subsidize its position in another.[2]

In industry after industry, companies that operated their local companies as independent profit centers found themselves at a disadvantage to competitors playing the global strategic game of cross-subsidizing markets. Companies that found no economic, technological, or market reason to manage their businesses globally were suddenly finding the urgent need to do so for reasons of competitive strategy.

By the early 1980s, there was little argument that all these diverse globalizing forces were transforming the nature of competition worldwide. But while few challenged the existence and widespread influence of such forces, some did question the unidimensionality of their influence and the universality of their strategic implications. They took issue, for example, with Levitt's suggestions that "the

---

[2]See the article by Hout, Porter, and Rudden in this volume.

world's needs and desires have been irrevocably homogenized," that "no one is exempt and nothing can stop the process," and that "the commonality of preference leads inescapably to the standardization of products, manufacturing, and the institution of trade and commerce." The critics argued that, while these might indeed be long-term trends in many industries, there were important short- and medium-term impediments and countertrends that had to be taken into account if companies were to operate successfully over the next decade or two as the international economy jolts along—*perhaps* eventually toward Levitt's "global village."

THE CULTURAL AND POLITICAL FORCES FOR LOCAL DIFFERENTIATION

There are many stories of multinational companies making major blunders in transferring successful products or ideas from their home countries to foreign markets. General Motors is believed to have faced some difficulties in selling the popular Chevrolet Nova in Mexico where the product name sounded like "no va" meaning "it does not go" in Spanish.[3] Similarly, when managers began investigating why its advertising campaign built around the highly successful "come alive with Pepsi" theme was not having the expected impact in Thailand, they discovered that the Thai copy translation read more like "come out of the grave with Pepsi." Although these and other such cases are widely cited, they represent the most extreme and simple-minded examples of an important strategic task facing managers of all MNCs: how to sense, respond to, and even exploit the differences in the environments of the many different countries in which their company operates.

National environments are different on many dimensions. For example, there are clear differences in the per capita GNP or the industry-specific technological capabilities in Japan, Australia, Brazil, and Poland. They also differ in terms of political systems, government regulation of domestic and foreign companies, social norms, and cultural values of their people. It is these national differences that force managers to be sensitive and responsive to national social, economic, and political differences in the host countries in which they operate around the globe.

Far from being overshadowed by the forces of globalization, by the early 1980s, the impact of these localizing forces were being felt with increasing intensity and urgency. In particular, many Japanese companies that had so successfully ridden the wave of globalization began to feel the strong need to become much more sensitive to host-country economic and political forces. Indeed, if the strategic implications of the globalizing trends have dominated management thinking in the West, the cultural and political forces for *localization* have become the preoccupation of top-level executives in Japan.

---

[3] For this and many other such examples of international marketing problems, see David A. Ricks, *Big Business Blunders* (Homewood, Ill.: Richard D. Irwin, 1983).

Cultural Differences

A large body of academic research provides strong evidence that nationality plays an important and enduring role in shaping the assumptions, beliefs, and values of individuals. Perhaps the most celebrated effort to date to describe and categorize these differences in the orientations and values of people in different countries is Geert Hofstede's study that described national cultural differences along four key dimensions: power distance, uncertainty avoidance, individualism, and "masculinity."[4]

This study demonstrates how distinct cultural differences across countries result in wide variations in social norms and individual behavior (for example, respect for elders or response to time pressure) and is reflected in the effectiveness of different organizational forms (for example, the French do not like the matrix organization) and management systems (the Swedes are accustomed to flatter organizations and smaller wage differentials).

However, cultural differences are also reflected in nationally differentiated consumption patterns: the way people dress or the foods they prefer. Take the simple example of tea as a beverage consumed around the globe. The British drink their tea as a light brew further diluted with milk, while Americans see it primarily as a summer drink to be served over ice, and Saudi Arabians drink theirs as a thick, hot brew heavily sweetened.

To succeed in a world of such diversity, companies often had to modify their quest for global efficiency through standardization and find ways to respond to the needs and opportunities created by cultural differences.

Government Demands

While cultural differences among countries have been an important localizing force, diverse demands and expectations of their home and host governments have perhaps been the most severe constraint to the global strategies of many companies.

Traditionally, the interactions between MNCs and the host governments have had many attributes of a classic love-hate relationship. The "love" of the equation was built on the benefits each could bring to the other. To the host government, the MNC represented an important source of funds, technology, and expertise that could help further national priorities such as regional development, employment, import substitution, and export promotion. To the MNC, the host government represented the key to local-market or resource access, which provided new opportunities for profit, growth, and improvement of its competitive position.

---

[4]For a more detailed exposition see Professor Hofstede's book *Culture's Consequences* (Beverly Hills, Calif.: Sage Publications, 1984). A brief overview of the four different aspects of national culture are presented in the reading "Culture and Organisation" at the end of this chapter. For organized and managerial implications of such differences in national culture, also see Nancy J. Adler, *International Dimensions of Organisational Behaviour* (Boston: Kent Publishing 1986).

The "hate" side of the relationship—though more often frustration than outright antagonism—arose from the differences in the motivations, objectives, and evaluation criteria adopted by the two partners. To be effective global competitors, MNCs typically tried to improve their economic efficiency (for example, through access to lower factor costs or through increased scale economies) and to gain strategic positions that gave them leverage over other companies (such as through cross-subsidization across markets). Ideally, therefore, the MNC sought three important operating objectives: unrestricted access to resources and markets throughout the world; the freedom to integrate manufacturing and other operations across national boundaries; and the unimpeded right to coordinate and control all aspects of the company on a worldwide basis.

The host government, on the other hand, sought to develop an economy that could survive and prosper in a competitive international environment. At times, this objective led to the designation of another company—perhaps a "national champion"—as its standard bearer in the specific industry, bringing it into direct conflict with the MNC. IBM, for example, faced such difficulties in its relationship with the French government, which spent decades trying to build a viable national computer industry.[5]

Even when the host government did not have such a national champion and was willing to permit and even support an MNC's operations within its boundaries, it would usually do so only at a price. Although both parties might be partners in the search for global competitiveness, the MNC hoped to achieve it within its global system while the host government strove to capture it within its national boundaries, thereby leading to conflict and mutual resentment.

The potential for conflict between the host government and the MNC arose not only from economic but also social, political, and cultural issues. MNC operations often cause social disruption in the host country through rural exodus, rising consumerism, rejection of indigenous values, or breakdown of traditional community structures. Similarly, even without the maliciousness of some MNCs that blatantly tried to manipulate host government structures or policies (for example, ITT's attempt to overthrow the Allende government in Chile), MNCs can still represent a political threat due to their size, power, and influence, particularly in developing economies.

Potential for conflict is also inherent in the different measurement systems adopted by the two partners. Because their objectives are fundamentally economic in nature, MNCs can assess their situation and measure their performance in essentially economic and competitive terms. The governments, on the other hand, define their goals in terms of social, political, and economic outcomes, and measure performance against socioeconomic and not just economic criteria. And, given the potential differences between economic and social returns, these

---

[5]For a more detailed discussion of this love-hate relationship, see Yves L. Doz, Christopher A. Bartlett, and C. K. Prahalad, "Global Competitive Pressures and Host Country Demands," *California Management Review,* vol. 23, no. 3, 1981.

differences in measurement criteria lead to significant differences in their evaluation of alternative courses of action. For example, most managers in the textile industry will readily acknowledge the economic advantage of power looms over hand looms because of their substantially higher labor efficiency. However, if the introduction of power looms will leave thousands of textile workers unemployed and dependent on government support, and if the more advanced machines not only have a higher capital cost but may also need to be imported using scarce foreign exchange, from the government's perspective, hand looms may show a higher social return.[6]

Because of these differences in objectives, motivations, and measures, MNC–host government relationships are often seen as a zero-sum game in which the outcome depends on the balance between the government's power (arising from its control over local market access and from competition among different MNCs for that access) and the MNC's power (arising from its financial, technological, and managerial resources and the competition among national governments for those resources). If, in the 1960s, multinational companies had been able to hold "sovereignty at bay" as one respected international researcher concluded,[7] by the 1980s, the balance seemed to have tipped in the other direction. The rapidly growing power of the global companies was perceived as a threat not only by other companies but also by various national governments that saw their social and economic policies being upset by the rising import penetration.

In an effort to stem the flood of imports, many countries began bending or side-stepping trade agreements signed in earlier years. By the early 1980s, even the U.S. government, traditionally one of the strongest advocates of free trade, began to negotiate a series of orderly marketing agreements and voluntary restraints on Japanese exports, while threats of sanctions were debated with increasing emotion in legislative chambers around the globe.

Furthermore, the new trade barriers were being reinforced by increasingly sophisticated industrial policies in developing and developed countries alike. Through such policies, governments were able to make trade restrictions more effective by preventing superficial responses such as the establishment of local plants to assemble knock-down kits exported from the MNCs home operations. Such "screwdriver plants" did little to respond to the host governments' concerns since they provided only limited low-skilled employment, resulted in little local value-added, and transferred minimal technology. Increasingly sophisticated foreign investment regulations defined specific levels of local content, technology transfer, and a variety of other conditions from re-export commitments to plant location requirements. The common objective of all such government intervention was to force MNCs to localize many activities that they might have otherwise preferred to carry out more centrally.

---

[6]See Louis T. Wells, Jr., "Social Cost-Benefit Analysis for MNCs," *Harvard Business Review,* March–April 1975.

[7]Raymond Vernon, *Sovereignty at Bay* (New York: Basic Books, 1971).

Growing Pressures for Localization

While there is no doubt that the increasing frequency of world travel and the ease with which communication linkages occur across the globe have lately done a great deal toward reducing the effect of national consumer differences, it would be naive to believe that worldwide tastes, habits, and preferences have become anywhere near homogeneous.

Furthermore, while many companies have succeeded in appealing to—and accelerating—such converging tastes and preferences by developing products that could be sold to consumers worldwide, even this trend toward standardized products designed to appeal to a lowest common denominator of consumer demand has a flip side. In industry after industry, a large group of consumers emerged that rejected the homogenized product design and performance of standardized global products. By reasserting traditional preferences for more differentiated products, they created openings—often very profitable ones—for companies that were willing to respond to, and even expand, the need for products and services that were more responsive to those needs.

The rapid growth of the upstart U.K. electronics company, Amstrad, is a good example of the phenomenon. Alan Sugar, the company's entrepreneurial founder, correctly perceived that many English consumers were unhappy about the transformation of traditional hi-fi equipment into global standard units that became known as "music centers." Many preferred the teak furniture exterior to the black or silver metal casing, and they missed the complex control panels that gave them a sense of technical wizardry that was absent in the simpler and more functional design of the new global products. Amstrad sensed this consumer preference and responded by designing a product line that put back the technical feel into the controls, reintroduced the component elements to the system, and enclosed it in teak cases. Locking in with the country's largest discount retailers, this upstart local company was able to capture market leadership from its larger global competitors. Using this product as a base, Amstrad expanded by applying the same market-sensitive logic to other consumer electronic products, and eventually to personal computers.

Other consumer and market trends are emerging to counterbalance the forces of global standardization of products. In an increasing number of markets from telecommunications to office equipment to consumer electronics, consumers are not so much buying individual products as selecting systems. A typewriter is linked into an integrated office system; the role of the TV set is changing as it becomes an integral part of a home entertainment and information system, connected to the VCR, the hi-fi system, the home computer, and perhaps an on-line databank and information network. This transformation is forcing companies to adapt their standard hardware-oriented products to more-flexible and locally differentiated systems consisting of hardware plus software and services. In such an environment, the competitive edge lies less with the company with the most scale-efficient global operation and more with the one that is sensitive and responsive to local requirements and able to develop the software and services to meet it.

In addition to the barriers and countertrends to globalization provided by local consumer needs and national market structures, there are also important impediments to the globalizing forces of scale economies that have been so widely discussed. While it is obvious that the benefits of scale economies must outweigh the additional costs of supplying markets from a central point, companies often ignore the fact that those costs consist of more than just freight charges. In particular, the administrative costs of coordinating and scheduling worldwide demand through global-scale plants is normally quite significant and must be taken into account. For some products, lead times are so short or market service requirements so high that these scale economies may well be offset by other costs.

More significantly, recent developments in computer-aided design and manufacturing, robotics, and other advanced production technologies have made the concept of flexible manufacturing a viable reality. Companies that previously had to produce tens or hundreds of thousands of standardized printed circuit boards (PCBs) in a central global-scale plant now find they can achieve minimum efficient scale in smaller distributed national plants closer to their customers. Flexible manufacturing technologies mean that there is little difference in unit costs between making 1,000 or 100,000 PCBs. When linked to the consumer's growing disenchantment with homogenized global products, this technology appears to offer multinational companies an important tool that will enable them to respond to localized consumer preferences and national political constraints without compromising their economic efficiency.

THE TECHNOLOGICAL AND COMPETITIVE FORCES FOR WORLDWIDE INNOVATION

The trends we have described have created an extremely difficult competitive environment in a large number of industries, and only those firms that have been able to adapt to these increasingly demanding and often conflicting forces for global coordination and national differentiation have been able to survive and prosper. In the global oligopolies that are emerging in many industries, new forces have surfaced in recent years that are influencing companies' strategies every bit as much as the globalizing and localizing trends that have been evolving during the past two or three decades.

As companies with extensive worldwide operations begin to match each other in global scale and international market positions, the competitive focus has shifted to a new set of forces that are redefining the battleground for world markets. In the emerging competitive game, victory goes to the company that can most effectively develop, diffuse, and implement innovative products and processes on a worldwide basis.

The trends that are driving this shift in the competitive game in many ways derive from the globalizing and localizing forces we described earlier. The increasing cost of R&D, coupled with shortening life cycles for new technologies and the products that they spawn, have combined to reinforce the need for companies to seek global volume in order to amortize the heavy investment as quickly as possible. The need to launch these new products on a worldwide basis is not only facilitated by the converging needs and preferences of consumers in various countries, but also tends to reinforce the trend.

At the same time, even the most advanced technology has diffused rapidly around the globe, particularly over the past few decades. In part, this trend has been in response to the demands, pressures, and coaxing of host governments as they bargain for increasing levels of national production and high levels of local content in the leading-edge products being sold in their markets. But the high cost of product and process development has also encouraged companies to transfer new technologies voluntarily, with licensing becoming an important source of funding, cross-licensing a means to fill technology gaps for many MNCs, and joint development programs and strategic alliances a strategy for rapidly building global competitive advantage.

When coupled with the converging consumer preferences worldwide, this diffusion of technology has had an important effect on both the pace and locus of innovation. No longer can U.S.–based companies assume, as they often did in the immediate postwar decades, that their domestic environment provided them with the most sophisticated consumer needs and the most advanced technological capabilities, and thus the most innovative environment in the world. Today, the newest consumer trend or market need can emerge in Australia or Italy, and the latest technologies to respond to the new needs may be located in Japan or Sweden. Innovations are springing up worldwide, and companies are recognizing that they can gain competitive advantage by sensing needs in one country, responding with capabilities located in a second, and diffusing the resulting innovation to markets around the globe.

Another trend is reinforcing the need for MNCs to sense, create, and diffuse innovation on a worldwide basis. We described how a gradual shift from free-standing products to integrated systems has increased the importance of locally differentiated software and market-responsive services in a number of industries. When combined with the rapid global diffusion of new products, a company's ability to link its products with others or to be compatible with complementary software has raised the importance of global standards and specifications to a new level. The winners in the battle for the globally accepted computer software standard, video-recording format, and even razor blade cartridge design can build and defend dominant competitive positions around the world that can endure for decades. First-mover advantages have increased substantially and have provided strong incentive for companies to focus attention not only on the internal task of rapidly creating and diffusing innovations within their own worldwide operations, but also on the external task of establishing the new product as an industry standard.

THE ENVIRONMENTAL CHALLENGE: RESPONDING TO THE DIVERSE FORCES SIMULTANEOUSLY

Trying to distill the key environmental demands in large and complex industries is a hazardous venture, but, at the risk of oversimplification, one can make the case that until recently most worldwide industries presented relatively unidimensional environmental requirements. But although this led to the development of industries with very different characteristics—those we distinguish as global, multinational, and international industries—more recently this differentiation has been eroding with important consequences for companies' strategies.

Global, Multinational, and International Industries

In some businesses, the economic forces of globalization were historically especially strong and dominated the other environmental demands. For example, in the consumer electronics industry, the four decades since invention of the transistor have witnessed an inexorable expansion in the benefits of scale economics: Successive rounds of technological change such as introduction of printed circuit boards and integrated circuits, and automation of component insertion, materials handling, assembly, packaging, and testing have led to an increase of the minimum efficient scale of operations from about 50,000 sets per annum to over 3 million sets per annum. In an environment of falling transportation and communications costs, relatively low tariffs and other protectionist barriers, and increasing homogenization of national markets, these huge scale economics have dominated the strategic task for managers of consumer electronics companies.

Such industries, in which the economic forces of globalization had been dominant, we call *global industries.* In such businesses, success typically belonged to companies that adopted classic *global strategies* of capitalizing on highly centralized scale-intensive manufacturing and R&D operations, and leveraging them through worldwide exports of standardized global products.

In some other businesses, the localizing forces of national, cultural, social, and political differences dominated the development of industry characteristics. In laundry detergents, for example, R&D and manufacturing costs were relatively small parts of a company's total expenses, and all but the smallest markets could justify the investment in a detergent tower and benefit from its scale economies. At the same time, sharp differences in laundry practices, perfume preferences, phosphate legislation, distribution channels, and other such attributes of different national markets led to significant benefits from differentiating products and strategies on a country-by-country basis.

This is typical of what we call *multinational industries*—worldwide businesses in which the dominance of national differences in cultural, social, and political environments made multiple national industry structures flourish. Success in such businesses typically belonged to companies that followed *multinational strategies* of building strong and resourceful national subsidiaries that were sensitive to local market needs and opportunities, and allowing them to manage their local businesses by developing or adapting products and strategies to respond to the powerful localizing forces.

Finally, in some other industries, technological forces were central, and the need for companies to develop and diffuse innovations was the dominant source of competitive advantage. For example, the most critical task for manufacturers of telecommunications switching equipment was the ability to develop and harness new technologies and to exploit them worldwide. While both the globalizing and localizing forces were historically strong, it was the ability to innovate and to appropriate the benefits of those innovations in multiple national markets that differentiated the winners from the losers in this highly complex business.

Such businesses, where the key to success lay in a company's ability to exploit the technological forces by creative new products and to leverage the international life cycles of the product by effectively transferring the technologies to overseas units, we call *international industries*. The name reflects the importance of the international product cycle that lay at the core of these industries' strategic demands. Success in these industries often accrued to companies that adopted *international strategies*—that of effectively managing the creation of new products and processes in their home markets and sequentially diffusing those innovations to their foreign affiliates.

Transition to Transnationality

Our portrayal of the traditional environmental demands of some major worldwide industries is clearly oversimplified. Different tasks in the value-added chains of the different businesses were subject to different levels of the economic, political, cultural, and technological forces. We have described what might be called the *center of gravity* of these activities—the environmental forces that had the most significant impact on the industry's strategic task demands.

By the late 1980s, however, these environmental demands were undergoing some important changes. In many industries, the earlier dominance of a single set of environmental forces was replaced by a much more complex environmental demand in which each of the different sets of forces were becoming strong simultaneously. Increasingly, new economics of scale and scope and intensifying competition among few competitors were enhancing the economic forces of globalization in many multinational and international industries. In the detergent business, for example, product standardization has become more feasible because of growing penetration and standardization of washing machines and because the increasing use of synthetic textiles has narrowed differences in washing practices across countries. Companies have leveraged this potential for product standardization by developing global or regional brands, uniform multilingual packaging, and common advertising themes, all of which have led to additional economies.

Similarly, localizing forces are growing in strength in global industries such as consumer electronics. While the strengths of the economic forces of scale and scope have continued to increase, host government pressures and renewed customer demand for differentiated products are forcing companies with global strategies to reverse their earlier strategies based on exporting standard products. To protect their competitive positions, they have begun to give more emphasis to local design and production of differentiated product ranges in different countries and for different international segments.

Finally, in the emerging competitive battle among a few large firms with comparable capabilities in global-scale efficiency and nationally responsive strategies, the ability to innovate and to exploit the resulting developments globally is becoming more and more important for building durable comparative advantage even in industries where global economic forces or local political and cultural influences had earlier been dominant.

In the emerging international environment, therefore, there are fewer and fewer examples of industries that are pure global, textbook multinational, or classic international. Instead, more and more businesses are driven by *simultaneous* demands for global efficiency, national responsiveness, and worldwide innovation. These are the characteristics of what we call a *transnational industry*. In such industries, companies will find it increasingly difficult to defend a competitive position based on only one dominant capability. They will need to develop their ability to respond effectively to all the diverse and conflicting forces at one and the same time so as to manage efficiency, responsiveness, and innovation without trading off any one for the other.

The emergence of transnational industry has not only made the needs for efficiency, responsiveness, and innovation simultaneous, but it has also led to the tasks for achieving each of these capabilities becoming more demanding and complex. World-scale economies through centralized production of standardized products are no longer adequate or appropriate in most businesses. Companies must instead build global efficiency through a worldwide infrastructure or distributed but specialized assets and capabilities that exploit comparative advantages, scale economies, and scope economies simultaneously. In most industries, a few global competitors now compete head-to-head in almost all major markets. To succeed in such an environment of global competition, low cost and high quality are essential but no longer sufficient. The infinitely more complex game of global chess has led to a new set of moves that all leading players must master: building and defending profit sanctuaries that are impenetrable to competitors, leveraging existing strengths to build new advantages through cross-subsidizing weaker products and market positions; making high-risk preemptive investments that raise the stakes and force out rivals with weaker stomachs or purse strings; and forming alliances and coalitions to isolate and outflank competitors. These and other similar maneuvers must now be combined with world-scale economies to develop and maintain global competitive efficiency.

Similarly, responsiveness through differentiated and tailor-made local-for-local products and strategies in each host environment is neither necessary nor feasible anymore. National customers no longer demand differentiation. They demand differentiation along with the level of cost and quality of standard global products that they have become used to. At the same time, host governments' desire to build their national competitiveness dominates economic policy in many countries, and

MNCs are increasingly viewed as key instruments in the implementation of national competitive strategies. And changes in labor costs, interest levels, materials availability, and foreign exchange rates across countries have become key instruments of national competitive strategies. Changes in regulations, tastes, exchange rates, and related factors have become less predictable and more frequent. In such an environment, mere responsiveness has become inadequate. The flexibility to continuously change product designs, sourcing patterns, and pricing policies in order to remain responsive to continually changing national environments has become essential for survival.

And, finally, exploiting centrally developed products and technologies is also no longer enough. MNCs must now build the capability to learn from many environments to which they are exposed and to appropriate the benefits of such learning throughout their global operations. While some products and processes must still be developed centrally for worldwide use and others must be created locally in each environment to meet purely local demands, MNCs must increasingly use their access to multiple centers of technologies and familiarity with diverse customer preferences in different countries to create truly transnational innovations. Similarly, environmental and competitive information acquired in different parts of the world must be collated and interpreted so as to become a part of the company's shared knowledge base, and be input to future strategy.

THE STRATEGIC AND ORGANIZATIONAL CHALLENGE

The increasing complexity of the environmental forces and the need to respond simultaneously to their diverse and often conflicting demands have created some major new challenges for many multinational companies. The global companies, such as many highly successful Japanese MNCs, with their competitive advantage rooted in a highly efficient and centralized system, have been forced to respond more effectively to the forces demanding national responsiveness and worldwide innovation. The multinational companies—many of them European—had the advantage of responsiveness but faced the challenge of exploiting the economic and technological forces more effectively. The U.S. companies, with their more international approach, struggled to build more understanding of the cultural and political forces and to respond to national differences more effectively while simultaneously enhancing efficiency through improved scale economies.

For most MNCs, the challenge of the 1990s is both strategic and organizational. On the one hand, they are now forced to develop a more complex array of strategic capabilities that allow them to capture the competitive advantages that accrue to efficiency, responsiveness, and innovations. At the same time, the traditional organizational approaches of these companies, developed to support their earlier global, multinational, or international approaches, have become inadequate for the more complex strategic tasks they now have to accomplish. In the following chapters, we discuss some of the ways in which companies can respond to these new strategic and organizational challenges.

Case 2–1 White Nights and Polar Lights: Investing in the Russian Oil Industry

The basis of the economic revival of Russia and Western Siberia will not be some political laws. It will be the existence of strong companies. They will influence the new structure of the laws to be adopted. The oil companies are very active now. They should not wait. If they wait for political stabilization, it may take 1,000 years.

Vladimir Spielman, *Deputy Director of the Western Siberian Geology Institute*

In the second half of the 1980s the collapse of the Soviet empire created an unprecedented opportunity for Western businesses. With dizzying speed, nearly all of the world's communist states embarked upon radical programs of economic liberalization and declared themselves open for capital flows and foreign investment. Among the first to heed this call were Western oil firms, who rushed to investigate the vast petroleum reserves of what was once the Soviet Union. In many respects, investment in Russian oil seemed a perfect match between East and West. Western firms promised to bring to Russia the capital, technology, and managerial talent that the country so desperately needed. They also had the ability—and desire—to restore production levels in Russia's long neglected fields and provide the fledgling government with a valuable source of hard currency. For decades, oil sales had financed the Soviet Union's ambitious program of industrialization. Now, the continued capacity of the oil sector to generate tax revenues was vital to the success of political reform.

The potential for the Western oil firms was similarly vast. Even divorced from the other republics of the Soviet Union, Russia was still the world's largest single producer of crude petroleum. Its reserves of petroleum were the seventh largest in the world, and its reserves of natural gas the largest. Unlike many other oil-rich countries, moreover, Russia was located directly next to the lucrative European and Japanese markets, and boasted an existing network of pipelines and refineries capable of serving Western Europe. Finally, investment in

Russian oil seemed relatively free of the currency constraints that dogged other potential investments, since oil exports could presumably be priced and sold in hard currency.

By the middle of the 1990s, however, a string of unforeseen events had significantly increased the risks of doing any business in Russia. The economy was in a shambles, the political situation remained unsettled, and, under nationalist pressure, the Yeltsin government had passed measures that taxed foreign-owned ventures nearly to the point of bankruptcy. The environment was particularly hostile for oil companies, which faced an onerous tax on export revenues. Still the sheer size of Russia's oil reserves and the oligopolistic structure of the international oil industry made it difficult for any Western firm to ignore Russia completely. Instead they ventured with varying degrees of caution, some anxious to grab the advantages of being first movers, others willing to exchange a smaller piece of the prize for a higher level of certainty. In all their calculations, though, the Western oil firms faced a common and generic, even if extreme, dilemma: how to balance the potential for very high reward with the possibility of very high risk. And in choosing their strategies, they all sought some means of defining and then hedging this risk.

The Russian Oil Industry

The petroleum industry in Russia dates from 1870, when the czarist regime recognized the market potential of the lands around the Caspian Sea and opened the entire area to competitive private enterprise. Because Russian industry at this time lagged significantly behind its Western counterparts, the first large-scale entrepreneurs were foreigners, who came to the region of Baku to develop the oil fields and export their production to serve a growing world demand. The Rothschilds and the Nobels built their fortunes in this way, as did Shell, which began as a trade and transportation company for Russian crude. By the turn of the century, Russian oil was a major factor in the world market. The state, however, remained largely aloof from the fields, intervening only to collect taxes from the foreign ventures.

This cozy relationship ended in 1905, when strikes in the Caucasus threw the oil fields into turmoil and launched the ill-fated Revolution of 1905. Subsequent discoveries in Kazakhstan and the Urals reignited Western interest in Russia but, for the most part, foreign investors began to pull out of the country, eager to cut their dependence on what was quickly becoming an unstable and uncertain supply. Between 1904 and 1913, Russia's share of world petroleum exports dropped from 31% to 9%.[1] By the time the Bolsheviks seized power in 1917, the foreigners were virtually gone, and Russian oil came under the sole direction of the state. It remained there for the next 70 years.

Oil in the Soviet Union

As with nearly all industries, oil in the Soviet Union was centrally controlled and hierarchically organized. Responsibility for the industry was divided among several ministries—Oil, Geology, and Pipelines—each of which handled its own segment of the production process and was rewarded on the basis of quantity. Thus, the Ministry of Geology and the regional geological associations tried to maximize the volume of reserves discovered; while

the Oil Ministry and its local subsidiaries, known as production associations, tried to maximize the production of crude petroleum. Costs and profits did not enter anywhere into the calculations, since inputs were allocated and prices set by the central planning agencies. Through yet another agency the Soviet state also controlled oil exports, which were critical to the country's balance of payments and its hard currency receipts. Throughout most of the post-war period, petroleum and gas accounted for roughly 90% of the Soviet Union's exports, and allowed the state to purchase the imported foodstuffs on which it increasingly depended.

The structure of this system—hierarchical authority, conflicting goals, and split responsibility—pushed the oil industry inevitably towards inefficiency and over-production. Since volume rather than efficiency was measured, officials tended to overestimate their output and stretch their resources to the breaking point. This tendency became even more pronounced whenever price shifts or bad harvests compelled the central authorities to sell more oil on world markets. Vast discoveries in western Siberia had eased this pressure somewhat in the mid-1960s, but by the 1970s a continuation of standard Soviet practices had reduced yields there as well. With an abandon unheard of in the West, Soviet managers would repeatedly drill new wells rather than repair existing ones, and flood oil fields with untreated water to push the oil flows as high and as fast as possible.[2] By the mid-1980s, the combined effect of these practices was evident in Soviet production and export figures. Production of crude petroleum, for example, fell from nearly 12 million barrels per day in

---

[1]Daniel Yergin, *The Prize* (New York: Simon & Schuster, 1991), p. 133.

[2]The technique of water-flooding involves injecting water into certain wells to increase the pressure and thus the yields of crude petroleum. If properly engineered and applied, water flooding will increase oil recovery. If performed incorrectly, however, there may be a short-term increase in production, but it will be followed by reservoir damage and actual decrease in ultimate reserves recovery.

1983 to 8.4 million in 1992, while exports fell from 2.6 million to 1.4 million.[3]

Simultaneously, the political structure of the Soviet Union was also rapidly unravelling.[4] With the ascension of Mikhail Gorbachev to power in 1985 the Soviet state entered the transition that would lead, ultimately, to its demise. In the process, the centrally planned economy was dismantled and industries such as oil were revamped and restructured. More importantly, they were also re-opened to the outside world and permitted again to woo foreign investment.

Russian Oil in Transition

During this transitional period the structure of the Russian oil industry remained fluid, changing shape with the changing political priorities of the new government. Basically, though, the Russian industry retained the broad outlines of its Soviet predecessor. The Ministry of Ecology and Natural Resources controlled exploration for petroleum; the Ministry of Fuel and Energy oversaw production, transportation, and refining; and 32 production associations (PAs) were established to manage oil operations at the provincial level. In a more radical departure from past practices, the Russian government also founded five new companies—LUKoil, YUKOS, Surgutneftegaz, Sidanco, and Rosneft—that were designed to mirror and behave like vertically integrated multinational energy firms.

To facilitate investment, meanwhile, the Russian government passed a series of new and fairly radical foreign investment laws.[5] The 1991 Law on Foreign Investment explicitly allowed for foreign participation in the exploration of natural resources, granting a legal right for joint ventures with 30% or greater foreign participation to export 100% of their oil, stipulating only that exploration and extraction licenses be granted on the basis of public bid or auction. It also pledged the "full and unconditional legal protection" of foreign investments.[6] In 1992, the Law on Mineral Resources formally ended the state's monopoly on resource development and instead ceded to local governments the right to develop and exploit their own subsoil reserves. The Russian government, however, retained ownership of all resources. The Law on Mineral Resources also laid out in considerable detail the procedures for obtaining exploration and extraction licenses, and divided the responsibility for licensing between federal and local authorities.[7]

The weight of legislation, however, did little to change the underlying conditions for investment. Russia remained a perilous place by nearly all measures, with an inchoate political system and a rapidly deteriorating economy. Both the Soviet Union and the Soviet bloc had splintered into their component states, leaving Russia in the midst of a now-defunct trading and distribution network. Outside Russia's borders, many of the republics were embroiled in violent ethnic conflicts, while inside the Russian

---

[3]Oil exports to the West have remained fairly stable. Most of the decline in total exports has come from sales to the former Soviet bloc and CIS countries. U.S. International Trade Commission, "Trade and Investment Patterns in the Crude Petroleum and Natural Gas Sectors of the Energy-Producing States of the Former Soviet Union," Investigation No. 332-338, Publication 2656, pp. 2–5 and 2–9. (Hereinafter cited as USITC Report)

[4]For a detailed description of the political and economic situation that prevailed in Russia at this time, see Alexander Dyck, *Russia 94: The Death of a System?*, HBS Case No. 794-107.

[5]A full review of all of the Russian legislation which affects foreign investment in the petroleum sector is beyond the scope of this paper. See "Russian property law, privatization, and the right of "full economic control," 107 *Harvard Law Review* 1044 (1994).

[6]See "Law on Foreign Investments in the RSFSR," 1991, at article 6.

[7]The law provides for five types of licenses: 5-year exploration licenses; 20-year extraction licenses; licenses for nonextractive uses; licenses for the protection of geological features; and licenses for the collection of mineral samples. See USITC, p. 3–2; and "Law of the Russian Federation on Sub-soil Resources," dated February 21, 1992, effective May 5, 1992, as amended June 26, 1992.

mafia was becoming a ubiquitous and ruthless presence. The ruble, pegged at 1.8/$1 during the communist days plunged to 150/$1 at the beginning of 1992, and then to roughly 3261/$1 by late 1994. The collapse of the communist system, moreover, had not been as clean as it had been elsewhere in eastern Europe, nor as controlled as it was in China. Instead, the system simply disintegrated, leaving little but the mafia and a handful of emerging private businesses to take its place. As price controls were gradually removed, inflation soared, letting loose a flood of popular discontent that often painted capitalism and foreigners as the source of Russia's woes. One of the few sectors that retained price controls, moreover, was energy, meaning that domestic fuel prices remained far below their international level, and even below the cost of production.

Most troubling of all for potential investors was the general uncertainty that surrounded any business venture in Russia. Despite rapid attempts to create a Western-style legal framework, Russia's legal system remained underdeveloped, lacking any serious foundation of contract, property, or corporate law. There were laws, to be sure, and courts, and jails, but no Western investor could be confident of how the laws would be interpreted, or on what grounds legal decisions would be made. Similarly, the pace of change in the country had tremendously complicated the old hierarchies of control, leaving investors—and oftentimes even officials—unclear about who had real power. This uncertainty was compounded in industries like oil, where finding the appropriate licensing agency was often critical. Even if the proper official was located, moreover, contracts for natural resource investments were notoriously difficult to implement, since the law required foreign firms to have domestic partners, and the partners were either the state or a state agency.

Uncertainty also plagued the Russian tax code which, to investors at least, seemed driven by politics and arbitrary decisions rather than any economic motivations. Taxes in Russia, particulary in the oil and gas sectors, changed quickly and unpredictably, and included a number of overlapping

components such as exports, production, profits, inputs, social costs, and repatriation. At times, the total tax burden on a venture was so high as to undermine any hope of profit—or even, in some cases, of recouping initial capital investments. In 1993, for example, officials from the Russian Subcommittee on Taxation acknowledged that taxes absorbed roughly 52% of the gross revenues of petroleum projects.[8] Price Waterhouse estimated the burden to be even higher, accounting for fully 75% of revenues and assuring a loss of $45 on each ton of petroleum produced in Russia.[9]

What made these taxes particularly ironic was that Russia was desperate for investment in its petroleum sector. The fields were in disrepair and the Russian production associations lacked access to the technology and expertise they needed to improve their yields. In 1993, 32,000 oil wells stood abandoned, even while the Russian government was critically short of hard currency and the Russian economy kept plummeting downwards. To bring Russia's energy sector back to the production levels of 1988–89, the industry needed an initial capital investment of $25 billion, and subsequent injections of around $6–7 billion a year.[10] The only realistic source for this capital was foreign investors, and particularly the large Western energy firms with an obvious interest in Russia's vast oil and gas reserves. But before these investors would come, they needed some means to protect themselves against the financial, political, and physical risks of doing business in Russia.

Opportunities and Constraints

Nearly since its creation, the oil industry had been international in scope. The largest firms, known

---

[8]Sergey Gorbachev, First Deputy Minister of Finance, Second annual Russian Oil Conference, "The Russian Oil Industry: Foreign Investment Opportunities," London, February 11–12, 1993, cited in USITC, p. 3–3.

[9]Byron Ratliff, Director of Petroleum Services, Price Waterhouse, Second Annual Russian Oil Conference, cited in ibid.

[10]Deutsche Bank estimates, published in *Focus: Eastern Europe,* Jan. 6, 1993, No. 66, p. 4.

generally as the "majors," ventured across the globe in search of new fields and in the hopes of bringing these fields under their sole control. Through a fluke of geography and development, the majors tended to be Western, while the world's largest reserves of crude petroleum were located elsewhere, primarily in the Middle East, Latin America, and Russia. To bridge this gap, the majors had developed early into vast and diversified firms, bringing the exploration, production, refining, and transportation functions into a vertically integrated whole. The size of these firms and the capital they required tended to reduce their number and drive the industry towards an oligopolistic structure. While the collusion that had marked the industry in its earlier days was gone, the big oil firms remained linked by their common interest in a global commodity that was still relatively hard to find and acquire. These links were made even stronger by the looming presence of the OPEC cartel which, even in its weaker periods, had a tremendous impact on petroleum supplies and prices.

Russia's position in the global industry was complex. Merely by virtue of the size of its reserves, it had been a player in the industry since the late nineteenth century. Once the early Western investors left, however, Russia's participation in international markets had been limited to the exports regularly channeled through its state trading agency. While this agency generally played by the rules of the international markets, and indeed often mimicked OPEC's price behavior, it was never really part of the global industry, and had no direct contact with the Western majors or service providers.

Once liberalization re-opened Russia to the outside world, therefore, it was virtually virgin territory for the oil firms, comparable in many ways to the earlier great discoveries in the Middle East and Africa. As in these territories, there was a tremendous incentive for each of the major firms to establish itself quickly in Russia, gaining control over the fields before its competitors could do likewise. Given the size and reputed productivity of the Siberian fields, the stakes were particularly high. If a firm did not invest in Russia, it risked being permanently excluded from one of the world's largest single sources of crude petroleum. In the highly competitive oil industry, this exclusion could leave a firm with a serious disadvantage—especially since most of the other large sources of crude were located in the perpetually unstable Middle East.

Balancing these potentially high rewards, however, were correspondingly high risks. Under the conditions that existed in Russia, any investment was vulnerable to arbitrary taxation and possibly even expropriation. Soaring inflation and a plummeting ruble compounded exchange rate risk and operating exposure, while the tenuous state of Russia's legal system threatened to render any contract moot. Under these conditions, oil companies contemplating a Russian investment faced three major choices:

- Should they venture early into Russia, with all of its concomitant risks, or should they wait until some of the country's uncertainties were resolved?
- If they decided to go, what kinds of deals would best enable them to reduce risk to an acceptable level?
- Once the deal was structured, how could they bind their various partners to the necessary contracts and commitments?

As of 1994, Western oil firms had responded to these questions in a wide range of ways. Some jumped eagerly in, confident that the advantages of being first mover would, over time, outweigh the risks. Others waited by the sideline, fearful of being left out of the Russian game, yet unwilling to accept the level of risk it entailed. Still others tried to manage the process more directly, attempting to craft institutions and sanctions to compensate for their absence in Russia.

The three companies and strategies described below reveal the range of decisions that Western firms made. Taken together, they begin to suggest how firms approach risk in highly unstable environments, and how they can manage it to their best advantage.

Phibro Energy: First Mover's Advantage?

Phibro Energy Production, Inc. is a wholly owned subsidiary of Salomon Inc., the New York-based investment firm. In late 1981, Phibro Corporation, a large international commodities trading group, joined with Salomon to create the firm Phibro/Salomon. The friendly merger was designed in part to consolidate trading activities under Salomon's roof and use Phibro's cash flow to fuel Salomon's growth.

The strategy appeared to make great sense in the 1980s, as Salomon rose to become the leading stock underwriter in the United States. In late 1983, Phibro Energy, Inc. was formed as Salomon's energy trading arm and subsequently purchased a series of refineries in Louisiana and Texas. Then, in 1990, Phibro Energy focused its sights on the newly opened Russian market and established Phibro Energy Production, Inc. ("Phibro") specifically to develop opportunities in Russia. If Phibro could enter the Russian market quickly, management calculated the company would gain both a significant source of crude petroleum and a key advantage over its larger rivals. With Russian oil, Phibro and Salomon could together build a web of oil transactions that extended from extraction, to refining, to the sale of oil futures.

Thus in November 1990, Phibro took the plunge. Together with the Russian state-owned production association Varyeganneftegaz ("VNG"), it formed the White Nights Joint Enterprise, a 50/50 Russian/American joint venture. The project, based in the Tyumen Region of Western Siberia, was granted licenses by the then Soviet government to develop and produce oil and gas reserves in three fields: Tagrinsk, West Varyegan and Roslavl. As one of the first major foreign oil joint ventures in the Soviet Union, White Nights received tremendous publicity in the international oil community and compelled other firms to hasten their own Russian involvement.

Financially, White Nights was established as a three-way partnership: VNG (50%); Phibro (45%); and Anglo-Suisse, Inc., a small Texas-based company, (5%). Technically, White Nights was con-

ceived as a field development project, with Phibro providing capital to fund the services and technology required to boost yields in the existing fields and VNG providing the fields and attendant infrastructure. The partners negotiated a "decline curve," which plotted the expected production from the existing wells. Under the terms of the joint venture agreement, all oil "under the curve," would go to VNG, which would sell the oil to its traditional Russian customers and use the proceeds to reimburse Phibro for the costs of producing this "under the curve" oil. All oil "above the curve" would be exported and remaining after-cost proceeds divided among the venture's partners in accordance with their ownership interest.

From the start, Phibro's management was well aware of the risks that faced their venture. Most critically, in 1990, the Soviet Union still lacked a comprehensive legal and fiscal framework for foreign investment. Phibro's management, however, determined that the rules and regulations already in place, while less than ideal, were sufficiently adequate to proceed. Company executives also felt reasonably confident that the investment climate would improve along with the fast-evolving political climate of the time. To secure Phibro's long-term interests, moreover, White Nights was consciously structured to maximize the incentives for cooperation among the partners. Since VNG's profits came from its share of production in excess of the decline curve, its natural objective would be to expand output as much as possible. To do this, it would need the Western technology and management skills that Phibro could provide. Indeed, central to the agreement was the $40 million in capital which Phibro was committed to put up as the Western party's share of the venture's $80 million charter fund. It was envisioned that this $40 million capital infusion would be used to provide the advanced oilfield technology, services, and management skills which VNG lacked and which would allow White Nights to remain a viable joint venture for its full 25 year duration. Thus, both VNG and Phibro conceived of White Nights not as a terminal project, but as a long-term partnership. If

VNG wanted continued access to Western technology for future projects, it would have a real incentive to do whatever was necessary to ensure the success of White Nights.

With this assurance, during 1991, Phibro committed $40 million in cash and VNG contributed $40 million in wells and infrastructure to the White Nights venture.

Early Setbacks

Shortly after White Nights began field operations in April 1991, the project encountered unexpected difficulties. The biggest problem was increased taxation. When the venture was formed in November 1990, it was subject to four taxes. By early 1992, however, the number of taxes had soared to a dozen, many of which were revenue-based, as opposed to the more benign profit-based taxes in effect at the outset. As a result, by the spring of 1992, White Nights was paying approximately 70% of its gross revenue in taxes to the Russian government, reducing its remaining cash receipts to an amount below actual production costs. The worst tax from White Nights' perspective was the export tax, levied at the arbitrary rate of 30 ECUs ($35) per metric ton (or approximately $5 per barrel).[11] Ostensibly, in accordance with a decree issued in July 1992, any foreign venture established prior to January 1992 was eligible for exemption from the export tax until it recouped the full amount of its initial investment. But despite repeated pleas by the foreign investment community, promises by the Russian government, and high-level bargaining between the U.S. and Russian governments, no producing foreign joint enterprise received an exemption under the 1992 Decree.

In addition to these tax and fiscal concerns, White Nights also ran into technical difficulties. To begin with, once operations were commenced in 1991, White Nights' two producing fields (Tagrinsk and West Varyegan) proved to be far less productive than the Russian geological surveys had indicated. In particular, recoverable reserves proved to be much lower than Phibro had been led to believe due to a combination of complex geology, overly optimistic Russian reserve projections, low well productivity, and years of poorly conceived reservoir management. As a result, Phibro's original strategy of boosting output with expensive, advanced imported equipment operated by Western crews did not make economic sense; the well production rates and reserves were simply not high enough to cover the costs. A second problem concerned VNG's domestic sales. As the Russian economy disintegrated, the state-owned enterprises found themselves locked into a system that no longer functioned. VNG was required by the state to sell oil to its traditional customers, most of whom were large state-owned refineries. But because these refineries were not being paid by their customers, they could no longer afford to pay VNG for their purchases, even at the extremely low, state-mandated prices that still prevailed in the market. As a result of these and other factors, the White Nights venture began running significant deficits, and Phibro was compelled to loan the project an additional $60 million beginning in late 1991. By the middle of 1992, the company braced itself for a potential $116-million pre-tax loss from the White Nights project.[12]

Staying the Course

Despite all these troubles, Phibro and Salomon remained committed to their Russian venture. The venture also began to show some signs of emerging from the Siberian morass. In June of 1992, White Nights exported its first full cargo of crude oil, and by mid-1993, Phibro had succeeded in boosting production at the venture by a third to over 26,000 barrels per day. More importantly, by negotiating a reduction in the decline curve in March 1994, the venture's exports—and thus Phibro's potential

---

[11]The Export Tax, initially imposed at a rate of 33.8 ECUs/ton on January 1, 1992, fluctuated broadly throughout 1992 between 21 ECUs/ton and 48 ECUs/ton before settling at 30 ECUs/ton for 1993 and 1994.

[12]*Petroleum Intelligence Weekly,* May 11, 1992.

ability to recoup its investment—eventually began to rise. As part of the renegotiation, White Nights also assumed from VNG all responsibility for domestic sales of below decline curve oil. Because White Nights was not tied into the network of old contracts that had bound VNG to the state-owned refineries, the venture's management felt confident that they would begin to receive payment for their local sales and, thus, that they could begin to reduce some of White Nights' accumulated debts.

On the political front, Phibro had also joined with other U.S. oil companies to exert pressure for an official exemption from the export tax. Chairman and CEO Brian Lavers, who had been recruited in mid-1992 following his retirement as Chairman of Shell Nigeria to restructure White Nights and make it profitable, remained guardedly optimistic. Like others involved in the Russian oil industry, Lavers found reassurance in a May 1994 decree that established a new procedure for exempting foreign ventures from the onerous export tax. Lavers also believed strongly that high-level lobbying by the U.S. Departments of Commerce, Energy, Treasury, and State, through the medium of the newly established Gore-Chernomyrdin commission, would convince the Russian government that it was in its own best interest to remove the tax.[13] This confidence was rewarded when, by Decree 1611R of October 11, 1994, the Russian government exempted six Western joint ventures from the export tax, including Phibro's White Nights project.

Mobil: Waiting by the Side

Founded in the late nineteenth century as the Standard Oil Company of New York, Mobil was one of the oldest and most influential players in the international oil market. In the 1920s, Mobil had been one of the first U.S. firms to enter the newly discovered oil fields of Iraq and in the mid-1940s it joined the American charge into Saudi Arabia. Over the years the company had diversified, extending its operations into all segments of the energy sector. In addition to its estimated reserves of 5.8 billions of barrels of oil,[14] Mobil also had significant refining and transportation facilities, and an international chain of service stations. Even at the production stage it was diversified, with massive gas fields supplementing its oil holdings.

From this vantage point, Mobil's enthusiasm for Russia was mixed from the start with a certain degree of caution. In 1988, the company's overriding objective was to cut costs, rather than increase reserves, especially in the face of sharply declining oil prices. Like many of the other majors, Mobil had discovered that exploration in the post-OPEC world was a trickier prospect, since increased oil production was keeping prices hovering at the $11–17/barrel mark. Below that, many exploration and development projects simply could not break even.

Thus, while Mobil was attracted by the huge reserves of Russia, and the potentially low costs of production, company executives were also reluctant to make any high risk investment in oil that they really did not need. And so, unlike Phibro, Mobil approached the Russian oil market with great caution. It sent investigative teams to Siberia, it established contacts within the Russian oil bureaucracy; and it tendered, and lost, bids for several projects. But as of the summer of 1994 it had not made any significant investments in the Russian petroleum sector.

What Mobil had done was to reorganize the way in which it approached uncertain but promising areas of the world. In 1992, the company formed a new organizational unit, the Strategic Ventures Group, and charged it with exploring and developing new activities in the former Soviet Union,

---

[13]U.S. Vice President Albert Gore and Russian Prime Minister Viktor S. Chernomyrdin signed a series of agreements on June 23, 1994, that established a major oil and gas exploration project by U.S. companies and called for joint development of a space station. The two parties also agreed to work together on various economic and environmental issues.

[14]The figure actually measures oil and its equivalents.

eastern Europe, Mexico, and Venezuela. Explicitly, Mobil's management recognized that the scope of business in these areas and the impact they could have on the global oil market was too large either to be ignored or to be handled within the customary corporate structure. So the decisions about whether and how to proceed in these high-risk/high-reward markets were spun off, directed, as Mobil's chairman and CEO described, towards the "hot pursuit of opportunities that may materialize."[15]

In Russia, however, the group moved slowly. Early in 1992, the company bid for a major exploration and production contract on Sakhalin Island in Russia's far east, but lost to the "3M" consortium of Mitsui, McDermott Engineering, and Marathon Oil. Soon thereafter, the Russian government asked the 3M group to consider including Mobil in the $10 billion project, but Mobil seemed in no great hurry to participate. Instead company officials reported that they were generally quite pessimistic about options in Russia, categorizing it as "one of the most politically risky countries in the world." Thus, even while acknowledging that there already was "not enough of the pie left to divide up," Mobil was content to wait.

Conoco: Crafting the Venture

In several respects, Conoco holds the middle ground between Phibro and Mobil. Whereas Mobil is one of the original majors and Phibro a recent entrant to the market, Conoco is part of the second tier of so-called independent firms, with a significant presence in the international oil market, but not the clout or network of a Mobil or Exxon. In Russia, it also chose a middle course, entering the country early but cautiously and committing to large projects while simultaneously trying to minimize its own financial exposure.

Conoco's involvement in the Soviet Union began late in 1989, when the company acquired several detailed geological studies and began to choose the most interesting targets for potential

investment. It soon narrowed its focus to three projects—Shtockman, West Siberia, and Timan Pechora—and attached an in-house task force to each. It also decided even at this early stage to structure the projects as separate "subsidiaries" with "headquarters support" provided by a single administrative staff.

Once this basic structure was established, Conoco's management tried to outline some basic strategies for dealing with the vast uncertainties of Russia. For instance, rather than just accepting the technical and geological information provided by the Russians, Conoco sent its own team to re-evaluate and test potential production sites. Likewise, to ward off the possibility of Russian expropriation or breach of contract, the company began to think about increasing their own leverage in any project by providing equipment—particularly pipeline—that would not be easily available to its partners. And finally, in a fairly radical departure, it started to investigate outside sources of financing.

In plotting its actual involvement in Russia, Conoco adopted a conscious strategy of sequential investment, striving to gain experience and contacts in Russia before making any major or irreversible commitments. It began, therefore, with the Shtockman project, a joint venture between Conoco, Norsk Hydro—three Finnish companies—and the Soviet Ministry of Oil & Gas. The project itself was straightforward, designed to produce gas from existing wells and then construct a pipeline to transport the gas to European export markets. Conoco's financial involvement in the deal was limited, as was its downside risk. In Western Siberia, its second project, Conoco also moved cautiously, launching major studies of the region's production potential and putting the project on a timetable of contingent approvals. First came a joint Conoco/Soviet feasibility study, then a six-month period for consideration, and only then the creation of an official joint venture.

Only after these initial forays did Conoco shift its attention to its largest and most significant venture. In June 1992, it signed an agreement with its Russian partner Archangelskgeologia to establish a

---

[15]Allen Murray, cited in *Energy Economist,* March 1992.

new joint venture named "Polar Lights." Located at the Arctic edge of the Timan-Pechora Basin, Polar Lights was considerably more ambitious than Conoco's earlier ventures, and indeed more ambitious than nearly any previous investment in the Russian oil sector. Unlike most earlier projects, Polar Lights was established in an area without any existing production capacity. The venture thus planned to design, build, and operate the total infrastructure that production would demand, for an ultimate cost of roughly $3 billion. To get even the initial phases of the project underway, Conoco and its partner needed to develop 24 drilling wells, install a central processing facility, and build a 37-mile pipeline capable of transporting 40,000 barrels a day of Russian oil. All of this was to occur, moreover, in a sparsely populated region with virtually no infrastructure and where temperatures regularly dropped to −40° Fahrenheit. Despite these obstacles, and despite the sheer magnitude of Polar Lights, Conoco's management continued to see the venture as an experimental foray. As the company's CEO, Constantine Nicandros, explained, "We chose to participate in developing this relatively small field with two goals in mind" to use the project as a test case to learn whether or not we could successfully do business in Russia and, if we could, to use it as a platform for future investments."[16]

The magnitude of the deal also forced Conoco to experiment with ways of reducing the company's financial and economic exposure. First, the number of middlemen involved with the project was sharply limited. Polar Lights would itself control the flow of oil from the well-head to the shipment point and would also operate and finance the pipeline.[17] This control, presumably, would allow the venture to increase its leverage with the Russian government even while maintaining a healthy distance between Polar Lights and the Oil Ministry in

Moscow. To increase its financial leverage and reduce its exposure meanwhile, Conoco went to great lengths to bring outside partners into the venture. It sought the active involvement of multilateral and U.S. government lending institutions and successfully lobbied the European Bank for Reconstruction and Development (EBRD) for a $90 million loan. The International Finance Corporation put up another $60 million, and the Overseas Private Investment Corporation an additional $50 million. Under the terms of the agreement, all partners to the venture would receive cash through the declaration of dividends by the Board of Founders, composed of Conoco and Russian members. By using institutional funds, Conoco clearly increased the pressure for production and hard currency revenues. But it also subtly changed the stakes of the Russian game. Once the international institutions were involved, the costs of violation, or even excessive intervention, rose higher, since lending institutions have much greater clout than any individual company. Or as Randall Fischer of the EBRD described: "The Bank has certain rights, most importantly to close the window on further operations with that country."

Moving Ahead

In 1994, it was still too early to predict the ultimate fate of Conoco's Polar Lights venture. On one hand, Polar Lights was being heralded as one of the most exciting and well-conceived forays into post-communist Russia. On the other hand, though, the same problems that had plagued Phibro and other Western investors were beginning to loom.

The taxation issue, for instance, remained painfully unresolved. Although Conoco had ultimately negotiated a formal exemption from Russia's onerous export tax, it was not clear whether, and for how long, the exemption would prove acceptable to the Subcommittee on Taxation. Moreover any significant increase in other taxes—on revenues, wages, or the like—could also jeopardize the project's future, especially at a time when oil prices remained stubbornly fixed at $11–17 a barrel.

---

[16]Constantine S. Nicandros, "The Russian Investment Dilemma," *Harvard Business Review,* May–June 1994, p. 40.

[17]See D. Schlegel, "Joint Venture Gets $200 Million in Loans to Develop Russian Oil Field" (1993).

EXHIBIT 1 Major Oil Fields in the Former Soviet Union

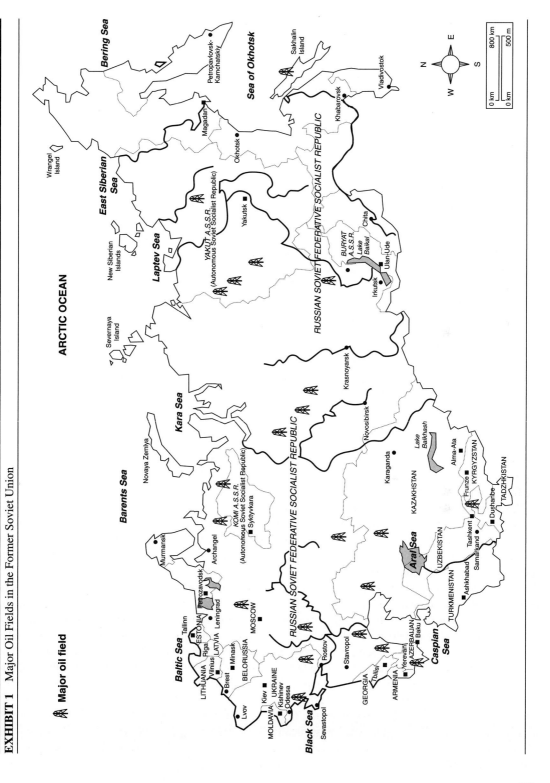

EXHIBIT 2   Structure of the Former Soviet Union's Petroleum and Natural Gas Industries

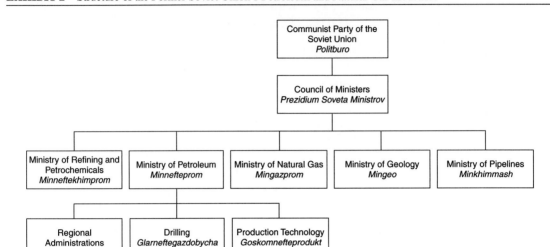

Source: Commonwealth of Independent States: Petroleum Industry Structure and Organization; and Canadian Energy Research Institute, *Oil in the Former Soviet Union.*

Meanwhile, even though production at Polar Lights had been slated to begin in 1994, Conoco's management was still wrestling with its partner and a host of Russian authorities over the details of its contractual terms. Negotiations were proceeding amicably for the most part, but many issues remained still unresolved. Export licenses, for instance, which were critical to the venture's commercial success, were being held up in Moscow, and the basic infrastructure at the fields remained wholly inadequate. Late in 1992, moreover, a little-known environmental group had brought suit against the Russian government, charging that it had undermined the national interest in approving the Polar Lights project. While the suit was subsequently dismissed, it created an air of uncertainty, and prompted even the chief engineer of Archangelskge-

ologia to complain that, "Patience is running out. If the Americans, after investing a bundle of money in the project, see that no work can be done this winter, they'll give up and go home."[18] Conoco had also suffered a blow in its Shtockman project: after the consortium had spent tens of millions of dollars surveying the region, the Russian government had summarily awarded the production concession to a hastily assembled Russian group. Conoco and its partners received no compensation for their efforts.[19] In the summer of 1994, CEO Nicandros

---

[18]Quoted in Vasily Zakharko, "World 'Shark' Is Near," *Izvestia,* December 17, 1992, p. 7. Reprinted in *The Current Digest,* vol XLIV, no. 50 (1992), p. 23.

[19]*Economist,* "Russia's Cold Shoulder", March 13, 1993, pp. 73–74.

EXHIBIT 3 Structure of the Russian Petroleum and Natural Gas Industries

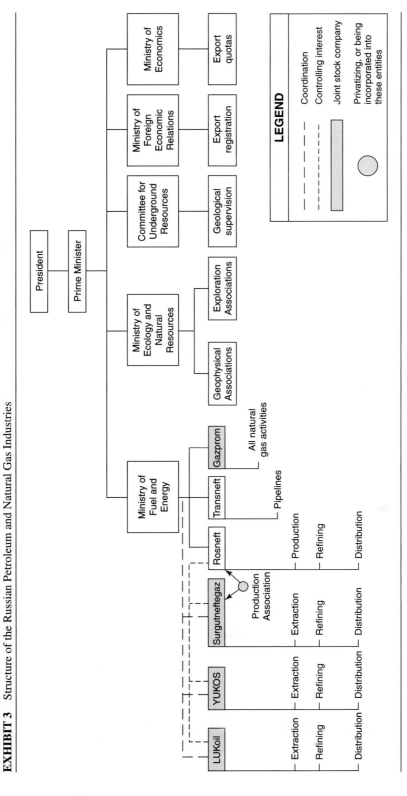

Source: Commonwealth of Independent States: Petroleum Industry Structure; Canadian Energy Research Institute, *Oil in the Former Soviet Union;* and Interfax-America, *Petroleum Report.*

EXHIBIT 4 World Crude Oil Production and Consumption, 1970–1992 (millions of barrels per day)

	1970	1975	1980	1985	1986	1987	1988	1989	1990	1991	1992
World production	45.7	53.3	59.3	53.3	55.5	55.7	57.8	59.0	59.7	59.4	59.5
World consumption	47.4	56.0	62.6	60.1	61.8	63.2	65.0	66.1	66.3	66.7	66.9

Source: Cambridge Energy Research Associates and Arthur Andersen & Co., *World Oil Trends 1994*, pp. 10, 24.

EXHIBIT 5 Average Prices of Crude Oil, 1970–1992 (U.S.$ per barrel)

	Mideast Light Official	Brent Spot	WII Spot	U.S. Average Spot	Wellhead
1970	1.35	1.21	NA	NA	3.18
1971	1.75	1.69	NA	NA	3.39
1972	1.90	1.82	NA	NA	3.39
1973	2.64	2.81	NA	NA	3.89
1974	9.56	10.98	NA	NA	6.87
1975	10.46	10.43	NA	NA	7.67
1976	11.51	11.63	NA	NA	8.19
1977	12.40	12.57	NA	NA	8.57
1978	12.70	12.91	NA	NA	9.00
1979	17.84	29.19	NA	NA	12.61
1980	29.38	36.01	NA	NA	21.61
1981	33.20	34.17	NA	NA	31.77
1982	33.77	31.76	NA	NA	28.52
1983	29.23	28.67	NA	NA	26.19
1984	28.75	28.10	NA	NA	25.88
1985	28.08	27.45	27.33	27.92	24.08
1986	28.00	13.33	14.56	15.14	12.60
1987	17.60	17.33	18.34	19.16	15.42
1988	17.52	13.40	14.94	16.01	12.57
1989	17.52	16.21	18.22	19.61	16.28
1990	17.52	20.71	23.39	24.30	19.98
1991	17.52	17.45	20.07	21.55	16.53
1992	17.52	17.86	19.28	20.52	16.00

Source: Cambridge Energy Research Associates and Arthur Andersen & Co., *World Oil Trends 1994*, p. 48.

broke from his customary enthusiasm to characterize the Russian investment climate as "one of complete disarray."[20]

To settle this disarray, Nicandros and other investors continued to stress the importance of a strong and transparent legal framework. Along with representatives from Western governments and lending institutions, they lobbied Russia's fledgling government to pass legislation that would clearly define the financial and legal basis for investment in the petroleum sector and create some mechanism for resolving disputes. In the summer of 1994, many industry insiders thought the legislation was only months or weeks away from passage.

But then in August, Russian President Boris Yeltsin dismissed the draft law under consideration by the parliament, claiming that the document

[20]Nicandros, p. 40.

EXHIBIT 6   Share of Crude Petroleum Production in the Former Soviet Union, 1991

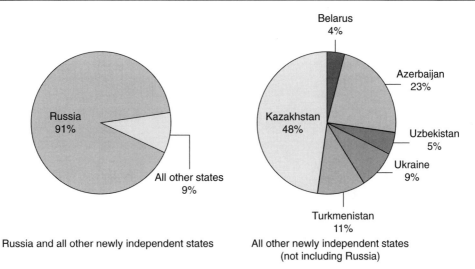

Russia and all other newly independent states

All other newly independent states
(not including Russia)

Source: U.S. Department of Energy, Policy Office.

EXHIBIT 7   Comparison of Crude Petroleum Production in the United States, Former
Soviet Union, and World (1982B92) (1,000 barrels per day)

Year	United States	Former Soviet Union	World
1982	8,649	11,912	53,481
1983	8,688	11,972	53,255
1984	8,879	11,861	54,488
1985	8,971	11,585	53,981
1986	8,680	11,895	56,227
1987	8,349	11,985	56,601
1988	8,140	11,978	58,662
1989	7,613	11,625	59,773
1990	7,355	10,880	60,471
1991	7,417	9,887	60,221
1992	7,153	8,354	60,141

Source: U.S. Department of Energy, Policy Office.

revealed an "anti-reform approach." Yeltsin argued that the existing legislation on mineral resources was specific enough to make any new law redundant. In interpreting this unexpected move, the *Financial Times* wrote: "Mr. Yeltsin's dismissal of the draft law, and his evident reluctance to propose an alternative, suggests he would prefer this area, as others, to be regulated by his decree."[21]

---

[21]John Lloyd, "Yeltsin Dismisses Draft Law to Build Up Oil Investment," *Financial Times,* August 5, 1994.

EXHIBIT 8 Former Soviet Union Imports and Exports of Crude Petroleum and Natural Gas, 1982–92 (1,000 barrels per day)

	Crude Petroleum		Natural Gas	
Year	Imports	Exports	Imports	Exports
1982	100	2,500	80	2,240
1983	140	2,600	80	2,185
1984	264	2,509	80	2,312
1985	262	2,275	105	2,510
1986	240	2,450	105	2,778
1987	291	1,684	78	2,973
1988	396	2,826	78	3,140
1989	167	2,554	36	3,618
1990	271	2,170	54	3,935
1991	0	1,215	NA	3,677
1992	0	1,390	NA	3,500

Source: Official statistics of the U.S. Department of Energy, Interfax *Petroleum Report,* and *Petroleum Intelligence Weekly.*

EXHIBIT 9 Relationship of the Former Soviet Union's Crude Petroleum Exports to Aggregate World Petroleum Prices, 1982–1992

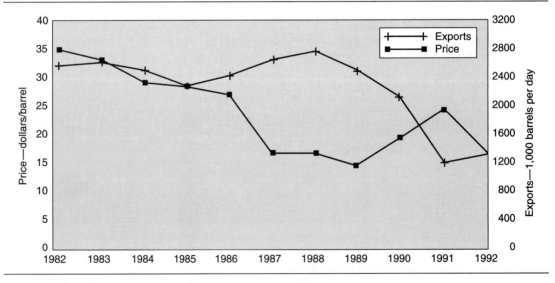

Source: U.S. Department of Energy.

EXHIBIT 10   Development Cost Profile for Western Siberia, 1992

	10M Barrels	60M Barrels	350M Barrels	1,000M Barrels
	Gross Cost (U.S.$ millions)			
Drilling	34	67	146	232
Facilities	48	110	401	868
Pipeline	45	50	56	66
Operations	63	221	851	2,121
Tariffs	11	70	408	1,165
Total	198	517	1,862	4,453
	Per Barrel Cost (U.S.$)			
Drilling	3.55	1.05	0.39	0.22
Facilities	4.77	1.73	1.08	0.82
Pipeline	4.69	0.78	0.15	0.06
Operations	6.54	3.49	2.30	2.00
Tariff	1.10	1.10	1.10	1.10
Total	20.66	8.15	5.03	4.21

Source: Spears and Associates.

EXHIBIT 11   Location of White Night Fields

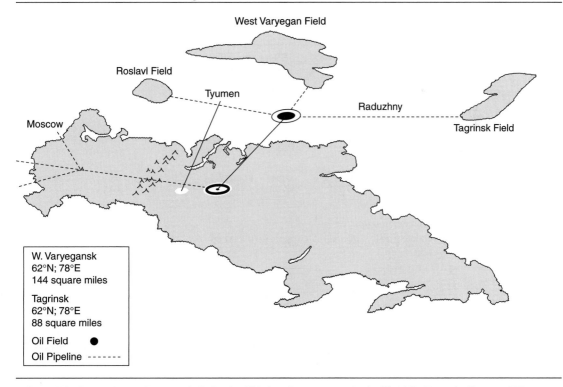

W. Varyegansk
62°N; 78°E
144 square miles

Tagrinsk
62°N; 78°E
88 square miles

Oil Field ●

Oil Pipeline - - - - - -

West Varyegan Field

Roslavl Field

Tyumen

Moscow

Raduzhny

Tagrinsk Field

Source: Brian Lavers, "Western Investment in the Russian Oil Industry," paper presented at the Oil and Gas Economics Finance and Management Conference (London), June 8–9, 1994.

EXHIBIT 12   White Nights Production

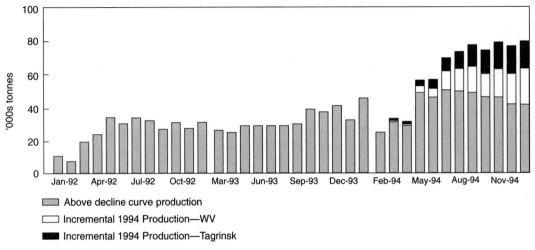

□ Above decline curve production

□ Incremental 1994 Production—WV

■ Incremental 1994 Production—Tagrinsk

The graph shows the effect of the change in the decline curve effective from April 1994.
Actual figures up to the end April 1994: estimates for May–December 1994 (in tonnes 000s)

Source: Brian Lavers, "Western Investment in the Russian Oil Industry," paper presented at the Oil and Gas Economics Finance and Management Conference (London), June 8–9, 1994.

EXHIBIT 13   White Nights Joint Enterprise Unit Cashflow, 1994

Urals Blend (revenue per barrel)	*$14.00*	*100.0%*
Taxes		
Export tax	$ 4.74	33.9%
Excise tax	1.44	10.3
Mineral usage tax	1.12	8.0
Resource renewal tax	0.60	4.3
Road use tax	0.06	0.4
VAT on pipeline fees	0.58	4.1
Social and accommodation tax	0.21	1.5
Property and land tax (est.)	0.20	1.4
Payroll-related taxes (est.)	0.16	1.2
Excess payroll tax (est.)	0.09	0.7
Total taxes	$ 9.19	65.7%
Pipeline costs (est.)	$ 2.50	17.9
Sales commission (est.)	0.09	0.7
Net remaining revenue for all operating and capital costs		
	$2.31	16.5%

Source: Brian Lavers, "Western Investment in the Russian Oil Industry," paper presented at Oil and Gas Economics Finance and Management Conference (London), June 8–9, 1994.

EXHIBIT 14   Financial Highlights, 1991–1994 (U.S.$ millions)

	1991	1992	1993	1994
Mobil Corporation				
Revenues from sales and services	62,359	63,564	63,474	66,757
Crude oil, products and operating supplies and expenses	35,735	36,639	35,622	36,665
Exploration expense	779	507	405	516
SG&A expenses	4,944	5,324	5,483	5,453
Interest and related income (expense)	155	(280)	177	165
Net income (loss)	1,920	862	2,084	1,079
Total assets	42,187	40,561	40,733	41,542
Current liabilities	13,602	12,629	12,351	13,418
Total liabilities	24,653	24,021	23,496	24,396
E. I. du Pont and Company (Conoco)				
Revenues	38,695	37,799	37,098	39,333
Cost of goods sold	22,528	21,856	21,396	21,977
Exploration expense	602	416	361	357
Research and development expense	1,298	1,277	1,132	1,047
SG&A expenses	3,576	3,553	3,081	2,888
Interest and related income (expense)	76	(90)	149	367
Net income (loss)	1,403	(3,927)	555	2,727
Total assets	36,559	38,870	37,053	36,892
Current liabilities	7,935	10,226	9,439	7,565
Total liabilities	19,655	26,928	25,636	23,873
Salomon Inc.				
Revenues	9,175	8,183	8,799	6,278
Interest expense	5,638	4,324	4,600	4,892
Total noninterest expenses	2,618	2,803	2,734	2,217
Net income (loss)	507	550	827	(399)
Total assets	97,402	159,459	184,835	172,732
Short-term borrowings	40,393	88,417	97,890	78,579
Total liabilities	93,387	155,151	179,589	168,240

Source: Company annual reports.

Case 2–2   Gerber Products Company: Investing in the New Poland

Tangible structural changes in the Polish economy will not emerge without more vigorous investment processes. They will certainly not be stimulated artificially and arbitrarily by the Government, which, even if it wished to, has no means to achieve that. There is a recession and the industry is weak. What is available is virtually only foreign aid, foreign credit, and foreign direct investment.

Dariusz Ledworowski, *Polish Minister of International Economic Cooperation*

If adults from different countries had as much in common as babies do, there would be fewer problems in the world.

Gerber official at an Alima press conference

In December of 1991, Fred Schomer and Steve Clark were caught in a delicate position. For months, Schomer, the chief financial officer of Gerber Products Company, and Clark, the company's general counsel, had been shuttling between Michigan and Warsaw, putting together a deal that would allow Gerber to acquire Alima S.A., one of Poland's largest and most successful food processing plants. On all sides, the deal had seemed to make sense. Gerber would modernize the aging plant, boost its sagging export trade, and give the Polish government $11 million of the hard currency it so desperately needed. In exchange, the world's largest baby food producer would gain a low-cost base for its European operations and an early advantage in the growing markets of Central and Eastern Europe.

Until this point, the negotiations had progressed smoothly. After winning a competitive bidding process sponsored by Poland's Ministry of Privatization, the Gerber officials had signed a Purchase and Sale agreement on October 1. Under the terms

of this agreement, Gerber had formally committed itself to the Alima deal and agreed to work with the government in resolving a series of complicated issues such as property ownership and taxation. Everyone involved in the negotiations had acknowledged that these issues were critical to the deal's success, but because the discussions were going so well both sides were confident that they could resolve all issues by the end of the year.

But then on October 27 politics had intervened. After months of internal squabbling Lech Walesa's Solidarity government had bowed to popular pressures and convened the country's first fully democratic elections since World War II. The results were chaotic. Twenty-nine parties, including such novices as the Beer Lover's party, the Give Us a Chance party, and the Alliance of Women Against the Hardships of Life party, won seats in the Sejm, none with more than 13% of the vote. Solidarity splintered into a number of rival factions, the communists emerged as the second strongest party in the nation, and for weeks the newly elected representatives could not even form a coalition capable of selecting a Cabinet. Most ominously of all perhaps, the elections had revealed a wellspring of discontent with Poland's economic reform. After two years spent on an ambitious "leap to the market,"

This case was prepared by Research Associate Allegra Young under the supervision of Professor Debora Spar.

Copyright © 1998 by the President and Fellows of Harvard College. Harvard Business School case 793-069.

many Poles had grown disenchanted with capitalism and wanted their new government to embrace policies of looser money, more social insurance, and fewer foreign investors.

And thus Fred Schomer and Steve Clark found themselves reconsidering their options. They knew that, at a minimum, the new government was going to want to renegotiate the Purchase and Sale agreement and take a tougher stance on the issues of ownership and taxation. Most likely, the government would also tinker with existing policies on profit repatriation, currency devaluation, privatization, and worker compensation—all of which could have a serious impact on Gerber's bottom line. Likewise, it was clear that the new government would be unable to deliver many of the promises that its predecessor had made in the October 1 agreement.

In principle, Schomer, Clark, and the rest of the Gerber team were still committed to Poland and the Alima plant. The facilities were in good shape, the enterprise was well managed, and the entire operation fit nicely with Gerber's plans for global expansion. But before they spent $25 million for an overseas acquisition, the Gerber officials needed to reevaluate the merits of investing in such an uncertain situation.

The Gerber Products Company

Founded in 1928, the Gerber Products Company specialized in the care of the world's smallest consumers: babies. Daniel Gerber, Sr. founded the company in 1928 in the small town of Fremont, Michigan. At the core of Gerber's line were the 165 varieties of jarred baby food that the company distributed worldwide. In addition, Gerber manufactured basic baby apparel under its own product name and children's wear under the Buster Brown label.

The location of Gerber's main plant in the small farming town of Fremont, Michigan (1991 pop. 3,800) was a critical element of the company's operations. Most of the fruits and vegetables used in the factory were grown within 100 miles of Fre-

mont, including 7.3 million pounds of peas, 60 million pounds of apples, 8.4 million pounds of peaches, and tons of pears, carrots, squash, green beans, blueberries, cherries, plums and wheat.[1] A nearby glass manufacturer provided glass for the approximately 600 million jars that the plant used each year.

Gerber employed 1,200 people at the Fremont site, which also served as its corporate headquarters. The offices of Gerber reflected the culture of the corporation: babies' pictures adorned the walls and desks of the employees, many of whom were also shareholders. Nameplates were created from children's blocks and automated toy soldiers guarded the entrance to the chairman's office. At one point in the company's 63-year history, corporate officers had considered a corporate office move to Chicago, but Fremont's loyalty to Gerber persuaded them to stay. As Robert Johnston, the company vice chairman explained, "It is a dedicated group of people. They used to blow the whistle when they needed people to come in to help process peas. People would give up whatever they were doing and come in to help out. That's pretty hard to walk away from."[2]

Since Gerber introduced processed baby food, the company had dominated the United States market, with a 1991 market share of 72%. The company's commitment to providing a child with nutritional food was central to its philosophy and paramount to its appeal. The company's managers prided themselves on the fact that doctors had been known to use Gerber's 1-800 number as an emergency resource for their patients, and focused on producing whatever was necessary to maintain the medical community's endorsement. The entire company was devoted to its founder's original determination to "do everything we can to deserve and maintain the

---

[1]"Gerber: Attention to Heritage and Values Has Defined and Helped Develop One of Michigan's Largest Multinational Corporation," *North Force Magazine*, Vol. 4, No. 2 (January 1991), p. 17.

[2]*North Force Magazine*, p. 17.

confidence mothers have in our products."[3] Or as one current executive vowed, "If the pediatrician says we need to make artichokes to provide a baby with a balanced diet, we'll make artichokes."

Gerber's commitment to quality paid off handsomely on its bottom line. Despite flattening birth rates in the United States, the company had managed an 11% increase in sales in FY 1991, propelling its superbrand to total sales of over $1.2 billion. Of the 4% of U.S. houses that had babies, Gerber reached a full 92% of them. Gerber's other U.S. competitors, Heinz and Beech-nut, shared about equal amounts of the rest of the market.[4]

With a dominant position in the American market, therefore, Gerber's challenge was to find some means of expansion or diversification. For awhile the company had experimented with ventures in day care centers and toys, but when these operations failed to provide any significant growth for the company, Gerber's management had decided to divest from all but the most basic lines of infant clothing, refocusing instead on the production of baby food. This streamlined strategy doubled Gerber's return on equity, taking it from 14.5% during the 1980s to around 29% since 1990.[5] Still the company wanted to grow.

The most obvious place for growth was the global market. In 1991, 90% of Gerber's sales were still occurring in the United States, a country with only 3% of the world's babies.[6] The company also did very well in Puerto Rico, Central America, and especially Mexico, where a joint venture with Pepsi controlled 100% of the local market. Elsewhere, though, Gerber's presence was limited. In Canada, Heinz effectively controlled the domestic market. And in Western Europe, Australia, the Middle East, and Africa, Gerber had already licensed their technology to local firms and thus were precluded from expanding their own sales operations. In the Far East, Gerber had had some success in penetrating the Korean and Taiwanese markets, but its success was limited by these countries' traditional reliance on cereal-based foods. In Japan, meanwhile, the company had encountered cultural barriers. Apparently many women felt that their mothers-in-law and husbands would look down at the use of commercially prepared baby food. Gerber executives were thinking of ways to market their product across this cultural divide, but prospects for the Japanese markets were still not overwhelming.

Against this backdrop, Al Piergallini, Gerber's chairman and CEO, had decided in 1990 to make Central and Eastern Europe a target for Gerber's international expansion. With the fall of communism, the markets of Central and Eastern Europe were positioned to grow rapidly, and consumers were eager for the Western-style goods that had been forbidden to them for so long. Despite a poor local economy Gerber was already doing well in the region, having exported around $3 million of baby food to Poland since 1988. Exports, though, were not the best means of servicing the Polish markets, since they left Gerber at the mercy of foreign exchange rates. If the company could instead establish a local plant, it would be able to minimize the vicissitudes of exchange rate swings and also develop an anchor for exports to neighboring countries, such as Hungary and Czechoslovakia. More importantly, a Polish plant would also help Gerber improve its sales in France. Since the French licensee's license had just expired, Gerber had recently entered more aggressively into the French market where per capita consumption of baby food was higher than in the United States. Gerber officials knew that they could be competitive in France in terms of quality. While many of their competitors' products tasted better because they included sugar and other seasonings, Gerber's more natural formulas had already won the endorsement of a majority of French pediatricians.[7] Gerber also needed, though, to make its

---

[3]Daniel Gerber, cited in *Gerber Annual Report*, 1992, p. 1.

[4]Margaret Littman, "Processor of the Year," *Prepared Foods*, September 1992, p. 30.

[5]Marcia Berss, "Limited Horizons," *Forbes*, October 12, 1992, P. 66.

[6]Berss, p. 66.

[7]Interview with Gerber executive, December 7, 1992.

food competitive on price, and a plant in Central Europe would do this. It would allow Gerber to move closer to the European market, gain valuable economies of scale, and avoid the duties that fell heaviest on goods imported from the United States.[8]

In order to gain this potentially lucrative opportunity, however, Gerber had to move fast. Already the CEO of Heinz had announced that his company was considering using Central Europe as a base of operations and was researching cites in Ukraine, Hungary, and Poland. Clearly, Gerber's competitors had also noticed the potential of Central Europe and they were beginning to act.

Then, in May of 1991, the investment firm of Wasserstein Perella called Gerber with an interesting prospect. John Simpson, a director in Wasserstein Perella's Chicago office, informed Fred Schomer that the Polish government was inviting bids for the acquisition of Alima S.A., a food processing plant located in the southeastern town of Rzeczow.[9] Simpson did not know a lot about the plant, but he knew that it was considered one of Poland's best businesses and that one of its products was baby food. Quickly Schomer called a meeting with Piergallini and senior managers from Gerber's International Division. After a brief strategy session they all agreed that the offer was intriguing but that they needed to learn much more about Poland and Alima before they went any further.

---

[8]Since 1989, Poland had been involved in a series of trade negotiations with the European Community. Early on, both sides had agreed to the elimination of most tariffs within five years. In December 1989, the EC extended its Generalized System of Preferences to Poland, waiving import duties for a broad array of goods. In December 1991, Poland was officially granted association status with the EC. Under the association agreement, tariffs on most Polish goods were substantially reduced. See Kalypso Nicolaïdis, "East European Trade in the Aftermath of 1989: Did International Institutions Matter?" in Robert O. Keohane, Joseph S. Nye and Stanley Hoffman, eds., *After the Cold War: International Institutions and State Strategies in Europe, 1989-1991* (Cambridge: Harvard University Press, 1993), pp. 196–245.

[9]Pronounced Zhes-hoff.

Country Risks: The Political Economy of Poland

Macroeconomics and the leap to the market. In January of 1990, the Polish government had launched an unprecedented program of economic reform. Under the leadership of Leszek Balcerowicz, the country's controversial Finance Minister, Poland had attempted to "leap to the market," moving as quickly as possible to stabilize its inflationary economy and establish the foundations of a market economy.[10] On the morning of January 1, the government had simultaneously lowered trade barriers, declared a convertible currency, and eliminated virtually all domestic price controls. Soon thereafter, it also announced an increase in taxes and a substantial decrease in the existing consumer subsidies.

The logic of the plan was tough but straightforward: to push Poland away from centralized control of its economy and towards the rigors of the market. Once wage and price controls were removed and the zloty allowed to trade openly on world markets, prices in Poland would converge gradually with those prevailing elsewhere. Likewise, once the government stopped subsidizing Polish consumers and financing industry, market mechanisms would have to develop in order to serve these needs. And once realistic prices and financial institutions were in place, the government could advance to the next stage of reform—the mass privatization of Poland's state-owned economy.

After nearly two years of austerity, though, Balcerowicz's plan had still not achieved all that its proponents had expected. On some fronts, the results were promising. The long lines and empty shelves of communism had disappeared, replaced by new establishments selling everything from personal computers to designer fashion. Restaurants and office buildings had sprouted up across Warsaw and a farmer's market flourished in the shadows

---

[10]For more detailed account of these changes, see Debora Spar, *Poland 1989,* Harvard Business School case 792–091 (Boston: Harvard Business School, 1992).

of the former Ministry of Culture. Polish exports were faring well on world markets and inflation, which had been 54% a month in 1989, had declined to a manageable 3%.

But other areas were disappointing. While the stores were stocked with luxury items, few Poles could afford to buy any of the merchandise because their savings had been deflated so severely by the currency conversion. Even basic items such as food and rent had become prohibitively expensive after the lifting of price controls. Energy prices alone had risen by 500% and government deficit rose to U.S.$400 million and was predicted to soar to $1 billion by 1993. Meanwhile, Poland's traditional industrial base was struggling to deal with the triple burdens of global competition, a cessation of government support, and the loss of their Eastern European market. Industrial production fell 30% in 1990, many smaller firms were forced out of business, and unemployment, which was virtually unknown under communism, was predicted to climb to 12% by early 1993. Most dramatically perhaps, the country was still critically short of the capital it needed to import technology and modernize its industrial base. The government was able to raise some funds on international markets and through institutions such as the World Bank and European Bank for Reconstruction and Development. But these sources were limited. Poland's outstanding debt of $41 billion in 1989 made it a poor risk for international lenders, and its lack of an adequate financial infrastructure made even the most generous donors wary of advancing much money. In the short run, at least, the transformation of Poland's economy depended on the capitalization of industry. And the capitalization of industry depended on foreign investors.

The climate for investment.   In many ways, the new Poland was an ideal target for foreign investment. There was a domestic market of nearly 40 million people, decades of pent-up demand, and a government desperate for hard currency and eager to sell its aging industrial assets. Because the Poles needed Western capital so badly, they were apparently willing to negotiate with anyone who offered and willing to make whatever concessions were necessary to attract potential investors.

Unlike the other countries of Central Europe, moreover, Poland had a relatively strong history of foreign investment. Officially, Poland had been open to foreign investment since 1976, when the Council of Ministers passed a regulation permitting the establishment of small-scale enterprises.[11] Then, in 1982 the Sejm had loosened the rules even further, formally recognizing the legal basis for foreign investment and creating a state guarantee for the invested capital.[12] The laws were liberalized again in 1986 and 1988 until, with the passage of still more legislation in 1991, the country had abolished virtually all legal restraints on foreign investment. There was no minimum set on the amount of the initial investment and permits were required only for a handful of industries such as defense, air and sea ports, real estate, and wholesale trade in imported goods. Foreign companies were allowed to repatriate all of their capital, including capital gains, and to remit full profits and dividends. For companies that made large investments (ECU two million or more) or large exporters (exporting 20% of their production), additional tax relief could be obtained. Foreigners were given full national treatment as well as investment guarantees, tax credits, and capital export allowances, which arguably were not available to the average Polish investor.

In effect, the Polish laws had placed foreign direct investment beyond the realm of government regulation. Foreigners were free to engage in any

---

[11]Under these laws, however, the investors were significantly constrained both in the scale of their operations and in their potential profitability. They were not eligible, for instance, for credit at any Polish banks; they had to make an advance deposit of 30% of their projects' cost to a Polish bank; and they were allowed to transfer 50% of their export profits out of the country. Under these conditions, only nine major firms chose to invest in Poland during the six years those regulations were in place.

[12]This section draws heavily on Debora Spar, "Foreign Direct Investment in Eastern Europe," in Keohane, Nye and Hoffmann, eds., *After the Cold War,* pp. 286–309.

business they desired, as long as they paid their taxes and brought hard currency with them. But still there were problems. Outside the government, many Poles were adamantly opposed to foreign investment, seeing it as just another form of foreign control over Poland's economic development. As of 1991, the opposition was relatively quiet, since even the most vehement opponents of investment recognized the country's desperate need for capital. If foreign investment grew too large however, or if it was seen as contributing in any way to the country's economic woes, then the critics would undoubtedly become louder, and bring their discontent directly into the political process.

Alima S.A.

The Alima food processing plant was located in a small Polish town that bore a certain resemblance to Gerber's headquarters in Fremont. Like Fremont, Rzeszow was an agricultural center, surrounded by thousands of farmers whose families had been selling fruits and vegetables to Alima for two or three generations. As was the case in most of Poland, the plots around Rzeszow had never been successfully collectivized, and thus their farmers tended to be more independent and financially better off than the rest of the population. The farmers were also technologically quite advanced, since they benefitted from an extensive system of university support for agriculture.[13] The crops around Rzeszow were not exactly what Gerber would want to use in the future—the apples were too tart and the carrots not right for baby food—but as long as the plant had a good relationship with the farmers, which seemed to be the case, Gerber believed it could work with the farmers to ensure that the right changes were made.

Physically, the Alima plant bore the strong imprint of centralized planning. It was an odd amalgamation of facilities and businesses lumped together by planners who had simply assigned them to the

---

[13]In the words of one Gerber official, the farmers of Rzeszow "have the book on the shelf and actually use it."

Alima site. Thus Alima produced everything from pickled beets to pureed raspberries. Baby food accounted for only about 10% of its total production, while 60% was composed of various fruit juices and nectars sold domestically under the "Bobo" label. The remainder of the plant's production was a random and varying mix of whatever the farmers had grown that year. In addition, Alima's facilities included a set of apartment complexes and a separate enterprise, Borek Stary, which specialized in the production of liquored peaches and "fortified" (alcoholic) fruit beverages.

Technically, Alima was rather up-to-date. While some of its equipment dated from the 1920s, the baby food lines contained state-of-the-art machinery imported from Italy in 1985. The lines lacked some key parts and were not perfectly aligned, but they still produced 300 to 400 jars of baby food per minute. This was far below Gerber's rate of 1,300 jars per minute, but still quite acceptable. Alima also had a stable source of high-quality glass jars, a crucial input for any baby food manufacturer. Located just 50 miles down the road, the Jaroslaw glassworks had supplied Alima for decades. Jaroslaw was well-run, technically proficient, and unusually fuel efficient, since it produced 50% of its fuel from a local gas well. Like most of Poland's state-owned enterprises, Jaroslaw was in transition and slotted to be sold as part of the government's privatization program. Until the sale took place, however, the plant would continue to provide Alima with glass jars.

Alima's final asset was its manager, Maria Potocka-Bielecka. Potocka-Bielecka had been chosen by a national search for the Alima position and knew her business well. By all accounts, she was extremely intelligent, flexible, and adept at heading off worker strikes.

Despite Potocka-Bielecka's skills, though, business at Alima still operated haphazardly. No one paid much attention to accounting procedures or financial reports, and orders were placed on an ad hoc basis: if raspberries had been delivered in the previous year, then Alima would order and process raspberries again, even if there was no demand for the fruit. Similarly, the plant had no sales force. It simply waited for requests to come by phone or during Poland's quarterly food processing fair. It never marketed its production in any way since Poland's "economy of shortage" had always meant that buyers would take whatever was available.

Though awkward by Western standards, this system had served Alima well. With $20 million in sales, Alima was one of the most successful enterprises in Poland. It employed 1,200 people, bought produce from thousands of farmers and produced one of Poland's most popular beverages. The question, though, was whether Alima could survive the transition to capitalism, and whether Western capitalists could ever make Alima worth their efforts.

Evaluation and Assessment

For Gerber, the evaluation process began in May of 1991, only days after Schomer had received the first phone call from Wasserstein Perella. In order to compete for Alima, Gerber had to meet the government's deadline for entering bids. That gave the company's executives two weeks to investigate everything from politics to radiation poisoning.

Right from the start, the Gerber team saw the logistical difficulties of doing business in Poland. First, Wasserstein Perella had never closed a deal in Poland. While they had done some previous work in Central Europe, this acquisition involved new issues and a very new territory. Second, few law firms were suitable to represent Gerber's interests. The Polish firms that Steve Clark interviewed did not really understand Western-style practices or the legal language that Gerber and its advisors would rely upon. And Gerber's lawyers in the United States were completely unfamiliar with Poland's changing investment laws. Finally, Gerber settled on the London office of Skadden, Arps, Meagher & Flom since they were representing the Polish government in several deals and at least knew the government officials.

In the meantime, teams of Gerber specialists flew to Poland to check into plant and environmental conditions. At Alima, they were mostly pleased with what they saw. Gerber's engineers found that while the plant lacked some technical expertise, it was basically sound. They confirmed that the equipment was in good repair and of top quality. As expected, they also reported that the plant had too much equipment and a number of auxiliary operations that would have to be jettisoned. The engineers also investigated the glassworks at Jaroslaw and judged it to be adequate for meeting Alima's short-term needs. Once the manufacturing process at Alima was brought up to Western speeds, the glass would have to be stronger, but until then Jaroslaw would be fine.

On the environmental front, Gerber's first priority was to ensure that the soil around Rzeszow had not been in any way contaminated by fallout from the 1987 disaster at Chernobyl. And on this score, they were lucky: after extensive sampling, consultants from the World Health Organization confirmed that the soil was completely clean. Simultaneously, however, Gerber's own engineers uncovered a number of potential environmental problems. First, the farmers were using too many pesticides for Gerber to accept their produce as "pure and natural." Second, the solid waste disposal system at the Alima plant was faulty and would need at least $3 million worth of repairs. And third, Alima's management permitted some practices—such as smoking on the production line—that simply violated existing EC and U.S. regulations. Still, Gerber's engineers did not consider these problems insurmountable. They would cost money and take time, but they could be solved.

A more troubling issue was how to evaluate the broader context of the Alima deal. Gerber's management knew that Poland was changing, but they had little sense of how specific changes might occur and what impact they could have on a Western investor. To learn more, Gerber's managers consulted with a number of academic specialists. They inquired into Poland's history, its culture, and its experience under communist rule. No one, of course, could predict how Poland would emerge from this period of transition, but the academics

EXHIBIT 1   Gerber Products Company and Subsidiaries—Consolidated Balance Sheet, 1990–1991 (thousands of nominal dollars)

	1990	1991
ASSETS		
Current Assets:		
Cash and cash equivalents	$ 32,097	$ 99,195
Short-term investments	19,941	29,892
Trade accounts receivable, less allowances	110,355	120,960
Inventories:		
Finished products	101,140	116,465
Work-in-process	37,835	30,691
Raw materials and supplies	59,428	44,667
Current assets of discontinued operations	2,574	
Total current assets	$363,370	$441,870
Other Assets:		
Investments held by insurance operations	$57,325	$66,794
Deferred policy acquisition costs	33,578	38,790
Prepaid pension costs	37,046	44,161
Miscellaneous other assets	22,405	31,891
Intangible assets, less accumulated amortization of $4,744	7,653	
Land, Buildings, and Equipment:		
Land	4,036	4,148
Buildings	88,670	89,133
Machinery and equipment	220,525	234,285
Construction in progress	19,278	21,502
Allowances for depreciation	(140,714)	(145,238)
Fixed assets of discontinued operations (net)	41,561	
Total assets	$754,733	$827,336
LIABILITIES AND SHAREHOLDERS' EQUITY		
Current Liabilities:		
Short-term borrowings	$7,032	$475
Trade accounts payable	59,868	56,770
Salaries, wages, and other compensation	36,634	43,992
Local taxes, interest, and other expenses	51,863	58,302
Income taxes	10,460	20,567
Policy claims and reserves	7,343	10,884
Current liabilities of discontinued operations	8,656	
Current maturities of long-term debt	424	1,117
Total current liabilities	$182,280	$192,107

(continued)

EXHIBIT 1   (*concluded*)

	1990	1991
LIABILITIES AND SHAREHOLDERS' EQUITY		
Current Liabilities:		
Long-term debt	146,221	164,491
Deferred income taxes	26,941	20,507
Future policy benefits	47,486	55,674
Shareholders' equity:		
Common stock, par value $2.50 a share—		
authorized 200M shares: (1992—37,196,959		
shares, 1991—37,392,560 shares)	104,134	93,481
Paid-in capital	6,390	5,382
Retained earnings	377,768	322,121
Foreign currency translation	(2,190)	(3,598)
Unearned stock comp.	(269)	(3,115)
Unearned ESOP compensation	(20,300)	(19,714)
Cost of common stock in treasury:		
(1990—3,956,768 shares)	(113,728)	
Total	$754,733	$827,336

Source: *Gerber Annual Report,* 1991, pp. 24–25.

EXHIBIT 2   Gerber Products Company and Subsidiaries—Consolidated Statement of Operations (thousands of nominal dollars)

	1990	1991
Net sales and revenue	$1,136,436	$1,178,942
Interest, royalties, and other income	14,366	24,264
Total income	$1,150,802	$1,203,206
Deductions from income:		
Cost of products sold, services provided	$678,216	$691,527
Marketing, distribution, administrative		
and general expenses	285,223	291,786
Restructuring charges	16,500	19,000
Interest expense	16,487	17,543
Total deductions	$996,426	$1,019,856
Earnings from continuing		
operations before income taxes	$154,376	$183,350
Income taxes	59,822	70,532
Loss from discontinued operations	(479)	
Net earnings	**$94,075**	**$112,818**
Net earnings per share	**2.49**	**3.00**

Source: *Gerber Annual Report,* 1991, p. 23.

EXHIBIT 3   Poland—National Income Accounts, 1985–1990 (billions of 1987 zlotys)

	1985	1986	1987	1988	1989	1990
Gross domestic product	15,803	16,585	16,940	17,626	17,675	15,630
Government consumption	1,560	1,508	1,516	1,445	1,056	1,160
Private consumption	9,752	10,137	10,157	10,063	9,145	8,431
Gross fixed capital formation	3,370	3,631	3,821	3,964	2,891	2,982
Increase in stocks	1,034	1,159	1,063	1,781	3,911	1,769
Exports	2,898	3,019	3,625	4,013	3,372	4,024
Imports	−2,672	−2,784	−3,218	−3,530	−2,630	−2,749

Figures may not add due to rounding.

Source: IMF, *International Financial Statistics Yearbook,* 1992, p. 581; World Bank, 1992, p. 493.

EXHIBIT 4   Poland—Balance of Payments, 1985–1990 (millions of 1985 $U.S.)

	1985	1986	1987	1988	1989	1990
A. Current Account						
Exports (fob)	10,945	11,612.5	11,3454.3	12,587.3	11,200.2	13,241.6
Imports (fob)	10,599	11,157.7	10,600.0	11,597.3	11,159.3	10,240.8
Trade balance	347	454.7	745.3	990	40.9	3,000.8
Services, credit	2,104	1,962.0	2,090.6	2,247.3	2,785.9	2,675.6
Services, debit	1,846	1,959.1	1,913.2	2,185.5	2,657.1	2,380.4
Services, net	258	2.9	177.4	61.8	128.8	295.2
Interest and dividends, credit	173	183.1	204.7	246.4	356.8	504.2
Interest and dividends, debit	2,730	2,785.8	2,954.7	2,932.7	3,153.2	3,335.3
Interest and dividends, net	−2,557	−2,602.7	−2,750	−2,686.4	−2,796.3	−2,831.1
Private transfers	970	1,068.2	1,469.8	1,537.3	1,323.8	1,844.5
Official transfers					76.6	255.1
Transfers, net	970	1,068.2	1,469.8	1,537.3	1,400.3	2,099.5
Current account balance	**−982**	**−1,076.9**	**−357.5**	**−97.2**	**−1,226.2**	**2,564.4**
B. Direct Investment						
	14	−5.8	3.4	−6.4	−6.1	74.4
C. Other Capital						
Resident official sector	−827	−799.4	−2,229.3	−423.6	−1,019.2	5,418.1
Deposit money banks	−797	−2,887.1	469.8	−1,851.8	−426.5	−2,880.4
Other sectors	134	21.4	−250.9	−398.2	−111.4	−5.8
D. Errors and Omissions						
	118	771.8	85.8	−242.7	−95.7	111.2
E. Reserves and Related Items						
Change in reserves	236	168.5	−751.8	−510	−225.4	−2,021.7
Exceptional financing	2,104	3,867.6	3,030.2	3,511.8	3,110.5	−3,685.6
Use of fund credit and loans						425.6

Source: IMF, *International Financial Statistics Yearbook,* 1992, p. 581.

EXHIBIT 5   Prices, Production, and Employment, 1985–1991 (1985 = 100)

	1985	1986	1987	1988	1989	1990	1991
Producer prices	100	117	149	238	745	5,385	7,976
Consumer prices	100	117	147	236	828	5,684	9,680
Wages:							
Average nominal earnings	100	121	147	270	1,035	4,817	7,696
Industrial production	100	104	107	112	111	82	69
Industrial employment	100	100	99	98	95	83	83

Source: IMF, *International Financial Statistics Yearbook,* 1992, p. 581.

EXHIBIT 6   Monthly Inflation and Exchange Rates

Year and Month	CPI Inflation	Nominal Exchange Rate (zloty/$)*	Year and Month	CPI Inflation	Nominal Exchange Rate (zloty/$)*
89:1	11.1	505.8	90:8	1.8	9500
89:2	7.9	525.9	90:9	4.6	9500
89:3	8.1	566.9	90:10	5.7	9500
89:4	8.9	631.3	90:11	4.9	9500
89:5	7.2	746.2	90:12	5.9	9500
89:6	6.1	848.7	91:1	12.7	9500
89:7	9.5	836.2	91:2	6.7	9500
89:8	39.5	988	91:3	4.5	9500
89:9	34.4	1339.5	91:4	2.7	9500
89:10	54.8	1970.3	91:5	4.9	10290
89:11	22.4	3076.7	91:6	.1	11498
89:12	17.7	5235.5	91:7	.6	11523
90:1	79.6	9500	91:8	4.3	11301
90:2	23.8	9500	91:9	4.3	11039
90:3	4.3	9500	91:10	3.2	11222
90:4	7.5	9500	91:11	3.2	11224
90:5	4.6	9500	91:12	3.1	10967
90:6	3.4	9500	92:1	7.5	11483
90:7	3.6	9500			

*The zloty was declared convertible on January 1, 1990, and was fixed until May 17, 1991, at which time it began following a crawling peg.

Source: Data from the Polish Central Statistical Office.

pointed out several trends and practices that gave Gerber reason for optimism. First, unlike some of its neighbors in central Europe, Poland had a tradition of commercial life that extended back to the Middle Ages. Even under communism, the Poles had retained a certain spirit of free enterprise. Polish farmers had never been collectivized and Polish laborers went on strike far more frequently than their counterparts in other countries of the Soviet bloc. Second, most Poles had always detested the

EXHIBIT 7   Poland—Consumer Prices, 1989–1992

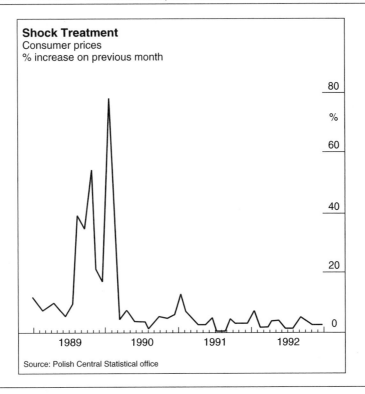

Source: *The Economist,* January 23, 1993, p. 21.

communist regime that was thrust upon them after World War II. They always saw it as a foreign intrusion and thus had never developed an indigenous ideology or a hard-core band of devotees. Thus, no matter how badly the economy deteriorated during the transition to a free market, it was unlikely that the Poles would choose to return to communism.

Finally, the academics underlined the importance of Poland's bid to enter the European Community. With 1992 fast approaching, most Poles wanted desperately to join the common market and register their status as full-fledged Europeans. Realistically, of course, membership in the EC was still many years away. But the desire to conform to European standards would act as a powerful constraint on the Poles, forcing them to acquiesce whenever possible to existing norms.

Forecast and Conclusions

While Schomer, Clark, and others from the Gerber team were interviewing the experts and visiting the Alima site at Rzeszow, Martin Lasher was back in Fremont trying to piece all the data together. As Director of Corporate Planning, Lasher's job was to evaluate the overall prospects of the Alima deal, and to recommend how much—if anything—Gerber should pay for this acquisition.

To arrive at this calculation, Lasher, in conjunction with Wasserstein Perella, constructed a basic capital budget model and tried to estimate the

EXHIBIT 8   Poland—Industrial Production, 1989–1992

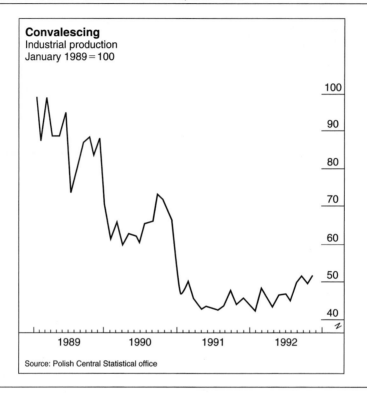

Convalescing
Industrial production
January 1989 = 100

Source: Polish Central Statistical office

Source: *The Economist,* January 23, 1993, p. 21.

EXHIBIT 9   Poland—Percent Share of the Private Sector, 1989–1991

	1989	1990	1991
GDP	29	31	42
Employment, incl. private agriculture	44	46	51
Employment, excl. private agriculture	22	23	27
Exports	—	5	22
Imports	—	14	50
Investment	35	42	41
Industrial production	16	18	24
Construction	33	32	55
Commerce	60	64	83
Transport	12	14	24

Source: *The Economist,* January 23, 1993, p. 22.

EXHIBIT 10   The Lower House of the Sejm, November 1991

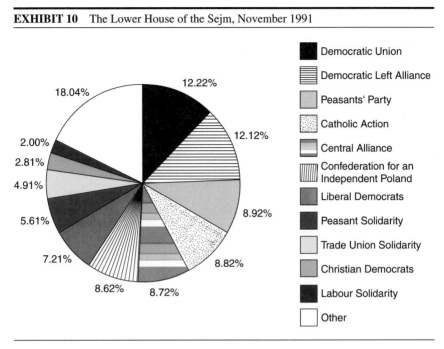

Legend:
- Democratic Union
- Democratic Left Alliance
- Peasants' Party
- Catholic Action
- Central Alliance
- Confederation for an Independent Poland
- Liberal Democrats
- Peasant Solidarity
- Trade Union Solidarity
- Christian Democrats
- Labour Solidarity
- Other

Source: "How many Polish parties does it take to make a cabinet?", *The Economist,* November 2, 1991, p. 43.

relevant variables as closely as possible (see Exhibit 11). In some cases, Lasher was able to derive his numbers from the usual sources. He projected revenues on the basis of current sales of Bobo fruit. Gerber expected to have sales of baby food in Poland and France, and future exports to Central and Eastern European markets. He based labor costs on existing wages plus expected inflation and used prevailing international prices to figure the cost of key inputs such as jars, caps, and labels. In all of these calculations Lasher was conservative, basing his assumptions on a worst case scenario.

Input prices, however, were the easy part. Lasher's real challenge lay in forecasting broader variables such as interest rates, inflation rates, and any tax credit that the government might allow under current conditions in Poland. These economic factors were liable to swing quickly and significantly, even over a short period. Unlike the financial variables, moreover, these factors were also particularly vulnerable to any shift in govern-

ment policy. If popular pressures mounted against Bakcerowicz's program of economic reform, for example, the government might be forced to reinstitute price controls or revalue the zloty. If foreign investors came under particular attack, the government might try to revoke any special privileges it had bestowed upon Gerber.

Thus, on all fronts, the Alima deal faced tremendous uncertainties. But somehow Marty Lasher had to convert these uncertainties into numbers and plug them into his model. So, as conservatively as he could, he guessed. The existing assets at Alima were valuable, but the other warehouses filled with old equipment were useless to Gerber and would have to be scrapped. Lasher then gathered current and predicted sales information, reduced the numbers, and then put them into his model. He assumed that the devaluation of the zloty would roughly keep pace with the inflation rate, and that both would stabilize over the next five years, eventually reaching levels similar to those of Spain, another

EXHIBIT 11 Gerber's Capital Budgeting Model: Volume, Price, and Revenue Forecast

	1992	1993	1994	1995	1996	1997	1998	1999	2000	2001
Volume:										
Bobo nectar business (dozens mn's)										
Domestic	8.0	8.0	8.0	8.0	8.0	8.0	8.0	8.0	8.0	8.0
Export	0.0	0.0	0.0	0.0	0.0	0.0	0.0	0.0	0.0	0.0
Gerber jar business (dozens mn's)										
Domestic	0.0	1.2	1.8	2.4	3.0	3.6	4.2	4.8	5.4	6.0
Export	0.0	5.0	7.0	9.0	11.0	13.0	15.0	17.0	17.0	17.0
Industrial products (tons 000's)										
Domestic	0.0	0.0	0.0	0.0	0.0	0.0	0.0	0.0	0.0	0.0
Export	10.0	13.8	17.51	21.3	25.0	28.8	32.5	36.3	40.0	43.8
Total Bobo and Gerber jar volume (dozens mn's)										
Domestic	8.0	9.2	9.8	10.4	11.0	11.6	12.2	12.8	13.4	14.0
Export	0.0	5.0	7.0	9.0	11.0	13.0	15.0	17.0	17.0	17.0
Prices:										
Bobo nectar business ($/dozen)										
Domestic	$1.91	$1.91	$1.91	$1.91	$1.91	$1.91	$1.91	$1.91	$1.91	$1.91
Export	0.00	0.00	0.00	0.00	0.00	0.00	0.00	0.00	0.00	0.00
Gerber jar business ($/dozen)										
Domestic	2.56	2.56	2.56	2.56	2.56	2.56	2.56	2.56	2.56	2.56
Export	2.12	2.12	2.12	2.12	2.12	2.12	2.12	2.12	2.12	2.12
Industrial products ($/ton)										
Domestic	0.00	0.00	0.00	0.00	0.00	0.00	0.00	0.00	0.00	0.00
Export	400.00	400.00	400.00	400.00	400.00	400.00	400.00	400.00	400.00	400.00

(continued)

EXHIBIT 11 Gerber's Capital Budgeting Model: Volume, Price, and Revenue Forecast

	1992	1993	1994	1995	1996	1997	1998	1999	2000	2001
					Total Revenues ($ MN's):					
Bobo nectar business										
Domestic	$15.3	$15.3	$15.3	$15.3	$15.3	$15.3	$15.3	$15.3	$15.3	$15.3
Export	0.0	0.0	0.0	0.0	0.0	0.0	0.0	0.0	0.0	0.0
Gerber jar business										
Domestic	0.0	3.1	4.6	6.1	7.7	9.2	10.8	12.3	13.8	15.4
Export	0.0	10.6	14.9	19.1	23.3	27.6	31.8	36.1	36.1	36.1
Industrial products										
Domestic	0.0	0.0	0.0	0.0	0.0	0.0	0.0	0.0	0.0	0.0
Export	4.0	5.5	7.0	8.5	10.0	11.5	13.0	14.5	16.0	17.5
Total Revenues	$19.3	$34.5	$41.8	$49.0	$56.3	$63.6	$70.9	$78.2	$81.2	$84.2
					Variable Costs ($ dozen):					
Bobo nectar business										
Ingredients	$0.36	$0.36	$0.36	$0.36	$0.36	$0.36	$0.36	$0.36	$0.36	$0.36
Jars/containers	0.45	0.45	0.45	0.45	0.45	0.45	0.45	0.45	0.45	0.45
Lid/caps	0.05	0.05	0.05	0.05	0.05	0.05	0.05	0.05	0.05	0.05
Cases, overwrap	0.06	0.06	0.06	0.06	0.06	0.06	0.06	0.06	0.06	0.06
Labels	0.06	0.06	0.06	0.06	0.06	0.06	0.06	0.06	0.06	0.06
Direct manufacturing overhead	0.08	0.08	0.08	0.08	0.08	0.08	0.08	0.08	0.08	0.08
Total Bobo nectar variable costs (dz. jars)	$1.05	$1.05	$1.05	$1.05	$1.05	$1.05	$1.05	$1.05	$1.05	$1.05
Gerber jar buisness										
Ingredients	$0.28	$0.28	$0.28	$0.28	$0.28	$0.28	$0.28	$0.28	$0.28	$0.28
Jars/containers	0.65	0.65	0.65	0.65	0.65	0.65	0.65	0.65	0.65	0.65
Lid/caps	0.33	0.33	0.33	0.33	0.33	0.33	0.33	0.33	0.33	0.33
Cases, overwrap	0.06	0.06	0.06	0.06	0.06	0.06	0.06	0.06	0.06	0.06
Labels	0.06	0.06	0.06	0.06	0.06	0.06	0.06	0.06	0.06	0.06
Direct manufacturing overhead	0.08	0.08	0.08	0.08	0.08	0.08	0.08	0.08	0.08	0.08
Total Gerber variable costs (dz. jars)	$1.46	$1.46	$1.46	$1.46	$1.46	$1.46	$1.46	$1.46	$1.46	$1.46

(*continued*)

EXHIBIT 11 *(concluded)*

Total Variable Costs ($MN's):

	1992	1993	1994	1995	1996	1997	1998	1999	2000	2001
Bobo nectar business										
Ingredients	$2.9	$2.9	$2.9	$2.9	$2.9	$2.9	$2.9	$2.9	$2.9	$2.9
Jars/containers	3.6	3.6	3.6	3.6	3.6	3.6	3.6	3.6	3.6	3.6
Lid/caps	0.4	0.4	0.4	0.4	0.4	0.4	0.4	0.4	0.4	0.4
Cases	0.5	0.5	0.5	0.5	0.5	0.5	0.5	0.5	0.5	0.5
Labels	0.5	0.5	0.5	0.5	0.5	0.5	0.5	0.5	0.5	0.5
Direct manufacturing overhead	0.6	0.6	0.6	0.6	0.6	0.6	0.6	0.6	0.6	0.6
Bobo nectar variable costs	$8.4	$8.4	$8.4	$8.4	$8.4	$8.4	$8.4	$8.4	$8.4	$8.4
Gerber jar business										
Ingredients	$0.0	$1.7	$2.4	$3.2	$3.9	$ 4.6	$ 5.3	$ 6.1	$ 6.2	$ 6.4
Jars/containers	0.0	4.0	5.7	7.4	9.1	10.8	12.5	14.2	14.6	15.0
Lid/caps	0.0	2.1	2.9	3.8	4.7	5.5	6.4	7.3	7.5	7.7
Cases	0.0	0.4	0.5	0.7	0.8	10.0	1.1	1.3	1.3	1.4
Labels	0.0	0.4	0.5	0.7	0.8	10.0	1.1	1.3	1.3	1.4
Direct manufacturing overhead	0.0	0.5	0.7	0.9	1.1	1.3	1.5	1.8	1.8	1.9
Gerber jar variable costs	$0.0	$9.1	$12.9	$16.7	$20.5	$24.3	$28.1	$31.9	$32.7	$33.0
Industrial variable costs (assume 10% margin)	3.6	5.0	6.3	7.7	9.0	10.4	11.7	13.1	14.4	15.8
Total variable costs	$12.0	$22.4	$27.6	$32.7	$37.9	$43.0	$48.2	$53.3	$55.6	$57.8

agrarian-based European economy. He also assumed that Gerber would price its exports in foreign currencies, borrow locally to meet its Polish capital requirements, and export its profits in the form of quarterly dividends. Finally, he assumed that the Polish government would give Gerber a significant tax credit during the first few years of its investment. With these assumptions in place, Lasher ran the model repeatedly, tinkering with the various numbers and running sensitivity analyses on the key political and economic variables. Each time the project produced a robust internal rate of return and a positive net present value. Barring political or economic catastrophes, Alima seemed like a very good deal.

On the basis of these calculations, Gerber entered its bid. It offered to purchase 60% of Alima's stock for an up-front purchase price of $11 million, and then to spend another $14 million over the next three to five years in reengineering the existing facility and upgrading its waste disposal system. The Gerber officials knew that their total capital commitment of $25 million was somewhat less than the Polish government had hoped for. But, combined with their technological expertise and their position in the industry, they thought it was a reasonable offer.

Anatomy of a Deal

Luckily for Gerber, the Ministry of Privatization also agreed that theirs was a reasonable offer and selected the company from among its 19 competitors. After Gerber's bid was accepted, negotiations began in earnest.

The government was clear in laying out its own objectives. It wanted to ensure that it got a reasonable selling price for Alima and a guaranteed level of future investment. It also wanted guarantees that Gerber would not immediately reduce employment at the Alima plant and that it would continue to purchase fruits and vegetables from its current suppliers. The government also wanted to make certain that the workers at Alima received some means by which to participate in the management of their new venture.

The Gerber negotiators accepted these demands unconditionally. They agreed to keep all employees for at least 18 months and to allow the Ministry of Privatization to reserve 40% of the new enterprise's stock for sale to Alima's employees and suppliers. Informally, Gerber also told the government that they intended to give the employees a considerable raise at the time of purchase and establish programs to teach these people how the stock market operated. As the negotiations progressed, Gerber made the stock option even more attractive by promising to subsidize purchases made by their new employees and to match up to certain levels the money employees spent for shares on a one-for-one basis.

Thus the government and Gerber amicably settled the core issues of the Alima deal. But still there were differences. Three points in particular became Gerber's grounds for negotiations:

The Borek Stary facility.   The Gerber officials expressly did not want this facility since its production of alcoholic beverages would not sit well with the company's predominant image as a "pure and natural" baby food manufacturer. In addition, Gerber's engineers had uncovered some environmental problems at the plant that were potentially quite complicated and expensive. If Gerber took possession of the plant even briefly, it risked being held responsible for any capital improvements that had to be made, including any environmental clean up. In an effort to avoid this additional burden, Gerber had requested that the Polish government sell Borek Stary independently. The government consented, and committed itself to the sale of Borek Stary under the terms of the October 1 Purchase and Sale agreement. Soon after the agreement was signed, however, it became clear that the government would not fulfill this commitment. The problem, it seemed, was that the people with whom Gerber was negotiating simply did not have the power to do as they had promised. They were not in a position to negotiate a separate deal for Borek Stary, and they had no authority over the *wojwewoda*, the local authority entrusted to handle these matters.

Property rights.   A broader and even riskier source of contention concerned the status of property rights at the Alima facility. Formally, of course, the land and the plant belonged to the state, and thus to the Ministry of Privatization that had been entrusted with its sale. Potentially, though, the land could be claimed by any of the thousands of people whose ancestors had farmed it sometime during Poland's past. One of the likeliest claimants, moreover, was a Catholic church that sat right beside the Alima plant and had historically owned a swath of land that ran directly through the middle of the facility.

For months Clark and the legal staff at Fremont had pored over maps of the property, trying to figure out who the claimants were and where their various slices of the property were located. Eventually, they decided not to wrestle with the ownership issue directly and to settle instead for a 99-year lease. Still, they were concerned that any lease signed with the federal government could be contested and even invalidated at the regional level, especially if the *wojwewodas* began to draw power away from the center.

Again, though, the Gerber team agreed to sign the Purchase and Sale agreement before the issue of ownership was completely resolved. It trusted that the Ministry officials would soon be able to secure the lease and protect it from any competing claims or regional interference.

Taxation.   For Gerber, the most important unresolved issue was taxation. According to the numbers generated by Marty Lasher's model, Alima's total long-term return depended significantly on the taxes it paid . If Gerber were granted the kind of tax credit that the Polish government had initially offered to foreign investors, it would enhance the potential return of the Alima deal. Thus the Gerber team was determined to secure a favorable tax break. Specifically, they wanted the Polish government to grant them a dollar-for-dollar exemption for all capital invested in the country over a three-year period. The government officials balked at these terms but eventually agreed. In the letter of intent, however, the

specifics of the tax credit were left open. Negotiators agreed to work out the financial details as quickly and as amicably as they could.

Gerber's Choice

Gerber's plans were derailed, however, by the political events that unfolded in October. For several weeks after the elections, policymaking effectively came to a halt in Poland as the new deputies scrambled to form a government and assemble a cabinet. Work in the ministries ground to a halt as bureaucrats waited for their instructions and newly appointed officials groped to learn the outline of their responsibilities. None of this boded well for Gerber, since it still needed the government officials to iron out the critical details of the Alima deal.

The Polish media, meanwhile, was making matters even worse. Emboldened by the nationalist bent of the elections, many of Warsaw's 70 papers were targeting foreigners as the source of Poland's economic problems. Because the Alima deal was so big and because the enterprise was already quite successful, the press attacked Gerber with a particular vengeance. Critics charged that the Ministry of Privatization had blundered the deal, that the government was "giving away a crown jewel," and that Gerber intended to fire the workers, close the Alima facility, and import its own products from the United States. The charges were false, but in the political turmoil that surrounded the elections, the Gerber officials had no chance to refute them.

More importantly, the Gerber team also no longer had any relationship with high ranking members of the Polish government or the Ministry of Privatization. All Gerber knew was that the new government was more conservative than its predecessor, it was under tremendous public pressure not to sell Poland's assets to foreigners, and that it had already considered abrogating the Alima deal entirely.

And thus Schomer and Clark were back in the Warsaw Marriott, reviewing the deal and wondering what to do with it. On the one hand, the Gerber officials felt that any Polish government would want to comply with normal contract laws and honor their contractual commitments. As long as Poland intended to move closer to the European Community it behooved the government to adhere as closely as possible to the norms of Western business. On the other hand, though, Schomer and Clark felt certain that political pressures in Poland would force the government to renegotiate the Alima deal and revoke the specific guarantees of nonexpropriation and repatriation that the previous government had extended. If the government went any farther, slowing economic reform or introducing price controls, Gerber's acquisition of Alima could quickly become a financial disaster. In addition, the turmoil that surrounded the deal made it increasingly unlikely that the Polish government

would find a buyer for Borek Stary, clarify the remaining issues of ownership, or grant the type of tax credit that Gerber had requested. Finally, inflation was also beginning to rise again in Poland and the government's deficit was mounting.

By the same token, Schomer and Clark still felt that the fundamentals of their deal were sound. The plant was good, the price was reasonable, and if Gerber walked away they risked losing their potentially lucrative markets of Central Europe to one of their traditional competitors. With flat birth rates in their core U.S. market and strong competition in Western Europe and Canada, Gerber's management clearly wanted to establish the company in Central Europe. But now they had to decide if the rewards of investment in Poland were worth the risk.

Case 2–3   Toys "R" Us Japan

I do not believe the Japanese have chosen freely to have these limitations. All we would have to do is open a large retail store where prices were 40% less and choices were very broad. If the Japanese consumer didn't like products offered in that fashion, then the store would not be a success. . . .

Carla Hills, *United States Trade Representative, February 1990*

In early 1991, Toys "R" Us seemed poised on the brink of a high-profile entry into the world's second largest toy market. A "category killer" that enjoyed phenomenal success in the United States and Europe, Toys "R" Us had tried for several years to crack the lucrative but forbidding Japanese market. At every step, the U.S. company had faced difficulty and opposition. Japanese retailers had tried repeatedly to block the chain's entrance, as had small shopkeepers from the area around Niigata,

site of the first Toys "R" Us store. The Japanese media had loudly denounced Toys "R" Us as the "black ship of Kawasaki," and a host of Japanese toy manufacturers, including Nintendo, had refused to deal directly with the U.S. retailer.[1] The very structure of Japan's multilayered distribution system also seemed to conspire against Toys "R" Us, thwarting the company's attempts and perpetuating Japan's infamously high consumer prices.

This case was prepared by Professor Debora Spar with the assistance of Jacqueline MacKenzie and Research Associate Laura Bures.

Copyright © 1995 by the President and Fellows of Harvard College. Harvard Business School case 796-077.

---

[1]The epithet referred to Commodore Matthew C. Perry's four black warships that sailed into the harbor at Edo (now Tokyo) in 1854, forcing the Shogun's government to end three centuries of self-imposed Japanese isolation. "Black ships" thus became symbolic of the opening of Japanese culture to Western influence. *Reuters,* December 19, 1991, and *The Toronto Star,* December 23, 1991.

Despite this litany of problems, though, success seemed finally within reach. Toys "R" Us had found an influential local partner, Den Fujita, and won approval from Japan's powerful Ministry of International Trade and Investment (MITI). Management also felt confident that some of the more restrictive aspects of Japanese retail regulation were about to change. But still some basic questions remained: Would Japanese customers, accustomed to small shops and personal service, ever accept a self-service discount warehouse? Would Japanese manufacturers risk damaging long-standing relationships with wholesalers and retailers by dealing directly with Toys "R" Us? And how quickly and efficiently could the chain hope to expand in the face of protracted local opposition?

The Toys "R" Us Company

Toys "R" Us was the brainchild of Charles Lazarus, a shop owner who founded the chain in 1957. Born in Washington, D.C., in 1923, Lazarus had learned about the retail business from his father, who rebuilt bicycles and sold them at the family store. When Lazarus asked why the store did not sell new bicycles, his father explained that the big chain stores could sell them much cheaper—a comment Lazarus would clearly recall later in his career.[2]

After a wartime career as a cryptographer, Lazarus inherited the family shop and turned to selling children's furniture in a market boosted by the post-war baby boom. Over time, he began to realize that because baby furniture did not wear out, repeat purchases of items such as cribs were rare.[3] Toys, by contrast, were frequently requested. Toys, he therefore decided, created a far superior business opportunity. After studying the U.S. discounter Korvettes, Lazarus decided to experiment with a self-service, supermarket-style format. In his new Children's Supermarket, he vowed to undercut competition and have a bigger, better selection than any single toy store. Discounting had arrived in the toy business.

Children's Supermarket quickly grew into a thriving chain of four stores, renamed Toys "R" Us after Lazarus decided he needed better signs with "shorter words, bigger letters."[4] He sold the chain to Interstate Stores in 1966 for $7.5 million, retaining a seat on the company's Board. When Interstate folded in 1978, Lazarus rescued his company, determined to build it into a nationwide chain. Over the next decade, Toys "R" Us sales compounded by 26% per year, with sales productivity per square foot double that of the retailer's nearest competitor.[5] By 1988, Toys "R" Us had captured 20% of the U.S. toy market, with sales surpassing the $4 billion mark.[6] Sourcing directly from manufacturers, the chain used its huge buying clout to offer goods at 10–20% discounts compared to smaller toy retailers. Year-round advertising campaigns encouraged consumers to buy toys at any time, instead of just at Christmas.

A typical Toys "R" Us store brought together 8–15,000 SKUs (stockkeeping units) of toys and children's products in a warehouse-sized (54,000 sq. ft.) self-service outlet. The presentation was simple and colorful, based on a "cookie cutter conformity" where stores resembled each other down to the layout of each aisle. Central control was a key feature of the organization, and extensive computer networks ensured almost automatic replacement of every toy sold once inventories dropped below pre-determined levels. The key to the sales and inventory formula, according to Lazarus, was that "No decisions are made in the field."[7]

In 1984, the company took its retailing concept global, opening its first international outlet in Canada and then moving quickly into Europe,

---

[2]David Owen, *The Man Who Invented Saturday Morning,* Villard, 1988.

[3]Ibid.

[4]*Newsmakers,* October 1992.

[5]*Business Quarterly,* June 22, 1989, and *Newsmakers,* October 1992.

[6]*Tokyo Business Today,* February 1990.

[7]*Newsweek,* November 11, 1991.

Hong Kong, and Singapore. As it had in the United States, the discount formula quickly proved popular with customers who flocked to the new Toys "R" Us outlets. Whenever the chain expanded abroad, however, it drew the ire of local retailers, who feared (correctly in many cases) that the giant discount stores would drive them out of business. German manufacturers, for example, refused to sell to Toys "R" Us in 1987 for fear of damaging their relationships with the thousands of small retailers and wholesalers who dominated toy distribution. And in the United Kingdom, retailers also protested, noting that the number of British toy stores had declined from 3,500 to 2,000 in the five years after Toys "R" Us first arrived.[8]

But Toys "R" Us regularly overcame the protests and its foreign outlets flourished. By 1991, the chain operated 97 stores abroad, with international operations accounting for 14% of the chain's total sales. Commenting on this spectacular growth, Larry Bouts, president of the chain's international division since 1991, suggested that the expansion of Toys "R" Us actually benefited foreign retailers as well as consumers. "Initially I think there was a fair amount of consternation from competitors," he acknowledged, "but now the industry has grown so much, there's really a lot warmer feeling. From the consumer's point of view, they're very happy . . . coming to us in droves. . . . People said it wouldn't work, but consumers want value today."[9] Confident that this formula applied broadly, Toys "R" Us management began to contemplate an entry into one of the world's toughest retail markets: Japan.

The Japanese Market for Toys

By any measure, Japan was an extremely attractive market for toys. Throughout the 1980s, the entire retail market in Japan had expanded dramatically, propelled by the economy's continued strength and a long-awaited increase in consumer spending. According to the Bank of Japan, annual retail sales

grew 94% during the 1980s, while Japan's GDP grew at an average annual rate of 7%.[10] Japan's children were particularly strong beneficiaries of this boom. Despite a rigorous education system that left children with little time for play, children's products accounted for a significant proportion of consumer spending in Japan. Perhaps to compensate for the constant pressure to excel in school, parents lavished expensive toys and clothes on their offspring.[11] Japan's falling birthrate also allowed parents and grandparents to focus their spending on fewer children; and fewer mouths to feed enabled families to spend less money on food and more on toys.[12]

Thus Japan's toy market had become the second largest in the world, lagging only behind the United States'. In 1991, the Japanese toy market was worth Y932 billion ($7.1 billion), up Y26 billion from the previous year. Responding to this boom, large retailers designed special formats to appeal to children. In October of 1990, Isetan opened a special section called "Dr. Kids Town" within one of its Tokyo department stores, while Seibu's flagship store opened a "Kids Farm," complete with a hollow miniature mountain amidst clothing racks and toy shelves.[13] A Sesame Street theme park was opened outside of Tokyo in 1990.

On the surface, these developments suggested that the Japanese toy market was ripe for Toys "R" Us. But as the chain's management quickly discovered, the structure of Japan's retail industry made it very difficult for new retailers—particularly foreign discount retailers—to establish a market position. Despite the rapid growth it had experienced, Japan's toy industry remained highly fragmented and locally focused. Though some estimates claimed that the number of toy stores had fallen from 8,000 in

---

[8]*Wall Street Journal,* September 10, 1990.
[9]*Europe,* September 1992.

[10]*Business Tokyo,* May 1992, and *International Marketing Data and Statistics 1995,* p. 183.
[11]*The Washington Post,* February 11, 1991.
[12]The average number of children per family had fallen from four in the early post-war years to just two by the early 1990s. *Washington Post,* February 11, 1991.
[13]Ibid.

1980, at least 6,000 remained in 1990.[14] A typical toy store was less than 3,200 square feet in area and sold 1–2,000 SKUs. Display areas were customarily cramped, inventories turned slowly, and most stores stocked very similar merchandise. Nearly all retail shops were domestically owned and bought their toys from local wholesalers, usually for 75–80% of the manufacturer's "suggested price."[15] Retailers then sold the toys for the "suggested price," deviating from it only rarely.[16] In exchange for maintaining prices, retailers were able to return their unsold goods to the wholesaler or manufacturer for full credit. In this tightly-knit system, only two national players existed: Chiyoda, which sold through the Hello Mac and Ace formats; and Marutomi, which operated a traditional toy chain, Banban, as well as a discount format, Toy Ryutsu Center. With a combined 700–800 stores, the two chains accounted for over Y100 billion in annual sales.[17]

At the wholesale level, the Japanese toy industry was again marked by its characteristic pattern of fragmentation and long-standing relationships. Even such giants as Nintendo, the Kyoto-based maker of Gameboy and other popular electronic games, distributed its products through a sprawling network of 70 affiliated distributors.[18] These distributors served as the key link between manufacturers and retailers, cementing long-term relationships based on personal commitments rather than competitive terms. They also served as a barrier to foreign firms, making it difficult for foreigners to achieve sufficient scale in either manufacturing or retailing to cover the costs of their investment. As a result, foreign firms were almost entirely absent from the Japanese domestic toy industry, and even imports accounted for only 9.2% of sales.[19]

Potentially, Toys "R" Us had the ability to change the Japanese toy industry and profit handsomely in the process. Merely by undercutting the "suggested price" it could capture the entire discount market. All it needed to do was to mimic precisely what it had done elsewhere: establish large-scale stores and use the buying power created by these stores to negotiate lower prices from toy manufacturers. Since 1987, the chain's management had been trying to implement this strategy. But in Japan, they came to realize, the very structure of the retail sector made their customary strategy almost inconceivable.

The Structure of Japanese Retail

A "Nation of Shops"

For years, Japan had been aptly described as a nation of small shopkeepers. Though the population of the four islands was approximately half that of the United States, the number of retail outlets in Japan was almost the same, resulting in twice as many outlets per capita.[20] Many of these outlets were the country's famous "mom and pop" stores. In 1988, over half of all retail outlets in Japan employed just one or two people; less than 15% of outlets employed more than five people.[21] In the early 1980s, such small stores accounted for a full 75% of retail spending. Nearly half of these outlets sold food, compared with 20% in the United States.[22]

The fragmentation of the retailers was matched by the fragmentation of the wholesalers who served them. Of the 436,421 wholesalers operating in 1988, less than half employed more than five people, and nearly all sold their products through a complex distribution system that typically involved between three and five layers of intermediaries. The primary wholesaler was often a subsidiary, or close affiliate,

---

[14]*Nihon Keizai Shimbun,* February 10, 1990.

[15]*Nikkei Weekly,* February 22, 1993.

[16]In 1989, 70% of toy retailers priced at the manufacturer's "suggested price," according to figures from Japan's Fair Trade Commission.

[17]*Nikkei Weekly,* February 22, 1993.

[18]*Nikkei Weekly,* June 29, 1991.

[19]*Nikkei Weekly,* June 20, 1992.

[20]Jack G. Kaikati, "Don't crack the Japanese distribution system—just circumvent it," *Columbia Journal of Business,* Summer 1993.

[21]MITI survey.

[22]*The Economist,* September 19, 1981.

of the manufacturer. The secondary wholesaler was a regional distributor, while the tertiary wholesaler operated on the local level. As in the toy industry, prices of goods were effectively controlled by the manufacturers, who sold to wholesalers at a pre-arranged discount of the "manufacturers' suggested price." With the added inducements of credit and generous payment terms, manufacturers throughout the Japanese system gained guaranteed distribution of their products, while wholesalers and retailers gained some measure of protection against economic swings and fluctuations in demand.

While Western observers tended to mock the Japanese retail system as cumbersome and archaic, most Japanese consumers genuinely seemed to enjoy and appreciate its benefits. As an article in *The Economist* explained, "The Japanese are as sentimental about their tiny shops as the French are about their peasants and the British about their old industries. Small Japanese shops are the centers of village neighborhoods in big cities. Small stores flourished before the rest of Japan modernized because merchants were restricted by law to their local patch, and retailers were encouraged to mop up labor from the land."[23]

In addition to its commercial function, small store retailing thus served a valuable social purpose. Described directly by some as a "social service," the retail sector was "filled with under-employed workers who in other societies might well be unemployed."[24] All together, the Japanese distribution system accounted for 18% of the nation's employees and 13% of its GNP.[25] In a 1980s survey, 26% of shopkeepers reported "security in old age" as a reason for opening a shop, and 10% said they opened a shop because their husbands would soon retire.[26] One quarter of owner-operators of stores were over 60. In a country with few pension provisions, small-scale retailing offered a safety net for retirement.

Supporters of the Japanese system further argued that small stores were a natural reflection of the Japanese way of life, that Japanese consumers preferred to shop every day for small quantities of fresh goods.[27] Small homes and kitchens allowed no space for storing large amounts of goods, and use of automobiles was impractical in Japan's congested streets.[28] High quality and personalized service, many claimed, were expected by Japanese consumers, who were willing to pay for the privilege.

Detractors, though, argued that small stores continued to exist simply because they were protected from more efficient competitors by laws restricting the construction of large stores and by tacit non-competition arrangements. Japanese consumers *would* accept less service in exchange for lower prices, they asserted, but by 1991, they had rarely been offered the choice.

Keiretsu Stores

In fact, choice of retail goods in some sectors was actively restricted by the activities of diversified conglomerates such as Matsushita and Toshiba. Working through their own distribution keiretsu (related groups of companies), these giant firms supported tens of thousands of small affiliate stores that stocked only "their" manufacturer's brand at manufacturer-specified prices. Where these stores prevailed, customers found no benefit in comparison-shopping, since price uniformity was nearly absolute. What they did get however, and what many Japanese reportedly preferred over low prices, was personal attention from the shop-owner and guaranteed repair or replacement service for the life of their purchase.

[23]Ibid.

[24]Ibid, and Hugh T. Patrick and Thomas P. Rohlen, "Small-Scale Family Enterprises," *The Political Economy of Japan: The Domestic Transformation,* Vol. 1, Stanford University Press, 1987, p. 350.

[25]*Business Asia*, January 4, 1993.

[26]Patrick and Rohlen, "Small-Scale Family Enterprises," p. 350.

[27]Takatoshi Ito, *The Japanese Economy,* MIT Press, 1992, p. 392.

[28]Japanese typically had 60% of the living space enjoyed by their U.S. counterparts. *Business Review Weekly,* January 12, 1990.

The operators of the small keiretsu stores also effectively made a trade-off between prices and personal loyalty. Simply by becoming a store owner, one gained a position of some visibility in the community, a position symbolized by the storefront pairing of the proprietor's name with that of a well-known manufacturer. Through the manufacturers' many affiliates, store operators also received financial and marketing advice and even information about their competitors' activities. In exchange for this assistance, they implicitly agreed to tie themselves closely to the keiretsu's lead manufacturer. Storekeepers who dared to meddle with the manufacturer's "suggested price" faced expulsion from the network and blacklisting by other manufacturers. In 1979, Yoshio Terada, a National (Matsushita) retailer in Tokyo, incurred the wrath of his supplier by discounting batteries by 20%. When he refused to remove the discount, a truck arrived instead to remove the National sign from his store and with it, his entire business.[29] Terada subsequently set up a no-service discount electrical appliance business called STEP and, despite Japanese consumers' alleged preferences for full-service stores, built a $100 million business in ten years. Yet, few keiretsu retailers at the time would have dared to defy the might of Matsushita. In 1991, over 20,000 keiretsu stores still existed, and the principle of loyalty to manufacturers remained strong in both retailing and wholesaling.

The Role of Regulation

In addition to customers' habits and personal loyalties, Japan's retail structure was also bolstered by a series of laws restricting the spread of larger retail stores. By sheer force of numbers, the country's 1.4 million store owners wielded considerable voting power. For decades, they had used this power to extract concessions and explicit protection from Japan's reigning political party, the Liberal Democratic Party (LDP). In 1990, the Chairman of the National Shopkeepers Promotion Association

described the political situation succinctly: "The big stores stuff the politicians with money, but we have the power of 20 million votes."[30]

The small store owners won their first victory in 1956, just after the LDP came to power. The 1956 Department Store Law required that a permit be obtained for each new department store, effectively allowing department store construction to be blocked by smaller retailers. By 1990, there were still only about 1,600 department stores in Japan— one for every 75,000 people. With the growth of department stores so severely limited, most innovation in Japanese retailing came through the emerging supermarkets—large, non-specialized, low-price stores with large grocery sections. But just as the supermarkets were starting to gain ground, they, too, encountered the shopkeepers' force.

In 1973, Japan's Ministry of International Trade and Investment (MITI) responded to the small retailers' demands by introducing the Large Scale Retail Law, legislation that subjected all would-be large retailers to a rigorous screening process. Before building any stores over 1,500 sq. m. (16,000 sq. ft.), retailers had to submit detailed plans to MITI and then allow these plans to be passed on to a local review board composed of consumers and retailers. In 1982, the law was made even more stringent, requiring large store operators to "explain" their plans to local retailers directly, even before notifying MITI. With this provision in place, small store owners could effectively delay the construction of large stores for years, simply by boycotting "explanation meetings" or raising objections to a myriad of small details. As a result, even powerful supermarket chains such as Daiei found themselves entangled for years in local negotiations.[31]

Innovations

If Japan's fragmented and hierarchical retail sector had remained unchanged in the 1980s, it is unlikely that even so powerful a force as Toys "R" Us would

[29]Kenichi Miyashita and David W. Russell, *Keiretsu,* McGraw-Hill, 1994, pp. 203–4.

[30]*East Asian Executive Reports,* May 15, 1990.
[31]*Business Week,* December 9, 1991.

have dared enter the market. But as the Japanese economy expanded and developed in the late 1980s, several cracks in the retail structure began to appear.

The Rise of Convenience Stores

The first major change in Japan's retail structure came from a quiet and unlikely source: convenience stores. Usually occupying no more than 1100 sq. ft., convenience stores were small enough to slip past restrictive laws and establish themselves in the very heart of Japan's towns and villages. By 1982, Japan had 23,235 convenience stores, accounting for 2.3% of total retail sales.[32] Between 1982 and 1985, convenience store sales rose faster than any other form of retailing sales;[33] and by 1992, they accounted for nearly 8% of Japan's total retail sales.[34]

The most successful convenience store was the 7-Eleven chain, licensed from its U.S. parent Southland in 1974 by Ito-Yokado. At first glance a 7-Eleven Japan store fit the profile of many Japanese stores: small, locally focused, and "open all hours." At the core of this business, however, was an information-oriented strategy unlike anything dreamed of by its "mom and pop" competitors. The key to 7-Eleven's strategy was close inventory control facilitated by early and comprehensive adoption of information technology. In the late 1970s, 7-Eleven cut its wholesale suppliers from 80 to 40 by closely supervising their inventory and eliminating goods which did not generate adequate sales. From 1985 onwards, the chain used point of sales equipment to track sales of each item and en-

sure timely replenishment. Employees also entered specific information about shoppers with each sale to predict product-specific shopping habits. Ito-Yokado used this information to refine product offerings and inventory replacement schedules to the point of providing fresh *o nigiri* (rice balls popular as lunch snacks) at lunch time in every store as well as adequate supplies of soft drinks for children on their way home from school in the afternoon. The information was also used as a bargaining chip with manufacturers, who could be persuaded to deliver according to 7-Eleven's precise requirements.

By 1990, almost 85% of goods in the chain's 94 wholly owned and 4,140 franchised stores throughout Japan were distributed through the chain's own elaborate regional distribution system, and 7-Eleven Japan had been described as one of the most efficient retailers in the world. As 7-Eleven grew, it also spawned a series of imitators, stores hoping to make similar use of information technologies and catering to the demands of Japan's aging population and increasing numbers of women in the workforce.

MITI's "Vision for the 1990s"

Just as the convenience stores were demonstrating the commercial potential of new retailing formats, the established format was also coming under pressure from Japan's changing demographics. Increasingly, young Japanese balked at the idea of taking over their parents' small shops and wanted instead to experiment with bolder ventures. With significantly greater international exposure than their parents, the younger generation also realized that they were paying highly inflated prices for many consumer goods. Slowly, their demands for fewer commercial restrictions and lower prices began to influence the political process.

In 1989, MITI quietly advocated reform of Japan's retailing sector. In a public document on Japan's distribution system, it first defended the existing retail structure, arguing that:

1. It cannot necessarily be said that our distribution system is inefficient; however, there is room for further rationalization as respects costs.

[32]*The Economist,* January 31, 1987.

[33]Frank Upsham, "Privatizing Regulation: The Implementation of the Large-Scale Retail Stores Law," in Gary D. Allison and Yasunori Sone, eds., *Political Dynamics in Contemporary Japan,* Ithaca, 1993, p. 265. Cited in Jeff Bernstein and Thomas K. McCraw, "Convenience-Store Retailing in Two Countries: Southland and Seven-Eleven Japan," HBS Case Number N9-395-092.

[34]Cited in Jeffrey Rayport, "Japanese Retailing System: Tokugawa Period to the Present," HBS Industry Note prepared for Professor Thomas K. McCraw, April 1991.

2. Though our country's distribution system is as a whole highly competitive, there are some factors which mitigate competition.

3. Due to unfamiliarity with commercial customs in Japan, foreign firms may feel difficulty attempting to gain access to the Japanese distribution sector; however, this system does not fundamentally discriminate against either domestic or foreign firms, and there are a large variety of distribution channels available to importing firms.

4. There are a variety of reasons for the gap in domestic and foreign prices, and some of them lie in the nature of the distribution system.[35]

MITI's document proceeded, though, to propose significant changes to the Large Scale Retail Stores Law, including limits on the amount of time each stage in the notification process could take. The law would remain in force, MITI explained, "since Japan still has a large number of retail stores and a limited amount of land, [and] giving large stores free rein to set up business would cause serious problems for regional communities."[36] Yet MITI did commit to "amending the system . . . to reflect recent changes in socio-economic circumstances" and to removing "all practices which deviate from the original intent of the system," noting in particular that "the purpose of [the "explanation" of store plans to relevant constituencies] is not to obtain the approval of local retailers."[37]

Accordingly, MITI proposed reducing the permissible time between pre-notification and approval to as little as 18 months. It even promised to re-examine restrictions on opening hours, which required large stores to close at 6 pm and for at least one full day per month. If MITI succeeded in implementing these proposed changes, small store owners would at last lose their power to hold back a tidal wave of space-hungry domestic retailers.

The Structural Impediments Initiative[38]

At the same time that MITI launched its re-evaluation of the retail system, it also began to respond to demands that Japan open its market to foreign investors. Even after half a decade of dramatically increased global investment flows, Japan's stock of foreign direct investment remained low. In manufacturing, for example, which attracted 65% of total foreign investment flows, foreign affiliated companies accounted for 2.1% of total capitalization and 2.3% of sales in 1988. By comparison, FDI in the United States at the same time accounted for 14.7% of capitalization and 12.2% of sales.[39] In 1990, Japan was host to less accumulated U.S. direct investment than Canada, the UK, Germany, Switzerland, or the Netherlands.[40]

For many in the United States, the imbalance in investment levels was evidence that the Japanese market remained unfairly closed to U.S. investors. Consequently, in the fall of 1989, U.S. negotiators launched a series of discussions with their Japanese counterparts "to identify and solve structural problems in both countries that stand as impediments to trade and to balance of payments adjustment with the goal of contributing to the reduction of payments imbalances."[41] Dubbed the Structural Impediments Initiative, the talks theoretically covered "structural impediments" in both countries. The bulk of the negotiation, however, was devoted to the perennial problem of perceived trade barriers to U.S. imports and investment in Japan. In particular, U.S. negotiators pushed their Japanese counterparts to address the prevalence of keiretsu structures and other interlocked relationships which, they argued, prevented foreign firms from

---

[35]*News from MITI,* September 1989.

[36]Ibid.

[37]Ibid.

---

[38]This section draws heavily on Ito, *The Japanese Economy,* Chapter 12.

[39]The retail sector was host to a tiny but growing fraction of foreign direct investment in Japan. Between 1985 and 1990 U.S. investment in Japanese retailing quadrupled to reach $340m. *Business Tokyo,* May 1992.

[40]Mark Mason, "United States Direct Investment in Japan: Trends and Prospects," *California Management Review,* Fall 1992.

[41]*Final Report of Structural Impediments Initiative.*

competing on equal terms. The U.S. team also suggested that consumer prices in Japan were higher than they should be, compared with prices in other markets, and that Japan's distribution system remained a major impediment to U.S. export sales.[42]

Toys "R" Us: The Move into Japan

For Toys "R" Us, both the Structural Impediments Initiative and MITI's changes to the Large Scale Retail Store Law came at a propitious time. Together with domestic developments in the retail sector, they seemed to indicate that the largest barriers to the chain's entry—the distribution sector and the legal restrictions on establishment—were at last about to change. And so long as they changed, Toys "R" Us felt confident that the chain could succeed in the Japanese market.

Because the Japanese market retained so many idiosyncracies, however, Toys "R" Us management decided to seek an alliance with a strong local partner. Initially, the chain followed the same strategy that most foreign retailers had adopted and launched negotiations with a major Japanese retailer. But once the negotiations were underway, the Toys "R" Us representatives realized that the two sides had fundamentally different assumptions of how to run a business. According to one Toys "R" Us executive, "they pushed traditional business practices on us, like using wholesalers. That would distort the basic principle of our business."[43] And so Toys "R" Us broke off the first round of talks and began to search for someone in Japan with a better grasp of U.S. retailing practices.

Den Fujita

In 1989, Joseph Baczko, then head of Toys "R" Us International, met Den Fujita, president of McDonalds Japan. Fujita, the son of an engineer, had grown up in Osaka, a city famous for its merchant tradition. He graduated from the Law Department of Tokyo University, the most prestigious university in Japan and traditional training ground for the country's political elite.[44] During the U.S. occupation of Japan, he had worked as a translator at McArthur's Headquarters in Tokyo, despite having lost his father and two sisters in U.S. bombing raids.

In 1950, he took the unusual step (for a Tokyo Law graduate) of starting his own trading venture, Fujita & Company, to import a range of items, such as Dior handbags, to a luxury-starved Japan.[45] Since post-war rationing and restrictions on imports had eliminated most other luxury goods, Fujita prospered, building one of Japan's strongest import businesses over the next two decades.

In 1971, McDonalds approached Fujita and asked him to join them in introducing U.S.-style fast food to Japan. Fujita agreed, arguing in public that McDonalds-style food would be good for Japan. As he later explained, "the Japanese are very hardworking, but very weak, very small . . . we had to strengthen ourselves."[46] Fellow retailers, though, were not amused—the Ginza Street Association was still attempting to evict the first McDonalds from its prestigious location more than 10 years after its establishment.[47] Fujita, undaunted, told Japanese teenagers that eating beef might give them the blond hair of their American counterparts.[48] Whatever the rationale, McDonalds' sales in Japan had topped Y50 billion by 1980 and reached Y208 billion ($1.6 billion) by 1991.

What Fujita had brought to McDonalds—retail experience, political influence, vision, and a unique understanding of both Japanese and American cultures—was equally attractive to Toys "R" Us. With strong links to influential government figures,

[42]The Large Scale Retail Law, for example, impeded the distribution of foreign goods by supporting the 1.6 million small family-run stores which were less likely to carry imported goods than were large stores.

[43]*Nikkei Weekly,* May 16, 1992.

[44]*New York Times,* March 22, 1992.

[45]Ibid.

[46]Ibid.

[47]*Nihon Keizai Shimbun,* October 11, 1983.

[48]*Reuters,* February 1, 1986.

Fujita also had unrivaled knowledge of real estate in Japan, boasting that "If you name a city, I can see the post office, the train station, everything."[49] Fujita's flamboyant style and frequent new ventures guaranteed publicity for each business. Often described as a heretic, he was quoted as wishing to "blow a hole in the under-developed structure of the Japanese retail industry."[50]

So impressed was Toys "R" Us with Fujita that Robert Nakasone, the American-born Vice Chairman of Toys "R" Us, described him as not only the first choice as a partner, but "our second, third, fourth, fifth, and so on. . . . We could see he was a bit of a maverick. He was not only bilingual, but bicultural."[51] Likewise Fujita regarded Toys "R" Us as a natural partner due to the similarities in the two companies' target markets. Soon after hearing of Toys "R" Us' plans, in fact, he began to think of ways to combine Toys "R" Us, McDonalds, and Blockbuster Entertainment, another foreign business seeking his help, in specially developed family shopping malls. In the spring of 1989, Toys "R" Us formally asked Fujita to cooperate with the company in a Japanese joint venture. McDonalds Japan took a 20% stake in the new subsidiary: Toys "R" Us Japan.

Criticism and Opposition

Almost as soon as plans for the new venture were announced, other retailers and manufacturers claimed that Toys "R" Us Japan was doomed to failure. Consumers would check out the stores initially, they elaborated, but Japanese consumers would not like warehouse stores, and it was "unrealistic" to consider bypassing wholesalers.[52]

Explicit opposition to Toys "R" Us emerged rapidly from those most threatened by the chain's expansion. In January 1990, Toys "R" Us applied to the municipal government of Niigata, a city of 500,000 on the Japan Sea coast, for permission to open the first of its Japanese superstores. Local toy

sellers were horrified. At 5,000 sq. m. (54,000 sq. ft.), the proposed store would be over 50 times larger than the average Niigata toy shop; projected first year revenues of Y2 billion represented half the combined sales of the city's existing toy merchants.[53] Mobilizing quickly, the Niigata toy sellers warned publicly that, "If Toys "R" Us comes in, Japanese toy shops will be wiped out."[54] The group's spokesman, owner of eight Niigata toy shops further argued that, "Toys "R" Us is making this a political problem. But toys are more than that. Toys are culture."[55]

The Niigata application was just one of ten applications that Toys "R" Us filed across Japan, many of which sparked opposition of some kind. Toy retailers and wholesalers in Fukuoka submitted a petition to their local government demanding a one-year delay to the opening of a proposed Toys "R" Us. The toy industry in Sagamihara (near Tokyo) reacted with similar defensiveness. After Toys "R" Us announced its intentions to open seven stores by 1993, with an eventual target as high as 100, a group of 520 small toy retailers formed the Japan Association of Specialty Toy Shops to help small retailers develop ways to compete with Toys "R" Us and other foreign retailers.

Central to this concern was the effect Toys "R" Us would have on the long-standing ties between Japan's toy manufacturers and toy wholesalers. To leverage the economies of scale inherent in their large stores, Toys "R" Us would have to replicate in Japan the same buying structure that had worked so effectively elsewhere. That is, the chain would have to buy directly from the manufacturers, using the sheer size of its outlets to circumvent the wholesalers and win price concessions from the toy makers. If Toys "R" Us had to rely on Japan's cumbersome system of wholesale distribution, it would inevitably have to charge much higher retail prices, undermining its whole competitive strategy. If the chain did not use the wholesalers, though, it risked

---

[49]*Business Week,* December 9, 1991.
[50]*Nikkei Weekly,* May 16, 1992.
[51]*New York Times*, March 22, 1992.
[52]Ibid.

[53]*The Economist,* June 16, 1990.
[54]*Wall Street Journal,* February 7, 1990.
[55]Ibid.

EXHIBIT 1   Toys "R" Us Inc. Balance Sheet (millions of U.S.$)

	January 1990	*January 1991*
Assets		
Cash and cash equivalents	40.9	35.0
Net receivables	53.1	73.2
Inventories	1,230.4	1,275.2
Prepaid expenses	14.0	21.0
Current assets—total	1,338.4	1,404.3
Net property, plant, and equipment	1,703.0	2,141.3
Other assets	33.4	36.8
Total assets	3,074.7	3,582.4
Liabilities		
Long-term debt due within year	1.4	1.6
Notes payable	205.5	386.5
Accounts payable	517.9	483.9
Taxes payable	96.0	81.6
Other current liabilities	279.1	274.0
Total current liabilities	1,100.0	1,227.6
Long-term debt	173.0	195.2
Deferred taxes	96.4	113.4
Equity		
Common stock	19.8	29.8
Capital surplus	322.7	352.6
Retained earnings	1,459.9	1,793.2
Less: treasury stock	97.0	129.3
Total equity	1,705.3	2,046.3
Total liabilities and equity	3,074.7	3,582.4

Note: Numbers may not add due to rounding.

Source: *Standard & Poor's Compustat, Compustat PC Plus.*

raising the ire of the manufacturers, who were tied so tightly to both the wholesalers and the small retail outlets. As one newspaper explained, "Japanese toy makers drool at the prospect of supplying Toys "R" Us, but worry they'll be locked out of their current distribution channels if they play ball with the U.S. company."[56] Accordingly, there were indications that toy manufacturers would resist, if not actually oppose, the U.S. discounter. Top toy manufacturers such as Bandai Co. refused to comment on whether they would deal directly with Toys "R" Us, insisting that anything they (Bandai) said could "have a great influence on toy

---

[56]*Japan Economic Journal,* February 16, 1991.

EXHIBIT 2   Toys "R" Us Inc. Income Statement (millions of U.S.$)

	January 1990	*January 1991*
Sales	4,787.8	5,510.0
Cost of goods sold	3,309.7	3,820.8
Gross profit	1,478.2	1,689.2
Selling, general, and administrative expense	866.4	1,024.8
Operating income before depreciation	611.8	664.4
Depreciation, depletion, and amortization	65.8	79.1
Operating profit	545.9	585.3
Interest expense	52.8	82.7
Non-operating income/expense	20.5	19.7
Special items	0.0	1.0
Pretax income	513.7	523.2
Total income taxes	192.6	197.2
Net income	321.1	326.0

Note: Numbers may not add due to rounding.

Source: *Standard & Poor's Compustat, Compustat PC Plus.*

EXHIBIT 3   Toys "R" Stock Price (U.S.$), 1979–1992

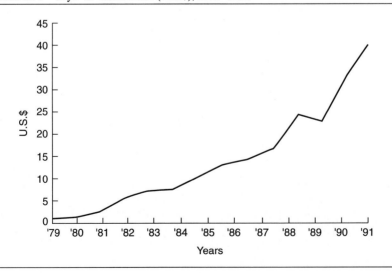

Source: *Standard & Poor's Compustat, Compustat PC Plus.*

EXHIBIT 4   Distribution of Toys "R" Us Stores, 1991

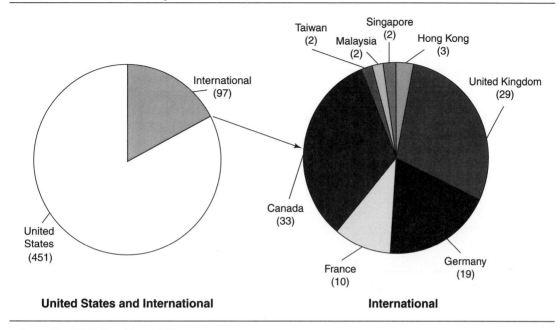

United States and International   **International**

Source: Toys "R" Us Annual Report, 1991.

EXHIBIT 5   Total Retail Sales of Toys and Games, Selected Countries, 1992

Country	Sales of Toys and Games (millions of U.S.$)	Country	Sales of Toys and Games (millions of U.S.$)
Canada	1,033.0	Mexico	220.0
China	140.0	Philippines	32.0
Hong Kong	200.0	Singapore	55.0
India	260.0	South Korea	425.0
Japan	7,884.0	Taiwan	375.0
Malaysia	20.0	United States	20,684.0

Source: *International Marketing Data and Statistics 1994.*

wholesalers. . . . [E]ven the smallest comments cause concern."[57]

Meanwhile, like all foreign retailers hoping to invest in Japan, Toys "R" Us still faced major problems in obtaining suitable real estate. With a population density of 322 people per square kilo-

meter and a land-mass filled 80% with mountains, Japan had very limited amounts of land suitable or desirable for retailing.[58] In the late 1980s, land prices around Tokyo were at an all time high, with a 540 sq. ft. shop in the exclusive Ginza area renting

---

[57]*Wall Street Journal,* September 10, 1990.

[58]The U.S. population density was only 26 people per square kilometer.

EXHIBIT 6   Index of Urban Land Prices in Japan, 1982–1991 (end of March 1990 = 100)

	1982	1983	1984	1985	1986	1987	1988	1989	1990	1991
					All urban land					
Total average	61.5	64.4	66.5	68.3	70.2	74.1	81.5	87.6	100.0	110.4
Commercial	55.6	58.0	59.8	61.7	64.2	69.2	78.4	86.3	100.0	111.5
Residential	64.6	68.3	70.7	72.7	74.2	77.6	84.0	88.7	100.0	109.7
Industrial	66.2	68.8	70.7	72.4	73.9	76.4	82.3	88.2	100.0	109.8
					6 major cities					
Total average	28.4	29.7	31.3	33.6	38.4	48.3	61.8	76.9	100.0	103.0
Commercial	19.5	20.8	22.7	25.6	33.0	44.2	62.6	78.3	100.0	103.3
Residential	33.5	34.8	36.0	38.0	41.7	52.9	65.2	75.1	100.0	102.1
Industrial	35.7	37.0	38.2	39.6	41.6	48.7	58.1	77.2	100.0	103.8

Source: *Japan Statistical Yearbook 1995.*

EXHIBIT 7   Monthly Living Expenditure Per Average Household in Japan, 1980–1991 (value in Yen)

	1980	1985	1990	1991
Food	66,923	73,735	78,956	82,130
Medical care	5,865	6,931	8,866	9,016
Transportation/communication	18,416	24,754	29,469	30,533
Education	8,325	10,853	14,471	14,211
Reading/recreation	19,620	24,191	30,122	31,442
Housing	10,682	12,686	14,814	16,712
Fuel/light/water	13,225	17,724	17,147	17,981
Furniture/household items	9,875	11,665	12,396	13,401
Clothes/footwear	18,163	19,606	22,967	23,814
Miscellaneous/personal	12,411	15,589	17,207	19,173
Pocket money	21,002	24,345	27,569	28,502
Social expenses	21,504	25,573	29,830	32,543
Annual rate of inflation (percent growth)	7.7	2.0	3.1	3.3

Note: Numbers may not add due to rounding.

Source: *Japan Statistical Yearbook 1995, International Marketing Data and Statistics 1995.*

for about $11,500 per month.[59] Finding local workers also presented a serious and potentially expensive challenge. With the Japanese economy in a state of virtual full employment, competition for top male graduates was intense, particularly for foreign firms, which remained less prestigious employers than their Japanese counterparts.[60] Searching for something positive to say on the labor front, one report could only comment that "for flexible firms willing to hunt around, there is a strong supply of bright, well-educated women."[61]

[59]*Business Tokyo,* May 1992.

[60]*Business Asia,* April 16, 1990.
[61]Ibid.

EXHIBIT 8   Employees and Establishments in Japan, 1970–1991

Year	Retail Establishments	Employees (000s)	Average/ Outlet	Wholesale Establishments	Employees (000s)	Average/ Business
1970	1,471,297	4926	3.35	255,974	2861	11.18
1972	1,495,510	5141	3.44	259,163	3008	11.61
1974	1,548,184	5303	3.43	292,155	3290	11.26
1976	1,614,067	5580	3.46	340,249	3513	10.32
1979	1,673,667	5960	3.56	368,608	3673	9.96
1982	1,721,465	6369	3.70	428,858	4091	9.54
1985	1,628,644	6329	3.89	413,016	3998	9.68
1988	1,619,752	6851	4.23	436,421	4332	9.93
1991	1,591,223	6937	4.36	475,983	4773	10.03

Source: Census of Commerce, MITI.

EXHIBIT 9   Number of Outlets in Japan by Format, 1988 and 1991

Outlet Format	1988	1991
Department store	433	455
General supermarket	1,478	1,549
Other general supermarket	373	375
Specialty supermarket	6,397	7,130
Convenience store	34,550	41,847
Other supermarket	53,834	67,473
Specialty store	1,007,756	1,000,166
Miscellaneous retail stores	513,338	470,289
Others	1,593	1,939
Total	1,619,752	1,591,223

Source: *Retail Trade International,* Euromonitor 1995.

A final set of concerns centered on the company's choice of partner: the maverick Fujita had his detractors. In a letter to *The New York Times,* he was accused of anti-Semitism and of supporting Communism to provoke the Americans.[62] These criticisms stemmed from Fujita's well-known claim that Osaka-born Japanese (like himself) were more business-oriented than their Tokyo cousins because Jews had settled in Osaka hundreds of years ago. He had also written several books on "the Jewish way of doing business" and described himself as "the Ginza Jew."

As a result of all the resistance that Toys "R" Us Japan faced, the schedule of store openings began to slip steadily. Though initial publicity had suggested six stores by the end of 1991, subsequent plans slated only the first store to open in December 1991.[63] Without direct distribution deals, the high land prices and labor costs would render the cost structure of the superstores almost insurmountable.

[62]Harold Solomon, "To the Editor: Beware the Agenda of Den Fujita," *New York Times,* April 12, 1992.

[63]*The Daily Yomiuri,* November 12, 1991.

EXHIBIT 10 Number of Outlets in Japan by Size, 1988 and 1991

Outlet Size (sq. m.)	1988	1991
Under 10	83,510	72,387
10–19	280,761	246,657
20–29	267,077	239,425
30–49	367,266	360,059
50–99	271,227	282,388
100–199	96,260	109,050
200–499	48,423	56,490
500–999	8,408	8,799
1,000–1,499	3,888	4,358
1,500–2,999	2,047	2,269
Over 3,000	2,107	2,371
Not reported	188,778	206,970
Total	1,619,752	1,591,223

Note: 1 sq. m. = 0.092 sq. ft.

Source: *Retail Trade International*, Euromonitor 1995.

EXHIBIT 11 Comparison of Price Levels by Store Type in Japan (manufacturer's suggested retail price = 100)

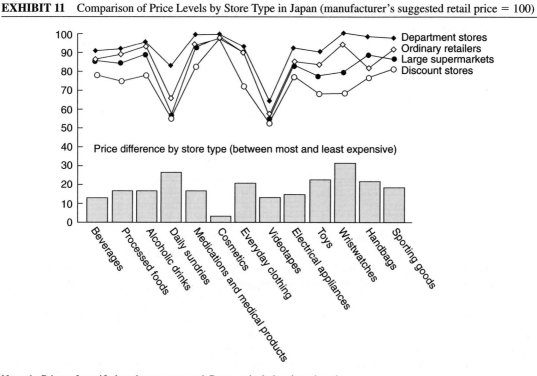

Notes 1: Prices of specific brands were surveyed. Does not include private brands.
2: 'Electrical appliances' is the average for TVs and air conditioners, and includes delivery, piping and installation charges.

Source: Adapted from the Japanese Economic Planning Agency, *Price Survey by Store Type,* July 1994.

EXHIBIT 12   Leading Foreign Retailers in Japan, 1991

Company	Year Opened	Number of Stores	Owners
		Clothing/Accessories	
Brooks Brothers (Japan)	1979	3	Brooks Brothers Inc. (51%)
			Daidoh Ltd. (49%)
Hermes Japan Co.	1979	1	Hermes S.A. (50%)
			Seibu Department Stores Ltd. (50%)
Laura Ashley Japan	1986	12	Aeon Group (40%)
			Laura Ashley Group Plc. (40%)
Louis Vuitton Japan	1981	1	Louis Vuitton Malletier (99%)
		Audio/Visual	
Blockbuster Japan	1990	1	Blockbuster Entertainment (50%)
			Fujita & Co. (50%)
HMV Japan	1990	3	HMV Group Ltd. (100%)
Tower Records	1980	14	MTS Inc. (100%)
Virgin Mega Stores Japan	1990	1	Virgin Group Ltd. (50%)
			Marui Co. (50%)
		Others	
Tireplus	1990	3	Sears, Roebuck & Co. (50%)
			Saison Group (50%)
Toys "R" Us	1991	0	Toys "R" Us Inc. (80%)
			McDonald's Co. (Japan) (20%)

Note: The first Toys "R" Us store in Japan opened on December 20, 1991.

Source: *Nikkei Weekly,* November 16, 1991.

EXHIBIT 13   Foreign Direct Investment in the United States and Japan, 1985 and 1991 (millions of U.S.$)

Year	United States		Japan	
	Total Stock of Foreign Investment	Stock of Japanese-owned Foreign Investment	Total Stock of Foreign Investment	Stock of U.S.-owned Foreign Investment
1985	184,615	19,313	6,397	3,067
1991	414,358	92,896	22,771	9,907

Source: *International Direct Investment Statistics Yearbook 1994.*

Case 2–4 Philips and Matsushita 1998: Growth of Two Global Companies

Throughout their long histories, N.V. Philips (Netherlands) and Matsushita Electric Industrial (Japan) had followed very different strategies and emerged with different organizational capabilities. Philips had built its success on a worldwide portfolio of responsive national organizations while Matsushita had built its global competitiveness on its centralized, highly efficient operations in Japan.

During the 1980s, both companies experienced major challenges to their historic approaches that forced major strategic and organizational changes, and throughout the 1990s, both companies were struggling to reestablish their competitiveness. With the twenty-first century around the corner, observers were divided on the effectiveness of the massive strategic and organizational changes both companies had taken, and how it would affect their long-running competitive battle.

Philips: Background

In 1892, Gerard Philips and his father opened a small light bulb factory in Holland. When their Eindhoven-based venture almost failed, they recruited Gerard's brother, Anton, an excellent salesman and manager, to join the company. By 1900, Philips was the third largest light bulb producer in Europe.

From its founding, Philips developed a tradition of caring for workers. In Eindhoven, it built company houses, bolstered education, and provided local services; and it paid its employees so well that other local employers complained. When Philips incorporated in 1912, it set aside 10% of profits for employees.

This case was prepared by Professor Christopher A. Bartlett.

Copyright © 1999 by the President and Fellows of Harvard College. Harvard Business School case 399-102.

Technological Competence and Geographic Expansion

While larger electrical products companies were racing to diversify, Philips & Co. made only light bulbs. This one-product focus and Gerard's technological prowess enabled the company to create significant innovations. Company policy was to scrap old plant and use new machines or factories whenever advances were made in new production technology. Anton wrote down assets rapidly and set aside substantial reserves for replacing outdated equipment. Philips also became a leader in industrial research, established physics and chemistry labs to address production problems as well as more abstract scientific ones. The labs developed a tungsten metal filament bulb that was a great commercial success and gave Philips the financial strength to compete against its giant rivals.

Holland's small size soon forced Philips to look beyond Dutch borders for enough volume to mass produce, and in 1899, Anton hired the company's first export managers. The managers spent 8 to 10 months a year traveling in such diverse places as Japan, Australia, Canada, Brazil, and Russia to establish new markets. In 1912, as the electric lamp industry started to show signs of overcapacity, Philips started building sales organizations in the United States, Canada, and France, and other cartel-free countries. All other functions remained highly centralized in Eindhoven. In many foreign countries, Philips created joint ventures with domestic companies to gain acceptance in local markets.

In 1919, Philips entered into the "Principal Agreement" with General Electric, giving each company the use of the other's patents. The agreement also divided the world into "three spheres of influence": General Electric would control North America; Philips would control Holland; both companies agreed to compete freely in the rest of the world. (General Electric also took a 20% stake in Philips.) After this time, Philips began evolving from a highly centralized company whose sales were conducted through third parties to a decentralized sales organization with autonomous marketing companies in 14 European countries, China, Brazil, and Australia.

During this period, the company also broadened its product line significantly. In 1918, it began producing electronic vacuum tubes; eight years later its first radios appeared, capturing a 20% world market share within a decade; and during the 1930s, Philips began producing X-ray tubes. The Great Depression brought with it trade barriers and high tariffs, and Philips was forced to build local production facilities to protect its foreign sales of these products.

Philips: Organizational Development

One of the earliest traditions at Philips was a shared but competitive leadership by the commercial and technical functions. Gerard, an engineer, and Anton, a businessman, began a subtle competition where Gerard would try to produce more than Anton could sell and vice versa. Nevertheless, the two agreed that strong research was vital to Philips' survival.

During the late 1930s, in anticipation of the impending war, Philips transferred its overseas assets to two trusts, British Philips and the North American Philips Corporation; it also moved most of its vital research laboratories to Redhill in Surrey, England, and its top management to the United States. Supported by the assets and resources transferred abroad, and isolated from their parent, the individual country organizations became more independent during the war.

Because waves of Allied and German bombing had pummeled most of Philips' industrial plant in the Netherlands, the management board decided to build the postwar organization on the strengths of the national organizations (NOs). Their greatly increased self-sufficiency during the war had allowed most to become adept at responding to country-specific market conditions—a capability

that became a valuable asset in the postwar era. For example, when international wrangling precluded any agreement on television transmission standards, each nation decided at different times whether to adopt PAL, SECAM, or NTSC standards. Furthermore, consumer preferences and economic conditions varied: in some countries, rich, furniture-encased TV sets were the norm; in others sleek, contemporary models dominated the market. In the United Kingdom, the only way to penetrate the market was to establish a rental business; in richer countries, a major marketing challenge was overcoming elitist prejudice against television. In this environment, the independent NOs had a great advantage in being able to sense and respond to the differences.

Eventually, responsiveness extended beyond adaptive marketing. As NOs built their own technical capabilities, product development often became a function of local market conditions. For example, Philips of Canada created the company's first color TV; Philips of Australia created the first stereo TV; and Philips of the United Kingdom created the first TVs with teletext.

While NOs took major responsibility for financial, legal, and administrative matters, fourteen product divisions (PDs), located in Eindhoven, were formally responsible for development, production, and global distribution. (In reality, the NOs' control of assets and the PDs' distance from the operations often undercut this formal role.) The research function remained independent and expanded internationally with eight separate laboratories in Europe and the United States.

While formal corporate-level structure was represented as a type of geographic/product matrix, it was clear that NOs had the real power. NOs reported directly to the management board, which Philips enlarged from 4 members to 10 to ensure that top management remained in control of the vital NO operations. To lead the expanded management board, a four-man "presidium" was created. The board encouraged interaction with the highly autonomous NOs. Each NO sent envoys to Eindhoven to represent its interests, and top management, most of whom had been with the company for their entire careers, typically including multiple foreign tours of duty, made frequent country visits. In 1954, the International Concern Council was established to formalize regular meetings among the principal managers from all the NOs and the board of management.

Within the NOs, the management structure mimicked the legendary joint technical and commercial leadership of the two Philips brothers. NOs were led by a technical manager and a commercial manager. In some locations, a finance manager filled out the top management triad that typically reached key decisions collectively. This cross-functional coordination capability was reflected throughout the organization. On the front lines, product teams, comprising junior managers from the commercial and technical functions, set product policies and carried out administrative functions. Cross-functional coordination also occurred at the product group level through group management teams, whose technical and commercial members met monthly to review progress and resolve inter-functional differences. Finally, the senior management committee of each subsidiary (with top commercial, technical and financial managers) reviewed progress to ensure that product group directions fit with national strategies and priorities.

The overwhelming importance of foreign operations to Philips, the commensurate status of the NOs within the corporate hierarchy, and even the cosmopolitan appeal of many of the subsidiaries' locations encouraged many Philips managers to take extended foreign tours duty, working in a series of two or three year posts. This elite group of expatriate managers identified strongly with each other and with the NOs as a group, and had no difficulty representing their strong, country-oriented views to corporate management.

Philips: Attempts at Reorganization

In the 1960s, the creation of the Common Market eroded trade barriers within Europe and diluted the rationale for maintaining independent, country-level subsidiaries. New transistor- and printed circuit-based technologies demanded larger production runs than most national plants could justify, and many of Philips' competitors were moving production of electronics to new facilities in low-wage areas in East Asia and Central and South America. Despite its many technological innovations, Philips' ability to bring products to market began to falter. In the 1960s, the company invented the audiocassette but let its Japanese competitors capture the mass market. Almost 20 years later, Philips developed the V2000 videocassette format—superior technically to Sony's Beta or Matsushita's VHS—but could not successfully market the product. Indeed, North American Philips rejected the V2000, choosing instead to outsource, brand, and sell a VHS product under license from Matsushita. Within three years, Philips was forced to abandon V2000 and produce a VHS product.

Over three decades, five chairman experimented with reorganizing the company to deal with its growing problems. Yet in the late 1990s, Philips' financial performance remained poor and its global competitiveness was still in question. (See Exhibits 1 and 2.)

Van Reimsdijk and Rodenburg Reorganizations, 1970s

Concerned about what *Management Today* described as "continued profitless progress," newly appointed CEO Hendrick van Reimsdijk created an organization committee to prepare a policy paper on the division of responsibilities between the PDs and the NOs. Their report, dubbed the "Yellow Booklet," outlined the disadvantages of Philips' matrix organization in 1971:

> Without an agreement [defining the relationship between national organizations and product divisions], it is impossible to determine in any given situation which of the two parties is responsible. . . . As operations become increasingly complex, an organizational form of this type will only lower the speed of reaction of an enterprise.

On the basis of this report, van Reimsdijk proposed rebalancing the managerial relationships

EXHIBIT 1 Philips Group Summary Financial Data, 1970–1997 (millions of guilders unless otherwise stated)

	1997	1996	1995	1990	1985	1980	1975	1970
Net sales	F76,453	F69,195	F64,462	F55,764	F60,045	F36,536	F27,115	F15,070
Income from operations (excluding restructuring)	5,065	2,537	4,090	2,260	3,075	1,577	1,201	1,280
Income from operations (including restructuring)	4,960	1,812	4,044	−2,389	NA	NA	NA	NA
As a percentage of net sales	6.5%	2.6%	6.3%	−4.3%	5.1%	4.3%	4.5%	8.5%
Income after taxes	3,278	685	2,889	F−4,447	F1,025	F532	F341	F446
Net income from normal business operations	3,291	723	2,684	−4,526	NA	328	347	435
Stockholders' equity (common)	19,457	13,956	14,055	11,165	16,151	12,996	10,047	6,324
Return on stockholders' equity	16.6%	5.0%	20.2%	−30.2%	5.6%	2.7%	3.6%	7.3%
Distribution per common share, par value F 10 (in guilders)	F2.00	F1.60	F1.60	F0.0	F2.00	F1.80	F1.40	F1.70
Total assets	59,441	55,072	54,683	51,595	52,883	39,647	30,040	19,088
Inventories as a percentage of net sales	18.6%	17.9%	18.2%	20.7%	23.2%	32.8%	32.9%	35.2%
Outstanding trade receivables in month's sales	1.7	1.7	1.6	1.6	2.0	3.0	3.0	2.8
Current ratio	1.7			1.4	1.6	1.7	1.8	1.7
Employees at year-end (in thousands)	270	263	265	273	346	373	397	359
Wages, salaries and other related costs				F17,582	F21,491	F15,339	F11,212	F5,890
Exchange rate (period end; guilder/$)	2.02	1.74	1.60	1.69	2.75	2.15	2.69	3.62
	Selected Data in Millions of Dollars:							
Sales	$39,207	$40,944	$40,039	$33,018	$21,802	$16,993	$10,098	$4,163
Operating profit	2,543	1,072	2,512	1,247	988	734	464	NA
Pretax income	2,174	541	2,083	−2,380	658	364	256	NA
Net income	2,940	(349)	1,667	−2,510	334	153	95	120
Total assets	29,426	31,651	32,651	30,549	19,202	18,440	11,186	5,273
Shareholders' equity (common)	9,632	8,021	8,784	6,611	5,864	6,044	3,741	1,747

Source: Annual reports; Standard & Poors' *Compustat*; Moody's Industrial and International Manuals.

EXHIBIT 2 Philips Group, Sales by Product and Geographic Segment, 1985–1997 (million guilders)

	1997		1996		1995		1990		1985	
Net Sales by Product Segment:										
Lighting	F10,024	13%	F8,860	13%	F8,353	13%	F7,026	13%	F7,976	12%
Consumer electronics	23,825	31	24,039	35	22,027	34	25,400	46	16,906	26
Domestic appliances	—		—		—				6,644	10
Professional products/systems	12,869	17	11,323	16	11,562	18	13,059	23	17,850	28
Components/semiconductors	15,003	20	11,925	17	10,714	17	8,161	15	11,620	18
Software/services	13,009	17	11,256	16	9,425	15				
Miscellaneous	1,723	2	1,783	3	2,381	4	2,118	4	3,272	5
Total	76,453	100%	69,195	100%	64,462	100%	F55,764	100%	F64,266	100%
Operating Income by Sector:										
Lighting	1,151	23%	702	39%	983	24%	419	18%	F 910	30%
Consumer electronics	772	16	10	1	167	4	1,499	66	34	1
Domestic appliances	—		—		—		—		397	13
Professional products/systems	502	10	0	0	157	4	189	8	1,484	48
Components/semiconductors	2,262	46	1,496	83	2,233	55	−43	−2	44	1
Software/services	1,173	24	490	27	886	22	—			
Miscellaneous	188	4	199	11	423	10	218	10	200	7
Increase not attributable to a sector	(1,090)	(22)	(1,085)	(60)	(805)	(20)	−22	−1	6	0
Total	4,960	100%	1,812	1,006	4,044	100%	2,260	100%	F3,075	100%

Notes: Totals may not add due to rounding.
Product sector sales after 1988 are external sales only, therefore no eliminations are made; sector sales before 1988 include sales to other sectors, therefore eliminations are made.
Data are not comparable to consolidated financial summary due to restating.

Source: Annual reports.

between PDs and NOs—"tilting the matrix" in his words—to allow Philips to increase the scale of production, decrease the number of products marketed, concentrate production, and increase the flow of goods among national organizations. He proposed closing the least efficient local plants and converting the best into International Production Centers (IPCs), each supplying many NOs. In so doing, van Reimsdijk hoped that PD managers would gain control over manufacturing operations. Due to the political and organizational difficulty of closing local plants, however, implementation was slow. By the end of the decade, several IPCs had been established, but the NOs seemed as powerful and independent as ever.

In the late 1970s, his successor CEO, Dr. Rodenburg, continued this thrust. He reinforced matrix simplification by replacing the dual commercial and technical leadership with single management at both the corporate and national organizational levels. Yet the power struggles continued.

Wisse Dekker Reorganization, 1982

Unsatisfied with the company's slow response and concerned by its slumping financial performance, upon becoming CEO in 1982, Wisse Dekker outlined a new global strategy. Aware of the cost advantage of Philips' Japanese counterparts, he created more IPCs and closed inefficient operations— particularly in Europe where 40 of the company's more than 200 plants were shut. He focused on core operations by selling some businesses (e.g., welding, energy cables, and furniture) while acquiring an interest in Grundig and Westinghouse's North American lamp activities. Dekker also supported technology-sharing agreements and pushed alliances in off-shore manufacturing.

To deal with the slow-moving bureaucracy, he continued his predecessor's initiative to replace dual leadership with single general managers. He also continued to "tilt the matrix" by giving PDs formal product management responsibility, but leaving NOs responsible for local profits. And, he energized the management board by reducing its size, bringing on directors with strong operating experience, and creating subcommittees to deal with difficult issues. Finally, Dekker redefined the product planning process to incorporate input from the NOs, but gave global PDs the final decision on long-range direction. Still sales declined and profits stagnated.

Van der Klugt Reorganization, 1987

When Cor van der Klugt succeeded Dekker as chairman, Philips had lost its long-held industry leadership position to Matsushita, and was one of only two non-Japanese consumer electronics companies in the world's top ten. Its profit margins of 1% to 2% not only lagged behind General Electric's 9%, but even its highly aggressive Japanese competitors' slim 4%. Van der Klugt set a profit objective of 3%–4% and made beating the Japanese companies a top priority.

As van der Klugt reviewed Philips' strategy, he designated various businesses as core (those that shared related technologies, had strategic importance, or were technical leaders) and non-core (stand-alone businesses that were not targets for world leadership and could eventually be sold if required). Of the four businesses defined as core, three were strategically linked: Components, Consumer Electronics, and Telecommunications and Data Systems. The fourth, Lighting, was regarded as strategically vital because cash flow funded development. The non-core businesses included domestic appliances and medical systems which van der Klugt spun off into joint ventures with Whirlpool and GE, respectively.

In continuing efforts to strengthen the PDs relative to the NOs, van der Klugt restructured Philips around the four core global divisions rather than the former 14 PDs. This allowed him to trim the management board, appointing the displaced board members to a new policy-making Group Management Committee. Finally, he sharply reduced the 3,000 strong headquarters staff, reallocating many of them to the PDs.

To link PDs more directly to markets, van der Klugt dispatched many product line managers to Philips' most competitive markets. For example, management of the digital audio tape and electric shaver product lines were relocated to Japan, while the medical technology and domestic appliances lines were moved to the United States.

Such moves, along with continued efforts at globalizing product development and production efforts required that the parent company gain firmer control over NOs, especially the giant North American Philips Corp. (NAPC). Although Philips had obtained a majority equity interest after World War II, the U.S. company did not always respond to directives from the center. Referring to its much publicized choice of Matsushita's VHS video cassette format over its parent's V2000 format, NAPC's chairman said, "We made the best decisions for the parochial interests of our stockholders. They were not always parallel with those of Philips worldwide." To prevent replays of such experiences, in 1987 van der Klugt repurchased publicly owned NAPC shares for $700 million.

Reflecting the growing sentiment among some managers that R&D was not market-oriented enough, van der Klugt halved spending on basic research to about 10% of total R&D. To manage R&D's tendency "to ponder the fundamental laws of nature," he made R&D the direct responsibility of the businesses being supported by the research. This required that each research lab become focused on specific business areas (see Exhibit 3).

Finally, van der Klugt continued the effort to build efficient, specialized, multi-market production facilities by closing 75 of the company's 420 remaining plants worldwide. He also eliminated 38,000 of its 344,000 employees—21,000 through divesting businesses, shaking up the myth of lifetime employment at the company. He anticipated that all these restructurings would lead to a financial recovery by 1990. Unanticipated losses for that year, however—more than 4.5 billion Dutch guilder ($2.5 billion)—provoked a class action law suit by angry American investors, who alleged that positive projections by the company had been misleading. In a surprise move, on May 14, 1990, van der Klugt and half of the management board were replaced.

Timmer Reorganization, 1990

The new president, Jan Timmer, had spent most of his 35-year Philips career turning around unprofitable businesses. In an early meeting with his top 100 managers he distributed a hypothetical—but fact-based—press release announcing that Philips was bankrupt. (There had already been rumors of a takeover or a government bailout.) "So what action can you take this weekend?" he challenged.

Under "Operation Centurion," headcount was reduced by 68,000 or 22% over the next 18 months, earning Timmer the nickname "The Butcher of Eindhoven." Because European laws required substantial compensation for layoffs—Eindhoven workers received 15 months' pay, for example—the first round of 10,000 layoffs alone cost Philips

EXHIBIT 3   Philips Research Labs by Location and Specialty, 1987

Location	Size (staff)	Specialty
Eindhoven, The Netherlands	2,000	Basic research, electronics, manufacturing technology
Redhill, Surrey, England	450	Microelectronics, television, defense
Hamburg, Germany	350	Communications, office equipment, medical imaging
Aachen, West Germany	250	Fiber optics, X-ray systems
Paris, France	350	Microprocessors, chip materials and design
Brussels, Belgium	50	Artificial intelligence
Briarcliff Manor, New York	35	Optical systems, television, superconductivity, defense
Sunnyvale, California	150	Integrated circuits

Source: Philips, in *Business Week,* March 21, 1988, p. 156.

$700 million. To spread the burden around the globe, and to speed the process, Timmer asked his PD managers to negotiate cuts with NO managers. According to one report, however, country managers were "digging in their heels to save local jobs." But the cuts came—many from overseas operations. In addition to the job cuts, Timmer vowed to "change the way we work." He established new performance rules and asked hundreds of top managers to sign contracts that committed them to specific financial goals. Those who broke those contracts were replaced—often with outsiders.

To focus resources further, Timmer sold off various businesses including integrated circuits to Matsushita, minicomputers to Digital, defense electronics to Thomson and the remaining 53% of appliances to Whirlpool. Yet profitability was still well below the modest 4% on sales he promised. In particular, consumer electronics lagged with slow growth in a price-competitive market. The core problem was identified by a 1994 McKinsey study that estimated that value added per hour in Japanese consumer electronic factories was still 68% above that of European plants.

After three years of cost-cutting, in early 1994 Timmer presented a new growth strategy to the board. His plan was to expand software, services and multimedia to become 40% of revenues by 2000. Earlier, he had recruited Frank Carrubba, Hewlett-Packard's director of research, and encouraged him to focus on developing 15 core technologies. The list, which included interactive compact disc (CD-i), digital compact cassettes (DCC), high-definition television (HDTV) and multimedia software, was soon dubbed "the president's projects." But his earlier divestment of some of Philips's truly high-tech businesses and a 37% cut in R&D personnel left the company with few who understood the technology of the new priority businesses.

Boonstra Reorganization, 1996

By 1996, it was clear that Philips's HDTV technology would not become industry standard, that its DCC gamble had lost out to Sony's Minidisc, and that CI-i was a marketing failure. While costs were lower, so too was morale, particularly among middle management. Critics claimed that the company's drive for cost-cutting and standardization had led it to ignore new worldwide market demands for more segmented products and higher consumer service. When Timmer stepped down in October 1996, the board decided to replace him with a radical choice for Philips—an outsider whose expertise was in marketing and Asia rather than technology and Europe.

Cor Boonstra was a 58-year-old Dutchman whose years as CEO of Sara Lee, the U.S. consumer products firm, had earned him a reputation as a hard driver and a marketing genius. Joining Philips in 1994, he had headed the Asia Pacific region and the lighting division before being tapped as CEO. Unencumbered by tradition, he immediately announced sweeping changes. "There are no taboos, no sacred cows," he said. "The bleeders must be turned around, sold or closed. And we must change an organization that has been a closed system."

Within six months Boonstra had sold off 18 businesses he described as "bleeders" and had reduced commitments to 13 more perpetual loss makers, including a withdrawal from troubled German giant, Grundig. To reach his target of increasing return on invested capital from 17% to 24% by 1999, he also initiated a major restructuring of Philips' worldwide operations, promising to transform a structure he described as "a plate of spaghetti" into "a neat row of asparagus." He said:

> How can we compete with the Koreans? They don't have 350 companies all over the world. Their factory in Ireland covers Europe and their manufacturing facility in Mexico serves North America. We need a more structured and simpler manufacturing and marketing organization to achieve a cost pattern in line with those who do not have our heritage. This is still one of the biggest issues facing Philips.

Within a year, he had begun to rationalize the global structure and redeploy its resources. Over and above the restructuring, 3,100 jobs were eliminated in North America and 3,000 employees were added in Asia Pacific during 1997, emphasizing

Boonstra's determination to shift production to low-wage countries and his broader commitment to Asia. ("With Europe's slow growth, Asia is key to our rebuilding task," he said.) And he restructured the company around 100 business units, each responsible for its profits, worldwide, effectively eliminating the old PD/NO matrix. Finally, to the shock of most employees, he announced that the 100-year-old Eindhoven headquarters would be relocated to Amsterdam.

By early 1998, he was ready to announce his strategy. Despite early speculation that he might abandon consumer electronics, he proclaimed it as the center of Philips's future. Betting on the "digital revolution," he planned to focus on established technologies such as cellular phones (through joint ventures with Marantz and Lucent), digital TV, digital videodisc and web TV. More radically, he committed major resources to marketing, including a 40% increase in advertising to raise awareness and image of the Philips brand.

Record profits in 1997 boosted spirits in Philips, but, as *The Financial Times* pointed out, from such a low profit base, "the first few percentage points are comparatively easy to achieve."

Matsushita: Background

In 1918, Konosuke Matsushita (or "KM" as he was affectionately known), a 23-year-old inspector with the Osaka Electric Light Company, invested ¥100 to start production of double-ended sockets in his modest home. The company grew rapidly, expanding into battery-powered lamps, electric irons, and radios. On May 5, 1932, Matsushita's 14th anniversary, KM announced to his 162 employees a 250-year corporate plan broken into 25-year sections, each to be carried out by successive generations. His plan was codified in a company creed and in the "Seven Spirits of Matsushita" (see Exhibit 4), which, along with the company song, continued to be woven into morning assemblies worldwide and provided the basis of the "cultural and spiritual training" all new employees received during their first seven months with the company.

In the post-war boom, Matsushita introduced a flood of new products: TV sets in 1952; transistor radios in 1958; color TVs, dishwashers and electric ovens in 1960. Capitalizing on its broad line of 5,000 products (Sony produced 80), the company opened 25,000 domestic retail distribution outlets. With more than six times the outlets of rival Sony, the ubiquitous "National Shops" represented about 40% of all appliance stores in Japan in the late 1960s. These not only provided assured sales volume, but also gave the company direct access to market trends and consumer product reaction.

When post-war growth slowed, however, Matsushita had to look beyond its expanding product line and excellent distribution system for growth. After trying many tactics to boost sales—even sending assembly line workers out as door-to-door salesmen—the company eventually focused on export markets.

The Organization's Foundation: Divisional Structure

Plagued by RI health, KM wished to delegate more authority than was typical in Japanese companies. In 1933, Matsushita became the first Japanese company to adopt the divisional structure, giving each division clearly defined profit responsibilities while creating a "small business" environment to maintain growth and flexibility. Under its "one-product-one division" system, each product line was managed by a separate autonomous division to be operated almost like an independent corporation. Corporate management provided it with initial funds, deliberately underestimating working capital requirements to motivate divisions to work hard for their retained earnings. Divisional profitability was determined after deductions for central services such as R&D, and interest on internal borrowings. KM expected uniform performance across the company's 36 divisions, and division managers whose operating profits fell below 4% of sales for two successive years were replaced.

Matsushita ran its corporate treasury like a commercial bank, reviewing divisions' loan requests for which it charged slightly higher-than-market

---

EXHIBIT 4 Matsushita Creed and Philosophy (excerpts)

Creed

Through our industrial activities, we strive to foster progress, to promote the general welfare of society, and to devote ourselves to furthering the development of world culture.

Seven Spirits of Matsushita

Service through Industry

Fairness

Harmony and Cooperation

Struggle for Progress

Courtesy and Humility

Adjustment and Assimilation

Gratitude

KM's Business Philosophy (Selected Quotations)

"The purpose of an enterprise is to contribute to society by supplying goods of high quality at low prices in ample quantity."

"Profit comes in compensation for contribution to society. . . . [It] is a result rather than a goal."

"The responsibility of the manufacturer cannot be relieved until its product is disposed of by the end user."

"Unsuccessful business employs a wrong management. You should not find its causes in bad fortune, unfavorable surroundings or wrong timing."

"Business appetite has no self-restraining mechanism. . . . When you notice you have gone too far, you must have the courage to come back."

Source: "Matsushita Electric Industrial (MEI) in 1987," Harvard Business School case 388-144.

---

interest, and accepting deposits on their excess funds. Each division paid 60% of earnings to headquarters and financed all additional working capital and fixed asset requirements from the retained 40%. Transfer prices were based on the market and settled through the treasury on normal commercial terms.

While basic technology was developed in a central research laboratory (CRL), product development and engineering occurred in each of the product divisions. Matsushita intentionally underfunded the CRL, forcing it to compete for additional funding from the divisions. Annually, the CRL publicized its major research projects to the product divisions, which then provided funding in exchange for technology for marketable applications.

This divisional structure generated competition among divisions, spurring them to drive growth by leveraging their technology assets into new products. After the innovating division had earned substantial profits on its new product, however, company policy was to spin it off as a new division to maintain the "hungry spirit."

Matsushita: Internationalization

Although the establishment of overseas markets was a major thrust of the second 25 years in the 250-year plan, in an overseas trip in 1951 KM had been unable to find any American company willing to collaborate with Matsushita. The best he could do was a technology exchange and licensing agreement with Philips. Nonetheless, the push to internationalize continued.

Expanding through Color TV

In the 1950s and 1960s, trade liberalization and lower shipping rates made possible a healthy export business built on black and white TV sets. In 1953, the company opened its first overseas branch office—the Matsushita Electric Corporation of America (MECA). With neither a distribution network nor a strong brand, the company could not access traditional retailers, and had to resort to selling its products under their private brands through mass merchandisers and discounters.

During the 1960s, pressure from national governments in developing countries led Matsushita to open manufacturing facilities in several countries in Southeast Asia and Central and South America. As manufacturing costs in Japan rose, Matsushita shifted more basic production to these low-wage countries, but almost all high-value components and subassemblies were still made in Japan. By the 1970s, projectionist sentiments in the West forced the company to establish plants in the Americas and Europe. In 1972, it opened a plant in Canada; in 1974, it bought Motorola's TV business and started manufacturing its Quasar brand in the United States; and in 1976, it built a plant in Cardiff, Wales to supply the Common Market.

Building Global Leadership: Dominating through VCRs

The birth of the videocassette recorder (VCR) propelled Matsushita into first place in the consumer electronics industry during the 1980s. Recognizing the potential mass-market appeal of the VCR—developed by Californian broadcasting company, Ampex, in 1956—engineers at Matsushita began developing VCR technology. After six years of development work, Matsushita launched its commercial broadcast video recorder in 1964, and introduced a consumer version two years later.

In 1975, Sony introduced the technically superior "Betamax" format, and the next year JVC launched a competing "VHS" format. Under pressure from

MITI, Matsushita agreed to give up its own format and adopt the more popular VHS. During Matsushita's 20 years of VCR product development, various members of the VCR research team had moved from central labs to the product divisions' development labs and eventually to the plant. In 1976, as sales at home and abroad began to take off, Matsushita celebrated the unit's first profitable year.

The company quickly built production to meet its own needs as well as OEM customers like GE, RCA and Zenith who decided to forego self-manufacture. Between 1977 and 1985, capacity was increased 33-fold to 6.8 million units. (In parallel, the company aggressively licensed the VHS format to other manufacturers, including Hitachi, Sharp, Mitsubishi and, eventually, Philips.) Increased volume enabled Matsushita to slash prices 50% within five years of product launch, while simultaneously improving quality on several carefully monitored dimensions. By the mid-1980s, VCRs accounted for 30% of sales—over 40% of overseas revenues—and provided 45% of profits.

Matsushita: Managing International Operations

In the mid-1980s, the growing number of overseas companies reported to Japan in one of two ways: wholly owned, single-product global plants reported directly to Matsushita's product divisions, while overseas sales and marketing subsidiaries and overseas companies producing a broad product line for local markets, reported to Matsushita Electric Trading Company (METC), a separate legal entity. (See Exhibit 5 or METC's organization.)

Changing Systems and Controls

Throughout the 1970s, the central product divisions maintained strong operating control over their offshore production units. Overseas operations used plant and equipment designed by the parent company, followed manufacturing procedures dictated by the center, and used materials from Matsushita's domestic plants. Growing trends toward

EXHIBIT 5   Organization of METC, 1985

1985 Organization:

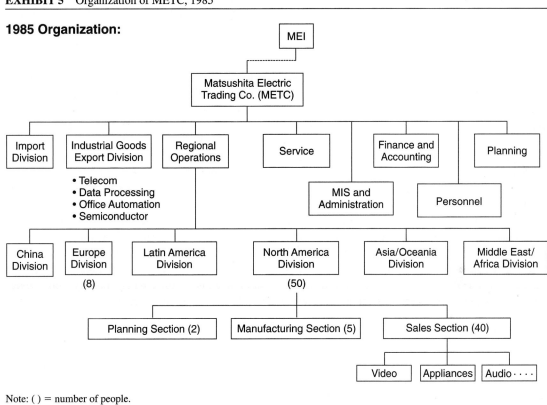

Note: ( ) = number of people.

Source: Harvard Business School case 388-144.

local sourcing, however, gradually weakened the divisions' direct control. By the 1980s, instead of controlling inputs, they began to monitor measures of output (e.g., quality, productivity, inventory levels).

About the same time, product divisions began receiving the globally consolidated return on sales reports that had previously been consolidated in METC statements. By the mid-1980s, as worldwide planning was introduced for the first time, corporate management required all its product divisions to prepare global product strategies.

Headquarters-Subsidiary Relations
Although METC and the product divisions set detailed sales and profits targets for their overseas subsidiaries, local managers were told they had complete autonomy on how to achieve the targets. "Mike" Matsuoko, president of the company's largest European production subsidiary in Cardiff, Wales, however, emphasized that failure to meet targets forfeited freedom: "Losses show bad health and invite many doctors from Japan who provide advice and support."

In the mid-1980s, Matsushita had over 700 expatriate managers and technicians on foreign assignment for four to eight years, but defended that high number by describing their pivotal role. "This vital communication role," said one manager, "almost always requires a manager from the parent company. Even if a local manager speaks Japanese, he would not have the long experience that is needed to build relationships and understand our management processes."

Expatriate managers were located throughout foreign subsidiaries, but there were a few positions that were almost always reserved for them. The most visible were subsidiary general managers whose main role was to translate Matsushita philosophy abroad. Expatriate accounting managers were expected to "mercilessly expose the truth" to corporate headquarters; and Japanese technical managers were sent to transfer product and process technologies and provide headquarters with local market information. These expatriates maintained relationships with senior colleagues at headquarters who acted as career mentors, evaluated performance (with some input from local managers), and provided expatriates with information about parent company developments.

General managers of foreign subsidiaries visited headquarters at least two or three times each year—some as often as every month. Corporate managers reciprocated these visits, and on average, major operations hosted at least one headquarters manager each day of the year. Face-to-face meetings were considered vital: "Figures are important," said one manager, "but the meetings are necessary to develop judgment." Faxes and after-hour phone calls between headquarters and expatriate colleagues were a vital management link.

In the mid-1980s, offshore production subsidiaries gained some flexibility. They were free to buy minor parts from local vendors as long as quality could be assured, but still had to buy key components from internal sources. Subsidiaries now carried out routine production tasks independently, calling on corporate technical personnel when plans called for major expansion or change. Similarly, sales subsidiaries had some choice over the products they sold. Each year the company held a two-week internal merchandising show and product planning meeting, where sales subsidiary managers negotiated over features, quantities, and even prices of the products they wanted to buy from the parent's product divisions. Corporate managers,

however, could overrule the subsidiary if they thought introduction of a particular product was strategic.

Yamashita's Operation Localization

Although international sales kept rising, as early as the early 1980s growing host country pressures caused concern about the company's highly centralized operations. In 1982, newly appointed company President Toshihiko Yamashita launched "Operation Localization" to boost offshore production from less than 10% of value added to 25%, or half of overseas sales, by 1990. To support the target, he set out a program of four localizations—personnel, technology, material, and capital.

Over the next few years, Matsushita increased the number of local nationals in key positions. In the United States, for example, U.S. nationals became the presidents of three of the six local companies while in Taiwan, the majority of production divisions were replaced by Chinese managers. In each case, however, local national managers were still supported by senior Japanese advisors who maintained a direct link with the parent company. To localize technology and material, the company developed its national subsidiaries' expertise to source equipment locally, modify designs to meet local requirements, and incorporate local components, and adapt corporate processes and technologies to accommodate these changes while maintaining the company's quality standards.

The overall localization thrust sparked opposition from managers in Japan. In a low-growth environment, increased foreign production would come at the expense of export sales. "What will that mean for employment in Japan?" said one senior manager. "Protecting the interests of employees is one of our greatest moral commitments. We cannot sacrifice that for any reason." Even some foreign subsidiary managers feared it would reduce their access to central resources and expertise. If localized operations caused export income to contribute less, they reasoned, the central product division managers could give priority to domestic needs over foreign operations.

Nonetheless, between 1980 and 1988, Matsushita added 21 manufacturing companies and 12 sales companies abroad to bring those respective totals to 60 and 41. In 1990, Matsushita employed 50,000 workers overseas, twice the number of a decade earlier. Despite these efforts, in 1990 overseas production stood at only ¥600 billion—still less than half Matsushita's 25% target.

President Yamashita had also hoped that Operation Localization would help Matsushita's overseas companies develop the innovative capability and entrepreneurial initiatives that he had long admired in the national organizations of rival Philips. (Past efforts to develop such capabilities abroad had failed. For example, when Matsushita acquired Motorola's TV business in the United States, its highly innovative technology group atrophied as American engineers resigned in response to what they felt to be excessive control from Japan's highly centralized R&D operations.) In an unusual act for a Japanese CEO, Yamashita publicly expressed his unhappiness with the lack of initiative at the TV plant in Cardiff. Despite the transfer of substantial resources and the delegation of many responsibilities, he felt that the plant remained too dependent on the center.

Tanii's Integration and Expansion

Yamashita's successor, Akio Tanii, expanded on his predecessor's initiatives. In part because Matsushita's product divisions received only 3% royalties for foreign production against at least 10% return on sales for exports from Japan, he felt that product divisions were not giving their full attention to developing operations outside Japan. To correct the situation, he brought all foreign subsidiaries of Matsushita under the control of METC in 1986, thus consolidating the company's international operations in one administrative entity. To further integrate domestic and overseas operations, in April 1988, Tanii merged METC into the parent company. Then, to shift operational control nearer to local markets, he relocated major regional headquarters functions from Japan to North America, Europe, and Southeast Asia. Yet still he was frustrated that the overseas subsidiary companies acted as the implementing agents of the Osaka-based product divisions.

Through all these changes, however, Matsushita's worldwide growth continued generating huge reserves. With $17.5 billion in financial assets at the end of 1989, the company was referred to as the "Matsushita Bank." Several top executives felt that if they could not develop innovative overseas companies, they should buy them. Flush with cash and international success, in early 1991 the company acquired MCA, the U.S. entertainment giant for $6.1 billion, with the objective of obtaining a media software source for its hardware. Within a year, however, Japan's bubble economy had burst, wiping out $2.6 trillion in stock market value and plunging the economy into recession. Almost overnight, Tanii had to shift the company's focus from expansion to cost containment.

Morishita's Restructuring

Despite Tanii's best efforts to cut costs, the problems ran too deep. The company's huge capacity, its full line of products, and its network of 27,000 retailers turned from assets to liabilities. With 1992 profits less than half their 1991 level, Tanii was forced to resign in February 1993.

His replacement, Yoichi Morishita—at 56 the most junior of the firm's executive vice presidents—immediately implemented a major restructuring designed "to eliminate laxness and extravagance." Central to his effort was a commitment to cut headquarters staff and decentralize responsibility to operating units, including overseas companies. Under the slogan "simple, small, speedy and strategic," over the next 18 months he eliminated a layer of management and transferred 6,000 corporate staff to operating jobs. To the shock of many, he even began questioning the sanctity of lifetime employment. By contrast, he consolidated 20 research centers into nine, centralizing decisions to speed up new product introductions. Unwilling to respond to MCI's management pressure for more funding and greater independence, Matsushita sold off 80% of the company to Seagram at a $1.2 billion loss in early 1995.

EXHIBIT 6 Matsushita, Summary Financial Data, 1990–1997*

	1997	1996	1995	1990	1985	1980	1975	1970
In Billions of Yen and Percent:								
Sales	¥7,676	¥6,795	¥6,948	¥6,003	¥5,291	¥2,916	¥1,385	¥932
Income before tax	332	77	232	572	723	324	83	147
As percentage of sales	4.3%	1.1%	3.3%	9.5%	13.7%	11.1%	6.0%	15.8%
Net income	¥138	¥(58)†	¥90	¥236	¥216	¥125	¥32	¥70
As percentage of sales	1.8%	(0.8%)	1.3%	3.9%	4.1%	4.3%	2.3%	7.6%
Cash dividends (per share)	12.50	12.50	13.50	¥10.00	¥9.52	¥7.51	¥6.82	¥6.21
Total assets	8,696	8,011	8,202	7,851	5,076	2,479	1,274	735
Stockholders' equity	3,696	3,398	3,255	3,201	2,084	1,092	573	324
Capital investment	415	381	316	355	288	NA	NA	NA
Depreciation	345	292	296	238	227	65	28	23
R&D	435	399	378	346	248	102	51	NA
Employees (units)	270,651	265,538	265,397	198,299	175,828	107,057	82,869	78,924
Overseas employees	116,279	107,530	112,314	59,216	38,380	NA	NA	NA
As percentage of total employees	43%	40%	42%	30%	22%	NA	NA	NA
Exchange rate (fiscal period end; ¥/$)	124	106	89	159	213	213	303	360
In Millions of Dollars:								
Sales	$61,902	$64,102	$78,069	$37,753	$24,890	$13,690	$4,572	$2,588
Operating income before depreciation	3,015	2,495	2,924	4,343	3,682	1,606	317	NA
Operating income after depreciation	2,678	723	2,609	2,847	2,764	1,301	224	NA
Pretax income	1,112	(536)	1,017	3,667	3,396	1,520	273	408
Net income	70,128	75,583	92,159	1,482	1,214	584	105	195
Total assets	29,804	32,053	36,575	49,379	21,499	11,636	4,206	2,042
Total equity				20,131	10,153	5,129	1,890	900

*Data prior to 1987 are for the fiscal year ending November 20; data 1988 and after are for the fiscal year ending March 31.
†1996 results include a write-off of ¥164 billion in losses stemming from the sale of MCA in June 1995.

Source: Annual reports; Standard & Poors' *Compustat*; Moody's Industrial and International Manuals.

EXHIBIT 7   Matsushita, Sales by Product and Geographic Segment, 1985–1990 (billion yen)

	1997		1996		1995		FY 1990		FY1985	
By Product Segment:										
Video equipment	¥1,342	17%	¥1,225	18%	¥1,272	18%	¥1,598	27%	¥1,947	37%
Audio equipment	576	8	518	8	555	8	561	9	570	11
Home appliances	1,026	13	914	13	916	13	802	13	763	14
Communication and industrial equipment	2,492	32	2,013	<30	1,797	26	1,375	23	849	16
Electronic components	1,055	14	1,020	15	893	13	781	13	573	11
Batteries and kitchen-related equipment	472	6	405	6	374	4	312	5	217	4
Others	710	9	700	10	530	8	573	10	372	7
Total	7,676	100%	6,795	100%	6,948	100%	¥6,003	100%	¥5,291	100%
By Geographic Segment:										
Domestic	4,046	53%	3,727	55%	3,455	50%	¥3,382	56%	¥2,659	50%
Overseas	3,630	47	3,068	45	3,493	50	2,621	44	2,632	50

Notes: Total may not add due to rounding.

Source: Annual reports.

Meanwhile, stimulated by a rising yen that raised the export prices, product divisions were aggressively moving value added offshore, particularly to Southeast Asia. Attracted by booming markets, lower costs and strong local partners, the company began investing in major production facilities, not just the knockdown assembly plants of the 1970s and 1980s. For example, production of all 1.5 million of Matsushita's export air conditioners was transferred to Malaysia. In that country alone, Matsushita had established 16 companies producing a wide range of products and employing 20,000 people. Subsequently, the air conditioning and television companies expanded their commitment by establishing substantial Malaysian design and development centers. Similar levels of commitment were also being made to facilities in China, India and Vietnam.

By fiscal year 1997, profit margins had risen from 2.8% when Morishita took over to 4.3%. Besides restructuring the company, he had successfully repositioned its product portfolio, reducing low margin consumer electronics from 50% to 35% of sales and moving into digital technologies such as cellular phones, digital cameras and digital video discs. Yet Morishita was still discouraged that still less than 50% of overseas sales were manufactured abroad. Equally troubling was the company's slow transition to local senior-level management in its overseas companies, and the even less successful attempts to integrate foreign managers at senior levels in the parent company

---

Reading 2–1

THE GLOBALIZATION OF MARKETS

Theodore Levitt

A powerful force drives the world toward a converging commonality, and that force is technology. It has proletarianized communication, transport, and travel. It has made isolated places and impoverished peoples eager for modernity's allurements. Almost everyone everywhere wants all the things they have heard about, seen, or experienced via the new technologies.

The result is a new commercial reality—the emergence of global markets for standardized consumer products on a previously unimagined scale

of magnitude. Corporations geared to this new reality benefit from enormous economies of scale in production, distribution, marketing, and management. By translating these benefits into reduced world prices, they can decimate competitors that still live in the disabling grip of old assumptions about how the world works.

Gone are accustomed differences in national or regional preference. Gone are the days when a company could sell last year's models—or lesser versions of advanced products—in the less-developed world. And gone are the days when prices, margins, and profits abroad were generally higher than at home.

The globalization of markets is at hand. With that, the multinational commercial world nears its end, and so does the multinational corporation.

The multinational and the global corporation are not the same thing. The multinational corporation operates in a number of countries, and adjusts its products and practices in each—at high relative costs. The global corporation operates with resolute constancy—at low relative cost—as if the entire world (or major regions of it) were a single entity; it sells the same things in the same way everywhere.

Which strategy is better is not a matter of opinion but of necessity. Worldwide communications carry everywhere the constant drumbeat of modern possibilities to lighten and enhance work, raise living standards, divert, and entertain. The same countries that ask the world to recognize and respect the individuality of their cultures insist on the wholesale transfer to them of modern goods, services, and technologies. Modernity is not just a wish but also a widespread practice among those who cling, with unyielding passion or religious fervor, to ancient attitudes and heritages.

Who can forget the televised scenes during the 1979 Iranian uprisings of young men in fashionable French-cut trousers and silky body shirts thirsting with raised modern weapons for blood in the name of Islamic fundamentalism?

In Brazil, thousands swarm daily from pre-industrial Bahian darkness into exploding coastal cities, there quickly to install television sets in crowded corrugated huts and, next to battered Volkswagens, make sacrificial offerings of fruit and fresh-killed chickens to Macumban spirits by candlelight.

During Biafra's fratricidal war against the Ibos, daily televised reports showed soldiers carrying blood stained swords and listening to transistor radios while drinking Coca-Cola.

In the isolated Siberian city of Krasnoyarsk, with no paved streets and censored news, occasional Western travelers are stealthily propositioned for cigarettes, digital watches, and even the clothes off their backs.

The organized smuggling of electronic equipment, used automobiles, Western clothing, cosmetics, and pirated movies into primitive places exceeds even the thriving underground trade in modern weapons and their military mercenaries.

A thousand suggestive ways attest to the ubiquity of the desire for the most advanced things that the world makes and sells—goods of the best quality and reliability at the lowest price. The world's needs and desires have been irrevocably homogenized. This makes the multinational corporation obsolete and the global corporation absolute.

Living in the Republic of Technology

Daniel J. Boorstin, author of the monumental trilogy, *The Americans,* characterized our age as driven by "the Republic of Technology [whose] supreme law . . . is convergence, the tendency for everything to become more like everything else."

In business, this trend has pushed markets toward global commonality. Corporations sell standardized products in the same way everywhere—autos, steel, chemicals, petroleum, cement, agricultural commodities and equipment, industrial and commercial construction, banking and insurance services, computers, semiconductors, transport, electronic instruments, pharmaceuticals, and telecommunications, to mention some of the obvious.

Nor is the sweeping gale of globalization confined to these raw material or high-tech products, where the universal language of customers and users facilitates standardization. The transforming winds whipped up by the proletarianization of communication and travel enter every crevice of life.

Commercially, nothing confirms this as much as the success of McDonald's from the Champs Elysées to the Ginza, of Coca-Cola in Bahrain and Pepsi-Cola in Moscow, and of rock music, Greek salad, Hollywood movies, Revlon cosmetics, Sony televisions, and Levi jeans everywhere. "High-touch" products are as ubiquitous as high-tech.

Starting from opposing sides, the high-tech and the high-touch ends of the commercial spectrum gradually consume the undistributed middle in their cosmopolitan orbit. No one is exempt and nothing can stop the process. Everywhere everything gets more and more like everything else as the world's preference structure is relentlessly homogenized.

Consider the cases of Coca-Cola and Pepsi-Cola, which are globally standardized products sold everywhere and welcomed by everyone. Both successfully cross multitudes of national, regional, and ethnic taste buds trained to a variety of deeply ingrained local preferences of taste, flavor, consistency, effervescence, and aftertaste. Everywhere both sell well. Cigarettes, too, especially American-made, make year-to-year global inroads on territories previously held in the firm grip of other, mostly local, blends.

These are not exceptional examples. (Indeed their global reach would be even greater were it not for artificial trade barriers.) They exemplify a general drift toward the homogenization of the world and how companies distribute, finance, and price products.[1] Nothing is exempt. The products and methods of the industrialized world play a single tune for all the world, and all the world eagerly dances to it.

Ancient differences in national tastes or modes of doing business disappear. The commonality of preference leads inescapably to the standardization of products, manufacturing, and the institutions of trade and commerce. Small nation-based markets transmogrify and expand. Success in world competition turns on efficiency in production, distribution, marketing, and management, and inevitably becomes focused on price.

The most effective world competitors incorporate superior quality and reliability into their cost structures. They sell in all national markets the same kind of products sold at home or in their largest export market. They compete on the basis of appropriate value—the best combinations of price, quality, reliability, and delivery for products that are globally identical with respect to design, function, and even fashion.

That, and little else, explains the surging success of Japanese companies dealing worldwide in a vast variety of products—both tangible products like steel, cars, motorcycles, hi-fi equipment, farm machinery, robots, microprocessors, carbon fibers, and now even textiles, and intangibles like banking, shipping, general contracting, and soon computer software. Nor are high-quality and low-cost operations incompatible, as a host of consulting organizations and data engineers argue with vigorous vacuity. The reported data are incomplete, wrongly analyzed, and contradictory. The truth is that low-cost operations are the hallmark of corporate cultures that require and produce quality in all that they do. High quality and low costs are not opposing postures. They are compatible, twin identities of superior practice.[2]

To say that Japan's companies are not global because they export cars with left-side drives to the United States and the European continent, while those in Japan have right-side drives, or because they sell office machines through distributors in the United States but directly at home, or speak Portuguese in Brazil, is to mistake a difference for a distinction. The same is true of Safeway and Southland retail chains operating effectively in the Middle East, and to not only native but also imported populations from Korea, the Philippines, Pakistan, India, Thailand, Britain, and the United States. National rules of the road differ, and so do distribution channels and languages. Japan's distinction is its unrelenting push for economy and value enhancement. That translates into a drive for standardization at high quality levels.

Vindication of the Model T

If a company forces costs and prices down and pushes quality and reliability up—while maintaining reasonable concern for suitability—customers will prefer its world-standardized products. The

[1]In a landmark article, Robert D. Buzzell pointed out the rapidity with which barriers to standardization were falling. In all cases they succumbed to more and cheaper advanced ways of doing things. See "Can You Standardize Multinational Marketing?" *HBR,* November–December 1968.

[2]There is powerful new evidence for this, even though the opposite has been urged by analysts of PIMS data for nearly a decade. See "Product Quality: Cost Production and Business Performance—A Test of Some Key Hypotheses" by Lynn W. Phillips, Dae Chang, and Robert D. Buzzell, Harvard Business School Working Paper No. 83–13.

theory holds, at this stage in the evolution of globalization, no matter what conventional market research and even common sense may suggest about different national and regional tastes, preferences, needs, and institutions. The Japanese have repeatedly vindicated this theory, as did Henry Ford with the Model T. Most important, so have their imitators, including companies from South Korea (television sets and heavy construction), Malaysia (personal calculators and microcomputers), Brazil (auto parts and tools), Colombia (apparel), Singapore (optical equipment), and yes, even from the United States (office copiers, computers, bicycles, castings), Western Europe (automatic washing machines), Rumania (housewares), Hungary (apparel), Yugoslavia (furniture), and Israel (pagination equipment).

Of course, large companies operating in a single nation or even a single city don't standardize everything they make, sell, or do. They have product lines instead of a single product version, and multiple distribution channels. There are neighborhood, local, regional, ethnic, and institutional differences, even within metropolitan areas. But although companies customize products for particular market segments, they know that success in a world with homogenized demand requires a search for sales opportunities in similar segments across the globe in order to achieve the economies of scale necessary to compete.

Such a search works because a market segment in one country is seldom unique; it has close cousins everywhere precisely because technology has homogenized the globe. Even small local segments have their global equivalents everywhere and become subject to global competition, especially on price.

The global competitor will seek constantly to standardize his offering everywhere. He will digress from this standardization only after exhausting all possibilities to retain it, and he will push for reinstatement of standardization whenever digression and divergence have occurred. He will never assume that the customer is a king who knows his own wishes.

Trouble increasingly stalks companies that lack clarified global focus and remain inattentive to the economics of simplicity and standardization. The most endangered companies in the rapidly evolving world tend to be those that dominate rather small domestic markets with high value-added products for which there are smaller markets elsewhere. With transportation costs proportionately low, distant competitors will enter the now-sheltered markets of those companies with goods produced more cheaply under scale-efficient conditions. Global competition spells the end of domestic territoriality, no matter how diminutive the territory may be.

When the global producer offers his lower costs internationally, his patronage expands exponentially. He not only reaches into distant markets, but also attracts customers who previously held to local preferences and now capitulate to the attractions of lesser prices. The strategy of standardization not only responds to worldwide homogenized markets but also expands those markets with aggressive low pricing. The new technological juggernaut taps an ancient motivation—to make one's money go as far as possible. This is universal—not simply a motivation but actually a need.

The Hedgehog Knows

The difference between the hedgehog and the fox, wrote Sir Isaiah Berlin in distinguishing between Dostoevski and Tolstoy, is that the fox knows a lot about a great many things, but the hedgehog knows everything about one great thing. The multinational corporation knows a lot about a great many countries and congenially adapts to supposed differences. It willingly accepts vestigial national differences, not questioning the possibility of their transformation, not recognizing how the world is ready and eager for the benefit of modernity, especially when the price is right. The multinational corporation's accommodating mode to visible national differences is medieval.

By contrast, the global corporation knows everything about one great thing. It knows about the absolute need to be competitive on a worldwide basis as well as nationally and seeks constantly to drive down prices by standardizing what it sells and how it operates. It treats the world as composed of few standardized markets rather than many customized markets. It actively seeks and vigorously works toward global convergence. Its mission is modernity and its mode, price competition, even when it sells top-of-the-line, high-end products. It knows about the one great thing all nations and people have in common: scarcity.

Nobody takes scarcity lying down; everyone wants more. This in part explains division of labor and specialization of production. They enable people and nations to optimize their conditions through trade. The median is usually money.

Experience teaches that money has three special qualities: scarcity, difficulty of acquisition, and transience. People understandably treat it with respect. Everyone in the increasingly homogenized world market wants products and features that everybody else wants. If the price is low enough, they will take highly standardized world products, even if these aren't exactly what mother said was suitable, what immemorial custom decreed was right, or what market-research fabulists asserted was preferred.

The implacable truth of all modern production—whether of tangible or intangible goods—is that large-scale production of standardized items is generally cheaper within a wide range of volume than small-scale production. Some argue that CAD/CAM will allow companies to manufacture customized products on a small scale—but cheaply. But the argument misses the point. If a company treats the world as one or two distinctive product markets, it can serve the world more economically than if it treats it as three, four, or five product markets.

Why Remaining Differences?
Different cultural preferences, national tastes and standards, and business institutions are vestiges of the past. Some inheritances die gradually; others prosper and expand into mainstream global prefer-

ences. So-called ethnic markets are a good example. Chinese food, pita bread, country and western music, pizza, and jazz are everywhere. They are market segments that exist in worldwide proportions. They don't deny or contradict global homogenization but confirm it.

Many of today's differences among nations as to products and their features actually reflect the respectful accommodation of multinational corporations to what they believe are fixed local preferences. They *believe* preferences are fixed, not because they are but because of rigid habits of thinking about what actually is. Most executives in multinational corporations are thoughtlessly accommodating. They falsely presume that marketing means giving the customer what he says he wants rather than trying to understand exactly what he'd like. So they persist with high-cost, customized multinational products and practices instead of pressing hard and pressing properly for global standardization.

I do not advocate the systemic disregard of local or national differences. But a company's sensitivity to such differences does not require that it ignore the possibilities of doing things differently or better.

There are, for example, enormous differences among Middle Eastern countries. Some are socialist, some monarchies, some republics. Some take their legal heritage from the Napoleonic Code, some from the Ottoman Empire, and some from the British common law; except for Israel, all are influenced by Islam. Doing business means personalizing the business relationship in an obsessively intimate fashion. During the month of Ramadan, business discussions can start only after 10 o'clock at night, when people are tired and full of food after a day of fasting. A company must almost certainly have a local partner; a local lawyer is required (as, say, in New York), and irrevocable letters of credit are essential. Yet, as Coca-Cola's Senior Vice President Sam Ayoub noted, "Arabs are much more capable of making distinctions between cultural and religious purposes on the one hand and economic realities on the other than is generally assumed. Islam is compatible with science and modern times."

Barriers to globalization are not confined to the Middle East. The free transfer of technology and data across the boundaries of the European Common Market countries are hampered by legal and financial impediments. And there is resistance to radio and television interference ("pollution") among neighboring European countries.

But the past is a good guide to the future. With persistence and appropriate means, barriers against superior technologies and economics have always fallen. There is no recorded exception where reasonable effort has been made to overcome them. It is very much a matter of time and effort.

A Failure in Global Imagination

Many companies have tried to standardize world practice by exporting domestic products and processes without accommodation or change—and have failed miserably. Their deficiencies have been seized on as evidence of bovine stupidity in the face of abject impossibility. Advocates of global standardization see them as examples of failures in execution.

In fact, poor execution is often an important cause. More important, however, is failure of nerve—failure of imagination.

Consider the case for the introduction of fully automatic home laundry equipment in Western Europe at a time when few homes had even semiautomatic machines. Hoover, Ltd., whose parent company was headquartered in North Canton, Ohio, had a prominent presence in Britain as a producer of vacuum cleaners and washing machines. Due to insufficient demand in the home market and low exports to the European continent, the large washing machine plant in England operated far below capacity. The company needed to sell more of its semiautomatic or automatic machines.

Because it had a "proper" marketing orientation, Hoover conducted consumer preference studies in Britain and each major continental country. The results showed feature preferences clearly enough among several countries (see Exhibit 1).

EXHIBIT 1   Consumer Preferences as to Automatic Washing Machine Features in the 1960s

Features	Great Britain	Italy	West Germany	France	Sweden
Shell dimensions*	34″ and narrow	Low and narrow	34″ and wide	34″ and narrow	34″ and wide
Drum material	Enamel	Enamel	Stainless steel	Enamel	Stainless steel
Loading	Top	Front	Front	Front	Front
Front porthole	Yes/no	Yes	Yes	Yes	Yes
Capacity	5 kilos	4 kilos	6 kilos	5 kilos	6 kilos
Spin speed	700 rpm	400 rpm	850 rpm	600 rpm	800 rpm
Water-heating system	No[†]	Yes	Yes[‡]	Yes	No[†]
Washing action	Agitator	Tumble	Tumble	Agitator	Tumble
Styling features	Inconspicuous appearance	Brightly colored	Indestructible appearance	Elegant appearance	Strong appearance

*34″ height was (in the process of being adopted as) a standard work-surface height in Europe.
[†]Most British and Swedish homes had centrally heated hot water.
[‡]West Germans preferred to launder at temperatures higher than generally provided centrally.

The incremental unit variable costs (in pounds sterling) of customizing to meet just a few of the national preferences were:

	£	s*	d†
Stainless steel versus enamel drum	1	0	0
Porthole window		10	0
Spin speed of 800 rpm versus 700 rpm		15	0
Water heater	2	15	0
6 versus 5 kilos capacity	1	10	0
	£6	10s	0d
	$18.20 at the exchange rate of that time.		

*s = shillings
†d = pence

Considerable plant investment was needed to meet other preferences.

The lowest retail prices (in pounds sterling) of leading locally produced brands in the various countries were approximately:

U.K.	£110
France	114
West Germany	113
Sweden	134
Italy	57

Product customization in each country would have put Hoover in a poor competitive position on the basis of price, mostly due to the higher manufacturing costs incurred by short production runs for separate features. Because Common Market tariff reduction programs were then incomplete, Hoover also paid tariff duties in each continental country.

How to Make a Creative Analysis

In the Hoover case, an imaginative analysis of automatic washing machine sales in each country would have revealed that:

1. Italian automatics, small in capacity and size, low-powered, without built-in heaters, with porcelain enamel tubs, were priced aggressively low and were gaining large market shares in all countries, including West Germany.
2. The best-selling automatics in West Germany were heavily advertised (three times more than the next most promoted brand), were ideally suited to national tastes, and were also by far the highest priced machines available in that country.
3. Italy, with the lowest penetration of washing machines of any kind (manual, semiautomatic, or automatic) was rapidly going directly to automatics, skipping the pattern of first buying hand-wringer, manually assisted machines and then semiautomatics.
4. Detergent manufacturers were just beginning to promote the technique of cold-water and tepid-water laundering then used in the United States.

The growing success of small, low-powered, low-speed, low-capacity, low-priced Italian machines, even against the preferred but highly priced and highly promoted brand in West Germany, was significant. It contained a powerful message that was lost on managers confidently wedded to a distorted version of the marketing concept according to which you give the customer what he says he wants. In fact the customers *said* they wanted certain features, but their behavior demonstrated they'd take other features provided the price and the promotion were right.

In this case it was obvious that, under prevailing conditions, people preferred a low-priced automatic over any kind of manual or semiautomatic machine and certainly over higher priced automatics, even though the low-priced automatics failed to fulfill all their expressed preferences. The supposedly meticulous and demanding German consumers violated all expectations by buying the simple, low-priced Italian machines.

It was equally clear that people were profoundly influenced by promotions of automatic washers; in West Germany, the most heavily promoted ideal machine also had the largest market share despite its high price. Two things clearly influenced customers to buy: low price regardless of feature preferences and heavy promotion regardless of price. Both factors helped homemakers get what they most wanted—the superior benefits bestowed by fully automatic machines.

Hoover should have aggressively sold a simple, standardized high-quality machine at a low price (afforded by the 17% variable cost reduction that the elimination of £6-10-0 worth of extra features made possible). The suggested retail prices could have been somewhat less than £100. The extra funds "saved" by avoiding unnecessary plant modifications would have supported an extended service network and aggressive media promotions.

Hoover's media message should have been: *this* is the machine that you, the homemaker, *deserve* to have to reduce the repetitive heavy daily household burdens, so that *you* may have more constructive time to spend with your children and your husband. The promotion should also have targeted the husband to give him, preferably in the presence of his wife, a sense of obligation to provide an automatic washer for her even before he bought an automobile for himself. An aggressively low price, combined with heavy promotion of this kind, would have overcome previously expressed preferences for particular features.

The Hoover case illustrates how the perverse practice of the marketing concept and the absence of any kind of marketing imagination let multinational attitudes survive when customers actually want the benefits of global standardization. The whole project got off on the wrong foot. It asked people what features they wanted in a washing machine rather than what they wanted out of life. Selling a line of products individually tailored to each nation is thoughtless. Managers who took pride in practicing the marketing concept to the fullest did not, in fact, practice it at all. Hoover asked the wrong questions, then applied neither thought nor imagination to the answers. Such companies are like the ethnocentricists in the Middle Ages who saw with everyday clarity the sun revolving around the earth and offered it as Truth. With no additional

data but a more searching mind, Copernicus, like the hedgehog, interpreted a more compelling and accurate reality. Data do not yield information except with the intervention of the mind. Information does not yield meaning except with the intervention of imagination.

Accepting the Inevitable

The global corporation accepts for better or for worse that technology drives consumers relentlessly toward the same common goals—alleviation of life's burdens and the expansion of discretionary time and spending power. Its role is profoundly different from what it has been for the ordinary corporation during its brief, turbulent, and remarkably protean history. It orchestrates the twin vectors of technology and globalization for the world's benefit. Neither fate, nor nature, nor God but rather the necessity of commerce created this role.

In the United States two industries became global long before they were consciously aware of it. After over a generation of persistent and acrimonious labor shutdowns, the United Steelworkers of America have not called an industrywide strike since 1959; the United Auto Workers have not shut down General Motors since 1970. Both unions realize that they have become global—shutting down all or most of U.S. manufacturing would not shut out U.S. customers. Overseas suppliers are there to supply the market.

Cracking the Code of Western Markets

Since the theory of the marketing concept emerged a quarter of a century ago, the more managerially advanced corporations have been eager to offer what customers clearly wanted rather than what was merely convenient. They have created marketing departments supported by professional market researchers of awesome and often costly proportions. And they have proliferated extraordinary numbers of operations and product lines—highly tailored products and delivery systems for many different markets, market segments, and nations.

Significantly, Japanese companies operate almost entirely without marketing departments or market research of the kind so prevalent in the West. Yet, in the colorful words of General Electric's chairman John F. Welch, Jr., the Japanese, coming from a small cluster of resource-poor islands, with an entirely alien culture and an almost impenetrably complex language, have cracked the code of Western markets. They have done it not by looking with mechanistic thoroughness at the way markets are different but rather by searching for meaning with a deeper wisdom. They have discovered the one great thing all markets have in common—an overwhelming desire for dependable, world-standard modernity in all things, at aggressively low prices. In response, they deliver irresistible value everywhere, attracting people with products that market-research technocrats described with superficial certainty as being unsuitable and uncompetitive.

The wider a company's global reach, the greater the number of regional and national preferences it will encounter for certain product features, distribution systems, or promotional media. There will always need to be some accommodation to differences. But the widely prevailing and often unthinking belief in the immutability of these differences is generally mistaken. Evidence of business failure because of lack of accommodation is often evidence of other shortcomings.

Take the case of Revlon in Japan. The company unnecessarily alienated retailers and confused customers by selling world-standardized cosmetics only in elite outlets; then it tried to recover with low-priced world-standardized products in broader distribution, followed by a change in the company president and cutbacks in distribution as costs rose faster than sales. The problem was not that Revlon didn't understand the Japanese market; it didn't do the job right, wavered in its programs, and was impatient to boot.

By contrast, the Outboard Marine Corporation, with imagination, push, and persistence, collapsed long-established three-tiered distribution channels in Europe into a more focused and controllable two-step system—and did so despite the vociferous warnings of local trade groups. It also reduced the number and types of retail outlets. The result was greater improvement in credit and product-installation service to customers, major cost reductions, and sales advances.

In its highly successful introduction of Contac 600 (the timed-release decongestant) into Japan, SmithKline Corporation used 35 wholesalers instead of the 1,000-plus that established practice required. Daily contacts with the wholesalers and key retailers, also in violation of established practice, supplemented the plan, and it worked.

Denied access to established distribution institutions in the United States, Komatsu, the Japanese manufacturer of lightweight farm machinery, entered the market through over-the-road construction equipment dealers in rural areas of the Sunbelt, where farms are smaller, the soil sandier and easier to work. Here inexperienced distributors were able to attract customers on the basis of Komatsu's product and price appropriateness.

In cases of successful challenge to prevailing institutions and practices, a combination of product reliability and quality, strong and sustained support systems, aggressively low prices, and sales-compensation packages, as well as audacity and implacability, circumvented, shattered, and transformed very different distribution systems. Instead of resentment, there was admiration.

Still, some differences between nations are unyielding, even in a world of microprocessors. In the United States almost all manufacturers of microprocessors check them for reliability through a so-called parallel system of testing. Japan prefers the totally different sequential testing system. So Teradyne Corporation, the world's largest producer of microprocessor test equipment, makes one line for the United States and one for Japan. That's easy.

What's not so easy for Teradyne is to know how best to organize and manage, in this instance, its marketing effort. Companies can organize by product, region, function, or by using some combination of these. A company can have separate marketing organizations for Japan and for the United States, or it can have separate product groups, one working largely in Japan and the other in the United States. A single manufacturing facility or marketing operation might service both markets, or a company might use separate marketing operations for each.

Questions arise if the company organizes by product. In the case of Teradyne, should the group handling the parallel system, whose major market is the United States, sell in Japan and compete with the group focused on the Japanese market? If the company organizes regionally, how do regional groups divide their efforts between promoting the parallel versus the sequential system? If the company organizes in terms of function, how does it get commitment in marketing, for example, for one line instead of the other?

There is no one reliably right answer—no one formula by which to get it. There isn't even a satisfactory contingent answer.[3] What works well for one company or one place may fail for another in precisely the same place, depending on the capabilities, histories, reputations, resources, and even the cultures of both.

The Earth Is Flat

The differences that persist throughout the world despite its globalization affirm an ancient dictum of economics—that things are driven by what happens at the margin, not at the core. Thus, in ordinary competitive analysis, what's important is not the average price but the marginal price; what happens not in the usual case but at the interface of newly erupting conditions. What counts in commercial affairs is what happens at the cutting edge. What is most striking today is the underlying similarities of what is happening now to national

---

[3]For a discussion of multinational reorganization, see Christopher A. Barlett, "MNCs: Get Off the Reorganization Merry-Go-Round," *HBR,* March–April 1983, p. 138.

preferences at the margin. These similarities at the cutting edge cumulatively form an overwhelming, predominant commonality everywhere.

To refer to the persistence of economic nationalism (protective and subsidized trade practices, special tax aids, or restrictions for home market producers) as a barrier to the globalization of markets is to make a valid point. Economic nationalism does have a powerful persistence. But, as with the present almost totally smooth internationalization of investment capital, the past alone does not shape or predict the future.

Reality is not a fixed paradigm, dominated by immemorial customs and derived attitudes, heedless of powerful and abundant new forces. The world is becoming increasingly informed about the liberating and enhancing possibilities of modernity. The persistence of the inherited varieties of national preferences rests uneasily on increasing evidence of, and restlessness regarding, their inefficiency, costliness, and confinement. The historic past, and the national differences respecting commerce and industry it spawned and fostered everywhere, is now subject to relatively easy transformation.

Cosmopolitanism is no longer the monopoly of the intellectual and leisure classes; it is becoming the established property and defining characteristic of all sectors everywhere in the world. Gradually and irresistibly it breaks down the walls of economic insularity, nationalism, and chauvinism. What we see today as escalating commercial nationalism is simply the last violent death rattle of an obsolete institution.

Companies that adapt to and capitalize on economic convergence can still make distinctions and adjustments in different markets. Persistent differences in the world are consistent with fundamental underlying commonalities; they often complement rather than oppose each other—in business as they do in physics. There is, in physics, simultaneously matter and anti-matter working in symbiotic harmony.

The earth is round, but for most purposes it's sensible to treat it as flat. Space is curved, but not much for everyday life here on earth.

Divergence from established practice happens all the time. But the multinational mind, warped into circumspection and timidity by years of stumbles and transnational troubles, now rarely challenges existing overseas practices. More often it considers any departure from inherited domestic routines as mindless, disrespectful, or impossible. It is the mind of a bygone day.

The successful global corporation does not abjure customization or differentiation for the requirements of markets that differ in product preferences, spending patterns, shopping preferences, and institutional or legal arrangements. But the global corporation accepts and adjusts to these differences only reluctantly, only after relentlessly testing their immutability, after trying in various ways to circumvent and reshape them as we saw in the cases of Outboard Marine in Europe, Smith-Kline in Japan, and Komatsu in the United States.

There is only one significant respect in which a company's activities around the world are important, and this is in what it produces and how it sells. Everything else derives from, and is subsidiary to, these activities.

The purpose of business is to get and keep a customer. Or, to use Peter Drucker's more refined construction, to *create* and keep a customer. A company must be wedded to the ideal of innovation—offering better or more preferred products in such combinations of ways, means, places, and at such prices that prospects *prefer* doing business with the company rather than with others.

Preferences are constantly shaped and reshaped. Within our global commonality enormous variety constantly asserts itself and thrives, as can be seen within the world's single largest domestic market,

the United States. But in the process of world homogenization, modern markets expand to reach cost-reducing global proportions. With better and cheaper communication and transport, even small local market segments hitherto protected from distant competitors now feel the pressure of their presence. Nobody is safe from global reach and the irresistible economies of scale.

Two vectors shape the world—technology and globalization. The first helps determine human preferences; the second, economic realities. Regardless of how much preferences evolve and diverge, they also gradually converge and form markets where economies of scale lead to reduction of costs and prices.

The modern global corporation contrasts powerfully with the aging multinational corporation. Instead of adapting to superficial and even entrenched differences within and between nations, it will seek sensibly to force suitably standardized products and practices on the entire globe. They are exactly what the world will take, if they come also with low prices, high quality, and blessed reliability. The global company will operate, in this regard, precisely as Henry Kissinger wrote in *Years of Upheaval* about the continuing Japanese economic success—"voracious in its collection of information, impervious to pressure, and implacable in execution."

Given what is everywhere the purpose of commerce, the global company will shape the vectors of technology and globalization into its great strategic fecundity. It will systematically push these vectors toward their own convergence, offering everyone simultaneously high-quality, more or less standardized products at optimally low prices, thereby achieving for itself vastly expanded markets and profits. Companies that do not adapt to the new global realities will become victims of those that do.

Reading 2–2

CULTURE AND ORGANIZATION

Intuitively, people have always assumed that bureaucratic structures and patterns of action differ in the different countries of the Western world and even more markedly between East and West. Practitioners know it and never fail to take it into account. But contemporary social scientists . . . have not been concerned with such comparisons.

Michel Crozier[1]

Just how does culture influence organization structure and process? To what extent do organizational structures and processes have an inherent logic which overrides cultural considerations? Given the nature of today's business demands, do we find convergence in the ways of organizing? To what extent will popular techniques such as team management and empowerment be adopted across cultures? With what speed and with what possible (re) interpretation? What cultural dimensions need to be recognized which may facilitate or hinder organizational change efforts?

In order to demonstrate the impact of culture on organizational structure, systems, and processes, we present the evidence for national differences and consider the cultural reasons for these differences. Examining the degree to which organizations have centralized power, specialized jobs and roles, and formalized rules and procedures, we find distinct patterns of organizing which prevail despite pressures for convergence. This raises concerns regarding the transferability of organizational forms across borders and questions the logic of universal "best practices."

Different Schools, Different Cultures

While many managers are ready to accept that national culture may influence the way people relate to each other, or the "soft stuff," they are less convinced that it can really affect the nuts and bolts of organization: structure, systems, and processes. The culture-free (or *emic*) argument is that structure is determined by *organizational* features such as size and technology. For example, the famous Aston studies,[2] conducted in the late 1960s in the United Kingdom and widely replicated, point to size as the most important factor influencing structure: larger firms tend to have greater division of labor (specialized) and more formal policies and procedures (formalized) but are not necessarily more centralized. Furthermore, the nature of technology, such as mass production, is considered to favor a more centralized and formal (mechanistic) rather than decentralized and informal (organic) approach.[3]

Other management scholars argue that the *societal* context creates differences in structure in

---

Excerpted from *Managing Across Cultures,* by Susan Schneider and Jean-Louis Barsoux. London: Prentice-Hall, 1997.

[1]Crozier, M. (1964) *The Bureaucratic Phenomenon,* Chicago: University of Chicago Press, p. 210.

---

[2]Pugh, D.S., Hickson, D.J., Hinings, C.R., and Turner, C. (1969) "The context of organization structure", *Administrative Science Quarterly,* 14, 91–114; Miller, G.A. (1987) "Meta-analysis and the culture-free hypothesis", *Organization Studies,* 8(4), 309–25; Hickson, D.J. and McMillan, I. (eds) (1981) *Organization and Nation: The Aston Programme IV,* Farnborough: Gower.

[3]Burns, T. and Stalker, G.M. (1961) *The Management of Innovation,* London: Tavistock.

different countries (*etic*).[4] In effect, the "structural-ists" argue that structure creates culture, while the "culturalists" argue that culture creates structure. The debate continues, with each side arming up with more sophisticated weapons: measurements and methodologies.

Taking an historical perspective, theories about how best to organize—Max Weber's (German) bureaucracy, Henri Fayol's (French) administrative model, and Frederick Taylor's (American) scientific management—all reflect societal concerns of the times as well as the cultural backgrounds of the individuals.[5] Today, their legacies can be seen in the German emphasis on structure and competence, the French emphasis on social systems, roles and relationships (unity of command), and the American emphasis on the task system or machine model of organization, now popularized in the form of re-engineering.

Indeed, many of the techniques of modern management—performance management, participative management, team approach, and job enrichment all have their roots firmly embedded in a particular historical and societal context: *scientific management* in the United States at the turn of the century; *human relations,* brought about by Hawthorne studies (1930s) in the United States; *socio-technical* brought by the Tavistock studies of the coal mines in the United Kingdom (1930s); and *human resources* brought about in Sweden (1970s) with Saab Scania's and Volvo's redesign of auto assembly into autonomous teams.

These approaches reflect different cultural assumptions regarding, for example, human nature and the importance of task and relationships. While the scientific management approach focused on how best to accomplish the task, the human relations approach focused on how best to establish relationships with employees. The human resources approach assumed that workers were self-motivated, while earlier schools assumed that workers needed to be motivated by more or less benevolent management.

These models of management have diffused across countries at different rates and in different ways. For example, mass-production techniques promoted by scientific management were quickly adopted in Germany, while practices associated with the human relations school transferred more readily to Spain.[6] For this reason the historical and societal context needs to be considered to understand the adoption and diffusion of different forms of organization across countries. While some theorists focus on the *institutional arrangements,*[7] such as the nature of markets, the educational system, or the relationships between business and government, to explain these differences, we focus here, more specifically, on the cultural reasons.

This does not mean that institutional factors are irrelevant. In effect, it is quite difficult to separate out the influence of institutions from culture as they have both evolved together over time and are thus intricately linked. For example, the strong role of the state and the cultural emphasis on power and hierarchy often go hand in hand, as in the case of France. Or in the words of the French *roi soleil*

[4]Child, J. (1981) "Culture, contingency and capitalism in the cross-national study of organizations" in L.L. Cummings and B.M. Staw (eds) *Research in Organizational Behavior,* Vol. 3, 303–356, Greenwich, CT: JAI Press; Scott, W.R. (1987) "The adolescence of institutional theory", *Administrative Science Quarterly,* 32, 493–511; Lincoln, J.R., Hanada, M. and McBride, K. (1986) "Organizational structures in Japanese and US manufacturing", *Administrative Science Quarterly,* 31, 338–64.

[5]Weber, M. (1947) *The Theory of Social and Economic Organization,* New York: Free Press; Fayol, H. (1949) *General Industrial Management,* London: Pitman; Taylor, F. (1947, first published 1912) *Scientific Management,* New York: Harper & Row.

[6]Kogut, B. (1991) "Country capabilities and the permeability of borders", *Strategic Management Journal,* 12, 33–47; Kogut, B. and Parkinson, D. (1993) "The diffusion of American organizing principles to Europe" in B. Kogut (ed.) *Country Competitiveness: Technology and the Organizing of Work,* Ch. 10, New York: Oxford University Press, 179–202; Guillen, M. (1994) "The age of eclecticism: Current organizational trends and the evolution of managerial models", *Sloan Management Review,* Fall, 75–86.

[7]Westney, D.E. (1987) *Imitation and Innovation,* Cambridge, MA: Harvard University Press.

Louis XIV, *L'étât, c'est moi* ("The state is me"). Our argument (the culturalist perspective) is that different forms of organization emerge which reflect underlying cultural dimensions.

Culture and Structure

Hofstede's Findings

One of the most important studies which attempted to establish the impact of culture differences on management was conducted by Geert Hofstede, first in the late 1960s, and continuing through the next three decades.[8] The original study, now considered a classic, was based on an employee opinion survey involving 116,000 IBM employees in 40 different countries. From the results of this survey, which asked people for their preferences in terms of management style and work environment, Hofstede identified four "value" dimensions on which countries differed: power distance, uncertainty avoidance, individualism/collectivism, and masculinity/femininity.

Power distance indicates the extent to which a society accepts the unequal distribution of power in institutions and organizations. **Uncertainty avoidance** refers to a society's discomfort with uncertainty, preferring predictability and stability. **Individualism/collectivism** reflects the extent to which people prefer to take care of themselves and their immediate families, remaining emotionally independent from groups, organizations, and other collectivities. And the **masculinity/femininity** dimension reveals the bias towards either "masculine" values of assertiveness, competitiveness, and materialism, or towards "feminine" values of nurturing, and the quality of life and relationships. Country rankings on each dimension are provided in Table 1.

Given the differences in value orientations, Hofstede questioned whether American theories could be applied abroad and discussed the consequences of cultural differences in terms of motivation, leadership, and organization.[9] He argued, for example, that organizations in countries with high power distance would tend to have more levels of hierarchy (vertical differentiation), a higher proportion of supervisory personnel (narrow span of control), and more centralized decision-making. Status and power would serve as motivators, and leaders would be revered or obeyed as authorities.

In countries with high uncertainty avoidance, organizations would tend to have more formalization evident in greater amount of written rules and procedures. Also there would be greater specialization evident in the importance attached to technical competence in the role of staff and in defining jobs and functions. Managers would avoid taking risks and would be motivated by stability and security. The role of leadership would be more one of planning, organizing, coordinating, and controlling.

In countries with a high collectivist orientation, there would be a preference for group as opposed to individual decision-making. Consensus and cooperation would be more valued than individual initiative and effort. Motivation derives from a sense of belonging, and rewards are based on being part of the group (loyalty and tenure). The role of leadership in such cultures is to facilitate team effort and integration, to foster a supportive atmosphere, and to create the necessary context or group culture.

In countries ranked high on masculinity, the management style is likely to be more concerned with task accomplishment than nurturing social relationships. Motivation will be based on the acquisition of money and things rather than quality of life. In such cultures, the role of leadership is to ensure bottom-line profits in order to satisfy shareholders, and to set demanding targets. In more feminine cultures, the role of the leader would be to safeguard employee well-being, and to demonstrate concern for social responsibility.

---

[8]Hofstede, G. (1980) *Cultures Consequences,* Beverly Hills, CA: Sage; Hofstede, G. (1991) *Cultures and Organizations: Software of the Mind,* London: McGraw-Hill.

[9]Hofstede, G. (1980) "Motivation, leadership, and organization: Do American theories apply abroad?", *Organizational Dynamics,* Summer, 42–63.

TABLE 1   Hofstede's Rankings

Country	Power Distance		Individualism		Masculinity		Uncertainty Avoidance	
	Index	Rank	Index	Rank	Index	Rank	Index	Rank
Argentina	49	35–6	46	22–3	56	20–1	86	10–15
Australia	36	41	90	2	61	16	51	37
Austria	11	53	55	18	79	2	70	24–5
Belgium	65	20	75	8	54	22	94	5–6
Brazil	69	14	38	26–7	49	27	76	21–2
Canada	39	39	80	4–5	52	24	48	41–2
Chile	63	24–5	23	38	28	46	86	10–15
Colombia	67	17	13	49	64	11–12	80	20
Costa Rica	35	42–4	15	46	21	48–9	86	10–15
Denmark	18	51	74	9	16	50	23	51
Equador	78	8–9	8	52	63	13–14	67	28
Finland	33	46	63	17	26	47	59	31–2
France	68	15–16	71	10–11	43	35–6	86	10–15
Germany (F.R.)	35	42–4	67	15	66	9–10	65	29
Great Britain	35	42–4	89	3	66	9–10	35	47–8
Greece	60	27–8	35	30	57	18–19	112	1
Guatemala	95	2–3	6	53	37	43	101	3
Hong Kong	68	15–16	25	37	57	18–19	29	49–50
Indonesia	78	8–9	14	47–8	46	30–1	48	41–2
India	77	10–11	48	21	56	20–1	40	45
Iran	58	19–20	41	24	43	35–6	59	31–2
Ireland	28	49	70	12	68	7–8	35	47–8
Israel	13	52	54	19	47	29	81	19
Italy	50	34	76	7	70	4–5	75	23
Jamaica	45	37	39	25	68	7–8	13	52
Japan	54	33	46	22–3	95	1	92	7
Korea (S)	60	27–8	187	43	39	41	85	16–17
Malaysia	104	1	26	36	50	25–6	36	46
Mexico	81	5–6	30	32	69	6	82	18
Netherlands	38	40	80	4–5	14	51	53	35
Norway	31	47–8	69	13	8	52	50	38
New Zealand	22	50	79	6	58	17	49	39–40
Pakistan	55	32	14	47–8	50	25–6	70	24–5
Panama	95	2–3	11	51	44	34	86	10–15
Peru	64	21–3	16	45	42	37–8	87	9
Philippines	94	4	32	31	64	11–12	44	44
Portugal	63	24–5	27	33–5	31	45	104	2
South Africa	49	36–7	65	16	63	13–14	49	39–40
Salvador	66	18–19	19	42	40	40	94	5–6
Singapore	74	13	20	39–41	48	28	8	53
Spain	57	31	51	20	42	37–8	86	10–15
Sweden	31	47–8	71	10–11	5	52	29	49–50
Switzerland	34	45	68	14	70	4–5	58	33
Taiwan	58	29–30	17	44	45	32–3	69	26

(continued)

TABLE 1   (concluded)

Country	Power Distance		Individualism		Masculinity		Uncertainty Avoidance	
	Index	Rank	Index	Rank	Index	Rank	Index	Rank
Thailand	64	21–3	20	39–41	34	44	64	30
Turkey	66	18–19	37	28	45	31–3	85	16–17
Uruguay	61	26	36	29	38	42	100	4
United States	40	38	91	1	62	15	46	43
Venezuela	81	5–6	12	50	73	3	76	21–2
Yugoslavia	76	12	27	33–5	21	48–9	88	8
Regions:								
East Africa	64	21–3	27	33–5	41	39	52	36
West Africa	77	10–11	20	39–41	46	30–1	54	34
Arab countries	80	7	38	26–7	53	23	68	27

Rank numbers: 1—Highest; 53—Lowest.

Source: G. Hofstede (1991) *Cultures and Organizations: Software of the Mind,* McGraw-Hill, Maidenhead.

Having ranked countries on each dimension, Hofstede then positioned them along two dimensions at a time, creating a series of cultural maps. He too found country clusters—Anglo, Nordic, Latin, and Asian—similar to those reported in the previous chapter.[10] While some concern has been voiced that the country differences found in Hofstede's research are not representative due to the single company sample, further research by him and others supports these dimensions and the preferences for different profiles of organization.

One such cultural map, as shown in Figure 1 (see also Table 2), is particularly relevant to structure in that it simultaneously considers power distance (acceptance of hierarchy) and uncertainty avoidance (the desire for formalized rules and procedures). Countries which ranked high both on power distance and uncertainty avoidance would be expected to be more "mechanistic"[11] or what is commonly known as bureaucratic. In this corner we find the Latin countries.

In the opposite quadrant, countries which rank low both on power distance and uncertainty avoidance are expected to be more "organic"[12]—less hierarchic, more decentralized, having less formalized rules and procedures. Here we find the Nordic countries clustered and to a lesser extent, the Anglo countries.

In societies where power distance is low but uncertainty avoidance is high, we expect to find organizations where hierarchy is downplayed, decisions are decentralized, but where rules and regulations are more formal, and task roles and responsibilities are more clearly defined. Thus there is no need for a boss, as the organization runs by routines. This is characteristic of the Germanic cluster.

In societies where power distance is high but uncertainty avoidance is low, organizations resemble families or tribes. Here, "the boss is the boss", and the organization may be described as paternalistic. Subordinates do not have clearly defined task roles and responsibilities (formalization), but instead social roles. Here we find the Asian countries where business enterprise is often characterized by centralized power and personalized relationships.

---

[10]Ronen, S. and Shenekar, O. (1985) "Clustering countries on attitudinal dimensions: A review and synthesis", *Academy of Management Review*, 10(3), 435–54.

[11]Burns and Stalker, *Op. cit.*

[12]*Ibid.*

FIGURE 1   Hofstede's Maps

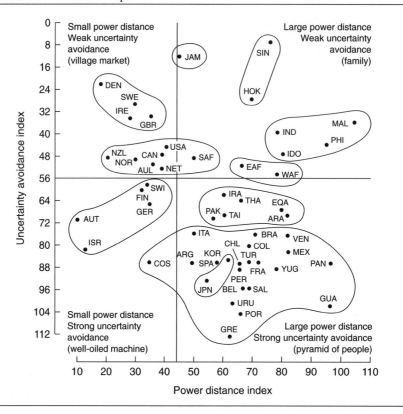

Source: G. Hofstede (1991) *Cultures and Organizations,* McGraw-Hill, Maidenhead.

Emerging Cultural Profiles:
Converging Evidence

These differences in structural preferences also emerged in a study conducted by Stevens[13] at IN-SEAD. When presented with an organizational problem, a conflict between two department heads within a company, MBA students from Britain, France, and Germany proposed markedly different solutions. The majority of French students referred the problem to the next level up, the president. The Germans argued that the major problem was a lack

of structure; the expertise, roles, and responsibilities of the two conflicting department heads had never been clearly defined. Their suggested solution involved establishing procedures for better coordination. The British saw it as an interpersonal communication problem between the two department heads which could be solved by sending them for interpersonal skills training, preferably together.

On the basis of these findings, Stevens described the "implicit model" of the organization held by each culture. For the French, the organization represents a "pyramid of people" (formalized and centralized). For the Germans, the organization is like a "well-oiled machine" (formalized but not centralized), in which management intervention is limited

---

[13]Stevens, O.J., cited in Hofstede, G. (1991) *Cultures and Organizations,* London: McGraw-Hill, 140–2.

TABLE 2   Abbreviations for the Countries and Regions Studied

Abbreviation	Country or Region	Abbreviation	Country or Region
ARA	Arab-speaking countries (Egypt, Iraq, Kuwait, Lebanon, Libya, Saudi Arabia, United Arab Emirates)	ITA	Italy
		JAM	Jamaica
		JPN	Japan
		KOR	South Korea
ARG	Argentina	MAL	Malaysia
AUL	Australia	MEX	Mexico
AUT	Austria	NET	Netherlands
BEL	Belgium	NOR	Norway
BRA	Brazil	NZL	New Zealand
CAN	Canada	PAK	Pakistan
CHL	Chile	PAN	Panama
COL	Colombia	PER	Peru
COS	Costa Rica	PHI	Philippines
DEN	Denmark	POR	Portugal
EAF	East Africa (Ethiopia, Kenya, Tanzania, Zambia)	SAF	South Africa
		SAL	Salvador
EQA	Equador	SIN	Singapore
FIN	Finland	SPA	Spain
FRA	France	SWE	Sweden
GBR	Great Britain	SWI	Switzerland
GER	Germany F.R.	TAI	Taiwan
GRE	Greece	THA	Thailand
GUA	Guatemala	TUR	Turkey
HOK	Hong Kong	URU	Uruguay
IDO	Indonesia	USA	United States
IND	India	VEN	Venezuela
IRA	Iran	WAF	West Africa (Ghana, Nigeria, Sierra Leone)
IRE	Ireland (Republic of)		
ISR	Israel	YUG	Yugoslavia

Source: G. Hofstede (1991) *Cultures and Organizations,* McGraw-Hill, Maidenhead.

to exceptional cases because the rules resolve problems. And for the British, it was more like a "village market" (neither formalized nor centralized) in which neither the hierarchy nor the rules, but rather the demands of the situation determine structure.

Going beyond questionnaires by observing the actual behavior of managers and company practices, further research reveals such cultural profiles as shown in Figure 2. Indeed, in studies comparing firms in France, Germany, and the United King-dom,[14] French firms were found to be more centralized and formalized with less delegation when compared with either German or British firms. The role of the PDG (French CEO) was to provide

[14]Brossard, A. and Maurice, M. (1976) "Is there a universal model of organization structure?", *International Studies of Management and Organizations,* 6, 11–45; Horovitz, J. (1980) *Top Management Control in Europe,* London: Macmillan; Stewart, R., Barsoux, J.-L., Kieser, A., Ganter, D. and Walgenbach, P. (1994) *Managing in Britain and Germany*, London: Macmillan.

FIGURE 2   Emerging Cultural Profiles

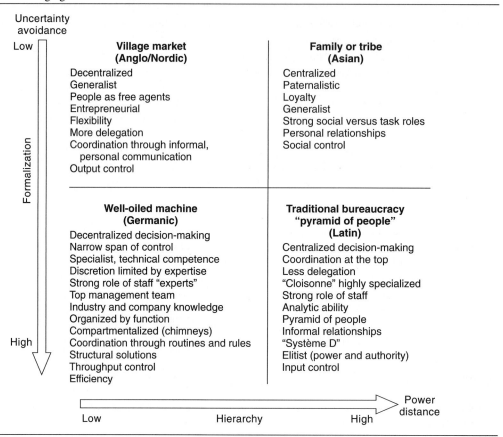

coordination at the top and to make key decisions, which demands a high level of analytical and conceptual ability that need not be industry- or company-specific. The staff function plays an important role in providing analytic expertise. These capabilities are developed in the elite *grandes écoles* of engineering and administration.

The research findings confirmed the image of German firms as "well-oiled machines" as they were more likely to be decentralized, specialized, and formalized. In fact, German managers were more likely to cite structure as a key success factor, having a logic of its own, apart from people. German firms were more likely to be organized by function (sometimes to the extent that they are referred to as "chimney" organizations) with coordination achieved through routines and procedures.

Although German organizations tended to be flatter and to have a broader span of control when compared with the French, middle managers had less discretion than their British counterparts as they were limited to their specific technical competence. The premium placed on competence was expressed in the concern to find competent people to perform specialized tasks, the strong role of staff to provide technical expertise, and expectations that top management not only has specific technical competence, but also in-depth company knowledge. Furthermore, top management typically consists of a managing board, *Vorstand,* which integrates the specialized knowledge of the various top managers (rather than in the head of a lone individual as in the case of France, Britain, or the United States).

In contrast to the well-oiled machine model with its greater concern for efficiency, the "village market" model reflects a greater concern for flexibility. Indeed, structure in British firms was found to be far more flexible, more decentralized and less formalized, when compared with the French and German firms. Organized by divisions, there is greater decentralization and delegation in the company and the role of central staff is far less important. Here, the burden of coordinating functions was placed on individual managers requiring a constant need for persuasion and negotiation to achieve cooperation.[15]

British managers, compared with Germans, were more ready to adapt the structure to the people working in it. Changes in personnel were often used as opportunities to reshuffle the jobs and responsibilities in order to accommodate available talent, and to create opportunities for personal development (free agents). Top management's role was to identify market opportunities and convince others to pursue them, underlining the importance of taking a more strategic view and of being able to communicate it persuasively.[16]

Studies in Asia have also found companies to fit the "family model," being more hierarchic and less formalized, with the exception of Japan. When compared with the Japanese, Hong Kong Chinese firms were less likely to have written manuals and Hong Kong Chinese bosses were also found to be more autocratic and paternalistic.[17] Another study of thirty-nine multinational commercial banks from fourteen different countries operating in Hong Kong found the Hong Kong banks to have the greatest number of hierarchical levels (eleven); the banks from Singapore, the Philippines, and India were also among those most centralized.[18]

A recent study of Chinese entrepreneurs found the Confucian tradition of patriarchal authority to be remarkably persistent. Being part of the family is seen as a way of achieving security. Social roles are clearly spelled out in line with Confucian precepts, which designate the responsibilities for the roles of father–son, brothers, and so on. Control is exerted through authority, which is not questioned. In 70 percent of the entrepreneurial firms studied, even large ones, the structure of Chinese organizations was found to resemble a hub with spokes around a powerful founder, or a management structure with only two layers.[19]

What begins to emerge from these various research studies is a converging and coherent picture of different management structures when comparing countries within Europe, as well as when comparing countries in Europe, the United States, and Asia. The primary cultural determinants appear to be those related to relationships between people in terms of power and status and relationship with nature, for example how uncertainty is managed and how control is exercised.

These underlying cultural assumptions are expressed in beliefs (and their subsequent importance, or value) regarding the need for hierarchy, for formal rules and procedures, specialized jobs and functions. These beliefs and values, in turn, are observable in behavior and artifacts, such as deference to the boss, the presence of executive parking and dining facilities ("perks"), and the existence of written policies and procedures, specific job descriptions, or manuals outlining standard operating procedures.

[15]Stewart *et al.*, *Op. cit.*

[16]*Ibid.*

[17]Redding, S.G. and Pugh, D.S. (1986) "The formal and the informal: Japanese and Chinese organization structures" in S. Clegg, D. Dunphy, and S.G. Redding (eds) *The Enterprise and Management in East Asia,* Hong Kong: Center of Asian Studies, University of Hong Kong, 153–168; Vertinsky, I., Tse, D.K., Wehrung, D.A. and Lee, K. (1990) "Organization design and management norms: A comparative study of managers' perceptions in the People's Republic of China, Hong Kong and Canada", *Journal of Management,* 16(4), 853–67.

[18]Wong, G.Y.Y. and Birnbaum-More, P.H. (1994) "Culture, context and structure: A test on Hong Kong banks", *Organization Studies,* 15(1), 99–23.

[19]Kao, J. (1993) "The worldwide web of Chinese business", *Harvard Business Review,* March–April, 24–35.

The research findings in the above-mentioned studies were based on observations as well as questionnaires and interviews of managers and companies in different countries. The same, of course, can be done comparing companies in different industries or within the same industry, and managers in different functions providing corresponding models of industry, corporate and/or functional cultures. From these findings, management scholars interpret underlying meaning.

The Meaning of Organizations:
Task Versus Social System

André Laurent argues that the country differences in structure described above reflect different conceptions (or understandings) of what is an organization.[20] These different conceptions were discovered in surveys which asked managers to agree or disagree with statements regarding beliefs about organization and management. A sample of the questions are shown in Table 3.

The results of this survey are very much in line with the discussion above in that they show similar cultural differences regarding power and uncertainty in views of organizations as systems of hierarchy, authority, politics, and role formalization. What would these different views of organization actually look like, were we to observe managers at work and even to question them? What arguments would managers from different countries put forth to support their responses?

Having a view of organizations as **hierarchical systems** would make it difficult, for example, to tolerate having to report to two bosses, as required in a matrix organization, and it would make it difficult to accept bypassing or going over or around the boss. The boss would also be expected to have precise answers to most of the questions that subordinates have about their work. Asian and Latin managers argue that in order for bosses to be

respected, or to have power and authority, they must demonstrate expert knowledge. And if the most efficient way to get things done is to bypass the hierarchical line they would consider that there was something wrong with the hierarchy.

Scandinavian and Anglo managers, on the other hand, argue that it is perfectly normal to go directly to anyone in the organization in order to accomplish the task. It would seem intolerable, for example, to have to go through one's own boss, who would contact his or her counterpart in a neighboring department before making contact with someone in that other department.

Furthermore, they argue that it is impossible to have precise answers, since the world is far too complex and ambiguous, and even if you could provide precise answers, this would not develop the capability of your subordinates to solve problems. Thus a Swedish boss with a French subordinate can anticipate some problems: the French subordinate is likely to think that the boss, not knowing the answers, is incompetent, while the Swedish boss may think that the French subordinate does not know what to do and is therefore incompetent.

Those who view the organization as a **political system** consider managers to play an important political role in society, and to negotiate within the organization. Thus obtaining power is seen as more important than achieving specific objectives. Here again, Latin European managers are more likely to adhere to this view than their Nordic and Anglo counterparts.

In France, for example, executives have often played important roles in the French administration before assuming top positions in companies. Furthermore, Latin managers are acutely aware that it is necessary to have power in order to get things done in the organization. Nordic and Anglo managers, however, tend to downplay the importance of power and therefore reject the need for political maneuvering.

When organizations are viewed as systems of **role formalization,** managers prefer detailed job descriptions, and well-defined roles and functions. These serve to clarify complex situations and tasks.

---

[20]Laurent, A. (1983) "The cultural diversity of western conception of management", *International Studies of Management and Organization,* 13(1–2), 75–96.

TABLE 3   Management Questionnaire

A = Strongly agree
B = Tend to agree
C = Neither agree, nor disagree
D = Tend to disagree
E = Strongly disagree

1. When the respective roles of the members of a department become complex, detailed job descriptions are a useful way of clarifying.	A	B	C	D	E
2. In order to have efficient work relationships, it is often necessary to bypass the hierarchical line.	A	B	C	D	E
8. An organizational structure in which certain subordinates have two direct bosses should be avoided at all costs.	A	B	C	D	E
13. The more complex a department's activities, the more important it is for each individual's functions to be well-defined.	A	B	C	D	E
14. The main reason for having a hierarchical structure is so that everyone knows who has authority over whom.	A	B	C	D	E
19. Most organizations would be better off if conflict could be eliminated forever.	A	B	C	D	E
24. It is important for a manager to have at hand precise answers to most of the questions that his/her subordinates may raise about their work.	A	B	C	D	E
33. Most managers have a clear notion of what we call an organizational structure.	A	B	C	D	E
38. Most managers would achieve better results if their roles were less precisely defined.	A	B	C	D	E
40. Through their professional activity, managers play an important role in society.	A	B	C	D	E
43. The manager of tomorrow will be, primarily, a negotiator.	A	B	C	D	E
49. Most managers seem to be more motivated by obtaining power than by achieving objectives.	A	B	C	D	E
52. Today there seems to be an authority crisis in organizations.	A	B	C	D	E

Source: A. Laurent. Reproduced by permission.

Otherwise it is difficult to know who is responsible for what and to hold people accountable. In addition they argue that lack of clear job descriptions or role definitions creates overlap and inefficiency. Nordic and Anglo managers, on the other hand, argue that the world is too complex to be able to clearly define roles and functions. Furthermore they say that detailed descriptions interfere with maintaining flexibility and achieving coordination.

From his research, Laurent concluded that underlying these arguments managers had different conceptions of organization: one which focused on the task, called **instrumental,** and one which focused on relationships, called **social.** For Latin European managers, organizations are considered as **social systems,** or systems of relationships, where personal networks and social positioning are important. The organization achieves its goals through relationships and how they are managed (as prescribed by Fayol). Roles and relationships are defined formally (by the hierarchy) and informally, based on authority, power, and status which are seen as attributes of the person, not the task or function. Personal loyalty and deference to the boss are expected.

However, getting things done means working around the system—using informal, personal networks to circumvent the hierarchy as well as the rules and regulations—what the French call, *Système D*. According to sociologist Michel Crozier, it is this informal system that gives the French "bureaucratic model" its flexibility.[21] Organizations are thus considered to be necessarily political in nature. When asked to diagnose organizational problems, French social scientists and consultants typically start by analyzing the power relationships and power games (*les enjeux*).[22]

In contrast, for Anglo-Saxon, and northern European managers, the organization is a system of tasks where it is important to know what has to be done, rather than who has power and authority to do so (as in the socio/political view). This instrumental or functionalist view of organizations (very much in keeping with Taylor's scientific management) focuses on what is to be achieved and whether objectives are met (achievement orientation). Structure is defined by activities—what has to be done—and the hierarchy exists only to assign responsibility. It follows that authority is defined by function and is limited, specific to the job not the person.

Here, coordination and control are impersonal, decentralized, and reside in the structure and systems. Rules and regulations are applied universally. If the rules and regulations are dysfunctional, then they are changed rather than circumvented or broken. Management consultants are called in to figure out the best way to devise strategy, design structure, classify jobs and set salary scales, and develop concrete programs such as "total quality" or "performance management."

These different conceptions of organization were confirmed recently when Trompenaars[23] asked 15,000 managers to choose between the following statements:

> A company is a system designed to perform functions and tasks in an efficient way. People are hired to fulfill these functions with the help of machines and other equipment. They are paid for the tasks they perform.
>
> A company is a group of people working together. The people have social relations with other people and with the organization. The functioning is dependent upon these relations.

He too found large differences between Anglo and Nordic managers compared with Latin and Asian managers, as shown in Figure 3. These different beliefs reveal the underlying cultural meaning of organizations as task versus social systems.

As We See Us . . . (Revisited)

These findings can be further corroborated by asking managers to describe the approach to management in their countries, or "how we see us," . . . For example, many of the research results discussed above place Scandinavian managers at one end of a continuum, with Latin and Asian managers at the other. Jan Selmer,[24] a Swedish management professor, proposed the following profile of "Viking Management." Compare this with the self-descriptions of Brazilian[25] and Indonesian managers in Table 4.

According to self-reports, clear differences and similarities emerge in terms of the nature of relationships (hierarchy) and the relationship with nature (uncertainty and control). For example, in keeping with the findings discussed above, Viking Management is characterized as decentralized (less

[21]Crozier, M. (1964) *The Bureaucratic Phenomenon,* Chicago: University of Chicago Press.

[22]Crozier, M. and Friedberg, E. (1977) *L'Acteur et le système: Les contraintes de l'action collective,* Paris: Seuil.

[23]Trompenaars, F. (1993) *Riding the Waves of Culture,* London: Nicholas Brealey.

[24]Selmer, J. (1988) Presentation, International Conference on Personnel and Human Resource Management Conference, Singapore.

[25]Amado, G. and Brasil, H.V. (1991) "Organizational behaviors and cultural context: The Brazilian 'Jeitiñho'", *International Studies of Management and Organization,* 21(3), 38–61.

FIGURE 3   Organizations as Task versus Social Systems

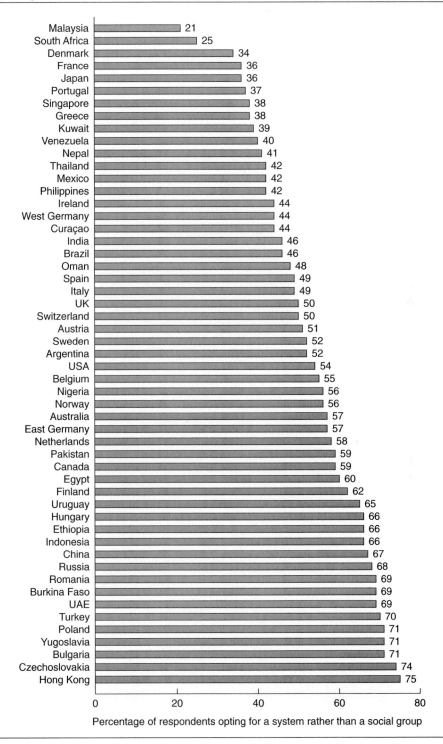

Percentage of respondents opting for a system rather than a social group

Source: F. Trompenaars (1993) *Riding the Waves of Culture: Understanding cultural diversity in business,* Nicholas Brealey, London.

TABLE 4   As We See Us . . . .

Viking Management

Decentralized decision-making
Organization structure is often ambiguous
Perceived by others to be indecisive
Goal formulation, long-range objectives, and performance evaluation criteria are vague and implicit
    informal channels of communication
Coordinate by values not rules (normative versus coercive)
Case by case approach versus standard procedures
Consensus-oriented
Avoid conflict
Informal relationships between foreign subsidiaries and headquarters (mother–daughter relationships)

Brazilian Management

Hierarchy and authority; status and power are important
Centralized decision-making
Personal relationships are more important than the task
Rules and regulations are for enemies
Flexible and adaptable (too much?) *Jeitiñho*
Anything is possible
Short-term oriented—immediatism
Avoid conflict—seen as win/lose
Rely on magic—low control over environment
Decisions based on intuition and feeling

Indonesian Management

Respect for hierarchy and elders
Family-oriented
Group- versus individual-oriented
Friendly and helpful, hospitable
Tolerant
Decisions based on compromise—"keep everyone happy"
Importance of religion—(Islam)
Five principles
Bhinneka Tunggal lka (unity through diversity)

---

hierarchy) when compared with the Brazilian and Indonesian views, which emphasize status and power or respect for elders.

On the other hand, in each case there is a strong emphasis on the importance of relationships: family (mother–daughter) and friends, avoiding conflict, being tolerant, seeking consensus, and "keeping everyone happy." For the Swedes, this corresponds to their keen concern for social well-being and quality of relationships, reflected in their number one ranking on Hofstede's femininity dimension.

In all three self-descriptions there is less emphasis placed on formalization. For the Swedes, organization goals and structures are experienced as vague and ambiguous. Uncertainty is managed with a "case by case" (and *not* a universal) approach, through informal communication channels, and "through values not rules." For the Indonesians, it is the "Five principles" established by President Suharto that provide the rules, rather than organizational ones. In comparison with the Swedes, however, the Indonesians perceive little control over their environment, *Insh'allah* (if God wills . . .)." Thus the Swedish approach to getting things done may be frustrated by the Indonesian sense of letting things happen.

Brazilian managers, faced with great uncertainty in the day-to-day business environment over which they feel they have little control, say that they have developed a finely tuned sense of intuition, having learned to trust their "gut" feel, as previously mentioned. For the Brazilians, the notion of *Jeitiñho* is similar to that of the French *Système D*, going around the system in order to get things done. This assures flexibility and adaptability such that anything is possible (although perhaps too much so as Brazilian managers themselves acknowledge).

Now imagine a Brazil–Sweden–Indonesia joint venture. This raises the possibility that three firms would have to resolve their differences on several fronts while using their similarities to create a shared sense of purpose. In particular, there would probably be a clash between the cultural assumptions underlying Swedish management—little concern with power and status and high perceived control over the environment—with those of Brazilian and Indonesian management—more emphasis on power and authority and less perceived control.

This would probably cause the biggest headaches for the Swedes when it came to efforts to delegate decision-making and to encourage individual responsibility and accountability. For the Indonesian and Brazilian managers, the frustration would come from confusion as to "who is the boss?" and "why isn't he/she making decisions?," and "how can I be held responsible when I have no control over what happens?" In decision-making, the Brazilians would find the Indonesians and Swedes interminably slow, seeking consensus or democratic compromise, while they in turn would see the Brazilians as impetuous, and too individualistic. On the other hand, the similarity in importance placed on relationships, on informal communication, and on avoiding conflict can help to work through these difficulties together, on a personal basis.

Although there are variations within countries, due to industry and corporate culture, as well as individual styles of key managers, the above research findings and self-descriptions point to different cultural profiles of organization. The underlying assumptions can be interpreted to reveal the nature of relationships, as seen in the importance of hierarchy, and control over nature, as seen in the need for formal or social rules and procedures. The underlying cultural meaning of the organization can then be interpreted as systems of tasks versus systems of relationships. These cultural profiles provide a starting point to explore different structural preferences and to begin to anticipate potential problems when transferring practices from one country to another or in forming joint ventures and strategic alliances.

On a less serious note, these differences have been caricatured in the organizational charts shown in Figure 4. Using these caricatures can provoke discussion of structural differences across countries in a humorous mode while allowing us to discover the grain of truth within and to imagine how our own organization chart might seem to others. Constructing cultural profiles enables us to appreciate the impact of culture on management as multidimensional. It would therefore be a mistake to base a prediction regarding structure or process on a single cultural dimension.

In addition, managers need to recognize that the relationships between cultural dimensions and structure (or processes) are not simple cause–effect links, but instead, are multidetermined. Similar approaches may exist for different cultural reasons, and different approaches may exist for the same reason. Thus formalized rules and procedures or participative management approaches may have a different *raison d'être* on different sides of the national border.

Having considered cultural differences in organization and structure, we can now turn our attention to organizational processes. In addition to cultural

FIGURE 4   The Organization Chart

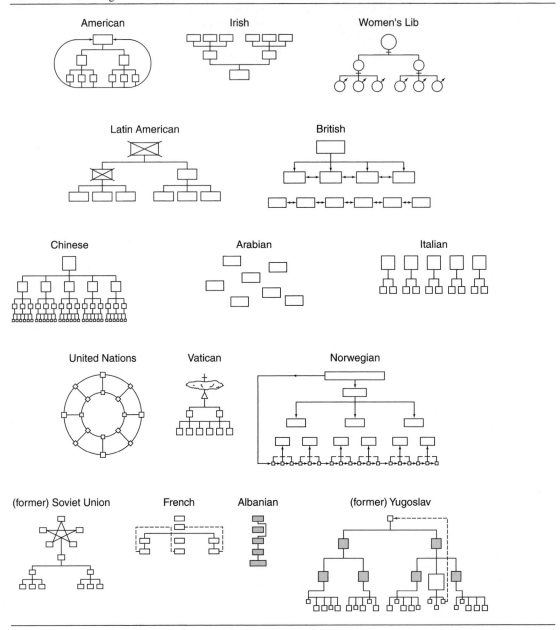

preferences regarding hierarchy and formalization, other cultural dimensions are considered to explain the reasons for some of the country differences that may seem contradictory. And to show why similar business practices may have different underlying cultural roots, or meaning.

Culture and Processes

The characterization of organizations as pyramids, well-oiled machines, village markets, and family tribes, and the structural correlates are further reflected in the organizational processes. In effect, structures are similar to fossils, as they bear the traces of organizational processes over time. Thus the influence of culture can also be seen in organizational processes such as the nature of policies and procedures, planning and control, information processing and communication, and decision-making.

Policies and Procedures

The formalization and standardization of policies and procedures may reflect low tolerance for uncertainty, as they can be clearly spelled out, leaving little room for doubt. Other cultural dimensions may also have a hand in explaining differences found between cultures. For instance, although the United States ranks low on uncertainty avoidance, European managers working for U.S. multinationals often complain about the formal reporting systems, and volume of written policies and procedures that come down from headquarters.

This is perhaps more understandable given the contractual view of employment in the United States, an instrumental view of the firm, and low-context communication. All of these dimensions encourage a high level of explicitness which is evident in the ubiquitous standard operating procedures. Policies and job descriptions are thus written down and standardized so that anyone can perform them. Information is embedded in the system not in the person, as the organization is thought to exist independently from its members. This might seem contrary to the primacy of the individual, but in fact it is this standardization which allows individuals to move easily in and out of jobs/organizations and guarantees their career mobility in the village market. Also, given U.S. commitment to universalism, rules and procedures are necessary to assure that all people are treated equally.[26]

A comparison of British and German firms[27] showed that all the British firms had detailed job descriptions while only one of the German firms did. This seems contrary to expectations, given the respective attitudes to uncertainty avoidance in the two countries (Germany high, Britain low). However, as German managers are specialists and tend to stay longer in one job, job descriptions are well-internalized, and there is less of a need to formalize them.

On the other hand, British managers are generalists, and tend to rotate jobs more often. One study found that in matched companies twenty-five out of thirty British managers had changed jobs within four years, compared with ten out of thirty German managers.[28] Therefore job descriptions are formalized to provide general guidelines to new incumbents.

Furthermore, British managers had a higher tolerance for mismatch between written expectations and actual responsibilities and thus did not feel constrained to follow the job descriptions. German resistance to written descriptions stemmed from the desire to preserve flexibility. Unlike the British managers, the German managers would have felt uncomfortable with any divergence between written procedures and practice (uncertainty).

Procedures or job descriptions are less likely to be made explicit where communication is more embedded in relationships and in situations (high context). Japanese managers tend to have broader general knowledge of the company, which is often tacit, having been gained through observation and on-the-job experience, like a craft.[29] In addition,

---

[26]Hampden-Turner, C. and Trompenaars, F. (1994) *Seven Cultures of Capitalism,* London: Piatkus.

[27]Stewart *et al., Op. cit.*

[28]*Ibid.*

[29]Nonaka, I. (1991) "The knowledge-creating company", *Harvard Business Review,* November–December, 96–104.

tasks are assigned to groups not individuals, and individual accountability remains vague. This creates a stronger link between people, the group, and the organization, making knowledge company-specific, thereby reducing career mobility outside the organization, keeping it all in the family.

Systems and Controls

Control systems also reflect different cultural assumptions regarding relationships with people (in terms of power and human nature) and relationship with nature (uncertainty and control). For example, French managers indicate that the most important function for a manager is to control, while British managers say it is to coordinate.[30] This reflects different attitudes towards power. For the French, control derives from the hierarchy; for the British, coordination is achieved through persuasion and negotiation, since the boss is not seen as all-powerful.

Furthermore, the nature of control depends on assumptions regarding human nature. When employees are seen as capable and self-directed (Theory Y),[31] there is more reliance on communication, rather than direct supervision. When managers assume that workers are basically lazy and need to be directed by others (Theory X), they are more likely to set up tight control processes.

Different types of control—input, throughout, and output—are also evident across cultures. The French are particularly careful about recruiting future senior managers from the top schools. This reflects input control—choosing the best and the brightest—and then assuming that they will manage and produce results. German companies are less concerned with hiring elites than with developing managers through rigorous apprenticeships and in-depth job-specific experience. The focus on detailed plans and operational controls also reflects the importance of throughput controls. In the United States and Britain, the emphasis is on budgets, financial controls, and reporting procedures, which reflects more output control.

This can be seen in different ideas regarding the purpose of budgets. One comparative study[32] of managers in U.S. and French subsidiaries of the same firm found that for the American managers, budgets were treated as useful tools which provided concrete objectives against which performance could be measured. French managers, on the other hand, were more concerned with the overall logic and perfection of the budgeting system. These differences reflect American managers' confidence in their ability to control events by being pragmatic (instrumental) and results (achievement)-oriented, while French managers rely more on their analytic (Cartesian) capability, or the quality of thinking.

Planning practices also reflect underlying cultural assumptions. A study by Horovitz[33] comparing planning practices in the United Kingdom, Germany and France found that planning practices in the United Kingdom were more strategic in focus, more long term (six year horizon), with more participation in the process. In Germany, planning was more operational (including stringent, detailed one year plans), more short term (three year horizon), with little participation from the ranks. In France, planning was also more short term (less than half of the firms had long-range planning), more administrative (three year financial forecasts), and also less participative. The shorter term and the more operational/administrative orientation reflects the need to limit uncertainty to more manageable time frames and with more concrete outcomes. Thus the need to reduce uncertainty and to impose controls will result in planning that is more operational than strategic, more short term, and less participative.

[30]Laurent, A. (1986) "The cross-cultural puzzle of global human resource management", *Human Resource Management,* 25(1), 91–102.

[31]McGregor, D. (1960) *The Nature of Human Enterprise,* New York: McGraw-Hill.

[32]Perret, M.S. (1988) "The impact of cultural differences in budgeting", unpublished Ph.D. dissertation, University of Western Ontario.

[33]Horovitz, *Op. cit.*

Information and Communication

Organizations must process information in order to make decisions, to communicate policies and procedures, and to coordinate across units. Yet what kind of information is sought or heeded, how information circulates, and what information is shared with whom, are likely to reflect cultural preferences for hierarchy, formalization, and participation.

For example, French companies are often characterized by French managers as *cloisonné* (compartmentalized), very clearly structured vertically as well as horizontally. This makes very clear the personal roles and responsibility, privileges and obligations, and hence the degree of discretion in performing one's job.[34] Thus the flow of information between groups is limited.

Furthermore, given the view of organization as a social system based on relationships, information may not be readily shared as it is viewed as personal, not public. Information is passed through personal connections. According to one French manager, "Information which is widely distributed is obviously useless."[35] In addition, the political nature of French organizations encourages information to be seen as a source of power, and therefore not easily given away.

For these reasons, it is not surprising that informal communication assumes considerable importance in French companies. A survey in the *Nouvel Economiste*[36] found that information was more likely obtained from rumours than from one's immediate boss. Informal channels compensate for the centralized, formalized, and limited participative nature of information flows.

In contrast, managers in Sweden, which is more egalitarian and more tolerant of uncertainty, pay very little attention to formal structure or hierarchy. Communication patterns are much more open and informal. This is supported in the research findings

of André Laurent that Swedish managers were far less inhibited than their French counterparts about bypassing the hierarchical line.[37] Given the Swedish view of organizations as instrumental rather than socio-political, there is a greater willingness to share information with anyone who has an interest in it. Information can be put to use; its value is instrumental, not social.

The Swedish insistence on transparency, or the open sharing of information, created initial difficulties for Electrolux when they acquired Italian company, Zanussi.[38] The Italian managers and labor unions, although first surprised by this transparency, came to respect and trust the "Viking" acquirers because of it. Nevertheless, Zanussi managers had trouble unlearning the previous habit of keeping information to themselves as a way of preserving power.[39]

In Japanese companies, intensive and extensive discussion is encouraged at all levels both within (among employees) and outside (with suppliers and customers) the organization. The adaptability of Japanese companies is often attributed to this cross-boundary, open flow of information. By maximizing the informal exchange of information, Japanese firms are able to generate and leverage knowledge, to create a "learning company."[40]

Consider the special case of Kao, the Japanese competitor of Proctor & Gamble and Unilever.[41] CEO Dr. Maruta strongly believes that,

> If everyone discusses on an equal footing, there is nothing that cannot be resolved . . . [As such,] the organization was designed to "run as a flowing system" which would stimulate interaction and the spread of ideas in every direction and at every

---

[34]D'Iribarne, P. (1989) *La logique de l'honneur,* Paris: Seuil.

[35]Orleman, P.A. (1992) "The global corporation: Managing across cultures", Masters thesis, University of Pennsylvania.

[36]"La communication dans l'entreprise", *Nouvel Economiste,* May 12, 1980, 42–7.

[37]Laurent, *Op. cit.*

[38]Haspeslagh, P. and Ghoshal, S. (1992) *Electrolux Zanussi,* INSEAD case.

[39]Lorenz, C. (1989) "The Italian connection—a stark contrast in corporate manners", *Financial Times,* June 23, 20.

[40]Nonaka, *Op. cit.;* Schütte, H. (1993) "Competing and cooperating with Japanese firms", Euro–Asia Center, INSEAD.

[41]Ghoshal, S. and Butler, C. (1991) KAO Corporation, INSEAD case.

level . . . [Thus] organizational boundaries and titles were abolished.

Kao's head office is indeed designed in such a way as to encourage the cross-fertilization of ideas.

> On the 10th floor, known as the top management floor, sat the Chairman, the President, four executive vice presidents, and a pool of secretaries. A large part of the floor was open space, with one large conference table and two smaller ones, and chairs, blackboards and overhead projectors strewn around; this was known as the Decision Space, where all discussions with and among the top management took place. Anyone passing, including the President, could sit down and join in any discussion on any topic . . . This layout was duplicated on the other floors . . . Workplaces looked like large rooms; there were no partitions, but again tables and chairs for spontaneous or planned discussions at which everyone contributed as equals. Access was free to all, and any manager could thus find himself sitting round the table next to the President, who was often seen waiting in line in Kao's Tokyo cafateria.

Furthermore, any employee can retrieve data on sales or product development, the latest findings from R&D, details of yesterday's production and inventory at every plant, and can even check up on the President's expense account.

Thus office design, building layout, and information technology can encourage managers to share information or to keep it to themselves, and can facilitate whether communication channels are open and multiple, or limited to a one-to-one basis, serial, and secretive. The Japanese scientists from Toshiba, assigned to a joint venture with IBM and Siemens, found it unproductive to be in separate little rooms. So they spent most of their time standing in the halls discussing ideas.[42] The German scientists preferred privacy.

This use of physical space and the consequent patterns of interaction are cultural artifacts which reveal different beliefs regarding the optimal degree of hierarchy, formalization, and level of participation. These beliefs influence the flow of information and communication within companies in different countries. Digging deeper, we find differences in the assumptions regarding the use of information under conditions of uncertainty, whether people are seen as trustworthy and capable, and whether information is used to preserve power or to be shared. In addition we find the underlying cultural meaning of information as serving instrumental versus political purposes.

Decision-making

The nature of decision-making is also culturally rooted. Who makes the decision, who is involved in the process, and where decisions are made (in formal committees or more informally in the hallways and corridors, or on the golf course) reflect different cultural assumptions. In turn, the very nature of the decision-making processes as well as different time horizons influences the speed with which decisions are taken.

It is perhaps not surprising that in countries such as Sweden and Germany, where power and hierarchy are played down, there is the greatest evidence of participation in decision-making. In Sweden, perhaps furthest along on the road of industrial democracy, union leaders often sit on the management board and are involved in making major strategic decisions, including decisions to relocate factories abroad. Everyone has the right to contribute to a decision. Decision-making means seeking consensus.

In The Netherlands and Germany, the works council, or labor representation, also plays an important role in deciding business affairs. The strong commitment to consensus, social equality, and human welfare reveals assumptions regarding collectivism and the importance of the quality of working life.[43]

In contrast, companies in cultures which emphasize power and hierarchy are more likely to

---

[42]Browning, E.S. (1994) "Computer chip project brings rivals together, but the cultures clash", *Wall Street Journal,* May 3, A7.

[43]Fry, J.A. (ed.) (1979) *Limits of the Welfare State: Critical Views on Post-war Sweden,* Farnborough: Saxon House.

centralize decision-making. In France, for example, the government plays an important role in determining company strategy and policy, often choosing top management. This has earned France the reputation of being "the father of industrial policy."[44] The PDG (CEO) may well have more experience in government than in business. Furthermore, he (in rare cases she) is expected to make decisions and is respected for it. Power is jealously guarded by each actor, such that management and unions often end up in violent confrontation, neither willing to concede to the other party. While industry is currently being privatized, and employees have become more involved through participation and through quality circles, French management is criticized for remaining centralized and elitist.[45]

The difference in decision-making between Nordic and Latin European firms was sharply illustrated when Sweden's Electrolux acquired Italy's Zanussi. The Swedish top management was often frustrated in its efforts to get Italian managers to arrive at a consensus among themselves in solving problems. The Italian managers, in turn, expected the senior management to settle problems such as transfer pricing between Italian product lines and the UK sales offices. According to one senior Italian manager, ". . . the key in this complex international organization is to have active mechanisms in place to create—and force—the necessary integration." However, the Swedish CEO preferred to let them solve their own problems; "Force is a word that is rarely heard in the Electrolux culture."[46]

Japanese firms, with their collectivist orientation, take yet another approach to decision-making. In the Japanese *Ringi* system, petitions (decision proposals) are circulated requiring individuals to "sign on." Signing, however, does not necessarily mean

approval, but means that if the decision is taken, the person agrees to support it. While the opinions of superiors are sought, these opinions tend to be more implicit than explicit. Therefore, Japanese managers devote extra time in trying to "read their boss" to find out what is actually desired. In this way, Japanese firms reconcile the importance placed on both collectivism and the hierarchy.

Northern European and American managers often complain about the "slowness" with which Japanese companies *make* decisions. Japanese managers, on the other hand, often complain about the time it takes American and European companies to *implement* decisions. Although in Japan more time is taken to reach decisions, once the decision is taken it can be implemented more quickly as everyone has been involved and understands why the decision has been taken, what has been decided, and what needs to be done. Americans may pride themselves on being "decisive," making decisions quickly on their own. However, they then have to spend more time back at the office selling these decisions, explaining why, what, and how, and gathering support. Inevitably, implementation takes longer.

These different approaches to decision-making therefore have repercussions on the time taken to reach decisions, even in countries that appear to share cultural assumptions. For example, one study comparing strategic decision-making in Sweden and Britain demonstrated that it took twice as long in Sweden, not just to identify strategic issues (37 months versus 17 months), but also to decide what to do about those issues (23 months versus 13 months).[47]

These differences in the amount of time for reaching decisions was explained by the degree of involvement of others in the process and desire for consensus. In Sweden, more participants are involved in contributing information and more time is taken to collect information and compare

[44]Aubert, N., Ramantsoa, B. and Reitter, R. (1984) "Nationalizations, managerial power, and societal change", Working paper Harvard Business School.

[45]Schmidt, V.A. (1993) "An end to French economic exceptionalism: The transformation of business under Mitterand", *California Management Review,* Fall, 75–98.

[46]Lorenz, *Op. cit.*

[47]Axelsson, R., Cray, D., Mallory, G.R. and Wilson, D.C. (1991) "Decision style in British and Swedish organizations: A comparative examination of strategic decision making", *British Journal of Management,* 2, 67–79.

alternatives. Also, strategic decisions were more often taken by the management board (a collective) in Sweden rather than, as in Britain, by the Managing Director (CEO), an individual. The Swedish consensus-driven approach (which includes government and union officials) results in the tendency to appoint commissions or special working groups which are often time-consuming.

The speed of decision-making reflects not just the process, but also the prevailing attitude towards time. Many Western managers complain that their sense of urgency is not shared in other parts of the world where the attitude seems to be "what's the big hurry?" Yet in Asia and the Middle East, a decision made quickly may indicate that it has little importance. Otherwise, more time for consideration, reflection, and discussion would be warranted. Thus taking quick decisions is not universally admired as a sign of determination and strong leadership but can be regarded as a sign of immaturity and irresponsibility, or even stupidity.

Furthermore, in cultures where the past plays an important role, traditions cannot be dismissed so quickly. Therefore, decisions need to be taken and implemented more slowly. While this may be more obvious in Asian cultures, important differences exist between countries with otherwise similar cultural profiles. American managers, who are less tradition-bound, may perceive European managers as rather slow in making decisions.

British society, for example, has been described as conservative and tradition-bound, with a marked reluctance to change.[48] The slower speed of decision-making in British firms is also attributed to its being more decentralized (assigned to standing committees) and more informal (guided by unwritten rules and procedures which are maintained through personal connections).[49]

A study comparing strategic decision-making in British and Brazilian firms found that Brazilian executives tend to take decisions more quickly.[50] This was attributed to their centralized power which enables them to take decisions individually. Also according to Brazilian managers, the greater perceived uncertainty and lack of control over the environment contributes to a strong sense of urgency (or as referred to in Table 3 "immediatism") and need for change.

Thus differences in approaches to decision-making can be attributed to multiple, interacting cultural dimensions. In addition to cultural preferences for hierarchy, and formalization, assumptions regarding time and change are important considerations in *how* and *how quickly* decisions will be made. In addition, the level of participation in decision-making may be similar but for different reasons. In some countries, such as the United States, participation may be seen as a way of integrating different individual perspectives and preserving everyone's right to decide. In other cultures, such as Japan, it is a way to preserve group harmony and relationships, while in The Netherlands and Sweden it serves to promote social welfare. This results in different underlying cultural reasons for empowerment.

In Sweden where interested parties have the "right to negotiate" (*forhandlingsratt*), and in Germany where they have the "right to decide" (*Mitbestimmung*),[51] "empowerment" signifies power sharing in order to arrive at a consensus regarding collective well-being. In countries such as the United States, where you are supposed to be self-sufficient and take care of yourself (high degree of individualism), labor and management relationships are more characterized by distributive bargaining. Each actor insists on safeguarding their own interests at the expense of the others and having the

[48]Tayeb, M.H. (1988) *Organizations and National Culture: A Comparative Analysis,* London: Sage.

[49]Mallory, G.R., Butler, R.J., Cray, D., Hickson, D.J. and Wilson, D.C. (1983) "Implanted decision making: American owned firms in Britain", *Journal of Management Studies,* 20, 191–211; Fry, *Op. cit.*

[50]Oliveira, B. and Hickson, D.J. (1991) "Cultural bases of strategic decision making: A Brazilian and English comparison", presented at EGOS conference, Vienna.

[51]Lawrence, P. and Spybey, T. (1986) *Management and Society in Sweden,* London: Routledge and Kegan Paul.

resources, support, and authority to pursue individual well-being independently.[52]

Transferability of Best Practice? Alternative Approaches

By pulling together the various experiences of managers and more systematic research studies, we have demonstrated how culture affects organization structure and process. We have proposed different profiles or models of organizing which evolve from different underlying cultural assumptions. This raises questions about what is considered to be "universal wisdom" and the transferability of "best practice." For the most part, arguments for transferability are in line with convergence notions which claim universality; "Management is management and best practice can be transferred anywhere." This was the rationale behind the 1980s rush to copy Japanese management practice and current rash of American-style restructuring and re-engineering.

Those that question transferability point to differences in the cultural or national (institutional) context. The culturalists question the effectiveness with which Japanese quality circles, say, can be transferred to individualist countries, such as the United States and France. The institutionalists stress the nature of ownership, and the role of government, and of labour unions in promoting such practices. Whether the success of Japanese management practices is due to cultural or institutional factors remains a matter of ongoing debate.[53]

The transfer of best practice nevertheless assumes, to some extent, universality. For example, matrix structures were heralded in the 1970s as a means of combining the benefits of product, geographic, and functional structures. In theory, decentralized decision-making, overlapping roles and responsibilities, and multiple information channels were all supposed to enable the organization to capture and analyze external complexity, to overcome internal parochialism, and to enhance response time and flexibility.[54]

While matrix management may have promised more than it could deliver, Laurent found deep resistance to matrix structures among both French and German managers, but for different reasons.[55] For the French, matrix structures violated the principle of "unity of command" and clear hierarchical reporting relationships. The idea of having two bosses was undesirable, as it created divided loyalties and caused unwelcome conflict. On the other hand, German managers resisted matrix structures, as they frustrated the need for clear-cut structure, information channels, roles and responsibilities. Again, the principles underlying matrix management ran counter to the German need to reduce uncertainty.

Thus cultural differences often undermine the best intentions and the assumed rationality of best practices. Different logics of organization exist in different countries, which can be equally effective, if not more so, given different societal contexts. In fact, there seems to be little doubt that some contexts are more favorable to the success of certain management practices, and it need not always be the country where that practice originated. Japanese quality-control methods originally came from the American gurus, Demming and Juran. Quality circles were the Japanese value-added.

Effectively transferring management structures and processes relies on the ability to recognize their inherent assumptions and to compare them with the cultural assumptions of the potential host country recipient. Countries also differ in their readiness to adopt or adapt foreign models, or to manifest a NIH (not invented here) syndrome. Throughout their history, the Japanese have borrowed models from China and then Europe. Other countries, such as Germany, may be more resistant to importing alien

---

[52]Irene Rodgers, Cross-cultural consultant, personal communication.

[53]See Whitley, R.D. (ed.) (1992) *Business Systems in East Asia: Firms, Markets and Societies,* London: Sage.

[54]Davis, S. and Lawrence, P.R. (1977) *Matrix,* Reading, MA: Addison-Wesley.

[55]Laurent, A. (1981) "Matrix organization and Latin cultures", *International Studies of Management and Organization,* 10(4), 101–14.

management practices. In eastern European countries, such as Poland, and in the developing Asian countries, such as Thailand, the eagerness to adopt foreign models is tempered by the desire to develop their own models which are more culturally appropriate.

For example, managers in eastern Europe may reject "team" approaches looking for strong leadership and a sense of clear direction in an effort to break with the more collective approach of the past.[56] Despite the prevailing wisdom that organizations need to be less hierarchical and more flexible, some managers argue that faced with competitive threats and conditions of economic decline or instability, greater centralization and stronger controls are needed.

Indeed, companies in Hong Kong, Japan, and Singapore, where the hierarchy remains firmly in place, have performed well in industries, such as banking, which are facing turbulent environments. Here, other value orientations, not readily apparent in Western business, may be at work. For example, when trying to replicate Hofstede's original study in China, another dimension was discovered—"Confucian dynamism," thrift, persistence and a long-term perspective. This added dimension was considered to account for the competitiveness of the "Five Asian Dragons": China, Hong Kong, Taiwan, Japan, and South Korea.[57]

Consider this testimony regarding the entrepreneurial, family model characteristic of the overseas Chinese business community which has been quite successful whether transplanted to Malaysia or Canada.

. . . The Confucian tradition of hard work, thrift and respect for one's social network may provide continuity with the right twist for today's fast-changing markets. And the central strategic question for all current multinationals—be they Chinese, Japanese or Western—is how to gather and integrate power through many small units. The evolution of a worldwide web of relatively small Chinese businesses, bound by undeniable strong cultural links, offers a working model for the future.[58]

Whatever the model of the future, be it team management or network organizations, we need to consider how culture may facilitate or hinder their diffusion. Will the more collective culture of Russia facilitate the team approach, while the greater relationship orientation of Chinese culture facilitates creating networks? Could it be that the greater emphasis on the task and the individual, which prevails in the performance management approach, will actually hinder American firms in their attempts to become more team- and network-oriented?

Given recent trends in the United States and Europe towards participative management and empowerment, the role of the leadership is changing. Rather than the more authoritarian notion of being the "boss," the role model is that of the "coach." (Rather than directing and controlling, the new role calls for facilitating and developing. Notions of empowerment and the leader as coach, however, may not readily transfer.

Take, for example, two items from the Management Questionnaire designed by Laurent regarding the role of the boss (hierarchy) and of power as shown in Figure 5. Comparing the responses of managers attending training seminars from 1990 to 1994 with the results reported in 1980, we find some signs of convergence. According to self-reports, managers are becoming less authoritarian and more concerned with achieving objectives than

---

[56]Cyr, D.J. and Schneider, S.C. (1996) "Implications for learning: human resources management in east-west joint ventures", *Organization Studies,* 17(2), 207–226.

[57]Hofstede, G. and Bond, M.H. (1988) "The Confucius connection: From cultural roots to economic growth", *Organizational Dynamics,* 16, 4–21; see also Hofstede, G. (1991) *Cultures and Organizations: Software of the Mind,* London: McGraw-Hill.

[58]Kao, *Op. cit.,* p. 36.

FIGURE 5   Convergence?

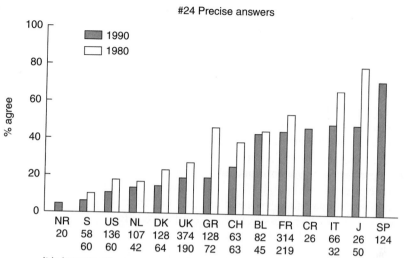

#24 Precise answers

It is important for a manager to have at hand precise answers to most of the questions his/her subordinates may raise about their work.

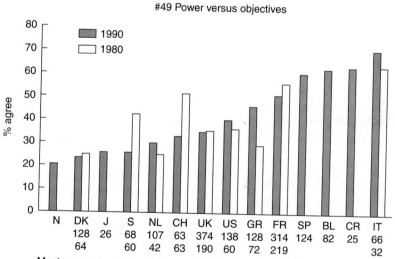

#49 Power versus objectives

Most managers seem to be more motivated by obtaining power than by achieving objectives.

Source: Reproduced by permission of A. Laurent.

g power. Nevertheless, while country differences may have eroded, the different country rankings remain in place.

Even in countries which supposedly do not put much stock in hierarchy, such as The Netherlands and the United Kingdom, this new leadership behavior may be difficult to achieve. Therefore, what will that mean for countries in Asia where the hierarchy is still revered? What would the Asian version of empowerment look like? Perhaps there are different means of achieving this end. In the case of Japanese firms, the hierarchy is clearly, albeit implicitly, present. Nevertheless, there are apparently high levels of participation.

And as hierarchies collapse and as cooperation between units becomes more of a necessity, there is a greater need for negotiation and persuasion. Managers will increasingly have to elicit the cooperation of people over whom they have no formal authority. In fact this may demand a more political view of organizations to which Latin firms may be more attuned.

These are the challenges facing many companies as they remodel their corporate structures. They must not lose sight of the impact of national culture in their search for a model of organization that can respond best to the demands of the rapidly changing business context, and the pressures for internationalization. They must also recognize that the "best models" are not necessarily "home grown," but that other ways of organizing may be equally, if not more, effective.

Reading 2–3

THE COMPETITIVE ADVANTAGE OF NATIONS

Michael E. Porter

National prosperity is created, not inherited. It does not grow out of a country's natural endowments, its labor pool, its interest rates, or its currency's value, as classical economics insists.

A nation's competitiveness depends on the capacity of its industry to innovate and upgrade. Companies gain advantage against the world's best competitors because of pressure and challenge. They benefit from having strong domestic rivals, aggressive home-based suppliers, and demanding local customers.

In a world of increasingly global competition, nations have become more, not less, important. As the basis of competition has shifted more and more to the creation and assimilation of knowledge, the role of the nation has grown. Competitive advantage is created and sustained through a highly localized process. Differences in national values, culture, economic structures, institutions, and histories all contribute to competitive success. There are striking differences in the patterns of competitiveness in every country; no nation can or will be competitive in every or even most industries. Ultimately, nations succeed in particular industries because their home environment is the most forward-looking, dynamic, and challenging.

These conclusions, the product of a four-year study of the patterns of competitive success in ten leading trading nations, contradict the conventional wisdom that guides the thinking of many companies and national governments—and that is pervasive today in the United States. (For more about the study, see the box "Patterns of National Competitive Success.") According to prevailing thinking, labor costs, interest rates, exchange rates, and economies of scale are the most potent determinants of competitiveness. In companies, the words of the day are merger, alliance, strategic partnerships, collaboration, and supranational globalization. Managers are pressing for more government support for particular industries. Among governments, there is a growing tendency to experiment with various policies intended to promote national competitiveness—from efforts to manage exchange rates to new measures to manage trade to policies to relax antitrust—which usually end up only undermining it. (See the box "What Is National Competitiveness?")

These approaches, now much in favor in both companies and governments, are flawed. They fundamentally misperceive the true sources of competitive advantage. Pursuing them, with all their short-term appeal, will virtually guarantee that the United States—or any other advanced nation—never achieves real and sustainable competitive advantage.

We need a new perspective and new tools—an approach to competitiveness that grows directly out of an analysis of internationally successful industries, without regard for traditional ideology or current intellectual fashion. We need to know, very simply, what works and why. Then we need to apply it.

How Companies Succeed in International Markets

Around the world, companies that have achieved international leadership employ strategies that differ from each other in every respect. But while every successful company will employ its own particular strategy, the underlying mode of operation—the character and trajectory of all successful companies—is fundamentally the same.

Companies achieve competitive advantage through acts of innovation. They approach innovation in its broadest sense, including both new technologies and new ways of doing things. They perceive a new basis for competing or find better means for competing in old ways. Innovation can be manifested in a new product design, a new production process, a new marketing approach, or a new way of conducting training. Much innovation is mundane and incremental, depending more on a cumulation of small insights and advances than on a single, major technological breakthrough. It often involves ideas that are not even "new"—ideas that have been around, but never vigorously pursued. It always involves investments in skill and knowledge, as well as in physical assets and brand reputations.

Some innovations create competitive advantage by perceiving an entirely new market opportunity or by serving a market segment that others have ignored. When competitors are slow to respond, such innovation yields competitive advantage. For instance, in industries such as autos and home electronics, Japanese companies gained their initial advantage by emphasizing smaller, more compact, lower capacity models that foreign competitors disdained as less profitable, less important, and less attractive.

In international markets, innovations that yield competitive advantage anticipate both domestic and foreign needs. For example, as international concern for product safety has grown, Swedish companies like Volvo, Atlas Copco, and AGA have succeeded by anticipating the market opportunity in this area. On the other hand, innovations that respond to concerns or circumstances that are peculiar to the home market can actually retard international competitive success. The lure of the huge U.S. defense market, for instance, has diverted the attention of U.S. materials and machine-tool companies from attractive, global commercial markets.

Information plays a large role in the process of innovation and improvement—information that either is not available to competitors or that they do not seek. Sometimes it comes from simple

Patterns of National Competitive Success

To investigate why nations gain competitive advantage in particular industries and the implications for company strategy and national economies, I conducted a four-year study of ten important trading nations: Denmark, Germany, Italy, Japan, Korea, Singapore, Sweden, Switzerland, the United Kingdom, and the United States. I was assisted by a team of more than 30 researchers, most of whom were natives of and based in the nation they studied. The researchers all used the same methodology.

Three nations—the United States, Japan, and Germany—are the world's leading industrial powers. The other nations represent a variety of population sizes, government policies toward industry, social philosophies, geographical sizes, and locations. Together, the ten nations accounted for fully 50% of total world exports in 1985, the base year for statistical analysis.

Most previous analyses of national competitiveness have focused on single nation or bilateral comparisons. By studying nations with widely varying characteristics and circumstances, this study sought to separate the fundamental forces underlying national competitive advantage from the idiosyncratic ones.

In each nation, the study consisted of two parts. The first identified all industries in which the nation's companies were internationally successful, using available statistical data, supplementary published sources, and field interviews. We defined a nation's industry as internationally successful if it *possessed competitive advantage relative to the best worldwide competitors.* Many measures of competitive advantage, such as reported profitability, can be misleading. We chose as the best indicators the presence of substantial and sustained exports to a wide array of other nations and/or significant outbound foreign investment based on skills and assets created in the home country. A nation was considered the home base for a company if it was either a locally owned, indigenous enterprise or managed autonomously although owned by a foreign company or investors. We then created a profile of all the industries in which each nation was internationally successful at three points in time: 1971, 1978, and 1985. The pattern of competitive industries in each economy was far from random: the task was to explain it and how it had changed over time. Of particular interest were the connections or relationships among the nation's competitive industries.

In the second part of the study, we examined the history of competition in particular industries to understand how competitive advantage was created. On the basis of national profiles, we selected over 100 industries or industry groups for detailed study; we examined many more in less detail. We went back as far as necessary to understand how and why the industry began in the nation, how it grew, when and why companies from the nation developed international competitive advantage, and the process by which competitive advantage had been either sustained or lost. The resulting case histories fall short of the work of a good historian in their level of detail, but they do provide insight into the development of both the industry and the nation's economy.

We chose a sample of industries for each nation that represented the most important groups of competitive industries in the economy. The industries studied accounted for a large share of total exports in each nation: more than 20% of total exports in Japan, Germany, and Switzerland, for example, and more than 40% in South Korea. We studied some of the most famous and important international success stories—German high-performance autos and chemicals, Japanese semiconductors and VCRs, Swiss banking and pharmaceuticals, Italian footwear and textiles, U.S. commercial aircraft and motion pictures—and some relatively obscure but highly competitive industries—South Korean pianos, Italian ski boots, and British biscuits. We also added a few industries because they appeared to be paradoxes: Japanese home demand for Western-character typewriters is nearly nonexistent, for example, but Japan holds a strong export and foreign investment position in the industry. We avoided industries that were highly dependent on natural resources: such industries do not form the backbone of advanced economies, and the capacity to compete in them is more explicable using classical theory. We did, however, include a number of more technologically

(continued)

intensive, natural-resource-related industries such as newsprint and agricultural chemicals.

The sample of nations and industries offers a rich empirical foundation for developing and testing the new theory of how countries gain competitive advantage. The accompanying article concentrates on the determinants of competitive advantage in individual industries and also sketches out some of the study's overall implications for government policy and company strategy. A fuller treatment in my book, *The Competitive Advantage of Nations,* develops the theory and its implications in greater depth and provides many additional examples. It also contains detailed descriptions of the nations we studied and the future prospects for their economies.

Michael E. Porter

---

investment in research and development or market research; more often, it comes from effort and from openness and from looking in the right place unencumbered by blinding assumptions or conventional wisdom.

This is why innovators are often outsiders from a different industry or a different country. Innovation may come from a new company, whose founder has a nontraditional background or was simply not appreciated in an older, established company. Or the capacity for innovation may come into an existing company through senior managers who are new to the particular industry and thus more able to perceive opportunities and more likely to pursue them. Or innovation may occur as a company diversifies, bringing new resources, skills, or perspectives to another industry. Or innovations may come from another nation with different circumstances or different ways of competing.

With few exceptions, innovation is the result of unusual effort. The company that successfully implements a new or better way of competing pursues its approach with dogged determination, often in the face of harsh criticism and tough obstacles. In fact, to succeed, innovation usually requires pressure, necessity, and even adversity: the fear of loss often proves more powerful than the hope of gain.

Once a company achieves competitive advantage through an innovation, it can sustain it only through relentless improvement. Almost any advantage can be imitated. Korean companies have already matched the ability of their Japanese rivals to mass-produce standard color televisions and VCRs; Brazilian companies have assembled technology and designs comparable to Italian competitors in casual leather footwear.

Competitors will eventually and inevitably overtake any company that stops improving and innovating. Sometimes early-mover advantages such as customer relationships, scale economies in existing technologies, or the loyalty of distribution channels are enough to permit a stagnant company to retain its entrenched position for years or even decades. But sooner or later, more dynamic rivals will find a way to innovate around these advantages or create a better or cheaper way of doing things. Italian appliance producers, which competed successfully on the basis of cost in selling midsize and compact appliances through large retail chains, rested too long on this initial advantage. By developing more differentiated products and creating strong brand franchises, German competitors have begun to gain ground.

Ultimately, the only way to sustain a competitive advantage is to *upgrade it*—to move to more sophisticated types. This is precisely what Japanese automakers have done. They initially penetrated foreign markets with small, inexpensive compact cars of adequate quality and competed on the basis of lower labor costs. Even while their labor-cost advantage persisted, however, the Japanese companies were upgrading. They invested aggressively to build large modern plants to reap economies of scale. Then they became innovators in process technology, pioneering just-in-time production and a host of other quality and productivity practices. These process improvements led to better product quality, better repair records, and better customer-

What Is National Competitiveness?

National competitiveness has become one of the central preoccupations of government and industry in every nation. Yet for all the discussion, debate, and writing on the topic, there is still no persuasive theory to explain national competitiveness. What is more, there is not even an accepted definition of the term *competitiveness* as applied to a nation. While the notion of a competitive company is clear, the notion of a competitive nation is not.

Some see national competitiveness as a macroeconomic phenomenon, driven by variables such as exchange rates, interest rates, and government deficits. But Japan, Italy, and South Korea have all enjoyed rapidly rising living standards despite budget deficits; Germany and Switzerland despite appreciating currencies; and Italy and Korea despite high interest rates.

Others argue that competitiveness is a function of cheap and abundant labor. But Germany, Switzerland, and Sweden have all prospered even with high wages and labor shortages. Besides, shouldn't a nation seek higher wages for its workers as a goal of competitiveness?

Another view connects competitiveness with bountiful natural resources. But how, then, can one explain the success of Germany, Japan, Switzerland, Italy, and South Korea—countries with limited natural resources?

More recently, the argument has gained favor that competitiveness is driven by government policy: Targeting, protection, import promotion, and subsidies have propelled Japanese and South Korean auto, steel, shipbuilding, and semiconductor industries into global preeminence. But a closer look reveals a spotty record. In Italy, government intervention has been ineffectual—but Italy has experienced a boom in world export share second only to Japan. In Germany, direct government intervention in exporting industries is rare. And even in Japan and South Korea, government's role in such important industries as facsimile machines, copiers, robotics, and advanced materials has been modest; some of the most frequently cited examples, such as sewing machines, steel, and shipbuilding, are now quite dated.

A final popular explanation for national competitiveness is differences in management practices, including management-labor relations. The problem here, however, is that different industries require different approaches to management. The successful management practices governing small, private, and loosely organized Italian family companies in footwear, textiles, and jewelry, for example, would produce a management disaster if applied to German chemical or auto companies, Swiss pharmaceutical makers, or American aircraft producers. Nor is it possible to generalize about management-labor relations. Despite the commonly held view that powerful unions undermine competitive advantage, unions are strong in Germany and Sweden—and both countries boast internationally preeminent companies.

Clearly, none of these explanations is fully satisfactory; none is sufficient by itself to rationalize the competitive position of industries within a national border. Each contains some truth; but a broader, more complex set of forces seems to be at work.

The lack of a clear explanation signals an even more fundamental question. What is a "competitive" nation in the first place? Is a "competitive" nation one where every company or industry is competitive? No nation meets this test. Even Japan has large sectors of its economy that fall far behind the world's best competitors.

Is a "competitive" nation one whose exchange rate makes its goods price competitive in international markets? Both Germany and Japan have enjoyed remarkable gains in their standards of living—and experienced sustained periods of strong currency and rising prices. Is a "competitive" nation one with a large positive balance of trade? Switzerland has roughly balanced trade; Italy has a chronic trade deficit—both nations enjoy strongly rising national income. Is a "competitive" nation one with low labor costs? India and Mexico both have low wages and low labor costs—but neither seems an attractive industrial model.

The only meaningful concept of competitiveness at the national level is *productivity*. The principal goal

(*continued*)

of a nation is to produce a high and rising standard of living for its citizens. The ability to do so depends on the productivity with which a nation's labor and capital are employed. Productivity is the value of the output produced by a unit of labor or capital. Productivity depends on both the quality and features of products (which determine the prices that they can command) and the efficiency with which they are produced. Productivity is the prime determinant of a nation's long-run standard of living; it is the root cause of national per capita income. The productivity of human resources determines employee wages; the productivity with which capital is employed determines the return it earns for its holders.

A nation's standard of living depends on the capacity of its companies to achieve high levels of productivity—and to increase productivity over time. Sustained productivity growth requires that an economy continually *upgrade itself.* A nation's companies must relentlessly improve productivity in existing industries by raising product quality, adding desirable features, improving product technology, or boosting production efficiency. They must develop the necessary capabilities to compete in more and more sophisticated industry segments, where productivity is generally high. They must finally develop the capability to compete in entirely new, sophisticated industries.

International trade and foreign investment can both improve a nation's productivity as well as threaten it. They support rising national productivity by allowing a nation to specialize in those industries and segments of industries where its companies are more productive and to import where its companies are less productive. No nation can be competitive in everything. The ideal is to deploy the nation's limited pool of human and other resources into the most productive uses. Even those nations with the highest standards of living have many industries in which local companies are uncompetitive.

Yet international trade and foreign investment also can threaten productivity growth. They expose a nation's industries to the test of international standards of productivity. An industry will lose out if its productivity is not sufficiently higher than foreign rivals' to offset any advantages in local wage rates. If a nation loses the ability to compete in a range of high-productivity/high-wage industries, its standard of living is threatened.

Defining national competitiveness as achieving a trade surplus or balance trade per se is inappropriate. The expansion of exports because of low wages and a weak currency, at the same time that the nation imports sophisticated goods that its companies cannot produce competitively, may bring trade into balance or surplus but lowers the nation's standard of living. Competitiveness also does not mean jobs. It's the *type* of jobs, not just the ability to employ citizens at low wages, that is decisive for economic prosperity.

Seeking to explain "competitiveness" at the national level, then, is to answer the wrong question. What we must understand instead is the determinants of productivity and the rate of productivity growth. To find answers, we must focus not on the economy as a whole but on *specific industries and industry segments.* We must understand how and why commercially viable skills and technology are created, which can only be fully understood at the level of particular industries. It is the outcome of the thousands of struggles for competitive advantage against foreign rivals in particular segments and industries, in which products and processes are created and improved, that underpins the process of upgrading national productivity.

When one looks closely at any national economy, there are striking differences among a nation's industries in competitive success. International advantage is often concentrated in particular industry segments. German exports of cars are heavily skewed toward high-performance cars, while Korean exports are all compacts and subcompacts. In many industries and segments of industries, the competitors with true international competitive advantage are *based in only a few nations.*

Our search, then, is for the decisive characteristic of a nation that allows its companies to create and sustain competitive advantage in particular fields—the search is for the competitive advantage of nations. We are particularly concerned with the determinants of international success in technology- and skill-intensive segments and industries, which underpin high and rising productivity.

(continued)

Classical theory explains the success of nations in particular industries based on so-called factors of production such as land, labor, and natural resources. Nations gain factor-based comparative advantage in industries that make intensive use of the factors they possess in abundance. Classical theory, however, has been overshadowed in advanced industries and economies by the globalization of competition and the power of technology.

A new theory must recognize that in modern international competition, companies compete with global strategies involving not only trade but also foreign investment. What a new theory must explain is why a nation provides a favorable *home base* for companies that compete internationally. The home base is the nation in which the essential competitive advantages of the enterprise are created and sustained. It is where a company's strategy is set, where the core product and process technology is created and maintained, and where the most productive jobs and most advanced skills are located. The presence of the home base in a nation has the greatest positive influence on other linked domestic industries and leads to other benefits in the nation's economy. While the ownership of the company is often concentrated at the home base, the nationality of shareholders is secondary.

A new theory must move beyond comparative advantage to the competitive advantage of a nation. It must reflect a rich conception of competition that includes segmented markets, differentiated products, technology differences, and economies of scale. A new theory must go beyond cost and explain why companies from some nations are better than others at creating advantages based on quality, features, and new product innovation. A new theory must begin from the premise that competition is dynamic and evolving; it must answer the questions: Why do some companies based in some nations innovate more than others? Who do some nations provide an environment that enables companies to improve and innovate faster than foreign rivals?

Michael E. Porter

---

satisfaction ratings than foreign competitors had. Most recently, Japanese automakers have advanced to the vanguard of product technology and are introducing new, premium brand names to compete with the world's most prestigious passenger cars.

The example of the Japanese automakers also illustrates two additional prerequisites for sustaining competitive advantage. First, a company must adopt a global approach to strategy. It must sell its product worldwide, under its own brand name, through international marketing channels that it controls. A truly global approach may even require the company to locate production or R&D facilities in other nations to take advantage of lower wage rates, to gain or improve market access, or to take advantage of foreign technology. Second, creating more sustainable advantages often means that a company must make its existing advantage obsolete—even while it is still an advantage. Japanese auto companies recognized this; either they would make their advantage obsolete, or a competitor would do it for them.

As this example suggests, innovation and change are inextricably tied together. But change is an unnatural act, particularly in successful companies; powerful forces are at work to avoid and defeat it. Past approaches become institutionalized in standard operating procedures and management controls. Training emphasizes the one correct way to do anything; the construction of specialized, dedicated facilities solidifies past practice into expensive brick and mortar; the existing strategy takes on an aura of invincibility and becomes rooted in the company culture.

Successful companies tend to develop a bias for predictability and stability; they work on defending what they have. Change is tempered by the fear that there is much to lose. The organization at all levels filters out information that would suggest new approaches, modifications, or departures from the norm. The internal environment operates like an immune system to isolate or expel "hostile" individuals who challenge current directions or established thinking. Innovation ceases, the company becomes stagnant; it is only a matter of time before aggressive competitors overtake it.

The Diamond of National Advantage

Why are certain companies based in certain nations capable of consistent innovation? Why do they ruthlessly pursue improvements, seeking an ever-more sophisticated source of competitive advantage? Why are they able to overcome the substantial barriers to change and innovation that so often accompany success?

The answer lies in four broad attributes of a nation, attributes that individually and as a system constitute the diamond of national advantage, the playing field that each nation establishes and operates for its industries. These attributes are:

1. *Factor Conditions.* The nation's position in factors of production, such as skilled labor or infrastructure, necessary to compete in a given industry.

2. *Demand Conditions.* The nature of home-market demand for the industry's product or service.

3. *Related and Supporting Industries.* The presence or absence in the nation of supplier industries and other related industries that are internationally competitive.

4. *Firm Strategy, Structure, and Rivalry.* The conditions in the nation governing how companies are created, organized, and managed, as well as the nature of domestic rivalry.

These determinants create the national environment in which companies are born and learn how to compete. (See the diagram "Determinants of National Competitive Advantage.") Each point on the diamond—and the diamond as a system—affects essential ingredients for achieving international competitive success: the availability of resources and skills necessary for competitive advantage in an industry; the information that shapes the opportunities that companies perceive and the directions in which they deploy their resources and skills; the goals of the owners, managers, and individuals in companies; and most important, the pressures on companies to invest and

Determinants of National Competitive Advantage

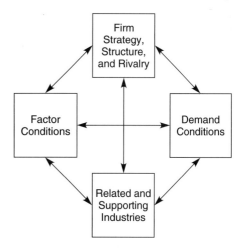

innovate. (See the box "How the Diamond Works: The Italian Ceramic Tile Industry.")

When a national environment permits and supports the most rapid accumulation of specialized assets and skills—sometimes simply because of greater effort and commitment—companies gain a competitive advantage. When a national environment affords better ongoing information and insight into product and process needs, companies gain a competitive advantage. Finally, when the national environment pressures companies to innovate and invest, companies both gain a competitive advantage and upgrade those advantages over time.

Factor Conditions

According to standard economic theory, factors of production—labor, land, natural resources, capital, infrastructure—will determine the flow of trade. A nation will export those goods that make most use of the factors with which it is relatively well endowed. This doctrine, whose origins date back to Adam Smith and David Ricardo and that is embedded in classical economics, is at best incomplete and at worst incorrect.

In the sophisticated industries that form the backbone of any advanced economy, a nation does not inherit but instead creates the most important

How the Diamond Works: The Italian Ceramic Tile Industry

In 1987, Italian companies were world leaders in the production and export of ceramic tiles, a $10 billion industry. Italian producers, concentrated in and around the small town of Sassuolo in the Emilia-Romagna region, accounted for about 30% of world production and almost 60% of world exports. The Italian trade surplus that year in ceramic tiles was about $1.4 billion.

The development of the Italian ceramic tile industry's competitive advantage illustrates how the diamond of national advantage works. Sassuolo's sustainable competitive advantage in ceramic tiles grew not from any static or historical advantage but from dynamism and change. Sophisticated and demanding local buyers, strong and unique distribution channels, and intense rivalry among local companies created constant pressure for innovation. Knowledge grew quickly from continuous experimentation and cumulative production experience. Private ownership of the companies and loyalty to the community spawned intense commitment to invest in the industry.

Tile producers benefited as well from a highly developed set of local machinery suppliers and other supporting industries, producing materials, services, and infrastructure. The presence of world-class, Italian-related industries also reinforced Italian strength in tiles. Finally, the geographic concentration of the entire cluster supercharged the whole process. Today foreign companies compete against an entire subculture. The organic nature of this system represents the most sustainable advantage of Sassuolo's ceramic tile companies.

The Origins of the Italian Industry

Tile production in Sassuolo grew out of the earthenware and crockery industry, whose history traces back to the thirteenth century. Immediately after World War II, there were only a handful of ceramic tile manufacturers in and around Sassuolo, all serving the local market exclusively.

Demand for ceramic tiles within Italy began to grow dramatically in the immediate postwar years, as the reconstruction of Italy triggered a boom in building materials of all kinds. Italian demand for ceramic tiles was particularly great due to the climate, local tastes, and building techniques.

Because Sassuolo was in a relatively prosperous part of Italy, there were many who could combine the modest amount of capital and necessary organizational skills to start a tile company. In 1955, there were 14 Sassuolo area tile companies; by 1962, there were 102.

The new tile companies benefited from a local pool of mechanically trained workers. The region around Sassuolo was home to Ferrari, Maserati, Lamborghini, and other technically sophisticated companies. As the tile industry began to grow and prosper, many engineers and skilled workers gravitated to the successful companies.

The Emerging Italian Tile Cluster

Initially, Italian tile producers were dependent on foreign sources of raw materials and production technology. In the 1950s, the principal raw materials used to make tiles were kaolin (white) clays. Since there were red- but no white-clay deposits near Sassuolo, Italian producers had to import the clays from the United Kingdom. Tile-making equipment was also imported in the 1950s and 1960s: kilns from Germany, America, and France; presses for forming tiles from Germany. Sassuolo tile makers had to import even simple glazing machines.

Over time, the Italian tile producers learned how to modify imported equipment to fit local circumstances: red versus white clays, natural gas versus heavy oil. As process technicians from tile companies left to start their own equipment companies, a local machinery industry arose in Sassuolo. By 1970, Italian companies had emerged as world-class producers of kilns and presses; the earlier situation had exactly reversed: They were exporting their red-clay equipment for foreigners to use with white clays.

The relationship between Italian tile and equipment manufacturers was a mutually supporting one, made even more so by close proximity. In the mid-1980s, there were some 200 Italian equipment manufacturers; more than 60% were located in the Sassuolo area. The equipment manufacturers competed fiercely for

(*continued*)

local business, and tile manufacturers benefited from better prices and more advanced equipment than their foreign rivals.

As the emerging tile cluster grew and concentrated in the Sassuolo region, a pool of skilled workers and technicians developed, including engineers, production specialists, maintenance workers, service technicians, and design personnel. The industry's geographic concentration encouraged other supporting companies to form, offering molds, packaging materials, glazes, and transportation services. An array of small, specialized consulting companies emerged to give advice to tile producers on plant design, logistics, and commercial, advertising, and fiscal matters.

With its membership concentrated in the Sassuolo area, Assopiastrelle, the ceramic tile industry association, began offering services in areas of common interest: bulk purchasing, foreign-market research, and consulting on fiscal and legal matters. The growing tile cluster stimulated the formation of a new, specialized factor-creating institution: In 1976, a consortium of the University of Bologna, regional agencies, and the ceramic industry association founded the Centro Ceramico di Bologna, which conducted process research and product analysis.

Sophisticated Home Demand

By the mid-1960s, per-capita tile consumption in Italy was considerably higher than in the rest of the world. The Italian market was also the world's most sophisticated. Italian customers, who were generally the first to adopt new designs and features, and Italian producers, who constantly innovated to improve manufacturing methods and create new designs, progressed in a mutually reinforcing process.

The uniquely sophisticated character of domestic demand also extended to retail outlets. In the 1960s, specialized tile showrooms began opening in Italy. By 1985, there were roughly 7,600 specialized showrooms handling approximately 80% of domestic sales, far more than in other nations. In 1976, the Italian company Piemme introduced tiles by famous designers to gain distribution outlets and to build brand name awareness among consumers. This innovation drew on another related industry, design services, in which Italy was world leader, with over $10 billion in exports.

Sassuolo Rivalry

The sheer number of tile companies in the Sassuolo area created intense rivalry. News of product and process innovations spread rapidly, and companies seeking technological, design, and distribution leadership had to improve constantly.

Proximity added a personal note to the intense rivalry. All of the producers were privately held, most were family run. The owners all lived in the same area, knew each other, and were the leading citizens of the same towns.

Pressures to Upgrade

In the early 1970s, faced with intense domestic rivalry, pressure from retail customers, and the shock of the 1973 energy crisis, Italian tile companies struggled to reduce gas and labor costs. These efforts led to a technological breakthrough, the rapid single-firing process, in which the hardening process, material transformation, and glaze-fixing all occurred in one pass through the kiln. A process that took 225 employees using the double-firing method needed only 90 employees using single-firing roller kilns. Cycle time dropped from 16 to 20 hours to only 50 to 55 minutes.

The new, smaller, and lighter equipment was also easier to export. By the early 1980s, exports from Italian equipment manufacturers exceeded domestic sales; in 1988, exports represented almost 80% of total sales.

Working together, tile manufacturers and equipment manufacturers made the next important breakthrough during the mid- and late 1970s: the development of materials-handling equipment that transformed tile manufacture from a batch process to a continuous process. The innovation reduced high labor costs—which had been a substantial selective factor disadvantage facing Italian tile manufacturers.

The common perception is that Italian labor costs were lower during this period than those in the United States and Germany. In those two countries, however, different jobs had widely different wages. In Italy, wages for different skill categories were compressed, and work rules constrained manufacturers from using

(continued)

overtime or multiple shifts. The restriction proved costly: Once cool, kilns are expensive to reheat and are best run continuously. Because of this factor disadvantage, the Italian companies were the first to develop continuous, automated production.

Internationalization

By 1970, Italian domestic demand had matured. The stagnant Italian market led companies to step up their efforts to pursue foreign markets. The presence of related and supporting Italian industries helped in the export drive. Individual tile manufacturers began advertising in Italian and foreign home-design and architectural magazines, publications with wide global circulation among architects, designers, and consumers. This heightened awareness reinforced the quality image of Italian tiles. Tile makers were also able to capitalize on Italy's leading world export posi-

tions in related industries like marble, building stone, sinks, washbasins, furniture, lamps, and home appliances.

Assopiastrelle, the industry association, established trade-promotion offices in the United States in 1980, in Germany in 1984, and in France in 1987. It organized elaborate trade shows in cities ranging from Bologna to Miami and ran sophisticated advertising. Between 1980 and 1987, the association spent roughly $8 million to promote Italian tiles in the United States.

Michael J. Enright and Paolo Tenti

Michael J. Enright, a doctoral student in business economics at the Harvard Business School, performed numerous research and supervisory tasks for *The Competitive Advantage of Nations.* Paolo Tenti was responsible for the Italian part of research undertaken for the book. He is a consultant in strategy and finance for Monitor Company and Analysis F.A.–Milan.

---

factors of production—such as skilled human resources or a scientific base. Moreover, the stock of factors that a nation enjoys at a particular time is less important than the rate and efficiency with which it creates, upgrades, and deploys them in particular industries.

The most important factors of production are those that involve sustained and heavy investment and are specialized. Basic factors, such as a pool of labor or a local raw-material source, do not constitute an advantage in knowledge-intensive industries. Companies can access them easily through a global strategy or circumvent them through technology. Contrary to conventional wisdom, simply having a general work force that is high school or even college educated represents no competitive advantage in modern international competition. To support competitive advantage, a factor must be highly specialized to an industry's particular needs—a scientific institute specialized in optics, a pool of venture capital to fund software companies. These factors are more scarce, more difficult for foreign competitors to imitate—and they require sustained investment to create.

Nations succeed in industries where they are particularly good at factor creation. Competitive advantage results from the presence of world-class institutions that first create specialized factors and then continually work to upgrade them. Denmark has two hospitals that concentrate in studying and treating diabetes—and a world-leading export position in insulin. Holland has premier research institutes in the cultivation, packaging, and shipping of flowers, where it is the world's export leader.

What is not so obvious, however, is that selective disadvantages in the more basic factors can prod a company to innovate and upgrade—a disadvantage in a static model of competition can become an advantage in a dynamic one. When there is an ample supply of cheap raw materials or abundant labor, companies can simply rest on these advantages and often deploy them inefficiently. But when companies face a selective disadvantage, like high land costs, labor shortages, or the lack of local raw materials, they *must* innovate and upgrade to compete.

Implicit in the oft-repeated Japanese statement, "We are an island nation with no natural resources," is the understanding that these deficiencies have only served to spur Japan's competitive innovation. Just-in-time production, for example, economized on prohibitively expensive space. Italian steel producers in the Brescia area faced a similar set of disadvantages: high capital costs, high energy costs, and no local raw materials. Located in Northern Lombardy, these privately owned companies faced staggering logistics costs due to their distance from southern ports and the inefficiencies of the state-owned Italian transportation system. The result: They pioneered technologically advanced minimills that require only modest capital investment, use less energy, employ scrap metal as the feedstock, are efficient at small scale, and permit producers to locate close to sources of scrap and end-use customers. In other words, they converted factor disadvantages into a competitive advantage.

Disadvantages can become advantages only under certain conditions. First, they must send companies proper signals about circumstances that will spread to other nations, thereby equipping them to innovate in advance of foreign rivals. Switzerland, the nation that experienced the first labor shortages after World War II, is a case in point. Swiss companies responded to the disadvantage by upgrading labor productivity and seeking higher value, more sustainable market segments. Companies in most other parts of the world, where there were still ample workers, focused their attention on other issues, which resulted in slower upgrading.

The second condition for transforming disadvantages into advantages is favorable circumstances elsewhere in the diamond—a consideration that applies to almost all determinants. To innovate, companies must have access to people with appropriate skills and have home-demand conditions that send the right signals. They must also have active domestic rivals who create pressure to innovate. Another precondition is company goals that lead to sustained commitment to the industry. Without such a commitment and the presence of active rivalry, a company may take an easy way around a disadvantage rather than using it as a spur to innovation.

For example, U.S. consumer-electronics companies, faced with high relative labor costs, chose to leave the product and production process largely unchanged and move labor-intensive activities to Taiwan and other Asian countries. Instead of upgrading their sources of advantage, they settled for labor-cost parity. On the other hand, Japanese rivals, confronted with intense domestic competition and a mature home market, chose to eliminate labor through automation. This led to lower assembly costs, to products with fewer components and to improved quality and reliability. Soon Japanese companies were building assembly plants in the United States—the place U.S. companies had fled.

Demand Conditions

It might seem that the globalization of competition would diminish the importance of home demand. In practice, however, this is simply not the case. In fact, the composition and character of the home market usually has a disproportionate effect on how companies perceive, interpret, and respond to buyer needs. Nations gain competitive advantage in industries where the home demand gives their companies a clearer or earlier picture of emerging buyer needs, and where demanding buyers pressure companies to innovate faster and achieve more sophisticated competitive advantages than their foreign rivals. The size of home demand proves far less significant than the character of home demand.

Home-demand conditions help build competitive advantage when a particular industry segment is larger or more visible in the domestic market than in foreign markets. The larger market segments in a nation receive the most attention from the nation's companies; companies accord smaller or less desirable segments a lower priority. A good example is hydraulic excavators, which represent the most widely used type of construction equipment in the Japanese domestic market—but which comprise a far smaller proportion of the market in other advanced nations. This segment is one of the few where there are vigorous Japanese international competitors and where Caterpillar does not hold a substantial share of the world market.

More important than the mix of segments per se is the nature of domestic buyers. A nation's companies gain competitive advantage if domestic buyers are the world's most sophisticated and demanding buyers for the product or service. Sophisticated, demanding buyers provide a window into advanced customer needs; they pressure companies to meet high standards; they prod them to improve, to innovate, and to upgrade into more advanced segments. As with factor conditions, demand conditions provide advantages by forcing companies to respond to tough challenges.

Especially stringent needs arise because of local values and circumstances. For example, Japanese consumers, who live in small, tightly packed homes, must contend with hot, humid summers and high-cost electrical energy—a daunting combination of circumstances. In response, Japanese companies have pioneered compact, quiet air-conditioning units powered by energy-saving rotary compressors. In industry after industry, the tightly constrained requirements of the Japanese market have forced companies to innovate, yielding products that are *kei-haku-tan-sho*—light, thin, short, small—and that are internationally accepted.

Local buyers can help a nation's companies gain advantage if their needs anticipate or even shape those of other nations—if their needs provide ongoing "early-warning indicators" of global market trends. Sometimes anticipatory needs emerge because a nation's political values foreshadow needs that will grow elsewhere. Sweden's long-standing concern for handicapped people has spawned an increasingly competitive industry focused on special needs. Denmark's environmentalism has led to success for companies in water-pollution control equipment and windmills.

More generally, a nation's companies can anticipate global trends if the nation's values are spreading—that is, if the country is exporting its values and tastes as well as its products. The international success of U.S. companies in fast food and credit cards, for example, reflects not only the American desire for convenience but also the spread of these tastes to the rest of the world. Nations export their values and tastes through media, through training foreigners, through political influence, and through the foreign activities of their citizens and their companies.

Related and Supporting Industries

The third broad determinant of national advantage is the presence in the nation of related and supporting industries that are internationally competitive. Internationally competitive home-based suppliers create advantages in downstream industries in several ways. First, they deliver the most cost-effective inputs in an efficient, early, rapid, and sometimes preferential way. Italian gold and silver jewelry companies lead the world in that industry in part because other Italian companies supply two-thirds of the world's jewelry-making and precious-metal recycling machinery.

Far more significant than mere access to components and machinery, however, is the advantage that home-based related and supporting industries provide in innovation and upgrading—an advantage based on close working relationships. Suppliers and end-users located near each other can take advantage of short lines of communication, quick and constant flow of information, and an ongoing exchange of ideas and innovations. Companies have the opportunity to influence their suppliers' technical efforts and can serve as test sites for R&D work, accelerating the pace of innovation.

The illustration of "The Italian Footwear Cluster" offers a graphic example of how a group of close-by, supporting industries creates competitive advantage in a range of interconnected industries that are all internationally competitive. Shoe producers, for instance, interact regularly with leather manufacturers on new styles and manufacturing techniques and learn about new textures and colors of leather when they are still on the drawing boards. Leather manufacturers gain early insights into fashion trends, helping them to plan new products. The

The Italian Footwear Cluster

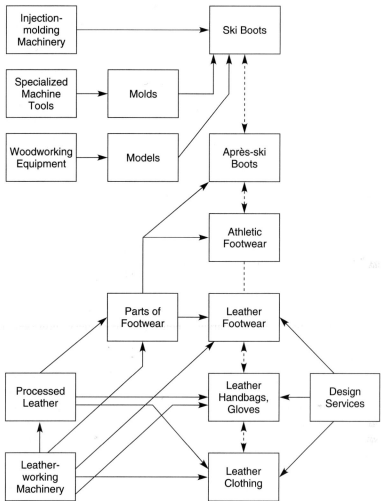

interaction is mutually advantageous and self-reinforcing, but it does not happen automatically: It is helped by proximity, but occurs only because companies and suppliers work at it.

The nation's companies benefit most when the suppliers are, themselves, global competitors. It is ultimately self-defeating for a company or country to create "captive" suppliers who are totally dependent on the domestic industry and prevented from serving foreign competitors. By the same token, a nation need not be competitive in all supplier industries for its companies to gain competitive advantage. Companies can readily source from abroad materials, components, or technologies without a major effect on innovation or performance of the industry's products. The same is true of other generalized technologies—like electronics or software—where the industry represents a narrow application area.

Home-based competitiveness in related industries provides similar benefits: Information flow and technical interchange speed the rate of innovation and upgrading. A home-based related industry also increases the likelihood that companies will embrace new skills, and it also provides a source of entrants who will bring a novel approach to competing. The Swiss success in pharmaceuticals emerged out of previous international success in the dye industry, for example; Japanese dominance in electronic musical keyboards grows out of success in acoustic instruments combined with a strong position in consumer electronics.

Firm Strategy, Structure, and Rivalry

National circumstances and context create strong tendencies in how companies are created, organized, and managed, as well as what the nature of domestic rivalry will be. In Italy, for example, successful international competitors are often small or medium-sized companies that are privately owned and operated like extended families; in Germany, in contrast, companies tend to be strictly hierarchical in organization and management practices, and top managers usually have technical backgrounds.

No one managerial system is universally appropriate—notwithstanding the current fascination with Japanese management. Competitiveness in a specific industry results from convergence of the management practices and organizational modes favored in the country and the sources of competitive advantage in the industry. In industries where Italian companies are world leaders—such as lighting, furniture, footwear, woolen fabrics, and packaging machines—a company strategy that emphasizes focus, customized products, niche marketing, rapid change, and breathtaking flexibility fits both the dynamics of the industry and the character of the Italian management system. The German man-

agement system, in contrast, works well in technical or engineering-oriented industries—optics, chemicals, complicated machinery—where complex products demand precision manufacturing, a careful development process, after-sale service, and thus a highly disciplined management structure. German success is much rarer in consumer goods and services where image marketing and rapid new-feature and model turnover are important to competition.

Countries also differ markedly in the goals that companies and individuals seek to achieve. Company goals reflect the characteristics of national capital markets and the compensation practices for managers. For example, in Germany and Switzerland, where banks comprise a substantial part of the nation's shareholders, most shares are held for long-term appreciation and are rarely traded. Companies do well in mature industries, where ongoing investment in R&D and new facilities is essential but returns may be only moderate. The United States is at the opposite extreme, with a large pool of risk capital but widespread trading of public companies and a strong emphasis by investors on quarterly and annual share-price appreciation. Management compensation is heavily based on annual bonuses tied to individual results. America does well in relatively new industries, like software and biotechnology, or ones where equity funding of new companies feeds active domestic rivalry, like specialty electronics and services. Strong pressures leading to underinvestment, however, plague more mature industries.

Individual motivation to work and expand skills is also important to competitive advantage. Outstanding talent is a scarce resource in any nation. A nation's success largely depends on the types of education its talented people choose, where they choose to work, and their commitment and effort. The goals a nation's institutions and values set for individuals and companies, and the prestige it attaches to certain industries, guide the flow of capital and human resources—which, in turn, directly affects the competitive performance of certain industries. Nations tend to be competitive in activities that people admire or depend on—the activities from which the nation's heroes emerge. In Switzerland, it is banking and pharmaceuticals. In Israel, the highest callings have been agriculture and defense-related fields. Sometimes it is hard to distinguish between cause and effect. Attaining international success can make an industry prestigious, reinforcing its advantage.

The presence of strong local rivals is a final, and powerful, stimulus to the creation and persistence of competitive advantage. This is true of small countries, like Switzerland, where the rivalry among its pharmaceutical companies, Hoffmann-La Roche, Ciba-Geigy, and Sandoz, contributes to a leading worldwide position. It is true in the United States in the computer and software industries. Nowhere is the role of fierce rivalry more apparent than in Japan, where there are 112 companies competing in machine tools, 34 in semiconductors, 25 in audio equipment, 15 in cameras—in fact, there are usually double figures in the industries in which Japan boasts global dominance. (See the table "Estimated Number of Japanese Rivals in Selected Industries.") Among all the points on the diamond, domestic rivalry is arguably the most important because of the powerfully stimulating effect it has on all the others.

Conventional wisdom argues that domestic competition is wasteful: It leads to duplication of effort and prevents companies from achieving economies of scale. The "right solution" is to embrace one or two national champions, companies with the scale and strength to tackle foreign competitors, and to guarantee them the necessary resources, with the government's blessing. In fact, however, most national champions are uncompetitive, although heavily subsidized and protected by their government. In many of the prominent industries in which there is only one national rival, such as aerospace and telecommunications, government has played a large role in distorting competition.

Estimated Number of Japanese Rivals in Selected Industries	
Air Conditioners	13
Audio Equipment	25
Automobiles	9
Cameras	15
Car Audio	12
Carbon Fibers	7
Construction Equipment*	15
Copiers	14
Facsimile Machines	10
Large-Scale Computers	6
Lift Trucks	8
Machine Tools	112
Microwave Equipment	5
Motorcycles	4
Musical Instruments	4
Personal Computers	16
Semiconductors	34
Sewing Machines	20
Shipbuilding[†]	33
Steel[‡]	5
Synthetic Fibers	8
Television Sets	15
Truck and Bus Tires	5
Trucks	11
Typewriters	14
Videocassette Recorders	10

*The number of companies varied by product area. The smallest number, 10, produced bulldozers. Fifteen companies produced shovel trucks, truck cranes, and asphalt-paving equipment. There were 20 companies in hydraulic excavators, a product area where Japan was particularly strong.
[†]Six companies had annual production exports in excess of 10,000 tons.
[‡]Integrated companies.

Sources: Field interviews, *Nippon Kogyo Shinbun, Nippon Kogyo Nenkan,* 1987, Yano Research, *Market Share Jitan,* 1987, researchers' estimates.

Static efficiency is much less important than dynamic improvement, which domestic rivalry uniquely spurs. Domestic rivalry, like any rivalry, creates pressure on companies to innovate and improve. Local rivals push each other to lower costs, improve quality and service, and create new products and processes. But unlike rivalries with foreign competitors, which tend to be analytical and distant, local rivalries often go beyond pure economic or business competition and become intensely personal. Domestic rivals engage in active feuds; they compete not only for market share but also for people, for technical excellence, and perhaps most important, for "bragging rights." One domestic rival's success proves to others that advancement is possible and often attracts new rivals to the industry. Companies often attribute the success of foreign rivals to "unfair" advantages. With domestic rivals, there are no excuses.

Geographic concentration magnifies the power of domestic rivalry. This pattern is strikingly common around the world: Italian jewelry companies are located around two towns, Arezzo and Valenza Po; cutlery companies in Solingen, West Germany, and Seki, Japan; pharmaceutical companies in Basel, Switzerland; motorcycles and musical instruments in Hamamatsu, Japan. The more localized the rivalry, the more intense. And the more intense, the better.

Another benefit of domestic rivalry is the pressure it creates for constant upgrading of the sources of competitive advantage. The presence of domestic competitors automatically cancels the types of advantage that come from simply being in a particular nation—factor costs, access to or preference in the home market, or costs to foreign competitors who import into the market. Companies are forced to move beyond them, and as a result, gain more sustainable advantages. Moreover, competing domestic rivals will keep each other honest in obtaining government support. Companies are less likely to get hooked on the narcotic of government contracts or creeping industry protectionism. Instead, the industry will seek—and benefit from—more constructive forms of government support, such as assistance in opening foreign markets, as well as investments in focused educational institutions or other specialized factors.

Ironically, it is also vigorous domestic competition that ultimately pressures domestic companies to look at global markets and toughens them to succeed in them. Particularly when there are economies of scale, local competitors force each other to look outward to foreign markets to capture greater efficiency and higher profitability. And having been tested by fierce domestic competition, the stronger companies are well equipped to win abroad. If Digital Equipment can hold its own against IBM, Data General, Prime, and Hewlett-Packard, going up against Siemens or Machines Bull does not seem so daunting a prospect.

The Diamond as a System

Each of these four attributes defines a point on the diamond of national advantage; the effect of one point often depends on the state of others. Sophisticated buyers will not translate into advanced products, for example, unless the quality of human resources permits companies to meet buyer needs. Selective disadvantages in factors of production will not motivate innovation unless rivalry is vigorous and company goals support sustained investment. At the broadest level, weaknesses in any one determinant will constrain an industry's potential for advancement and upgrading.

But the points of the diamond are also self-reinforcing: They constitute a system. Two elements, domestic rivalry and geographic concentration, have especially great power to transform the diamond into a system—domestic rivalry because it promotes improvement in all the other determinants and geographic concentration because it elevates and magnifies the interaction of the four separate influences.

The role of domestic rivalry illustrates how the diamond operates as a self-reinforcing system. Vigorous domestic rivalry stimulates the development of unique pools of specialized factors, particularly if the rivals are all located in one city or region: The University of California at Davis has become the world's leading center of wine-making research, working closely with the California wine industry. Active local rivals also upgrade domestic demand in an industry. In furniture and shoes, for example,

Italian consumers have learned to expect more and better products because of the rapid pace of new product development that is driven by intense domestic rivalry among hundreds of Italian companies. Domestic rivalry also promotes the formation of related and supporting industries. Japan's world-leading group of semiconductor producers, for instance, has spawned world-leading Japanese semiconductor-equipment manufacturers.

The effects can work in all directions: Sometimes world-class suppliers become new entrants in the industry they have been supplying. Or highly sophisticated buyers may themselves enter a supplier industry, particularly when they have relevant skills and view the new industry as strategic. In the case of the Japanese robotics industry, for example, Matsushita and Kawasaki originally designed robots for internal use before beginning to sell robots to others. Today they are strong competitors in the robotics industry. In Sweden, Sandvik moved from specialty steel into rock drills, and SKF moved from specialty steel into ball bearings.

Another effect of the diamond's systemic nature is that nations are rarely home to just one competitive industry; rather, the diamond creates an environment that promotes *clusters* of competitive industries. Competitive industries are not scattered helter-skelter throughout the economy but are usually linked together through vertical (buyer-seller) or horizontal (common customers, technology, channels) relationships. Nor are clusters usually scattered physically; they tend to be concentrated geographically. One competitive industry helps to create another in a mutually reinforcing process. Japan's strength in consumer electronics, for example, drove its success in semiconductors toward the memory chips and integrated circuits these products use. Japanese strength in laptop computers, which contrasts to limited success in other segments, reflects the base of strength in other compact, portable products and leading expertise in liquid-crystal display gained in the calculator and watch industries.

Once a cluster forms, the whole group of industries becomes mutually supporting. Benefits flow forward, backward, and horizontally. Aggressive rivalry in one industry spreads to others in the cluster, through spin-offs, through the exercise of bargaining power, and through diversification by established companies. Entry from other industries within the cluster spurs upgrading by stimulating diversity in R&D approaches and facilitating the introduction of new strategies and skills. Through the conduits of suppliers or customers who have contact with multiple competitors, information flows freely and innovations diffuse rapidly. Interconnections within the cluster, often unanticipated, lead to perceptions of new ways of competing and new opportunities. The cluster becomes a vehicle for maintaining diversity and overcoming the inward focus, inertia, inflexibility, and accommodation among rivals that slows or blocks competitive upgrading and new entry.

The Role of Government

In the continuing debate over the competitiveness of nations, no topic engenders more argument or creates less understanding than the role of the government. Many see government as an essential helper or supporter of industry, employing a host of policies to contribute directly to the competitive performance of strategic or target industries. Others accept the "free market" view that the operation of the economy should be left to the workings of the invisible hand.

Both views are incorrect. Either, followed to its logical outcome, would lead to the permanent erosion of a country's competitive capabilities. On one hand, advocates of government help for industry frequently propose policies that would actually hurt companies in the long run and only create the demand for more helping. On the other hand, advocates of a diminished government presence ignore the legitimate role that government plays in shaping the context and institutional structure surrounding companies and in creating an environment that stimulates companies to gain competitive advantage.

Government's proper role is as a catalyst and challenger; it is to encourage—or even push—

companies to raise their aspirations and move to higher levels of competitive performance, even though this process may be inherently unpleasant and difficult. Government cannot create competitive industries; only companies can do that. Government plays a role that is inherently partial, that succeeds only when working in tandem with favorable underlying conditions in the diamond. Still, government's role of transmitting and amplifying the forces of the diamond is a powerful one. Government policies that succeed are those that create an environment in which companies can gain competitive advantage rather than those that involve government directly in the process, except in nations early in the development process. It is an indirect, rather than a direct, role.

Japan's government, at its best, understands this role better than anyone—including the point that nations pass through stages of competitive development and that government's appropriate role shifts as the economy progresses. By stimulating early demand for advanced products, confronting industries with the need to pioneer frontier technology through symbolic cooperative projects, establishing prizes that reward quality, and pursuing other policies that magnify the forces of the diamond, the Japanese government accelerates the pace of innovation. But like government officials anywhere, at their worst Japanese bureaucrats can make the same mistakes: attempting to manage industry structure, protecting the market too long, and yielding to political pressure to insulate inefficient retailers, farmers, distributors, and industrial companies from competition.

It is not hard to understand why so many governments make the same mistakes so often in pursuit of national competitiveness: Competitive time for companies and political time for governments are fundamentally at odds. It often takes more than a decade for an industry to create competitive advantage; the process entails the long upgrading of human skills, investing in products and processes, building clusters, and penetrating foreign markets. In the case of the Japanese auto industry, for instance, companies made their first faltering steps toward exporting in the 1950s—yet did not achieve strong international positions until the 1970s.

But in politics, a decade is an eternity. Consequently, most governments favor policies that offer easily perceived short-term benefits, such as subsidies, protection, and arranged mergers—the very policies that retard innovation. Most of the policies that would make a real difference either are too slow and require too much patience for politicians or, even worse, carry with them the sting of short-term pain. Deregulating a protected industry, for example, will lead to bankruptcies sooner and to stronger, more competitive companies only later.

Policies that convey static, short-term cost advantages but that unconsciously undermine innovation and dynamism represent the most common and most profound error in government industrial policy. In a desire to help, it is all too easy for governments to adopt policies such as joint projects to avoid "wasteful" R&D that undermine dynamism and competition. Yet even a 10% cost saving through economies of scale is easily nullified through rapid product and process improvement and the pursuit of volume in global markets—something that such policies undermine.

There are some simple, basic principles that governments should embrace to play the proper supportive role for national competitiveness: encourage change, promote domestic rivalry, stimulate innovation. Some of the specific policy approaches to guide nations seeking to gain competitive advantage include the following:

Focus on specialized factor creation. Government has critical responsibilities for fundamentals like the primary and secondary education systems, basic national infrastructure, and research in areas of broad national concern such as health care. Yet these kinds of generalized efforts at factor creation rarely produce competitive advantage. Rather, the factors that translate into competitive advantage are advanced, specialized, and tied to specific industries or industry groups. Mechanisms such as specialized apprenticeship programs, research efforts in universities connected with an industry, trade association activities, and, most important, the private investments of companies ultimately create the factors that will yield competitive advantage.

Avoid intervening in factor and currency markets. By intervening in factor and currency markets, governments hope to create lower factor costs or a favorable exchange rate that will help companies compete more effectively in international markets. Evidence from around the world indicates that these policies—such as the Reagan administration's dollar devaluation—are often counterproductive. They work against the upgrading of industry and the search for more sustainable competitive advantage.

The contrasting case of Japan is particularly instructive, although both Germany and Switzerland have had similar experiences. Over the past 20 years, the Japanese have been rocked by the sudden Nixon currency devaluation shock, two oil shocks, and, most recently, the yen shock—all of which forced Japanese companies to upgrade their competitive advantages. The point is not that government should pursue policies that intentionally drive up factor costs or the exchange rate. Rather, when market forces create rising factor costs or a higher exchange rate, government should resist the temptation to push them back down.

Enforce strict product, safety, and environmental standards. Strict government regulations can promote competitive advantage by stimulating and upgrading domestic demand. Stringent standards for product performance, product safety, and environmental impact pressure companies to improve quality, upgrade technology, and provide features that respond to consumer and social demands. Easing standards, however tempting, is counterproductive.

When tough regulations anticipate standards that will spread internationally, they give a nation's companies a head start in developing products and services that will be valuable elsewhere. Sweden's strict standards for environmental protection have promoted competitive advantage in many industries. Atlas Copco, for example, produces quiet compressors that can be used in dense urban areas with minimal disruption to residents. Strict standards, however, must be combined with a rapid and streamlined regulatory process that does not absorb resources and cause delays.

Sharply limit direct cooperation among industry rivals. The most pervasive global policy fad in the competitiveness arena today is the call for more cooperative research and industry consortia. Operating on the belief that independent research by rivals is wasteful and duplicative, that collaborative efforts achieve economies of scale, and that individual companies are likely to underinvest in R&D because they cannot reap all the benefits, governments have embraced the idea of more direct cooperation. In the United States, antitrust laws have been modified to allow more cooperative R&D; in Europe, mega-projects such as ESPRIT, an information-technology project, bring together companies from several countries. Lurking behind much of this thinking is the fascination of Western governments with—and fundamental misunderstanding of—the countless cooperative research projects sponsored by the Ministry of International Trade and Industry (MITI), projects that appear to have contributed to Japan's competitive rise.

But a closer look at Japanese cooperative projects suggests a different story. Japanese companies participate in MITI projects to maintain good relations with MITI, to preserve their corporate images, and to hedge the risk that competitors will gain from the project—largely defensive reasons. Companies rarely contribute their best scientists and engineers to cooperative projects and usually spend much more on their own private research in the same field. Typically, the government makes only a modest financial contribution to the project.

The real value of Japanese cooperative research is to signal the importance of emerging technical areas and to stimulate proprietary company research. Cooperative projects prompt companies to explore new fields and boost internal R&D spending because companies know that their domestic rivals are investigating them.

Under certain limited conditions, cooperative research can prove beneficial. Projects should be in areas of basic product and process research, not in subjects closely connected to a company's proprietary sources of advantage. They should constitute only a modest portion of a company's overall research program in any given field. Cooperative research should be only indirect, channeled through independent organizations to which most industry participants have access. Organizational structures, like university labs and centers of excellence, reduce management problems and minimize the risk to rivalry. Finally, the most useful cooperative projects often involve fields that touch a number of industries and that require substantial R&D investments.

Promote goals that lead to sustained investment. Government has a vital role in shaping the goals of investors, managers, and employees through policies in various areas. The manner in which capital markets are regulated, for example, shapes the incentives of investors and, in turn, the behavior of companies. Government should aim to encourage sustained investment in human skills, in innovation, and in physical assets. Perhaps the single most powerful tool for raising the rate of sustained investment in industry is a tax incentive for long-term (five years or more) capital gains restricted to new investment in corporate equity. Long-term capital gains incentives should also be applied to pension funds and other currently untaxed investors, who now have few reasons not to engage in rapid trading.

Deregulate competition. Regulation of competition through such policies as maintaining a state monopoly, controlling entry into an industry, or fixing prices has two strong negative consequences: It stifles rivalry and innovation as companies become preoccupied with dealing with regulators and protecting what they already have; and it makes the industry a less dynamic and less desirable buyer or supplier. Deregulation and privatization on their own, however, will not succeed without vigorous domestic rivalry—and that requires, as a corollary, a strong and consistent antitrust policy.

Enforce strong domestic antitrust policies. A strong antitrust policy—especially for horizontal mergers, alliances, and collusive behavior—is fundamental to innovation. While it is fashionable today to call for mergers and alliances in the name of globalization and the creation of national champions, these often undermine the creation of competitive advantage. Real national competitiveness requires governments to disallow mergers, acquisitions, and alliances that involve industry leaders. Furthermore, the same standards for mergers and alliances should apply to both domestic and foreign companies. Finally, government policy should favor internal entry, both domestic and international, over acquisition. Companies should, however, be allowed to acquire small companies in related industries when the move promotes the transfer of skills that could ultimately create competitive advantage.

Reject managed trade. Managed trade represents a growing and dangerous tendency for dealing with the fallout of national competitiveness. Orderly marketing agreements, voluntary restraint agreements, or other devices that set quantitative targets to divide up markets are dangerous, ineffective, and often enormously costly to consumers. Rather than promoting innovation in a nation's industries, managed trade guarantees a market for inefficient companies.

Government trade policy should pursue open market access in every foreign nation. To be effective, trade policy should not be a passive instrument; it cannot respond only to complaints or work only for those industries that can muster enough political clout; it should not require a long history of injury or serve only distressed industries. Trade policy should seek to open markets wherever a nation has competitive advantage and should also actively address emerging industries and incipient problems.

Where government finds a trade barrier in another nation, it should concentrate its remedies on dismantling barriers, not on regulating imports or exports. In the case of Japan, for example, pressure to accelerate the already rapid growth of manufactured imports is a more effective approach than a shift to managed trade. Compensatory tariffs that punish companies for unfair trade practices are better than market quotas. Other increasingly important tools to open markets are restrictions that prevent companies in offending nations from investing in acquisitions or production facilities in the host country—thereby blocking the unfair country's companies from using their advantage to establish a new beachhead that is immune from sanctions.

Any of these remedies, however, can backfire. It is virtually impossible to craft remedies to unfair trade practices that avoid both reducing incentives for domestic companies to innovate and export and harming domestic buyers. The aim of remedies should be adjustments that allow the remedy to disappear.

The Company Agenda

Ultimately, only companies themselves can achieve and sustain competitive advantage. To do so, they must act on the fundamentals described above. In particular, they must recognize the central role of innovation—and the uncomfortable truth that innovation grows out of pressure and challenge. It takes leadership to create a dynamic, challenging environment. And it takes leadership to recognize the all-too-easy escape routes that appear to offer a path to competitive advantage, but are actually short-cuts to failure. For example, it is tempting to rely on cooperative research and development projects to lower the cost and risk of research. But they can divert company attention and resources from proprietary research efforts and will all but eliminate the prospects for real innovation.

Competitive advantage arises from leadership that harnesses and amplifies the forces in the diamond to promote innovation and upgrading. Here are just a few of the kinds of company policies that will support that effort:

Create pressures for innovation. A company should seek out pressure and challenge, not avoid them. Part of strategy is to take advantage of the home nation to create the impetus for innovation. To do that, companies can sell to the most sophisticated and demanding buyers and channels; seek out those buyers with the most difficult needs; establish norms that exceed the toughest regulatory hurdles or product standards; source from the most advanced suppliers; treat employees as permanent in order to stimulate upgrading of skills and productivity.

Seek out the most capable competitors as motivators. To motivate organizational change, capable competitors and respected rivals can be a common enemy. The best managers always run a little scared; they respect and study competitors. To stay dynamic, companies must make meeting challenge a part of the organization's norms. For example, lobbying against strict product standards signals the organization that company leadership has diminished aspirations. Companies that value stability, obedient customers, dependent suppliers, and sleepy competitors are inviting inertia and, ultimately, failure.

Establish early-warning systems. Early-warning signals translate into early-mover advantages. Companies can take actions that help them see the signals of change and act on them, thereby getting a jump on the competition. For example, they can find and serve those buyers with the most anticipatory needs; investigate all emerging new buyers or channels; find places whose regulations foreshadow emerging regulations elsewhere; bring some outsiders into the management team; maintain ongoing relationships with research centers and sources of talented people.

Improve the national diamond. Companies have a vital stake in making their home environment a better platform for international success. Part of a company's responsibility is to play an active role in forming clusters and to work with its home-nation buyers, suppliers, and channels to help them upgrade and extend their own competitive advantages. To upgrade home demand, for example, Japanese musical instrument manufacturers, led by Yamaha, Kawai, and Suzuki, have established music schools. Similarly, companies can stimulate and support local suppliers of important specialized inputs—including encouraging them to compete globally. The health and strength of the national cluster will only enhance the company's own rate of innovation and upgrading.

In nearly every successful competitive industry, leading companies also take explicit steps to create specialized factors like human resources, scientific knowledge, or infrastructure. In industries like wool cloth, ceramic tiles, and lighting equipment, Italian industry associations invest in market information, process technology, and common infrastructure. Companies can also speed innovation by putting their headquarters and other key operations where there are concentrations of sophisticated buyers, important suppliers, or specialized factor-creating mechanisms, such as universities or laboratories.

Welcome domestic rivalry. To compete globally, a company needs capable domestic rivals and vigorous domestic rivalry. Especially in the United States and Europe today, managers are wont to complain about excessive competition and to argue for mergers and acquisitions that will produce hoped-for economies of scale and critical mass. The complaint is only natural—but the argument is plain wrong. Vigorous domestic rivalry creates sustainable competitive advantage. Moreover, it is better to grow internationally than to dominate the domestic market. If a company wants an acquisition, a foreign one that can speed globalization and supplement home-based advantages or offset home-based disadvantages is usually far better than merging with leading domestic competitors.

Globalize to tap selective advantages in other nations. In search of "global" strategies, many companies today abandon their home diamond. To be sure, adopting a global perspective is important to creating competitive advantage. But relying on foreign activities that supplant domestic capabilities is always a second-best solution. Innovating to offset local factor disadvantages is better than outsourcing; developing domestic suppliers and buyers is better than relying solely on foreign ones. Unless the critical underpinnings of competitiveness are present at home, companies will not sustain competitive advantage in the long run. The aim should be to upgrade home-base capabilities so that foreign activities are selective and supplemental only to over-all competitive advantage.

The correct approach to globalization is to tap selectively into sources of advantage in other nations' diamonds. For example, identifying sophisticated buyers in other countries helps companies understand different needs and creates pressures that will stimulate a faster rate of innovation. No matter how favorable the home diamond, moreover, important research is going on in other nations. To take advantage of foreign research, companies must station high-quality people in overseas bases and mount a credible level of scientific effort. To get anything back from foreign research ventures, companies must also allow access to their own ideas—recognizing that competitive advantage comes from continuous improvement, not from protecting today's secrets.

Use alliances only selectively. Alliances with foreign companies have become another managerial fad and cure-all: They represent a tempting solution to the problem of a company wanting the advantages of foreign enterprises or hedging against risk, without giving up independence. In reality, however, while alliances can achieve selective benefits, they always exact significant costs: They involve coordinating two separate operations, reconciling goals with an independent entity, creating a competitor, and giving up profits. These costs ultimately make most alliances short-term transitional devices, rather than stable, long-term relationships.

Most important, alliances as a broad-based strategy will only ensure a company's mediocrity, not its international leadership. No company can rely on another outside, independent company for skills and assets that are central to its competitive advantage. Alliances are best used as a selective tool, employed on a temporary basis or involving noncore activities.

Locate the home base to support competitive advantage. Among the most important decisions for multinational companies is the nation in which to locate the home base for each distinct business. A company can have different home bases for distinct businesses or segments. Ultimately, competitive advantage is created at home: It is where strategy is set, the core product and process technology is created, and a critical mass of production takes place. The circumstances in the home nation must support innovation; otherwise the company has no choice but to move its home base to a country that stimulates innovation and that provides the best environment for global competitiveness. There are no half-measures: the management team must move as well.

The Role of Leadership

Too many companies and top managers misperceive the nature of competition and the task before them by focusing on improving financial performance, soliciting government assistance, seeking stability, and reducing risk through alliances and mergers.

Today's competitive realities demand leadership. Leaders believe in change; they energize their organizations to innovate continuously; they recognize the importance of their home country as integral to their competitive success and work to upgrade it. Most important, leaders recognize the need for pressure and challenge. Because they are willing to encourage appropriate—and painful—government policies and regulations, they often earn the title "statesmen," although few see themselves that way. They are prepared to sacrifice the easy life for difficulty and, ultimately, sustained competitive advantage. That must be the goal, for both nations and companies: not just surviving, but achieving international competitiveness.

And not just once, but continuously.

Author's note: Michael J. Enright, who served as project coordinator for this study, has contributed valuable suggestions.

Chapter 3

Building Strategic Capabilities: The Competitive Challenge

The turbulent international competitive environment of the 1980s led to a number of different perspectives and prescriptions on how companies can build competitive advantage in worldwide businesses. Some of the most well known of these analyses are included in the readings, and each is reasonable and intuitively appealing.[1] What soon becomes clear, however, is that the respective prescriptions are very different and, at times, contradictory:

- Levitt, for example, argues that effective global strategy is not a bag of many tricks but the successful practice of just one: product standardization. According to him, the core of a global strategy lies in developing a standardized product to be produced and sold the same way throughout the world.
- According to Hout, Porter, and Rudden, on the other hand, effective global strategy requires the approach not of a hedgehog, who knows only one trick, but that of a fox, who knows many. Exploiting economies of scale through global volume, taking preemptive positions through quick and large investments, and managing interdependently to achieve synergies across different activities are, according to these authors, some of the more important moves that a winning global strategist must muster.
- Hamel and Prahalad's prescription for a global strategy contradicts that of Levitt even more sharply. Instead of a single standardized product, they recommend a broad product portfolio, with many product varieties, so that investments in technologies and distribution channels can be shared. Cross-subsidization across products and markets and the development of a strong worldwide distribution system are the two moves that find the pride of place in these authors' views on how to succeed in the game of global chess.

---

[1]Levitt's article is included as part of the reading for the preceding section. The articles by Hout, Porter, and Rudden, and Hamel and Prahalad are reproduced as readings for the section.

These different analyses and prescriptions only highlight the complexity of the strategic challenge facing managers in large, worldwide companies. As we described in the preceding chapter, to achieve sustainable competitive advantage, these companies need to develop, *at one and the same time,* global-scale efficiency, multinational flexibility, and the ability to develop innovations and leverage knowledge on a worldwide basis. Each of the different prescriptions focus on one or the other of these different strategic objectives: The challenge for most companies is to achieve all the objectives simultaneously.

In this chapter, we first present a broad framework that relates the different strategic objectives and the different means available to a company for achieving these objectives. From such a juxtaposition of goals and means, we highlight some specific issues that managers must consider for developing worldwide competitive advantage. We then use this framework to describe some of the key characteristics of multinational, international, and global strategies—the three traditional approaches to worldwide management we introduced in the previous two chapters—and to highlight the respective strengths and vulnerabilities of each of these approaches.

We conclude by showing how the framework helps us to understand some of the requirements for developing a transnational strategy—the approach companies need to respond to the new environmental challenges. And we highlight some of the ways companies can build such transnational strategies, or if they are either unable or unwilling to develop such a comprehensive strategic approach and infrastructure, how they might defend themselves against the transnational's onslaughts.

WORLDWIDE COMPETITIVE ADVANTAGE: GOALS AND MEANS

As we have described in the preceding chapter, to develop worldwide advantage, a company must achieve three strategic objectives. It must build global-scale efficiency in its existing activities, it must develop multinational flexibility so as to manage diverse country-specific risks and opportunities, and it must create the ability to learn from its international exposure and opportunities and to exploit that learning on a worldwide basis. Competitive advantage is developed by taking strategic actions that optimize a company's achievement of these different and, at times, conflicting goals.

In developing each of these capabilities, the MNC can utilize three very different tools and approaches, which we also described briefly in Chapter 1 as the main forces motivating companies to internationalize. It can exploit the differences in sourcing and market opportunities among the many countries in which it operates; it can capitalize on the diversity of its activities and operations to create synergies or develop economies of scope; and it can leverage the scale economies that are potentially available in its different worldwide activities.

The MNC's strategic challenge, then, is to exploit all three sources of global competitive advantage—national differences, scope economies, and scale economies—in order to optimize global efficiencies, multinational flexibility, and worldwide learning. And this means that the key to worldwide, competitive advantage lies in managing the interactions between the different goals and the different means. In the following pages, we first provide a fuller description of the different strategic objectives—the goals—and the different sources of competitive advantage—the means. We then turn our attention to some of the opportunities and constraints of using the different means for achieving the different goals.

The Goals: Efficiency, Flexibility, and Learning

In Chapter 2, we argued that to respond effectively to the new environmental challenges a company must develop global competitiveness, multinational flexibility, and the capability of worldwide learning. Let us now consider each of these strategic goals in a little more detail.

Global Efficiency.   Viewing an MNC as an input-output system, we can think of its overall efficiency as the ratio of the value of its outputs to the value of its inputs. In this simplified view of the firm its efficiency could be enhanced by increasing the value of outputs (i.e., by securing higher revenues), by lowering the value of its inputs (i.e., by lowering its costs), or by doing both. This is a simple point but one that is often overlooked: Efficiency improvement is not just cost reduction, but also revenue enhancement.

To help understand the concept of global efficiency, we will use the global integration–national responsiveness framework proposed by Professors C. K. Prahalad and Yves Doz (see Figure 3–1).[2] The vertical axis represents the potential benefits from global integration of activities—benefits that largely translate into lower costs through scale and scope economies. The horizontal axis represents the benefits of national responsiveness—those that result from country-by-country differentiation of product, strategies, and the way activities are carried out. These benefits essentially translate into better revenues from more-effective differentiation to respond to national differences in tastes, industry structures, distribution systems, and government regulations.

As illustrated in Figure 3–1, the framework can be used to understand differences in the benefits of integration and responsiveness at the aggregate level of industries, as well as to identify and describe differences in the strategic approaches of companies competing in the same industry. We have plotted several of the industries whose characteristics we discussed in Chapter 2.

It is important to recognize that industry characteristics alone do not determine company strategies. In automobiles, for example, Fiat has long pursued a classical multinational strategy, helping establish national auto industries through its joint venture partnerships and host government support in Spain, Yugoslavia, Poland, and many other locations. Toyota, by contrast, succeeded by developing products and manufacturing them in centralized globally scaled facilities in Japan.

---

[2]For a detailed exposition of this framework, see C. K. Prahalad and Yves Doz, *The Multinational Mission* (New York: Free Press, 1988).

FIGURE 3–1 The Integration-Responsiveness Framework

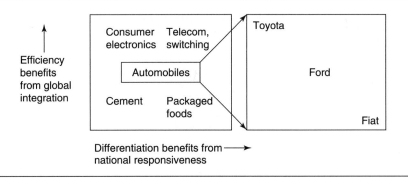

While the popular conception is that Toyota has achieved global-scale efficiency while Fiat has lost the opportunity to do so, a closer examination of their strategy reveals that each has important actual and potential assets and vulnerabilities on this score. Toyota's globally scaled product development and manufacturing facilities in Toyota City, Japan, are clearly a major asset that Fiat cannot match. Yet Fiat's more-dispersed manufacturing facilities in low–labor cost countries where host governments are often willing to subsidize operations offers Fiat some potential to offset Toyota's scale. On the revenue side, Toyota relies on a strong brand built on a quality reputation to help it increase its volume and price. Fiat's strategy enhances revenues by providing it with a portfolio of largely protected markets and a constant flow of revenue from the technology licensing agreements it has with its joint venture partners.

We can debate which of the two strategies is more sustainable competitively, but the point we want to emphasize is that every MNC must develop the infrastructures and capabilities for managing both costs and revenues simultaneously. Efficient and specialized facilities for research, production, logistics, and sourcing are the requirements for managing the cost side; strong portfolio of brands, powerful distribution facilities, access to key markets, and local resources to create or adapt products and brands are some of the main requirements for managing the revenue side.

Multinational Flexibility. A worldwide company faces an environment characterized by its diversity and volatility. Some of the opportunities and risks generated by this environment are endemic to all firms; others, however, are unique to companies operating across national borders. A key element of worldwide competitiveness, therefore, is multinational flexibility—the ability of a company to manage the risks and to exploit the opportunities that arise from the diversity and volatility of the global environment.[3]

---

[3]This issue of multinational flexibility is discussed more fully in Bruce Kogut, "Designing Global Strategies: Profiting from Operating Flexibility," *Sloan Management Review,* Fall 1985, pp. 27–38.

Although there are many sources of the diversity and volatility that characterizes the MNC's operating context, we will focus on four that we regard as particularly important. Since opportunities and risks are often two sides of the same coin, we will review the four environmental forces in terms of the risks, even though the arguments can be easily translated to the corresponding opportunities.

First, an MNC faces certain macroeconomic risks that are completely outside its control, and which may be country-specific, regional, or worldwide in scope. These include cataclysmic events such as wars and natural calamities, and also equilibrium-seeking or even random movements in wage rates, interest rates, exchange rates, commodity prices, and so on.

Second, the company faces what is usually referred to as *political risks* but may be more appropriately called *policy risks* to emphasize that they arise from policy actions of national governments. The net effect of such policy actions may often be indistinguishable from the effect of macroeconomic forces; for example, both may lead to changes in the exchange rate of a particular currency. But, from a management perspective, the two must be distinguished, since the former is uncontrollable, but the latter may be partially controllable or at least influenceable.

Third, the company also faces certain competitive risks arising from the uncertainties of competitors' responses to its own strategies. Since both monopolies and perfect competition are rare, all companies face such risks to some extent. In the context of global strategies, however, their implications are particularly complex, since competitors may respond in many different forms and in many different markets.

Finally, the MNC also faces what may be called *resource risks.* This is the risk that its adopted strategy will require resources that the company does not have, cannot acquire, or cannot spare. A key scarce resource for most firms is managerial talent, but resource risks can also arise from lack of appropriate technology, or even capital.

In all four categories, the common characteristic of the various types of risks is that they all vary across countries and change over time. This makes flexibility the key strategic management requirement, since the diversity and volatility create attendant opportunities that must be considered jointly.

In Fiat, for example, the opening up of Eastern bloc economies, the EEC's program to harmonize markets beginning in 1992, the rapid expansion of Japanese auto manufacturers into Europe, and the parent company's resource constraints due to an aggressive diversification strategy represent examples of each class of risk/opportunity Fiat managers faced in the early 1990s. The implications in terms of plant investment and sourcing strategy alone were mind-boggling: whether to acquire majority share in a plant in Spain—a growth market with low-cost labor and access to the EEC market; whether to enter a new technology licensing agreement with the Soviets to help them modernize their auto industry; or whether to pursue Poland as a potential regional source for high labor content parts, and components.

The company could not resolve any of these in isolation, since the optimization of one (e.g., the Polish sourcing strategy) might compromise the ability to implement the others (e.g., the Spanish joint venture and the Russian licensing deal). Yet it also had to be more flexible in its approach, trying to keep each option alive and viable, but without compromising the other two.

In general, multinational flexibility requires management to scan its broad environment to detect the changes and discontinuities that present new risks and opportunities. It then demands that they respond to that new situation, albeit in the context of the worldwide business. In this mode, incrementalism and opportunism may be given greater emphasis in the company's strategy development than preemptive resource commitments and long-term planning. These MNCs exploit their exposure to diverse and dynamic environments to develop strategies in more-general and more-flexible terms, so as to be robust to different international environmental scenarios. Furthermore, they lay side bets to cover contingencies and to create strategic options that might be exercised in the future.

Worldwide Learning.   Most existing theories of the MNC view it as an instrument to extract additional revenues from internalized capabilities. The assumption is that the firm goes abroad to make more profits by exploiting its technology, brand name, or management capabilities in different countries around the world. But, according to the theory, the key competencies always resided at the MNC's center.

While the search for additional profits or the desire to protect existing revenues may explain why MNCs come to exist, they do not provide an equally complete explanation of why some of them continue to grow and flourish. As we suggested in Chapter 1, an alternative view may well be that a key asset of the multinational is the diversity of environments in which it operates. This diversity exposes the MNC to multiple stimuli, allows it to develop diverse capabilities, and provides it with a broader learning opportunity than is available to a purely domestic firm. The enhanced organizational learning that results from the diversity internalized by the multinational is often a key source of its ongoing success. Furthermore, its initial stock of knowledge provides the MNC with the strength that allows it to create such organizational diversity in the first place.

Exposure to a broad range of stimuli and the consequent development of a diversity of resources and competencies appears to have a direct impact on the firm's ability to create joint innovations, and to exploit them in multiple locations. One example of such benefits of diversity was recently described in *The Wall Street Journal:*

> P&G [Procter & Gamble] recently introduced its new Liquid Tide, but the product has a distinctly international heritage. A new ingredient that helps suspend dirt in wash water came from the company's research center near P&G's Cincinnati headquarters. But the formula for Liquid Tide's surfactants, or cleaning agents, was developed by P&G technicians in Japan. The ingredients that fight mineral salts present in hard water came from P&G's scientists in Brussels.[4]

---

[4] *The Wall Street Journal,* April 29, 1985, p. 1.

The same *WSJ* article described how P&G's research center in Brussels developed its special capability in water-softening technology largely due to the fact that water in Europe contains more than twice the level of mineral content compared to wash water available in the United States. (The history is described more fully in the case Procter & Gamble Europe: Vizir Launch, page 632). Similarly, surfactant technology is particularly advanced in Japan because Japanese consumers wash their clothes in colder water than do consumers in the United States or Europe, and this makes greater demands on the cleaning ability of the surfactants. The advantage of P&G as a multinational is that it is exposed to these different operating environments and has learned, in each environment, the skills and knowledge that coping with that environment specially requires. Liquid Tide is an example of the strategic advantages that accrue from such diverse learning.

The mere existence of diversity, however, does not ensure that learning will occur—it only creates the potential. To exploit this potential, the organization must make learning an explicit objective, and create mechanisms and systems to facilitate the learning process.

In companies where most organizational resources are centralized and where the national subsidiaries are relegated to the role of implementors of centrally developed strategies and products in local markets, little worldwide learning is likely to occur. In the first place, without the resources or responsibility to sense, analyze, and respond to their local environments, subsidiaries develop little ability or incentive to learn. In the second place, because centralized decision processes are often insensitive to knowledge accumulated outside the corporate headquarters, even when subsidiaries do make suggestions or requests, the proposals rarely result in corporate learning.

Other companies, in which overseas subsidiaries enjoy high levels of local resources and autonomy, may also fail to exploit global learning benefits. Their inability to transfer and synthesize knowledge and expertise developed in different organizational components is usually due more to local loyalties, turf protection, and the "not-invented-here" (NIH) syndrome—the three handmaidens of decentralization.

Those that wish to develop genuine worldwide learning capabilities must overcome the limitations of processes in which either centralization or decentralization dominates. They must develop the organization structures and systems that allow them to do as P&G did—to sense consumer needs and market opportunities worldwide and to tap into the appropriate corporate resources wherever they exist to develop innovative responses.

The Means: National Differences, Scope, and Scale Economies

As we described in Chapter 1, there are three fundamental tools for building worldwide competitive advantage: exploiting differences in sourcing and market potential across countries, exploiting economies of scope, and exploiting economies of scale.

National Differences. The comparative advantage of locations in terms of differences in labor and material costs is perhaps the most discussed, and also the best understood, source of competitive advantage in international business.

In the absence of efficient markets, the fact that different nations have different factor endowments (for example, abundance of labor, land, materials) leads to intercountry differences in factor costs. Because different activities of the firm, such as R&D, production, or marketing, use various factors to different degrees, a firm can gain cost advantages by configuring its value chain so that each activity is located in the country that has the least cost for its most intensively used factor. R&D facilities may be placed in England due to the available supply of high-quality, yet modestly paid scientists, while manufacturing of labor-intensive components may be undertaken in Taiwan to capitalize on the low-cost, efficient labor force. This is the core concept of comparative advantage–based competitive advantage—a concept for which highly developed analytical tools are available from the discipline of international economics.

National differences may also exist in output markets. As we have discussed, customer tastes and preferences may be different in different countries, as may distribution systems, government regulations applicable to the concerned product markets, or the effectiveness of different promotion strategies and other marketing techniques. A firm can obtain higher prices for its output by tailoring its offerings to fit the unique requirements in each national market.

In the traditional economics view, comparative advantages of countries are determined by their relative factor endowments. From a strategic perspective, however, it is increasingly necessary to replace this static and purely economic view of national differences with a more dynamic view of comparative advantage and to broaden the economics-dominated framework to encompass factors that are more socially based.

One lesson of the past four decades is that comparative advantages change more rapidly than had historically been assumed, increasingly in response to government-driven industrial policies designed to effect such changes. Thus, for any nation, the availability and cost of capital change, as do the availability of technical workers and the wages of skilled and unskilled labor. In the long run, such changes take place to accommodate differences in the economic and social performance of nations, but in the short run they occur in response to specific policies and regulations of national governments.

This dynamic aspect of comparative advantages adds considerable complexity to the strategic considerations of the firm. At the simplest level, increases in wage rates, interest rates, or currency exchange rates in a particular country will affect the viability of a company located in that country with a strategy based on the historic levels of these economic variables. But there can also be a more intriguing second-order effect. If an activity is located in an economically inefficient environment, and if the firm is able to achieve a higher level of efficiency in its own operations compared to the rest of the local economy, its competitive advantage may actually increase as the local economy slips lower and lower. This is because the macroeconomic variables such as wage or exchange rates may change to reflect the overall performance of the economy relative to the rest of the world and, to the extent that the firm's performance is better than this national aggregate, it may benefit from these macrolevel changes.

Consistent with the discipline that gave birth to the concept, the usual view of comparative advantage is limited to factors that an economist admits into the production function, such as the costs of labor and capital. However, from a managerial perspective, it may be more appropriate to take a broader view of societal comparative advantages to include all the relative advantages conferred on a society by the quality, quantity, and configuration of its material, human, and institutional resources. This would include "soft" resources such as interorganizational linkages (with government, suppliers, and even competitors), the nature of its educational system, and organizational and managerial know-how. These soft societal factors, if absorbed in the overall organizational system, can provide benefits as real to a multinational as those provided by such economic factors as cheap labor or low-cost capital.[5]

While the concept of comparative advantage is quite clear, available evidence on its actual effect on the overall competitiveness of firms is surprisingly weak and conflicting. For example, it has often been claimed that one source of competitive advantage for Japanese firms is the lower cost of capital in Japan. However, some systematic studies have shown that there is practically no difference in the risk-adjusted cost of capital in the United States and Japan and that capital-cost advantages of Japanese firms, if any, arise from complex interactions between government subsidies and corporate ownership structures. Similarly, historically low wage rates in Japan have also been proposed as the primary reason Japanese companies were able to penetrate the U.S. market. But, as the U.S. plants of companies such as Honda and Nissan were able to develop practically the same levels of cost advantages over U.S. manufacturers as they had for their production in Japan, such arguments have become increasingly suspect. Overall, there is increasing evidence that while comparative advantages of countries can provide competitive advantages to firms, the realization of such benefits is not automatic but depends on complex organizational factors and processes.

Scale Economies.   Microeconomic theory provides a strong basis for evaluating the effect of scale on cost reduction, and the use of scale as a competitive tool is common in practice. Its implication for strategy is simple: Unless a firm expands the volume of its output so as to achieve available scale benefits, a competitor who can achieve such volume can build cost advantages. And in recent decades, the reality and relevance of that simple theoretical construct had become painfully clear to numerous companies in industries ranging from roller bearings to semiconductors.

While scale, by itself, is a static concept, there may be dynamic benefits of scale through what has been variously described as the *experience* or *learning effect*. The higher volume that helps a firm to exploit scale benefits also allows it to accumulate learning, and this leads to progressive cost reduction as the firm moves

---

[5]Porter's study of the international competitiveness of companies led him to conclude that home-country competitive intensity had an important influence on a firm's success in the global marketplace. See Michael E. Porter, *The Competitive Advantage of Nations* (New York: Free Press, 1990).

down its learning curve. So while emerging Korean electronics firms were able to match the scale of experienced Japanese competitors, they were unable to compensate for the innumerable process-related efficiencies the Japanese had learned after decades of operating their global-scale plants.

The concept of the value-added chain popularized by Professor Michael Porter also adds considerable richness and sophistication to the analysis of scale as a source of competitive advantage.[6] This conceptual apparatus allows a disaggregated analysis of scale benefits in different value-creating activities of the firm. Efficient scale may vary widely by activity—being higher for component production, say, than for assembly. In contrast to a unitary view of scale, this disaggregated view permits the firm to configure different elements of its value chain to attain optimum scale economies in each.

Historically, scale has often been perceived as an unmixed blessing—something that always helps and never hurts. Recently, however, many researchers have begun to argue otherwise. While scale efficiencies can be obtained through increased specialization and through creation of dedicated assets and systems, the same processes may also result in inflexibilities and limit the firm's ability to cope with change. The large global-scale textile plant built in 1972 to capitalize on low Japanese wages and an undervalued yen looked very different 15 years later when labor rates had increased fivefold and the dollar-yen exchange rate had more than doubled.

As environmental turbulence has increased, therefore, so too has the need for strategic and operational flexibility. At the extreme, this line of argument has led to predictions of a reemergence of the craft form of production to replace the scale-dominated assembly form.[7] A more typical argument has been to emphasize the need to balance scale and flexibility, through the use of modern technologies such as CAD/CAM and flexible manufacturing systems.

Scope Economies.   Relatively speaking, the concept of scope economies is much newer and less well understood. It is based on the notion that certain economies arise from the fact that the cost of the joint production (or development, or distribution) of two or more products can be less than the cost of producing them separately.[8] Such cost reductions can take place due to many reasons—for example, resources such as information or technologies once acquired for use in producing one item may be available without cost for production of other items.

The strategic importance of scope economies arises from a diversified firm's ability to share investments and costs across the same or different value chains—a source of economies competitors without such internal and external diversity cannot match. Such sharing can take place across segments, products, or markets, and may involve joint use of different kinds of assets (see Table 3–1).

---

[6]Michael E. Porter, *Competitive Advantage: Creating and Sustaining Superior Performance* (New York: Free Press, 1985).

[7]The textile industry in Italy is a classic example of such a craft form of production. See Michael Piore and Chuck Sabel, *The Second Industrial Divide* (New York: Basic Books, 1985).

[8]For a detailed exposition of scope economies, see W. J. Baumol, J. C. Panzer, and R. D. Willig, *Contestable Markets and the Theory of Industry Structure* (New York: Harcourt Brace Jovanovich, 1982).

TABLE 3–1   Scope Economies in Product and Market Diversification

	Sources of Scope Economies	
	Product Diversification	*Market Diversification*
Shared physical assets	Factory automation with flexibility to produce multiple products (Ford)	Global brand name (Coca-Cola)
Shared external relations	Using common distribution channels for multiple products (Matsushita)	Servicing multinational customers worldwide (Citibank)
Shared learning	Shared R&D in computer and communications business (NEC)	Pooling knowledge developed in different markets (Procter & Gamble)

A diversified firm may share physical assets such as production equipment, financial resources, or brand names across different businesses and markets. For example, Ford has made major investments in flexible manufacturing systems using robots, to allow individual pieces of equipment and even whole lines to be adapted for the production of different parts, systems, and entire models. Coca-Cola is perhaps the best example of a company that has captured scope economies in a very different way through the exploitation of a single brand name across diverse markets.

A second important source of scope economies is shared external relations with customers, suppliers, distributors, governments, and other institutions. A multinational bank like Citibank can provide relatively more effective service to a multinational customer than can a bank that operates in a single country. Similarly, as argued by Professors Hamel and Prahalad (see reading in this chapter), companies such as Matsushita have benefited considerably from their ability to market a diverse range of products (radios, TVs, tape recorders, VCRs) through the same distribution channel. In another variation, Japanese trading companies have expanded into new businesses to meet different requirements of their existing customers.

The third important component of scope economies is shared knowledge. The fundamental thrust of NEC's global strategy is "C&C"—computers and communication. The company firmly believes that its even strengths in the two technologies and resulting capabilities of merging them in-house to create new products give it a competitive edge over global giants such as IBM and AT&T who have technological strength in only one of these two areas. Another example of the scope advantages of shared learning is the case of Liquid Tide described earlier in this chapter.

Even scope economies, however, may not be costless. Different segments, products, or markets of a diversified company face different environmental demands. To succeed, a firm needs to differentiate its management systems and processes so that each of its activities can develop external consistency with the requirements of its own environment. The search for scope economies, on the other hand, is a search for internal consistencies within the firm and across its different activities. The effort to create such internal synergies may result in some compromise with the search for external consistency in each activity.

However, even where a company is able to achieve internal synergies while meeting the external needs, the organizational cost of doing so may exceed the economic benefits. The strains of leveraging existing capabilities to meet new product and market needs can sometimes overwhelm an organization. The appropriate lesson might be that it is unwise to attempt to capture scope economies where they require linking parts of a company's portfolio of businesses or markets that are inherently very different from each other. In a variation of this same theme, IBM has "externalized" the PC business by setting up an almost stand-alone organization, instead of trying to exploit scope benefits by integrating this business within the structure of its existing organization.

Mapping Ends and Means: Building Blocks for Worldwide Advantage

Table 3–2 shows a mapping of the different goals and the different means for achieving worldwide competitiveness. Each goals-means intersection suggests some of the factors that can enhance a company's strategic position. The factors are only illustrative, and since they follow from our preceding arguments, they need no elaboration. It may be useful, however, to study these factors carefully and to compare them against the proposals of the different articles included in the

TABLE 3–2   Worldwide Advantage: Goals and Means

	Sources of Competitive Advantage		
Strategic Objectives	*National Differences*	*Scale Economies*	*Scope Economies*
Achieving efficiency in current operations	Benefiting from differences in factor costs—wages and cost of capital	Expanding and exploiting potential scale economies in each activity	Sharing of investments and costs across markets and businesses
Managing risks through multinational flexibility	Managing different kinds of risks arising from market- or policy-induced changes in comparative advantages of different countries	Balancing scale with strategic and operational flexibility	Portfolio diversification of risks and creation of options and side bets
Innovation, learning, and adaptation	Learning from societal differences in organizational and managerial processes and systems	Benefiting from experience—cost reduction and innovation	Shared learning across organizational components in different products, markets, or businesses

readings for this chapter. It will become apparent that each author is focusing on a specific subset of factors—essentially, some of the different goals-means combinations—and the differences among their prescriptions can probably be understood in terms of the differences in the particular aspect of worldwide competitive advantage that they focus on.

MULTINATIONAL, INTERNATIONAL, GLOBAL, AND TRANSNATIONAL STRATEGIES

In Chapter 2, we described some of the traditional approaches to managing worldwide operations that we designated multinational, international, global, and transnational strategies. The distinction among these different approaches as well as their respective strengths and vulnerabilities can be explained in terms of the different goals-means combinations we have just described.

Multinational Strategy

The multinational strategic approach focuses primarily on one of the different means—national differences—to achieve most of its strategic objectives. Companies adopting this approach try to enhance their economic efficiency primarily by focusing on the revenue side, usually by differentiating their products and services in response to national differences in customer preferences, industry characteristics, and government regulations. This leads most of such companies to depend on local-for-local innovations, a process requiring the subsidiary not only to identify local needs but also to use its own local resources to respond to those needs. Carrying out most activities within each country on a local-for-local basis also allows those adopting a multinational strategy to match costs and revenues on a currency-by-currency basis.

Many European companies such as Unilever, ICI, Philips, and Nestlé have traditionally followed this strategic model. In these companies, assets and resources historically were widely dispersed, allowing overseas subsidiaries to carry out a wide range of activities from development and production to sales and services. Their self-sufficiency was typically accompanied by considerable local autonomy. But, while such independent national units were unusually flexible and responsive to their local environments, they inevitably suffered problems of inefficiencies and an inability to exploit the knowledge and competencies of other national units.

International Strategy

Companies adopting this broad approach focus on creating and exploiting innovations on a worldwide basis, using all the different means to achieve this end. As we describe in the next chapter, MNCs headquartered in large and technologically

advanced countries often adopted this strategic approach but limited it pr
to exploiting home-country innovations to develop competitive positions abroad.
The international product cycle theory we described in Chapter 1 describes both
the strategic motivation and competitive posture of these companies: At least initially, their internationalization process relied heavily on transferring new products, processes, or strategies developed from the home country to less-advanced
overseas markets.

This approach was common among U.S.–based MNCs such as Kraft, Pfizer,
Procter & Gamble, and General Electric. While these companies built considerable strengths out of their ability to create and leverage innovations, many suffered from deficiencies of both efficiency and flexibility since they did not
develop either the centralized and high-scale operations of companies adopting
global strategies, nor the very high degree of local responsiveness that multinational companies could muster through their autonomous, self-sufficient, and entrepreneurial local operations.

Global Strategy

Companies adopting the classic global strategic approach, as we have defined it,
depend primarily on developing global efficiency. They use all the different
means to achieve the best cost and quality positions for their products.

This has been the classic approach of many Japanese companies such as Toyota,
Canon, Komatsu, and Matsushita. As several of these companies, and many others, have found, however, such efficiency comes with some compromise of both
flexibility and learning. For example, concentrating manufacturing to capture
global scale may also result in a high level of intercountry product shipments that
can raise risks of policy intervention, particularly by host governments in major
importer countries. Similarly, companies that centralize R&D for efficiency reasons often find they are constrained in their ability to capture new developments
in countries outside their home markets or to leverage innovations created by
foreign subsidiaries in the rest of their worldwide operations. And finally, the
concentration (most often through centralization) of activities like R&D and
manufacturing to achieve global scale exposes such companies to high exchange
rate risks.

Transnational Strategy

Beneath each of these traditional approaches lies some implicit assumptions on
how best to build worldwide competitive advantage. The global company assumes that the best cost position is the key source of competitiveness; the multinational company sees differentiation as the primary way to enhance performance; and the international company expects to use innovations to reduce costs,
enhance revenues, or both.

Companies adopting the transnational strategy recognize that each of these traditional approaches is partial: that each has its own merits but none represents the whole truth. To achieve worldwide competitive advantage, costs and revenues have to be managed simultaneously, efficiency and innovation are both important, and innovations can arise in many different parts of the organization. Therefore, instead of focusing on any subpart of the set of issues shown in Table 3–2, the transnational company focuses on exploiting each and every goals-means combination so as to develop efficiency, flexibility, and learning simultaneously.

To achieve this ambitious strategic approach, however, the transnational company must develop a very different configuration of assets and capabilities than is typical of the traditional multinational, international, and global company structures.

The global company tends to concentrate all its resources—often locating them in its home country—so as to exploit the scale economies available in each activity. The multinational company typically disperses its resources among its different national operations so as to be able to respond to local needs. And the international company tends to centralize those resources that are key to developing innovations, but decentralizes others to allow its innovations to be adapted worldwide.

The transnational, however, must develop a more sophisticated and differentiated configuration of assets and capabilities. It first decides which key resources and capabilities are best centralized within the home-country operation, not only to realize scale economies but also to protect certain core competencies and to provide the necessary supervision of corporate management. Basic research, for example, is often viewed as such a capability, with core technologies kept at home for reasons of strategic security as well as competence concentration. For different reasons, the treasury function or international management development responsibility may be located centrally to facilitate top-management control over these key corporate resources.

Certain other resources may be concentrated but not necessarily at home—a configuration that might be termed *excentralization* rather then *decentralization.* World-scale production plants for labor-intensive products may be built in a low-wage country such as Mexico or Singapore. The advanced state of a particular technology may demand concentration of relevant R&D resources and activities in Japan, Germany, or the United States. Such flexible specialization—or excentralization—complements the benefits of scale economies with the flexibility of accessing low input costs or scarce resources, and the responsiveness of accommodating national political interests.

Some other resources may be best decentralized on a regional or local basis, either because potential economies of scale are smaller than the benefits to be gained from greater differentiation or market responsiveness, or because of the need to create flexibility and reduce risks by avoiding exclusive dependence on a single facility. Local or regional facilities may not only afford protection against exchange rate shifts, strikes, natural disasters, and other disruptions, but also reduce logistical and coordination costs. An important side benefit provided by such facilities is the

TABLE 3–3   Strategic Orientation and Configuration of Assets and Capabilities in Multinational, International, Global, and Transnational Companies

	Multinational	*International*	*Global*	*Transnational*
Strategic orientation	Building flexibility to respond to national differences through strong, resourceful, and entrepreneurial national operations	Exploiting parent-company knowledge and capabilities through worldwide diffusion and adaptation	Building cost advantages through centralized, global-scale operations	Developing global efficiency, flexibility, and worldwide learning capability simultaneously
Configuration of assets and capabilities	Decentralized and rationally self-sufficient	Sources of core competencies centralized, others decentralized	Centralized and globally scaled	Dispersed, interdependent, and specialized

impact they can have in building the motivation and capability of national subsidiaries, an impact that can easily make small efficiency sacrifices worthwhile.

The result is a complex configuration of assets, resources, and capabilities that centralizes some resources at home, excentralizes some abroad, and distributes yet others among its many national operations. Furthermore, the company integrates these dispersed yet specialized resources through strong interdependencies. World-scale component plants in Taiwan and Mexico may supply specialized manufacturing plants in Singapore, Germany, and the United States. Furthermore, within Europe, subsidiary operations may be set up in a reciprocal supply relationship: The British subsidiary may depend on France for one range of final products, while the French depend on the British for others. By such a complex configuration, the transnational can leverage many more of the ways for building competitive advantage shown in Table 3–2 than its multinational, international, or global counterparts. Table 3–3 summarizes the differences in the asset configuration that support the different strategic approaches of the various MNC models.

WORLDWIDE COMPETITIVE ADVANTAGE: THE STRATEGIC TASKS

Having developed a framework to suggest *what* a company needs to do to build worldwide advantage, we now must confront the question of *how* a company can respond to the strategic challenges we have described. The task will clearly be very different depending on the company's international posture and history. Companies that are among the major worldwide players in their businesses must focus on defending their dominance. For companies that are smaller but aspire to worldwide competitiveness, the task is one of building the resources and capabilities needed to challenge the entrenched leaders. And, for companies that are focused on their national markets and lack either the resources or the motivation for international expansion, the challenge is to protect their domestic positions from others that have the advantage of being MNCs.

Defending Worldwide Dominance

The new environmental forces we have described resulted in severe difficulties even for those MNCs that had enjoyed strong historical positions in their businesses worldwide. Typically, most of these companies pursued the traditional multinational, international, or global strategies, and their past successes were built on the fit between their specific strategic capability and the dominant environmental force in their industries. In multinational industries such as branded packaged products where forces for national responsiveness were dominant, companies such as Unilever developed strong worldwide positions by adopting multinational strategies.

In contrast, in global industries like consumer electronics or semiconductor chips, companies such as Matsushita or Hitachi built leadership positions by adopting global strategies that matched the dominant need for global efficiency to succeed in these businesses.

In the emerging competitive environment, however, these companies could no longer rely on their ability to exploit either global efficiency, multinational flexibility, or worldwide learning. As an increasing number of industries developed what we have termed *transnational characteristics,* companies faced the need to master all three capabilities simultaneously. The challenge for the leading companies was to protect and enhance the particular strength they had, while simultaneously building the other capabilities.

For many companies, the initial response to this new strategic challenge was to try to restructure the configuration of their assets and activities to develop the capabilities they lacked. Global companies with highly centralized resources sought to develop flexibility by dispersing resources among their national subsidiaries; multinational companies, in contrast, tried to emulate their global competitors by centralizing R&D, manufacturing, and other scale-intensive activities. In essence, these companies tried to find a new "fit" configuration by drastic restructuring of their existing configuration.

Such a zero-based search for the ideal configuration not only led to external problems such as conflict with host governments over issues such as plant closures, but also resulted in a great deal of trauma inside the company's own organization. The greatest problem of such an approach, however, was that it tended to erode the particular competency the company already had without adding the new strengths they sought.

The complex balancing act of protecting existing advantages while building new ones required companies to follow two fairly simple principles. First, they had to concentrate at least as much on defending and reinforcing their existing assets and capabilities as on developing new ones. Instead of launching crash programs for structural change, these companies adopted a much longer-term vision of the changes that were required and a much more gradual process of managing those changes with the least possible disruption of ongoing activities. Their approach tended to be one of building on—and eventually modifying—their existing infrastructure instead of radical restructuring. To the extent possible, they relied on modernizing existing facilities rather than dismantling the old and creating new ones.

Second, to the extent that they needed to create new capabilities, these companies looked first for ways to compensate for their deficiency or approximate a competitor's source of advantage, rather than trying to imitate its asset structure or task configuration. In searching for efficiency, multinational companies with a decentralized and dispersed resource structure found it easier to develop efficiency by adopting new flexible manufacturing technologies in some of their existing plants in relatively high-cost countries than to close those plants and shift production to low-cost countries to match the structure of competing global companies. Similarly, global companies found it more effective to develop responsiveness and flexibility by creating internal linkages between their national sales subsidiaries and their centralized development or manufacturing units than by dispersing their resources to each country operation that would strongly undermine their core strength of efficiency.

Challenging the Global Leader

Over the last two decades, a number of U.S., European, and Japanese companies have managed to evolve from relatively small national players to major worldwide competitors, challenging the dominance of traditional leaders in their businesses. Digital Equipment Corporation (DEC) in the computer industry, Electrolux in the domestic appliances business, and Komatsu in the earth-moving equipment industry are some examples of companies that have evolved from relative obscurity to global visibility within relatively short periods of time.

The actual processes adopted to manage such dramatic transformations vary widely from company to company. Electrolux, for example, grew almost exclusively through acquisitions while DEC and Komatsu built their capabilities largely through internal development. Similarly, while Komatsu built its growth on the basis of cost advantages, DEC expanded internationally due to its revolutionary computer architecture and technological ability to develop products and services around that concept. Despite wide differences in their specific approaches, however, most of these new champions appear to have followed a similar step-by-step approach to building their competitive positions.

Each developed an initial toehold in the market by focusing on a narrow niche—often one specific product within one specific market—and by developing a strong competitive position within that niche. That competitive position was built on multiple sources of competitive advantage rather than on a single strategic capability. Through a sequential process, each of these companies developed both cost and product quality advantages.

Next, the toehold was expanded to a foothold by limited and carefully selected expansion along both product and geographic dimensions, and by extending the step-by-step improvement of both cost and quality to this expanded portfolio. Such expansion was typically focused on products and markets that were not of central importance to the established leaders in the business. By staying outside the range of the leaders' peripheral vision, the challenger could remain relatively invisible, thereby building up its strength and infrastructure without incurring direct retaliation from competitors with far greater resources. For example, given the preoccupation of many industry leaders with upscale, high-margin products and with large, sophisticated markets in North America and Western Europe, emerging companies often focused initially on relatively low-margin products such as small-screen TV sets or subcompact cars and first entered secondary markets in Latin America, Southeast Asia, or Eastern Europe.

While developing its own product portfolio, technological capabilities, geographic scope, and marketing expertise, challengers were often able to build up manufacturing volume and the resulting cost efficiencies by becoming original equipment manufacturer (OEM) suppliers to their larger competitors. Although this allowed the larger competitor to benefit from the challenger's cost advantages, it also developed the supplying company's understanding of customer needs and marketing strategies in the advanced markets served by the leading companies.

Once these building blocks for worldwide advantage were in place, the challenger typically moved rapidly to convert its low-profile foothold into a strong permanent position in the worldwide business. Dramatic scaling up of production facilities—increasing capacity 30-fold in five years as Matsushita did for VCRs—typically preceded a wave of new-product introduction and expansion into the key markets through multiple channels and own brand names. (The Hamel and Prahalad reading in this chapter provides a more detailed description of how some companies have managed this step-by-step process of challenging and dethroning established leaders in their businesses.)

Protecting Domestic Niches

Finally, for reasons of resource or other constraints, some national companies may not be able to aspire to such worldwide expansion. Such companies are not insulated from the impact of global competition, however. Their major challenge is to protect their domestic niches from worldwide players with superior resources and multiple sources of competitive advantage.

There are three broad alternative courses of action that can be pursued by such national competitors. The first approach is to *defend* against the competitor's global advantage. MNCs do not have the exclusive rights to analyze industry trends or to influence competitive conditions. Just as MNC managers can act to facilitate the globalization of industry structure, so their counterparts in national companies can use their influence in the opposite direction. An astute manager of a national company might be able to foil the attempts of a global competitor by taking action to influence industry structure or market conditions to the national company's advantage. This might involve influencing consumer preference to demand a more locally adapted or service-intensive product; it could imply tying up key distribution channels; or it might mean preempting local sources of critical supplies. Many companies trying to enter the Japanese market claim to have faced this type of defensive strategy by local firms.

A second strategic option would be to *offset* the competitor's global advantage. The simplest way to do this is to lobby for government assistance in the form of tariff protection. A more ambitious approach would be to gain government sponsorship to develop equivalent global capabilities through funding of R&D, subsidizing exports, and financing capital investments. As a "national champion," the company would theoretically be able to compete globally. The normal expectation is that eventually the government supports would be unnecessary, although this rarely seems to be the reality in implementation. The French government's sponsorship of a national electronics industry and several other key sectors designated in its five-year plans provide a good example of such an approach.

The third alternative would be to *approximate* the competitors' global advantages by linking up in some form of alliance or coalition with a viable global company. Numerous such linkages have been formed with the purpose of sharing the risks and costs of operating in a high-risk global environment. By pooling or exchanging market access, technology, and production capability, smaller competitors can gain some measure of defense against global giants. One example of such an approach would be the way in which Siemens, ICL, and Amdahl have all entered into agreements and joint projects with Fujitsu to enable them to maintain viability against the classic transnational global competitor, IBM.

Case 3–1   Caterpillar Tractor Co.

It was late afternoon on the twentieth of October 1981, and a positive mood pervaded the corporate headquarters of Caterpillar Tractor Co. (Cat) in Peoria, Illinois. Preliminary reports showed that Cat, the world's largest manufacturer of earthmoving equipment (EME), was headed for the best

This case was prepared by U. Srinivasa Rangan, Research Associate, under the supervision of Associate Professor Christopher A. Bartlett.

Copyright © 1985 by the President and Fellows of Harvard College. Harvard Business School case 385-276.

financial results in its history. Sales in 1981 were projected to reach $9.2 billion, exceeding the previous high of $8.6 billion achieved in 1980, and profits were expected to jump from the previous year's $565 million to about $580 million. A top management meeting had been called by Lee Morgan, chairman and chief executive officer, to review the preliminary results and appraise Caterpillar's competitive strategy for the next several years. Morgan wanted to know what measures were required to ensure that the company's impressive performance continued.

World Earth-Moving Equipment Industry in 1981

EME represented about 70% of the dollar sales of the construction equipment industry in 1981, encompassed a diverse range of machines such as excavators, bulldozers, graders, loaders, off-highway tractors and haulers. Some of these machines were available with wheels or crawler tracks, and most were available in a wide range of sizes and horsepower (hp) ratings.

The Market

Worldwide demand for EME had doubled between 1973 and 1980. Overall the United States exported roughly one-third of its production. (See Exhibit 1 for shipments by year including exports.) Estimates of worldwide market size varied between $14 and $15 billion for 1981, depending on the type of machines included.

Besides the original equipment, the world market for parts and attachments was substantial, accounting for as much as one-third of construction machinery sales volume. Most attachments were sold along with the prime mover at the time of sale and were included in the initial sales figures. Generally, profit margins were substantially higher for parts and attachments than for whole machines.

The Users

The construction and mining industries were the key users of EME, the former representing over 60% of the market and the latter for almost 30%. Forestry accounted for the balance.

The term *construction industry* usually included work relating to buildings, dams, airports, roads, waste disposal, and so forth. The United States accounted for roughly 5% of world new-construction expenditures, or an estimated $230 billion in 1980.

EXHIBIT 1   U. S. Industry Shipments, Including Exports (number of units)

	Total Shipments					Export				
	1977	*1978*	*1979*	*1980*	*1981**	*1977*	*1978*	*1979*	*1980*	*1981**
Tractors										
Crawler	19,847	22,058	19,468	16,446	15,785	NA[†]	8,850	6,902	7,063	7,466
Wheel	2,798	6,013	4,962	6,895	4,254	1,591	2,285	2,289	1,381	1,733
Loaders										
Crawler	6,146	7,040	6,321	4,455	3,286	NA[†]	1,270	1,117	1,211	1,422
Wheel	14,331	18,214	21,628	17,103	13,168	3,626	3,352	3,213	5,710	4,645
Track Shovel	21,011	23,401	29,409	23,837	16,915	3,431	3,645	5,364	6,633	4,678
Hauler										
Rear Dump	2,816	2,330	2,486	1,877	1,930	1,007	816	1,051	1,163	1,190
Bottom Dump	60	2,775	NA[†]	3,187	2,855	NA[†]	388	NA[†]	NA[†]	NA[†]
Scrapers	4,898	5,012	4,075	2,571	2,403	1,211	1,187	1,253	1,156	1,317
Graders	6,117	7,372	7,257	7,165	5,947	2,606	2,537	2,183	3,074	3,062
Excavators										
Crawler	4,207	5,007	5,084	3,562	2,338	783	790	1,167	857	722
Wheel	855	995	645	410	460	145	150	NA[†]	66	69
Cable	214	127	165	82	60	46	46	31	62	30

*Estimated.
[†]Not available.

Source: Bureau of the Census; CIMA, *Outlook 1984*.

EXHIBIT 2   New Construction Output Indicators for the United States

| Year | Total Value | | As Percentage of GNP | | Value Per Capita Constant 1972$ | Construction Index 1972 = 100 |
	Current $ ($ bil.)	Constant $ ($ bil.)	Current $ (%)	Constant $ (%)		
1970	94.9	107.0	9.7	9.9	522	88.6
1971	110.0	116.0	10.3	10.3	560	94.8
1972	124.1	123.9	10.6	10.4	593	100.0
1973	137.9	126.9	10.6	10.1	603	108.7
1974	138.5	109.1	9.8	8.7	515	126.9
1975	134.5	97.2	8.8	7.9	455	138.4
1976	151.1	105.0	8.9	8.1	488	143.9
1977	174.0	111.3	10.9	8.3	513	156.3
1978	205.5	116.9	9.7	8.1	535	175.7
1979	229.0	114.7	9.5	7.7	520	199.0
1980	228.7	103.5	8.7	6.9	465	221.7

Source: *Construction Review,* June 1981.

Repairs and maintenance expenditures were believed to be another $75 billion worldwide.

Since 1979, the construction industry in the United States had faced a major downturn. The Commerce Department considered the industry depressed, with a 12% drop in aggregate hours worked by construction workers and a seasonally adjusted unemployment rate of 16% in late 1981. (See Exhibit 2 for some data relating to the industry.) The end of the interstate highways program in the late 1960s had shrunk the road construction market considerably.

The EME demand depended largely on the pace at which machines were substituting for labor. Thus, demand had traditionally been higher in developed countries than in developing ones. Recent trends, however, were changing the overall demand pattern. (See Table A.) Since the mid-1970s, the oil-rich Middle Eastern countries had witnessed a massive rise in construction activity. Among the less developed countries (LDCs) in general, considerable potential existed, since they required extensive infrastructure. Many, however, faced financing problems.

The construction industry was highly concentrated and U.S. dominated—although both these characteristics were changing. All of the industrialized nations had indigenous construction capabilities, and many had successfully expanded their operations overseas. Several of the "advanced developing countries" were also upgrading their construction services and entering the international market. Until recently, the U.S. contractors, who had a large domestic base and assured U.S. government-sponsored construction work abroad, had also won a

TABLE A   Worldwide Construction Expenditure (1981)

Region	Expenditure Percent	Projected Real Annual Growth Rates, 1982–1986
United States	50.0%	1%
Canada	3.5	2
Latin America	7.5	4
Europe	5.0	2
Middle East	7.5	5
Asia and Australia	26.5	6
Total	100.0%	

Source: Compiled data from various 1981 issues of *Engineering News Record* and *First Boston Research.*

large portion of the overseas construction contracts. A survey indicated that 29 companies accounted for 94% of non-U.S. construction and 54% of U.S. construction in 1980. But these firms were facing increasing competition from Third World construction firms, which tended to use their low-cost labor as their main competitive weapon, shifting work crews to construction sites worldwide. Many observers felt that non-U.S. companies were better placed to bid for and perform contracts in developing countries since they did not face curbs similar to the U.S. Foreign Corrupt Practices Act (FCPA) of 1977 which forbade U.S. companies from indulging in unethical activities such as bribery and kickbacks in overseas dealings.

Third World contractors also benefited by being more flexible. A vice president of the leading Filipino construction firm was quoted as saying that his company looked for joint ventures with local firms in developing countries, since these arrangements enabled his company "to enjoy government treatment normally reserved for indigenous contractors." Many U.S. companies also noted that foreign companies received financial and diplomatic support from their home governments when bidding and favorable tax treatment on earnings outside their own countries. The South Korean government established an overseas construction fund of about $500 million "to help finance development of new markets and technology." Similarly, India coordinated the efforts of the Indian companies in pooling information on working conditions abroad and in pooling resources for joint ventures. (See Table B for Asian success in Middle Eastern contracts in recent years. For purposes of comparison, it should be noted that as late as 1975, U.S. companies claimed more than one-third of Middle Eastern construction contracts in dollar terms.)

Usually, in overseas projects, the machinery was brought in by the sole contractor or by one of the partners in a consortium, who also took responsibility for disposing of machines at the end of the contract. Frequently the heavy equipment was sold locally or shipped to nearby markets; sometimes it was moved to another site where the operating company or members of a consortium were working.

TABLE B Middle Eastern Construction Contracts Awarded to Companies of Different Nationalities

Country or Region of Origin	1979	1980
1. Middle East	16.52%	27.38%
2. United States	16.86	6.88
3. Japan	17.32	9.89
4. France	14.84	19.67
5. West Germany	12.69	8.94
6. South Korea	9.45	12.82
7. United Kingdom	6.87	7.16
8. Eastern Europe	4.52	5.07
9. Philippines	0.93	2.19
	100.00%	100.00%
Amount (in $ millions)	$39,429	$33,967

Source: *Constructor,* January 1982.

This "overhang" of used equipment was large in the Middle East. The equipment's value was written off over varying periods, ranging from one to five years.

Construction companies all over the world operated under severe cost and time constraints. Scheduling machine use efficiently and minimizing downtime were considered vital for success, and some companies used computerized systems to schedule parts changes. In the United States, high capital and energy costs had led some construction companies to use their equipment longer, and to rent, rather than buy, more equipment.

Equipment purchase decisions were generally made by committees of high-level management and technical personnel in large construction companies, and by a few top executives in smaller ones. A survey conducted in the late 1970s indicated that the manufacturer's reputation, machine performance and dealer capability were the most important criteria for decision making, followed closely by price and parts availability.

Governments were generally more price-sensitive than contractors and placed more reliance on the manufacturer's ability to deal directly with them to provide direct maintenance and repair facilities. In many developing countries, particularly in the Far East, the major buyers were a few large, state-owned enterprises. Their bids for machines specifically sought quotations which included prices for parts needed over the next two years.

The mining industry was another important user of EME. All types of open-pit mining made use of these machines, and new markets appeared as the search for energy alternatives to oil intensified with coal, oil from oil shale sands and nuclear power. But forecasting the demand for EME in the energy sector was extremely difficult. Four countries—the United States, USSR, China, and Australia—accounted for 60% of world reserves and current production of coal. Much of the coal production was by open-pit surface mining which was less costly, but also more capital-intensive and demanded more skilled labor. The U.S. coal industry, the world's largest and most export-oriented, was operating at 77% of installed capacity in 1981. Surface mining faced many environmental constraints, as did other fuel minerals such as oil-shale-sands development and uranium mining.

Six nonfuel minerals—iron, copper, aluminum, zinc, nickel and lead—accounted for roughly three-quarters of the total value of world mineral production in 1976. Since the late 1960s, mining of these minerals in almost all the developing countries had come under state control. The related expropriations of foreign mining companies' assets had led to the development of new mines in politically safe countries like Canada and Australia. The state-owned mining enterprises, lured by very high mineral prices in the early 1970s, had also undertaken large expansion and new capacity-creation projects.

One UN study on new mine-opening expenditures concluded that between 1978 and 1990 about $12 billion (1977 dollars) would be spent annually in the developed and developing countries, of which the latter's share would be $4 billion.

Distribution

Internationally, EME manufacturers sold through dealers, who provided direct and after-sales service. Even when the sale was made direct, it was often the dealer who provided the service. The rule

of thumb was that a crawler tractor, over its six-year economic life, would require service and parts equal to its initial cost.

Normal competitive practice had been to franchise dealers by means of a separate sales agreement for each product line handled. Many manufacturers believed that a full-line franchise not only hindered dealer specialization, but also limited the manufacturer's ability to get maximum market coverage for all its products.

Because most dealerships carried their inventories on their own accounts, they were characterized by high capitalization and required relatively high dollar sales volume. Individual sales had high per unit value and generally demanded greater service than, say, agricultural equipment. Customers stressed dealer relationships and/or dealer reputation as an important factor in their purchasing decisions.

The Suppliers

The EME industry began in the late 1800s with the development of steam-powered equipment, developing as a derivative of the agricultural tractor. Except for Cat, most of the world's major EME manufacturers were also leaders in the agricultural equipment market.

Rather than high-technology breakthroughs, the industry had focused more on constant improvement of existing products to make them more energy efficient, comfortable, or suitable for specific kinds of jobs. In 1981, U.S. construction equipment manufacturers spent $432 million on sales of about $17 billion. In comparison, the automobile industry spent 4.9% of sales on R&D, and heavy machinery manufacturers 2.3%.

About two-thirds of the total product cost of construction equipment was in heavy components—engines, axles, transmissions, and hydraulics—whose manufacturing was capital intensive and highly sensitive to economies of scale. Because of the secrecy surrounding the operations of EME manufacturers, it was difficult to quantify scale effects. Some industry observers tended to compare the EME industry with the agricultural tractor industry, however, where it was estimated that the optimum scale of operation was about 90,000 units a year and the costs fell by 11% between 60,000 and 90,000 units. Although others questioned the validity of the comparison, there appeared to be general agreement that economies of scale did exist up to a level of 90,000 units, but there was considerable disagreement over the extent of cost disadvantage resulting from lower output levels.

The cost structure of a typical large bulldozer appears in Table C. Except for some highly specialized products, the basis for profitable operation was believed to be volume production. Many manufacturers had also integrated backward into components such as engines and axles. Steel purchases were particularly important since they represented approximately 15% of the product cost. Steel prices varied widely, with Japanese steel costing on average about 30% less than U.S.-made steel.

Several large developing countries, such as Mexico, Brazil, Argentina and India, had demanded at least partial manufacture of EME sold in their markets. Other countries erected nontariff barriers, such as specification requirements, that pressured EME companies to build offshore plants.

Competition

In 1981 there were seven major contenders in the EME industry and a myriad of smaller, local specialists. The majors—Caterpillar (Cat), J.I. Case (a division of Tenneco), John Deere, Clark Equipment, Fiat-Allis, International Harvester and Komatsu (of Japan)—accounted for more than 90% of dollar sales worldwide. Their market shares through the 1970s are shown in Exhibit 3.

All companies had to contend with Cat's dominance in almost all market segments. This had encouraged the smaller firms to approach these markets indirectly. As one industry participant put it, their strategy was to "nibble away, moving in as Cat moved up to bigger equipment, forcing Cat to protect its heels here and head there." Some manufacturers chose to offer a full line of only one type of product, such as loaders or scrapers, while others chose to offer one product of each type. Often competitors brought out either a larger or a smaller version of a Cat product. (The major competitors' positions in various product segments appear in Exhibit 4.)

International Harvester (IH). IH was a large U.S. firm with its basic products in three industries: heavy-duty trucks, agricultural equipment and construction equipment. In the heavy-duty truck sector (45% of sales in 1980), it faced tough competitors such as GM and Ford, who were low-cost producers in an industry where competition was often on price. In the mature and cyclical agricultural equipment sector, competition centered on having a strong dealer network. IH was second to John Deere in market share in the U.S., with 30%, compared with Deere's 36%. In 1980, 40% of IH's sales came from the farm sector. In construction equipment, IH competed head-on with Cat. It had a strong distribution system, with 70 dealers and 200 outlets worldwide, but particularly strong in Asia and in Eastern Bloc countries. After Cat, IH had the second broadest product line. It produced some components, like engines, castings, fasteners and bearings, and purchased 50-70% of its parts requirements. In 1980, IH's sales in EME were $750 million (12% of sales). IH's results in recent years had been poor, and the company was reported to be in financial difficulty.

TABLE C Cost Structure of a Large Bulldozer (Equivalent to Cat D-6)

	Percent of Cost
Labor	35.0%
Components and subassemblies	12.4
Overhead	18.0
Assembly	4.6
Purchased materials and components	49.6
Overhead	15.4
	100.0%

Source: Boston Consulting Group.

EXHIBIT 3 Market Share Positions of Major Earth-moving Equipment Producers

	1971	1972	1973	1974	1975	1976	1977	1978	1979	1980
Caterpillar*	56.0%	55.0%	53.0%	53.0%	54.4%	56.1%	53.6%	51.9%	50.0%	53.3%
Komatsu	10.3	10.9	11.6	9.0	9.2	11.3	11.8	14.3	14.8	15.2
J.I. Case	6.7	6.9	8.9	8.3	7.2	7.4	8.5	9.4	10.5	10.3
Fiat-Allis[†]	4.3	4.0	3.8	7.3	7.7	6.3	6.5	6.1	5.8	5.7
Deere	5.8	6.2	6.3	6.1	4.7	5.2	6.6	6.7	7.1	6.6
International Harvester	11.0	10.0	10.1	9.7	10.0	7.6	7.2	6.6	7.1	5.1
Clark	5.9	6.0	6.3	6.6	6.8	6.1	5.8	5.0	4.7	3.8
Total	100.0%	100.0%	100.0%	100.0%	100.0%	100.0%	100.0%	100.0%	100.0%	100.0%
IBH[‡]	—	—	—	—	0.5	0.5	0.6%	0.7	1.4	4.2
Total sales (millions)[§]	$4,063	$4,954	$6,190	$7,651	$8,840	$8,773	$10,130	$12,841	$14,027	$14,916
Year-to-year change		21.3%	24.9%	23.6%	15.5%	−0.8%	15.5%	26.8%	9.2%	6.3%
Price increase‖	4%	5%	12%	10%	18%	6%	8%	9%	11%	12%
Real growth‖	—	16	13	13	(3)	(7)	7	18	(2)	(6)

Note: The figures relating to Massey-Ferguson Limited have not been included in this table. MF held less than 2% of the market in 1980, and in the previous years, it seldom held more than 3.5%.

*Includes sales from Caterpillar-Mitsubishi joint venture net of sales to and from Caterpillar.

[†]Allis-Chalmers only prior to 1974.

[‡]IBH Holding AG—founded in 1975 with growth through acquisitions of ten European equipment manufacturers through 1980. In 1980 IBH acquired Hymac (U.K.) and Hanomag (Germany). In 1981 IBH acquired Terex from General Motors.

[§]Excludes IBH.

‖Wertheim & Co., Inc. estimates.

Source: Wertheim & Co., Inc.

EXHIBIT 4   Position of Competitors in Product Segments

	Cat	Komatsu	J.I. Case*	Int'l. Harv.	Deere	IBH†	Fiat-Allis	Clark
Backhoes‡			XXX	X	XX	XX	X	
Excavators§	XXX	XX	XX		XX			
Tractors								
Crawler over 90 hp	XXX	XX	X	XX	X	X	XX	
Crawler under 90 hp	XX	XX	XX	XX	XXX	X	X	
Wheel‖	XXX	X	X	XX	X	X	X	XX
Graders	XXX	X			XX		X	X
Loaders								
Crawler	XXX	XX	X	X	XX	X	X	
Wheel	XXX	XX	X	XX	XX	X	X	XX
Off-highway trucks#	XX	X	X	XX	X	XX	X	XX
Scrapers	XXX	X		X	X	X	X	X
Other**	XXX	XX	X	XX	X	X	X	XX

Note: XXX denotes leading position; XX denotes major participation; X denotes minor participation.
*A subsidiary of Tenneco, Inc.
†IBH Holding, A.G.-founded in 1975 with growth through acquisitions of ten European equipment manufacturers through 1980.
‡Other participants include J.C. Bamford in the U.K., Ford Motor, and Volvo in Sweden.
§Other participants include Koehring Co., Poclain (40% owned by J.I. Case) in France, Hitachi and Mitsubishi in Japan, Orenstein & Koppel (O&K) and Liebherr in Germany, and J.C. Bamford and Priestman (Acrow) in the U.K.
‖Other participants include Ford Motor, Volvo, O&K, J.C. Bamford, and Leyland.
#Other participants include Unit Rig & Equipment Co. (private), Volvo, Euclid (Daimler-Benz), and Leyland.
**Includes skidders, compactors and attachments.

Source: Wertheim & Co., Inc.

J. I. Case.   Case was an independent farm equipment company before it was purchased by Tenneco in 1970. It had since diversified away from the very competitive, highly cyclical farm equipment industry. By 1981, construction equipment represented 67% of Case's sales. Many of the company's eleven plants in the U.S. produced components and finished products for both agricultural and construction equipment, and the same distribution channels were used to distribute both. Case's network of 1,200 independent dealers and 219 company-owned retail outlets were almost all in the United States and Canada. Its product strategy focused on a few products and offered a wide array of machines in each category. For instance, in the hydraulic excavator segment, Case offered 13 models, with horsepowers ranging from 120 to 445. This compared with Cat's offering of five models between 85 and 325 hp and John Deere's two models within the same range. Acquiring a 40% interest in Poclain of France in 1977, Case gained access to the technology of a leading hydraulic excavator producer. Poclain's European marketing subsidiaries and Brazilian excavator assembly operation came with the acquisition.

John Deere.   Deere led the world in farm equipment manufacture, offering a full line with a concentration on large horsepower tractors. More than 85% of Deere's sales of $5,450 million in 1981 came from farm equipment, and the balance from construction equipment. In the latter the company offered a full line, but only one or two models for each product. Deere reportedly has over 25% of the U.S. crawler market. The company's loyal 2,300 dealer network was a major asset, and according to one report, Deere was rapidly expanding its small base of overseas distributors. The same report said that Deere aimed to be number two in the United States in construction equipment and number four worldwide. In the farm sector, the company was reputed to be a low-cost producer. Although Deere depended heavily on outside sourcing for components, there was extensive integration of manufacturing, especially in engines, transmissions, and components linked to Deere designs and specifications. Deere had manufacturing and/or assembly operations in a number of countries, including France, Germany, Brazil, South Africa, Australia, and Spain, although only the French operation was related to construction equipment. Deere spent heavily on R&D, devoting 4.4% of sales to it in 1981. The company had industry production "firsts" such as the dual-path hydrostatic drive for tracked equipment and microcomputers to control some transmission functions. It was implementing CAD/CAM programs to lower its manufacturing costs further.

Komatsu.   This company dominated the Japanese construction equipment industry and was the second largest EME company worldwide. It held 60% market share within Japan, but was a distant second to Caterpillar worldwide. Until the late 1960s, Komatsu had been a small Japanese EME producer with a limited line of inferior-quality products. In the mid-1960s, when Caterpillar announced a joint venture with Mitsubishi, Komatsu's management was motivated to revitalize the company. Through licensing agreements with Cummins for diesel engines, International Harvester for large wheel loaders and Bucyrus-Erie for excavator designs, the company developed its technology. With the benefit of a labor cost advantage relative to U.S. and European competitors, and the postwar Japanese construction boom, Komatsu not only survived but also prospered over the next decade. When domestic demand slowed in the mid-seventies, the company looked towards export markets. Komatsu exported mainly whole machines although, responding to government requests, it had set up as-

sembly plants in Mexico and Brazil in the 1970s. It cultivated cordial relationships with governments in communist and Third World countries.

Outside Japan, Komatsu lacked an effective dealer network. In the large U.S. market, for instance, it had to rely on nonexclusive dealerships which generally catered to small contractors. Komatsu's machines were often cheaper than Cat's. Said Lee Morgan, Cat's CEO, "Generally speaking, Komatsu's products are priced at least 10% to 15% below Caterpillar's. That says clearly what they believe our value is versus theirs."

Other Competitors.   Among other major manufacturers, Clark Equipment focused on one type of product, the loader. The company faced severe competition from low-cost producers, and the recession had not helped. Fiat-Allis competed with a full line, emphasizing heavier models. The company tended to compete on price but was not considered a serious competitive threat due to its poor reputation for quality and reliability.

Since 1975, a new German-based company, IBH Holding Company (IBH), burgeoned. It had been put together through the acquisition of a handful of money-losing French, German, and American operations by a 37-year-old entrepreneur and Harvard MBA, Dieter Esch. He planned to make the company a full-line competitor and felt that it would be "the No. 2 company in the industry after Caterpillar." In early 1981 IBH acquired Terex Corporation, a GM subsidiary that specialized in making a wide range of EME, giving IBH a much-needed U.S. manufacturing and marketing base. Only six months after the acquisition, IBH had already turned Terex around. IBH had integrated several sets of distributors (some 600 worldwide) and found it difficult to manage spare parts inventories and to keep service levels high. Moreover, IBH did not make most parts itself, and it had an equity base of only $70 million.

Besides these larger companies, smaller national competitors were particularly strong in some countries. J.C. Bamford, for instance, held a 40% share of the U.K. market. The company planned to increase its overseas sales, taking advantage of the falling pound sterling.

Cat's Background

Headquartered in Peoria, Illinois, Cat was a multinational company that designed, manufactured, and marketed products in two principal categories: (1) earth-moving, construction, and materials-handling machinery and equipment and related parts; and (2) engines for earth-moving and construction machines, on-highway trucks, and for marine, petroleum, agricultural, industrial, and other applications, and electric power generation systems. Cat was the world's largest manufacturer of EME. Of the company's expected $9.2 billion in sales in 1981, 57% would be overseas. (See Exhibits 5, 6, and 7.) Products and components manufactured in the United States accounted for 68% of these non-U.S. sales. Cat's large geographic base and its broad product line were intended to protect it from a dependence on the domestic business cycle. Estimated parts sales represented about 35% to 45% of total revenue, although their exact contribution was never revealed by the company.

Cat's rise to global dominance stemmed from a mixture of good luck, shrewd judgment and world history. The company was fortunate to be based in the United States, where the proliferation of highways that followed the development of the auto industry led to strong demand for EME. In the late 1920s Raymond Force, a far sighted chief executive, pulled Cat out of the overcrowded farm equipment business to concentrate on this growing EME segment. World War II created tremendous demand for earth-moving machines, and the U.S. Army decided to standardize on Cat's bulldozers. From 1941 to 1944, Cat's sales tripled. When the U.S. Army withdrew from Europe and Asia after the war, it left behind the bulky machines for local use. Foreign users became familiar with Cat machines and foreign mechanics learned to service Cat equipment, thereby laying the foundation for the emergence of a formidable worldwide EME producer.

The company's management engaged in careful strategic analysis and tried to take a long-term view of its business. In more than half a century, Cat had suffered only one year of loss; and that was 1932, the height of the Depression. The strength of the company's classic strategic posture of high-quality products backed by effective service was well understood throughout the company, and management was committed to its maintenance and defense. A senior executive said in an interview: "Our management strengths are a hell of a hurdle for competitors to overcome. We not only have a strong defensible strategic position, we just know our business better than anyone else, and we work harder at it."

Marketing

Cat seized the postwar opportunity with both hands, establishing independent dealerships to service the machines left in Europe and Asia. These dealers quickly became self-sustaining, and along with the strong U.S. dealership network, they became the core of Cat's marketing strategy. In 1981, the company had 129 full-line independent dealers overseas operating 605 branches worldwide, each branch capable of providing service and spare parts backup. In the United States, the corresponding figures were 87 dealers and 284 branches. These dealers' combined net worth was nearly equal to that of Caterpillar itself (see Exhibit 8).

Cat tied the dealers close to it by enhancing their position as entrepreneurs. When one of the U.S. dealers had established a production line to rebuild Cat engines, and a shop that refurbished track shoes and other tractor parts, Cat management supported the efforts despite the fact that customers could buy rebuilt parts that lasted about 80% as long as new ones at half the cost.

Cat helped the dealers maintain appropriate inventory levels. The company established a national computer network that enabled its U.S. dealers to order any part from the central distribution depot in Illinois for delivery the next day. Cat offered to repurchase parts or equipment dealers could not sell. When introducing new products, the company first built up a two-month supply of spare parts. Cat guaranteed that if parts were not delivered within 48 hours anywhere in the world, the customer got them free.

EXHIBIT 5 Income Statement ($ millions)

Fiscal Year	1976 $	1976 %	1977 $	1977 %	1978 $	1978 %	1979 $	1979 %	1980 $	1980 %	1981* $	1981* %
Net sales	$5,042.30	(100.0)	$5,848.90	(100.0)	$7,219.20	(100.0)	$7,613.20	(100.0)	$8,597.80	(100.0)	$9,154.50	(100.0)
Cost of goods sold	3,720.20	(73.8)	4,312.00	(73.7)	5,349.30	(74.1)	5,888.50	(77.3)	6,627.10	(77.1)	6,933.30	(75.7)
SG&A†	453.20	(9.0)	489.20	(8.4)	586.00	(8.1)	662.00	(9.7)	769.50	(8.9)	868.70	(9.5)
Depreciation and amortization	184.10	(3.7)	210.50	(3.6)	257.10	(3.6)	311.80	(4.1)	370.20	(4.3)	448.40	(4.9)
Net operating income	684.80	(13.6)	837.20	(14.3)	1,026.80	(14.2)	750.90	(9.9)	831.00	(9.7)	904.1	(9.9)
Nonoperating income (Expense)	0.00		0.00		48.00		80.00		112.60		107.30	
Interest expense	42.50	(0.8)	60.10	(1.0)	111.90	(1.6)	139.10	(1.8)	173.20	(2.0)	224.80	(2.5)
Pretax income	643.30	(12.8)	779.20	(13.3)	963.20	(13.3)	725.50	(9.5)	796.70	(9.3)	802.80	(8.8)
Income taxes	260.10	(5.2)	334.10	(5.7)	396.90	(5.5)	233.90	(3.1)	231.90	(2.7)	223.90	(2.4)
Current taxes	271.60		308.30		395.90		271.60		243.50		240.30	
Deferred income taxes	(11.50)		25.80		1.00		(37.70)		(11.60)		(16.40)	
Profit after tax	383.20	(7.6)	445.10	(7.6)	566.30	(7.8)	491.60	(6.5)	564.80	(6.6)	578.90	(6.3)
Common dividends per share	$ 1.46		$ 1.58		$ 1.88		$ 2.10		$ 1.33		NA‡	

*Estimated.
†Selling, general, and administrative expenses.
‡NA means not available.

Source: Annual reports.

(continued)

EXHIBIT 5 Caterpillar Balance Sheet ($ millions) (concluded)

As of December 31:	1976	1977	1978	1979	1980	1981*
Assets						
Current assets						
Cash and equivalents	$2,096.90	$2,252.30	$2,628.30	$2,606.90	$2,932.90	$3,544.40
Receivables	88.10	209.40	244.50	147.20	104.00	81.00
Inventories	604.60	648.10	767.80	692.70	912.40	994.30
Other current assets	1,244.90	1,288.60	1,522.30	1,670.20	1,749.60	2,213.80
	159.30	106.20	93.70	96.80	166.90	255.30
Fixed assets						
Long-term investments	1,797.00	2,093.30	2,402.80	2,796.40	3,165.30	3,740.50
Net plant	78.30	72.50	58.80	35.30	103.50	120.00
Accumulated depreciation	1,698.60	1,999.10	2,281.40	2,687.80	3,008.50	3,396.20
Deferred charges	1,082.60	1,222.10	1,418.50	1,638.00	1,822.90	2,154.60
Intangibles	0.00	0.00	0.00	23.50	0.00	0.00
Other assets	0.00	0.00	0.00	0.00	0.00	146.40
	20.10	21.70	62.60	49.80	53.30	77.90
Total assets	3,893.90	4,345.60	5,031.10	5,403.30	6,098.20	7,284.90
Liabilities and stockholders' equity						
Current liabilities						
Short-term debt	821.20	955.80	1,237.10	1,386.10	1,711.50	2,369.50
Notes payable	59.90	99.90	146.90	463.20	446.60	847.60
Current long-term debt	30.90	87.30	112.60	404.20	430.30	747.00
Accounts payable	29.00	12.60	34.30	59.00	16.30	100.60
Income taxes payable	622.70	677.70	724.00	645.00	890.00	1,120.90
Other current liabilities	138.60	178.20	236.70	133.40	198.10	189.40
	0.00	0.00	129.50	144.50	176.80	211.60
Deferred taxes	11.30	36.00	23.90	0.00	23.10	97.70
Long-term debt	1,034.10	1,011.00	1,018.00	951.90	931.60	960.90
Total liabilities	1,866.60	2,002.80	2,279.00	2,338.00	2,666.20	3,428.10
Stockholders' equity	2,027.30	2,342.80	2,752.10	3,065.30	3,432.00	3,856.80
Total liabilities and net worth	3,893.90	4,345.60	5,031.10	5,403.30	6,098.20	7,284.90

*Estimated.

Source: Annual reports.

EXHIBIT 6   Distribution of Caterpillar's Overseas Sales

	1973	*1977*	*1978*	*1979*	*1980*	*1981*
Africa and Middle East	14%	30%	25%	23%	26%	36%
Asia/Pacific	12	14	17	20	19	19
Europe	50	25	27	28	26	19
Latin America	13	20	19	17	18	17
Canada	11	11	12	12	11	9
Total	100%	100%	100%	100%	100%	100%
Overseas sales as percent of Cat's total sales	49.1%	50.7%	48.1%	53.8%	57.1%	56.6%

Source: Form 10-K reports.

EXHIBIT 7   Mix of Caterpillar Sales by Third World Region ($ millions)

	1977	*1978*	*1979*	*1980*	*1981*
Latin America					
Exports from U.S.	$ 438	$ 506	$ 476	$ 617	$ 654
Sales of foreign mfd. pdt.	162	168	240	262	249
Total sales	600	674	716	879	903
Exports percent of total sales	73%	75%	66%	70%	72%
Africa/Mideast					
Exports from U.S.	$ 509	$ 497	$ 580	$ 765	$1,236
Sales of foreign mfd. pdt.	376	370	380	517	650
Total sales	885	867	960	1,282	1,886
Exports percent of total sales	58%	57%	60%	60%	66%
Asia/Pacific*					
Exports from U.S.	$ 291	$ 398	$ 528	$ 641	$ 687
Sales of foreign mfd. pdt.	119	168	236	280	239
Total sales	410	566	764	921	929
Exports percent of total sales	71%	70%	69%	70%	74%
Third World Total					
Exports from U.S.	$1,238	$1,401	$1,584	$2,023	$2,577
Sales of foreign mfd. pdt.	557	706	856	1,059	1,138
Total sales	1,795	2,107	2,440	3,082	3,715
Exports percent of total sales	65%	66%	65%	66%	69%
Caterpillar worldwide sales	$5,848	$7,219	$7,613	$8,598	$9,154
Exports to Third World percent of Cat	21%	19%	21%	24%	28%
Third World sales percent of Cat	30%	29%	32%	36%	40%

*Includes Australia and New Zealand.

Source: Form 10-K reports.

EXHIBIT 8   Data on Caterpillar Dealers in 1981

Cat Dealers	Inside U.S.	Outside U.S.	Worldwide
Full-line dealers	87	129	216
Lift-truck dealers exclusively	12	4	16
Branch stores	284	605	889
Employees	24,913	53,657	78,570
Service bays	4,708	5,117	9,825
Investment in new facilities and equipment in last five years ($ millions)	$ 375	$ 515	$ 890
Floor space added for sales, service, and parts in last five years (square feet in millions)	7.4	5.2	12.6
Total dealer floor space (square feet in millions)	16.4	16.9	33.3
Combined net worth ($ millions)	$1,400	$2,197	$3,597

Source: Annual report.

The company conducted regular training programs for dealers and product demonstrations for their customers. It even conducted a course in Peoria for dealers' children to encourage them to remain in the family business. Caterpillar's chairman summed up his company's attitude: "We approach our dealers as partners in the enterprise, not as agents or middlemen. We worry as much about their performance as they do themselves."

An average Cat dealer had a net worth of $4 million and annual sales of $100 million in the United States. The field population of Cat machines approached 20 times that of the nearest competitor. Because of his financial strength, an average dealer could expand his selling and service capabilities at the same pace that Cat expanded its product line. In 1980, Cat dealers spent more than $200 million on new buildings and equipment. No Cat dealer had failed in recent years. In fact some of the largest dealerships abroad were held by other multinationals, like General Electric (in Colombia and Venezuela) and Unilever (in Africa). Although no reliable figures were available, it was believed that dealers received a margin of 25% on list (retail)

prices of Caterpillar machines, and considerably higher margins on parts.

Cat advertised its products heavily in specialist magazines like the *Engineering News Record*. Mostly its advertisements focused on a single product, often a new introduction.

Manufacturing

The second leg of Cat's strategy was its concentration on manufacturing excellence. All Cat products were substantially the same, wherever made. Cat invested heavily in a few large-scale, state-of-the-art component manufacturing facilities—many of them near Peoria—to meet worldwide demand. The company then used these centralized facilities to supply overseas assembly plants that also added local features. Local plants not only avoided the high transportation cost of end products but also helped the company respond to the demands of local governments for manufacturing investment.

The company manufactured in 22 plants in the United States, three in the United Kingdom, two each in Brazil, Canada, and France, and one each in Australia and Belgium. It also manufactured

TABLE D Cat's Capital Expenditure Program ($ millions)

Year	Capital Expenditures	Gross Plant	Cap. Exp. as Percent Gross Plant (at previous year-end)
1981*	$713.2	$5,454.3	15.0%
1980	749.2	4,750.8	17.8
1979	675.9	4,209.7	18.6
1978	543.4	3,637.0	17.2
1977	516.5	3,165.6	18.9
1976	495.0	2,734.5	21.8
1975	446.0	2,266.9	24.0
1974	349.7	1,856.4	22.6
1973	263.7	1,543.2	20.2
1972	132.8	1,303.5	9.8
1971	123.6	1,361.1	9.9
1970	$113.2	$1,251.5	9.7%

*Estimated.

Source: First Boston.

through 50%-owned ventures in Japan and India and a 49%-owned company in Mexico. Another 50/50 joint venture was being negotiated in Indonesia. Five of the U.S. plants made mainly engines, both for incorporation into Cat's machines, and for sale to other equipment manufacturers and dealers. Five U.S. plants made only turbine-engine and related system components for Solar Turbines Incorporated, a wholly owned subsidiary. All other U.S. plants produced various EME machines.

Throughout the 1970s, Cat continued to expand its plants, although it typically operated at less than 75% capacity. In 1981 Cat had an estimated $12 billion of sales capacity (both machines and engines). To achieve break-even the company had to sell about $6.8 billion each year. According to senior management, it was better to shave profit margins in times of soft demand than to risk losing customers because shipments were late or products were poorly made. The company was highly integrated backward, with nearly 90% of its components and parts made in-house.

Cat's commitment to manufacturing excellence showed in its capital spending program. (See Table D for recent trends in capital expenditure programs.) Much of the capital spending was motivated by an internal Caterpillar study in late 1970s that concluded there was enormous growth potential in the earth-moving industry. Another aspect of this ambitious capital spending program was Caterpillar's commitment to flexible manufacturing systems. Obsolete equipment was being replaced by more up-to-date, electronically controlled equipment.

Quality control also attracted management's attention. In 1980, Cat started experimenting with quality circles, an approach that encouraged assembly line workers to form problem-solving groups to identify and analyze problems and recommend solutions. The company had also used employee newsletters to emphasize the importance of increasing productivity in order to meet foreign competition, especially from Japan.

Cat's use of automation to achieve productivity gains was not well received by its workers. In 1979, the company and the United Auto Workers union (UAW) went through an unusually bitter strike which led to an 11-week walkout by 40,000 workers in Peoria, and a 7-week stoppage at other U.S. plants. In 1980, the company laid off 5,600 workers, further souring management-labor relations. Many observers felt that labor relations was Cat's Achilles' heel. In recent press releases, Cat contended that its workers were paid an average of $20 per hour, compared to the $11 Komatsu paid its workers. Since labor costs accounted for nearly two-thirds of the value added at Caterpillar, management felt it was imperative that costs be contained. (See Table E for a comparison of the value-added structures.)

Cat's manufacturing system was not without its critics. One industry observer remarked:

> Cat's engineers are terrific in engineering but not in organizing. They know that if they let production go overseas, the U.S. operations will have to act as a buffer, causing production to yo-yo. They would prefer to use exports from the United States to keep production levels constant. Their approach is to keep volume concentrated so that they can automate and cut labor.

The observer also criticized Cat's production system, terming it as being "five years behind the production systems used in Japan" resulting in "high overheads and setup costs."

TABLE E Value-Added Structure at Caterpillar and Komatsu

	Cat	Komatsu*
Labor costs	66.4%	50.2%
Depreciation	10.2	10.4
Interest expenses	5.1	−4.8
Net income	13.2	17.1
Taxes	5.1	25.2
Other	—	1.9
Total	100.0%	100.0%

*About half of the total domestic sales of Komatsu were derived from direct sales to end-users who usually purchased machines under installment credit. This enabled Komatsu to earn interest at a rate higher than its borrowings. Further, Komatsu had substantial marketable securities as liquid assets.

Source: Nomura Securities.

Overseas Expansion

Cat's top management had developed a world view of their business. Initially, overseas dealers depended on the parts business of U.S. construction companies, shuttling machines around the world from job to job. Through its long-term commitment to international markets, however, Cat cemented its relationship with its dealers and encouraged them to devote primary attention to Cat products. The typical overseas dealer did more than half of his business in Cat's products. In the United States and Canada, the proportion was 80%.

During the 1950s and 1960s Cat opened offices in the United Kingdom, Europe, Brazil, Canada, Mexico, and Australia. It built manufacturing facilities in the United Kingdom, France, and Canada in the mid-1950s, and in Brazil, Belgium, and Australia in the early 1960s. The late 1960s saw the establishment of the Mexican joint venture. Although some of the foreign expansion was motivated by the fear of being locked out of markets through protectionist measures, most moves were the result of a management belief that wherever a market existed in an industrially advanced country, a local competitor would eventually emerge to serve it and later move abroad. Thus, unless Cat itself were on the scene, it would not be able to compete effectively.

In the early 1960s the company tried to enter the Japanese market. First it attempted to link up with Komatsu, but Komatsu wanted only a licensing agreement. Cat then began talking to Mitsubishi. Immediately, Komatsu went to the Ministry of International Trade and Industry (MITI) and asked it to block the new venture until Komatsu upgraded its product line. MITI obliged. After Komatsu had concluded a deal with Cummins Engine for the manufacture of engines under license, MITI permitted the Cat-Mitsubishi joint venture.

Because it saw its domestic and international operations as being closely linked, Cat preferred to maintain complete managerial control over all subsidiaries through 100% ownership. It agreed to joint ventures only when required by host government policies, and until 1981, had not set up a minority-owned subsidiary abroad. Furthermore, Cat ensured strategic unity in the worldwide operations by sending some of its best senior managers abroad to manage the operations of its subsidiaries. When they returned to Peoria, these managers took more of a world view of the company's operations. The executive compensation system for expatriates put considerable stress on their contribution to Cat's worldwide performance.

Cat's international marketing operations viewed the world in three parts. North and South America were served by the U.S. operation as well as by the Brazilian, Mexican, and Canadian facilities. Europe, the Middle East, and Africa were served by the European facilities. The Far East received its products from Japan, Australia, and India, although the large Australian market was served mostly from the United States. Despite these regional options, many of the large machines and a number of key components, such as transmissions, were sourced only from the United States.

This division of the world led to friction between Mitsubishi and Cat. For instance, in the 1970s an independent dealer in British Columbia imported Mitsubishi-Cat machines and started selling them at a lower price and yet making profits. The regular Cat dealer for the region complained to Peoria, and Cat management directed the Japanese venture to refrain from selling direct in North America. In Australia, a similar situation prevailed.

The company's international sales efforts were coordinated by the sales managers based in Peoria, directing Cat's field representatives who in turn, communicated with the dealers. The sales managers tried to maintain consistent worldwide pricing and dealer policies, but industry observers felt that Cat's prices in the United States were consistently higher than in overseas markets. "They have never known an acceptable return on European production—even in the best years," said one analyst. In 1981, according to the same analyst, Caterpillar's operating margin abroad was about 7% vs. 20% in the United States.

Product Development

Research and development expenditures at Cat were substantial—$363 million in 1981. Most research was targeted directly toward product development, product improvement, and applied research. Cat undertook basic research when it needed materials or components that its suppliers could not provide. For instance, it developed a beadless tire for its big loaders, then licensed the technology to Goodyear.

A senior executive summed up the company's approach to product development: "Unless a product is highly capital-intensive, will benefit from high technology, and is marketable through our current distribution system, it will not fit our product development strategy." Cat was rarely the first with a new offering, preferring to let other companies go through the trial-and-error stage, then following quickly with the most trouble-free product in the market. One of the company's vice presidents said: "Market share for us is not an objective. Building sophisticated, durable, reliable products and providing good support is." By constant adaptation, Cat engineers had created 120 different machines serving almost as many market segments.

Pricing

Cat's products were usually priced at a premium of 10% to 20% over the nearest competitive model, but management felt that its product quality and service excellence merited such a premium. It tried to avoid overpricing, and did not factor in some costs, such as new plant start-up costs, into its pricing calculations. This had meant lower profit margins in recent years of major capacity expansion. Because of Cat's uniform pricing policy, dealers all over the world were billed in dollars, irrespective of the origin of the machines. The prices were often based on U.S. manufacturing cost, but when the dollar was strong, Cat had to be flexible.

In the EME industry, a large part of the profit was in spare parts. A large crawler tractor cutting into rocks in an iron ore mine will use up parts worth as much as the original equipment within two years or so. Although Cat never revealed the data, one industry estimate was that Cat's profit margin on parts was at least twice that on original equipment.

Diversification

Cat's stated objective was to grow 6% to 7% a year in real terms throughout the 1980s. Because its domestic construction business was becoming increasingly mature, the company decided to achieve this through related diversification. In mid-1981, the company purchased the Solar Turbines Division from financially troubled IH for $505 million. Solar made turbine engines, natural gas compressors, generators and power drives; 80% of its sales went to the oil and natural gas industry with more than 50% outside the United States.

Cat's competitive strategy in engines built on a huge captive base; the company was the world's largest consumer of engines over 400 hp. In addition, since the late 1960s, it had developed and supplied engines for Ford trucks, and by 1981 supplied over a third of Ford's truck engine needs. It aimed to become the low-cost producer by using up-to-date technologies and factories. The capital expenditure record of the engines division detailed in Exhibit 9 shows the company's commitment.

Cat's purchase of Solar Turbines came 16 years after its previous acquisition (in 1965, it bought Towmotor to gain a foothold in the lift truck business). Lee Morgan explained why his company had not followed the acquisition route of competitors like Clark Equipment and Massey-Furguson:

> Most companies look at diversification as a proliferation of products in many different lines, but that misses the point. A tractor does not really care whether it works in agriculture, oil exploration, or road building, and that is the essence of diversification—being involved in many sectors of the economy.

Financial Policies

Cat was a financially conservative company with a low dependence on debt. It traditionally offered low dividend payout ratios, using retained earnings for financing. The company used the last-in, first-out (LIFO) method of inventory valuation, and treated its R&D costs as expenses in the years incurred.

Cat's balance sheet was not as tight as some competitor's due to the company's manufacturing policies. One supplier estimated that half of his and

---

EXHIBIT 9   Caterpillar Engine Division's Operating Record ($ millions)

Year Ends December 31	Net Sales	Operating Profit	Operating Margin (%)	Total Engine Sales*	Engine Division Capital Spending	Outside Sales As % Cat's Sales
1981[†]	2,049	364	17.8	2,983[‡]	410	22/24[‡]
1981[§]	1,805	389[‖]	21.6	2,492	NA	20
1980	1,400	218	15.6	2,156	214	16
1979	1,138	124	10.9	1,680	183	15
1978	1,057	234	22.1	1,644	146	15
1977	771	156	20.1	1,259	168	17
1975	482	NA	NA	NA	NA	10
1970	174	NA	NA	NA	NA	8

Note: NA means not available.
*Including internal usage at transfer price.
[†]Including Solar, estimated.
[‡]As if Solar, purchased in July 1981, had been present for a full year.
[§]Excluding; Solar, estimated.
[‖]Estimated; reflects absence of $25 million write-down at Solar after acquisition.

Source: First Boston.

Cat's work-in-progress inventory maintained by Cat and its suppliers resulted from a safety stock to guard against quality problems. In early 1981, Lee Morgan singled out the Japanese inventory control systems as one of the keys to Japanese success in manufacturing. "What the factory needs today should be either made today or delivered today."

Personnel and External Relations Policies

Cat hired only individuals who expressed a willingness to work their way up from the factory and dedicate their entire careers to the company. It hired management recruits directly from college, often people with technical degrees. As a rule, the company did not hire MBAs. Over two-thirds of Caterpillar's top executives were born in Illinois or neighboring states. Morgan joined the company in 1946, after graduating from the University of Illinois, and spent most of his career in sales. The company president, Robert Gilmore, was a forty-four-year company veteran who rose through the ranks via an apprenticeship in manufacturing after graduating from high school. The company conducted its own in-house management development programs.

This approach to recruitment and training had led to a close-knit management group (inbred in the view of critics) who worked, lived, and socialized together. They were so dedicated to their work that they were sometimes described as having "yellow paint in their veins," a reference to the ubiquitous yellow of Cat's machines. This approach was carried abroad as well. Most employees in the company's sales subsidiary in Geneva lived in one suburb referred to locally as "Caterpillar Village." In Japan, all of the company's American employees were housed in one Tokyo apartment complex and traveled to work together in one bus. This clubbiness was reinforced by the company's close-mouthed conduct of its business. It routinely refused to provide information to the press unless it thought it absolutely necessary. The same treatment was meted out to security analysts and even the industry association, the Construction Industry Manufacturers Association (CIMA). The company also discouraged its dealers from joining the Association of Equipment Distributors.

An important feature of Cat's operations was the extent to which the company dominated the economy of Illinois in general and Peoria in particular. Cat's high wages had provided the region with Illinois' third highest per-capita income. Cat was proud of its contribution to the local community, and its senior managers often reiterated the company's commitment to Peoria. In 1981, the company was in the midst of constructing a training center in downtown Peoria as well as a huge addition to its Morton worldwide parts distribution center nearby. With considerable reluctance, Cat reduced its local work force from a peak of 36,000 in 1979 to its 1981 level of 33,500. This represented over 20% of the area's work force, and was more than 15 times the payroll of Peoria's second-largest employer.

Management Systems and Style

The key element in Cat's management systems was what the company called being "severally responsible." Under this value system, all staff and operating people in a department were responsible for obtaining results. The company believed this promoted a cooperative, team-building approach. "This is no place for individual star performers," said Morgan. "We encourage an uncommon amount of subordination of personal wishes to the good of the company." In keeping with that tradition of excising the cult of personality, the public relations department put out no personal profile of Lee Morgan or any other top manager.

Cat was one of the first companies to respond constructively to the Lee emerging criticisms of multinational corporations. Morgan said: "At Caterpillar, we seek friendly, cooperative relationships with governments. To that end, we are willing to make some substantial commitments—not only in terms of capital, but also in terms of operating principles." Those operating principles were spelled out in the *Caterpillar Code of Worldwide Business Conduct,* first published in 1974, two years before the OECD guidelines on multinational enterprises came into being. The code set a high standard of behavior for its business managers and set forth the company's expectations of fair treatment by host governments.

Another aspect of Cat's management style had been its consistent willingness to take a long-term view of the company's fortunes and spend today for tomorrow's growth. Lee Morgan again: "In our business, the lead times are long. It takes ten years or more to develop and introduce a new product. To us, short-term planning means the next five years." To further the long-term approach, the company strove toward a simple management structure that encouraged easy and informal communications. Said Morgan: "The root of our organizational process is the ability of anyone to walk into my office. . . . We try to see to it that the rate of bureaucracy does not get out of hand here."

Cat had long resisted the idea of a separate corporate planning office, believing that its line managers throughout the organization understood the company's well-established strategic principles and functional policies. At the core of its strategy was a defense of its dominant competitive position through continuous product development and long-term investment in its production facilities and marketing channels.

Typically, top management decisions were arrived at by consensus. For instance, product development was monitored through a product control department comprising representatives from manufacturing, marketing, and engineering that assessed potential competition and forecast sales volumes for five years. The final decision rested with a committee composed of the chairman, some executives from his office, and several key vice presidents. "People begin bouncing ideas off one another in a series of meetings," said Morgan. "I am presumably the guy who makes the decision, but I am greatly influenced by the consensus."

There was no question, however, that Peoria dominated the entire company. Besides maintaining strong central financial and production controls, headquarters kept constant tabs on the company's operation worldwide, and no problem was considered undeserving of its attention. In fact, no management promotion above the level of department head was authorized without the chairman's personal approval.

Situation in October 1981

In late 1981 Caterpillar faced an unsettled economic environment. Since 1979, the U.S. economy had been in a downturn. The Federal Reserve's anti-inflationary tight money policy, which had raised interest rates, had severely affected the construction industry. The 1982 consensus forecast among economists predicted deeper recession and gradually declining interest rates. Having benefited from the depreciation of the dollar in the late 1970s, Cat management was also concerned about forecasts of a continued strengthening of the U.S. currency.

The 1979 oil shock had stimulated construction in some of the oil-rich countries. By late 1981, however, the oil price rise had forced a recession on non-oil-developing countries. Meanwhile, demand for crude had softened, and some economists predicted an oil glut in the 1980s. This threatened to upset the massive development plans of countries like Nigeria and Mexico.

In late 1981 much talk also circulated in the world financial press about the global debt crisis. Many large developing countries, such as Mexico, Brazil, Argentina, Nigeria, and South Korea, were facing a severe liquidity crunch, and international banks were reportedly reluctant to increase their already large exposure to LDCs. Simultaneously, developed countries were proposing reductions in foreign aid, and commodity prices were also registering steep declines.

The Far East and Australia was the only region showing hopeful signs. The ASEAN countries—Singapore, Malaysia, Indonesia, the Philippines, and Thailand—had been growing impressively over the last five years, and this trend was expected to continue. South Korea, Taiwan, and Japan were also prospering. Australia's minerals-led boom, temporarily dampened by the world recession, was expected to reassert itself through the 1980s.

In 1981 the U.S. EME industry was operating at about 60% of capacity. Capacity utilization rates for the last few years had been around 65%. In 1980, the industry had employed about 190,000 people; it was estimated that by the end of 1981, the number would have fallen to about 152,000.

Future Strategy

Morgan opened his management meeting with the news that the UAW delegates had given advance notice that in light of Cat's outstanding financial results, the union would be asking for substantial increases at next year's triennial contract negotiation. It also expected to recoup the benefits lost after the bitter 1979 strike.

As well as beginning to think about the company's approach to these demands, Morgan also wanted to engage his managers in a discussion of how Cat might respond to the changing industry and emerging competitive environment.

Case 3–2 Komatsu Limited

In late January 1985 Chairman Ryoichi Kawai of Komatsu Limited, the world's second-largest earth-moving equipment (EME) company, saw the quarterly financial results of Caterpillar Tractor Co. (Cat), its archrival. With his understanding of the industry and of his competitor's problems, he was not surprised to see Cat's losses continuing but was not expecting the figure to be so high. The $251 million fourth-quarter loss brought the company's full-year loss to $428 million, closing out Cat's third straight unprofitable year. Although it meant that Komatsu appeared to be closing in on a competitor that had dominated the industry for so long, Kawai knew his competitor well enough to understand that Cat would fight hard to regain its preeminent position.

The realization that the industry structure was changing led Kawai to reflect on Komatsu's position. Since his company had become a major player in the industry, it might be necessary to reappraise its competitive strategy. "After all," mused Kawai, "one important lesson to be drawn from Cat's decline is that success today does not necessarily imply success tomorrow."

World EME Industry

The demand for EME depended mainly on the general level of construction and mining activities, and both industries had undergone considerable change during the 1970s.[1] In the construction industry, for example, it became increasingly clear that in most developed countries the major nonrecurring construction expenditures such as highway programs, water management programs, land clearing, and housing had been largely completed. In the last quarter of the century, developing countries would probably provide most of the large remaining infrastructure projects.

Among developing countries, financing considerations played a significant part in buying decisions for all capital equipment. Further, the state sector was often a significant buyer, and for EME, the buying behavior typically stressed up-front bidding procedures that regularly included not only

---

This case was prepared by Associate Professor Christopher A. Bartlett and Research Associate U. Srinivasa Rangan.

Copyright © 1985 by the President and Fellows of Harvard College. Harvard Business School case 385-277.

[1]A detailed industry review is contained in the companion case, "Caterpillar Tractor, Co." HBS Case No. 9-385-276, and only a brief summary of the key issues is presented here.

machines but also spare parts for a period of two years or more.

The mining industry had also undergone considerable change during the 1970s. In many less developed countries (LDCs) mining belonged to the state sector. This contributed to the surplus production and widely gyrating prices of many minerals. The economic uncertainty and political instability in several of the traditional source countries caused mining companies to explore mineral development in developed countries such as Australia. In the energy sector, the oil crises of 1973 and 1979 triggered a construction boom in the Middle East, and major developments elsewhere as other sources of energy were tapped.

The worldwide EME industry had traditionally been dominated by a handful of firms, almost all of them North American. The industry giant was Cat, based in Peoria, Illinois. Throughout the 1960s and the 1970s the company held a market share of over 50%. (Exhibit 1 shows the market share trend from 1971 to 1984.) The company built an unmatched reputation for quality and service in construction equipment. Its dealer network in North America and abroad, particularly in Europe and Latin America, had been an important source of its strength. The company's carefully planned competitive strategy emphasized the building of advanced, enduring machines using components made in specialized plants (mostly in the United States), selling them at premium prices, and offering fast, high-quality field service. Cat's high point came in 1981, when the sales and profits hit record levels of $9.2 billion and $580 million, respectively.

Industry Developments Since 1981

As the U.S. recession deepened in the early 1980s, the value of contracts signed by the top 400 U.S. construction companies fell by a third from $170 billion in 1981 to $115 billion in 1983. Much of Europe and Latin America was also in the throes of a recession, and the overseas portion of U.S. construction companies' contracts fell by 45% from 1981 to 1983.

During the same period many LDCs, particularly in Latin America and Africa, faced uncertain economic environments with low commodity prices, problems associated with debt servicing and new borrowing, and recession in their principal export markets such as the United States and Western Europe. Furthermore, the softening of oil prices meant that the Middle East no longer remained the center of activity for large construction contracts as it had been in the 1970s. The only economies with much economic resilience were in the Far East.

The competition in the EME industry had intensified during this period. The substantial capacity built during the more prosperous years of the late 1970s far exceeded industry demand. IBH, a German firm formed through the acquisition of many smaller European companies, registered extraordinary growth for several years. By 1983, however, this major European competitor faced bankruptcy proceedings. International Harvester (IH), an industry veteran, was forced to sell its EME business to Dresser in 1983. Almost all the companies had suffered losses since 1981, with U.S. exporters particularly hurt by a dollar that appreciated 40% between 1981 and 1984 in trade-weighted terms.

Cat's performance, however, held the attention of most industry observers. Although it had been known to pay generous hourly rates to its workers, Cat's labor relations had deteriorated. In the October 1982 wage negotiations, the company, citing the labor cost differential of more than 45% compared with its Japanese rival, sought to contain costs. Cat's treasurer was quoted as saying, "We can handle a 10% to 15% differential but not 45%."

The United Auto Workers union (UAW) would have none of it. Citing Cat's extraordinarily good performances in prior years, the UAW demanded a share in the prosperity. However, considering the company's worries about future prospects, the UAW made what in other days would have been a generous offer: to continue the old contract for three years with cost-of-living allowances (COLAs) continued as before plus 3% raises annually, but no new add-ons. The company turned down the union

EXHIBIT 1 Market Shares of Major EME Producers

	1971	1972	1973	1974	1975	1976	1977	1978	1979	1980	1981	1982	1983	1984‖
Cat*	56.0%	55.0%	53.0%	53.0%	54.4%	56.1%	53.6%	51.9%	50.0%	53.3%	50.8%	45.7%	43.9%	43.0%
Komatsu	10.3	10.9	11.6	9.0	9.2	11.3	11.8	14.3	14.8	15.2	16.1	19.6	23.6	25.0
J.I. Case	6.7	6.9	8.9	8.3	7.2	7.4	8.5	9.4	10.5	10.3	9.7	9.9	9.6	10.0
Fiat-Allis†	4.3	4.0	3.8	7.3	7.7	6.3	6.5	6.1	5.8	5.7	5.3	5.8	4.8	4.3
Deere	5.8	6.2	6.3	6.1	4.7	5.2	6.6	6.7	7.1	6.6	5.0	4.8	5.9	6.5
International Harvester	11.0	10.0	10.1	9.7	10.0	7.6	7.2	6.6	7.1	5.1	4.7	3.5	3.3	3.0
Clark	5.9	6.0	6.3	6.6	6.8	6.1	5.8	5.0	4.7	3.8	3.2	2.9	3.1	3.5
Total	100%	100%	100%	100%	100%	100%	100%	100%	100%	100%				
IBH‡	—	—	—	—	0.5	0.5	0.6	0.7	1.4	4.2	5.3	7.8	5.8	4.7
Total industry sales (mil.)§	$4,063	$4,954	$6,190	$7,651	$8,840	$8,773	$10,130	$12,841	$14,027	$14,916	$14,788	$12,098	$10,956	$13,956
Year-to-year change	—	21.3%	24.9%	23.6%	15.5%	−0.8%	15.5%	26.8%	9.2%	6.3%	−0.9%	−23.3%	−9.4%	27.3%
Price increase‖	4%	5%	12%	10%	18%	6%	8%	9%	11%	12%	9%	5%	3%	0%
Real growth‖	—	16	13	13	(3)	(7)	7	18	(2)	(6)	(10)	(28)	(12)	27

*Includes sales from Mitsubishi-Cat joint venture net of sales to and from Cat.

†Allis-Chalmers only before 1974.

‡IBH Holding AG—founded in 1975 with growth through acquisitions of 10 European equipment manufacturers through 1980. In 1980 IBH acquired Hymac (U.K.) and Hanomag (Germany). In 1981 IBH acquired Terex from General Motors.

§Excludes IBH up to 1980 but includes it thereafter.

‖Wertheim & Co., estimates.

Source: Wertheim & Co., Inc.

proposal and stuck to its offer: no basic pay increases for three years; COLA for two of the three years but at a trimmed-down rate. Further, Cat wanted reductions in paid time off and more management flexibility in work scheduling between areas without having to consider workers' seniority.

A bitter 204-day strike (one of the largest on record against a major U.S. company) was finally broken in May 1983. Facing inventory shortages and the prospect of its dealer network not being able to meet customer demand, Cat conceded to almost all the union's demands except the additional 3% annual increase in COLA. Said one industry analyst, "The settlement will do little to ameliorate what has become a hostile relationship between Cat and the UAW."

With the strike behind it, the company was optimistic that it would post a profit in 1984. Indeed, a robust U.S. economic recovery lifted Cat's domestic sales 30% above 1983 levels. Foreign sales also increased 11% in 1984, with strong gains in Canada, Australia, Japan, and Europe offsetting overall declines in developing countries. Although total physical volume increased 26% over 1983 levels, sales revenue rose by only 21% due to "intense price competition." Cat managers blamed excess industry capacity and the strength of the U.S. dollar for this situation.

In response to continuing losses, Cat initiated a cost-reduction program in 1982, and management claimed that its 1984 costs were 14% below 1981 levels adjusted for inflation and volume. Furthermore, the company consolidated the operations of five U.S. plants and halted the construction of a national parts warehouse, resulting in 1984 write-offs of $226 million. In late 1984 management decided to close five other facilities. The full benefits of the consolidations and closings were not reflected in 1984's results, but management indicated that its efforts "could permit the company to be moderately profitable in 1985," acknowledging that this implied gaining sales at the expense of competitors. (Selected financial data for the period from 1979 to 1984 appear in Exhibit 2.)

Komatsu Limited

In 1983 Komatsu Limited, the Osaka-based Japanese company with its headquarters in Tokyo, had consolidated net sales of $3.2 billion, with 81% of the sales emanating from the EME sector and the balance from a diversified base of manufactures, such as diesel engines, presses, machine tools, industrial robots, solar batteries, and steel castings. Yet, only two decades earlier, Komatsu had been just one of many small local equipment manufacturers living in the shadow of Cat.

Background

Komatsu was established in 1921 as a specialized producer of mining equipment. The company's basic philosophy since its earliest days emphasized the need to export. The founder of the company, Mr. Takeuchi, had stressed in his management goals statement as early as 1921 the requirement for management to have two important perspectives—an "overseas orientation" and a "user orientation." A year later Komatsu acquired an electric furnace and started producing steel castings. In 1931 the company successfully produced a two-ton crawler type of agricultural tractor, the first in Japan. During the Second World War Komatsu became an important producer of bulldozers, tanks, howitzers, and so forth.

In the postwar years the company reoriented itself toward industrial EME. The company's bulldozer was much in demand in the late 1950s as Japan's postwar reconstruction started in earnest. There was little competitive pressure on Komatsu either to augment its product line or to improve the quality of products. The company president acknowledged, "The quality of our products in terms of durability during that period was only half that of the international standards." Unable to persuade dealers to sell its equipment, the company set up its own branch sales offices and authorized small local repair shops to be Komatsu service agents. Given the poor quality of the machines, it is not surprising that customers complained of the company's poor service capability. Thus, despite the booming

EXHIBIT 2 Selected Financial Data on Caterpillar ($ in millions, except per share amounts)

	1984	1983	1982	1981	1980	1979
Sales	$6,576	$5,424	$6,469	$9,154	$8,598	$7,613
Profit (loss) for year—consolidated	$(428)	$(345)	$(180)	$579	$565	$492
Profit (loss) per share of common stock	$(4.47)	$(3.74)	$(2.04)	$6.64	$6.53	$4.92
Return on average common stock equity	(138.8)%	(10.0)%	(4.9)%	15.9%	17.4%	16.9%
Dividends paid per share of common stock	$1.25	$1.50	$2.40	$2.40	$2.325	$2.10
Current ratio at year-end	1.5:1	2.5:1	2.87:1	1.50:1	1.71:1	1.88:1
Total assets at year-end	$6,223	$6,968	$7,201	$7,285	$6,098	$5,403
Long-term debt due after one year at year-end	$1,384	$1,894	$2,389	$961	$932	$952
Capital expenditures for land, buildings, machinery, and equipment	$234	$324	$534	$836	$749	$676
Depreciation and amortization	$492	506	$505	$448	$370	$312
Research and engineering costs	$345	$340	$376	$363	$326	$283
Average number of employees	59,776	58,402	73,249	83,455	86,350	89,266
Average number of shares of common stock outstanding	95,919,938	92,378,405	87,999,086	87,178,522	86,458,748	86,406,162

Source: Annual reports.

demand and the tariff-sheltered market, by 1963, Komatsu remained a puny, $168 million manufacturer of a limited line of EME, lacking technical know-how to produce sophisticated machines.

The turning point came in 1963, when the Japanese Ministry of International Trade and Investment (MITI) decided to open the EME industry to foreign capital investment. MITI felt it was necessary to continue to protect the emerging Japanese auto and electronics industries. As a quid pro quo, the EME industry was to be opened up since MITI officials believed that Japan did not possess a long-run competitive advantage in this industry. Cat decided to take advantage of the opportunity, and Komatsu was suddenly faced with a formidable competitor in its own backyard. Komatsu opposed the proposed Mitsubishi-Cat joint venture, but MITI was only willing to delay the project for two years. Yashinari Kawai, Komatsu's president, decided he must immediately take advantage of the Japanese government's policies, which demanded that foreign companies help the Japanese companies in return for access to Japan's markets. He planned to make his company a competitor of world standards.

The 1960s

In his single-minded drive for survival, Kawai set two goals: the acquisition of the necessary advanced technology from abroad and the improvement of product quality within the company. A manager who had been at Komatsu during this time recalled:

> Our mission was made very clear by the president. There was no question that the rapid upgrading of quality standards was the priority task that had to be promoted. It was the only way Komatsu could survive the crisis.

The company entered licensing arrangements with two major EME manufacturers in the United States—International Harvester and Bucyrus-Erie. The former was well known for its wheel-loader technology, and the latter was a world leader in excavator technology. Komatsu also concluded a licensing and technology collaboration agreement with Cummins Engine in the United States, which led the world in diesel engine development. Komatsu paid a substantial price for this technological access, not only in financial payments but also in restrictions on exports that it had to agree to as part of the arrangements. Recognizing that its dependence on these licensees left it vulnerable, the company established its first R&D laboratory in 1966 to focus on the application of electrical engineering developments.

Komatsu also launched a quality upgrading program in its factories. The program, one of the first to reflect the Total Quality Control (TQC) concept, was an adaptation and extension of the well-known Japanese quality-control-circles system in manufacturing operations. The objective of TQC was to ensure the highest quality in every aspect of Komatsu's operations. A company spokesperson explained, "The TQC umbrella spreads over all our activities. Virtually everything necessary to develop, to produce, and to service our products—and to keep customers around the world satisfied with those products' high performance, reliability, and durability—is incorporated into our scheme of Total Quality Control." All personnel—from top management to every worker on the assembly line—was expected to strive for TQC. Komatsu management was proud of receiving the highly coveted 1964 Deming Prize for quality control within three years of launching TQC.

In 1964 the company also began Project A. The project aimed to upgrade the quality of the small and medium-sized bulldozers, Komatsu's primary domestic market product. A top manager recalled, "The president commanded the staff to ignore the costs and produce world-standard products. He told us to disregard the Japanese Industrial Standards [JIS]." The first batch of upgraded products reached the market in 1966. The project produced spectacular results. The durability of the new products was twice that of the old ones, and despite the fact that Komatsu doubled the length of its warranty period, the number of warranty claims actually decreased by 67% from the previous level.

At this stage the company launched the second phase of Project A as cost reductions took precedence. Every aspect of design, production facilities, parts assembly, assembly-line systems, and the operation processes was subjected to thorough scrutiny, and costs were pared down. Between 1965 and 1970 the company increased its domestic market share from 50% to 65% despite the advent of the Mitsubishi-Caterpillar joint venture in Japan.

The company also benefited in other ways as reflected by the company president's comments:

> The product quality improvement activities greatly improved the quality of work within the company. A crisis atmosphere prevailed in the company when the project was being implemented, resulting in a spirit of unity between the management and staff. This was perhaps the most valuable achievement of the project.

The Early 1970s

By the early 1970s Komatsu's management sensed the need for aggressive expansion abroad. The company had achieved dominance within Japan. With domestic construction activity leveling off, however, it appeared as if the EME market was reaching maturity with little prospect of substantial growth. Meanwhile, management was aware of the rise of natural resources activities throughout the world, and particularly the construction boom in the Middle East in the post-1974 period.

Up until the 1960s the company's exports were largely based on inquiries received from abroad. The first large export order came from Argentina in 1955. During the early 1960s the company began opening a market in Eastern bloc countries. Yashinari Kawai was committed to promoting Japan's trade relations with the USSR and China. He and his son Ryoichi, a promising young Komatsu manager, conducted extensive negotiations in both countries and developed excellent relations with many high-level officials.

In the mid-1960s the company turned its attention to Western Europe. Large-scale shipments to Italy were followed by exports to other countries. In 1967 Komatsu Europe was established as a European marketing subsidiary, to better coordinate the delivery of parts and the provision of field service. In the same year the first Komatsu machines were exported to the United States. In 1970

Komatsu America was established to develop business in the huge North American market. In most of these markets Komatsu concentrated on selling a limited product line, typically crawler-tractors and crawler-loaders, which were the most common equipment on construction sites. By pricing 30% to 40% below similar Cat equipment, the company soon established a foothold in most target markets.

Unlike Cat, whose servicing dealer network covered the globe, Komatsu had no such sales and service system. Even in Japan the company was trying to supplement its company-owned branches and small repair shops with an independent dealer structure. Overseas, Komatsu found it even more difficult to establish strong sales and service capabilities. Companies with the resources and skills to be strong dealers were already locked into one of the competitive EME distribution networks. To ensure good service by those dealers it had signed up, Komatsu maintained extensive parts inventories in each country—"a deliberate overkill," according to one dealer. When it could not get dealers, however, Komatsu handled the sales function directly, at least initially. Its links with Japanese trading companies helped to locate important projects, and the company's overseas subsidiaries would often follow these up to sell directly to government agencies or large companies.

In 1972 Komatsu launched a new project called Project B. This time the focus was on the exports. The large bulldozer, the company's main export item, was chosen for improvement. The aim was similar to Project A's: to upgrade the quality and reliability of its large bulldozer models and bring them up to world standards, then work on cost reductions. Once these aims were realized, the company planned to launch similar efforts for the other lines of export products such as power shovels. Although Project B's main objective was to develop the company's overseas markets, the new machines were also offered in Japan and further reinforced Komatsu's domestic position.

The mid-1970s also saw the beginnings of efforts to penetrate the markets of LDCs, and in particular the fast-growing industrializing countries in Asia and Latin America. In 1974 the company established a new presale service department that provided assistance from the earliest stage of planned development projects in LDCs. The services that the department made available to LDCs free of cost included advice on issues such as site investigation, feasibility studies, planning of projects, selections of machines, training of operators, and so on. Komatsu also started developing its own exclusive dealer network in some of the large LDCs. In Southeast Asia and Africa, where payment terms for imported machines often involved some form of countertrade, the company also used the services of Japanese trading companies. With all these efforts, Komatsu's ratio of exports to total sales grew from 20% in 1973 to 41% in 1974 and to 55% in 1975.

During the early 1970s the company's R&D efforts continued apace with some attention to basic research as well as product development. Much of the effort, however, focused on the needs of the domestic market since the licensing arrangements constrained export efforts in some important new product areas. New excavator models were brought onto the market in this period, as were completely new products such as pipe layers, large dump trucks, and hydroshift vehicles.

The Late 1970s

By 1976 the Japanese market was highly concentrated, with Komatsu taking a 60% share and the Mitsubishi-Cat joint venture left with slightly over 30%. However, there was no indication of much market growth in the near future, since worldwide demand for construction equipment was slowing. Komatsu management decided to focus on improving the competitiveness of its products.

A four-part cost-reduction plan was initiated, the first part being dubbed the "V-10 campaign." The V-10 goal was to reduce the cost by 10% while maintaining or improving product quality. The second part of the overall plan called for reducing the number of parts by over 20%. The third part aimed at value engineering, specifically focusing on redesigning the products to gain economies in materials or manufacturing. The fourth part was a rationalization of the manufacturing system. By the end of the decade the company was well on its way to achieving all these goals.

As Komatsu planned this ambitious cost-reduction plan, an unexpected development occurred that required immediate management attention. In the fall of 1977 the Japanese yen began appreciating rapidly against most major currencies. For example, the yen/dollar exchange rate went from 293 at the end of 1976 to 240 a year later. Management responded by adopting a policy of using a pessimistic internal yen/dollar exchange rate of 180 for planning purposes. Manufacturing was responsible for achieving a cost structure that could be profitable even at this "worst-scenario" rate. After trading at a high of ¥179 to the dollar in mid-1978, the yen weakened considerably against the dollar and most other currencies in 1979 (see Figure A).

During the late 1970s Komatsu also accelerated its product development program. Between 1976 and 1981 the number of models offered in the five basic categories of EME (bulldozers, excavators, dump trucks, loaders, and graders) increased from 46 to 77. When Komatsu introduced its off-highway dump trucks and hydraulic excavators earlier than Cat, management proudly hailed the company's new leadership in technical development and innovation. "We are not content to produce the same type of equipment year after year," said one technical manager, "but are always looking at the latest technical developments and are trying to see how we can adapt them to our products." An example of this approach was the application of electronic technology to all types of machinery. Komatsu had the distinction of introducing the world's first radio-controlled bulldozer, amphibious bulldozer, and remote-controlled underwater bulldozer. These unique products were aimed at special uses such as toxic dump sites and underwater mining.

The 1980s

Until 1980 Komatsu was impeded by the narrow product line it offered abroad. According to a senior manager, the market for EME could be divided into the bidding market (dominant in most developing

FIGURE A   Currency Movements: Effective Exchange Rates (1975 average = 100)

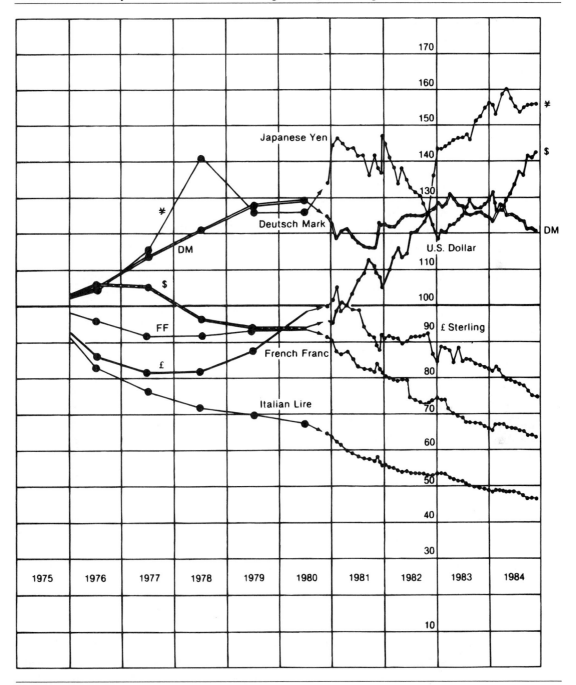

countries) and the commercial market (dominant in most developed countries). Although Komatsu's bulldozers and loaders were generally adequate to meet the needs of the former, demand in such markets was highly erratic. Any company that aspired to become a global competitor needed to gain a strong foothold in the commercial market, and to do so, it was almost a competitive necessity to be a full-line manufacturer with an extensive sales and service network.

The decision to become a full-line supplier, however, meant that Komatsu had to reevaluate its licensing relationships with technology suppliers. In exchange for help in obtaining essential know-how from Bucyrus-Erie and International Harvester for the manufacture of excavators and loaders, Komatsu signed agreements giving American licensers a tight grip over Komatsu's exports of its products and a veto over the introduction of competing products in Japan. In 1980 Komatsu objected to Bucyrus-Erie's terms restricting the export of two new products using the latter's technology. When Bucyrus demurred, Komatsu appealed to Japan's fair trade commission. After appropriate deliberations, the government agency agreed with Komatsu that it was a restrictive business practice that impaired competition. This finding allowed Komatsu to buy its way out of the contract, paying Bucyrus $13.6 million to get the data it wanted and another $6 million for royalties on the balance of the contract in May 1981. In early 1982 Komatsu had an opportunity to buy out of its obligations to International Harvester. When financially strapped Harvester was looking for cash, Komatsu bought back IH's half interest in its loader business for $52 million.

One senior manager of Komatsu summed up the approach very matter-of-factly, "Komatsu had digested its licensed technology and had established its own technology. Therefore, we just got out of the various licensing agreements." Freed of the constraints of the licensing agreements, Komatsu could sell hydraulic excavators and wheel loaders to world markets. The company emerged as a full-line competitor.

In the early 1970s Komatsu started to reorganize its distributor network worldwide, aiming to supplement the direct sales offices with more servicing dealers similar to Cat's. In 1983 the company had 8 marketing subsidiaries abroad, more than 20 overseas offices, and some 160 distributors in foreign countries. It maintained liaison offices in Havana, Warsaw, Moscow, and Peking (Beijing). In the United States, its established five regional centers for parts distribution and service. At each of these centers Japanese engineers were available to help dealers' repair departments with significant problems.

Komatsu management recognized that its 56 dealers in the United States were no match for the Cat distribution system. On average, only 30% of a Komatsu-America dealer's sales were of the company's products. Without exception, they all carried other lines as well, such as Clark and Fiat-Allis. Dealers were reluctant to become exclusive, often citing the small field population of Komatsu machines and its narrow product line. As the company broadened its product range, it began a heavy advertising campaign in specialist trade magazines, stressing its full-line capability and its product reliability.

Komatsu celebrated its sixtieth anniversary in 1981. That year it launched a new product called "EPOCHS," which stood for "Efficient Production-Oriented Choice Specifications." The project's theme was reconciliation of two contradictory demands. The aim was to "improve production efficiency without reducing the number of product specifications required by the market." The overseas expansion in the 1970s taught management that customer requirements varied widely by market and by application. For example, in Australia prospects were excellent in coal and iron-ore mining, but the tough operating requirements surpassed the capabilities of machines designed for Japanese construction applications. Komatsu responded by designing bulldozers, power shovels, and dump trucks adapted to mining conditions in Australia. To better its competition, it sent field engineers to survey Australian miners and elicited their comments and complaints about the equipment. The company then incorporated the needed improvements into its products.

As its export market increased, the company faced demands to adapt its products to suit the user requirements in different countries and diverse applications. These requirements varied with each country's environmental conditions and legal requirements. Such adaptations, however, were costly in terms of production efficiency, parts inventory, and field service management. The purpose of the EPOCHS project was to allow the company to respond to the diverse market needs without compromising its cost position.

The project focused attention on the linkages between production and marketing requirements, thereby reinforcing the spirit of TQC, which emphasized the connection between user needs and product development. The EPOCHS project led to the development of a standardized core module for major products and the required number of parts to create the market-determined variety of finished models. This approach was expected to reconcile the contradictory needs of the production and marketing departments.

By the end of 1983 the company's manufacturing had become fully integrated, producing almost all of its components and parts in-house (it was the largest producer of steel castings in Japan, for example). Komatsu prided itself on what it called the "integrated" and "concentrated" production system. From the selection of raw materials to the production and assembly of finished products, it was all part of a single, coordinated system. Further, main components of Komatsu products, regardless of size, were manufactured exclusively in individual plants.

Komatsu products were manufactured in 14 separate plants, 13 of them in Japan. The fully owned Brazilian subsidiary produced medium-sized bulldozers for Brazil and other countries in the region. In 1975 the company established a 49%-owned Mexican joint venture for the production of large-scale bulldozers for Mexico and neighboring countries.

Komatsu continued to emphasize its commitment to R&D. By 1982 four separate research labs specialized in production engineering, design

engineering, electrical applications, and electronic applications. Product development centers were located in four major plants. A new research laboratory integrating the engineering and electrical labs was in the offing in 1982. The R&D expenditures as a percentage of sales increased from 4.3% in 1981 to 5.3% in 1982 and to 5.8% in 1983. In comparison, the average for the Japanese mechanical equipment industry was 1.7% in 1982.

The R&D staff was elated when the company decided in 1981 that it was ready to participate in the International Construction Equipment Exposition (Conexpo) in Houston. Komatsu displayed some machines not previously seen—prototypes of products that would be marketed in 1982 or later. One of the main attractions at Conexpo was Komatsu's 1,000 hp bulldozer, bigger than Cat's top-of-the-line 700 hp machine. Officially, Cat's response was cool, saying that it had no plans to follow suit. But according to Komatsu managers, the most interested observers at their exhibit were Cat technicians. One Komatsu manager reportedly photographed four Cat managers examining and measuring the company's equipment at the exposition. "Ten years ago," he smiled, "we would have been the ones caught doing that."

Nonetheless, concern persisted about the depressed state of the construction industry worldwide, and Komatsu managers began talking increasingly about other business opportunities. In 1979 top management launched a companywide project called "F and F." The abbreviation stood for "Future and Frontiers," and its objective was to develop new products and new businesses. The project encouraged suggestions from all employees, asking them to consider both the needs of society and the technical know-how of the company. Management followed up on many of the 3,500 suggestions submitted, eventually leading to the development of such diverse new products as arc-welding robots, heat pumps, an excavating system for deep-sea sand, and amorphous silicon materials for efficient exploitation of solar energy.

Komatsu's R&D laboratories played an important role in this new diversification thrust, and the company planned to quadruple the number of research professionals within five years. Further, a joint research agreement with Cummins Engine provided for the sharing of information on diesel equipment improvements, including a heat pump Komatsu had developed that reportedly cut fuel costs by about 40%. The company also announced a breakthrough in developing a cast-iron alloy that was superior to the conventional aluminum alloy in heat resistance, noise generation, and fuel economy for use in high-speed diesel engines.

In the early 1980s Japanese-made industrial robots accounted for 80% of the world market, and Komatsu was already one of the top manufacturers focusing on arc-welding and material-handling robots, which it also put to use in its own factories.

Komatsu in 1984

By 1984 Komatsu managers had good reason to be proud of their company's record of the previous two decades. (See Exhibit 3 for a summary of the financial results of the company.) It still held a 60% market share in Japan, helped in part by sales to its fully owned construction and real estate subsidiaries. The company's domestic sales and service network was acknowledged to be the most extensive and efficient in Japan. Sales activities were conducted by 10 regional offices, 50 branch offices, and over 100 other sales offices. In addition, 100 independent dealers handled Komatsu products and were backed by the company's computerized parts supply system, which guaranteed a replacement part within 48 hours anywhere in the world.

Exports expanded so that they represented well over half of Komatsu's total sales in 1983. The company continued to strengthen its relationships with the Eastern bloc and had a backlog of orders for equipment for the Siberian natural resource project. The Reagan administration's embargo in December 1981 on the sale of Cat pipe-laying equipment to Russia handed the total business to the Japanese company. Komatsu also signed a contract with the Soviets to develop a scraper based on a Russian design, using Japanese components, and was collaborating with the Russians on a big crawler-dozer and dump truck. Komatsu's sales to the Soviet Union were soon expected to overtake Cat's.

Worldwide, the company's marketing efforts gathered momentum. In Australia, its products were well received in mining circles. Referring to his company's decision to buy Komatsu's machines, the managing director of one of the largest mining companies in Australia said:

> Having come to consider the market its monopoly, Caterpillar became very offhand with its customer relations. Our analysis suggested that the Komatsu machines offered significant dollar savings and outperformed the equivalent Caterpillar equipment. Komatsu's spares backup should be rated good. The operators also seemed to like the machines.

Despite competitors' suggestions to the contrary, Komatsu dealers generally denied that they were still competing mainly on price. A U.S. dealer commented:

> When you're selling against number one, you need some price advantage. But we tell contractors we can give them 10% more machine for 10% less money. That's not selling price in my book.

Although Komatsu had undoubtedly been highly successful over the previous two decades, the company's senior management felt that stagnant world demand would lead to fierce competition in the EME industry and could threaten Komatsu's growth. The internal consensus was that the existing distribution network represented a point of vulnerability. Almost inevitably, a senior Komatsu marketing executive compared his company with Cat:

> We have some gaps in our overseas sales network. Caterpillar's distribution network surpasses that of Komatsu in terms of capital, assets, number of employees, and experience. Caterpillar has greater strength in user financing and sales promotion. Indeed, some of our major dealers went bankrupt in the 1980 recession, and that taught us a major lesson about the need for financially strong dealers.

Managers hoped that Komatsu's continued efforts to produce new and differentiated products

EXHIBIT 3 Selected Consolidated Financial Data on Komatsu Limited (millions of yen)

	1984	1983	1982	1981	1980	1979	1978
Net sales	¥713,472	¥750,530	¥810,379	¥703,705	¥647,773	¥558,229	¥479,732
Net income	22,642	26,265	32,639	33,257	27,766	23,746	19,617
Earnings per common share	27.2	32.6	41.9	44.0	37.8	32.8	27.6
Cash dividends per common share	8.0	8.0	8.0	8.0	8.0	8.0	8.5
Working capital at year-end	154,466	120,829	119,695	63,705	58,469	43,496	26,927
Property, plant and equipment at year-end	157,617	143,182	134,223	120,225	110,579	107,767	110,459
Total assets at year-end	943,806	888,324	930,685	877,544	830,773	792,847	739,031
Long-term debt—less current maturities at year-end	80,722	57,442	67,731	48,443	62,755	76,925	70,871
Exchange rates				*Yen per U.S. Dollar*			
Rate at year-end	252	232	234	220	203	239	191
Average rate	239	238	248	222	225	220	204
Range of high and low rate	223–252	227–247	230–278	206–240	203–251	200–249	179–240

Note: Komatsu had a number of subsidiaries involved in construction, real estate development, overseas sales, and other activities in addition to the parent company, which was involved in earth-moving equipment manufacture.

Source: Annual reports and Form 20F reports.

EXHIBIT 4 Komatsu's Sales by Geographic Region

	1977	1978	1979	1980	1981	1982	1983
Japan	57.7%	62.4%	62.6%	56.7%	50.7%	41.8%	46.1%
Asia and Oceania	11.2	11.6	15.8	18.3	22.5	30.6	30.5
America (North and South)	18.7	15.7	12.3	11.8	11.8	7.8	7.5
Europe, Middle East, and Africa	12.4	10.3	9.3	13.2	15.0	19.8	15.9
Total	100.0	100.0	100.0	100.0	100.0	100.0	100.0

Source: Form 20F reports.

would help it to build a network of exclusive distributors overseas. Although the company could point to some progress on this objective in Europe, Asia, and Australia, it faced a much tougher task in the United States, where its market share was only 5% in 1983 (see Exhibit 4).

Responding to the demands of local governments, the company had commenced assembly operations in Brazil and Mexico. It was also working on a joint-venture proposal with its local dealer in Indonesia, where it held a 70% market share in the EME business. But Komatsu's preference had consistently been to design, manufacture, and export machines from Japan, despite the potential problems related to such a highly centralized production system. The rise of trade frictions between the European Community and the United States on the one hand and Japan on the other represented the most obvious risk in the early 1980s. A dumping complaint had been filed against Komatsu in Europe, and the EEC Commission was considering the imposition of countervailing duties. Another risk for a centrally sourced company was the possible loss of competitive position due to adverse exchange-rate movements. And finally, the logistical economics of shipping heavy equipment around the world could become a burden. According to the president of Komatsu-America Corporation, freight for bulldozers and loaders amounted to 6% to 7% of Komatsu's landed cost in the United States. For other machines it could be 10% or more.

Again, Komatsu managers compared their company with Cat:

Caterpillar has production throughout the world. It is easier for them to shift production in response to protectionism, exchange-rate fluctuations, and changes in other competitive factors. Komatsu has production plants only in a few developing countries, where it had to establish them [due to local government pressures]. Consequently, Komatsu has less flexibility in the face of changes in competitive factors.

Komatsu's market approach continued to emphasize the twin orientations toward overseas markets and consumer satisfaction laid down 60 years earlier by the founder. During the 1970s two additional themes had emerged. A senior manager described them succinctly, "The first is vertical integration based on the philosophy that you must start with good raw materials if you want to manufacture good machines. The second is the Total Quality Control [TQC] practices that pervade all our actions."

At Komatsu TQC went beyond just management practice. It epitomized management philosophy, representing the value system of the workers and managers alike. According to one top manager:

It is the spirit of Komatsu. For every issue or problem, we are encouraged to go back to the root cause and make the necessary decisions. Not only does TQC help us resolve short-run management problems, but it also lays the foundation for future growth. Thus, it is a key to management innovation.

Komatsu extended its quality commitment to its dealers and suppliers. Working closely with suppliers, the company trained them in adopting its TQC system. The dealers were also encouraged to take advantage of its offer of free services to help implement such a system in their companies. In 1981 Komatsu achieved the distinction of being awarded the Japan Quality Control Prize, considered by many to be the world's supreme quality-control honor. Furthermore, its quality-control circle at the Osaka plant had twice won gold medals from the Union of Japanese Scientists and Engineers, topping the 178,000 quality-control circles of all companies in Japan.

The management practice of relying on the TQC system was supplemented by another system called the "PDCA" management cycle. The initials stood for Plan, Do, Check, and Act. The starting point for the PDCA cycle was the long-term plan announced by the top management team, and the company president's policy statement issued at the beginning of the year. Company president Ryoichi Kawai referred to this as "management by policy." He said:

> Personally, I believe that a company must always be innovative. To this end, the basic policy and value of the target must be clarified so that all the staff members can fully understand what the company is aiming for in a specific time period. This is the purpose of the management by policy system.

The policy statements became the basis for management focus and follow-up action. As one of the managers described the PDCA system:

> A plan is made, it is executed, its results are checked, and then new actions are planned. Every activity is based on this cycle, including companywide management control systems, production, marketing, and R&D. Because of this, the corporate ability to achieve the targets set improves. These steps also improve the workers' morale and management's leadership.

The management team at Komatsu believed that the intertwined system of TQC, PDCA, and management by policy contributed to company performance and employee development. In the words of one senior manager:

> Tangible results from these systems have been twofold—increasing market share through quality improvement and productivity improvement leading to cost reduction. But equally important is the achievement of the intangibles such as improved communications among departments and setting up of clear common goals.

Ryoichi Kawai again:

> A human being donates his energy to work in order to enjoy and lead an enriched and satisfying life. . . . We think that it is necessary to satisfy the workers' monetary as well as other needs simultaneously. First of all, there is the satisfaction of achievement in work. Second, there is the satisfaction of cooperating with a colleague and receiving the approval of others. Third, there is the satisfaction of witnessing an institution grow and achieve maturity. It is satisfaction, pride, and consciousness toward participation that make workers feel that they are contributing to a great objective and are doing important work in the company.

As a result, Komatsu had a long history of good labor relations, and the company believed this had been important in its ability to improve productivity and achieve cost competitiveness. Statistics compiled by Nomura Securities showed that between 1976 and 1981 labor productivity rose at an annual compound rate of 15.2% at Komatsu compared with the 10.6% annual rate at Cat. Both companies were investing heavily in plant capital expenditure during the period.

Despite the high productivity of its workers, the average Komatsu employee earned only 55% of the wages paid to Cat employees. Together with lower raw material costs (particularly steel), this low-cost, high-productivity labor force was clearly one of Komatsu's basic assets (see Tables A and B).

Pondering the Future

It was quite in character for Ryoichi Kawai, the chairman of Komatsu, to ponder the future direction for the company that he had headed since 1964, succeeding his father, Yashinari Kawai. Like

TABLE A   Cost Structure of a Large Bulldozer
(equivalent to CAT D-6)

		Percent of Cost
Labor		35.0%
Components and subassemblies	12.4	
Overhead	18.0	
Assembly	4.6	
Purchased materials and components		49.6
Overhead		15.4
		100.0%

Source: Boston Consulting Group.

TABLE B   Steel Price Comparison: U.S./Japan ($/ton)

	U.S.	Japan*	Japan/U.S.
Hot-rolled mill coil	494	359	73%
Hot-rolled steel plate	635	445	70%

Note: Assumed yen-dollar rate is $1 = ¥220.
*Contracted price. Actual prices are often lower due to negotiations between suppliers and the users.

Source: Boston Consulting Group.

his father, he had graduated from the elite Tokyo University and had served in the government bureaucracy. He became the youngest department head in MITI's history before joining Komatsu in 1954. Like every other company executive, he had spent time with workers on the factory floor and was familiar with the company's products and production processes.

Kawai had been described in the press as a "workaholic," who often spent his lunch time at his desk partaking of the $3 box lunch from the company cafeteria. He traveled abroad frequently to pursue business deals. Although considered a mild and gentle person, he reportedly had a tight grip on the company. In an interview with *Fortune* magazine, he hinted at his philosophy of life. "In the government you are only requested to do your best. In a company, it is one's duty to earn money and pay your workers. You can't get there by just doing your best."

Kawai greatly admired Cat and often spoke of modeling his company after it. Despite his generous praise of his American competitor, however, he seemed to cherish the idea of beating Cat some day. He likened the competition to a tennis match. "As you know, in a tennis tournament, you can be losing in the middle of the game but win at the late stage." This spirit of competition with Cat pervaded the entire company. Komatsu's in-house slogan was "Maru-C," which roughly translated meant "Encircle Caterpillar." Reportedly, the company continuously monitored events in Peoria, and one of the main jobs of Komatsu's executives in the United States was to keep tabs on any and all relevant press reports. Cat's monthly in-house letter to its employees, which featured new product introductions and other company-related news, was required reading for all Komatsu executives, and copies were sent by express mail to Tokyo for analysis at the corporate headquarters.

As Kawai continued to think about the possible changes in Komatsu's competitive strategy, he kept reminding himself that complacency is one vice his company had to guard against. "Eternal vigilance is not the price of liberty alone. It is also the price of prosperity."

Case 3–3   Komatsu Ltd.: Project G's Globalization

On a breezy spring day in 1991, passers-by on the bustling street in front of Komatsu's world headquarters stopped, pointed, and stared at the spectacle atop the building. Ten stories above, workers were dismantling one of central Tokyo's most notable landmarks—a giant, yellow Komatsu bulldozer precariously perched on a tall pole. For 25 years, this corporate icon had symbolized Komatsu's overriding strategic aim to surpass Caterpillar (Cat) and become the world's premier construction equipment manufacturer.

President Tetsuya Katada had carefully timed the removal of this corporate symbol to mark recent changes in the company in preparation for Komatsu's spring celebration of its 70th anniversary. Soon, a new electronic beacon would flash a new logo and a new corporate slogan ("The Earth Company, Unlimited"), confirming the changes in strategy and management practices that Katada and his management had started to implement. The new company president explained:

> Pulling down the bulldozer is just one example showing the strong determination of the president to outsiders and, more importantly, employees that we can't single-mindedly pursue production of the bulldozer. . . . Instead, we have challenged the organization with a new slogan, "Growth, Global, Groupwide"—or "the Three Gs" for short. It's a much more abstract challenge than one focused on catching and beating Cat, but I hope it will stimulate people to think and discuss creatively what Komatsu can be.

Katada's Three Gs slogan challenged managers in all parts of Komatsu to reignite growth through a renewed commitment to global expansion, and an increase in group-wide leveraging of resources.

This case was prepared by Professor Christopher A. Bartlett.
Copyright © 1997 by the President and Fellows of Harvard College. Harvard Business School case 398-016.

For the core construction equipment business, it implied nothing less than a revolution. After three decades of focusing on the goal "to catch up and surpass Cat," this group was now being told to broaden their perspective and define the business on its own terms. In particular, Katada's challenge would require even further expansion of the company's three regionally based operations in the Americas, Europe, and Asia-Pacific. Furthermore, although several parts of this organization were new and untried, management felt it must try to integrate these operations more into a worldwide network of resources. Finally, those in Tokyo recognized that unless they began to elicit the ideas and leverage the expertise of these international operations, Project G would be little more than rhetoric.

Komatsu Company and Management History

Established in 1921 as a specialized producer of mining equipment, Komatsu expanded into agricultural machinery during the 1930s and, during the Second World War, into the production of military equipment. The heavy-machinery expertise the company developed positioned it well to expand into earth-moving equipment needed for postwar reconstruction. Soon, construction equipment dominated Komatsu's sales.

In the high-demand and capital-constrained Japanese environment, Komatsu held a market share of more than 50%, despite the low quality of its equipment at that time. This comfortable situation changed in 1963 when, after the government decided to open the industry to foreign investors, Cat announced it would enter the market in partnership with Mitsubishi. At this time, Komatsu had sales of $168 million and a product line well below world standards. Local analysts predicted three years of struggle before Cat bankrupted the puny, local company.

Emergence and Expansion: The Kawai Era (1964–1982)[1]

It was in this context that Ryoichi Kawai assumed the presidency of Komatsu from his father in 1964. The older man had prepared the company by initiating a Total Quality Control (TQC) program in 1961. Building on this base, Ryoichi Kawai's strategy for the company was straightforward—to acquire and develop advanced technology, to raise quality, and to increase efficiency to the level necessary to "catch up with and surpass Cat." To galvanize the company around his challenge and to focus management on his strategic priorities, Kawai introduced a style of management which he called "management by policy." Kawai explained the philosophy behind his strongly focused and directive approach:

> Personally, I believe that a company must always be innovative. To this end, the basic policy and value of the target must be clarified so that all the staff members can fully understand what the company is aiming for in a specific time period. This is the purpose of the management-by-policy system.

Under the umbrella of the TQC philosophy that was now deeply ingrained in Komatsu, management by policy began with Kawai's statement of an overriding, focused priority for the company. Launched the year after Cat announced its entry into the Japanese market, his first policy, "Project A," sought to raise the quality of Komatsu's middle-sized bulldozers to Cat's level. To support this goal, Kawai began an aggressive program to license technology from leading companies such as Cummins, International Harvester, and Bucyrus-Erie. As he implemented his "management by policy" approach, the young CEO instituted a new system of control, the "Plan, Do, Check, Act" (PDCA) cycle. Once Kawai announced the projects and priorities at the beginning of the year, the continuous PDCA cycle concentrated efforts within the company on attaining the broad policy objective until it was fully implemented (see Exhibit 1).

Kawai's new management approach, as reflected in Project A, was an immediate and outstanding success. Project A enabled Komatsu to double its warranty period within two years while cutting claim rates by two-thirds. And, in the face of Cat's entry into Japan, it triggered an increase in sales that raised Komatsu's market share from 50% to 65% by 1970, thereby confounding the experts' forecasts of an early demise.

An avalanche of policies followed, steering Komatsu through the turbulent environment. In response to the economic stagnation that hit Japan in 1965, Kawai targeted a "cost down" program at slashing costs. In 1966, his five-year "World A" campaign sought to make Komatsu internationally competitive in cost and quality, thus reducing Komatsu's potentially dangerous reliance on domestic sales. And, in rapid succession, Kawai launched Projects B, C, and D to improve reliability and durability in large bulldozers and shovels, payloaders, and hydraulic excavators, respectively. Throughout the 1970s, not a year went by without a major project, campaign, or program aimed at catching and surpassing Cat.

By the early 1980s, Komatsu had emerged as the major challenger in the construction equipment industry, putting Cat clearly on the defensive (see Exhibit 2). Nowhere were Cat's concerns clearer than in its 1982 annual report, which opened with a picture of a Komatsu bulldozer and a stern warning that Cat would not be able to compete against its Japanese rival at prevailing exchange and wage rates.

Struggle and Turmoil: The Nogawa Era (1982–1987)

Having guided the organization through an 18-year period of extraordinary growth, Ryoichi Kawai handed over operating leadership to Shoji Nogawa in 1982. Unfortunately for Nogawa, this date also marked the beginning of an era of falling demand, worldwide price wars, a rapidly appreciating yen,

---

[1]For a detailed description of the Kawai era, see "Komatsu: Ryoichi Kawai's Leadership," HBS case No. 390-037.

EXHIBIT 1 Company Description of "Plan, Do, Check, Act" Control Cycle

	Stage	*Actual Activities*
What is Control? The term "control" is explained in the concept of a plan-do-check-action circle. Please understand that the concept of control is practice. In short, control means the plan-do-check-action circle.	**Plan** **(P)**	• In a work shop: arranging daily operation, preparing operation standards, equipment, jigs and tools, and planning for cost reduction. • In a technical department: planning for research and establishing design policy. • In a sales department: preparation of daily or monthly sales and visiting plans according to a given target. • Working out countermeasures for any defects or debts. • Understanding the problem through facts. One must grasp the facts of the matter in order to know the problem. Never adopt false data. To grasp the facts • See the place where the problem exists. • Overserve the job and operation. • Investigate the actual problem. • Examine the data. • Listen to people. • Priority principle. Treat the gathered facts and problem points on a priority principle, stressing those which are more important in view of expected effects. The Pareto diagram described later will be very helpful. -Maximum effect with minimum labor- 70% of the problem is solved if the planning is properly done.
	Do **(D)**	Put the plan into practice and operate according to the rules and standards. This includes training on rules and standards.
	Check **(C)**	• It is your responsibility to check your own work. (Self-inspection as well as error checks for drawings, documents, and business forms produce quality products.) Do not hand trouble on to the next person. • Check the result in comparison with the plan.
	Action **(A)**	• If a result deviates from the standard, correct it. • If any abnormality is found, investigate and remove the cause, and take action to prevent its reoccurrence. (Emergency and preventive measures are necessary.)

Source: Company records.

	1991	1990	1989	1988	1987	1986	1985	1984	1983	1982	1981	1980	1979	1978	1977	1976	1975
Komatsu																	
Company sales	6,915	7,013	5,615	5,961	6,121	4,992	3,581	2,831	3,235	3,434	3,199	2,944	2,736	1,999	2,118	1,680	1,506
Construction equipment sales	4,356	4,685	3,824	4,131	4,389	3,592	3,023	2,177	2,585	2,733	2,488	2,338	2,214	1,597	1,655	1,252	1,137
Net income	82	222	173	157	79	93	110	90	113	138	141	126	116	82	66	63	60
Percent of sales outside Japan	30%	30%	31%	31%	39%	47%	49%	46%	54%	58%	49%	43%	37%	38%	42%	41%	45%
Percent of sales from construction equipment	63%	67%	68%	69%	72%	72%	76%	77%	80%	80%	81%	79%	81%	80%	76%	75%	75%
Caterpillar																	
Sales (companywide)	9,838	11,103	10,882	10,255	8,180	7,321	6,725	6,576	5,424	6,469	9,154	8,598	7,613	7,219	5,849	5,042	4,964
Net income	(404)	21	497	616	350	76	198	428	345	180	578	564	491	566	445	383	399
Percent of sales from outside the United States	59%	55%	53%	50%	48%	46%	44%	42%	46%	57%	57%	57%	54%	48%	51%	58%	57%
Sales of Other Major Construction and Agricultural Equipment Manufacturers																	
Clark Equipment	1,190	1,445	1,392	1,278	1,055	954	964	878	702	824	1,077	1,534	1,732	1,503	1,309	1,261	1,425
Deere[†] (FY Oct. 31)	5,060	6,780	6,234	5,365	4,135	3,516	4,061	4,399	3,968	4,608	5,447	5,470	4,933	4,155	3,604	3,134	2,995
Hitachi Construction Machinery (FY Mar. 31)	1,812	1,780	1,777	1,725	1,195	824	602										
Ingersoll-Rand[‡]	1,363	1,445	1,328	1,140	969	865	929	876	771	988	1,292	772	686	676	676	615	529
International Harvester[†,§]	NR	NR	NR	NR	NR	NR	NR	NR	NR	NR	NR	NR	4,069	3,200	3,065	2,930	2,992
J I Case (Division of Tenneco)	4,449	5,396	5,069	4,309	3,676	3,369	2,697	1,741	1,752	NR	NR	NR	NR	1,386	1,149	1,054	964
Shin-Caterpillar Mitsubishi (FY Mar. 31)	1,519	1,810	1,728														

NR means business segment data not reported.

*Komatsu fiscal year ended on Mar. 31 between 1989 and 1991 and on Dec. 31 between 1975 and 1987. Data from 1988 are for the period April to March and correspond with January to December of other companies.

[†] Construction and agricultural machinery segments only.

[‡] Standard machinery segment only. Includes some nonconstruction and agricultural equipment.

[§] J I Case acquired agricultural equipment division of International Harvester in 1985. Komatsu data are converted from yen-denominated data at fiscal year-end exchange rates.

Sources: Annual reports, Yamaichi Research Institute, company records, forms 10-K, Moody's Industrial Manuals, various years.

and heightened trade frictions throughout the industry.

Nogawa was an engineer who had risen through the manufacturing side of the construction equipment division. A reputed strong-willed, hands-on manager, he had high expectations of his managers, and drove them hard to meet those expectations. In spite of the growing challenges facing the industry, Nogawa was initially reluctant to change Komatsu's traditional policies, including the company's reliance on its highly efficient, centralized, global production facilities. As conditions worsened and external pressures increased (see Exhibit 3), the new president seemed to focus more on cost-cutting and aggressive pricing than on shifting production overseas or reducing Komatsu's dependence on the stagnating construction industry. As the company implemented its aggressive sales strategy worldwide, political pressure mounted. Faced with several antidumping suits, Nogawa introduced new strategic goals in 1984, including faster product introduction and expansion of nonconstruction industrial machinery businesses.

The situation reached a crisis pitch in 1985 and 1986, when the value of the yen surged alarmingly. (See Exhibit 3.) With domestic markets in turmoil, a 25% rise in the value of the yen in nine months exposed Komatsu's foreign exchange vulnerability, putting Nogawa under pressure to internationalize production more rapidly. His short-term strategy included raising prices abroad, expanding overseas parts procurement, and cutting production costs. His medium-term strategy called for developing more marketable construction equipment products through increased R&D spending and capital investments in manufacturing facilities. In the long-term, he told shareholders, "Komatsu is gearing itself toward new business areas of high-growth potential."

In addition, in 1985 he responded to the growing internal and external pressures for internationalization, approving the establishment of two important overseas plants—one in Chattanooga, Tennessee, and the other in a closed Cat facility in Birtley, United Kingdom. "As a drastic means of efficiently managing the sensitive trade friction and volatile foreign exchange environments," he told shareholders, "we have secured manufacturing bases in the world's major markets." Even after the plants were established, however, Nogawa seemed reluctant to embrace them fully into Komatsu's strategy. For example, when U.S. distributors began lobbying the head office to move additional production overseas, he rejected their proposals outright, finally relenting only when the yen appreciated even further to ¥140 per dollar.

The rising tide of problems, rapidly deteriorating results, Nogawa's apparent resistance to faster and more dramatic change, and the deleterious influence of his unpopular autocratic management style eventually resulted in his replacement. Chairman Kawai explained: "With this serious appreciation of the yen . . . we have no time to lose. We need to have a complete change in people's attitudes so that we can build a new organization, aiming at progress in the 1990s and the twenty-first century."

Steadying the Ship: The Tanaka Transition (1987–1989)

In June 1987, Ryoichi Kawai chose Masao Tanaka to replace Nogawa as president. A former general manager of the domestic sales division and, more recently, three-year general manager of the overseas division, Tanaka responded quickly to the competitive crisis in the domestic market. Chosen, in part, for his diplomatic skills, Tanaka demonstrated his conciliatory approach by emphasizing the need to end price discounting and high-pressure sales practices. In one of his many public statements on the topic, he argued:

> Market share is certainly a source of profit, but there can be no such thing as market share that ignores long-term profitability. We are trying to establish a situation where we can recoup the money spent on development and investment. If Komatsu cannot do this, there is no other company in Japan that can. If business conditions become worse, we should cover this not by carrying out a price war, but by reducing production.

Slowly, the industry responded and Tanaka's efforts culminated in a spate of collective OEM

EXHIBIT 3 Conditions for Komatsu and the Japanese Construction Industry, 1966–1990

	1990†	1989†	1987	1986	1985	1984	1983	1982	1980	1970	1966
Average exchange rate (¥/$)	158	133	121	158	200	252	232	236	204	360	360
Domestic construction investment expenditures											
¥ trillion	72.6	67.4	61.5	53.6	50.0	48.5	47.6	50.2			
percent of GNP	17.7	17.4	17.3	15.8	15.4	15.9	16.6	18.3			
Komatsu construction equipment (CE)											
¥ CE segment sales (¥ billion)	603.9	549.5	531.1	567.5	604.5	548.7	546.6	646.6	505.3	183.2	64.5
¥ Overseas CE production (percent total CE)	30.2	12.2	8.9	2.4	3.2						
¥ Overseas share of CE sales (%)	40.9	38.9	47.9	55.4	58.5	54.3	62.8	67.0	43.3	13.9	10.2
¥ Japanese CE industry, export ratio	27.2	27.8	36.2	44.2	52.3	49.9	55.1	57.0	36.8	10.6	7.6
Global unit demand (excl. Japan) for selected types of CE*											
• Bulldozers	18,000	22,000	25,000	22,000	21,000	21,000	22,000	20,000			
¥ yearly percent change	−18	−4	+14	+5	0	−5	+10				
• Hydraulic excavators	39,000	40,000	33,000	29,000	29,000	24,000	23,000	20,000			
¥ yearly percent change	−3	+8	+14	0	+21	+4	+15				
Global unit demand (excl. Japan) all types of CE	110,500	121,000	112,000	104,000	107,000	98,000	96,000	86,000			
¥ yearly percent change	−9	+3	+8	−3	+9	+2	+12				
Komatsu results:											
Sales (¥ billion)	887	793	741	789	796	713	751	810	648	264	28
Income (¥ billion)	27	21	10	15	22	23	26	33	28	13	2
Income (% of sales)	3.0	2.6	1.3	1.9	2.8	3.2	3.5	4.1	4.3	4.9	7.1

*Bulldozers are large pieces of equipment used primarily in road construction, earth moving, agricultural engineering, forestry, mining and waste management. Hydraulic excavators are lighter machinery used in these areas as well as river maintenance, building and demolition, water and sewer main construction, landscaping, and cargo-handling.

†Komatsu's results are for year ending December 31 up to 1987, and year ending March 31 from 1989 on.

Sources: MITI, company records, *Komatsu Fact Book* (various years), Yamaichi Research Institute of Securities and Economics.

supply agreements within the industry and the creation of the Japan Construction Equipment Manufacturers Association in March 1990. More important from Komatsu's perspective, restoring market order improved the bottom line. In the hydraulic excavator market segment alone, for example, while Komatsu's market share fell from 35% to 31%, overall profits rose.

Tanaka's pricing and sales policies were controversial within the company. When Komatsu developed the first mini-excavator that used advanced microelectronic controls, for example, some managers contended that with its traditional lower prices and aggressive sales methods, the company could capture a 50% market share. But Tanaka's philosophy prevailed, and the product was introduced at a 10% premium to existing prices.

Tanaka also pursued internationalization much more aggressively than his predecessor. More than internationalizing sales or market exposure, Tanaka wished to establish autonomous bases with regional capabilities in manufacturing, sales, and finance in the three core markets—Japan, the United States, and Europe. Explained Tanaka: "On the assumption that the yen will further appreciate to, let's say, ¥100 per U.S. dollar, I believe any extension of conventional measures such as management and production rationalization will no longer be effective." Extending its conservative domestic pricing strategy, in 1988 the company raised U.S. prices 7%, the seventh mark-up since September 1985. (Collectively, these represented a 40% aggregate price increase.)

Much of the driving force behind this emerging strategy came from Tanaka's director for corporate planning, Tetsuya Katada. Concerned about Komatsu's dwindling growth prospects in construction equipment and its dangerous reliance on domestic production, Katada pushed the company toward regionalizing production in Europe and the United States.

In Europe, Komatsu pursued a number of initiatives to reduce its yen exposure, respond to political pressure, and flesh out its product line. In response to an antidumping suit, the company began producing wheel loaders in its U.K. plant. It began sourcing mini-excavators for the European market—the subject of another antidumping suit—from the Italian company, FAI, using engines made by Perkins, a British diesel manufacturer. And it began sourcing articulated dump trucks from Brown (U.K.) and vibratory rollers from ABG Werke (Germany), marketing them around the world under its own name. It even imported backhoe loaders from FAI into Japan.

In the United States, the company's moves were even bolder. In September 1988, Komatsu's U.S. company entered into a 50/50 joint venture with Dresser, the American oil services company that had acquired International Harvester's constructions equipment business in 1983. The new $1.4-billion company (Komatsu Dresser Corp., or KDC) combined the U.S.-based finance, engineering, and manufacturing operations of both companies, while maintaining separate sales and marketing organizations in KDC. Using all four of the two parent companies' plants in the United States and Brazil, the joint venture produced most major construction products including hydraulic excavators, bulldozers, wheel loaders, and dump trucks.

The joint venture was controversial within Komatsu, partly because many within the company had heard the industry speculation that Dresser entered the joint venture as a means of exiting this money-losing business segment in which it had a neglected product line, lagging quality, and out-of-date plants. Furthermore, it represented a radical departure from several of Komatsu's closely held strategic maxims and traditional management policies: centralized production, total control over product development, whole ownership of subsidiaries, and Japanese management throughout the Komatsu group. In this way, the KDC deal served notice that the company was committed to a major change in the way it managed its international operations.

Entering the 1990s

New Leadership: Tetsuya Katada

In June 1989, Masao Tanaka stepped down as president and was replaced by his internationally oriented vice president of corporate planning, Tetsuya Katada. With a degree from Kyoto University of Law, Katada had risen through Komatsu's ranks in personnel, labor relations, and corporate planning. After 36 years in the company, Katada was well-known. Colleagues saw him as a "quiet and cool-headed commander," who spoke freely and honestly with superiors and subordinates alike. His introduction in the press signaled that he intended to take bold action. In response to questions about yet another change in Komatsu's leadership, the new president differentiated his strategy and style from his predecessor's:

> Mr. Tanaka placed defense above anything else in his management policy. [Defense] was necessary because of the persistent high-yen environment. I, however, will be on the offensive in my own management policy.

When pressed on his relationship with Ryoichi Kawai, Mr. Katada added: "I have never hesitated to talk straight with my superiors. . . . [Chairman] Kawai is indispensable at Komatsu. He is, however, nothing more or nothing less than an important advisor."

Questioning the Past

The situation Katada inherited was anything but promising. Despite Komatsu's recent yet belated internationalization, sales were virtually unchanged from their level seven years prior, and profits were only half those of 1982 (see Exhibit 4). This stagnation was made all the more painful by the incredible growth taking place all around Komatsu. In the same 1982 to 1989 period, while Komatsu's profits plunged, Japan's GNP grew 43%. Although the worldwide demand for construction equipment had rebounded since the 1982/1983 downturn, a simultaneous shift toward smaller, lighter, and therefore, less expensive equipment such as the hydraulic excavator and the mini-excavator had dampened the impact of the recovery (see Exhibit 5).

Worse still, worldwide industry demand was expected to dip again, at least over the next few years (see Exhibits 2 and 5). With the global political

economy in the midst of major upheaval and large-scale development projects on the wane, Katada was concerned about the stability of a strategy tightly focused on this declining sector:

> There are doubts about the future demand for construction equipment. Central and South America and Africa are having problems with accumulated debt; the Soviet Union and China also have their problems; and the price of oil is [depressing demand for construction equipment]. In the places where there is latent demand, the market is dormant. As a result, 90% of our demand is in America, Japan, and Europe. . . .
>
> We cannot hope for growth by relying simply on construction equipment. We need to take an objective look at the world economic situation and to discuss future moves within the company. In other words, I want everyone to stop concentrating simply on catching up with Caterpillar.

This call to abandon Komatsu's long-established competitive slogan surprised many observers. But Katada went even further. He openly challenged many of the company's deeply ingrained organizational processes and even much of the management philosophy that had made Komatsu the textbook example of management by "strategic intent."[2] The new president expressed his views openly:

> The company is now stagnating. It has become stereotyped and bureaucratic. The spirit of enterprise and challenge has been lost. . . . When Mr. Kawai was president, the time and our situation allowed him to employ a top-down approach to lead the company. But times have changed. . . . First, the world economy is more and more borderless, and companies must play an important role in developing international harmony. Also, the values of the young people in Japan are changing, and increasingly they question narrow, top-down directions.

A New Culture; A New Direction

Managers at Komatsu confirmed that Katada was less autocratic than prior leaders. Said one colleague, "Mr. Katada believes that one can't manage

---

[2]See Gary Hamel and C. K. Prahalad, "Strategic Intent," *Harvard Business Review,* Volume 67, Number 3, p. 63.

EXHIBIT 4 Komatsu Financial Highlights, 1982–1989 (consolidated, ¥ million)

				FY Ending Decemebr 31: (to 1987) and March 31 (1989 onward)					
	1991	1990	1989	1987	1986	1985	1984	1983	1982
Net sales	988,897	887,108	792,809	740,599	788,726	796,235	713,472	750,530	810,379
Net income	31,258	27,282	20,833	9,504	14,701	21,915	22,642	26,265	32,639
Net income per share	31.20	27.54	22.71	11.02	17.68	26.49	27.76	32.40	40.78
Total assets	1,319,189	1,230,636	1,128,957	1,027,475	983,682	1,003,560	943,806	894,549	930,685
Shareholders' equity	524,790	490,596	444,975	398,609	381,969	374,320	355,376	337,084	315,701
As a percentage of total assets (%)	39.8	39.9	39.4	38.8	38.8	37.3	37.7	37.7	33.9
Number of consolidated subsidiaries	51	43	37	37	35	36	35	33	30
Number of companies included in account	34	33	28	25	25	24	27	26	26
CE sales (as percent total sales)	63.6	68.1	69.3	71.7	71.9	75.9	76.9	72.8	79.8

Source: Komatsu, *Fact Book*, 1992.

EXHIBIT 5   Global Trends in Construction Equipment Demand by Region and Type of Equipment

	1991		*1990*		*1989*	
Region	*Number of Units*	*Growth Rate*	*Number of Units*	*Growth Rate*	*Number of Units*	*Growth Rate*
The Americas	28,000	−30%	40,000	−22%	51,000	−6%
Europe	42,000	−7%	45,000	−4%	47,000	4
Middle East and Africa	9,000	0	9,000	29	7,000	0
Asia and Oceania	13,000	−24	17,000	6	16,000	33
Total	92,000	−17	111,000	−8	121,000	3

	1991		*1990*		*1989*	
Equipment Type	*Number of Units*	*Growth Rate*	*Number of Units*	*Growth Rate*	*Number of Units*	*Growth Rate*
Bulldozers	14,000	−22%	18,000	−18%	22,000	−4%
Dozer shovels	2,000	−33	3,000	−40	5,000	−17
Wheel loaders	35,000	−10	39,000	−7	42,000	2
Hydraulic excavators	32,000	−20	40,000	0	40,000	8
Motor graders	7,000	−13	8,000	0	8,000	4
Dump trucks	2,000	−33	3,000	0	3,000	0
Motor scrapers	0	0	0	0	1,000	0
Total	92,000	−17	111,000	−8	121,000	3

Note: Figures in both tables exclude those for the Japanese market and show totals for bulldozers, dozer shovels, wheel loaders, hydraulic excavators, motor graders, dump trucks, and motor scrapers only.

Source: Komatsu, *Fact Book,* 1992.

from top down, and that any important idea or concept should be fully understood by everyone before a campaign proceeds. . . . His style of free discussion is new in Komatsu."

In keeping with his participatory style, Katada encouraged debate over the company's future direction. In off-site meetings and other forums, he invited a broad spectrum of managers to help shape Komatsu's new mission. During a June 1989 off-site meeting (billed as a "directors' free-discussion camp-out"), Katada proposed a new slogan to help crystallize the nascent consensus of the company's new strategic thrusts: "Growth, Global, Group-wide," or the "Three Gs." Katada explained:

Top-down management by policy is becoming obsolete. Although it is still useful, we can no longer

have TQC at the center of the management process. The future outlook for the industry is not bright. Managers can no longer operate within the confines of a defined objective. They need to go out and see the needs and opportunities, and operate in a creative and innovative way, always encouraging initiative from below. . . .

Although the "three G" slogan is something I came up with when I became president, there's nothing new or unusual about it given the economic conditions we were in—stagnant sales and a bureaucratic and rigidly structured company. These three simple words were intended to promote discussions, directions and policies at the board level and throughout the organization. The slogan may seem abstract, but it was this abstract nature that stimulated people to ask what they could do, and respond creatively.

1988		1987		1986	1985	1984	1983	1982
Number of Units	Growth Rate	Number of Units	Growth Rate	Number of Units	Number of Units	Number of Units	Number of Units	Number of Units
54,000	−2%	55,000	10%	50,000	50,000	45,000	35,000	23,000
45,000	15	39,000	11	35,000	33,000	30,000	30,000	28,000
7,000	−13	8,000	−20	10,000	13,000	13,000	21,000	23,000
12,000	33	10,000	11	9,000	10,000	9,000	9,000	12,000
118,000	5	112,000	8	104,000	106,000	97,000	95,000	86,000

1988		1987		1986	1985	1984	1983	1982
Number of Units	Growth Rate	Number of Units	Growth Rate	Number of Units	Number of Units	Number of Units	Number of Units	Number of Units
23,000	−8%	25,000	14%	22,000	21,000	21,000	22,000	20,000
6,000	−14	7,000	0	7,000	6,000	6,000	6,000	5,000
41,000	14	36,000	6	34,000	37,000	34,000	34,000	31,000
37,000	12	33,000	14	29,000	28,000	24,000	22,000	19,000
7,000	−13	8,000	−11	9,000	10,000	8,000	8,000	7,000
3,000	50	2,000	0	2,000	3,000	3,000	2,000	3,000
1,000	0	1,000	0	1,000	1,000	1,000	1,000	1,000
118,000	5	112,000	8	104,000	106,000	97,000	95,000	86,000

Stimulating New Initiatives

Stimulated by the new open organizational forums, and encouraged by Katada's participative and challenging management style, Komatsu executives struggled to give meaning and definition to the "Three Gs" slogan in a series of meetings that cascaded down the organization from September 1989 to March 1990. By this time, Katada and his top team were ready to formally adopt the new slogan and operationalize it in a long-term strategic plan, known as "Project G."

The most basic element of Project G was that the organization committed itself to return to growth, the first of the three Gs. Following the months of intensive negotiation and debate during 1989–1990, Katada announced that the company would aim at achieving a sales level of ¥1,400 billion by the mid-1990s—a level almost double its 1989 revenue level.

The core task in achieving this objective was to begin to grow construction equipment sales that had been stagnating (as reported in yen) since the early 1980s. This was to be the company's major globalization task—the second G—and Katada predicted that by the year 2000, the overseas operations of this business would manufacture over half of Komatsu's total output. To signal his continued commitment to his core business, Katada announced plans to triple the company's capital investment in construction equipment to ¥50 billion per annum, and challenged his managers to develop the proposals to justify that commitment.

Beyond revitalizing construction equipment, the third major element in Project G was a belief that Komatsu had to reduce its dependence on its traditional business through the groupwide leveraging of existing assets and resources to apply them to new product and business opportunities. Katada planned to encourage his organization to grow business such as electronics, robotics, and plastics, so that by the mid-1990s the nonconstruction part of Komatsu would account for 50% of its sales. (For a representation of Komatsu's diverse business holdings, see Exhibit 6.)

To communicate this new vision, Katada began referring to the company not as a construction equipment manufacturer (and certainly not as one that defined itself in terms of its old rival Caterpillar), but rather as "a total technology enterprise." And the old Japan-centered, engineering-dominated organization was now redefined in futuristic terms as "a globally integrated high-tech organization that integrates hardware and software as systems."

Globalizing Construction Equipment

The implications of Project G for Komatsu's core construction equipment business were profound. It implied a commitment to globalization that would build on and expend the thrust that had begun in the late 1980s under Katada's urging when he was director for corporate planning. Mr. Aoyama, Katada's new director for corporate planning, commented on the business's new long-term strategic objectives outside Japan:

> We don't want our strategic position to depend just on exchange rate fluctuations or the latest trade frictions. We want a stable, perpetual system of being in the construction equipment business around the world in a more integrated way, starting from development through marketing and sales.

Katada wanted to change the way the construction equipment business was managed, loosening the traditional company policy of whole ownership and control over subsidiaries to allow much more flexibility and local participation. Under his guidance, Komatsu Dresser Corporation (KDC) had not only been structured as a 50/50 joint venture, but was managed jointly. Indeed, despite the fact that it contributed half of the joint venture's equity, Komatsu asked for only two seats on KDC's 12-person board—and it asked Dresser to provide the CEO. (It did, however, still maintain equal management representation on KDC's six-person management committee that oversaw operations and decided the basic policy for the joint venture.) Katada explained the change in thinking behind the new organization:

> We have begun to doubt whether it is possible to become a "localized and international enterprise" using only the capital, management, and engineers of Komatsu. I consider the joint venture to be a combination of Japanese technology with American management and marketing. Of course, Japanese also have pride and confidence in their administrative and marketing skills, but these cannot be fully effective in an American environment. At the same time, Dresser is behind in development and capital investment, so we plan to combine Komatsu's design and development technology with American management and marketing to achieve localization.

With a major presence in North America, attention next focused on Europe. In July 1989, one month after Katada became president, Komatsu acquired an interest in the 154-year-old German niche producer of construction equipment, Hanomag. In addition, the company finalized a supply arrangement with FAI spa, the Italian producer of miniexcavators. Over the next three years, Komatsu signed no fewer than 18 agreements establishing various partnership and alliances with local firms. Again, the objective was to obtain a local marketing and management capability.

To oversee the growing number of operations, Katada agreed to the proposal to form Komatsu Europe International SA (KEISA) in November 1989 to develop a more integrated group of European

EXHIBIT 6 The Komatsu Group

The Komatsu Group consists of 185 related companies.
The list below shows the major affiliates and subsidiaries.

KOMATΣY

Domestic

Machinery manufacturing—4 companies
Komatsu Forklift Co., Ltd*
Komatsu Zenoah Co.*
Komatsu Est Corporation
Komatsu MEC Corp.

Electronics manufacturing—3 companies
Komatsu Electronic Metals Co., Ltd.
Komatsu Electronics Inc.
Unizon Corporation

Real estate, construction and housing—4 companies
Komatsu Construction Ltd.
Komatsu Plastics Industry Co., Ltd.
Komatsu House Ltd.
Komatsu Building Co., Ltd.

Materials-related business—4 companies
Tedori Heavy Industry Co., Ltd.
Komatsu Shearing Co., Ltd.
Komatsu-Howmet, Ltd.
Komatsu Metal Ltd.

Engineering-related business—9 companies
Komatsu Systex Corp.
Komatsu Cast Engineering Co. Ltd.
Komatsu Engineering Ltd.
Komatsu Seiki Ltd.
Komatsu Press Engineering Service Ltd.
Komatsu Press Technology & Service Co.
Daltex Co., Ltd.
Komatsu Tokki Corporation
Komatsu Techno Brain Ltd.

Trading—2 companies
Komatsu Trading Corporation
Komatsu Trading International, Inc.

Transport-related business—2 companies
Komatsu Logistics Corp.
Komatsu Building Unso Ltd.

Security procedures—1 company
Komatsu Security Service Co.

Software business—2 companies
Komatsu Soft Ltd.
Komatsu Tec Corp.

Personnel education—2 companies
Staff & Brain Co.
Komatsu Career Creation Ltd.

Printing and publishing—1 company
KIP Ltd.

Finance—1 company
Komatsu Finance Co., Ltd.

Service related operations—3 companies
Nihon Hananotomo Co., Ltd.
Komatsu General Services Ltd.
Komatsu Trading & Service Ltd.

Companies selling construction and industrial equipment—54 companies
31 domestic distributors
Komatsu Driving School of Construction Machinery Ltd.
Komatsu Business Support Ltd.
Komatsu VIC Ltd.
Komatsu Diesel Co., Ltd.
Komatsu Used Equipment Corp.
Komatsu Dredge System Corp.
17 other sales-related companies

*Listed companies.

Source: Company records.

Overseas

North and South America

Manufacturing and sales—6 companies
Komatsu Dresser Company
Dina Komatsu Nacional S.A. de. C.V.
Husky Injection Molding Systems, Ltd.
Danly Komatsu Limited Partnership
Komatsu Do Brasil S.A.
Komatsu-Cybermation, Inc.

Sales and other services—2 companies
Komatsu America Corp.
Komatsu America Industries Corp.

Europe

Coordination—1 company
N.V. Komatsu Europe International Corp.

Manufacturing and sales—3 companies
Komatsu UK Ltd.
Hanomag A.G.
Moxy Trucks AS

Sales—3 companies
Komatsu Europe
Komatsu Baumaschinen Deutschland G.m.b.H.
Komatsu Industries Europe G.m.b.H.

Finance—2 companies
Komatsu Overseas Finance PLC
Komatsu Finance (Netherlands) B.V.

Southeast Asia and Oceania

Manufacturing and sales—1 company
P.T. Komatsu Indonesia

Sales—3 companies
Komatsu Singapore Pte., Ltd.
Komatsu Australia Pty., Ltd.
NS Komatsu Pty., Ltd.

operations, and to coordinate the "mutual supply" of parts and increasingly specialized products. Under KEISA's guidance, for example, Hanomag took over Komatsu's U.K.'s (KUK) production of wheel loaders. This arrangement capitalized both on Hanomag's 20% share of the German market for wheel loaders and its 100-outlet-strong distribution network in Europe. It also freed KUK to specialize in hydraulic excavators. Extending the specialized sourcing network, Italian licensee FAI supplied mini-excavators to all European markets. Exhibit 7 shows the resulting regionalization and specialization that emerged.

As a result of the aggressive expansion of offshore operations, the company's overseas production of construction equipment rose from ¥11.7 billion, or 2.4% of total production in 1987, to ¥256.5 billion, or 32.5% of the total in 1991 (see Exhibit 8). This growth in offshore production, together with an overall slowdown in the market, led to a major decline in the importance of parent company export sales. Accounting for 67% of sales at its peak in 1982 Komatsu Limited's export ratio had fallen to 37.7% by 1992. Nonetheless, exports still remained an important part of Komatsu's sales to all three global regions (see Exhibit 9).

Expanding Overseas Responsibilities

Beyond developing its resource base abroad, the construction equipment management group also began to expand the roles and responsibilities of these offshore operations. With an overall vision of building a three-part, regional geographic structure, these overseas units began to develop not only manufacturing and sales functions, but also purchasing and development capabilities.

In the late 1980s, international production facilities mushroomed from a handful of offshore assembly plants to a worldwide network of sophisticated manufacturing facilities as described briefly above. Much more gradual was the shift in responsibilities for product design and development. The company's traditionally centralized development and applications policies were challenged when Hanomag's operations were found to have excellent engineering and development capabilities. The company decided to build on this asset by delegating clear development responsibility to the German company, and eliminating some duplication of effort with Tokyo. For example, management gave Hanomag full responsibility to develop all small wheel loaders for Europe, and a joint-development role with Tokyo on larger models.

In its U.K. company, however, the decision was a more basic one. Up until 1988, KUK had a three-person product engineering office headed by a Japanese manager, whose main task was to make minor modifications to Japanese drawings. Gradually, however, Komatsu began transferring responsibility for the redevelopment of the PW170 wheel excavator to a new development facility in KUK, expanding the department to include 27 design engineers and 12 test engineers by 1992.

Such responsibility transfer had considerable immediate and tangible benefits. Starting with an existing undercarriage from Europe, KUK engineers designed and modified a wheel excavator to satisfy European safety regulations and new work range requirements. Aware of strict local standards on braking and steering performance, these British engineers reduced the engine size and thus maximum speed, avoiding a far more costly redesign of the braking system. German engineers at Hanomag, too, modified basic product dimensions of a different vehicle to meet European road-width standards, creating a model better-suited to local conditions than Tokyo's. Generally, local engineers were also able to simplify the manufacturing process design, and bring the new product to market far faster than if it had been engineered in Tokyo. By operating according to centrally mandated standards covering parts and serviceability concepts, designers ensured that parts for the locally designed product were compatible with others in its product line. Said one former KUK manager.

> Before, if manufacturing had a concern about a drawing, they had no way to complain. Three engineers could not solve the problem. Information had to be transferred to Tokyo asking for a solution from the Osaka test center. Now, locals can decide on

EXHIBIT 7 Specialization of Manufacturing Operations by Region and by Plant, 1992

Plant Komatsu Share (year stake taken)	Komatsu Ownership Percent	Number of Employees (= Japanese expatriates)	Main Product	Local Content	Regions Supplied
Europe:					
Komatsu UK (1985)	100%	370 (10)*	Hydraulic excavators	70–75%	Europe, North Africa
Hanomag, Germany (1988)	64.1	1,600 (5)*	Wheel loaders	60–65	Europe, North Africa
FAI, spa, Italy (1991)	10	600	Mini-excavators	85	Europe, North Africa
Asia (non-Japan):					
Indonesia (1982)	50	530	Bulldozers, wheel loaders	15–25	Indonesia, SE Asia, cast metal for Japan
		(24)*	Hydraulic excavators, motor graders, casting and forging products, sheet metal (for Japan)		
Americas:					
Komatsu Dresser Corp. (1988)†	50	2,779 (15)†	Wheel loaders, hydraulic excavators, dump trucks, motor graders	50–65	U.S., Canada
Mexico (1974)	68.4	190 (10)*	Small presses, sheet metal to USA	NA	Small presses to U.S.; sheet metal
Brazil (1973)	100	1,010 (10)*	Hydraulic excavators, bulldozers, wheel loaders, motor graders	8–95	South America, U.S., Indonesia

*Number of Japanese employees as of year-end 1991.
†Includes companies in Peoria (1,020 employees), Chattanooga (261), Galion (330), Candiac, Canada (110).

Source: Company records; *Komatsu Fact Book*, 1992.

EXHIBIT 8   Construction Equipment, Overseas Production (¥ million)

Overseas Production Subsidiaries	1986	1987	1988	1989	1990	1991	1992
Komatsu Dresser Co.					¥182,000[†]	¥199,000	¥136,000
Komatsu America Mfg. Corp.	NM*	¥600	¥17,100	¥25,400	NM	NM	NM
Komatsu Do Brasil SA	¥7,100	7,000	11,700	9,200	NM	NM	1,100[‡]
Komatsu UK Ltd.	NM*	100	4,400	12,600	19,000	19,200	18,600
Dina Komatsu Nacional SA de CV	6,400	1,600	1,900	1,800	2,200	NM	NM
PT Komatsu Indonesia	3,100	2,400	6,400	5,500	8,600	11,600	9,300
Hanomag AG	NM	NM	NM	NM	NM	26,700	26,300
Overseas production	16,600	11,700	41,500	54,500	211,800	256,500	191,600
Domestic production	500,800	475,500	427,500	447,600	489,400	533,200	437,200
Overseas production as percentage of total production	3.2	2.4	8.9	12.2	30.2	32.5	30.5

NM = not meaningful (see Notes)
Notes: *Production began in the United States and the United Kingdom at the end of 1986.
[†]After 1989, Komatsu America Mfg. Corp. and Komatsu Brasil SA were reported as part of the Komatsu Dresser joint venture.
[‡]In October 1991, Komatsu Brasil SA was again separated from Komatsu Dresser.

Source: Company records.

design changes as long as they meet commonality requirements.

KUK's recently opened test center, and its newly assigned responsibility for two additional projects, pointed to a continually expanding role for the group. The impact on local morale was immediate and visible.

Localizing Management

To have enduring value, it was clear to Komatsu's top-management—and constantly emphasized by Katada—that this transfer of responsibility had to be accompanied by an equally strong commitment to the recruitment, development, and promotion of local managers. This strong belief was formalized in a July 1989 human resources policy that required a substantial increase in the number of foreign nationals in management positions. Komatsu Europe, for example, reduced the number of Japanese managers from 26 out of 180 employees in 1986 to 13 out of 260 by 1992, and planned to reduce that number to 6 within two years.

Despite the transfer of responsibilities and the replacement of expatriates with locals, Komatsu managers expressed surprise at how long the transition was taking. For example, their strong belief that "bottom-up problem solving" was an essential ingredient of the spirit of Komatsu, led to frustration at the lack of initiative at the local level as responsibility was expanded. When one senior executive routinely began to answer employee reports of problems with the question, "How do you propose we fix it?", he was disappointed to find that typically the employees were surprised—and without answer. Other managers commented on fundamental differences in attitudes toward core values such as quality and customer service, and how long it took for such values to take deep root in Komatsu subsidiaries.

Those running the business found several causes of these problems and several areas where they needed to take action. Part of the challenge of localizing management entailed changing the way headquarters communicated with the subsidiaries.

EXHIBIT 9 Komatsu, Export Sales Trends by Region (consolidated)

	The Americas			Europe, Middle East, and Asia			Asia and Oceania			Total		
	Net Sales		Company	Net Sales		Company	Net Sales		Company	Net Sales		Exchange
	Yen in billions	U.S.$ in millions	Export Share (%)	Yen in billions	U.S.$ in millions	Export Share (%)	Yen in billions	U.S.$ in millions	Export Share (%)	Yen in billions	U.S.$ in millions	Rate in millions (yen/dollar)
1979	¥49	$205	26.8	¥88	$ 367	48.0	¥46	$192	25.2	¥183	$ 764	240
1980	51	248	21.8	128	628	55.3	53	260	22.9	232	1,136	204
1981	57	261	18.7	203	920	66.0	47	214	15.3	307	1,396	220
1982	31	131	7.4	274	1,163	65.9	111	471	26.7	416	1,753	236
1983	41	177	10.9	268	1,157	71.3	67	288	17.7	376	1,621	232
1984	107	423	34.1	149	591	47.6	57	227	18.3	313	1,240	252
1985	103	517	31.8	145	723	44.4	78	388	23.8	325	1,627	200
1986	94	594	29.2	180	1,140	56.1	47	299	14.7	321	2,032	158
1987	87	718	36.3	98	812	41.1	54	445	22.6	239	1,976	121
1989	67	505	33.6	80	605	40.2	53	395	26.2	200	1,505	133
1990	61	385	28.1	81	513	37.4	75	472	34.5	216	1,370	158
1991	50	354	21.6	94	667	40.7	87	617	37.7	231	1,638	141
1992	38	282	19.2	97	728	49.7	61	456	31.1	195	1,466	133

Notes: 1. The exchange rate for each year reflects the Federal Reserve Bank of New York fiscal year-end average.
2. This table excludes the three-month fiscal period ended March 31, 1988, because it represented an extraordinary term caused by the change in the fiscal period.

Source: Company records.

Mr. Suketomo, a director and former president of KUK, explained his difficulty motivating non-Japanese employees in an environment where all high-level documents were written in Japanese:

> When I became KUK's president, there was a real difficulty with the language problem because all important communication with Tokyo was in Japanese. So my first job was to send a letter to Tokyo explaining that *all* communication from Tokyo would be in English, or I would ignore it! Soon, all official letters to me were in English. It not only allowed me to distribute copies to local managers, but more importantly, it forced expatriate staff to improve their English skills.

The other major problem was that many of the local nationals recruited in the earlier era were not strong managers. The main need prior to the late 1980s was for loyal implements—"yes men," as one Japanese executive described them. As a result, many were not equal to the new challenges being given to them, and overseas units had to undertake major efforts to upgrade their personnel. In 1987, for example, Komatsu Europe had recruited only one university graduate; by 1991, it had recruited 23, including its first two MBAs.

Localization created another unforeseen problem. As the number of Japanese nationals in the oversees operations decreased, the local entities' ability to coordinate their activities with the parent company—and even with each other—began to deteriorate noticeably. Numerous examples of miscommunication began to surface regularly, on issues ranging from market forecasts to product specifications. Said one observer:

> Just at the time they need more coordination than ever, they are reducing the number of Japanese managers abroad. For many Japanese companies, the most difficult task for local nationals has been to operate effectively in a linkage or coordinative role due to the high language and cultural barriers within the organization. As they increase their global integration, the intensity of such a role is going to increase dramatically.

Despite these difficulties adjusting, in 1992 some managers believed that Japanese and Western management practices were converging, with each group learning from the other. Said one manager who spent four years in KDC:

> Our partner's style is very different from ours. The Komatsu style represents the typical Japanese emphasis on growth potential and market share for long-term survival. Dresser puts the highest priority on ROI and profit measures. Because of these differences, we encountered some friction at first. Recently, Komatsu managers have learned the importance of ROI; and those in Dresser came to understand that they must think beyond the short-term. In the future, I think we can expect a hybrid system of management.

Management also began to recognize that their localization program was only one step on a long road to fully internationalizing their management process. As Katada told the Japanese press in November 1990:

> Out goal is to transfer management from Tokyo to overseas outlets run by local nationals. As far as nationalities are concerned, this has already been accomplished in such key units as Komatsu Dresser and Hanomag. . . . But this is not enough for doing business. In this regard, what we really need to do is internationalize our headquarters in Tokyo.

Two full years later, Mr. Suketomo felt pride in the achievements, but echoed Katada's concerns:

> We have been successful increasing the local management of KUK, but there is a danger here in our thinking. If you ask, "Could the top of KUK or KDC become top of the home office in Japan, I would have to express my doubt. That reflects a limitation on our part, and I think we should see that as a challenge.

Achievements and Challenges

After three years of growth, Komatsu's construction equipment business experienced a sharp downturn in 1992. Overseas sales fell 10.6% to ¥246 billion, while domestic sales in this segment slipped even further, falling 13.5% to ¥334 billion. Worse, its operating income from construction equipment plummeted 60%.

Management attributed the setback to the downturn in industry demand associated with a recession that seemed to be deepening worldwide in 1992. To some industry observers, however, the continued performance problems also hinted at deeper problems with Komatsu's overall globalization strategy. Said one:

> There are clear risks in basing international expansion so heavily on joint ventures with and acquisitions of local and regional players each of which has different products, capabilities, and

approaches. It's going to be hard for them to achieve the same product quality, efficiency, and strategic focus as they had a decade ago. The task is made all the more difficult if we continue to withdraw experienced Japanese expatriates from our overseas operations in the name of localization.

Nonetheless, Katada remained confident. In response to the downturn, the confirmed that Komatsu would continue its long-term globalization investments and its commitment to localization. In the short term, he was preparing a major new sales drives for hydraulic excavators, wheel loaders, and dump trucks in all three regional markets. He was clearly prepared to stay the course.

Case 3–4   Canon: Competing on Capabilities

In 1961, following the runaway success of the company's model 914 office copier, Joseph C. Wilson, President of Xerox Corporation, was reported to have said, "I keep asking myself, when am I going to wake up? Things just aren't this good in life." Indeed, the following decade turned out to be better than anything Wilson could have dreamed. Between 1960 and 1970, Xerox increased its sales 40 percent per year from $40 million to $1.7 billion and raised its after-tax profits from $2.6 million to $187.7 million. In 1970, with 93 percent market share worldwide and a brand name that was synonymous with copying, Xerox appeared as invincible in its industry as any company ever could.

When Canon, "the camera company from Japan," jumped into the business in the late 1960s, most observers were skeptical. Less than a tenth the

This case was prepared by Mary Ackenhusen, Research Associate, under the supervision of Sumantra Ghoshal, Associate Professor at INSEAD.

Copyright © 1992 INSEAD, Fontainebleau, France.

size of Xerox, Canon had no direct sales or service organization to reach the corporate market for copiers, nor did it have a process technology to bypass the 500 patents that guarded Xerox's Plain Paper Copier (PPC) process. Reacting to the spate of recent entries in the business including Canon, Arthur D. Little predicted in 1969 that no company would be able to challenge Xerox's monopoly in PPC's in the 1970s because its patents presented an insurmountable barrier.

Yet, over the next two decades, Canon rewrote the rule book on how copiers were supposed to be produced and sold as it built up $5 billion in revenues in the business, emerging as the second largest global player in terms of sales and surpassing Xerox in the number of units sold. According to the Canon Handbook, the company's formula for success as displayed initially in the copier business is "synergistic management of the total technological capabilities of the company, combining the full measure of Canon's know-how in fine optics, precision mechanics, electronics and fine chemicals."

Canon continues to grow and diversify using this strategy. Its vision, as described in 1991 by Ryuzaburo Kaku, president of the company, is "to become a premier global company of the size of IBM combined with Matsushita."

Industry Background

The photocopying machine has often been compared with the typewriter as one of the few triggers that have fundamentally changed the ways of office work. But, while a mechanical Memograph machine for copying had been introduced by the A.B. Dick company of Chicago as far back as 1887, it was only in the second half of this century that the copier market exploded with Xerox's commercialization of the "electrophotography" process invented by Chester Carlson.

Xerox

Carlson's invention used an electrostatic process to transfer images from one sheet of paper to another. Licensed to Xerox in 1948, this invention led to two different photocopying technologies. The Coated Paper Copying (CPC) technology transferred the reflection of an image from the original directly to specialized zinc-oxide coated paper, while the Plain Paper Copying (PPC) technology transferred the image indirectly to ordinary paper through a rotating drum coated with charged particles. While either dry or liquid toner could be used to develop the image, the dry toner was generally preferable in both technologies. A large number of companies entered the CPC market in the 1950s and 1960s based on technology licensed from Xerox or RCA (to whom Xerox had earlier licensed this technology). However, PPC remained a Xerox monopoly since the company had refused to license any technology remotely connected to the PPC process and had protected the technology with over 500 patents.

Because of the need for specialized coated paper, the cost per copy was higher for CPC. Also, this process could produce only one copy at a time, and the copies tended to fade when exposed to heat or light. PPC, on the other hand, produced copies at a lower operating cost that were also indistinguishable from the original. The PPC machines were much more expensive, however, and were much larger in size. Therefore, they required a central location in the user's office. The smaller and less expensive CPC machines, in contrast, could be placed on individual desks. Over time, the cost and quality advantages of PPC, together with its ability to make multiple copies at high speed, made it the dominant technology and, with it, Xerox's model of centralized copying, the industry norm.

This business concept of centralized copying required a set of capabilities that Xerox developed and which, in turn, served as its major strengths and as key barriers to entry to the business. Given the advantages of volume and speed, all large companies found centralized copying highly attractive and they became the key customers for photocopying machines. In order to support this corporate customer base, Xerox's product designs and upgrades emphasized economies of higher volume copying. To market the product effectively to these customers, Xerox also built up an extensive direct sales and service organization of over 12,000 sales representatives and 15,000 service people. Forty percent of the sales reps' time was spent "hand holding" to prevent even minor dissatisfaction. Service reps, dressed in suits and carrying their tools in briefcases, performed preventative maintenance and prided themselves on reducing the average time between breakdown and repair to a few hours.

Further, with the high cost of each machine and the fast rate of model introductions, Xerox developed a strategy of leasing rather than selling machines to customers. Various options were available, but typically the customers paid a monthly charge on the number of copies made. The charge covered not only machine costs but also those of the paper and toner that Xerox supplied and the service visits. This lease strategy, together with the carefully cultivated service image, served as key safeguards from competition, as they tied the customers into Xerox and significantly raised their switching costs.

Unlike some other American corporations, Xerox had an international orientation right from the beginning. Even before it had a successful commercial copier, Xerox built up an international presence through joint ventures which allowed the company to minimize its capital investment abroad. In 1956, it ventured with the Rank Organization Ltd. in the U.K. to form Rank Xerox. In 1962, Rank Xerox became a 50 percent partner with Fuji Photo to form Fuji Xerox which sold copiers in Japan. Through these joint ventures, Xerox built up sales and service capabilities in these key markets similar to those it had in the United States. There were some 5,000 salespeople in Europe, 3,000 in Japan and over 7,000 and 3,000 service reps, respectively. Xerox also built limited design capabilities in both the joint ventures for local market customization, which developed into significant research establishments in their own rights in later years.

Simultaneously, Xerox maintained high levels of investment in both technology and manufacturing to support its growing market. It continued to spend over $100 million a year in R&D, exceeding the total revenues from the copier business that any of its competitors were earning in the early 70s, and also invested heavily in large-size plants not only in the U.S., but also in the U.K. and Japan.

Competition in the 1970s

Xerox's PPC patents began to expire in the 1970s, heralding a storm of new entrants. In 1970, IBM offered the first PPC copier not sold by Xerox, which resulted in Xerox suing IBM for patent infringement and violation of trade secrets. Canon marketed a PPC copier the same year through the development of an independent PPC technology which they licensed selectively to others. By 1973, competition had expanded to include players from the office equipment industry (IBM, SCM, Litton, Pitney Bowes), the electronics industry (Toshiba, Sharp), the reprographics industry (Ricoh, Mita, Copyer, 3M, AB Dick, Addressograph/Multigraph), the photographic equipment industry (Canon, Kodak, Minolta, Konishiroku) and the suppliers of copy paper (Nashua, Dennison, Saxon).

By the 1980s many of these new entrants, including IBM, had lost large amounts of money and exited the business. A few of the newcomers managed to achieve a high level of success, however, and copiers became a major business for them. Specifically, copiers were generating 40 percent of Canon's revenues by 1990.

Canon

Canon was founded in 1933 with the ambition to produce a sophisticated 35 mm camera to rival that of Gemany's world-class Leica model. In only two years' time, it had emerged as Japan's leading producer of high-class cameras. During the war, Canon utilized its optics expertise to produce an X-ray machine which was adopted by the Japanese military. After the war, Canon was able to successfully market its high-end camera, and by the mid-1950s it was the largest camera manufacturer in Japan. Building off its optics technology, Canon then expanded its product line to include a mid-range camera, an 8 mm video camera, television lenses and micrographic equipment. It also began developing markets for its products outside of Japan, mainly in the U.S. and Canada.

Diversification was always very important to Canon in order to further its growth, and a new products R&D section was established in 1962 to explore the fields of copy machines, auto-focusing cameras, strobe-integrated cameras, home VCRs and electronic calculators. A separate, special operating unit was also established to introduce new non-camera products resulting from the diversification effort.

The first product to be targeted was the electronic calculator. This product was challenging because it required Canon engineers to develop new expertise in microelectronics in order to incorporate thousands of transistors and diodes in a compact, desk model machine. Tekeshi Mitarai, President of Canon at that time, was against developing the product because it was seen to be too difficult and risky. Nevertheless, a dedicated group of engineers believed in the challenge and developed the calculator in secrecy. Over a year later, top management gave their support to the project. In 1964, the result of the development effort was introduced as the Canola 130, the world's first 10-key numeric pad calculator. With this product line, Canon dominated the Japanese electronic calculator market in the 1960s.

Not every diversification effort was a success, however. In 1956, Canon began development of the synchroreader, a device for writing and reading with a sheet of paper coated with magnetic material. When introduced in 1959, the product received high praise for its technology. But, because the design was not patented, another firm introduced a similar product at half the price. There was no market for the high-priced and incredibly heavy Canon product. Ultimately, the firm was forced to disassemble the finished inventories and sell off the usable parts in the "once-used" components market.

Move into Copiers

Canon began research into copier technology in 1959, and, in 1962, it formed a research group dedicated to developing a plain paper copier (PPC) technology. The only known PPC process was protected by hundreds of Xerox patents, but Canon felt that only this technology promised sufficient quality, speed, economy and ease of maintenance to successfully capture a large portion of the market. Therefore, corporate management challenged the researchers to develop a new PPC process which would not violate the Xerox patents.

In the meantime, the company entered the copier business by licensing the "inferior" CPC technology in 1965 from RCA. Canon decided not to put the name of the company on this product and marketed it under the brand name Confax 1000 in Japan only. Three years later, Canon licensed a liquid toner technology from an Australian company and combined this with the RCA technology to introduce the CanAll Series. To sell the copier in Japan, Canon formed a separate company, International Image Industry. The copier was sold as an OEM to Scott Paper in the U.S. who sold it under its own brand name.

Canon's research aiming at developing a PPC technical alternative to xerography paid off with the announcement of the "New Process" (NP) in 1968. This successful research effort not only produced an alternative process but also taught Canon the importance of patent law: how not to violate patents and how to protect new technology. The NP process was soon protected by close to 500 patents.

The first machine with the NP technology, the NP1100, was introduced in Japan in 1970. It was the first copier sold by Canon to carry the Canon brand name. It produced 10 copies per minute and utilized dry toner. As was the standard in the Japanese market, the copier line was sold outright to customers from the beginning. After two years of experience in the domestic market, Canon entered the overseas market, except North America, with this machine.

The second generation of the NP system was introduced in Japan in 1972 as the NPL7. It was a marked improvement because it eliminated a complex fusing technology, simplified developing and cleaning, and made toner supply easier through a new system developed to use liquid toner. Compared with the Xerox equivalent, it was more economical, more compact, more reliable and still had the same or better quality of copies.

With the NP system, Canon began a sideline which was to become quite profitable: licensing. The first generation NP system was licensed to AM, and Canon also provided it with machines on an OEM basis. The second generation was again licensed to AM as well as to Saxon, Ricoh, and Copyer. Canon accumulated an estimated $32 million in license fees between 1975 and 1982.

Canon continued its product introductions with a stream of state-of-the-art technological innovations throughout the seventies. In 1973 it added colour to the NP system; in 1975, it added laser beam printing technology. Its first entry into high volume copiers took place in 1978 with a model which was targeted at the Xerox 9200. The NP200 was introduced in 1979 and went on to win a gold medal at the Leipzig Fair for being the most economical and productive copier available. By 1982, copiers had surpassed cameras as the company's largest revenue generator (see Exhibits 1 and 2 for Canon's financials and sales by product line).

EXHIBIT 1 Canon, Inc.—Ten-Year Financial Summary (millions of yen except per share amounts)

	1990	1989	1988	1987	1986	1985	1984	1983	1982	1981
Net sales:										
Domestic	¥ 508,747	413,854	348,462	290,382	274,174	272,966	240,656	198,577	168,178	144,698
Overseas	1,219,201	937,063	757,548	686,329	615,043	682,814	589,732	458,748	412,322	326,364
Total	1,727,948	1,350,917	1,106,010	976,711	889,217	955,780	830,388	657,325	580,500	471,262
Percentage to previous year	127.9%	122.1	113.2	109.8	93.0	115.1	126.3	113.2	123.2	112.5
Net income	61,408	38,293	37,100	13,244	10,728	37,056	35,029	28,420	22,358	16,216
Percentage to sales	3.6%	2.8	3.4	1.4	1.2	3.9	4.2	4.3	3.9	3.4
Advertising expense	72,234	54,394	41,509	38,280	37,362	50,080	51,318	41,902	37,532	23,555
Research and development	86,008	75,566	65,522	57,085	55,330	49,461	38,256	28,526	23,554	14,491
Depreciation	78,351	64,861	57,627	57,153	55,391	47,440	39,995	30,744	27,865	22,732
Capital expenditure	137,298	107,290	83,069	63,497	81,273	91,763	75,894	53,411	46,208	54,532
Long-term debt	262,886	277,556	206,083	222,784	166,722	134,366	99,490	60,636	53,210	39,301
Stockholders' equity	617,566	550,841	416,465	371,198	336,456	333,148	304,310	264,629	235,026	168,735
Total assets	1,827,945	1,636,380	1,299,843	1,133,681	1,009,504	1,001,044	916,651	731,642	606,101	505,169

(*continued*)

EXHIBIT 1 *(concluded)*

	1990	1989	1988	1987	1986	1985	1984	1983	1982	1981
Per share data:										
Net income										
Common and common equivalent share	78.29	50.16	51.27	19.65	16.67	53.38	53.63	46.31	41.17	34.04
Assuming full dilution	78.12	49.31	51.26	19.64	16.67	53.25	53.37	45.02	38.89	33.35
Cash dividends declared	12.50	11.93	11.36	9.09	11.36	11.36	9.88	9.43	8.23	7.84
Stock price:										
High	1,940	2,040	1,536	1,282	1,109	1,364	1,336	1,294	934	1,248
Low	1,220	1,236	823	620	791	800	830	755	417	513
Average number of common and common equivalent shares in thousands	788,765	780,546	747,059	747,053	746,108	727,257	675,153	645,473	564,349	515,593
Number of employees	54,381	44,401	40,740	37,521	35,498	34,129	30,302	27,266	25,607	24,300
Average exchange rate ($1 =)	143	129	127	143	167	235	239	238	248	222

Source: Canon 1990 Annual Report.

EXHIBIT 2   Canon—Sales by Product (millions of yen)

Year	Cameras	Copiers	Other Business Machines	Optical and Other Products	Total
1981	201,635	175,389	52,798	40,222	470,044
1982	224,619	242,161	67,815	45,905	580,500
1983	219,443	291,805	97,412	48,665	657,325
1984	226,645	349,986	180,661	73,096	830,388
1985	197,284	410,840	271,190	76,466	955,780
1986	159,106	368,558	290,630	70,923	889,217
1987	177,729	393,581	342,895	62,506	976,711
1988	159,151	436,924	434,634	75,301	1,106,010
1989	177,597	533,115	547,170	93,035	1,350,917
1990	250,494	686,077	676,095	115,282	1,727,948

Source: Canon Annual Report, 1981–1990

EXHIBIT 3   Office Size Distribution, Japan 1979

Copier Market Segment	Number of Office Workers	Number of Offices	Working Population
A	300+	200,000	9,300,000
B	100–299	30,000	4,800,000
C	30–99	170,000	8,300,000
D	5–29	1,820,000	15,400,000
E	1–4	4,110,000	8,700,000

Source: Breakthrough: The Development of the Canon Personal Copier, Teruo Yamanouchi, *Long Range Planning,* Vol. 22, October 1989, P. 4.

The Personal Copier

In the late 1970s, top management began searching for a new market for the PPC copier. They had recently experienced a huge success with the introduction of the AE-1 camera in 1976 and wanted a similar success in copiers. The AE-1 was a very compact single-lens reflex camera, the first camera that used a microprocessor to control electronically functions of exposure, film rewind and strobe. The product had been developed through a focused, cross-functional project team effort which had resulted in a substantial reduction in the number of components, as well as in automated assembly and the use of unitized parts. Because of these improvements, the AE-1 enjoyed a 20 percent cost advantage over competitive models in the same class.

After studying the distribution of offices in Japan by size (see Exhibit 3), Canon decided to focus on a latent segment that Xerox had ignored. This was the segment comprised of small offices (segment E) who could benefit from the functionality offered by photocopiers but did not require the high-speed machines available in the market. Canon management believed that a low-volume "value for money" machine could generate a large demand in this segment. From this analysis emerged the business concept of a "personal side desk" machine which could not only create a new market in small offices, but potentially also induce decentralization of the copy function in large offices. Over time, the machine might even create demand for a personal copier for home use. This would be a copier that up to now no one had thought possible. Canon felt that, to be successful in this market, the product had to cost half the price of a conventional copier (target price $1,000), be maintenance free, and provide ten times more reliability.

Top management took their "dream" to the engineers, who, after careful consideration, took on the challenge. The machine would build off their previous expertise in microelectronics but would go much further in terms of material, functional component, design and production engineering technologies. The team's slogan was "Let's make the AE-1 of copiers!," expressing the necessity of know-how transfer between the camera and copier divisions as well as their desire for a similar type of success. The effort was led by the director of the Reprographic Production Development Center. His cross-functional team of 200 was the second largest ever assembled at Canon (the largest had been that of the AE-1 camera).

During the development effort, a major issue arose concerning the paper size that the new copier would accept. Canon Sales (the sales organization for Japan) wanted the machine to use a larger-than-letter-size paper which accounted for 60 percent of the Japanese market. This size was not necessary for sales outside of Japan and would add 20–30 percent to the machine's cost as well as make the copier more difficult to service. After much debate worldwide, the decision was made to forego the ability to utilize the larger paper size in the interest of better serving the global market.

Three years later the concept was a reality. The new PC (personal copier) employed a new cartridge-based technology which allowed the user to replace the photoreceptive drum, charging device, toner assembly and cleaner with a cartridge every 2,000 copies, thus eliminating the need to maintain the copier regularly. This enabled Canon engineers to meet the cost and reliability targets. The revolutionary product was the smallest, lightest copier ever sold, and created a large market which had previously not existed. Large offices adjusted their copying strategies to include decentralized copying, and many small offices and even homes could now afford a personal copier. Again, Canon's patent knowledge was utilized to protect this research, and the cartridge technology was not licensed to other manufacturers. Canon has maintained its leadership in personal copiers into the 1990s.

Building Capabilities

Canon is admired for its technical innovations, marketing expertise, and low-cost quality manufacturing. These are the result of a long-term strategy to become a premier company. Canon has frequently acquired outside expertise so that it could better focus internal investments on skills of strategic importance. This approach of extensive outsourcing and focused internal development has required consistent direction from top management and the patience to allow the company to become well grounded in one skill area before tasking the organization with the next objective.

Technology

Canon's many innovative products, which enabled the company to grow quickly in the seventies and eighties are in large part the result of a carefully orchestrated use of technology and the capacity for managing rapid technological change. Attesting to its prolific output of original research is the fact that Canon has been among the leaders in a number of patents issued worldwide throughout the eighties.

These successes have been achieved in an organization that has firmly pursued a strategy of decentralized R&D. Most of Canon's R&D personnel are employed by the product divisions where 80–90 percent of the company's patentable inventions originate. Each product division has its own development center which is tasked with short- to medium-term product design and improvement of production systems. Most product development is performed by cross-functional teams. The work of the development groups is coordinated by an R&D headquarters group.

The Corporate Technical Planning and Operation centre is responsible for long-term strategic R&D planning. Canon also has a main research centre which supports state-of-the-art research in optics, electronics, new materials and information technology. There are three other corporate research centres which apply this state-of-the-art research to product development.

Canon acknowledges that it has neither the resources nor the time to develop all necessary technologies and has therefore often traded or bought specific technologies from a variety of external partners. Furthermore, it has used joint ventures and technology transfers as a strategic tool for mitigating foreign trade tensions in Europe and the United States. For example, Canon had two purposes in mind when it made an equity participation in CPF Deutsch, an office equipment marketing firm in Germany. Primarily, it believed that this move would help develop the German market for its copiers; but it did not go unnoticed among top management that CPF owned Tetras, a copier maker who at that time was pressing dumping charges against Japanese copier makers. Canon also used Burroughs as an OEM for office automation equipment in order to acquire Burroughs software and know-how and participated in joint development agreements with Eastman Kodak and Texas Instruments. Exhibit 4 provides a list of the company's major joint ventures.

Canon also recognizes that its continued market success depends on its ability to exploit new

EXHIBIT 4   Canon's Major International Joint Ventures

Category	Partner	Description
Office Equipment	Eastman Kodak (U.S.) exports copiers to Kodak	Distributes Kodak medical equipment in Japan;
	CPF Germany	Equity participation in CPF which markets Canon copiers
	Olivetti (Italy) Lotte (Korea)	Joint venture for manufacture of copier
Computers	Hewlett-Packard (U.S.)	Receives OEM mini-computer from HP; supplies laser printer to HP
	Apple Computer (U.S.)	Distributes Apple computers in Japan; supplies laser printer to Apple
	Next, Inc. (U.S.)	Equity participation; Canon has marketing rights for Asia
Semiconductors	National Semiconductor (U.S.)	Joint development of MPU and software for Canon office equipment
	Intel (U.S.)	Joint development of LSI for Canon copier, manufactured by Intel
Telecommunications	Siemens (Germany)	Development of ISDN interface for Canon facsimile; Siemens supplies Canon with digital PBX
	DHL (U.S.)	Equity participation; Canon supplies terminals to DHL
Camera	Kinsei Seimitsu (Korea)	Canon licenses technology on 35 mm camera
Other	ECD (U.S.)	Equity participation because Canon values its research on amorphous materials

Source: Canon Asia, Nomura Management School.

research into marketable products quickly. It has worked hard to reduce the new product introduction cycle through a cross-functional programme called TS 1/2 whose purpose is to cut development time by 50 percent on a continuous basis. The main thrust of this programme is the classification of development projects by total time required and the critical human resources needed so that these two parameters can be optimized for each product depending on its importance for Canon's corporate strategy. This allows product teams to be formed around several classifications of product development priorities of which "best sellers" will receive the most emphasis. These are the products aimed at new markets or segments with large potential demands. Other classifications include products necessary to catch up with competitive offerings, product refinements intended to enhance customer satisfaction, and long-run marathon products which will take considerable time to develop. In all development classifications, Canon emphasizes three factors to reduce time to market: the fostering of engineering ability, efficient technical support systems, and careful reviews of product development at all stages.

Canon is also working to divert its traditional product focus into more of a market focus. To this end, Canon R&D personnel participate in international product strategy meetings, carry out consumer research, join in marketing activities, and attend meetings in the field at both domestic and foreign sales subsidiaries.

Marketing

Canon's effective marketing is the result of step-by-step, calculated introduction strategies. Normally, the product is first introduced and perfected in the home market before being sold internationally. Canon has learned how to capture learning from the Japanese market quickly so that the time span between introduction in Japan and abroad is as short as a few months. Furthermore, the company will not simultaneously launch a new product through a new distribution channel—its strategy is to minimize risk by introducing a new product through known channels first. New channels will only be created, if

necessary, after the product has proven to be successful.

The launch of the NP copier exemplifies this strategy. Canon initially sold these copiers in Japan by direct sales through its Business Machines Sales organization, which had been set up in 1968 to sell the calculator product line. This sales organization was merged with the camera sales organization in 1971 to form Canon Sales. By 1972, after three years of experience in producing the NP product line, the company entered into a new distribution channel, that of dealers, to supplement direct selling.

The NP copier line was not marketed in the U.S. until 1974, after production and distribution were running smoothly in Japan. The U.S. distribution system was similar to that used in Japan, with seven sales subsidiaries for direct selling and a network of independent dealers.

By the late 1970s, Canon had built up a strong dealer network in the U.S. which supported both sales and service of the copiers. The dealer channel was responsible for rapid growth in copier sales, and, by the early 1980s, Canon copiers were sold almost exclusively through this channel. Canon enthusiastically supported the dealers with attractive sales incentive programmes, management training and social outings. Dealers were certified to sell copiers only after completing a course in service training. The company felt that a close relationship with its dealers was a vital asset that allowed it to understand and react to customers' needs and problems in a timely manner. At the same time, Canon also maintained a direct selling mechanism through wholly owned sales subsidiaries in Japan, the U.S. and Europe in order to target large customers and government accounts.

The introduction of its low-end personal copier in 1983 was similarly planned to minimize risk. Initially, Canon's NP dealers in Japan were not interested in the product due to its low maintenance needs and inability to utilize large paper sizes. Thus, PCs were distributed through the firm's office supply stores who were already selling its personal calculators. After seeing the success of the PC, the NP dealers began to carry the copier.

In the U.S., the PC was initially sold only through existing dealers and direct sales channels due to limited availability of the product. Later, it was sold through competitors' dealers and office supply stores, and, eventually, the distribution channels were extended to include mass merchandisers. Canon already had considerable experience in mass merchandising from its camera business.

Advertising has always been an integral part of Canon's marketing strategy. President Kaku believes that Canon must have a corporate brand name which is outstanding to succeed in its diversification effort. "Customers must prefer products because they bear the name Canon," he says. As described by the company's finance director, "If a brand name is unknown, and there is no advertising, you have to sell it cheap. It's not our policy to buy share with a low price. We establish our brand with advertising at a reasonably high price."

Therefore, when the NP-200 was introduced in 1980, 10 percent of the selling price was spent on advertising; for the launch of the personal copier, advertising expenditure was estimated to be 20 percent of the selling price. Canon has also sponsored various sporting events including World Cup football, the Williams motor racing team, and the ice dancers Torvill and Dean. The company expects its current expansion into the home automation market to be greatly enhanced by the brand image it has built in office equipment (see Exhibit 1 for Canon's advertising expenditures through 1990).

Manufacturing

Canon's goal in manufacturing is to produce the best quality at the lowest cost with the best delivery. To drive down costs, a key philosophy of the production system is to organize the manufacture of each product so that the minimum amount of time, energy and resources are required. Canon therefore places strong emphasis on tight inventory management through a stable production planning process, careful material planning, close supplier relationships, and adherence to the **kanban** system of inventory movement. Additionally, a formal waste elimination programme saved Canon 177 bil-

lion yen between 1976 and 1985. Overall, Canon accomplished a 30 percent increase in productivity per year from 1976 to 1982 and over 10 percent thereafter through automation and innovative process improvements.

The workforce is held in high regard at Canon. A philosophy of "stop and fix it" empowers any worker to stop the production line if he or she is not able to perform a task properly or observes a quality problem. Workers are responsible for their own machine maintenance governed by rules which stress prevention. Targets for quality and production and other critical data are presented to the workers with on-line feedback. Most workers also participate in voluntary "small group activity" for problem solving. The result of these systems is a workforce that feels individually responsible for the success of the products it manufactures.

Canon sponsors a highly regarded suggestion programme for its workers in order to directly involve those most familiar with the work processes in improving the business. The programme was originally initiated in 1952 with only limited success, but in the early 1980s, participation soared with more than seventy suggestions per employee per year. All suggestions are reviewed by a hierarchy of committees with monetary prizes awarded monthly and yearly depending on the importance of the suggestion. The quality and effectiveness of the process are demonstrated by a 90 percent implementation rate of the suggestions offered and corporate savings of $202 million in 1985 (against a total expenditure of $2 million in running the programme, over 90 percent of it in prize money).

Canon chooses to backward integrate only on parts with unique technologies. For other components, the company prefers to develop long-term relationships with its suppliers and it retains two sources for most parts. In 1990, over 80 percent of Canon's copiers were assembled from purchased parts, with only the drums and toner being manufactured in-house. The company also maintains its own in-house capability for doing pilot production of all parts so as to understand better the technology and the vendors' costs.

Another key to Canon's high quality and low cost is the attention given to parts commonality between models. Between some adjacent copier models, the commonality is as high as 60 percent.

Copier manufacture was primarily located in Toride, Japan, in the early years but then spread to Germany, California and Virginia in the U.S., France, Italy and Korea. In order to mitigate trade and investment friction, Canon is working to increase the local content of parts as it expands globally. In Europe it exceeds the EC standard by 5 percent. It is also adding R&D capability to some of its overseas operations. Mr. Kaku emphasizes the importance of friendly trading partners:

> Frictions cannot be erased by merely transferring our manufacturing facilities overseas. The earnings after tax must be reinvested in the country; we must transfer our technology to the country. This is the only way our overseas expansion will be welcomed.

Leveraging Expertise

Canon places critical importance on continued growth through diversification into new product fields. Mr. Kaku observed,

> Whenever Canon introduced a new product, profits surged forward. Whenever innovation lagged, on the other hand, so did the earnings . . . In order to survive in the coming era of extreme competition, Canon must possess at least a dozen proprietary state-of-the-art technologies that will enable it to develop unique products.

While an avid supporter of diversification, Mr. Kaku was cautious.

> In order to ensure the enduring survival of Canon, we have to continue diversifying in order to adapt to environmental changes. However, we must be wise in choosing ways toward diversification. In other words, we must minimize the risks. Entering a new business which requires either a technology unrelated to Canon's current expertise or a different marketing channel than Canon currently uses incurs a 50 percent risk. If Canon attempts to enter a new business which requires both a new technology and a new marketing channel which are unfamiliar to Canon, the risk

entailed in such ventures would be 100 percent. There are two prerequisites that have to be satisfied before launching such new ventures. First, our operation must be debt-free; second, we will have to secure the personnel capable of competently undertaking such ventures. I feel we shall have to wait until the twenty-first century before we are ready.

Combining Capabilities

Through its R&D strategy, Canon has worked to build up specialized expertise in several areas and then link them to offer innovative, state-of-the-art products. Through the fifties and sixties, Canon focused on products related to its main business and expertise, cameras. This prompted the introduction of the 8-mm movie camera and the Canon range of mid-market cameras. There was minimal risk because the optics technology was the same and the marketing outlet, camera shops, remained the same.

Entrance into the calculator market pushed Canon into developing expertise in the field of microelectronics, which it later innovatively combined with its optics capability to introduce one of its most successful products, the personal copier. From copiers, Canon utilized the replaceable cartridge system to introduce a successful desktop laser printer.

In the early seventies, Canon entered the business of marketing micro-chip semiconductor production equipment. In 1980, the company entered into the development and manufacture of unique proprietary ICs in order to strengthen further its expertise in electronics technology. This development effort was expanded in the late eighties to focus on optoelectronic ICs. According to Mr. Kaku:

> We are now seriously committed to R&D in ICs because our vision for the future foresees the arrival of the opto-electronic era. When the time arrives for the opto-electronic IC to replace the current ultra-LSI, we intend to go into making large-scale computers. Presently we cannot compete with the IBMs and NECs using the ultra-LSIs. When the era of the opto-electronic IC arrives, the technology of designing the computer will be radically transformed; that will be our chance for making entry into the field of the large-scale computer.

Creative Destruction

In 1975 Canon produced the first laser printer. Over the next fifteen years, laser printers evolved as a highly successful product line under the Canon brand name. The company also provides the "engine" as an OEM to Hewlett Packard and other laser printer manufacturers which when added to its own branded sales supports a total of 84 percent of worldwide demand.

The biggest threat to the laser printer industry is substitution by the newly developed bubble jet printer. With a new technology which squirts out thin streams of ink under heat, a high-quality silent printer can be produced at half the price of the laser printer. The technology was invented accidentally in the Canon research labs. It keys on a print head which has up to 400 fine nozzles per inch, each with its own heater to warm the ink until it shoots out tiny ink droplets. This invention utilizes Canon's competencies in fine chemicals for producing the ink and its expertise in semiconductors, materials, and electronics for manufacturing the print heads. Canon is moving full steam forward to develop the bubble jet technology, even though it might destroy a business that the company dominates. The new product is even more closely tied to the company's core capabilities, and management believes that successful development of this business will help broaden further its expertise in semiconductors.

Challenge of the 1990s

Canon sees the office automation business as its key growth opportunity for the nineties. It already has a well-established brand name in home and office automation products through its offerings of copiers, facsimiles, electronic typewriters, laser printers, word processing equipment and personal computers. The next challenge for the company is to link these discrete products into a multifunctional system which will perform the tasks of a copier, facsimile, printer, and scanner and interface with a computer so that all the functions can be performed from one keyboard. In 1988, with this target, Canon introduced a personal computer which incorporated a PC, a fax, a telephone and a word processor. Canon has also introduced a colour laser copier which hooks up to a computer to serve as a colour printer. A series of additional integrated OA offerings are scheduled for introduction in 1992, and the company expects these products to serve as its growth engine in the first half of the 1990s.

Managing the Process

Undergirding this impressive history of continuously building new corporate capabilities and of exploiting those capabilities to create a fountain of innovative new products lies a rather unique management process. Canon has institutionalized corporate entrepreneurship through its highly autonomous and market-focused business unit structure. A set of powerful functional committees provide the bridge between the entrepreneurial business units and the company's core capabilities in technology, manufacturing and marketing. Finally, an extraordinarily high level of corporate ambition drives this innovation engine, which is fuelled by the creativity of its people and by top management's continuous striving for ever higher levels of performance.

Driving Entrepreneurship: The Business Units

Mr. Kaku had promoted the concept of the entrepreneurial business unit from his earliest days with Canon, but it was not until the company had suffered significant losses in 1975 that his voice was heard. His plan was implemented shortly before he became president of the company.

Mr. Kaku believed that Canon's diversification strategy could only succeed if the business units were empowered to act on their own, free of central controls. Therefore, two independent operating units were formed in 1978, one for cameras and one for office equipment, to be managed as business units. Optical Instruments, the third business unit, had always been separate. Since that time, an additional three business units have been spun off. The original three business units were then given clear profitability targets, as well as highly ambitious growth objectives, and were allowed the freedom to devise their own ways to achieve these goals. One immediate result of this decentralization was the recognition that Canon's past practice of mixing production of different products in the same manufacturing facility would no longer work. Manufacturing was reorganized so that no plant produced more than one type of product.

Mr. Kaku describes the head of each unit as a surrogate of the CEO empowered to make quick decisions. This allows him, as president of Canon, to devote himself exclusively to his main task of creating and implementing the long-term corporate strategy. In explaining the benefits of the system, he said:

> Previously, the president was in exclusive charge of all decision making; his subordinates had to form a queue to await their turn in presenting their problems to him. This kind of system hinders the development of the young managers' potential for decision-making.
>
> Furthermore, take the case of the desktop calculator. Whereas, I can devote only about two hours each day on problems concerning the calculator, the CEO of Casio Calculator could devote 24 hours to the calculator . . . In the fiercely competitive market, we lost out because our then CEO was slow in coping with the problem.

In contrast to the Western philosophy of stand-alone SBUs encompassing all functions including engineering, sales, marketing and production, Canon has chosen to separate its product divisions from its sales and marketing arm. This separation allows for a clear focus on the challenges that Canon faces in selling products on a global scale. Through a five-year plan initiated in 1977, Seiichi Takigawa, the president of Canon Sales (the sales organization for Japan), stressed the need to "make sales a science." After proving the profitability of this approach, Canon Sales took on the responsibility for worldwide marketing, sales and service. In 1981, Canon Sales was listed on the Tokyo stock exchange, reaffirming its independence.

Canon also allows its overseas subsidiaries free rein, though it holds the majority of stock. The philosophy is to create the maximum operational leeway for each subsidiary to act on its own initiative. Kaku describes the philosophy through an analogy:

> Canon's system of managing subsidiaries is similar to the policy of the Tokugawa government, which established secure hegemony over the warlords, who were granted autonomy in their territory. I am "shogun" [head of the Tokugawa regime] and the subsidiaries' presidents are the "daimyo" [warlords]. The difference between Canon and the Tokugawa government is that the latter was a zero-sum society; its policy was repressive. On the other hand, Canon's objective is to enhance the prosperity of all subsidiaries through efficient mutual collaborations.

Canon has also promoted the growth of intrapreneurial ventures within the company by spinning these ventures off as wholly owned subsidiaries. The first venture to be spun off was Canon Components, which produces electronic components and devices, in 1984.

Building Integration: Functional Committees

As Canon continues to grow and diversify, it becomes increasingly difficult but also ever more important to link its product divisions in order to realize the benefits possible only in a large multi-product corporation. The basis of Canon's integration is a three-dimensional management approach in which the first dimension is the independent business unit, the second a network of functional committees, and the third the regional companies focused on geographic markets (see Exhibit 5).

Kaku feels there are four basic requirements for the success of a diversified business: (1) a level of competence in research and development; (2) quality, low-cost manufacturing technology; (3) superior marketing strength; and (4) an outstanding corporate identity, culture and brand name. Therefore, he has established separate functional committees to address the first three requirements of development, production and marketing, while the fourth task has been kept as a direct responsibility of corporate management. The three functional committees, in turn, have been made responsible for company-wide administration of three key management systems:

- The Canon Development System (CDS) whose objectives are to foster the research and creation

EXHIBIT 5   Canon Organization Chart

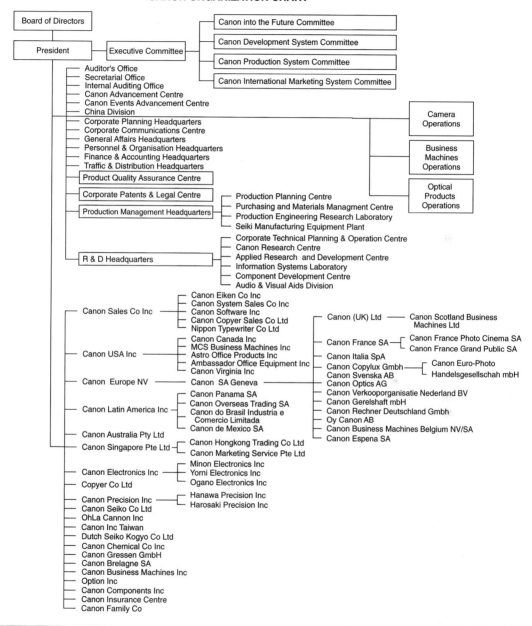

CANON ORGANIZATION CHART

(continued)

EXHIBIT 5   (*concluded*)

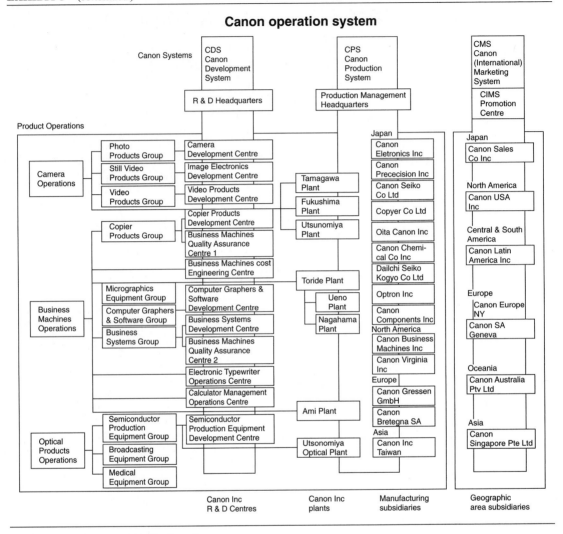

Canon operation system

Source: Canon Handbook, published by Canon, Inc.

of new products and technologies by studying and continuously improving the development process;

- The Canon Production System (CPS) whose goal is to achieve optimum quality by minimizing waste in all areas of manufacturing;
- The Canon Marketing System (CMS), later renamed the Canon International Marketing System (CIMS), which is tasked to expand and strengthen Canon's independent domestic and overseas sales networks by building a high quality service and sales force.

Separate offices have been created at headquarters for each of these critical committees, and over time their role has broadened to encompass general improvement of the processes used to support their functions. The chairpersons of the committees are members of Canon's management committee, which gives them the ability to ensure consistency and communicate process improvements throughout the multiproduct, multinational corporation.

Using information technology to integrate its worldwide operations, Canon began development of the Global Information System for Harmonious Growth Administration (GINGA) in 1987. The system will consist of a high-speed digital communications network to interconnect all parts of Canon into a global database and allow for the timely flow of information among managers in any location of the company's worldwide organization. GINGA is planned to include separate but integrated systems for computer integrated manufacturing, global marketing and distribution, R&D and product design, financial reporting, and personnel database tracking, as well as some advances in intelligent office automation. As described by Mr. Kaku, the main objective of this system is to supplement Canon's efficient vertical communications structure with a lateral one that will facilitate direct information exchange among managers across businesses, countries, and functions on all operational matters concerning the company. The system is being developed at a total cost of 20 billion yen and it is targeted for completion in 1992.

Managing Renewal: Challenges and Change

Mr. Kaku was very forthright about some of the management weaknesses of Canon prior to 1975:

> In short, our skill in management—the software of our enterprise—was weak. Management policy must be guided by a soundly created software on management; if the software is weak, the firm will lack clearly defined ideals and objectives. In the beginning we had a clearly defined objective, to overtake West Germany's Leica. Since then our management policy has been changing like the colours of a chameleon.
>
> In the past our management would order employees to reach the peak of Mount Fuji, and

then before the vanguard of climbers had barely started climbing, they would be ordered to climb Mount Tsukuba far to the north. Then the order would again be suddenly changed to climb Mount Yatsugatake to the west. After experiencing these kind of shifts in policy, the smarter employees would opt to take things easy by taking naps on the bank of the river Tamagawa. As a result, vitality would be sapped from our workforce—a situation that should have been forestalled by all means.

Mr. Kaku's first action as President of Canon was to start the firm on the path to global leadership through establishing the first "premier company plan," a six-year plan designed to make Canon a top company in Japan. The plan outlined a policy for diversification and required consistently recurring profits exceeding 10 percent on sales.

> The aim of any Japanese corporation is ensuring its perpetual survival. Unlike the venture businesses and U.S. corporations, our greatest objective is not to maximize short-term profits. Our vital objective is to continually earn profits on a stable basis for ensuring survival. To implement this goal, we must diversify.

By the time the original six-year plan expired in 1981, Canon had become a highly respected company in Japan. The plan was then renewed through 1986 and then again into the 1990s. The challenge was to become a premier global company, defined as having recurring profits exceeding 15 percent of sales. R&D spending was gradually increased from 6 percent of sales in 1980 to 9 percent in 1985 as a prerequisite for global excellence. As described by Mr. Kaku:

> By implementing our first plan for becoming a premier company we have succeeded in attaining the allegorical top of Mount Fuji. Our next objective is the Everest. With a firm determination, we could have climbed Fuji wearing sandals. However, sandals are highly inappropriate for climbing Everest; it may cause our death.

According to Mr. Kaku, such ambitions also require a company to build up the ability to absorb temporary reversals without panic; ambition without stability makes the corporate ship lose its way. To illustrate, he described the situation at Canon during the time the yen depreciated from 236 to the dollar in 1985 to 168 to the dollar in 1986. With 74 percent of Canon's Japanese production going to export markets, this sudden change caused earnings to fall to 4.6 billion yen, one tenth of the previous year. Some board members at Canon sought drastic action such as a major restructuring of the company and cutting the R&D budget. Mr. Kaku had successfully argued the opposite:

> What I did was calm them down. If a person gets lost in climbing a high mountain, he must avoid excessive use of his energy; otherwise his predicament will deepen . . . Our ongoing strategy for becoming the premier company remains the best, even under this crisis; there is no need to panic. Even if we have to forego dividends for two or three times, we shall surely overcome this crisis.

While celebrating the company's past successes, Mr. Kaku also constantly reminds his colleagues that no organizational form or process holds the eternal truth. The need to change with a changing world is inevitable. For example, despite being the creator of the product division–marketing company split, he was considering rejoining these two in the nineties.

> In the future, our major efforts in marketing must be concentrated on clearly defining and differentiating the markets of the respective products and creating appropriate marketing systems for them. In order to make this feasible, we may have to recombine our sales subsidiaries with the parent company and restructure their functions to fully meet the market's needs.

While constantly aware of the need to change, Kaku also recognizes the difficulties managers face in changing the very approaches and strategies that have led to past successes:

> In order for a company to survive forever, the company must have the courage to be able to deny at one point what it has been doing in the past; the biological concept of "ecdysis"—casting off the skin to emerge to new form. But it is difficult for human beings to deny and destruct what they have been building up. But if they cannot do that, it is certain that the firm cannot survive forever. Speaking about myself, it is difficult to deny what I've done in the past. So when such time comes that I have to deny the past, I inevitably would have to step down.

Case 3–5   S.A. Chupa Chups

Abstract

Spain is renowned for its sunshine, beaches, tapas and other wonderful things which attract millions of foreign tourists each year. But despite the size of Spain's economy, Europe's fifth largest, the country is not renowned for its multinational corporations. One exception is S.A. Chupa Chups.

Founded in 1957, S.A. Chupa Chups is the original company of the Barcelona-based Chupa Chups Group which now includes subsidiaries in distribution, trading, banking, marketing, confectionery machine manufacturing and insurance. (See Appendix A: The Chupa Chups Group.) The group trades in more than 130 countries and has manufacturing facilities in 5 countries with plans for further expansion. It had consolidated turnover of US$194 million in 1994. All activities have been developed around an empire built on one product—a lollipop.

Achieving Domestic Market Leadership

> "What is the key to such sweet success? Chupa Chups are just better. *Enrique Bernat*

The company's success story begins with the vision and drive of Chupa Chups founder and President, Enrique Bernat Fontlladosa. He was born in Barcelona in 1924 into a family with a confectionery tradition. His grandfather had one of the first sweet manufacturing plants in Spain, and his father and uncles had confectionery shops in Barcelona.

During the tough post–Civil War period in Spain, Bernat combined his studies with an apprenticeship in a retail store. In 1955 he traveled to Asturias (central north Spain) to work as General Manager for a sweets manufacturer. The company, S.A. Granja Asturias, was founded in 1940 but was experiencing financial difficulties. About one and a half years after his appointment the company started to flour-

This case was written by Regina S. Kilfoyle, Sloan Fellow of the London Business School, under the supervision and guidance of Professor Sumantra Ghoshal. The research support of Norma Enright, Juan F. Iturri and Wolf Waschkuhn—all students in the LBS Sloan Fellowship Programme—is gratefully acknowledged, as is the advice of Mr. Dominic Houlder and the cooperation of the management and staff of S.A. Chupa Chups.

ish and the first profits were reported. Bernat chose this moment to propose a radical change in strategy: instead of producing hundreds of different sweets for one market, would the company consider producing just one product for several markets? It was necessary to find an innovative product for the Spanish market. It would have to add something new to the end customer (the child) and, principally, to the buyer (the mother). Bernat remembered how children were admonished because they had stained their hands, faces and clothes with their sweets. He proposed the idea of a sweet with a stick—what is now known around the world as a lollipop.

The board took a skeptical view of this plan, judging it to be the madness of an ambitious youngster. But Bernat had faith in his idea, so progressively he bought the shares of the company. In 1957, he took over as the sole shareholder. The first lollipop, under the Chups brand was introduced in 1958. Triggered by the success of the first radio commercial where the musical slogan prompted "Chupa un Chups" (suck a sucker), the product name was changed three years later to Chupa Chups.

The Product

An early technical difficulty in developing the product was the quality of the stick. It had to be strong enough to resist manipulation but soft enough not to hurt children's mouths. In a period when Spain was still largely closed to foreign trade, Bernat found the quality of wood required in Central Europe. Later, in 1960, when plastic technology was developed, the company was one of the first in the world to develop a plastic stick that was safer and more resistant to splintering than wood. In another innovation in 1962, the first whistling lollipop in the market was introduced. A version of this lollipop, Melody Pop, was still being sold around the world in the mid-1990s.

Product adaptation has been kept to the minimum, but some local tastes have prevailed over the decades. For example, sugar free lollipops sell well in Scandinavia, while Finnish consumers snap up the salted liquorice pops developed specifically for them. Japanese buyers enjoy the original flavours, but a recently developed green tea flavour is now popular, while in China, lighter colours are considered lucky. For the Saharan Desert region, the company adjusts its formulas of natural ingredients to prolong product shelf life. Wrappers and presentation materials also are adapted by printing in the languages of the many local markets.

There have been very few complaints about the company's products. Indeed, it is only when Chupa Chups is completely confident about its quality that a new product is introduced under the Chupa Chups brand name. One of the very few complaints they have received was from a New York woman who claimed to have fallen because she slipped on a Chupa Chups' stick. She requested $500 as compensation and, without further investigation, the company paid up.

Process Technology

The popularity of Chupa Chups quickly grew in the company's early years, with production averaging circa 3,000 kgms. per day, and a corresponding increase in the number of points of sale. Having developed the product, Bernat decided that the company had to develop its own process technology. In order to do this Chupa Chups bought a company in the metal-mechanic sector called Construcciones Mecánicas Seuba. The name was subsequently changed to Confipack.

Within a few years Confipack developed the machinery, first, to produce spherical sweets, later, a "hole puncher" to introduce the stick, and, lastly, the paper wrapping machine that enabled production capacity to expand from 500 to 4,800 units per hour. This technology enabled production to reach 4,500 kg/day in the early 1960s, the equivalent to 80 million chupa chups per year, and a turnover of 28 millions ptas (nearly half a million U.S. dollars).

Marketing and Distribution

The company started advertising its product very early in its life through radio and later TV campaigns, as well as through intensive use of point of sale publicity. In 1969 Chupa Chups charged renowned Catalán artist Salvador Dali with the design of its brilliant red and yellow wrapper, an identifying mark that has been adapted to local markets and continues to be used today. (See Appendix B.)

In an unusual move, the company developed its own distribution system. During this period an innovative system of 'cash on delivery' was instituted. The sales representative traveled with supplies of the product, executing the sale, delivery and cash settlement simultaneously. Following a careful adaptation of inexpensive SEAT cars, salesmen were able to carry sufficient volume to visit between 40 to 50 customers per day. To facilitate the cash settlement, the product was packaged in envelopes of 140 units with a price of 100 ptas, thus eliminating the need to give change to the retailer. This sales and distribution system proved to be vital in enabling the rapid expansion of the company in Spain. In 1962, the company instituted a parallel distribution system for the whistling pop which mirrored this format. The director of Coca Cola in Spain was recruited to manage these successful distribution operations.

Moving Beyond Home Shores

In 1968 we made our first visit to Japan, making contacts with Japanese manufacturers/distributors who were very surprised to meet a Spaniard selling sweets on a chop stick. It took a long time for the Japanese to overcome their initial revulsion to sucking in public to become one of Chupa Chups' biggest customers. *Enrique Bernat*

With a dominant presence in the Spanish market, the company faced a dilemma concerning further growth. The options were either to leverage the existing national distribution network to diversify into other confectionery and food products or to develop new geographic markets which would enable the sale of a narrow product range such as Chupa Chups.

Chupa Chups elected the latter course. The company began exporting to France, replicating its successful distribution system which it built in partnership with a French manufacturer. The partner was reimbursed by Chupa Chups via combined payments for products sold plus shipping costs according to weight. Two hundred French salesmen in small cars quickly gained Chupa Chups a strong share of the French lollipop market. Its distribution partner was soon exposed as a cheat, however. The French company was weighting the Chupa Chups containers with stones to inflate its reimbursement.

Chups Chups management bided its time, establishing alternative systems before responding with legal action. This situation, in combination with the 20% export fees imposed by the Franco government in Spain, had determined Chupa Chups management to begin some manufacturing abroad. In 1970, the company offered to purchase the facilities and brand name of a renowned but bankrupt French confectionery company. But the French courts blocked the sale, citing the potential for a lollipop monopoly! Nevertheless, Chupa Chups eventually bought a large share in this company while acquiring another suitable plant in Bayonne for production of Chupa Chups branded products intended for Common Market countries.

Growing Pains
During the years 1960 to 1967, Chupa Chups followed an expansion plan in Spain, France, Germany and the United States, replicating the formula of a single appealing, top-quality product distributed by its own salesforce. In 1966, the first foreign commercial office was opened in the Champs Elysées in Paris, followed by an office in New York one year later. By 1968, the first foreign wholly owned subsidiary, Societe Bernat et Cie, was established in France.

During this period, Chupa Chups also was looking eastwards. It entered the Japanese market in 1968. The company contemplated entering the Chinese market, but the Cultural Revolution of 1967 put a hold on this move.

These ambitious expansion plans met more than one setback along the way, however. While experiencing success in France, despite the vagaries of its partnership, the company's first entry into the German market was a failure. The company exited after one year, although it re-entered in 1970 and Germany has since emerged as one of Chupa Chups' largest markets, served through its subsidiary Uniconfis GmbH.

After some trial and error, the Chupa Chups formula also met great success in the United States. New York was to be the test case, and it provided a salutary lesson. Perhaps naively, the company saw the U.S. and New York as culturally similar to Spain. A Cuba-born distributor was chosen, and soon he was managing a large group of salesmen who were in touch with the vast numbers of corner shops in the city. The salesmen were remunerated with a small base salary and a sales-based commission. The direct sales system took hold just as in Europe. But soon after, although sales flattened, the salesmen continued working without complaint. Puzzled by this behaviour, Enrique Bernat made an unannounced midnight trip to New York. He found a distribution system which had been adapted to the sale of marijuana! Chups Chups selected another distributor.

1968–1987: Some Structural Changes
By the late 1970s, the Spanish lollipop market was becoming saturated and rising labour costs were putting pressure on the dedicated distribution network. In 1970, the sales and distribution network had grown to more than 500 people representing

nearly two thirds of the company payroll. Following the difficult recognition that this self-distribution structure was incompatible with rapid foreign expansion, Chupa Chups reduced its distribution staff to eight people, spinning the rest of the group off as another wholly owned subsidiary, Chupa Chups Diversificación, which managed independent salesmen in Spain for both Chupa Chups confections and imported products, including Trebor (part of Cadbury) and Mon Cheri chocolates, Wrigley's and Lamy-Tutti chewing gums, and mints from Vivil, a German producer.

The "downsizing" was well managed with many of the company's former sales representatives becoming very successful distributors/businessmen. And Chupa Chups Diversificación has been highly successful. In the late 1989s, Chupa Chups joined forces with McLane USA (part of the WalMart Group) and Repsol (Spain's largest industrial group) to establish a sophisticated distribution company to convenience stores, petrol stations, mini-markets and fast food franchises, including Burger King and Pizza Hut. In 1982, an additional subsidiary called Uniconfis Corporation, USA, was established in Atlanta dedicated to product distribution.

"But the 1970s were hard years," recounted Executive Vice President Xavier Bernat, eldest son of company founder Enrique Bernat. "'Struggling' is the word to describe us during that period. We were dismantling our own distribution business and building an external system. In addition, our sales had flattened. We couldn't grow any more in our home market. We were working to increase foreign sales, but there were strong trade barriers in many markets. How did we get through this time? Sales in Japan began climbing and we had great success in the USA. We certainly were helped by the popularity of "Kojak," the television series about the detective with a lollipop perpetually in his mouth. Plus some luck, perhaps."

Or perhaps persistence. During these years, the company was learning, sometimes the hard way, exactly how best to market and distribute its product. In the 1980s, commercial subsidiaries were established in Bonn, London and Atlanta. Worldwide sales began to climb again in the mid-1980s. A significant change at headquarters underpinning this expansion was the beginning of a more formal planning process. By the mid-1980s, the company had reached an annual production level of 1,000 million units, with the USA (200 m units), France (120 m units), Japan (120 m units), Spain (80 m units), and Italy (40 m units) emerging as its principal markets.

Up to the late 1980s all production took place in the Spanish and French plants, namely:

- Villamayor in Asturias, northern Spain—6,500 sq. meters with a capacity for 20 metric tons per day.
- San Esteve de Sesrovires near Barcelona—9,000 sq. meters with a capacity for 60 metric tons per day.
- Bayonne in south east France—7,000 sq. meters producing 1 million sweets per day.

This was complemented by a factory in Elche in Spain owned by S.A. Regalin (82% owned by S.A. Chupa Chups) manufacturing liquorice products. This factory was later relocated to Slovenia for more cost-effective production.

Taking on the World

Commenting on reported Mafia problems in the Russian market:

> Problems are everywhere, and the Mafia may be everywhere. But consumers are everywhere, also, and they eat every day. *Enrique Bernat*

Following its success in developed countries, Chupa Chups began to target less developed countries during the late 1980s. "In this period," Xavier Bernat stated, "we began to attack the world."

As mentioned previously, the Chinese market seemed the most attractive. The liberalisation of foreign investment which began in 1979 under Mr. Deng's rule was likely to continue. The market had the potential to be extraordinarily large, and it was mostly untapped territory for foreign confectionery makers. However, finding the right Chinese partner proved difficult and research went on for several years. Ironically China was not the site for Chupa Chups' first joint venture. While Chupa Chups was continuing its opportunity search in China, the Soviet market began to open.

Entering Russia

The Soviet Union allowed foreign investment from 1987. The new law stipulated that foreign ventures work with a Soviet partner. In 1990, Chupa Chups' long-standing Soviet shipping associate put them in touch with the Soviet Foods Minister. He recommended contacting a confectioner in Leningrad with a factory, a strong brand, and an interest in partnership. While the Soviet producer, Azart, would continue manufacturing its own line of products, Chupa Chups financed 60% of a new Chupa Chups production line at Azart's plant. A two-tiered deal was struck. With financing from its Dutch Antilles finance subsidiary, Chupa Chups bought into the partnership. A second deal was arranged for the partner to rent production equipment from Chupa Chups. Chupa Chups retained title to the equipment because Soviet property rights were unclear.

The financial risks to providing the equipment were minimal: Chupa Chups shipped slower, older machinery obsolete for the Spanish plants but suitable for Soviet workers unused to working with or maintaining high-tech, computerised equipment. (The factory workers were subcontracted from Azart to Neva Chupa Chups.) It was planned that twenty-five Soviet employees would be trained in Spain in the operation of the older equipment. Locally produced items would be limited to the "Chupa Chups Classic," with other products shipped in from Spain. Supplies of sugar and glucose would be sourced locally, adhering to centrally established, stringent quality specifications. All other production supplies, from flavouring to packaging, would be sourced from Barcelona.

Chupa Chups staff were installing the last pieces of the production line in Leningrad on the day of the Russian coup. All communications with the staff were cut off. Reports of a potential revolution filled the news. Was the Leningrad location secure?

Back in headquarters, a worried Enrique Bernat waited for some news. Three long days later, the staff reported in safe. Six months later, the Russian economy was wide open. Neva Chupa Chups was in production, and opportunities were rife in the new Russia. So were the problems.

Russian Accounting System. "We entered at the right time," said Miguel Otero, Manager, International Investments, for S.A. Chupa Chups. "But the situation was a shock to us because developments there were so unexpected and so fast." Learning as they went, Chupa Chups and their Russian partner weathered a series of economic crises including hyperinflation and losses due to currency devaluation and non-existent banking systems. For example, payments wired from outlying regions took weeks to reach St. Petersburg (Leningrad had re-adopted its original name following the collapse of the USSR), by which time inflation had greatly diminished the transaction value. Checking accounts did not exist, so many local payments were made in cash; customers would arrive at the plant with sacks of roubles slung over their shoulders. Reacting to needs, Neva Chupa Chups quickly developed contracts allowing payment terms in roubles but which were valued at the U.S. dollar rate on the date of payment. The situation improved in 1993 when the raw materials and dollar markets were liberalised and inflation dropped to a mere 1,000%.

The economy was cooling, relatively, but change at Neva Chupa Chups seemed endemic: that year their Russian partner, Nikolai Azarov, had to raise capital to privatise the state-owned Azart. He sold 15% of Azart's share of Neva Chupa Chups to S.A. Chupa Chups, and a further 10% to a St. Petersburg bank (of which Neva Chupa Chups owned 5%). His company retained only 15% ownership but Azarov still had an influential voice at Board meetings. For instance, despite his lamentations that after four years Azart had no money to show for its work with Neva Chupa Chups, Azarov had been an outspoken proponent of reinvesting Neva Chupa Chups profits into a new factory with greatly increased capacity. And it was he who arranged discussions in 1995 between Neva Chupa Chups' general manager and the owner of Russia's largest bread baker and distributor. As a result, by 1996 a new line of cakes baked on the Russian's premises was ready for marketing in Russia under the Chupa Chups brand. In typical Bernat fashion, this newest joint venture involved family: Enrique Bernat's brother, representing the maternal, bakers branch of the family, visited Russia regularly to advise on the start-up.

Neva Chupa Chups Takes the Market.   A Spanish General Manager was sent to Leningrad for the start-up in 1991, along with a Finance Director and a Russian-speaking Logistics Manager. However, while great strides were made in organising production, other problems continued to dog Russian operations. For instance, the Russian press galloped with a negative publicity campaign concerning the "Painted Chupa Chups." This temporarily tongue-dying lollipop was labeled carcinogenic by the Russian media and had to be withdrawn.

The growing power of the Russian "Red Mafia" also posed a potential threat to the venture's success. Three other major Spanish manufacturers operating in Russia—sausage maker Campofrio and cava (Catalán sparkling wine) producers Codorniu and Freixenet—were likewise dealing with security threats and demands for "security payments." In fact, Freixenet had to reach agreement with the hard-core of the Mafia which controls the distribution of alcohol and tobacco, and Codorniu withdrew from the market after thieves murdered four of the company's security guards and pilfered 230,000 cases of cava. Market conditions were, as they say, difficult.

The Spanish General Manager established an efficient production line and was effective in dealing with the slow-moving Soviet bureaucracy (as for example, when Confipack technicians required full investigation and a permit from the KGB before entering the Soviet Union). But the accelerating new Russian economy was making it difficult to plan company development or to make profits.

Neva Chupa Chups' situation improved suddenly following the September 1993 "Sweet Expo" in Moscow. Xavier Bernat attended this gathering. Encountering representatives from every major Western confectioner from Cadbury to Wrigley, he fully realised the potential of the Russian market and wasted no time in allocating resources to shore up the money-losing subsidiary. A new General Manager, Walter Borio Almo, was sent from headquarters in 1993 along with a new Spanish Financial Director. A Mexican of Italian-Spanish heritage, Borio spoke five languages fluently and quickly gained a working knowledge of Russian. But with years of commercial experience throughout Europe with S.A. Chupa Chups and other multinationals, even he was challenged by the situation at Neva Chupa Chups.

"Our 'offices' contained one desk, one chair, and eight salesmen in a queue for our one telephone," he related with animation. "Our production line was completely ready but was functioning at 50% of capacity due to lack of demand. Customers would arrive, purchase one $25 box of lollipops, then drive 10 kilometres down the road and sell our products from the back of their cars. Our own fledgling sales system relied on the efforts of eight independent salesman paid $185 per month to walk from kiosk to kiosk in all weather conditions promoting our goods. They were wearing out their shoes selling one box of lollipops a day to each kiosk. And without a car, Russia is a big country!"

He continued: "Our warehouse consisted of only 200 square metres located on the fifth floor and equipped with shelves too narrow for our boxes. The lift couldn't hold more than one box of lollipops, so it took two hours to load a truck, box by box—when the lift was working, that is. But we had faith in our product, so we quickly made some changes."

Organisational Systems.   Borio and his team began planning their expansion in the Russian market. As a priority, relations with Azarov were improved and more Azart space was freed for the joint venture. ("After the first time Nikolai and I got drunk together, the ice began to melt," confided Borio.) Equally critically, the team established commercial systems, such as setting prices and minimum sales orders, targeting customers and distributors, and planning promotions.

Direct sales to kiosks were stopped in January 1994. Minimum orders were raised from $25 to $1,000 and later, in 1995, to $5,000. Partial credit for the enlarged order size was given to customers meeting three criteria, viz, (i) they had been Neva Chups Chups customers for more than six months; (ii) they had established corporate structures which allowed them to move the product, such as warehouses and computers; and (iii) they already distributed for other quality companies such as Mars, etc.

Concerning distribution, the usual Chupa Chups approach of distributing through top manufacturers was modified for Russia: since Western companies were not manufacturing at that time in Russia, Neva Chupa Chups selected Russian third-party distributors with a track record of distribution for the best confectioners. Borio aimed to have a distributor in each of the 65 Russian cities with a population of 300,000 or more. By 1995, he had appointed distributors in 43 cities, and these provided hubs to penetrate all parts of Russia until such time as the total goal was achieved.

Advertising adapted to the Russian media was held back until distribution was assured, but a television campaign released to run through April, May and June led to spiraling demand. A popular feature of the Russian television ads was the genuine footage of Russian cosmonauts sucking on Chupa Chups while on duty in the Mir Space Station. The cosmonauts had requested supplies of their favourite candy—Chupa Chups—as a substitute for cigarettes which were forbidden in the space station. (Xavier Bernat knew the Director of the Mir Programme who facilitated videotaping in space of Chupa Chups—truly a universal product.) With the growth in sales, larger warehouses had been acquired which allowed sufficient stocks to meet demand. By April 1994, the production line was working at full capacity for two shifts. That June, a third shift was added.

Similarly, corporate structures had to be built from the ground up. A 25-year-old Russian, formerly a lieutenant in the Soviet army, was hired immediately as Sales Manager to build the commercial team. The new territory was divided into five regions, each headed by a young Russian product market manager, most with international experience or experience in other multinational corporations within Russia, and most formerly with the Soviet military. A new Marketing Director, an American, arrived from Barcelona in November 1995, but the remainder of the 100 member staff also were Russian, including managers, secretaries, line foremen, the quality control scientist, and mechanical engineers.

Situation in November 1995. Neva Chupa Chups bought a satellite dish in 1994 to improve telephone access. Although still Spartan, the offices had been modernised using $50,000 from the parent company. Separate desks were made available for everyone and a computer was placed on each desk. Multiple telephone lines rang constantly, and the interaction of sales staff, secretaries, uniformed factory staff and managers was carried on in the open plan office in a mixture of Russian, Spanish and English. (In fact, the environment had become exactly like headquarters in Barcelona which likewise has an open floor plan, a multinational staff and an energetic atmosphere.) In the center of this humming activity sat Walter Borio with a large bust of Vladimir Lenin holding a Chupa Chups Classic lollipop on the corner of his desk.

By 1995, the venture had emerged as a roaring success. Dividends to the partner were related to production, so the facility ran at one hundred percent capacity. However, sales exceeded even this capacity, so Chupa Chups' new Chinese plant was required to ship products to Russia to meet demand. Sales had climbed steadily: $6 million in 1992; $13 million in 1993; $25 million in 1994; and $35 million in 1995. Operations achieved break-even in 1994, with the first profits coming in 1995. The Russian staff worked hard, according to Chupa Chups management, and they had been fully trained in Chupa Chups production techniques. A new factory was under construction, and plans were in hand to install new, more sophisticated equipment by the summer of 1996. The locally manufactured product line was planned for expansion beyond the "Chupa Chups Classic" to include "Melody Pops" and other more complex lollipops, inaugurating production of these outside the Spanish and French plants.

Even the Mafia had been dealt with in a creative fashion: low margin confectionery products were not so attractive to the Mafia as alcohol, tobacco or banknotes, anyway, but Neva Chupa Chups counter-offered the Mafia's overtures with a 5% reduction off the wholesale price of lollipops.

China Opens Up

On Chupa Chups' persistence:

Looked at China—the cultural revolution. More negotiations!
Looked at China—Mao dies. More negotiations!
Looked at China—Mao's widow came to power. More negotiations!
Looked at China—Mao's widow 'resigns.' More negotiations!
Looked at China—Tianenmen Square. More negotiations!. *Enrique Bernat.*

While pleased with developments in the Russian market, Chupa Chups management continued looking for opportunities to enter the Chinese market. Following the fruitless negotiations with Bei Jing First Confectionery Company, another delegation from the Chinese government arrived in Barcelona in 1994 seeking Spanish business partners for Chinese enterprises. One such enterprise was Tian Shan, a subsidiary of Guan Sheng Yuan of Shanghai, the largest Chinese confectionery producer. Following up on this contact, Chupa Chups' managers visited Shanghai and a joint venture agreement was quickly developed between the two companies.

In opening its Chinese venture, Chupa Chups adhered to its expansion model: it partnered with a local organisation in a country with an underdeveloped distribution network; took the majority share of the partnership (67%); and provided the equipment. "It's possible to have a 100% foreign owned company in China, but it's the work of a crazy person,"

commented Xavier Bernat. "You must pay to get clearance from fourteen commissions at least—for the real estate, the buildings, the firemen's health insurance, and so on. We've found a good partner, a serious company that had the only lollipop production line in the market. We work together on everything."

Organisational Systems.   In November 1994, the Shanghai Chupa Chups Guan Sheng Yuan Food Co., Ltd., opened its doors. Building on their Russian experiences, Chupa Chups established a production and management structure similar to that of Neva Chupa Chups. The local plant focused on producing the "Chupa Chups Classic" only, using proven Chupa Chups technology. Their partner continued to maintain its own successful confectionery line. Raw materials such as glucose and sugar were sourced locally while other materials, packaging and complex lollipops were shipped from Spain. Management consisted of a mixture of expatriots and national staff. The General Manager was the former head of Chupa Chups' highly successful German subsidiary, the Finance Director was Spanish, while the Deputy General Manager was recruited locally in China and dealt principally with Chinese finances and managed the accounting systems.

Marketing and Sales.   Like the Russian operation, marketing and distribution also was developed with national staff, although in a slightly more complex fashion: Chinese law forbade wholesale distribution by foreign firms of any goods not produced within China. But Chupa Chups intended to export to China its more complex products and some supplies. Management was on the point of inking a contract with a Chinese distributor. But Enrique Bernat strongly advised the Executive Group not to rely on the efforts of a single distributor, but to develop its own direct distribution system in this market with its vast potential. So Chupa Chups set up a commercial sales company based in Singapore and Hong Kong with mainland Chinese who had previously worked for Mars and Pepsi Cola in China. This group provided inward distribution of Chupa Chups products and also some supporting marketing services in exchange for a commission. While acknowledging that developing distribution in a country the size of China has been challenging, Xavier Bernat and the Executive Committee believed that the decision to maintain direct control of distribution in China was correct.

Expanding into India and Beyond

In 1996, Chupa Chups continues to eye new markets, especially those with exploding populations. Many of these developing markets, however, present trade barriers to foreign companies, leading Chupa Chups to develop local partnerships instead of relying on imports. Chupa Chups signed a joint venture agreement in 1994 with a company based in Madras, India, to begin production of the "Chupa Chups Classic." As with the previous joint ventures, Chupa Chups contributes the technology and marketing expertise to the venture and the partner provides the site. The new plant was expected to be operational by late 1996. In addition, Chupa Chups has plans to enter Mexico with a local partner who will hold 10% of the joint venture. The facility will capitalise on low labour costs and the recently unified, duty-free North American market. Plans for constructing a facility in Brazil were announced at the end of 1995. The company fully intends to continue all of its joint venture partnerships, even after operations are well established, according to Xavier Bernat.

In comparing the three established joint ventures, International Investment General Manager Miguel Otero contrasted the bureaucracy and the banking systems. In Russia, he said, dealing with the government is no problem. Permission for entry and expansion is easily obtained. The Chinese government also will facilitate foreign ventures. The Indian government, apparently, is quite another matter. "The British left behind many wonderful systems," he said, "including a very large bureaucracy."

On the other hand, banking systems range from sophisticated (India) to bureaucratic (China) to chaotic (Russia). The company even had provisions for "bad bank transactions" in Russia. At one point the currency situation became so bad in the former USSR that Neva Chupa Chups staved off a cash crisis by distributing sunflower seeds from the Ukraine to Spain and the USA to earn the hard currency required by the Soviets of all foreign companies. This system was functional until the former USSR was broken up, the Ukraine gained independence, and the deal had to be abandoned.

Financing the International Expansion

Prior to Spain's entry to the European Union (EU), Chupa Chups' international expansion was financed by preferential bank lines of credit and, after Franco's death, tax incentives offered by Spain to foster the development of export activities. In addition, the Chupa Chups Group and in particular, the Bernat family, could provide start-up support. More recently, Chupa Chups continues to fund its expansion through a shrewd combination of company funds and grants/low interest loans offered by the EU and other government agencies, as well as through its partnership arrangements. These activities, combined with a successful track record of negotiating with Russian, Chinese and Indian governments reveal Chupa Chups' strengths in managing government relations.

Financing arrangements are somewhat different for each situation. Flexibility and adaptation to local conditions are crucial. Chupa Chups' philosophy has been to share financial responsibility. With joint ventures, its intention is to seek partnerships but retain majority share.

Russia. Early funding for Neva Chupa Chups was provided by the Chupa Chups Group. In 1996, however, given the established track record of the Russian subsidiary, external financing for this subsidiary was being, sought from the European Bank of Reconstruction and Development (EBRD) for the new 10,000 sq. meter factory plus warehouse on the outskirts of St. Petersburg. Construction and working capital costs were estimated at $25M. If EBRD funding was not forthcoming, Neva Chupa Chups would finance the project through profit reinvestment and slowed payments to S.A. Chupa Chups for supplies.

China. The Chinese subsidiary also was financed with relatively risk-free capital. The China State Bank provided long-term financing at market rates directly to the partner in Shanghai with no backing required from Chupa Chups. The China State Bank also financed working capital requirements and could authorise up to $30M of financing without central government approval.

India. The Indian venture partner had agreed to invest its share, with the backing of an Indian bank, primarily to construct the factory. Chupa Chups would contribute the dedicated equipment to the venture, but due to order backlogs at Confipack, these could not be delivered until mid-1996 at the earliest.

Management of International Operations

Once a subsidiary had been established, Chupa Chups management approach focused on putting financial control systems in place. Any new manufacturing subsidiary was also embedded into the global procurement system and in Chupa Chups' system of plant specialisation. All subsidiaries were involved in developing marketing, advertising and distribution. (See Appendix C for Chupa Chups Group sales for 1994.)

The Financial System
In addition to information circulated by frequent telephone conversations and faxes, financial reports from subsidiaries included daily updates taxed to Barcelona with information on production, sales, cash/financial situation, stocks and debtors. These were brief, one-page reports which Walter Borio, GM of Neva Chupa Chups, contrasted a bit smugly with the onerous paperwork required of the GMs of other multinationals' subsidiaries. "It's incredible the reports they have to send to headquarters. The other GMs have no time to do anything but prepare reports, while I am able to work" he stated.

Monthly reports provided deeper sales information as well as P&L and balance sheet information. Frequent meetings took place between subsidiary management and headquarters staff. Finally, annual sales, financials and monthly milestones were established via annual budget forecasts. It was expected that the entire financial system, including all the daily and monthly reports would be integrated in the future via a new linked global IT system.

The Procurement System
The central procurement system provided the global operations with all raw material (aside from sugar and glucose) necessary to ensure the production of Chupa Chups in a standard format. This was particularly true for the packaging materials such as the wrappers, tins and cartons in which the lollipops were presented. All these items were produced in Spain, labeled in multiple languages where appropriate, and shipped to subsidiaries.

Plant Specialisation and Transfer of Technology
All the Spanish plants and the plant in Bayonne in southern France produced the sophisticated lollipops (i.e. Melody Pops, Fantasy Balls, Tattoo Pops, etc.) and shipped them to other markets. The new Neva Chupa Chups plant was the first outside of Spain and France that was scheduled to produce some of the sophisticated products beginning in 1996. However, the "Chupa Chups Classic" was produced in all plants.

The proprietary process technology, one of the competitive advantages of Chupa Chups, was transferred only gradually from the centre to subsidiary plants. The level of sophistication of the equipment shipped was increased over time: at the beginning very robust, used machinery was shipped to new plants, followed later by the high technology equipment developed more recently by Confipack.

A procedure of prudence, risk minimisation and acknowledgment of local skills could be discerned on the part of Chupa Chups in this approach. First,

Chupa Chups' entire capability of process technology was revealed only after a certain period of a mutual trust and co-operation. Second, workers could gain experience with, for them, new process technology before operating and maintaining more sophisticated machinery. In turn, Chupa Chups could easily develop potential local sales of "Classic" products through older, fully amortised equipment, while sophisticated machines could be employed only when their output could be maximally exploited.

Marketing

In 1996, worldwide marketing efforts of Chupa Chups were directed by Willem van Brakel, a Dutchman. At least a dozen other nationalities were represented on the marketing team. All spoke multiple languages although marketing meetings were conducted in English as a courtesy to the U.K. manager who spoke no other language. The team consisted of 12 area marketing managers each responsible for 5–10 countries. They were all based in Barcelona but traveled about 40% of the time. In this way they stayed in touch with country distributors and salespeople, and could make customer calls with the salespeople. They were intentionally not called sales managers. If an area market manager returned from an exploratory trip to a new territory with a full order book, the trip was considered a failure. The staff aimed to agree on marketing plans with an exclusive distributor, not to make direct sales.

In addition, there were nine product managers who worked directly with areas where there was either a subsidiary or a joint venture. All marketing staff participated in an unofficial and constant flow of information facilitated by the office's open floor plan. The company also had an open door policy which facilitated decision making, and Executive Vice President Xavier Bernat was in daily touch with area marketing managers. The decision process was therefore short and direct, typically involving the area manager and Xavier Bernat, with input sometimes from two to three other marketing staff.

The second arm of the marketing department was responsible for product and packaging development, advertising/promotions, and consumer research. Children remained the primary customers, so product and packaging innovation was seen as a critical success factor in maintaining the customers' interest, especially since the product range was limited to one item. Recent new products have included the Fantasy Ball (bubblegum and rub-on tattoos) and Wind Ball (a game with candy). Until recently, Enrique Bernat himself participated directly in product introductions: he would sit behind the counters of small stores, observing customer reactions to the new product and listening to their comments. Staff also served constantly as test marketers: They dipped into open dishes of new products placed throughout the offices and gave feedback on them.

Distribution

Given the nature of the product and the vision of Enrique Bernat, to have the brand name Chupa Chups etched in people's minds, the product had to be displayed on as many shelves as possible. From its early days, Chupa Chups planned to internationalise. It had preferred to do so through exclusive distributors wherever possible, rather than creating new subsidiaries. But apart from nationalistic trade barriers, another barrier to entering markets was access to the right distribution channels. According to Xavier Bernat, the 'right' distributors were those with excellent local market knowledge, and with wide sales networks (wholesale and retail level) at the appropriate locations and not too many products in their portfolio. Chupa Chups' early lessons were reflected in its clarity of action in distribution through its threefold approach:

- Chupa Chups operated through its own distribution company only in key markets

- Exclusivity was sought after in any contracts with foreign distributors
- The foreign distributors were carefully selected

Chupa Chups undertook an in-depth analysis of the existing distribution structure in a country and its competitive forces. It focused on that country's top distributors (e.g., Cadbury, Unilever, Nabisco, etc.). Once this research was complete, area managers then would approach the top national distributors with a detailed marketing plan. It was reported that their high level of knowledge about the local market conditions regularly flabbergasted local partners during negotiations.

There was a clear preference to select distributors who had their own manufacturing facilities, usually other confectioners. Thus these manufacturers could spread their fixed distribution costs over a bigger volume. Chupa Chups' rationale was to have a dedicated distributor who was not distracted by thousands of others' product lines. Chupa Chups also believed that a distributor who was also a manufacturer had a better fit to the culture of Chupa Chups, itself a manufacturer with strong distribution skills.

Advertising

As part of the distribution agreement, Chupa Chups sought the physical and psychological involvement of the distributors. This was particularly true of the advertising and promotion process. The distributors' participation in advertising and promotions not only resulted in more opinions, but also in more potential solutions to issues. With distributors all over the world, creative ideas abounded, although Chupa Chups screened them carefully to ensure all promotions protected its brand.

Chupa Chups contracted with an advertising agency in Spain but also worked with many different agencies abroad, in particular linking with the distributors' agencies. Chupa Chups typically selected medium or even small advertising agencies. The Chupa Chups account was therefore significant

to the agencies. The advertising and promotion brief was many times directed by headquarters but creative ideas often were initiated elsewhere.

The Changing Focus of Marketing

Chupa Chups' advertising acknowledged the fact that within their traditional markets birth rates were falling. Consequently, there were fewer children eating lollipops. Chupa Chups recognised a long time ago that if there was a Chupa Chups at home, an adult would eat it but they would not go out and buy it. Therefore the company was changing its advertising focus towards teenagers and adult customers. Late teens were important targets since their activities often were mimicked by younger, pre-teens who otherwise might stop eating lollipops at around age 10. In Australia, for example, the company launched a successful campaign to college and university students with the slogan Smoke a Chupa Chups, and they sponsor Light Fridays in discos with sweets as opposed to cigarettes. Chupa Chups also has launched a new mouth freshening product, Smints, aimed at adults.

Flow of Promotional Ideas

Chupa Chups' marketing philosophy was to develop goals and advertising campaigns centrally and then allow subsidiaries to adopt portions selectively as appropriate to their markets. Promotional ideas were initiated anywhere within the company and discussed with headquarters, subsidiaries and distributors before a campaign was developed further at headquarters. The campaigns across most countries tended to follow the main theme of displaying a Chupa Chups to the viewer, though within Spain, where knowledge of the product was high, Chupa Chups had developed advertising which did not show the product to the viewer.

The Chupa Chups Philosophy

We don't have to tell the General Managers what to do. They know the company strategy. *Xavier Bernat*

Decisions

All strategic moves and investments were decided by consensus by the Executive Committee, which included three family members—Xavier, Marcos and Ramon—and two other senior general managers. Enrique Bernat, while withdrawing himself from most daily operations of S.A. Chupa Chups, still spent about 10% of his time on Chupa Chups activities, and he retained a strong influence on the Committee, illustrated by his advice to establish direct distribution in China.

The Executive Committee reported to the Board, which was comprised entirely of family members. Therefore all Board members shared common objectives and points of view. Actually, there were no formal Board meetings. This speeded decision making which could be reduced to 24 hours, as opposed to a month or more with other corporate boards. Chupa Chups' speed and decisiveness was demonstrated when senior staff returned the Chinese delegation's visit within a month of their initial meeting in Barcelona to explore real joint venture possibilities.

Once subsidiaries or joint ventures were established, the placement of appropriate staff was a major mechanism by which headquarters helped the subsidiaries. Once installed, the subsidiaries' managers were encouraged to make decisions on the ground. In return, they were expected to achieve financial self-sufficiency for the subsidiary within 2–3 years. The threshold of a 15 percent profit margin was a means by which the performance of the subsidiary management was measured.

Formal reports were demanded (see Finance section), but the lines of communication between management and staff and between headquarters and subsidiaries remained open and informal. For example, the family was highly accessible. Enrique Bernat was nearly always available for discussion although the best time to catch him informally, according to a junior staff member, was on Saturdays between 10:00 and 2:00 when he was always in his office. Executive Vice President Xavier Bernat was a lot more involved and accessible. Product market managers rang him directly from field visits to discuss ideas and problems, as did subsidiary managers.

"We are not like some other multinationals with a formal top group and seven reporting divisions," exclaimed Xavier Bernat. "We have a structure, yes, but we really are a conglomeration of companies developing products. We have sold 30 billion lollipops and we believe we will sell 30 billion more, maybe in more sophisticated ways, but with the same focus as always."

Staff Development

> I have always taken care that people feel good about working with us. It is vitally important that they feel happy at work; that they like the job.
> *Enrique Bernat*

"I am a Chupa Chups boy," explained one production engineer. He described the characteristics of a true Chupa Chups staff member: "First, they're crazy because they work very long hours, but they like it. Second, it's a happy company. Third, they live the philosophy of a Basque saying, 'We always do the impossible and a miracle a day.'" Finally, a family-owned business, it retained the feel of family. After about three years with the company, staff gained the full confidence of the top—the Bernats—and of the other managers. They then were authorised to make decisions, and failure was accepted so long as the decisions were taken based on defensible logic.

The Bernat family had consciously developed an enthusiastic environment within the company. "The consumer market is very competitive, so we must maintain a super-motivation among the staff," explained Xavier Bernat. "In some sectors you must be conservative, but not in this one. We don't sell a product. We sell a world, a philosophy, an attitude." Indeed, the atmosphere in offices and factories was palpably energetic and friendly. And many staff members walked around the office or factory floor with a Chupa Chups in their mouths.

Enrique Bernat attributed the company's success to its ability to recruit talented staff and admitted to paying above-average salaries. There were many nationalities represented within the company, yet typically after three years they all shared the Chupa Chups mentality. The exchange of staff between headquarters and subsidiaries, as well as between subsidiaries, facilitated the transfer of the Chupa Chups culture. For example, following on the great success in Germany, the German manager was transferred into the GM role in Shanghai. The management team at Neva Chupa Chups likewise consisted of experienced Chupa Chups staff members.

Although not actually Chupa Chups employees, factory staff at the joint ventures were involved in problem solving, such as machine installation or repairs, as well as quality control programmes. All staff also shared in celebrations, such as the annual lunches hosted by the general managers of Neva Chupa Chups and Azart to celebrate their birthdays.

Chupa Chups staff, however, attributed the company's success to the role that the Bernat family played in the day to day operations of the company. Company legends were frequently repeated concerning the vision and drive of founder Enrique as well as the acumen of son, Xavier. "Their involvement is fundamental to the company's success," explained a staff member. Why? "Because the Bernats like this company!"

APPENDIX A   The Chupa Chups Group

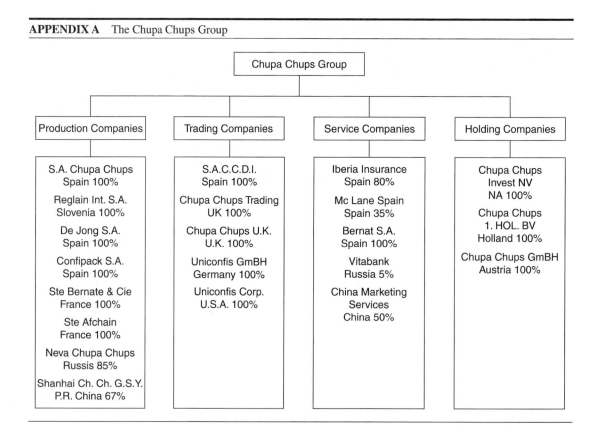

APPENDIX B   The Chupa Chups logo

APPENDIX C Chupa Chups Group 1994 Estimated Consolidated Sales

| | | | | Consolidated Figures (Estimated) at the End of 1994 | | | | |
Company	(%) Ownership	Currency	Total Sales*	Exchange Rate	Intercompany Sales (%)	Total Sales in Ptas†	Intercompany Sales (Ptas)†	Consolidated Sales (Ptas)†
S.A. Chupa Chups	100%	Ptas	13,588,900	1.0	40%	13,588,900	5,435,560	8,153,340
Regalin Int. S.A.	100%	Ptas	356,000	1.0		356,000		356,000
Ste. Bernat et Cie	100%	F.F.	70,000	24.5		1,715,000		1,715,000
Conf Afchain S.A.	100%	F.F.	9,837	24.5		241,007		241,007
Neva Ch Ch A/O	85%	$US	25,681	130.0		2,837,751		2,837,751
De Jong S.A.	90%	Ptas	331,000	1.0		297,900		297,900
Confipack S.A.	100%	Ptas	522,000	1.0		522,000		522,000
S.A. Ch Ch Distribution	100%	Ptas	2,731,000	1.0		2,731,000		2,731,000
Uniconfis GmbH	100%	D.M.	38,363	85.0		3,260,855		3,260,855
Uniconfis Corp	100%	$US	18,200	130.0		2,366,000		2,366,000
Ch Ch Trading	100%	$US	27,032	130.0	40%	3,514,160	1,405,664	2,108,496
Total Confectionery						**31,430,572**	**6,841,224**	**24,589,348**
McLane—Spain	35%	Ptas	5,321,000	1.0		1,862,350		1,862,350
Iberia Insurance	80%	Ptas	8,233,000	1.0		6,586,400		6,586,400
Total Other						**8,448,750**		**8,448,750**
Total						**39,879,322**	**6,841,224**	**33,038,098**

*all figures in 000s
†in 000s Ptas

APPENDIX D   Chupa Chups Group Projected Sales 1994–2000

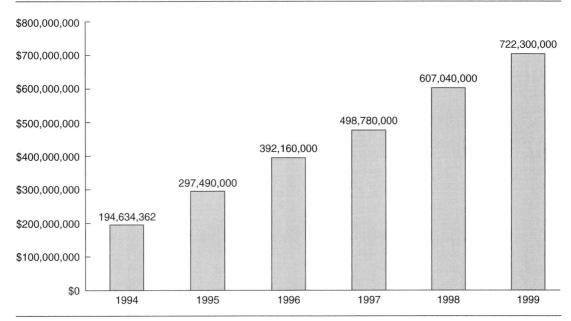

APPENDIX E   Opening Letter to a Company Brochure

A message from the President:

Everything started almost 40 years ago when I undertook the thrilling objective of specialising in lollipops, in order to obtain a unique product of better quality than any other lollipop known in the world. The achievement of this objective has been extremely rewarding not only in terms of the benefits to my company but also because it has brought enormous satisfaction and enjoyment to many millions of consumers.

The Chupa Chups history is acknowledged as a classic example of creative intuition and state-of-the-art technology. With the expansion of the Group such essential elements for success are no longer limited only to S.A. Chupa Chups.

As this booklet shows, many new companies have joined the group. All of them, be it manufacturing, commercial or service companies, share one main characteristic: Faith.

The absolute faith in a product, in inexhaustible creativity, in professional honesty, the unshakable faith in the consumer, and faith that the body and soul of a product must be an object loved by the consumer.

And nobody knows better than the staff of our Company, that there is nothing more exigent than Faith.

Enrique Bernat Fontlladosa
President

Reading 3–1

HOW GLOBAL COMPANIES WIN OUT

Thomas Hout, Michael E. Porter, and Eileen Rudden

Hold that obituary on American manufacturers. Some not only refuse to die but even dominate their businesses worldwide. At the same time Ford struggles to keep up with Toyota, Caterpillar thrives in competition with another Japanese powerhouse, Komatsu. Though Zenith has been hurt in consumer electronics, Hewlett-Packard and Tektronix together profitably control 50% of the world's industrial test and measurement instrument market. American forklift truck producers may retreat under Japanese pressure, but two U.S. chemical companies—Du Pont and Dow—dramatically outperform their competitors.

How do these American producers hold and even increase profitability against international competitors? By forging integrated, global strategies to exploit their potential, and by having a long-term outlook, investing aggressively, and managing factories carefully.

The main reason is that today's international competition in many industries is very different from what it has been. To succeed, an international company may need to change from a multidomestic competitor, which allows individual subsidiaries to compete independently in different domestic markets, to a global organization, which pits its entire worldwide system of product and market position against the competition.

The global company—whatever its nationality—tries to control leverage points, from cross-national

Reprinted by permission of *Harvard Business Review.* "How Global Companies Win Out" by Thomes Hout, Michael E. Porter, and Eileen Rudden, (September/October 1982).

production scale economies to the foreign competitors' sources of cash flow. By taking unconventional action, such as lowering prices of an important product or in key markets, the company makes the competitor's response more expensive and difficult. Its main objective is to improve its own effectiveness while eroding that of its competitors.

Not all companies can or should forge a global strategy. While the rewards of competing globally are great, so are the risks. Major policy and operating changes are required. Competing globally demands a number of unconventional approaches to managing a multinational business to sometimes allow:

Major investment projects with zero or even negative ROI.

Financial performance targets that vary widely among foreign subsidiaries.

Product lines deliberately overdesigned or underpriced in some markets.

A view of country-by-country market positions as interdependent and not as independent elements of a worldwide portfolio to be increased or decreased depending on profitability.

Construction of production facilities in both high and low labor cost countries.

Not all international businesses lend themselves to global competition. Many are multidomestic in nature and are likely to remain so, competing on a domestic-market-by-domestic-market basis. Typically these businesses have products that differ greatly among country markets and have high transportation costs, or their industries lack sufficient scale economies to yield the global competitors a significant competitive edge.

Before entering the global arena, you must first decide whether your company's industry has the right characteristics to favor a global competitor. A careful examination of the economies of the business will highlight its ripeness for global competition.[1] Simply put, the potential for global competition is greatest when significant benefits are gained from worldwide volume—in terms of either reduced unit costs or superior reputation or service—and are greater than the additional costs of serving that volume.

Identifying potential economies of scale requires considerable insight. Advantages to increased volume may come not only from larger production plants or runs but also from more efficient logistics networks or higher volume distribution networks. Worldwide volume is also particularly advantageous in supporting high levels of investment in research and development; many industries requiring high levels of R&D, such as pharmaceuticals or jet aircraft, are global. The level of transport or importing costs will also influence the business's tendency to become global. Transport is a relatively small portion of highly traded optical goods, for example, while it is a barrier in trading steel reinforcing bars.

Many businesses will not be able to take the global step precisely because their industries lack these characteristics. Economies of scale may be too modest or R&D spending too closely tied to particular markets. Products may differ significantly across country boundaries, or the industry may emphasize distribution, installation, and other local activities. Lead times may be short, as in fashion-oriented businesses and in many service businesses, including printing. Also, transportation costs and government barriers to trade may be high, and distribution may be fragmented and hard to penetrate. Many consumer nondurable businesses or low-technology assembly companies fall into this category, as do many heavy raw-material

processing industries and wholesaling and service businesses.

Our investigation into the strategies of successful global companies leads us to believe that a large group of international companies have global potential, even though they may not know it. Almost every industry that is now global—automobiles and TV sets, for example—was not at one time. A company must see the potential for changing competitive interaction in its favor to trigger a shift from multidomestic to global competition. And because there is no guarantee that the business can become global, the company must be willing to risk the heavy investment that global competition requires.

A company that recognizes its business as potentially global, but not yet so, must ask itself whether it can innovate effectively and must understand its impact on the competition to find the best answers to these three questions:

What kind of strategic innovation might trigger global competition?

Is it in the best position among all competitors to establish and defend the advantages of global strategy?

What kind of resources—over how long a period—will be required to establish the leading position?

The Successful Global Competitor

If your industry profile fits the picture we've drawn, you can better judge your ability to make these kinds of unconventional decisions by looking at the way three global companies have succeeded. These organizations (American, European, and Japanese) exemplify the global competitor. They all perceive competition as global and formulate strategy on an integrated, worldwide basis. Each has developed a strategic innovation to change the rules of the competitive game in its particular industry. The innovation acts as a lever to support the development of an integrated global system but demands a market position strong enough to implement it.

---

[1]For a more detailed look at globalization, see Michael E. Porter, *Competitive Strategy.*

Finally, the three companies have executed their strategies more aggressively and effectively than their competitors. They have built barriers to competitive responses based on careful assessment of competitors' behavior. All three have the financial resources and commitment needed to compete unconventionally and the organizational structure to manage an integrated system.

We will take a careful look at each of these three and how they developed the strategic innovation that led, on the one hand, to the globalization of their industries and, on the other, to their own phenomenal success. The first company's innovation was in manufacturing; the second, in technology; and the third, in marketing.

The Caterpillar Case: Warring with Komatsu

Caterpillar Tractor Company turned large-scale construction equipment into a global business and achieved world leadership in that business even when faced with an able Japanese competitor. This accomplishment was difficult for a variety of reasons. For one thing, specifications of construction equipment varied widely across countries. Also, machines are expensive to transport, and field distribution—including user financing, spare parts inventories, and repair facilities—is demanding and best managed locally.

Navy Seabees who left their Caterpillar equipment in other countries following World War II planted the seeds of globalization. The company established independent dealerships to service these fleets, and this base of units provided a highly profitable flow of revenue from spare parts, which paid for inventorying new units. The Caterpillar dealers quickly became self-sustaining and to this day are larger, better financed, and do a more profitable parts business than their competitors. This global distribution system is one of Cat's two major barriers against competition.

The company used its worldwide production scale to create its other barrier. Two-thirds of the total product cost of construction equipment is in heavy components—engines, axles, transmissions, and hydraulics—whose manufacturing costs are capital intensive and highly sensitive to economies of scale. Caterpillar turned its network of sales in different countries into a cost advantage by designing product lines that use identical components and by investing heavily in a few large-scale, state-of-the-art component manufacturing facilities to fill worldwide demand.

The company then augmented the centralized production with assembly plants in each of its major markets—Europe, Japan, Brazil, Australia, and so on. At these plants Cat added local product features, avoiding the high transportation cost of end products. Most important, Cat became a direct participant in local economies. The company achieved lower costs without sacrificing local product flexibility and became a friend rather than a threat to local governments. No single "world model" was forced on the customer, yet no competitor could match Caterpillar's production and distribution cost.

Not that they haven't tried. The most recent—and greatest—challenge to Caterpillar has come from Komatsu (see Exhibit I, for a financial comparison). Japan's leading construction equipment producer forged its own global strategy based on exporting high-quality products from centralized facilities with labor and steel cost advantages. Over the last decade Komatsu has gained some 15% of the world construction-equipment market, with a significant share of sales in nearly every product line in competition with Cat.

Caterpillar has maintained its position against Komatsu and gained world share. The two companies increasingly dominate the market vis-á-vis their competitors, who compete on a domestic or regional basis. What makes Caterpillar's strategy so potent? The company has fostered the development of four characteristics essential to defending a leading world position against a determined competitor:

1. *A global strategy of its own.* Caterpillar's integrated global strategy yields a competitive advantage in cost and effectiveness. Komatsu simply plays catch-up ball rather than pulling ahead. Facing a competitor that has consciously devised a global strategy, Komatsu is in a much weaker

---

EXHIBIT I   Financial Comparison of Caterpillar and Komatsu

	Caterpillar	*Komatsu*
1980 estimated sales of construction equipment	$7.2 billion	$2.0 billion
1974–1979 averages:		
Return on capital employed	13.6%	4.0%
Debt/equity	0.4 times	2.1 times
Return on equity	19.1%	12.2%
Percent of earnings retained	69%	65%
Spare parts as percent of total revenue (estimated)	30% to 35%	16% to 20%
Cash flow available from operations	$681 million	$140 million

Source: Financial statements.

---

position than were Japanese TV and automobile manufacturers when they took off.

2. *Willingness to invest in manufacturing.* Caterpillar's top management appears committed to the kind of flexible automated manufacturing systems that allow full exploitation of the economies of scale from its worldwide sales volume.

3. *Willingness to commit financial resources.* Caterpillar is the only Western company that matches Komatsu in capital spending per employee; in fact, its overall capital spending is more than three times that of the Japanese company. Caterpillar does not divert resources into other businesses or dissipate the financial advantage against Komatsu by paying out excessive dividends. Because Komatsu's profitability is lower than Caterpillar's, it must exhaust debt capacity in trying to match Cat's high investment rates.

4. *Blocking position in the Japanese market.* In 1963, Caterpillar formed a joint venture in Japan with Komatsu's long-standing but weaker competitor, Mitsubishi. Operationally, the venture serves the Japanese market. Strategically, it acts as a check on the market share and cash flow of Komatsu. Japan accounts for less than 20% of the world market but yields over 80% of Komatsu's worldwide cash flow. The joint venture is number two in market position, serving to limit Komatsu's profits. Japanese tax records indicate that the Cat-Mitsubishi

joint venture has earned only modest profits, but it is of great strategic value to Caterpillar.[2]

L.M. Ericsson: Can Small Be Beautiful?

L.M. Ericsson of Sweden has become a successful global competitor by developing and exploiting a technological niche. Most major international telephone-equipment producers operated first in large, protected home markets that allowed the most efficient economies of scale. The additional profits helped underwrite R&D and provided good competitive leverage. Sweden's home market is relatively small, yet Ericsson translated the advent of electronic switching technology into a powerful global lever that befuddled competitors in its international market niche. In the electromechanical era of the 1960s, the telephone switching equipment business was hardly global. Switching systems combine hardware and software. In the electromechanical stage, 70% of total installed costs lay in hardware and 70% of hardware cost was direct labor, manufacturing overhead, and installation of the equipment.

Each country's telephone system was unique, economies of scale were low, and the wage rate was

---

[2]For more on this subject, see Craig M. Watson, "Counter-Competition Abroad to Protect Home Markets," *HBR*, January–February 1982, p. 40.

more important than the impact of volume on costs. In the late 1960s, major international companies (including Ericsson) responded by moving electroswitching production to LDCs not only to take advantage of cheaper labor but also to respond to the desire of government telephone companies to source locally.

Eventually, each parent company sourced centrally only the core software and critical components and competed on a domestic-market-by-domestic-market basis. For its part, Ericsson concentrated investment in developing countries without colonial ties to Europe and in smaller European markets that lacked national suppliers and that used the same switching systems as the Swedish market.

The telecommunicatons industry became global when, in the 1970s, electronic switching technology emerged, radically shifting cost structures and threatening the market position Ericsson had carved for itself. Software is now 60% of total cost; 55% of hardware cost is in sophisticated electronic components whose production is highly scale sensitive. The initial R&D investment required to develop a system has jumped to more than $100 million, which major international companies could have amortized more easily than Ericsson. In addition, the move to electronics promised to destroy the long-standing relationships Ericsson enjoyed with smaller government telephone companies. And it appeared that individual electronic switching systems would require a large fixed-cost software investment for each country, making the new technology too expensive for the smaller telephone systems, on which Ericsson thrived.

Ericsson knew that the electronic technology would eventually be adapted to small systems. In the meantime, it faced the possibility of losing its position in smaller markets because of its inability to meet the ante for the new global competition.

The company responded with a preemptive strategic innovation—a modular technology that introduced electronics to small telephone systems. The company developed a series of modular software packages that could be used in different combinations to meet the needs of diverse telephone systems at an acceptable cost. Moreover, each successive system required fewer new modules. As Exhibit II shows, the first system—Södertalje in Sweden—required all new modules, but by the third year, the Ābo system in Finland required none at all. Thus the company rapidly amortized development costs and enjoyed economies of scale that steepened as the number of software systems sold increased. As a result, Ericsson was able to compete globally in small systems.

Ericsson's growth is accelerating as small telephone systems convert to electronics. The company now enjoys an advantage in software cost and variety that continually reinforces itself. Through this technology Ericsson has raised a significant entry barrier against other companies in the small-system market.

Honda's Marketing Genius

Before Honda became a global company, two distinct motorcycle industries existed in the world. In Asia and other developing countries, large numbers of people rode small, simple motorcycles to work. In Europe and America, smaller numbers of people

---

EXHIBIT II Ericsson's Technology Lever: Reduction of Software Cost through Modular Design

	Representative Systems	New Modules Required	Existing Modules Used
Year 1	Södertalje, Sweden	57	0
Year 2	Orleans, France	22	57
Year 3	Ābo, Finland	0	77

Source: Boston Consulting Group, *A Framework for Swedish Industries Policy* (Stockholm: Uberforlag, 1978).

drove big, elaborate machines for play. Since the Asian motorcycle was popular as an inexpensive means of transportation, companies competed on the basis of price. In the West, manufacturers used styling and brand image to differentiate their products. No Western market exceeded 100,000 units; wide product lines and small volumes meant slight opportunities for economies of scale. Major motorcycle producers such as Harley-Davidson of the United States, BMW of West Germany, and Triumph and BSA of the United Kingdom traded internationally but in only modest volumes.

Honda made its industry global by convincing middle-class Americans that riding motorcycles could be fun. Because of the company's marketing innovations, Honda's annual growth rate was greater than 20% from the late 1950s to the late 1960s. The company then turned its attention to Europe, with a similar outcome. Honda invested for seven full years before sustaining profitability in Europe, financing this global effort with cash flows earned from a leading market position at home and in the United States.

Three crucial steps were decisive in Honda's achievement. First, Honda turned market preference around to the characteristics of its own products and away from those of American and European competitors. Honda targeted new consumers and used advertising, promotions, and trade shows to convince them that its motorbikes were inexpensive, reliable, and easy to use. A large investment in the distribution network—2,000 dealerships, retail missionaries, generous warranty and service support, and quick spare-parts availability—backed up the marketing message.

Second, Honda sustained growth by enticing customers with the upper levels of its product line. Nearly half of new bike owners purchased larger, more expensive models within 12 months. Brand loyalty proved very high. Honda exploited these trends by expanding from its line of a few small motorcycles to one covering the full range of size and features by 1975. The result: self-sustaining growth in dollar volume and a model mix that allowed higher margins. The high volume reduced marketing and distribution costs and improved the position of Honda and other Japanese producers who invaded the 750cc "super bike" portion of the market traditionally reserved for American and European companies. Here Honda beat the competition with a bike that was better engineered, lower priced, and whose development cost was shared over the company's wide product line.

The third step Honda took was to exploit economies of scale through both centralized manufacturing and logistics. The increasing volume of engines and bike assemblies sold (50,000 units per month and up) enabled the company to use less costly manufacturing techniques unavailable to motorcycle producers with lower volumes (see Exhibit III). Over a decade, Honda's factory productivity rose at an average annual rate of 13.1%—several times

EXHIBIT III   The Effect of Volume on Manufacturing Approaches in Motorcycle Production

Cost Element	Low Volume	High Volume
Machine tools	Manual, general purpose	Numerical control, special purpose
Changeover time	Manual, slow (hours)	Automatic positioning, fast (minutes)
Work-in-process inventory	High (days of production)	Low (hours of production)
Materials handling	Forklift trucks	Automated
Assembly	Bay assembly	Motorized assembly line
Machine tool design	Designed outside the company, available throughout industry	Designed in-house, proprietary
Rework	More	Less

Source: *Strategy Alternatives for the British Motorcycle Industry,* a report prepared for the British Secretary of State for Industry by the Boston Consulting Group, July 30, 1975.

higher than European and American producers. Combined with lower transportation cost, Honda's increased output gave it a landed cost per unit far lower than the competition's. In turn, the lower production cost helped fund Honda's heavy marketing and distribution investment. Finally, economies of scale in marketing and distribution, combined with low production cost, led to the high profits that financed Honda's move into automobiles.

What Can We Learn?

Each of these successful global players changed the dynamics of its industry and pulled away from its major competitors. By achieving economies of scale through commonality of design, Caterpillar exploited both its worldwide sales volume and its existing market for parts revenues. Competitors could not match its costs or profits and therefore could not make the investment necessary to catch up. Ericsson created a cost advantage by developing a unique modular technology perfectly adapted to its segment of the market. Its global strategy turned electronics from a threat to Ericsson into a barrier to its competitors. Honda used marketing to homogenize worldwide demand and unlock the potential for economies of scale in production, marketing, and distribution. The competition's only refuge was the highly brand-conscious, small-volume specialty market.

In each case, the industry had the potential for a worldwide system of products and markets that a company with a global strategy could exploit. Construction equipment offered large economies of scale in component manufacture, allowing Caterpillar to neutralize high transportation costs and government barriers through local assembly. Ericsson unlocked scale economies in software development for electronic switches. The modular technology accommodated local product differences and governments' desire to use local suppliers. Once Honda's marketing techniques raised demand in major markets for products with similar characteristics, the industry's economies of scale in production combined with low transportation costs and low tariff barriers to turn it into a global game.

In none of the cases did success result from a "world product." The companies accommodated local differences without sacrificing production costs. The global player's position in one major market strengthened its position in others. Caterpillar's design similarities and central component facilities allowed each market to contribute to its already favorable cost structure. Ericsson's shared modules led to falling costs each time a system was sold in a new country. Honda drew on scale economies from the centralized production of units sold in each market and used its U.S. marketing and distribution experience to succeed in Europe.

In addition to superior effectiveness and cost advantages, a winning global strategy always requires abilities in two other dimensions. The first is timing. The successful global competitor uses a production cost or distribution advantage as a leverage point to make it more difficult or expensive for the competitor to respond. The second is financial. The global innovator commits itself to major investment before anyone else, whether in technology, facilities, or distribution. If successful, it then reaps the benefits from increased cash flows from either higher volume (Honda and Ericsson) or lower costs (all three companies). The longer the competitor takes to respond, the larger the innovator's cash flows. The global company can then deploy funds either to increase investment or lower prices, creating barriers to new market entrants.

A global player should decide against which of its major competitors it must succeed first in order to generate broad-based success in the future. Caterpillar located in the Far East not only to source products locally but also to track Komatsu. (Cat increasingly sources product and manufacturing technology from Japan.) Ericsson's radical departure in technology was aimed squarely at ITT and Siemens, whose large original market shares would ordinarily have given them an advantage in the smaller European and African markets. Honda created new markets in the United States and Europe because its most powerful competitors, Yamaha and Kawasaki, were Japanese. By exploiting the global opportunity first, Honda got a head start, and it remained strong even when competitors' own international ambitions came to light.

Playing the Global Chess Game

Global competition forces top management to change the way it thinks about and operates its businesses. Policies that made sense when the company was multidomestic may now be counterproductive. The most powerful moves are those that improve the company's worldwide cost position or ability to differentiate itself and weaken key worldwide competitors. Let us consider two potential moves.

The first is preempting the leading positions in major newly industrializing countries (NICs). Rapid growth in, for example, Mexico, Brazil, and Indonesia has made them an important part of the worldwide market for many capital goods. If its industry has the potential to become global, the company that takes a leading position in these markets will have made a decisive move to bar its competitors. Trade barriers are often prohibitively high in these places, and a company that tries to penetrate the market through a *self-contained* local subsidiary is likely to fall into a trap.

The astute global competitor will exploit the situation, however, by building a specialized component manufacturing facility in an NIC which will become an integral part of a global sourcing network. The company exports output of the specialized facility to offset importing complementary components. Final assembly for the domestic and smaller, neighboring markets can be done locally. (Having dual sources for key items can minimize the risk of disruption to the global sourcing network.)

A good illustration of this strategy is Siemens' circuit breaker operation in Brazil. When the company outgrew its West German capacity for some key components, it seized the opportunity presented by Brazilian authorities seeking capital investments in the heavy electrical equipment industry. Siemens now builds a large portion of its common components there, swaps them for other components made in Europe, and is the lowest-cost and leading supplier of finished product in Brazil.

Another move that can be decisive in a global industry is to establish a solid position with your largest customers to block competitors. Many businesses have a few customers that dominate the global market. The global competitor recognizes their importance and prevents current or prospective competitors from generating any sales.

A good example is a British company, BSR, the world's largest producer of automatic record changers. In the 1970s, when Japanese exports of audio equipment were growing rapidly, BSR recognized that it could lose its market base in the United States and Europe if the Japanese began marketing record changers. BSR redesigned its product to Japanese specifications and offered distributors aggressive price discounts and inventory support. The Japanese could not justify expanding their own capacity. BSR not only stalled the entry of the Japanese into the record-changer market but it also moved ahead of its existing competitor, Garrard.

A global company can apply similar principles to block the competition's access to key distributors or retailers. Many American companies have failed to seize this opportunity in their unwillingness to serve large, private-label customers (e.g., Sears, Roebuck) or by neglecting the less expensive end of their product line and effectively allowing competitors access to their distributors. Japanese manufacturers in particular could then establish a toehold in industries like TV sets and farm equipment.

The decision on prices for pivotal customers must not be made solely on considerations of ROI. Equally important in global competition is the impact of these prices on prospective entrants and the cost of failing to protect and expand the business base. One way to control the worldwide chess game in your favor is to differentiate prices among countries.

Manage Interdependently

The successful global competitor manages its business in various countries as a single system, not a portfolio of independent positions. In the view of portfolio planning theory, a market's attractiveness and the strength of a company's position within it determine the extent of corporate resources devoted to it. A company should defend strong positions and try to turn weak ones around or abandon them. It will pursue high-profit and/or high-growth markets more aggressively than lower-profit or lower-growth ones, and it will decide on a stand-alone basis whether to compete in a market.

Accepting this portfolio view of international competition can be disastrous in a global industry. The global competitor focuses instead on its ability to leverage positions in one country market against those in other markets. In the global system, the ability to leverage is as important as market attractiveness; the company need not turn around weak positions for them to be useful.

The most obvious leverage a company obtains from a country market is the volume it contributes to the company's overall cost or effectiveness. Du Pont and Texas Instruments have patiently won a large sales volume in the sophisticated Japanese market, for example, which supports their efforts elsewhere. Winning a share of a market that consistently supports product innovation ahead of other markets—like the United States in long-haul jet aircraft—is another leverage point. The competitor with a high share of such a market can always justify new product investment. Or a market can contribute leverage if it supports an efficient scale manufacturing facility for a region—like Brazil for Siemens. Finally, a market can contribute leverage if a position in it can be used to affect a competitor's cash flow.

Organization: The Achilles' Heel

Organizational structure and reporting relationships present subtle problems for a global strategy. Effective strategic control argues for a central product-line organization; effective local responsiveness, for a geographic organization with local autonomy. A global strategy demands that the product-line organization have the *ultimate* authority, because without it the company cannot gain systemwide benefits.

Nevertheless, the company still must balance product and area needs. In short, there is no simple solution. But there are some guidelines to help.

No one organization structure applies to all of a company's international businesses. It may be unnecessarily cumbersome, for example, to impose a matrix structure on all business. Organizational reporting lines should probably differ by country market depending on that market's role. An important market that offers high leverage, as in the foregoing examples, must work closely with the global business-unit managers at headquarters. Coordination is crucial to success. But the manager of a market outside the global system will require only sets of objectives under a regional reporting system.

Another guideline is that organizational reporting lines and structures should change as the nature of the international business changes. When a business becomes global, the emphasis should shift toward centralization. As countries increase in importance, they must be brought within the global manager's reach. Over time, if the business becomes less global, the company's organization may emphasize local autonomy.

The common tendency to apply one organizational structure to all operations is bound to be a disadvantage to some of them. In some U.S. companies, this approach inhibited development of the global strategy their industries required.

Match Financial Policies to Competitive Realities

If top management is not careful, adherence to conventional financial management and practices may constrain a good competitive response in global businesses. While capital budgeters use such standard financial tools as DCF return analysis or risk profiles to judge investments and creditors and stock analysts prefer stable debt and dividend policies, a global company must chart a different course.

Allocating Capital

In a global strategy, investments are usually a long-term, interdependent series of capital commitments, which are not easily associated with returns or risks. The company has to be aware of the size and timing of the total expenditures because they will greatly influence competitors' new investment response. Most troublesome, however, is that revenues from investments in several countries may have to build up to a certain point before the company earns *any* return on investment.

A global strategy goes against the traditional tests for capital allocation: project-oriented DCF risk-return analysis and the country manager's record of credibility. Global competition requires a less mechanical approach to project evaluation. The successful global competitor develops at least two levels of financial control. One level is a profit and cost center for self-contained projects; the other is a strategy center for tracking interdependent efforts and competitors' performance and reactions. Global competitors operate with a short time frame when monitoring the execution of global strategy investments and a long time frame when evaluating such investments and their expected returns.

Debt and Dividends

Debt and dividend policies should vary with the requirements of the integrated investment program of the whole company. In the initial stages, a company with a strong competitive position should retain earnings to build and defend its global position. When the industry has become global and growth slows or the returns exceed the reinvestment needed to retain position, the company should distribute earnings to the rest of the corporation and use debt capacity elsewhere, perhaps in funding another nascent global strategy.

Honda's use of debt over the last 25 years illustrates this logic (see Exhibit IV). In the mid-1950s, when Honda held a distant second place in a rapidly growing Japanese motorcycle industry, the company had to leverage its equity 3.5 times to finance growth. By 1960, the Japanese market had matured and Honda emerged dominant. The debt-equity ratio receded to 0.5 times but rose again with the company's international expansion in motorcycles. In the late 1960s, Honda made a major move to the automobile market, requiring heavy debt. At that time, motorcycle cash flows funded the move.

Which Strategic Road to Take?

There is no safe formula for success in international business. Industry structures continuously evolve. The Caterpillar, Ericsson, and Honda approaches will probably not work forever. Competitors will try to push industrial trends away from the strengths

---

EXHIBIT IV   Honda Motor Company's Financial Policy from 1954 to 1980

Period	*Interest-Bearing Debt-to-Equity Ratio*	*Strategic Phase*
1954–55	3.5 times	Rapid growth in domestic motorcycle market; Honda is low-margin, number two producer
1959–60	0.5	Domestic motorcycle market matured; Honda is dominant, high-margin producer
1964–65	0.7	Honda makes major penetration of U.S. motorcycle market
1969–70	1.6	Honda begins major move in domestic auto market
1974–75	1.3	Investment pause due to worldwide recession; motorcycle is major cash generator
1978–80	1.0	Auto exports are highly profitable, as are motorcycles

Source: Annual reports.

of the industry leaders, and technological or political changes may force the leading companies to operate in a multidomestic fashion once again.

Strategy is a powerful force in determining competitive outcomes, whether in international or domestic business. And although adopting a global strategy is risky, many companies can dramatically improve their positions by fundamentally changing the way they plan, control, and operate their businesses. But a global strategy requires that managers think in new ways. Otherwise the company will not be able to recognize the nature of competition, justify the required investments, or sustain the change in everyday behavior needed.

If the company can successfully execute a global strategy, it may find itself joining the ranks of the truly successful international companies. Whether they be Japanese, American, European, or otherwise, the strategic thread that ties together companies like IBM, Matsushita, K. Hattori (Seiko), Du Pont, and Michelin clearly shows that the rules of the international competitive game have changed.

Reading 3–2

THE CORE COMPETENCE OF
THE CORPORATION

by C. K. Prahalad and Gary Hamel

The most powerful way to prevail in global competition is still invisible to many companies. During the 1980s, top executives were judged on their ability to restructure, declutter, and de-layer their corporations. In the 1990s, they'll be judged on their ability to identify, cultivate, and exploit the core competencies that make growth possible—indeed, they'll have to rethink the concept of the corporation itself.

Consider the last ten years of GTE and NEC. In the early 1980s, GTE was well positioned to become a major player in the evolving information technology industry. It was active in telecommunications. Its op-

C. K. Prahalad is professor of corporate strategy and international business at the University of Michigan. Gary Hamel is lecturer in business policy and management at the London Business School. Their most recent *Harvard Business Review* article, "Strategic Intent" (May–June 1989), won the 1989 McKinsey Award for excellence. This article is based on research funded by the Gatsby Charitable Foundation. *Harvard Business Review* (May–June 1990).

erations spanned a variety of businesses including telephones, switching and transmission systems, digital PABX, semiconductors, packet switching, satellites, defense systems, and lighting products. And GTE's Entertainment Products Group, which produced Sylvania color TVs, had a position in related display technologies. In 1980, GTE's sales were $9.98 billion, and net cash flow was $1.73 billion. NEC, in contrast, was much smaller, at $3.8 billion in sales. It had a comparable technological base and computer businesses, but it had no experience as an operating telecommunications company.

Yet look at the positions of GTE and NEC in 1988. GTE's 1988 sales were $16.46 billion, and NEC's sales were considerably higher at $21.89 billion. GTE has, in effect, become a telephone operating company with a position in defense and lighting products. GTE's other businesses are small in global terms. GTE has divested Sylvania TV and Telenet, put switching, transmission, and digital PABX into joint ventures, and closed down semiconductors. As a result, the international position of GTE has eroded. Non-U.S. revenue as a percent of total revenue dropped from 20% to 15% between 1980 and 1988.

NEC has emerged as the world leader in semiconductors and as a first-tier player in telecommunications products and computers. It has consolidated its position in mainframe computers. It has moved beyond public switching and transmission to include such lifestyle products as mobile telephones, facsimile machines, and laptop computers—bridging the gap between telecommunications and office automation. NEC is the only company in the world to be in the top five in revenue in telecommunications, semiconductors, and mainframes. Why did these two companies, starting with comparable business portfolios, perform so differently? Largely because NEC conceived of itself in terms of "core competencies," and GTE did not.

Rethinking the Corporation

Once, the diversified corporation could simply point its business units at particular end product markets and admonish them to become world leaders. But with market boundaries changing ever more quickly, targets are elusive and capture is at best temporary. A few companies have proven themselves adept at inventing new markets, quickly entering emerging markets, and dramatically shifting patterns of customer choice in established markets. These are the ones to emulate. The critical task for management is to create an organization capable of infusing products with irresistible functionality or, better yet, creating products that customers need but have not yet even imagined.

This is a deceptively difficult task. Ultimately, it requires radical change in the management of major companies. It means, first of all, that top managements of Western companies must assume responsibility for competitive decline. Everyone knows about high interest rates, Japanese protectionism, outdated antitrust laws, obstreperous unions, and impatient investors. What is harder to see, or harder to acknowledge, is how little added

momentum companies actually get from political or macroeconomic "relief." Both the theory and practice of Western management have created a drag on our forward motion. It is the principles of management that are in need of reform.

NEC versus GTE, again, is instructive and only one of many such comparative cases we analyzed to understand the changing basis for global leadership. Early in the 1970s, NEC articulated a strategic intent to exploit the convergence of computing and communications, what it called "C&C."[1] Success, top management reckoned, would hinge on acquiring *competencies,* particularly in semiconductors. Management adopted an appropriate "strategic architecture," summarized by C&C, and then communicated its intent to the whole organization and the outside world during the mid-1970s.

NEC constituted a "C&C Committee" of top managers to oversee the development of core products and core competencies. NEC put in place coordination groups and committees that cut across the interests of individual businesses. Consistent with its strategic architecture, NEC shifted enormous resources to strengthen its position in components and central processors. By using collaborative arrangements to multiply internal resources, NEC was able to accumulate a broad array of core competencies.

NEC carefully identified three interrelated streams of technological and market evolution. Top management determined that computing would evolve from large mainframes to distributed processing, components from simple ICs to VLSI, and communications from mechanical cross-bar exchange to complex digital systems we now call ISDN. As things evolved further, NEC reasoned, the computing, communications, and components businesses would so overlap that it would be very hard to distinguish among them, and that there would be enormous opportunities for any company that had built the competencies need to serve all three markets.

---

[1]For a fuller discussion, see our article, "Strategic Intent," *HBR* (May–June 1989), p. 63.

NEC top management determined that semiconductors would be the company's most important "core product." It entered into myriad strategic alliances—over 100 as of 1987—aimed at building competencies rapidly and at low cost. In mainframe computers, its most noted relationship was with Honeywell and Bull. Almost all the collaborative arrangements in the semiconductor-component field were oriented toward technology access. As they entered collaborative arrangements, NEC's operating managers understood the rationale for these alliances and the goal of internalizing partner skills. NEC's director of research summed up its competence acquisition during the 1970s and 1980s this way: "From an investment standpoint, it was much quicker and cheaper to use foreign technology. There wasn't a need for us to develop new ideas."

No such clarity of strategic intent and strategic architecture appeared to exist at GTE. Although senior executives discussed the implications of the evolving information technology industry, no commonly accepted view of which competencies would be required to compete in that industry were communicated widely. While significant staff work was done to identify key technologies, senior line managers continued to act as if they were managing independent business units. Decentralization made it difficult to focus on core competencies. Instead, individual businesses became increasingly dependent on outsiders for critical skills, and collaboration became a route to staged exits. Today, with a new management team in place, GTE has repositioned itself to apply its competencies to emerging markets in telecommunications services.

The Roots of Competitive Advantage

The distinction we observed in the way NEC and GTE conceived of themselves—a portfolio of competencies versus a portfolio of businesses—was repeated across many industries. From 1980 to 1988, Canon grew by 264%, Honda by 200%. Compare that with Xerox and Chrysler. And if Western managers were once anxious about the low cost and high quality of Japanese imports, they are now overwhelmed by the pace at which Japanese rivals are inventing new markets, creating new products, and enhancing them. Canon has given us personal copiers; Honda has moved from motorcycles to four-wheel off-road buggies. Sony developed the 8 mm camcorder, Yamaha, the digital piano. Komatsu developed an underwater remote-controlled bulldozer, while Casio's latest gambit is a small-screen color LCD television. Who would have anticipated the evolution of these vanguard markets?

In more established markets, the Japanese challenge has been just as disquieting. Japanese companies are generating a blizzard of features and functional enhancements that bring technological sophistication to everyday products. Japanese car producers have been pioneering four-wheel steering, four-valve-per-cylinder engines, in-car navigation systems, and sophisticated electronic engine-management systems. On the strength of its product features, Canon is now a player in facsimile transmission machines, desktop laser printers, even semiconductor manufacturing equipment.

In the short run, a company's competitiveness derives from the price/performance attributes of current products. But the survivors of the first wave of global competition, Western and Japanese alike, are all converging on similar and formidable standards for product cost and quality—minimum hurdles for continued competition, but less and less important as sources of differential advantage. In the long run, competitiveness derives from an ability to build, at lower cost and more speedily than competitors, the core competencies that spawn unanticipated products. The real sources of advantage are to be found in management's ability to consolidate corporatewide technologies and production skills into competencies that empower individual businesses to adapt quickly to changing opportunities.

Senior executives who claim that they cannot build core competencies either because they feel the autonomy of business units is sacrosanct or because their feet are held to the quarterly budget fire should think again. The problem in many Western companies is not that their senior executives are any less capable than those in Japan nor that Japanese companies possess greater technical capabilities. Instead, it is their adherence to a concept of the corporation that unnecessarily limits the ability of individual businesses to fully exploit the deep reservoir of technological capability that many American and European companies possess.

The diversified corporation is a large tree. The trunk and major limbs are core products, the smaller branches are business units; the leaves, flowers, and fruit are end products. The root system that provides nourishment, sustenance, and stability is the core competence. You can miss the strength of competitors by looking only at their end products, in the same way you miss the strength of a tree if you look only at its leaves. (See the chart "Competencies: The Roots of Competitiveness.")

Core competencies are the collective learning in the organization, especially how to coordinate diverse production skills and integrate multiple streams of technologies. Consider Sony's capacity to miniaturize or Philips's optical-media expertise. The theoretical knowledge to put a radio on a chip does not in itself assure a company the skill to produce a miniature radio no bigger than a business card. To bring off this feat, Casio must harmonize know-how in miniaturization, microprocessor design, material science, and ultrathin precision

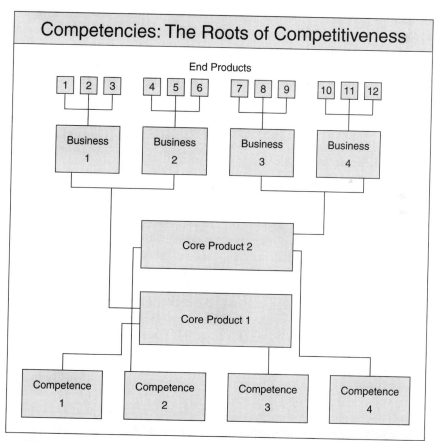

The corporation, like a tree, grows from its roots. Core products are nourished by competencies and engender business units, whose fruit are end products.

casing—the same skills it applies in its miniature card calculators, pocket TVs, and digital watches.

If core competence is about harmonizing streams of technology, it is also about the organization of work and the delivery of value. Among Sony's competencies is miniaturization. To bring miniaturization to its products, Sony must ensure that technologists, engineers, and marketers have a shared understanding of customer needs and of technological possibilities. The force of core competence is felt as decisively in services as in manufacturing. Citicorp was ahead of others investing in an operating system that allowed it to participate in world markets 24 hours a day. Its competence in systems has provided the company the means to differentiate itself from many financial service institutions.

Core competence is communication, involvement, and a deep commitment to working across organizational boundaries. It involves many levels of people and all functions. World-class research in, for example, lasers or ceramics can take place in corporate laboratories without having an impact on any of the businesses of the company. The skills that together constitute core competence must coalesce around individuals whose efforts are not so narrowly focused that they cannot recognize the opportunities for blending their functional expertise with those of others in new and interesting ways.

Core competence does not diminish with use. Unlike physical assets, which do deteriorate over time, competencies are enhanced as they are applied and shared. But competencies still need to be nurtured and protected; knowledge fades if it is not used. Competencies are the glue that binds existing businesses. They are also the engine for new business development. Patterns of diversification and market entry may be guided by them, not just by the attractiveness of markets.

Consider 3M's competence with sticky tape. In dreaming up businesses as diverse as "Post-it" notes, magnetic tape, photographic film, pressure-sensitive tapes, and coated abrasives, the company has brought to bear widely shared competencies in substrates, coatings, and adhesives and devised various ways to combine them. Indeed, 3M has invested consistently in them. What seems to be an extremely diversified portfolio of businesses belies a few shared core competencies.

In contrast, there are major companies that have had the potential to build core competencies but failed to do so because top management was unable to conceive of the company as anything other than a collection of discrete businesses. GE sold much of its consumer electronics business to Thomson of France, arguing that it was becoming increasingly difficult to maintain its competitiveness in this sector. That was undoubtedly so, but it is ironic that it sold several key businesses to competitors who were already competence leaders—Black & Decker in small electrical motors, and Thomson, which was eager to build its competence in microelectronics and had learned from the Japanese that a position in consumer electronics was vital to this challenge.

Management trapped in the strategic business unit (SBU) mind-set almost inevitably finds its individual businesses dependent on external sources for critical components, such as motors or compressors. But these are not just components. They are core products that contribute to the competitiveness of a wide range of end products. They are the physical embodiments of core competencies.

How Not to Think of Competence

Since companies are in a race to build the competencies that determine global leadership, successful companies have stopped imagining themselves as bundles of businesses making products. Canon, Honda, Casio, or NEC may seem to preside over portfolios of businesses unrelated in terms of customers, distribution channels, and merchandising strategy. Indeed, they have portfolios that may seem idiosyncratic at times: NEC is the only global company to be among leaders in computing, telecommunications, and semiconductors *and* to have a thriving consumer electronics business.

But looks are deceiving. In NEC, digital technology, especially VLSI and systems integration skills, is fundamental. In the core competencies underlying them, disparate businesses become coherent. It is Honda's core competence in engines and power trains that gives it a distinctive advantage in car, motorcycle, lawn mower, and generator businesses. Canon's core competencies in optics, imaging, and microprocessor controls have enabled it to enter, even dominate, markets as seemingly diverse as copiers, laser printers, cameras, and image scanners. Philips worked for more than 15 years to perfect its optical-media (laser disc) competence, as did JVC in building a leading position in video recording. Other examples of core competencies might include mechantronics (the ability to marry mechanical and electronic engineering), video displays, bioengineering, and microelectronics. In the early stages of its competence building, Philips could not have imagined all the products that would be spawned by its optical-media competence, nor could JVC have anticipated miniature camcorders when it first began exploring videotape technologies.

Unlike the battle for global brand dominance, which is visible in the world's broadcast and print media and is aimed at building global "share of mind," the battle to build world-class competencies is invisible to people who aren't deliberately looking for it. Top management often tracks the cost and quality of competitors' products, yet how many managers untangle the web of alliances their Japanese competitors have constructed to acquire competencies at low cost? In how many Western boardrooms is there an explicit, shared understanding of the competencies the company must build for world leadership? Indeed, how many senior executives discuss the crucial distinction between competitive strategy at the level of a business and competitive strategy at the level of an entire company?

Let us be clear. Cultivating core competence does *not* mean outspending rivals on research and development. In 1983, when Canon surpassed Xerox in worldwide unit market share in the copier business, its R&D budget in reprographics was but a small fraction of Xerox's. Over the past 20 years, NEC has spent less on R&D as a percentage of sales than almost all of its American and European competitors.

Nor does core competence mean shared costs, as when two or more SBUs use a common facility—a plant, service facility, or sales force—or share a common component. The gains of sharing may be substantial, but the search for shared costs is typically a post hoc effort to rationalize production across existing businesses, not a premeditated effort to build the competencies out of which the businesses themselves grow.

Building core competencies is more ambitious and different than integrating vertically, moreover. Managers deciding whether to make or buy will start with end products and look upstream to the efficiencies of the supply chain and downstream toward distribution and customers. They do not take inventory of skills and look forward to applying them in nontraditional ways. (Of course, decisions about competencies *do* provide a logic for vertical integration. Canon is not particularly integrated in its copier business, except in those aspects of the vertical chain that support the competencies it regards as critical.)

Identifying Core Competencies—And Losing Them

At least three tests can be applied to identify core competencies in a company. First, a core competence provides potential access to a wide variety of markets. Competence in display systems, for example, enables a company to participate in such diverse businesses as calculators, miniature TV sets, monitors for laptop computers, and automotive dashboards—which is why Casio's entry into the handheld TV market was predictable. Second, a core competence should make a significant contribution to the perceived customer benefits of the end product. Clearly, Honda's engine expertise fills this bill.

Finally, a core competence should be difficult for competitors to imitate. And it *will* be difficult if it is a complex harmonization of individual technologies and production skills. A rival might acquire some of the technologies that comprise the core competence, but it will find it more difficult to duplicate the more or less comprehensive pattern of internal coordination and learning. JVC's decision in the early 1960s to pursue the development of a videotape competence passed the three tests outlined here. RCA's decision in the late 1970s to develop a stylus-based video turntable system did not.

Few companies are likely to build world leadership in more than five or six fundamental competencies. A company that compiles a list of 20 to 30 capabilities has probably not produced a list of core competencies. Still, it is probably a good discipline to generate a list of this sort and to see aggregate capabilities as building blocks. This tends to prompt the search for licensing deals and alliances through which the company may acquire, at low cost, the missing pieces.

Most Western companies hardly think about competitiveness in these terms at all. It is time to take a tough-minded look at the risks they are running. Companies that judge competitiveness, their own and their competitors', primarily in terms of the price/performance of end products are courting the erosion of core competencies—or making too little effort to enhance them. The embedded skills that give rise to the next generation of competitive products cannot be "rented in" by outsourcing and OEM-supply relationships. In our view, too many companies have unwittingly surrendered core competencies when they cut internal investment in what they mistakenly thought were just "cost centers" in favor of outside suppliers.

Consider Chrysler. Unlike Honda, it has tended to view engines and power trains as simply one more component. Chrysler is becoming increasingly dependent on Mitsubishi and Hyundai: between 1985 and 1987, the number of outsourced engines went from 252,000 to 382,000. It is difficult to imagine Honda yielding manufacturing responsibility, much less design, of so critical a part of a car's function to an outside company—which is why Honda has made such an enormous commitment to Formula One auto racing. Honda has been able to pool its engine-related technologies; it has parlayed these into a corporatewide competency from which it develops world-beating products, despite R&D budgets smaller than those of GM and Toyota.

Of course, it is perfectly possible for a company to have a competitive product line up but be a laggard in developing core competencies—at least for a while. If a company wanted to enter the copier business today, it would find a dozen Japanese companies more than willing to supply copiers on the basis of an OEM private label. But when fundamental technologies changed or if its supplier decided to enter the market directly and become a competitor, that company's product line, along with all of its investments in marketing and distribution, could be vulnerable. Outsourcing can provide a shortcut to a more competitive product, but it typically contributes little to building the people-embodied skills that are needed to sustain product leadership.

Nor is it possible for a company to have an intelligent alliance or sourcing strategy if it has not made a choice about where it will build competence leadership. Clearly, Japanese companies have benefited from alliances. They've used them to learn from Western partners who were not fully committed to preserving core competencies of their own. As we've argued in these pages before, learning within an alliance takes a positive commitment of resources—travel, a pool of dedicated people, test-bed facilities, time to internalize and test what has been learned.[2] A company may not make this effort if it doesn't have clear goals for competence building.

Another way of losing is forgoing opportunities to establish competencies that are evolving in existing businesses. In the 1970s and 1980s, many American and European companies—like GE, Motorola, GTE, Thorn, and GEC—chose to exit the color television business, which they regarded as mature. If by "mature" they meant that they had run out of new product ideas at precisely the moment global rivals had targeted the TV business for entry, then yes, the industry was mature. But it certainly wasn't mature in the sense that all opportunities to enhance and apply video-based competencies had been exhausted.

In ridding themselves of their television businesses, these companies failed to distinguish between divesting the business and destroying their video media-based competencies. They not only got out of the TV business but they also closed the door on a whole stream of future opportunities reliant on video-based competencies. The television industry, considered by many U.S. companies in the 1970s to be unattractive, is today the focus of a fierce

---

[2]"Collaborate with Your Competitors and Win," *HBR* (January–February 1989), p. 133, with Yves L. Doz.

public policy debate about the inability of U.S. corporations to benefit from the $20-billion-a-year opportunity that HDTV will represent in the mid- to late 1990s. Ironically, the U.S. government is being asked to fund a massive research project—in effect, to compensate U.S. companies for their failure to preserve critical core competencies when they had the chance.

In contrast, one can see a company like Sony reducing its emphasis on VCRs (where it has not been very successful and where Korean companies now threaten), without reducing its commitment to video-related competencies. Sony's Betamax led to a debacle. But it emerged with its videotape recording competencies intact and is currently challenging Matsushita in the 8 mm camcorder market.

There are two clear lessons here. First, the costs of losing a core competence can be only partly calculated in advance. The baby may be thrown out with the bath water in divestment decisions. Second, since core competencies are built through a process of continuous improvement and enhancement that may span a decade or longer, a company that has failed to invest in core competence building will find it very difficult to enter an emerging market, unless, of course, it will be content simply to serve as a distribution channel.

American semiconductor companies like Motorola learned this painful lesson when they elected to forgo direct participation in the 256 k generation of DRAM chips. Having skipped this round, Motorola, like most of its American competitors, needed a large infusion of technical help from Japanese partners to rejoin the battle in the 1-megabyte generation. When it comes to core competencies, it is difficult to get off the train, walk to the next station, and then reboard.

From Core Competencies to Core Products

The tangible link between identified core competencies and end products is what we call the core products—the physical embodiments of one or more core competencies. Honda's engines, for example, are core products, linchpins between design and development skills that ultimately lead to a proliferation of end products. Core products are the components or subassemblies that actually contribute to the value of the end products. Thinking in terms of core products forces a company to distinguish between the brand share it achieves in end product markets (for example, 40% of the U.S. refrigerator market) and the manufacturing share it achieves in any particular core product (for example, 5% of the world share of compressor output).

Canon is reputed to have an 84% world manufacturing share in desktop laser printer "engines," even though its brand share in the laser printer business is minuscule. Similarly, Matsushita has a world manufacturing share of about 45% in key VCR components, far in excess of its brand share (Panasonic, JVC, and others) of 20%. And Matsushita has a commanding core product share in compressors worldwide, estimated at 40%, even though its brand share in both the air-conditioning and refrigerator businesses is quite small.

It is essential to make this distinction between core competencies, core products, and end products because global competition is played out by different rules and for different stakes at each level. To build or defend leadership over the long term, a corporation will probably be a winner at each level. At the level of core competence, the goal is to build world leadership in the design and development of a particular class of product functionality—be it compact data storage and retrieval, as with Philips's optical-media competence, or compactness and ease of use, as with Sony's micromotors and microprocessor controls.

To sustain leadership in their chosen core competence areas, these companies *seek to maximize their world manufacturing share in core products.* The manufacture of core products for a wide variety of external (and internal) customers yields the revenue and market feedback that, at least partly, determines the pace at which core competencies can be enhanced and extended. This thinking was behind JVC's decision in the mid-1970s to establish VCR supply relationships with leading national consumer electronics companies in Europe and the United States. In supplying Thomson, Thorn, and Telefunken (all independent companies at that time) as well as U.S. partners, JVC was able to gain the cash and the diversity of market experience that ultimately enabled it to outpace Philips and Sony. (Philips developed videotape competencies in parallel with JVC, but it failed to build a worldwide network of OEM relationships that would have allowed it to accelerate the refinement of its videotape competence through the sale of core products.)

JVC's success has not been lost on Korean companies like Goldstar, Sam Sung, Kia, and Daewoo, who are building core product leadership in areas as diverse as displays, semiconductors, and automotive engines through their OEM-supply contracts with Western companies. Their avowed goal is to capture investment initiative away from potential competitors, often U.S. companies. In doing so, they accelerate their competence-building efforts while "hollowing out" their competitors. By focusing on competence and embedding it in core products, Asian competitors have built up advantages in component markets first and have then leveraged off their superior products to move downstream to build brand share. And they are not likely to remain the low-cost suppliers forever. As their reputation for brand leadership is consolidated, they may well gain price leadership. Honda has proven this with its Acura line, and other Japanese car makers are following suit.

Control over core products is critical for other reasons. A dominant position in core products allows a company to shape the evolution of applications and end markets. Such compact audio disc-related core products as data drives and lasers have enabled Sony and Philips to influence the evolution of the computer-peripheral business in optical-media storage. As a company multiplies the number of application arenas for its core products, it can consistently reduce the cost, time, and risk in new product development. In short, well-targeted core products can lead to economies of scale *and* scope.

The Tyranny of the SBU

The new terms of competitive engagement cannot be understood using analytical tools devised to manage the diversified corporation of 20 years ago, when competition was primarily domestic (GE versus Westinghouse, General Motors versus Ford) and all the key players were speaking the language of the same business schools and consultancies. Old prescriptions have potentially toxic side effects. The need for new principles is most obvious in companies organized exclusively according to the logic of SBUs. The implications of the two alternate concepts of the corporation are summarized in "Two Concepts of the Corporation: SBU or Core Competence."

Obviously, diversified corporations have a portfolio of products and a portfolio of businesses. But we believe in a view of the company as a portfolio of competencies as well. U.S. companies do not lack the technical resources to build competencies, but the top management often lacks the vision to build them and the administrative means for assembling resources spread across multiple businesses. A shift in commitment will inevitably influence patterns of diversification, skill deployment, resource allocation priorities, and approaches to alliances and outsourcing.

We have described the three different planes on which battles for global leadership are waged: core competence, core products, and end products. A corporation has to know whether it is winning or losing on each plane. By sheer weight of investment, a company might be able to beat its rivals to blue-sky technologies yet still lose the race to build core competence leadership. If a company is winning the race to build core competencies (as opposed to building leadership in a few technologies), it will almost certainly outpace rivals in new business development. If a company is winning the race to capture world manufacturing share in core products, it will probably outpace rivals in improving product features and the price/performance ratio.

Determining whether one is winning or losing end product battles is more difficult because measures of product market share do not necessarily reflect various companies' underlying competitiveness. Indeed, companies that attempt to build market share by relying on the competitiveness of others, rather than investing in core competencies and

Two Concepts of the Corporation: SBU or Core Competence

	SBU	*Core Competence*
Basis for competition	Competitiveness of today's products	Interfirm competition to build competencies
Corporate structure	Portfolio of businesses related in product-market terms	Portfolio of competencies, core products, and businesses
Status of the business unit	Autonomy is sacrosanct; the SBU "owns" all resources other than cash	SBU is a potential reservoir of core competencies
Resource allocation	Discrete businesses are the unit of analysis; capital is allocated business by business	Businesses and competencies are the unit of analysis: top management allocates capital and talent
Value added of top management	Optimizing corporate returns through capital allocation trade-offs among businesses	Enunciating strategic architecture and building competencies to secure the future

world core-product leadership, may be treading on quicksand. In the race for global brand dominance, companies like 3M, Black & Decker, Canon, Honda, NEC, and Citicorp have built global brand umbrellas by proliferating products out of their core competencies. This has allowed their individual businesses to build image, customer loyalty, and access to distribution channels.

When you think about this reconceptualization of the corporation, the primacy of the SBU—an organizational dogma for a generation—is now clearly an anachronism. Where the SBU is an article of faith, resistance to the seductions of decentralization can seem heretical. In many companies, the SBU prism means that only one plane of the global competitive battle, the battle to put competitive products on the shelf *today,* is visible to top management. What are the costs of this distortion?

Underinvestment in Developing Core Competencies and Core Products. When the organization is conceived of as a multiplicity of SBUs, no single business may feel responsible for maintaining a viable position in core products nor be able to justify the investment required to build world leadership in some core competence. In the absence of

a more comprehensive view imposed by corporate management, SBU managers will tend to underinvest. Recently, companies such as Kodak and Philips have recognized this as a potential problem and have begun searching for new organizational forms that will allow them to develop and manufacture core products for both internal and external customers.

SBU managers have traditionally conceived of competitors in the same way they've seen themselves. On the whole, they've failed to note the emphasis Asian competitors were placing on building leadership in core products or to understand the critical linkage between world manufacturing leadership and the ability to sustain development pace in core competence. They've failed to pursue OEM-supply opportunities or to look across their various product divisions in an attempt to identify opportunities for coordinated initiatives.

Imprisoned Resources. As an SBU evolves, it often develops unique competencies. Typically, the people who embody this competence are seen as the sole property of the business in which they grew up. The manager of another SBU who asks to borrow talented people is likely to get a cold rebuff. SBU managers are not only unwilling to lend their competence carriers but they may actually hide talent to prevent its redeployment in the pursuit of new opportunities. This may be compared to residents of an underdeveloped country hiding most of their cash under their mattresses. The benefits of competencies, like the benefits of the money supply, depend on the velocity of their circulation as well as on the size of the stock the company holds.

Western companies have traditionally had an advantage in the stock of skills they possess. But have they been able to reconfigure them quickly to respond to new opportunities? Canon, NEC, and Honda have had a lesser stock of the people and technologies that compose core competencies but could move them much quicker from one business unit to another. Corporate R&D spending at Canon is not fully indicative of the size of Canon's core competence stock and tells the casual observer nothing about the velocity with which Canon is able to move core competencies to exploit opportunities.

When competencies become imprisoned, the people who carry the competencies do not get assigned to the most exciting opportunities, and their skills begin to atrophy. Only by fully leveraging core competencies can small companies like Canon afford to compete with industry giants like Xerox. How strange that SBU managers, who are perfectly willing to compete for cash in the capital budgeting process, are unwilling to compete for people—the company's most precious asset. We find it ironic that top management devotes so much attention to the capital budgeting process yet typically has no comparable mechanism for allocating the human skills that embody core competencies. Top managers are seldom able to look four or five levels down into the organization, identify the people who embody critical competencies, and move them across organizational boundaries.

Bounded Innovation.   If core competencies are not recognized, individual SBUs will pursue only those innovation opportunities that are close at hand—marginal product-line extensions or geographic expansions. Hybrid opportunities like fax machines, laptop computers, hand-held televisions, or portable music keyboards will emerge only when managers take off their SBU blinkers. Remember, Canon appeared to be in the camera business at the time it was preparing to become a world leader in copiers. Conceiving of the corporation in terms of core competencies widens the domain of innovation.

Developing Strategic Architecture

The fragmentation of core competencies becomes inevitable when a diversified company's information systems, patterns of communication, career paths, managerial rewards, and processes of strategy development do not transcend SBU lines. We believe that senior management should spend a significant amount of its time developing a corporatewide strategic architecture that establishes objectives for competence building. A strategic architecture is a road map of the future that identifies which core competencies to build and their constituent technologies.

By providing an impetus for learning from alliances and a focus for internal development efforts, a strategic architecture like NEC's C&C can dramatically reduce the investment needed to secure future market leadership. How can a company make partnerships intelligently without a clear understanding of the core competencies it is trying to build and those it is attempting to prevent from being unintentionally transferred?

Of course, all of this begs the question of what a strategic architecture should look like. The answer will be different for every company. But it is helpful to think again of that tree, of the corporation organized around core products and, ultimately, core competencies. To sink sufficiently strong roots, a company must answer some fundamental questions: How long could we preserve our competitiveness in this business if we did not control this particular core competence? How central is this core competence to perceived customer benefits? What future opportunities would be foreclosed if we were to lose this particular competence?

The architecture provides a logic for product and market diversification, moreover. An SBU manager would be asked: Does the new market opportunity add to the overall goal of becoming the best player in the world? Does it exploit or add to the core competence? At Vickers, for example, diversification options have been judged in the context of becoming the best power and motion control company in the world (see the insert "Vickers Learns the Value of Strategic Architecture").

The strategic architecture should make resource allocation priorities transparent to the entire organization. It provides a template for allocation decisions by top management. It helps lower-level managers understand the logic of allocation priorities and disciplines senior management to maintain consistency. In short, it yields a definition of the company and the markets it serves. 3M, Vickers, NEC, Canon, and Honda all qualify on this score. Honda *knew* it was exploiting what it had learned from motorcycles—how to make high-revving, smooth-running, lightweight engines—when it entered the car business. The task of creating a strategic architecture forces the organization to identify and commit to the technical and production linkages across SBUs that will provide a distinct competitive advantage.

It is consistency of resource allocation and the development of an administrative infrastructure appropriate to it that breathes life into a strategic architecture and creates a managerial culture, teamwork, a capacity to change, and a willingness to share resources, to protect proprietary skills, and to think long term. That is also the reason the specific architecture cannot be copied easily or overnight by competitors. Strategic architecture is a tool for communicating with customers and other external constituents. It reveals the broad direction without giving away every step.

Redeploying to Exploit Competencies

If the company's core competencies are its critical resource and if top management must ensure that competence carriers are not held hostage by some particular business, then it follows that SBUs should bid for core competencies in the same way they bid for capital. We've made this point glancingly. It is important enough to consider more deeply.

Once top management (with the help of divisional and SBU managers) has identified overarching competencies, it must ask businesses to identify the projects and people closely connected with them. Corporate officers should direct an audit of the location, number, and quality of the people who embody competence.

This sends an important signal to middle managers: core competencies are *corporate* resources and may be reallocated by corporate management. An individual business doesn't own anybody. SBUs are entitled to the services of individual employees so long as SBU management can demonstrate that the opportunity it is pursuing yields the highest possible pay-off on the investment in their skills. This message is further underlined if each year in the strategic planning or budgeting process, unit managers must justify their hold on the people who carry the company's core competencies.

Elements of Canon's core competence in optics are spread across businesses as diverse as cameras, copiers, and semiconductor lithographic equipment and are shown in "Core Competencies at Canon." When Canon identified an opportunity in digital laser printers, it gave SBU managers the right to raid other SBUs to pull together the required pool of talent. When Canon's reprographics products division undertook to develop microprocessor controlled copiers, it turned to the photo products group, which had developed the world's first microprocessor-controlled camera.

Also, reward systems that focus only on product-line results and career paths that seldom cross SBU boundaries engender patterns of behavior among unit managers that are destructively competitive. At NEC, divisional managers come together to identify next-generation competencies. Together they decide how much investment needs to be made to build up each future competency and the contribution in capital and staff support that each division will need to make. There is also a sense of equitable

Vickers Learns the Value of Strategic Architecture

The idea that top management should develop a corporate strategy for acquiring and deploying core competencies is relatively new in most U.S. companies. There are a few exceptions. An early convert was Trinova (previously Libbey Owens Ford), a Toledo-based corporation, which enjoys a worldwide position in power and motion controls and engineered plastics. One of its major divisions is Vickers, a premier sup-

plier of hydraulics components like valves, pumps, actuators, and filtration devices to aerospace, marine, defense, automotive, earth-moving, and industrial markets.

Vickers saw the potential for a transformation of its traditional business with the application of electronics disciplines in combination with its traditional technologies. The goal was "to ensure that change in

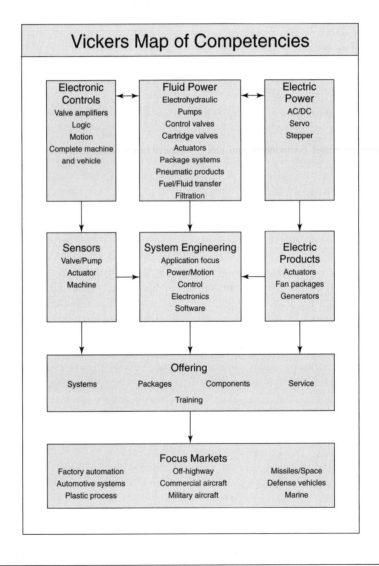

(*continued*)

technology does not displace Vickers from its customers." This, to be sure, was initially a defensive move: Vickers recognized that unless it acquired new skills, it could not protect existing markets or capitalize on new growth opportunities. Managers at Vickers attempted to conceptualize the likely evolution of (a) technologies relevant to the power and motion control business, (b) functionalities that would satisfy emerging customer needs, and (c) new competencies needed to creatively manage the marriage of technology and customer needs.

Despite pressure for short-term earnings, top management looked to a 10- to 15-year time horizon in developing a map of emerging customer needs, changing technologies, and the core competencies that would be necessary to bridge the gap between the two. Its slogan was "Into the 21st Century." (A simplified version of the overall architecture developed is shown here.) Vickers is currently in fluid-power components. The architecture identifies two additional competencies, electric-power components and electronic controls. A systems integration capability that would unite hardware, software, and service was also targeted for development.

The strategic architecture, as illustrated by the Vickers example, is not a forecast of specific products or specific technologies but a broad map of the evolving linkages between customer functionality requirements, potential technologies, and core competencies. It assumes that products and systems cannot be defined with certainty for the future but that preempting competitors in the development of new markets requires an early start to building core competencies. The strategic architecture developed by Vickers, while describing the future in competence terms, also provides the basis for making "here and now" decisions about product priorities, acquisitions, alliances, and recruitment.

Since 1986, Vickers has made more than ten clearly targeted acquisitions, each one focused on a specific component or technology gap identified in the overall architecture. The architecture is also the basis for internal development of new competencies. Vickers has undertaken, in parallel, a reorganization to enable the integration of electronics and electrical capabilities with mechanical-based competencies. We believe that it will take another two to three years before Vickers reaps the total benefits from developing the strategic architecture, communicating it widely to all its employees, customers, and investors, and building administrative systems consistent with the architecture.

---

exchange. One division may make a disproportionate contribution or may benefit less from the progress made, but such short-term inequalities will balance out over the long term.

Incidentally, the positive contribution of the SBU manager should be made visible across the company. An SBU manager is unlikely to surrender key people if only the other business (or the general manager of that business who may be a competitor for promotion) is going to benefit from the redeployment. Cooperative SBU managers should be celebrated as team players. Where priorities are clear, transfers are less likely to be seen as idiosyncratic and politically motivated.

Transfers for the sake of building core competence must be recorded and appreciated in the corporate memory. It is reasonable to expect a business that has surrendered core skills on behalf of corporate opportunities in other areas to lose, for a time, some of its competitiveness. If these losses in performance bring immediate censure, SBUs will be unlikely to assent to skills transfers next time.

Finally, there are ways to wean key employees off the idea that they belong in perpetuity to any particular business. Early in their careers, people may be exposed to a variety of businesses through a carefully planned rotation program. At Canon, critical people move regularly between the camera business and the copier business and between the copier business and the professional optical-products business. In mid-career, periodic assignments to cross-divisional project teams may be necessary, both for diffusing core competencies and for loosening the bonds that might tie an individual to one business even when brighter opportunities beckon elsewhere. Those who embody critical core competencies should know that their careers are tracked and guided by corporate human resource professionals.

Core Competencies at Canon

	Precision Mechanics	Fine Optics	Micro-electronics
Basic camera	■	■	
Compact fashion camera	■	■	
Electronic camera	■	■	
EOS autofocus camera	■	■	■
Video still camera	■	■	■
Laser beam printer	■	■	■
Color video printer	■		■
Bubble jet printer	■		■
Basic fax	■		■
Laser fax	■		■
Calculator			■
Plain paper copier	■	■	■
Battery PPC	■	■	■
Color copier	■	■	■
Laser copier	■	■	■
Color laser copier	■	■	■
NAVI	■	■	■
Still video system	■	■	■
Laser imager	■	■	■
Cell analyzer	■	■	■
Mask aligners	■		■
Stepper aligners	■		■
Excimer laser aligners	■	■	■

Every Canon product is the result of at least one core competency.

In the early 1980s at Canon, all engineers under 30 were invited to apply for membership on a seven-person committee that was to spend two years plotting Canon's future direction, including its strategic architecture.

Competence carriers should be regularly brought together from across the corporation to trade notes and ideas. The goal is to build a strong feeling of community among these people. To a great extent, their loyalty should be to the integrity of the core competence area they represent and not just to particular businesses. In traveling regularly, talking frequently to customers, and meeting with peers, competence carriers may be encouraged to discover new market opportunities.

Core competencies are the wellspring of new business development. They should constitute the focus for strategy at the corporate level. Managers have to win manufacturing leadership in core products and capture global share through brand-building programs aimed at exploiting economies of scope. Only if the company is conceived of as a hierarchy of core competencies, core products, and market-focused business units will it be fit to fight.

Nor can top management be just another layer of accounting consolidation, which it often is in a regime of radical decentralization. Top management must add value by enunciating the strategic architecture that guides the competence acquisition process. We believe an obsession with competence building will characterize the global winners of the 1990s. With the decade underway, the time for rethinking the concept of the corporation is already overdue.

Reading 3–3

BUILDING A VISIONARY COMPANY

James C. Collins
Jerry I. Porras

Above all, there was the ability to build and build and build—never stopping, never looking back, never finishing—the institution. . . . In the last analysis, Walt Disney's greatest creation was Walt Disney [the company].

Richard Schickel, *The Disney version*[1]

I have concentrated all along on building the finest retailing company that we possibly could. Period. Creating a huge personal fortune was never particularly a goal of mine.

Sam Walton, *Founder, Wal-Mart*[2]

Imagine you met a remarkable person who could look at the sun or stars at any time of day or night and state the exact time and date: "It's April 23, 1401, 2:36 A.M., and 12 seconds." This person would be an amazing time teller, and we'd probably revere that person for the ability to tell time. But wouldn't that person be even more amazing if, instead of telling the time, he or she *built a clock* that could tell the time forever, even after he or she was dead and gone?[3]

Having a great idea or being a charismatic visionary leader is "time telling"; building a company that can prosper far beyond the presence of any single leader and through multiple product life

cycles is "clock building." The builders of visionary companies tend to be clock builders, not time tellers. They concentrate primarily on building an organization—building a ticking clock—rather than on hitting a market just right with a visionary product idea and riding the growth curve of an attractive product life cycle. And instead of concentrating on acquiring the individual personality traits of visionary leadership, they take an architectural approach and concentrate on building the organizational traits of visionary companies. The primary output of their efforts is not the tangible implementation of a great idea, the expression of a charismatic personality, the gratification of their ego, or the accumulation of personal wealth. Their greatest creation is *the company itself* and what it stands for.

We came upon this finding when the evidence from our research punched holes in two widely held and deeply cherished myths that have dominated popular thinking and business school education for years: the myth of the great idea and the myth of the great and charismatic leader. In one of the most fascinating and important conclusions from our research, we found that creating and building a visionary company absolutely does not require *either* a great idea or a great and charismatic

[1]Richard Schickel, *The Disney Version* (New York, NY: Simon & Schuster, 1968), pp. 44, 363.

[2]Sam Walton with John Huey, *Sam Walton: Made in America* (New York, NY: Doubleday, 1992), p. 234.

[3]The original inspiration for this analogy came from a lecture series on intellectual history and the Newtonian Revolution entitled "The Origin of the Modern Mind," taught by Alan Charles Kors, Professor of History, University of Pennsylvania, and captured on audiotape as part of the Superstar Teacher Series from the Teaching Company, Washington, D.C.

leader. In fact, we found evidence that great ideas brought forth by charismatic leaders might be *negatively correlated* with building a visionary company. These surprising findings forced us to look at corporate success from an entirely new angle and through a different lens than we had used before. They also have implications that are profoundly liberating for corporate managers and entrepreneurs alike.

The Myth of the "Great Idea"

On August 23, 1937, two recently graduated engineers in their early twenties with no substantial business experience met to discuss the founding of a new company. However, they had no clear idea of what the company would make. They only knew that they wanted to start a company with each other in the broadly defined field of electronic engineering. They brainstormed a wide range of initial product and market possibilities, but they had no compelling "great idea" that served as the founding inspiration for the fledgling company.

Bill Hewlett and Dave Packard decided to first start a company and *then* figure out what they would make. They just started moving forward, trying anything that might get them out of the garage and pay the light bills. According to Bill Hewlett:

> When I talk to business schools occasionally, the professor of management is devastated when I say that we didn't have any plans when we started—we were just opportunistic. We did anything that would bring in a nickel. We had a bowling foul-line indicator, a clock drive for a telescope, a thing to make a urinal flush automatically, and a shock machine to make people lose weight. Here we were, with about $500 in capital, trying whatever someone thought we might be able to do.[4]

The bowling foul-line indicator didn't become a market revolution. The automatic urinal flushers and fat-reduction shock machines didn't go any-

where, either. In fact, the company stumbled along for nearly a year before it got its first big sale—eight audio oscilloscopes to Walt Disney for work on the movie *Fantasia*. Even then, Hewlett-Packard continued its unfocused ways, sputtering and tinkering with a variety of products, until it got a boost from war contracts in the early 1940s.

Texas Instruments, in contrast, traces its roots to a highly successful initial concept. TI began life in 1930 as Geophysical Service, Inc., "the first independent company to make reflection seismograph surveys of potential oil fields, and its Texas labs developed and produced instruments for such work."[5] TI's founders, unlike Hewlett and Packard, formed their company to exploit a *specific* technological and market opportunity.[6] TI started with a "great idea." HP did not.

Neither did Sony. When Masaru Ibuka founded his company in August of 1945, he had no specific product idea. In fact, Ibuka and his seven initial employees had a brainstorming session—*after* starting the company—to decide what products to make. According to Akio Morita, who joined the company shortly after its founding, "The small group sat in conference . . . and for weeks they tried to figure out what kind of business this new company could enter in order to make money to operate."[7] They considered a wide range of possibilities, from sweetened bean-paste soup to miniature golf equipment and slide rules.[8] Not only that, Sony's first product attempt (a simple rice cooker) failed to work properly and its first significant product (a tape recorder) failed in the marketplace. The company kept itself alive in the early days by stitching wires on cloth to make crude, but sellable, heating pads.[9] In

---

[4]Hewlett-Packard Company Archives, "An Interview with Bill Hewlett," 1987, p. 4.

[5]"Research Packed with Ph.D.s," *Business Week,* December 22, 1956, p. 58.

[6]John McDonald, "The Men Who Made T.I.," *Fortune* (November 1961), p. 118.

[7]Akio Morita, *Made in Japan* (New York, NY: Dutton, 1986), pp. 44–57.

[8]Nick Lyons, *The Sony Vision* (New York, NY: Crown, 1976), pp. 4–5.

[9]Morita, op. cit., pp. 44–57.

comparison, Kenwood's founder, unlike Ibuka at Sony, appeared to have a specific category of products in mind. He christened his company with the name "Kasuga Wireless Electric Firm" in 1946 and "since its foundation," according to the *Japan Electronics Almanac,* "Kenwood has always been a specialist pioneer in audio technology."[10]

Like fellow legendaries Ibuka and Hewlett, Sam Walton also started without a great idea. He went into business with nothing other than the desire to work for himself and a little bit of knowledge (and a lot of passion) about retailing. He didn't wake up one day and say, "I have this great idea around which I'm going to start a company." No. Walton started in 1945 with a single Ben Franklin franchise five-and-dime store in the small town of Newport, Arkansas. "I had no vision of the scope of what I would start," Walton commented in a *New York Times* interview, "but I always had confidence that as long as we did our work well and were good to our customers, there would be no limit to us."[11] Walton built incrementally, step by step, from that single store until the "great idea" of rural discount popped out as a natural evolutionary step almost two decades after he started his company. He wrote in *Made in America:*

> Somehow over the years folks have gotten the impression that Wal-Mart was something that I dreamed up out of the blue as a middle-aged man, and that it was just this great idea that turned into an over-night success. But [our first Wal-Mart store] was totally an outgrowth of everything we'd been doing since [1945]—another case of me being unable to leave well enough alone, another experiment. And like most over-night successes, it was about twenty years in the making.[12]

In a twist of corporate irony, Ames Stores (Wal-Mart's comparison in our study), had a four-year head start over Sam Walton's company in rural discount retailing. In fact, Milton and Irving Gilman founded Ames in 1958 specifically to pursue the "great idea" of rural discount retailing. They "believed that discount stores would succeed in small towns" and the company achieved $1 million in sales in its first year of operation.[13] (Sam Walton didn't open his first rural discount retail store until 1962; until then, he had simply operated a collection of small, main-street variety stores.)[14] Nor was Ames the only other company that had a head start over Walton. According to Walton biographer Vance Trimble, "Other retailers were out there [in 1962] trying to do just what he was doing. Only he did it better than nearly anyone."[15]

HP, Sony, and Wal-Mart put a large dent in the widely held mythology of corporate origins—a mythology that paints a picture of a far-seeing entrepreneur founding his or her company to capitalize on a visionary product idea or visionary market insight. This mythology holds that those who launch highly successful companies usually begin first and foremost with a brilliant idea (technology, product, market potential) and then ride the growth curve of an attractive product life cycle. Yet this mythology—as compelling and pervasive as it is—does not show up as a general pattern in the founding of the visionary companies.

Indeed, few of the visionary companies in our study can trace their roots to a great idea or a fabulous initial product. J. Willard Marriott had the desire to be in business for himself, but no clear idea of what business to be in. He finally decided to start his company with the only viable idea he could think of: take out a franchise - license and open an A&W root beer stand in Washington, D.C.[16] Nordstrom started as a small, single-outlet shoe store in downtown Seattle (when John Nordstrom, just returned from the Alaska

---

[10]*Japan Electronics Almanac,* 1988, p. 282.

[11]Vance Trimble, *Sam Walton* (New York, NY: Dutton, 1990), p. 121.

[12]Walton with Huey, op. cit., p. 35.

[13]*Hoover's Handbook of Corporation,* 1991.

[14]Trimble, op. cit., pp. 102–104.

[15]Ibid., pp. 121–122.

[16]Robert O'Brien, *Marriott: The J. Willard Marriott Story* (Salt Lake City, UT: Deseret, 1987).

Gold Rush, didn't know what else to do with himself).[17] Merck started merely as an importer of chemicals from Germany.[18] Procter & Gamble started as a simple soap and candle maker—one of eighteen such companies in Cincinnati in 1837.[19] Motorola began as a struggling battery eliminator repair business for Sears radios.[20] Philip Morris began as a small tobacco retail shop on Bond Street in London.[21]

Furthermore, some of our visionary companies began life like Sony—with outright failures. 3M started as a failed corundum mine, leaving 3M investors holding stock that fell to the barroom exchange value of "two shares for one shot of cheap whiskey."[22] Not knowing what else to do, the company began making sandpaper. 3M had such a poor start in life that its second president did not draw a salary for the first eleven years of his tenure. In contrast, Norton Corporation, 3M's comparison in the study, began life with innovative products in a rapidly growing market, paid steady annual dividends in all but one of its first fifteen years of operations, and multiplied its capital fifteenfold during the same time.[23]

Bill Boeing's first airplane failed ("a handmade, clumsy seaplane copied from a Martin seaplane" which flunked its Navy trials), and his company faced such difficulty during its first few years of operations that it entered the furniture business to keep

itself aloft![24] Douglas Aircraft, in contrast, had superb initial success with its first airplane. Designed to be the first plane in history to make a coast-to-coast nonstop trip and to lift more load than its own weight, Douglas turned the design into a torpedo bomber which he sold in quantity to the Navy.[25] Unlike Boeing, Douglas never needed to enter the furniture business to keep the company alive.[26]

Walt Disney's first cartoon series *Alice in Cartoon Land* (ever heard of it?) languished in the theaters. Disney biographer Richard Schickel wrote that it was "by and large a limp, dull and cliché ridden enterprise. All you could really say for it was that it was a fairly ordinary comic strip set in motion and enlivened by a photographic trick."[27] Columbia Pictures, unlike Disney, attained substantial success with its first theater release. The film, *More to Be Pitied Than Scorned* (1922), cost only $20,000 and realized income of $130,000, thus launching Columbia forward with a sizable cash cushion that funded the making of ten additional profitable movies in less than two years.[28]

Waiting for "The Great Idea" Might Be a Bad Idea

In all, *only three* of the visionary companies began life with the benefit of a specific, innovative, and highly successful initial product or service—a "great idea": Johnson & Johnson, General Electric, and Ford. And even in the GE and Ford cases, we found some slight dents in the great idea theory. At GE, Edison's great idea turned out to be inferior to Westinghouse's great idea. Edison pursued direct current (DC) system, whereas Westinghouse promoted the vastly superior alternating current (AC)

[17]John W. Nordstrom, *The Immigrant in 1887* (Seattle, WA: Dogwood Press, 1950), pp. 44–50; "Nordstrom History," company publication, November 26, 1990.

[18]*Values and Visions: A Merck Century* (Rahway, NJ: Merck, 1993), pp. 13–15.

[19]"Procter & Gamble Chronology," company publication; Oscar Schisgall, *Eyes on Tomorrow: The Evolution of Procter & Gamble* (New York, NY: Doubleday, 1981), pp. 1–14; Alfred Lief, *It Floats: The Story of Procter & Gamble* (New York, NY: Rinehart, 1958), pp. 14–32.

[20]Harry Mark Petrakis, *The Founder's Touch* (New York, NY: McGraw-Hill, 1965), pp. 62–63.

[21]*The Philip Morris History*, company publication, 1988.

[22]*Our Story So Far* (St. Paul, MN: 3M Company, 1977), p. 51.

[23]Charles W. Cheape, *Norton Company: A New England Enterprise* (Cambridge, MA: Harvard University Press, 1985), p. 12.

[24]Robert J. Serling, *Legend and Legacy: The Story of Boeing and Its People* (New York, NY: St. Martin's Press, 1992), pp. 2–6.

[25]"Take off for the Business Jet," *Business Week*, September 28, 1963.

[26]Rene J. Francillon, *McDonnell Douglas Aircraft Since 1920* (Annapolis, MD: Naval Institute Press, 1988), pp. 1–12.

[27]Schickel, op. cit., pp. 106–107.

[28]Clive Hirschhorn, *The Columbia Story* (New York, NY: Crown, 1989), pp. 7–16.

system, which eventually prevailed in the U.S. market.[29] In Ford's case, contrary to popular mythology, Henry Ford didn't come up with the idea of the Model T and *then* decide to start a company around that idea. Just the opposite. Ford was able to take full advantage of the Model T concept because he already had a *company* in place as a launching pad. He founded the Ford Motor Company in 1903 to capitalize on his automotive engineering talent—his third company in as many years—and introduced five models (Models A, B, C, F, and K) before he launched the famous Model T in October of 1908.[30] In fact, Ford was one of 502 firms founded in the United States between 1900 and 1908 to make automobiles—hardly a novel concept at the time. In contrast to the visionary companies, we traced the founding roots of eleven comparison companies much closer to the great-idea model: Ames, Burroughs, Colgate, Kenwood, McDonnell Douglas, Norton, Pfizer, R.J. Reynolds, Texas Instruments, Westinghouse, and Zenith.

In other words, we found that the visionary companies were much less likely to begin life with a "great idea" than the comparison companies in our study. Furthermore, whatever the initial founding concept, we found that the visionary companies were less likely to have early entrepreneurial success than the comparison companies. In only three of eighteen pairs did the visionary company have greater initial success than the comparison company, whereas in ten cases, the comparison company had greater initial success than the visionary company. Five cases were indistinguishable. *In short, we found a negative correlation between early entrepreneurial success and becoming a highly visionary company.* The long race goes to the tortoise, not the hare.

If you are a prospective entrepreneur with the desire to start and build a visionary company but have not yet taken the plunge because you don't have a "great idea," we encourage you to lift from your shoulders the burden of the great-idea myth. Indeed, the evidence suggests that it might be better to *not* obsess on finding a great idea before launching a company. Why? Because the great-idea approach shifts your attention away from seeing the company as your ultimate creation.

The Company Itself Is the Ultimate Creation

In courses on strategic management and entrepreneurship, business schools teach the importance of starting first and foremost with a good idea and well-developed product/market strategy, and *then* jumping through the "window of opportunity" before it closes. But the people who built the visionary companies often didn't behave or think that way. In case after case, their actions flew in the face of the theories being taught at the business schools.

Thus, early in our project, we had to reject the great idea or brilliant strategy explanation of corporate success and consider a new view. We had to put on a different lens and look at the world backward. We had to *shift from seeing the company as a vehicle for the products to seeing the products as a vehicle for the company.* We had to embrace the crucial difference between time telling and clock building.

To quickly grasp the difference between clock building and time telling, compare GE and Westinghouse in their early days. George Westinghouse was a brilliant product visionary and prolific inventor who founded fifty-nine other companies besides Westinghouse.[31] Additionally, he had the insight that the world should favor the superior AC electrical system over Edison's DC system, which it eventually did.[32] But compare George Westinghouse to Charles Coffin, GE's first president. Coffin invented not a single product. But he sponsored an innovation of great significance: the establishment of the General Electric Research Lab, billed as

[29]Grover and Lagai, *Development of American Industries,* 4th Edition, 1959, p. 491.

[30]Robert Lacey, *Ford: The Men and the Machine* (New York, NY: Ballantine Books, 1986), pp. 47–110.

[31]*Centennial Review,* Internal Westinghouse Document, 1986.
[32]Ibid.

"America's first industrial research laboratory."[33] George Westinghouse told the time; Charles Coffin built a clock. Westinghouse's greatest creation was the AC power system; Coffin's greatest creation was the General Electric Company.

Luck favors the persistent. This simple truth is a fundamental cornerstone of successful company builders. The builders of visionary companies were highly persistent, living to the motto: Never, never, *never* give up. But what to persist *with?* Their answer: The company. *Be prepared to kill, revise, or evolve an idea* (GE moved away from its original DC system and embraced the AC system), *but never give up on the company.* If you equate the success of your company with success of a specific idea—as many businesspeople do—then you're more likely to give up on the company if that idea fails; and if that idea happens to succeed, you're more likely to have an emotional love affair with that idea and stick with it too long, when the company should be moving vigorously on to other things. But if you see the ultimate creation as the company, not the execution of a specific idea or capitalizing on a timely market opportunity, then you can persist beyond any specific idea—good or bad—and move toward becoming an enduring great institution.

For example, HP learned humility early in its life, due to a string of failed and only moderately successful products. Yet Bill Hewlett and Dave Packard kept tinkering, persisting, trying, and experimenting until they figured out how to build an innovative company that would express their core values and earn a sustained reputation for great products. Trained as engineers, they could have pursued their goal *by being* engineers. But they didn't. Instead, they quickly made the transition from designing products to designing an organiza-

tion—creating an environment—conducive to the creation of great products. As early as the mid-1950s, Bill Hewlett displayed a clock-building perspective in an internal speech:

> Our engineering staff [has] remained fairly stable. This was by design rather than by accident. Engineers are creative people, so before we hired an engineer we made sure he would be operating in a stable and secure climate. We also made sure that each of our engineers had a long-range opportunity with the company and suitable projects on which to work. Another thing, we made certain that we had adequate supervision so that our engineers would be happy and would be productive to the maximum extent. . . . *[The process of] engineering is one of our most important products* [emphasis added]. . . . we are going to put on the best engineering program you have ever seen. If you think we have done well so far, just wait until two or three years from now when we get all of our new lab people producing and all of the supervisors rolling. You'll see some real progress then![34]

Dave Packard echoed the clock-building orientation in a 1964 speech: "The problem is, how do you develop an environment in which individuals can be creative? . . . I believe that you have to put a good deal of thought to your organizational structure in order to provide this environment."[35] In 1973, an interviewer asked Packard what specific product decisions he considered the most important in the company's growth. Packard's response didn't include one single product decision. He answered entirely in terms of organizational decisions: developing an engineering team, a pay-as-you-go policy to impose fiscal discipline, a profit-sharing program, personnel and management policies, the "HP Way" philosophy of management, and so on. In a fitting twist, the interviewer titled the article,

---

[33]Leonard S. Reich, *The Making of American Industrial Research: Science and Business at GE and Bell, 1876–1926* (Cambridge: Cambridge University Press, 1985), pp. 69–71. (*Author's note:* We cannot verify that GE's lab was definitely America's first, but we do know that it preceded Bell Labs, one of the other early labs, by a full twenty-five years.)

[34]Bill Hewlett internal speech, 1956. Courtesy Hewlett-Packard Company Archives.

[35]Dave Packard, "Industry's New Challenge: The Management of Creativity," Western Electronic Manufacturers' Association, San Diego, September 23, 1964, Courtesy Hewlett-Packard Company Archives.

"Hewlett Packard Chairman Built Company by Design, Calculator by Chance."[36]

Similarly, Masaru Ibuka's greatest "product" was not the Walkman or the Trinitron; it was Sony the company and what it stands for. Walt Disney's greatest creation was not *Fantasia,* or *Snow White,* or even Disneyland; it was the Walt Disney Company and its uncanny ability to make people happy. Sam Walton's greatest creation wasn't the Wal-Mart concept; it was the Wal-Mart Corporation—an organization that could implement retailing concepts on a large scale better than any company in the world. Paul Galvin's genius lay not in being an engineer or inventor (he was actually a self-educated but twice-failed businessman with no formal technology training),[37] but in his crafting and shaping of an innovative engineering organization that we've come to call the Motorola Company. William Procter and James Gamble's most significant contribution was not hog fat soap, lamp oils, or candles, for these would eventually become obsolete; their primary contribution was something that can never become obsolete: a highly adaptable organization with a "spiritual inheritance"[38] of deeply ingrained core values transferred to generation after generation of P&G people.

We ask you to consider this crucial shift in thinking—the shift to seeing the company itself as the ultimate creation. If you're involved in building and managing a company, this shift has significant implications for how you spend your time. It means spending less of your time thinking about specific product lines and market strategies, and spending more of your time thinking about organization design. It means spending less of your time thinking like George Westinghouse, and spending more of your time thinking like Charles Coffin, David Packard, and Paul Galvin. It means spending less of your time being a time teller, and spending more of your time being a clock builder.

We don't mean to imply that the visionary companies never had superb products or good ideas. They certainly did. And most of them view their products and services as making useful and important contributions to customers' lives. Indeed, these companies don't exist just to "be a company"; they exist to do something useful. But we suggest that *the continual stream of great products and services from highly visionary companies stems from them being outstanding organizations, not the other way around.* Keep in mind that all products, services, and great ideas, no matter how visionary, eventually become obsolete. But a visionary company does not necessarily become obsolete, not if it has the organizational ability to continually change and evolve beyond existing product life cycles.

Similarly, all leaders, no matter how charismatic or visionary, eventually die. But a visionary company does not necessarily die, not if it has the organizational strength to transcend any individual leader and remain visionary and vibrant decade after decade and through multiple generations.

This brings us to a second great myth.

The Myth of the Great and Charismatic Leader

When we ask executives and business students to speculate about the distinguishing variables—the root causes—in the success of the visionary companies, many mention "great leadership." They point to George W. Merck, Sam Walton, William Procter, James Gamble, William E. Boeing, R.W. Johnson, Paul Galvin, Bill Hewlett, Dave Packard, Charles Coffin, Walt Disney, J. Willard Marriott, Thomas J. Watson, and John Nordstrom. They argue that these chief executives displayed high levels of persistence, overcame significant obstacles, attracted dedicated people to the organization, influenced groups of people toward the achievement of goals, and played key roles in guiding their companies through crucial episodes in their history.

But—and this is the crucial point—so did their counterparts at the comparison companies! Charles

---

[36]"Hewlett-Packard Chairman Built Company by Design, Calculator by Chance," *The AMBA Executive* (September 1977), pp. 6–7.

[37]Petrakis, op. cit., pp. x–63.

[38]Schisgall, op. cit., p. xii.

Pfizer, the Gilman brothers (Ames), William Colgate, Donald Douglas, William Bristol, John Myers, Commander Eugene F. McDonald (Zenith), Pat Haggarty (TI), George Westinghouse, Harry Cohn, Howard Johnson, Frank Melville—these people *also* displayed high levels of persistence. They *also* overcame significant obstacles. They *also* attracted dedicated people to the organization. They *also* influenced groups of people toward the achievement of goals. They *also* played key roles in guiding their companies through crucial episodes in their history. A systematic analysis revealed that the comparison companies were just as likely to have solid "leadership" during the formative years as the visionary companies.

In short, we found no evidence to support the hypothesis that great leadership is the distinguishing variable during the critical, formative stages of the visionary companies. Thus, as our study progressed, we had to reject the great-leader theory; it simply did not adequately explain the *differences* between the visionary and comparison companies.

Charisma Not Required

Before we describe what we see as the crucial difference between the early shapers of visionary companies versus the comparison companies (for we do think there is a crucial difference), we'd like to share an interesting corollary: *A high-profile, charismatic style is absolutely not required to successfully shape a visionary company.* Indeed, we found that some of the most significant chief executives in the history of the visionary companies did not have the personality traits of the archetypal high-profile, charismatic visionary leader.

Consider William McKnight. Do you know who he is? Does he stand out in your mind as one of the great business leaders of the twentieth century? Can you describe his leadership style? Have you read his biography? If you're like most people, you know little or nothing about William McKnight. As of 1993, he had not made it onto *Fortune* magazine's "National Business Hall of Fame."[39] Few articles have ever been written about him. His name doesn't appear in the *Hoover's Handbook* sketch of the company's history.[40] When we started our research, we're embarrassed to say, we didn't even recognize his name. Yet the company McKnight guided *for fifty-two years* (as general manager from 1914 to 1929, chief executive from 1929 to 1949, and chairman from 1949 to 1966) earned fame and admiration with businesspeople around the world; it carries the revered name Minnesota, Mining, and Manufacturing Company (or 3M for short). 3M is famous; McKnight is not. We suspect he would have wanted it exactly that way.

McKnight began work in 1907 as a simple assistant bookkeeper and rose to cost accountant and sales manager before becoming general manager. We could find no evidence that he had a highly charismatic leadership style. Of the nearly fifty references to McKnight in the company's self-published history, only one refers to his personality, and that described him as "a soft-spoken, gentle man."[41] His biographer described him as "a good listener," "humble," "modest," "slightly stooped," "unobtrusive and soft-spoken," "quiet, thoughtful, and serious."[42]

McKnight is not the only significant chief executive in the history of the visionary companies who breaks the archetypal model of the charismatic visionary leader. Masaru Ibuka of Sony had a reputation as being reserved, thoughtful, and introspective.[43] Bill Hewlett reminded us of a friendly, no-nonsense, matter-of-fact, down-to-earth farmer from Iowa. Messrs. Procter and Gamble were stiff, prim, proper, and reserved—even deadpan.[44] Bill Allen—the most significant CEO in Boeing's

---

[39]"National Business Hall of Fame Roster of Past Laureates," *Fortune,* April 5, 1993, p. 116.

[40]*Hoover's Handbook, 1991,* p. 381.

[41]*Our Story So Far* (St. Paul, MN: 3M Company, 1977), p. 59.

[42]Mildred Houghton Comfort, *William L. McKnight, Industrialist* (Minneapolis: T.S. Denison, 1962), pp. 35, 45, 182, 194, 201.

[43]Morita, op. cit., p. 147.

[44]Schisgall, op. cit., pp. 1–15.

history—was a pragmatic lawyer, "rather benign in appearance with a rather shy and infrequent smile."[45] George W. Merck was "the embodiment of 'Merck restraint.'"[46]

We've worked with quite a few managers who have felt frustrated by all the books and articles on charismatic business leadership and who ask the sensible question, "What if high-profile charismatic leadership is just not my style?" Our response: Trying to develop such a style might be wasted energy. For one thing, psychological evidence indicates that personality traits get set relatively early in life through a combination of genetics and experience, and there is little evidence to suggest that by the time you're in a managerial role you can do much to change your basic personality style.[47] For another—and even more important— our research indicates that you don't need such a style anyway.

Please don't misunderstand our point here. We're not claiming that the architects of these visionary companies were poor leaders. We're simply pointing out that a high-profile, charismatic style is clearly not required for building a visionary company. (In fact, we speculate that a highly charismatic style might show a slight negative correlation with building a visionary company, but the data on style are too spotty and soft to make a firm statement.) We're also pointing out—and this is the essential point of this section—that *both* sets of companies have had strong enough leaders at formative stages that great leadership, be it charismatic or otherwise, cannot explain the superior trajectories of the visionary companies over the comparison companies.

We do not deny that the visionary companies have had superb individuals atop the organization at critical stages of their history. They often did. Furthermore, we think it unlikely that a company can remain highly visionary with a continuous string of mediocre people at the top. In fact, as we will discuss in a later chapter, we found that the visionary companies did a better job than the comparison companies at developing and promoting highly competent managerial talent from inside the company, and they thereby attained greater *continuity* of excellence at the top through multiple generations. But, as with great products, perhaps *the continuity of superb individuals atop visionary companies stems from the companies being outstanding organizations, not the other way around.*

Consider Jack Welch, the high-profile CEO at General Electric in the 1980s and early 1990s. We cannot deny that Welch played a huge role in revitalizing GE or that he brought an immense energy, drive, and a magnetic personality with him to the CEO's office. But obsessing on Welch's leadership style diverts us from a central point: Welch grew up in GE; he was a product of GE as much as the other way around. Somehow GE *the organization* had the ability to attract, retain, develop, groom, and select Welch the leader. GE prospered long before Welch and will probably prosper long after Welch. After all, Welch was not the first excellent CEO in GE's history, and he probably will not be the last. Welch's role was not insignificant, but it was only a small slice of the entire historical story of the General Electric Company. The selection of Welch stemmed from a good corporate architecture—an architecture that traces its roots to people like Charles Coffin, who, in contrast to George Westinghouse, took an architectural approach to building the company.

An Architectural Approach: Clock Builders at Work

As in the case of Charles Coffin versus George Westinghouse, we did see in our study differences between the two groups of early shapers, but the differences were more subtle than "great leader" versus "not great leader." The key difference, we believe, is one of orientation—the evidence suggests to us that the key people at formative stages of the visionary

[45]Serling, op. cit., p. 70.

[46]*Values and Visions: A Merck Century* (Rahway, NJ: Merck, 1993), p. 12.

[47]Camille B. Wortman and Elizabeth F. Loftus, *Psychology* (New York, NY: McGraw-Hill, 1992), pp. 385–418.

companies had a stronger organizational orientation than in the comparison companies, regardless of their personal leadership style. As the study progressed, in fact, we became increasingly uncomfortable with the term "leader" and began to embrace the term "architect" or "clock builder." The following contrasts further illustrate what we mean by an architectural, or clock-building, approach.

Citicorp Versus Chase

James Stillman, Citicorp's president from 1891 to 1909 and chairman to 1918, concentrated on organizational development in pursuit of his goal to build a great national bank.[48] He transformed the bank from a narrow parochial firm into "a fully modern corporation."[49] He oversaw the bank as it opened new offices, instituted a decentralized multidivisional structure, constructed a powerful board of directors composed of leading CEOs, and established management training and recruiting programs (instituted three decades earlier than at Chase).[50] *Citibank 1812–1970* describes how Stillman sought to architect an institution that would thrive far beyond his own lifetime:

> Stillman intended National City [precursor to Citicorp] to retain its position [as the largest and strongest bank in the United States] even after his death, and to ensure this he filled the new building with people who shared his own vision and entrepreneurial spirit, people who would build an organization. He would step aside himself and let them run the bank.[51]

Stillman wrote in a letter to his mother about his decision to step aside, to the role of chairman, so that the company could more easily grow beyond him:

I have been preparing for the past two years to assume an advisory position at the Bank and to decline re-election as its official head. I know this is wise and it not only relieves me of the responsibility of details, but gives my associates an opportunity to make names for themselves [and lays] the foundation for limitless possibilities, greater even for the future than what has been accomplished in the past.[52]

Albert Wiggin, Stillman's counterpart at Chase (president from 1911 to 1929), did not delegate at all. Decisive, humorless, and ambitious, Wiggin's primary concern appeared to be with his own aggrandizement. He sat on the boards of fifty other companies and ran Chase with such a strong, centralized controlling hand that *Business Week* wrote, "The Chase Bank is Wiggin and Wiggin is the Chase Bank."[53]

Wal-Mart Versus Ames

No doubt Sam Walton had the personality characteristics of a flamboyant, charismatic leader. We cannot help but think of his shimmy-shaking down Wall Street in a grass skirt and flower leis backed by a band of hula dancers (to fulfill a promise to employees for breaking 8 percent profit), or his leaping up on store counters and leading hundreds of screaming employees through a rousing rendition of the Wal-Mart Cheer. Yes, Walton had a unique and powerful personality. *But so did thousands of other people who didn't build a Wal-Mart.*

Indeed, the key difference between Sam Walton and the leaders at Ames is not that he was a more charismatic leader, but that he was much more of a clock builder—an architect. By his early twenties, Walton had pretty much settled upon his personality style; he spent the bulk of his life in a never-ending quest to build and develop the capabilities of the Wal-Mart organization, not in a quest to

---

[48]Harold van B. Cleveland and Thomas F. Huertas, *Citibank 1812–1970* (Cambridge, MA: Harvard University Press, 1985), p. 32.

[49]Ibid., p. 301.

[50]Ibid., pp. 41, 301; and John Donald Wilson, *The Chase* (Boston, MA: Harvard Business School Press, 1986), p. 25.

[51]Cleveland and Huertas, op. cit., p. 54.

[52]Anna Robeson Burr, *Portrait of a Banker: James Stillman, 1850–1918* (New York, NY: Duffield, 1927), p. 249.

[53]"Wiggin Is the Chase Bank and the Chase Bank Is Wiggin," *Business Week*, April 30, 1930.

develop his leadership personality.[54] This was true even in Walton's own eyes, as he wrote in *Made in America:*

> What nobody realized, including a few of my own managers at the time, was that we were really trying from the beginning to become the very best operators—the most professional managers—that we could. There's no question that I have the personality of a promoter. . . . But underneath that personality, I have always had the soul of an operator, somebody who wants to make things work well, then better, then the best they possibly can. . . . I was never in anything for the short haul; I always wanted to build as fine a retailing organization as I could.[55]

For example, Walton valued change, experimentation, and constant improvement. But he didn't just preach these values, he instituted concrete *organizational* mechanisms to stimulate change and improvement. Using a concept called "A Store Within a Store," Walton gave department managers the authority and freedom to run each department as if it were their own business.[56] He created cash awards and public recognition for associates who contribute cost saving and/or service enhancements ideas that could be reproduced at other stores. He created "VPI (Volume Producing Item) Contests" to encourage associates to attempt creative experiments.[57] He instituted merchandise meetings, to discuss experiments that should be selected for use throughout the entire chain, and Saturday morning meetings, which often featured an individual employee who tried something novel that worked really well. Profit sharing and employee stock ownership produced a direct incentive for employees to come up with new ideas, so that the whole company might benefit. Tips and ideas generated by associates got published in the Wal-Mart internal

magazine.[58] Wal-Mart even invested in a satellite communications system "to spread all the little details around the company as soon as possible."[59] In 1985, stock analyst A.G. Edwards described the ticking Wal-Mart clock:

> Personnel operate in an environment where change is encouraged. For example, if a . . . store associate makes suggestions regarding [merchandising or cost savings ideas], these ideas are quickly disseminated. Multiply each suggestion by over 750 stores and by over 80,000 employees (who can potentially make suggestions) and this leads to substantial sales gains, cost reductions and improved productivity.[60]

Whereas Walton concentrated on creating an organization that would evolve and change on its own, Ames leaders dictated all changes from above and detailed in a book the precise steps a store manager should take, leaving no room for initiative.[61] Whereas Walton groomed a capable successor to take over the company after his death (David Glass), the Gilmans had no such person in place, thus leaving the company to outsiders who did not share their philosophy.[62] Whereas Walton passed along his clock-building orientation to his successor, post-founder CEOs at Ames recklessly pursued disastrous acquisitions in a blind, obsessive pursuit of raw growth for growth's sake, gulping down 388 Zayre stores in one bite. In describing Wal-Mart's key ingredient for future success, David Glass said "Wal-Mart associates will find a way" and "Our people are relentless."[63] Ames CEO of the same era said, "The real answer and the only issue is market share."[64] In a sad note, a 1990 *Forbes* article on Ames noted, "Co-founder Herbert Gilman has seen

---

[54]Trimble, op. cit., see pp. 1–45 for a good account of Walton's early life.

[55]Walton with Huey, op. cit., pp. 78–79.

[56]"America's Most Successful Merchant," *Fortune,* September 23, 1991.

[57]Much of the detail in this section comes from Walton with Huey, op. cit., pp. 225–232.

---

[58]Trimble, op. cit., p. 274.

[59]Walton with Huey, op. cit., p. 225.

[60]Trimble, op. cit., p. 121.

[61]"Industry Overview," *Discount Merchandiser* (June 1977).

[62]"Gremlins Are Eating up the Profits at Ames," *Business Week,* October 19, 1987.

[63]"David Glass Won't Crack Under Fire," *Fortune,* February 8, 1993, p. 80.

[64]"Pistner Discusses Ames Strategy," *Discount Merchandiser* (July 1990).

his creation destroyed."[65] On a happier note, Sam Walton died with his creation intact and the belief that it could prosper long beyond him, stronger than ever. He knew that he would probably not live to the year 2000, yet shortly before he died in 1992, he set audacious goals for the company out to the year 2000, displaying a deep confidence in what the company could achieve independent of his presence.[66]

Motorola versus Zenith

Motorola's founder, Paul Galvin, dreamed first and foremost about building a great and lasting company.[67] Galvin, architect of one of the most successful technology companies in history, did not have an engineering background, but he hired excellent engineers. He encouraged dissent, discussion, and disagreement, and gave individuals "the latitude to show what they could do largely on their own."[68] He set challenges and gave people immense responsibility so as to stimulate the organization and its people to grow and learn, often by failures and mistakes.[69] Galvin's biographer summarized, "He was not an inventor, but a builder whose blueprints were people."[70] According to his son, Robert W. Galvin, "My father urged us to reach out . . . to people—to all the people—for their leadership contribution, yes their creative leadership contribution. . . . Early on, [he] was obsessed with management succession. *Ironically, he did not fear his own demise. His concern was for the company* [emphasis ours]."[71]

In contrast, Zenith's founder, Commander Eugene F. McDonald, Jr., had no succession plan, thus leaving a void of talent at the top after his unexpected death in 1958.[72] McDonald was a tremendously charismatic leader who moved the company forward primarily through the sheer force of his gigantic personality. Described as "the volatile, opinionated mastermind of Zenith," McDonald had "colossal self-assurance . . . based on a very high opinion of his own judgment."[73] He expected all except his closest friends to address him as "Commander." A brilliant tinkerer and experimenter who pushed many of his own inventions and ideas, he had a rigid attitude that almost caused Zenith to miss out on television.[74] A history of Zenith states:

> McDonald's flamboyant style was echoed in the company's dramatic advertising methods and this style, coupled with innovative genius and an ability to sense changes in public tastes, meant that for more than three decades, in the public perception McDonald *was* Zenith.[75]

Two and a half years after McDonald's death, *Fortune* magazine commented: "[Zenith] is still growing and reaping profits from the drive and imagination of its late founder. McDonald's powerful personality remains a palpable influence in the company. But Zenith's future now depends on its ability and new drive to meet conditions McDonald never anticipated."[76] A competitor commented, "As time goes on, Zenith will miss McDonald more and more."[77]

Galvin and McDonald died within eighteen months of each other.[78] Motorola sailed successfully into new arenas never dreamed of by Galvin; Zenith languished and, as of 1993, it never regained the energy and innovative spark that it had during McDonald's lifetime.

---

[65]"James Harmon's Two Hats," *Forbes,* May 28, 1990.

[66]Goals for the year 2000 from a letter we received from a Wal-Mart director in 1991.

[67]Petrakis, op. cit., pp. 49, 61.

[68]Ibid., pp. 69, 88.

[69]Ibid., pp. 114–115.

[70]Ibid., p. xi.

[71]Robert W. Galvin, *The Idea of Ideas* (Schaumburg, IL: Motorola University Press, 1991), pp. 45, 65.

[72]"Zenith Bucks the Trend," *Fortune* (December 1960).

[73]"At the Zenith and on the Spot," *Forbes,* September 1, 1961.

[74]"Zenith Bucks the Trend," *Fortune* (December 1960); "Irrepressible Gene McDonald," *Reader's Digest* (July 1944); and "Commander McDonald of Zenith," *Fortune* (June 1945).

[75]*International Directory of Corporate Histories* (Chicago, IL: St. James Press, 1988), p. 123.

[76]"Zenith Bucks the Trend," *Fortune* (December 1960).

[77]Ibid.

[78]Galvin died in November of 1959; McDonald died in May of 1958.

Walt Disney versus Columbia Pictures

Quick, stop and think: Disney. What comes to mind? Can you create a clear image or set of images that you associate with Disney? Now do the same thing for Columbia Pictures. What comes to mind? Can you put your finger on distinct and clear images? If you're like most people, you can conjure up images of what Disney means, but you probably had trouble with Columbia Pictures.

In the case of Walt Disney, it is clear that Walt brought immense personal imagination and talent to building Disney. He personally originated many of Disney's best creations, including *Snow White* (the world's first-ever full-length animated film), the character of Mickey Mouse, the Mickey Mouse Club, Disneyland, and EPCOT Center. By any measure, he was a superb time teller. But, even so, in comparison to Harry Cohn—Disney's counterpart at Columbia Pictures—Walt was much more of a clock builder.

Cohn "cultivated his image as a tyrant, keeping a riding whip near his desk and occasionally cracking it for emphasis, and Columbia had the greatest creative turnover of any major studio due largely to Cohn's methods."[79] An observer of his funeral in 1958 commented that the thirteen hundred attendees "had not come to bid farewell, but to make sure he was actually dead."[80] We could find no evidence of any concern for employees by Cohn. Nor could we find any evidence that he took steps to develop the long-term capabilities or distinct self-identity of Columbia Pictures as an institution.

The evidence suggests that Cohn cared first and foremost about becoming a movie mogul and wielding immense personal power in Hollywood (he became the first person in Hollywood to assume the titles of president *and* producer) and cared little or not at all about the qualities and identity of the Columbia Pictures Company that might endure beyond his lifetime.[81] Cohn's personal purpose propelled Columbia Pictures forward for years, but such personal and egocentric ideology could not possibly guide and inspire a company after the founder's death. Upon Cohn's death, the company fell into listless disarray, had to be rescued in 1973, and was eventually sold to Coca-Cola.

Walt Elias Disney, on the other hand, spent the day before he died in a hospital bed thinking out loud about how to best develop Disney World in Florida.[82] Walt would die, but Disney's ability to make people happy, to bring joy to children, to create laughter and tears would not die. Throughout his life, Walt Disney paid greater attention to developing his company and its capabilities than did Cohn at Columbia. In the late 1920s, he paid his creative staff more than he paid himself.[83] In the early 1930s, he established art classes for all animators, installed a small zoo on location to provide live creatures to help improve their ability to draw animals, invented new animation team processes (such as storyboards), and continually invested in the most advanced animation technologies.[84] In the late 1930s, he installed the first generous bonus system in the cartoon industry to attract and reward good talent.[85] In the 1950s, he instituted employee "You Create Happiness" training programs and, in the 1960s, he established Disney University to orient, train, and indoctrinate Disney employees.[86] Harry Cohn took none of these steps.

Granted, Walt did not clock build as well as some of the other architects in our study, and the Disney film studio languished for nearly fifteen years after his death as Disneyites ran around asking themselves, "What would Walt do?"[87] But the fact remains that Walt, unlike Cohn, created an

---

[79]*International Directory of Company Histories* (Chicago, IL: St. James Press, 1988), Volume 2, p. 135.

[80]Ibid., p. 135.

[81]Hirschhorn, op. cit.

[82]Schickel, op. cit., p. 362.

[83]*The Disney Studio Story* (Hollywood, CA: Walt Disney, 1987), p. 18.

[84]Ibid., and Schickel, op. cit., p. 180.

[85]*The Disney Studio Story* (Hollywood, CA: Walt Disney, 1987), p. 42.

[86]*Personnell* (December 1989), p. 53.

[87]John Taylor, *Storming the Magic Kingdom* (New York, NY: Ballantine Books, 1987), p. 14.

institution much bigger than himself, an institution that could still deliver the "Disney Magic" to kids at Disneyland decades after his death. During the same time period that Columbia ceased to exist as an independent entity, the Walt Disney Company mounted an epic (and ultimately successful) fight to prevent a hostile takeover. To the Disney executives and family, who could have made a tidy multimillion-dollar profit on their stock had the raiders been successful, Disney had to be preserved as an independent entity *because it was Disney.* In the preface to his book *Storming the Magic Kingdom,* a superb account of the Disney takeover attempt, John Taylor wrote:

> To accept [the takeover offer] was unthinkable. Walt Disney Productions was not just another corporate entity . . . that needed to be rationalized by liquidation of its assets to achieve maximum value for its shareholders. Nor was Disney just another brand name. . . . The company's executives saw Disney as a force shaping the imaginative life of children around the world. It was woven into the very fabric of American culture. Indeed, its mission—and it did, they believed, have a mission as important as making money for its stockholders—was to celebrate American values.[88]

Disney went on in the 1980s and 1990s to rekindle the heritage installed by Walt decades earlier. In contrast, Cohn's company had little to save or rekindle. No one felt Columbia had to be preserved as an independent entity; if the shareholders could get more money by selling out, then so be it.

The Message for CEOs, Managers, and Entrepreneurs

One of the most important steps you can take in building a visionary company is not an action, but a shift in perspective. We're doing nothing less than asking you to make a shift in thinking as fundamental as those that preceded the Newtonian revolution, the Darwinian revolution, and the founding of the United States.

Prior to the Newtonian revolution, people explained the world around them primarily in terms of a God that made specific decisions. A child would fall and break his arm, and it was an act of God. Crops failed; it was an act of God. People thought of an omnipotent God who made each and every specific event happen. Then in the 1600s people said. "No, that's not it! What God did was to put in place a universe with certain principles, and what we need to do is figure out how those principles work. God doesn't make all the decisions. He set in place processes and principles that would carry on."[89] From that point on, people began to look for basic underlying dynamics and principles of the entire system. That's what the Newtonian revolution was all about.

Similarly, the Darwinian revolution gave us a dramatic shift in thinking about biological species and natural history—a shift in thinking that provides fruitful analogies to what we've seen in the visionary companies. Prior to the Darwinian revolution, people primarily presumed that God created each and every species intact and for a specific role in the natural world: Polar bears are white because God created them that way; cats purr because God created them that way; robins have red breasts because God created them that way. We humans have a great need to explain the world around us by presuming that someone or something must have had it all figured out—something must have said, "We need robins with red breasts to fit here in the ecosystem." But if the biologists are right, it doesn't work that way. Instead of jumping directly to robins with red breasts (time telling), we have instead an *underlying process* of evolution (the genetic code, DNA, genetic variation and mutation, natural selection)

---

[88]Ibid., p. viii.

[89]We have paraphrased from the lecture series "The Origin of the Modern Mind," by Alan Charles Kors, Professor of History, University of Pennsylvania, for this paragraph.

which eventually produces robins with red breasts that appear to fit perfectly in the ecosystem.[90] The beauty and functionality of the natural world springs from the success of its underlying processes and intricate mechanisms in a marvelous "ticking clock."

Likewise, we're asking you to see the success of visionary companies—at least in part—as coming from underlying processes and fundamental dynamics embedded in the organization and not primarily the result of a single great idea or some great, all-knowing, godlike visionary who made great decisions, had great charisma, and led with great authority. If you're involved in building and managing a company, we're asking you to think less in terms of being a brilliant product visionary or seeking the personality characteristics of charismatic leadership, and to think more in terms of being an *organizational* visionary and building the characteristics of a visionary company.

Indeed, we're asking you to consider a shift in thinking analogous to the shift required to found the United States in the 1700s. Prior to the dramatic revolutions in political thought of the seventeenth and eighteenth centuries, the prosperity of a European kingdom or country depended in large part on the quality of the king (or, in the case of England, perhaps the queen). If you had a good king, then you had a good kingdom. If the king was a great and wise leader, then the kingdom might prosper as a result.

Now compare the good-king frame of reference with the approach taken at the founding of the United States. The critical question at the Constitutional Convention in 1787 was not "Who should be president? Who should lead us? Who is the wisest among us? Who would be the best king?" No, the founders of the country concentrated on such questions as "What *processes* can we create that will give us good presidents long after we're dead and gone? What type of enduring country do we want to build? On what principles? How should it operate? What guidelines and mechanisms should we construct that will give us the kind of country we envision?"

Thomas Jefferson, James Madison, and John Adams were not charismatic visionary leaders in the "it all depends on me" mode.[91] No, they were organizational visionaries. They created a constitution to which they and all future leaders would be subservient. They focused on building a country. They rejected the good-king model. They took an architectural approach. They were clock builders!

But notice: In the case of the United States, it's not a cold, mechanistic Newtonian or Darwinian clock. It's a clock based on human ideals and values. It's a clock built on human needs and aspirations. It's a clock with a *spirit.*

And that brings us to the second pillar of our findings: It's not just building any random clock; it's building *a particular type of clock.* Although the shapes, sizes, mechanisms, styles, ages, and other attributes of the ticking clocks vary across visionary companies, we found that they share an underlying set of fundamental characteristics. The important thing to keep in mind is that once you make the shift from time telling to clock building, most of what's required to build a visionary company *can be learned.* You don't have to sit around waiting until you're lucky enough to have a great idea. You don't have to accept the false view that until your company has a charismatic visionary leader, it cannot become a visionary company. There is no mysterious quality or elusive magic. Indeed, once you learn the essentials, you—and all those around you—can just get dwn to the hard work of making your company a visionary company.

---

[90]For the best coverage of the theory of evolution, we suggest Norman K. Wessells and Janet L. Hopson, *Biology* (New York, NY: Random House, 1988) chapters 9–15, pp. 19, 41–43.

[91]For an excellent description of the personalities and processes of the constitutional convention see Catherine Drinker Bowen, *Miracle at Philadelphia—The Story of the Constitutional Convention: May to September, 1787* (Boston, MA: Little, Brown, 1966).

Reading 3–4

GLOBAL STRATEGY . . . IN A WORLD OF NATIONS?

George S. Yip

Whether to globalize and how to globalize, have become two of the most burning strategy issues for managers around the world. Many forces are driving companies around the world to globalize by expanding their participation in foreign markets. Almost every product market in the major world economies—computers, fast food, nuts and bolts—has foreign competitors. Trade barriers are also falling; the recent United States/Canada trade agreement and the impending 1992 harmonization in the European Community are the two most dramatic examples. Japan is gradually opening up its long barricaded markets. Maturity in domestic markets is also driving companies to seek international expansion. This is particularly true of U.S. companies that, nourished by the huge domestic market, have typically lagged behind their European and Japanese rivals in internationalization.

Companies are also seeking to globalize by integrating their worldwide strategy. Such global integration contrasts with the multinational approach whereby companies set up country subsidiaries that design, produce, and market products or services tailored to local needs. This multinational model

(also described as a "multidomestic strategy") is now in question.[1] Several changes seem to increase the likelihood that, in some industries, a global strategy will be more successful than a multidomestic one. One of these changes, as argued forcefully and controversially by Levitt, is the growing similarity of what citizens of different countries want to buy.[2] Other changes include the reduction of tariff and nontariff barriers, technology investments that are becoming too expensive to amortize in one market only, and competitors that are globalizing the rules of the game.

Companies want to know how to globalize—in other words, expand market participation—and how to develop an integrated worldwide strategy. As depicted in Figure 1, three steps are essential in developing a total worldwide strategy:

- Developing the core strategy—the basis of sustainable competitive advantage. It is usually developed for the home country first.

George S. Yip is visiting associate professor at the School of Business Administration, Georgetown University, and also director of the PIMS Global Strategy Program. Dr. Yip holds the B.A. and M.A. degrees from Cambridge University, the M.B.A. degree from Cranfield Institute of Technology, and the M.B.A. and D.B.A. degrees from the Graduate School of Business Administration, Harvard University. His business experience includes marketing and advertising responsibilities with Unilever and Lintas and management consulting with Price Waterhouse and the MAC Group. He is the author of *Barriers to Entry* and of numerous articles.

---

[1]See T. Hout, M. E. Porter, and E. Rudden, "How Global Companies Win Out," *Harvard Business Review,* September–October 1982, pp. 98–108. My framework, developed in this article, is based in part on M. E. Porter's pioneering work on global strategy. His ideas are further developed in M. E. Porter, "Competition in Global Industries: A Conceptual Framework," in *Competition in Global Industries,* ed. M. E. Porter (Boston: Harvard Business School Press, 1986). Bartlett and Ghoshal define a "transnational industry" that is somewhat similar to Porter's "global industry." See: C. A. Bartlett and S. Ghoshal, "Managing across Borders: New Strategic Requirements," *Sloan Management Review,* Summer 1987, pp. 7–17.

[2]T. Levitt, "The Globalization of Markets," *Harvard Business Review,* May–June 1983, pp. 92–102.

FIGURE 1 Total Global Strategy

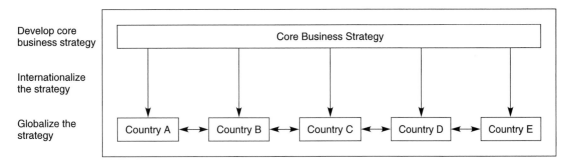

• Internationalizing the core strategy through international expansion of activities and through adaptation.

• Globalizing the international strategy by integrating the strategy across countries.

Multinational companies know the first two well. They know the third step less well since globalization runs counter to the accepted wisdom of tailoring for national markets.[3]

This article makes a case for how a global strategy might work and directs managers toward opportunities to exploit globalization. It also presents the drawbacks and costs of globalization. Figure 2 lays out a framework for thinking through globalization issues.[4]

Industry globalization drivers (underlying market, cost, and other industry conditions) are external determined, while global strategy levers are choices available to the worldwide business. Drivers create the potential for a multinational business to achieve the benefits of global strategy. To achieve these benefits, a multinational business

needs to set its *global strategy levers* (e.g., use of product standardization) appropriately to industry drivers, and to the position and resources of the business and its parent company.[5] The organization's ability to implement the strategy affects how well the benefits can be achieved.

What Is Global Strategy?

Setting strategy for a worldwide business requires making choices along a number of strategic dimensions. Table 1 lists five such dimensions or "global strategy levers" and their respective positions under a pure multidomestic strategy and a pure global strategy. Intermediate positions are, of course, feasible. For each dimension, a multidomestic strategy seeks to maximize worldwide performance by maximizing local competitive advantage, revenues, or profits: a global strategy seeks to maximize worldwide performance through sharing and integration.

Market Participation

In a multidomestic strategy, countries are selected on the basis of their stand-alone potential for revenues and profits. In a global strategy, countries need to be selected for their potential contribution

---

[3]These obstacles are laid out in one of the rejoinders provoked by Levitt's article. See: S. P. Douglas and Y. Wind, "The Myth of Globalization," *Columbia Journal of World Business,* Winter 1987, pp. 19–29.

[4]For a more theoretical exposition of this framework see: G. S. Yip, "An Integrated Approach to Global Competitive Strategy," in *Frontiers of Management,* ed. R. Mansfield (London: Routledge, forthcoming).

[5]The concept of the global strategy lever was first presented in: G. S. Yip, P. M. Loewe, and M. Y. Yoshino, "How to Take Your Company to the Global Market," *Columbia Journal of World Business,* Winter 1988, pp. 37–48.

FIGURE 2   Framework of Global Strategy Forces

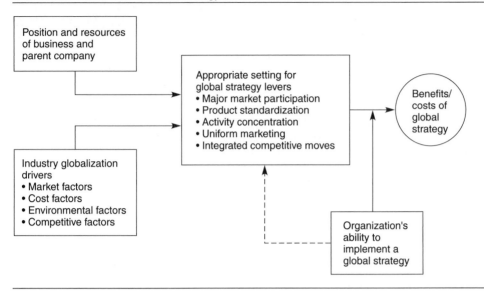

TABLE 1   Globalization Dimensions/Global Strategy Levers

Dimension	Setting for Pure Multidomestic Strategy	Setting for Pure Global Strategy
Market participation	No particular pattern	Significant share in major markets
Product offering	Fully customized in each country	Fully standardized worldwide
Location of value-added activities	All activities in each country	Concentrated—one activity in each (different) country
Marketing approach	Local	Uniform worldwide
Competitive moves	Stand-alone by country	Integrated across countries

to globalization benefits. This may mean entering a market that is unattractive in its own right, but has global strategic significance, such as the home market of a global competitor. Or it may mean building share in a limited number of key markets rather than undertaking more widespread coverage. A pattern of major share in major markets is advocated in Ohmae's USA-Europe-Japan "triad" concept.[6] In

contrast, under a multidomestic strategy, no particular pattern of participation is required—rather, the pattern accrues from the pursuit of local advantage. The Electrolux Group, the Swedish appliance giant, is pursuing a strategy of building significant share in major world markets. The company aims to be the first global appliance maker. In 1986, Electrolux took over Zanussi Industries to become the top producer of appliances in Western Europe. Later that year, Electrolux acquired White Consolidated Industries, the third largest American appliance manufacturer.

---

[6]K. Ohmae, *Triad Power: The Coming Shape of Global Competition* (New York: Free Press, 1985).

Product Offering

In a multidomestic strategy, the products offered in each country are tailored to local needs. In a global strategy, the ideal is a standardized core product that requires minimal local adaptation. Cost reduction is usually the most important benefit of product standardization. Levitt has made the most extreme case for product standardization. Others stress the need for flexibility, or the need for a broad product portfolio, with many product varieties in order to share technologies and distribution channels.[7] In practice, some multinationals have pursued product standardization to a greater or lesser extent.[8] Differing worldwide needs can be met by adapting a standardized core product. In the early 1970s, sales of the Boeing 737 began to level off. Boeing turned to developing countries as an attractive new market, but found initially that its product did not fit the new environments. Because of the shortness of runways, their greater softness, and the lower technical expertise of their pilots, the planes tended to bounce a great deal. When the planes bounced on landing, the brakes failed. To fix this problem, Boeing modified the design by adding thrust to the engines, redesigning the wings and landing gear, and installing tires with lower pressure. These adaptations to a standardized core product enabled the 737 to become the best-selling plane in history.

Location of Value-Added Activities

In a multidomestic strategy, all or most of the value chain is reproduced in every country. In another type of international strategy—exporting—most of the value chain is kept in one country. In a global strategy, costs are reduced by breaking up the value chain so each activity may be conducted in a different country. One value chain strategy is partial concentration and partial duplication. The key feature of a global position on this dimension is the strategic placement of the value chain around the globe.

Many electronics companies now locate part or all of their manufacturing operations in Southeast Asia because of that region's low-cost, skilled labor. In addition, a key component (the semiconductor chip) is very cheap there. Under the United States-Japan Semiconductor Agreement, the Japanese agreed not to sell chips in the United States below cost. But in an industry plagued by overcapacity, the chips had to go somewhere. The agreement resulted in Japanese chips being sold below cost in Southeast Asia. The lower cost of chips combined with the lower labor cost has attracted many manufacturers of computers and other electronic equipment to Southeast Asia.

Marketing Approach

In a multidomestic strategy, marketing is fully tailored for each country, being developed locally. In a global strategy, a uniform marketing approach is applied around the world, although not all elements of the marketing mix need be uniform.[9] Unilever achieved great success with a fabric softener that used a globally common positioning, advertising theme, and symbol (a teddy bear), but a brand name that varied by country. Similarly, a product that serves a common need can be geographically expanded with a uniform marketing program, despite differences in marketing environments.

Competitive Moves

In a multidomestic strategy, the managers in each country make competitive moves without regard for what happens in other countries. In a global strategy, competitive moves are integrated across

---

[7]G. Hamel and C. K. Prahalad, "Do You Really Have a Global Strategy?" *Harvard Business Review,* July–August, 1985, pp. 139–148; B. Kogut, "Designing Global Strategies: Profiting from Operational Flexibility," *Sloan Management Review,* Fall 1985, pp. 27–38.

[8]P. G. P. Walters, "International Marketing Policy: A Discussion of the Standardization Construct and Its Relevance for Corporate Policy," *Journal of International Business Studies,* Summer 1986, pp. 55–69.

[9]For a discussion of the possibilities and merits of uniform marketing see: R. D. Buzzell, "Can You Standardize Multinational Marketing?" *Harvard Business Review,* November–December 1968, pp. 102–13; and J. A. Quelch and E. J. Hoff, "Customizing Global Marketing," *Harvard Business Review,* May–June 1986, pp. 59–68.

countries. The same type of move is made in different countries at the same time or in a systematic sequence: A competitor is attacked in one country in order to drain its resources for another country, or a competitive attack in one country is countered in a different country. Perhaps the best example is the counterattack in a competitor's home market as a parry to an attack on one's own home market. Integration of competitive strategy is rarely practiced, except perhaps by some Japanese companies.[10]

Bridgestone Corporation, the Japanese tire manufacturer, tried to integrate its competitive moves in response to global consolidation by its major competitors—Continental AG's acquisition of Gencorp's General Tire and Rubber Company, General Tire's joint venture with two Japanese tire makers, and Sumitomo's acquisition of an interest in Dunlop Tire. These competitive actions forced Bridgestone to establish a presence in the major U.S. market in order to maintain its position in the world tire market. To this end, Bridgestone formed a joint venture to own and manage Firestone Corporation's worldwide tire business. This joint venture also allowed Bridgestone to gain access to Firestone's European plants.

Benefits of a Global Strategy

Companies that use global strategy levers can achieve one or more of these benefits (see Figure 3):[11]

- cost reductions;
- improved quality of products and programs;
- enhanced customer preference; and
- increased competitive leverage.

Cost Reductions

An integrated global strategy can reduce worldwide costs in several ways. A company can increase the benefits from economies of scale by *pooling production or other activities* for two or more countries. Understanding the potential benefit of these economies of scale, Sony Corporation has concentrated its compact disc production in Terre Haute, Indiana, and Salzburg, Austria.

A second way to cut costs is by *exploiting lower factor costs* by moving manufacturing or other activities to low-cost countries. This approach has, of course, motivated the recent surge of offshore manufacturing, particularly by U.S. firms. For example, the Mexican side of the U.S.-Mexico border is now crowded with "maquiladoras"—manufacturing plants set up and run by U.S. companies using Mexican labor.

Global strategy can also cut costs by *exploiting flexibility*. A company with manufacturing locations in several countries can move production from location to location on short notice to take advantage of the lowest costs at a given time. Dow Chemical takes this approach to minimize the cost of producing chemicals. Dow uses a linear programming model that takes account of international differences in exchange rates, tax rates, and transportation and labor costs. The model comes up with the best mix of production volume by location for each planning period.

An integrated global strategy can also reduce costs by *enhancing bargaining power*. A company whose strategy allows for switching production among different countries greatly increases its bargaining power with suppliers, workers, and host governments. Labor unions in European countries are very concerned that the creation of the single European market after 1992 will allow companies to switch production from country to country at will. This integrated production strategy would greatly enhance companies' bargaining power at the expense of unions.

Improved Quality of Products and Programs

Under a global strategy, companies focus on a smaller number of products and programs than under a multidomestic strategy. This concentration can improve both product and program quality. Global focus is one reason for Japanese success in

---

[10]P. Kotler et al., *The New Competition* (Englewood Cliffs, N.J.: Prentice-Hall, 1985), p. 174.

[11]Figure 3 is also presented in Yip (forthcoming).

FIGURE 3 How Global Strategy Levers Achieve Globalization Benefits

Global Strategy Levers	Benefits				Major Drawbacks
	Cost Reduction	Improved Quality of Products and Programs	Enhanced Customer Preference	Increased Competitive Leverage	All Levers Incur Coordination Costs, Plus
Major market participation	Increases volume for economies of scale		Via global availability, global serviceability, and global recognition	Advantage of earlier entry Provides more sites for attack and counterattack, hostage for good behavior	Earlier or greater commitment to a market man warranted on own merits
Product standardization	Reduces duplication of development efforts Allows concentration of production to exploit economies of scale	Focuses development and management resources	Allows consumers to use familiar product while abroad Allows organizations to use same product across country units	Basis for low-cost invasion of markets	Less responsive to local needs
Activity concentration	Reduces duplication of activities Helps exploit economies of scale Exploits differences in country factor costs Partial concentration allows flexibility versus currency charges, and versus bargaining parties	Focuses effort Allows more consistent quality control		Allows maintenance of cost advantage independent of local conditions	Distances activities from the customer Increases currency risk
Uniform marketing	Reduces design and production costs of marketing programs	Focuses talent and resources Leverages scarce, good ideas	Reinforces marketing messages by exposing customer to same mix in different countries		Reduces adaptation to local customer behavior and marketing environment
Integrated competitive moves				Provides more options and leverage in attack and defense	Local competitiveness may be sacrificed

automobiles. Toyota markets a far smaller number of models around the world than does General Motors, even allowing for its unit sales being half that of General Motors's. Toyota has concentrated on improving its few models while General Motors has fragmented its development funds. For example, the Toyota Camry is the U.S. version of a basic worldwide model and is the successor to a long line of development efforts. The Camry is consistently rated as the best in its class of medium-sized cars. In contrast, General Motors's Pontiac Fiero started out as one of the most successful small sports cars, but was recently withdrawn. Industry observers blamed this on a failure to invest development money to overcome minor problems.

Enhanced Customer Preference

Global availability, serviceability, and recognition can enhance customer preference through reinforcement. Soft drink and fast food companies are, of course, leading exponents of this strategy. Many suppliers of financial services, such as credit cards, must have a global presence because their service is travel-related. Manufacturers of industrial products can also exploit this benefit. A supplier that can provide a multinational customer with a standard product around the world gains from worldwide familiarity. Computer manufacturers have long pursued this strategy.

Increased Competitive Leverage

A global strategy provides more points from which to attack and counterattack competitors. In an effort to prevent the Japanese from becoming a competitive nuisance in disposable syringes, Becton Dickinson, a major U.S. medical products company, decided to enter three markets in Japan's backyard. Becton entered the Hong Kong, Singapore, and Philippine markets to prevent further Japanese expansions.[12]

---

[12]M. R. Cvar, "Case Studies in Global Competition," in Porter (1986).

Drawbacks of Global Strategy

Globalization can incur significant management costs through increased coordination, reporting requirements, and even added staff. It can also reduce the firm's effectiveness in individual countries if overcentralization hurts local motivation and morale. In addition, each global strategy lever has particular drawbacks.

A global strategy approach to *market participation* can incur an earlier or greater commitment to a market than is warranted on its own merits. Many American companies, such as Motorola, are struggling to penetrate Japanese markets, more in order to enhance their global competitive position than to make money in Japan for its own sake.

Product standardization can result in a product that does not entirely satisfy *any* customers. When companies first internationalize, they often offer their standard domestic product without adapting it for other countries, and suffer the consequences. For example, Procter & Gamble stumbled recently when it introduced Cheer laundry detergent in Japan without changing the U.S. product or marketing message (that the detergent was effective in all temperatures). After experiencing serious losses, P&G discovered two instances of insufficient adaptation. First, the detergent did not suds up as it should because the Japanese use a great deal of fabric softener. Second, the Japanese usually wash clothes in either cold tap water or bath water, so the claim of working in all temperatures was irrelevant. Cheer became successful in Japan only after the product was reformulated and the marketing message was changed.

A globally standardized product is designed for the global market but can seldom satisfy all needs in all countries. For instance, Canon, a Japanese company, sacrificed the ability to copy certain Japanese paper sizes when it first designed a photocopier for the global market.

Activity concentration distances customers and can result in lower responsiveness and flexibility. It also increases currency risk by incurring costs and revenues in different countries. Recently volatile exchange rates have required companies that concentrate their production to hedge their currency exposure.

Uniform marketing can reduce adaptation to local customer behavior. For example, the head office of British Airways mandated that every country use the "Manhattan Landing" television commercial developed by advertising agency Saatchi and Saatchi. While the commercial did win many awards, it has been criticized for using a visual image (New York City) that was not widely recognized in many countries.

Integrated competitive moves can mean sacrificing revenues, profits, or competitive position in individual countries, particularly when the subsidiary in one country is asked to attack a global competitor in order to send a signal or to divert that competitor's resources from another country.

Finding the Balance

The most successful worldwide strategies find a balance between overglobalizing and underglobalizing. The ideal strategy matches the level of strategy globalization to the globalization potential of the industry. In Figure 4 both Business A and Business C achieve balanced global and national strategic advantage. Business A does so with a low level of strategy globalization to match the low globalization potential of its industry (e.g., frozen food products). Business C uses a high level of strategy globalization to match the high globalization potential of its industry (e.g., computer equipment). Business B is at a global disadvantage because it uses a strategy that is less globalized than the potential offered by its industry. The business is failing to exploit potential global benefits

FIGURE 4   Globalization Potential of Industry versus Globalization Strategy

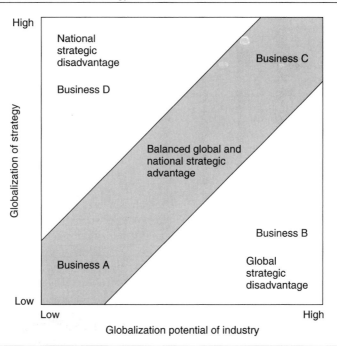

such as cost savings via product standardization. Business D is at a national disadvantage because it is too globalized relative to the potential offered by its industry. The business is not tailoring its products and programs as much as it should. While there is no systematic evidence, executives' comments suggest that far more businesses suffer from insufficient globalization than from excessive globalization. Figure 4 is oversimplified in that it shows only one overall dimension for both strategy and industry potential. As argued earlier, a global strategy has five major dimensions and many subdimensions. Similarly, the potential of industry globalization is multidimensional.

Industry Globalization Drivers

To achieve the benefits of globalization, the managers of a worldwide business need to recognize when industry globalization drivers (industry conditions) provide the opportunity to use global strategy levers. These drivers can be grouped in four categories: market, cost, governmental, and competitive. Each industry globalization driver affects the potential use of global strategy levers (see Figure 5).

Market Drivers

Market globalization drivers depend on customer behavior and the structure of distribution channels. These drivers affect the use of all five global strategy levers.

• *Homogeneous Customer Needs.* When customers in different countries want essentially the same type of product or service (or can be so persuaded), opportunities arise to market a standardized product. Understanding which aspects of the product can be standardized and which should be customized is key. In addition, homogeneous needs make participation in a large number of markets easier because fewer different product offerings need to be developed and supported.

• *Global Customers.* Global customers buy on a centralized or coordinated basis for decentralized use. The existence of global customers both allows

and requires a uniform marketing program. There are two types of global customers: national and multinational. A national global customer searches the world for suppliers but uses the purchased product or service in one country. National defense agencies are a good example. A multinational global customer also searches the world for suppliers, but uses the purchased product or service in many countries. The World Health Organization's purchase of medical products is an example. Multinational global customers are particularly challenging to serve and often require a global account management program. Companies that implement such programs have to beware of global customers using the unified account management to extract lower global prices. Having a single global account manager makes it easier for a global customer to negotiate a single global price. Typically, the global customer pushes for the lowest country price to become the global price. But a good global account manager should be able to justify differences in prices across countries.

• *Global Channels.* Analogous to global customers, channels of distribution may buy on a global or at least a regional basis. Global channels or middlemen are also important in exploiting differences in prices by buying at a lower price in one country and selling at a higher price in another country. Their presence makes it more necessary for a business to rationalize its worldwide pricing. Global channels are rare, but regionwide channels are increasing in number, particularly in European grocery distribution and retailing.

• *Transferable Marketing.* The buying decision may be such that marketing elements, such as brand names and advertising, require little local adaptation. Such transferability enables firms to use uniform marketing strategies and facilitates expanded participation in markets. A worldwide business can also adapt its brand names and advertising campaigns to make them more transferable, or, even better, design global ones to start with. Offsetting risks include the blandness of uniformly acceptable brand names or advertising, and the vulnerability of relying on a single brand franchise.

FIGURE 5 Effects of Industry Globalization Drivers on the Potential Use of Global Strategy Levers

Industry Drivers	Major Market Participation	Product Standardization	Strategy Levers		
			Activity Concentration	Uniform Marketing	Integrated Competitive Moves
Market					
Homogeneous needs	Fewer varieties needed to serve many markets	Standardized product is more acceptable			Allows sequenced invasion of markets
Global customers			Marketing process has to be coordinated	Marketing content needs to be uniform	
Global channels			Marketing process has to be coordinated	Marketing content needs to be uniform	
Transferable marketing	Easier to expand internationally			Allows use of global brands advertising, etc.	
Cost					
Economies of scale and scope	Multiple markets needed to reach economic scale	Standardization needed to reach economic scale	Conentration helps reach economic scale	Uniform marketing cuts program development and production costs	Country interdependence affects overall scale economies
Learning and experience	Multiple markets accelerate learning	Standardization accelerates learning	Concentration accelerates learning		
Sourcing efficiencies			Centralized purchasing exploits efficiencies		
Favorable logistics	Easier to expand internationally		Allows concentrated production		Allows export competition

(continued)

FIGURE 5 (concluded)

Industry Drivers	Strategy Levers				
	Major Market Participation	Product Standardization	Activity Concentration	Uniform Marketing	Integrated Competitive Moves
Cost					
Differences in country costs and skills			Exploited by activity concentration		Increase vulnerability of high-cost countries
Product development costs	Multiple markets needed to pay back investment	Standardization reduces development needs	Concentration cuts cost of development		
Government					
Favorable trade policies	Affects nature extent of participation	May require or prevent product features	Local content rules affect extent of concentration possible		Integration needed to deal with competitive effects of tariffs/subsidies
Compatible technical standards	Affects markets that can be entered	Affects standardization possible			
Common marketing regulations				Affects approaches possible	
Competitive					
Interdependence of countries	More participation leverages benefits	Accept tradeoffs to get best global product	Locate key activities in lead countries	Use lead country to develop programs	Integration needed to exploit benefits
Competitors globalized or might globalize	Expand to match or preempt	Match or preempt	Match or preempt	Match or preempt	Integration needed to exploit benefits

Cost Drivers

Cost drivers depend on the economics of the business; they particularly affect activity concentration.

• *Economies of Scale and Scope.* A single-country market may not be large enough for the local business to achieve all possible economies of scale or scope. Scale at a given location can be increased through participation in multiple markets combined with product standardization or concentration of selected value activities. Corresponding risks include rigidity and vulnerability to disruption.

In the past few years, the economics of the electronics industry have shifted. As the cost of circuits has decreased, the economic advantage has gone to companies that can produce the lowest-cost components. Size has become a major asset. Thomson, the French electronics firm, understands the need to have a worldwide presence in an industry characterized by economies of scale. In 1987, Thomson greatly increased both its operating scale and its global coverage by acquiring the RCA television business from General Electric.

• *Learning and Experience.* Even if economies of scope and scale are exhausted, expanded market participation and activity concentration can accelerate the accumulation of learning and experience. The steeper the learning and experience curves, the greater the potential benefit will be. Managers should beware, though, of the usual danger in pursuing experience curve strategies—overaggressive pricing that destroys not just the competition but the market as well. Prices get so low that profit is insufficient to sustain any competitor.

• *Sourcing Efficiencies.* Centralized purchasing of new materials can significantly lower costs. Himont began as a joint venture between Hercules Inc. of the United States and Montedison Petrolchimica SpA of Italy, and is the leader in the global polypropylene market. Central to Himont's strategy is global coordination among manufacturing facilities in the purchase of raw materials, particularly monomer, the key ingredient in polypropylene production. Rationalization of raw material orders significantly strengthens the venture's low-cost production advantage.

• *Favorable Logistics.* A favorable ratio of sales value to transportation cost enhances the company's ability to concentrate production. Other logistical factors include nonperishability, the absence of time urgency, and little need for location close to customer facilities. Even the shape of the product can make a crucial difference. Cardboard tubes, such as those used as cores for textiles, cannot be shipped economically because they are mostly air. In contrast, cardboard cones are transportable because many units can be stacked in the same space.

• *Differences in Country Costs and Skills.* Factor costs generally vary across countries; this is particularly true in certain industries. The availability of particular skills also varies. Concentration of activities in low-cost or high-skill countries can increase productivity and reduce costs, but managers need to anticipate the danger of training future offshore competitors.[13]

Under attack from lower-priced cars, Volkswagen has needed to reduce its costs. It is doing so by concentrating its production to take advantage of the differences in various country costs. In Spain, hourly labor costs are below DM 20 per hour, while those in West Germany are over DM 40 per hour. To take advantage of this cost differential, the company moved production of Polos from Wolfsburg to Spain, freeing up the high-wage German labor to produce the higher-priced Golf cars. Another example of this concentration occurred when Volkswagen shut down its New Stanton, Pennsylvania, plant that manufactured Golfs and Jettas. The lower end of the U.S. market would be served by its low-wage Brazilian facility that produced the Fox. The higher end of the product line (Jetta and Golf) would be exported from Europe. This concentration and coordination of production has enabled the company to lower costs substantially.

---

[13]See: C. C. Markides and N. Berg, "Manufacturing Offshore Is Bad Business," *Harvard Business Review,* September–October 1988, pp. 113–20.

• *Product Development Costs.* Product development costs can be reduced by developing a few global or regional products rather than many national products. The automobile industry is characterized by long product development periods and high product development costs. One reason for the high costs is duplication of effort across countries. The Ford Motor Company's "Centers of Excellence" program aims to reduce these duplicating efforts and to exploit the differing expertise of Ford specialists worldwide. As part of the concentrated effort, Ford of Europe is designing a common platform for all compacts, while Ford of North America is developing platforms for the replacement of the midsized Taurus and Sable. This concentration of design is estimated to save "hundreds of millions of dollars per model by eliminating duplicative efforts and saving on retooling factories."[14]

Governmental Drivers

Government globalization drivers depend on the rules set by national governments and affect the use of all global strategy levers.

• *Favorable Trade Policies.* Host governments affect globalization potential through import tariffs and quotas, nontariff barriers, export subsidies, local content requirements, currency and capital flow restrictions, and requirements on technology transfer.[15] Host government policies can make it difficult to use the global levers of major market participation, product standardization, activity concentration, and uniform marketing; they also affect the integrated-competitive-moves lever.

National trade policies constrain companies' concentration of manufacturing activities. Aggressive U.S. government actions including threats on

---

[14]"Can Ford Stay on Top?" *Business Week,* 28 September 1987, pp. 78–86.

[15]Three public sector activities that can protect domestic competitors are blocking access to the domestic market, providing subsidies, and creating spillovers in research and development. See: M. A. Spence, "Industrial Organizational and Competitive Advantage in Multinational Industries," *American Economic Review* 74 (May 1984): 356–60.

tariffs, quotas, and protectionist measures have helped convince Japanese automakers and other manufacturers to give up their concentration of manufacturing in Japan. Reluctantly, Japanese companies are opening plants in the United States. Honda has even made a public relations virtue out of necessity. It recently gave great publicity to the first shipment of a U.S.-made Honda car to Japan.

The easing of government restrictions can set off a rush for expanded market participation. European Community regulations for banking and financial services will be among those harmonized in 1992. The European Community decision to permit the free flow of capital along member countries has led European financial institutions to jockey for position. Until recently, the Deutsche Bank had only 15 offices outside of Germany, but it has recently established a major presence in the French market. In 1987, Deutsche Bank also moved into the Italian market by acquiring Bank of America's 100 branches there. Other financial organizations, such as J. P. Morgan of the United States, Swiss Bank Corporation, and the S. P. Warburg Group in Britain have increased their participation in major European markets through acquisitions.

• *Compatible Technical Standards.* Differences in technical standards, especially government-imposed standards, limit the extent to which products can be standardized. Often, standards are set with protectionism in mind. Motorola found that many of their electronics products were excluded from the Japanese market because these products operated at a higher frequency than was permitted in Japan.

• *Common Marketing Regulations.* The marketing environment of individual countries affects the extent to which uniform global marketing approaches can be used. Certain types of media may be prohibited or restricted. For example, the United States is far more liberal than Europe about the kinds of advertising claims that can be made on television. The British authorities even veto the depiction of socially undesirable behavior. For example, British television authorities do not allow scenes of children pestering their parents to buy a product. And, of course, the use of sex is different. As one extreme,

France is far more liberal than the United States about sex in advertising. Various promotional devices, such as lotteries, may also be restricted.

Competitive Drivers

Market, cost, and governmental globalization drivers are essentially fixed for an industry at any given time. Competitors can play only a limited role in affecting these factors (although a sustained effort can bring about change, particularly in the case of consumer preferences). In contrast, competitive drivers are entirely in the realm of competitor choice. Competitors can raise the globalization potential of their industry and spur the need for a response on the global strategy levers.

• *Interdependence of Countries.* A competitor may create competitive interdependence among countries by pursuing a global strategy. The basic mechanism is through sharing of activities. When activities such as production are shared among countries, a competitor's market share in one country affects its scale and overall cost position in the shared activities. Changes in that scale and cost will affect its competitive position in all countries dependent on the shared activities. Less directly, customers may view market position in a lead country as an indicator of overall quality. Companies frequently promote a product as, for example, "the leading brand in the United States." Other competitors then need to respond via increased market participation, uniform marketing, or integrated competitive strategy to avoid a downward spiral of sequentially weakened positions in individual countries.

In the automobile industry, where economies of scale are significant and where sharing activities can lower costs, markets have significant competitive interdependence. As companies like Ford and Volkswagen concentrate production and become more cost competitive with the Japanese manufacturers, the Japanese are pressured to enter more markets so that increased production volume will lower costs. Whether conscious of this or not, Toyota has begun a concerted effort to penetrate the German market: Between 1984 and 1987, Toyota doubled the number of cars produced for the German market.

• *Globalized Competitors.* More specifically, attaching or preempting individual competitor moves may be necessary. These moves include expanding into or within major markets, being the first to introduce a standardized product, or being the first to use a uniform marketing program.

The need to preempt a global competitor can spur increased market participation. In 1986, Unilever, the European consumer products company, sought to increase its participation in the U.S. market by launching a hostile takeover bid for Richardson-Vicks Inc. Unilever's global archrival, Procter & Gamble, saw the threat to its home turf and outbid Unilever to capture Richardson-Vicks. With Richardson-Vicks's European system, P&G was able to greatly strengthen its European positioning. So Unilever's attempt to expand participation in a rival's home market backfired to allow the rival to expand participation in Unilever's home markets.

In summary, industry globalization drivers provide opportunities to use global strategy levers in many ways. Some industries, such as civil aircraft, can score high on most dimensions of globalization.[16] Others, such as the cement industry, seem to be inherently local. But more and more industries are developing globalization potential. Even the food industry in Europe, renowned for its diversity of taste, is now a globalization target for major food multinationals.

Changes over Time

Finally, industry evolution plays a role. As each of the industry globalization drivers changes over time, so too will the appropriate global strategy change. For example, in the European major appliance industry, globalization forces seem to have reversed. In the late 1960s and early 1970s, a regional standardization strategy was successful for some key competitors.[17] But in the 1980s the situation

---

[16]M. Y. Yoshino, "Global Competition in a Salient Industry: The Case of Civil Aircraft," in Porter (1986).

[17]Levitt (May–June 1983).

appears to have turned around, and the most successful strategies seem to be national.[18]

In some cases, the actions of individual competitors can affect the direction and pace of change; competitors positioned to take advantage of globalization forces will want to hasten them. For example, a competitor with strong central manufacturing capabilities may want to accelerate the worldwide acceptance of a standardized product.

More Than One Strategy Is Viable

Although they are powerful, industry globalization drivers do not dictate one formula for success. More than one type of international strategy can be viable in a given industry.

Industries vary across drivers. No industry is high on every one of the many globalization drivers. A particular competitor may be in a strong position to exploit a driver that scores low on globalization. For example, the dominance of national government customers offsets the globalization potential from other industry drivers, because government customers typically prefer to do business with their own nationals. In such an industry a competitor with a global strategy can use its other advantages, such as low cost from centralization of global production, to offset this drawback. At the same time, another multinational competitor with good government contacts can pursue a multidomestic strategy and succeed without globalization advantages, and single-country local competitors can succeed on the basis of their very particular local assets. The hotel industry provides examples both of successful global and of successful local competitors.

Global effects are incremental. Globalization drivers are not deterministic for a second reason: The appropriate use of strategy levers adds competitive advantage to existing sources. These other sources may allow individual competitors to thrive

with international strategies that are mismatched with industry globalization drivers. For example, superior technology is a major source of competitive advantage in most industries, but can be quite independent of globalization drivers. A competitor with sufficiently superior technology can use it to offset globalization disadvantages.

Business and parent company position and resources are crucial. The third reason that drivers are not deterministic is related to resources. A worldwide business may face industry drivers that strongly favor a global strategy. But global strategies are typically expensive to implement initially even though great cost savings and revenue gains should follow. High initial investments may be needed to expand within or into major markets, to develop standardized products, to relocate value activities, to create global brands, to create new organization units or coordination processes, and to implement other aspects of a global strategy. The strategic position of the business is also relevant. Even though a global strategy may improve the business's long-term strategic position, its immediate position may be so weak that resources should be devoted to short-term, country-by-country improvements. Despite the automobile industry's very strong globalization driver, Chrysler Corporation had to deglobalize by selling off most of its international automotive businesses to avoid bankruptcy. Lastly, investing in nonglobal sources of competitive advantage, such as superior technology, may yield greater returns than global ones, such as centralized manufacturing.

Organizations have limitations. Finally, factors such as organization structure, management processes, people, and culture affect how well a desired global strategy can be implemented. Organizational differences among companies in the same industry can, or should, constrain the companies' pursuit of the same global strategy. Organization issues in globalization are a major topic, and cannot be covered in the space here.[19]

---

[18]C. Baden Fuller et al., "National or Global?" *The Study of Company Strategies and the European Market for Major Appliances* (London: London Business School Centre for Business Strategy, working paper series, No. 28, June 1987).

[19]See: Yip et al. (1988); and C. K. Prahalad and Y. L. Doz. *The Multinational Mission: Balancing Local Demands and Global Vision* (New York: Free Press, 1987).

Chapter 4

Managing across Boundaries: The Collaborative Challenge

In the 1970s and early 1980s, the strategic challenge for a company was viewed primarily as one of protecting its potential profits from erosion through either competition or bargaining. Such erosion of profits could be caused not only by the actions of competitors but also by the bargaining powers of customers, suppliers, and governments. The key challenge facing a company was assumed to be its ability to maintain its independence by maintaining firm control over its activities. Furthermore, this strategic approach emphasized the defensive value of making other entities depend on it by capturing critical resources, building switching costs, and exploiting other vulnerabilities.[1]

This view of strategy underwent a sea change in the late 1980s. The need to pursue multiple sources of competitive advantage simultaneously (see Chapter 2) led not only to the need for building an interdependent and integrated network organization within the company (Chapter 6), but also to the need for building collaborative relationships externally with governments, competitors, customers, suppliers, and a variety of other institutions.

The change in perspective was triggered by a variety of factors including rising R&D costs, shortening product life cycles, growing barriers to market entry, increasing need for global-scale economies, and the expanding importance of global standards. Such dramatic and simultaneous changes forced managers to recognize they may not have all the human, financial, or technological resources necessary to respond effectively. This led many to shift their strategic focus away from an all-encompassing obsession with preempting competition to a broader

---

[1]For the most influential exposition of this view, see Michael E. Porter, *Competitive Strategy* (New York: Free Press, 1980).

view of building competitive advantage through selective and often simultaneous reliance on both collaboration and competition.

The previously dominant focus on value appropriation that characterized all dealings across a company's organizational boundary changed to simultaneous consideration of both value creation and value appropriation. Instead of trying to enhance their bargaining power over customers, companies began to build partnerships with them, thereby bolstering the customer's competitive position and, at the same time, leveraging their own competitiveness and innovative capabilities. Instead of challenging or, at best, accommodating the interests of host governments, many MNCs began actively pursuing cooperative relationships with government agencies and administrators.

The latest and also perhaps the most visible manifestation of this growing role of collaborative strategies lies in the phenomenon often described as *strategic alliances:* the increasing propensity of MNCs to form cooperative relationships with their global competitors. As described by Carlo de Benedetti, the ex-chairman of Olivetti and the key instigator of the variety of partnerships that Olivetti had developed with companies such as AT&T and Toshiba, "We have entered the age of alliances. . . . In the high-tech markets of the 1990s, we will see a shaking out of the isolated and a shaking in of the allied."

The causes and consequences of such collaborative strategies are the topic of our discussion in this chapter. While our analysis focuses on the phenomenon of strategic alliances among global competitors, some of our arguments can be applied to a broader range of cooperative relations including those with customers, suppliers, and governments. We begin with a discussion of the key motivations for forming strategic alliances and show how global competition, competitive convergence, economies of scale, need for risk management, and technology exchange have acted as driving forces in the recent growth of cooperative agreements. However, such alliance arrangements carry considerable risks, which we describe in the second section. In the third part of the chapter, we suggest some of the key challenges and tasks for managers who have to carry the responsibility for building and managing such alliances. The final section provides some brief conclusions.

WHY STRATEGIC ALLIANCES?

The term *strategic alliance* has become widely used to describe a variety of different interfirm cooperation agreements ranging from shared research to formal joint ventures and minority equity participation. But regardless of the definitional vagueness, a variety of recent studies have shown that large numbers of firms worldwide, including many industry leaders, are becoming increasingly involved in strategic alliances. Furthermore, several of these surveys have suggested that the recent wave of partnerships is distinguishable from the traditional foreign investment joint ventures in several important ways.

Classically, the traditional joint ventures were formed between a senior multinational headquartered in an industrialized country and a junior local partner in a less developed or less industrialized country. The primary goal that dominated their formation was to gain new market access for existing products. In this classic contractual agreement, the senior partner provided existing products while the junior partner provided the local marketing expertise, the means to overcome any protectionist barriers, and the governmental contacts to deal with national regulations. Both partners benefited: The multinational achieved increased sales volume, and the local firm gained access to new products and often learned important new skills from its partner.

In contrast, the scope and motivations for the modern form of strategic alliances seem to be broadening. There are three trends that are particularly noteworthy. First, present-day strategic alliances are increasingly between firms in industrialized countries. Second, the focus is on the creation of new products and technologies rather than the distribution of existing ones. And third, the present-day strategic alliances are often forged during industry transitions when competitive positions are shifting and the very basis for building and sustaining competitive advantage is being defined.

All of these characteristics make the new form of strategic alliances considerably more strategically important than the classic joint ventures they succeeded, and today the opportunity for competitive gain and loss through partnering is substantial. In the following paragraphs, we discuss in more detail why this rapidly developing form of business relationship is becoming so important by focusing on four key motivations that are driving the formation of strategic alliances: technology exchange, global competition, industry convergence, and economies of scale and reduction of associated risks.

Technology Exchange

Various studies have confirmed that technology transfer or R&D collaboration is the major objective of over half the strategic alliances formed in recent years. Indeed, it will become clear that the need to share technology resources has emerged as the single most powerful common thread linking all of the motivating factors we describe in the following pages. The reason that technological exchange has become such a strong driver of alliances is simple. In recent years, breakthroughs and major innovations increasingly have been based on interdisciplinary and interindustry advances that blur the formerly discrete boundaries between different industrial sectors and technologies. Because the necessary capabilities and resources are often beyond the scope of a single firm, it has become increasingly difficult to compete effectively on the strength of one's own internal R&D efforts. The need to collaborate is further intensified by increasingly short product life cycles that increase both the time pressure and risk exposure while reducing the potential payback of massive R&D investments.

As a result, all the major technology-intensive sectors such as telecommunications, computer and office equipment, electronics, pharmaceuticals, and special chemicals have become the central arenas for major and extensive cooperative agreements. Companies in these industries face an environment of accelerating change, short product life cycles, small market windows, and multiple vertical and lateral dependencies for market success. Because interfirm cooperation has often provided a solution to many of these difficulties, much of the technological development in each of these industries is now being driven by some form of R&D partnership.

Global Competition

In the 1990s, there is a fast-growing and widespread perception that global competitive battles will increasingly be fought out between teams of players aligned in strategic partnerships. Robert P. Collin, head of the U.S. subsidiary of a joint venture between General Electric and Fanuc, the Japanese robot maker, understood the urgency with which many now view the challenge: "To level out the global playing field, American companies will have to find partners." In the new game of global networks, successful MNCs may be those who have chosen the best set of corporate allies.

Particularly in industries where there is a dominant worldwide market leader, strategic alliances and networks allow coalitions of smaller partners to compete more effectively against a global "common enemy" rather than each other. This strong motivation for strategic alliances was voiced by the top-level Japanese manager heading Fujitsu's computer operations who stated that his major strategic goal was, "to find strong allies to fight IBM."

Strategic alliances have also played a major role in the global technology race. MNCs face the dual challenge of competing in global markets while attempting to produce tailored local solutions to compete effectively against local competitors. This challenge is further complicated by the need to coordinate and deploy discrete pools of technological resources. Strategic alliances have been used by multinationals to meet this challenge without sacrificing R&D and commercialization scale advantages. For example, advanced material suppliers can assist global automotive companies in transferring technology across geographic borders; GEC played a key role in transferring the Ford Xenoy bumper technology from Europe and adapting it to the U.S. market.

Industry Convergence

Many high-technology industries are converging and overlapping in a way that seems destined to create a huge competitive traffic jam. Producers of computers, telecommunications, and components are merging; bio and chip technologies are intersecting; and advanced materials applications are creating greater overlaps in diverse applications from the aerospace to the automotive industry. Nowhere are the implications of this convergence clearer than in the case of high-definition television (HDTV).

As with many other strategically critical technologies of the future—biotechnology, superconductivity, advanced ceramics, artificial intelligence—HDTV not only dwarfs previous investment requirements, but also extends beyond the technological capabilities of even the largest and most diversified MNCs. As a result, the development of this important new industry segment has been undertaken almost exclusively by alliances of large powerful companies sharing technological and financial resources. In Japan, companies allied together to develop the range of products necessary for a system offering. At the same time, a European HDTV consortium was banded together to develop a competitive system. But in the United States, the various legal and cultural barriers that prevented companies working together in such partnerships threatened to compromise U.S. competitiveness in this major new industry.

Strategic alliances are sometimes the only way to develop the complex and interdisciplinary skills necessary in the competitive time frame required. Through such collaboration, alliances also become a way of shaping competition by reducing competitive intensity by excluding potential entrants and isolating particular players, and by building complex integrated value chains that can act as a barrier to those who chose to go it alone.

Economies of Scale and Reduction of Risk

There are several ways in which strategic alliances and networks allow participating firms to reap the benefits of scale economies or learning. First, partners can pool their resources and concentrate their activities to raise the scale of activity or the rate of learning within the alliance significantly over that of each firm operating separately. Second, alliances allow partners to share and leverage the specific strengths and capabilities of each of the other participating firms. Third, trading different or complementary resources between companies can also result in mutual gains and save each partner the high cost of duplication.

At the same time that product life cycles are shortening and technological complexity is increasing, R&D expenses are being driven sharply higher by personnel and capital costs. Because none of the participating firms bear the full risk and cost of the joint activity, alliances are often seen as an attractive risk-hedging mechanism.

THE RISKS AND COSTS OF COLLABORATION

Because of these different motivations, there was an initial period of euphoria in which partnerships were seen as the panacea for most of the MNCs' global strategic problems and opportunities. Particularly in the early and mid-1980s, a large number of companies rushed to form polygamous relationships with a variety of partners around the world. The euphoria was fueled by two fashionable management concepts of the period: *triad power*[2] and *stick to your knitting.*[3]

The triad power concept emphasized the need to develop significant positions in the three key markets of the United States, Western Europe, and Japan as a prerequisite for competing in global industries. Given the enormous costs and difficulties of independently accessing any one of these developed and highly competitive markets, many companies with unequal legs to their geographic stool saw alliances as the only feasible way to develop this triadic position.

The stick-to-your-knitting prescription in essence urged managers to disaggregate the value chain and focus their investments, efforts, and attention on only those tasks in which the company had a significant competitive advantage. Other operations were to be externalized through outsourcing or alliances.

The seductive logic of both these arguments, coupled with the rapidly evolving environmental demands, led to an explosion in the formation of such alliances as illustrated in Figure 4–1.

Since then, the experience companies gathered through such collaborative ventures highlighted some of the costs and risks of such partnerships. Some risks arise from the simultaneous presence of both collaborative and competitive aspects in such relationships and the resulting possibility of one partner using the collaboration as a way of developing competitive advantages over the other. Other risks and costs arise from the higher levels of strategic and organizational complexity of managing cooperative relationships outside the company's own boundaries. As described in one of the readings in this book, it has now become clear that "alliances are like marriages—they work only when both partners do."

The Risks of Competitive Collaboration

Many strategic alliances—including some of the most visible—involve partners who are fierce competitors outside the specific scope of the cooperative venture. Such relationships create the possibility that the collaborative venture might be used by one or both partners to develop a competitive edge over the other, or at least that the benefits from the partnership would be asymmetrical to the two parties, thereby changing their relative competitive positions. There are several factors that might cause such asymmetry.

In an extreme situation, there is always the possibility that one of the companies might join the alliance with the explicit objective of using the venture to exploit its partner company. It may try to extract core competencies from the venture, or it could use its influence over the investment and development processes to reduce its partner's competitiveness.

---

[2]See Kenichi Ohmae, *Triad Power* (New York: Free Press, 1985).

[3]One of the lessons developed in the highly influential book by Thomas Peters and Robert Waterman, *In Search of Excellence* (New York: Harper & Row, 1982).

FIGURE 4–1   Cooperative Agreements, 1979–1985

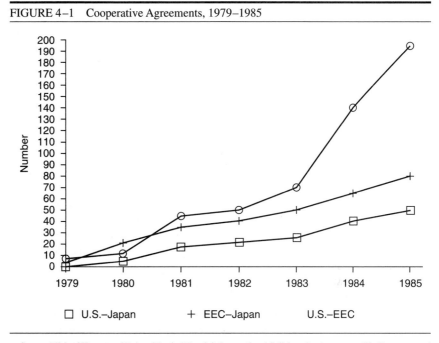

Source: Michael Hergert and Deigan Morris, "Trends in International Collaborative Agreements," in Contractor and Lorange (eds.), *Cooperative Strategies in International Business* (Lexington, Mass.: Lexington Books, 1988), p. 101.

A partnership is often motivated by the desire to join and leverage complementary skills and resources. For example, the two partners may have access to different technologies that can be combined to create new businesses or products. This, for example, was the main motivation for the alliance between Digital Equipment Corporation and Ericsson: the two companies hoped to pool some aspects of their computer (DEC) and communication (Ericsson) technologies to create new products at the interface of these two converging businesses. The alliance between Chrysler and Maserati represents an alternative form of such competency pooling in which Maserati's skills in designing luxury sports cars was intended to be combined with Chrysler's mass production capabilities to develop a new TC coupe model.

Such an arrangement for competency pooling inevitably entails the possibility that, in the course of the partnership, one of the partners will learn and internalize the other's skills while carefully protecting its own, thereby creating the option of ultimately discarding the partner and appropriating all the benefits created by the partnership. This possibility becomes particularly salient when the skills and competencies of one of the partners are tacit and deeply embedded in complex organizational processes (and thereby being difficult to learn or emulate) while those of the other partner are explicit and embodied in specific individual machines or drawings (and thereby being liable to relatively easy observation and emulation).

The other predatory tactic might involve capturing investment initiative in order to use the partnership to erode the other's competitive position. In this scenario, the company ensures that it, rather than the partner, makes and keeps control over the critical investments. Such investments can be in the domain of product development, manufacturing, marketing, or wherever the most strategically vital part of the business value chain is located. Through such tactics, the aggressive company can strip its partner of the necessary infrastructure for competing independently and create one-way dependence on the collaboration that can be exploited at will.

Although they provide lively copy for magazine articles, such Machiavellian intentions and actions remain the exception, and the vast majority of cross-company collaborations are founded on a basis of mutual trust and shared commitment. Yet, experience has shown that even the most carefully constructed strategic alliances can become highly risky and problematic ventures. While many provide short-term solutions to some strategic problems, they can also serve to hide the deeper and more fundamental deficiencies that cause those problems. The short-term solution takes the pressure off the problem without solving it and makes the company highly vulnerable when the problem finally resurfaces, now in a more extreme and immediate form.

Furthermore, because such alliances typically involve sharing of tasks, each company almost inevitably loses some of the benefits from "learning by doing" for the tasks that it externalizes to its partner. Finally, even in the best-case scenario of a partnership that fully meets all expectations, the very success of partnership leads to some benefits for each partner and, therefore, to some strengthening of one's competitor. Behind the success of the alliance, therefore, lies the ever-present possibility that a competitor's newly acquired strength will be used against its alliance partner in some future competitive battle.[4]

The Cost of Strategic and Organizational Complexity

Cooperation is difficult to attain even in the best of circumstances. One of the strongest forces facilitating such behavior within a single company's internal operations is the understanding that the risks and rewards ultimately accrue to the company's own accounts, and therefore, either directly or indirectly, to the participants. This basic motivation is absent in strategic alliances that require cooperation across organizational boundaries that are also boundaries for the accounting of risks and rewards. This fundamental problem of cooperation in the context of divided loyalties inevitably creates additional strategic and organizational complexity and, therefore, involves additional costs for managing those complexities.

---

[4]These potential risks of competitive collaboration are the focus for the article by Gary Hamel, C. K. Prahalad, and Yves L. Doz, "Collaborate with Your Competitor and Win," *Harvard Business Review.*

In addition, organizational problems are exacerbated by differences in the administrative heritages of the partner companies, each of which brings its own strategic mentality and managerial practices to the venture. Furthermore, the scope of most alliances and the environmental uncertainties they inevitably face often prevent clear understanding of the nature, extent, and distribution of risks that might be incurred or rewards that might accrue in the course of the partnership's evolution, or even a clear definition of each partner's roles and tasks.

International partnerships bring together companies that are often products of vastly different economic, political, social, and cultural systems. Protected against take-over possibilities by a variety of legal and institutional factors, many Dutch, Swiss, or Japanese companies have been bewildered by what they have perceived as the "accounting mentality" of their British or U.S. partners. Subject to the expectations of "The City" or "The Street" and forever under the threat of a hostile bid, the British and U.S. partners have been equally puzzled by their foreign partners' insensitivity to stock price effects of announcements and actions and by what they have perceived as the partners' naivete in financial and planning matters. Tensions between Xerox and Fuji-Xerox—a successful but often troubled relationship documented in a case later in this chapter—were as much an outgrowth of the differences in the business systems in which each was located as differences in the corporate culture between the U.S. company and its Japanese joint venture.

Organizational complexity due to the very broad scope of operations that is typical of many strategic alliances also contributes to the added difficulties. As we described in the introduction to this chapter, one of the distinguishing characteristics of present-day alliances is that compared to the narrower and more focused goals of earlier joint ventures, they often cover a broad range of activities involving product development, manufacturing, marketing, and related supporting tasks. This expansion of scope requires partners not only to manage the many areas of contact within the alliance, but also to coordinate the different alliance-related tasks within its own organization.

Finally, additional complexity is generated because of growing environmental uncertainties. The strategic rather than tactical goals of the alliances make them relatively more sensitive to environmental changes. The combination of higher environmental sensitivity and growing environmental uncertainty means that the goals, tasks, and management processes for the alliance must be constantly monitored and adapted to changing conditions. This involves additional investments both for monitoring and also for renegotiations, adding to the overall risks and costs of the alliance.

BUILDING AND MANAGING COLLABORATIVE VENTURES

As we have described in the preceding sections, alliances are neither conventional organizations with fully internalized activities, nor are they well-specified transaction relationships through which externalized activities are linked by contracts. Instead, they combine elements of both. The participating companies retain their own competitive strategies and performance expectations as well as their national ideological and administrative identities. Yet, to obtain the required benefits out of the partnership, diverse organizational units in different companies and in different countries must effectively and flexibly coordinate their activities.

There are numerous reasons why such collaborative ventures inevitably present some very significant management challenges: strategic and environmental disparities among the partners, lack of a common experience and perception base, difficulties in interfirm communication, conflicts of interest and priorities, and inevitable personal differences among individuals who manage the interface. As a result, while it is manifest to most managers that strategic alliances can provide great benefits and must play an increasingly important role in the global strategies of their companies, they have also begun to realize that there is a big difference between making alliances and making them work.

These challenges of building and managing strategic alliances can be considered in two parts, reflecting the two stages of prealliance tasks of analysis, negotiation, and decision making and the postalliance tasks of coordination, integration, and adaptation.

Building Cooperative Ventures

Alliances are like marriages. Just as the foundations of the relationship established during the dating process influences the quality and durability of the marriage, so the quality of the prealliance processes of partner selection and negotiation influence the clarity and reciprocity of mutual expectations from the alliance.

There are three aspects of the prealliance process to which managers must pay close attention if the alliance is to have the best possible chance of success: partner selection, escalating commitment, and alliance scope.[5]

Partner Selection: Strategic and Organizational Analysis.   The process of analyzing a potential partner's strategic and organizational capabilities is perhaps the most important yet also the most difficult of the prealliance tasks. Several factors impede the quality of the choice-making process.

The most important constraint lies in the availability of information required for an effective evaluation of the potential partner. Effective prealliance analysis needs data on the partner's relevant physical assets (such as the condition and productivity of plant and equipment), as well as on less-tangible assets (including the strength of brands, the quality of customer relationships, and the level of technological expertise) and organizational capabilities (such as managerial competence, employee loyalty, and shared values). The difficulty of obtaining such

---

[5]The prealliance process is in many ways similar to the preacquisition process and shares the same needs. See the article by David B. Jamison and Sam B. Sitkin, "Acquisition: The Process Can Be a Problem," *Harvard Business Review,* no. 2 (1986): 107–14.

information is made even more problematic by the short time limits in which most alliances are finalized.

The one key lesson from the history of strategic alliances is that each partner's competitive positions and strategic priorities change over time and such changes have crucial impacts on the viability of the alliance. Even if the strategic trajectories of two companies cross at a particular point of time creating complementarities and the potential for a partnership, their paths may be so divergent as to make such complementarities too transient for the alliance to have any lasting value. While it is difficult enough to make a static assessment of a potential partner's strategic and organizational capabilities, it is almost impossible to make an effective prealliance analysis of how those capabilities are likely to evolve over time.

While there is probably no solution to this problem, companies that recognize alliances as a permanent and important part of their future organization have made monitoring for partners an ongoing rather than ad hoc process. Some have linked such activities into their integrated business intelligence system set up to monitor competitors. By having this group not only to analyze their competitors' potential strategies but also to assess their value as acquisition or alliance candidates, these companies find themselves much better prepared when a specific alliance opportunity arises.

Escalating Commitment: Thrill of the Chase. The very process of alliance planning and negotiations can cause unrealistic expectations and wrong choices. In particular, some of the managers involved in the process can build up a great deal of personal enthusiasm and expectations in trying to internally sell the idea of the alliance to their own organization. This escalation process is similar to a process observed in many acquisition decisions where, in one manager's words, "The thrill of the chase blinds pursuers to the consequences of the catch." Because the champions of the idea who become caught in a spiral of escalating commitment often are different from the operational managers who are later given responsibility for making the alliance work, major problems arise when the latter are confronted with inevitable pitfalls and less-visible problems.

The most effective way to control this escalation process is to ensure that at least the key operating managers likely to be involved in the implementation stage of the alliance are involved in the predecision negotiation process. Their involvement not only ensures greater commitment but also creates a continuity between the pre- and postalliance actions. But the greatest benefit accrues to the long-term understanding that must develop between the partners. By ensuring that the broader strategic goals that motivate the alliance are related to specific operational details in the negotiation stage, the companies can enhance the clarity and the consistency of both the definition and the understanding of the alliance's goals and tasks.

Alliance Scope: Striving for Simplicity and Flexibility. All too often, in an effort to show commitment at the time of the agreement, partners press for broad and all-encompassing corporate partnerships and equity participation or exchange.

Available experience, on the other hand, suggests that the key to successful alliance building lies in defining as simple and focused a scope for the partnership as is adequate to get the job done, and to retain at the same time the possibility to redefine and broaden the scope if experience suggests the need. This is because alliances that are more complex also require more management attention to succeed and tend to be more difficult to manage.

Three factors add to the management complexity of a partnership: complicated cross-holdings of ownership or equity, the need for cross-functional coordination or integration, and breadth in the number and scope of joint activities. Before involving any alliance in such potentially complicated arrangements, management should ask the question: "Are these conditions absolutely necessary, given our objectives?" If a simple OEM arrangement can suffice, it is not only unnecessary to enter into an equity alliance but it is also undesirable since the added complexity will increase the likelihood of problems and difficulties in achieving the objectives of the partnership.

At the same time, it might be useful to provide some flexibility in the terms of the alliance for renegotiating and changing the scope, if and when found necessary. Even when a broad-based and multifaceted alliance is seen as the ultimate goal, many companies have found that it is preferable to start with a relatively simple and limited partnership whose scope is expanded gradually as both partners develop both better understanding of and greater trust in each other's motives, capabilities, and expectations.

Managing Cooperative Ventures

In personal relationships, while the mutual understanding and shared expectations developed during the courtship period affect the quality of the relationship after marriage, it is the ongoing commitment and flexibility of each partner that has the greater influence on determining the durability and success of such a union. Similarly, in corporate relationships, while the prealliance analysis and negotiation processes are important, it is a company's ability to manage the ongoing relationship that tends to be the key determining factor for the success or failure of an alliance. Among the numerous issues that influence a company's ability to manage a cooperative venture, there are three that appear to present the greatest challenges: managing the boundary, managing knowledge flows, and providing strategic direction.

Managing the Boundary: Structuring the Interface.   There are many different ways in which the partners can structure the boundary of the alliance and manage the interface between this boundary and their own organizations. At one extreme, an independent legal organization can be created and given complete freedom to manage the alliance tasks. Alternatively, the alliance's operations can be managed by one or both parents with more substantial strategic, operational, and/or administrative controls. In many cases, however, the creation of such a distinct entity is not necessary, and simpler, less bureaucratic governance mechanisms such as joint committees may often be enough to guide and supervise shared tasks.

The choice among alternative boundary structures depends largely on the scope of the alliance. When the alliance's tasks are characterized by extensive functional interdependencies, there is a need for a high level of integration in the decision-making process relating to those shared tasks. In such circumstances, the creation of a separate entity is often the only effective way to manage such dense functional interlinkages. But while an alliance to develop, manufacture, and market a new product on a worldwide basis is probably best managed through an organization with a relatively independent decision-making structure, an alliance between two companies with the objective of marketing each other's existing products in noncompetitive markets may only need a few simple rules determining marketing parameters and financial arrangements, and a single joint committee to periodically review the outcomes.

Managing Knowledge Flows: Integrating the Interface. Irrespective of the specific objectives of any alliance, the very process of collaboration creates flows of information across the boundaries of the participating companies and creates the potential for learning from one another. For technology collaborations, such knowledge flows may be the central purpose of the alliance. But even for alliances that may be focused on achieving scale economies through joint production or managing risks through co-investment, such knowledge flows are inevitable.

Managing these knowledge flows involves two kinds of tasks for the participating companies. First, they must ensure full exploitation of the learning potential so created. Second, they must also prevent outflow of any information or knowledge they do not wish to share with their alliance partners.

While such information and knowledge flow from one company to the other, the individuals managing the interface may often not be the best users for such knowledge. To maximize its learning from the partnership, a company must effectively integrate its interface managers into the rest of its organization. The gatekeepers must have knowledge of and access to the different individuals and management groups within the company who are likely to benefit most from the diverse kinds of information that flow through an alliance boundary. Managers familiar with the difficulties in managing information flows within the company's boundaries will readily realize that such cross-boundary learning is unlikely to occur unless specific mechanisms are created to make it happen.

Selection of appropriate interface managers is perhaps the single most important factor for facilitating such learning. Interface managers should have at least three key attributes: They must be well versed in the company's internal organizational process; they must have the personal credibility and status necessary to access key managers in different parts of the organization; and they must have a sufficiently broad understanding of the company's business and strategies to be able to recognize useful information and knowledge that might cross their path.

Merely placing the right managers at the interface is not sufficient to ensure effective learning, however. Supportive administrative processes must also be developed to facilitate systematic transfer of such information and to monitor the effectiveness of such transfers. Such support is often achieved most effectively through simple means such as the creation of task forces or the holding of periodic review meetings.

While exploiting the alliance's learning potential, however, each company must also manage the interface to prevent unintended flows of information to its partner. It is a delicate balancing task for those playing the gatekeeper role to ensure the free flow of information across the organizational boundaries while effectively regulating the flow of people and data to ensure that sensitive or proprietary knowledge is appropriately protected.

Providing Strategic Direction: The Governance Structure.   The key to providing leadership and direction, ensuring strategic control, and resolving interorganizational conflicts is an effective governance structure. Unlike acquisitions, alliances are often premised on the equality of both partners, but an obsession to protect such equality often prevents companies from creating an effective governance structure for the partnership. Committees consisting of an equal number of participants from both companies and operating under strict norms of equality are often incapable of providing clear directions or forcing conflict resolution at lower levels. Indeed, many otherwise well-conceived alliances have floundered because of their dependence on such committees for their leadership and control.

To find their way around such problems, partners need to negotiate on the basis of what is termed "integrative" rather than "distributive" equality. Under such an agreement, each committee would be structured with clear single-handed leadership, but with each company taking the lead responsibility for different tasks. However, such delicately balanced arrangements can only work if the partners can agree on specific individuals, delegate the overall responsibility for the alliance to these individuals, and protect their ability to work to the best interests of the alliance itself rather than those of the parents.

CONCLUDING COMMENTS

Perspectives on strategic alliances have oscillated between the extremes of euphoria and disillusionment. Finally, however, there seems to be a recognition that while many such partnerships may not represent perfect solutions, they are often the best solution available to a particular company, at a particular point in time.

Easy but Not the Best Solution

Perhaps the biggest danger for many companies is to pretend that the "quick and easy" option of partnership is also the best or the only option that is available. Cooperative arrangements are perhaps too tempting in catch-up situations where the partnership might provide a façade of recovery that masks serious or even terminal problems.

Yet, while going it alone may well be the best option for any specific objective or task in the long term, almost no company can afford to meet all of its objectives in this way. When complete independence and self-sufficiency are not possible because of resource scarcity, lack of expertise or time, or any other such reason, strategic alliances often become the second-best option.

Alliances Need Not Be Permanent

Another important factor that is commonly misunderstood is that dissolution of a partnership is not synonymous with failure. Many companies appear to have suffered because of their unwillingness or inability to terminate partnership arrangements when changing circumstances made those arrangements inappropriate. All organizations create internal pressures for their own perpetuation, and an alliance is no exception to this enduring reality. One important task for senior managers of the participating companies is to periodically ask the question why the alliance should not be terminated and to continue with the arrangement only if they can find compelling reasons to continue.

Flexibility Is Key

The original agreement for a partnership is typically based on limited information and unrealistic expectations. Experience from the actual process of working together provides the opportunity for fine-tuning and often for finding better ways of achieving higher levels of joint value creation. In such circumstances, the flexibility to adapt the goals, scope, and management of the alliance to changing conditions is essential. Besides, changing environmental conditions often make obsolete the original intentions and plans. Effective partnering requires the ability to monitor these changes and to allow the partnership to evolve in response.

An Internal Knowledge Network: Basis for Learning

Finally, learning is one of the main benefits that a company can derive from a partnership, irrespective of whether it is one of the formal goals. For such learning to occur, however, a company must be receptive to the knowledge and skills available from the partner and must have an organization able to diffuse and leverage such learning. In the absence of an internal knowledge network, information obtained from the partner cannot be made use of irrespective of poten-tial value. Thus, building and managing an integrated network organization are essential prerequisites for effective management across organizational boundaries.

Case 4–1   Xerox and Fuji Xerox

We are committed to strengthening the strategic and functional coordination of Xerox and Fuji Xerox so that we will compete effectively against strong and unified global competitors.

Paul Allaire, *president and CEO of Xerox Corporation*
Yotaro Kobayashi, *president and CEO of Fuji Xerox*

Fuji Xerox, the joint venture between Xerox and Fuji Photo Film, was at a pivotal point in its 28-year history in 1990. Many considered it the most successful joint venture in history between an American and a Japanese company. Originally a sales organization for Xerox products in Japan, Fuji Xerox had evolved into a fully integrated operation with strong research, development, and manufacturing capabilities. As its sales and capabilities evolved, so did its importance within the Xerox Group: Its 1989 revenues of $3.6 billion represented 22% of the Xerox Group's worldwide revenue.[1] Furthermore, Fuji Xerox supplied the rest of the Xerox Group with low- to mid-range copiers. In Japan, the home country of Xerox's major competitors, Fuji Xerox held 22% of the installed base of copiers and 30% of revenues in the industry.

Yotaro "Tony" Kobayashi, Fuji Xerox's president and CEO, ascribed a good deal of the company's success to the autonomy that the joint venture had enjoyed from the beginning. Fuji Xerox was not "the norm" for joint ventures, he contended, adding that "the degree to which Xerox let us run was very unusual." Yet, paradoxically, as the company grew

to represent a larger portion of Xerox's worldwide business (Exhibit 1), this situation seemed to be changing. "We have to begin to pay more attention to what our actions mean to Xerox," explained Kobayashi.

Paul Allaire, Xerox's president and CEO, added that Fuji Xerox's autonomy had been an important factor not only in its own success, but also in its growing contribution to the Xerox Group:

> The fact that we had this strong company in Japan was of extraordinary importance when other Japanese companies started coming after us. Fuji Xerox was able to see them coming earlier, and understood their development and manufacturing techniques.
>
> We have excellent relationships with Fuji Xerox at the research, development, manufacturing, and managerial levels. Yet, because of this close relationship, there is a greater potential for conflict. If Fuji Xerox were within our organization, it would be easier, but then we would lose certain benefits. They have always had a reasonable amount of autonomy. I can't take that away from them, and I wouldn't want to.

Over the years, Fuji Xerox saw its local competitors grow rapidly through exports. The terms of its technology licensing agreements with Xerox, however, limited Fuji Xerox's sales to Japan and certain Far Eastern territories. As Canon, in particular, grew to challenge Xerox worldwide in low-end copiers, laser printers, and color copiers, Fuji Xerox began to feel constrained by the relationship. "Fuji Xerox has aspirations to be a global company in marketing, manufacturing, and research," explained Jeff Kennard, who had managed the

This case was prepared by Benjamin Gomes-Casseres and Krista McQuade.

Copyright © 1991 by the President and Fellows of Harvard College. Harvard Business School case 391-156.

[1]The Xerox Corporation (XC) is referred to in this case simply as Xerox. The combination of Rank Xerox (RX), Fuji Xerox (FX), and the Xerox Corporation is referred to as the Xerox Group. The revenues of Rank Xerox were consolidated into those of Xerox Corporation, but Fuji Xerox revenues were not. As described below, Xerox Corporation received 66% of RX earnings, which in turn included half of FX earnings.

EXHIBIT 1   Growth of Xerox Corporation and Fuji Xerox, 1968–1989

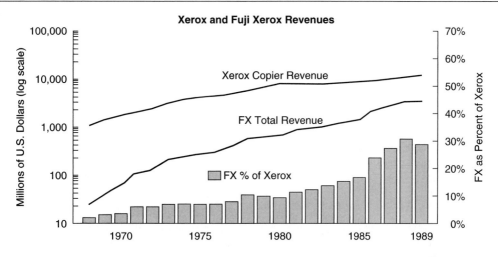

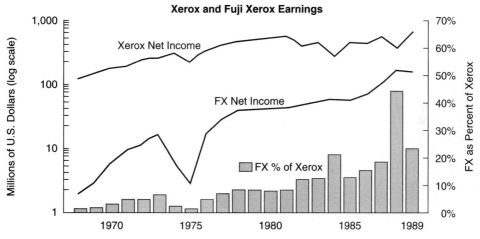

Notes: Top: The Xerox revenues shown include Rank Xerox but not Fuji Xerox. Bottom: Xerox earnings include 33% of FX earnings.

Source: Xerox and Fuji Xerox annual reports.

relationship between Xerox and Fuji Xerox since 1977. Kobayashi elaborated:

> The goals of Xerox and Fuji Xerox can be described as mostly compatible and partly conflicting. There *are* serious issues facing us. We often compare our situation with that of Canon or Ricoh, companies that have a single management organization in Japan. Are we as efficient and effective in the worldwide management of our business as we could be?
>
> Some of Fuji Xerox's products, such as facsimile machines, are managed like Canon's—with single-point design and manufacturing. But now there are external conditions in the United States and Europe that call for local manufacturing and development. Rank Xerox and Xerox are able to reach efficient volumes in their marketplaces. If Fuji Xerox manufactures only for Japan and adjacent markets, our volume will be too small, but Xerox is insisting on this. It is a tough challenge that we have to face together.

How should Fuji Xerox's aspirations be managed within the context of the Xerox Group? This was one of the questions facing the Codestiny Task Force commissioned in 1989 to review the capabilities and goals of Xerox and Fuji Xerox. Composed of senior managers from both companies, the task force would seek ways to enhance the strategic relationship between Xerox and Fuji Xerox for the 1990s. This was the third such review; Codestiny I (1982) and Codestiny II (1984) had both resulted in changes in contracts and agreements between the firms. With the basic technology licensing contract between Xerox and Fuji Xerox due to be renegotiated in 1993, participants in Codestiny III knew that their analysis could well lead to a substantial restructuring of the strategic relationship between the companies.

Xerox's International Expansion

When Chester Carlson tried to sell the rights to the revolutionary xerographic technology that he invented in 1938, GE, IBM, RCA, and Kodak all turned him down. Instead, the Haloid Corporation— a small photographic paper firm in Rochester, NY— agreed in 1946 to fund further research, and 10 years later acquired the full rights to the technology. By the time the company introduced its legendary 914 copier in 1959, xerographic products had come to dominate its business; in 1961 Haloid's name was changed to Xerox Corporation. The 914 was the world's first automatic plain paper copier (PPC), and produced high-quality copies four times faster than any other copier on the market. These advantages, coupled with an innovative machine rental scheme, led Xerox to dominate the industry for nearly 20 years. Company revenues rose from $40 million in 1960 to nearly $549 million in 1965, and to $1.2 billion in 1968, breaking the American record for the fastest company to reach $1 billion in sales. Net income grew from $2.6 million in 1960 to $129 million in 1968. In a mere decade, the name Xerox had become synonymous with copying.

Xerox moved quickly to establish an international network. Lacking the funds to expand alone, it formed a 50/50 joint venture in 1956 with the Rank Organization of Britain. Xerox would be entitled to about 66% of the profits of Rank Xerox. Rank operated a lucrative motion picture business and was seeking opportunities for diversification. Rank Xerox (RX), the new joint venture, was to manufacture xerographic products developed by Xerox and market them exclusively worldwide, except in the United States and Canada. By the early 1960s, Rank Xerox had established subsidiaries in Mexico, Italy, Germany, France, and Australia. In 1964, Xerox bought back the right to market xerographic products in the Western hemisphere.

Japanese firms immediately inquired about obtaining xerography licenses from Rank Xerox, but they were refused on the grounds that the technology was not commercially mature. By 1958, however, RX executives had turned their sights to the Japanese market. Aware of Japanese government regulations that required foreign firms to sell through local licensees or joint ventures, they sought a strong partner. Twenty-seven Japanese firms jockeyed for the position; Fuji Photo Film (FPF) was the only nonelectronics firm in this group. Still, the company was chosen, partly because of the personal relationship and trust that had developed between RX President Thomas Law and FPF Chairman Setsutaro Kobayashi.

Fuji Photo Film was a manufacturer of photographic film since the early 1930s and second only to Kodak in that field. The company was trying to diversify its business away from silver-based photography, and was convinced that its technical expertise was well suited to the requirements of xerography. Under the direction of Nobuo Shono, the company had already begun experimenting with xerography; by 1958, it had invested 6 million yen in research and manufacturing facilities for the copiers that it hoped to license from Rank Xerox. As negotiations between the two companies intensified, Rank Xerox insisted on a joint venture instead of simply a license to Fuji Photo Film.

The Establishment of Fuji Xerox

Fuji Xerox, the 50/50 joint venture established by Fuji Photo Film and Rank Xerox in 1962, was originally intended to be a marketing organization to sell xerographic products manufactured by Fuji Photo Film. When the Japanese government refused to approve a joint venture intended solely as a sales company, however, the agreement was revised to give Fuji Xerox manufacturing rights. Fuji Xerox—not Fuji Photo Film—then became the contracting party with Rank Xerox, and received exclusive rights to xerographic patents in Japan. Fuji Xerox, in turn, subcontracted Fuji Photo Film to manufacture the products. As part of its technology licensing agreements with Rank Xerox, Fuji Xerox had exclusive rights to sell the machines in Japan, Indonesia, South Korea, the Philippines, Taiwan, Thailand, and Indochina. In return, Fuji Xerox would pay Rank Xerox a royalty of 5% on revenues from the sale of xerographic products. Rank Xerox would also be entitled to 50% of Fuji Xerox's profits.

Nobuo Shono became Fuji Xerox's first senior managing director, and Setsutaro Kobayashi, its president. Shono and Kobayashi drew their core executive staff, later known as the "Seven Samurai," from the ranks of Fuji Photo Film. A board of directors consisting of representatives from Rank Xerox and Fuji Photo Film was established to decide policy matters, while day-to-day operations were left to the Japanese management. The Xerox Corporation itself was to have no direct relationship with Fuji Xerox, and would participate in the profits of the joint venture only through its share in Rank Xerox.

Although Fuji Xerox adopted a number of business practices from Xerox, including organizational structure and the rental system, it remained distinctly Japanese throughout its history. Hideki Kaihatsu, managing director and chief staff officer at Fuji Xerox, explained:

> Employees are typically rotated through many functions before rising to the level of general management, and compensation and lifetime employment practices are similar to those of other Japanese firms. We emphasize long-term planning, teamwork, and we follow bottom-up decision making, including the "ringi" system. Furthermore, in procuring parts we follow the Japanese practice of qualifying a small group of vendors and working closely with them.

The Development of Fuji Xerox's Capabilities

Well before negotiations for the joint venture were finalized, engineers at Fuji Photo Film geared up for the production of Xerox copiers. Xerox machines were disassembled and studied to determine the equipment and supplies necessary for production. Three FPF engineers spent two months touring Xerox and Rank Xerox production facilities. At the establishment of the joint venture, a specific schedule was agreed upon, calling first for the sale of imported machines, then the assembly of imported knocked-down kits, and finally the domestic production of copiers. Import restrictions in Japan and government pressure to source locally accelerated this schedule, and the first Japanese-produced Xerox 914 was completed in September 1962; by 1965, 90% of the parts for the 914 came from local suppliers.

Fuji Xerox's first sales plan targeted financial institutions, large manufacturing corporations, and central government agencies. At the time of the introduction of the 914, 85% of the market was held by the inexpensive diazo type of copier. Although these copiers were difficult to operate and produced poor quality copies, they had been enormously successful in Japan, as the large number of characters in the Japanese language made typewriters difficult to use, and made copiers essential even for small offices. Ricoh, Copyer, and Mita had sold diazo copiers since the 1940s. By the early 1960s, Ricoh held an estimated 75% share of the market. A diazo copy was often referred to as a "Ricopy" in Japan.

Though Fuji Xerox had intended to sell the 914 copier outright, at Rank Xerox's insistence it implemented Xerox's trademark rental system. Within a year, the back-order list for the copier was five months' long. Output rose fivefold in five years, and Fuji Photo Film soon built a second production facility. In 1967, Fuji Xerox's sales passed those of Rank Xerox's French and German subsidiaries. Fuji Xerox's product line expanded to include other models, including a faster version of the 914, and a smaller desktop model. The 2400, capable of making 40 copies per minute (cpm),[2] was introduced in 1967. Sales subsidiaries were established throughout Fuji Xerox's licensed territory.

By the late 1960s, Fuji Xerox dominated the high-volume segment of the Japanese copier market. Ricoh, however, had made great inroads into the middle segment with an electrostatic copier based on an RCA technology, and was squeezing Fuji Xerox's market from below. In addition to the threat of substitute technologies, Fuji Xerox faced the end of its monopoly in plain paper copying; some of Xerox's core patents were scheduled to expire between 1968 and 1973. FX managers were already aware of efforts by several Japanese firms to develop plain paper copiers. In response to these pressures, Peter McColough, Xerox's president and CEO at the time, proposed to transfer the manufacture of copiers from Fuji Photo Film to Fuji Xerox, and in

this way combine manufacturing and marketing activities under one roof. McColough described the rationale for this decision:

> Fuji Xerox had to develop its own manufacturing capability. It had built up a good marketing organization, but had no assured source of supply. That left the company vulnerable. Fuji Photo Film initially resisted this idea because it would lose manufacturing volume and product revenues. They realized in the end that the issue went to the heart of the joint venture. Looking back, that was the most difficult period in our relationship.

In 1971, Fuji Photo Film transferred its copier plants to Fuji Xerox. That same year, Fuji Xerox completed the construction of a 160,000-square-foot manufacturing and engineering facility. From then on, Fuji Photo Film had little direct role in Fuji Xerox's operations. Yoichi Ogawa, senior managing director at Fuji Xerox in 1989 and one of the Seven Samurai, explained why Fuji Photo Film remained a passive partner after 1971:

> According to Fuji Photo Film's agreement with Xerox, the company, as a shareholder, could collect information from Fuji Xerox, but it could not use it in its own operations. In addition, a technology agreement between Fuji Xerox and Xerox provided that any technology acquired by Fuji Xerox from outside sources (including from Fuji Photo Film) could be freely passed on to Xerox.

In a separate development, Rank Xerox also lost much of its direct role in Fuji Xerox's operations. In December 1969, Xerox bought an additional 1% share of Rank Xerox from the Rank Organization, giving it 51% control of that joint venture. From then on, Rank Xerox would be managed as a Xerox subsidiary. Moto Sakamoto, an FX resident at Rank Xerox at the time, noticed an immediate change: "Things changed instantly as the Americans started coming in . . . gone was the old British style of management." Sakamoto was transferred to Xerox's main facility in Rochester, NY, as Fuji Xerox began to deal directly with Xerox. Rank Xerox's ownership share in Fuji Xerox remained at 50%, and the Xerox Corporation continued to receive 66% of

---

[2]The copier market was typically divided into low-, mid-, and high-volume segments. In the 1960s, the 2400 was considered a high-volume model; the original 914 copier made seven copies per minute. In the 1980s, copiers making less than 25 cpm were generally considered low-volume, while those making over 90 cpm were considered high-volume.

Rank Xerox's profits, and therefore 33% of Fuji Xerox's.

Product Development at Fuji Xerox

The transfer of production facilities to Fuji Xerox and the direct relationship established between Fuji Xerox and Xerox contributed to a continued strengthening of FX technical capabilities. Fuji Photo Film engineers had already been making modifications to Xerox designs in order to adapt the copiers to the local market; Japanese offices, for example, used different sized paper than American offices. Nobuo Shono, however, advocated the development of long-term R&D capabilities that would enable the company to develop its own products. In particular, he envisioned a high-performance, inexpensive, compact machine that could copy books. At the time, Xerox's priorities were different. Tony Kobayashi explained:

> We had been insisting that the Xerox Group needed to develop small copiers as an integral part of its worldwide strategy. However, Xerox's attitude was that the low end of the market was not a priority. . . . On the other hand, we were seeing rising demand for small copiers in Japan.[3]

Shono's development group produced four experimental copiers, each with projected manufacturing costs approximately half those of Xerox's smallest machine. When they first heard of the effort, engineers at Rank Xerox and Xerox doubted that these models could become commercially viable. Shono persisted, and in 1970 took a working prototype to London, where its performance amazed Rank Xerox executives. The machine was slow (5 cpm), but substantially smaller and lighter than comparable Xerox models. This demonstration immediately boosted Fuji Xerox's technical reputation within the Xerox Group, and for the first time Xerox allowed Fuji Xerox a small budget for R&D. In 1973, the FX2200—the world's smallest copier—

was introduced in Japan with the slogan: "It's small, but it's a Xerox." The speed of the FX2200 was doubled in 1977 by the FX2202, and the basic model was improved further by the FX2300 and the FX2305.

Mushrooming Competition

The FX2200 appeared just in time to face an avalanche of new and serious competition. Canon was the first Japanese company to enter the plain paper copier market, introducing its low end "New Process" copiers in 1970; these machines were developed in-house and did not infringe on any Xerox patent. Ricoh and Konica, Fuji Photo Film's chief Japanese rivals in film, followed with their own technologies. In 1972, Canon made another major move by introducing copiers using liquid instead of dry toner. This technology was later licensed to Saxon, Ricoh, and Copyer. Liquid-toner copiers had the advantage of being smaller and less expensive to manufacture than dry-toner copiers like Xerox's, but they were cumbersome to use. They were introduced as a cheap alternative to Xerox dry copiers. Minolta, Copia, Mita, Sharp, and Toshiba also entered the plain paper copier industry; by 1975, 11 companies competed in the Japanese market.

In addition to developing small machines for its local market, Fuji Xerox tried to stem the competitive onslaught with more aggressive sales strategies. The company began to offer two- and three-year rental contracts as well as its standard one-year contract, and provided price incentives that were tied to contract length. It also began to offer three of its new low-priced copiers for outright sale, as the competition had been doing. Matazo Terada, one of the Seven Samurai, recalled that when the company tried to sell copiers before, Xerox management resisted:

> Xerox insisted on uniform policies—every country had to be managed like the U.S. firm. That was successful only while we were protected from competitors because of our monopoly. If Xerox had been more flexible from the beginning, we might have captured a larger market. That was a lost opportunity.

---

[3] Quoted in "Fuji Xerox Company, Ltd." Translation of a case study prepared by the Nomura School of Advanced Management in Tokyo.

By 1977, Ricoh accounted for 34% of the number of copiers installed in Japan. Fuji Xerox followed with 25%, Canon with 15%, and Konica with 10%. In terms of copy volume, however, Fuji Xerox led the competition with more than 50% of the market, followed by Ricoh with 20%, and Canon and Konica with 10% each. In the low end of the market, Ricoh accounted for 50% of copy volume, compared to 10% for Fuji Xerox.

Fuji Xerox's TQC Movement

Partly as a response to the new competition of the 1970s, as well as the oil shock and recession of 1973–1975, Fuji Xerox launched a Total Quality Control (TQC) program. Fuji Photo Film had operated a successful statistical quality control program, and in 1956 won the prestigious Deming Prize, awarded to companies that had shown outstanding quality management throughout their organization. Fuji Xerox's New Xerox Movement had three primary aims: to speed up the development of products that matched customer needs; to reduce costs and eliminate waste; and to adopt aggressively the latest technologies.

The focal point of the campaign was the development of "dantotsu," roughly translated as the "Absolute No. 1 Product." Company executives challenged the marketing and engineering departments to develop a product fitting this description in less time and at a lower cost than the competition. For six months, project proposals were turned down until the basic concept for the new product emerged in 1976: a compact, 40-cpm machine manufactured for half the price of any comparable machine, with half the number of parts of previous models, and developed in two years, compared to Xerox's typical four. Setsutaro's son, Tony Kobayashi, who became FX president in 1978 after his father died, explained:

> This was the first time Fuji Xerox had developed a copier based on our own design concept. The FX2200 copier we previously developed was an improved adaptation of a model developed in the United States. The American system of development was well established in our company. However, the U.S. way of developing new products on a step-by-

step basis was too time consuming for our dynamic environment. The competition in the Japanese market required us to study the development systems of our rivals. . . . We found that we had been spending too much time in development. That is why we formulated the design concept for the new model and committed the entire company's resources to its development within a very limited timetable.[4]

The FX3500 was indeed introduced two years later, and by 1979, it had broken the Japanese record for the number of copiers sold in one year. Ricoh and Canon rushed to develop copiers that could compete in the FX3500's market segment. Largely because of Fuji Xerox's effort to develop the FX3500, the company won the Deming Prize in 1980. In addition, the FX3500 firmly established Fuji Xerox as a technologically competent member of the Xerox Group. David Kearns, who would become Xerox's president in 1977, was amazed when he first saw a demonstration of the FX3500 prototype, and spontaneously broke out in applause.

Later, some observers labeled the FX3500 Fuji Xerox's "declaration of independence." The FX3500 project came after Xerox canceled a series of low- to mid-volume copiers on which Fuji Xerox was depending. Code-named SAM, Moses, Mohawk, Elf, Peter, Paul, and Mary, they were each canceled in mid-development, even though Fuji Xerox had gaps in its product range in the Japanese market. Jeff Kennard remembered that when Tony Kobayashi was told about the cancellation of Moses, he was also asked to stop work on the FX3500 project. "Tony refused," Kennard recalled, adding that Kobayashi said, in effect, "As long as I am responsible for the survival of this company, I can no longer be totally dependent on you for developing products. We are going to have to develop our own."

Xerox's Lost Decade

During the 1970s, competition in the U.S. and European copier markets changed radically. Prior to that period, Xerox had had a virtual monopoly

---

[4]Quoted in "Fuji Xerox Company, Ltd."

because of its xerography patents. But beginning in 1970, one competitor after another entered the industry, often with new and improved PPC technologies. The Xerox Group share of worldwide PPC revenues fell from 93% in 1971 to 60% in 1975, and 40% in 1985 (Exhibit 2). This was Xerox's "lost decade"—an era of increasing competition, stagnating product development, and costly litigation.

New Competition High and Low

The proliferation of PPC vendors that started in Japan in the early 1970s soon appeared in the United

EXHIBIT 2 Copier Sales of Leading Vendors Worldwide, 1975–1985 (millions of U.S. dollars except share data)

	1975	1980	1985
Xerox Group	$3,967	$ 7,409	$ 8,903
U.S. and Americas	2,340	3,866	4,770
Rank Xerox	1,350	2,856	2,400
Fuji Xerox	277	687	1,733
Canon	87	732	2,178
Ricoh	290	1,092	1,926
Kodak	1	300	900
IBM	310	680	700
Minolta	25	387	743
3M	380	575	400
Oce	178	680	600
Savin	52	430	448
Konishiroku	85	302	470
Nashua	155	401	278
Agfa	115	268	200
Pitney Bowes	52	129	204
A.B. Dick	35	55	60
Saxon	56	127	20
AM International	59	23	10
Other Japanese	155	1,220	2,846
Other	596	792	1,115
Total	$6,598	$15,602	$22,001

Shares of Leading Firms in World Total

Xerox Group	60%	47%	40%
Americas	35	25	22
Rank Xerox	20	18	11
Fuji Xerox	4	4	8
Canon	1	5	10
Ricoh	4	7	9
Kodak	0	2	4
IBM	5	4	3
Minolta	0	2	3

Source: Donaldson, Lufkin & Jenrette, Inc.

States and Europe. By 1975, approximately 20 PPC manufacturers operated worldwide, including reprographic companies (Xerox, Ricoh, Mita, Copyer, A.B. Dick, AM, and 3M), paper companies (Dennison, Nashua, and Saxon), office equipment companies (IBM, SCM, Litton, and Pitney Bowes), photographic equipment companies (Canon, Konica, Kodak, and Minolta), and consumer electronics companies (Sharp and Toshiba).

Canon's New Process copiers were the first to hit the U.S. market, followed by a wave of liquid-toner copiers. The new Japanese machines were priced aggressively, and sold outright through independent dealers. On average, these machines broke down half as often as Xerox copiers. Canon sold under its own brand name, taking advantage of its reputation for quality photographic products, and supported its dealers through extensive financing, and sales and service training. Ricoh sold its machines through Savin Business Machines and the Nashua Corporation. Savin, primarily a marketing company, had funded the Stanford Research Institute's development of a liquid-toner copier, and subsequently had licensed Ricoh to manufacture the machines. The first Ricoh machines using this new technology were introduced in 1975 and were an instant success. Konica, Toshiba, Sharp, and Minolta entered the U.S. market through OEM relationships, as well as with their own brands.

Despite the entrance of so many Japanese competitors into the U.S. market, Xerox initially did little to respond to them. These competitors targeted the low end of the market, leaving Xerox's most important segments seemingly unaffected. Furthermore, Xerox continued to dominate the world copier market, with revenues that rose each year by more than Savin's total copiers sales. Xerox executives were more concerned by the entrance of IBM and Eastman Kodak into the copier industry, as these companies targeted the mid- and high-volume segments. (See Exhibit 3.)

IBM's introduction of its Copier I in 1970 signaled the end of Xerox's monopoly in its home market. Although IBM's first model was not successful because of a combination of high price and performance problems, the Copier II, introduced in 1972, began to take market share away from Xerox. These machines were marketed by IBM's office products sales force on a rental basis, supported by heavy advertising. IBM introduced the Copier II in Europe and Japan in 1975, and by 1976 had installed 80,000 copiers worldwide, against Xerox's estimated 926,000. IBM's high-volume Copier III came out in 1976, but was withdrawn because of reliability problems. It was reintroduced as a mid-volume machine early in 1978, but IBM's copier business suffered permanently from the setback.

Eastman Kodak's main facilities were located across town from Xerox's in Rochester, NY. Kodak's success as a high-technology, chemistry-based, American firm had been a model for Xerox's founders and early leaders. When Kodak introduced the high-end Ektaprint 100 copier in 1975, however, admiration quickly turned to intense rivalry. Unlike the IBM Copier I, Kodak's first machine was extremely innovative. In particular, it featured a microcomputer that monitored the performance of the copier and alerted operators to problems through a digital display. A central computer at Kodak monitored the trouble signals and dispatched service people to a machine before breakdown. The machines were also capable of excellent reproduction. The Ektaprint series was well accepted in the marketplace, and quickly gained a reputation for the highest-quality image reproduction in the field.

Xerox's Stagnation

In its first competitive actions against IBM, Kodak, and the Japanese entrants, Xerox could not come up with a winning strategy. It focused R&D on developing a super-high-speed copier and field-tested its first color copier in 1971; neither became a commercial success. Xerox's mid-volume 4000 and 3100 series, introduced in the early 1970s, suffered from reliability problems and were also commercial failures. Even when the price of the 3100 was slashed from $12,000 to $4,400, it did not sell well. Ricoh/Savin became the top seller in the U.S. market in 1976, and Xerox's market share in the United

EXHIBIT 3 Copier Unit Placements of Xerox and Major Competitors

	Thousands of Units Placed by Market Segment (net)*					Share of Net Placements in Each Market Segment*				
	PCs	*Low*	*Mid*	*High*	*Total*	*PCs*	*Low*	*Mid*	*High*	*Total*
In the United States:										
Xerox										
1975	—	9	−8[†]	1	2	—	29%	—	100%	6%
1980	—	34	6	6	46	—	11	22	52	13
1985	—	66	27	15	108	0%	10	21	53	10
1989	12	101	53	13	179	5	14	27	45	15
Kodak and IBM										
1975	—	—	10	—	10	—	0	213	0	27
1980	—	—	5	5	11	—	0	20	48	3
1985	—	—	2	13	14	0	0	2	46	1
1989	—	—	5	9	13	0	0	2	31	1
Canon										
1975	—	3	—	—	3	—	10	0	0	8
1980	—	46	4	—	50	—	15	14	0	14
1985	176	107	17	—	300	86	16	13	0	29
1989	141	106	19	4	270	62	15	10	13	23
Others										
1975	—	19	3	—	22	—	61	55	0	59
1980	—	237	12	—	249	—	75	44	0	70
1985	30	514	81	—	625	14	75	64	0	60
1989	75	513	123	3	714	33	71	61	11	61
Total for all vendors										
1975	—	31	5	1	37					
1980	—	317	27	11	355					
1985	206	687	126	28	1,047					
1989	227	710	200	29	1,176					
In Western Europe:										
Rank Xerox										
1980	—	40	4	4	48	—	11	22	100	13
1984	—	54	19	9	82	0	9	25	74	10
1989	18	73	49	4	144	7	10	29	34	12
Kodak										
1980	—	—	4	—	4	—	0	22	0	1
1984	—	—	—	3	3	0	0	0	26	0
1989	—	—	2	2	3	0	0	1	13	0
Canon										
1980	—	36	4	—	40	—	10	21	0	11
1984	115	81	8	—	204	90	15	10	0	26
1989	130	110	25	3	268	49	15	15	26	22

(continued)

EXHIBIT 3   (concluded)

	Thousands of Units Placed by Market Segment (net)*					Share of Net Placements in Each Market Segment*				
	PCs	Low	Mid	High	Total	PCs	Low	Mid	High	Total
In Western Europe:										
Total for all vendors										
1980	—	351	19	4	374					
1984	128	578	76	12	794					
1989	268	752	168	11	1,199					
In Japan:										
Fuji Xerox										
1986					112					20
1989					142					21
Canon										
1986					138					25
1989					195					28
Others[‡]										
1986					311					55
1989					354					51
Total for all vendors										

*"Net Placements" are sales and new rentals minus old rentals returned to the vendor. Volume segments are defined as follows:

> PC = Less than 12 cpm (average price about $1,000)
> Low = 12 to 30 cpm (average price about $3,000)
> Mid = 31 to 69 cpm (average price about $8,500)
> High = Over 70 cpm (average price about $55,000)

[†]Indicates that, on balance, 8,000 rental units were returned.
[‡]Ricoh was particularly strong in Japan, with a 32% share in 1989.

Source: Dataquest Incorporated.

States continued to fall. However, the seriousness of Xerox's situation was slow to sink in, according to David Kearns:

> We dominated the industry we had created. We were convinced that we were providing the world with high-quality machines, and our convictions were reinforced by the broad acceptance of Xerox products by our customers. We had always been successful, and we assumed that we would continue to be successful. Our success was so overwhelming that we became complacent.[5]

About 1978, Fuji Xerox offered to sell its FX2202 copier to Xerox and Rank Xerox to help them counter Japanese competition in the United States and Europe. Rank Xerox purchased 25,000 of the machines, but Xerox Corporation refused to buy any.[6] Bill Glavin, the managing director at Rank Xerox at that time, noted:

> We had never placed such a large order before and expected to sell them in 12 months. Two thousand

[5]David T. Kearns, "Leadership Through Quality," *Academy of Management Executive,* vol. 4 (1990): 86–89.

[6]Although Xerox had acquired equity control of Rank Xerox in 1969, the line operations of the two firms were not integrated until 1978. Rank Xerox could thus make this decision in relative autonomy.

machines per month was an incredible rate of sales, but we did it. For Tony Kobayashi, that order must have represented a substantial part of his production that year. We worked closely with them, and they gave us top-notch support.

This first successful cooperation led Rank Xerox to import more of the FX machines. In addition, Kodak had delayed its entry into Europe by two years, giving Rank Xerox time to formulate a defensive marketing strategy for the high end. As for IBM, its excellent distribution network and reputation in Europe could not make up for a generally inferior product. As Wayland Hicks, the general manager of Rank Xerox's U.K. operating company in the late 1970s, noted, "If IBM had Kodak's product, Xerox would have been dead." Rank Xerox was able to defend its market share while Xerox's U.S. share continued to decline.

In 1979, largely because of Rank Xerox's success with the FX product, Xerox began to import the FX2202, and later the FX2300 and the FX2350. Typically, in the year that the products were introduced in the U.S. market, the machines were assembled by Fuji Xerox before export. Then, acceding to union demands in the United States, Fuji Xerox exported them as knock-down units to be assembled at Xerox. "Some of our people had been reluctant to import FX machines," recalled Peter McColough. "Our engineers felt that they had developed xerography, and that the first FX machines weren't good enough."

Courtroom Battles

Xerox became involved in the 1970s in a series of courtroom battles. Immediately after IBM came out with its Copier I in 1970, Xerox sued for patent infringement, and IBM countersued. The companies argued 12 separate counts in the United States and Canada. Xerox won some of these suits and the rest were settled in 1978, when the firms agreed to an exchange of patents covering all information-handling products and to a $25 million payment to Xerox. Two other American firms, the SCM Corporation and Van Dyk Research, sued Xerox for alleged antitrust violations in 1973 and 1975, respectively, each claiming $1.5 billion in damages. Both lost their suits in 1978–1979.

More damaging still, the Federal Trade Commission (FTC) initiated action against Xerox in 1973, charging that the firm controlled 95% of the plain paper copier industry, and that its pricing, leasing, and patent-licensing practices violated the Sherman Antitrust Act. The FTC demanded that Xerox offer unrestricted, royalty-free licenses on all its copier patents, that it divest itself of Rank Xerox and Fuji Xerox, and that it allow third parties to service, maintain, and repair copiers leased from Xerox. In 1975, Xerox settled out of court by signing a consent decree with the FTC, in which it agreed to license more than 1,700 past and future patents for a period of 10 years. Competitors were permitted to license up to three patents free of royalties, to pay 0.5% of revenues on the next three, and to license additional patents royalty free. Xerox also agreed to forgive past patent infringements, to cease offering package-pricing plans on machines and supplies, and to begin outright sales of machines.

Kodak, IBM, Canon, Ricoh, and other Japanese firms were among the firms to secure Xerox licenses under this arrangement. At this point, the Japanese firms that had entered the market with liquid-toner copiers switched to Xerox's dry-toner process.

Adjusting the Relationship between Xerox and Fuji Xerox

As Fuji Xerox's business grew and Xerox's came under increasing pressure at home, the relationship between the two companies changed. The original joint venture and technology assistance agreements of the early 1960s were updated in 1976 and in 1983, and numerous interim agreements were signed to adjust policies on such issues as procurement and relations to third parties (Exhibit 4). Bob Meredith, a lawyer by training and Xerox's resident director in Tokyo, described the role of these contracts:

> The legal contracts are flexible. We don't follow an adversarial, arm's-length approach, where you might try to gain short-term advantage or act opportunistically. The equity commitment focuses our relationship on one main objective: What is the profit-maximizing thing to do?

EXHIBIT 4   Major Agreements between Xerox and Fuji Xerox

1960 Joint Enterprise Contract and Articles of Incorporation (1962)

- Established equal ownership of FX by Rank Xerox and Fuji Photo Film
  - Defined FX's exclusive license to Xerography in its territory: Japan, Taiwan, Philippines, the Koreas, Indonesia, Indochina
  - FX nonexclusive license to nonxerographic products in territory
  - Specifies terms of technology assistance: royalty due Rank Xerox—5% of net sales of xerographic products

1976 Joint Enterprise Contract (JEC)

- Agreement between Rank Xerox and Fuji Photo Film, updating 1960 JEC
- Specified Board of Directors composition
- FX management to be appointed by Fuji Photo Film
- Agreements on technology transfer, royalties, and transfer pricing
- Identified matters requiring Xerox concurrence, including:
  Financial policy, including major capital expenditures
  Business and operating plans
  Relations with third parties
  Sales outside of FX licensed territory

1976 Technological Assistance Contract (TAC)

- 10-year agreement between Xerox and Fuji Xerox
- Revised technology assistance agreements of 1960, 1968, and 1971
- Maintained 5% royalty on xerographic products

1978 R&D Reimbursement Agreement

- Defines reimbursement to FX for R&D on FX products marketed by Xerox: 100% to 120% of design cost

1983 Technology Assistance Agreement (TAA)

- 10-year agreement between Xerox and Fuji Xerox
- Replaced 1976 technology transfer agreements
- Revised royalty rates:
  Basic Royalty on total FX revenue, plus
  Royalty on xerographic revenues to decline annually from 1983 to 1993

1983 Product Acquisition Policy

- Provided guidelines for intercompany transfer pricing
- Established concept of reciprocal Manufacturing License Fee (MLF), designed to reimburse FX for development and manufacturing costs:
  Up to 25% markup on assembled machines supplied by FX
  Up to 20% markup on unit cost for FX machines assembled by XC
  Specific designs and services required by Xerox reimbursed 100%

1985 Procurement Policy

- Provided guidelines for Xerox procurement in FX licensed territory:
  FX right to bid first
  Procurement from third party to be coordinated with FX

1986 Arrangements Strategy Agreement

- Defined parameters for negotiating alliances with third parties

---

Source: Compiled from Xerox Corporation documents.

Technology agreements and other contracts between Xerox and Fuji Xerox provided guidelines for the relationship. In addition, the contracts specified royalties and transfer pricing procedures. In 1976, a Technology Assistance Contract (TAC) had been signed by Xerox and Fuji Xerox, which maintained the 5% royalty that Xerox received from Fuji Xerox's xerographic sales, and that was to last 10 years. During the Codestiny I discussions, however, the royalty structure of the contract was revised. The 1983 TAA established a basic royalty on Fuji Xerox's total sales, representing Fuji Xerox's right to use the Xerox tradename and technology in its licensed territory. The royalty on xerographic sales, however, was set to decline annually between 1983 and 1993. In addition, for the first time Fuji Xerox would begin receiving a manufacturing license fee (MLF), designed to compensate it for its development and manufacturing investments. In particular, an MLF of up to 20% could be added to the unit costs of FX machines exported in knocked-down form and assembled and sold by Xerox.

These and other subtle changes in the relationship between the two firms tended to reinforce Fuji Xerox's autonomy. David Kearns recalled how he worked to "unfetter" Fuji Xerox in the late 1970s:

> Xerox was attempting to control so many aspects of Fuji Xerox's operations. We were reviewing their marketing strategies, what products they were going to develop, and so on. But it didn't make sense to me to try to run the business from thousands of miles away. So, I encouraged them to pursue their own strategies and develop their own products. Of course, they were moving in that direction anyway.

Turning Around Xerox

In 1979, Xerox began to formalize a strategy based on the reality of its declining position in the copier industry. Kearns recalled the initial shock of the necessity to do so:

> The Japanese were selling products in the United States for what it cost us to *make* them. We were losing market share rapidly, but didn't have the cost structure to do anything about it. I was not sure if Xerox would make it out of the 1980s.

One of Xerox's strategies was to diversify out of copiers by acquiring a number of financial services companies between 1983 and 1988. Financial services, Kearns believed, would provide "an anchor in a nonmanufacturing business, and one in which Japanese companies were not active overseas." Before the financial services industry went sour at the end of the decade, this line of business was a steady source of earnings for Xerox, providing more than $2 billion in profits in five years. In 1989, however, financial services' earnings declined significantly and substantial assets were written off.

Kearns also began to take a closer look at the strategies of Fuji Xerox and other Japanese companies. Upon importing the first FX products, Xerox engineers had been amazed by a reject rate for parts that was a mere fraction of the American rate, and by substantially lower manufacturing costs. Visits to FX facilities introduced Xerox executives to the practice of "benchmarking," or systematically tracking costs and performance in all areas of operations against those of the best in the field. The findings from Xerox's own benchmarking efforts helped fuel Kearns's efforts to infuse his organization with new vision and determination.

In 1981, Kearns announced a companywide initiative for "business effectiveness," and two years later formally launched Xerox's Leadership Through Quality program. Xerox's program was based on the experience of Fuji Xerox, and throughout the effort, Kearns called upon Kobayashi and others at Fuji Xerox for help. Xerox hired Japanese consultants recommended by Fuji Xerox, and some 200 high-level Xerox and Rank Xerox managers visited Fuji Xerox in later years to learn first-hand about its TQC management and philosophy. The Leadership Through Quality program emphasized high employee involvement in attaining five major goals: (1) increased market research and competitive benchmarking; (2) just-in-time manufacturing to decrease costs; (3) faster product development; (4) development of state-of-the-art technology; and (5) a devotion to quality in all areas.

The rallying point for Xerox's quality movement was the development of the 10 Series, a new family of copiers. Wayland Hicks, in charge of this development effort, stated: "The Xerox turnaround started on September 22, 1982, at the announcement of the 1075 in New York." Led by this mid-volume machine, the 10 Series became the most successful line of copiers in Xerox history, and served to restore the company's finances and morale. The series—dubbed the "Marathon" family of copiers—represented a new generation of machines aimed primarily at the mid-volume segment of the market. Altogether, 14 models were introduced between 1982 and 1986, 6 of which were still sold in 1990. Fuji Xerox designed and produced the low end models in the 10 Series—the 1020, 1035, and the 1055, the latter drawing on basic technologies developed for the FX3500. The 1075 became the first American-made product to win Japan's Grand Prize for Good Design. Because at that time Xerox's Japanese competitors were not strong in mid-volume copiers, the 10 Series forestalled their move into that segment of the market and helped Xerox win back market share. The company regained 2–3 percentage points in 1983, and 12 points in 1984. By the end of 1985, more than 750,000 10 Series machines had been rented or sold, accounting for nearly 38% of Xerox's worldwide installed base.

Throughout the 1980s, Xerox continued to change the way it did business. For example, over 100,000 employees went through three days of off-site training to unite the entire organization behind the quality effort. The program achieved significant improvements in Xerox operations. After reducing its supplier base, the company reduced its purchased parts' costs by 45% and their quality was improved dramatically. Xerox's average manufacturing costs were reduced by 20% and the time-to-market for new products was cut by 60%. Xerox's progress was recognized by the U.S. Commerce Department in 1989, when the company's Business Products and Systems division received the Malcolm Baldrige National Quality Award for its "preeminent quality leadership." (Xerox's 1971–1989 financial results are in Exhibit 5.)

Xerox and Fuji Xerox in the 1990s

The Canon Challenge

A number of factors were expected to continue to draw Fuji Xerox and Xerox closer to each other in the 1990s. One was the continuously rising capabilities of the Xerox Group's competitors, particularly Canon. While Xerox's precipitous decline in the 1970s had been stemmed and many of the competitors from that decade had faded away, Canon's copier business continued to expand. From 1980 to 1989, Canon's total sales grew from $2.9 billion to $9.4 billion, a growth rate of 14% per year. Canon's R&D spending grew even more rapidly at 24% per year, from $77 million to $525 million. By 1989, Canon was no longer primarily a camera company—40% of its revenues came from copiers, and 20% from laser printers.

In the second half of the 1980s, Canon developed a dominating presence in the low end laser printers that were becoming ubiquitous companions to microcomputers. Laser printing technology was closely related to plain paper copying technology, and as digital copying systems were introduced, the importance of laser printing in the PPC market was bound to increase. Canon's laser printing engines were the core of the highly successful Hewlett-Packard Laserprinter series, which accounted for about 50% of laser printer sales in the United States. This OEM business was thought to yield Canon some $1 billion in revenues. In the rest of the world, Canon sold printers under its own brand name.

In copiers, Canon was strong in the low end of the market, and had recently developed a growing business in color copiers, where it held 50% of the market by 1989. Analysts pointed out that Canon was introducing twice as many products as the Xerox Group, although it spent less than $600 million on R&D annually, compared to Xerox's $800 million and Fuji Xerox's $300 million. Canon's goal was to become a $70 billion company by the year 2000, implying a 22% annual growth rate in the 1990s. A significant portion of this growth was projected to come from Xerox's heartland—high- and mid-volume copiers and printers.

EXHIBIT 5 Key Financial Data for Xerox and Fuji Photo Film (millions of U.S. dollars except financial ratios and where noted)

	1971	1976	1981	1982	1983	1984	1985	1986	1987	1988	1989
Xerox Corporation											
Total revenues	1,954	4,515	8,180	8,073	10,463	11,400	11,994	13,287	15,108	16,441	17,635
Document processing			8,013	7,895	8,223	8,714	9,068	9,744	10,834	11,688	12,431
Financial services			167	178	2,240	2,686	2,926	3,543	4,274	4,753	5,204
Operating income	785	1,486	2,071	1,654	1,444	1,557	1,502	1,327	1,376	2,154	2,031
Net income	213	365	598	424	466	291	475	465	578	388	704
Total assets	2,250	4,959	7,674	7,668	14,064	15,154	16,838	19,050	22,450	26,441	30,088
Long-term debt	425	1,000	870	850	1,461	1,614	1,583	1,730	1,539	5,379	7,511
Stockholders' equity	1,052	2,179	3,728	3,724	4,664	4,543	4,828	5,129	5,547	5,667	6,116
R&D expenses	96	226	511	541	529	555	597	650	722	794	809
Employees (millions)	66	100	112	103	108	111	113	112	112	113	111
Earnings/Share (U.S. dollars)	2.85	4.35	6.25	4.06	4.5	3.26	3.42	4.48	5.3	3.49	6.56
Dividend/Share (U.S. dollars)	0.80	1.10	3.00	3.00	3.00	3.00	3.00	3.00	3.00	3.00	3.00
Document processing revenues as share of total	*	*	98%	98%	79%	76%	76%	73%	72%	71%	70%
Operating income/Revenue	40%	33%	25%	20%	14%	14%	13%	10%	9%	13%	12%
Operating income/Assets	35	30	27	22	10	10	9	7	6	8	7

(continued)

EXHIBIT 5 (concluded)

	1971	1976	1981	1982	1983	1984	1985	1986	1987	1988	1989
					Xerox Corporation						
Operating income/Equity	75	68	56	44	31	34	31	26	25	38	33
Net income/Revenue	10.9	8.1	7.3	5.3	4.5	2.6	4.0	3.5	3.8	2.4	4.0
Net income/Assets	9.5	7.4	7.8	5.5	3.3	1.9	2.8	2.4	2.6	1.5	2.3
Net income/Equity	20.2	16.8	16.0	11.4	10.0	6.4	9.8	9.1	10.4	6.8	11.5
R&D expense/Revenue	4.9	5.0	6.2	6.7	5.1	4.9	5.0	4.9	4.8	4.8	4.6
Long-term debt/Assets	19	20	11	11	10	11	9	9	7	20	25
Equity/Assets	47	44	49	49	33	30	29	27	25	21	20
Dividends/Earnings	28	25	48	74	67	92	88	67	57	86	46
					Fuji Photo Film						
Total revenue							3,136	4,504	5,636	6,833	6,732
Net income							600	801	1,030	1,217	1,210
Dividends							21	30	35	41	36
Net income/Revenue							19%	18%	18%	18%	18%
Dividends/Earnings							3.5%	3.7%	3.4%	3.4%	3.0%

*Practically 100%.

Source: Company annual reports.

Xerox, however, was determined to be aggressive in its response. Hicks, who in 1989 had become the executive vice president for worldwide marketing at Xerox, hung a framed blow-up of a 1984 *Fortune* article on Canon in his office. It was entitled "And Then We Will Attack"; below it Hicks hung a sign that read: "And Then They Will Lose."

Xerox Group strategists saw the relationship between Xerox and Fuji Xerox as a critical element in competing worldwide against Canon. Canon had a strong presence in all major world markets, as did the Xerox companies (Exhibit 6). But Xerox CEO Paul Allaire highlighted a major difference in the two firms' global networks: "When we negotiate with Fuji Xerox, we can't just represent ourselves. We need to find what is fair and equitable to essentially three partners. Canon is 100% owned by one company."

The Fuji Xerox Challenge

Another trend drawing Fuji Xerox and Xerox closer was the growth of Fuji Xerox itself (Exhibit 7). Fuji Xerox's dollar revenues grew faster than Xerox's in the 1980s, and represented a more significant portion of the Xerox Group's worldwide revenues than it had previously. Fuji Xerox's financial contribution to Xerox's net earnings in the form of royalties and profits had also grown sharply—from 5% in 1981 to 22% in 1988. And throughout the decade, Fuji Xerox had been an important source of low end copiers for Xerox. Between 1980 and 1988, Fuji Xerox's sales to Xerox and Rank Xerox grew from $32 million to $620 million (Exhibit 8). "Fuji Xerox is a critical asset of Xerox," concluded Allaire.

Fuji Xerox developed its technological capabilities further in the 1980s, investing heavily in R&D (Exhibit 9). While it continued to rely on Xerox for basic research on new technologies, by the late 1980s very few of the models sold by Fuji Xerox in Japan had been designed by Xerox (Exhibit 10). For the most part, they were high end models, working at speeds of above 120 cpm. Heavy investment by Fuji Xerox during the late 1980s had produced many low end models, and even a few in the 60–90 cpm

range. Many of these were exported to or manufactured by Xerox and Rank Xerox. In 1980, 70% of the low-volume units sold by Xerox and Rank Xerox were of their own design, and 30% were of Fuji Xerox design; by 1987, 94% were of Fuji Xerox design. Even in 1989, however, all of Xerox and Rank Xerox's mid- and high-volume copiers were of their own design.

All these factors led Fuji Xerox and Xerox to intensify their cooperation on research, product development, manufacturing, and planning in the 1980s. Bill Glavin and Jeff Kennard worked together to launch "strategy summits." Glavin described why:

> We needed the senior management of research, engineering, manufacturing, and planning from both companies to come together, and begin discussing the issues that affected them jointly. The talks included people from all product lines—copiers, printers, and systems. We tried to agree on common strategies and allocate who should do what.

These top management summits were held about twice a year during the 1980s, and led to further meetings between the functional organizations on each side. Fuji Xerox's organization mirrored Xerox's: A corporate research group did basic and applied research; machines were designed and built by the development and manufacturing organization; and products were sold and serviced by the marketing organization. Collaboration between Xerox and Fuji Xerox seemed to be most successful in research, and harder to implement in development and manufacturing; there was no coordination at all between marketing groups, as each had a different licensed territory. Of course, there was some tendency to protect traditional turfs. "On both sides you cannot totally dismiss the NIH syndrome," commented Tony Kobayashi. "It is another form of parochialism." Still, where the incentives for collaboration were high, the companies launched joint projects, agreeing on who would take "lead" and "support" roles and eliminating overlapping activities. Bill Spencer, Xerox vice president of technology at the time, described the rationale behind one

EXHIBIT 6 Global Configuration of Xerox Group and Canon in 1989

	United States	Japan	Western Europe	Other
Share of world GNP	26%	14%	21% (4 largest countries)	39%
Share of world PPC market (units)	33%	20%	34%	14%

Xerox Group

	United States	Japan	Europe	Americas
Revenues	$6.6 billion	$3.5 billion	$4.0 billion	$1.7 billion
Employees	54,000	19,600	29,000	16,000
Production:				
PPC	149,000	180,000	176,400	39,100
Printers	15,000	60,000	15,700	—
Systems	8,000	18,000	1,900	—
Faxes	—	95,000	—	—
Percent of market (units):				
PPCs	15%	22%	12%	
R&D centers	2	1	1	1
Alliances	—	Fuji Photo Film	Rank Organization	

Canon

	North America	Japan	Europe	Other
Revenues	$2.9 billion	$2.9 billion	$2.9 billion	
Employees	4,500	27,500	6,500	
Production:				
PPC	60,000	700,000	370,000	
Other	Laser printers and engines	Cameras, printers		Cameras in China
Percent of market (units):				
PPCs	23%	26%	23%	
Laserprinting	70			
Color PPCs	50			
R&D centers	0	1	0	
Alliances	HP ($1B OEM) Kodak, NeXT	—	Olivetti	

Source: Xerox and industry sources.

EXHIBIT 7 Key Financial Data for Fuji Xerox (millions of U.S. dollars at yearly average exchange rates, except financial ratios and where noted)

	1971	1976	1981	1982	1983	1984	1985	1986	1987	1988	1989
Revenues	107	307	872	962	1,111	1,282	1,456	2,303	2,955	3,570	3,554
Operating expenses	79	259	754	813	970	1,125	1,304	2,093	2,673	3,197	3,180
R&D	—	13	49	47	84	109	117	151	194	242	292
S, G, and A	38	119	308	333	399	443	507	801	1,041	1,296	1,324
Operating income	27	47	117	150	141	157	152	210	282	373	374
Net income	10	17	46	50	56	61	59	71	106	173	162
Total assets	176	405	897	931	1,046	1,199	1,276	1,883	2,457	3,186	3,093
Total equity	49	121	324	325	388	440	487	744	959	1,237	1,285
Retained earnings	33	84	270	277	338	390	439	680	885	1,154	1,131
Depreciation and amortization	16	63	131	113	130	155	153	218	266	271	278
Capital expenditure	65	64	196	178	230	217	244	296	284	297	512
Employees (thousands)	4.9	7.7	9.8	11.3	12.6	13.9	15.1	16.5	17.2	18.0	19.6
Dividends paid out	1	7	9	8	8	8	8	12	14	18	30
Financial Ratios											
Operating income/Revenues	25%	15%	13%	16%	13%	12%	10%	9%	10%	10%	11%
Operating income/Assets	15	12	13	16	13	13	12	11	11	12	12
Net income/Revenues	9.1	5.6	5.3	5.2	9.1	4.8	4.1	3.1	3.6	4.9	4.5
Net income/Assets	5.5	4.3	5.1	5.3	5.4	5.1	4.6	3.7	4.3	5.4	5.2
Net income/Equity	19.9	14.3	14.2	15.3	14.6	13.8	12.2	9.5	11.1	14.0	12.6
R&D expense/Revenues	—	4.4	5.6	4.9	7.6	8.5	8.0	6.5	6.6	6.8	8.2
Capital expenditure/Revenues	61.2	20.9	22.5	18.5	20.7	16.9	16.8	12.9	9.6	8.3	14.4
Total equity/Assets	28	30	36	35	37	37	38	40	39	39	42
Dividends paid/Total equity	1.6	6	3	2	2	2	2	2	1	1	2
Dividends/Earnings	8.2	41	20	16	14	13	14	17	13	10	19
Average exchange rate (yen per U.S. dollar)	348	297	221	249	238	238	239	169	145	128	138

Note: Fiscal year ending October 20.

Source: Fuji Xerox annual reports; exchange rate from the IMF.

EXHIBIT 8   Intra-Firm and Bilateral Trade in Copiers

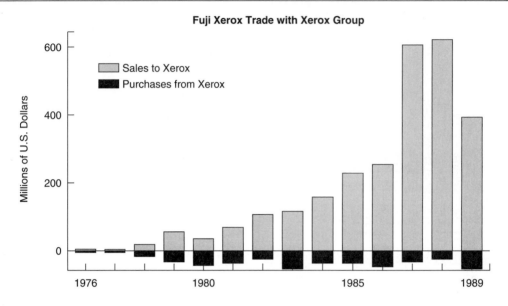

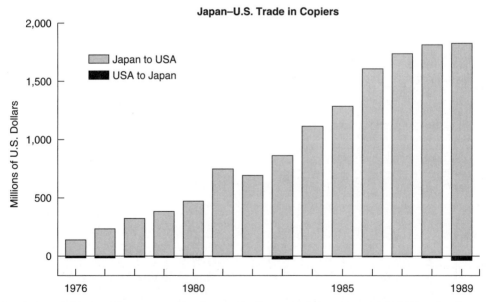

Notes: Top: Includes finished machines, parts, and knock-down kits. Bottom: Includes copiers (SITC 75182) and copier parts and accessories (SITC 75919).

Source: Fuji Xerox annual report; and United Nations, *SITC Trade Data Base*.

EXHIBIT 9   Fuji Xerox Technology Spending and Receipts, 1968–1989

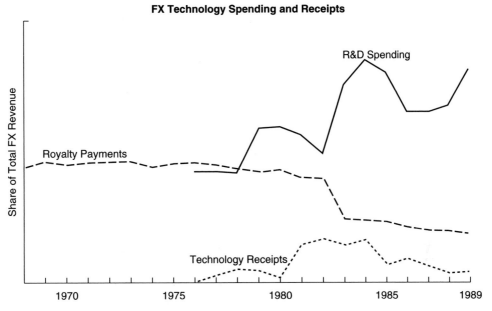

Note: Technology receipts represent reimbursement to Fuji Xerox for special design and customization work on machines sold by XC and RX.

Source: Fuji Xerox annual reports.

of these joint research projects:

> It is an attempt to combine American ingenuity with the manufacturing skills of the Japanese. Xerox has excellent basic research and software capabilities, and Fuji Xerox is good at development and hardware design. Together, we should be able to develop better products quicker than alone.

The functional collaboration between the companies was reinforced by exchanges of personnel and by an evolving communication process. Since the 1970s, personnel from Fuji Xerox had spent time as residents at Xerox and engineers from both companies had frequently crossed the Pacific to provide on-the-spot assistance. These personnel exchanges had, in fact, been an important channel for the transfer of technology from Xerox to Fuji Xerox. By 1989, an estimated 1,000 young, high-potential FX employees had spent three years each

as residents at Xerox, and some 150 Xerox people had done this at Fuji Xerox. These residents were directly involved in the work of their host companies. Every year there were also some 1,000 shorter visits by engineers and managers. These exchanges and the summit meetings contributed to a constructive relationship. "Whenever a problem came up, we established a process to manage it," explained Jeff Kennard. "The trust built up between the companies has been a key factor in the success of this relationship. It enables one to take on short-term costs in the interest of long-term gains for the group."

By the mid-1980s, most Xerox managers also had mixed feelings of challenge and admiration toward Fuji Xerox, which were echoed by Kennard:

> It seems that every time Xerox blinks and retracts, Fuji Xerox forges ahead. Fuji Xerox continues to be the agent for change. They have great corporate vision and they target what is strategically important.

EXHIBIT 10   Growth of Fuji Xerox's Technical Capabilities, 1970–1989

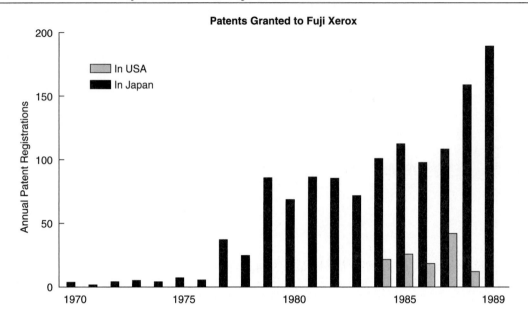

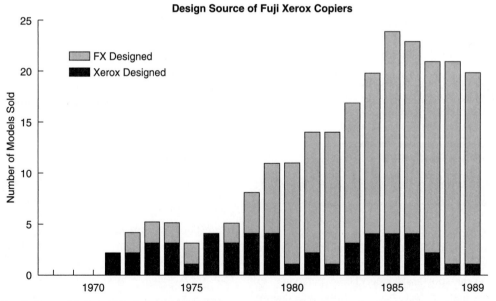

Notes: Top: Utility models included in Japan. Bottom: Based on product introductions, assuming that every product has a commercial life of four years.

Source: Fuji Xerox.

Then they take tough decisions and make the needed investment.

The Management Challenge

In this context, Allaire and Kobayashi commissioned the Codestiny III Task Force, charging it with developing a framework for cooperation between the two companies in the 1990s. The task force consisted of top planners in each company and was to report to the two CEOs within a year of its formation. Roger Levien, Xerox's vice president for strategy and head of the Codestiny III talks, described the motivation for the project:

> Fuji Xerox had certain issues they wanted to discuss, and we agreed to do so in the Codestiny process. One of their desires was to get the worldwide market for the low end. They also wanted to develop a more symmetric relationship with us. We wanted to spell everything out, identify all of the alternatives, and leave the final decision to top management.

One of the issues to be addressed by the Codestiny team was Fuji Xerox's aspirations to expand its markets in Asia. Under the existing technology licensing contracts, Fuji Xerox had the right to sell in Indonesia, South Korea, the Philippines, Taiwan, and Thailand (total GDP in 1989: $570 billion), and it had indeed established sales subsidiaries in each of these markets. But Rank Xerox in London was responsible for managing sales in what it called the South Pacific Operations—Australia (1989 GDP: $280 billion), New Zealand ($45 billion), Singapore ($28 billion), Malaysia ($37 billion), China ($420 billion), and Hong Kong ($63 billion). Since the early 1980s, Fuji Xerox had argued that this arrangement led to inefficiencies in serving the South Pacific markets. At that time, knock-down kits were sometimes shipped from Fuji Xerox to Britain for assembly, and then shipped back to Asia for sale. Furthermore, Rank Xerox followed a very different marketing strategy in these markets than Fuji Xerox did in its neighboring Asian markets. Rank Xerox emphasized high profit margins and sales of high-end machines, whereas Fuji Xerox put greater emphasis on market share and low-end

products. As a result, when Fuji Xerox urged Rank Xerox in the late 1970s to adopt a more aggressive sales strategy in Australia before Canon entered that market, Rank Xerox refused. Although Rank Xerox managed the South Pacific countries out of a regional office in Hong Kong, Fuji Xerox's sales subsidiaries were usually joint ventures with local partners, and so drew more on local management talent.

Another key issue for the Codestiny team was how the Xerox Group should manage the low end laser printer business in the United States. This market segment was receiving renewed attention in 1989, following the appointment of Bill Lowe as Xerox's executive vice president for development and manufacturing. Lowe came to Xerox from IBM, where he had been in charge of the personal computer business. Soon after arriving at Xerox, he began to focus on the problems in the low end copier and printer businesses, where Fuji Xerox typically developed and manufactured products sold by Xerox.

> Both companies were trying to get full profit out of it, even though the margins were slim. Fuji Xerox's policy was to mark up costs; Xerox's was to get an acceptable gross profit. Furthermore, each product had a different mark-up scheme, and many sideline deals confounded the issues. This fostered sharp dealings between the partners. So, most of our energy was focussed on each other, not on Canon. We were pointing fingers and frustrating ourselves.

The Codestiny team analyzed these specific issues within a broad framework, and began by outlining the various options available for cooperation in marketing, research, and development and manufacturing (Exhibit 11). The team considered the advantages and disadvantages of each of these options and began to develop possible strategies for the South Pacific Operations and for the low end printer business in the United States.

But there was much more at stake than decisions in these two areas. The central question facing Xerox and Fuji Xerox was: How should the relationship between the two companies be structured and managed in the new global environment of the 1990s?

EXHIBIT 11   Relationship Options Identified by Codestiny Task Force

---

Marketing

A. Independent and overlapping

Act as two separate companies serving the world market, with some coordination on business direction and strategy. No geographic constraints.

B. Independent and separate

Concentrate efforts on licensed territories for core products, with multinational business as required.

C. Separate with exceptions

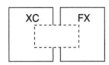

Same as B, but with joint or overlapping activities across territorial boundaries on case-by-case basis.

D. Coordinated global product mandates

Worldwide and exclusive responsibility for products or product ranges manufactured under special licenses.

Research

A. Independent

Each pursues own interest and becomes self-sufficient.

B. Coordinated

Coordinated group research programs of XC and FX, with both self-sufficiency and overlap.

C. Joint

Single research organization without overlap.

D. Complementary

Separate organizations operating on exclusive products.

(continued)

EXHIBIT 11   (*concluded*)

Development and Manufacturing

A. Independent

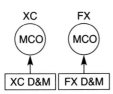

Each development and manufacturing (D&M) organization supplies its own marketing organization (MCO).

B. Complementary without overlap

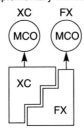

Assign development roles to each organization, with no overlap allowed in development projects.

C. Complementary with overlap

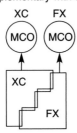

Same as B, but with overlap in development projects.

D. Joint

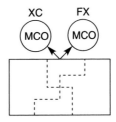

Single development and manufacturing organization with individual projects targeted to needs of separate marketing organizations.

Source: Compiled from Xerox documents.

Case 4–2   Swissair's Alliances

It was a cloudy Saturday morning in November 1990, and Otto Loepfe was alone in his office at the Zurich Airport headquarters of Swissair, Switzerland's flagship airline. Loepfe, Swissair's president, opened his briefcase and pulled out a list of important topics to be covered in his upcoming meeting in Singapore. The meeting was the third between chief executives of Swissair, Delta, and Singapore Airlines (SIA), a three-partner global alliance established in 1989.

Alliances had been the centerpiece of Swissair's strategy for the 1990s. In addition to the global alliance with Delta and SIA, Swissair developed the European Quality Alliance (EQA) in 1989 with Scandinavian Air Services (SAS), Finnair, and Austrian Airlines. EQA carriers would cooperate in fleet purchases and maintenance, and would coordinate their routes, similar to the global alliance. The ultimate goal of these alliances was to provide customers with seamless service as well as create a framework for broader sharing of activities.

Much progress had been made in solidifying the alliances during the previous eleven months, but several unanswered questions lingered in Loepfe's mind. Was it the correct strategy for the competitive environment confronting Swissair? Were Swissair and its allies sufficiently committed to the strategy? And what obstacles remained and how could the CEOs resolve them?

Swissair

The Swiss Air Transport Co. Ltd., was founded in 1931 to fly between Switzerland and a handful of

This case was prepared by Eric J. Vayle (under the direction of David B. Yoffie).

central European locations. By 1949, the company had become the Swiss flag airline, and had inaugurated long-haul intercontinental service over the North Atlantic. By 1970, Swissair also served destinations in Asia, Africa, and South America.

In 1990, Swissair was among the top 20 airlines in international revenue-passenger-kilometers flown and among the top ten in international passengers carried. The carrier had revenues of $2.2 billion in 1989, with strong enough cash flow to self-finance between 50% and 100% of its expenditures for aircraft and other capital equipment each year. It owned several subsidiaries, including two charter airlines and the largest travel agent in Switzerland. Unlike many of its European competitors, Swissair was not owned by the national government. Only about 22% of its equity was owned by various Swiss authorities, with the rest owned by private investors. Swissair was widely considered as "the most Swiss of Swiss companies" and management worked to maintain Swissair's close identification with Swiss national culture and pride. Swissair's main hub was Zurich's Kloten airport, with European traffic also routed through Geneva.

About seven million people lived in Switzerland. Its two major cities, Zurich and Geneva, were important global business and financial centers, helping Switzerland become the wealthiest nation, per capita, in Europe. Switzerland's gross domestic product was forecast to reach nearly $175 billion in 1990, having grown steadily at between 2% and 3% per year over the previous five years. Labor markets were extremely tight in Switzerland during the period, with unemployment as low as 0.5 percent. Despite this, Swiss inflation was low and stable; prices rose an average of 2% per year in the 1980s. Although Switzerland had not joined the European Community (EC), almost 60% of imports and over 70% of exports were traded with her European neighbors.

Swissair's route structure in 1990 consisted of flights to over 100 destinations. Most flights were "short hauls" within Europe (Swissair carried 5.9% of European traffic in 1990), but it also flew to destinations on every continent except Australia. According to Paul Mueller, executive in charge of External Relations, "Swissair is stretched to its geographic limits. Going forward, our strategy is not to expand the number of routes we fly, but to strengthen our market share on existing routes, especially Asia and North America."

Products
Government-approved prices for short haul flights between Western Europe and Switzerland were among the most expensive in Europe. Swissair concentrated on attracting international business travellers. Despite high fares, 5.4% of passengers travelled first class on Swissair, compared to 2.0% for the average European airline. Similarly, 38.5% of Swissair's passengers flew full fare economy, while 34.8% did so on the average European carrier. Swissair's passengers were willing to pay premium fares for what one Swissair executive called "guaranteed quality from one of the premier air carriers in the world." Swissair repeatedly won awards and strong praise from the air transport and business media for excellence in customer service and overall product superiority. *Quality Wins,* Swissair's motto, reminded staff members of their responsibility to maintain Swissair's "fetish for excellence from maintenance to housekeeping to cuisine." Airport caterers' kitchens were supervised by Swissair's own chefs. First class meals on intercontinental flights were full-course dinners that cost Swissair almost $100 per passenger, featuring Beluga caviar and fine wines. Flight attendants were required to be fluent in French, German, and English. The airline provided unique extra comforts to passengers as well; when not showing movies, video screens showed the flight's progress along a route map, as calculated by an on-board computer. Surveys showed that route maps helped most passengers to relax. Lavatories were equipped with make-up

necessities and with diaper changing stations. Onboard telephones were not available because Swissair feared they would make for a less restful flight.[1]

Third Party Services
Swissair employed several measures to generate incremental revenues from fixed investments. Personnel in Swissair's kitchens in Zurich, Geneva, and Karachi performed contract catering for 40 other air carriers. Maintenance professionals were also subcontracted to do technical and maintenance work for other air companies. In international locations where Swissair did not have maintenance or ground-handling personnel, it typically subcontracted with local carriers to do the work. Contract services netted 12% of Swissair's revenues in 1989. About 50% of the capacity of Swissair's Engineering and Maintenance Division was used to work on aircraft from other airlines. Swissair performed major overhaul work in Zurich on McDonnell Douglas aircraft, on Pratt & Whitney engines, and in Airbus frames and engines. It also maintained aircraft in a joint venture with Lufthansa.

Cost Structure
Swissair faced higher wages and operating costs than most other European airlines (see Exhibit 1). Most employees were represented by unions. The 1,000 pilots and flight engineers bargained collectively, as did the 2,500 flight attendants. Two unions represented the 17,000 ground personnel. Swissair had not experienced labor difficulties, but Swissair's personnel policy was generous. "It is very hard to get fired or laid off at Swissair," one senior official admitted.

Swissair's fleet structure mirrored the nature of its route structure (see Exhibit 2). Although the majority of its aircraft were from McDonnell Douglas, the carrier purchased nine aircraft frames from four

---

[1]Swissair's revenues depended heavily on cargo transport (see Exhibit 1) and expected its cargo business to continue growing throughout the 1990s. This case, however, focuses on passenger travel.

EXHIBIT 1 Airline Financial and Operating Statistics (1989) (all items are in millions of U.S. dollars unless otherwise specified)

	Swissair	Delta	SIA	SAS	American	United	BA	Lufthansa	JAL
Passenger revenues	$1,920.2	$8,042.0	$1,928.1	$1,484.8	$9,107.3	$8,536.0	$6,401.7	$6,234.7	$5,710.1
Total revenues	3,004.3	8,582.0	2,503.0	2,125.8	10,479.6	9,794.0	7,194.3	6,948.2	8,269.5
Salaries and related costs	1,043.5	3,426.0	432.0	944.6	3,446.2	3,158.0	1,749.2	2,221.2	NA
Aircraft fuel	258.4	1,233.0	324.6	170.1	1,392.0	1,352.0	NA	NA	NA
Depreciation and amortization	228.6	459.0	232.2	141.8	612.7	517.0	NA	568.8	794.9
Total operating expenses	2,945.3	8,163.0	1,905.7	2,059.3	9,735.6	9,329.0	6,626.5	6,797.1	7,616.8
Pretax income	NA	468.0	760.0	90.3	718.4	539.0	452.9	157.1	394.4
Net income	58.8	303.0	635.2	NA	454.8	324.0	295.8	72.9	147.5
Capital expenditures	544.8	1,425.0	559.4	806.9	2,394.8	1,568.0	1,052.9	NA	793.6
Current assets	1,736.0	1,018.0	1,844.9	1,369.9	2,091.2	2,738.0	1,428.1	1,827.1	3,360.1
Fixed assets (net)	1,933.5	5,399.0	2,512.6	1,581.1	7,819.6	3,898.0	4,049.2	4,810.6	4,459.4
Total assets	3,669.6	7,227.0	4,357.6	2,951.1	10,877.4	7,207.0	5,815.3	6,649.4	9,220.1
Current liabilities	893.8	1,833.0	1,173.9	902.5	3,479.1	3,224.0	2,942.3	NA	2,886.0
Long-term debt	1,182.6	1,181.0	273.9	937.2	808.9	946.0	1,497.3	NA	3,688.2
Shareholders' equity	891.9	2,596.0	2,909.7	1,026.8	3,765.8	1,564.0	1,210.0	1,930.0	2,037.0
Passengers (millions)	8.6	67.2	6.8	14	NA	54.9	22.6	20.4	19.7
Available-seat-KMs (millions)	24,057.8	154,340.8	39,236.4	23,320.0	184,355.2	167,275.2	82,984.0	54,731.9	94,507.7
Revenue-passenger-KMs (millions)	15,804.0	94,379.2	30,737.0	15,229.0	117,604.8	111,422.4	57,795.0	36,203.9	69,085.1
Passenger yield (cents)	12.2	8.5	6.3	9.7	7.7	7.7	11.1	17.2	8.3
Passenger load factor	65.7%	61.1%	78.3%	65.3%	63.8%	66.6%	69.6%	66.1%	73.1%

(continued)

EXHIBIT 1 *(concluded)*

	Swissair	Delta	SIA	SAS	American	United	BA	Lufthansa	JAL
Available-ton-KMs (millions)	3,751.6	19,999.5	6,280.0	3,060.4	24,531.2	NA	11,404.0	11,169.9	11,731.2
Revenue-ton-KMs (millions)	2,474.6	10,710.1	4,643.5	1,876.5	13,182.4	NA	7,636.0	7,550.3	8,197.0
Total yield (cents)	121.4	80.1	53.9	113.3	79.5	NA	94.2	92.0	100.9
Total load factor	66.0%	53.6%	73.9%	61.3%	53.7%	NA	67.0%	67.6%	69.9%
Breakeven load factor	64.7%	50.9%	56.3%	59.4%	49.9%	NA	61.7%	66.1%	64.4%
Percent of passenger revenues:									
Salaries and related costs	54.3%	42.6%	22.4%	63.6%	37.8%	37.0%	27.3%	35.6%	NA
Aircraft fuel	13.5	15.3	16.8	11.5	15.3	15.8	NA	NA	NA
Depreciation and amortization	11.9	5.7	12.0	9.6	6.7	6.1	NA	9.1	13.9
Total operating expenses	153.4	101.5	98.8	138.7	106.9	109.3	103.5	109.0	133.4
Pretax income	NA	5.8	39.4	6.1	7.9	6.3	7.1	2.5	6.9
Net income	3.1	3.8	32.9	NA	5.0	3.8	4.6	1.2	2.6
Percent of total revenues:									
Salaries and related costs	34.7	39.9	17.3	44.4	32.9	32.2	24.3	32.0	NA
Aircraft fuel	8.6	14.4	13.0	8.0	13.3	13.8	NA	NA	NA
Depreciation and amortization	7.6	5.3	9.3	6.7	5.8	5.3	NA	8.2	9.6
Total operating expenses	98.0	95.1	76.1	96.9	92.9	95.3	92.1	97.8	92.1
Pretax income	NA	5.5	30.4	4.2	6.9	5.5	6.3	2.3	4.8
Net income	2.0	3.5	25.4	NA	4.3	3.3	4.1	1.0	1.8
Personnel cost per employee ($000s)	64	54	33	NA	NA	NA	42	53	NA
Total operating expenses per ATK (cents)	78.5	40.8	30.3	67.3	39.7	NA	58.1	60.9	64.9

Sources: 1989 annual reports and Swissair documents.

EXHIBIT 2   Comparison of Fleet Structures of Global Alliance Partners

Manufacturer	Segment Type	Number of Aircraft Used (ordered)		
		Swissair	*Delta Air*	*Singapore Air*
Boeing				
747-400	Long range	0	0	5 (24)
747-300	Long range	2	0	11
747-300 combined	Long range	3	0	3
747-200	Long range	0	0	7
767	Medium range	0	9	0
767-ER	Long range	0	3 (6)	0
757	Short range	0	60 (18)	0
737	Short range	0	72 (57)	0
727	Short range	0	129	0
Airbus Industries				
A310-300	Medium range	4	0	6 (3)
A310-200	Medium range	5	0	6
McDonnell Douglas				
MD-11	Long range	(12)	(9)	(5)
DC-10 ER	Long range	4	0	0
DC-10	Medium range	6	0	0
DC-9	Short range	0	36	0
MD-80	Short range	22 (2)	63 (28)	0
Fokker				
100	Short range	8 (22)	0	0
Lockheed				
L-1011	Medium range	0	40	0

Note: Amounts include aircraft owned and leased in 1989–90.

Source: Company annual reports.

different manufacturers to accommodate its need for a wide variety of distance capabilities. Swissair used Boeing 747's to fly intercontinental routes to North America and Asia. These craft had maximum ranges of over 10,000 km, but due to the cargo configurations that Swissair used, Asia-bound 747's from Zurich could fly nonstop only as far as Bangkok, Thailand, about an hour and a half short of Singapore. Swissair also invested heavily in aircraft maintenance. Eduard Meier, general manager for planning in Swissair's Engineering and Maintenance Division explained, "we probably put more maintenance into planes than most of our competitors and we often do routine maintenance overnight so that our planes are out of service far less and for shorter periods of time. We also sell our planes very young (average age for a Swissair plane was 7 years in 1990, compared to an industry average of 12 years)."

Like most major international airlines, Swissair invested heavily in computerized reservation systems (CRSs) during the 1980s, which it rented to travel agents to access its flight and fare schedules. It developed Traviswiss, a domestic and international CRS for use in Switzerland. Ongoing development of Traviswiss cost Swissair SFr 20 million (about $16 million) in 1989, and installation in travel agencies cost about SFr 22 million. By 1990, Traviswiss was in 95% of Swiss travel agencies. Management estimated that Traviswiss generated about SFr 40 million in revenues in 1990.[2] Swissair was also a founding member of Galileo, a CRS developed jointly by several European international carriers and marketed to travel agents worldwide. Annual costs associated with Galileo were about SFr 12 million. The third CRS employed by Swissair was Apollo, developed by United Airlines. Swissair owned 11% of Covia, the company that ran the Apollo CRS.

Historically, Swissair's central location in Europe combined with its strong reputation for service allowed the airline to prosper. In an internationally regulated industry where prices and competition were controlled, Swissair had successfully differentiated itself from major competitors. But deregulation of airlines in the U.S. set in motion new economic and political forces in the international airline business in the late 1980s. These forces would change Swissair's competitive position forever.

The International Airline Industry

In 1989, there were 157 member airlines in the International Air Transport Association (IATA). They transported approximately 858 million passengers in 1989, of which 25% flew internationally. Operating revenues of the world's airlines had grown 10.1% annually between 1984 and 1989, reaching $182.5 billion in 1989. The industry had been profitable on an operating basis every year since 1983. (See Exhibit 3 for travel demand growth.)

Government Regulations

Perhaps the most significant issue for Swissair was the possibility that deregulation would spread globally. In fact, by 1990, limited global deregulation became a reality: governments of many industrialized nations in Europe and Asia were loosening restrictions on operating rights and fare pricing, while retaining regulation of traffic safety and security.

Historically, the disbursement of operating rights to a foreign carrier for international travel was subject to a bilateral aviation service agreement (ASA) between the governments of the host country and the carrier's country. ASAs delineated which of the five internationally recognized "freedoms of the air" would be recognized between the two countries. (See Exhibit 4 for a graphical representation of the five freedoms.) ASAs also outlined the number of carriers and flights operating between the nations, restrictions on pricing, and other operational matters. In 1990, ASAs did not allow carriers from one country the right to *cabotage,* or domestic travel, within another country. Swissair, for example, could fly Zurich–Boston and Zurich–New York, but not New York–Boston.

Leverage in government-to-government negotiations over ASAs typically varied with market size and location: the United States, for example, had substantial leverage in negotiations because most foreign carriers wanted access to U.S. gateways.[3] Yet Switzerland, noted one Swissair manager, "has little leverage in ASA negotiations, partly because we have little new to offer partner countries, and partly because the government has a very liberal attitude toward signing agreements." By 1990, Switzerland had 102 ASAs, 36 of which went unused by Swissair.

ASAs also determined how airlines could set fares. Carriers could neither charge more nor less than the approved fare. In addition, fares collected by the carriers flying between two countries in Europe used to be pooled and divided equally among carriers of both nations, regardless of what percentage of traffic each airline carried. Although pooling was phased out on most European routes in the late 1980s, most fares remained subject to approval by the country of the flight's origin. Increasingly, ASAs were using more liberal "double disapproval"

---

[2]Swissair estimated that annual operating costs of Traviswiss were SFr 22 million and annual depreciation was around SFr 18 million.

[3]Until 1989, for instance, Swissair had a monopoly on ground handling for all flights in Zurich and Geneva. The United States demanded that this monopoly be broken up in exchange for landing rights for Swissair in Atlanta and Los Angeles.

EXHIBIT 3   World Travel Demand

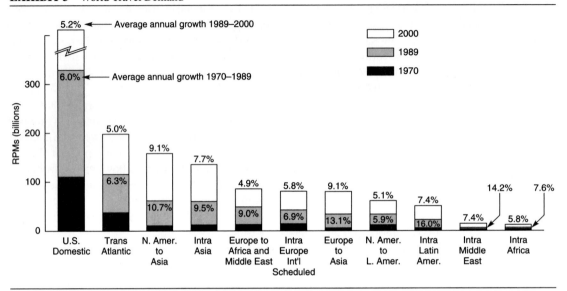

Source: *Boeing Current Market Outlook* (1990).

EXHIBIT 4   Five Freedoms of the Air

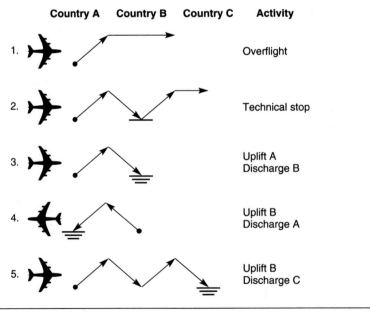

	Country A	Country B	Country C	Activity
1.				Overflight
2.				Technical stop
3.				Uplift A Discharge B
4.				Uplift B Discharge A
5.				Uplift B Discharge C

Source: R. B. McKern, *Evolving Strategies in the International Airline Industry* (Stanford GSB, 1990).

structures, where both governments could disapprove a fare, but neither had to approve it.

Industry Economics

Pricing was only one variable that affected a firm's profitability. It was standard for most air carriers to manage several variables, represented in the following accounting identity:

$$\left[\frac{\text{Revenues/}}{\text{RPK}} \times \frac{\text{RPKs/}}{\text{ASKs}}\right] - \frac{\text{Expenses/}}{\text{ASK}} = \frac{\text{Operating income/}}{\text{ASK}}$$

or

$$\left[\text{Yield} \times \frac{\text{Load}}{\text{factor}}\right] - \text{Unit Cost} = \frac{\text{Unit Operating Income}}{}$$

Using this identity, airlines could track the load factor needed to maintain profitability:

Unit cost/Yield = Breakeven load factor

The variables were defined as follows: An "available seat kilometer" (ASK) was the total number of kilometers traveled by one seat. A "revenue passenger kilometer" (RPK) was the number of kilometers traveled by an occupied seat. The amount of revenue provided by one seat was known as the *yield* (Revenues/RPKs). Unit costs were defined as operating expenses/ASKs (operating costs were examined on an ASK basis because in the short run, most of the operating expenses of an airline—wages/benefits, fuel, equipment depreciation costs, airport access charges, etc.—varied by capacity offered rather than by the number of passengers served). A measure of occupancy rate, known as the *load factor* (RPKs/ASKs) related yield to capacity.

Product Lines

Although most air carriers had cargo business, over two-thirds of all traffic tonnage transported in 1989 was passenger traffic. Most domestic fliers offered two classes of service, "coach" or economy class, and first class. The price differential between the two was substantial, and grew wider during the

1980s. A coach ticket from New York to London was $1,044 in 1980, while a first class ticket cost $1,856. By 1989, the economy class fare had risen to $1,616 (with discounts, often, to well below $1,000), and the price of a first class ticket had jumped to $4,880. International carriers added a third segment to the passenger market, usually known as "business" or "club" class. Business class fares were intermediate of economy and first class fares, with New York–London fares of $1,938 in 1983 and $3,196 in 1989.

Beyond different classes of service, airlines found other ways, often hidden from the passenger, to segment the travel market. Many carriers developed highly complex computer algorithms for manipulating fares, discounts, and special offers to optimize load factors while minimizing the dilution of yields. Computers analyzed current and historical data regarding each flight in a carrier's route structure and made recommendations as to how many seats should be available at a given fare level. These recommendations changed dynamically, and were fed to travel agents via the CRS link. Commenting on the remarkable advance of yield management technology, the CEO of KLM predicted that "in the not distant future, we [will] see daily and hourly prices for our products and services."[4] Strong yield management programs were formidable weapons for carriers like American, United, and BA during the 1980s. As CRSs advances spread globally, yield management techniques did as well.

Production Inputs

The major portions of an airline's cost structure were labor, fuel, maintenance, and fleet procurement. The largest single item was personnel: salaries, benefits, and other related expenses could make up as much as one-third of a carrier's costs of operations. In 1989, airlines employed about 114 employees per aircraft flown, and one employee for every 885 passengers served. In most major international airlines,

---

[4]Speech by JFA De Soet, Stockholm, Sweden, September 27, 1990.

employees belonged to one of several different labor unions. During the 1980s, several airlines started in the U.S., hoping that their nonunionized labor force would give them a cost advantage. Many of these small carriers went bankrupt or were acquired by the end of the decade. By 1990, nonunion carriers were beginning to emerge in Europe.

The second largest component of the cost structure of most carriers was consumed fuel. Airlines had almost no leverage vis-à-vis fuel suppliers in the short term, for airlines had no way of controlling the price, or their consumption, of fuel. Maintenance and ground services also made up a substantial portion of carrier expenses. Each body and engine type required repair personnel with specialized expertise. In general, routine maintenance was performed at home bases, but airlines needed repair capabilities across their route structure. Typically, international carriers purchased local repair capacity from competitors, or maintained satellite repair facilities. International carriers sold subcontracting services at a profit, even when they were handling the work of partners. Unlike their global counterparts, U.S. airlines handled all of their own ground services. Finally, three firms dominated the commercial plane market in 1989. Boeing was the leader, with about half the world's market; Airbus Industries, a consortium of European government-backed manufacturers, had a 28% share; and McDonnell Douglas had 20%.

Distribution

Computerized Reservation Systems (CRSs) were the chief methods by which airlines influenced the air carrier selections of travel agents and passengers. Prior to United Airline's introduction of Apollo in 1976, travel agents reserved seats for passengers using an Official Airlines Guide, a monthly book that outlined all flights into airports across the globe. Apollo was designed to give up-to-date information on flights, seat availability, and fares to travel agents who were hooked into its network. Soon, other American carriers followed with similar systems. Those carriers that had developed CRSs also rented space on them to competitors

who needed to allow travel agents real-time access as well. "Co-hosts," as carriers which rented CRS space were called, paid an average $1.75 per flight segment for each flight booked on the hosts's CRS. By 1990, almost every travel agent in the United States used an automated system, and about 80% of airline tickets in the United States were sold through a CRS. Virtually every U.S. carrier had invested millions of dollars to create a reservation system and to induce travel agents to use that system instead of competitors' systems. The most successful CRS, American Airlines's Sabre system, generated about 200 bookings per month for each terminal. With millions of terminals in its network, Sabre provided rates of return close to 70% for American Airlines.

As U.S. carriers expanded, the technology quickly spread globally. Most U.S. carriers owned CRSs, and rented the technology to travel agents across the world. European and Asian carriers feared that if their travel agents used American CRS technology, it would lead to greater inroads by U.S. carriers. Two European airline consortia formed to develop independent CRS technology. In 1990, two CRS networks, Amadeus and Galileo, displayed the flight information of the various European carriers that owned them. A similar consortium of Asian carriers developed a CRS network called Abacus. Several of these CRSs were linked to one another, providing even wider global reservation capabilities (see Exhibit 5).

Route Structure

After the U.S. domestic industry was deregulated in 1978, most airlines scrapped their government-mandated domestic route structure and replaced it with a hub-and-spoke route system. The hub-and-spoke system consisted of using airports in strategic locations as central hubs, through which passengers from several flights could be fed, and then transferred to outbound flights to their final destinations. Hub-and-spoke systems were adopted by carriers outside the United States, though in a more limited fashion; like Swissair, most European carriers had single hubs from which all flights radiated.

EXHIBIT 5 Major CRS Networks Worldwide

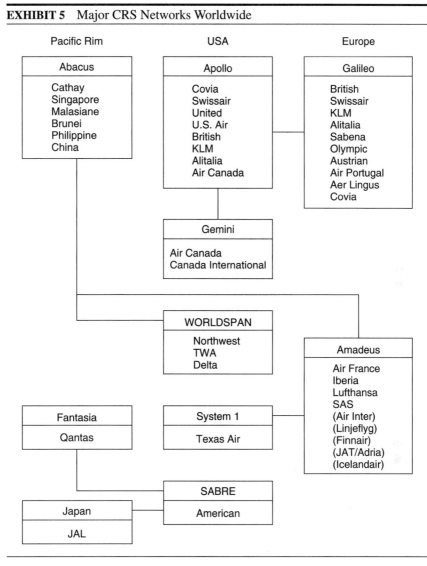

Source: Swissair documents.

Swissair's Major European International Competitors

On one level, Swissair competed with all carriers that flew in and out of Switzerland; i.e., most major carriers in the world. All of Swissair's routes were served by at least one other airline. However, Swissair's management viewed its primary competition as large quality-oriented European firms. They were Air France, Lufthansa, British Air, KLM, and SAS.[5]

---

[5]Since SAS was also a partner, it will be discussed later in the case.

Air France.   Air France was the government-owned flag carrier of the French republic, and one of the largest, most active carriers in Europe. Its route structure connected Paris to wide-ranging destinations in Europe, Africa, Asia, and the Americas. In 1989, Air France acquired majority interests in UTA and Air Inter, competitors for domestic passengers and for traffic between France and other European countries. Combined, the three companies had revenues in 1989 of about $8 billion and controlled 9.2% of European traffic in 1990. Unlike Swissair, Air France was not regarded as having superior in-flight service. Business travelers did note, however, innovative amenities such as free ground transport after arrival in Paris. After its purchases of UTA and Air Inter, Air France controlled more than 60% of traffic at Paris's two major airports. France occupied a strong geographic, political, and financial position in the EC.

Deutsche Lufthansa.   Lufthansa was the flag carrier for West Germany, and also carried passengers to 160 destinations on all continents. Lufthansa had hubs in both Frankfurt and Munich, and received about 45% of its revenues on flights among European countries. It carried 11.9% of European passengers in 1990. Flights to North America and Asia each generated about 20% of revenues. Lufthansa was known in the international travel industry for two unique strengths. First, it was a leader in the international transport of cargo. Reasons for its strength in cargo transport included high technology support services and an international CRS agreement with Air France and Japan Airlines to reach cargo customers around the world. Lufthansa's second strength was its capability in maintenance. One quarter of its employees were in maintenance. The carrier sold technical capacity and expertise on a contract basis. Lufthansa was also consulted by aircraft manufacturers in improving old frame designs or building new ones. Since 1988, Lufthansa had been aggressively buying market-share on many of its routes, especially travel between Eastern and Western Europe. Moreover, it was an investor or partner in over 30

European businesses. These included a German commuter airline, a charter carrier in Spain, and joint ventures in China and the USSR.

British Airways.   British Airways (BA) was the furthest-reaching international carrier in the world. In 1989 it carried almost 25 million passengers to destinations on every populated continent. It controlled 50% of traffic at its hub, London's Heathrow airport, and 15.5% of traffic in Europe in 1990. Heathrow was the busiest airport in Europe. The carrier also used airports in Singapore, Bombay, and Kuwait as secondary, intermediate hubs for trips between London and the Pacific Rim. Formerly government owned, the British flag carrier was privatized in 1987. In the years leading up to its privatization, the carrier strongly improved the services it provided, especially to international business travellers. The resulting jump in reputation turned the carrier's dismal financial situation into a profitable, competitive one. After privatization, BA was also aggressive in pursuing strategic opportunities. In addition to interairline agreements with Aeroflot, Interflug, Sabena, and United, the carrier's international partnerships included a meshed schedule arrangement with Delta through Dallas–Fort Worth airport, and cargo service to the Far East in conjunction with Singapore Airlines. It also owned a 25% share in Covia, the partnership that ran the Apollo CRS. In 1987, BA acquired its main domestic competitor, British Caledonian, and in 1990 it was negotiating to buy the Belgian airline, Sabena.

KLM Royal Dutch.   Based in the Netherlands, KLM was similar in size to Swissair. In 1989, KLM flew passengers between Amsterdam and 140 other destinations in 77 countries. Almost half of KLM's destinations were in Europe, and it carried 4.2% of European travellers in 1990. The majority of its traffic flew between Amsterdam and North America or between Amsterdam and the Far East. Load factors on these intercontinental flights averaged between 72% and 75%. KLM enjoyed a strong reputation for customer service. According to

Swissair's Mueller, "KLM's reputation for quality service and punctuality made them a strong candidate as an ally during our search. Unfortunately, their route structure overlapped ours to too great a degree for an alliance to be fruitful." Nonetheless, KLM expressed interest in joining the EQA while launching several partnerships of its own, including a 5% equity investment in Northwest Airlines. KLM's ownership of Northwest Airlines was restricted by U.S. regulations, which prohibited foreign carriers from owning more than 25% of one of its carriers.

Interline Cooperation

The international airline business had always been a mixture of competition and cooperation: during the 1960s, 1970s, and 1980s, virtually every major international air carrier regularly entered cooperative ventures with other carriers to expand route networks, to circumvent political and capital obstacles to growth, and to gain operating synergies. Historically, these arrangements were focused agreements, limited to one area of operations. In the late 1980s, airline alliances exploded both in number and in breadth of activities (see Exhibit 6).

Two of the most common alliances were joint purchasing arrangements and maintenance agreements. A classic example of this was a European alliance, begun in the 1970s, called KSSU. KSSU was a division of labor between KLM, SAS, Swissair, and UTA, started in 1975 to coordinate the purchase and maintenance of airframes (handled by Swissair and SAS), engines (which KLM maintained), and landing gear (serviced by UTA). Each airline specialized in the repair of a particular portion, and was responsible for the upkeep of that portion of partners' aircraft as well. At the outset of the arrangement, fleets were similar enough that KSSU carriers could combine purchases and maintenance. This became more complicated by 1990, as the partners' strategies diverged and resulting fleet requirements no longer matched. However, Swissair and SAS continued to coordinate their purchases in the European Quality Alliance (discussed below), as did Air France and Lufthansa.

In addition to cooperation on purchasing and operations, some airlines operated joint ventures (JVs) and coordinated marketing activities. Joint ventures took a variety of forms. BA, for instance, used JVs to penetrate previously unavailable markets, such as a 49%/51% joint venture with Aeroflot, the Soviet airline, to set up an independent airline serving routes between the Soviet Union and Western Europe, and between the Soviet Union and North America. Late in 1990, BA was also negotiating a minority investment in Interflug, the former state airline of East Germany. Another common JV was buying dedicated seats on a competitor airline; Swissair, for instance, flew from Zurich to Tokyo, but JAL "owned" a particular block of seats. JAL would pay the prorated costs of operating those seats, while selling them to its customer base.

In the marketing arena, alliances proliferated in the 1980s. Perhaps the most widely known were joint frequent flyer programs, where two or more airlines agreed to share the costs and benefits of giving passengers credit towards upgrades and free flights. "Code sharing" was yet another form of cooperation that became popular in the late 1980s. If two airlines shared their reservation codes, passengers could easily connect between airlines without the hassles of multiple fares and multiple check-ins. One of the innovators in code sharing was a 1987 agreement between United and BA: they assigned a single code for feeder flights, rearranged terminal locations to create complementary transfer points, and manipulated CRS technology to allow seamless passenger handling on transfer flights.[6] Air France and Lufthansa signed a similar agreement in September 1989 to weave together their European route schedules, and to create new long haul routes together. In addition to code sharing, Air France and Lufthansa agreed to start a catering joint venture, engage in fleet purchases together, and create permanent links between management

---

[6]The BA–United alliance was placed in jeopardy in late 1990 when United bought Pan Am's London routes.

EXHIBIT 6 Interline Agreements

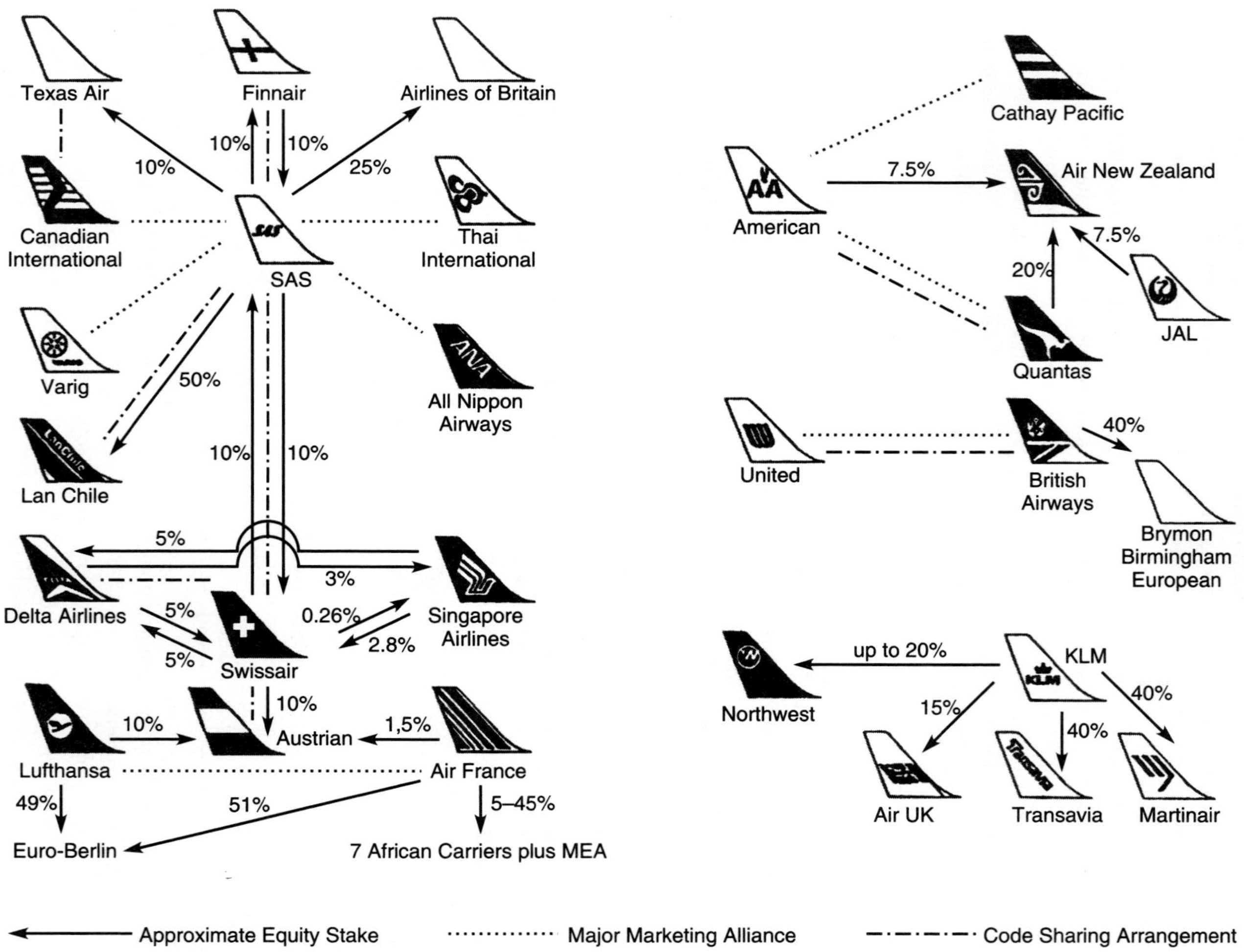

Source: Avmark Aviation Economist and casewriter estimates.

including joint board meetings every six months. There was no exchange of equity, but the two carriers publicly mentioned this as a future possibility.

Swissair's 1992 Fears

As Swissair's management readied themselves for the changing economics of the international airline business, they also faced the prospect of a radically new political environment in Europe. When the European Community (EC) passed the Single European Act in 1985, they set in motion plans to integrate the area into a single, unified trading zone, with reduced regulation by the end of 1992. From Swissair's perspective, the 1992 program had both regulatory and political repercussions. The government regulations of the airline industry would be completely overhauled, except regulations on public safety. The first step in the overhaul was a directive which would deregulate the structure of fare pricing on international flights within the EC by 1993. The measures included provisions for deep-discount fares. In 1990, Swissair believed that international fares were already being undercut by a developing "gray market." In the future, carriers were likely to be more aggressive in offering discount prices for flights originating in the EC.

Freeing prices was only one consequence of 1992 for Swissair: if Switzerland did not join the EC, the Swiss government might have to renegotiate European ASAs with EC representatives, rather than representatives of the individual member nations. This prospect of political dislocation was alarming to Swissair's Paul Mueller. "EC carriers will have opportunities and flexibility that we won't have as a non-member. Equilibrium among 12 different economies will change; relationships built up with members of the power structures in 12 countries would be useless. They will have a home market of 350 million, compared to our seven million. Negotiations on tariffs, market access, and capacity will be lopsided and we'll be over a barrel." If flights by non-EC carriers between London and Munich could be considered "EC cabotage," Swissair would be significantly disadvantaged.

To address the prospect of a radically new competitive environment, the company took drastic actions. The first change was a wholesale restructuring of its organization in 1988. In the words of one Swissair official, management felt that "the airline was too centralized in 1988, with all strategic decisions made in Zurich. We needed more flexibility to adapt to new competitive situations quickly. We needed to be closer to the market." In order to move decision-making capabilities further down the organizational structure, Swissair eliminated three of nine layers of management. The carrier also separated its route network into three separate geographic teams, then gave sixteen route managers bottom line responsibilities for timetable planning, staffing, and marketing.

The second change was an attempt to strengthen Swissair's position in the global market. The internal task force assembled under Mueller recommended several alternatives to the board which could strengthen the carrier's position in the global travel market. Although they considered a variety of alternatives ranging from business-as-usual to mergers, the task force recommended in July 1988 pursuing alliances with another European carrier, an American carrier, and an Asian carrier. The board accepted the recommendation with one caveat: to maintain Swissair's strength in the premium-priced segment of the market, no ally could be chosen that would dilute Swissair's reputation of premium quality and dedication to customer service.

Swissair's Alliances

After the task force recommendation in 1988, management at Swissair turned to Paul Mueller's external relations group to negotiate and implement alliances. Potential partners were examined relative to a checklist of 85 strengths and weaknesses that would complement Swissair's. The criteria examined related to technical capabilities—both maintenance and CRS/yield management; marketing opportunities and commercial strengths; financial capabilities; the complementary nature of fleet and route structures with Swissair's; and reputation for quality in terms of punctuality, ground service, and air service among others.

By the end of 1988, external relations had completed the first steps of the task force's recommendation. In March 1989, Swissair and Delta signed an agreement for transatlantic cooperation. Swissair and SAS signed a cooperation agreement which led to the formation of the European Quality Alliance with Austrian Airlines and Finnair in October 1989. In December, Swissair signed the third agreement, an intercontinental alliance with Singapore Airlines. (See Exhibit 7 for alliance partners' route destinations.)

The Global Alliance

Delta Airlines. In 1990, Delta was the third largest carrier in the U.S., with revenues over $8.5 billion. The airline flew to 174 destinations in 1990, of which 148 were destinations in the domestic United States, and in 1990, 12.9% of domestic travelers flew on Delta. In 1990, it combined its CRS called Datas II with the Pars system run by TWA and Northwest Airlines into a CRS called Worldspan. Worldspan was also connected with Abacus in Asia. Delta was one of the pioneers of the domestic U.S. hub-and-spoke routing system, and it had hubs in airports in Atlanta, Boston, Cincinnati, Dallas–Fort Worth, Los Angeles, Orlando, and Salt Lake City.

Delta acquired Western Airlines, a regional U.S. carrier, in 1987. After the acquisition, Delta management saw international travel as the major growth opportunity in the 1990s. "We believed that we had filled out our domestic route structure pretty much as well as we could when we bought Western," explained W. Whitley Hawkins, Delta's executive vice president of marketing, "but we had no existing base of international traffic. We knew that growth in the 1990s was going to come in transatlantic and

transpacific markets, so we needed to start building an international route structure. International marketing agreements seemed like a perfect way to grow into the market, and we had undertaken similar arrangements with a variety of offshore carriers in the past, including British Caldedonian and Lufthansa. When we were approached by Swissair in 1988, the concept made a lot of sense to us. We see a large advantage in being able to market a Zurich vacation to a passenger in Mobile, Alabama. Yet an alliance, rather than a merger, keeps each of us from having to sacrifice our corporate culture and style. We each liked that." In 1990, the carrier had destinations in England, France, Ireland, the Netherlands, and West Germany, and management expected to service the growth of traffic markets in Asia as well. Analysts generally believed that Delta's priorities were first in the U.S., followed by developing routes in the Pacific, and then Europe. On some routes, Delta and Swissair remained competitors. Delta management's expansion plans also emphasized routes between "nontraditional" gateway airports in the U.S., Europe, and Asia, such as between Cincinnati and Shannon, Ireland.[7]

U.S. airline stocks had been hot takeover candidates in 1988 and 1989. To resist a takeover, Delta sought the assistance of "white squires," financial partners who would invest in the carrier without demanding a role in running it. At the same time they announced a code-sharing and marketing partnership, Delta and Swissair also announced that each would purchase 5% of the other carrier's common stock. Delta management denied, however, that Delta's alliance moves were motivated by fears of a takeover. "The driving force behind the alliance was the opportunity to substantially extend our market of destinations," Hawkins maintained, "the

---

[7]Delta was also opportunistic about international expansion. Despite a strategy focused on nontraditional gateways, it was considering a bid for the L.A.–London routes of Pan Am if and when Pan Am filed for bankruptcy.

EXHIBIT 7 Destinations of the Global Alliance

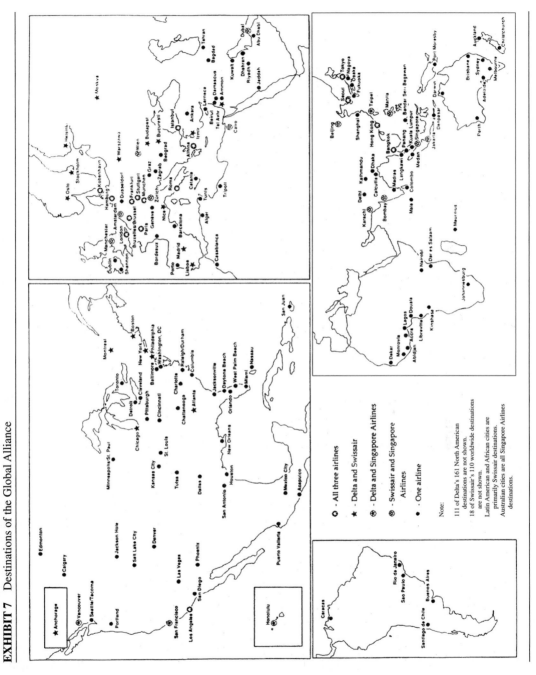

◇ - All three airlines
★ - Delta and Swissair
⊛ - Delta and Singapore Airlines
⊘ - Swissair and Singapore Airlines
● - One airline

Note:

111 of Delta's 161 North American destinations are not shown.
18 of Swissair's 110 worldwide destinations are not shown.
Latin American and African cities are primarily Swissair destinations.
Australian cities are all Singapore Airlines destinations.

Source: Partner airline documents.

459

stock swap certainly made sense in that environment, but it was not the driving force."

Neither carrier had strong access to the base market of the other, and the two planned to develop code-shared routes for transatlantic passengers through Atlanta, Boston, and Los Angeles, the three hubs/gateways that they shared. Along with code meshing, the two carriers planned to link their CRSs to enlarge scheduling capabilities and to provide several customer handling conveniences, like through check-in and baggage handling. Although both had participated in prorate arrangements in the past, managers like Peter Luethi, Swissair's route manager–North America, expected this to be different. "The routing portions of the alliance are based on mutual incentives. When we prorated with United in Chicago, they basically told us their flight schedule. We were welcome to mesh our schedule or not, as we pleased. In the Delta arrangement, we have rearranged the schedules of *both* carriers to create the most connections possible. In Atlanta, our first meshed gateway, we now have 35 Delta connections for our passengers within an hour of arrival."

The two carriers also had similar fleet types, although Delta's was far larger. Many of the planes that each carrier had purchased were made by McDonnell Douglas, and they planned to coordinate technical operations where possible, examining areas of overlap in their repair and maintenance expertise. There were discussions, for example, of doing routine overhaul work on Delta's narrow-body fleet at Swissair's facility in Shannon, Ireland. The two also expressed hope that they could standardize the cockpit configurations of future aircraft purchases, facilitating both technical maintenance and the transfer of flight crews.

Singapore International Airlines SIA. Like Swissair, SIA was constantly chosen by travel and business magazines as one of the premier airlines in the world. Its cabin staffs were lauded as being among the best-trained, most attentive and accommodating in the world. Its aircraft were among the youngest and best maintained, and were filled with innovative customer comforts. Finally, its financial

management was superior to most. It combined the advantage of having a relatively low personnel cost structure with scheduling efficiency (its load factor was 78.9%). SIA had followed the strong growth of its home country, and was one of the fastest growing carriers in the Far East. SIA was a founder of the Asian CRS called Abacus. Abacus was based in Singapore. SIA, like other international carriers, also had a variety of collaborative arrangements: for instance, it operated joint cargo services with BA, KLM, and Lufthansa, among others.

The Swissair–SIA alliance was modeled on the agreements that Delta had made with both of them. Equity holdings were cross-purchased. While management did not believe that such investments precluded SIA from working with other airlines, it decided to swap up to 5% equity in Swissair to cement the relationship. As with Delta, the carriers aimed to create a marketing alliance of high-quality service, code-sharing routes between Europe and Asia, and close collaboration in operational areas. SIA's primary motivation in the alliances, according to T. A. Hwang, SIA's senior vice president–Americas, was "to find a way to compete with mega-carriers while retaining our unique identity. We looked for partners with complementary route structures and like-minded management emphasis, and Swissair was a very good fit." T. A. Hwang elaborated, "our objective is to compete with the big boys and gain strategic advantages by reaching out to markets that we could never economically serve ourselves. Furthermore, through working with Delta and Swissair, we hope to give customers real value by offering 'seamless' service from Singapore to virtually all areas of the world. Our second priority is to develop 'operating efficiencies.' For instance, it may not be commercially efficient for Swissair or Delta to fly to some Southeast Asian destinations a few times each week; since SIA flies many daily services to many Southeast Asian locations, it may be more sensible for partner airlines to buy a block of seats on some SIA flights. The same would be true for SIA marketing to some major offline cities in the U.S. or Europe. Moreover, in the future we will develop joint products, work towards sharing ticket offices and airport handling, and ultimately have similar cockpit designs that allow Swissair to utilize our aircraft during long stopovers in Zurich or allow us to utilize their aircraft from Singapore." Even before the alliance was contemplated, SIA and Swissair operated seven flights weekly between Singapore and Zurich. Once the alliance was consummated, the two airlines planned to double the number of services between Zurich and Singapore within three years. As with Delta and Swissair, there was not yet any code sharing, but the two carriers had attempted to mesh schedules to allow connecting flights in Zurich and Singapore.

A Trilateral Venture. Although the relationships between the three carriers had started as separate ventures, all three were quick to see the value of melding the bilateral partnerships into a trilateral "Global Alliance." By the end of 1990, the three had created a marketing campaign that highlighted the alliance, the carriers' excellent customer service, and specific products such as Switzerland skiing packages and vacation packages in both the U.S. and Europe. It was planned for Swissair to be the first and only European airline to accompany SIA's move to a new terminal at Singapore's Changi airport. Delta planned to be the first American carrier.

Among Swissair's first priorities was aligning the reservation systems: as one executive put it, "if the passenger could not see a benefit to the alliance, there would be no competitive advantage." Furthermore, explained Peter Luethi, "if you want to be global and offer choices, you must be able to reach your partner's reservation system." Other areas of coordination included personnel exchanges. Swissair, lacking flight attendants for new routes, "borrowed" 74 flight attendants from Delta for a three-month period. Both carriers found that the information exchange and marketing opportunities available through personnel swaps were valuable, as was the flexibility of additional swing capacity. They planned exchanges for middle managers and headquarters personnel, as well as continued swaps of in-flight crews. Although they had not

fully accomplished code-sharing arrangements by the end of 1990, they had made progress in CRS access. Delta purchased a "host-to-host" link from Swissair, allowing direct access of Worldspan by Swissair. Travel agents with Swissair's system were able to access Delta flights and were able to book passengers and check in passengers on flights connecting with Swissair flights. Accomplishing the direct link had taken Swissair technicians about 3.5 man-years.[8] Accomplishing the customer service aspects like through-check-in and baggage transfer had taken about 150 man-years. Technicians expected Swissair-Singapore links to follow quickly.

The airlines also expected to tighten operating coordinations even further in the future (see Exhibit 8), but Delta was cautious and wanted to go slowly, especially when it came to rationalizing fixed assets. According to Hawkins, "expenditures to alter terminals and frequent flier lounges, and to develop joint CRSs for the alliance are sunk costs, and we want to make sure that we're totally aligned on an idea before we spend vast sums for it." Hawkins went on to say that "we don't want to make mistakes. We recognize that giving Swissair or Singapore complete access to our database would enhance customer service, but we need to tread lightly and be cautious before we allow any airline access to our 8.5 million frequent flier travel records." Until November 1990, Delta had nobody in charge of alliance planning. More experienced in making international operating arrangements, Swissair had managers overseeing the relationships with both Delta and Singapore for over a year. Swissair was also anxious to rationalize operations. "We see opportunities for tremendous economies of scale," explained Luethi, "with relatively little cost. Take the coordination of baggage handling and aircraft

---

[8]There were 190 man-days in one man-year, and Swissair estimated the cost of one man-day at about SFr 1,700, or $1,063. Swissair expected to link with other carriers like United and British Airways in the future. Because the link was already established, the cost of linking additional carriers was nil.

EXHIBIT 8   Alliance Activities as of November 1990

	Delta	Singapore
Ground organization:		
Common passenger handling	x	p
Common lounge availability	p	p
Through check-in	x	p
Passenger transfer services	x	p
Timetables:		
Product joint timetable	x	x
Coordinated schedules	x	p
Reciprocal sales representation:		
Off-line stations	p	p
General sales agent agreements	p	p
Tariffs:		
Pro-rate tariffs	x	x
Around the world fare	x	x
Personnel:		
Flight attendant exchange	x	x
Junior management exchange	p	p
Marketing:		
Advertising/joint logo	x	x
Sales promotions		x
Joint pricing	p	p
Joint tour programs	x	p
Block source agreements	p	p
Code sharing	x	p
Meshed frequent flier program	x	x
Aircraft procurement:		
Common purchasing	p	p
Exchange of aircraft/fleet planning	p	p
Technology and maintenance sharing	p	p
Air freight:		
Link cargo systems	p	p
Joint development of systems	p	p

x = Activities in process; p = Planned.

Source: Swissair internal documents.

servicing. We want to make sure that the carrier doing ground handling for the partner can handle it with their own equipment. Coordinating this should cost about a million or two million dollars in software adjustments. However, it only needs to be done once. We fly into 108 destinations worldwide, and after the first adjustments are made, Delta can fly into any of these virtually overnight. Also, we can get much better use out of service counters and passenger lounges that are used for thirty or forty flights per day than we can out of assets that service one or two flights a day." While Singapore agreed in principle with most of these ideas, Delta was unwilling to move quickly. One Swissair executive wondered aloud, "how do you get share of mind of the local employees in alliance from a huge company like Delta, where international expansion is driven by domestic concerns?"

The European Quality Alliance

SAS was a European carrier similar to Swissair. The airline was owned by a consortium of the national airlines and governments of Denmark, Norway, and Sweden, with a "home" population of about 17 million people. Because Denmark was an EC member nation, SAS was under the auspices of the EC. SAS had been on the verge of financial collapse in the late 1970s. A new charismatic CEO, Jan Carlzon, introduced a corporate culture which called for dedication to the customer. Carlzon targeted the business traveler, developing innovations like separate check-ins, lounges with business amenities, and the first business class. By 1990, SAS had returned to operating profitability and its load factor had grown from 59.4% to 61.5% (intercontinental load factors averaged 71%). In 1990, SAS flew to 82 destinations in 36 countries, down from 102 destinations in 1979. In Europe, SAS handled 8.8% of traffic. Although some overlap with Swissair, SAS's route structure concentrated on Scandinavia, Eastern and Western Europe, and North America, making it complementary to Swissair's in many areas, especially Asia, India, Africa, and the Middle East. SAS also had an aggressive alliance strategy. Jan Carlzon believed that there would be only five European airlines by the end of the 1990s, and "we want to be one of the five [surviving] European airlines . . . [To do this] we must reach critical mass . . . B.A., Lufthansa, and Air France [will] survive] and there will be a union among the others to form the fourth and fifth carriers." Carlzon went on to say, "the reservation system is critical; 95% of all tickets sold are shown on the CRS's first screen . . . [In addition,] we have to transform

ourselves into a U.S. carrier [to reach critical mass]."[9] This philosophy led SAS to take a large ownership position in Continental Airlines as well as form an alliance with Thai International.

Swissair and SAS had been bitter competitors for several decades, and had been partners in purchasing and maintenance ventures since 1958. In September 1989, executives at the two airlines decided to invest in one another and coordinate many of their activities. Not long after this, they were joined by Austrian Airlines, another long-time Swissair ally, and Finnair. Together they proclaimed the European Quality Alliance. Among them, the four members accounted for more than 40% of all connections available between Eastern and Western Europe on Western carriers. Their route structures linked the four European countries and points in North America, South America, Western Europe, Africa, the Middle East, Eastern Europe, and Asia. As with Delta and Singapore, Swissair expected to coordinate code-sharing and connected flight arrangements with its EQA partners.

Years of coordination on technical matters proved advantageous to the carriers. Twenty SAS flight crews were able to temporarily pilot Swissair flights in Swissair planes; Swissair cockpit specifications were the same as in SAS aircraft. In 1990, work progressed on a project to combine the carriers' CRSs. Technical managers estimated that having Swissair and SAS on the same CRS would save the two carriers between $60 million and $120 million per year. Swissair and SAS also planned to consolidate customer service and ground support personnel.

As 1990 ended, the four airlines had also signed an agreement to coordinate a purchase of over 200 aircraft for delivery in the mid-1990s. Swissair and Austrian Airlines had combined their fleets of other McDonnell Douglas aircraft. Based on the commonality of their fleets and of the proximity of their

---

[9]Jan Carlzon at the Harvard Business School, 1988. By 1990, European airlines were beginning to believe that only four airlines would survive the 1990s.

home base airports, EQA partners were confident that there would be ample opportunities for joint maintenance.

Swissair's Dilemma

Swissair was clearly on the move. Its network of alliances had patched together a formidable combination of global competitors. Yet for Leopfe and his senior management team, many questions remained. Perhaps the two most important issues were: Would the economics and politics of international airlines mirror the structure which deregulation had produced in the U.S. or would some alternative structure emerge? And would Swissair's multiple alliances position the company to weather whatever competitive storms were brewing?

Case 4–3 STAR TV (A, B, and C Condensed)

In the summer of 1993, 25-year-old Richard Li was considering the future of STAR TV, the Pan-Asian satellite television service which he had launched less than two years ago. STAR TV broadcast five channels of English- and Chinese-language programming without charge throughout Asia and swiftly became immensely popular. It now boasted about 45 million viewers in more than 38 countries. The plan had been to fund the service entirely by advertising, but revenues were not covering costs. Some estimates put losses as high as $5 million per week. In addition, the prospects of new competitors and greater satellite capacity threatened to undercut STAR's position. To increase revenues and stave off competitors, Richard Li had at least two options. One was introducing "pay-TV": to begin charging viewers for the service. Another was to increase the amount of in-house programming. Either strategy might have to involve some sort of alliance because STAR had little experience in these areas. Complicating the decisions was the interest that several media companies had reportedly expressed in acquiring a stake in STAR. Thus, Richard Li was faced with an unusual dilemma. He had created a phenomenon:

now he needed to find out how to turn the phenomenon into profit.

Background: Li Ka Shing, Richard Li, and Hutchison Whampoa

Li Ka Shing, "Superman Li," was the richest man in Hong Kong, personally worth an estimated U.S.$4 billion, with his companies valued at about U.S.$22 billion. His businesses were now centered around a core of property, retail, shipping, telecommunications, and energy. His flagships were Hutchison Whampoa and the holding company Cheung Kong.

Li Ka Shing was described as combining "the instincts of a gambler with the calculations of an actuary."[1] Yet he was never reckless, preferring to share risks when possible, with friends and allies. The importance of allies and long-term relationships was central to his business philosophy, which was: "Behave honorably; never cheat on a deal; buy low and sell high, but always try to take less, even if you can take more, because that way a hundred more deals will come to you."

Richard Li, one of Li Ka Shing's two sons, was born in 1967. He went to prep school in America and earned a degree in computer engineering from Stanford. After graduation, he worked in investment

---

This case was prepared by Research Associate Henry Laurence under the supervision of Professor Michael Y. Yoshino and Peter Williamson.

[1]Louis Kraar, "A Billionaire's Global Strategy," *Fortune,* June 29, 1992.

banking in Canada for four years and returned to Hong Kong in 1990.

Satellite Television

Direct broadcast satellite television (DBS) involved a terrestrial transmitter sending a program signal up to a satellite in geostationary orbit, from where it would be broadcast down to a variety of receiving devices. The "footprint" each satellite could cover varied according to its power. (See Exhibit 1.) The most common types of reception were Television Receive Only (TVRO), in which a single household picked up the signal with a single antenna dish; Community Antenna Television (CATV), in which the signal was picked up by one antenna and redistributed by cable to multiple households, usually for a subscription fee; and Satellite Master Antenna Television (SMATV) in which one antenna served multiple households within one building, such as an apartment complex.

In both America and Europe, the experience of DBS T.V. had been almost uniformly disappointing.[2] No venture had proved particularly profitable, and most had been outright failures, including United Satellite Communications, Inc., Crinson Satellite Associates, and News Corporation's aborted Skyband Inc. In Europe, British Satellite Broadcasting and Sky Television were losing money at a combined rate of almost £10 million per week.[3]

Television in Asia

Relative to the United States or Europe, most Asian countries were underserved by television. TV ownership rates were growing, and as high as 98% in many urban areas. In rural or less well developed regions, however, penetration was much lower, averaging about 50% in China for example. The overall choice and quality of programming were generally perceived as poor, however, and competi-

tion was minimal. On average, Asian viewers could watch two to four channels, compared with about 25 for Western audiences. Most stations were government controlled or strictly regulated, often being used to relay government propaganda. Cable TV was beginning to appear in parts of Asia, but was in its infancy. DBS was virtually nonexistent. There was no satellite with a footprint extending over all of Asia, and there were no commercial DBS ventures. However, since satellites were used to retransmit terrestial station broadcasts in many areas including China and Indonesia, there was a small base of satellite reception dish owners in the region.

The largest Asian TV company outside Japan was the Hong Kong–based Television Broadcasts Ltd., (TVB) which churned out low-budget Cantonese-language films and shows. A much smaller rival producer to TVB in Hong Kong was Asian Television Ltd.

Western media companies including the news service CNN and sports channel ESPN were beginning to enter the Asian market, but had not yet achieved significant penetration.

The STAR Concept

Background on AsiaSat 1.[4] In 1985, an American communications satellite was recovered by NASA after an abortive private launch. It was sold to a AsiaSat, a consortium consisting of Hutchison Whampoa, Cable and Wireless Plc, and China International Trust and Investment Corporation, an investment arm of the Chinese government. Renamed AsiaSat 1, the satellite was relaunched in April 1990. Li Ka Shing's main interest was telecommunications, but for the first time ever there was spare transponder space for commercial use in Asia. AsiaSat 1 had two beams, creating a huge footprint. (See Exhibits 2 and 3.)

Hutchison Whampoa and Li Ka Shing jointly provided the equity for HutchVision, which in turn was to operate Satellite Television Asia Region

---

[2]This section draws, in part, upon David Hartshorn, "DBS vs. cable: Is time running out?" *Satellite Communications,* Vol. 16, No. 6, June 1992.

[3]More detail is found in "British Satellite Broadcasting versus Sky Television," Harvard Business School case No. 794-031.

[4]This section draws on "Hutchison Whampoa's Decision to Launch STAR TV," a paper prepared by Jean-Luc de Fanti, Monique Maddy, Amedeo Serra, and Nancy Ward.

EXHIBIT 1

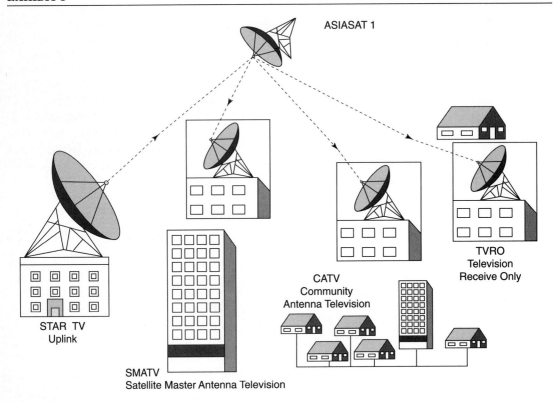

ASIASAT 1

STAR TV
Uplink

SMATV
Satellite Master Antenna Television

CATV
Community
Antenna Television

TVRO
Television
Receive Only

(STAR TV) to investigate the economical feasibility of satellite television. A small team was recruited to develop the concept, with the best people lured from all around the world. The original team was notable for its youth, mix of Asians and Westerners, and wide variety of career backgrounds.

Richard Li explained:

> Hutchison Whampoa regarded AsiaSat 1 as venture capital. The amount of money was relatively small in relation to the Group's overall activities. Cable television was the big deal . . . So STAR started out as a weekend project.

Technological Issues. AsiaSat 1 had 24 transponders of which 12 were leased out. This left STAR with capacity to broadcast six TV channels (one channel per transponder per beam). Each channel could theoretically carry four different soundtracks for the same picture, making multiple-language broadcasts possible.

For reception, TVRO viewers would need an antenna dish. Although the consumer market for reception equipment in Asia was small, almost all of the necessary parts were manufactured in the region for export. Scrambling the signal was possible, but U.S. experience had been that even the best scrambling technology could be pirated. An estimated 40% of all U.S. TV signals were pirated in the late 1980s.

Target Audience. Catering to the 2.7 billion people under the footprint presented difficulties, as there were such vast cultural, linguistic, religious

EXHIBIT 2

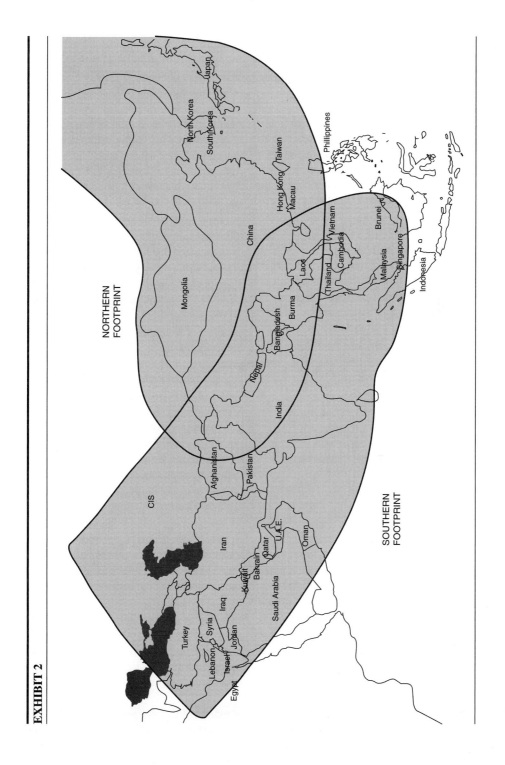

NORTHERN FOOTPRINT

SOUTHERN FOOTPRINT

Japan
North Korea
South Korea
Hong Kong
Macau
Taiwan
Phillippines
China
Mongolia
Vietnam
Brunei
Cambodia
Singapore
Laos
Thailand
Malaysia
Burma
Indonesia
Bangladesh
Nepal
India
CIS
Afghanistan
Pakistan
U.A.E.
Iran
Qatar
Oman
Bahrain
Kuwait
Iraq
Saudi Arabia
Turkey
Syria
Lebanon
Jordan
Israel
Egypt

EXHIBIT 3

Northern Footprint	Southern Footprint
Bhutan	Afghanistan
China (P.R.C.)	Bahrain
*Hong Kong	Bangladesh
Japan	Brunei
Macau	Burma (Myanmar)
Mongolia	Cambodia
Nepal	Cyprus
North Korea	Egypt
*Philippines	*India
Soviet Union	*Indonesia
*South Korea	Iran
*Taiwan (R.O.C.)	Iraq
	Israel
	Jordan
	Kuwait
	Laos
	Lebanon
	*Malaysia
	Oman
	*Pakistan
	Qatar
	Saudi Arabia
	*Singapore
	Sri Lanka
	Syria
	*Thailand
	Turkey
	U.A.E.
	Vietnam

*An asterisk is placed before the 10 primary targeted markets.

and political differences among so diverse an audience. STAR had the choice of trying to tailor its programming to specific local audiences or adopting a regional strategy appealing across the linguistic and cultural divisions. It chose the latter, a Pan-Asian strategy targeted demographically at the wealthiest 5% of the population. This group, rich and cosmopolitan and international, would be an appealing audience for advertisers.

Programming. STAR's concept was to broadcast in both English and Chinese. Producing its own programming did not appear attractive: it involved enormous costs, a long lead-time, and lots of experience, which the company did not have. Ready-made programming was the other option. To keep down start-up costs, alliances with program suppliers (revenue or profit-sharing agreements) were sought. Many Western program makers were initially unenthusiastic. They were worried in part by the copyright violations associated with parts of Asia, where copyright laws were often weak or poorly enforced and piracy was widespread and sophisticated. Some producers were already planning alternative routes into the Asian market. Most were hesitant to commit to an untested product. But finally STAR was able to put together a package of programming.

Each channel was an independent company, with STAR TV itself acting as a holding company and providing technical, administrative, and marketing services. The channels STAR offered in 1993 were the following:

News: BBC World Service Television. An offshoot of the British Broadcasting Corporation's World Service radio. A straight buy-in rather than a joint venture, it was expensive (about £10 million per year), and the BBC kept complete editorial control, but the BBC's prestige and existing popularity in places such as India and Hong Kong had been important in establishing credibility with both viewers and advertisers.

Sports: Prime Sports. A profit-sharing joint venture with Prime Network, a Denver-based partnership, which gave STAR access to a wide variety of sports shows and events.

Chinese-language: *The Mandarin Channel.* A joint venture with Asian Television Ltd., which took a 30% profit share in return for Chinese-language programming. ATV had the option to drop out if revenues were less than 85% of projections.

Music: *MTV.* A revenue-sharing arrangement with America's Music Television Company. It was more of a franchise—STAR "Asianised" the channel with local presenters and much more local music such as Mandarin love songs, but used the well-known MTV name and image.

General Entertainment: *STAR Plus.* Because STAR could not find a suitable partner, it decided to produce its own channel by purchasing and packaging individual shows. Dated American soap operas were a fruitful source of cheap and surprisingly popular programming.

Hindi-language: *Zee TV.* Zee TV, a production company created by a group of nonresident Indians, it leased transponder space from STAR in a "condo in space" type of arrangement (reportedly for about (£15 million for five years). Attempts by STAR to set up a joint venture foundered. Nonetheless, Zee's presence was a valuable way for STAR to attract Indian viewers to its satellite, and thus to the other channels.

Free-to-Air versus Pay-TV. A major dilemma was how to make money, by advertising or by subscriptions. Conventionally a Western cable company would expect a revenue breakdown of 60% subscriptions and 40% advertising. No satellite or cable company had ever made money solely from advertising.

Yet, pay-TV presented considerable difficulties. The lack of any legal or technical infrastructure in much of the region, added to STAR's total lack of organization outside Hong Kong, would make collecting revenues and monitoring and enforcing compliance difficult or impossible. It would take time and money to establish a local presence, and in countries where redistribution of nonauthorized TV was illegal, it would be impossible. Currency conversion would often be tricky. Faced with these problems STAR opted for a free-to-air strategy in which it would broadcast unscrambled, and anyone could tune in.

Advertising. The Pan-Asian elite-focused programming strategy was pitched especially at international advertisers of luxury goods. It offered a precisely targeted, fast-growing and wealthy audience. Television had proved to be a powerful advertising medium in America and Europe, and it offered a cheap way to penetrate the exciting new markets of Asia. CPM (Cost per thousand) rates were projected at about $10, much lower than those using international print media. (*Fortune's* CPM was $184, *Time's* $116.) Satellite also offered a way to evade certain local advertising restrictions.

But advertisers were very reluctant to commit themselves. The enormous diversity of the audience made it unimaginable that a programming strategy could be found to appeal to everyone, and Asia was littered with stories of advertising ventures that had ended in disaster because of unforeseen cultural sensitivities. The second objection was that the project was totally untested. Validated viewing figures were the currency of television advertising. STAR did not have any. Moreover, the logistics of collecting reliable viewing figures would still be problematic, even after broadcasting started, because the organizations to collect such statistics were as yet nonexistent in most countries. Finally, the Pan-Asian strategy cut across the "country manager" structure of many multinational advertisers. Marketing was usually a key responsibility of local country managers, and many were reluctant to have their autonomy undermined.

To help attract advertisers, STAR offered heavily discounted "trial rates." Founding advertisers could lock in CPMs of $5 for two years. As viewership grew, CPMs were projected to fall further. Warrants (one quarter of 1% of the equity in HutchVision) were offered to early advertisers. There were 60 advertisers committed at the launch. (See Exhibit 4.)

Distribution Hurdles. Even broadcasting free-to-air, there were distribution problems. Viewers would need to buy a reception dish costing around $1,000 to $3,000, (and up to $10,000). Then there was the question of who would produce and sell the dishes. Manufacturing might present fewer problems, because almost all of the requisite components were already manufactured in Asia for export. The retail network would have to be

---

EXHIBIT 4 List of Advertisers on STAR TV as of December 1, 1991

San Francisco Academy of Arts	Mandarin Singapore Hotel
Ambassador Hotel	MasterCard International
Bank of China Group	Merrill Lynch
Banque Paribas	Mitsui & Company
Brand's Essence of Chicken	Mitsubishi Electric (HK)
Canadian Imperial Bank of Commerce	Mobil Oil
Cathay Pacific Airways	Movado Watch
Chase Manhattan Bank	Nike International Ltd.
China Resources Holdings	Nishimatsu Construction
Citibank	Pioneer
Dao Heng Bank	Remy Nicholas
Durffee Watch	Satchi Leather Products
Forum Restaurant	Shell Oil
Giordano Fashions	Sumitomo Electric
Goldlion Fashions (Far East)	Swatch Watch
Hennessy XO	Tse Sui Luen Jewellery
Hong Kong Bank	Volvo
Jùvenia Watch	Watson's Distilled Water
Kowloon Panda Hotel	Yoahan International
Levi Strauss (Far East)	Yue Hwa
Lippo Group	

---

developed from scratch, however. In addition, redistributors would need technical advice and support.

The possibility of redistribution raised another dilemma. If the service was free-to-air, then redistributors (legal or illegal) could get STAR's programming for no charge, but charge subscribers for it. If redistribution was not controlled STAR would lose control of its product, and its audience would be cannibalized. Problems such as deterioration of picture quality could go unchecked. It also might be harder to introduce a pay-TV service later on in the absence of a large base of committed TVRO viewers. Trying legally to control redistributors would be difficult in some countries.

On the other hand, redistribution might help to expand the viewer base (although STAR's advertising strategy emphasized quality rather than quantity of viewership). Still, many at STAR were of the opinion that redistribution would be impossible to stop, but would result in more viewers and should therefore be encouraged or tolerated.

Regulatory Hurdles. There were three levels of regulation. As an international satellite broadcaster, STAR would come under the regulations of the United Nations–sponsored International Telecommunications Union, which could be satisfied fairly straightforwardly by providing a "point-to-point" service between an uplink and a downlink. Next would come the regulations from its home base, Hong Kong, although STAR could avoid these by choosing to site the uplink facility elsewhere. (Thailand was considered as an alternative.) Last were the different national regulations. Private satellite TV broadcasting and private ownership of dishes were illegal in some countries (e.g., South Korea, Singapore). The status in other countries was unclear. Many governments had strict regulations on program content or advertising. On the one hand, there was not much that national regulators could do to prevent STAR from broadcasting whatever it wanted. On the other hand, antagonistic governments could cause problems: a hostile government could, for instance, ban the sale of reception dishes and effectively keep STAR out of its country.

STAR thus faced another dilemma: Should it attempt simultaneously to satisfy the programming restrictions of each country in the footprint? To do so would drastically reduce its programming options. Not to do so would risk retaliation and the possibility of losing entire countries full of viewers.

Economics. STAR commissioned Price Waterhouse Management Consultants to estimate both the potential viewership of a satellite TV service and the likely advertising revenues that could be expected. With so many unknowns, the study could provide only very crude estimates of potential viewership and advertising revenue, but it was intended to give some baseline numbers on which to make projections.

Potential Audience. Price Waterhouse took a number of approaches towards estimating potential viewing figures, modelling likely satellite dish ownership as a function of both income and video-cassette recorder (VCR) ownership. Their best and most conservative estimate, based on the VCR approach, was that viewership would be close to two million after one year of broadcasting, four million after two years, and about 18 million after ten years. (See Exhibits 5 and 6.)

In addition, STAR commissioned a series of focus group studies in three different Asian countries to gauge qualitatively the level of interest in satellite TV.[5] The studies generally revealed that among wealthy households, there was dissatisfaction with existing TV and strong interest in satellite TV.

Potential Costs and Revenues. Accurate financial projections were very difficult to make in this new and completely untested market. STAR was able to form only very rough estimates of probable costs and revenues.

_____

[5]These focus group discussion studies were conducted by Frank Small and Associates in Taiwan, Thailand, and South Korea, July–August 1990.

Costs could be on the order of $80 million for the first full year of operation. Of this amount, the largest single component would be programming costs, accounting for about half of the total. Costs could be expected to rise to perhaps $90 to $100 million by the third or fourth year—more if programming costs increased dramatically. Revenues could be estimated by making assumptions about total advertising in the 10 target countries and by further assumptions about the proportion of that total that could be captured by satellite television and how much of this amount that in turn could be captured by STAR. As a rough guide, satellite television could be expected to capture anything from 0.5% to 1.5% of total advertising spending in the region by the third or fourth year of operations. At a conservative estimate, STAR could win from 20% to 40% of this satellite television advertising.

From such assumptions and from using what data were available, potential revenues could be put on the order of $50 million to $100 million by the third year of operations and up to $150 million by the fourth. Thereafter, the upside potential was enormous, with revenues potentially rising to about $500 million by the year 2000. STAR could thus expect to be breaking even or in profit by the third or fourth year of operations.

Launch

Star's purchase and launch of the AsiaSat 1 satellite had been accomplished for about $120 million. The Hong Kong Government had granted a license to broadcast in late 1990. Following months of frenetic activity, a preview channel began broadcasting in April 1991. By December of that year, STAR was fully operational. Zee TV was launched in 1992. The original team of seven grew rapidly to about 700 in 1993.

Potential viewers were blitzed with an intense consumer awareness campaign. Once broadcasting began, program listings were widely distributed. With an 800,000 circulation, STAR's listings guide claimed to be the largest English-language publication in Asia. STAR used local entrepreneurs to boost circulation by providing free program

EXHIBIT 5   Potential Viewing Households

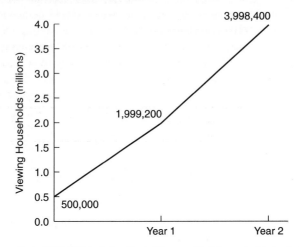

- Of the more than 4,350,000 existing "satellite capable" households in Asia (source: Business International and multinational advertising agencies), it is projected that 500,000 will be capable and willing to view STAR TV programs from day one of broadcasting
- Strong correlation between viewers' motivation to purchase VCRs and satellite dishes
- Within one year, 15 percent of current VCR-owning households in ten target countries (total: 13,328,000 households, source: Price Waterhouse) will have access to the STAR TV satellite television service
- Within two years, 30 percent of current VCR-owning households in ten target countries (total: 13,328,000 households, source: Price Waterhouse) will have access to the STAR TV satellite television service
- Projections do not include methods of program redistribution

information to local publishers. Hotels were especially targeted in order to reach the well-travelled business classes directly.

Developments Postlaunch

Growth in Viewership.   Viewing figures wildly exceeded expectations, as shown in Exhibit 7. One of the many surprises was STAR's enormous popularity in India and mainland China. Another was the depth of penetration it had achieved in certain markets, most notably Taiwan and Israel. Average incomes of STAR viewers were about 40% higher than the average in both Hong Kong and India. In Taiwan, because STAR reached more than 50% of the population, viewers had average incomes that were only 7% higher than normal.

Richard Li later remarked:

One of our biggest surprises was Indonesia. We had expected to do better there because our secondary research told us that there were already a lot of individuals with satellite dishes. But we didn't do well there. We were also genuinely surprised by our success in India, which we had discounted at first. In some ways, the total liberalization of satellite dishes was bad for us because it discouraged the cable operators.

Redistribution.   The extent of redistribution was the greatest surprise of all. STAR had expected most

EXHIBIT 6

Income Approach
Total Number of Satellite Capable Households ('000)

	Taiwan	Hong Kong	South Korea	Singapore	Indonesia	Thailand	Malaysia	Philippines	India	Pakistan	Total	Total Excludes India
1990	0	0	0	0	0.00	0.00	0	0	0	0	0	0
1991	270	131	432	46	37.99	59.49	30	16	584	0	1,608	1,023
1992	806	384	1,258	136	77.49	126.13	62	40	1,069	0	3,959	2,890
1993	1,631	696	2,880	254	128.21	264.21	125	94	1,931	1	8,004	6,074
1994	2,473	961	4,887	363	298.05	514.12	236	171	3,399	2	13,305	9,906
1995	3,203	1,121	6,673	434	474.77	923.24	412	335	5,779	3	19,360	13,581
1996	3,676	1,207	8,032	475	806.37	1,498.28	642	512	9,430	5	26,285	16,854
1997	3,963	1,268	8,938	504	1,079.15	2,179.42	883	597	14,377	8	33,796	19,419
1998	4,147	1,308	9,513	523	1,375.65	2,823.70	1,098	732	20,390	12	41,923	21,534
1999	4,287	1,346	9,944	543	1,832.85	3,355.91	1,290	812	26,773	16	50,201	23,427
2000	4,418	1,384	10,314	564	2,053.71	3,862.16	1,451	866	32,826	19	57,758	24,932

VCR Approach
Total Number of Satellite-Capable Households ('000)

	Taiwan	Hong Kong	South Korea	Singapore	Indonesia	Thailand	Malaysia	Philippines	India	Pakistan	Total
1990	0	0	0	0	0	0	0	0	0	0	0
1991	142	60	107	27	67	109	59	47	73	17	707
1992	349	147	264	66	164	269	146	115	182	42	1,743
1993	775	326	589	147	364	601	328	256	409	95	3,888
1994	1,444	608	1,104	274	680	1,128	618	476	770	180	7,284
1995	2,167	914	1,666	413	1,022	1,703	938	713	1,167	274	10,977
1996	2,706	1,143	2,093	516	1,277	2,141	1,182	889	1,477	348	13,772
1997	3,029	1,280	2,356	578	1,431	2,411	1,336	993	1,675	396	15,485
1998	3,218	1,361	2,518	615	1,522	2,578	1,433	1,053	1,801	427	16,525
1999	3,344	1,414	2,632	641	1,583	2,695	1,503	1,091	1,892	451	17,246
2000	3,457	1,462	2,735	664	1,638	2,802	1,568	1,125	1,975	473	17,897

(continued)

EXHIBIT 6 (concluded)

Total Number of VCR Households ('000)

	Taiwan	Hong Kong	South Korea	Singapore	Indonesia	Thailand	Malaysia	Philippines	India	Pakistan	Total
1990	2,695	1,127	2,017	507	1,260	2,048	1,101	892	1,368	313	13,328
1991	2,765	1,159	2,081	521	1,295	2,116	1,143	915	1,424	327	13,748
1992	2,838	1,192	2,146	536	1,332	2,187	1,187	938	1,480	342	14,176
1993	2,911	1,224	2,214	551	1,368	2,258	1,232	961	1,536	357	14,612
1994	2,986	1,258	2,283	567	1,406	2,332	1,278	984	1,592	372	15,056
1995	3,061	1,291	2,354	583	1,444	2,406	1,325	1,008	1,648	388	15,508
1996	3,138	1,325	2,427	598	1,481	2,482	1,371	1,031	1,713	404	15,971
1997	3,216	1,359	2,502	614	1,519	2,560	1,418	1,054	1,778	420	16,441
1998	3,295	1,393	2,578	630	1,558	2,639	1,467	1,078	1,844	437	16,919
1999	3,375	1,427	2,656	647	1,598	2,720	1,516	1,101	1,909	455	17,404
2000	3,457	1,462	2,735	663	1,638	2,802	1,568	1,125	1,975	473	17,897

EXHIBIT 7   STAR TV Validated Viewing Figures by Household—Launch Date: ALL Five Channels Operational by December 1991

	January 1992	May 1992	January 1993	Penetration Rate STAR TV Homes as Percentage of Total Households
Taiwan	1,059,369	1,191,419	1,980,140	41%
India	412,500	1,282,500	3,300,500	17*
Israel	198,500	272,000	410,000	41
Hong Kong	116,925	154,459	306,837	19
Indonesia	14,335	14,335	36,211	< 1
Philippines		70,474	137,141	4
Pakistan		30,145	60,300	3
South Korea		18,945	18,945	6
China			4,800,000	3
Thailand			24,517	< 1
Saudi Arabia			200,000	NA
UAE			72,809	18
Kuwait			12,280	5
Total (number of households)	1,801,629	3,034,327	11,360,180	
Projections:	500,000		2,000,000)	
Hotel rooms	37,519	66,300	116,363	

*In selected urban areas over 500,000 population.

Source: Frank Small and Associates, State Statistical Office of China STAR TV.

of its audience would be in the Television Receive Only (TVRO) category, individual households using individually owned reception dishes. No one had foreseen the extent to which redistribution would take off. Yet by 1993, 80% to 90% of the audience was paying to receive a redistributed signal from CATV (cable) or SMATV operators.

Redistributors ranged widely in size and scope of operation. The region had a few large cable companies, serving thousands of subscribers. For these existing operators, STAR was quite literally a gift from the heavens. Where there were no existing redistribution channels, STAR had created a new business opportunity. Reception dishes were soon being "banged out" from scrap metal or nickel-painted concrete for as little as $100. Anyone who could afford a dish, a few hundred yards of cheap coaxial cable, and some connectors could pick up STAR's free broadcast and resell it. Such individual

entrepreneurs typically hooked up the TVs of a few neighbors, charging them a small subscription to retransmit STAR's signal. The economic and legal details varied, but the costs of entry (buying the reception and retransmission equipment) could be as low as $500, up to $2,000, or higher. Subscribers were charged whatever the market would bear: from approximately $2 per month in China to $5 in India and up to $100 in parts of the Middle East.

No one knew how many such operators there were—STAR estimated about 70,000, with about 15,000 "cable wallahs" in India alone. In China, an official ban on ownership of private satellite dishes was not enforced. There were an estimated 500,000 dishes sold in China in 1992, and by the end of that year there were about 1,400 cable systems operating.

STAR also entered rebroadcasting agreements with existing terrestrial stations in the Philippines,

Malaysia, Thailand, Egypt, and elsewhere, as an additional revenue source and a way of entering new markets.

Government Responses. Both Singapore and Malaysia banned the manufacture, sale, or import of reception equipment, effectively keeping STAR out. The Chinese government was known to be unhappy with the BBC but took no action. In some countries, including India, the growth of redistribution prompted governments to take steps to regularize the laws relating to TV redistribution.

Advertising. STAR found it increasingly easy to attract new advertisers. Richard Li declared, "In advertising, you can break every rule except one: your client has to see increased sales, and ours did."

As STAR's penetration into individual countries deepened beyond the target 5%, a new selling pitch took shape: the idea of deep penetration into specific markets. Its ad rates were often more attractive even than those of alternative national media. (Isracard, a charge card used exclusively in Israel, still found it worthwhile to advertise on STAR.) As a bonus, advertisers enjoyed automatic international exposure. Several companies advertising for a specific country found themselves inundated with export orders.

STAR began to customize its programming in order to back up the pitch stressing deep penetration of individual markets rather than its Pan-Asian appeal. That the footprint covered seven hours of time zones meant considerable room for programming flexibility based on the different tastes in different time zones. By 1993 it had increased the number of advertisers to 360. (See Exhibit 8.)

Competitor Responses. STAR's success created a gateway for competitors. It created a demand for TV and built a large—but not necessarily loyal—satellite-capable viewer base. The redistribution and legal infrastructure was stimulated and developed and the market attractiveness clearly demonstrated.

STAR still controlled AsiaSat 1, but more satellite capacity was coming. APT Satellite, a Chinese consortium, was planning to launch Apstar One with a footprint covering most of southeast Asia in mid-1994. Both AsiaSat 1 and APT were planning to launch second satellites in late 1994 or early 1995. In addition, many countries were planning either to launch or replace their own national satellites.

Many of these planned satellites would have greater capacity than AsiaSat 1. Additionally, digital compression technology, allowing about 10 channels to be squeezed onto a single transponder, was well advanced.[6] Finally BSkyB (the British company created by the merger of BSB and Sky TV) had developed advanced encryption technology to prevent pirating of scrambled satellite signals.

Cable systems were developing all over Asia. In Hong Kong, years of negotiations ended in February 1993, when Wharf Cable[7] was granted an exclusive license to establish a cable system covering the entire colony. Wharf, which was planning an initial service of 20 pay channels, to be operational by October 1993, aspired to service the fast developing Guangdong Province on the Chinese mainland. STAR was in negotiations over the rights to supply programming to the group and to provide pay-TV in the colony.

CNN, ESPN, and HBO had established pay-TV services, using encryption, on Indonesia's Palapa satellite in 1992. In addition, CNN was broadcasting from other satellites in the region. In February 1993 it had set up new bureaus in Bangkok and New Delhi to cope with its 6.9 million Asian subscribers, growing at 30% per year.

TVB had been developing a Chinese-focused strategy that was to include a "Superstation" capable of broadcasting terrestrially from Hong Kong to Taiwan and parts of mainland China. It was also making contact with 120 of the largest cable operators in Taiwan to negotiate a pay-TV satellite channel in Mandarin. As the largest producer of Chinese

---

[6]Raymond Snoddy, "Surfing Across the Screen," *Financial Times*, February 27, 1993.

[7]A consortium of the giant Hong Kong–based Wharf Group, the U.S. telephone company Nynex, and the media group United International Holdings.

EXHIBIT 8   Partial List of On-Air Advertisers on STAR TV as of December 18, 1992

Academy of Arts (San Francisco)
Adornica
Airfreight
Ambassador Hotel, Hong Kong
Amrut Distilleries
Aristocrat Marketing
Asia Financial Holdings
Associated Breweries
Australian Tourist Commission

Bajaj Auto
Bank of China Group
Banque Paribas
Benetton
Benzer Classics
Big Video Company
Bisleri Beverages
Bombay Dyeing & MFG Company
Borosil Glass Works
Brand's Essence of Chicken
British Airways
Brooke Bond India
Business Week International

Cadbury Chocolates
Canadian Imperial Bank of
   Commerce
Castrol
Ceat Tyres
Chee Shing Foundation Company
China Resources Holdings
China Travel Service
CIBA Vision Taiwan Company
Citibank
Clorets
Colgate-Palmolive
Complan
Consolidated Footwear

Da Ka Yuen
Dean-Jiang Record Company
Dey's Medical Stores
Dukes & Sons
Durffee Watches

E.M.A. Lubricants
Emirates Airlines
Evergo

Far Eastern Economic Review
Ferrero Chocolates
Ford Cars
Fu Hui Jewelry

G-2000 Apparel
Giordano Fashions
Goldlion Fashions
Goldman Sachs Asia
Gramaphone Company of India
Gulf Air

Hasmukhrai & Company
Hennessy
Hero Cycles
Hey-Song Corporation
Hindustan Lever
Holiday Inn Crowne Plaza
Hong Kong Bank
Hutchison AT&T Network
   Services

ICI Dulux Paint Asia Pacific
International Herald Tribune
Isracard

J.K. Helene Curtis
Jiannanchun Wine
Juvenia Watches

K-Swiss
Kinetic Engineering
Kong Wah Holdings
Kraft Foods
Kymco Motorcycle

L & S Synthetics
Lakme
Levi Strauss
Lexus Cars
Lippo Group
Lotte Ice Cream
Lucky Enterprises Corporation

M/S Racold Appliances
Malaysia Airlines
Maria's Bakery Company
Martell
McDowells Whisky
Mercuries Department Store

Metro Shoes
Milkfood
Mitsubishi Corporation
Mitsubishi Heavy Industries
Mitsui & Company
Motorola
MRF Tyres

NEC
Netlon India
Newsweek International
Nice Group
Nikko Securities
Nishimatsu Construction Company
Nissan Motors
Northwest Airlines

Omega Watches
Optonica VCR
Otard Cognac

Pak Fah Yeow
Pan Pacific Hotel, Singapore
Parfums Christian Dior
Pepsi-Cola
Peugeot Cars
Philips Electric
Polaroid
Pro Sport Agency

Quanxing Distillery

Raffles Hotel, Singapore
Raymonds Woolen
Recon Enterprises
Remy Nicholas Fine Wines
Rivon Food
Rolex Watches
Rosa Food
Rover Cars
Royal Cliff Beach Resort, Thailand
Royal Pacific Hotel, Hong Kong

Sampo Corporation
Samsung Refrigerator
Sanyo Electric Trading
Sha-ger Record
Shaw Wallace & Company
Sheng Di Property

(continued)

EXHIBIT 8 *(concluded)*

Sichuan Tou Pai Distillery	Titan Watches	United Distillers
Singapore Tourist Promotion	Tokyo Electric	Vitalon Foods
Board	Toys R' Us	VXL India
Siyaram Silk Mills	Tribhovandas Bhimji Zaveri	Watsons Chemist Taiwan
Sony Corporation	TTK Pharma	Weekender
Standard Chartered Bank	Two Girls	Weston Hotels & Resorts
Sun Chlorella	Ube Industries	Wipro
Swatch Watches	UIP International Services	
Swiss-Hao Company	UNI Foods	Yaohan International
		Yuh Cheng Construction
Taiwan Tourism Bureau	Unisys Computers	Company
Time Magazine	United Airlines	

language programming, with an immense library (100,000 hours) of dramas and films, TVB was potentially a formidable competitor.

In June 1993, came the shocking news of News Corporation's agreed purchase of 23% of TVB, at a cost of $385 million. The marriage of News Corporation's satellite TV experience and film and television programming with TVB's domination of Chinese-language programming would create what Rupert Murdoch described as "the premier Asian [television] company."[8] Two weeks later, though, the deal was dropped. Under Hong Kong law, foreign corporations were limited to a 10% stake in a TV broadcaster. News Corporation had sought an exemption unsuccessfully.

Later in June 1993, TVB announced the creation of the "Gang of Five"—a consortium consisting of TVB International, HBO Asia, CNN International, ESPN Asia, and Australian Television International (ATVI).[9] It had jointly leased space on the Apstar 1 satellite, due for launch in mid-1994. For the time being, the consortium would broadcast from Palapa. The package was a direct threat to STAR, for as TVB's S.K. Fong remarked, in the television industry, "Product is where you win or lose the war, and we've got it."[10] If programming was ammunition, he derided STAR as "a gun with no bullets."

Another kind of threat came at the national level, with improvements in the quality of existing terrestrial and government stations. The response of the Indian government was most striking. It planned to privatize the Doordarshan (state broadcaster) and was attempting to boost its attractiveness with a sustained effort to improve programming, (for instance by buying the hit American series "Dallas"). In 1993, the Indian Parliament was even considering its own satellite television venture and planned to broadcast three channels from a foreign satellite. In discussions about the legalization and rationalization of cable operators, Parliament debated a requirement that all cable redistributors carry at least one Doordarshan channel.

STAR was apparently unconcerned. One executive quoted a Chinese proverb that "In business, the one who goes first is a genius; the one who goes second is a fool." STAR claimed some first-mover

---

[8] *Financial Times,* June 17, 1993.

[9] Cable News Network (CNN), a U.S. 24-hour news service controlled by Turner Broadcasting Systems with revenues from subscriptions and advertising; ESPN, a U.S. sports channel. Home Box Office (HBO) Asia, a Movie channel; a joint venture between Time Warner and Paramount Communications with revenues solely from subscriptions; and Australian Television International, an arm of Australian Television, the government broadcaster.

---

[10] Jonathan Karp, "Catch a Rising STAR," *Far East Economic Review,* August 5, 1993.

advantages, including extensive name recognition and considerable viewer loyalty based in part on simple inertia: most reception dishes in use in the region, especially the cheapest ones, could be tuned to pick up signals from only one satellite at a time. Returning to a different satellite was usually technically and physically difficult and sometimes impossible. A rival satellite package would need to offer extremely attractive programming to induce viewers away from AsiaSat 1. In addition, STAR had locked in several years of programming from its existing suppliers. Finally, rivals such as the "Gang" would be likely to face other difficulties such as internal competition for the best time slots.

Issues

A central issue for STAR was negative cash flow. The fixed costs of running such a technologically sophisticated operation were high. Rapid growth in organization size and in employees had added further costs. Although advertising revenues were improving with both rates and numbers of advertisers increasing, they did not yet cover those costs. Reports put losses at anywhere between $1 million and $5 million per week. By the spring of 1993, it was clear that the issue of raising revenues must be addressed.

Moving to Pay-TV

Introducing pay-TV was the most obvious option. In Europe both SES and BSkyB, Rupert Murdoch's newly-merged satellite venture, were becoming successful. The model for satellite TV revenues was about 80% subscription and 20% advertising. In America, the cable companies all charged viewer fees, with a 60:40 fee-to-advertising-revenue split being typical.

Digital compression technology, which would allow about 10 times as many channels to be broadcast from the same satellite, had improved to the point that it was commercially viable. STAR, which had been testing the technology since late 1992 and made a considerable investment in it, thought it was technically possible to be broadcasting up to 180

channels by 1995. Another technological advance was the development of cheaper decoding boxes. In 1992, a digital decoder box cost about $2,000. By 1993, STAR had a deal with a supplier to provide them at about $400.

However, there were still considerable logistical and legal hurdles to be overcome before pay-TV could be made feasible. Piracy and illegal redistribution were still major problems. As well as reducing STAR's revenues, piracy would deter outside producers, especially movie studios, from releasing their most popular and newest programs to STAR. The organization required to monitor broadcasting in more than 38 separate countries with 70,000 legal and illegal redistributors and 45 million viewers would be immense—thousands of people would be needed in advance of any increase in revenues.

If STAR was to adopt pay-TV, it seemed likely that it would have to work with the burgeoning network of redistributors rather than directly with individual viewers. The regulatory environment in many countries, including Taiwan and India, was maturing toward recognition of the redistributors, which would make it easier to contract with them. STAR had established contact with the largest ones already. One approach could be to try to drive the rationalization of cable operators in each country by selecting specific large operators and giving them enhanced programming for a price—perhaps a fixed monthly fee, regardless of how many subscribers they had connected. Selected redistributors would then have an advantage, which might enable them to absorb smaller rivals.

However, there was considerable debate within the company about the wisdom of shifting to pay-TV. Obviously, a major cause of STAR's rapid viewer growth was the entrepreneurial activity of the small redistributors who had sprung up all over Asia. The free-to-air service played into the entrepreneurial spirit by creating a profit opportunity that many individuals had seized. Charging for the service would blunt this spirit and risk killing the engine of new viewer growth. As long as STAR relied primarily on advertising, high viewing numbers were essential, and introducing pay-TV at the expense of the free-to-air service would be counterproductive.

Improving Programming

The other way to increase revenues was through more advertisers, which could be attracted either by higher viewing figures or by greater propensities to view. Both would require improvements in the quality and relevance of STAR's programming, a need which was being made more acute by the "boredom factor" afflicting the increasingly sophisticated and demanding viewers.

Another issue was the continued viability of the regional programming strategy. The deep penetration that STAR had achieved in markets such as Taiwan, Israel, and certain urban areas of India meant that the audience was no longer the wealthy elite, but a much broader, less prosperous, and much more heterogenous group. These viewers presumably would prefer to watch programs in their own language and with content relevant to their own taste and experience. They would be a less appealing audience for international advertisers. With greater competition likely from both local terrestrial stations and rivals on other satellites targeting specific countries, it was possible that the Pan-Asian strategy could be seriously undercut. Should STAR attempt to customize its programming by offering channels to appeal to specific countries or language groups? If so, how?

STAR thus faced two programming dilemmas: how to raise quality, and whether to switch from a Pan-Asian strategy to a more customized one in which it would target individual countries with individual channels.

One way for STAR to address these issues would be to increase its degree of vertical integration in production. Already, it was doing most of the production of MTV-Asia and the packaging for STAR Plus. Costs would increase in the short term, and it would be months or even years before it could build a critical mass of programming, but these were less crucial issues now than during the prelaunch phase.

STAR estimated that to build its own production facilities would cost about $150 million, plus the costs of hiring skilled staff. The cost of a drama series was between $50,000 and $150,000 per episode. Coproduction with Japanese and Chinese studios, already being done for STAR Plus, was a cheaper alternative.

Another way for STAR to acquire high-quality programming was through alliances. Its sister company, Media Assets Ltd., had acquired the rights to Chinese-language programming from the Hong Kong–based Golden Harvest Group, a relatively small film producer. STAR's management was also in talks with several program suppliers, including many big Hollywood studios. The company had memoranda of understanding with Walt Disney studios, MCA International, Columbia/TriStar International, and Metro Goldwyn Mayer. It was discussing a business channel with CNBC of the United States, Pearson Plc of Great Britain, and Mitsui and Co. of Japan.

Partnership?

Complicating the decisions STAR faced were the advances of a number of potential partners, at least some of which wanted control of the company. According to press reports, STAR had already been approached by two international media groups, Pearson Plc and News Corporation, and was in negotiations with them. It was also reportedly in serious talks with three other interested parties. Both Pearson and News were interested, ultimately, in a controlling equity stake.

Pearson Plc

Pearson was an extremely diversified group, with interests including publishing and media, entertainment, banking, fine china, and oil services. Publishing interests included the Financial Times Group and *The Economist.* Entertainment interests included a 17.5% stake in BSkyB (the British satellite television company formed by the merger of BSB and Sky TV) and a 14% stake in Yorkshire

Tyne Tees (a small U.K. television company). In April 1993, Pearson acquired Thames Television, a major British television producer, which held a 10% stake in the European Astra satellite. The only common thread to this patchwork of holdings was quality: each business was a leader in its field. Pearson adopted a conservative and hands-off approach towards its various managers.

An alliance with STAR TV would be a tremendous boost to Pearson's aspirations to become a major media player. What Pearson could bring to such a venture included its satellite TV experience BSB and then BSkyB, a supply of top-quality English-language TV programming, the possibility of an educational channel through its educational publishing interests, and input for a business news channel through the *Financial Times* and *The Economist*. STAR was already talking to Thames about securing programming. Money would not be a problem for Pearson, especially because the group was planning to raise about $900 million through the sale of its oil and china divisions.

It was rumored that Pearson, during talks with STAR, had offered up to $300 million for roughly a one-third stake, but would prefer to control up to 70%. It reportedly wanted the company to remain private and was very anxious that the Li family agree to retain at least a minority share for several years to come. With little experience in Asia and with Hong Kong due to revert to Communist Chinese rule in 1997, Pearson apparently wanted to lock in the family's local influence.

News Corporation[11]

News Corporation had its origins in Australia and owned the world's largest and most extensive collection of newspaper holdings, with more than 100 newspapers and a combined weekly circulation of more than 60 million. Hands-on management, operating efficiencies (often involving extensive staff

layoffs) and a commitment to high technology characterized News Corporation's publishing style. Sensationalism was said to be a key factor in the success of its many newspapers.

Television interests included the Seven Network in Australia and a 50% holding in BSkyB, whose success could be attributed partly to the successful development of a cheap and secure digital encryption system (Videocrypt), over which News Corporation exercised proprietary control. In the United States, the company controlled the movie studio 20th Century Fox and the Fox Television network. Murdoch was also considering a cable television service in South America and expansion of the pay-TV satellite service in Europe, with German- and Spanish-language channels.

News Corporation's aggressive acquisition strategy had been based on extraordinarily high leverage, which went sour in 1990. The company almost collapsed under debts exceeding $7 billion. Extensive restructuring followed, and by 1993, it was restored to financial health and back on the expansion trail.

Rupert Murdoch's strategy was to become a truly international media giant, controlling both software and distribution. A global distribution network would provide enormous economies of scale by greatly leveraging the earnings for company programming. Asia was the big gap in the distribution network, and STAR was therefore an attractive prize. From STAR's point of view, the chief attractions of a partnership with News Corporation were the wealth of popular programming from Fox TV and the 20th Century Fox film library, and the satellite TV experience gained at BSkyB. The legal restrictions on foreign ownership which had stymied News Corporation's bid for TVB did not apply because STAR was regulated as a telecommunications rather than a television company by the Hong Kong authorities. There were, however, disadvantages of a deal with News Corporation. Murdoch wanted control. He was never comfortable when not in charge of a project. His hands-on management, outspoken style, and

[11]This section draws on "BSB versus Sky Television," HBS case No. 794-031.

confrontational tactics were not always popular and might not be suitable in politically sensitive countries.

What to Do?

STAR TV was at a crossroads. The service was enormously popular, but it was losing money fast. New competitors and increases in satellite capacity threatened to undercut STAR's lead. Richard Li somehow had to raise revenues and defend his competitive position. Pay-TV and greater in-house production were two possible strategies. Both might involve an alliance of some sort. Complicating these decisions were the attentions of up to five would-be partners. If an alliance was necessary, the choice of partner was not obvious. News Corporation, for example, offered more and better programming, greater satellite TV experience than did, say, Pearson. On the other hand, it reportedly was not the highest bidder. Moreover, the benefits of a deal with News Corporation could come at the price of giving up managerial control. If Richard Li wanted to keep control of STAR, then Pearson or one of the others, could be a better choice.

Reading 4–1

THE GLOBAL LOGIC OF STRATEGIC ALLIANCES

Kenichi Ohmae

Companies are just beginning to learn what nations have always known: in a complex, uncertain world filled with dangerous opponents, it is best not to go it alone. Great powers operating across broad theaters of engagement have traditionally made common cause with others whose interests ran parallel with their own. No shame in that. Entente—the striking of an alliance—is a responsible part of every good strategist's repertoire. In today's competitive environment, this is also true for corporate managers.

But managers have been slow to experiment with genuinely strategic alliances. A joint venture here and there, yes, of course. A long-term contractual relationship, certainly. But the forging of entente,

Reprinted by permission of *Harvard Business Review.* "The Global Logic of Strategic Alliances" by Kenichi Ohmae, (March/April 1989).

Copyright © 1989 by the President and Fellows of Harvard College; all rights reserved.

rarely. A real alliance compromises the fundamental independence of economic actors, and managers don't like that. After all, for them, management has come to mean total control. Alliances mean sharing control. The one precludes the other.

In stable competitive environments, this allergy to loss of control exacts little penalty. Not so, however, in a changeable world of rapidly globalizing markets and industries—a world of converging consumer tastes, rapidly spreading technology, escalating fixed costs, and growing protectionism. I'd go further. Globalization mandates alliances, makes them absolutely essential to strategy. Uncomfortable, perhaps—but that's the way it is. Like it or not, the simultaneous developments that go under the name of globalization make alliances—entente—necessary.

Why, then, the reluctance of so many companies either to experiment with alliances or to stick with them long enough to learn how to make them work? To some extent, both foot dragging and early exit are born of fear—fear that the alliance will turn out to be a Trojan horse that affords potential competitors easy access to home markets. But there is also an impression that alliances represent, at best, a convenience, a quick-and-dirty means of entry into foreign markets. These attitudes make managers skittish and impatient.

Unless you understand the long-run strategic value of entente, you will grow frustrated when it proves—as it must—not to be a cheap and easy way of responding to the uncertainties of globalization. If you expect more of your partners than is reasonable, you will blame them too quickly when things do not go as planned. Chances are your impatience will make you much less tolerant of them than you would be of your own subsidiary overseas.

When you expect convenience, you rarely have much patience for the messy and demanding work of building a strong competitive position. Nor do you remember all the up-front overseas investments that you did *not* have to make. And without memory or patience, you risk precipitating exactly what you fear most: an unhappy or unsatisfied partner that decides to bow out of the alliance and try to tackle your markets on its own.

Alliances are not tools of convenience. They are important, even critical, instruments of serving customers in a global environment. Glaxo, the British pharmaceutical company, for example, did not want to establish a full business system in each country where it did business. Especially given its costly commitment to topflight R&D, it did not see how it could—or why it should—build an extensive sales and service network to cover all the hospitals in Japan and the United States. So it decided to link up with first-class partners in Japan, swap its best drugs with them, and focus its own resources on generating greater sales from its established network in Europe. *That* kind of value creation and delivery is what alliances make possible.

Few companies operating in the Triad of Japan, the United States, and Europe can offer such topflight levels of value to all their customers all the time all by themselves. They need partners. They

need entente. They might wish things were otherwise. But deep down they know better. Or they should.

The Californiaization of Need

To understand why alliances are a necessity and not just a fad or a fashion, you first have to understand *why* globalization makes them essential as vehicles for customer-oriented value.

The explanation begins with a central, demonstrable fact: the convergence of consumer needs and preferences. Whatever their nationality, consumers in the Triad increasingly receive the same information, seek the same kinds of life-styles, and desire the same kinds of products. They all want the best products available, at the lowest prices possible. Everyone, in a sense, wants to live—and shop—in California.

Economic nationalism flourishes during election campaigns and infects what legislatures do and what particular interest groups ask for. But when individuals vote with their pocketbooks—when they walk into a store or showroom anywhere in the Triad—they leave behind the rhetoric and the mudslinging and the trappings of nationalism.

Do you write with a Waterman or a Mont Blanc pen or travel with a Vuitton suitcase because of national sentiments? Of course not. It does not matter if you live in Europe or Japan or the United States. You buy these pens or pieces of luggage because they represent the kind of value that you're looking for.

At the cash register, you don't care about country of origin or country of residence. You don't think about employment figures or trade deficits. You don't worry about where the product was made. It does not matter to you that a "British" sneaker by Reebok (now an American-owned company) was made in Korea, a German sneaker by Adidas in Taiwan, or a French ski by Rossignol in Spain. All you care about is the product's quality, price, design, value, and appeal to you as a customer.

This is just as true for industrial customers. The market for IBM computers or Toshiba laptops is not defined by geographic borders but by the inherent appeal of the product to users, regardless of where they live. And with the proliferation of trade journals, trade shows, and electronic databases, users have regular access to the same sources of product information.

Chip makers buy Nikon steppers because they are the best, not because they are made by a Japanese company. Manufacturers buy Tralfa industrial robots for the same reason and not because they happen to be Norwegian. The same goes for robots made by De Vilbiss in the United States. Companies around the world use IBM's MRP and CIM systems to shorten production times and cut work-in-process. Because of the demands of contemporary production modes, they use Fujitsu Fanuc's machine tools made in Japan. In fact, this one company dominates the numerically controlled (NC) machine-tool market worldwide: its market share in Japan is 70%; around the globe, 50%. This is neither accident nor fashion. These NC machines deliver value, and everyone knows it. But the national identity of these products has effectively disappeared.

The Dispersion of Technology

Today's products rely on so many different critical technologies that most companies can no longer maintain cutting-edge sophistication in all of them. The business software that made IBM PCs such an instant hit—1–2–3—was not, of course, an IBM product. It was a creation of Lotus Development Corporation. Most of the components in the popular-priced IBM PC itself were outsourced as well. IBM simply could not have developed the machine in anywhere near the time it did if it had tried to keep it 100% proprietary. In fact, the heart of IBM's accomplishment with the PC lay precisely in its decision—and its ability—to approach the development effort as a process of managing multiple external vendors.

Lotus provided applications software, and Microsoft wrote the operating system on an Intel microprocessor. Of course, Lotus, Microsoft, and Intel don't want to sell only to IBM. Naturally, they want to sell their products to as wide a range of customers as possible. Just as IBM needs to rely on an army of external vendors, so each vendor needs to sell to a broad array of customers. The inevitable result is the rapid dispersion of technology. No one company can do it all, simultaneously. No one company can keep all relevant technologies in-house, as General Motors did during the 1930s and 1940s. And that means no one can truly keep all critical technologies out of the hands of competitors around the globe.

Even original equipment manufacturers with captive technology are not immune to this dispersion. NEC may develop a state-of-the-art memory chip for its own mainframes, but it can sell five times the volume to other computer makers. This generates cash, lowers unit costs, and builds up the experience needed to push the technology still further. It also gets them better information about its products: external customers provide tougher feedback than do internal divisions. To be a world-class producer, NEC must provide the best new technology to global customers.

In short order, the technology becomes generally available, making time even more of a critical element in global strategy. Nothing stays proprietary for long. And no one player can master everything. Thus, operating globally means operating with partners—and that in turn means a further spread of technology.

The Importance of Fixed Costs

The convergence of customer need, together with this relentless dispersion of technology, has changed the logic by which managers have to steer. In the past, for example, you tried to build sustainable competitive advantage by establishing dominance in all of your business system's critical areas. You created barriers to entry where you could, locked away market share whenever possible, and used every bit of proprietary expertise, every collection of nonreplicable assets to shore up the wall separating you from competitors. The name of the game in most industries was simply beating the competition. If you discovered an ounce of advantage, you strengthened it with a pound of proprietary skill or knowledge. Then you used it to support the defensive wall you were building against competitors.

The forces of globalization turn this logic on its head. You can't meet the value-based needs of customers in the Triad entirely on your own. You can't do without the technology and skills of others. You can't even keep your own technology to yourself for very long. Having a superior technology is important, of course, but it is not sufficient to guarantee success in the market. Meeting customer needs is the key—no matter what the source of the technology. No wall you erect stands tall. No door you slam stays shut. And no road you follow is inexpensive.

To compete in the global arena, you have to incur—and somehow find a way to defray—immense fixed costs. You can't play a variable-cost game anymore. You need partners who can help you amortize your fixed costs, and with them you need to define strategies that allow you to maximize the contribution to your fixed costs.

The evidence for this lesson is overwhelming. As automation has driven the labor content out of production, manufacturing has increasingly become a fixed-cost activity. And because the cost of developing breakthrough ideas and turning them into marketable products has skyrocketed, R&D has become a fixed cost too. In pharmaceuticals, for instance, when it takes $50 million or more to come up with an effective new drug, R&D is no longer a variable-cost game. And you can't count on being able to license a new drug—a variable cost—from companies not operating in your primary markets. Not unless you have your own proprietary drug to offer in return. With globalization, all major players in your industry are—or may become—direct competitors. You can't be sure in advance that they (or you) will want to share a particular piece of technology. You need partners, but you need your own people and your own labs too. That's fixed cost.

In much the same way, building and maintaining a brand name is a fixed cost. For many products, a brand name has no value at all if brand recognition falls below certain levels. When a company decides to buy a paper copier, for example, it usually calls up two or three producers in the order of their brand familiarity. If your copier is not among them, you don't even get a chance to try to sell your product. You simply *have* to be there to enjoy a high level of awareness among customers. And that means you have to pay for the privilege.

Trying to save money on brand promotion makes no sense if what you're selling is a consumer "pull" product: you spend a little money but not enough to realize any "pull" benefits. And a half-baked, half-supported brand is worse than no brand at all. With some products, you can better use the same money to enhance commissions so that the sales force will push them. In branded competition, if you want to play, you have to ante up the fixed costs of doing so.

The past decade has seen a comparable movement toward fixed costs in sales and distribution networks. Sure, you can try to play the variable-cost game by going through dealers. You can, at least, to an extent. But your sales force still has to provide the support, the training, and the manuals. And all these are fixed costs.

You can also try to make some of these costs variable on your own. You can chase low-cost labor, for example, by moving production to developing countries, but that won't get you very far these days. In the past, you could make costs variable with your computers and management information systems by time-sharing. But experience has shown that you can't use time-sharing if you want a system that's dedicated to your own needs, a system capable of providing competitive advantage. So today, information technology is pretty much a fixed cost. Over the long term, of course, all these fixed costs become variable through adjustments in investment (capital expenditure) levels. But for the short term, they remain fixed. And the need to bolster contribution to them points in a single, clear direction: toward the forging of alliances to share fixed costs.

This is a fundamental change from the competitive world of 15 or even 10 years ago. And it demands a new logic for management action. In a variable-cost environment, the primary focus for managers is on boosting profits by reducing the cost of materials, wages, labor hours. In a fixed-cost environment, the focus switches to maximizing marginal contribution to fixed cost—that is, to boosting sales.

This new logic forces managers to amortize their fixed costs over a much larger market base—and this adds yet more fuel to the drive toward globalization. It also forces managers to rethink their strategies as they search for ways to maximize contribution to these fixed costs. Finally, this logic mandates entente—alliances that both enable and facilitate global, contribution-based strategies.

In practice, this means that if you don't have to invest in your own overseas sales force, you don't do it. If you run a pharmaceutical company with a good drug to distribute in Japan but no sales force to do it, find someone in Japan who also has a good product but no sales force in your country. You get double the profit by putting two strong drugs through your fixed-cost sales network, and so does your new ally. Why duplicate such huge expenses all down the line? Why go head-to-head? Why not join forces to maximize contribution to each other's fixed costs?

Maximizing the contribution to fixed costs does not come naturally. Tradition and pride make companies want to be the best at everything, to do everything themselves. But companies can no longer afford this solitary stance. Take the machine-tool market. If a German manufacturer clearly excels in custom-made segments, why should highly automated Japanese producers like Mori Seiki and Yamazaki tackle those segments too? Why not tie up with the Germans and let them dominate those segments worldwide? Why not try to supply them with certain common components that you can make better—or more cheaply—than they do? Why not disaggregate the product and the business system and put together an alliance that delivers the most value to customers while making the greatest contribution to both partners' fixed costs?

Why not do this? Companyism gets in the way. So does a competitor-focused approach to strategy. So does not knowing what it takes to operate globally and how alliances help with fixed costs. Managers must overcome these obstacles. And that will not happen by chance.

Dangers of Equity

Global alliances are not the only valid mechanisms for boosting contribution to fixed costs. A strong brand umbrella can always cover additional products. You can always give heightened attention to, say, an expensive distribution system that you've already built in Japan or Europe. And there is always the possibility of buying a foreign company. Experience shows, however, that you should look hard—and early—at forging alliances. In a world of imperfect options, they are often the fastest, least risky, and most profitable way to go global.

You can expand brands and build up distribution yourself—you can do everything yourself—with enough time, money, and luck. But all three are in short supply. In particular, you simply do not have the time to establish new markets one-by-one throughout the Triad. The "cascade" model of expansion no longer works. Today you have to be in all important markets simultaneously if you are going to keep competitors from establishing their positions. Globalization will not wait. You need alliances and you need them now. But not the traditional kind.

In the past, companies commonly approached international expansion by doing it on their own, acquiring orders, or establishing joint ventures. Now, the latter two approaches carry important equity-related concerns. Let equity—the classic instrument of capitalism—into the picture, and you start to worry about control and return on investment. There is pressure to get money back fast for the money you put in and dividends from the paper you hold.

It's a reflex. The analysts expect it of you. So do the business press, colleagues, and stockholders. They'll nod politely when you talk about improved sales or long-term strategic benefits. But what everybody really wants in short order is chart-topping ROI.

No one's going to argue that dividends aren't nice to tuck in your pocket. Of course they are. But the pressure to put them there can wreak havoc with your initial goals, especially if they include competing successfully in global markets by maximizing the contribution to fixed costs.

Managers must also overcome the popular misconception that total control increases chances of success. Companies that have enjoyed successful joint ventures for years can have things quickly go sour when they move to a literal, equity- and contract-based mode of ownership. Naturally, details vary with the particular case, but the slide into disarray and disappointment usually starts with the typical arguments that broke up one transnational chemical joint venture.

(Soon-to-Be) New Owner:

You guys never make decisions on time.

(Soon-to-Be) Former Partner:

Speedy decisions are not everything. Consensus is more important.

NO:

Well, just tell the dealers that our products are the best in the world. Tell them that they sell everywhere except here.

FP:

But the dealers complain that your products are just okay, not great. Even worse, they are not really tailored to the needs or aesthetic preferences of local customers.

NO:

Nonsense. What customers buy, everywhere in the world, is the physical performance of the product. No one matches us in performance.

FP:

Perhaps. Still, the dealers report that your products are not neatly packaged and often have scratches on the surface.

NO:

But that has no effect on performance.

FP:

Tell that to the dealers. They say they cannot readily see—or sell—the performance difference you're talking about, so they have to fall back on aesthetics, where your products are weak. We'll have to reduce price.

NO:

Don't you dare. We succeeded in the United States and in Europe by keeping our prices at least 5% above those of our competitors. If we're having trouble in Japan it's because of you. Your obvious lack of effort, knowledge, even confidence in our products—that's what keeps them from selling. Besides, your parent keeps on sending our joint venture group a bunch of bumbling old incompetents for managers. We rarely get the good people. Maybe the idea is to kill off our relationships entirely so they can start up a unit of their own making imitation products.

FP:

Well, if you feel that way, there is not much point in our continuing on together.

NO:

Glad you said that. We'll buy up the other 50% of the equity and go it on our own.

FP:

Good luck. By the way, how many Japanese-speaking managers do you have in your company—that is, after we pull out all the "bumbling old incompetents" from our joint venture?

NO:

None. But don't worry. We'll just hire a bunch of headhunters and get started up in record time.

This is a disaster waiting—no, rushing—to happen. Back when this arrangement was a functioning joint venture, however, both partners, and especially the middle managers, really made an effort to have things work. Under a cloud of 100% control, things are different. You can buy a company's equity, but you cannot buy the mind or the spirit or the initiative or the devotion of its people. Nor can you just go hire replacements. In different environments, the availability of key professional services—managerial, legal, and so on—varies considerably.

The lesson is painful but inescapable: having control does not necessarily mean a better managed company. You cannot manage a global company through control. In fact, control is the last resort. It's what you fall back on when everything else fails and you're willing to risk the demoralization of workers and managers.

This need for control is deeply rooted. The tradition of Western capitalism lies behind it, a tradition that has long taught managers the dangerously incorrect arithmetic that equates 51% with 100% and 49% with 0%. Yes, of course, 51% buys you full legal control. But it is control of activities in a foreign market, about which you may know little as you sit far removed from the needs of customers in your red-carpeted office in Manhattan, Tokyo, or Frankfurt.

When Americans and Europeans come to Japan, they all want 51%. That's the magic number because it ensures majority position and control over personnel, brand decisions, and investment choices. But good partnerships, like good marriages, don't work on the basis of ownership or control. It takes effort and commitment and enthusiasm from both sides if either is to realize the hoped-for benefits. You cannot own a successful partner any more than you can own a husband or a wife.

In time, as the relationship between partners deepens and as mutual trust and confidence build, there may come a point when it no longer makes sense to remain two separate entities. Strategy, values, and culture might all match up so well that both sides want to finish the work of combination. Hewlett-Packard's presence in Japan started out in 1963, for example, as a 51–49 joint venture with Yokogawa Electric. Over two decades, enough confidence had built up that in 1983, Yokogawa Electric gave Hewlett-Packard another 24%.

The point is, it took two decades for Hewlett-Packard to reach a significant ownership position. Control was never the objective. All along, the objective was simply to do things right and serve customers well by learning how to operate as a genuine insider in Japan. As a result, Hewlett-Packard now owns 75% of a $750 million company in Japan that earns 6.6% net profit after tax.

An emphasis on control through equity, however, immediately poisons the relationship. Instead of focusing on contribution to fixed costs, one company imperialistically tells the other, "Look, I've got a big equity stake in you. You don't give me all the dividends I want, so get busy and distribute my product. I'm not going to distribute yours, though. Remember, you work for me."

This kind of attitude problem prevents the development of intercompany management skills, which are critical for success in today's global environment. But these skills must be learned. Peter L. Bonfield, chairman and managing director of International Computers Ltd., has a plastic name-card holder that he distributes to all his people who are in touch with Fujitsu, ICL's mainframe computer partner in Japan. On one side there is a place for the cards; on the other, a proven list of "*Do*s" for making such collaborative arrangements work. (See "ICL's *Do*s for Successful Collaboration.") Nothing here about 51% or establishing control.

Equity by itself is not the problem in building successful alliances. In Japan, we have a lot of "group companies," known as *keiretsu,* where an equity stake of, say, 3% to 5% keeps both partners interested in each other's welfare without threatening either's autonomy. Stopping that far short of a controlling position keeps the equity holder from treating the other company as if it were a subsidiary. Small equity investments like these may be the way to go.

Joint ventures may also work, but there are two obstacles that can trip them up. First, there is a contract, and contracts—even at their best—can only reflect an understanding of costs and markets and technologies at the moment companies sign them. When things change, as they always do, the partners don't really try to compromise and adjust. They look to the contract and start pointing fingers. After all, managers are human. They are sweet on their own companies and tolerant of their own mistakes. Tolerance goes way down when partners cause mistakes.

The second problem with joint ventures is that parent companies behave as parents everywhere

---

ICL's Dos for Successful Collaboration

1. Treat the collaboration as a personal commitment. It's people that make partnerships work.
2. Anticipate that it will take up management time. If you can't spare the time, don't start it.
3. Mutual respect and trust are essential. If you don't trust the people you are negotiating with, forget it.
4. Remember that both partners must get something out of it (money, eventually). Mutual benefit is vital. This will probably mean you've got to give something up. Recognize this from the outset.
5. Make sure you tie up a tight legal contract. Don't put off resolving unpleasant or contentious issues until "later." Once signed, however, the contract should be put away. If you refer to it, something is wrong with the relationship.
6. Recognize that during the course of a collaboration, circumstances and markets change. Recognize your partner's problems and be flexible.
7. Make sure you and your partner have mutual expectations of the collaboration and its time scale. One happy and one unhappy partner is a formula for failure.
8. Get to know your opposite numbers at all levels socially. Friends take longer to fall out.
9. Appreciate that cultures—both geographic and corporate—are different. Don't expect a partner to act or respond identically to you. Find out the true reason for a particular response.
10. Recognize your partner's interests and independence.
11. Even if the arrangement is tactical in your eyes, make sure you have corporate approval. Your tactical activity may be a key piece in an overall strategic jigsaw puzzle. With corporate commitment to the partnership, you can act with the positive authority needed in these relationships.
12. Celebrate achievement together. It's a shared elation, and you'll have earned it!

Postscript
Two further things to bear in mind:

1. If you're negotiating a product OEM deal, look for a quid pro quo. Remember that another product may offer more in return.
2. Joint development agreements must include joint marketing arrangements. You need the largest market possible to recover development costs and to get volume/margin benefits.

---

often do. They don't give their children the breathing space—or the time—they need to grow. Nor do they react too kindly when their children want to expand, especially if it's into areas the parents want to keep for themselves. "Keep your hands off" is the message they send, and that's not a good way to motivate anyone, let alone their own children.

This is not to say that joint ventures cannot work. Many work quite well. Fuji Xerox, for example, a very successful 50–50 arrangement between Rank Xerox and Fuji Film, earns high profits on its $3 billion annual sales and attracts some of the best people in Japan to work for it. Equally important, it has enough autonomy to get actively involved in new areas like digital-imaging technology, even though both parents have strong interests there themselves.

The head of Fuji Xerox, Yotaro Kobayashi, who is the son of the founder of Fuji Film, now sits on the board of Xerox, which has benefited greatly from Fuji Xerox's experience in battling the Japanese companies that have attacked Xerox's position in the medium- to low-end copier segments in the United States.

On balance, however, most parents are not so tolerant of their joint ventures' own ambitions. There have to be better ways to go global than a regular sacrifice of the firstborn. There are.

Going global is what parents should do together—through alliances that address the issue of fixed costs. They work. Nissan distributes Volkswagens in Japan; Volkswagen sells Nissan's four-wheel drive cars in Europe. Mazda and Ford swap cars in the Triad; GM and Toyota both collaborate and compete in the United States and Australia. Continental Tire, General Tire (now owned by Continental), Yokohama Rubber, and Toyo Tire share R&D and swap production. In the United States, for example, General Tire supplies several Japanese transplants on behalf of Yokohama and Toyo, both of which supply tires on behalf of General and Continental to car companies in Japan. No equity changes hands.

In the pharmaceutical industry, where both ends of the business system (R&D and distribution) represent unusually high fixed costs, companies regularly allow their strong products to be distributed by (potential) competitors with excellent distribution systems in key foreign markets. In the United States, Marion Laboratories distributes Tanabe's Herbesser and Chugai's Ulcerim; Merck, Yamanouchi's Gaster; Eli Lilly, Fujisawa's Cefamezin. In Japan, Shionogi distributes Lilly's Ceclor as Kefral (1988 sales: $700 million). Sankyo distributes Squibb's Capoten; Takeda, Bayer's Adalat; Fujisawa, SmithKline's Tagamet. Sales in Japan of each of these medicines last year were in the order of $300 million.

The distribution of drugs is a labor- and relationship-intensive process. It takes a force of more than 1,000 detail people to have any real effect on Japanese medicine. Thus, unless you are committed to building and sustaining such a fixed cost in Japan, it makes sense to collaborate with someone who has such a force already in place—and who can reciprocate elsewhere in the Triad.

Despite the typical "United States versus Japan" political rhetoric, the semiconductor industry has given rise to many forms of alliances. Most companies feel shorthanded in their R&D, so they swap licenses aggressively. Different forces prompted cooperative arrangements in the nuclear industry. General Electric, Toshiba, Hitachi, ASEA, AMU, and KWU (Siemens) banded together during the late 1970s to develop an improved nuclear boiling-water reactor. They shared their upstream R&D on a global basis but kept downstream construction

and local customer relationships to themselves. During the 1980s, the first three (core) members of the alliance continued their R&D collaboration and, in fact, developed an advanced boiling-water reactor concept. This time around, they split the orders from Tokyo Electric Power, among others, one-third each. As confidence builds, the activities open to joint participation can begin to encompass the entire business system.

Hitachi Kenki, a maker of construction equipment, has a loose alliance in hydraulic excavators with Deere & Company in North America and with Fiat Allis in Europe. Because Hitachi's product line was too narrow for it to set up its own distribution networks throughout the Triad, it tied up with partners who have strong networks already in place, as well as good additional products of their own, like bulldozers and wheel loaders, to fill in the gaps in Hitachi's product line. So effective have these arrangements been that the partners are now even committed to the joint development of a new wheel loader.

In the oligopolistic sheet glass industry, there is a noteworthy alliance between PPG and Asahi Glass, which began in 1966 with a joint venture in Japan to produce polyvinyl chloride. In 1985, the same pair formed a joint automotive-glass venture in the United States in hopes of capturing the business of Japanese automakers with U.S. production facilities. They built a second such plant in 1988. That same year they set up a chloride and caustic soda joint venture in Indonesia, along with some local participants and Mitsubishi Trading Company. During all this time, however, they remained fierce global competitors in the sheet-glass business.

Another long-term relationship is the one between Brown Shoe and Nippon Shoe, which introduced a new technology back in 1962 to produce Brown's "Regal" shoes. Today the relationship encompasses several other brands of Brown's shoes. For Brown, this has proven a most effective way to participate in a Japanese market for leather goods that would be otherwise closed to them for both social reasons (historically, Japanese tanners have been granted special privileges) and reasons of appropriate skill (Brown's expertise in, for example, managing its own retail chains is not so relevant in an environment where sky-high real estate prices make direct company ownership of retail shops prohibitively expensive).

There are more examples, but the pattern is obvious: a prudent, non–equity-dependent set of arrangements through which globally active companies can maximize the contribution to their fixed costs. No surprise here. These alliances are an important part of the way companies get back to strategy.

The Logic of Entente

One clear change of mind necessary to make alliances work is a shift from a focus on ROI to a focus on ROS (return of sales). An ROS orientation means that managers will concern themselves with the ongoing business benefits of the alliance, not just sit around and wait for a healthy return on their initial investment. Indeed, equity investments almost always have an overtone of one company trying to control another with money. But few businesses succeed because of control. Most make it because of motivation, entrepreneurship, customer relationships, creativity, persistence, and attention to the "softer" aspects of an organization, such as values and skills.

An alliance is a lot like a marriage. There may be no formal contract. There is no buying and selling of equity. There are few, if any, rigidly binding provisions. It is a loose, evolving kind of relationship. Sure, there are guidelines and expectations. But no one expects a precise, measured return on the initial commitment. Both partners bring to an alliance a faith that they will be stronger together than either would be separately. Both believe that each has unique skills and functional abilities the other lacks. And both have to work diligently over time to make the union successful.

When one partner is weak or lazy or won't make an effort to explore what the two can do together,

things can come apart. One-sidedness and asymmetry of effort and attention doom a relationship. If a wife goes out and becomes the family's breadwinner *and* does all the housework *and* raises the children *and* runs the errands *and* cooks the meals, sooner or later she will rebel. Quite right. If the husband were in the same position, he'd rebel too. As soon as either partner starts to feel that the situation is unfair or uneven, it will begin to come apart. Alliances are like that. They work only when the partners do.

It's hard work. It's all too easy for doubts to start to grow. A British whiskey company used a Japanese distributor until it felt it had gained enough experience to start its own sales operation in Japan. Japanese copier makers and automobile producers have done this to their U.S. partners. It happens. There's always the danger that a partner is not really in it for the long haul.

But the odds run the other way. There is a tremendous cost—and risk—in establishing your own distribution, logistics, manufacturing, sales, and R&D in every key market around the globe. It takes time to build skills in your own people and develop good relations with vendors and customers. Nine times out of 10, you will want to stay in the alliance.

Inchcape, a British trading house with a strong regional base in Asia, distributes Toyota cars in China, Hong Kong, Singapore, elsewhere in the Pacific region, and in several European countries. It also distributes Ricoh copiers in Hong Kong and Thailand. This arrangement benefits the Japanese producers, which get access to important parts of the world without having to set up their own distribution networks. It also benefits Inchcape, which can leverage its traditional British connections in Asia while adding new, globally competitive products to its distribution pipeline to replace the less attractive offerings of declining U.K.–based industries.

In practice, though, companies do start to have doubts. Say you've started up a Japanese alliance, not invested all that much, and been able to boost your production at home because of sales in Japan. Then you look at the actual cash flow from those sales, and it doesn't seem all that great. So you compare it with a competitor's results—a competitor that has gone into Japan entirely on its own. It's likely that you've forgotten how little effort you've put in when compared with the blood, sweat, and tears of your competitor. All you look at are the results.

All of a sudden you start to feel cheated; you remember every little inconvenience and frustration. You yield to the great temptation to compare apples with oranges, to moan about revenues while forgetting fixed costs. You start to question just how much the alliance is really doing for you.

It's a bit like going to a marriage counselor and complaining about the inconveniences of marriage because, had you not married, you could be dating anyone you like. You focus on what you think you're missing, on the inconveniences, and forget entirely about the benefits of being married. It's a psychological process. Alliance partners can easily fall into this kind of destructive pattern of thought, complaining about the annoyances of coordination, of working together, of not having free rein. They forget the benefits.

Actually, they forget to *look* for the benefits. And most accounting and control systems only make this worse. For instance, if you are running your own international sales operation in Japan, you know where to look for accurate measures of performance. You know how to read an income statement, figure out the return on invested capital, consolidate the performance of subsidiaries.

But when you're operating through a partner in Japan and you're asking yourself how that Japanese operation is doing, you forget to look for the benefits at home in the contribution to the fixed costs of R&D, manufacturing, and brand image. The financials don't highlight them; they usually don't even capture them. Most of the time, these contributions—like the extra production volume for OEM export—are simply invisible, below the line of sight.

Companies in the United States, in particular, often have large, dominant home country opera-

tions. As a result, they report the revenues generated by imports from their overseas partners as their own domestic sales. In fact, they think of what they're doing not as importing but as managing procurement. Exports get recorded as overseas sales of the domestic divisions. In either case, the contribution of the foreign partner gets lost in the categories used by the U.S.–based accounting system.

It takes real dedication to track down the domestic benefits of a global alliance. And you're not even going to look for them if you spend all your time complaining. The relationship is never going to last. That's too bad, of course, if the alliance really does contribute something of value. But even when alliances are good, you can outgrow them. Needs change, and today's partner might not be the best or the most suitable tomorrow.

Financial institutions shift about like this all the time. If you're placing a major issue, you may need to tie up with a Swiss bank with deep pockets. If you need help with retail distribution, you may turn to Merrill Lynch or Shearson Lehman Hutton. In Japan, Nomura Securities may be the best partner because of its size and retail strength. You don't need to be good at everything yourself as long as you can find a partner who compensates for your weak points.

Managing multiple partners is more difficult in manufacturing industries but still quite doable. IBM in the United States has a few important allies; in Japan it has teamed up with just about everyone possible. (There has even been a book published in Japanese, entitled *IBM's Alliance Strategy in Japan.*) It has links with Ricoh in distribution and sales of low-end computers, with Nippon Steel in systems integration, with Fiji Bank in financial systems marketing, with OMRON in CIM, and with NTT in value-added networks. IBM is not a jack-of-all-trades. It has not made huge fixed-cost investments. In the eyes of Japanese customers, however, it has become an all-around player. No wonder IBM has achieved a major "insider" position in the fiercely competitive Japanese market, along with handsome sales ($7 billion in 1988) and profits ($1.2 billion).

Sure, individual partners may not last. Every business arrangement has its useful life. But maintaining a presence in Japan by means of alliances *is* a permanent endeavor, an enduring part of IBM's strategy. And acting as if current arrangements are permanent helps them last longer. Just like marriage. If you start cheating on day two, the whole thing gets shaky fast.

Why does the cheating start? You're already pretty far down the slippery slope when you say to yourself, "I've just signed this deal with so-and-so to distribute my products. I don't need to worry about that anymore as long as they send me my check on time." You're not holding up your half of the relationship. You're not working at it. More important, you're not trying to learn from it—or through it. You're not trying to grow, to get better as a partner. You start to imagine all sorts of grievances. And your eye starts to wander.

One of Japan's most remarkable success stories is 7-Eleven. Its success, however, is not due to the efforts of its U.S. owner, Southland Corporation, but rather to the earnest acquisition of "know-how" by Ito-Yokado, the Japanese licensee. Faced with a take-over threat, Southland management collected something on the order of $5 billion through asset stripping and junk bond issues. The high-interest cost of the LBO caused the company to report a $6 million loss in 1987. Meanwhile, since the Japanese had completely absorbed the know-how for running 7-Eleven, the only thing Southland had left in Japan was its 7-Eleven brand.

When Southland's management asked Ito-Yokado to buy the 7-Eleven brand name for half a billion dollars, Ito-Yokado's counterproposal was to arrange an interest-free loan of ¥41 billion to Southland in exchange for the annual royalty payment of $25 million, with the brand name as collateral. Should something happen to Southland so that it cannot pay back the debt, it will lose the brand and its Japanese affiliation completely.

Yes, Southland got as much as a half a billion dollars out of Japan in exchange for mundane know-how, so they should be happy as a Yukon River gold miner. On the other hand, the loss of business connections in Japan means that Southland is permanently out of one of the most lucrative retail markets in the world. That's not a marriage. It's just a one-night stand.

Another company, a U.S. media company, took 10% of the equity of a good ad agency in Japan. When the agency went public, the U.S. investor sold off 3% and made a lot of money over and above its original investment. It still had 7%. Then the stockholders started to complain. At Tokyo's crazy stock market prices, that 7% represented about $40 million that was just sitting in Japan without earning dividends. (The dividend payout ratio of Japanese companies is usually very low.) So the stockholders pushed management to sell off the rest and bring the money back to the United States, where they could get at least a money-market level of return. No growth, of course. No lasting position in the booming Japanese market. Just a one-time killing.

Much the same logic seems to lie behind the sale by several U.S.–based companies of their equity positions in Japanese joint ventures. McGraw-Hill (Nikkei–McGraw-Hill), General Electric (Toshiba), B.F. Goodrich (Yokohama Rubber), CBS (CBS–Sony), and Nabisco (Yamazaki–Nabisco), among others, have all realized handsome capital gains in this fashion. If they had not given up their participation in so lucrative a market as Japan, however, the value of their holdings would now be many times greater still. GE, for example, probably realized more than $400 million from its sale of Toshiba shares during the early 1980s. But those same shares would be worth roughly $1.6 billion today. Similarly, B.F. Goodrich's investment in Yokohama Rubber would now be worth nearly $300 million, compared with an estimated $36 million that it realized from selling its shares during the late 1970s and early 1980s. Of course, such funds have since found other opportunities for profitable investment, but they would have to do very well indeed to offset the loss of so valuable an asset base in Japan.

This kind of equity-based mind-set makes the eye wander. It sends the message that alliances are not a desirable—or effective—means of coping with the urgent and inescapable pressures of globalization or of becoming a genuine insider throughout the Triad market. It reinforces the short-term orientation of managers already hard-pressed by the uncertainties of a new global environment.

When a dispute occurs in a transnational joint venture, it often has overtones of nationalism, sometimes even racism. Stereotypes persist. "Americans just can't understand our market," complain some frustrated partners. "The Germans are too rigid," complain others. "Those mechanical Japanese may be smart at home, but they sure as hell are dumb around here." We've all heard the comments.

It does not take companies with radically different nationalities to have a "clash of cultures" in a joint venture. Most of the cross-border mergers that took place in Europe during the 1970s have resulted in divorce or in a takeover by one of the two partners. In Japan, mergers between Japanese companies—Dai-Ichi Kangyo Bank and Taiyo Kobe Bank, for example—have journalists gossiping about personal conflicts at the top between, say, ex-Kangyo and ex-Dai-Ichi factions lingering on for 10 years or more.

Good combinations—Ciba-Geigy and Nippon Steel (a combination of Yawata and Fuji), for example—are the exception, not the rule. Two corporate cultures rarely mesh well or smoothly. In the academic world, there is a discipline devoted to the study of interpersonal relationships. To my knowledge, however, there is not even one scholar who specializes in the study of *intercompany* relationships. This is a serious omission, given the importance of joint ventures and alliances in today's competitive global environment. We need to know much more than we do about what makes effective corporate relationships work.

Having been involved with many multicomplex situations, I do not underestimate this task. Still, we must recognize and accept the inescapable subtleties and difficulties of intercompany relationships. That is the essential starting point. Then we must focus not on contractual or equity-related issues but on the quality of the people at the interface between organizations. Finally, we must understand that success requires frequent, rapport-building meetings at least at three organizational levels: top management, staff, and line management at the working level.

This is hard, motivation-testing work. No matter what they say, however, many companies don't really care about extending their global reach. All they want is a harvesting of the global market. They are not interested in the hard work of serving customers around the world. They are interested in next quarter's ROI. They are not concerned with getting back to strategy or delivering long-term value or forging entente. They want a quickie. They want to feel good today and not have to work too hard tomorrow. They are not serious about going global or about the painstaking work of building and maintaining the alliances a global market demands.

Yet the relentless challenges of globalization will not go away. And properly managed alliances are among the best mechanisms that companies have found to bring strategy to bear on these challenges. In today's uncertain world, it is best not to go it alone.

Reading 4–2

COLLABORATE WITH YOUR COMPETITORS—AND WIN

Gary Hamel, Yves L. Doz, and C. K. Prahalad

Collaboration between competitors is in fashion. General Motors and Toyota assemble automobiles, Siemens and Philips develop semiconductors, Canon supplies photocopiers to Kodak, France's Thomson and Japan's JVC manufacture videocassette recorders. But the spread of what we call "competitive collaboration"—joint ventures, outsourcing agreements, product licensings, cooperative research—has triggered unease about the long-term consequences. A strategic alliance can strengthen both companies against outsiders even as it weakens one partner vis-à-vis the other. In particular, alliances between Asian companies and Western rivals seem to work against the Western partner. Cooperation becomes a low-cost route for new competitors to gain technology and market access.[1]

Yet the case for collaboration is stronger than ever. It takes so much money to develop new products and to penetrate new markets that few companies can go it alone in every situation. ICL, the British computer company, could not have developed its current generation of mainframes without Fujitsu. Motorola needs Toshiba's distribution capacity to break into the Japanese semiconductor market. Time is another critical factor. Alliances can provide shortcuts for Western companies racing to improve their production efficiency and quality control.

We have spent more than five years studying the inner workings of 15 strategic alliances and monitoring scores of others. Our research (see the insert "About Our Research") involves cooperative ventures between competitors from the United States and Japan, Europe and Japan, and the United States and Europe. We did not judge the success or failure of each partnership by its longevity—a common mistake when evaluating strategic alliances—but by the shifts in competitive strength on each side. We focused on how companies use competitive collaboration to enhance their internal skills and technologies while they guard against transferring competitive advantages to ambitious partners.

There is no immutable law that strategic alliances *must* be a windfall for Japanese or Korean partners. Many Western companies do give away more than they gain—but that's because they enter partnerships without knowing what it takes to win. Companies that benefit most from competitive collaboration adhere to a set of simple but powerful principles.

Collaboration is competition in a different form. Successful companies never forget that their new partners may be out to disarm them. They enter alliances with clear strategic objectives, and they also understand how their partners' objectives will affect their success.

Harmony is not the most important measure of success. Indeed, occasional conflict may be the best evidence of mutually beneficial collaboration. Few alliances remain win-win undertakings forever. A partner may be content even as it unknowingly surrenders core skills.

Reprinted by permission of *Harvard Business Review.* "Collaborate With Your Competitors and Win" by Gary Hamel, C. K. Prahalad, and Yves Doz, January/February 1989.

[1]For a vigorous warning about the perils of collaboration, see Robert B. Reich and Eric D. Mankin, "Joint Ventures with Japan Give Away Our Future," *HBR,* March–April 1986, p. 78.

About Our Research

We spent more than five years studying the internal workings of 15 strategic alliances around the world. We sought answers to a series of interrelated questions. What role have strategic alliances and outsourcing agreements played in the global success of Japanese and Korean companies? How do alliances change the competitive balance between partners? Does winning at collaboration mean different things to different companies? What factors determine who gains most from collaboration?

To understand who won and who lost and why, we observed the interactions of the partners firsthand and at multiple levels in each organization. Our sample included four European–U.S. alliances, two intra-European alliances, two European–Japanese alliances, and seven U.S.–Japanese alliances. We gained access to both sides of the partnerships in about half the cases and studied each alliance for an average of three years.

Confidentiality was a paramount concern. Where we did have access to both sides, we often wound up knowing more about who was doing what to whom than either of the partners. To preserve confidentiality, our article disguises many of the alliances that were part of the study.

Cooperation has limits. Companies must defend against competitive compromise. A strategic alliance is a constantly evolving bargain whose real terms go beyond the legal agreement or the aims of top management. What information gets traded is determined day to day, often by engineers and operating managers. Successful companies inform employees at all levels about what skills and technologies are off-limits to the partner and monitor what the partner requests and receives.

Learning from partners is paramount. Successful companies view each alliance as a window on their partners' broad capabilities. They use the alliance to build skills in areas outside the formal agreement and systematically diffuse new knowledge throughout their organizations.

Why Collaborate?

Using an alliance with a competitor to acquire new technologies or skills is not devious. It reflects the commitment and capacity of each partner to absorb the skills of the other. We found that in every case in which a Japanese company emerged from an alliance stronger than its Western partner, the Japanese company had made a greater effort to learn.

Strategic intent is an essential ingredient in the commitment to learning. The willingness of Asian companies to enter alliances represents a change in competitive tactics, not competitive goals. NEC, for example, has used a series of collaborative ventures to enhance its technology and product competences. NEC is the only company in the world with a leading position in telecommunications, computers, and semiconductors—despite its investing less in R&D (as a percentage of revenues) than competitors like Texas Instruments, Northern Telecom, and L.M. Ericsson. Its string of partnerships, most notably with Honeywell, allowed NEC to leverage its in-house R&D over the last two decades.

Western companies, on the other hand, often enter alliances to avoid investments. They are more interested in reducing the costs and risks of entering new businesses or markets than to acquiring new skills. A senior U.S. manager offered this analysis of his company's venture with a Japanese rival: "We complement each other well—our distribution capability and their manufacturing skill. I see no reason to invest upstream if we can find a secure source of product. This is a comfortable relationship for us."

An executive from this company's Japanese partner offered a different perspective: "When it is necessary to collaborate, I go to my employees and say, 'This is bad, I wish we had these skills ourselves. Collaboration is second best. But I will feel worse if after four years we do not know how to do what our partner knows how to do.' We must digest their skills."

The problem here is not that the U.S. company wants to share investment risk (its Japanese partner does too) but that the U.S. company has no ambition *beyond* avoidance. When the commitment to learning is so one-sided, collaboration invariably leads to competitive compromise.

Many so-called alliances between Western companies and their Asian rivals are little more than sophisticated outsourcing arrangements (see the box "Competition for Competence"). General Motors buys cars and components from Korea's Daewoo. Siemens buys computers from Fujitsu. Apple buys laser printer engines from Canon. The traffic is almost entirely one way. These OEM deals offer Asian partners a way to capture investment initiative from Western competitors and displace customer competitors from value-creating activities. In many cases this goal meshes with that of the Western partner: to regain competitiveness quickly and with minimum effort.

Consider the joint venture between Rover, the British automaker, and Honda. Some 25 years ago, Rover's forerunners were world leaders in small car design. Honda had not even entered the automobile business. But in the mid-1970s, after failing to penetrate foreign markets, Rover turned to Honda for technology and product-development support. Rover has used the alliance to avoid investments to design and build new cars. Honda has cultivated skills in European styling and marketing as well as multinational manufacturing. There is little doubt which company will emerge stronger over the long term.

Troubled laggards like Rover often strike alliances with surging latecomers like Honda. Having fallen behind in a key skills area (in this case, manufacturing small cars), the laggard attempts to compensate for past failures. The latecomer uses the alliance to close a specific skills gap (in this case, learning to build cars for a regional market). But a laggard that forges a partnership for short-term gain may find itself in a dependency spiral: as it contributes fewer and fewer distinctive skills, it must reveal more and more of its internal operations to keep the partner interested. For the weaker company, the issue shifts from "Should we collaborate?" to "With whom should we collaborate?" to "How do we keep our partner interested

as we lose the advantages that made us attractive to them in the first place?"

There's a certain paradox here. When both partners are equally intent on internalizing the other's skills, distrust and conflict may spoil the alliance and threaten its very survival. That's one reason joint ventures between Korean and Japanese companies have been few and tempestuous. Neither side wants to "open the kimono." Alliances seem to run most smoothly when one partner is intent on learning and the other is intent on avoidance—in essence, when one partner is willing to grow dependent on the other. But running smoothly is not the point; the point is for a company to emerge from an alliance more competitive than when it entered it.

One partner does not always have to give up more than it gains to ensure the survival of an alliance. There are certain conditions under which mutual gain is possible, at least for a time.

The partners' strategic goals converge while their competitive goals diverge. That is, each partner allows for the other's continued prosperity in the shared business. Philips and Du Pont collaborate to develop and manufacture compact discs, but neither side invades the other's market. There is a clear upstream/downstream division of effort.

The size and market power of both partners is modest compared with industry leaders. This forces each side to accept that mutual dependence may have to continue for many years. Long-term collaboration may be so critical to both partners that neither will risk antagonizing the other by an overtly competitive bid to appropriate skills or competence. Fujitsu's 1 to 5 disadvantage with IBM means it will be a long time, if ever, before Fujitsu can break away from its foreign partners and go it alone.

Each partner believes it can learn from the other and at the same time limit access to proprietary skills. JVC and Thomson, both of whom make VCRs, know that they are trading skills. But the two companies are looking for very different things. Thomson needs product technology and manufacturing prowess; JVC needs to learn how to succeed in the fragmented European market. Both sides believe there is an equitable chance for gain.

Competition for Competence

In the article "Do You Really Have a Global Strategy?" (*HBR* July–August 1985), Gary Hamel and C. K. Prahalad examined one dimension of the global competitive battle: the race for brand dominance. This is the battle for control of distribution channels and global "share of mind." Another global battle has been much less visible and has received much less management attention. This is the battle for control over key technology-based competences that fuel new business development.

Honda has built a number of businesses, including marine engines, lawn mowers, generators, motorcycles, and cars, around its engine and power train competence. Casio draws on its expertise in semiconductors and digital display in producing calculators, small-screen televisions, musical instruments, and watches. Canon relies on its imaging and microprocessor competences in its camera, copier, and laser printer businesses.

In the short run, the quality and performance of a company's products determine its competitiveness. Over the longer term, however, what counts is the ability to build and enhance core competences—distinctive skills that spawn new generations of products. This is where many managers and commentators fear Western companies are losing. Our research helps explain why some companies may be more likely than others to surrender core skills.

Alliance or Outsourcing?

Enticing Western companies into outsourcing agreements provides several benefits to ambitious OEM partners. Serving as a manufacturing base for a Western partner is a quick route to increased manufacturing share without the risk or expense of building brand share. The Western partners' distribution capability allows Asian suppliers to focus all their resources on building absolute product advantage. Then OEMs can enter markets on their own and convert manufacturing share into brand share.

Serving as a sourcing platform yields more than just volume and process improvements. It also generates low-cost, low-risk market learning. The downstream (usually Western) partner typically provides

information on how to tailor products to local markets. So every product design transferred to an OEM partner is also a research report on customer preferences and market needs. The OEM partner can use these insights to read the market accurately when it enters on its own.

A Ratchet Effect

Our research suggests that once a significant sourcing relationship has been established, the buyer becomes less willing and able to reemerge as a manufacturing competitor. Japanese and Korean companies are, with few exceptions, exemplary suppliers. If anything, the "soft option" of outsourcing becomes even softer as OEM suppliers routinely exceed delivery and quality expectations.

Outsourcing often begins a ratchetlike process. Relinquishing manufacturing control and paring back plant investment leads to sacrifices in product design, process technology, and, eventually, R&D budgets. Consequently, the OEM partner captures product-development as well as manufacturing initiative. Ambitious OEM partners are not content with the old formula of "You design it and we'll make it." The new reality is, "You design it, we'll learn from your designs, make them more manufacturable, and launch our products alongside yours."

Reversing the Verdict

This outcome is not inevitable. Western companies can retain control over their core competences by keeping a few simple principles in mind.

A competitive product is not the same thing as a competitive organization. While an Asian OEM partner may provide the former, it seldom provides the latter. In essence, outsourcing is a way of renting someone else's competitiveness rather than developing a long-term solution to competitive decline.

Rethink the make-or-buy decision. Companies often treat component manufacturing operations as cost centers and transfer their output to assembly

(continued)

units at an arbitrarily set price. This transfer price is an accounting fiction, and it is unlikely to yield as high a return as marketing or distribution investments, which require less research money and capital. But companies seldom consider the competitive consequences of surrendering control over a key value-creating activity.

Watch out for deepening dependence. Surrender results from a series of outsourcing decisions that individually make economic sense but collectively amount to a phased exit from the business. Different managers make outsourcing decisions at different times, unaware of the cumulative impact.

Replenish core competencies. Western companies must outsource some activities; the economics are just too compelling. The real issue is whether a company is adding to its stock of technologies and competences as rapidly as it is surrendering them. The question of whether to outsource should always provoke a second question: Where can we outpace our partner and other rivals in building new sources of competitive advantage?

How to Build Secure Defenses

For collaboration to succeed, each partner must contribute something distinctive: basic research, product development skills, manufacturing capacity, access to distribution. The challenge is to share enough skills to create advantage vis-à-vis companies outside the alliance while preventing a wholesale transfer of core skills to the partner. This is a very thin line to walk. Companies must carefully select what skills and technologies they pass to their partners. They must develop safeguards against unintended, informal transfers of information. The goal is to limit the transparency of their operations.

The type of skill a company contributes is an important factor in how easily its partner can internalize the skills. The potential for transfer is greater when a partner's contribution is easily transported (in engineering drawings, on computer tapes, or in the heads of a few technical experts); easily interpreted (it can be reduced to commonly understood equations or symbols); and easily absorbed (the skill or competence is independent of any particular cultural context).

Western companies face an inherent disadvantage because their skills are generally more vulnerable to transfer. The magnet that attracts so many companies to alliances with Asian competitors is their manufacturing excellence—a competence that is less transferable than most. Just-in-time inventory systems and quality circles can be imitated, but this is like pulling a few threads out of an oriental carpet.

Manufacturing excellence is a complex web of employee training, integration with suppliers, statistical process controls, employee involvement, value engineering, and design for manufacture. It is difficult to extract such a subtle competence in any way but a piecemeal fashion.

There is an important distinction between technology and competence. A discrete, stand-alone technology (for example, the design of a semiconductor chip) is more easily transferred than a process competence, which is entwined in the social fabric of a company. Asian companies often learn more from their Western partners than vice versa because they contribute difficult-to-unravel strengths, while Western partners contribute easy-to-imitate technology.

So companies must take steps to limit transparency. One approach is to limit the scope of the formal agreement. It might cover a single technology rather than an entire range of technologies; part of a product line rather than the entire line; distribution in a limited number of markets or for a limited period of time. The objective is to circumscribe a partner's opportunities to learn.

Moreover, agreements should establish specific performance requirements. Motorola, for example, takes an incremental, incentive-based approach to technology transfer in its venture with Toshiba. The agreement calls for Motorola to release its microprocessor technology incrementally as Toshiba delivers on its promise to increase Motorola's penetration in the Japanese semiconductor market. The greater Motorola's market share, the greater Toshiba's access to Motorola's technology.

Many of the skills that migrate between companies are not covered in the formal terms of collaboration. Top management puts together strategic alliances and sets the legal parameters for exchange. But what actually gets traded is determined by day-to-day interactions of engineers, marketers, and product developers: who says what to whom, who gets access to what facilities, who sits on what joint committees. The most important deals ("I'll share this with you if you share that with me") may be struck four or five organizational levels below where the deal was signed. Here lurks the greatest risk of unintended transfers of important skills.

Consider one technology-sharing alliance between European and Japanese competitors. The European company valued the partnership as a way to acquire a specific technology. The Japanese company considered it a window on its partner's entire range of competences and interacted with a broad spectrum of its partner's marketing and product-development staff. The company mined each contact for as much information as possible.

For example, every time the European company requested a new feature on a product being sourced from its partner, the Japanese company asked for detailed customer and competitor analyses to justify the request. Over time, it developed a sophisticated picture of the European market that would assist its own entry strategy. The technology acquired by the European partner through the formal agreement had a useful life of three to five years. The competitive insights acquired informally by the Japanese company will probably endure longer.

Limiting unintended transfers at the operating level requires careful attention to the role of gatekeepers, the people who control what information flows to a partner. A gatekeeper can be effective only if there are a limited number of gateways through which a partner can access people and facilities. Fujitsu's many partners all go through a single office, the "collaboration section," to request

information and assistance from different divisions. This way the company can monitor and control access to critical skills and technologies.

We studied one partnership between European and U.S competitors that involved several divisions of each company. While the U.S. company could only access its partner through a single gateway, its partner had unfettered access to all participating divisions. The European company took advantage of its free rein. If one division refused to provide certain information, the European partner made the same request of another division. No single manager in the U.S. company could tell how much information had been transferred or was in a position to piece together patterns in the requests.

Collegiality is a prerequisite for collaborative success. But *too much* collegiality should set off warning bells to senior managers. CEOs or division presidents should expect occasional complaints from their counterparts about the reluctance of lower level employees to share information. That's a sign that the gatekeepers are doing their jobs. And senior management should regularly debrief operating personnel to find out what information the partner is requesting and what requests are being granted.

Limiting unintended transfers ultimately depends on employee loyalty and self-discipline. This was a real issue for many of the Western companies we studied. In their excitement and pride over technical achievements, engineering staffs sometimes shared information that top management considered sensitive. Japanese engineers were less likely to share proprietary information.

There are a host of cultural and professional reasons for the relative openness of Western technicians. Japanese engineers and scientists are more loyal to their company than to their profession. They are less steeped in the open give-and-take of university research since they receive much of their training from employers. They consider themselves team members more than individual scientific contributors. As one Japanese manager noted, "We don't feel any need to reveal what we know. It is not an issue of pride for us. We're glad to sit and listen. If we're patient we usually learn what we want to know."

Controlling unintended transfers may require restricting access to facilities as well as to people. Companies should declare sensitive laboratories and factories off-limits to their partners. Better yet, they might house the collaborative venture in an entirely new facility. IBM is building a special site in Japan where Fujitsu can review its forthcoming mainframe software before deciding whether to license it. IBM will be able to control exactly what Fujitsu sees and what information leaves the facility.

Finally, which country serves as "home" to the alliance affects transparency. If the collaborative team is located near one partner's major facilities, the other partner will have more opportunities to learn—but less control over what information gets traded. When the partner houses, feeds, and looks after engineers and operating managers, there is a danger they will "go native." Expatriate personnel need frequent visits from headquarters as well as regular furloughs home.

Enhance the Capacity to Learn

Whether collaboration leads to competitive surrender or revitalization depends foremost on what employees believe the purpose of the alliance to be. It is self-evident: to learn, one must *want* to learn. Western companies won't realize the full benefits of competitive collaboration until they overcome an arrogance borne of decades of leadership. In short, Western companies must be more receptive.

We asked a senior executive in a Japanese electronics company about the perception that Japanese companies learn more from their foreign partners than vice versa. "Our Western partners approach us with the attitude of teachers," he told us. "We are quite happy with this, because we have the attitude of students."

Learning begins at the top. Senior management must be committed to enhancing their companies' skills as well as to avoiding financial risk. But most learning takes place at the lower levels of an alliance. Operating employees not only represent the front lines in an effective defense but also play a vital role in acquiring knowledge. They must be well briefed on the partner's strengths and weaknesses and understand how acquiring particular skills will bolster their company's competitive position.

This is already standard practice among Asian companies. We accompanied a Japanese development engineer on a tour through a partner's factory. This engineer dutifully took notes on plant layout, the number of production stages, the rate at which the line was running, and the number of employees. He recorded all this despite the fact that he had no manufacturing responsibility in his own company, and that the alliance didn't encompass joint manufacturing. Such dedication greatly enhances learning.

Collaboration doesn't always provide an opportunity to fully internalize a partner's skills. Yet just acquiring new and more precise benchmarks of a partner's performance can be of great value. A new benchmark can provoke a thorough review of internal performance levels and may spur a round of competitive innovation. Asking questions like, "Why do their semiconductor logic designs have fewer errors than ours?" and "Why are they investing in this technology and we're not?" may provide the incentive for a vigorous catch-up program.

Competitive benchmarking is a tradition in most of the Japanese companies we studied. It requires many of the same skills associated with competitor analysis: systematically calibrating performance against external targets; learning to use rough estimates to determine where a competitor (or partner) is better, faster, or cheaper; translating those estimates into new internal targets; and recalibrating to establish the rate of improvement in a competitor's performance. The great advantage of competitive collaboration is that proximity makes benchmarking easier.

Indeed, some analysts argue that one of Toyota's motivations in collaborating with GM in the much-publicized NUMMI venture is to gauge the quality of GM's manufacturing technology. GM's top manufacturing people get a close look at Toyota, but the reverse is true as well. Toyota may be learning whether its giant U.S. competitor is capable of closing the productivity gap with Japan.

Competitive collaboration also provides a way of getting close enough to rivals to predict how they will behave when the alliance unravels or runs its course. How does the partner respond to price changes? How does it measure and reward executives? How does it prepare to launch a new product? By revealing a competitor's management orthodoxies, collaboration can increase the chances of success in future head-to-head battles.

Knowledge acquired from a competitor-partner is only valuable after it is diffused through the organization. Several companies we studied had established internal clearinghouses to collect and disseminate information. The collaborations manager at one Japanese company regularly made the rounds of all employees involved in alliances. He identified what information had been collected by whom and then passed it on to appropriate departments. Another company held regular meetings where employees shared new knowledge and determined who was best positioned to acquire additional information.

Proceed with Care—But Proceed

After World War II, Japanese and Korean companies entered alliances with Western rivals from weak positions. But they worked steadfastly toward independence. In the early 1960s, NEC's computer business was one-quarter the size of Honeywell's, its primary foreign partner. It took only two decades for NEC to grow larger than Honeywell, which eventually sold its computer operations to an alliance between NEC and Group Bull of France. The NEC experience demonstrates that dependence on a foreign partner doesn't automatically condemn a company to also-ran status. Collaboration may sometimes be unavoidable; surrender is not.

Managers are too often obsessed with the ownership structure of an alliance. Whether a company controls 51% or 49% of a joint venture may be much less important than the rate at which each partner learns from the other. Companies that are confident of their ability to learn may even prefer some ambiguity in the alliance's legal structure. Ambiguity creates more potential to acquire skills and technologies. The challenge for Western companies is not to write tighter legal agreements but to become better learners.

Running away from collaboration is no answer. Even the largest Western companies can no longer outspend their global rivals. With leadership in many industries shifting toward the East, companies in the United States and Europe must become good borrowers—much like Asian companies did in the 1960s and 1970s. Competitive renewal depends on building new process capabilities and winning new product and technology battles. Collaboration can be a low-cost strategy for doing both.

Chapter 5

Developing Coordination and Control: The Organizational Challenge

In the earlier chapters we described how changes in the international operating environment have forced MNCs to optimize global efficiency, national responsiveness, and worldwide learning simultaneously. For most companies, this new challenge implied not only a fundamental strategic reorientation, but also a major change in organizational capability.

Implementing such a complex three-pronged strategic objective would be difficult under any circumstances, but in a worldwide company the task is complicated even further. The very act of "going international" multiplies a company's organizational complexity. Most companies find it difficult enough balancing product divisions that carry overall responsibility for achieving operating efficiency and strategic focus with corporate staffs whose functional expertise allows them to play an important counterbalance and control role. The thought of adding capable geographically oriented management and maintaining a three-way balance of organizational perspectives and capabilities among product, function, and area is intimidating. The difficulty is further increased because the resolution of tensions among the three different management groups must be accomplished in an organization whose operating units are often divided by distance and time and whose key members are separated by barriers of culture and language.

BEYOND STRUCTURAL FIT

Because the choice of a basic organizational structure has such a powerful influence on the management process in an MNC, much of the earlier attention of managers and researchers alike was focused on trying to find which formal structure

FIGURE 5–1   Stopford and Well's International Structural Stages Model

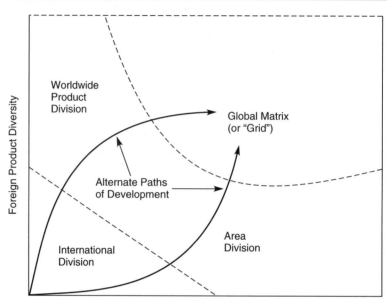

Source: Adapted from John M. Stopford and Louis T. Wells, *Strategy and Structure of the Multinational Enterprise* (New York: Basic Books, 1972).

provided the right "fit" under various conditions. The most widely recognized study on this issue was John Stopford's research on the 187 largest U.S.–based MNCs in the late 1960s.[1] His work resulted in a "stages model" of international organization structure that became the benchmark for most work that followed.

Stopford defined two variables to capture strategic and administrative complexity that faced most companies as they expanded abroad: the number of products sold internationally ("foreign product diversity," shown on the vertical axis in Figure 5–1) and the importance of international sales to the company ("foreign sales as a percentage of total sales," shown on the horizontal axis). Plotting the structural change in his sample of 187 companies, he found that worldwide corporations typically adopt different organizational structures at different stages of international expansion.

According to this model, worldwide companies typically manage their international operations through an international division at the early stage of foreign expansion, when both foreign sales and the diversity of products sold abroad are limited. Subsequently, those companies that expand their sales abroad without

---

[1]See John M. Stopford and Louis T. Wells, *Strategy and Structure of the Multinational Enterprise* (New York: Basic Books, 1972).

significantly increasing foreign product diversity typically adopt an area structure. Other companies that expand by increasing their foreign product diversity tend to adopt the worldwide product division structure. Finally, when both foreign sales and foreign product diversity are high, companies resort to the global matrix.

Although these ideas were presented as a descriptive model, consultants, academics, and managers alike soon began to apply them prescriptively. For many companies, it seemed that structure followed fashion more than strategy. And in the process, the debate was often reduced to generalized discussions of the comparative value of product- versus geography-based structures and to simplistic choices between "centralization" and "decentralization."

Confronted with the increasing complexity, diversity, and change in the 1980s, managers in many worldwide companies looked for ways to restructure. Conventional wisdom provided a ready solution: the global matrix. But for most companies, the result was disappointing. The promised land of the global matrix turned out to be an organizational quagmire from which they were forced to retreat.

FAILURE OF THE MATRIX

In theory, the solution should have worked. Having front-line managers report simultaneously to different organizational groups (such as business managers reporting to both the area and the functional groups or area managers reporting along functional and business lines) should have enabled the companies to maintain the balance among centralized efficiency, local responsiveness, and worldwide knowledge transfer. The multiple channels of communication and control promised the ability to nurture diverse management perspectives, and the ability to shift the balance of power within the matrix theoretically gave it great flexibility. The reality turned out to be otherwise, however, and the history of companies that built formal global matrix structures was an unhappy one.

Dow Chemical, a pioneer of global matrix organization, eventually returned to a more conventional structure with clear lines of responsibility being given to geographic managers. Citibank, once a textbook example of the global matrix, similarly discarded this mode of dual reporting relationships after a few years of highly publicized experimentation. And so too did scores of other companies that experimented with this complex and rather bureaucratic structure.

Most encountered the same problems. The matrix amplified the differences in perspectives and interests by forcing all issues through the dual chains of command so that even a minor difference could become the subject of heated disagreement and debate. While this strategy had proven useful in highly concentrated domestic operations, the very design of the global matrix prevented the resolution of differences among managers with conflicting views and overlapping responsibilities. Dual reporting led to conflict and confusion; the proliferation of channels created informational logjams; and overlapping responsibilities resulted in turf battles and a loss of accountability. Separated by barriers of distance, time, language, and culture, managers found it virtually impossible to clarify the confusion and resolve the conflicts.

As a result, the management process was slow, acrimonious, and costly. Communications were routinely duplicated, approval processes were time-consuming, and constant travel and frequent meetings raised the company's administrative costs dramatically. In company after company, the initial appeal of the global matrix structure quickly faded into a recognition that a different solution was required.

BUILDING ORGANIZATIONAL CAPABILITY

The basic problem underlying a company's search for a structural fit was that it focused on only one organizational variable—formal structure—and this single tool proved to be unequal to the task of capturing the complexity of the strategic task facing most MNCs. First, as indicated earlier, this focus often forced managers to ignore the multidimensionality of the environmental forces as they made choices between product- versus geographically-based structures and debated the relative advantages of centralization versus decentralization. Furthermore, structure defined a static set of roles, responsibilities, and relationships in a dynamic and rapidly evolving task environment. And finally, restructuring efforts often proved harmful, as organizations were bludgeoned into a major realignment of roles, responsibilities, and relationships overnight.

In an increasing number of companies, managers now recognize that formal structure is a powerful but blunt instrument of strategic change. Moreover, given the complexity and volatility of environmental demands, structural fit is becoming both less relevant and harder to achieve. Success in coping with managers' multidimensional strategic task now depends rather more on building strategic and organizational flexibility.

To develop multidimensional and flexible strategic capabilities, a company must go beyond structure and expand its fundamental organizational capabilities. The key tasks become to reorient managers' thinking and reshape the core decision-making systems. In doing so, the company's entire management process—the administrative system, communication channels, and interpersonal relationships—become the tools for managing such change.

In this chapter, we will explore some of the more subtle and sophisticated ways of thinking about and dealing with the organizational challenges facing managers in worldwide companies. As a first step, we will examine how administrative heritage—a company's history and its embedded management culture—influences its organization and its ability and willingness to change. Next, we will describe the characteristics of the transnational organization that can operate effectively in the complex international environment. Finally, we will describe the tools and processes that can be used to develop the required organizational capability and suggest how these tools might be used to manage the process of strategic and organizational change.

ADMINISTRATIVE HERITAGE

While industry analysis can reveal a company's strategic challenges and market opportunities, its ability to fulfill that promise will be greatly influenced—and often constrained—by existing asset configurations, its historical definition of management responsibilities, and the ingrained organizational norms. A company's organization is shaped not only by current external task demands but also by past internal management biases. In particular, each company is influenced by the path by which it developed—its organizational history—and the values, norms, and practices of its management—its management culture. Collectively, these factors constitute a company's *administrative heritage.* It can be, at the same time, one of the company's greatest assets—the underlying source of its key competencies—and also a significant liability, since it resists change and thereby prevents realignment or broadening of strategic capabilities. As managers in many companies have learned, often at considerable cost, while strategic plans can be scrapped and redrawn overnight, there is no such thing as a zero-based organization. Companies are, to a significant extent, captives of their past, and any organizational transformation has to focus at least as much on where the company is coming from—its administrative heritage—as on where it wants to get to.

The importance of a company's administrative heritage can be illustrated by contrasting the development of a typical European MNC whose major international expansion occurred in the decades of the 1920s and 1930s, a typical American MNC that expanded abroad in the 1940s and 1950s, and a typical Japanese company that made its main overseas thrust in the 1960s and 1970s. Even if these companies were in the same industry, the combined effects of the different historical contexts in which they developed and the disparate internal cultural norms that influenced their management processes led to their adopting some very different strategic and organizational models.

Decentralized Federation

Expanding abroad in a period of rising tariffs and discriminatory legislation, the typical European company found its budding export markets threatened by local competitors. To defend its various market positions, it was forced to build local production facilities. With their own plants, various national subsidiaries were able to modify products and marketing approaches to meet widely differing local market needs. The increasing independence of these fully integrated national units was reinforced by the transportation and communications barriers that existed in that era, limiting the headquarters' ability to intervene in the management of the company's spreading worldwide operations.

The emerging configuration of distributed assets and delegated responsibility fit well with the ingrained management norms and practices in many European companies. Because of the important role of owners and bankers in corporate-level decision making, European companies, particularly those from the United Kingdom, the Netherlands, and France, developed an internal culture that emphasized personal relationships rather than formal structures, and financial controls more than coordination of technical or operational detail. This management style, philosophy, and capability tended to reinforce companies' willingness to delegate more operating independence and strategic freedom to their foreign subsidiaries. Highly autonomous national companies were often managed more as a portfolio of offshore investments rather than as a single international business.

The resulting organization and management pattern was a loose federation of independent national subsidiaries, each focused primarily on its local market. As a result, many of these companies adopted what we have described in the earlier chapters as the *multinational* strategy and developed a *decentralized federation* organization model that is represented in Figure 5–2(a).

FIGURE 5–2   Organizational Configuration Models

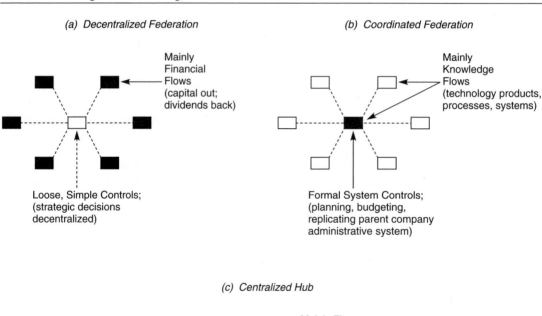

(a) Decentralized Federation

Mainly Financial Flows (capital out; dividends back)

Loose, Simple Controls; (strategic decisions decentralized)

(b) Coordinated Federation

Mainly Knowledge Flows (technology products, processes, systems)

Formal System Controls; (planning, budgeting, replicating parent company administrative system)

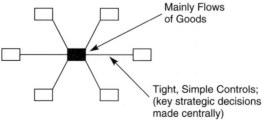

(c) Centralized Hub

Mainly Flows of Goods

Tight, Simple Controls; (key strategic decisions made centrally)

Coordinated Federation

U.S. companies, many of which enjoyed their fastest international expansion in the 1950s and 1960s, developed under very different circumstances. Their main strength lay in the new technologies and management processes they had developed as a consequence of being located in the world's largest, richest, and most technologically advanced market. After the war, their foreign expansion focused primarily on leveraging this strength, particularly in response to demands generated by postwar reconstruction and the granting of independence to previously colonized nations. So pervasive was this pattern of internationalization that it gave rise to the international product cycle theory referred to in Chapter 1.

Reinforcing this strategy was a professional managerial culture in most U.S.–based companies that contrasted with the "old boy network" that typified the European companies' processes. The management approach in most U.S.–based companies was built on a willingness to delegate responsibility, while retaining overall control through sophisticated management systems and specialist corporate staffs. The systems provided channels for a regular flow of information, to be interpreted by the central staff. Holding the managerial reins, top management could control the free-running team of independent subsidiaries and guide the direction in which they were headed.

The main handicap such companies faced was that parent-company management often adopted a parochial and even superior attitude toward international operations, perhaps because of the assumption that new ideas and developments all came from the parent. Despite corporate management's increased understanding of its overseas markets, it often seemed to view foreign operations as appendages whose principal purpose was to leverage the capabilities and resources developed in the home market.

Nonetheless, the approach was highly successful in the postwar decades, and many U.S.–based companies adopted what we have described as the *international* strategy and a *coordinated federation* organizational model shown in Figure 5–2(b). Their foreign subsidiaries were often free to adapt products or strategies to reflect market differences, but their dependence on the parent company for new products, processes, and ideas dictated a great deal more coordination and control by headquarters than in the decentralized federation organization. This was facilitated by the existence of formal systems and controls in the headquarters-subsidiary link.

Centralized Hub

In contrast, the typical Japanese company, making its main international thrust since the 1970s, faced a greatly altered external environment and operated with very different internal norms and values. With limited prior overseas exposure, it chose not to match the well-established local marketing capabilities and facilities that its European and U.S. competitors had built up. (Indeed, well-established Japanese trading companies often provided it with an easier means of entering foreign markets.) However, it had new, efficient, scale-intensive plants, built to serve its rapidly expanding domestic market, and it was expanding into a global environment of declining trade barriers. Together, these factors gave it the incentive to develop a competitive advantage at the upstream end of the value-added chain. Its competitive strategy emphasized cost advantages and quality assurance and required tight central control of product development, procurement, and manufacturing. A centrally controlled, export-based internationalization strategy represented a perfect fit with the external environment and the company's competitive capabilities.

Such an approach also fit the cultural background and organizational values in the emerging Japanese MNC. At the foundation of the internal processes were the strong national cultural norms that emphasized group behavior and valued interpersonal harmony. These values had been enhanced by the paternalism of the *zaibatsu* and other enterprise groups. They were also reflected in the group-oriented management practices of *nemawashi* and *ringi* that were at the core of Japanese organizational processes. By keeping primary decision making and control at the center, the Japanese company could retain this culturally dependent management system that was so communications-intensive and people-dependent.

Cultural values were also reflected in one of the main motivations driving the international expansion of Japanese MNCs. As growth in their domestic market slowed and became increasingly competitive, these companies needed new sources of growth so they could continue to attract and promote employees. In a system of lifetime employment, growth was the engine that powered organizational vitality and self-renewal. It was this motivation that reinforced the bias toward an export-based strategy managed from the center rather than the decentralized foreign investment approach of the European. As a result, these companies adopted what we have described as a *global* strategy, and developed a *centralized hub* organizational model, shown in Figure 5–2(c), to support this strategic orientation.

The Transnational Challenge

In Chapters 2 and 3, we advanced the hypothesis that many worldwide industries have been transformed in the 1980s from traditional multinational, international, and global forms toward a transnational form. Instead of demanding efficiency, responsiveness, or learning as the key capability for success, these businesses now require participating firms to achieve the three capabilities simultaneously to remain competitive.

Table 5–1 summarizes the key characteristics of the decentralized federation, coordinated federation, and centralized hub organizations we have described in this chapter as the supporting forms for companies pursuing the multinational, international, and global strategies. A review of these characteristics immediately reveals the problems each of the three archetypal company models might face in responding to the transnational challenge.

TABLE 5–1 Organizational Characteristics of Decentralized Federation, Coordinated Federation, and Centralized Hub Organizations

	Decentralized Federation	*Coordinated Federation*	*Centralized Hub*
Strategic approach	Multinational	International	Global
Key strategic capability	National responsiveness	Worldwide transfer of home country innovations	Global-scale efficiency
Configuration of assets and capabilities	Decentralized and nationally self-sufficient	Sources of core competencies centralized, others decentralized	Centralized and globally scaled
Role of overseas operations	Sensing and exploiting local opportunities	Adapting and leveraging parent-company competencies	Implementing parent-company strategies
Development and diffusion of knowledge	Knowledge developed and retained within each unit	Knowledge developed at the center and transferred to overseas units	Knowledge developed and retained at the center

With its resources and capabilities consolidated at the center, the global company achieves efficiency primarily by exploiting potential scale economies in all its activities. In such an organization, however, the national subsidiaries' lack of resources and responsibilities may undermine their motivation and their ability to respond to local market needs. Similarly, while the centralization of knowledge and skills allows the global company to be highly efficient in developing and managing innovative new products and processes, the central groups often lack adequate understanding of the market needs and production realities outside their home market. Limited resources and the narrow implementation role of its overseas units prevent the company from tapping into learning opportunities outside its home environment. These are problems that a global organization cannot overcome without jeopardizing its trump card of global efficiency.

The classic multinational company suffers from other limitations. While its dispersed resources and decentralized decision making allows national subsidiaries to respond to local needs, the fragmentation of activities also leads to inefficiency. Learning also suffers, because knowledge is not consolidated and does not flow among the various parts of the company. As a result, local innovations often represent little more than the efforts of subsidiary management to protect its turf and autonomy, or reinventions of the wheel caused by blocked communication or the not-invented-here (NIH) syndrome.

In contrast, the international company is better able to leverage the knowledge and capabilities of the parent company. However, its resource configuration and operating systems make it less efficient than the global company, and less responsive than the multinational company.

THE TRANSNATIONAL ORGANIZATION

There are three important organizational characteristics that distinguish the transnational organization from its multinational, international, or global counterparts: It builds and legitimizes multiple diverse internal perspectives able to sense the complex environmental demands and opportunities; its physical assets and management capabilities are distributed internationally but are interdependent; and it has developed a robust and flexible internal integrative process. In the following paragraphs, we will describe and illustrate each of these characteristics.

Multidimensional Perspectives

Managing in an environment in which strategic forces are both diverse and changeable, the transnational company must develop the ability to sense and analyze the numerous and often conflicting opportunities, pressures, and demands it faces worldwide. Having a limited or biased management perspective through which to view developments can constrain a company's ability to understand and respond to some potential problems or opportunities.

The transnational organization must have broad sensory capabilities able to reflect the diverse environmental opportunities and demands in the internal management process. Strong national subsidiary management is needed to sense and represent the changing needs of local consumers and the increasing pressures from host governments; capable global business management is required to track the strategy of global competitors and to provide the coordination necessary to respond appropriately; and influential functional management is needed to concentrate corporate knowledge, information, and expertise, and facilitate its transfer among organizational units.

Unfortunately, however, in many companies, power is concentrated with the particular management group that has historically represented the company's most critical strategic tasks—often at the cost of allowing other groups representing other needs, to atrophy. For example, in multinational companies, key decisions were usually dominated by the country management group since they made the most critical contribution to achieving national responsiveness, which lay at the center of the strategic approach of such companies. In global companies, by contrast, managers in worldwide product divisions were typically the most influential, since strong business management played the key role in the company's efforts to seek global efficiency. And in international companies, functional management groups often came to assume this position of dominance because of their roles in building, accumulating, and transferring the company's skills, knowledge, and capabilities.

In transnational companies, however, biases in the decision-making process are consciously reduced by building up the capability, credibility, and influence of the less powerful management groups while protecting the morale and capabilities of the dominant group. The objective is to build a multidimensional organization in which the influence of each of the three management groups is balanced. Some of the cases in this book focus explicitly on this issue of developing and maintaining such a balanced and multidimensional organization and illustrate how this capability may be developed.

Distributed, Interdependent Capabilities

Having sensed the diverse opportunities and demands it faces, the transnational organization must then be able to make choices among them and respond in a timely and effective manner to those that are deemed strategically important. When a company's decision-making process and organizational capabilities are concentrated at the center—as they are in the global organization's centralized hub configuration—it is often difficult to respond appropriately to diverse worldwide demands. Being distant from the front-line opportunities and threats, the central group's ability to act in an effective and timely manner is constrained by its reliance on complex and intensive international communications. Furthermore, the volume and diversity of demands made on the central group often result in central capabilities being overloaded, particularly where scarce technological or managerial resources are involved.

On the other hand, multinational organizations with their response capabilities spread throughout the decentralized federation of independent operations suffer from duplication of effort (the reinventing-the-wheel syndrome), inefficiency of operations (the "locally self-sufficing scale" problem), and barriers to international learning (the not-invented-here syndrome).

In transnational organizations, management breaks away from the restricted view that assumes the need to centralize activities for which global scale or specialized knowledge is important. They ensure that viable national units achieve global scale by giving them the responsibility of becoming the company's world source for a given product or expertise. And they tap into important technological advances and market developments wherever they are occurring around the globe. They do this by securing the cooperation and involvement of the relevant national units in upgrading the company's technology, developing its new products, and shaping its marketing strategy.

One major consequence of the distribution of assets and responsibilities is that the interdependence of worldwide units automatically increases. Simple structural configurations like the decentralized federation, the coordinated federation, and the centralized hub are inadequate for the task facing the transnational corporation. What is needed is a structure we term the *integrated network* (see Figure 5–3).

FIGURE 5–3 Integrated Network Model

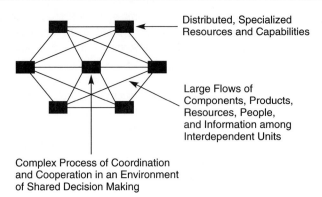

Distributed, Specialized Resources and Capabilities

Large Flows of Components, Products, Resources, People, and Information among Interdependent Units

Complex Process of Coordination and Cooperation in an Environment of Shared Decision Making

---

In the integrated network configuration, national units are no longer viewed only as the end of a delivery pipeline for company products, or as implementors of centrally defined strategies, or even as local adapters and modifiers of corporate approaches. Rather, the assumption behind this configuration is that management should consider each of the worldwide units as a source of ideas, skills, capabilities, and knowledge that can be harnessed for the benefit of the total organization. Efficient local plants may be converted into international production centers; innovative national or regional development labs may be designated the company's "center of excellence" for a particular product or process development; and creative subsidiary marketing groups may be given a lead role in developing worldwide marketing strategies for certain products or businesses. The company becomes a truly integrated network of distributed and interdependent resources and capabilities.

Flexible Integrative Process

Having established management groups representing multiple perspectives to reflect the variety of environmental demands and pressures and a configuration based on distributed and interdependent assets and organizational capabilities, the transnational organization requires a management process that can resolve the diversity of interests and perspectives and integrate the dispersed responsibilities. However, it cannot be bound by the symmetry of organizational process that follows when the task is seen in simplistic or static terms (e.g., "Should responsibilities be centralized or decentralized?"). It is clear that the benefits to be gained from central control of worldwide research or manufacturing activities may be much more important than those related to the global coordination of the sales and service functions. We have also seen how the pattern of functional coordination varies by business and by geographic area (aircraft engine companies need central control of more decisions than multinational food packagers; operations in developing countries may need more central support than those in advanced countries). Furthermore, all coordination needs change over time due to changes in the international operating environment, the life cycles of products and technologies, or the company's stage of development.

Thus, management must be able to differentiate its operating relationships and change its decision-making roles by function, across businesses, among geographic units, and over time. The management process must be able to change from product to product, from country to country, and even from decision to decision.

This requires the development of rather sophisticated and subtle decision-making machinery based on three different but interdependent management processes. The first is a supportive but constrained escalation process that allows top management to intervene directly in the content of certain decisions—a subtle and carefully managed form of *centralization.* The second is a managed organizational process in which the key management task is to structure individual roles and supportive systems to influence specific key decisions through *formalization.* The third is a self-regulatory capability in which top management's role is to establish a broad culture and set of relationships that provide an appropriate organizational context for delegated decisions—a sophisticated management process driven by *socialization.*

ANATOMY, PHYSIOLOGY, AND PSYCHOLOGY OF THE TRANSNATIONAL

The kind of organization we have described as a transnational clearly represents something quite different from its predecessors—the multinational, international, and global organizations. Building such an organization requires much more than choosing between a product or a geographic organization structure; and managing it implies much more than centralizing or delegating decisions. The tools and techniques employed in developing and managing this kind of organization are different in kind and application from those typically used in the traditional organizations.

Different Tools

By viewing the organizational challenge as one of creating and managing a decision process that responds to the company's critical task demands, the MNC manager is forced to adopt a very different approach from someone who defines the problem as one of discovering and installing the ideal structure. But if the structural stages model no longer provides a helpful description of international organization development, we need a different way to conceptualize the more complex array of tools and processes discussed in our earlier descriptions of transnational organizations.

The simple but useful framework adopted here is to describe the organization in terms of a physiological model. This analogy helps emphasize that while formal structure is critical in defining the basic anatomy, its role is by no means dominant. To be effective, change in an organization's anatomy (the formal structure of its assets, resources, and responsibilities) must be accompanied and complemented by appropriate adaptations to its physiology (the organization's systems and decision processes) and to its psychology (the organization's culture and management mentality). The different tools and processes used to build and manage the transnational will be described using this physiological model.

Structuring the Organizational Anatomy.   The traditional approach to MNC organization problems not only had a strong structural bias, but it also took a very narrow view of formal structure as a management tool: The prescribed organizational forms tended to be defined in *macro* terms that focused on dominant *line* relationships. Thus, they focused on simple but rather superficial choices, such as the classic product versus area structure debate.

As we have seen, however, the development of a transnational organization needs a different approach. It requires management not only to define the characteristics of the dominant line organization, but emphasizes the importance of designing and developing a surrounding structure that ensures that the innate power of the line structure does not lead to unidimensional management of multidimensional problems.

Having carefully defined the structure and responsibilities of all management groups, the next challenge is to ensure that particularly those without line authority have appropriate access to and influence in the mainstream of the management process. This is difficult to achieve using only the powerful but blunt instrument of macrostructure. Much more effective in achieving this task are *micro*structural tools such as task forces or committees that become important supplemental decision-making forums. It is in these microstructures that nonline managers can assume responsibility and be given authority in a way that is not possible within the formal line organization.

Where once task forces and special committees were considered ad hoc, or quick-fix devices useful primarily in reacting to short-term problems, now companies building transnational organizations have used them as legitimate and important structural tools through which top management can modify or fine-tune their basic structure. To stretch our anatomical analogy, if the formal line structure is the organization's backbone, then the nonline structure is its rib cage, and these microstructural tools are the muscle and the cartilage that give the organizational skeleton its flexibility.

Building the Organizational Physiology.   With its ability to shape classic hierarchical line relationships, dotted-line staff relationships, and off-line decision forum relationships, management clearly has the means available to influence the structure of the communication channels through which much of the organization's decision-making process operates. Yet, by adapting the various administrative systems, hierarchical channels, and informal relationships, they can exert an even more extensive and direct control over the volume, content, and direction of information flows. We term this flow of information that is the basis of all management processes the *organizational physiology.*

Many researchers have shown the link between the need for information and the complexity and uncertainty of the tasks to be performed. In the integrated network configuration, task complexity and uncertainty are very high. Operating an interdependent system in an environment of diverse, changeable, and often contradictory needs for national responsiveness and global coordination requires large volumes of complex information to be gathered, exchanged, and processed. We have seen a great deal of evidence that transnational organizations need a large number of sophisticated administrative, operational, and strategic systems. However, it is equally clear to those in such organizations that formal systems alone cannot support their information processing needs. Again, companies have been forced to look beyond the traditional tools and the conventional approaches in order to develop and manage their new organizational form.

For years, managers have recognized that a great deal of information exchange and even decision making—perhaps the majority—occurs through the organization's innumerable informal channels and relationships. Yet this part of the management process has often been dismissed as either unimportant ("office gossip" or "rumor mill") or unmanageable ("disruptive cliques" or "unholy alliances"). In the management of transnational organizations, such biases need to be reexamined. Not only is it more important for managers of international operations to exert some control and influence over informal systems, in most cases it is also more feasible to do so.

The highly complex and uncertain management processes in a transnational organization require more information than can be reasonably channeled through the formal systems. Furthermore, because organizational units are widely separated and because information is scarce and uncertainty is high, informal systems become an important source of information (and often, misinformation). However, the widespread distribution of organizational units and the relative infrequency of direct contacts mean that management has a better opportunity to shape and manage the informal systems in an international organization. Top managers are increasingly aware that it is legitimate and often important for them to try to do so.

Getting started is often remarkably easy, requiring little more than a conscious effort to shape the nature and quality of communications patterns and relationships through their daily involvement in the ongoing management processes. Such top-management influence on the nature and intensity of informal relationships can be shaped more deliberately by influencing the frequency and agenda of management trips, corporate meetings, or committee assignments, and by defining an individual's career development process. In addition, management can also recognize, legitimize, and reinforce those existing informal relationships that are already contributing to the corporate objective.

Developing the Organizational Psychology. In addition to an anatomy and a physiology, each organization also has a psychology (i.e., a set of explicit or implicit corporate values and shared beliefs) that greatly influences the way it operates. For companies operating in an international environment, this is a particularly important organizational attribute. With employees coming from a variety of different national backgrounds, management cannot assume that all will share common values and relate to common norms. Furthermore, in an operating environment in which managers are separated by distance and time barriers, shared management understanding is often a much more powerful tool than formal structure and systems in coordinating diverse activities. Yet, managers faced with the task of organizational change tend to reach for the more familiar and tangible tools of structural reorganization and systems redesign.

Of the numerous tools and techniques that can affect an organization's psychology, our review of transnational organizations has highlighted three that are particularly important. The first is the need for a clear, shared understanding of the company's mission and objectives. Matsushita's 250-year vision of its role in a world society, NEC's commitment to communications and computers (C&C), and Komatsu's objective to surround Caterpillar ("Maru C") represent variants of this approach applied at different strategic and operational levels.

The second important tool is the visible behavior and public actions of senior management. Particularly in a transnational organization where other signals may be diluted or distorted by the sheer volume of information being sent to foreign outposts, top management's actions speak louder than words and tend to have a powerful influence on the company's culture. They represent the clearest role model of behavior and a signal of the company's strategic and organizational priorities. When Sony Corporation founder and CEO, Akio Morita, relocated to New York to build the company's U.S. operations personally, he sent a message about Sony's commitment to its overseas businesses that could not have been conveyed as strongly by any other means.

The third and most commonly used set of tools for modifying organizational psychology in the transnational organization is nested in the company's personnel policies, practices, and systems. A company can develop a multidimensional and flexible organization process only if its personnel systems develop and reinforce the appropriate kinds of people. In Eli Lilly, we saw a good example of such an approach. Its recruiting and promotion policies emphasized the importance of good interpersonal skills and flexible, nonparochial personalities; its career path management was used not only to develop skills and knowledge, but also to broaden individual perspectives and interpersonal relationships; and its measurement and reward systems were designed to reinforce the thrust of other organization-building efforts.

Although the process of adapting an organization's culture, values, or beliefs is slow and the tools and techniques are subtle, this tool plays a particularly important role in the development of a transnational organization, because change in the organizational anatomy and physiology without complementary modifications to its psychology can lead to severe organizational problems.

MANAGING THE PROCESS OF CHANGE

Many managers have assumed that organizational change was driven and dominated by changes in the formal structure. This belief was particularly strong in U.S.–based companies, whose heritage favored the formalization of management processes. One of the most dramatic examples was Westinghouse's reorganization of its operations. Dissatisfied with the worldwide product organization it had installed eight years earlier in 1979, top management assigned a team of executives to study the company's international organization problems for 90 days. Its proposal that Westinghouse adopt a global matrix was accepted, and the team was then given three months to "install the new structure."

The example is far from unusual—literally hundreds of other companies have done the same thing. The managers involved seemed to assume that changes in formal roles and reporting relationships would force changes in the organizational linkages and decision processes, which in turn would reshape the way individual managers think and act. This model of the process of organizational change is illustrated in Figure 5–4.

It is tempting to view the task of managing change as one of sketching alternative chart structures by moving boxes and redrawing lines. Such a view loses sight of the real organization behind those structural representations. The boxes that are casually shifted around represent people with abilities, motivations, and interests, not just formal positions with specified roles. The lines that are redrawn are not just formal reporting channels, but interpersonal relationships that may have taken years to develop. As a result, forcing changes in organizational process and management mentality by altering the formal structure can have a high cost. The new relationships defined in the reorganized structure will often take months to establish at the most basic level, and a year or more to become truly effective. Developing new individual attitudes and behaviors will take even longer, since

---

FIGURE 5–4   Model I: The Traditional Change Process

Change in formal structure and responsibilities
(Anatomy)
↓
Change in interpersonal relationships and processes
(Physiology)
↓
Change in individual attitudes and mentalities
(Psychology)

---

many employees will be frustrated, alienated, or simply unequal to the new job requirements.

Most European and Japanese companies tend to adopt a very different approach in managing organizational change. Top management in these companies consciously uses personnel assignments as an important mechanism of organizational change. Building on the informal relationships that dominated their earlier management processes, European companies use assignments and transfers to forge interpersonal links, build organizational cohesion, and develop policy consistency. Such mechanisms are at least as important as structural change for developing their desired international processes.

Japanese companies place enormous emphasis on socializing the individual into the organization and shaping his or her attitudes to conform with overall corporate values. Organizational change in these companies is often driven more by intensive education programs than by reconfigurations of structure or systems.

Although the specific change process and sequence must vary from one company to the next, the overall process adopted in these companies for managing change is very different from the process driven by structural realignment. Indeed, the sequence is often the reverse. The first objective for many European and Japanese companies seeking major change is often to influence the understanding and the perceptions of individuals, particularly those in key positions. Then follows a series of changes aimed at modifying the communication flows and decision-making processes. Only in a final stage are the changes consolidated and confirmed by structural realignment. This process is represented by the model in Figure 5–5.

Of course, these two models of organizational change in worldwide companies are both oversimplifications of the process and overgeneralizations of national difference. All change processes inevitably involve substantial overlap and interaction in the alterations in organizational autonomy, physiology, and psychology; the two sequences merely reflect differences in the relative emphasis on each set of tools during the process. Furthermore, while the two models reflect historical national biases, those differences seem to be eroding. U.S., European, and Japanese companies appear to be learning from one another with the Americans recognizing the power of socialization processes and the others developing greater structural and systems sophistication.

While the emerging change process is much less organizationally traumatic and therefore less likely to result in major problems or even outright rejection, it will

---

FIGURE 5–5   Model II: The Emerging Change Process

Change in individual attitudes and mentalities
↓
Change in interpersonal relationships and processes
↓
Change in formal structure and responsibilities

sometimes be appropriate to employ the traditional approach, relying first on changes in formal structure. Particularly in times of crisis—chronic poor performance, a badly misaligned structure, or major structural change in the environment, for example—it may be necessary to achieve rapid and sweeping restructuring. For most organizations, however, dramatic structural change is also highly traumatic and can distract managers from their external tasks as they focus on the internal realignment. Fortunately, most change processes can be managed in a more evolutionary manner. When a company focuses first on modification of individual perspectives and interpersonal relationships before tackling the formal redistribution of responsibilities and power, the process seems to have a greater chance of success.

Case 5–1   *Corning Glass Works International (A)*

It was early spring 1975 and Forrest Behm, president of Corning International Corporation (CIC), the international operations of Corning Glass Works (CGW), was reviewing the organization structure of CIC as he had often done over the previous few weeks. The coordination of the overseas subsidiaries and affiliates and their integration with the domestic organization were still not being achieved to his satisfaction, and he wondered if there was any way the situation could be improved. The major risk in trying to improve coordination and integration, in Behm's mind, was that increasing centralized decision making could weaken the strong subsidiary organizations he had built, thus possibly compromising CIC's ability to respond to local needs.

The company had been through several organizational modifications over the last few years, some of which had been less successful than Behm had hoped. He realized that some managers in both the domestic and the international organizations had

become somewhat frustrated with continuing problems, and that they were growing skeptical of the company's organization changes designed to alleviate the problems. For the sake of the management group's morale and confidence, Behm knew that any further restructuring would have to provide a more effective and more durable solution to the problems.

Company Background

Although Corning Glass Works had been in operation for almost 125 years, in 1975 the company was still very much family owned and operated. Amory Houghton, Jr., the great-great-grandson of the founder, had become president in 1961 at age 35 and in 1964 was appointed chairman of the board. His brother James had been named vice chairman in 1971, assuming responsibility for the company's international operations and many of its corporate staff groups. The Houghton family still owned more than 10% of the stock that was listed on the New York Stock Exchange. This long history of family involvement, together with the location of the company headquarters in Corning, a small town in upstate New York, created a corporate environment

This case was prepared by Assistant Professor Christopher A. Bartlett and Professor M. Y. Yoshino.

Copyright © 1981 by the President and Fellows of Harvard College. Harvard Business School case 381-160.

that was personal and informal. Many of the managers were social friends during nonworking hours, and the company itself played a major role in local civic affairs.

Since its establishment in 1851, the company had built a strong reputation as a manufacturer and marketer of specialty glasses with properties adapted to specific end uses. CGW's stated corporate objective was "to pursue excellence in glass worldwide, making this family of materials, its related products, and its corollary technologies the most unusual and useful in our civilization." This strategy, built around a material and its applications, led Corning in 1908 to become one of the country's first companies to establish a research laboratory; from then on, technology-based research was at the center of the company's operation.

The way in which R&D led Corning's growth and diversification is illustrated by the following examples:

- Corning's turn of the century research to find a railroad lantern glass that would not crack in snowstorms led to the development of a low-expansion glass that became the company's Pyrex® bakeware and laboratory glassware. The entry into the laboratory market gave the company the opportunity in the 1960s and 1970s to develop a line of sophisticated medical products, including diagnostic reagents and biomedical instruments.

- Thomas Edison approached Corning to develop a glass envelope for his first incandescent lamp, launching the company as a major supplier of lighting products. The product line was extended to sealed beam headlamps for Detroit, and this industry relationship led to the development of ceramics for auto emission-control devices in the 1970s.

Through expansion of existing businesses and diversification into new products, Corning's sales were growing at around 10% annually, and by 1974 sales had surpassed the $1 billion mark (see Exhibit 1). The company had 46,000 employees worldwide, and it operated 90 plants in 20 countries.

Corning's Businesses

Through the research efforts described, Corning had developed over 300 different glasses that it converted into over 60,000 products. These products were consolidated into 10 major business groupings, each of which was managed by one of CGW's product divisions in the United States. However, only the following six product groups had significant foreign sales.

Television Products

Corning got into the television bulb business after gaining experience in manufacturing radar tubes in World War II. By continually developing the product through research and development efforts, particularly on the color picture tube, Corning became one of the two major suppliers to the television original equipment manufacturers (OEMs) in the United States. By subsequently starting up bulb manufacturing facilities in France, Brazil, Mexico, and Taiwan, Corning was able to capitalize on the international purchases of major customers such as Philips, RCA, and Sylvania. Competitive pricing was important, but product development and delivery were also critical. The bulb differed in specification between regions due to the differences in TV transmission characteristics. In France and Brazil, TV bulb manufacturing facilities were a part of larger broad product line plants. Technology was becoming fairly well established by the 1970s and was not subject to the rapid changes it had been through in the 1950s and 1960s. A substantial percentage of the company's sales were overseas. Competitors tended to be regional, some being licensees of Corning technology, such as Schott in Europe and Asahi in Japan.

Electronics Products

These were largely resistors and capacitors for electronic equipment manufacturers such as the OEMs of computers, communications, home entertainment, and military equipment. Most of the products were mature commodities, but the technology was changing and product development had to keep up

EXHIBIT 1 Summary of Financial Data, 1970–1974 ($ thousands except per share amounts)

	1974	1973	1972	1971	1970
Consolidated Statements of Income					
Net sales	$1,050,962	$945,785	$714,631	$603,382	$609,251
Cost of sales	797,528	656,746	496,043	427,792	429,657
	253,434	289,039	218,588	175,590	179,594
Selling, general, and administrative expenses	160,925	140,300	107,302	92,820	92,571
Research and development expenses	37,628	35,172	29,987	25,781	26,099
	198,553	181,472	137,289	118,601	118,670
Income from operations	54,881	107,567	81,299	56,989	60,924
Royalty, interest, and dividend income	15,272	19,066	16,884	16,218	15,748
Interest expense	[19,571]	[15,193]	[9,101]	[10,156]	[8,840]
Other income [deductions], net	[1,611]	[7,542]	[2,923]	[835]	[304]
Taxes on income	[19,182]	[50,076]	[41,372]	[31,938]	[31,949]
Income before minority interest and equity earnings	29,789	53,822	44,787	30,278	35,579
Minority interest in [earnings] loss of subsidiaries	1,832	[1,258]	[906]	2,112	[124]
Equity in earnings of associated companies	16,504	17,818	9,565	4,786	8,435
Income before extraordinary items	48,125	70,382	53,446	37,176	43,890
Extraordinary items			828	[3,126]	
Net income	$48,125	$70,382	$54,274	$34,050	$43,890
Per Share of Common Stock					
Income before extraordinary items	$2.73	$4.00	$3.04	$2.12	$2.50
Net income	$2.73	$4.00	$3.09	$1.94	$2.50
Dividends	$1.40	$1.40	$1.35	$1.30	$1.30
Average shares outstanding [thousands]	17,601	17,573	17,558	17,554	17,542
Consolidated Statements of Financial Condition					
Working capital	$222,349	$233,491	$192,789	$177,652	$160,185
Investments	110,852	91,252	84,309	76,695	74,392
Plant and equipment, at cost [net]	403,582	336,602	245,731	242,277	251,966
Goodwill and other assets	35,318	24,746	31,928	33,256	26,307
	772,101	686,091	554,757	529,880	512,850
Loans payable beyond one year	183,029	120,316	64,415	68,453	61,554
Other liabilities and deferred credits	53,322	54,769	31,640	33,374	34,774
Stockholders' equity	$535,750	$511,006	$458,702	$428,053	$416,522
Additions to plant and equipment	$136,596	$119,213	$48,638	$35,873	$44,284
Depreciation and amortization	$54,430	$44,642	$39,463	$39,723	$38,282
Dividends paid	$24,672	$24,623	$23,728	$22,759	$22,531
Current earnings retained in the business	$23,453	$45,759	$30,546	$11,291	$21,359
Number of stockholders at last dividend date	16,321	14,654	13,537	14,799	14,818
Owens-Corning Fiberglas Corporation unremitted earnings					
Total	$5,691	$9,080	$6,525	$3,572	$3,142
Per share	$.32	$.52	$.37	$.20	$.18

Source: Company document.

with customer needs. Manufacturing value added was the major cost component of most products, and price competition forced managers in this business to focus attention on manufacturing cost reductions. Manufacturing abroad was concentrated heavily in two separate manufacturing and marketing organizations set up as joint ventures in the early 1960s: Electrosil in the United Kingdom and Sovcor in France. A few key customers accounted for a substantial part of Corning's sales, and several of these were multinational. Most users sourced components multinationally, with price being a major decision factor. About one third of CGW's total sales were in foreign markets.

Consumer Products

Pyrex® bakeware, the company's first major consumer product, was launched in 1915 in the United States and within a few years spread globally through export sales and licensing agreements. In the 1950s, Corning research developed a glass ceramics material with properties that allowed freezer-to-oven-to-table cookware to be developed from it. This product became Corning Ware®, which was soon the leading cookware product in the United States. Other recent developments were Centura® and Corelle® tableware, and flat-top glass ceramic cooking surfaces. As the company moved into foreign markets, it began to realize that different markets demanded different product shapes and designs, such as the soufflé dishes and demitasse cups that were popular in France. The high cost of new molds and equipment, however, limited Corning's ability to respond to all local demands, since sales of $3 million were required to break even on a new product shape. Pyrex manufacturing facilities existed in many markets—including France, the United Kingdom, Argentina, and Australia—usually within a large multiproduct plant. However, facilities for Corning Ware manufacture outside North America existed only in Holland in a plant built solely for the product in 1963. There were two broad groups of customers: the mass home market and commercial food operations. The types of retail outlets used to reach the former varied by country as did the distribution channels to the retailer. For example, in Argentina, distributors sold to independent retailers, while in the United Kingdom a direct sales force fought for shelf space in mass merchandisers and national chains. A few global competitors existed, such as the popular Noritake line, but most were local or regional. The competitive combination of price, promotion, and advertising also varied by market. About one third of consumer product sales were overseas.

Medical Products

These were scientific instruments such as blood-gas analyzers and white-cell analyzers, and the reagents required to calibrate them, mainly used to determine body chemistry. In addition, the company had a line of single test diagnostic reagent materials and kits used, for example, to test patients' blood for thyroid-related disorders. Some of the instrumentation technology had come with the 1970 Evans Electroselenium acquisition in the United Kingdom, with most of the instruments being high value added products, manufactured in small numbers in highly technical, specialized operations. The product life cycle of many instruments and tests was relatively short, and identification, specification, and development of new products were a key task. Although most products had application in worldwide markets, some local differences in medical practice or physical facilities such as electric current complicated product development. Some global competitors existed along with specialist local instrument companies. Direct sales forces demonstrated products to potential customers in labs and hospitals. Approximately one quarter of all sales were outside the United States.

Science Products

The two major science businesses were scientific glassware and chemical systems. The former was special *lab glassware,* usually manufactured from Pyrex glass. It was an old, mature product line with competition based mainly on price and delivery. End users were small and widely spread, and Corning generally sold through local distributors. Foreign sales were almost 40% of the CGW total. The second major science products business was *chemical systems,* consisting of process systems designed for specific applications. Pyrex® heat exchangers and process piping were designed into specific applications. Overseas markets—particularly France, Germany, and the United Kingdom—were large and represented over two thirds of CGW's total process systems business.

Technical Products

Two very different businesses were included under this grouping. First there were *ophthalmic products,* which were principally eyeglass blanks produced to a variety of thickness, curvature, and periphery specifications, and made from either fixed or photochromic glass. The latter was a recent Corning research breakthrough that caused the lens to darken when exposed to bright light. Although manufacturing facilities existed only in the United States, France, and Brazil, exports were shipped to markets worldwide. Due to the variety of shapes, sizes, colors, and materials that could be used, sourcing decisions were complex and important. High value to weight made export sales attractive to all major manufacturers in the world, however, and competition took on global implications. A few large lens finishers generally dominated each national market, and these were Corning's main customers. Approximately one third of all Corning's ophthalmic sales were overseas. The second part of technical products was known as *technical materials,* a highly varied business that basically involved supplying specialty subassemblies to a variety of industrial and government OEMs. Corning generally designed the product specifically for the customer's application. Products varied from substrates for disc memories for computer companies to refrigerator heater components and oven-window glass for appliance manufacturers. Overseas materials business accounted for perhaps 15% of the total.

International Operations

Company Development

Although Corning began exporting Pyrex® products as early as 1918, its primary strategic focus remained on the U.S. market over the next four decades. While export sales continued to be the company's primary foreign revenue generator, licensing agreements were also quite lucrative. Only rarely did Corning take an equity position in its foreign ventures, and even then it would exchange a minority shareholding position for technology.

After assuming the chairman's responsibility in 1964, however, Amory Houghton, Jr., made it clear that he intended to increase significantly the company's international position. His goal was to transform Corning from a U.S. company into a truly international corporation that developed, manufactured, and sold its products to worldwide markets.

The impact of this strategic change can be seen immediately in Exhibit 2. Over the next decade, there was hardly a year when some major new foreign venture was not being launched. From 1965 to 1974 international sales increased almost tenfold from $35 million to $336 million. Although the French and English affiliates were clearly the most important, a wide diversity of product markets had been developed as illustrated by Exhibit 3. By the early 1970s Corning had become an important international company, and it was feeling some of the management and organizational strains that flowed from the new strategy. Country operations that had been fiercely independent and often in direct competition against each other (Jobling, Corning's U.K. affiliate, and Sovirel, the French subsidiary, had a bitterly competitive history over half a century long) now had to give up some of their independence and back off from their internal competitive battles.

Organization until 1972: Area Orientation

Two men held major responsibility for implementating Corning's overseas expansion in the 1960s and early 1970s. Ambassador Robert D. Murphy was elected International Division president in

EXHIBIT 2 Major Foreign Operations, 1974

Operation and Location	Ownership	Facilities	Employment	Markets Served	Major Products
Sovirel, S.A. (established 1922 as Le Pyrex—joint venture) Paris, France	100% in 1972 (majority 1969)	4 plants 4 sales offices 1 lab	4,500	France EEC exports	Television bulbs, optical products, housewares, scientific glass, and a variety of other specialty glass products
Sovcor, S.A. (established 1964 as joint venture with Sovirel) Paris, France	100% in 1972 (majority 1968)	1 plant 1 sales office	400	France EEC	Electronic components (resistors, capacitors)
James A. Jobling & Co. (established 1858; Corning licensee 1922; joint venture 1954) Sunderland, England	100% in 1973	7 U.K. plants 3 foreign plants (Germany, Spain, and Australia) 6 sales offices	4,600	U.K. Western Europe exports	Lab glassware, chemical process equipment, housewares, and other products (2,500 total)
Electrosil Ltd. (established 1960) Sunderland, England	100% in 1973	1 plant/ sales office	400	U.K. Scandinavia and other ECC markets	Electronic components (resistors, potentiometers)
Evans Electroselenium (established 1940; acquired 1970) Halstead, England	100% in 1970	2 plants/ sales offices	350	U.K. Commonwealth West Europe	Scientific instruments
Corning Netherlands Fabrieken (established 1963) Groningen, Holland	100%	1 plant/ sales office	100	U.K. EEC	Glass-ceramic cookware
Corning Glass Works of Canada (established 1945) Toronto, Canada	100%	2 plants/ sales offices	350	Canada U.K.	TV bulbs, Corning Ware cookware

(continued)

526

EXHIBIT 2 Major Foreign Operations, 1974 (*concluded*)

Operation and Location	Ownership	Facilities	Employment	Markets Served	Major Products
Cristalerias Rigolleau (established 1906, Corning interest 1943) Buenos Aires, Argentina	55% in 1966	4 plants/sales offices	3,400	Argentina exports to Europe Latin America	Vials and specialty containers, lab and technical glass, cookware, dinnerware
Productos Corning de Mexico (established 1965) Monterrey, Mexico	75%	1 plant/sales office	250	Mexico Latin America Australia	TV bulbs, lab glassware
Vidros Corning Brazil (established 1944) Suzano, Brazil	100%	3 plants/sales offices	580	Brazil Latin America Australia	TV bulbs, lab glassware, ophthalmic
Iwaki Glass Co. Ltd. (established 1965) Tokyo, Japan	49.8%	2 plants/sales offices	600	Japan	Sealed beam, foam glass, Pyrex for lab, consumer, and industrial use
Pacific Glass Corp. (established 1972) Taipei, Taiwan	60%	1 plant/sales office	650	Taiwan	TV bulbs
Crown Corning Ltd. (established 1972) Sydney, Australia	50%	3 plants/sales offices	1,150	Australia exports	Consumer products, TV bulbs, labs and scientific glass, ophthalmic
Borosil Glass Works Ltd. (established 1962) Bombay, India	48.9%	1 plant/sales office	900	India	Tubing, lab and consumer products

EXHIBIT 3   Distribution of Sales by Major Product and Subsidiary, 1973–1974

Major Subsidiaries	Television	Science Products			Technical Products		Electronic Components	Medical Instruments
		Scientific Glass	Process Systems	Consumer Products	Optical Products	Industrial Materials		
France								
Sovirel	A	C	C	C	B	C		
Sovcor							C	
United Kingdom								
James A. Jobling		B	B	B		C		
Electrosil							C	
Evans Electro-selenium								C
Netherlands								
Corning Nederlandse Fabrieken				C				
Canada								
CGW of Canada	B			C				
Brazil								
Vidros Corning	C				C			
Mexico								
Productos Corning	C	C						
Argentina								
Rigolleau		C	C					
Taiwan								
Pacific Glass	C							

Key: Percentage of total International Division sales.
A = More than 10% total CIC sales.
B = 5% to 10% total CIC sales.
C = Less than 5% total CIC sales.

1960 when he joined the company after retiring from a 40-year diplomatic career. In 1965 Murphy became chairman of Corning Glass International and Forrest Behm was appointed division president. Behm, a 20-year veteran with CGW, had had both sales and manufacturing management experience and, before his appointment to International, had been general manager of the old Lamp Division.

From the mid-1960s until 1972 the organization within the International Division was largely structured around geography (see Exhibit 4). Reporting to Forrest Behm were three area managers, one each for Europe, Asia–Pacific, and Latin America. All three were located in international headquarters, along with their individual area staffs for sales, marketing and distribution, and manufacturing and engineering.

EXHIBIT 4   International Division Organization Chart, 1970

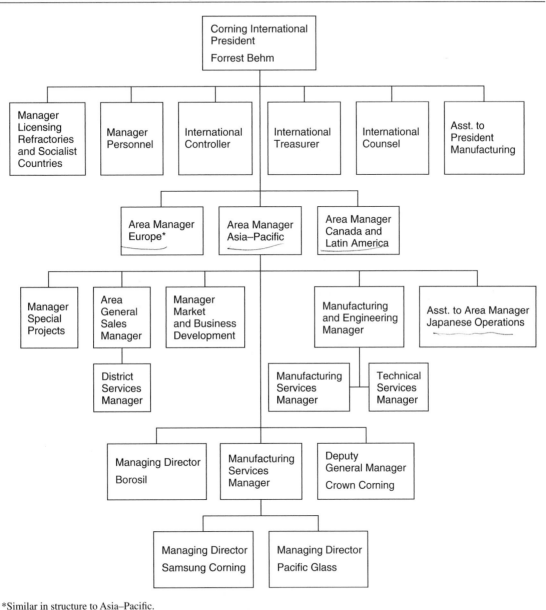

*Similar in structure to Asia–Pacific.

In 1971 a change of leadership and structure occurred in the parent company when Thomas MacAvoy, previously vice president and general manager of the Technical Products Group, was named president and chief operating officer of Corning Glass Works. MacAvoy had a doctorate in science and had entered Corning through its research laboratory. Under the reorganization, all product divisions and internal staff groups reported to him. In the same reorganization, James Houghton moved from his position as vice president and general manager of the Consumer Products Division to become vice chairman of Corning Glass Works, with responsibility for corporate staff groups and international operations, where he had gained previous experience as European area manager from 1965 to 1968. Both men reported to the chairman (see Exhibit 5).

At this time, the legal structure of the international organization was overhauled and Corning International Corporation (CIC) was created as a separate legal entity and a subsidiary of CGW. The separate international corporation was designed in part to emphasize the growing importance of Corning's overseas business, and that image of growth and separateness was strongly advocated within CIC. The separate corporate status was intended, at least partially, to upgrade the role of international managers and to help them feel more accepted within Corning.

The creation of CIC as a separate company, however, was insufficient by itself to change relationships between senior managers in the parent company and the international corporation. Within Corning, vice presidents in CIC (the area manager level) never really achieved the status and importance of vice presidents in CGW (the product division manager level). Nevertheless, relationships were generally cordial, even if contact between division managers and area managers was infrequent. More regular contact was taking place both above and below this level of management. Above, the president of CIC was pushing his key projects with corporate management to win his share of company resources; and below, strong informal technical links had been established between plant management and technical experts in the domestic product divisions. Expertise, assistance, and advice were exchanged along these channels, sometimes being billed in intercompany charges if a substantial amount of time or expense was involved.

Management Systems and Process until 1972

Before the international strategy shift of the mid-1960s, there was little need for elaborate management systems or processes to control foreign operations. Minority positions did not have to be consolidated for reporting purposes, so individual foreign affiliates could be left with their own individual reporting and control systems. Without a majority share, CGW could not intervene in operating issues such as global sourcing or manufacturing coordination, nor did it want to. Each subsidiary operated as an independent entity, maximizing its own position. Following the strategic shift of the mid-1960s, however, the management systems and processes began to change. With the decision to take majority positions in foreign operations wherever possible, financial results of these operations had to be consolidated. This, in turn, required the integration of their accounting systems into the parent company's—a move that created some problems according to Bill Hudson, president of the major French subsidiary, Sovirel, at the time of its consolidation:

> When I first arrived in Sovirel, we were a nonconsolidated operation, and the parent company really exercised very little direct control over us. Basically, they were interested only in how much our dividend payment to them would be, and when they could expect it. Otherwise, we were pretty much out of the corporate information and control system. We did have our own internal information, control, and planning systems, but they weren't heavy and they were only for our own use. But in 1969, when Corning's equity share went from 49% to 73%, the whole corporate information system was dumped on us. Everything was in English and in the American accounting system format, so from a local standpoint it was hardly helpful or meaningful to us at all. I couldn't replace our existing systems, so we just ran the corporate system in parallel.

With the availability of regular standardized reports and the growth of a staff group at international headquarters, controls on subsidiaries began

EXHIBIT 5   Corning Glass Works Organization Chart, 1971

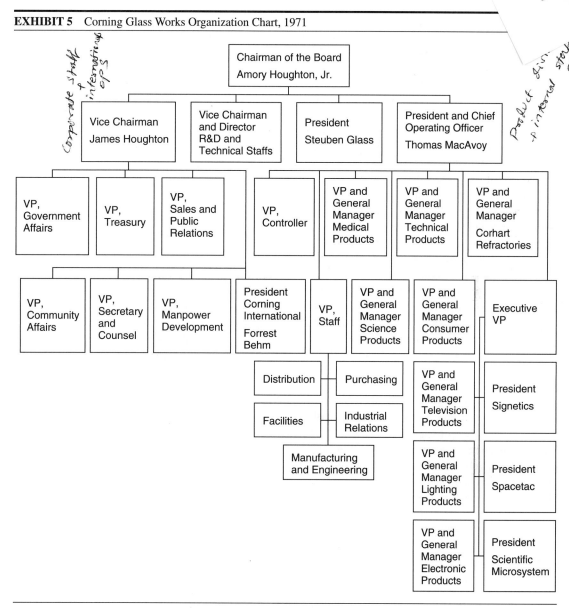

to increase. Bill Hudson explained that while the change in information systems was felt immediately, controls grew a little more gradually and subtly:

> Fast on the heels of centralized information came centralized control. We would receive telexes from CIC in the U.S. stating that "by month's end your receivables will be at X number of days' sales, and

your inventories will be at Y level." The availability of data tempted people back in Corning to second-guess subsidiary managers.

Most controls were still in the form of personal contacts, however, rather than systems, since the accounting system was more financial than management oriented. Behm, president of CIC, built up a strong internal budgeting system and a management-by-objectives style. He would visit subsidiaries regularly and review progress on financial goals set by the budget, and project goals set by the individual manager with Behm. International's budget was consolidated and presented to corporate headquarters as a package, and although data were available on an entity basis, there was rarely a line-by-line review at that level by corporate management.

The capital allocation process also changed as majority shareholding was taken in a foreign entity. One country manager referred to it as "part of the colonization that accompanies majority ownership." He explained that before consolidation the decision process used to consist of a meeting of key local managers who could discuss and decide the issue among themselves, then go out and raise the capital. Once the entity was consolidated, however, it was required to submit a formal capital appropriation request, prepared in English. This form had to be reviewed and agreed to by the area manager who then passed it on to the president of CIC for his approval. In this phase, several CIC accountants and technicians could be asked for their evaluation of the project. Once it had Behm's support, the request would pass to the corporate level where it would again be evaluated by corporate controllers, technical advisers, and senior managers. Because there was no overall capital budgeting system as such, individual appropriation requests had to be sold on their merits and this typically required the subsidiary general manager to "ride his request document through the system." One country manager observed that this allocation system also had other implications for the management process between the subsidiary and the parent company: "Our relationship with technical managers changed as a result. Whereas previously their role was simply to provide us with assistance on projects we had decided on, they now became part of the judge and jury system to decide if the project was feasible. As a result, they tended to become a lot more conservative with their advice and assistance, since they knew their judgment was on the line with the project."

The acquisition of majority shareholdings also encouraged management to begin to coordinate and integrate some of the foreign operations. The appointment of area managers provided the structure to achieve this, at least at a regional level. Jack Allen, who had spent most of his 25 years with Corning in plant management, division controllership, and corporate personnel positions, was appointed area manager for Europe in 1971. He recalled that his major tasks at that time were to unify and coordinate the European operations, and to integrate them into the parent company:

> It was a difficult time in Europe. We were trying to bring under control a number of long-established independent companies. Although tensions and rivalries between Jobling in the United Kingdom and Sovirel in France were perhaps the most extreme and best recognized, the lack of coordination and cooperation existed at every level. The parent company in the United States was exporting into Europe as were other Corning subsidiaries and affiliates as far away as Argentina and Australia. Furthermore, each of the European companies had export customers and often sales offices in several other European countries. When I became area manager, Corning had 31 legal entities operating in Europe. In Germany alone there were seven. My first job had to be to put some kind of operating order into that confusion.

It quickly became clear to Allen that he and his staff had to be located closer to the operating management level. He relocated his area office to Paris and built up an area staff of 25 to 30 people in sales and marketing services, administration, control and computer services, manufacturing, and engineering services. Yet, coordination and unification of the European operations were hard to achieve. Country affiliates tended to be well established and extremely knowledgeable about their national environment. The newly arrived area office staff managers simply did not have the market or product expertise to counter arguments against the consolidation of manufacturing operations that were based on detailed technical or market knowledge.

1972 Organization Problems and Changes: Product Dimension

As growth and expansion continued internationally, three major problems developed with the CIC organization structure and management processes; by 1972, CIC top management was struggling to find organizational or systems solutions to these problems. First, with management organized primarily around a geographic dimension, major decisions tended to be taken on a country-by-country basis, or on an area basis. Country managers and area managers promoted their own projects and protected their local interests. As a result, conflict would arise when the Japanese entity, for example, would want to manufacture the electronic components being exported to its market by the French electronics plant. Such conflicts could only be resolved by the president of CIC, and arguments were usually detailed and technical on both sides. Behm explained the impact this had on his job:

> During the late 1960s and early 1970s, there were large numbers of new facilities coming onstream, and capacity expansion and sourcing decisions were becoming infinitely more complex. Many of these were in potential conflict, and the only place they could be resolved was at my desk. In addition, I was the only one with sufficient position and connections at the corporate level to communicate our plans to the organization and get the resources to support them. Of necessity, I was spending 50% of my time traveling to the subsidiaries to get a good understanding of our problems and opportunities, and the other 50% pushing my ideas through corporate, and that left precious little time for coordination. I was the only one in a position to take a global perspective of our various businesses, yet my ability to do that was being threatened by the large number of demands on my time.

A second major difficulty was becoming evident in the company's ineffectiveness at transferring its technology to its foreign operations. Until the late 1960s, this generally had been achieved through informal but strong direct links that developed between the various overseas plants and individual technical experts in U.S. plants or product division staffs. As the number of foreign operations and transferred technologies multiplied, however, these informal relationships were unable to meet the demands placed on them and more reliance was placed on the formal channels within the international organization. This led to frustrations both at the subsidiary and within Corning's U.S. organization as Bill Hudson, Sovirel's general manager at the time, explained:

> There was a manufacturing and engineering manager located in the United States on the area manager's staff, and he was supposed to be our technical liaison with the parent company. But with so many products and processes to know, and so many countries to service, we found that our priorities just weren't being attended to. Finally, I put an English-speaking Sovirel man in Corning to act as our technical liaison to try to keep open our channels of communication to the technical experts in the divisions and in corporate. But the only way to really get things done was for me to visit Corning personally for a week or so every couple of months—not only to get technical help but also to see what new products were being developed and to push our appropriation requests through.

Dick Dulude, vice president and general manager of the Technical Products Division at the time, discussed the technology transfer problem from the domestic division perspective:

> In the early 1970s we were developing an excellent new product opportunity in photochromic glass—the eyeglass lens that darkens with increased light intensity. Nobody in International really understood the product, its potential applications, or how to manufacture it, and I could see that we were not capitalizing on this major corporate opportunity. So, largely through the efforts of my domestic organization, we got the project moving in France. Then, several months later I asked how things were developing on the project, and the French subsidiary told me that their capital appropriation request had been blocked. I certainly had no responsibility or authority to get photochromic glass established overseas, but the business represented such a major opportunity for the company that I decided I would chase the French project through personally. It turned

out that some corporate controller was deliberately holding up the appropriation approval documents as a lever to get the French to bring expenses under control. The whole problem was that nobody had a worldwide business responsibility or perspective.

A third set of organizational problems centered on the inability of the area-based structure to provide the global marketing coordination necessary in some businesses. In the television bulb business, for example, most of Corning's customers were multinational organizations such as Philips, RCA, or Sylvania. When the Corning subsidiary in Brazil defended its local position by reducing prices, the impact was felt throughout the company's worldwide television bulb business. Yet, nobody was coordinating global actions relating to price, product, or sourcing. Furthermore, because there was an area rather than a product focus within CIC, no consensus on product development needs for International was being communicated to the research group. Since Corning's R&D effort was oriented toward specific problems or applications, this meant that it was responding less to international development needs.

To try to resolve these various problems, Behm decided in 1972 to supplement his area-based international organization with a global business perspective. To do this, he appointed three international business managers with the status of vice

president of CIC, each being responsible for developing one or two lines of business worldwide. Each business manager built up a staff of three to six product and project managers and reported to the president of CIC. Although no job description existed for these new positions, a CIC publication described the relationship between functional, area, and business managers: "Responsibility for Corning International Corporation operations rests with three groups: *staff* services are provided largely by the parent company in a consulting and coordinating capacity; *area managers* are responsible for day-to-day operations within their respective geographical limits; *business managers* are responsible for developing business strategies for specific product lines worldwide." This structure is shown in Exhibit 6.

The first business manager appointed was made responsible for consumer products and he was given a rather general mandate "to straighten things out in consumer products in International." In particular, there was some concern over the state of the consumer products business in Europe. Following the outstanding success of Corning Ware in the United States, the company decided to make a major launch of its freezer-to-oven-to-table product line in Europe. In the mid-1960s, it had built a plant in Holland to manufacture Corning Ware, thereby bypassing its joint ventures in France and the United Kingdom. The product had never taken off in

EXHIBIT 6   Corning International Organization Representation

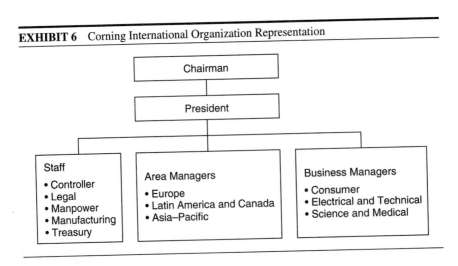

Europe as it had in the United States, however, and one of the new consumer business manager's major assignments was to help overcome this situation.

The man appointed to the job was a 25-year veteran of Corning who had spent much of his career in sales and sales management, particularly in the Consumer Products Division. Before his appointment as business manager, he had been president of a small division called Corning Packaging Company. He explained his view of his new task: "I'm trying to get some consumer-oriented thinking into subsidiaries overseas. As far as I'm concerned, they can take my role as advisory or directive or any way they want as long as the job gets done. But if my role is to be done right, then I've got to have clout in it, so I lean on the subsidiaries. I can't just allow them to sit there. You have got to let these people understand they are in a worldwide company, not a local one."

The second business manager was given responsibility for science and medical products. There was still no written job description, but he was told that his task would be "to put together a worldwide strategy for these products." The first half of his 20-year Corning experience had been in sales and mostly within the international organization. From 1965 until his appointment as a business manager, however, he had been manager of market planning for International. His sales and marketing background convinced him that his role was to assume worldwide marketing responsibility for his product lines, and he viewed the area managers as being mainly responsible for manufacturing.

The third business manager was given responsibility for electrical products (mainly television). He had previously worked in domestic manufacturing and engineering positions in his 15 years with the company. In carrying out his assignment, he adopted the view that his main role was that of a strategic planner for his product line, and secondly, as a conduit between the domestic operation and the area and subsidiary managers. In his view, the area managers needed to retain sole line authority to be effective, while his contribution could be through integrating the overseas and domestic parts of the operation.

Although there had been general agreement within the international organization that changes were necessary to provide some coordination and integration of product lines worldwide, almost from the outset the international business manager concept seemed to fall short of many of the expectations held for it. From the subsidiary management's viewpoint, the business managers were seen largely as an interference, although some were viewed less favorably than others. In discussions with subsidiary personnel, one gained the impression that the electrical products manager was generally seen as "helpful" because he "provided coordination in a truly worldwide business." The consumer products manager, on the other hand, was seen as "a total disaster," due to his efforts at "interfering in purely local issues such as how to promote and sell Corning Ware on the French market."

A variety of explanations were given for the limited success of the new organization. One country manager felt that some of the problems experienced by the business managers were due to the way the change was introduced to the organization: "The first I knew about worldwide business managers was from the yellow sheet announcing the appointment of the consumer products manager. People in my subsidiary were asking what this meant, who they would be reporting to, and how the whole thing would work. I had to answer that I honestly didn't know. As a result there was a certain defensiveness from the outset on the part of subsidiary personnel."

The European area manager at the time saw the major problem as being the strain put on the existing organization by the additional demands for managers' time and information.

> We all knew something had to be done to integrate business worldwide, but the problem with this solution was that the business managers' role was never properly defined and nobody knew how to relate to them. For me it meant a huge increase in the number of visits and other communications requirements, and these were a distraction from ongoing operations. With all the missions, safaris, and junkets to Europe, I was spending at least two nights a week entertaining visiting Americans.

Behm agreed that the change was not as effective as he had hoped. The main problem he saw was the business managers' inability to provide strong links to the domestic product divisions—to replace the liaison role he had undertaken personally for so long. In this view, this was at least partially due to the fact that some domestic managers wanted to control the fast-growing overseas part of their businesses themselves. In effect, the domestic division managers were saying, "If we have to provide you with all this support, why don't we just run the worldwide business ourselves?"

Dick Dulude, general manager of Technical Products Division at the time, replied that in his view the problem lay in the people appointed to the business manager position:

> Most of them just didn't have the status or credibility within the organization to do the job effectively. Forry Behm may have appointed these positions with the status equivalent of vice president, but I don't think there was a single vice president in the domestic corporation who saw them as equals. That's the reason they had difficulty liaising with the domestic organization—they simply lacked the power and credibility to get things done.

1974 Organization Change: World Boards

By the end of 1973, it was clear that the business manager concept was not meeting the demands it had been created to fill. Behm realized that he would have to integrate CIC more with the domestic organization if Corning was to manage its businesses on a truly global basis. With this objective in mind, he formulated the idea of *world boards* and developed it with his boss, James Houghton. The concept was to bring together managers with geographic, product, and functional expertise from the parent and the international companies, and to give them joint responsibility for developing strategies for the company's worldwide businesses. Six world boards were set up, one for each of the company's major worldwide businesses (television, consumer, electronics, and so forth). Each board determined its own membership, agenda, and meeting time, place, and frequency. In effect, the world boards were to be a vehicle that allowed the business manager to perform an integrative role between the domestic and international organizations. Typically, membership would include the U.S. product division general

manager, key members of the product division technical and marketing staff, subsidiary product division managers and/or subsidiary general managers, and the CIC business manager. As chairman of the world board, the business manager theoretically had the opportunity to involve the domestic division general managers in international developments, and to give area and subsidiary managers a communication link to the parent company.

In a major speech to Corning's top 300 managers attending a conference in January 1974, Houghton explained how world boards would operate and what their objectives were:

> Each world board is composed of the key people from each geographic area for the product line, domestic and overseas, plus the international business managers. These business managers, jobs created less than two years ago, are a vital link between our domestic and international operations. They are a key interface between all organizations on a day-to-day basis and furnish much of the staff work and initiative for the world boards. But the business managers can't do it all alone, and this is where the world boards fit in.
>
> The charter of each world board is to concern itself with all aspects of business as it relates to the present and future activity of the Corning group. It is in no way intended to supplant local management in its business activities. It is intended to supplement local management by providing a global strategy and a harmonization of all group activities. With the creation of world boards, we hope to move a step further toward becoming a truly international company.
>
> Thus we expect world boards to understand, help, communicate, question, plan, reassure, review, measure, and recommend, but *not* to manage or control. They will meet regularly in a *shared responsibility* to hammer out our world strategies and plan the future of our businesses.

Six world boards were established, one for each major worldwide business, and Houghton was explicit in his expectations for these new bodies. They were expected to (1) provide business marketing and operating planning on a world scale, (2) take advantage of global sourcing possibilities, (3) assure that Corning technology was developed on a worldwide scale, (4) make investment recommendations, and (5) develop international management. On this last point, Houghton emphasized the need for the non–U.S. personnel to become involved in Corning's worldwide management.

Some of the world boards appeared to meet these objectives admirably, and the example most frequently cited was the Optical Products World Board. The business manager responsible was Bill Hudson, former general manager of Sovirel. Having been appointed later than the other three business managers, he had had the chance to learn from their difficulties. "There were two main reasons why the optical world board worked," he explained. "First, it was to a substantial extent a worldwide business with opportunities and problems that had global implications. Second, the domestic division manager and I worked as a team, and always sorted out our differences *before* the world board met, and this prevented the board from becoming a political tool or a battleground."

In most of the other world boards, one or both of these requirements were missing. As a result, they either slipped into a "debating society" role in which issues were aired but never resolved, or they simply stopped meeting. The Consumer Products world board, for example, met only once, then lapsed. The domestic division manager was not even a board member.

Houghton reflected on the reasons why some of the world boards did not meet his expectations:

> First, I think the proposal had a skeptical reception, particularly given the difficulties the business manager concept had created. The overseas managers saw this as a first step in the collapse of the area organization, while the domestic division managers were concerned that the international business manager still seemed to be in the way. Second, I think you need perfect people to make the concept work: the business manager must be a great integrator, the domestic manager must be a team player, and the area managers must be willing to cooperate, even when their local interests are not fully satisfied.

Behm diagnosed the problem in these terms: "The world boards simply became too large and clumsy.

The television board had 15 people or more, and science had over 20. As a result, there were too many parochial views, special interests, and local problems represented, and the big issues didn't get resolved. The other major problem was that some domestic division managers did not cooperate, and were still trying to find ways to control the worldwide business directly."

MacAvoy, president of Corning Glass, attributed the failure in part to a lack of the domestic organization's involvement in the formation of the world boards:

> Despite the clear need for strong involvement by the domestic division managers reporting to me, I was not consulted on the form or the function of the world boards. I felt that continued independent action by either the international or domestic organization was disastrous for the company. We were a technology-based company whose strength lay in applying the technologies it developed to businesses and products that could benefit from them. It was crazy to have organizational barriers between the technology resources which were under my control, and a large part of our potential market which was not.

Need for Change

As Behm reviewed the organization's structure, he realized that neither the business manager concept nor the world board experiment had provided the effective device he needed to coordinate subsidiary operations worldwide and to integrate them into the company's domestic businesses. Yet, the lessons from those two experiences were not altogether clear. Was it the structure that was inappropriate, or were the organization processes and systems the reason for failure? Could either of these solutions have been more effective had they been implemented differently, or been given more time to succeed?

In thinking about these issues, the president of CIC knew that several of the domestic product division managers had been suggesting that the company divide up its international operations into individual product businesses and hand them over to the product divisions to manage globally. But Behm believed the solution was not as simple as that. Many of the businesses shared production facilities within a subsidiary, and could not be carved up into discrete operations. Furthermore, that would mean having six or eight separate Corning subsidiaries in major countries like France or the United Kingdom, and thereby losing the efficiencies of a single operation. In Behm's view, a single country operation with one strong general manager could be more effective in providing critical labor negotiations, government relations, and key customer contacts than a multiplicity of smaller subsidiaries.

At the same time, he recognized the need for CIC's operations to be better coordinated and more integrated with the U.S. operations. Yet the two attempts he had made to correct this situation had not met his expectations. He knew that if he wanted to restructure his organization again, it was going to be more difficult because of these past problems. He also knew that a third unsuccessful attempt to change the organization could have serious effects on his managers' morale. There was a good deal of pressure on Behm to ensure that his analysis of the previously encountered problems was correct, and that his proposal for future changes effectively dealt with these problems.

Case 5–2   *Lufthansa: The Challenge of Globalisation*

Deutsche Lufthansa AG—The Company

In 1991, Lufthansa was the national airline carrier of the Federal Republic of Germany, state owned, heavily subsidised and unprofitable. By 1996, Lufthansa was an independent, privately owned, profitable company; the flag carrier of a united Germany with aspirations to become a key global player in the airline industry.

Over this period, Lufthansa went from a record loss of DM 444 million in 1991 to a record profit of DM 302 million in 1994. By 1994, Lufthansa was carrying 37.7 million passengers and 1.26 million tonnes of freight. It was the global leader in air cargo and carried the second largest number of scheduled passengers in the world. It was serving 221 destinations in 85 countries and every 37 seconds a Lufthansa plane took off or landed somewhere in the world.

History

Deutsche Lufthansa AG was formed on January 6, 1926, as a result of a merger between Deutsche Aero Lloyd and Junkers Luftverkehr AG. When war broke out in 1939, Lufthansa was forced to abandon international flights and, in 1945, went into liquidation after the Potsdam Treaty prohibited all German flights. In 1953, the Aktiengesellschaft für Luftverkehrsbedarf (Luftag) was founded in Cologne to establish a new German air transport system. A year later, Luftag changed its name to Deutsche Lufthansa AG, and in 1955, the first scheduled services began. The company grew rapidly with the number of passengers exceeding 10 million for the first time 20 years later.

The mid-1980s saw a fundamental reorganisation of Lufthansa to give sales and marketing departments greater flexibility. A new "warmer" corporate identity was adopted with new livery for the aircraft, lounges, and offices. The company also began to expand its fleet, arguing that consolidation in the industry would only allow the largest airlines to survive. After many years of commitment to a policy of independence from other airlines, it signed its first co-operation agreements in 1989 with Air

This case was prepared by Annette Gardner, Rebecca Hansen, Louise Marchant, Hanno Ronte, and Indira Thambiah under the supervision of Professor Sumantra Ghoshal.

© London Business School, April 1996

France, Varig (Brazil) and United Airlines (USA). In 1990, just 25 days after reunification, Lufthansa resumed its scheduled services to Berlin.

Crisis in the Early 1990s

At the beginning of the 1990s, Lufthansa was organised into functional departments, each led by a member of the Vorstand (the executive board). The Vorstand was responsible for the running of the company and reported to the Aufsichtsrat (the supervisory board), comprising representatives from management, staff, and the government. The outbreak of the Gulf War in 1991 and economic recession impacted Lufthansa's financial performance. To senior managers, it became clear that these factors were not the sole causes of the problem. Despite rising volumes, the company's yield (revenues per km) was falling at a rate of up to 7% pa. Management saw that Lufthansa was nearing bankruptcy while most of the staff were unaware of the impending crisis.

The Turnaround

In 1991, Jürgen Weber replaced Heinz Rühnau as chairman of Lufthansa and in early 1992 the company embarked on Phase 1 of the turnaround. The first priorities were to communicate the gravity of the situation to Lufthansa managers and staff and to stem the losses. The 'Samurai of Change,' 25 middle managers, began to communicate this message within the company. A 'Sanierungsworkshop' (restructuring workshop) followed. Comprising many of the company's managers, it developed 123 key actions aimed at cutting costs and staff numbers and increasing revenues in order to reduce Lufthansa's losses by DM 1.3 billion. A smaller team, 'the Ops team' was then appointed to oversee the implementation of the proposed changes. In all, Lufthansa suffered losses for the three years from 1991 to 1993 before returning to profitability in 1994. Over this period, a pay freeze and a reduction of 8,500 staff was successfully negotiated with the unions.

Lufthansa recognised, however, that such actions would not be sufficient. At the outset of Phase 2 of the turnaround, it embarked on negotiations with the

German government to become a private company and to withdraw from the government pension fund which further tied it to the State. In 1994, the government diluted its holdings to 36% and a new organisational structure was announced. From January 1995, five new independent companies were created: Cargo, Technik (maintenance), Systems, Ground Service, and Flight Operations. These joined the existing Lufthansa subsidiaries: Condor (charter flights), Lufthansa City Lines (domestic flights) and LSG Skychef (catering). All the subsidiaries report to the main Lufthansa executive board but only the passenger airline business (Passenger Services and Passenger Operations) and central functions have remained in its direct control (see Appendix 1). Each subsidiary is wholly accountable for its results and is increasingly able to purchase services from external third parties if those offered by other subsidiaries are not competitive.

The turnaround made 1994 Lufthansa's most profitable year in its history. However, despite this success, the crisis for Lufthansa is not over—yields continue to fall at around 2% pa and pressures from the intensely competitive airline industry remain.

The Airline Industry

In 1994, the global annual turnover for scheduled passenger services was $231 billion.[1] The top 10 companies comprised six U.S. carriers and four others, British Airways, Lufthansa, Japan Airlines, and Air France (see Appendix 2). Over the next 20 years, growth in scheduled passenger traffic and cargo is expected to rise by 5% pa and 7% pa respectively. The fastest growing region is expected to be Southeast Asia.

Deregulation

In 1978, the U.S. led the way in deregulating the airline industry. The European carriers persuaded the European Union to begin deregulation in 1987. They recognised the threat to the European market from U.S. carriers' new-found strength. By 1997,

---

[1]*IATA*, Geneva.

deregulation in Europe will be complete; price fixing will have been eliminated and European airlines will have access to all European airports and the freedom to operate within any European country and between any two European countries. For Lufthansa, this is both an opportunity and a threat. For example, Deutsche BA, a subsidiary of British Airways, has already begun operating domestic flights within Germany. The impact of European deregulation, however, may be limited by the large national carriers who control the landing slots at their major domestic airports. On a global level, the industry remains highly regulated with routes usually negotiated by governments who are likely to act in the interests of their national carriers.

Increased Competition

The lower barriers to entry coupled with the effects of the Gulf War and the subsequent recession has led to industry over-capacity and intense price competition. This has been compounded by state subsidisation of some national carriers in Europe and Asia and by U.S. Chapter 11 insolvency legislation which have allowed some airlines to operate at a loss.

International airlines have found it difficult to respond to this increase in competition because their cost structures are relatively similar. Attempts to improve in-flight service are easily replicated by others and many airlines have turned to frequent flier programs to increase customer loyalty. They have also begun to compete through the control of Computer Reservation Systems (CRS) which allow greater access to customers, increase pricing flexibility, and enable closer links between airlines through route and code sharing.

Emerging Industry Structure

Regional deregulation and increased competition have led to a polarisation within the industry between small regional carriers and large global carriers. The larger carriers have retained control of the key regional hubs and have formed alliances with the smaller carriers which act as feeders, carrying passengers and cargo from locations throughout the region to the hubs. The lack of global deregulation

has meant that the larger carriers have difficulty expanding outside their original regions. To overcome this, they are forging partnerships either through equity investment or alliances with other major carriers from different regions which have similar service levels and complementary skills.

Lufthansa and Globalisation

In March 1995, the *Economist* commented that British Airways' chairman had "correctly bet in the late 1980s that the aviation world would be dominated by a handful of very large airlines."[2] This view of the airline industry's future is shared by all the major carriers. Lufthansa, like many others, is determined to be one of the global players that will lead the industry into the twenty-first century. The question for Lufthansa is how it can best achieve this. The answer has frequently been encapsulated in the word 'globalisation.' But as a director of Condor commented "there was never an explanation of the word globalisation."

Lufthansa has yet to explore the full implications of its goal of globalisation. Five of the key issues it will need to address in exploring globalisation are:

- Continuing development of the strategy to create a global network through alliances.
- Further realisation of the benefits of the restructuring programme.
- Internationalisation of costs to balance the increasing revenues originating outside Germany.
- Development of managers willing and able to operate successfully in a wide variety of markets and with people from different cultures.
- Development of a service culture geared to meeting the expectations of increasingly diverse customers.

Alliances

For international airlines seeking to globalise there are two distinct strategic options: firstly, indepen-

---

[2]*Economist,* 4 March 1995.

dent growth through equity investment abroad; and secondly, the formation of alliances with other airlines. British Airways (BA) has chosen the first option buying a 24.6% stake in USAir to gain a foothold in the U.S., the source of approximately 50% of the world's airline passengers. Lufthansa's limited resources have led it to forge non-equity partnerships with, amongst others, Thai Airways in Southeast Asia, United Airlines in the U.S., and the Scandinavian airline, SAS, in Europe, abandoning its previous policy of independence "Alliances are carefully sought and built on trust. It is like an engagement, not a marriage," Senior VP, Lufthansa.

Alliances are generally formed by a bilateral agreement between two companies. However as the network of alliances broadens, operational interdependencies are intensified. Currently, Lufthansa's important partners are allied with each other, (e.g., Thai Airways is also allied with SAS and United). However, bilateral agreements between one member of the alliance network and a third party are possible, with inevitable operational and branding implications.

Principles of Alliance Networks

The principles of alliances may be illustrated by Lufthansa's agreement with SAS, their most recent alliance partner (1 February, 1996). "SAS and Lufthansa will base their alliance on a close cooperation with no equity bonds. The two carriers remain fully independent and retain their identities. The alliance works on the principle of 'two restaurants-one kitchen.'" This was part of a statement issued in 1996 to SAS and Lufthansa staff by President and CEO of the SAS Group , Jan Stenbergin, in what he described as "a year of alliances for SAS."

Stations. Lufthansa handles SAS passengers and aircraft at German airports, and vice-versa. There is common baggage handling and check-in. Lounges are open to each other's customers.

Products. Products and procedures are harmonised including newspapers, in-flight service procedures, meals and meal times, and announcements.

Traffic system. All revenues and costs are shared between SAS and Lufthansa on shared routes. There is joint planning of international routes and harmonisation of fare structures within the European Union to give the customer a more frequent 'joint' schedule. There is a Lufthansa or SAS flight available at almost all times. Frequent flyer programmes are also coordinated both in terms of points collection and redemption.

IT systems. IT systems are harmonised to support code sharing, reservations and CRS displays.

Operational Implications

Whilst the stated goals of partnerships are clear, implementation is by no means simple. "Alliances bring all sorts of detailed issues to light . . . in the U.S. you can have two pieces of hand luggage while in Europe only one. Thus the passenger boarding a UA flight will be told on transfer to Lufthansa that he can only have one. These can be irritating issues for the client," Operations Manager, Frankfurt.

Customers expect similar service from all of the partners, particularly as these partnerships are generally invisible to the customer. For example, a customer booking a flight from Europe to Australia on 'Lufthansa' may fly the Tokyo to Sydney leg on a Thai Airways plane. This requires firstly, an agreement on service levels and secondly, a uniformity in hiring and training staff to ensure that the agreed level of service is maintained.

The alliance network brings with it a broader customer base with a wide variety of expectations. Meeting these expectations has been one of the reasons prompting Lufthansa to hire non-German cabin crew from India and Thailand. However, the costs and benefits of hiring non-German staff are still open to debate.

Merging Cultures

The key issues for Lufthansa and its partners will be to internationalise training activities and merge corporate cultures.

"In order to understand our strategic partners we need to have employees from other cultures

. . . people from different cultures bring new ideas although we need to protect our own culture—we must not deny our own history," Senior Manager, Condor.

But implementation is not without problems: "When we brought a group of Thai and Indian flight attendants to Frankfurt for training, everyone in the cafeteria looked at them because they were so different," HR Manager, Lufthansa AG.

"The problem is to convince people that Lufthansa cannot survive in this world alone. Weber emphasises the importance of alliances but it is hard for employees to accept—the mental change is still going on but we have to work hard to make it happen," Operations Manager, Frankfurt.

Although there is much to be gained from globalisation and the alliance partners many feel that "we must not give up our identity."

Vision of the Future

Lufthansa has already demonstrated a strength in its ability to develop powerful industry partnerships; its alliance strategy is a critical element of this quest for globalisation. The continuing development and cohesion of these relationships will be essential for the success of these networks in the future. Some are clear about the vision of the future: "We want to offer a seamless global connection for the global passenger," Senior VP, Lufthansa AG.

Nevertheless, the extent of integration remains an issue of debate. Employees have commented that "there is no clear strategy for integration." Perhaps the ultimate vision might be, " . . . a global umbrella brand, e.g. 'Leading Airlines of the World,' which would include Lufthansa, SAS, United and Thai. But we must remember that each of these has unique strengths that they do not want to lose," Senior VP, Passenger Division. A clear picture has yet to emerge.

Restructuring for Globalisation

Implementation of the New Structure

A global strategy must be supported by an appropriate organisational structure. For Lufthansa, Phase 2 of the turnaround brought the introduction of inde-pendent companies within the overall Lufthansa Group. Plans for this change were finalised in January 1994, leaving just 12 months for the first three new subsidiaries to complete preparations for formal separation on 1 January 1995. These subsidiaries, Cargo, Technik, and Systems, each appointed a team to develop a different organisational structure designed for their unique business and customers.

Principles of Restructuring

"The company was split to create entrepreneurial responsibility within manageable entities," Senior VP, Lufthansa AG.

Restructuring was based around certain key principles:

- **Responsibility**—Subsidiaries face the challenges and rewards of the market in which they compete; reducing the opportunity for cross-subsidisation or masking poor performance.
- **Accountability**—Costs and revenues are 'transparent'; it is clear which part of the organisation is successful and which must be changed or removed.
- **Alliance possibilities**—Each individual subsidiary can seek partners of value to their own area of business. New partners will not be discouraged by unrelated parts of the business.
- **Third party business**—Subsidiaries may seek customers beyond the Lufthansa umbrella.
- **Flexibility**—Each business is able to respond to business opportunities and local market needs.
- **Customer orientation**—Subsidiaries address their own customers and remain externally focused.

Operational Impact of Restructuring

For many of the subsidiaries, the changes have brought about a significant shift in business emphasis, mode of operation, and performance measurement. "Discipline only happens in small business units, when you replace the functional boundaries with business boundaries," Senior Manager, Cargo.

By establishing independent profit centres, companies and individuals have been forced into a greater business awareness: "Previously this was like an institute for air transport not a company . . . we had no clearly defined responsibility for business results," whereas now, "results are what count."

" . . . no one was interested in how much anything cost . . . we had internal billing but it was not visible. There was only one company result that mattered and that was Lufthansa AG! We had goals, but not business ones . . ." VP, Lufthansa Systems.

During the restructuring there was pressure to continue the cost reduction initiated in Phase 1 of the turnaround. This was achieved by several means including a reduction in the number of managers, redesigning processes and eliminating waste.

The new structure allows regional managers within the same business unit to communicate directly with each other. Information no longer has to pass up the line, possibly to managers less familiar with the market, before it travels back down the organisational hierarchy. "I now have much more freedom to make decisions—results are what count. There are fewer managers and people don't have to refer decisions upwards. Relations with my boss have changed; he is no longer my customer—the people who pay are," HR Manager, Lufthansa AG.

Communication between the subsidiaries is as a customer to a supplier. For some this has led to confusion as they search for the appropriate contacts and build new informal networks. Each subsidiary has its own independent management meetings which can mean that the information sharing across companies is limited. This has been accompanied by the development of a new corporate identity within each subsidiary, "I work for Lufthansa Systems not Lufthansa!" A potential danger of this is that the subsidiaries will start to do everything themselves, duplicating corporate or other subsidiary functions. For instance, some of the subsidiaries have started to develop internal systems houses.

Effects of Restructuring on Individuals

The restructuring has affected individuals differently. This is due to differences in role, position and level of seniority, and also because of differences in individual personality and motivation. For some, the effect of transformation has been negligible:

"Globalisation has not been an issue for me in the short term—I have not been affected by these changes," Senior Manager, Cargo. Others have discovered new opportunities, responsibilities, and freedom.

In many cases, authority has been pushed down the ranks to local managers who now have greater power to make decisions. The entrepreneurial spirit is encouraged. "I have learnt to rely on people—I give them targets, a framework, and tools and act as their coach," Operations Manager, Frankfurt.

"I have to educate them carefully toward more independence. If they come to me and say 'I have this problem' I answer, 'do you think I know the answer? Of course not! What are your solutions? Let's work on it together.' I have the philosophy that you need to tell people what the goal is, but let them find their own way there," Manager, Training Institute.

Lufthansa uses an inverted triangle to describe the new philosophy: senior managers supporting the 'front line' regional managers, closest to the customer. They limit their involvement with operational issues, allowing more time to concentrate on strategic decision making.

Middle managers have been given the freedom to make changes to respond to local market needs, "probably more freedom than they realise." For some, accustomed to following the rules and succeeding by doing things perfectly, the new responsibility has meant an uncomfortable shift in practice. They have had the "shock of being born." But others have embraced the changes and the opportunities they offer: "There is more work to be done now because there are so many projects going on . . . its become like a fever," General Manager Marketing, USA. "Its so exciting! . . . I never thought I would feel this good about my job!" Regional Director, Lufthansa Cargo.

With freedom comes new challenges, but the downside for individuals is pressure and risk. In some cases, rapid changes have not yet been supported by fully developed structures and systems. Cost reductions have left staff with fewer resources and, although productivity has risen, for many this has meant increased pressure. There is no book of rules; people are pointed in the right direction and allowed to get on with it. Generally senior managers are sympathetic: "If someone makes a mistake there are only rubber walls—the concrete walls come up after three or four mistakes," Senior VP, Lufthansa Cargo.

Nevertheless, many feel a sense of loss of security. "What I used to like best about Lufthansa was the safety . . . by the age of 27 I had a job for life . . . My attitude changed when I began to see the risks and the work became more interesting and challenging. People now feel and act more like owners," Senior Manager, Condor. The increased sense of risk has had implications on individuals' careers: "Contracts will change and people will have to work longer hours for less money . . ." HR Manager, Lufthansa AG.

The changes have led to a greater emphasis on career development for senior managers, controlled centrally by the Lufthansa Group. However, as the subsidiaries have become more independent, middle managers have sensed that it will be harder to move between them: "In some ways the potential scope of my career has expanded—however the restructuring has meant that each subsidiary has been very keen to keep its own people and so is restricting moves." Individuals realise that experiences in different subsidiaries offer them opportunities for learning. "There is danger now that managers will stay in one company. It is important to have the transfer of knowledge . . . We do not get much news about the Lufthansa Group these days," General Manager, Lufthansa Technik.

Internationalisation of Costs

As Lufthansa reaches ever more destinations and markets, revenues increasingly come from outside Germany while costs remain rooted in the high-cost German economy. "Germany as the cost centre is a problem. Only approximately half of our revenues come from Germany, but 65% of our costs and 80% of our staff do," Hemjö Klein, Lufthansa Board member, March 7, 1996.[3]

Lufthansa is subject to fierce global competition with the result that yields and revenues are reduced. "Global competition also makes it necessary to internationalise costs. It is a fact of life that global pricing requires global costing. If the market forces New York and Singapore prices on us, we must be able to respond accordingly. Our first step in this respect will be to employ regional flight attendants at local rates. We are very pleased that an agreement with our trade unions and employee representatives was signed on this issue a few days ago . . . In the future we shall not be able to produce everything in Germany. The slogan 'Made in Germany' will evolve into 'Made by Lufthansa,'" Jürgen Weber, Chairman Lufthansa, May 16, 1995.[4]

Following the reorganisation which has made costs more transparent, there now seems to be little doubt for senior managers that Lufthansa must internationalise costs in order to survive.

Where Can Lufthansa Internationalise Costs?
Some managers outside Germany resent the high German costs: "Let's take our Miles&More programme . . . We have 150 people sitting in Germany, on German salaries running this programme. Miles&More is a global programme. It can be run from anywhere in the world. Why must we run it from Germany?" Manager, UK.

Lufthansa has already taken significant steps toward internationalising costs including relocating operations overseas and hiring non-German cabin crew.

Recognising that planes can fly anywhere for maintenance or overhaul, Lufthansa Technik has built a base in Shannon, Ireland, to take advantage of lower local wages. The intention is to develop other strategically based centres with teams led by skilled German staff who could coach local technicians. Hence, the company would capitalise on its competitive advantage of technical excellence without suffering the full cost implications. A potential barrier to this change is the German civil

[3]"Servicewüste Deutschland," *Wirtschaftswoche,* 7 March 1996, p. 58.

[4]"Lufthansa, *Facts and Figures,* 1995, p. 30.

aviation authority which requires technicians to have particular qualifications.

When developments in IT systems allowed the relocation of ticket processing from Hamburg to New Delhi, Lufthansa was able to hire local, highly trained, computer specialists. A move which reduced costs without risking a reduction in quality. Despite claims that this exploits Indian staff by paying them so much less than the German staff, counter claims are made that salaries of DM 8,000–10,000 pa are good compared to local salary levels.

For Lufthansa Cargo, creating secondary hubs around the world, for instance in Sharjah and Bangkok, has as much to do with meeting customer needs as reducing costs. As its customers become increasingly global and industry growth predominates within Asia, Cargo can ensure a local presence while at the same time taking advantage of lower overheads.

The passenger business has made moves to internationalise the cost of its 8,000 member cabin crew. Arduous union negotiations have resulted in the concession that 10% of the cabin crew can be hired outside Germany. The first 'local' cabin crew, based in India, will start operations in April 1996 after undergoing training in Germany. The crew is not required to learn German, but must speak English.

Operational Implications

Although labour costs only represent 30% of total costs, they remain the most emotive cost issue. Not only do they directly impact job security in Germany, but they are the easiest lever for management to use. Lufthansa managers foresee tensions as the disparity between the Indian and German cabin crew's salary and benefits becomes known.

Cost was the primary impetus for hiring local cabin crews but some managers maintain that there is also a quality argument, "Germans don't want to do service jobs; foreigners tend not to have a problem with them. If I think about who always has issues with guests, disagreements, it's mainly the German staff, not the foreign staff," Manager, Training Institute.

On some routes to the Asia/Pacific, over half of the passengers are non-German, and it makes mar-

keting and strategic sense for Lufthansa to have local cabin crew. For example, on the Japanese routes Lufthansa has had local cabin crew for some time, based on the premise that an airline must have Japanese service staff to operate in Japan effectively. In Japan "salary issues were not important because the costs of living are higher in Tokyo than in Germany."

For some managers service quality remains the main reason for local cabin crew, "For me the argument for quality would have been better for promoting local cabin crew hires. Regional staff make customers from that region feel more at home and this therefore improves service quality. As a side effect, Lufthansa would have a windfall gain in terms of cost," VP, Lufthansa AG.

Although there is a balance to be reached, managers still feel a social responsibility to Germany: "I feel ambivalent about this. We need some regional cabin crew to offer the service, but also we cannot destroy employment at home. What is good for the company may not be good for the [German] economy. This issue is just what the whole country is facing now. Who will fly Lufthansa if we don't employ anyone [German] anymore?" VP, Lufthansa AG.

Issues for the Future

Ultimately, the internationalisation of costs represents a conundrum: it is necessary to 'export' jobs to remain competitive but may cost Lufthansa its German advantage: "People like Lufthansa because it's German. I don't think that it is necessary to employ people from all over the world to be a global airline," HR Manager, Lufthansa AG. "Lufthansa's critical success factors for the future is to cut costs and keep its German identity."

Employee representatives recognise the pressure Lufthansa and the German economy is under and try to work in partnership with management: "We have to negotiate with the unions. It is possible to retain the 'Made in Germany' concept and be competitive on costs. The realistic scenario is that we will internationalise all costs other than staff costs [and increase productivity]," Senior VP, Lufthansa AG.

"If you have local cabin crew, you lose German employment because you export jobs; if you don't have local cabin crew, you lose German employees because you are not competitive," VP, Corporate HR. The senior managers at Lufthansa face the challenge of deciding which costs to internationalise and to what degree, while preserving and improving the existing quality standards, cultural identity, and employee morale.

Internationalisation of Management

The majority of Lufthansa's managers are German and have only worked in Germany. This is illustrated by the backgrounds of the Executive Board members, Appendix 3. Some managers believe that in order to successfully implement a strategy of globalisation, the company's managers must become 'global.' What it means to be a global manager, the extent to which Lufthansa's managers must become global and the process by which this may be achieved are open to debate. "Jürgen Weber considers the internationalisation of management as a critical factor in the race for global markets."[5]

Currently there is no consensus on the definition of a 'global manager.' Some managers believe that they simply need to be trained to understand and respect cultural differences whilst others maintain that experience of working outside Germany is essential. Other managers argue that in order to create global management a greater number of Lufthansa's future managers will need to be non-German and all will need experience of working in several countries including Germany.

Advantages

Some managers believe that a more heterogeneous management will help Lufthansa to be successful by:

- Broadening and deepening the network of alliances with airlines from different regions of the world;
- Developing service strategies that meet the needs of increasingly culturally diverse customers;

- Predicting and reacting to the strategic moves of global competitors;
- Expanding Lufthansa's markets and increasing its market share by adapting marketing strategies to reflect local differences; and
- Managing staff that will be drawn from an increasingly wide range of countries.

Disadvantages

There are concerns that larger numbers of non-German managers may weaken management cohesion and the company's culture and image. "In order to understand our strategic partners we need to have people from other cultures . . . they bring new ideas but I think we need to protect our own culture—we must not deny our own history," Senior Manager, Condor. There is also reluctance to employ non-Germans in some posts abroad for fear of financial mismanagement and corruption.

Barriers

If Lufthansa adopts a policy of internationalising its management, it will need to introduce new systems and overcome cultural barriers. Such a policy might require significant financial investment at a time when there is continuing pressure to reduce costs. For some subsidiaries with less global interests, there may be little incentive to invest in such managers.

Currently, all management training courses are conducted in German and some non-German managers, although fluent in German, are frustrated with the company's limited acceptance of English. "Globalisation means that we must communicate internationally in English," Manager, U.K.

Many managers are reluctant to work abroad. "It is hard to encourage good managers to work abroad; in the past the people who were sent abroad were the people with problems. The organisation forgets about the people it has sent abroad. If you go away for three years you could miss opportunities. Managers here don't think in advance about what job someone should be given when they return from abroad," Manager, Lufthansa Technik.

---

[5]"I'm a Bavarian," *managermagazin*, April 1996.

Much will depend on whether Lufthansa decides that it will only need global managers in country positions or that it will eventually need global managers in all senior positions.

Developing a Service Culture

In response to increased competition airlines are seeking ways of differentiating themselves. Lufthansa has traditionally focused on the more technical aspects of service: reliability, punctuality, and safety. However, these aspects are now easily imitated by key competitors. "At the moment, we concentrate on safety and reliability and we are not customer focused. Now these are taken for granted; most airlines can offer them," Senior VP, Lufthansa AG. The quality and nature of the interaction between customers and staff (both in flight and on the ground) has become an increasingly important differentiator.

Lufthansa's Current Service Culture

In particular, Lufthansa has begun to recognise the importance of customer service through its alliances with airlines such as Thai Airways. There is a growing concern that Lufthansa must not only meet the expectations of its own customers but also the often different expectations of its partners' customers.

Some customers perceive Lufthansa staff to be unsmiling, unfriendly, and too concerned with company procedures. " . . . a Lufthansa airport lounge in Germany was due to close at 10.30 p.m. However, a Lufthansa flight was delayed and would not depart until 11 p.m. A German member of parliament refused to leave the lounge when the Lufthansa staff asked all the passengers to leave at the appointed time of 10.30 p.m. Despite the customer's request for the lounge to be kept open it was closed on time . . . Another example is that of a very good customer of Cargo who commented that, for him, Lufthansa was the greatest; better than all its competitors . . . but only if he follows Lufthansa's rules," Senior Manager, The Americas.

The company's focus on technical excellence and its attitude towards customer service is reflected in the aspects of service that the company chooses to measure. "In our customer service index, there are 15 points, but only one refers to whether employees were friendly and helpful, the others are more technical, like seat space." Appendix 4 shows the Lufthansa Service Index.

The need to develop a more customer-focused service culture has become a major issue for Lufthansa. "The message is that if the culture doesn't change, the customer will go elsewhere. The customer will always determine who wins and who loses. This decision will be made on very subtle differences in attitude, service, and treatment," Senior Manager, The Americas.

What Is High-Quality Service?

The dilemma for Lufthansa is how to define high-quality service. Does high-quality service mean the same thing to all customers? And should Lufthansa, as a German airline, strive to offer the same kind of service as Asian airlines or should it offer something different which is equally valuable and reflects its 'Germanness'?

"Germany has a style. Just because a Singapore International Airlines stewardess is willing to do anything for a customer doesn't mean that a Lufthansa stewardess should be. Some aspects of the service provided by Asian airlines are in their culture. Yes, we can insist on plastic smiles, but I think that it is better not to smile if you are German. Service is all about expectations and I'm not sure that it will work if we are exactly like the other airlines," Senior VP, Lufthansa AG.

Some managers believe that Lufthansa's image has a global appeal. "Lufthansa is an excellent brand world-wide and customers do want to buy some of the Germanness." But others think that Lufthansa may not meet all the needs of even its German customers. "The German mentality is slightly schizophrenic; wanting the almond-eyes type of devout service combined with German engineering efficiency. Globalisation means that it is not enough to be on time anymore; we must deliver the guest happy as well," Operation Manager, Condor. It is very difficult to meet this range of customer expectations. "The Americans perceive this [German] form of service as lacking warmth. Germans on the other hand find Americans too forward," General Manager, USA.

Hiring the Right Skills

If Lufthansa is to make the transition to being more customer focused, it needs the right people. The company is approaching this challenge in two ways. Selection criteria for personnel recruited in Germany have changed and the company has begun to hire flight attendants from India and Thailand.

The first approach reflects the view that people with appropriate service skills can be found in Germany. "A few years ago we employed more teachers as flight attendants than were employed in German schools. Now we are hiring people who have worked in service industries and are empathic even if they are less well educated . . . The important issue is not which country people come from but whether they have the right personalities. In Germany it is easy to find appropriate people . . . because of the high unemployment we are getting a good standard of applicants," HR Manager, Lufthansa AG.

The hiring of foreign nationals is particularly supported by those who believe that only by having personnel from a wide variety of backgrounds can Lufthansa meet the needs of its increasingly diverse customers. "People who have always worked in Germany have too narrow a perspective. When I look for new personnel they have to be willing to work in a foreign country . . . this is a main selection criteria," Senior Manager, Lufthansa Technical Training.

Measuring and Rewarding Service

For customer service to be a priority with employees, it must be a priority with the company. To reinforce the move towards a service culture, Lufthansa is in the process of developing ways of measuring and rewarding managers' contribution to customer service.

"Service quality has to be added to cost and revenue as a managerial performance measure.

Lufthansa has created a quality index which is reviewed each month. It measures friendliness, amount and quality of information, punctuality, luggage delivery, etc. By measuring service quality people can see what to do. Bearing in mind that service is different things to different people, Lufthansa has also developed different schemes or ways to measure quality region by region. The regions flown to most often receive most attention. The Executive Board has said quality is equal in importance to cost and revenues. The idea of 'service industry' has to come from the top and the top has to live by what they say. The board members have town meetings [meetings with staff] all over the world. This is where the service quality imperative comes down," Senior VP, Lufthansa AG.

Conclusion

Is Change Sustainable?

Although Lufthansa achieved record profits in 1995, senior management recognise that there is still a long way to go if the company is to become a successful global airline. Yields continue to fall at 2% pa and deregulation gives rise to ever-increasing competition.

Recently, Jürgen Weber informed unions that Lufthansa needs another DM 5 billion in savings over the next 5 years simply to maintain its current level of performance. Meanwhile, the company continues to broadcast its message of "more work for less money." This is heard and heeded by some but not all: "Lufthansa was a world-wide operating company with a good reputation. We found out that it was near bankruptcy. Some people still don't believe this," Senior Manager, Lufthansa Technical Training.

Despite apparent financial health, many of the indicators of strategic health are not good; Lufthansa does not have a clear positioning, a reputation for customer service, or a seamless alliance network. Coupled with an inherently high cost structure, and a culture traditionally focused on technical excellence, the future is not assured. Phase 3 of the Lufthansa turnaround, the change in the company's culture and mindset, will be arguably the hardest to achieve. "Lufthansa is now at a point where it will have to bleed a little—this next period will be more painful than the first," General Manager, USA.

Many managers have welcomed the changes so far. "Before it was not that interesting. Now, things change every day. We need to be so much more flexible. The changes have made every manager's job more interesting. I think this is my best time in the company." For them, the freedom and challenge has transformed their attitude to work. But for others the pressure, risk, and fear of job security has proved difficult.

Many employees feel that, given the company's return to profitability, they are entitled to a pay rise or more training and development. The full implications of the challenges ahead may only be visible to a few and so it may be difficult to maintain momentum "People think that as long as they are out there flying, they are making money for the company and that is all they have to do. They have not been included in the thinking of the company. When the company is doing well, this is an even greater problem," Operations Manager, Condor.

Communication

Essential to continuing the momentum for change is communicating the need for it. However, communication is made difficult when relationships change and when established channels are altered. Thus the restructuring has in itself made communication more difficult. "Lufthansa employees are not very optimistic at the moment. Senior managers need to convey the message that the change is here to stay . . . [but] the changes destroyed the informal networks and people are tired out from the changes. They don't understand why their colleagues keep changing every six months," Senior Manager, Condor.

Despite these difficulties, Lufthansa's willingness and ability to communicate is enhanced by the clear lead exhibited by its chairman. "You communicate the necessity of change the hard way or the Weber way—talk, and talk and talk about it. There is no other way than for managers to go to their people and talk about it and be a living example. 50% of a manager's time should be spent with his people," Senior Manager, Lufthansa Technical Training.

Questions

As Lufthansa enters the Phase 3 of the turnaround and faces the challenge of globalisation, senior management must address some critical issues:

- What does globalisation mean for Lufthansa and how can they globalise effectively?
- Are non-equity alliances the best way forward?
- Does Lufthansa have the best structure to complement its strategy? How can the company realise the full benefits of the new organisational structure?
- To what extent should Lufthansa internationalise its costs? What are the trade-offs?
- What is the value of a more international management for Lufthansa? How can this be achieved and what are the implications?
- How can Lufthansa develop a reputation for service?
- How can Lufthansa keep the momentum for change to become a leading global airline into the twenty-first century?

APPENDIX 1 Lufthansa Organizational Structure

Corporate Organizational Structure Deutsche Lufthansa AG. 01. Jan. 1995

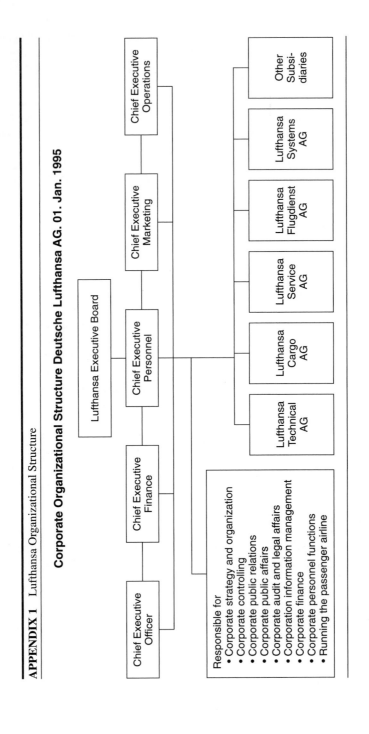

APPENDIX 2   Total International and Domestic Services of 20 Top World Airlines in 1993*

Airline	Revenue Passenger KM (£bn)	Freight Tonne KM (billion)
United Airlines	163.0	2.9
American Airlines	156.3	2.1
Delta Airlines	133.5	1.9
Northwest Airlines	94.5	3.5
British Airways	92.7	3.0
Lufthansa Group	**67.0**	**5.0**
Continental Airlines	64.6	1.0
US Air Group	56.7	0.4
Japan Airlines	56.7	3.5
Air France Group	55.4	3.8
Singapore Airlines	42.3	3.0
Quantas	40.6	1.4
KLM Royal Dutch Airlines	38.6	3.0
All Nippon Airlines	36.9	0.7
Trans World Airlines	36.7	0.6
Southwest Airlines	30.3	0.0
Cathay Pacific Airlines	29.1	2.0
Atlitalia	28.4	1.4
Korean Airlines	29.0	3.3
Iberian	22.8	0.6

*Excluding Russia

Source: *Airline Business*, September 1994.

Top 10 Airlines According to the Number of Passengers Carried on Nondomestic Flights

Airline	Passengers ('000)
British Airways	22,377
Lufthansa	**16,262**
American Airlines	14,305
Air France	12,620
United Airlines	10,942
KLM	9,855
SAS	9,337
Singapore Airlines	9,305
Cathay Pacific	8,605
Delta Airlines	8,202

Source: Reuters News Service.

APPENDIX 3 Internalisation of German Management: International Experience in the Top Management of 50 Large German Corporations

Company	Vorstand Members	International Experience*				Foreigners	Chairman CEO	International Experience
		none	<4	<9	>10			
ABB	6	4		1		1	Pohr	
Alianz	7	3	1	1	1	1	Schulte-Noelle	
AMB	5	4	1				Kaske	
BASF	9	5	2		2		Strube	10 yrs, Brazil
Bayer	8	4	2	1		1	Schneider	
Bay, Vereinsbank	9	6	1		1	1	Schmidt	
Bertelsmann	8	6	1		1		Woessner	
BMW	7	5	1	1			Pischetsreider	3 yrs, S. Africa
BP	3	1	2	2			Vogler	$ yrs, England
Colonia	8	5	1	4	1		Kleyboldt	
Commerzbank	11	5	1	2			Kohlhaussen	6 yrs, USA, Japan
Continental	6	2	2	1	2		von Gruenberg	9 yrs, Brazil, USA
Daimler - Benz	7	2	2				Schrempp	13 yrs, S. Africa, USA
Degussa	5	3	2				Bufe	4 yrs, USA
Deutshe Bahn	13	13		3			Duerr	
Deutsche Bank	12	6	2			1	Kopper	1 yr, USA
Deutsche Post	8	7	1				Zumwinkel	5 yrs, England, USA
Deutsche Telekom	8	6	1	1	1	1	Sommer	4 yrs, USA
DG Bank	10	8					Theiman	
Edeka	2	2		2			Neuhas	
Esso	4		1	3		1	Siemer	5 yrs, England, USA
Ford	10	1	3			3	Casoers	6 yrs, England, USA
Gerling	7	1	5				Zech	2 yrs, USA
Haniel	6	4	2		1		Schadt	2 yrs, France
Henkel	9	2	5	1	1	2	Winkhaus	
Hoechst	9	3	3	2		2	Dirmann	2 yrs, France
Holzmann	6	3	1	1			Mayer	2 yrs, France
IBM	4		2	1			Hug	
Krupp	5	3	1	1	1		Cromme	
Lufthansa	5	2	2		1		Weber	
MAN	9	6	1				Goette	
Mannesmann	7	5	1				Funk	
Metallgesekkschaft	4	2	2	3	1		Neukirchen	
Muenchner Rueck	11	5	2				Schinzler	
Opel	7	3	2			2	Herman	(Foreigner)
Otto	11	9	2				Otto	
Philips	3	2				1	Schmidt	
Peussag	8	6	2				Frenzel	
Rewe	3	3					Reischl	
Ruhrgas	6	5		1			Liesen	

(continued)

APPENDIX 3 (*concluded*)

Company	Vorstand Members	International Experience*					Chairman CEO	International Experience
		none	<4	<9	>10	Foreigners		
Ruhrkohle	5	5					Neipp	
RWE	10	9	1				Kuhnt	
Shell	4		2	1		1	Duncan	(Foreigner)
Siemens	14	7	3	4			von Pierer	
Thyssen	7	7					Vogel	
Veba	4	3	1				Hartman	
VIAG	5	3	1		1		Obermeier	
Volkswagen	7	1	2	1		3	Piech	(Foreigner)
Walter Holding	3	3					Walter	
WestLB	10	7	1	2			Neuber	
Total	355	207	71	41	15	21		

*International management experience abroad was only considered for German Vorstaende. Short placements of less than a year and education abroad were not considered. All information from the companies themselves. Status: 19 March 1996.

Source: *Managermagazin*, April 1996.

APPENDIX 4 Customer Service Index

The CSI is an important part of Lufthansa quality measurement. The 15 parameters are:
> Telephone availability in Germany
> Telephone availability internationally
> Service quality/sales
> Waiting time at check in
> Friendliness and efficiency/check in
> Take-off punctuality/continental
> Take-off punctuality/intercontinental
> Delay caused by maintenance
> Information during delay
> Condition of cabin
> Friendliness and attention/cabin
> Seat comfort
> Menus (including snacks and gate buffet)
> Waiting time/baggage reclaim Germany
> Miles&More mileage crediting

Source: *Lufthanseat,* 23 February 1996.

Case 5–3   *Rudi Gassner and the Executive Committee of BMG International (A)*

Rudi Gassner, CEO of BMG International, paused and glanced around the hotel suite at the members of his executive committee. They were not coming to any consensus on the issue at hand. It was May 1993 and the BMG International executive committee was gathered for one of its quarterly meetings, this time in Boca Raton, Florida, during the annual Managing Directors Convention.

Gassner had just congratulated Arnold Bahlmann, a regional director and executive committee member, on his recent negotiation of a reduced manufacturing transfer price for the upcoming year's production of CDs, records, and cassettes. Because business plans for the year had been established in March based on the assumption of a higher manufacturing cost, the new price would realize an unanticipated savings of roughly $20 million.

As a result of these savings, the executive committee now faced some tough decisions. First, they had to decide whether or not to change the business targets for each country to reflect the new manufacturing price. If they chose to alter the targets, they had to address the even more delicate matter of whether managing directors' bonuses, which were based principally on the achievement of these targets, should be based on the old or new figures.

Gassner had already discussed this issue with Bahlmann and CFO Joe Gorman, who had run calculations on the impact of the new price for each operating company. These had been distributed to the executive committee before the meeting. Through previous discussions and evaluation of the

financial impact, Gassner had formulated his opinion about what should be done.

In his mind, the issues were clear. BMG International had achieved tremendous success and growth in its short lifetime of six years, and the regional directors (RDs) and managing directors (MDs)[1] had every right to feel good about their exceptional performance. (See Exhibits 1 and 2 for company organization charts.) But now Gassner wanted to guard against the company becoming a victim of its own success. He knew that they would have to carefully monitor the economics of the business and maintain their agility in order to meet the challenges of the future. In light of these concerns, Gassner felt that the MDs should be held accountable for the savings from the reduced manufacturing price. The executive committee needed seriously to consider not only adjusting the targets, but also the bonus basis. As he explained, "It seemed fair to me. These were windfall profits coming to the managing directors, and they didn't even have to lift a finger to get them. I didn't want them to become complacent during the year."

The executive committee, however, seemed unwilling even to entertain this possibility. Gassner suspected that some of the RDs were taking the "path of least resistance" because they did not want to return to their MDs and announce that the bonus targets had been changed. His frustration mounting, Gassner wondered if he should drop the issue for now or provoke them by saying what was on his mind: "Listen guys, you're thinking too much like MDs. You should be thinking about what is good for the whole company."

Research Associate Katherine Seger Weber prepared this case under the supervision of Professor Linda A. Hill.

[1]Managing Directors managed local operations in a particular country; each MD reported to one of five Regional Directors.

EXHIBIT 1   Bertelsmann Music Group Organization Chart

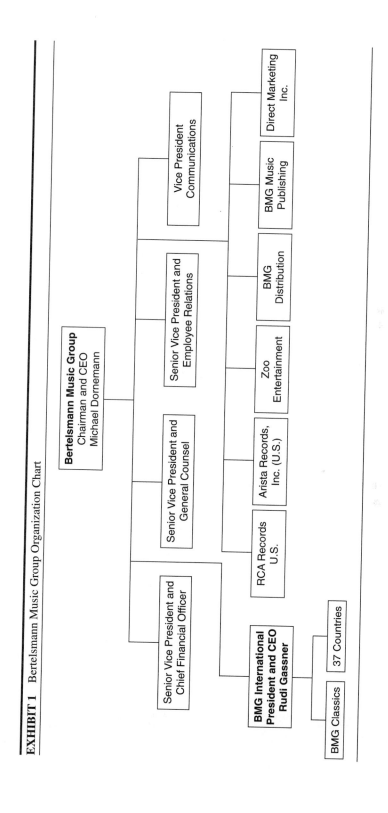

EXHIBIT 2 BMG International Organization Chart, 1993

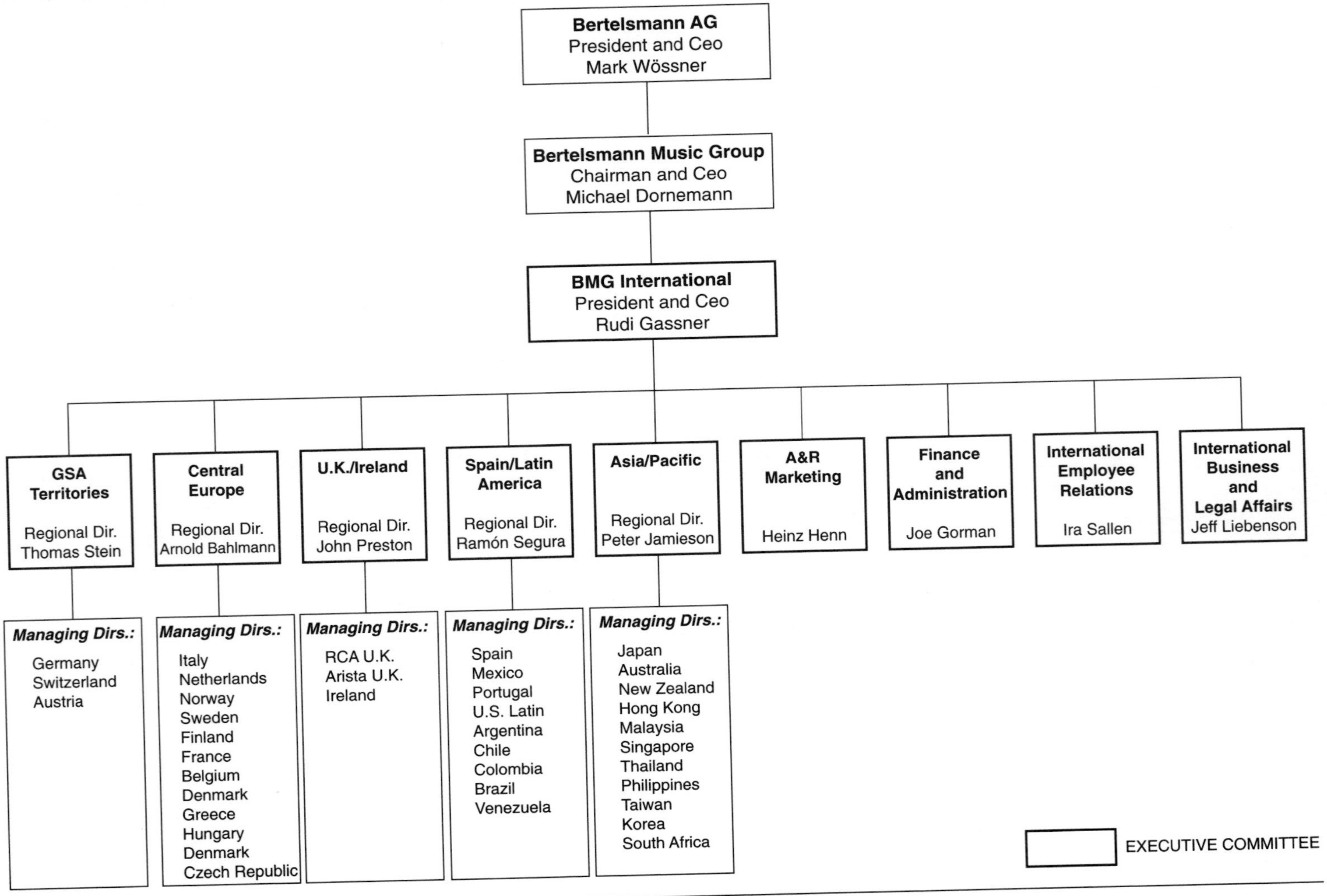

Bertelsmann AG
President and Ceo
Mark Wössner

Bertelsmann Music Group
Chairman and Ceo
Michael Dornemann

BMG International
President and Ceo
Rudi Gassner

A&R Marketing
Heinz Henn

Finance and Administration
Joe Gorman

International Employee Relations
Ira Sallen

International Business and Legal Affairs
Jeff Liebenson

GSA Territories
Regional Dir.
Thomas Stein

Managing Dirs.:
Germany
Switzerland
Austria

Central Europe
Regional Dir.
Arnold Bahlmann

Managing Dirs.:
Italy
Netherlands
Norway
Sweden
Finland
France
Belgium
Denmark
Greece
Hungary
Denmark
Czech Republic

U.K./Ireland
Regional Dir.
John Preston

Managing Dirs.:
RCA U.K.
Arista U.K.
Ireland

Spain/Latin America
Regional Dir.
Ramón Segura

Managing Dirs.:
Spain
Mexico
Portugal
U.S. Latin
Argentina
Chile
Colombia
Brazil
Venezuela

Asia/Pacific
Regional Dir.
Peter Jamieson

Managing Dirs.:
Japan
Australia
New Zealand
Hong Kong
Malaysia
Singapore
Thailand
Philippines
Taiwan
Korea
South Africa

☐ EXECUTIVE COMMITTEE

EXHIBIT 3   Rudi Gassner Career Highlights

Rudi Gassner
President and CEO, BMG International
German, 51 years old

- 1984–1987:   Executive VP, PolyGram International, London
- 1983–1984:   President, Polydor International (PolyGram), Hamburg
- 1980–1983:   President, Deutsche Grammophon (PolyGram), Hamburg
-   Fall 1979:   Harvard Business School Program for Management Development (PMD)
- 1977–1980:   Managing Director, Metronome (PolyGram), Hamburg
- 1969–1977:   Sales Manager, Deutsche Grammophon (PolyGram), Munich
- 1964–1969:   Music Wholesaling, Munich

Company Background

BMG International was a subsidiary of Bertelsmann AG, a German media conglomerate with over 200 companies and 50,000 employees operating in 37 countries. Founded in 1835 as a lithographic printing company in Guetersloh, Germany, Bertelsmann's interests had grown to include businesses in music, film, television, radio, book, magazine, and newspaper publishing and distribution, as well as printing and manufacturing operations. Still headquartered in the small rural town, Bertelsmann had become the second-largest media enterprise in the world, with 1992 sales of $9.7 billion.

Bertelsmann's corporate charter mandated autonomous business divisions and entrepreneurial operating management, and emphasized respect for the cultural traditions of each country in which it operated. Each business unit had its own, usually local, entrepreneurial management with operating control over its business plan, the development of its assets, its human resources, and its contribution to overall profitability. Delegation of responsibility and authority was supported by performance-linked compensation for managers and profit-sharing by all employees.

In 1986, Bertelsmann entered the U.S. market with its purchases of Doubleday and Dell, two large publishing houses, and RCA Records, which had made music history with Elvis Presley in the 1950s. On acquiring RCA, Bertelsmann organized its worldwide music holdings—which also included the American record label Arista, the German label Ariola, and various smaller labels and music publishing and marketing operations—into the Bertelsmann Music Group (BMG). With RCA, BMG entered the ranks of the "Big Six" record companies—CBS, Warner, BMG, Capitol-EMI, PolyGram, and MCA—which supplied 80% of worldwide music sales.[2]

BMG was headquartered in New York under German Chairman and CEO Michael Dornemann, who split the company's operations into two divisions: the United States and the rest of the world. In the United States, BMG's priority was to stem the losses from RCA (which posted a $35 million deficit in 1987) and build market share for the flagging U.S. labels.[3]

With BMG's overseas holdings, Dornemann formed an international division and hired German-born Rudi Gassner, then executive vice president of PolyGram International, as president and CEO (see Exhibit 3). According to Dornemann, Gassner "had the right background in the music business and the right international experience. He best fit the

---

[2]Purkiss, Alan, "Let's Hear It for the Unsung Hero," *Accountancy,* June 1992, pp. 70–73.

[3]Dannen, Frederick, *Hit Men: Power Brokers and Fast Money Inside the Music Business* (New York: Vintage Books, 1991), pp. 246–261.

leadership qualities we were looking for."[4] At its inception in 1987, the international division, also headquartered in New York, comprised operations in 17 countries across the globe. Gassner described the fledgling organization as "a patchwork of companies around the world. It had no mission, no goals, and in total, it didn't make any money. . . . The only way from there was up."[5]

In his first six years, Gassner led the company, which he named BMG International, through a tremendous period of growth. By launching new satellite companies, purchasing small labels, and forming joint ventures, BMG International's presence had expanded by 1993 to include 37 countries. Sales had increased an average of 20% annually, reaching $2 billion in 1993 (two-thirds of BMG's overall revenue that year). International market share, which was near 11% in 1987, was a healthy 17%, and as high as 25% in some territories.[6]

BMG International was responsible for marketing and distributing top-selling U.S. artists such as Whitney Houston and Kenny G across the globe.[7] In addition, the company developed such artists as Annie Lennox and Lisa Stansfield (Britain) and Eros Ramazzotti (Italy) in their local territories to be marketed worldwide. On a local level, groups such as B'z (Japan) and Bronco (Mexico) were extremely successful, selling in excess of 1 million units in their respective countries. The company also

had extensive classics and jazz catalogues, with artists such as James Galway and Antonio Hart. (See Exhibit 4 for roster of top-selling artists.)[8]

Rudi Gassner and BMG International

In 1987, at the age of 45, Gassner became the CEO of the newly formed BMG International. "It was a once-in-a-lifetime opportunity," he reflected, "to build what I think a global company should look like." When he arrived at BMG, Gassner adapted quickly to the Bertelsmann culture. "My 17 years at PolyGram gave me the experience to run a global business; that was my know-how," he explained. "But on the other hand, I very much liked the Bertelsmann style. It was very close to my personal style." One of his colleagues at BMG described Gassner's transition:

> Rudi came from PolyGram, which had a very different culture. The Philips PolyGram culture is highly politically charged; it is much more "stand by your beds when the senior management comes in." Rudi changed a lot when he came to BMG. He saw the value in the Bertelsmann managing style; he saw the freedom to do things, and he took it. He passed it on as well.

Building BMG International

One of Gassner's first priorities was to instill this culture in the newly acquired companies. He reflected on what he inherited when he joined BMG:

> My first step was basically to get to know the companies and the problems hands-on myself. RCA had been centrally managed out of New York, and the managers in the companies had the attitude that "I'm not doing anything unless somebody tells me what to do." I would find them hiding under tables. I spent the first two years preaching my gospel and saying to the managers, "You are

---

[4]"BMG's Five Year Man," *Music Business International,* Vol. 3, No. 1 (January 1993), p. 18.

[5]Ibid.

[6]According to Gassner, a 1% worldwide market share gain was worth around $250 million in revenue. ("Charting the Future" speech, May 1993, Boca Raton, Florida.)

[7]The "prestige market" of the U.S. was the most important supplier of recorded music around the world, and BMG's Arista, led by long-time music executive Clive Davis, had launched two global superstars, Whitney Houston and Kenny G, who reached No. 1 and 2 on the *Billboard* album chart. In 1993, Houston's soundtrack for *The Bodyguard* sold 20 million copies and became one of the top-selling albums of all time, fueling a significant portion of BMG's revenue in the U.S. and abroad. (Lander, Mark, "An Overnight Success—After Six Years," *Business Week,* April 19, 1993, pp. 52–54.)

[8]In addition, BMG International had an agreement with MCA/Geffen to market and distribute that company's products outside the U.S. The MCA/Geffen deal gave BMG International access to such stars as Guns 'N' Roses, Nirvana, Aerosmith, Bobby Brown, and Cher.

EXHIBIT 4   Selected BMG International Top-Selling Artists, 1993

Artist	Country of Origin	Units Sold 1992/1993 (in thousands)
Global Superstars:		
Whitney Houston	United States	11,800
Kenny G	United States	2,200
Annie Lennox	United Kingdom	1,200
David Bowie	United Kingdom	700
SNAP	Germany	700
Dr. Alban	Germany	600
Regional Superstars:		
Vaya Con Dios	Belgium	1,300
Juan Luis Guerra	Spain	1,100
Eros Ramazzotti	Italy	1,100
Die Prinzen	Germany	900
Take That	United Kingdom	700
Bonnie Tyler	Germany	500
Local Superstars:		
B'z	Japan	5,700
Bronco	Mexico	1,300
Joaquin Sabina	Spain	500
Jose Jose	Mexico	400
Lucio Dalla	Italy	250

responsible. I can give you advice, but don't send me a memo asking me to sign off here. You are in charge: you are Mr. Italy; you are Mr. France; you are Mr. Belgium."

At the same time, Gassner also began to communicate his vision for BMG International. "There were basically two strategic targets in my mind," he explained:

> One was globalization. Globalization allows you to serve a bigger world market. Every time we added a new country, we would increase our revenue accordingly. The other strategic target was domestic repertoire. I had a great fear of being too dependent on English-speaking repertoire. I made it clear to the managers that their foremost responsibility was

developing domestic talent. Joint ventures and acquisitions were another way to add local repertoire.

Gassner also instituted yearly business plans with each of his managing directors. He described the process:

> We [Gassner and each MD] do a budget once a year. The budget is between you and me. I want to know where you are going and how much investment you will need. We talk about revenues and profits. I make a very aggressive bonus plan for them to be able to make a lot of money; if they exceed their targets significantly, they can make up to half their salary as a bonus. In America, this might not have been so sensational, but for those countries who were not used to that, it was pretty new.

According to Gassner, "the majority of the guys came through with flying colors." For those who did not fit with the new program, Gassner held "career counseling sessions," as one colleague referred to them: "When Rudi conducts a career counseling session, it's pretty much over. But he's so smooth and so good at it, that it takes them about a week to figure out that they may have just been fired."

Gassner also turned his attention inward, focusing on his corporate management structure. "One advantage, obviously, was that nothing existed. I could do it any way I wanted. That was fantastic." He made Joe Gorman, who had been the senior finance executive for RCA's international arm, the chief financial officer of BMG International. During Gassner's first two years, Gorman accompanied him as he travelled around the world assessing each operating company.

Gassner's next corporate hire was Heinz Henn to coordinate global A&R marketing.[9] Henn had spent 17 years at EMI in international positions. He described his job interview with Gassner:

Rudi and I met for the first time on February 17, 1987, at the Park Lane Hotel and had breakfast together. What got me the job was that I ate two breakfasts—I was really hungry that day. He was impressed that somebody could eat two full breakfasts on a job interview.

Seriously, Rudi asked me what I would do if he gave me the job, and I told him that I would do things differently than they had been done so far in the industry, particularly [the companies] where we had both come from. I wanted to cultivate local talent in individual markets to build hot acts which we could launch globally. He totally agreed with me. Ever since, he's let me do what I wanted to do.

Gassner described the need for Henn's role:

Heinz has a dual role: he not only has to break local artists worldwide, he also has to sell Whitney

---

[9]"A&R" was a record industry term that stood for "artist and repertoire," record company products. In record companies, investing in A&R to develop talent was analogous to a manufacturing concern investing in R&D. "A&R marketing" was essentially product marketing.

Houston to all the local companies. We need Heinz because the interests of the countries and the regions stop at the borders, and we need a global view on artists. This will give us the competitive advantage; there's more money to be made outside the borders if you do it right.

Henn added:

You have to have coordination between the regions as far as marketing and promotion activities are concerned because recording and marketing expenses are far too great these days for any one [local] company to be able to earn back its investment in one country only. It requires coordination between regions and also globally.

To round out his corporate staff, Gassner added a human resource executive, Ira Sallen, and legal counsel, Jeff Liebenson. Sallen would be responsible for negotiating and maintaining the managing directors' contracts, as well as for worldwide personnel and organizational policies. Liebenson would serve as in-house counsel, assisting in the intricate contracts that were part of operating a complex global enterprise.

Gassner also instituted an annual Managing Directors' Convention in which Dornemann, Gassner, the corporate staff, and all of the MDs and joint-venture partners (JVs) would converge from around the world. A major objective of the annual MD Convention was to provide a forum for the MDs and JVs to give repertoire presentations to each other in an attempt to sell their local repertoire to the other countries.

Creating a Regional Structure
As BMG International's number of operating companies continued to grow, it became impossible for Gassner directly to oversee them all. By 1989, he concluded it was time to aggregate the countries into five regions and hire a regional director for each, a plan he had had in mind from the beginning. (See Exhibit 2 for organization chart and Exhibit 5 for revenue and profit distribution by region.) The role of the RD would be "to provide leadership for the region; to oversee the strategic development of the

EXHIBIT 5   BMG International Revenue and Operating Result Distribution by Region

Net Revenue by Region:

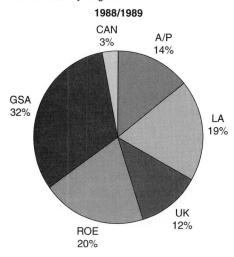

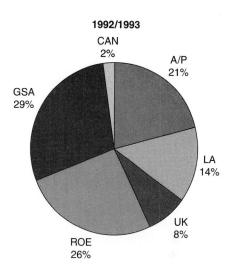

Operating Result (Betriebsergebnis) by Region:

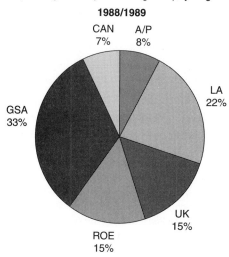

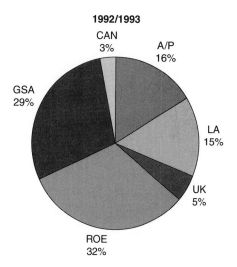

Legend
A/P = Asia/Pacific;
CAN = Canada;
LA = Latin America;
GSA = Germany/Switzerland/Austria;
ROE = Rest of Europe;
UK = United Kingdom.

region, in conjunction with the whole company; and to manage the managing directors." He explained:

I divided Europe into three different categories: the United Kingdom, German-speaking territories, and the rest of Europe. At that time, the German-speaking territories contributed about 50% of our profit, so they were a very important group unto themselves. I promoted Thomas Stein, who was the managing director of the German company, to regional director.

The United Kingdom, despite its relatively small profits, was our largest source of repertoire, a major supplier. I promoted John Preston, who was the MD of RCA Records U.K., to be the regional director of that region.

The MD for Ariola Spain, Ramon Segura, was an outstanding executive who also had, at that time, regional responsibilities for Ariola's Latin American companies. So I kept Spain/Latin America together as a region and made Segura the RD.

Now I needed someone for the rest of Europe. I hired Arnold Bahlmann, who was working in strategic analysis for Michael Dornemann. He was not one of the music managers coming through the ranks. He had never had a line job in his life. Still, I thought, you don't necessarily need the detailed day-to-day experience of running a company to manage a regional territory. It was an organizational task, and I thought Arnold had very good people skills. I thought he was ideal, though it was a hell of a risk to put him in.

At the same time as I promoted John Preston to RD in the United Kingdom, I asked the chairman of the RCA U.K. label, Peter Jamieson, to go out and establish our Asia/Pacific market. I remember a British competitor in the industry joking with me that "wasn't I worried about sending one of my best men out to the colonies?" I thought Jamieson was just the right person for the job. He accepted, and he's done a brilliant job building companies and repertoire in that region.

Gassner maintained the annual business planning system he had established with the MDs, but he now worked through the RDs. As Segura described it, "We are involved throughout the process, but Rudi has final approval." BMG International's fiscal year started July 1 and ran through June 30. In January, the MDs began to prepare their business plans,

developing targets for critical measures such as revenue, *betriebsergebnis,*[10] return on sales, market share, revenue per employee, days inventory, and days sales outstanding. Gassner was as much interested in the assumptions used to arrive at the targets as the figures themselves; MDs were expected to include an in-depth analysis of the risks and opportunities they faced based on the current economic climate and market, new A&R releases, and their priority artists.

In February, the MDs met with the RDs to review their plans; the RDs then met with Gassner to discuss regional as well as local goals. Gorman described Gassner's stance in these meetings: "Rudi has a reputation for being tough—fair, but tough. One of the reasons he has that reputation is that he makes you do things which you know you should do, but which you don't want to do." One RD described these sessions as "the famous February meetings. Rudi and I dislike each other a lot in February. But by March we usually agree."

In March, the RDs returned to the MDs with a final plan and targets; Gassner and Gorman joined many of these sessions (see Exhibit 6). At this point, the MDs would have a final opportunity to discuss their plans and the targets would be agreed upon. Gorman described these meetings:

March is the critical planning month for us. We tell everybody, look, when the meeting is over, we all walk out of here with the same goals. Period. We can sit in the room an hour, or we can sit there for two days, but in the end nobody is going to leave this room disagreeing on what the goals are. In these meetings, MD bonus criteria are also defined, since *betriebsergebnis* is the primary criterion for bonuses.

One RD described Gassner's approach:

Rudi plays a different role with each MD, depending on their personality and where he wants the country

---

[10]*Betriebsergebnis* was a German accounting term roughly translated to mean profit plus interest costs. The official language at BMG International was English (German was never spoken if a non-speaker was present); *betriebsergebnis* was the only German word the company used.

EXHIBIT 6   March 1992 Business Planning Meetings Attended by Rudi Gassner and Joe Gorman

Location:	Date:	Review:	
Munich	March 1	10:00 AM	Belgium
		11:30 AM	Netherlands
		2:00 PM	Italy
	March 2	10:00 AM	UK–RCA
		2:00 PM	UK–Arista
		4:00 PM	UK–Distrib.
	March 3	10:00 AM	GSA Overview
		11:30 AM	Munich Ariola
		2:00 PM	Germany Ariola
		3:45 PM	Hamburg Ariola
	March 4	10:00 AM	Germany Ariola
		11:30 AM	Austria
		2:00 PM	Switzerland
	March 5	10:00 AM	France Ariola
		11:30 AM	France Vogue
		1:30 PM	France RCA
		4:00 PM	European Regional Overview
New York	March 10	10:00 AM	Canada
		2:00 PM	Home Office
Hong Kong	March 16	10:00 AM	Australia
		3:00 PM	Hong Kong
	March 17	10:00 AM	Japan
		3:00 PM	Taiwan
	March 18	10:00 AM	South Africa
		3:00 PM	Malaysia
	March 19	10:00 AM	Asia/Pacific Regional Overview
New York	March 24	10:00 AM	Mexico
		2:00 PM	U.S. Latin
		4:00 PM	Portugal
	March 25	10:00 AM	Brazil
		2:00 PM	Spain
	March 26	10:00 AM	Latin America Regional Overview

to go. Sometimes he plays the good cop, and other times he plays the bad cop. He's very versatile, and very results-oriented. When necessary, he knows how to hit people's hot buttons and make them squirm.

According to one MD:

Rudi knows the business inside and out, and he has an amazing grasp of the details. When he is going

through these plans, he will go into particular line items if he wants to. These business plans are like contracts between Rudi and me. Face-to-face with him, I am committing to try to make this target. It's like a moral imperative to get it done.

According to Bahlmann, "The business plans serve their purpose well. If you ask me if I enjoy them—no. It's not enjoyable. I hate the process. But it works." Stein concurred: "The business plans help me explain what I think should be done in my region. It's a fair process because it's based on an objective financial measure." Another RD, however, commented on the danger inherent in the system:

> The business plan process is a necessary and effective tool. But the danger is that it becomes too inflexible. Instead of a jacket which guides, a sort of loose piece of clothing which shapes the way we operate, it becomes a straightjacket and restricts the way we operate.

Even with the addition of the regional directors, Gassner maintained close contact with the local companies around the world. "I emphasize what I call a very flat hierarchical structure," he explained. "I'm never too far removed from what's really happening." While he was primarily in contact with the RDs, Gassner always reserved the right to call the MDs directly, and they "feel absolutely free to call me about anything," according to Gassner. "But they all know that it is a two-way information system. Whatever they tell me, they know I will pass on to their regional director. And whatever they tell the RD, they know he passes on to me." When possible, Gassner made it a point to reach further into the organization by talking informally with local employees "just to double-check that my messages come through."

Gassner's style of running a global business was extremely demanding. Travel was a way of life: he and his corporate staff spent 50% or more of their time away from New York headquarters, and the regional directors traveled constantly throughout their regions. According to Gorman,

> Rudi believes that you are not managing an international company unless you travel extensively, because it's all about people. The financial statements are fine, the statistics are fine. But in the end, you have to sit down with somebody in a room and talk to them to get a real sense for the people and for what's going on. There are things that always come out "by the way. . . ." When you go out to dinner or you're at a concert until 4:00 in the morning, a lot of this comes out.

The Executive Committee and the ECMs

In 1989, after he had established his corporate staff and the regional structure, Gassner formally created an Executive Committee consisting of the five regional directors, the four senior staff members, and himself as the leader (see Exhibit 7). He recalled:

> I had always intended to have an executive committee. I always wanted to run a business on the basis of a European board system, like a *vorstand:*[11] although it is chaired by one person and members have their own portfolios [regions], the committee decides business issues jointly.
>
> The way I see it, the board should decide about important issues strategically or from an investment point of view. And I wanted everybody to be involved in the process, despite the fact that some issues may not have a direct consequence for their region.
>
> You cannot run a global organization without breaking it down into regions—it just becomes impossible. On the other hand, you have to have a global strategy. In our business, the regions are interlinked by artist agreements and by the exchange of repertoire. So it needs both a regional organization and a global vision.

Bahlmann recalled Gassner introducing the concept of an executive committee by describing it as "the group which will lead BMG International." Gassner decided that the committee would meet four times per year at the New York headquarters to discuss current operating issues, and once a year outside of New York to examine long-term strategy. Before each executive committee meeting (ECM), members were polled for agenda items; Gassner then, as he described it, "edited" the suggestions to create the agenda, which was circulated to the group.

---

[11]A *vorstand* was a German managing board consisting of full-time executive members who carried out the day-to-day operation of the company. It was distinguished from the supervisory board (*aufsichtsrat*), which consisted of shareholders and employee representatives. (Parkyn, Brian, *Democracy, Accountability, and Participation in Industry* (Bradford, West Yorkshire, England: MCB General Management Ltd., 1979), p. 105; and Kennedy, Thomas, *European Labor Relations* (Lexington, Massachusetts: Lexington Books, 1980), p. 185.

EXHIBIT 7   BMG International Executive Committee

From left to right: Arnold Bahlmann, Thomas Stein, John Preston, Rudi Gassner, Heinz Henn, Peter Jamieson, Ramon Segura, Joe Gorman (not pictured: Ira Sallen, Jeff Liebenson).

| *Regional Directors* | *New York Corporate Staff* |

Regional Directors

Arnold Bahlmann

Senior VP, Central Europe

- German, 41 years old.
- Promoted from: Senior VP Operations, BMG.
- 3 years strategic planning, Bertelsmann.
- Doctorate in Political Science.
- Master of Business Administration.

Thomas Stein

President, GSA Territories

- German, 44 years old.
- Promoted from: Managing Director, BMG Ariola, Munich.
- 14 years sales, marketing, and management in record business.

New York Corporate Staff

Heinz Henn

Senior VP, A&R/Marketing

- German, 38 years old.
- Promoted from: Director of International Division, Capitol/EMI America Records.
- 17 years A&R/marketing, promotion, and management in record business.

Joe Gorman

Senior VP, Finance and Administration

- American, 50 years old.
- Promoted from: Director, Operations Planning, RCA Records (U.S.).
- 10 years finance at RCA Records.
- 5 years Arthur Young & Company.
- Master of Business Administration.
- Military service, Captain, U.S. Army.

(continued)

EXHIBIT 7   *(Concluded)*

Regional Directors	*New York Corporate Staff*

John Preston
Chairman, BMG Records (U.K.) Ltd.
- Scottish, 43 years old.
- Promoted from: Managing Director, RCA Records, U.K.
- 19 years retail, marketing, and management in record business.

Ramon Segura
President, Spain and Sr. VP, Latin America
- Spanish, 52 years old.
- Promoted from: MD, Spain, and VP Latin American Region, Ariola Eurodisc.
- 31 years sales, A&R, marketing, and management in record business.

Peter Jamieson
Senior VP, Asia/Pacific
- English, 48 years old.
- Promoted from: Chairman, BMG Records U.K.
- 26 years marketing, sales, and management in record business.

Ira Sallen
VP, International Human Resources, BMG
- American, 39 years old.
- Promoted from: VP, Human Resources, Clean Harbors, Inc.
- 4 years corporate human resources.
- 2 years Consultant, Arthur Young & Company.
- 5 years research and clinical psychology.
- Master of Business Administration.

Jeff Liebenson
VP, Int'l. Legal and Business Affairs, BMG
- American, 40 years old.
- Promoted from: Director, Legal and Business Affairs, Sports Channel America.
- 15 years legal experience, including 12 in entertainment industry.
- J.D and LL.M. law degrees.

Gassner described the first ECM:

We needed to define the limitations and boundaries of authority among ourselves and the MDs. What should we allow our MDs to do without our approval? What should they have to bring to your level? What should you then bring to my level? We needed certain regulations; it makes our lives easier. It was interesting because of the history of the group coming together—they had not been organized before in a way that had these limitations, and they didn't like it.

I also had to explain the role of the New York staff. There was a lot of theoretical discussion about, for example, Heinz's responsibility. What can Heinz say about my repertoire and my country? How can Heinz say I have to spend a certain amount of money on an artist that is not valid for my region? My answer to that was always that Heinz cannot say. He can only sit down with you and try to convince you that this is the right thing for you. You've got to see the staff as somebody helping you; it is not some

governing body who tells you what to do. They have a dotted-line relationship with your people.

Preston described his perspective on the early meetings:

At first, there was no role for the RDs. Rudi had things he wanted to do; the agenda was laid out, and we would discuss ways of implementing the agenda. The staff people went into the meetings very well prepared and tried to establish a couple of policies with the help of Rudi in order to structure the business. It took us a certain amount of time to find a way of really working together.

Bahlmann echoed the same point:

Rudi needed to establish himself and the regional structure; it was like him telling us, via the agenda, what we're going to do. It was as our "educational process." Although I think we sometimes found it frustrating, we were so busy with our own companies [regions], there was not a lot of resistance.

Gassner found this lack of "resistance" somewhat disconcerting. According to Gorman,

> I remember after the first two ECMs, Rudi saying to me, "Everybody's too nice." He expects strong dissenting opinions. He doesn't want a bunch of people just sitting there mildly accepting anything. To him, a heated argument over an opinion is part of the fun of the job, I suppose. But if you're not used to this, and when I first started with him I wasn't, it jars you a little.

In time, however, the RDs became more vocal. According to Henn, "It took quite some time until the group felt comfortable enough with each other that they dared to say what they really wanted to say." According to the RDs, the shift in the ECMs was due to their growing confidence and success in running their regions. As Bahlmann noted:

> About two years ago it turned around. The regional directors and the managing directors make the decisions about the operating businesses and acquisitions. Today in the ECMs, we go more into other issues. More and more, we are finally making decisions together and running the business as a team.

Preston also commented on this shift in emphasis: "In the beginning, the staff and Rudi were more dominant. But now, it's more balanced between Rudi and the RDs, and then the staff."

Working Together

By 1993, the executive committee and the ECMs had been in place for four years, and the meetings had fallen into a fairly regular pattern. Each agenda would include a presentation by Gorman on current financial results relative to targets; a discussion by Henn about A&R developments, new releases, and priority artists; a briefing by Sallen on significant worldwide human resource issues; and an update on each region by the RDs. Gassner described the importance of these regional reviews: "I want to give them room to explain to their colleagues what they're up to. Even though it's not relevant to somebody running South America, for example, he should listen, in my opinion, to what happened in

Korea and how we do business in Korea. Here is where I try to get them involved in the global strategy."

Outside the ECMs there was frequent contact between Gassner and each RD. Contact among the RDs varied, and was most frequent among three of the European directors: Bahlmann, Stein, and Preston. Because they shared so many of the same circumstances and concerns, Gassner established a European subcommittee in 1991. As he explained,

> I created a European board because I didn't want to be in the middle of those discussions all the time. It seemed natural to make Arnold the chairman, since he is also the head of European-wide manufacturing and distribution. I told them: "You guys deal with European issues. Europe is your baby. If you cannot agree, I get the minutes and then I will make a ruling."

Since its inception, the European board had been very effective in achieving the purpose he had intended, according to Gassner:

> They deal with issues that are really not relevant to anybody else before they get to the ECM. They even discuss the ECM agenda before the meetings, and they sometimes come over with what I call a "prefabricated opinion." So now sometimes I have to work to break this group up a little bit.

Depending on their regional circumstances, the roles of the RDs varied significantly. Bahlmann, Preston, and Stein, for example, focused on continuing to carve out market share and bring costs down in their increasingly mature markets. Because of his region's importance as a repertoire supplier, Preston was seen as the "repertoire expert"; Bahlmann, on the other hand, was the "strategy expert." Segura and Jamieson were most concerned with establishing new companies and developing talent in the relatively undeveloped markets of Asia and Latin America. Jamieson commented on the satisfaction of being a "pioneer," as he called it: "Asia/Pacific is a huge, multicultural, diverse, economically varied region which is on exactly the opposite side of the world from America. It has the most growth potential and the most musical excitement, really. It's a very, very exciting place to be." Segura described the unique challenges in his region: "I am constantly battling against the terrible political and economic instability that affects some of the countries in my region. These situations cannot be solved with easy solutions or off-the-shelf business recipes."

Over time, the executive committee members developed a strong sense of mutual respect for one another. According to Henn:

> Everybody in that room is the *best* at what he does. The absolute best, and we all know it. It's pretty amazing. We're also total egomaniacs, the whole group of us. But in this company we still work as a team because we give each other the space to be the fool that everyone can be sometimes. Nobody's perfect.

Another RD commented, "I wouldn't necessarily choose these guys as my friends, but when we get together it's pretty awesome."

The group maintained a balanced mix of camaraderie and competition. Gassner, who himself used to play professional soccer, described the committee as "more like a soccer team than [an American] football team"; they frequently played heated games of golf or soccer when they were together. Stein remarked with a laugh, "It's all healthy competition—it's very healthy as long as I'm on top of the others. But seriously, it's a good sort of competitiveness. We are all ambitious people, but we respect each other; there is no jealousy."

Another executive committee member mentioned a different aspect of competition: "Rudi is only 51 [years old], far from the required retirement age of 60; but chances are good that he could move on to other things at Bertelsmann. As a result, there is a certain amount of jockeying for position within the executive committee, and people wonder if a non-German could ever be tapped to run this company."

As for Gassner's role in the ECMs, committee members had varying perspectives. Stein commented that "Rudi has a good relationship with the team. He knows when to be part of the team, and when to say yes or no. But he's always open-minded, and you can discuss things with him; it's like a partnership with him." According to Sallen, "Rudi does a lot of consensus-taking. He floats ideas by people, testing them on the group. He does impose his will, but not often. While he does not hand down many edicts, it is generally clear to all what his feelings are on most issues."

Jamieson, however, observed: "Debates in the ECMs are very rare. Rudi's not a man who needs or wants too many debates. I have never had an informal brainstorming session with him, a relaxed, almost agenda-less discussion. Rudi's management style is essentially autocratic." Henn commented:

> Rudi's brilliant. He's a tyrant; no, not a tyrant, a dictator. He has to be. You don't have a leader if you don't have a dictator. If you don't have a dictator, you won't be successful. Show me a company run by democracy, and I'll show you a loser. There's always got to be one chief and plenty of Indians.
>
> He's very smooth. If he thinks we're coming to a conclusion that is not what his opinion is, he will make sure the whole thing will turn his way. He has the ability to make you feel it was your idea, and if that doesn't work, he'll tell you to go and do it anyway.

Many committee members agreed that it could be difficult to change Gassner's mind. According to Stein, "To influence Rudi, you have to convince him. You have to be prepared properly with logical arguments." Preston added: "You have to be prepared to stand up for your argument. A lot of what he is testing is how much you really believe in what you are saying."

One RD noted that "Rudi usually does not allow himself in any way to be influenced by people who are not speaking directly about the areas for which they are responsible. In other words, he'll be very receptive to me for everything within my area, but when I stray into areas of the general good, I find him very unreceptive. I also find that I can influence him more one-on-one than I can in the ECMs."

Stein commented that he used the ECMs "as a tool to influence things in a way that I think they should go and to make the other RDs aware of things. Whether or not the committee agrees with me is another question." Preston agreed, explaining that he viewed participation in the ECMs as an important responsibility, even if it was sometimes hard to have much influence: "I believe that I have a job in the context of the group to say the things that I believe in order to get the group to behave in ways that I think are the right ones."

Bahlmann described the ECM as "an opinion-building exercise," explaining that:

Real decisions about who gets money for what acquisitions occur outside of the meetings. The other thing is that there has always been money there to do what we wanted. So for me, the group has never been tested to see whether we can really work as a team under pressure when it comes to a fight over who will get funds for what investment.

Jamieson commented:

Sometimes I feel that the main benefit of my coming all the way from Hong Kong to New York for the ECM is the ability (a) to meet my colleagues and chat with them from time to time, and (b) to have my separate meeting with Rudi, which is my best opportunity to influence him.

We have had some good meetings, and we have had some terrible meetings. Rudi occasionally runs them in an open way in which debate is invited and variations to policy are considered. In reality, there is not a team "working together" at the top; there are executives implementing predetermined policies in different areas. The enormous geography makes it difficult to manage by consensus. With Rudi, you know what you have to do, and you have the freedom to execute the policies in your own region with your own style. Nevertheless, you have to realize that Rudi's style works for him; the proof is his incredible success over the past six years.

Gassner suspected these feelings and opinions in the group. "Many of them probably think I am influencing them more than I should," he commented.

Sometimes I hear grumblings and they say that they can't always express their long-term ideas at the meetings because the meetings are so focused. I think they feel a lot of things are a bit too prepared or precooked. It's true—they have a difficult time convincing me. I am a person who likes to win an argument.

But my opinions are not just invented on the spot. I usually discuss issues one-to-one with certain people beforehand. If I have a subject on the agenda, I almost always have an opinion of what I think the outcome should be. And then in the ECM, I see if my belief is confirmed. Occasionally, I may not go ahead with my original idea because I see that the entire group is going in another direction. In that case, I will take a step back and try to analyze it one more time, and I may change my mind. But if I see that they agree, or if it's just very important to me, then I obviously try to push it along.

Reflecting on his original hopes for the role of the executive committee, Gassner commented:

It turned out to be a little bit different than I thought. I thought there would be more interface on strategic issues. I had hoped that they would contribute to problems which went beyond their ultimate responsibility.

In part, I guess it's because it's such a diverse group of people. Segura, for example, is an outstanding executive, but because he thinks his English is limited, he would rather discuss issues separately with me than in an open meeting. Bahlmann, on the other hand, is very interested in global strategy though sometimes he doesn't have as much impact as he would like to have. Stein and Jamieson are somewhere in the middle, and they are driven primarily by the success of their own regions. Preston is highly intellectual; he is also the biggest repertoire supplier, and sometimes he thinks we're not paying enough attention to his repertoire. It's a combination of very diverse people. That's probably why the results are still so much influenced by me.

And it may very well have to do with me and the way I run things. I think I know what is good for us. Therefore, when I'm convinced that that's the right way to go, it takes a great effort to get me off that route. However, because it has been successful, it has been hard to say that I should change my style.

The May 1993 ECM

Gassner opened the 1993 Managing Director's Convention in Boca Raton with a speech in which he stressed that the company's key success factor for the future was creating repertoire. "It's local artist development, it's joint ventures, it's acquisitions. That is the way we are going to grow. That is how we will reach our goal of becoming Number 1," he told the audience. He also congratulated them on another year of success in surpassing their business targets, but joked that "I am so naive; you must be lowballing your plans every time, because you have never missed them."

The week-long convention also included a session by Henn on developing A&R; a financial presentation from Gorman in which he emphasized the need to reduce costs and improve efficiency as markets matured and growth in the record business leveled off; a presentation about new recording and media technologies; and a speech by Dornemann about the future of the emerging Entertainment Group at BMG.[12] While the RDs attended, they played no formal role in the convention.

Whereas the focus in past conventions had been primarily on growth, the topics which formed the agenda for the 1993 MD Convention—global artist development, new technologies, BMG's expansion into new entertainment arenas, and cost control—emphasized disciplined management to position BMG International for the next phase. The MDs were excited about the important new role that BMG International could take on in the future. As Gassner told them, "We're the only company in Bertelsmann that is really global; we're the only ones in Japan, and we have over 300 people there. If Bertelsmann wants to sell film or video games globally, we are there. We have something Bertelsmann can build on."

On the other hand, many of the MDs expressed skepticism about Gassner's "conflicting messages." As one stated, "You can't grow market share unless you're willing to spend money, and you can't cut back on investing in new acts, because you never know who might be the next Rolling Stones." Gassner, however, did not see his goals in conflict: "Yes—it's inconvenient on the one hand to grow and on the other hand to control your costs. It's a difficult task, but I expect both. I cannot allow anyone to just charge ahead regardless of cost. I expect a balance; and I know they can do it."

These issues also figured heavily into Gassner's agenda at the May ECM, which took place during the convention. He knew that the future challenges would demand more cooperation and global strategic thinking on the part of the executive committee. They had all been extremely successful so far in their own regions, but a regional focus alone would no longer be enough to guide BMG International through the uncertain and ever-changing terrain of the next five years.

The Reduced Manufacturing Price

The reduced manufacturing price was a result of negotiations undertaken by Bahlmann with Sonopress, Bertelsmann's central manufacturing operation in Europe, which supplied product to the European countries. These countries were required to purchase a certain percentage of their CDs, records, and cassettes from Sonopress, and as part of his responsibilities as the head of central manufacturing,

---

[12]In response to trends toward multimedia entertainment technology, Dornemann had begun to look toward expanding BMG's reach in the entertainment industry to include television and even film. Industry analysts speculated that Dornemann was interested in purchasing an independent film studio, but such a deal had not yet materialized. In September 1993, BMG announced a joint venture with Tele-Communications, Inc., the largest cable system operator in the U.S., to launch a hybrid music video/home shopping cable channel that would rival MTV and VH-1. (Robichaux, Mark and Johnnie L. Roberts, "TCI, Bertelsmann Join to Launch Music, Shopping Cable Channel," *Wall Street Journal,* September 17, 1993.)

Bahlmann negotiated the transfer prices annually by comparing Sonopress's bid to those of outside vendors. Because the non-European countries did not source through Sonopress, they would not be affected by the new price.

As Gassner might have predicted, when he brought up the issue at the ECM by congratulating Bahlmann, Preston shot Stein a knowing glance. Preston was required to source his manufacturing through Sonopress even though he could get a better price by using a U.K. vendor. As he explained:

> Because the United Kingdom is such a large repertoire supplier, I have volume benefits which I offer Arnold. He takes my volume, combines it with the other European countries, and negotiates a manufacturing rate with Sonopress in Munich, and then I buy the product back with the exchange rate working against me. Austria pays the same price as I do, getting the benefit of my volume scale.

Gassner then raised the question of what to do in response to the new prices. There was a long pause at the table. Bahlmann responded first by suggesting that the "extra" profit from the regions be placed in investment funds for each territory. Stein argued that this was not necessary "since the money's always there if the investment is good anyway." The group agreed that the money did not need to be placed in a separate fund, but be left to each company to decide how to use.

"OK, so what about the targets?" Gassner asked. Looking down at his copy of the calculations that Gorman had distributed before the meeting, he continued, "There are significant variances here. An MD's *betriebsergebnis* in some cases could be increased by as much as 50% due solely to the price reduction."

Segura then spoke up: "This doesn't affect me in my region, so I can be objective.[13] We have never before changed targets once they have been set. Not for any reason. So I don't see why we should change them this time." Preston added: "I agree. Some years, I'm hurt by the transfer pricing and exchange rate, but our targets have never been eased to reflect this. So why would we change them now that it's working the other way? It doesn't seem fair."

Indeed, many of the executive committee members found the issue an unusual one for the ECM agenda. As Gorman explained,

> To tell you the truth, I was a little surprised when Rudi asked me to calculate adjusted business targets to reflect the new manufacturing price. I know I'm the one who has been pushing reexamination of our cost structure. But we've never changed the targets. Whether you acquired a company, lost a company, lost a customer, had a major bankruptcy, an artist didn't release—we've had everything you can imagine happen, and I do not remember ever adjusting the targets for anybody, for any reason.

Gassner said, however, that he was concerned that some of the MDs might become "complacent" because their *betriebsergebnis* target would be substantially easier to meet if it were not adjusted. "I want to maintain the challenge of an aggressive bonus target, I want the MDs to be held accountable for the savings. I want them to realize that it isn't just a Christmas gift," he explained to the group.

No one at the table responded or looked in Gassner's direction. Gassner then wondered how he could get them to address the question of changing the targets, a possibility they seemed unwilling even to consider.

---

[13]Since the Latin American region included Spain and Portugal, Segura was affected minimally by the reduced price.

Case 5–4   Acer, Inc.: Taiwan's Rampaging Dragon

With a sense of real excitement, Stan Shih, CEO of Acer, Inc., boarded a plane for San Francisco in early February 1995. The founder of the Taiwanese personal computer (PC) company was on his way to see the Aspire, a new home PC being developed by Acer America Corporation (AAC) Acer's North American subsidiary. Although Shih had heard that a young American team was working on a truly innovative product, featuring a unique design, voice recognition, ease-of-use, and cutting-edge multimedia capabilities, he knew little of the project until Ronald Chwang, President of AAC had invited him to the upcoming product presentation. From Chwang's description, Shih thought that Aspire could have the potential to become a blockbuster product worldwide. But he was equally excited that this was the first Acer product conceived, designed, and championed by a sales-and-marketing oriented regional business unit (RBU) rather than one of Acer's production-and-engineering focused strategic business units (SBUs) in Taiwan.

Somewhere in mid-flight, however, Shih's enthusiasm, was tempered by his well-known pragmatism. Recently, AAC had been one of the company's more problematic overseas units, and had been losing money for five years. Was this the group on whom he should pin his hopes for Acer's next important growth initiative? Could such a radical new product succeed in the highly competitive American PC market? And if so, did this unit—one of the company's sales-and-marketing-oriented RBUs—have the resources and capabilities to lead the development of this important new product, and, perhaps, even its global rollout?

Birth of the Company

Originally known as Multitech, the company was founded in Taiwan in 1976 by Shih, his wife, and three friends. From the beginning, Shih served as CEO and chairman, his wife as company accountant. With $25,000 of capital and 11 employees, Multitech's grand mission was "to promote the application of the emerging microprocessor technology." It grew by grasping every opportunity available—providing engineering and product design advice to local companies, importing electronic components, offering technological training courses, and publishing trade journals. "We will sell anything except our wives," joked Shih. Little did the founders realize that they were laying the foundations for one of Taiwan's great entrepreneurial success stories. (See Exhibit 1.)

Laying the Foundations

Because Multitech was capital constrained, the new CEO instituted a strong norm of frugality and created a constant sense of crisis in the firm. Acting on what he described as "a poor man's philosophy," he leased just enough space for current needs (leading to 28 office relocations over the next 20 years) and encouraged early employees to supplement their income by "moonlighting" at second jobs. Yet while Multitech paid little, it offered new recruits equity, leading to a situation where key employees could hold substantial ownership positions in subsidiary companies.

Frugality was one of many business principles Shih had learned while growing up in his mother's tiny store. He told employees that high-tech products, like his mother's duck eggs, had to be priced

Professor Christopher A. Bartlett and Research Associate Anthony St. George prepared this case. Much of the historical information was drawn from Robert H. Chen, "Made in Taiwan: The Story of Acer Computers," Linking Publishing Co., Taiwan, 1996, and Stan Shih, "Me-too Is Not My Style," Acer Foundation, Taiwan, 1996. We would like thank Eugene Hwang for his assistance in coordinating company contacts and to Professor Robert H. Hayes for his advice.

EXHIBIT 1 Selected Financials: Sales, Net Income, and Headcount, 1976–1994

	1976	1977	1978	1979	1980	1981	1982	1983	1984	1985
Sales ($M)	0.003	0.311	0.80	0.77	3.83	7.08	18.1	28.3	51.6	94.8
Net Income ($M)	NA	NA	NA	NA	NA	NA	NA	1.4	0.4	5.1
Employees	11	12	18	46	104	175	306	592	1,130	1,632

	1986	1987	1988	1989	1990	1991	1992	1993	1994
Sales ($M)	165.3	331.2	530.9	688.9	949.5	985.2	1,259.8	1,883	3,220
Net Income ($M)	3.9	15.3	26.5	5.8	(0.7)	(26.0)	(2.8)	85.6	205
Employees	2,188	3,639	5,072	5,540	5,711	5,216	5,352	7,200	5,825

with a low margin to ensure turnover. He preached the importance of receiving cash payment quickly and avoiding the use of debt. But above all, he told them that customers came first, employees second, and shareholders third, a principle later referred to as "Acer 1-2-3."

Shih's early experience biased him against the patriarch-dominated, family-run company model that was common in Taiwan. "It tends to generate opinions which are neither balanced nor objective," he said. He delegated substantial decision-making responsibility to his employees to harness "the natural entrepreneurial spirit of the Taiwanese." With his informal manner, bias for delegation, and "hands-off" style—an approach many saw as the polar opposite of the classic Chinese entrepreneur—Shih trusted employees to act in the best interests of the firm. "We don't believe in control in the normal sense . . . We rely on people and build our business around them," he said.

This philosophy was reflected in Shih's commitment to employee education and his belief that he could create a company where employees would constantly be challenged to "think and learn." In the early years, superiors were referred to as "shifu," a title usually reserved for teachers and masters of the martial arts. The development of strong teaching relationships between manager and subordinate was encouraged by making the cultivation and grooming of one's staff a primary criterion for promotion. The slogan, "Tutors conceal nothing from their pupils" emphasized the open nature of the relationship and reminded managers of their responsibility.

This created a close-knit culture, where coworkers treated each other like family, and the norm was to do whatever was necessary for the greater good of the company. But is was a very demanding "family," and as the patriarch, Stan Shih worked hard to combat complacency—what he called "the big rice bowl" sense of entitlement—by showering subordinates with ideas and suggestions for their examination and follow-up. As long as the managers took responsibility for their actions—acted as responsible older sons or daughters—they had the freedom to make decisions in the intense, chaotic, yet laissez-faire organization. Besides the suggestions, Shih's guidance came mainly in the form of the slogans, stories, and aphorisms he constantly communicated.

This philosophy of delegation extended to organizational units, which, to the extent possible, Shih forced to operate as independent entities and to compete with outside companies. Extending the model externally, Shih began experimenting with joint ventures as a way of expanding sales. The first such arrangement was struck with a couple of entrepreneurs in central and southern Taiwan. While capturing the partners' knowledge of those regional markets, this approach allowed Multitech to expand its sales without the risk of hiring more people or raising more capital.

Early successes through employee ownership, delegated accountability, management frugality, and joint ventures led to what Shih called a "commoner's culture." This reflected his belief that the way to succeed against wealthy multinationals—"the nobility"—was to join forces with other "commoners"—mass-market customers, local distributors, owner-employees, small investors and supplier-partners, for example. The "poor man's" values supported this culture and guided early expansion. As early as 1978, Shih targeted smaller neighboring markets that were of lesser interest to the global giants. At first, response to Multitech's promotional letters was poor since few foreign distributors believed that a Taiwanese company could make quality hi-tech products. Through persistence, however, Multitech established partnerships with dealers and distributors in Indonesia, Malaysia, Singapore, and Thailand.[1] Shih discribed this early expansion strategy:

> It is like the strategy in the Japanese game *Go*—one plays from the corner, because you need fewer resources to occupy the corner. Without the kind of resources that Japanese and American companies had, we started in smaller markets. That gives us the advantage because these smaller markets are becoming bigger and bigger and the combination of many small markets is not small.

Expansion abroad was greatly helped by a growing number of new products. In 1981, Multitech introduced its first mainstream commercial product, the "Microprofessor" computer. Following the success of this inexpensive, simple computer (little more than an elaborate scientific calculator), Shih and his colleagues began to recognize the enormous potential of the developing PC market. In 1983, Multitech began to manufacture IBM-compatible PCs—primarily as an original equipment manufacturer (OEM) for major brands but also under its own Multitech brand. In 1984 sales reached $51 million, representing a sevenfold increase on revenues three years earlier.

By 1986, the company felt it was ready to stake a claim in Europe, establishing a marketing office in Dusseldorf and a warehouse in Amsterdam. Multitech also supplemented its commission-based purchasing office in the United States with a fully fledged sales office.

Birth of the Dragon Dream

By the mid-1980s, Multitech's sales were doubling each year and confidence was high. As the company approached its tenth anniversary, Shih announced a plan for the next ten years that he described as "Dragon Dreams." With expected 1986 revenues of $400 million, employees and outsiders alike gasped at his projected sales of $5 billion by 1996. Critics soon began quoting the old Chinese aphorism, "To allay your hunger, draw a picture of a big cake." But Shih saw huge potential in overseas expansion.

After only a few years of international experience, the company's overseas sales already accounted for half the total. In several Asian countries Multitech was already a major player: in Singapore, for example, it had a 25% market share by 1986. To build on this Asian base and the new offices in Europe and the United States, Shih created the slogan, "The Rampaging Dragon Goes International." To implement the initiative, he emphasized the need to identify potential overseas acquisitions, set up offshore companies, and seek foreign partners and distributors.

In another major activity during the tenth year anniversary, Shih invited the board and vice presidents to a "Renewal of Company Culture Seminar," in which participants were asked to identify and evaluate the philosophies that had guided Multitech in its first ten years. Middle-level managers were then invited to participate in the process, reviewing, debating, and eventually voting on the key principles that would carry the company forward. The outcome was a statement of four values that

---

[1] About the same time, Shih enlisted an old classmate to open a purchasing unit in the United States, offering 60% share of the tiny venture. Working purely on commission based on the discounts he could obtain from suppliers, this individual became the company's low-cost beachhead in the United States.

captured the essence of their shared beliefs: an assumption that human nature is essentially good; a commitment to maintaining a fundamental pragmatism and accountability in all business affairs; a belief in placing the customer first; and a norm of pooling effort and sharing knowledge. (A decade later, these principles could still be found on office walls worldwide.)

Finally, the anniversary year was capped by another major achievement: Acer became the second company in the world to develop and launch a 32-bit PC, even beating IBM to market. Not only did the product win Taiwan's Outstanding Product Design Award—Acer's fifth such award in seven years—it also attracted the attention of such major overseas high-tech companies as Unisys, ICL and ITT, who began negotiations for OEM supply, and even technology licensing agreements.

Rebirth as Acer: Going Public

Unfortunately, Multitech's growing visibility also led to a major problem. A U.S. company with the registered name "Multitech" informed its Taiwanese namesake that they were infringing its trademark. After ten years of building a corporate reputation and brand identity, Shih conceded he had to start over. He chose the name "Acer" because its Latin root meant "sharp" or "clever," because it played on the English word "Ace," and because it would be first in alphabetical listings. Despite advice to focus on the profitable OEM business and avoid the huge costs of creating a new global brand, Shih was determined to make Acer a globally recognized name.

Beyond branding, the success of the 32-bit PC convinced Shih that Acer would also have to maintain its rapid design, development and manufacturing capability as a source of competitive advantage. Together with the planned aggressive international expansion, these new imperatives—to build a brand and maintain its technological edge—created investment needs that exceeded Acer's internal financing capability. When officials from Taiwan's Securities and Exchange Commission approached Shih about a public offering, he agreed to study the possibility although he knew that many Taiwanese were suspicious of private companies that went public.

A program that allowed any employee to purchase shares after a year in the company had already diluted the original 50% equity Shih and his wife owned to about 35%, but in 1987 he felt it may be time to go further. (Shih had long preached that it was "better to lose control but make money" and that "real control came through ensuring common interest.") An internal committee he asked to study the issue of going public concluded that the company would not only raise needed funds for expansion but also would provide a market for employee-owned shares. In 1988, Acer negotiated a complex multi-tiered financing involving investments by companies (such as Prudential, Chase Manhattan, China Development Corporation, and Sumitomo), additional sales to employees and, finally, a public offering. In total, Acer raised NT $2.2 billion (US $88 million).[2] Issued at NT $27.5, the stock opened trading at NT $47 and soon rose to over NT $100.

The Professionalization of Acer

While the public offering had taken care of Acer's capital shortage, Shih worried about the company's acute shortage of management caused by its rapid growth. In early 1985, when the number of employees first exceeded 1,000, he began to look outside for new recruits "to take charge and stir things up with new ideas." Over the next few years, he brought in about a dozen top-level executives and 100 middle managers. To many of the self-styled "ground troops" (the old-timers), these "paratroopers" were intruders who didn't understand Acer's culture or values but were attracted by the soaring stock. For the first time, Acer experienced significant turnover.

Paratroopers and Price Pressures

Because internally grown managers lacked international experience, one of the key tasks assigned to

_____

[2] After the IPO, Acer employees held about 70% of the equity including the Shihs' share, which had fallen to about 25%.

the "paratroopers" was to implement the company's ambitious offshore expansion plans. In late 1987, Acer acquired Counterpoint, the U.S.-based manufacturer of low-end minicomputers—a business with significantly higher margins than PCs. To support this new business entry, Acer then acquired and expanded the operations of Service Intelligence, a computer service and support organization. Subsequently, a dramatic decline in the market for minicomputers caused Acer's first new product for this segment, the Concer, to become a dismal disappointment. Worse still, the substantial infrastructure installed to support it began generating huge losses.

Meanwhile, changing competitive dynamics in the PC market created another problem for the company. In the closing years of the 1980s, Packard Bell made department and discount stores into major computer retailers, while Dell established its direct sales model. In the face of dramatic PC price reductions, Acer's historic gross margin of about 35% began eroding rapidly, eventually dropping 10 percentage points. Yet despite these problems, the spirits were high, and in mid-1989 the

company shipped its one millionth PC. Flush with new capital, the company purchased properties and companies within Taiwan worth $150 million. However, Acer's drift from its "commoner's culture" worried Shih, who felt he needed help to restore discipline to the "rampaging dragon." The ambition to grow had to be reconciled with the reality of Acer's financial situation.

Enter Leonard Liu

Projected 1989 results indicated that the company overextended itself and was in a tailspin. Earnings per share were expected to fall from NT $5 to NT $1.42. (See Exhibit 2.) The share price, which had been as high as NT $150, fell to under NT $20. Concerned by the growing problems, Shih decided to bring in an experienced top-level executive. After more than a year of courting in late 1989, he signed Leonard Liu, Taiwan-born, U.S.-based, senior IBM executive with a reputation for a no-nonsense professional management style. In an announcement that caught many by surprise, Shih stepped down as president of the Acer Group, handing over that day-to-day management role to Liu. In

EXHIBIT 2   Acer Share Price History, November 1988–January 1995

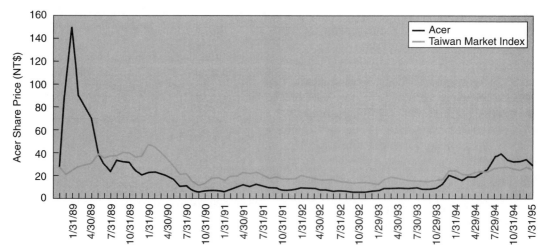

Note: Acer stock price in Taiwan dollars.

Source: Datastream.

addition, Liu was named CEO and chairman of AAC, the company's North American subsidiary.

Given Shih's desire to generate $5 billion in sales by 1996, Liu began to focus on opportunities in the networking market in the United States. Despite the continuing problems at Counterpoint and Service Intelligence, he agreed with those who argued that Acer could exploit this market by building on its position in high-end products, particularly in the advanced markets of the United States and Europe. In particular, Liu became interested in the highly regarded multi-user minicomputer specialist, Altos. Founded in 1977, this Silicon Valley networking company had 700 employees, worldwide distribution in 60 countries, and projected sales of $170 million for 1990. Although it had generated losses of $3 million and $5 million in the previous two years, Liu felt that Altos's $30 million in cash reserves and $20 million in real estate made it an attractive acquisition. For $94 million, Acer would get the respected Altos brand, its technology and its distribution network.[3] As if to remind management of the eclipse of Counterpoint's minicomputers, powerful new PCs soon offered an alternative means of multi-user networking, and within a year of its purchase in August 1990, Altos was losing $20 million. Through the 1990s, AAC's losses increased.

In addition to this strategic thrust, Liu also began working on Acer's established organization and management approaches. For example, under Shih's leadership, while managers had been given considerable independence to oversee their business units, they had not been given profit and loss responsibility. Furthermore, because of the family-style relationship that existed among long-time company members in Taiwan buying and selling between production and marketing units was conducted on an informal trading basis. Inter-company

transfers were often priced to do friends a favor and ensure that a buyer did not "lose face" on a transaction. Even outsourced products were often bought at prices negotiated to make long-term suppliers look good. With no accountability for the profits of their business units, managers had little incentive to ensure quality or price, and would let the group absorb the loss. As one Acer observer noted, the company was "frugal and hard-working, but with little organizational structure or procedure-based administration."

As Shih had hoped, Liu brought to Acer some of IBM's professional management structures, practices and systems. To increase accountability at Acer, the new president reduced management layers, established standards for efficient intra-company communications, and introduced productivity and performance evaluations. Most significantly, he introduced the Regional Business Unit/Strategic Business Unit (RBU/SBU) organization. Acer's long-established product divisions became SBUs responsible for the design, development, and production of PC components and system products, including OEM product sales. Simultaneously, the company's major overseas subsidiaries and marketing companies became RBUs responsible for selling product to customers in their region. RBUs were to develop distribution channels, provide support for dealers, distributor networks, and customers, and work to establish JVs in neighboring markets. All SBUs and RBUs had full profit responsibility.

By 1992, in addition to the four core SBUs, five RBUs had been established: Acer Sertek covering China and Taiwan; Acer Europe headquartered in the Netherlands; Acer America (AAC) responsible for North America; and Acer Computer International (ACI), headquartered in Singapore and responsible for Asia, Africa, and Latin America. (See Exhibits 3a and 3b.) One of the immediate effects of the new structures and systems was to highlight the considerable losses being generated by AAC, for which Liu was directly responsible. While no longer formally engaged in operations, Shih was urging the free-spending Altos management to adopt the more frugal Acer norms, and even began preaching his "duck egg" pricing theory. But

---

[3]Because this was a much larger deal than either Counterpoint (acquired for $1 million plus a stock swap) or Service Intelligence (a $500,000 transaction), Shih suggested the deal be structured as a joint venture to maintain the Altos managers' stake in the business. However, Liu insisted on an outright acquisition to ensure control, and Shih demurred.

EXHIBIT 3a   The Acer Group in 1994

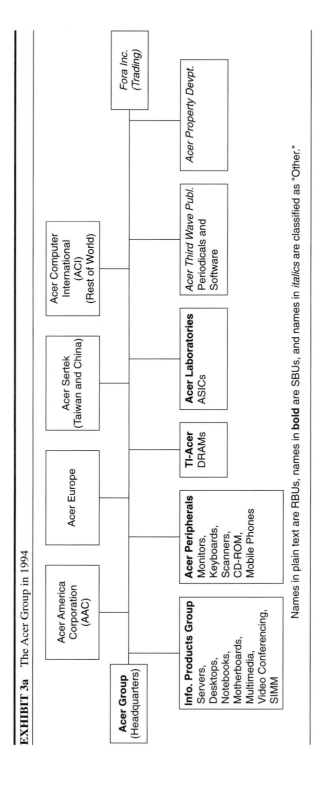

Names in plain text are RBUs, names in **bold** are SBUs, and names in *italics* are classified as "Other."

EXHIBIT 3b   Acer's Geographical Distribution in 1994

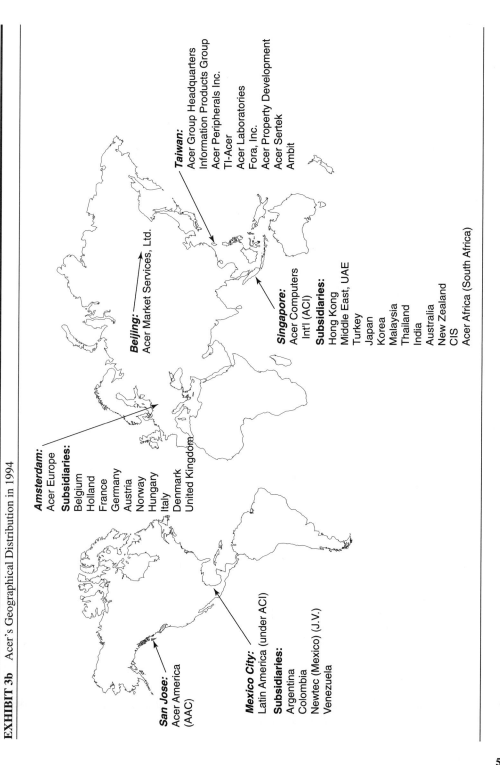

San Jose:
Acer America
(AAC)

Mexico City:
Latin America (under ACI)
Subsidiaries:
Argentina
Colombia
Newtec (Mexico) (J.V.)
Venezuela

Amsterdam:
Acer Europe
Subsidiaries:
Belgium
Holland
France
Germany
Austria
Norway
Hungary
Italy
Denmark
United Kingdom

Beijing:
Acer Market Services, Ltd.

Taiwan:
Acer Group Headquarters
Information Products Group
Acer Peripherals Inc.
TI-Acer
Acer Laboratories
Fora, Inc.
Acer Property Development
Acer Sertek
Ambit

Singapore:
Acer Computers
Int'l (ACI)
Subsidiaries:
Hong Kong
Middle East, UAE
Turkey
Japan
Korea
Malaysia
Thailand
India
Australia
New Zealand
CIS
Acer Africa (South Africa)

EXHIBIT 4   Acer Combination Income Statement, 1988–1994

Income Statement ($ millions)	1988	1989	1990	1991	1992	1993	1994
Turnover	530.9	688.9	949.5	985.2	1,260	1,883	3,220
Cost of sales	(389.4)	(532.7)	(716.7)	(737.7)	(1,000)	(1,498)	(2,615)
Gross profit	141.6	156.3	232.8	247.5	260	385	605
SG&A expenses	(88.2)	(118.2)	(192.2)	(217.2)	(217)	(237)	(316)
R&D and other expenses	(17.9)	(25.4)	(47.7)	(42.3)	(38)	(48)	(59)
Operating profit/(loss)	35.6	12.7	(7.1)	(12.0)	5	100	230
Non-operating profit/(loss)	(8)	(6.3)	(1.5)	(15)	(4)	(11)	(19)
Profit before tax	27.6	6.4	(8.6)	(27.0)	1	89	212
Tax	(1.2)	(1)	(1.2)	1	(3)	(3)	(7)
Profit (loss) after tax	26.4	5.4	(9.8)	(26.0)	(3)	86	205

Sales by Region (%)

North America	NA	31	31	31	38	44	39
Europe	NA	32	28	28	22	23	17
Rest of World	NA	37	41	41	40	33	44

Combination Revenue by Product (%)

Portables	NA	NA	3.2	2.9	7.9	18 ⎫	60%
Desktops and motherboards	NA	NA	60.9	56.3	54.9	47 ⎭	
Minicomputers	NA	NA	13.9	11.3	6.6		
Peripherals and other	NA	NA	22	29.5	30.6	35	40%

Combination Revenue by Business (%)

Brand	NA	53	47	NA	58	68	56%
OEM	NA	34	22	NA	18	32	36%
Trading	NA	13	31	NA	24	NA	7%

Source: Company Annual Reports year ending December 31.

demand was dropping precipitously and Liu decided stronger measures were required. He implemented tight controls and began layoffs.

Meanwhile, the company's overall profitability was plummeting. (See Exhibits 4 and 5.) A year earlier, Shih had introduced an austerity campaign that had focused on turning lights off, using both sides of paper, sharing transportation, and travelling economy. By 1990, however, Liu felt sterner measures were called for, particularly to deal with a payroll that had ballooned to 5,700 employees from only 2,200 in 1986. Under an initiative dubbed

Metamorphosis, managers were asked to rank employee performance, identifying the top 15% and lowest 30%. In January 1991, 300 of the Taiwan-based "thirty percenters" were terminated. (Previously, 100 AAC employees had been let go.)

The impact of the operating problems, the layoffs, the "paratroopers," and particularly the new iron-fisted management style had a predictable impact on Acer's culture and morale. In contrast to Shih's supportive, family-oriented approach, Liu's "by-the-numbers" management model proved grating. There was also growing resentment of his

EXHIBIT 5   Consolidated Balance Sheet, 1988–1994

	1988	1989	1990	1991	1992	1993	1994
Current assets	277.30	448.80	579.50	600.90	700.20	925.00	1,355.00
Fixed Assets							
Land, plant, and equipment (after depreciation)	53.10	126.90	191.10	161.50	179.60	590.00	645.00
Deferred charges and other assets	11.50	22.90	60.90	239.50	212.30	69.00	82.00
Total assets	341.90	598.60	831.50	1,001.90	1,092.10	1,584.00	2,082.00
Total current liabilities	189.40	248.60	464.60	505.80	504.20	752.00	1,067.00
Long-term liabilities	11.20	16.60	43.70	168.50	214.30	342.00	312.00
Total liabilities	200.6	265.20	508.40	674.30	718.50	1,094.00	1,379.00
Stockholders equity and minor: interest	141.30	333.40	323.10	327.60	373.60	490.00	703.00

Source: Company documents.

tendency to spend lavishly on top accounting and law firms and hire people who stayed at first-class hotels, all of which seemed out of step with Acer's "commoner's culture." Soon, his credibility as a highly respected world-class executive was eroding and Acer managers began questioning his judgment and implementing his directives half-heartedly.

In January 1992, when Shih realized the company would report losses of NT $607 million (almost $22 million) on sales on NT $33 billion ($1.26 billion) for 1991, he offered his resignation. The board unanimously rejected the offer, suggesting instead that he resume his old role as CEO. In May 1992, Leonard Liu resigned.

Rebuilding the Base

Shih had long regarded mistakes and their resulting losses as "tuition" for Acer employees' growth—the price paid for a system based on delegation. He saw the losses generated in the early 1990s as part of his personal learning, considering it an investment rather than a waste. ("To make Acer an organization that can think and learn," he said, "we must continue to pay tuition as long as mistakes are

unintentional and long-term profits exceed the cost of the education.") As he reclaimed the CEO role, Shih saw the need to fundamentally rethink Acer's basic business concept, the organizational model that reflected it, and the management philosophy that implemented it.

The Fast-Food Business Concept

In May 1992 Compaq announced a 30% across-the-board price reduction on its PCs. Given Acer's financial plight some urged the company to focus on OEM sales only, while others suggested a retreat from the difficult U.S. market. But Shih believed that crisis was a normal condition in business and that persistence usually paid off. His immediate priority was to reduce AAC's 5 months of inventory, a major liability in a business with a 6- to 9-month product cycle.

Under Shih's stimulus, various parts of the organization began to create new back-to-basics initiatives. In 1991, the System PC unit headed by Johnny Shih developed the "ChipUp" system. This patented technology allowed a motherboard to accept different types of CPU chips—various versions of Intel's 386 and 486 chips, for example—drastically reducing inventory of both chips and motherboards. Another unit, Home Office Automation led by Simon Lin, developed the "2-3-1 System" to reduce the new product introduction process to two months for development, three months for selling and one month for phase-out. And about the same time, a cross-unit initiative to support the launch of Acer's home PC, Acros, developed a screwless assembly process, allowing an entire computer to be assembled by snapping together components, motherboard, power source, etc.[4] All these initiatives culminated in the Uniload concept, a standard parts palette that configured components for easy unpacking, assembly, and testing and facilitated the transfer of assembly to overseas operations.

Shih's decision to manufacture motherboards in Taiwan—which he had been urging Liu to implement for more than a year—coupled with Uniload's ability to assemble products quickly and simply close to the customer led the CEO to start thinking of this push for efficiency as a "fast-food" business model. Under this approach, small, expensive components with fast-changing technology that represented 50%–80% of total cost (e.g., motherboards, CPUs, hard disc drives) were airshipped "hot and fresh" from SBU sources to RBUs in key markets, while less-volatile items (e.g., casings, monitors, power supplies) were shipped by sea. Savings in logistics, inventories and import duties easily offset higher local labor assembly cost, which typically represented less than 1% of product cost.

As Shih began promoting his fast-food business concept, he met with some internal opposition, particularly from SBUs concerned that giving up systems assembly would mean losing power and control. To convince them that they could increase competitiveness more by focusing on component development, he developed a presentation of the value-added elements in the PC industry. "Assem-

bly means you are making money from manual labor," he said. "In components and marketing you add value with your brains." To illustrate the point, Shih developed a disintegrated value-added chart that was soon known as "Stan's Smiling Curve." (See Exhibit 6.)

Client-Server Organization Model

To emphasize the activity redistribution implied in his new business concept, in 1993, Shih unveiled his client-server organization model. Using the metaphor of the network computer, he described the role of the Taiwan headquarters as a "server" that used its resources (finance, people, intellectual property) to support "client" business units, which controlled key operating activities. Under this concept of a company group "network," headquarters was there to help and mediate, not dictate or control, and business units could leverage their own ideas or initiatives directly through other RBUs or SBUs without having to go through the corporate center. Shih believed that this model would allow Acer to develop speed and flexibility as competitive weapons.

While the concept was intriguing, it was a long way from Acer's operating reality. Despite the long-established philosophy of decentralization and the introduction of the SBU and RBU structures in 1992, even the largest RBUs were still viewed as little more than the sales and distribution arms of Acer's Taiwan operations. Once again, Shih had a lot of selling to do. To operationalize the client-server concept, he emphasized several key principles. "Every man is lord of his castle," became his battle cry to confirm the independence of SBU and RBU heads. For example, when two SBUs—Acer Peripherals (API) and Information Products (IPG) both decided to produce CD-ROM drives, Shih did not force on them the corporate logic that competing internally was inefficient. Instead, he opted to let the market decide, with the result that both units succeeded, eventually supplying CD-ROMs to almost 70% of PCs made in Taiwan, by far the world's leading source of OEM and branded PCs.

---

[4]To promote the innovative idea, Shih sponsored internal contests to see who could assemble a computer the fastest. Although his personal best time was more than a minute, some accomplished the task in 30 seconds.

EXHIBIT 6   Stan Shih's PC Industry Conceptualization

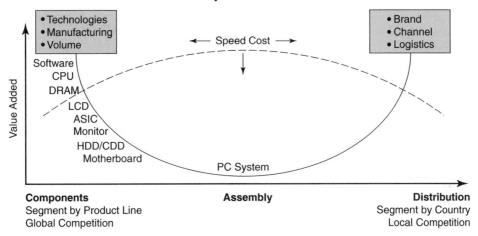

Stan Shih's Smiling Curve

PC Industry Value-Added Curve

Through another principle, "If it doesn't hurt, help," Shih spread a doctrine that favored internal suppliers. Although the "lord of the castle" principle prevented him from forbidding outsourcing, by urging that at least half of all Acer products and components be sold outside the Group, Shih hoped to ensure internal sources were competitive. However, if an RBU decided to improve its bottom line by sourcing externally, it could do so. But it was equally clear that the affected SBU could then find an alternative distributor for its output in that RBU's region. (Within Acer, this mutual deterrence was referred to as the "nuclear option"—the strategy of last resort that was rarely exercised.)

"Global Brand, Local Touch" Philosophy

As Acer's fast-food business concept and client-server organizational model were evolving, so was the overarching management philosophy. At Acer's 1992 International Distributors Meeting in Cancun, Mexico, Shih articulated a commitment to linking the company more closely to its national markets and its local partners, describing his vision as "Global Brand, Local Touch." Under this vision, he wanted Acer to evolve from a Taiwanese company to a truly global organization.

Building on the company's long tradition of taking minority positions in expansionary ventures, Shih began to offer established Acer distributors equity partnerships in the RBU they served. Four months after the Cancun meeting, Acer acquired a 19% interest in Computec, its Mexican distributor. Because of its role in building Acer into Mexico's leading PC brand, Shih invited Computec to form a joint venture company responsible for all Latin America. The result was Acer Computec Latin America (ACLA), a company subsequently floated on the Mexican stock exchange. Similarly, Acer Computers International (ACI), the company responsible for sales in Southeast Asia planned an initial public offering in Singapore in mid-1995. And in Taiwan, Shih was even considering taking some of Acer's core SBUs public.

As these events unfolded, Shih began to articulate an objective of "21 in 21," a vision of the Acer Group as a federation of 21 public companies, each with significant local ownership, by the twenty-first century. It was what he described as "the fourth way," a strategy of globalization radically different from the control-based European, American or Japanese models, relying instead on mutual interest and voluntary cooperation.

The Turnaround

For almost two years, Shih traveled constantly, taking his message to the organization. (He described his role as "to provide innovative stimulus, to materialize the new strategy which first emerges in vague ideas, then to communicate it, form consensus, and agree on action.") By late 1993, the impact of the changes began to appear. Most dramatically, the fast-food business concept (supported by Liu's systems) caused inventory turnover to double by late 1993. Not only did this result in reducing carrying costs, it dramatically lowered the obsolescence risk. By 1994, the Group returned to profit for the first time in three years.

Acer America and the Aspire

After Liu's resignation in April 1992, Shih named Ronald Chwang to head AAC. With a Ph.D. in Electrical Engineering, Chwang joined Acer in 1986 in technical development. After overseeing the start-up of Acer's Peripherals Business Unit, in 1991 he was made president of the Acer/Altos Business Unit, where he was responsible for integrating the newly acquired Altos into AAC.

Because AAC had been losing money since 1987, Chwang's first actions as CEO focused on stemming further losses. With Shih's full support, he tightened receivables, cut inventories, wrote off bad debt, terminated 200 employees, changed the product mix to increase economies of scale, and focused R&D spending on PC products. He also embraced the dramatic changes being initiated in Taiwan, making AAC's Palo Alto plant the first test site of the Uniload system. Under the new system, manufacture and delivery time was cut from 80 days to

45 days, reducing inventory levels by almost 45% and keeping product offerings technologically up-to-date. To adapt and apply the company's knowledge and expertise, AAC established a department of approximately 20 engineers, primarily to manage component testing, but also to adapt software design. By 1994, AAC was breaking even. (See Exhibit 7.)

Birth of Aspire

Despite the improvements these changes made to AAC's market responsiveness, local sales staff still felt that Acer's Taiwan-based SBUs were too distant to develop current relevant product configurations that would appeal to diverse consumer and competitive situations around the globe. What might sell well in Southeast Asia, for example, was likely to be at least a year out of date in the United States. However, the emerging "global brand, local touch" philosophy and the client-server organization model supporting it gave them hope that such problems might be remedied.

In January 1994, Mike Culver was promoted to become AAC's Director of Product Management, a role that gave him responsibility for the product development mandate he felt came with the new client-server model. The 29-year-old electrical engineer and recent MBA graduate had joined Acer America just $2\frac{1}{2}$ years earlier as AAC's product manager for notebook computers. Recently, however, he had become aware of new opportunities in home computing.

Several factors caught Culver's attention. First, data showed an increasing trend to working at home—from 26 million people in 1993 to a projected 29 million in 1994. In addition, there was a rapidly growing interest in the Internet. And finally, developments in audio, telecom, video, and computing technologies were leading to industry rumblings of a new kind of multimedia home PC. Indeed, rumor had it that competitors like Hewlett Packard were already racing to develop new multimedia systems. Sharing this vision, Culver believed the time

EXHIBIT 7   AAC Selected Financials (1990–1994)[5]

	1990	1991	1992	1993	1994
Revenue	161	235	304	434	858
Cost of sales	133	190	283	399	764
Selling and marketing	27	61	25	23	55
General administration	20	16	17	19	20
Research and development	5	8	6	4	4
Operating profit/(loss)	(24)	(40)	(26)	(11)	15
Non-operating profit/(loss)	(1)	(7)	(3)	(5)	(3)
Profit/(loss) before tax	(25)	(47)	(29)	(16)	12
Tax	1	(2)	0	0	1
Net income/(loss)	(26)	(45)	(29)	(16)	11
Current assets	155	153	123	144	242
Fixed assets (net)	39	43	28	25	25
Other assets (net)	37	37	31	19	11
Total assets	231	233	182	188	278
Current liabilities	155	169	154	136	218
Long-term debt	17	15	18	58	47
Stockholder equity (including additional capital)	58	50	10	(6)	12
Total liabilities	231	233	182	188	278

[5]Totals may not add due to rounding.

was right to create "the first Wintel-based PC that could compete with Apple in design, ease-of-use, and multimedia capabilities."

In October of 1994, Culver commissioned a series of focus groups to explore the emerging opportunity. In one of the groups, a consumer made a comment that had a profound impact on him. She said she wanted a computer that wouldn't remind her of work. At that moment, Culver decided that Acer's new home PC would incorporate radically new design aesthetics to differentiate it from the standard putty-colored, boxy PCs that sat in offices throughout the world.

By November, Culver was convinced of the potential for an innovative multimedia consumer PC,

and began assembling a project team to develop the concept. While the team believed the Acer Group probably had the engineering capability to develop the product's new technical features, they were equally sure they would have to go outside to get the kind of innovative design they envisioned. After an exhaustive review, the team selected Frog Design, a leading Silicon Valley design firm that had a reputation for "thinking outside of the box." Up to this point, Culver had been using internal resources and operating within his normal budget. The selection of Frog Design, however, meant that he had to go to Chwang for additional support. "The approval was incredibly informal," related Culver, "it literally took place in one 20-minute discussion in the hallway in late November. I told Ronald we would need $200,000 for outside consulting to create the cosmetic prototype." Chwang agreed on the spot, and the design process began.

In 1994, Acer was in ninth place in the U.S. market, with 2.4% market share, largely from sales of the Acros, Acer's initial PC product, which was an adaptation of its commercial product, the Acer Power. (See Exhibit 8 for 1994 market shares.) Culver and Chwang were convinced they could not only substantially improve that share, but also create a product with global potential. In 1994 Acer's share of the world market was 2.7% 278,000 units of a global multimedia desktop market estimated at 10.4 million units and growing at more than 20% annually, primarily in Europe and Asia.

Working jointly with designers from Frog Design, the project team talked to consumers, visited computer retail stores and held discussions to brainstorm the new product's form. After almost two months, Frog Design developed six foam models of possible designs. In January 1995, the Acer team chose a striking and sleek profile that bore little resemblance to the traditional PC. Market research also indicated that customers wanted a choice of colors, so the team decided that the newly named Aspire product would be offered in charcoal grey and emerald green. (See Exhibit 9.)

Meanwhile, the team had been working with AAC software engineers and a development group in Taiwan to incorporate the new multimedia capabilities into the computer. One significant introduction was voice-recognition software that enabled users to open, close, and save documents by voice commands. However, such enhancements also required new hardware design: to accommodate the voice-recognition feature, for example, a microphone had to be built in, and to properly exploit the machine's enhanced audio capabilities, speakers had to be integrated into the monitor. The multimedia concept also required the integration of CD-ROM capabilities, and a built-in modem and answering machine incorporating fax and telephone capabilities. This type of configuration was a radical innovation for Acer, requiring significant design and tooling changes.

In early 1995 the price differential between upper-tier PCs (Compaq and IBM, for example) and lower-end products (represented by Packard Bell) was about 20%. Culver's team felt the Aspire could be positioned between these two segments offering a high-quality innovative product at a less-than-premium price. They felt they could gain a strong foothold by offering a product range priced from $1,199 for the basic product to $2,999 for the highest-end system with monitor. With a September

---

EXHIBIT 8   Top Ten PC Manufacturers in the U.S. and worldwide in 1994

Company	U.S. Market Share	Worldwide Market Share
Compaq	12.6%	9.8%
Apple	11.5%	8.1%
Packard Bell	11.4%	5.1%
IBM	9.0%	8.5%
Gateway 2000	5.2%	2.3%
Dell	4.2%	2.6%
AST	3.9%	2.7%
Toshiba	3.6%	2.4%
Acer	2.4%	2.6%
Hewlett Packard	2.4%	2.5%

Source: *Los Angeles Times,* January 31, 1996.

EXHIBIT 9   First Generation Aspire Design Features and Marketing Materials

launch, they budgeted sales of $570,000 for 1995, rising to well over $1 million in 1996.

Stan Shih's Decisions

On his way to to San Jose in February 1995, Stan Shih pondered the significance of the Aspire project. Clearly, it represented the client-server system at work: this could become the first product designed and developed by an RBU, in response to a locally sensed market opportunity. Beyond that, he had the feeling it might have the potential to become Acer's first global blockbuster product.

Despite its promise, however, Shih wanted to listen to the views of the project's critics. Some pointed out that AAC had just begun to generate profits in the first quarter of 1994, largely on the basis of its solid OEM sales, which accounted for almost 50% of revenues.

Given its delicate profit position, they argued that AAC should not be staking its future on the extremely expensive and highly competitive mass distribution consumer business. Established competitors were likely to launch their own multimedia home PCs—perhaps even before Acer. Building a new brand in this crowded, competitive market was extremely difficult as proven by many failed attempts, including the costly failure of Taiwan-based Mitac, when it launched its own brand PC in the early 1990s.

Even among those who saw potential in the product, there were several that expressed concern about the project's implementation. With all the company's engineering and production expertise located in Taiwan, these critics argued that the task of coordinating the development and delivery of such an innovative new product was just too risky to leave with an inexperienced group in an RBU with limited development resources. If the project were to be approved, they suggested it be transferred back to the SBUs in Taiwan for implementation.

Finally, some wondered whether Acer's client-server organization model and "local touch" management would support Aspire becoming a viable global product. With the growing independence of the RBUs worldwide, they were concerned that each one would want to redesign the product and marketing strategy for its local market, thereby negating any potential scale economies.

As his plane touched down in San Francisco, Shih tried to resolve his feelings of excitement and concern. Should he support the Aspire project, change it, or put it on hold? And what implications would his decisions have for the new corporate model he had been building?

Reading 5–1

TAP YOUR SUBSIDIARIES FOR GLOBAL REACH

Christopher A. Bartlett and Sumantra Ghoshal

In 1972, EMI developed the CAT scanner. This technological breakthrough seemed to be the innovation that the U.K.–based company had long sought in order to relieve its heavy dependence on the cyclical music and entertainment business and to strengthen itself in international markets. The medical community hailed the product, and within four years EMI had established a medical electronics business that was generating 20% of the company's worldwide earnings. The scanner enjoyed a

dominant market position, a fine reputation, and a strong technological leadership situation.

Nevertheless, by mid-1979 EMI had started losing money in this business, and the company's deteriorating performance eventually forced it to accept a takeover bid from Thorn Electric. Thorn immediately divested the ailing medical electronics business. Ironically, the takeover was announced the same month that Godfrey Hounsfield, the EMI scientist who developed the CAT scanner, was awarded a Nobel Prize for the invention.

How could such a fairy-tale success story turn so quickly into a nightmare? There were many contributing causes, but at the center were a structure and management process that impeded the company's ability to capitalize on its technological assets and its worldwide market position.

The concentration of EMI's technical, financial, and managerial resources in the United Kingdom made it unresponsive to the varied and changing needs of international markets. As worldwide demand built up, delivery lead times for the scanner stretched out more than 12 months. Despite the protests of EMI's U.S. managers that these delays were opening opportunities for competitive entry, headquarters continued to fill orders on the basis of when they were received rather than on how strategically important they were. Corporate management would not allow local sourcing or duplicate manufacturing of the components that were the bottlenecks causing delays.

The centralization of decision making in London also impaired the company's ability to guide strategy to meet the needs of the market. For example, medical practitioners in the United States, the key market for CAT scanners, considered reduction of scan time to be an important objective, while EMI's central research laboratory, influenced by feedback from the domestic market, concentrated on improving image resolution. When General Electric eventually brought out a competitive product with a shorter scan time, customers deserted EMI.

In the final analysis, it was EMI's limited organizational capability that prevented it from capitalizing on its large resource base and its strong global competitive position. The company lacked:

The ability to sense changes in market needs and industry structure occurring away from home.

The resources to analyze data and develop strategic responses to competitive challenges that were emerging worldwide.

The managerial initiative, motivation, and capability in its overseas operations to respond imaginatively to diverse and fast-changing operating environments.

While the demise of its scanner business represents an extreme example, the problems EMI faced are common. With all the current attention being given to global strategy, companies risk underestimating the organizational challenge of managing their global operations. Indeed, the top management in almost every one of the MNCs we have studied has had an excellent idea of what it needed to do to become more globally competitive; it was less clear on how to organize to achieve its global strategic objectives.

United Nations Model and HQ Syndrome

Our study covered nine core companies in three industries and a dozen secondary companies from a more diverse industrial spectrum. They were selected from three areas of origin—the United States, Europe, and Japan. Despite this diversity, most of these companies had developed their international operations around two common assumptions on how to organize. We dubbed these well-ingrained beliefs the "U.N. model assumption" and the "headquarters hierarchy syndrome."

Although there are wide differences in importance of operations in major markets like Germany, Japan, or the United States, compared with subsidiaries in Argentina, Malaysia, or Nigeria, for example, most multinationals treat their foreign subsidiaries in a remarkably uniform manner. One executive we talked to termed this approach "the U.N. model of multinational management." Thus, it is common to see managers express subsidiary roles and responsibilities in the same general terms, apply their planning control systems uniformly systemwide, involve country managers to a like degree in planning, and evaluate them against standardized criteria. The uniform systems and procedures tend to paper over any differences in the informal treatment of subsidiaries.

When national units are operationally self-sufficient and strategically independent, uniform treatment may allow each to develop a plan for dealing with its local environment. As a company reaches for the benefits of global integration, however, there is little need for uniformity and symmetry among units. Yet the growing complexity of the corporate management task heightens the appeal of a simple system.

The second common assumption we observed, the headquarters hierarchy syndrome, grows out of and is reinforced by the U.N. model assumption. The symmetrical organization approach encourages management to envision two roles for the organization, one for headquarters and another for the national subsidiaries. As companies moved to build a consistent global strategy, we saw a strong tendency for headquarters managers to try to coordinate key decisions and control global resources and have the subsidiaries act as implementers and adapters of the global strategy in their localities.

As strategy implementation proceeded, we observed country managers struggling to retain their freedom, flexibility, and effectiveness, while their counterparts at the center worked to maintain their control and legitimacy as administrators of the global strategy. It's not surprising that relationships between the center and the periphery often became strained and even adversarial.

The combined effect of these two assumptions is to severely limit the organizational capability of a company's international operations in three important ways. First, the doctrine of symmetrical treatment results in an overcompensation for the needs of smaller or less crucial markets and a simultaneous underresponsiveness to the needs of strategically important countries. Moreover, by relegating the national subsidiaries to the role of local implementers and adapters of global directives, the head office risks grossly underutilizing the company's worldwide assets and organizational capabilities. And finally, ever-expanding control by headquarters deprives the country managers of outlets for their skills and creative energy. Naturally, they come to feel demotivated and even disenfranchised.

Dispersed Responsibility

The limitations of the symmetrical, hierarchical mode of operation have become increasingly clear to MNC executives, and in many of the companies we surveyed we found managers experimenting with alternative ways of managing their worldwide operations. And as we reviewed these various approaches,

we saw a new pattern emerging that suggested a significantly different model of global organization based on some important new assumptions and beliefs. We saw companies experimenting with ways of selectively varying the roles and responsibilities of their national organizations to reflect explicitly the differences in external environments and internal capabilities. We also saw them modifying central administrative systems to legitimize the differences they encountered.

Such is the case with Procter & Gamble's European operations. More than a decade ago, P&G's European subsidiaries were free to adapt the parent company's technology, products, and marketing approaches to their local situation as they saw fit—while being held responsible, of course, for sales and earnings in their respective countries. Many of these subsidiaries had become large and powerful. By the mid-1970s, economic and competitive pressures were squeezing P&G's European profitability. The head office in Cincinnati decided that the loose organizational arrangement inhibited product development, curtailed the company's ability to capture Europewide scale economies, and afforded poor protection against competitors' attempts to pick off product lines country by country.

So the company launched what became known as the Pampers experiment—an approach firmly grounded in the classic U.N. and HQ assumptions. It created a position at European headquarters in Brussels to develop a Pampers strategy for the whole continent. By giving this manager responsibility for the Europewide product and marketing strategy, management hoped to be able to eliminate the diversity in brand strategy by coordinating activities across subsidiary boundaries. Within 12 months, the Pampers experiment had failed. It not only ignored local knowledge and underutilized subsidiary strengths but also demotivated the country managers to the point that they felt no responsibility for sales performance of the brand in their areas.

Obviously, a different approach was called for. Instead of assuming that the best solutions were to be found in headquarters, top management decided to find a way to exploit the expertise of the national units. For most products, P&G had one or two European subsidiaries that had been more creative, committed, and successful than the others. By extending the responsibilities and influence of these organizations, top management reasoned, the company could make the success infectious. All that was needed was a means for promoting intersubsidiary cooperation that could offset the problems caused by the company's dispersed and independent operations. For P&G the key was the creation of "Eurobrand" teams.

For each important brand the company formed a management team that carried the responsibility for development and coordination of marketing strategy for Europe. Each Eurobrand team was headed not by a manager from headquarters but by the general manager and the appropriate brand group from the "lead" subsidiary—a unit selected for its success and creativity with the brand. Supporting them were brand managers from other subsidiaries, functional managers from headquarters, and anyone else involved in strategy for the particular product. Team meetings became forums for the lead-country group to pass on ideas, propose action, and hammer out agreements.

The first Eurobrand team had charge of a new liquid detergent called Vizir. The brand group in the lead country, West Germany, had undertaken product and market testing, settled on the package design and advertising theme, and developed the marketing strategy. The Eurobrand team ratified all these elements, then launched Vizir in six new markets within a year. This was the first time the company had ever introduced a new product in that many markets in so brief a span. It was also the first time the company had gotten agreement in several subsidiaries on a single product formulation, a uniform advertising theme, a standard packaging line, and a sole manufacturing source. Thereafter, Eurobrand teams proliferated; P&G's way of organizing and directing subsidiary operations had changed fundamentally.

On reflection, company managers feel that there were two main reasons why Eurobrand teams succeeded where the Pampers experiment had failed.

First, they captured the knowledge, the expertise, and most important, the commitment of managers closest to the market. Equally significant was the fact that relationships among managers on Eurobrand teams were built on interdependence rather than on independence, as in the old organization, or on dependence, as with the Pampers experiment. Different subsidiaries had the lead role for different brands, and the need for reciprocal cooperation was obvious to everyone.

Other companies have made similar discoveries about new ways to manage their international operations—at NEC and Philips, at L. M. Ericsson and Matsushita, at ITT and Unilever, we observed executives challenging the assumptions behind the traditional head office–subsidiary relationship. The various terms they used—lead-country concept, key-market subsidiary, global-market mandate, center of excellence—all suggested a new model based on a recognition that their organizational task was focused on a single problem: the need to resolve imbalances between market demands and constraints on the one hand and uneven subsidiary capabilities on the other. Top officers understand that the option of a zero-based organization is not open to an established multinational organization. But they seem to have hit on an approach that works.

Black Holes, Etc.

The actions these companies have taken suggest an organizational model of differentiated rather than homogeneous subsidiary roles and of dispersed rather than concentrated responsibilities. As we analyzed the nature of the emerging subsidiary roles and responsibilities, we were able to see a pattern in their distribution and identify the criteria used to assign them. Exhibit 1 represents a somewhat oversimplified conceptualization of the criteria and roles, but it is true enough for discussion purposes.

The strategic importance of a specific country unit is strongly influenced by the significance of its national environment to the company's global strategy. A large market is obviously important, and so is a competitor's home market or a market that is particularly sophisticated or technologically advanced.

EXHIBIT 1   Roles for National Subsidiaries

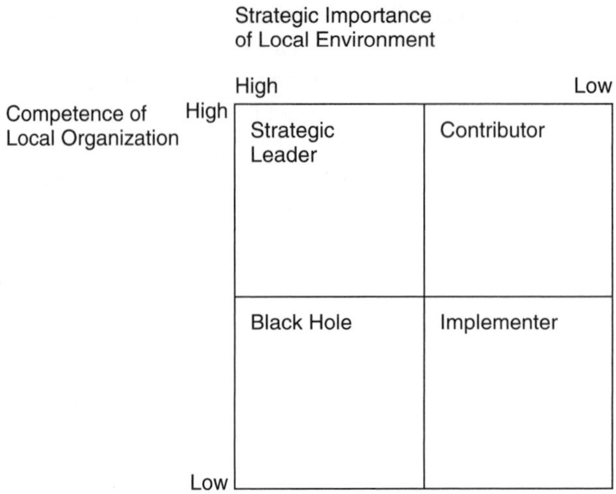

Strategic Importance
of Local Environment

	High	Low
Competence of Local Organization — High	Strategic Leader	Contributor
Low	Black Hole	Implementer

The organizational competence of a particular subsidiary can, of course, be in technology, production, marketing, or any other area.

Strategic Leader.   This role can be played by a highly competent national subsidiary located in a strategically important market. In this role, the subsidiary serves as a partner of headquarters in developing and implementing strategy. It must not only be a sensor for detecting signals of change but also a help in analyzing the threats and opportunities and developing appropriate responses.

The part played by the U.K. subsidiary of Philips in building the company's strong leadership position in the teletext-TV business provides an illustration. In the early 1970s, the BBC and ITV (an independent British TV company) simultaneously launched projects to adapt existing transmission capacity to permit broadcast of text and simple diagrams. But teletext, as it was called, required a TV receiver that would accept and decode the modified transmissions. For TV set manufacturers, the market opportunity required a big investment in R&D and production facilities, but commercial possibilities of teletext were highly uncertain, and most producers decided against making the investment.

They spurned teletext as a typical British toy— fancy and not very useful. Who would pay a heavy premium just to read text on a TV screen?

Philips' U.K. subsidiary, however, was convinced that the product had a future and decided to pursue its own plans. Its top officers persuaded Philips' component manufacturing unit to design and produce the integrated-circuit chip for receiving teletext and commissioned their Croydon plant to build the teletext decoder.

In the face of poor market acceptance (the company sold only 1,000 teletext sets in its first year), the U.K. subsidiary did not give up. It lent support to the British government's efforts to promote teletext and make it widely available. Meanwhile, management kept up pressure on the Croydon factory to find ways of reducing costs and improving reception quality—which it did.

In late 1979, teletext took off, and by 1982 half a million sets were being sold annually in the United Kingdom. Today almost three million teletext sets are in use in Britain, and the concept is spreading abroad. Philips has built up a dominant position in markets that have accepted the service. Corporate management has given the U.K. subsidiary formal responsibility to continue to exercise leadership in the development, manufacture, and marketing of teletext on a companywide basis. The Croydon plant is recognized as Philips' center of competence and international sourcing plant for teletext-TV sets.

Contributor. Filling this role is a subsidiary operating in a small or strategically unimportant market but having a distinctive capability. A fine example is the Australian subsidiary of L. M. Ericsson, which played a crucial part in developing its successful AXE digital telecommunications switch. The down-under group gave impetus to the conversion of the system from its initial analog design to the digital form. Later its engineers helped construct several key components of the system.

This subsidiary had built up its superior technological capability when the Australian telephone authority became one of the first in the world to call for bids on electronic telephone switching equipment. The government in Canberra, however, had insisted on a strong local technical capability as a condition for access to the market. Moreover, heading this unit of the Swedish company was a willful, independent, and entrepreneurial country manager who strengthened the R&D team, even without full support from headquarters.

These various factors resulted in the local subsidiary having a technological capability and an R&D resource base that was much larger than subsidiaries in other markets of similar size or importance. Left to their own devices, management worried that such internal competencies would focus on local tasks and priorities that were unnecessary or even detrimental to the overall global strategy. But if the company inhibited the development activities of the local units, it risked losing these special skills. Under the circumstances, management saw the need to co-opt this valuable subsidiary expertise and channel it toward projects of corporate importance.

Implementer. In the third situation, a national organization in a less strategically important market has just enough competence to maintain its local operation. The market potential is limited, and the corporate resource commitment reflects it. Most national units of most companies are given this role.

They might include subsidiaries in the developing countries, in Canada, and in the smaller European countries. Without access to critical information, and having to control scarce resources, these national organizations lack the potential to become contributors to the company's strategic planning. They are deliverers of the company's value added; they have the important task of generating the funds that keep the company going and underwrite its expansion.

The implementers' efficiency is as important as the creativity of the strategic leaders or contributors—and perhaps more so, for it is this group that provides the largest leverage that affords MNCs their competitive advantage. The implementers produce the opportunity to capture economies of scale and scope that are crucial to most companies' global strategies.

In Procter & Gamble's European introduction of Vizir, the French company played an important contributing role by undertaking a second market test and later modifying the advertising approach. In the other launches during the first year, Austria, Spain, Holland, and Belgium were implementers; they took the defined strategy and made it work in their markets. Resisting any temptation to push for change in the formula, alteration of the package, or adjustment of the advertising theme, these national subsidiaries enabled P&G to extract profitable efficiencies.

The Black Hole. Philips in Japan, Ericsson in the United States, and Matsushita in Germany are black holes. In each of these important markets, strong local presence is essential for maintaining the company's global position. And in each case, the local company hardly makes a dent.

The black hole is not an acceptable strategic position. Unlike the other roles we have described, the objective is not to manage it but to manage one's way out of it. But building a significant local presence in a national environment that is large, sophisticated, and competitive is extremely difficult, expensive, and time consuming.

One common tack has been to create a sensory outpost in the black hole environment so as to exploit the learning potential, even if the local business potential is beyond reach. Many American and European companies have set up small establishments in Japan to monitor technologies, market trends, and competitors. Feedback to headquarters, so the thinking goes, will allow further analysis of the global implications of local developments and will at least help prevent erosion of the company's position in other markets. But this strategy has often been less fruitful than the company had hoped. Look at the case of Philips in Japan.

Although Philips had two manufacturing joint ventures with Matsushita, not until 1956 did it enter Japan by establishing a marketing organization. When Japan was emerging as a significant force in the consumer electronics market in the late 1960s, the company decided it had to get further into that market. After years of unsuccessfully trying to penetrate the captive distribution channels of the principal Japanese manufacturers, headquarters settled for a Japan "window" that would keep it informed of technical developments there. But results were disappointing. The reason, according to a senior manager of Philips in Japan, is that to sense effectively, eyes and ears are not enough. One must get "inside the bloodstream of the business," he said, with constant and direct access to distribution channels, component suppliers, and equipment manufacturers.

Detecting a new development after it has occurred is useless, for there is no time to play catch-up. One needs to know of developments as they emerge, and for that one must be a player, not a spectator. Moreover, being confined to window status, the local company is prevented from playing a strategic role. It is condemned to a permanent existence as a black hole.

So Philips is trying to get into the bloodstream of the Japanese market, moving away from the window concept and into the struggle for market share. The local organization now sees its task as winning market share rather than just monitoring local developments. But it is being very selective and focusing on areas where it has advantages over strong local competition. The Japanese unit started with coffee makers and electric shavers. Philips' acquisition of Marantz, a hi-fi equipment producer, gives it a bid to expand on its strategic base and build the

internal capabilities that will enable the Japanese subsidiary to climb out of the black hole.

Another way to manage one's way out of the black hole is to develop a strategic alliance. Such coalitions can involve different levels of cooperation. Ericsson's joint venture with Honeywell in the United States and AT&T's with Philips in Europe are examples of attempts to fill up a black hole by obtaining resources and competence from a strong local organization in exchange for capabilities available elsewhere.

Shaping, Building, Directing

Corporate management faces three big challenges in guiding the dispersion of responsibilities and differentiating subsidiaries' tasks. The first is in setting the strategic direction for the company by identifying its mission and its business objectives. The second is in building the differentiated organization, not only by designing the diverse roles and distributing the assignments but also by giving the managers responsible for filling them the legitimacy and power to do so. The final challenge is in directing the process to ensure that the several roles are coordinated and that the distributed responsibilities are controlled.

Setting the Course.   Any company (or any organization, for that matter) needs a strong, unifying sense of direction. But that need is particularly strong in an organization in which tasks are differentiated and responsibilities dispersed. Without it, the decentralized management process will quickly degenerate into strategic anarchy. A visitor to any NEC establishment in the world will see everywhere the company motto "C&C," which stands for computers and communications. This simple pairing of words is much more than a definition of NEC's product markets; top managers have made it the touchstone of a common global strategy. They emphasize it to focus the attention of employees on the key strategy of linking two technologies. And they employ it to help managers think how NEC can compete with larger companies like IBM and AT&T, which are perceived as vulnerable insofar as they lack a balance in the two technologies and markets.

Top management at NEC headquarters in Tokyo strives to inculcate its worldwide organization with an understanding of the C&C strategy and philosophy. It is this strong, shared understanding that permits greater differentiation of managerial processes and the decentralization of tasks.

But in addition to their role of developing and communicating a vision of the corporate mission, the top officers at headquarters also retain overall responsibility for the company's specific business strategies. While not abandoning this role at the heart of the company's strategic process, executives of many multinational companies are co-opting other parts of the organization (and particularly its diverse national organizations) into important business strategy roles, as we have already described. When it gives up its lead role, however, headquarters management always tracks that delegated responsibility.

Building Differentiation.   In determining which units should be given the lead, contributor, or follower roles, management must consider the motivational as well as the strategic impact of its decisions. If unfulfilled, the promise offered by the new organization model can be as demotivating as the symmetrical hierarchy, in which all foreign subsidiaries are assigned permanent secondary roles. For most national units, an organization in which lead and contributor roles are concentrated in a few favorite children represents little advance from old situations in which the parent dominated the decision making. In any units continually obliged to implement strategies developed elsewhere, skills atrophy, entrepreneurship dies, and any innovative spark that existed when it enjoyed more independence now sputters.

By dealing out lead or contributing roles to the smaller or less developed units, even if only for one or two strategically less important products, the headquarters group will give them a huge incentive. Although Philips N.V. had many other subsidiaries closer to large markets or with better access to corporate know-how and expertise, headquarters awarded the Taiwan unit the lead role in the small-screen monitor business. This vote of confidence gave the Taiwanese terrific motivation

to do well and made them feel like a full contributing partner in the company's worldwide strategy.

But allocating roles isn't enough; the head office has to empower the units to exercise their voices in the organization by ensuring that those with lead positions particularly have access to and influence in the corporate decision-making process. This is not a trivial task, especially if strategic initiative and decision-making powers have long been concentrated at headquarters.

NEC discovered this truth about a decade ago when it was trying to transform itself into a global enterprise. Because NTT, the Japanese telephone authority, was dragging its feet in converting its exchanges to the new digital switching technology, NEC was forced to diverge from its custom of designing equipment mainly for its big domestic customer. The NEAC 61 digital switch was the first outgrowth of the policy shift; it was aimed primarily at the huge, newly deregulated U.S. telephone market.

Managers and engineers in Japan developed the product; the American subsidiary had little input. Although the hardware drew praise from customers, the switch had severe software deficiencies that hampered its penetration of the U.S. market.

Recognizing the need to change its administrative setup, top management committed publicly to becoming "a genuine world enterprise" rather than a Japanese company operating abroad. To permit the U.S. subsidiary a greater voice, headquarters helped it build a local software development capability. This plus the unit's growing knowledge about the Bell operating companies—NEC's target customers—gave the American managers legitimacy and power in Japan.

NEC's next-generation digital switch, the NEAC 61-E, evolved quite differently. Exercising their new influence at headquarters, U.S. subsidiary managers took the lead in establishing its features and specifications and played a big part in the design.

Another path to empowerment takes the form of dislodging the decision-making process from the home office. Ericsson combats the headquarters hierarchy syndrome by appointing product and functional managers from headquarters to subsidiary boards. The give-and-take in board meetings is helpful for both subsidiary and parent. Matsushita holds an annual review of each major worldwide function (like manufacturing and human resource management) in the offices of a national subsidiary it considers to be a leading exponent of the particular function. In addition to the symbolic value for employees of the units, the siting obliges officials from Tokyo headquarters to consider issues that the front lines are experiencing and gives local managers the home-court advantage in seeking a voice in decision making.

Often the most effective means of giving strategy access and influence to national units is to create entirely new channels and forums. This approach permits roles, responsibilities, and relationships to be defined and developed with far less constraint than through modification of existing communication patterns or through shifting of responsibility boundaries. Procter & Gamble's Eurobrand teams are a case in point.

Directing the Process.   When the roles of operating units are differentiated and responsibility is more dispersed, corporate management must be prepared to deemphasize its direct control over the strategic content but develop an ability to manage the dispersed strategic process. Furthermore, headquarters must adopt a flexible administrative stance that allows it to differentiate the way it manages one subsidiary to the next and from business to business within a single unit, depending on the particular role it plays in each business.

In units with lead roles, headquarters plays an important role in ensuring that the business strategies developed fit the company's overall goals and priorities. But control in the classic sense is often quite loose. Corporate management's chief function is to support those with strategy leadership responsibility by giving them the resources and the freedom needed for the innovative and entrepreneurial role they have been asked to play.

With a unit placed in a contributor role, the head-office task is to redirect local resources to programs outside the unit's control. In so doing, it has to

counter the natural hierarchy of loyalties that in most national organizations puts local interests above global ones. In such a situation, headquarters must be careful not to discourage the local managers and technicians so much that they stop contributing or leave in frustration. This has happened to many U.S. companies that have tried to manage their Canadian subsidiaries in a contributor role. Ericsson has solved the problem in its Australian subsidiary by attaching half the R&D team to headquarters, which farms out to these engineers projects that are part of the company's global development program.

The head office maintains tighter control over a subsidiary in an implementor role. Because such a group represents the company's opportunity to capture the benefits of scale and learning from which it gets and sustains its competitive advantage, headquarters stresses economy and efficiency in selling the products. Communication of strategies developed elsewhere and control of routine tasks can be carried out through systems, allowing headquarters to manage these units more efficiently than most others.

As for the black hole unit, the task for top executives is to develop its resources and capabilities to make it more responsive to its environment. Managers of these units depend heavily on headquarters for help and support, creating an urgent need for intensive training and transfer of skills and resources.

Firing the Spark Plugs

Multinational companies often build cumbersome and expensive infrastructures designed to control their widespread operations and to coordinate the diverse and often conflicting demands they make. As the coordination and control task expands, the typical headquarters organization becomes larger and more powerful, while the national subsidiaries are increasingly regarded as pipelines for centrally developed products and strategy.

But an international company enjoys a big advantage over a national one: it is exposed to a wider and more diverse range of environmental stimuli.

The broader range of customer preferences, the wider spectrum of competitive behavior, the more serious array of government demands, and the more diverse sources of technological information represent potential triggers of innovation and thus a rich source of learning for the company. To capitalize on this advantage requires an organization that is sensitive to the environment and responsive in absorbing the information it gathers.

So national companies must not be regarded as just pipelines but recognized as sources of information and expertise that can build competitive advantage. The best way to exploit this resource is not through centralized direction and control but through a cooperative effort and co-option of dispersed capabilities. In such a relationship, the entrepreneurial spark plugs in the national units can flourish.

Reading 5–2

MAKING GLOBAL STRATEGIES WORK

W. Chan Kim
Renée A. Mauborgne

What most motivates the top managers of multinational subsidiaries to execute the global strategies formulated at headquarters? Is it compensation, monitoring systems, or the magnitude and precision of rewards and punishment? It's none of these, argue the authors. Subsidiary top managers are most concerned that the global strategic decision-making process employs due process. That is, they want an open process that is consistent and fair and that allows for their input. The authors describe their research on this subject and urge companies to pay more attention to how they make strategic decisions.

It is hardly a novel insight that global competitive forces compel multinationals to fully leverage the distinctive resources, knowledge, and expertise residing in their subsidiary operations. Questions of what are "winning" global strategic moves for the modern multinational have increasingly intoxi-cated international executives.[1] Yet for all the fanfare about global strategies and their increasingly undeniable link to multinational success, little has been said or written about how to make global strategies work. The key question we address here is just that: What does it take for multinationals to successfully execute global strategies?

Our research results paint a striking picture of the importance of the strategy-making process itself for effective global strategy execution. Over the last four years, we have done extensive research

W. Chan Kim is associate professor of strategy and international management, INSEAD. Renée A. Mauborgne is research associate of management and international business, INSEAD.

Special thanks are due to Sumantra Ghoshal, Philippe Haspeslagh, and Michael Scott Morton. Their comments greatly improved this paper. Special thanks are also due to INSEAD, especially Associate Dean Yves Doz, for generous financial support of this research.

[1] For an excellent review of the literature on global strategy, see: S. Ghoshal, "Global Strategy: An Organizing Framework," *Strategic Management Journal* 8 (1987): 425–440.

to understand how multinationals can successfully implement global strategies. Because subsidiary top managers are the key catalysts for, or obstacles preventing, global strategy execution, we asked them directly just what it was that motivated them to execute or to defy their companies' global strategic decisions.

Subsidiary top managers were quick to rattle off a series of well-established implementation mechanisms: incentive compensation, monitoring systems, and rewards and punishments. They were equally quick to add that they did not believe these control mechanisms alone to be either sufficient or that effective. The general consensus was that these mechanisms were not particularly motivating and were easy to dodge and cheat. Even more recurrent in our discussions, however, were the dynamics of the global strategic decision-making process itself. When deciding whether or to what extent to carry out global strategies, subsidiary top managers accorded great importance to the way in which those strategies were generated. Their overriding concern involved a deceptively simple though evidently profound principle: due process should be exercised in the global strategic decision-making process.

In practical terms, due process means: (1) that the head office is familiar with subsidiaries' local situations; (2) that two-way communication exists in the global strategy-making process; (3) that the head office is relatively consistent in making decisions across subsidiary units; (4) that subsidiary units can legitimately challenge the head office's strategic views and decisions; and (5) that subsidiary units receive an explanation for final strategic decisions.

In short, we observed that, in the absence of these factors, subsidiary top managers were often upset and negatively disposed toward resulting strategic decisions. However, in the presence of these factors, the reaction was just the reverse. Subsidiary top managers were favorably disposed toward resulting decisions, thought them wise, and were motivated to implement them even if, and here is the biggest benefit of all, these decisions were not in line with their individual subsidiary units' interests.

We begin this paper by probing in depth just what subsidiary top managers mean by due process and why they judge its exercise important in the global strategy-making process. Next we examine what leads subsidiary top managers to view traditional implementation mechanisms as increasingly insufficient for global strategies. Finally, we trace the real effects of due process in global strategy making on global strategy execution and explore why they are so profound.

The Meaning of Due Process

To get to the heart of how multinationals can make global strategies work, we held extensive interviews with sixty-three subsidiary presidents.[2] Our initial objective was to get subsidiary presidents' honest evaluation of the factors that drove them to carry out or resist their organizations' global strategic decisions. As the interviews progressed, the one tendency that stood out was the subsidiary presidents' natural inclination to discuss how global strategies were generated. Time and again, the dynamics of the global strategy-making process itself were the centerpiece of their discussions. Their principal concern was whether due process was exercised. That is, was the strategy-making process fair from the subsidiary unit perspective?

Through these interviews, we identified the five characteristics above that, taken together, defined due process in global strategic decision making (see Figure 1).[3] What is interesting is that these five characteristics were important regardless of the

---

[2]For an extensive discussion on our field study, see:

W.C. Kim and R.A. Mauborgne, "Implementing Global Strategies: The Role of Procedural Justice," *Strategic Management Journal* 12 (1991): 125–143; and

W.C. Kim and R.A. Mauborgne, "Procedural Justice Theory and the Multinational Organization," in *Organization Theory and the Multinational Corporation,* eds. S. Ghoshal and E. Westney (London: MacMillan, 1993a).

[3]The Q-sort technique was used to define the meaning of due process in global strategic decision making. For a detailed explanation of this process, see:

Kim and Mauborgne (1991 and 1993a).

FIGURE 1   What Is Due Process in Global Strategic Decision Making?

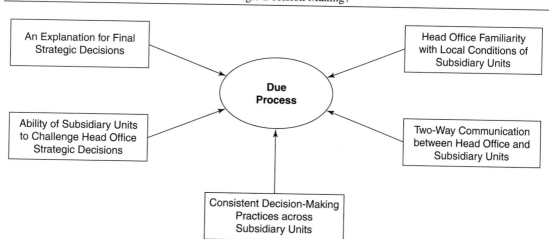

industry or the subsidiary's strategic importance. Appendix A profiles our sixty-three subsidiary presidents and discusses how they were selected. Here we discuss each of the characteristics and examine through the eyes of subsidiary top managers what makes each of them vital.

Head Office's Familiarity with Local Conditions

> The head office does not know a damn thing about what's going on down here. They tell me to further push their global "core" products even at the expense of our existing product lines. And you know what I tell them? I tell them they're crazy. They don't realize that not only don't these "core" products sell in our local market but that we are already losing sales on our existing product lines from tough local competitors due to our lack of push on them.

This statement indicates subsidiary top managers' attitudes when the head office lacks knowledge of the local market. One manager explains why local familiarity is important:

> The head office needs to invest in understanding the local market. How can I respect their decisions and follow them if I don't believe that they are made with an understanding of the local market?

When subsidiary managers believe the head office has a reasonable grasp of the local situation, they are apt to make statements like this one:

> I have tremendous faith and trust in the head office's strategic decisions. They know the local market. When they make a decision, they understand the ramifications of that decision, be those ramifications good or bad. Whether I like their decisions or not, there's at least a method to their madness.

What it comes down to is that in the absence of local familiarity, subsidiary top managers do not judge the head office to be competent and sincere. They tend to think of the head office instead as incapable and apathetic toward their foreign operation. As a consequence, these managers have little respect for the decisions coming down. They quickly become skeptical of the soundness and quality of the resulting global strategies. This provides an excellent excuse for not only why they do not implement global strategies but why they should not. As one executive put it, "To not follow the global strategic decisions handed down to a subsidiary unit is not a curse but a blessing in disguise. Those decisions aren't based on reality; they are based on air." At the most, local familiarity gives confidence that global strategies are based on thoughtful analyses; at the least, it prevents subsidiary managers from using this seemingly reasonable justification for not executing global strategic decisions.

Two-Way Communication

When global strategic decisions are being made that affect a subsidiary unit, subsidiary top managers value the ability to voice their opinion and work back and forth with the head office in decision formulation. This communication symbolizes the respect the head office has for subsidiary units as well as the confidence it places in subsidiary managers' opinions and insights.

Our observation is that this respect and confidence is quickly reciprocated by subsidiary top managers as well. Although two-way communication often results in heated debates, it also builds a profound spirit of comradeship, unity, and mutual trust among the head office and subsidiary top management teams. Moreover, when subsidiary managers participate in global strategic decision making, they come to view the decisions as their own. As a result, they often defend and uphold these decisions. As one executive commented:

> The open exchange of information and ideas is critical in global strategy making. It opens the ears of managers in both the head office and subsidiary units and typically results in better value judgments. When we [subsidiary managers] feel that our views are given sufficient attention, we are less likely to be dissatisfied with global strategic decisions or to feel antagonistic toward the head office and are better motivated to act rigorously to carry out the agreed-upon plan of action.

Consistent Decision-Making Practices

Consider two opposing comments made by different executives. One says:

> Our global strategic decision making is a very political process. If you are on the "inside track," the head office treats you as a relatively important element of global strategic decision making. But if not, you and your unit are likely to be completely overlooked and just slapped with a set of strategic decisions that are supposed to be implemented. At

times, I think the whole process is just a scam, a politicians' arena where strategic decisions reflect not competitive and economic dynamics but the dynamics of political interplay.

The other says:

> Admittedly subsidiary units don't walk away with symmetric decision outcomes—one subsidiary unit may get what seems to be a windfall allocation of resources while another may take a cut. But all subsidiary units are treated relatively consistently when it comes to how these decisions are reached. It's a fair process. There doesn't seem to be much favoritism or political jockeying in this decision-making process.

These two comments shed light on why consistent decision-making practices across subsidiary units are a prized aspect of due process. Basically, they are thought to minimize the degree of politics and favoritism in the strategy generation process. Subsidiary managers are confident that there is a level playing field across subsidiary units. And this is important. Subsidiary managers do not expect the strategic decisions made across subsidiary units to be identical, as they understand that units are not equally important for the organization. But they do view the consistent application of decision-making rules as an essential element of due process.

In the absence of consistency, subsidiary managers are quick to judge the decision-making process as arbitrary, politically rigged, and hence not to be trusted. They find the confusion and uncertainty extremely frustrating, and they are inclined to attribute unfavorable strategic decisions to unfair decision rules as opposed to competitive and economic dynamics. Consequently, they become bitter and resentful and more apt to want to undermine resulting decisions.

Ability to Refute Decisions

Having the ability to refute the head office's strategic views and decisions also makes subsidiary managers feel that due process is being exercised. Admittedly this can be traced in part to managers' perceived increase in influence over strategic decisions, but our discussions suggest another reason why the ability to refute is important. It makes managers feel that the process is fair simply because they can clearly point out possible misperceptions or wrong assumptions made by head office managers concerning local conditions or subsidiary operations. But more than this, the ability to challenge head office decisions inspires subsidiary managers to more willingly follow these decisions because they know that if the decisions should prove unreasonable or wrongheaded, the possibility always exists to correct them. As one executive explained:

> When I know I have the right to openly challenge the head office's decisions, that automatically tells me that the head office is confident in their decisions, that they have faith that their underlying logic and analyses can stand the test of open scrutiny. But it also tells me that, despite the head office's confidence, they also recognize that being removed from the local market opens up the possibility that they will judge the local situation incorrectly. Not only do I respect the head office for this, but it in turn gives me confidence that the intentions and global strategic decisions of the head office are truly made in the interests of the overall organization and not based on politics.

An Explanation for Final Decisions

Subsidiary top managers think it only fair that the head office give them an explanation for final global strategic decisions. And they consider it an important aspect of due process. In short, subsidiary managers need an intellectual understanding of the rationale driving ultimate decisions. They want to know why they should carry out the decisions. This is especially true if those decisions override their expressed views or seem unfavorable to their own unit. To quote one executive:

> When the head office provides an explanation for why decisions are made as they are, they provide evidence that they acted in a fair and impartial manner. This signals to me that the head office has at least considered the subsidiary point of view before they may have rejected it. When I understand why final strategic decisions are made

as they are, I'm more inclined to implement those decisions even if I don't particularly view them as favorable.

What Makes Due Process Important for Global Strategy Execution

As our interviews with subsidiary presidents progressed and the meaning of due process became clear, a second equally important trend became visible: those managers who believed that due process was exercised in the firms' global strategy-making process were the same executives who trusted their head offices significantly, who were highly committed to their organizations, who felt a sense of comradeship or unity with the corporate center, and who were motivated to execute not only the letter but also the spirit of the decisions. That is, not only did subsidiary presidents articulate the importance of due process in global strategy making, but their attitudes and behavior were significantly affected by its perceived presence or absence. And not just any attitudes or behavior, but attitudes and behavior that determine the success or failure of global strategy execution.

A review of some of the most popular global strategic prescriptions makes this point clear. They are as follows: locate each value-added activity in the country that has the least cost for the factor that activity uses most intensely;[4] dexterously shift capital and resources across national markets, cross-subsidizing global units, to knock out global competitors;[5] institutionalize fully standardized product offerings, marketing approaches, and commonly

---

[4]B. Kogut, "Designing Global Strategies: Comparative and Competitive Value-Added Chains," *Sloan Management Review,* Summer 1985, pp. 15–28; and

M.E. Porter, "Competition in Global Industries: A Conceptual Framework," in *Competition in Global Industries.* ed. M.E. Porter (Boston: Harvard Business School Press, 1986).

[5]G. Hamel and C.K. Prahalad, "Do You Really Have a Global Strategy?" *Harvard Business Review,* July–August 1985, pp. 139–148; and

W.C. Kim and R.A. Mauborgne, "Becoming an Effective Global Competitor," *The Journal of Business Strategy,* January–February 1988, pp. 33–37.

used distribution systems worldwide to allow for maximum global efficiencies;[6] and, as argued recently, consciously consolidate worldwide knowledge, technology, marketing, and production skills to build reservoirs of distinctive core competencies that can act as engines for continuous new business development, innovation, and enhanced customer value.[7]

Each of these global strategic prescriptions is different. There is no one formula for success. Different global competitive and economic dynamics will always dictate different and multiple routes to success. Yet a fundamental thread runs through and unites each of these prescriptions, and that is the underlying condition necessary for the effective execution of each strategy.

Ask about any of these purported global strategies: What does it take to successfully execute it? Time and again the answer involves three underlying requirements: (1) the increasing sacrifice of subsystem for system priorities and considerations; (2) swift actions in a globally coordinated manner; and (3) effective and efficient exchange relations among the nodes of the multinational's global network. Which is to say that to implement global strategies, multinationals need subsidiary managers with a sense of commitment, trust, and social harmony. Organizational commitment inspires these managers to identify with the multinational's global objectives and to exert effort, accept responsibility, and exercise initiative on behalf of the overall organization—despite potential "costs" at the subsidiary unit level. Trust is essential to work out mutual wills in the multinational. It inspires subsidiary managers to more readily accept in good faith the intentions, actions, and decisions of the

head office instead of second guessing, procrastinating, and opportunistically haggling over each directive. Which is to say that trust is necessary for quick and coordinated global actions. Lastly, social harmony is essential to strengthen the social fabric among members of global units. It encourages efficient and effective exchange relations, which have fast become indispensable to effective global strategy execution.

These salutary attitudes, however, are not in and of themselves sufficient to make global strategies work. Beyond this, multinationals need to ensure that subsidiary managers actually engage in not only compulsory but also voluntary execution of strategic decisions. By compulsory execution, we mean carrying out the directives of global strategic decisions in accordance with the multinational's formally required standards—satisfying, to the letter, the stipulated responsibilities. In contrast, by voluntary execution, we mean exerting effort beyond that which is formally required to execute decisions to the best of one's abilities. Put differently, it is the effort subsidiary top managers exert beyond the call of duty to implement global strategic decisions.[8]

What all this suggests is that the exercise of due process in global strategic decision making represents a potentially powerful though unexplored route to the implementation of global strategies. Not only do subsidiary top managers emphasize the importance of fairness and impartiality in global strategic decision making, they are so obsessed by the existence or nonexistence of due process that it profoundly affects their attitudes and behavior—attitudes and behavior that are virtually indispens-

[6]T. Levitt, "The Globalization of Markets," *Harvard Business Review,* May–June 1983, pp. 92–102; and

G.S. Yip, "Global Strategy . . . In a World of Nations?" *Sloan Management Review,* Fall 1989, pp. 29–41.

[7]C.K. Prahalad and G. Hamel, "The Core Competence of the Corporation," *Harvard Business Review,* May–June 1990, pp. 79–91.

[8]For an extensive discussion of these two forms of compliance, both the conceptual distinction between them and their theoretical root, see:

C. O'Reilly and J. Chatman, "Organizational Commitment and Psychological Attachment: The Effects of Compliance, Identification, and Internalization on Prosocial Behavior," *Journal of Applied Psychology* 71 (1986): 492–499; and

P.M. Blau and W.R. Scott, *Formal Organizations* (San Francisco, California: Chandler Publishing Company, 1962), pp. 140–141.

able to making global strategies work. We are talking about commitment, trust, social harmony, and the motivation to execute not only the letter but also the spirit of decisions—that is, to engage in compulsory and voluntary execution of strategic decisions.

But what about other implementation mechanisms? Are traditional implementation mechanisms alone not sufficient for the effective execution of global strategies? If not, how does due process support these traditional mechanisms to make global strategies work?

Traditional Implementation Mechanisms

As mentioned earlier, when we asked subsidiary presidents what motivated them to implement or to defy global strategic decisions, they typically began with a list of well-established administrative mechanisms. Most of them mentioned incentive compensation, monitoring systems, the fist of the head office, and the magnitude and precision of rewards and punishments. But as our discussions progressed, we found subsidiary presidents eager to add that they did not believe these implementation tools alone to be either sufficient or effective. For one thing, they were not particularly motivating. For another, the tools were increasingly easy to dodge and cheat.

Not Motivating?

I am not saying that rewards and punishments and auditing systems are useless in the implementation process. They certainly are useful. If the head office could assess exactly to what extent I followed global strategic decisions and rewarded me based precisely on that behavior, it would be a lie to say that this would not act as an incentive to execute global strategies. It would. It's just that this would not motivate me to do more than is absolutely necessary to satisfy the minimum requirements of global strategic decisions. It wouldn't inspire me to exert energy, exercise initiative, or to take on tasks that I am not directly compensated for in the execution of global strategies.

This comment, made by one executive, is representative of the general opinion of most of the subsidiary presidents we interviewed. Save for a few specific cases, we discovered that a reliance on instrumental approaches produced a utilitarian, contractual attitude toward compliance.[9] Stated succinctly: to the extent that subsidiary top managers judge that the head office can carefully monitor their behavior and will accurately allocate rewards and punishments, managers have an incentive to satisfy the minimum requirements of global strategic decisions. No more, no less. Instrumental approaches have the power to encourage only compulsory execution—execution to the letter, not to the spirit, of the decisions. The trouble, as we have already argued, is that to make global strategies work, subsidiary managers cannot simply "execute this" or "undertake that" in some highly prescribed manner. Their actions must be secured less by rational calculations of individual gain than by kinship obligations. What we are talking about is voluntary execution. An example will bring this to life.

The Case of Global Learning

Global learning—the ability of a multinational to transfer the knowledge and expertise developed in each part of its global network to all other parts worldwide—has fast become an essential strategic asset.[10] For global learning to be actualized, we argue that nothing less than an affirmative attitude toward cooperation will suffice—that is, voluntary execution. One reason for this is that knowledge and expertise are often viewed as power and as such are

---

[9]That a reliance on instrumental approaches to compliance leads to utilitarian contractual attitude toward involvement relations finds strong support in the award-winning article:

J. Kerr and J.W. Slocum, "Managing Corporate Culture through Reward Systems," *Academy of Management Executive* 1 (1987): 99–108.

[10]C.A. Bartlett and S. Ghoshal, "Managing across Borders: New Strategic Requirements," *Sloan Management Review,* Summer 1987, pp. 7–16; and

S. Ghoshal and C.A. Bartlett, "Creation, Adoption, and Diffusion of Innovations by Subsidiaries of Multinational Corporations," *Journal of International Business Studies,* Fall 1988, pp. 365–388.

not easily shared. Another reason is that the major benefits of internal diffusion of know-how accrue to recipients, not transmitters. Of course, were it possible for subsidiary units to "sell" their knowledge and expertise to other subsidiary units, these problems might be overcome. However, this is often and perhaps usually infeasible. As know-how is largely an intangible asset, its value to a "purchasing" unit cannot be known until the purchaser has it, but once the knowledge is disclosed, the purchaser has acquired it without cost.[11] In the absence of economic incentives and with the presence of perceived power disincentives to diffuse knowledge and expertise, it follows that full-blown global learning will not transpire as long as quid pro quo attitudes toward strategy execution prevail. Rather, the hoarding and withholding of knowledge and expertise are far more likely.

Easy to Dodge and Cheat?

Beyond the fact that subsidiary managers do not consider these instrumental approaches to be that motivating is the reality that managers increasingly find these tools easy to dodge and cheat. And if they are easy to dodge and cheat, they are truly ineffective. Basically, the decline in their effectiveness can be explained by the collapse of the three distinctive features of hierarchy in the modern multinational. These three features are: (1) appraisal and control capability; (2) the power of the head office; and (3) common values and expectations.[12] Traditional implementation tools are increasingly easy to dodge as these hierarchical features collapse.[13] Let us take

a quick look at the forces leading to the demise of these features.

Collapse of Appraisal and Control Capability. International executives are witnessing a collapse in the multinationals' appraisal and control capability. Although, in theory, information systems can be designed to meet the complexity of any organization or situation, in reality, they are having a tough time meeting the modern multinational's demands. The predominant reason for this is the rapid increase in horizontal linkages and interdependencies across subsidiary units. As subsidiary units increasingly share resources and work together on single projects to realize global economies of scale and scope, the unique performance and contribution of each subsidiary unit is increasingly difficult to decipher.[14] Distinctions between faulty and meritorious performance are becoming tenuous. Confusion opens the door for shirking, opportunistic behavior and conflict. Moreover, this problem is made even more severe by the escalating size of most multinationals. The corporate center is limited in its ability to make accurate evaluations of each subsidiary unit.

Eroding Power of the Head Office. No longer do centrally directed orders elicit easy obedience from subsidiary units. One reason for the erosion in the head office's hierarchical power is subsidiary units' increasing size and resource parity. Subsidiaries are less reliant on the head office, and the head office is more dependent on subsidiary units. To the extent that dependence decreases power, the corporate center and overseas units are converging in power.[15] This situation is aggravated further by

---

[11]K.J. Arrow, "The Organization of Economic Activity," *The Analysis and Evaluation of Public Expenditure: The PPB System* (Joint Economic Committee, Ninety-first Congress, First Session, 1969), pp. 59–73.

[12]For a brilliant discussion on the distinctive powers of hierarchy and internal organization, see:

O.E. Williamson, *Markets and Hierarchies: Analysis and Antitrust Implications* (New York: Free Press, 1975).

[13]See the perspicacious article by Hedlund for further support for this argument:

G. Hedlund, "The Hypermodern MNC-A Heterarchy?" *Human Resource Management* 25 (1986): pp. 9–25.

[14]For an extensive discussion on the ways in which interdependencies and joint efforts confound accountability and create monitoring difficulties, see:

G.R. Jones and C.W.L. Hill, "Transaction Cost Analysis of Strategy-Structure Choice," *Strategic Management Journal* 9 (1988): 159–172.

[15]For an excellent discussion on the inverse relationship between power and dependence, see, for example:

R.M. Emerson, "Power-Dependence Relations," *American Sociological Review* 27 (1962): 31–41.

FIGURE 2   The Collapse of Hierarchy in the Modern Multinational Corporation

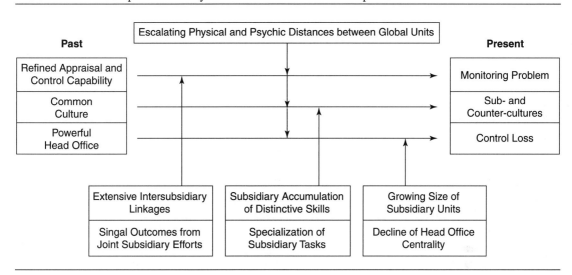

the mounting intensity of direct subsidiary-to-subsidiary linkages, which lessens the head office's centrality.[16]

Decline in Common Values and Expectations. As subsidiary units have increasingly accumulated distinct resources and capabilities in response to their different task environments, they have developed values and behavioral norms distinct from those in the home office.[17] On top of this, the nontrivial physical and psychic distances increasingly separating overseas units from corporate centers fuel even further the emergence of subcultures and countercultures within the modern multinational. The result is more antagonistic relations between head office and subsidiary top management teams and a natural inclination on the part of subsidiary managers to pursue subsidiary-level objectives.[18]

The upshot of all this is that the distinctive features of hierarchy in the multinational used to support traditional implementation mechanisms are increasingly collapsing. As shown in Figure 2, the emergence of a monitoring problem, the intensification of sub- and countercultures, and mounting control loss increasingly plague the multinational, making its traditional implementation tools less and less effective.

How Does Due Process Support Traditional Implementation Mechanisms?

Although traditional implementation tools have become on the whole less effective, the extent to which this is true appears to be contingent in part on whether due process is exercised. Recall for a moment the due process characteristics. Two-way communication, the ability to refute the head office's

---

[16]For a discussion on the ways in which centrality affects power relations, see:

L.C. Freeman, "Centrality in Social Networks: Conceptual Clarification," *Social Networks* 2 (1979): 215–239.

[17]That business units or divisions accumulation of distinct capabilities and tasks reinforces distinct values and behavioral norms was empirically validated. See:

P.R. Lawrence and J.W. Lorsch. *Organization and Environment* (Boston: Harvard University Press, 1967).

[18]See Hedlund (1986) for further elaboration of this point.

viewpoints, and an accounting for final strategic decisions all foster open interaction and intensive information exchange between head office and subsidiary top managers. This open interaction almost forces the head office to keep rewards, punishments, and appraisal and control systems aligned with strategic decisions. An example will make this point clear.

One subsidiary president we interviewed had been requested to institute an aggressive price-reductions policy in his local market. The strategic aim was to counter an assertive price attack launched by global competitor in his company's home market. The subsidiary president understood that the execution of such a policy would benefit the overall organization—it would drain the resources of the global competitor's profit sanctuary, its home market. He also knew, however, that the policy would likely result in negative financial performance by his local operation.

The open interaction between him and the head office allowed him to address his concern directly. He stated that he understood why it was necessary for his unit to institute such a policy and that he would accept such a global strategic mission. But he argued that the execution of this mission would invalidate a sole reliance on "stand-alone" financial criteria for assessing his subsidiary unit's performance. He proposed having his unit's performance evaluated also by the strategic contribution it made to the overall organization. The head office managers and subsidiary president were able to develop a mutually acceptable set of performance evaluation criteria for his unit. In this way, the exercise of due process spurs the head office to keep traditional implementation tools aligned with strategic decisions.

Lessons from Our Field Observations

We can draw two overriding lessons from our field observations. The first is that the multinational increasingly faces a dilemma in executing its global strategies. On the one hand, the effective implementation of global strategies requires a sense of community and cooperation among all the nodes of the multinational's global network. On the other hand,

multinationals are experiencing a loss in hierarchical control and an increasing independence of subsidiary units, which creates an environment of calculative, utilitarian, and frictional interunit relations. This is not particularly conducive to efficient and effective exchange. In the face of this *multinational dilemma,* we need more than traditional implementation mechanisms to make global strategies work.

The second lesson is that the exercise of due process in global strategy making seems to be a powerful, yet unexplored, way to overcome the multinational dilemma and make global strategies work. This is traceable to two sources. The first is that due process helps to overcome the exchange difficulties in the multinational by inspiring a sense of commitment, trust, and social harmony among subsidiary top managers. The second is that, beyond these salutary attitudes, the exercise of due process inspires subsidiary top managers to more readily execute strategic decisions to not only the letter but also the spirit with which they were set forth.

The Tangible Effect of Due Process

At the end of our interviews, we presented our findings to the subsidiary presidents' head office managers. These head office managers found our results fascinating and provocative. They were intrigued by our proposition that instrumental calculations of gains and losses were not the dominant driver behind subsidiary managers' actions and found it particularly interesting that subsidiary managers had placed so much emphasis on the importance of due process in global strategy making. According to these executives, it was a challenging proposition that the presence or absence of due process had the power to influence not only the important attitudes of commitment, trust, and social harmony but also subsidiary managers' actual execution of resulting decisions.

Nonetheless, despite the executives' overall excitement with our findings, underneath this ran a current of hesitation. To quote one executive:

> Your findings are provocative. But to institute
> due process in global strategy making is a time-
> consuming, difficult task. Before I start to embark on

such an attempt, I would like to have more evidence of the tangible benefits of due process than just the observations made and insights gained from your field research.

This hesitation was valid. It challenged us to go beyond our field work and empirically test our propositions. This meant conducting an extensive mail survey to develop a bigger database that could test the validity of our field observations. In short, we set out to examine whether due process exercised a positive overall effect not only on the commitment, trust, and social harmony of subsidiary top managers but also on compulsory and voluntary execution. We also set out to test whether these effects were significantly stronger or particularly potent in those subsidiary managers who received unfavorable strategic decision outcomes vis-à-vis those who received favorable outcomes. Appendix B presents a profile of our sample population, the measurements used to estimate each variable, and the type of analyses we employed.

The Results

The results of our regression analyses confirmed our observation that due process in global strategy making is indeed positively related to subsidiary managers' sense of organizational commitment, trust in head office management, and social harmony between them and the head office. All slope coefficients proved to be statistically significantly ($p < .01$),[19] which is to say that the more subsidiary managers believe that due process is exercised in the global strategy-making process, the more positive

attitudes they have toward head office management and the organization as a whole.

Beyond this, we also found a positive relationship between due process and compulsory and voluntary execution. All slope coefficients again proved to be statistically significant ($p < .01$). This provides evidence that the exercise of due process does more than inspire positive attitudes. It also triggers subsidiary managers to "go the extra mile" and carry out the spirit of global strategic decisions.

More interesting from an implementation perspective, however, are the results of another analysis. We wanted to see the effect of due process when subsidiary managers judged strategic decisions to be favorable or unfavorable for their unit. By strategic decisions we mean the strategic roles, resources, and responsibilities received by subsidiary units as a result of the last annual global strategy-making process.

During the course of our interviews, one of the most fascinating things we observed was that the effect of due process on subsidiary managers' attitudes and behavior was particularly strong precisely in those individuals who received decision outcomes viewed as unfavorable. Put differently, due process provided an especially strong "cushion of support" that mitigated the negative ramifications of unfavorable decisions by significantly inflating positive attitudes and behavior within recipients of unfavorable outcomes.[20] Figures 3a through 3c show the average commitment, trust, and social harmony scores for subsidiary top managers receiving favorable versus unfavorable strategic decision outcomes. As the figures consistently reveal, when decision outcomes were viewed as unfavorable, the exercise of due process did much to check discontent and to give "loser"

---

[19]That the exercise of due process or, as it is often referred to, procedural justice, has the power to effectuate the higher-order attitudes of commitment, trust, and social harmony finds theoretical and empirical support in other settings. See, for example:

S. Alexander and M. Ruderman, "The Role of Procedural and Distributive Justice in Organizational Behavior," *Social Psychology Research* 1 (1987): 177–198; and

R. Folger and M. Konovsky, "Effects of Procedural and Distributive Justice on Reactions to Pay Raise Decision," *Academy of Management Journal* 32 (1989): 115–130; and

E.A. Lind and T.R. Tyler, *The Psychology of Procedural Justice* (New York: Plenum, 1988).

[20]This "cushion of support" effect not only finds support in the existing procedural justice literature but is recognized to be one of the most important effects of procedural justice or due process. See, for example:

Lind and Tyler (1988); and

T.R. Tyler, *Why People Obey the Law: Procedural Justice, Legitimacy, and Compliance* (New Haven, Connecticut: Yale University Press, 1990).

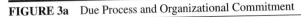

FIGURE 3a   Due Process and Organizational Commitment

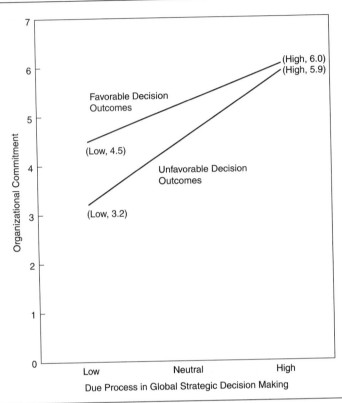

subsidiary managers powerful reasons to stay committed to their organization (in Figure 3a, the mean commitment score increases from 3.2 to 5.9; p < .01), to have trust in head office management (in Figure 3b, the mean trust score increases from 2.0 to 5.3; p < .01), and to cultivate an atmosphere of social harmony between them and the head office (in Figure 3c, the mean social harmony score increases from 2.3 to 4.7; p < .01). On the other hand, when outcomes were viewed as favorable, the due process effect, although undeniably present, was not as potent as with unfavorable outcomes. In particular, as due process heightened, the mean score for commitment increased from 4.5 to 6.0 (p < .01), that for trust from 4.4 to 5.6 (p < .05), and that for social harmony from 3.5 to 4.8 (p < .05). For all three salutary attitudes, the

slope coefficient differential between the favorable outcome and the unfavorable outcome group also proved to be statistically significant (p < .01).[21]

---

[21]We examined and confirmed the statistical difference in the due process effect between the favorable outcome and the unfavorable outcome group for organizational commitment, trust in head office management, and social harmony. This was done using what econometricians call the Chow test, which is able to examine the statistical significance in slope differentials between the groups. In our case, test statistics of F values for all three salutary attitudes were significant at the 1 percent level and hence indicated to reject the null hypotheses that no slope coefficient difference exists between the favorable outcome and the unfavorable outcome group. For a detailed discussion on the Chow test, see:

G.C. Chow, "Tests of Equality between Subsets of Coefficients in Two Linear Regression," *Econometrica* (1960): 591–605.

FIGURE 3b   Due Process and Trust in Head Office Management

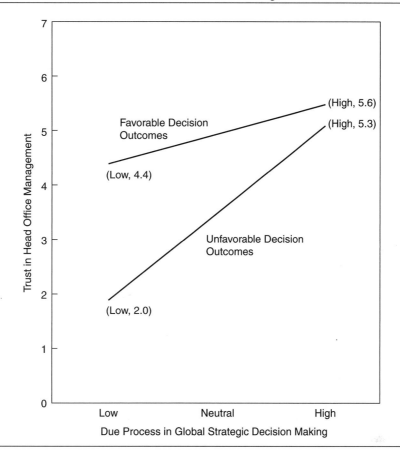

Figures 4a and 4b present the average compulsory and voluntary execution scores for subsidiary top managers receiving favorable versus unfavorable strategic decision outcomes. As Figure 4a reveals, the use of due process in global strategic decision making indeed appears to boost compulsory execution in managers who receive unfavorable decision outcomes to a greater extent than in those who received favorable outcomes. Specifically, when decision outcomes were judged unfavorable, the exercise of due process did much to motivate subsidiary managers to perform the strategic roles and responsibilities assigned to their unit in accordance with the organization's formal requirements (mean compulsory execution score increased from 3.8 to 5.7; p < .01). On the other hand, when outcomes were viewed as favorable, the due process effect on compulsory execution, although undeniably present, was not as potent (mean score increased from 5.2 to 6.2; p < .05). The slope coefficient differential between the favorable outcome and the unfavorable outcome group proved to be statistically significant (p < .05).[22]

---

[22] The F value for compulsory execution was significant at the 5 percent level and hence indicated to reject the null hypothesis that no slope coefficient difference exists between the favorable outcome and the unfavorable outcome group. Ibid.

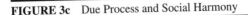

FIGURE 3c   Due Process and Social Harmony

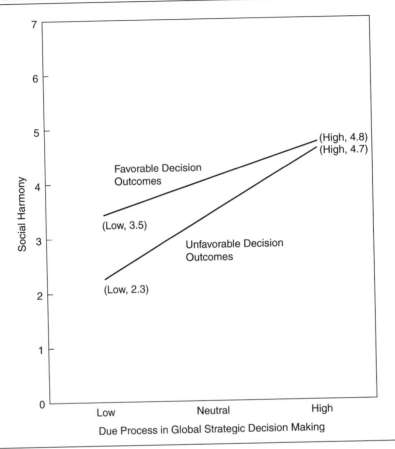

The same cannot be said, however, for voluntary execution. On the one hand, the voluntary execution of all subsidiary top managers significantly escalates as due process increases (in Figure 4b, mean voluntary execution score increases from 2.4 to 5.2 for recipients of unfavorable outcomes and from 2.9 to 5.5 for recipients of favorable outcomes; both significant at p < .01). On the other hand, the effect of due process on voluntary execution does not vary whether the decision outcomes are favorable or not. For voluntary execution, the slope coefficient differential between the favorable outcome and the unfavorable outcome group proved to be statistically not significant

(p > .10).[23] These findings indicate that although decision outcomes do not seem to affect subsidiary managers' voluntary execution, the exercise of due process does inspire these managers to go beyond the call of duty to implement strategic decisions. This is further supported by our regression result that decision outcomes had no relationship with voluntary execution; the regression coefficient for this relationship was not statistically significant (p > .10).

---

[23]The F value for voluntary execution was not significant (p > .10) and hence indicated not to reject the null hypothesis that no slope coefficient difference exists between the favorable outcome and the unfavorable outcome group. Ibid.

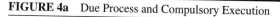

FIGURE 4a   Due Process and Compulsory Execution

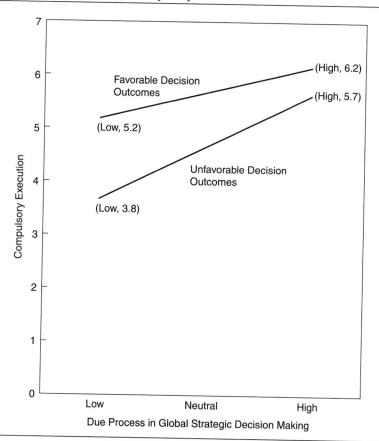

In summary, except in the case of voluntary execution, with a low level of due process, there is a big gap between the attitudes and behavior of subsidiary top managers with favorable and unfavorable decision outcomes.[24] As expected, with a low level of due process, subsidiary managers with unfavorable decision outcomes were generally dissatisfied with the head office and the overall organization and consequently felt a low level of commitment, trust, and social harmony. Not surprisingly, these same managers were not highly motivated to execute global strategic decisions to the letter or spirit with which they were set forth.

However, with a high level of due process, the picture was different. There was little gap between those managers who had received favorable and unfavorable decision outcomes in their reported scores of commitment, trust, and social harmony and compulsory and voluntary execution; all these gaps proved to be statistically not significant $(p > .10)$. Hence, the gap was significantly reduced as due process heightened. Which is to say that the power of due process is strong enough to overcome the negative ramifications of unfavorable outcomes and even inspires in those subsidiary top managers the positive disposition necessary for global strategy

[24]Variance analysis was employed to assess the statistical significance in the mean difference between the groups.

FIGURE 4b   Due Process and Voluntary Execution

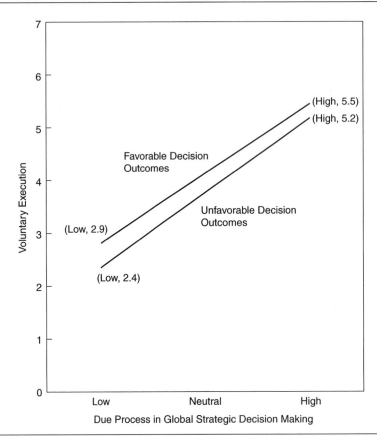

execution. Moreover, whether managers received favorable or unfavorable outcomes, their degree of commitment, trust, and social harmony and compulsory and voluntary execution was much higher when due process was exercised in global strategy making than when it was not. Hence, our empirical tests strongly support our field observations.

Conclusion

How can multinationals make global strategies work? The results of this research suggest that the answer resides in the quality of the global strategy-making process itself. When deciding whether or not or to what extent to carry out global strategic decisions, subsidiary top managers accord great importance to the way in which global strategies are generated. Their overriding concern: Is due process exercised in the global strategy-making process?

In the presence of due process, subsidiary managers are motivated to implement global strategies. They feel a strong sense of organizational commitment, trust in head office management, and social harmony with their head office counterparts. These attitudes are not only important, they are the fundamental requirements for making global strategies work. Further, the exercise of due process translates directly into a high level of compulsory and voluntary execution, which is to say that due process motivates managers not only to fulfill corporate standards but also to exert voluntary effort to implement strategic decisions to the best of their ability. The power of due process in this regard is more remarkable when we consider our finding that voluntary execution was induced only by due process and not by the instrumental value of decision outcomes. In the absence of due process, the effect is just the reverse. Subsidiary top managers are frustrated with the head office, the overall organization, and the resulting global strategic decisions. This diminishes fast their willingness to execute global strategies.

But beyond this, what makes due process particularly significant for global strategy execution is that its effect on salutary attitudes and implementation behavior is especially strong in managers who receive unfavorable decision outcomes. This is one of the most critical tasks for global strategy execution. After all, it is precisely those managers who are inclined to subvert, undermine, and even sabotage global strategic decisions. This is a significant issue because the intensity of global competition and the requirements of winning global strategies require an increasing number of decisions that are perceived as unfavorable.

Examples Abound

There are many examples of unfavorable decisions. In one multinational we studied, subsidiary units were recently asked to forgo their national products in favor of global core products that many units considered to be either overstandardized or overpriced for their national markets. In another multinational, the U.S. subsidiary was required to transfer a large portion of its export sales to its sister European subsidiaries. Although this substitution substantially increased capacity utilization rates in Europe and decreased the losses suffered from overcapacity there,

as one U.S. executive put it, "The transfer was nothing but a loss for us." And so the list goes, endlessly on. To cite one executive:

> Our modern enterprises live in a world of global competition. The key to win here is to think globally and fully leverage our globally dispersed resources, skills, and knowledge. It is important to maximize our efficiency at the global level. To achieve this, it is unavoidable that an increasing number of subsidiaries will end up receiving unfavorable decision outcomes from their individual standpoints. No doubt, these subsidiary units will be more inclined to foot-drag and exert counterefforts than to execute global strategies. The question is then, how can we turn around these negative attitudes and inspire subsidiary units to follow and implement a global approach?

To make global strategies work, head office executives need to pay greater attention to the way they generate global strategic decisions. Although the exercise of due process by itself does not make difficult head office–subsidiary issues vanish, it does motivate subsidiary managers to accept and implement global strategies. The image of the subsidiary manager that emerges here stands in marked contrast with that of the organization man who is driven overridingly by concerns of instrumental and economic maximization. It seems that subsidiary managers are both sensitive and responsive to issues of fairness in decision-making processes. Given that both our field observations and our empirical study consistently support the importance of due process, maybe it is time that companies seriously reflect on just what they have been doing to motivate their subsidiary top managers to implement global strategies. They need to pay more heed to the importance of due process in global strategy making.

Appendix A

How did we conduct our field research? We solicited the participation of twenty-five multinationals by means of direct and indirect personal contacts with head office senior executives. Nineteen of these multinationals agreed to support this research, and they gave us the names of the subsidiary presidents heading their ten largest subsidiary operations in terms of annual sales. The dominant industries of these nineteen multinationals were: computers (five firms), packaged foods (four), electrical products (four), pharmaceuticals (three), automobiles (one), paper and wood products (one), and textiles (one).

We were able to successfully contact, via telephone, 141 of the subsidiary presidents. We guaranteed that all comments would be held strictly confidential and used solely for scientific research and that their head office managers would not be informed as to which subsidiary presidents ultimately participated in our study. Sixty-three of these subsidiary presidents were willing to participate. The remaining subsidiary presidents declined, most frequently because of a lack of time. We then held extensive interviews.

Appendix B

Sample Population

We distributed the mail questionnaire to 195 subsidiary top managers. This pool comprised the 63 subsidiary presidents who participated in our field research and 132 other subsidiary top managers who directly participated in the last annual global strategic decision-making process between the head office and their national unit. The latter were also members of our nineteen original participation multinationals; their names were supplied by the 63 subsidiary presidents.[25] The titles of the subsidiary top managers ranged from president to executive vice president to director. These executives were considered to represent the key catalysts for global strategy execution in their national units.

––––––––
[25]For an extensive discussion on the design and administration of our mail questionnaire, see:
Kim and Mauborgne (1991 and 1993a).

We distributed the questionnaire within six weeks of the completion of the last annual global strategic decision-making process of our nineteen participating multinationals. Of the 195 questionnaires distributed, 142 were returned to the researchers. The questionnaire assessed the extent of due process in the last strategy-making process, subsidiary top managers' attitudes of organizational commitment, trust, and social harmony, and the perceived favorability of strategic decision outcomes.

Ten months later, just before the start of another annual global strategic decision-making process, we distributed a second questionnaire to the 142 managers who responded to our first-round questionnaire. In this one, we assessed subsidiary top managers' compulsory and voluntary execution of the global strategic decisions resulting from the preceding annual strategy-making process. Of these, 119 questionnaires were returned to the researchers and used in our analysis of the relationship between due process and compulsory and voluntary execution.[26]

Measurements

Due Process. To assess whether or to what extent due process was exercised in global strategic decision making, we used a five-item measure in our survey questionnaire.[27] This involved having subsidiary top managers evaluate on a seven-point Likert-type scale each of the five identified aspects of due process, in short: (1) the extent to which the head office is knowledgeable of the subsidiary unit's local situation; (2) the extent to which two-

––––––––
[26]For an extensive discussion on the design and administration of the second-wave questionnaire of our longitudinal study on subsidiary top managers' strategy execution, see:
W.C. Kim and R.A. Mauborgne, "Procedural Justice, Attitudes, and Subsidiary Top Management Compliance with Multinationals' Corporate Strategic Decisions," *Academy of Management Journal,* forthcoming, June 1993b.
[27]Kim and Mauborgne (1991 and 1993a).

way communication exists in the process; (3) the extent to which the head office is fairly consistent in making global strategic decisions across subsidiary units; (4) the extent to which subsidiary top managers can legitimately challenge the strategic views and decisions of the head office; and (5) the extent to which subsidiary top managers receive a full explanation for global strategic decisions.[28] The Cronbach's coefficient alpha for this five-item scale was .86.[29]

Organizational Commitment.

Nine items were used to assess the top managers' organizational commitment.[30] Sample items include, "I am willing to put in a great deal of effort beyond that normally expected in order to help this organization be successful," and "This organization really inspires the very best in me in the way of job performance." All items were assessed on a seven-point scale with anchors labeled (1) strongly disagree and (7) strongly agree. The Cronbach's coefficient alpha for this nine-item scale was .91.

Trust in Head Office Management.

To measure the trust subsidiary top managers have in the head office, we used four questions.[31] These are:

1. How much confidence and trust do you have in head office management?
2. Head office management at times must make decisions that seem to be against the interests of your unit. When this happens, how much trust do you have that your unit's current sacrifice will be justified by the head office's future support for your unit?
3. How willing are you to accept and follow those strategic decisions made by head office management?
4. How free do you feel to discuss with head office management the problems and difficulties faced by your unit without fear of jeopardizing your position or having your comment "held against" you later on?

Again, all four items were measured on seven-point scales. The Cronbach's coefficient alpha for this four-item scale was 94.

Social Harmony.

A four-item measure assessed the perceived social harmony between head office and subsidiary top managers.[32] The managers were asked to think of their relations with head office

---

[28]We averaged the scores for these multiple items to estimate our due process measure. The same procedure was used for all of our other multi-item measures: organizational commitment, trust, social harmony, and strategic decision outcome favorability. For a detailed discussion on why this simple averaging approach yields an unbiased estimate, see:

H.M. Blalock, "Multiple Indicators and the Causal Approach to Measurement Error," *American Journal of Sociology* 75 (1969): 264–272.

[29]The Cronbach's coefficient alpha indicates the internal consistency reliability of a scale. Generally, a multi-item scale can be judged to be reliable when the value of its Cronbach alpha exceeds 0.70. Notice here that besides our due process measure, all of our other multi-item scales can be said to be reliable. For a detailed discussion on a measure's reliability, see:

J. Nunnally, *Psychometric Methods* (New York: McGraw-Hill, 1978).

[30]The nine-item measure used to assess organizational commitment was developed by:

R.T. Mowday, R.M. Steers, and L.W. Porter, "The Measurement of Organizational Commitment," *Journal of Vocational Behavior* 14 (1979): 224–247.

[31]The items used to measure trust were drawn from the interpersonal trust measures of:

W.H. Read, "Upward Communication in Industrial Hierarchies," *Human Relations* 15 (1962): 3–15; and

R. Likert, *The Human Organization* (New York: McGraw-Hill, 1967).

[32]The indicators used to measure social harmony were drawn from the cohesiveness index developed by:

S.E. Seashore, *Group Cohesivenss in the Industrial Work Group* (Ann Arbor: University of Michigan Press, 1954); and

C. Cammann, M. Fichman, G. Douglas, and J.R. Klesh, "Assessing Attitudes and Perceptions of Organizational Members," in *Assessing Organizational Change,* eds. S.E. Seashore, E.E. Lawler, P.H. Mirvis, and C. Cammann (New York: John Wiley & Sons, 1983).

management when answering the following items: (1) how well they help each other out; (2) how well they get along with one another; (3) how well they stick together; and (4) the extent to which conflict characterizes their relations. These items were measured on seven-point scales with the fourth item reversely scored. The Cronbach's coefficient alpha for this four-item scale was .87.

Strategic Decision Outcome Favorability. Four items assessed the perceived favorability of global strategic decisions received by subsidiary units as a result of the last annual global strategic decision-making process.[33] Subsidiary top managers were asked to assess the extent to which the global strategic roles, responsibilities, and resources allocated to their unit: (1) reflected their unit's individual performance achieved; (2) mirrored their unit's relative contribution to the overall organization; (3) exceeded their unit's expectations; and (4) were absolutely favorable. All four items were measured on seven-point scales. The Cronbach's coefficient alpha for this four-item scale was .83.

Compulsory Execution. To assess the extent to which each subsidiary top manager carried out global strategic decisions in accordance with their formally required corporate standards, two questions were posed. First, for each of eight major activities (marketing and sales, research and development, manufacturing, purchasing, cost-reduction programs, general cash-flow utilization, human resource management, and other administrative activities), subsidiary top managers were asked to respond on a seven-point (1 = not at all, 7 = completely) scale to the following question: "Please try to recall as accurately as possible your overall behavior and actions taken since the preceding annual global strategic-decision process between the head office and your national unit. Then for each of the eight outlined activities indicate the extent to which

you executed these decisions in accordance with your organization's required standards. Note that you should not include in this assessment any efforts that may have been extended beyond your organization's required standards in order to achieve optimum performance in these activities." Organization was defined here as the multinational.

For each of these eight activities, we then had subsidiary top management rate on a five-point scale, ranging from "1 = not important" to "5 = extremely important," the degree of importance of each of these activities to the successful fulfillment of their overall job requirements. This assessment is important because although each of our respondents was a top manager with overarching responsibilities for and involvement in overall subsidiary unit operations across these activities, many reported having full responsibility for some activities but having only limited responsibility in the sense of giving final approval in other activities. Accordingly, to assess the extent of each manager's compulsory execution, these importance ratings were used as weights to reflect each activity's relative contribution or importance to the fulfillment of each manager's overall job requirements. Using these weights, we then obtained each manager's weighted-average compulsory execution score. Specifically, for each manager, we first multiplied the manager's compulsory execution score on each of the eight activities by his or her corresponding importance ratings and then added these weighted execution scores. Finally, we divided this added figure back by the sum of these importance ratings to arrive at each manager's weighted-average compulsory execution score.[34]

---

[33]The four-item measure used to assess strategic decision outcome favorability was originally developed by:
Kim and Mauborgne (1991).

---

[34]The use of a multidimensional approach with criterion weights to measure both compulsory and voluntary execution is in line with Steer's advice and seemed particularly appropriate for taking into account subsidiary top managers' different levels of involvement in carrying out these activities and hence their different levels of contribution to the execution of these activities in accordance with their formal job requirements. See:
R.M. Steers, "Problems in the Measurement of Organizational Effectiveness," *Administrative Science Quarterly* 20 (1975): 546–558.

Voluntary Execution. To assess the extent to which subsidiary top managers exerted voluntary effort to carry out global strategic decisions to the best of their abilities, we used a similar approach to that used in our assessment of compulsory execution. First, for each of the eight major activities, the managers were asked to respond on a seven-point scale (1 = not at all, 7 = greatly) to the following question: "Please try to recall as accurately as possible your overall behavior and actions taken since the preceding annual global strategic decision process between the head office and your national unit. Then for each of the eight outlined activities indicate the extent to which you voluntarily exerted effort beyond the formally required standards of your organization to execute global strategic decisions to the best of your abilities. Rephrased, to what extent did you willingly exert energy, exercise initiative, and devote your effort beyond that which is formally required to achieve optimum performance in your execution of global strategic decisions in each of these activities?"

Using the same question on dimensional importance described above for compulsory execution to obtain weights, we derived a weighted-average measure of each manager's voluntary execution of global strategic decisions. The process used to derive this weighted-average measure of voluntary execution mirrors that used to arrive at our weighted-average measure of compulsory execution.[35]

Analyses

We used two tests to establish the effect of due process on the managers' attitudes and behavior. First, we performed regression analyses to see whether due process positively correlated with the managers' attitudes of organizational commitment,

---

[35]Ibid.

trust in head office management, and social harmony between them and head office management and whether due process was also related to the managers' compulsory and voluntary execution of the resulting decisions.

Second, we tested whether due process produces a "cushion of support" that enhances salutary attitudes and execution to a greater extent in those managers who received unfavorable decision outcomes than those who received favorable outcomes. To perform this test, we first divided respondents into two groups based on the perceived favorability or unfavorability of strategic decision outcomes received in the last annual strategy-making process. Those managers with outcome favorability scores above the sample mean were classified as recipients of favorable strategic-decision outcomes; those below the sample mean were classified as recipients of unfavorable outcomes. We then further split our respondents based on the perceived degree of due process exercised. Respondents with due process scores above the sample mean were treated as experiencing a high level of due process, whereas those having due process scores below the sample mean were treated as experiencing a low level of due process. Finally, we calculated and compared the mean levels of reported organizational commitment, trust in head office management, social harmony, and compulsory and voluntary execution for each of our four groups: the high outcome favorability–high due process group; the high outcome favorability–low due process group; the low outcome favorability–high due process group; and the low outcome favorability–low due process group. As is described in the article, we used variance analysis and the slope coefficient differential test to test differences between these four groups. We observed no evidence for systematic differences in contextual variables such as industry type and subsidiary size across these four groups.

Chapter 6

Creating and Leveraging Knowledge: The Worldwide Learning Challenge

In Chapter 3, we described how companies competing in today's global competitive environment could no longer rely on a single dominant source of competitive advantage. Increasingly, they are being required to build layers of competitive advantage—in particular, the ability to capture global scale efficiencies, local market responsiveness, and worldwide learning capability. For most companies, the first two of these three core strategic capabilities were familiar attributes, although sometimes difficult to manage. But in the closing years of the 20th century, as MNCs found ways to match each other in global scale efficiency and local responsiveness, the leading-edge competitive battles shifted to companies' ability to link and leverage their resources to capture advantage through worldwide learning.

In the midst of a knowledge revolution amplified by an explosion of new information technologies, MNCs can no longer regard their overseas operations simply as the means to access low-cost labor or capture incremental markets. In an environment in which the ability to develop and rapidly diffuse innovation around the world is vital, offshore subsidiaries must act as the sensors of new market trends or technological developments wherever they occur; they must be able to attract scarce talent and expertise on a worldwide basis, tapping their knowledge to develop creative responses to the emerging opportunities and threats; and they must be able to act collectively with other subsidiaries to exploit the resulting new products and initiatives worldwide, regardless of where they originated.

Yet developing this capability to create, leverage, and apply knowledge worldwide is not a simple task for most large MNCs. Despite the fact that people are innately curious and naturally motivated to learn from each other, most modern corporations are constructed in a way that constrains and sometimes kills this natural human instinct. Focused on short-term static efficiency as a primary

618

objective, they end up sacrificing not only the long-term dynamic efficiencies that come from developing individual expertise, but also the embedded organizational capabilities to link and leverage it. In this chapter, we will focus on one of the most important current challenges facing management of most MNCs—how to develop and diffuse knowledge in a way that supports effective worldwide innovation and learning.

CENTRAL, LOCAL, AND TRANSNATIONAL INNOVATION

Traditionally, MNCs' innovative capabilities were dominated by one of two classic processes. In the *center-for-global* innovation model, the new opportunity or risk that triggered an innovation was usually sensed in the home country; the centralized resources and capabilities of the parent company were brought to bear to create the new product or process; and implementation involved driving the innovation through subsidiaries whose role was to introduce it to their local market. The process that led to NEC's global rollout of its NEAC 61 digital telecommunications switch or Matsushita's development and worldwide introduction of its VCRs are two classic examples of this model.

In contrast, *local-for-local* innovation relies on subsidiary-based knowledge development. Responding to perceived local opportunities, these local entities use their own resources and capabilities to create innovative responses that are then implemented in the local market. Unilever's development of a detergent bar for the Indian market's need for a product suitable for stream washing is a good illustration of the process, as is Philippines-based Jollibee's strategy of adapting its fast-food products to local market preferences of each country it entered.

While most MNCs have tried to develop elements of both models of innovation, the tension that exists between the knowledge management processes supporting each usually means that one dominates. Not surprisingly, the center-for-global innovation tends to dominate in companies we described as global in Chapter 3 where the quest for cross-market efficiency dominates the need for local flexibility. On the other hand, local-for-local processes fit more easily into the multinational strategic model where responsiveness to local needs is seen as the key to success in the marketplace.

However, in recent years the traditional strategic mentalities have been evolving into new ways of developing and diffusing knowledge and innovative ideas. These new *transnational innovation* processes fall into two broad categories we describe as *locally leveraged* and *globally linked*. The former involves ensuring that the special resources and capabilities of each national subsidiary are available not only to that local entity, but also to other MNC units worldwide. The latter process of innovation pools the resources and capabilities of many different units—at both the parent company and subsidiary level—to jointly create and manage an activity.

These are fundamentally different models of innovation that require new management mentalities and new organizational capabilities. They rest on a sophisticated ability to take market intelligence developed in one part of the organization, perhaps link it to specialized expertise located in a second entity and a scarce resource in a third, before eventually diffusing the new product or proposal rapidly throughout the organization's units worldwide. This was the kind of innovative process Procter and Gamble first developed through the Eurobrand initiative that resulted in the creation of the heavy-duty liquid detergent, Vizir. Recognizing the power of this cross-unit innovation and learning capability, the company gradually built it into a core competence that it now regards as the centerpiece of its global competitive strategy and a major source of advantage over other companies.

While the two more sophisticated processes that result in transnational innovations are becoming more widespread, they have supplemented rather than replaced the traditional central and local innovation processes. In a competitive environment, most companies recognize the need to engage their resources and capabilities in as many ways as they can. In other words, they must maximize the number of processes through which they can develop new knowledge, build new capabilities, and deploy new ideas rapidly around the globe. The challenge is to build an organization that can simultaneously facilitate all four processes of innovation and learning. This requires that they understand not only the power of each, but also their limitations—and, particularly, their mutually debilitating characteristics:

- The greatest risk of center-for-global innovation is market insensitivity and the accompanying resistance of local subsidiary management to what they view as inappropriate new products and processes.
- Local-for-local innovations, by contrast, often suffer from needless differentiation and "reinvention of the wheel" caused by resource-rich subsidiaries trying to protect their independence and autonomy.
- Locally leveraged innovations can be threatened by the "not-invented-here" syndrome that often blocks the successful transfer of products and processes from the innovative subsidiary to others in the company.
- And the major impediment to globally-linked innovation tends to be the high coordination cost required to link widely dispersed assets, resources, and capabilities into an effective integrated network of free-flowing ideas and innovations.

THE MANAGEMENT CHALLENGE: BUILDING MULTIPLE INNOVATION PROCESSES

Building a portfolio of innovative processes to drive worldwide learning requires that the companies overcome two related but different problems. First, for each process, they must avoid the different pitfalls we have described. Second, to manage operations simultaneously through all the different processes, companies must find ways to overcome the contradictions among the organizational factors that facilitate each of these processes.

Making Central Innovations Effective

The key strength on which many Japanese companies built their global leadership positions in a diverse range of businesses, from zippers to automobiles, lies in the effectiveness of their center-for-global innovations. This is not to say that they do not use some of the other operative modes, but in general, the Japanese are today's champion managers of centralized activities and tasks.

Three factors stand out as the most important explanations of their outstanding success in managing the center-for-global process: (1) gaining the input of subsidiaries into centralized activities, (2) ensuring that all functional tasks are linked to market needs, and (3) integrating value chain functions such as development, production, and marketing by managing the transfer of responsibilities among them.

Gaining Subsidiary Input: Multiple Linkages.   The two most important problems facing a company with highly centralized operations are that those at the center who are responsible for developing the new product or process may not understand market needs, and that those in the subsidiaries required to implement the central innovation in different national markets are not committed to it. (Philips learned both lessons very well when it tried to introduce its technologically superb V2000 video recorder in competition with Matsushita's VHS system and Sony's Beta format.) Managers in Japanese companies are very conscious of this problem and spend a great deal of time building multiple linkages between headquarters and overseas subsidiaries. These linkages are designed not only to give headquarters managers a better understanding of country-level needs and opportunities, but also to give subsidiary managers greater access to and involvement in centralized decisions and tasks.

Matsushita, for example, recognizes the importance of market sensing as a stimulus to innovation and does not want its centrally driven development and manufacturing processes to reduce its environmental sensitivity. They do not try to limit the number of linkages between headquarters and subsidiaries or focus them through a single point as many companies do for the sake of efficiency. Rather, they try to preserve the different perspectives, priorities, and even prejudices of its diverse groups worldwide, and ensure that they have linkages to those in the headquarters who can represent and defend their views.

The organizational systems and processes that connect different parts of the Matsushita organization in Japan with the video department of MECA, the U.S. subsidiary of the company, are illustrative of these multifaceted linkages. The vice president in charge of this department has his roots in Matsushita Electric Trading Company (METC), the organization that has overall responsibility for Matsushita's overseas business. Although formally posted to the United States, he continues to be a member of the senior management committee of METC and spends about a third of his time in Japan. This allows him to be a full member of the top management team of METC that finalizes overall product strategy for the U.S. market, including priorities for new product development. In his role as the vice president of MECA, he ensures that the local operation implements the agreed video strategy effectively. The general manager of this department is a company veteran who worked for 14 years in the video product division of Matsushita Electric, the production and domestic marketing company in Japan. He maintains strong connections with the central product division and acts as its link to the local U.S. market. Two levels below the department general manager is the assistant product manager, the junior-most expatriate in the organization. Having spent five years in the company's main VCR plant in Japan, he acts as the local representative of the factory and handles all day-to-day communication with factory personnel.

None of these linkages is accidental. They are deliberately created and maintained and they reflect the company's open acknowledgement that the parent company is not one homogeneous entity, but a collection of different constituencies and interests, each of which is legitimate and necessary. Collectively, these multiple-linkages enhance the subsidiary's ability to influence key headquarters decisions relating to its market, and particularly decisions about product specifications and design. The multiple links not only allow local management to reflect the local market needs, they also give headquarters managers the ability to coordinate and control implementation of their strategies and plans, including their innovations.

Responding to National Needs: Market Mechanisms.   Like many other companies, Matsushita's efforts to ensure that centralized activities are linked to local market needs do not stop at the input stage. The company created an integrative process that ensures that headquarters managers responsible for R&D, manufacturing, marketing, and so on are not sheltered from the pressures, constraints, and demands felt by managers in the front line of the operations. One of the key elements in achieving this difficult organizational task is the company's willingness to use internal "market mechanisms" for directing and regulating the central activities.

Research projects undertaken by the central research laboratories (CRL) of Matsushita can be categorized into two broad groups. The first group consists of "company total projects," which involve developing technologies that are important for Matsushita's long-term strategic position and that may be applicable across many different product divisions. Such projects are decided jointly by the research laboratories, the product divisions, and top management of the company, and are funded directly by the corporate board.

The second group of CRL research projects consists of relatively smaller projects that are relevant to the activities of particular product divisions. The budget for such research activities, which amount to approximately half of the total research budget of the company, is allocated not to the research laboratories but to the product divisions.

The purpose of the split budget is to create a context in which technologically driven and market-led ideas can compete for attention. Each year, the product divisions suggest a set of research projects that they would like to sponsor. At the same time, the various research laboratories hold annual exhibitions and write specific proposals to highlight research projects that they would like to undertake. The engineering and development groups of the product divisions mediate the subsequent contracting and negotiation process through which the expertise and interests of the laboratories and the needs of the product divisions are finally matched. Specific projects are sponsored by the divisions and are allocated to the laboratories or research groups of their choice, along with requisite funds and other resources.

The system creates intense competition for projects (and the budgets that go with them) among the research groups, and it is the mechanism that forces researchers to keep a close market orientation. At the same time, the product divisions are conscious that it is their money being spent on product development and they become less inclined to make unreasonable or uneconomical demands of R&D.

The market mechanism also works to determine annual product styling and features, which are responsibilities of the manufacturing division. Each year the company holds merchandising meetings that are, in effect, giant internal trade shows. Senior marketing managers from Matsushita's worldwide sales companies visit their manufacturing divisions and see on display the proposed product line for the new model year. Relying on their understanding of their individual markets, these managers pick and choose among proposed models, order specific modifications for their local markets, or simply veto products they feel are unsuitable. Individual products or even entire product lines might need to be redesigned as a result of input from the hundreds of managers at the merchandising meeting.

Managing Responsibility Transfer: Personnel Flow.   In local-for-local innovation processes, cross-functional integration across research, manufacturing, and marketing is facilitated by the smaller size and closer proximity of the units responsible for each stage of activity. Because this is not true where parent company units take the lead role in the development and manufacture of new products and processes, more centralized organizations must build alternative means for integrating the different tasks.

At Matsushita, for example, the integrative systems rely heavily on the transfer of people. First, the career paths of research engineers are structured so as to ensure that a majority of them spend about five to eight years in the central research laboratories engaged in pure research, then another five years in the product divisions in applied research and development, and finally in a direct operational function, such as production or marketing, wherein they take line-management positions for the rest of their working lives. More important, each engineer usually makes the transition from one department to the next along with the transfer of the major project on which he has been working.

In other companies, it is common for research engineers to move to development, but without their projects, thereby depriving the companies of one of the most important learning benefits of such moves. Furthermore, in most Western companies, engineers rarely take the next step of actually moving to the production or marketing functions. This last step, however, is perhaps the most critical in integrating the different functions, both in terms of building a network that connects managers across these functions, and transferring knowledge, expertise, and a set of common values that facilitates implementation of central decisions.

Another mechanism for cross-functional integration in Matsushita works in the opposite direction. Wherever possible, the company tries to identify the manager who will head the production task for a new product under development and makes him or her a full-time member of the research team from the initial stage of the development process. This system not only injects direct production expertise into the development team, but also facilitates transfer of the project after the design is completed. Matsushita also uses this mechanism as a way of transferring product expertise from headquarters to its worldwide sales subsidiaries. Although this is a common practice in other MNCs, in Matsushita it has additional significance because of its effect on internationalizing products as well as management.

Making Local Innovations Efficient

If the classic global companies in Japan are the champion managers of central innovation, the archetypal multinational companies from Europe are often masters at managing local innovations. This does not imply that the European companies are not successful in managing central innovation. But for reasons related to their unique administrative heritage, European companies have a track record of local adaptation and functional excellence unmatched by other companies of comparable size, diversity, and maturity. They have had unique success in blending with their local environment—developing, manufacturing, and marketing tailor-made products; establishing close links with local customers, suppliers, government, and other institutions; and attracting local management and technical talent—to the extent that many European MNCs are often thought to be a domestic company in the countries in which they operate.

Of the many factors that facilitate local-for-local innovations in European companies, there are three that are the most significant—their ability to empower local management in the different national organizations, to establish effective mechanisms for linking the local managers to corporate decision-making processes, and to force tight cross-functional integration within each subsidiary.

Empowering Local Management.   Perhaps the most important factor supporting local innovations in decentralized federation companies is the dispersal of their organizational assets and resources and the decentralization of authority. Together, these factors empower local management to experiment and to seek novel solutions to local problems.

As we described in Chapter 5, the decentralized organizational structure and dispersed resources in many European companies are the outcomes of a historical process and have deep roots in the companies' management philosophy. Since it was founded in 1891, for example, Philips has recognized the need to expand its operations beyond its small domestic market, but the successive barriers—poor transport and communication linkages in the early decades of the century, protectionist pressures in the 1930s, and the disruption of World War II—encouraged the company to build national organizations with a substantial degree of autonomy and self-sufficiency. Such dispersed managerial and technological resources coupled with local autonomy and decentralized control over the resources enable subsidiary managers to be more effective in managing local development, manufacturing, and other functional tasks.

Linking Local Managers to Corporate Decision-Making Processes. While local resources and autonomy make it feasible for subsidiary managers to be creative and entrepreneurial in designing and implementing local initiatives, linkages to corporate decision-making processes are necessary to make these local-for-local tasks effective for the company as a whole. In many European companies, a cadre of entrepreneurial expatriates play a key role in developing and maintaining such linkages.

Expatriate positions, particularly in the larger subsidiaries, have been very attractive for managers in many European companies. For example, in Philips, many of the national subsidiaries contribute much larger shares of the company's total revenues than the parent company (only 6 to 8 percent of total sales come from Holland). As a result, foreign operations enjoy higher organizational status than those in most large worldwide companies. Furthermore, Philips's formal management development system always requires considerable international experience as a prerequisite for top corporate positions. Finally, the corporate headquarters are located in a small Dutch town in a rural setting. After living in London, New York, Sydney, or Rio, many managers find it hard to return to Eindhoven.

As a result, the best and the brightest of Philips's managers spend most of their careers in national operations, working for three to four years in a series of subsidiaries. In most Japanese companies, by contrast, an expatriate manager spends four to six years in a particular national subsidiary and then returns to headquarters. This difference in the career systems has an important influence on managerial attitudes and organizational relationships.

In Philips, the expatriate managers tend to identify strongly with the national organization's point of view, and this shared identity creates a strong bond and distinct subculture within the company. On the other hand, in companies such as Matsushita there is very little interaction among the expatriate managers, and they tend to regard themselves as parent-company executives temporarily on assignment in a foreign company.

Expatriate managers in Matsushita are, therefore, far more likely to take a custodial approach that resists making local changes in standard products and policies, while expatriate managers in Philips are much more willing to advocate local views. Their willingness to rock the boat and their openness to experimentation and change are the characteristics that fuel innovative and effective management of local initiatives.

Because Philips has created an attractive environment in the national organizations, it has little difficulty in recruiting very capable local management. Whereas local managers in many Japanese companies often feel excluded from the decision-making process, local managers in Philips know their ideas are listened to and defended at headquarters. This, too, creates a supportive environment for the effective management of local innovations.

Integrating Subsidiary Functions.   Finally, local innovativeness of decentralized federation organizations is enhanced because of strong cross-functional integration within each national operation. Just as various means of cross-functional integration within the headquarters organization enhance the effectiveness of center-for-global innovations in Matsushita, integrative mechanisms for linking technical and marketing functions at multiple levels within the subsidiary improve the efficiency of local-for-local initiatives in Philips

Most Philips subsidiaries use integration mechanisms at three organizational levels. First, for each project, there is what Philips calls an article team consisting of relatively junior managers from the commercial and technical functions. It is the responsibility of this team to evolve product policies and to prepare annual sales plans and budgets. Subarticle teams may be formed to supervise day-to-day activities and to carry out special projects, such as preparing capital investment plans, if it seems major new investments are needed to manufacture and market a new product effectively.

At the product-group level, cross-functional coordination is accomplished through the group management team. This team, including technical and commercial representatives, meets once a month to review results, suggest corrective actions, and resolve any interfunctional differences. Keeping control and conflict resolution at this low level facilitates sensitive and rapid response to initiatives and ideas generated at the local level.

The highest-level coordination forum within the subsidiary is the senior management committee (SMC), consisting of the top commercial, technical, and financial managers in the subsidiary. Acting essentially as a local board, the SMC coordinates effort among the functional groups and ensures that the national operation retains primary responsibility for its own strategies and priorities. Again, local management has a forum where actions are decided on and issues resolved without escalation for approval or arbitration.

Making Transnational Processes Feasible

The complexity of the innovation and learning processes in a multinational corporation is significantly enhanced by the fact that the location of an opportunity is often different from the location where the complementary capability of the company is located. For example, while a company's hardware technology and main research laboratories may be in Japan, and its most-skilled software engineers may be in the United States, its fastest growth market opportunities may be in Europe. The locally leveraged and globally linked processes in the transnational company use linkages among different units of the company to leverage existing resources and capabilities, regardless of their locations, to exploit opportunities that arise in any part of the company's dispersed operations.

In many MNCs, three simplifying assumptions block organizational capabilities necessary for managing such transnational operations. The need to reduce organizational and strategic complexity has made these assumptions extremely widespread among large MNCs, regardless of industry, national origin, or management culture:

- A widespread, often implicit assumption is that roles of different organizational units are uniform and symmetrical. This leads companies to manage very different businesses, functions, and national operations in essentially the same way.
- One assumption, whether conscious or unconscious, is that internal interunit relationships should be based on clear and unambiguous patterns of dependence or independence.
- Finally, there is the assumption that one of corporate management's principal tasks is to institutionalize clearly understood mechanisms for decision making and to implement simple means of exercising control.

Companies that are most successful in developing transnational innovations challenge these assumptions and replace them with some very different attitudes and norms. Instead of treating different businesses, functions, and subsidiaries similarly, they systematically differentiate tasks and responsibilities. Instead of seeking organizational clarity by basing relationships on dependence or independence, they build and manage interdependence among the different units of the companies. And, instead of considering control their key task, corporate managers search for complex mechanisms to coordinate and co-opt the differentiated and interdependent organizational units into sharing a vision of the company's strategic tasks.

From Symmetry to Differentiation.   Like many other companies, Unilever built its international operations with an implicit assumption of organizational symmetry. Managers of diverse local operating companies, with products ranging from packaged foods to chemicals and detergents, all reported to strongly independent national managers, who in turn reported through regional directors to the board. In the post–World War II era, the company began to recognize a need to supplement this geographically dominated structure with an organizational ability to capture potential economies and to transfer learning across national boundaries. To meet this need, a few product-coordination groups were formed at the corporate center. But the assumption of organizational symmetry ensured that all businesses were similarly managed, and the number of coordination groups grew from three in 1962 to six in 1969 to ten by 1977.

By the early 1980s, however, the entrenched organizational symmetry was threatened. Global economic disruption caused by the oil crisis dramatically highlighted the very substantial differences in the company's businesses and markets and forced management to recognize the need to differentiate its organizational structures and administrative processes. While standardization, coordination, and integration paid high dividends in the chemical and detergent businesses, for example, important differences in local tastes and national cultures impeded the same degree of coordination in foods. As a result, the roles, responsibilities, and powers of the central product-coordination groups eventually began to diverge as the company tried to shake off the constraint of the symmetry assumption.

However, as Unilever tackled the challenge of managing some businesses in a more globally coordinated manner, it was confronted with the question of what to coordinate. Historically, the company's philosophy of decentralized capabilities and delegated responsibilities resulted in most national subsidiaries becoming fully integrated, self-sufficient operations. Although they were free to draw on product technology, manufacturing capabilities, and marketing expertise developed at the center, they were not required to do so, and most units chose to develop, manufacture, and market products as they thought appropriate. Thus, functions also tended to be managed symmetrically.

Over time, decentralization of all functional responsibilities became increasingly difficult to support. For example, when archcompetitor Procter & Gamble's subsidiaries launched a new line of laundry detergents based on the rapeseed formula created by the parent company, most of Unilever's national detergent companies responded with their own products. The cost of developing 13 different formulations was extremely high, and management soon recognized that not one of its local innovations was as good as P&G's centrally developed product. For the sake of cost control and competitive effectiveness, Unilever needed to break with tradition and begin centralizing European product development. The company has since created a system in which central coordination is more normal, although very different for different functions such as basic research, product development, manufacturing, marketing, and sales.

Just as they saw the need to change symmetrical structures and homogeneous processes imposed on different businesses and functions, most companies eventually recognized the importance of differentiating the management of diverse geographic operations. Despite the fact that various national subsidiaries operated with very different external environments and internal constraints, they all traditionally reported through the same channels, operated under similar planning and control systems, and worked under a set of common and generalized mandates.

However, managers increasingly recognized that such symmetrical treatment can constrain strategic capabilities. At Unilever, for example, it became clear that Europe's highly competitive markets and closely linked economies meant that its operating companies in that region required more coordination and control than those in, say, Latin America. Little by little, management increased groups' role in Europe until they had direct line responsibility for all operating companies in their businesses. Elsewhere, however, national management maintained its historic line-management role, and product coordinators acted only as advisors. Unilever has thus moved in sequence from a symmetrical organization to a much more differentiated one: differentiating by product, then by function, and finally by geography.

Recently, within Europe, differentiation by national units has proceeded even further. Operations in key countries such as France, Germany, and the United

Kingdom are allowed to retain considerably more autonomy than in "receiver countries" such as Switzerland, Sweden, Holland, and Denmark. While the company's overall commitment to decentralization is maintained, receiver countries have gradually come to depend more on the center for direction and support, particularly in the areas of product development and competitive strategy.

The detergent business must be managed in a more globally integrated manner than packaged foods, but also needs a more nationally differentiated strategy than the chemicals business. However, all tasks do not need to be managed in this differentiated yet coordinated manner: There is little need for national differentiation in research or for global coordination of sales management. Even functions such as marketing that exhibit the more complex simultaneous demands do not need to be managed in this way in all national markets. Marketing strategy for export sales can be highly coordinated, while approaches taken in closed markets like India and Brazil can be managed locally. Only in key strategic markets like Germany, the United Kingdom, and France is there a need for differentiated yet coordinated marketing strategies. This flexible and differentiated management approach stands in marked contrast to the standardized, symmetrical approach shown in Unilever's earlier blanket commitment to decentralized responsibility.

From Dependence or Independence to Interdependence. As we described in Chapter 5, national subsidiaries in decentralized federation organizations enjoyed considerable *independence* from the headquarters, while those in centralized hub organizations remained strongly *dependent* on the parent company for resources and capabilities. As we discussed in that chapter, the emerging strategic demands make organizational models of simple interunit dependence or independence inappropriate. The reality of today's worldwide competitive environment demands collaborative information sharing and problem solving, cooperative support and resource sharing, and collective action and implementation.

Independent units risk being picked off one by one by competitors whose coordinated global approach gives them two important strategic advantages—the ability to integrate research, manufacturing, and other scale-efficient operations, and the opportunity to cross-subsidize the losses from battles in one market with funds generated by profitable operations in home markets or protected environments. On the other hand, foreign operations, that depend totally on a central unit must deal with problems reaching beyond the loss of local market responsiveness. They also risk being unable to respond effectively to strong national competitors or to sense potentially important local-market or technical intelligence.

But it is not easy to change relationships of dependence or independence that were built over a long history. Many companies tried to address the increasing need for interunit collaboration by adding layer upon layer of administrative mechanisms to foster greater cooperation. Top managers extolled the virtues of teamwork and even created special departments to audit management response to this need. In most cases, these efforts to obtain cooperation by fiat or by administrative mechanisms were disappointing. The independent units feigned compliance while fiercely protecting their independence. The dependent units found that the new cooperative spirit bestows little more than the right to agree with those on whom they depend.

To create an effective interdependent organization, two requirements must be met. First, the company must develop a configuration of resources that is neither centralized nor decentralized, but is both dispersed and specialized. Such a configuration lies at the heart of the transnational company's integrated network mode of operations, as we have already discussed in Chapter 5.

The second requirement is to build interunit integration mechanisms to ensure that task interdependencies lead to the benefits of synergy rather than the paralysis of conflict. Above all else, interunit cooperation requires good interpersonal relations among managers in different units. The experiences of Ericsson, the Swedish telecommunications company, suggest some ways in which such relations can be built.

Movement of people is one of the strongest mechanisms for breaking down local dogmas, and Ericsson achieved this with a long-standing policy of transferring large numbers of people back and forth between headquarters and subsidiaries. It differs from the more common transfer patterns in both direction and intensity, as a comparison with NEC's transfer process will demonstrate. Where NEC may transfer a new technology through a few key managers sent on temporary assignment, Ericsson will send a team of 50 or 100 engineers and managers for a year or two; while NEC's flow is primarily from headquarters to subsidiary, Ericsson's is a balanced two-way flow with people coming to the parent company not only to learn but also to bring their expertise; and while NEC's transfers are predominantly Japanese, Ericsson's multidirectional process involves all nationalities.

However, any organization in which there are shared tasks and joint responsibilities requires additional decision-making and conflict-resolution forums. In Ericsson, often-divergent objectives and interests of the parent company and the local subsidiary are exchanged in the national company's board meetings. Unlike many companies whose local boards are pro forma bodies whose activities are designed solely to satisfy national legal requirements, Ericsson uses its local boards as legitimate forums for communicating objectives, resolving differences, and making decisions. At least one and often several senior corporate managers are members of each board, and subsidiary board meetings become an important means for coordinating functional tasks such as manufacturing, marketing, and personnel management across national lines.

From Unidimensional Control to Differentiated Coordination.   The simplifying assumptions of organizational symmetry and dependence (or independence) allowed the management processes in many companies to be dominated by simple controls—tight operational controls in subsidiaries that depend on the center, and a looser system of administrative or financial controls in decentralized units. When companies began to challenge the assumptions underlying organizational relationships, however, they found they also needed to adapt their management processes. The growing interdependence of organizational units strained the simple control-dominated systems and underlined the need to supplement existing processes with more-sophisticated ones. Furthermore, the differentiation of organizational tasks and roles amplified the diversity of management perspectives and capabilities and forced management to differentiate management processes.

As organizations became, at the same time, more diverse and more interdependent, there was an explosion in the number of issues that had to be linked, reconciled, or integrated. But the costs of coordination are high, both in financial and human terms, and coordinating capabilities are always limited. Most companies, though, tended to concentrate on a primary means of coordination and control—"the company's way of doing things."

In analyzing how managers might develop a coordination system that would best fit the needs for various functions and tasks, it is helpful to think about the various flows between organization units that are involved in the execution of each task. Three flows are the lifeblood of any organization, but are of particular importance in a transnational company. The first is the flow of goods: the complex interconnections through which companies source their raw materials and other supplies, link flows of components and subassemblies, and distribute finished goods throughout an integrated network of specialized purchasing units, focused sourcing plants, broad-line assembly operations, and localized sales subsidiaries. The second is the flow of resources, which encompasses not only the allocation of capital and repatriation of dividends, but also the transfer of technology and the movement of personnel throughout the system. The third is the flow of information: raw data, analyzed information, and accumulated knowledge, which companies must diffuse throughout the worldwide network of national units.

It can be very difficult to coordinate the flows of goods in a complex integrated network of interdependent operations. But in most companies, this coordination process can be managed effectively at lower levels of the organization when clear procedures and strong systems are set up. Although the cost of establishing the coordination process may be high, in both financial and managerial terms, it should require limited resources to operate. The fact that such flows are reasonably constant or can be adequately forecast makes this a classic candidate for a formalized management process. For example, within its network of 15 plants in different countries, Ericsson learned to coordinate product and materials flows by standardizing as many procedures as possible and formalizing the logistics control, primarily through the use of telex reports. Establishment of such formal systems and procedures helped the company understand how to operate highly interdependent yet widely separated worldwide facilities without developing burdensome coordination processes.

It is more difficult to coordinate flows of financial, human, and technological resources. Allocation of these scarce resources represents the major strategic choices the company makes and must therefore be controlled at the corporate level. We have described the transnational company as an organization of diverse needs and perspectives, many of which are conflicting and all of which are changing. In such an organization, only managers with an overview of the total situation can make the critical decisions on the funding of projects, the sharing of scarce technological resources, and the allocation of organizational skills and capabilities. Managing the flows of resources is a classic example of the need for coordination by centralization.

Perhaps the most difficult task is to coordinate the huge flow of strategic information and proprietary knowledge required to operate a transnational organization. The diversity and changeability of the flow make it impossible to coordinate through formalized systems or standardized policies; and the sheer volume and complexity of information would overload headquarters if coordination were centralized. The most effective way to ensure that worldwide organizational units are analyzing their diverse environments appropriately is to sensitize local managers to the broader corporate objectives and priorities and to other units' needs and capabilities. That goal is best reached by transferring personnel with the relevant knowledge or creating organizational forums that allow for the free exchange of information and foster interunit learning. In short, the socialization process is the classic solution for the coordination of information flows.

Naturally, none of these broad characterizations of the fit between flows and processes is absolute, and companies use a variety of coordinative mechanisms in managing all three flows. Goods flows may be centrally coordinated, for example, for products under allocation, when several plants are operating at less than capacity or if cost structures or host government demands change; many routine information flows can be coordinated through formalization if appropriate management information systems are installed.

Case 6–1   Procter & Gamble Europe: Vizir Launch

Charlie Ferguson, Procter & Gamble's (P&G) European vice president, faced three critical decisions in June 1981 as he reviewed the German test-market results for Vizir, the company's new heavy-duty liquid (HDL) detergent.

- Should he follow the recommendation of Wolfgang Berndt, Germany's new advertising manager for laundry and cleaning products, and his

This case was prepared by Professor Christopher A. Bartlett.
Copyright © 1983 by the President and Fellows of Harvard College. Harvard Business School case 384-139.

German team and authorize a national launch on the basis of four months of test results? Or should Ferguson ask Berndt to wait until final test-market results were in, or perhaps even rethink the entire HDL product strategy?

- If and when the decision was made to launch Vizir, to what extent could this be considered a European rather than just a German product? If a coordinated European rollout was planned, to what degree should the company standardize its product formulation, packaging, advertising, and promotion?
- Finally, what organizational implications would these decisions have? For example, to what

extent should the individual country subsidiary managers retain the responsibility to decide when and how this new product would be introduced in their national markets?

Procter & Gamble: Company Background

P&G's strong and long-established culture was reflected in its corporate values, policies, and practices, and the following paragraphs provide some background on each of these areas.

Corporate Values

Established in 1837 by two men of strong religious faith and moral conviction, P&G soon developed an explicit set of corporate standards and values. Prospective employees quickly learned of P&G's fundamental belief that the company's interests were inseparable from those of its employees. Over the years, this broad philosophy had been translated into various widely shared management norms such as the following:

- P&G should hire only good people of high character;
- P&G must treat them as individuals with individual talents and life goals;
- P&G should provide a work environment that encourages and rewards individual achievement.

These shared beliefs soon became part of the company's formal management systems. General managers knew that they were evaluated on their achievements in three areas: volume, profit, and people. P&G also tried to attract people who were willing to spend their entire careers with the company. Promotions were made from within, and top management was chosen from career P&G people rather than from outside the company.

Management Policies

Over its almost 150-year history, P&G had also accumulated a broad base of industry experience and business knowledge. Within the company, this ac-

cumulated knowledge was recognized as an important asset and much of it had been formalized and institutionalized as management principles and policies. According to previous Chairman Ed Harness, "Though our greatest asset is our people, it is the consistency of principle and policy which gives us direction."

These operating principles and management policies were strategically important in the marketing area, for P&G had a reputation as a premier consumer marketer. A basic policy was that P&G's products should provide "superior total value" and should meet "basic consumer needs." This led to a strong commitment in research to create products that were demonstrably better than the competition when compared in blind tests. (One manager said, "Before you can launch a new brand, you must have a win in a white box.")

Furthermore, P&G highly valued market research. In a business where ill-conceived new product launches could be very expensive, and sometimes not very successful, continuous and detailed market research was seen as insurance against major mistakes. Harness described the market research objectives as being "to spot a new trend early, then lead it."

For similar reasons, P&G also believed in extensive product and market testing before making major brand decisions. Having spotted a trend through market research, the company typically spent two or three years testing the product and the marketing strategy it had developed before committing itself to a full-scale launch. One paper-goods competitor said, "P&G tests and tests and tests. They leave no stone unturned, no variable untested. You can see them coming for months and years, but you know when they get there, it is time for you to move."

Finally, P&G believed that through continual product development and close tracking of consumer needs and preferences, brands could be managed so that they remained healthy and profitable in the long term. Their rejection of the conventional product-life-cycle mentality was demonstrated by Ivory Soap, which was over 100 years old; Crisco shortening, which was over 70; and Tide detergent, which was over 35. Yet each product was still a leader in its field.

Organization Practices

Besides strong corporate values and clear management principles, P&G's culture was also characterized by well-established organization practices and processes. Its internal operations had been described as thorough, creative, and aggressive by some; and as slow, risk averse, and rigid by others.

Perhaps the most widely known of P&G's organizational characteristics was its brand manager structure. Created in 1931, the brand management system provided each brand with management focus, expertise, and drive at a low level in the organization. By legitimizing and even reinforcing the internal competition that had existed since Camay soap began to compete with Ivory in 1923, the brand manager system tended to restrict lateral communication. This fostered a norm among P&G managers that information was shared on a need-to-know basis only.

Although the brand manager system impaired lateral communication, vertical communication within P&G was well established. Proposals on key issues were usually generated at the lower levels of management, with analysis and recommendations working their way up the organization for concurrence and approval. At P&G, top management was intimately involved in most large decisions (for example, all new brand launches; capital appropriations exceeding $100,000; and personnel appointment and promotion decisions three levels down). Although the approval system could be slow and, at times, bureaucratic (one manager claimed that a label change on Head and Shoulders shampoo had required 55 signatures), it was designed to minimize risk in the very risky and expensive consumer marketing business. When a project was approved, however, it would have the company's full commitment. As one manager said, "Once they sign off [on the new brand launch], they will bet the farm."

Another characteristic of the P&G management process was that proposals were committed to paper, usually as one- or two-page memos. This encouraged thoroughness and careful analysis on the part of the proposal originators and objectivity and rationality from the managers who reviewed the document. Written documents could also easily circulate through the organization, either building suport or eliciting comments and suggestions for improvement or rejection.

P&G International: European Operations

Expansion Principles

Although P&G acquired a small English soap company in 1926, it did not build a substantial European presence until the postwar years. In 1954, a French detergent company was acquired; two years later, a Belgian plant was opened; and by the end of the decade, P&G had established operations in Holland and Italy. A Swiss subsidiary served as a worldwide export center. In the 1960s, subsidiaries were opened in Germany, Austria, Greece, Spain, and the Scandinavian countries. The European Technical Center (ETC) was established in Brussels in 1963 to provide R&D facilities and a small regional management team.

By 1981, Europe represented about 15% of P&G's $11 billion worldwide sales, with almost all of that substantial volume having been built in the previous two and a half decades. The German and U.K. subsidiaries were the largest, each representing about one-fifth of the company's European sales. France and Italy together accounted for another 30%, and Belgium, Holland, Spain, Austria, and Switzerland made up the balance.

As international operations grew, questions arose as to how the new foreign subsidiaries should be managed. As early as 1955, Walter Lingle, P&G's overseas vice president, laid down some important principles that guided the company's subsequent development abroad. Recognizing that consumer needs and preferences differed by country, Lingle emphasized the importance of acquiring the same intensive knowledge of local consumers as was required in the United States. Lingle said, "Washing habits . . . vary widely from country to country. We must tailor products to meet consumer demands in each nation. We cannot simply sell products with U.S. formulas. They won't work. They won't be accepted."

But Lingle insisted that the management policies and practices that had proven successful for P&G in the United States would be equally successful overseas. He declared, "The best way to succeed in other countries is to build in each one as exact a replica of the U.S. Procter & Gamble organization as it is possible to create."

European Industry and Competitive Structure

From their earliest exposure to the European market for laundry detergents, managers from the parent company realized how important the first of these principles would be. Washing habits and market structures not only differed from the familiar home country market but also varied from one country to another within Europe. Among the obvious differences in laundry characteristics were the following:

- Typical washing temperatures were much higher in Europe, and the "boil wash" (over 60°C) was the norm in most countries. However, lower washing temperatures were commonplace in some countries where washing machines did not heat water (for example, in the United Kingdom) or where hand washing was still an important segment (for example, in Spain and Italy).
- European washing machines were normally front loading with a horizontal rotating drum—very different from the U.S. norm of an agitator action in a top-loaded machine. The European machine also had a smaller water capacity (3 to 5 gallons versus 12 to 14 gallons in the United States) and used a much longer cycle (90 to 120 minutes versus 20 to 30 minutes for the United States).
- Europeans used more cottons and less synthetics than Americans and tended to wear clothes longer between washes. Average washing frequency was 2 to 3 times per week versus 4 to 5 times in the United States. Despite the lower penetration of washing machines, much higher detergent dosage per load resulted in the total

European laundry detergent consumption being about 30% above the U.S. total.

Market structures and conditions were also quite different from the United States and also varied widely within Europe, as the following examples illustrate:

- In Germany, concentration ratios among grocery retailers were among the highest in the world. The five largest chains (including co-ops and associations) accounted for 65% of the retail volume, compared with about 15% in the United States. In contrast, the independent corner store in Italy was still very important, and hypermarkets had not made major inroads.
- Unlimited access to television, similar to the United States, was available only in the United Kingdom (and even there it was much more expensive). In Holland, each brand was allowed only 46 minutes of TV commercial time per annum; in Germany and Italy, companies had to apply for blocks of TV time once a year. Allocated slots were very limited.
- National legislation greatly affected product and market strategies. Legislation in Finland and Holland limited phosphate levels in detergent; German laws made coupons, refunds, and premium offers all but impossible; elsewhere local laws regulated package weight, labeling, and trade discounts.

The competitive environment was also different from P&G's accustomed market leadership position in the United States. In Europe, P&G shared the first-tier position with two European companies, Unilever and Henkel. By the early 1970s, each company claimed between 200% and 25% of the European laundry detergent market. P&G's old domestic market rival, Colgate, had a 10% share and was in a second tier. Several national competitors fought it out for the remaining volume at a third level. Henkel competed in most European markets but was strongest in Germany, its home market; Unilever was also international, dominating in Holland and the United Kingdom. Colgate's presence in Europe was spottier, but it had built up a powerful position in France. Typically, national companies were strong at the lower-priced end of their local markets.

Each company had its own competitive characteristics. Unilever had long been a sleeping giant but was becoming much more aggressive in the late 1970s and early 1980s. Henkel was a fierce competitor and could be relied on to defend its home market position tenaciously. Colgate was trying to elbow its way in and tended to be more impulsive and take bigger risks, often launching products with only minimal testing. As a result of this diverse activity, P&G's market share varied considerably by national market (see Table A).

By the mid-1970s, the rapid growth of the previous two decades dropped to a standstill. Not only did the oil crisis add dramatically to costs, but almost simultaneously, washing machines approached the 85% penetration rate that many observers regarded as the saturation point. In the late 1970s, volume was growing at only 2% per annum. As market growth slowed, competitive pressures increased.

P&G Europe's Strategy and Organization

These differences in consumer habits, market conditions, and competitive positions led to the development of strong national subsidiaries with the responsibility for developing products and marketing programs to match the local environment. Each subsidiary was a miniature P&G, with its own brand management structure, product development capability, advertising agencies, and typically, man-

TABLE A   Laundry Detergent Market ($ million)

	Total Market	P&G Share
Germany	$950	$200
United Kingdom	660	220
France	750	160
Italy	650	140
Spain	470	90
Total Europe	$3,750	$950

ufacturing capability. The subsidiary general manager directed the growth of the business and the organization (see Exhibit 1).

Each subsidiary attacked the task of establishing P&G in the basic detergent and soap business in its national market differently. The general manager tried to select the best volume and profit opportunity from over 200 products in the company's portfolio, then adapt them to the local situation. The general manager of the Italian subsidiary described the choices he faced when he took over in 1974:

> Given the limits of P&G Italy's existing brands [a laundry detergent, a bar soap, and a recently acquired coffee business], our priority was to build volume and profit and broaden our base. The choices we had were almost limitless. Pampers had been very successful in Germany and Belgium, but Italy couldn't afford such an expensive launch; Motiv, a new dishwashing liquid, was being launched in France and Germany, but we were unconvinced of its potential here. Mr. Propre [Mr. Clean in the United States] was successful in three European countries, but competition in Italy was strong. Finally, we decided to launch Monsavon, the French bar soap. It represented an affordable new product launch in a traditionally good profit line.

Since 1961, each of the country general managers had reported to Tom Bower, an Englishman who had headed up P&G's European operations. Bower had a reputation as an entrepreneur and an excellent motivator. He believed that by selecting creative and entrepreneurial country general managers and giving them the freedom to run their businesses, results would follow. Bower made sure that his small headquarters staff understood that they were not to interfere unduly in subsidiary decisions. Primarily, it was the subsidiary general manager's responsibility to call on ETC if a problem arose.

The strategy was most successful for P&G, and sales and profits grew rapidly throughout the 1960s and into the early 1970s. Growth was aided by P&G's entry into new national markets and additional product categories and by the rapid growth of the core detergent business with the penetration of washing machines into European homes.

EXHIBIT 1   Abbreviated Organization Chart, P&G Europe

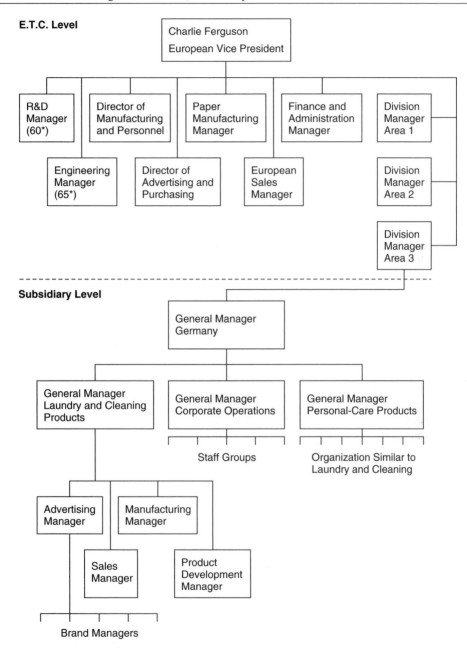

*Number of managerial and technical/professional staff. (Total number of managerial/technical/professional staff at ETC was 175.)

When Bower retired in 1975, his successor, Ed Artzt, faced a situation different from the one that existed in the 1950s and 1960s. As growth slowed, competition intensified, prices weakened, and profits dipped. Artzt felt that if profit and sales growth were to be rekindled, the diverse country operations would have to be better coordinated.

Over the next five years, under his leadership, the role of ETC took on new importance. (Exhibit 1 shows an abbreviated organization chart.) As increased competition led to declining margins, Artzt moved to strengthen the ETC finance manager's role in controlling costs. The finance manager described the problems:

> Largely because of duplication of marketing and administrative groups in each subsidiary, our overhead expense per unit was almost 50% higher than in the U.S. parent. We needed to get it under control. Our problem was that we couldn't get meaningful or comparable costs by subsidiary. Our introduction of better cost and reporting systems helped put pressure on subsidiaries to control their costs. It had a very beneficial effect.

Artzt was also concerned about the slowing of innovation in P&G Europe. He felt that the scarcity of new product development and their haphazard introductions contributed to the sales and profit problem. Under the able leadership of Wahib Zaki, Artzt's new R&D manager, ETC's role in product development shifted dramatically.

Previously each subsidiary initiated its own local product development. For example, the R&D group in the French subsidiary was around 30, while Germany's technical staff was perhaps twice that size. Responding to its own local market, the subsidiary defined and developed products with the appropriate characteristics, drawing on the parent company's basic technology and perhaps calling on ETC for specialized technical support or backup. Because subsidiaries were not required to use standard formulations or technology, products varied widely from country to country. As a result, Ariel detergent had nine different formulas throughout Europe. For example, it was positioned diversely as a low- and a high-suds powder and for low- and high-temperature usage, depending on the country.

Zaki concluded that developing products in this way provided insufficient focus, prioritization, or strategic direction for the work. Thus, the strong technical capabilities housed in the ETC, as well as in the United States, were not being fully or effectively utilized. Furthermore, local country management did not appreciate their efforts and tended to view the Technical Center as a high-cost, perfectionist group that did not respond rapidly enough to market needs.

Zaki aimed to change this by having ETC take a stronger leadership role in R&D and to assume responsibility for coordinating the new product development efforts among the subsidiaries. His analysis indicated that national differences in consumer practices and preferences were narrowing, and they no longer justified product differences that then existed from country to country. He wanted to establish priorities, to coordinate efforts, and as much as possible, to standardize products Europe-wide. To achieve these goals, he needed the involvement and cooperation of the subsidiaries.

In 1977, Zaki reorganized European R&D by creating European Technical Teams to work on products and technologies that had multiple market potential. In his vision, European products would be superior to existing local national products but without compromising performance or increasing cost. The objective was to focus the resources of the total European R&D community around key brands and to define a long-term European approach to product development.

As roles became clarified, the ETC technical groups were seen as the developers of new technologies ("putting the molecules together," as one R&D manager described it), while the subsidiaries took responsibility for testing and refining the products in the field. After a couple of painful years, the new process seemed to be working. "Lead countries" were named for each of the key products, thereby giving more local subsidiary responsibility and ownership for the development process, and also ensuring ongoing coordination among subsidiaries. Transfer of technical staff between ETC and subsidiaries further encouraged interdependence and cooperation.

An experimental attempt at "Europeanization" in marketing, however, had been less successful. In a break from the philosophy of product adaptation, a group of managers in Cincinnati concluded that "a baby is a baby" worldwide and that the laborious market-by-market evaluations that had been assumed necessary for cleaning products would not be needed for disposable diapers. Therefore, it was decided to gain experience by managing key elements of Pampers (such as product and copy strategy) on a Europe-wide basis. A senior manager was transferred from the German subsidiary, where Pampers was launched in 1973, to ETC, where he was made responsible for leading key activities on Pampers in all subsidiaries.

The brand promotion manager, responsible for Pampers in France at the time, recalled the experiment:

> As soon as it was known I would be principally working with the European Pampers manager in ETC and not the subsidiary GM, my local support dried up. I couldn't get a brand manager or even an assistant to work with me. The French subsidiary manager was preoccupied with the Motiv [dishwashing liquid] launch and was trying to regain leadership with Ariel [laundry powder]. The Pampers situation was a disaster. Eventually Pampers was given back to the subsidiaries. It was the only way to get their support.

This experience conveyed an important lesson to P&G's top management. It appeared that although coordination and planning could be effectively centralized and implemented on a European basis, the day-to-day management of the business had to be executed at the local subsidiary level.

In 1980, Artzt was transferred back to Cincinnati as executive vice president of P&G, and Charlie Ferguson was named group vice president, Europe. Ferguson was an energetic, creative, and intelligent manager with a reputation for getting things done. Impressed by the effectiveness of the European approach to technical development, Ferguson was convinced that a similar approach could succeed in product marketing.

With the encouragement and support of his boss, Artzt, who remained a strong advocate of Europeanization, Ferguson began to test the feasibility of developing Europe-wide brand and marketing strategies. In pursuing the Eurobrand concept, as it was becoming known, Artzt and Ferguson saw Vizir, the new HDL being prepared for launch in Germany, as a good test case.

The Vizir Project

Product Development

Following Lever's success in the United States with Wisk, P&G launched Era in 1974 as their entrant in the fast-growing HDL detergent segment. As a late entrant, however, it was unable to match Wisk's dominant share. P&G managers, watching developments from Europe, realized that if the HDL product concept was transferable to their market, the first company to stake out the territory would have an advantage. The success of liquids in other product categories (for example, household cleansers), the trend toward low-temperature washes, and the availability of liquid-product plant capacity, all provided additional incentives to proceed with the project.

ETC initiated its HDL project in late 1974 by testing the U.S. product Era against European powders in a small-scale test panel. Given the differences in laundry habits on either side of the Atlantic, it was not surprising that Era was evaluated poorly. The panel reported problems not only with the product's washing performance (for example, whitening ability, suds level) but also with its form. European washing machines had drawers that allowed different powdered products (pretreatment, main wash detergent, fabric softener) to be activated at different times in the typical 90-minute cycle. To win acceptance of a laundry liquid would be difficult. Consumers would have to be convinced that this product would achieve similar results; then, their washing habits would have to be changed.

Undeterred, a group at ETC began to work on a HDL product that would be more suitable to European laundry practices. It was with high hopes and considerable corporate visibility that the modified European HDL product was placed in six full-scale blind tests in Germany, France, and the United Kingdom. The results were disastrous in all tests. Given the high expectations that had been created within P&G, many insiders felt that the product was dead because it would be impossible to rebuild internal support and credibility.

However, the scientists at ETC were convinced that they could capitalize on the intrinsic ability of a liquid detergent to incorporate three times the level of surfactants as compared to a powder. (The surfactant is the critical ingredient that removes greasy stains.) In addition to surfactants, laundry detergents contained builders (to prevent redisposition of dirt) and phosphates (to soften water). Unlike U.S. products, however, European powdered detergents also contained enzymes (to break down proteins) and bleach (to oxidize stains). Unfortunately, it was not then possible to incorporate enzymes and bleach into a liquid detergent, and this limited capability was behind the new product's blind-test failure against European powders.

Overcoming these deficiencies challenged P&G's scientists at ETC and in the United States. Eventually they did patent a method to give enzymes stability in liquid form. Soon afterward, a bleach substitute that was effective at lower temperatures was developed. These product modifications led to improved consumer blind-test results. In late 1976, the new HDL product won a blind test against the leading French powder, Ariel; the following year, it won against Persil, the German market leader.

Although the project was still on shaky ground within P&G, these successes resulted in the establishment of an HDL brand group in Germany. The group reported to Germany's newly appointed advertising manager for laundry and cleaning products, Wolfgang Berndt, a 34-year-old Austrian, who was recognized as one of the promising young managers in Europe. He began his career 10 years earlier in the company's Austrian subsidiary. After gaining training and experience in brand management in Austria, the United Kingdom, and Germany, Berndt spent two years in Cincinnati as a brand manager in the parent company's Toilet Goods Division. He returned to Europe in 1973 as brand promotion manager at P&G Italy, before transferring to Germany a year later.

Soon after he was appointed advertising manager in 1977, Berndt was given responsibility to supervise this important, but delicate, new HDL responsibility. The main reason for the assignment, he believed, was that he and his German team had expressed their confidence in this new product's potential.

In early 1977, Colgate began test marketing Axion, an HDL formula that was similar to its U.S. product, Dynamo. Axion showed excellent initial results, gaining almost 4% share in three months. However, sales declined from this peak, and within 18 months, Colgate closed down the test market and withdrew Axion.

Meanwhile P&G's research team had developed three important breakthroughs: a fatty acid that provided similar water-softening performance to phosphate, a suds suppressant so that the product would function in European drum washing machines, and a patented washing machine anticorrosion ingredient. By 1979, P&G's European development efforts had shifted to product aesthetics, and the search began for perfumes compatible with the newly formulated HDL-Formula SB, as it was known.

Henkel was also reformulating its leading powder and relaunched it as New Persil. Blind tests of Formula SB against New Persil in early 1980 broke even. Finally, in October 1980, with a new fragrance, Procter's Formula SB won a blind test against New Persil by 53 to 47. The product's superiority was confirmed in subsequent tests against the main competitive powders in France (a 58 to 42 win for Formula SB) and in the United Kingdom (a 61 to 39 win).

Berndt and his German brand group were ready to recommend a full-scale test market. During the previous 18 months, they had cleared the proposed brand name (Vizir), appointed an advertising agency (Grey), designed packaging (bottles and labels), and collected and analyzed the masses of consumer and market data that were necessary to justify any new product launched by P&G. Management, up to the highest level, was interested and involved. Although an initial capital approval had been received for $350,000, to buy molds and raw materials, the test-market plan for Berlin was expected to involve a further investment of $1.5 million plus $750,000, for original advertising production and research. A national launch would involve an additional $1.5 million in capital investment and $16 million in marketing costs. It would pay out in about three years if the product could gain a 4% market share. A Europe-wide launch would be five or six times that amount.

Although Berndt and his team decided to proceed with the test market, uncertainty still surrounded Vizir. Some individuals in the company wondered whether it made sense to launch this product in Germany, particularly with the proposed marketing positioning and copy strategy. Other personnel were less concerned about the German launch but strongly opposed making Vizir a Eurobrand and launching it in all key European markets.

Vizir Launch Decision

Vizir's positioning in the detergent market concerned P&G's senior management. Vizir gave superior cleaning performance on greasy stains at low temperatures and (following the product improvements) matched powder performance on enzymatic stains and whiteness. The problem was that P&G's Ariel, the leading low-temperature laundry powder in Germany, made similar performance claims, and management feared that Vizir would cannibalize Ariel's sales. These similarities were highlighted when two advertising agencies, operating independently, produced almost identical commercials for Vizir and Ariel in early 1981 (see Exhibit 2).

The German brand group favored this positioning for Vizir, because these characteristics had resulted in high trials during the Axion test. To position Vizir as a pretreatment product would severely limit its sales potential, and emphasizing its peripheral bene-fits, such as fabric care or softness, would not have broad appeal. They argued that it had to be seen by consumers as a main wash product with superior cleaning performance at lower temperatures.

Some managers worried that P&G was creating a product segment that could result in new competitive entries and price erosion in the stagnant heavy-duty detergent market. Compared to powders, liquids were much easier to make and required less capital investment. ("For powders, you need a detergent tower. Liquids can be made in a bath tub," according to one manager.) Although P&G had patented many of its technological breakthroughs, they were not effective barriers to entry. One product development manager explained:

> Our work on Vizir was very creative but not a very effective barrier to competition. Often, it's like trying to patent a recipe for an apple pie. We can specify ingredients and compositions in an ideal range or a preferred range, but competitors can copy the broad concepts and work around the patented ranges. And, believe me, they are all monitoring our patents! Even if they don't, or can't, copy our innovations, there are other ways to solve the problems. If enzymes are unstable in liquid form, you could solve that by dumping in lots of enzymes so that enough will still be active by the estimated usage data.

If capital costs were low and products could be imitated, then new entrants could open up a market for "white labels" (generic products). Without either the product or the market development costs of P&G, they probably could undercut P&G's prices. The Germans' proposed pricing strategy was to price at an equivalent "cost-per-job" as the leading powders. This pricing strategy afforded a slightly higher gross profit margin for Vizir compared to powders. A premium price was justified on two counts: it was consistent with the product's image, and it would avoid overall profit erosion, assuming that Vizir would cannibalize some sales of the company's low-temperature laundry detergent brands.

At this time, P&G held a strong number-two position in the German detergent market—the largest in Europe. Henkel's leading brand, Persil, was positioned as an all-temperature, all-purpose powder,

EXHIBIT 2   Comparative Scripts: Vizir and Ariel Commercials

Vizir ("Peter's Pants") *(Woman in laundry examining newly washed pants on her son)*	*Ariel ("Helen Hedy")* *(Woman in laundry holding up daughter's blouse)*
Announcer: Hey, Peter's things look pretty nice.	**Announcer:** Looks beautifully clean again, doesn't it?
Woman: Thanks.	**Helen:** Yes, sure.
Announcer: Too bad they're not completely clean.	**Announcer:** Also close up?
Woman: What?	**Helen:** Well, no. When you really look up close—that's gravy. A stain like that never comes out completely.
Announcer: There's still oily dirt from his bicycle.	**Announcer:** Why is that?
Woman: I can't boil modern fabrics. And without boiling they don't get cleaner.	**Helen:** Because you just can't boil these modern things. I can't get Barbel's blouse really clean without boiling.
Announcer: Oh yes! Here is Vizir, the new liquid detergent Vizir, the liquid powder that gets things cleaner. Without boiling!	**Announcer:** Then use Ariel. It can clean without boiling.
Woman: Bicycle oil will come out? Without boiling?	**Helen:** Without boiling? Even these stains? That I want to see.
Announcer: Yes, one cap of Vizir in the main wash and on tough soil pour a little Vizir on directly. Then wash. Let's test Vizir against boil wash powder. These make-up stains were washed in powder at 60°—not clean. On top we put this unwashed dirty towel, then pour on Vizir. Vizir's liquid power penetrates the soil and dissolves it, as well as the stain that boil wash powder left behind.	**Announcer:** The Test: With prewash and main wash at low temperature we are washing stubborn stains like egg and gravy. The towel on the right had Ariel's cleaning power.
Woman: Incredible. The bicycle oil—gone! Without boiling. Through and through cleaner.	**Helen:** Hey, it's really true. The gravy on Barbel's blouse is completely gone. Even against the light—deep down clean. All this without boiling.
Announcer: Vizir—liquid power to get things cleaner.	**Announcer:** Ariel—without boiling, still clean!

and held a 17% share.[1] P&G's entrant in the all-temperature segment was Dash, and this brand had $5\frac{1}{2}$% share. However, the company's low-temperature brand, Ariel, had an 11% share and was a leader in its fast-growing segment, far ahead of Lever's Omo ($4\frac{1}{2}$%) and Henkel's new entrant, Mustang ($2\frac{1}{2}$%).

The opponents' final argument was that even if these risks were ignored, there were serious doubts that Vizir represented a real market opportunity. P&G's marketing of its HDL in the United States had not been an outstanding success. Furthermore

---

[1]These share data represented the total detergent market (including dishwashing liquid). The heavy-duty segment (that is, laundry detergent) represented about two-thirds of this total.

Colgate's experience with their European test market had been very disappointing.

In early 1981, Berndt's attention was drawn to an article that had been presented to an industry association congress in September in 1980 by Henkel's director of product development and two other scientists. They concluded that HDLs would continue to expand their penetration of the U.S. market, due to the less-demanding comparison standard of American powder detergents and also to the compatibility of HDLs with American washing practices. The paper claimed that in Europe, however, liquids were likely to remain specialty products with a small market share (1% compared with 20% in the United States). This limited HDL market potential was due to the superiority of European powder detergents and the different European washing habits (higher temperatures, washing machine characteristics, and so forth).

While managers in Brussels and Cincinnati wrestled with these strategic issues, Berndt's nervousness increased. He and his Vizir brand group were excited by the product and committed to its success. Initial test-market readings from Berlin were encouraging (see Exibit 3), but Berndt and his associates were certain that Henkel was also monitoring the test-market results. Vizir had been in development and testing for seven years. The German group

---

EXHIBIT 3   Selected Test-Market Results: Vizir Berlin Test Market

A. Total Shipments and Share

| | Shipments: MSU (volume index) | | Share (percent) | |
	Actual	Target	Actual	Target
Month				
February	4.6	1.8		
March	5.2	2.5	2.2	1.8
April	9.6	4.5	5.2	2.7
May	3.1	3.1	3.4	3.4

B. Consumer Research Results

Use and Awareness (at 3 months; 293 responses)			Attitude Data (at 3 months; including free-sample-only users)		
	Vizir	*Mustang**		*Vizir*	*Mustang**
Ever used (%)[†]	28	22	Unduplicated comments on:		
Past 4 weeks	15	9	Whiteness, brightness,		
Ever purchased[†]	13	15	cleaning or stain removal	65/11[‡]	58/8[‡]
Past 4 weeks	8	6	Cleaning or stain removal	49/8	52/4
Twice or more	4	n.a.	Cleaning	12/2	17/n.a.
Brand on hand	15	11	Stain removal	37/6	35/n.a.
Large sizes	3	5	Odor	30/4	15/3
Advertising awareness	47	89	Effect on clothes	7/–	13/6
Brand awareness	68	95	Form (liquid)	23/11	n.a.

n.a. = Not available.

*Mustang was a recently launched Henkel low-temperature powder on which comparable consumer data were available. It was judged to have been only moderately successful, capturing $2\frac{1}{2}$% market share compared to Ariel's 11% share as low-temperature segment leader.

[†]Difference between use and purchase data due to introductory free-sample program.

[‡]Number of unduplicated comments, favorable/unfavorable, about the product in user interviews. (For example, among Vizir users interviewed, 65 commented favorably about whiteness, brightness, cleaning, or stain removal, while 11 commented negatively about one or more of those attributes.)

believed that Henkel knew of their intentions and that it would counterattack to protect its dominant position in its home market. By the early summer of 1981, rumors began to spread in the trade that Henkel was planning an important new product. Henkel salespeople were recalled from vacation, and retailers were being sounded out for support on promotional programs.

On three occasions, Berndt or an associate presented the group's analysis of the test market and their concerns about a preemptive strike, but on each occasion, approval for a national launch was delayed. Senior management, on both sides of the Atlantic, explained that it was too risky to invest in a major launch, based on only three or four months of test results. Experience had shown that a one-year reading was necessary before deciding to act.

Eurobrand Decision

Another critical decision concerned the scope of the product launch. Within P&G's European organization, the budding Eurobrand concept was controversial. Although it fostered coordination of marketing strategies of brands in Europe, some managers thought that it conflicted with the existing philosophy that allowed country subsidiary managers to decide what products were most likely to succeed in their local markets, in what form, and when.

Artzt, Ferguson, and other managers countered by arguing that the time was ripe for a common European laundry detergent. Although widely differing washing practices among countries had justified national products tailored to local habits, the market data indicated a converging trend in consumer laundry habits (see Exhibit 4).

EXHIBIT 4   Selected Market Research Data

A. Selected Washing Practices

	Germany		United Kingdom		France		Italy		Spain	
	1973	1978	1973	1978	1973	1978	1973	1978	1973	1978
Washing Machine Penetration										
Households with drum machines (percent)	76	83	10	26	59	70	70	79	24	50
Washing Temperature										
To 60° (including handwash)	51	67	71	82	48	68	31	49	63	85
Over 60°	49	33	29	18	52	32	69	51	37	15
Fabric Softener Use										
Loads with fabric softener (percent)	68	69	36	47	52	57	21	35	18	37

B. Selected Consumer Attitude Data (German survey only)

	Laundry Cleaning Problems (percent respondents claim)*		
	Grease-Based	Bleach-Sensitive	Enzyme-Sensitive
Most frequent stains	61	53	34
Desired improvement	65	57	33
In washes to 60°	78	53	25
In washes above 60°	7	36	65

*Does not add to 100% because multiple responses allowed.

Opponents quickly pointed out that, despite the trends, the differences in washing habits still outweighed the similarities. For example, Spain and Italy still had large handwash segments; in the United Kingdom and Belgium, top-loading washers were still important; and in Southern Europe, natural-fiber clothing still predominated. Besides, the raw statistical trends could be misleading. Despite the trend to lower-temperature washing, even in Germany, over 80% of the households still used the boilwash (over 60°C) for some loads. In general, the boilwash was the standard by which consumers judged washing cleanliness.

Some subsidiary managers also emphasized differences other than consumer preferences. Their individual market structures would prevent any uniform marketing strategy from succeeding. They cited data on differences in television cost and access, national legislation on product characteristics and promotion-tool usage, and distribution structure and competitive behavior. All these structural factors would impede standardization of brands and marketing strategies across Europe.

The second point raised by Artzt and Ferguson was that greater coordination was needed to protect subsidiaries' profit opportunities. (However, they emphasized that subsidiary managers should retain ultimate profit responsibility and at least a concurrence role in all decisions affecting their operations.) Increasingly, competitors imitated P&G's new and innovative products and marketing strategies, and preempted them in national markets, where the local subsidiary was constrained by budget, organization, or simple poor judgment from developing the new-product category or market segment. For example, Pampers was introduced in Germany in 1973 but was not launched in France until 1978. Meanwhile, in 1976, Colgate launched a product named Calline (a literal French translation of Pampers). Its package color, product position, and marketing strategy were similar to Pampers, and it quickly won dominant market share. Late introduction also cost Pampers market leadership in Italy. The product was not introduced in the United Kingdom until 1981. Lenor provided an equally striking example. Similar to Downy in the United States, this new brand was launched in 1963 in Germany and created the new fabric-softener product category. It quickly became an outstanding market success. Nineteen years later, Lenor debuted in France as the number-three entrant in the fabric-softener category and consequently faced a much more difficult marketing task.

Determined to prevent similar recurrences, particularly for new brands, Artzt and Ferguson wanted to ensure that product development and introduction were coordinated with a consistent Pan-European approach. Furthermore, they wanted marketing strategies to be thought through from a European perspective. This meant a thorough analysis of the possibility of simultaneous or closely sequenced European product introductions.

At the country level, many managers quickly pointed out that because the company wanted to keep the subsidiary as a profit center, this concept was not feasible. To establish a new brand—or even more so, to create a new product category such as disposable diapers—was incredibly expensive and highly risky. Many country general managers questioned whether they should gamble their subsidiary's profitability on costly, chancy launches, especially if they were not at all convinced that their local markets were mature enough to accept the product. In many markets, subsidiary managers felt that their organizations should not be diverted from the primary goal of building a sound base in heavy- and light-duty detergents and personal products.

The third set of arguments put forward by the advocates of the Eurobrand concept was related to economics. They cited numerous examples: there were nine different Dash formulas in Europe; Mr. Clean (known as Mr. Propre, Meister Proper, and so forth) was sold in nine sizes throughout Europe. To go to a single formula, standard-size packs, and multilingual labels could save the company millions of dollars in mold costs, line downtime for changeovers, sourcing flexibility, and reduced inventory levels.

Other managers pointed out that the savings could easily be offset by the problems that standardization would create. The following were comments made at a country general managers' meeting when

Ferguson raised the Eurobrand issue for discussion:

> We have to listen to the consumer. In blind tests in my market that perfume cannot even achieve breakeven.
>
> The whole detergent market is in 2 kilo packs in Holland. To go to a European standard of 3 kg and 5 kg sizes would be a disaster for us.
>
> We have low phosphate laws in Italy that constrain our product formula. And we just don't have hypermarkets, like France and Germany, where you can drop off pallet loads.

One general manager put it most forcefully in a memo to ETC management:

> There is no such thing as a Eurocustomer, so it makes no sense to talk about Eurobrands. We have an English housewife whose needs are different from a Gerrman hausfrau. If we move to a system that allows us to blur our thinking, we will have big problems.
>
> Product standardization sets up pressures to try to meet everybody's needs (in which case you build a Rolls Royce that nobody can afford) and countervailing pressures to find the lowest-common-denominator product (in which case you make a product that satisfies nobody and which cannot compete in any market). These pressures probably result in the foul middle compromise that is so often the outcome of committee decision.

Organization Decision

The strategic questions of whether to launch Vizir and, if so, on what scale, also raised some difficult questions about the existing organization structure and internal decision-making processes. If product market decisions were to be made in relation to Europe-wide strategic assessments and less in response to locally perceived opportunities, what implications did that have for the traditional role and responsibility of the country general manager? And if the Eurobrand concept was accepted, what organizational means were necessary to coordinate activities among the various country subsidiaries?

By the time Ferguson became vice president of P&G Europe, the nontechnical staff in ETC had grown substantially from the 20 or so people that worked with Bower in the early 1970s. Ferguson was convinced that his predecessor, Artzt, had been moving in the right direction in trying to inject a Pan-European perspective into decisions and by aiming to coordinate more activities among subsidiaries. Ferguson wanted to reinforce the more integrated perspective by changing the responsibilities of the three geographic division managers that reported to him.

Besides their existing responsibilities for several subsidiaries, Ferguson gave each of these managers Europe-wide responsibility for one or more lines of business. For example, the division manager responsible for the British, French, Belgian, and Dutch subsidiaries was also given responsibility for packaged soaps and detergents for Europe as a whole. Although the new roles were clearly coordinative, the status and experience of these managers meant that their advice and recommendations would carry significant weight, particularly on strategic and product planning issues.

For the first time, this change permitted clear Europe-wide objectives and priorities to be set by line of business, product group, or brand. Some country subsidiary managers naturally wondered whether their authority and autonomy were being eroded. Partly to deal with this problem and partly because the division managers had neither the time nor the resources to adequately manage their product responsibilities, Ferguson proposed an organizational forum he termed the Euro Brand Team.

Borrowing from the successful technical team concept, Ferguson would assign each key brand a team headed by a "lead country." Typically the country subsidiary with the most resources, the leading market positions, or the most commitment to a product would be given the lead role so that it could spread its knowledge, expertise, and commitment. The charter of the lead country would be to coordinate the analysis of opportunities for the standardization of the product formula, its promotion, and its packaging. The team concept also aimed at coordinating activities across subsidiaries and eliminating needless duplication of the brand's management.

The main forum for achieving this responsibility would be the Euro Brand Team meetings. Various managers from the regional office and the subsidiaries would be invited to these meetings. From ETC, the appropriate European division manager and European functional managers (for example, technical, manufacturing, purchasing, advertising, and so forth) would be invited. Advertising and brand managers from all the countries that sold the product would also be invited. It was proposed that the meeting would be chaired by the brand manager from the lead country. Thus, a typical team might have twenty or more invited participants.

At the subsidiary level, the idea received mixed reviews. Some saw an opportunity for increased local-management participation in Eurobrand decisions. These individuals viewed the European technical teams as evidence that such an approach could work and felt that this was a better solution than having such decisions dominated by an enlarged staff group at ETC. Other individuals felt that the Euro Brand Teams posed a further risk to the autonomy of the country manager. They also saw it as a threat, rather than an aid, to intersubsidiary relations. One general manager from a smaller country subsidiary explained:

> When a big, resource-rich subsidiary like Germany is anointed with the title of Lead Country, as it probably will be for a large number of brands, I am concerned that they will use their position and expertise to dominate the teams. The rich will become more powerful, and the small subs will wither. I believe this concept will generate further hostility between subsidiaries. Pricing and volume are the only tools

we have left. The general manager's role will be compromised if these are dissipated in team discussions.

Another concern was that team meetings would not be an effective decision-making forum. With individual subsidiaries still responsible for and measured by their local profitability, it was felt that participants would go in with parochial views that they would not be willing to compromise. Some managers claimed that, because the teams' roles and responsibilities were not clear, it would become another time-consuming block to decision making rather than a means to achieve progress on Eurobrands. A subsidiary general manager commented:

> The agenda for the Euro Brand Teams is huge, but its responsibilities and powers are unclear. For such a huge and emotionally charged task, it is unrealistic to expect the "brand manager of the day" to run things. The teams will bog down, and decisions will take forever. How many of these meetings can we attend without tying up our top management? Our system is all checks and no balances. We are reinforcing an organization in which no one can say yes—they can only veto. With all the controls on approvals, we've lost the knack to experiment.

At least one manager at ETC voiced frustration, "If we were serious [about standardization], we would stop paying lip service, and tell everyone 'Like it or not, we're going to do it.'"

Ferguson remained convinced that the concept made sense and felt that *if* Vizir was launched and *if* it was considered a Eurobrand, it might provide an early test for his Euro Brand Team concept.

Case 6–2 Skandia AFS: Developing Intellectual Capital Globally

Jan R. Carendi, deputy chief executive officer (CEO) of Skandia Insurance Company Ltd. (Skandia) and chief operating officer (COO) of Skandia's Assurance and Financial Services (AFS) division, smiled as he reviewed a report on his unit's growth during his 10 years at the helm. Over this time, AFS's sales of private long-term savings and insurance products had grown 45% per year. Once a small unit in the international division of the 140-year-old Stockholm-based insurance and financial services company, AFS currently accounted for almost 50% of Skandia's gross premium revenues. (See Exhibit 1 for Skandia and AFS results 1986–1995.)

Yet to many, Carendi was a maverick who had continually defied conventional wisdom. By redefining the nature of the business, and restructuring it around alliances, some thought he had hollowed out the business and made it less robust than conventional and fully integrated companies. Others in this traditional industry questioned his radical approach of refocusing his managers on intellectual capital—looking at the organization's knowledge rather than finances as its key resources. While the payoffs of his approach were evident, the critics insisted there were also risks.

Carendi recognized that his bold actions were likely to raise eyebrows, but to date AFS's strong performance had been sufficient to quiet his critics. However, he was aware that in the turbulent segment of the market his company had carved out, past performance was no guarantee of future success. While financial analysts were focused on the 30% fall in

premium income of AFS's flagship U.K. operation in 1995, to Carendi, premium growth was a relative measure, and only one indicator of long-term success. His immediate concern was AFS's ability to maintain service quality when resources were constrained by rapid expansion. And long term, he was uncertain how the ability of the Internet to provide increasingly sophisticated consumers with direct access to insurance products would affect the broker-based distribution network his organization had spent a decade building.

Skandia Company Background

Skandia was founded in 1855 and almost immediately began expanding internationally, opening offices in Norway, Denmark, Russia, Germany, and the Netherlands within a year. It entered the U.S. market in 1900, becoming the first non-British insurance company to do so. However, following the losses incurred in the 1906 San Francisco earthquake and World War I, Skandia's interest in international markets waned, remaining fairly dormant until the 1960s when it entered another period of growth, at home and abroad. Despite some acquisitions of a few small foreign life assurance companies, most of Skandia's international business was in reinsurance.[1] The few foreign operations were managed as a portfolio of companies through International Life Operations, a small division of Skandia International.

In keeping with common industry practice, Skandia had developed as a fully integrated organization, focused primarily on its domestic market. The com-

---

This case was prepared by Professor Christopher A. Bartlett and Research Associate Takia Mahmood.

Copyright © 1996 by the President and Fellows of Harvard College. Harvard Business School case 396–412.

---

[1]Reinsurance was business accepted from another company to allow it to distribute its risk.

EXHIBIT 1 Financial Results for Skandia and AFS: 1986–1995

Million Swedish Kronor (MSEK)	1986	1987	1988	1989	1990	1991	1992	1993	1994	1995
Kronor per U.S.$	7.1	6.3	6.1	6.4	5.9	6.0	5.8	7.8	7.7	7.1
Gross Premium Income (MSEK)*										
Skandia Group	4,381	4,731	5,282	18,519	24,853	29,031	36,525	43,503	52,248	52,241
AFS:	—	1,919	1,524	1,979	2,868	5,483	7,891	17,240	25,888	23,961
Unit-link assurance	—	1,841	1,464	1,807	2,683	4,306	6,089	16,939	23,898	20,706
Life assurance	—	78	60	172	185	1,083	1,664	119	1,754	3,016
Management Operating Result (MSEK)†										
Skandia Group	4,773	(1,013)	4,410	4,044	(3,205)	(1,098)	(3,721)	4,069	(1,715)	815
AFS:	—	33	28	3	(33)	110	100	389	625	707
Unit-link assurance	—	25	15	(13)	(47)	88	80	386	530	595
Life assurance	—	8	13	16	14	22	20	3	91	99
Return on Net Asset Value (percent)										
Skandia Group	60	(10)	38	24	(19)	(10)	(30)	31	(8)	7
AFS	—	NA	NA	NA	NA	NA	6.5	17.6	19.2	17.6

*Beginning in 1989, Skandia Group results include Skandia International. Results in years 1989–1992 include American Skandia Reinsurance (Life Insurance sold in 1993), and in 1994–1995 include Intercaser (Spanish Life Insurance Company).
†Management operating results include changes in surplus values for investments.

Source: Skandia.

pany was comprised of four core value-adding activities, undertaken by a corporate staff located in Stockholm:

- An actuarial function whose key role was to make the risk assessments required to design insurance products to meet targeted consumer needs
- A sales and marketing group that identified market opportunities and sold products to consumers primarily through company representatives and exclusive agents
- An investment management function that invested premium income, and applied earnings to fund benefit payment, cover operating expenses, and generate profits

- An administrative group that managed the substantial customer, accounting, and regulatory paperwork generated by the system

Like most other insurance companies, Skandia had been a pioneer in the use of computer technology to facilitate the complex actuarial calculations, track huge investment portfolios, and support the heavy customer service and other administrative requirements. From the 1960s through the 1980s, it had followed the industry trend of building massive mainframe capacity at the central office, a location through which all data flowed. Many in the industry saw these huge infrastructure investments and the complex systems required to manage them as a barrier to entry in this highly regulated environment. Even for existing companies, it was estimated that the support structure and systems required for new market entry could cost millions of dollars and involve hundreds of man years of effort to establish.

In the late 1980s, however, many of Skandia's existing practices and management assumptions were being challenged by a newcomer to the corporate headquarters. In less than a decade, Jan Carendi had built an organization that had created a whole new business for Skandia. His international rollout of the unit-linked assurance annuity business grew to represent almost half the company's premium income by 1994, and become its dominant engine of future growth.[2]

Jan Carendi and the Rebirth of AFS

Born in Argentina of Swedish parents, Jan Carendi spoke fluent Spanish and felt more comfortable in the free-wheeling Latin environment than in the more restrictive Swedish culture. With a degree from the School of Economics in Gothenberg, Sweden, Carendi had joined Skandia as an executive trainee in 1970, taking an entry-level job in Skandia's Mexican regional headquarters in 1971. Based on his open and flexible style, he developed a great deal of trust within the Mexican entity and worked his way up to become controller and, ultimately, deputy chief executive in 1981.

In 1974, Carendi met Lars Lekander, a manager at Skandia and well-respected internal expert in organizational design, who had been sent to Mexico to help straighten out the subsidiary's managerial and organizational problems. Lekander immedi-

---

[2]Unit-linked (or mutual fund-linked) assurance is a variable life assurance product that allows the policyholder to invest the savings portion of the premium in a variety of investment vehicles offered by the company (various combinations of stock, bond, and money market investments with different risk-return profiles). While broadening the appeal of insurance products, these instruments created more complex demands on product development, sales, investment, and administration than the standard life assurance policies.

ately recognized Carendi as a highly effective manager and a "natural problem solver" who had taken responsibilities far beyond his controller's job. Carendi appeared to delegate responsibility easily, perhaps too easily at times—a trait that often made him impatient with traditional organizational forms and management practices. When the unexpected death of the head of Skandia's International Life Operations (ILO) in 1986 led to the search for a replacement, Lekander recommended Carendi, who by that time had become the president and CEO of Skandia's subsidiary in Colombia.

Lessons from the United Kingdom

ILO was a small division of Skandia International which had over 90% of its business in the high-risk reinsurance sector and was losing money. Carendi's plan was to clean up this core business, using the proceeds to fund growth in the primary life assurance business. However, when corporate management decided to spin off the reinsurance operation, ILO was viewed as an organization orphan. Its business portfolio consisted of a 50% share of a primary insurance company in Spain, with 37 shareholders fighting over its future direction, and a 60% share of an entrepreneurial life assurance venture in the United Kingdom.

The U.K. organization had been established in 1979 by a group of young entrepreneurs who had left an established insurance company to start a new business. Their objective was to take advantage of the opportunity created by regulatory changes that allowed savings to be linked to investment-backed variable life assurance policies. The entrepreneurs approached Skandia for financial backing for a venture to sell variable unit-linked annuities directly to the public. As the new company grew increasingly successful, the founders became ferociously independent and strongly resisted any intervention from the parent company. But Carendi wanted to learn more about the innovative unit-linked product that he saw as having potential in other markets.

He decided to gain control of the U.K. company by buying back 100% of the equity, and to support the U.K. team as it continued to develop its innovative product. One problem that the young company experienced was that its best in-house funds managers often left for higher pay elsewhere. It also experienced similar turnover problems with a sales force of dedicated agents. To stem the outflow of talent, the U.K. managers decided to externalize both the fund management and sales functions. They selected local retailers (independent brokers and banks), who were well known to the market, and entered into cooperative alliances with them for customer networking and distribution. They did the same with a wide range of highly visible local unit-trust (mutual fund) investment managers who had superior track records.

Eventually, Carendi began to see in this alliance-based structure, the foundation of a new business model upon which he could build a new worldwide Assurance and Financial Service (AFS) business. In this new configuration, he saw that AFS would

need to redefine its role as the linkage between the distribution and investment functions. It would add value by packaging long-term savings products for brokers and their clients, and by bringing wholesale distribution to brand name money managers. In describing his new business concept, he said, "We must begin to think of ourselves less as insurance specialists, and more as 'specialists in collaboration'." (See Exhibit 2.)

Transferring the Model: The U.S. Start-Up

By the late 1980s, the insurance industry was undergoing major change worldwide. In many countries, deregulation was opening the industry to banks and other financial and nonfinancial institutions. At the same time, cuts in government sponsored pension and social security schemes were leading many people to question their ability to depend on such programs for their retirement security. In some

---

EXHIBIT 2 The "Specialists in Collaboration" Organization Concept

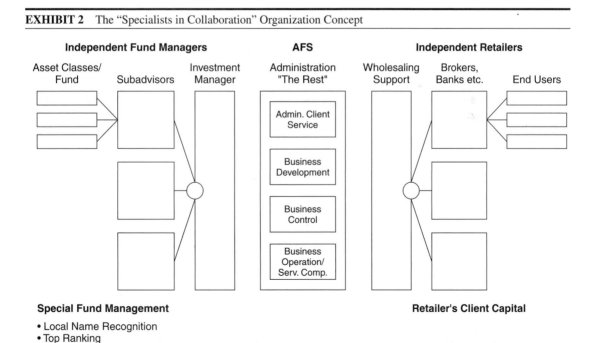

Source: Skandia

countries, governments were actively encouraging greater long-term self-reliance by creating tax incentives for insurance-backed long-term savings. Behind all of these changes was a worldwide demographic trend towards an aging population that was not only contributing to the crisis in social security programs, but simultaneously creating new insurance market opportunities. It was against this background that Carendi wanted to expand his business abroad as quickly and aggressively as he could, initially aiming at one new market entry a year.

Based on a feasibility study done by the U.K. company, in 1988 Carendi decided to leverage the U.K.'s success to enter the very competitive American life assurance market. To build the new business, he hired an experienced U.S. industry manager and gave him the support of three relocated executives with specialized expertise—the two U.K. executives who had headed the U.S. market study, and Leif Reinius, AFS's international systems controller.

Reinius had been working on a PC-based, modular, software system, designed to support the U.K. investment-linked product and its "partnership model" of management. The software was designed to capture the company's essential administrative processes and coordinative mechanisms, such as policyholder applications, fund selection, daily pricing, commission management, and statements of accounts. Unfortunately, when he tested it in the U.S. environment, Reinius found that the system was inflexible and inappropriate in a market with a different set of consumer needs and regulatory requirements.

At the same time, American Skandia was having difficulty establishing the external visibility it needed to attract new customers and the internal credibility it needed to obtain continued corporate support. The newly established U.S. company had spent $5 million per year in 1988 and 1989, but had booked no business and had few prospects. Some in the parent company were beginning to question whether AFS should continue to invest in the struggling operation. Carendi decided it was time for a shakeup. In 1989, he removed the U.S. head and some other managers and took on the role of subsidiary president himself.

Formalizing the Prototype

Although the initial transfer of the U.K.-based systems had not been successful, Carendi became increasingly convinced of the power of the concept of a transportable software package that Reinius was developing. By capturing cumulative experience, the huge start-up costs of new market entry—to define new products, support distribution efforts, and provide an administrative infrastructure—could be greatly reduced. As he explained: "Applying prototype concepts to business development should enable us to design products and develop administrative processes for a specific market in half the time, and at a quarter of the cost."

At the end of 1989, Reinius returned to Stockholm to continue working on the "core prototype system." His objective was to make it parameter-driven—so that those in new operations could input variables on risk factors, savings percentage, charges, and other factors—and to make it more flexible—so that it could be adapted to local restrictions, reporting requirements, and language. The first chance to use the new prototype came in 1990 when AFS expanded into the Swiss market. Breaking away from the model of traditional insurance companies, the AFS prototype was designed to operate on smaller IBM/AS400 computers rather than large mainframes. Its core chassis of various financially and administratively oriented modules—for applications such as policy administration, product definition, distribution, asset management, accounting, billing, and collection—now comprised a comprehensive yet flexible operating framework. (See Exhibit 3.)

Despite the excitement that the growth was generating within AFS, Carendi's unconventional approach found its detractors within Skandia. Senior level IT executives were concerned about his investments in nonmainframe-based systems development; others saw his reliance on loose, unfocused teams as a risk in a structured, financially conservative company. These doubts gained additional credibility because AFS was still reporting negative results. Because sales of these products typically generated more expenses than premiums income in early years (due to the heavy front loading of com-

EXHIBIT 3 Systems Prototype: Components and Integration

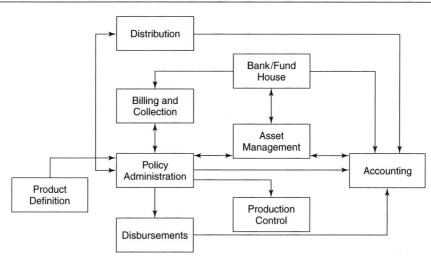

Component	Function
Product definition	Defines products (e.g., charges, cost factors, risk cover, calculation methods)
Distribution	Supports sales by maintaining field organization information, agent license information, sales performance and paying commissions
Billing and collection	Bills for and collects premiums
Policy administration	Governs all policy activity over the life of a policy, (e.g., underwriting, contract issue, financials, changes and terminations)
Disbursements	Pays claims, benefits, commissions and expenses
Bank/fund house	Supports wire transfers, international exchange rates, unit values, corporate financial transactions and balance reporting
Asset management	Controls balancing policyholder liabilities and fund assets, calculates required purchases or redemptions, provides reporting on funds
Production control	Provides management information at an operational level, (e.g., policies awaiting issue, premiums due and not paid, death claims pending)
Accounting	Controls all financial events, (e.g., maintains ledgers, performs compliance reporting, prepares corporate statements)

Source: Skandia.

missions, administrative set-up expenses, etc.), Carendi faced the dilemma that the faster he grew, the more losses he created. Despite American Skandia's sales growth from $6.3 million in 1989 to $141 million in 1991, Hans Dalborg, the head of Skandia International, of which AFS was still a part, continued to express concern about the ongoing negative results in the United States. It was only in 1991, when Dalborg left the company and AFS was made a separate unit reporting directly to Björn Wolrath, the president and CEO of Skandia Group and a strong supporter of AFS strategy, that Carendi won full support for his radically different approach to international expansion.

Leveraging the Model: The European Thrust

In 1991, with the fall of the Berlin wall, Carendi and his team decided to open a company in Germany. To develop some expertise in analyzing new market entry and starting up new subsidiaries, Carendi tapped Ann-Christin Pehrsson, a young woman he had met at a conference. Impressed by the quality of her thinking, he pursued her until he could convince her to leave her job and join AFS. Looking for a role that would challenge her and use her talents, he named Pehrsson AFS's Director of Business Development, a one-person function based in Stockholm. With the help of local contacts, she developed a three-phase analysis of the new market opportunity: a market study, a legal requirements analysis, and a report on local distribution and money management networks. Pehrsson described why the analysis was so important for the German startup:

> Germans hesitate to speculate and take financial risks. This is a problem which is conditioned by culture, so it's important to interest people in the advantages of a variable annuity—still a relatively unknown form of long-term savings. . . . We faced similar challenges in changing the distribution channels. The German market is traditionally a captive agent market, and the agents cooperate loyally with domestic companies and sell traditional life insurance products. Broker distribution is a new activity we had to help grow.

With the lessons taken from the Swiss entry and with the understanding generated by Pehrsson's business development analysis, Reinius and his team improved the systems prototype, allowing even greater flexibility to adapt to Germany's tax regulations and reporting requirements. Eventually, each local company hired its own IT people to make such adjustments and to maintain its systems, although the staff was kept quite small—three in Germany, three in Switzerland.

Managing the New Business Model

As he pursued his international expansion strategy built on the three-legged stool of unit-linked annuity products, the partnership-based business model, and the prototype-based learning processes, Carendi started to articulate a management philosophy that was radically different from the traditional Skandia approach. He became convinced that AFS would have to compete on its ability to maintain what he called a "permanent state of advanced readiness." He told his organization:

> Today, creating bullet-proof products isn't as important as building the ability to constantly develop and deploy new products that responded to changing customer needs. You have to be able to get in and out of products and services with the competitive energy of a kid playing a video game rather than with the analytical consistency of a grand master trying to hang on in a three-day chess match.

To create such a flexible and dynamic capability, he believed he had to create different internal organization framework, new performance metrics, and radically different ways of managing people.

The Federative Organization

For years Carendi had been working to transform AFS into Lekander's ideal of a "federative organization." The concept fit well with Carendi's evolving management philosophy based on delegated responsibility and individual initiative. As a result, when a local company began to develop particular capabilities in a vital function or activity from which other units might learn, Carendi recognized its achievements by designating it a strategic competence center. For instance, Spain became a competence center for bank product design, the United States for information technology, and Colombia for administrative support and back-office functions. But no designation was permanent and lasted only until another local company sped by it on the learning curve.

Since there was no formal structural linkage to connect the federation of national units in which AFS's expertise resided, Carendi worked hard to create informal connections that encouraged information and knowledge sharing across units. One common way was to draw people together to work on project teams not only in the startup of new subsidiaries, but also in the ongoing management of the business. The project team Carendi assembled to define the specifications of a system to deliver payouts for annuities was typical. Representatives from several subsidiaries not only captured diverse expertise from multiple country units, but also ensured that the system was designed so that the amount of adaptation required when it was deployed would be minimal.

Insisting that vital information available in any part of the organization should be accessible by all AFS companies, Carendi commissioned the IT units at AFS in Stockholm and Shelton, Connecticut to create an integrative global area network (GAN) infrastructure. Initially providing the capability for electronic mail and document and file sharing, even to those traveling within AFS offices, the GAN later expanded to serve as a conduit for core business applications and to provide an electronic venue for the exchange of ideas and experiences. For instance, the Austrian subsidiary ran part of its operations on the server in Switzerland, while Mexico used the GAN to access programs housed in the United States.

As he developed this linked federation, Carendi was careful to keep the AFS Stockholm staff at a minimum. Consisting of approximately 40 of the company's 1,700 employees, this group worked on the construction of the IT infrastructure, cross-border sales and marketing projects, business development, and accounting and financial control, leveraging resources decentralized to the country units. For example, there were five major centers in the IT federation, located in Germany, Colombia, Spain, England, and the United States, each of which not only supported its local operation but also contributed to the broader AFS development priorities. The Stockholm staff also organized knowledge-sharing activities and functioned as the center of AFS communications, particularly of its values. "We don't refer to Stockholm as the *head* office," said one senior manager. "The brain power is out in the field. If anything, the center acts as the *heart* office, maintaining the values of the group and helping pump information—our lifeblood—around the

organization. It certainly avoids prescribing how businesses should be conducted around the world."

Measuring Intellectual Capital

The more Carendi became convinced of the competitive value of AFS's knowledge assets, the more he became frustrated with the inability of traditional financial reports to focus management on the critical task of building and leveraging intellectual capital. Because traditional accounting measures did not even recognize, let alone try to measure such assets, he gave top priority to finding a way of describing and measuring the effectiveness of investments in noncapital assets and resources.

To help him with this challenge, in 1991, Carendi hired Leif Edvinsson, Senior Vice President of Training and Development at a Swedish bank, with an MBA from the University of California at Berkeley, and named him the world's first director of Intellectual Capital. Edvinsson observed that many companies on the Stockholm Stock Exchange were valued at three to eight times their book value, and in the United States at even higher multiples. He argued that these huge hidden values were largely accounted for by a company's intellectual capital:

> Hidden value is the root system of the corporate tree. Healthy, strong roots provide the nutrients and nourishment necessary for its growth and production of fruit. The quality of the fruit—the results you can see—is dependent on the roots, which you cannot see. . . . From this perspective, the bottom-line financial results are really the top-line results. The real bottom-line is renewal and development, which is the foundation for the future.

To help him translate the broad concept of "intellectual capital" into management specifics, Edvinsson classified it into human capital (the knowledge, skill, and capability of employees in meeting the needs of customers) and structural capital (codified brainpower embedded over time in databases, customer files, software, manuals, trademarks, and organizational structures). (See Exhibit 4.) Edvinsson believed that the key management task was developing intellectual capital, which involved leveraging

EXHIBIT 4   The Building Blocks of Intellectual Capital

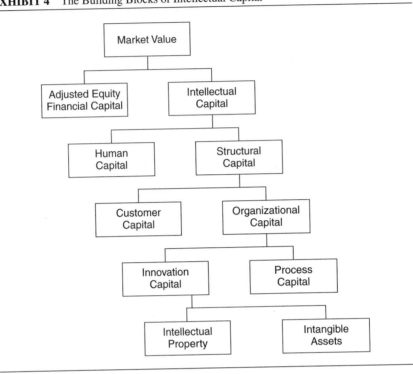

Source: Skandia.

its human capital, and transforming it into structural capital, thereby creating value for customers, investors, and other stakeholders. Said Edvinsson, "The real aim is to convert IQ into ECU [the European Currency Unit]. Focusing on managing financial resources using only information from their accounting systems is a bit like driving into the future while looking in the rearview mirror."

Edvinsson realized, however, that his task extended far beyond defining terms and developing concepts. To implement his ideas and influence into the ongoing decision-making processes, he obtained Carendi's approval to employ the world's first controller for Intellectual Capital whose full-time job was to define measures, gather data, and publish reports that would calibrate AFS's effectiveness in developing and exploiting its human and

structural capital. Beginning with modest quarterly reports, Edvinsson and his controller gradually expanded the number of categories of intellectual capital and the means of measuring them, culminating in the publication of AFS's first annual report on intellectual assets for 1993. The report provided baseline measurements of many nontraditional inputs and performance measures including information technology as a percentage of total expenses, the number of IT-literate employees as a percentage of all employees, gross insurance premiums per employee, and changes in savings per account.

Edvinsson's work touched off a debate within AFS about the utility of using scarce resources, first to identify and define the new indicators, (which were less universal and less readily apparent than traditional financial measures), and then to develop the infrastructure to capture the new data and analyze it. Some suggested that although they understood the effort conceptually, they were unclear about how the additional data would be used—in setting priorities, allocating resources, or determining compensation, for example. Even those who saw the value of highlighting the "hidden assets" in their operations, wondered if that would not be better managed by focusing on the knowledge-building process itself, rather than on creating a standardized "intellectual" balance sheet. "The concept of intellectual capital helps you see what else to do to stay competitive," said one senior manager. "But accounting for intellectual assets in the same way year after year—that would just be boring."

Despite the skepticism, Edvinsson continued his mission, eventually developing a new measurement model called the Business Navigator. This tool tracked changes in performance ratios on five key dimensions:

- The financial focus which represented yesterday's performance;
- The customer focus, the human focus, and the process focus, which represented today's performance;
- The renewal and development focus, which represented tomorrow's performance.

Edvinsson pointed out, "What's interesting is to measure not just the numbers, but the changes—because direction is more important than precision. It is better to be roughly right than precisely wrong. That is why we call it navigation."

In 1993, Carendi announced that each AFS unit would begin to report quarterly performance according to intellectual capital measures along with the standard financial ones, and that both sets of data would be used in resource allocation and priority setting decisions. (See Exhibit 5 for its application in American Skandia.) Use of the measures soon started to spread outside AFS, and Skandia's top management team decided to make this a corporate-wide initiative. In 1994, Skandia became the first company in the world to publish a formal report on intellectual capital (IC), as a supplement to its annual report.

Managing Employees as Volunteers

Carendi's commitment to developing intellectual capital was reflected in his attitude to AFS employees: "All my assets are in their heads, yet they can walk away. If I want them to give me their best ideas and share their biggest dreams, I have to treat them as volunteers."

Carendi described his own role as having two key functions—coach of the team and agent of change. Far from seeing his job as sitting at the apex of the organization, he took on multiple jobs, infiltrating the organization at all levels. In addition to his job as head of AFS, he served as a member of the parent company's five-person executive committee (the Direktionen), as CEO of American Skandia, and as Board Chairman of AFS's holding companies: a continental company that controlled the Swiss, German, and Austrian group; a Mediterranean company that managed the Spanish and Italian groups; a South American company responsible for the group in Colombia; and an American company that controlled the U.S. and Mexican groups. (See Exhibit 6.) Describing himself as "a civil servant in his own organization," Carendi spent 90% of his time internally, and only 10% of his time on outside-focused activities. (However, he expected all of his company managers to be highly attuned to their external environments.) He traveled constantly, more than 200 days a year by his estimate, spending approximately 40% of his time in the United States, 30% in Sweden, and 30% in the rest of the world.

By taking on so many roles and traveling, Carendi believed he had to manage his various formal positions with a light hand, leaving lots of room for others. In a management style he described as "thrust and trust," he outlined the board priorities or thrust, then empowered people to take action. If someone raised an issue, he was likely to recall an old Swedish adage that if you asked a question you owned the question. When things went wrong, Carendi encouraged open discussion of the problems amongst

---

EXHIBIT 5   The AFS Business Navigator

Indicators of American Skandia Life

In this report we have decided to excerpt and illustrate a sampling of indicators for one of AFS's units, the U.S. operating unit American Skandia Life Assurance Corporation.

Since its start in 1989, American Skandia has seen gross premium volume rise to more than MSEK 10,240. The company is thus the 14th largest in the U.S. variable annuity market. The rate of development is high and has resulted in the launching of two to four significant new products or services a year.

Financial Focus

	1994	1993	1992
Return on net asset value	12.2%	24.3%	16.5%
Result of operations (MSEK)	115	96	19
Value added/empl. (SEK 000)	1,666	1,982	976

Comments: American Skandia's growth remains strong, despite slowing growth in the overall market.

Customer Focus

	1994	1993	1992
Number of contract	59,089	31,997	12,123
Savings/contract (SEK 000)	333	371	281
Surrender ratio	4.2%	3.6%	8.0%
Points of sale	11,573	4,805	2,768
Number of fund managers	19	11	8
Number of funds	52	35	24

Comments: American Skandia has a growing network of brokers, banks and fund managers. All of these have shown growth of about 100 percent since last year. This growth adds to American Skandia's structural capital.

Human Focus

	1994	1993	1992
Number of employees (full-time)	220	133	94
Number of managers	62	n.a.	n.a.
of whom, women	13	n.a.	n.a.
Training exp./employee (SEK 000)	9.8	10.6	4.0

Comments: American Skandia's work force has grown rapidly. Many new employees are young. 72 percent of the employees are under 40 years of age.

Process Focus

	1994	1993	1992
Contracts/employee	269	241	129
Adm. expense/gross premium	2.9%	2.6%	4.8%
PC/employee	1.3	1.4	1.1
IT expense/adm. expense	8.8%	4.7%	13.3%

Comments: An aggressive IT focus during the year has resulted in low administrative expenses despite a concurrent growth in volume.

(*continued*)

EXHIBIT 5   *(concluded)*

Renewal & Development Focus

	1994	1993	1992
Premium from new launches	11.1%	5.2%	49.7%
Increase in net premium	17.8%	204.8%	159.1%
Business development exp./ administrative expense	11.6%	9.8%	3.0%
Share of empl. below age 40	72%	74%	n.a.

Comments: American Skandia has sustained its rapid pace of growth and presence in a highly competitive total market. The rate of business development is very high, which has become a hallmark of American Skandia. The rate of renewal can be credited among other things to IT investments and the build-up of the federative structure

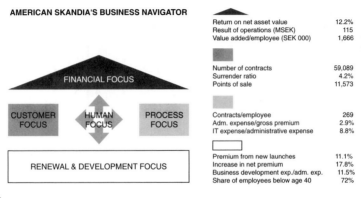

AMERICAN SKANDIA'S BUSINESS NAVIGATOR

Return on net asset value	12.2%
Result of operations (MSEK)	115
Value added/employee (SEK 000)	1,666

Number of contracts	59,089
Surrender ratio	4.2%
Points of sale	11,573

Contracts/employee	269
Adm. expense/gross premium	2.9%
IT expense/administrative expense	8.8%

Premium from new launches	11.1%
Increase in net premium	17.8%
Business development exp./adm. exp.	11.5%
Share of employees below age 40	72%

* n.a. = not available

Source: Skandia.

---

peers, giving rise to a culture in which people owned up to their errors and the lessons to be drawn from them. "As long as it's based on good faith and careful thinking, it's OK to make a mistake," he explained.

Carendi believed that this strong philosophy of delegation and learning by mistakes put a high premium on recruiting excellent people. "You hire the best people and leave them alone," he said. "If you're not going to leave them alone, you don't need to hire the best people." He often signed on people ahead of any defined need, as he did with Pehrsson, and let them poke around the organization until they

found a role. Viewing people selection as his greatest strength, Carendi retained the right to veto hiring decisions two levels below him. Beyond openness, honesty, willingness to question, and an ability to release the potential in others, he looked for personal "chemistry," asking himself "Would I like to have dinner with this person?"

Carendi also established a well-understood norm that "individuals had the responsibility to develop their own capabilities, and the company had the responsibility not to waste them." In keeping with that belief, people could volunteer to be on one of the numerous teams that were constantly being assembled

EXHIBIT 6 Skandia and AFS: Organizational Structure

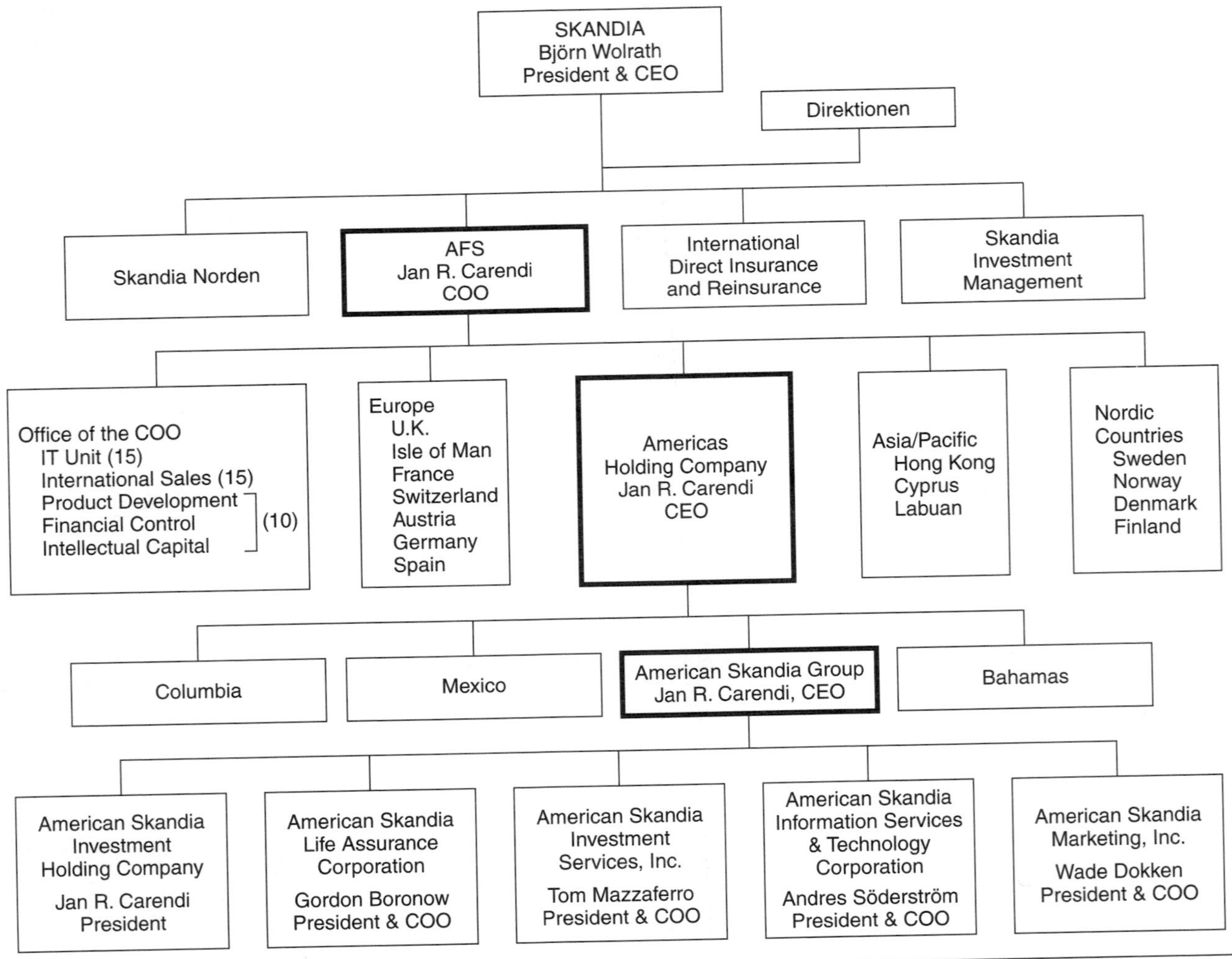

Source: Skandia.

in AFS, even if they were in areas outside their own expertise. When forming teams, managers typically sent out e-mail messages to relevant departments, and people nominated themselves. Before defining the final team, managers held an informal election among the nominees to get their input on who could best serve the team.

To fully utilize the potential of those he recruited, developed, and empowered, Carendi believed he had to maintain AFS's informal and entrepreneurial culture—one that was distinctly different from that of the parent company. "We are a tent in a palace pitched right on top of the Iranian carpet," he said. "When circumstances change, we just take our tent down and put it up somewhere else." Starting in 1992, Carendi began to formalize and communicate his ideas about how the organization should work in a series of "white papers" published in the internal newspaper. Among the key aspirations of the management model he wrote about were:

- A "high trust" culture characterized by shared values, transparent communications, and the encouragement for people to accept responsibility and take risk.
- A challenging work environment in which learning was driven by people pushing each other in open, honest disagreement.
- An organization built on identifying and improving processes that were unique to AFS, and could become a source of competitive differentiation.

Current Operations, New Challenges

As the functional units in some AFS companies began to adapt and apply IC measures into their front-line operations, the new structure, processes, and culture were affecting the way front-line managers made decisions.

Changes in American Skandia

After modifying the Business Navigator for his unit, Anders Söderström, the head of American Skandia's IT unit, discovered that he was not investing enough in training his employees in new rapidly changing technologies. (See Exhibit 7 for his unit's Business

EXHIBIT 7   The American Skandia IT Business Navigator

**AMERICAN SKANDIA'S
IT BUSINESS NAVIGATOR**

IT expense/administrative expense	19%
Value added*/IT-employees	117
Investments in IT	2,927
Number of internal IT customers	552
Number of external IT customers	14
Number of contracts/IT-employees	1,906
Corporate IT-literacy	+7%

IT capacity (CPU & DASD)		
AS/400	168,300 trans./hour	47 GB
PC/LAN	14,055 MIPS	199 GB
Change in IT inventory		3,639

IT development expense/IT expense	60%
IT expenses on training/IT expense	1%
R&D resources/total resources	5%

All amount in USD 000s.

*Change in IT inventory.

Source: Skandia.

Navigator.) "We noticed that our ratio of IT training expenses to IT expense was certainly lower than what we had planned, and lower relative to where we thought our competitors were," said Söderström. "The IC measures pointed me in exactly the opposite direction than the financial measures. While I was minimizing my expenses, I was putting at risk the knowledge and competence of my people at using current and future technologies to their fullest. The Business Navigator let me see that sometimes what looks good is bad, short-term thinking."

Other American Skandia units were doing likewise. The customer service area began to work on the customer focus dimension of the Navigator, developing measures and monitoring trends relating to the promptness and accuracy of responses to telephone requests from the wholesalers and brokers. It was piloting a project where, based on the results, representatives could win instant cash awards, based upon the performance of their customer service team. And in the marketing and sales department, management was trying to measure and monitor the development of customer capital. For instance, they started tracking number of brokers who wrote new business, or became inactive, each quarter, displaying the results on a bulletin board. Just by highlighting the data, they believed they made it manageable.

Reflecting his belief that "strategic ability begins and ends with serving the needs of the customer," Carendi urged the American Skandia marketing organization to redirect the bulk of systems development efforts towards meeting the needs of the company's key brokers and banks. At first, the focus was simply on providing them with excellent service and support. One initiative was the creation of a "concierge desk" to help brokers with whatever they needed: hotel reservations, lost credit cards, theater tickets. "Now the broker thinks of American Skandia when he has a problem to solve," said Carendi. "And the likelihood is that he will also think of us when he has business to write." At the same time, the customer-service function was reorganized into teams with the objective of providing personal service and building lifetime relationships with their assigned brokers and wholesalers. Carendi also invested in the professional development of his sales partners, establishing a Leaders College offering bimonthly sessions in an array of financial and professional development topics.

Envisioning a day when a broker would provide much greater perceived value to the client by filtering and interpreting the confusing amount of information in the marketplace, American Skandia developed a PC-based software product called ASSESS. Launched in 1994, ASSESS helped brokers become experts on 35 different investment

options by providing access to a variety of data sources, including analyst reports, stock listings, and standard indices. It also included an in-depth on-line questionnaire that helped the broker understand the client's needs, and educate them about the relationship of risk and return and the benefits of long-term investing. The software, which was mailed free to 20,000 brokers in the United States, freed them of tedious administrative tasks and allowed them to spend more time advising the client—addressing questions, completing paperwork, and closing the deal right away, rather than weeks later when interest might have cooled off.

To reduce the rate of turnover in its sales networks, American Skandia's sales and marketing division also made a sizable investment in creating a database on 250,000 brokers. The largest such repository in the industry, the database tracked by broker, the types of annuities sold, the commission structure, annual sales, and even the type of software each preferred. The area was also developing systems ranging from one that that signaled a slowdown in a broker's underwriting activity, predicted the need for support, and even sent out automatic thank-yous. "I want to create a process where we're communicating and building an emotional tie with the broker," said the subsidiary's marketing chief Dokken. "I want to make him think twice about leaving us."

Staying Ahead

Despite AFS's successful growth, Carendi was continually trying to identify and test strategic opportunities—what he described as a "dress rehearsal for the future." Recognizing that the world was becoming too complex and dynamic for him to develop clear foresight alone, he began more aggressively tapping into the ideas of his employees who were not only closer to the market, but also knew more about AFS and its capabilities. The more he thought about it, the more Carendi wanted to structure a formal process around future scanning. To help him implement, he enlisted the help of his Director of Intellectual Capital, Edvinsson.

Edvinsson hand-picked a pilot team of nine people from the United States, the United Kingdom,

Colombia, Germany, and Sweden, deliberately focusing on AFS's "Generation X," the twenty-somethings who were the seed corn of the future leadership. He gave them a full-time three-month assignment to develop scenarios of the future for the company and the industry and to be prepared to present their conclusions to the company's Strategic Advisory Board (SAB). After an initial brainstorming session, the team settled on four areas of investigation: the customer, the "Egonomy" (economy at both the personal and macro levels), corporate reality (AFS's resources and constraints), and "valutics," (political systems and national values).

After weeks of intensive reading and discussion to flesh out their ideas, the team made their presentation to the SAB in Stockholm. The Generation Xers foresaw a future in which the customer would be more knowledgeable, have access to information at any time and any place, and demand product flexibility to fit their fast-paced and changing lifestyles. "We will have to offer a totally customized product," said one member of the team. "In other words, there will be no product. There will be as many products as there are clients. The client will be the creator." They then challenged senior managers to accept their scenarios at face value, and to come up with the best response for AFS. The Generation X team and the SAB then compared notes and were surprised at how convergent their ideas were—with one major exception. While the generation Xers could foresee a fragmented market undermining AFS's carefully designed network, top management believed that there was still value to be added by brokers because they made clients aware of the need for financial planning.

With the success of the pilot attempt in 1995, Carendi supported and enlarged the concept of future scanning through the creation of the Skandia Future Centers (SFC) division, appointing Edvinsson in charge. The Centers would act as a meeting place and "greenhouse" for dialog and collaboration. The first iteration created five "future teams," each composed of five full-time members drawn from three populations—the "in power" generation, the "potential" generation, and "Generation X." The groups would meet over several months, convening frequently for a day or two to discuss their assigned issues—the future of information technology, organization and leadership, changing demographics, changes in the insurance market, and the future of the world economy. In addition, the groups would invite "rolodex groups" of outside experts to present their perspectives on broad conceptual issues in a variety of fields related or not to insurance and financial services. The knowledge gained would be shared throughout the organization via the GAN. The first future center was to be inaugurated near Stockholm in May 1996, and other locations were planned.

Current Issues

In 1996, AFS was a worldwide organization, with an impressive array performance statistics. Despite a downturn in 1995, premium income had grown 45% annually during the past five years. Between 1992 and 1995, its customer base had grown from 100,000 to 785,000, its alliance network of brokers, fund managers, and other partners had expanded from 15,000 to 46,000, and its employee base had expanded from 1,130 to 1,700. With only one out of twenty-seven people working for it on its payroll, some began to describe AFS as a "virtual corporation." By its own estimate, the company's network-based organization and its use of cutting-edge information technology had reduced its administrative costs to one-third those of its competitors.

Yet, despite these accomplishments, Carendi was focused on how to defend and improve AFS's position as a leader in its chosen business. Many of AFS's practices were now being imitated widely as other companies built cooperative alliances for money management and distribution. Still others had released their own versions of the ASSESS software, and cloned AFS's products. Furthermore, deregulation had lowered barriers to entry into the market, and most major mutual fund families now offered annuity insurance products. All of this meant that customer loyalty was eroding. As Carendi explained:

> Competition could come from anywhere. Today, we compete with mutual funds. Tomorrow, we are going to compete with software houses. . . .

Consumers couldn't care less about established relationships today if they can get it cheaper elsewhere, and at the time of day that suits their schedule rather than when the banker or broker's office is open.

Carendi was particularly intrigued by the ideas generated by the "Generation X" pilot team's future scenario in which potential policyholders would buy insurance very differently than they did in the past. Was the AFS model he had so carefully constructed still viable? if not, how should it be changed? And how should such profound decisions be made?

Case 6–3   McKinsey & Company: Managing Knowledge and Learning

In April 1996, halfway through his first three-year term as managing director of McKinsey & Company, Rajat Gupta was feeling quite proud as he flew out of Bermuda, site of the firm's second annual Practice Olympics. He had just listened to twenty teams outlining innovative new ideas they had developed out of recent project work, and, like his fellow senior partner judges, Gupta had come away impressed by the intelligence and creativity of the firm's next generation of consultants.

But there was another thought that kept coming back to the 47-year-old leader of this highly successful $1.8 billion consulting firm (see Exhibit 1 for a twenty-year growth history). If this represented the tip of McKinsey's knowledge and expertise iceberg, how well was the firm doing in developing, capturing, and leveraging this asset in service of its clients worldwide? In his mind, the task of knowledge development had become much more complex over the past decade or so due to three intersecting forces. First, in an increasingly information and knowledge-driven age, the sheer volume and rate of change of new knowledge made the task much more complex; second, clients' ex-

pectations of and need for leading-edge expertise were constantly increasing; and third, the firm's own success had made it much more difficult to link and leverage the knowledge and expertise represented by 3,800 consultants in 69 offices worldwide. Although the Practice Olympics was only one of several initiatives he had championed, Gupta wondered if it was enough, particularly in light of his often stated belief that "knowledge is the lifeblood of McKinsey."

The Founders' Legacy[1]

Founded in 1926 by University of Chicago professor, James ("Mac") McKinsey, the firm of "accounting and engineering advisors" that bore his name grew rapidly. Soon Mac began recruiting experienced executives and training them in the integrated approach he called his General Survey outline. In Saturday morning sessions he would lead consultants through an "undeviating sequence" of analysis—goals, strategy, policies, organization, facilities, procedures, and personnel—while still encouraging them to synthesize data and think for themselves.

This case was prepared by Prof. Christopher A. Bartlett.

Copyright © 1996 by the President and Fellows of Harvard College. Harvard Business School case 396–357.

[1]The Founders' Legacy section draws on Amar V. Bhide, "Building the Professional Firm: McKinsey & Co., 1939–1968," HBS Working Paper 95–010.

EXHIBIT 1 McKinsey & Company: 20-Year Growth Indicators

Year	Number Office Locations	Number Active Engagements	Number of CSS*	Number of MGMs[†]
1975	24	661	529	NA
1980	31	771	744	NA
1985	36	1823	1248	NA
1990	47	2789	2465	348
1991	51	2875	2653	395
1992	55	2917	2875	399
1993	60	3142	3122	422
1994	64	3398	3334	440
1995	69	3559	3817	472

*CSS = Client Service Staff (All professional consulting staff)
[†]MGM = Management Group Members (Partners and directors)

Source: Internal McKinsey & Company documents.

In 1932, Mac recruited Marvin Bower, a bright young lawyer with a Harvard MBA, and within two years asked him to become manager of the recently opened New York office. Convinced that he had to upgrade the firm's image in an industry typically regarded as "efficiency experts" or "business doctors," Bower undertook to imbue in his associates the sense of professionalism he had experienced in his time in a law partnership. In a 1937 memo, he outlined his vision for the firm as one focused on issues of importance to top-level management, adhering to the highest standards of integrity, professional ethics, and technical excellence, able to attract and develop young men of outstanding qualifications, and committed to continually raising its stature and influence. Above all, it was to be a firm dedicated to the mission of serving its clients superbly well.

Over the next decade, Bower worked tirelessly to influence his partners and associates to share his vision. As new offices opened, he became a strong advocate of the One Firm policy that required all consultants to be recruited and advanced on a firm-wide basis, clients to be treated as McKinsey & Company responsibilities, and profits to be shared from a firm pool, not an office pool. And through dinner seminars, he began upgrading the size and

quality of McKinsey's clients. In the 1945 New Engagement Guide, he articulated a policy that every assignment should bring the firm something more than revenue—experience or prestige, for example.

Elected Managing Partner in 1950, Bower led his ten partners and 74 associates to initiate a series of major changes that turned McKinsey into an elite consulting firm unable to meet the demand for its services. Each client's problems were seen as unique, but Bower and his colleagues firmly believed that well-trained, highly intelligent generalists could quickly grasp the issue, and through disciplined analysis find its solution. The firm's extraordinary domestic growth through the 1950s provided a basis for international expansion that accelerated the rate of growth in the 1960s. Following the opening of the London Office in 1959, offices in Geneva, Amsterdam, Düsseldorf, and Paris followed quickly. By the time Bower stepped down as Managing Director in 1967, McKinsey was a well-established and highly respected presence in Europe and North America.

A Decade of Doubt

Although leadership succession was well planned and executed, within a few years, the McKinsey growth engine seemed to stall. The economic turmoil of the oil crisis, the slowing of the division-alization process that had fueled the European expansion, the growing sophistication of client management, and the appearance of new focused competitors like Boston Consulting Group (BCG) all contributed to the problem. Almost overnight, McKinsey's enormous reservoir of internal self-confidence and even self-satisfaction began to turn to self-doubt and self-criticism.

Commission on Firm Aims and Goals

Concerned   that the slowing growth in Europe and the U.S. was more than just a cyclical market downturn, the firm's partners assigned a committee of their most respected peers to study the problem and make recommendations. In April 1971, the Commission on Firm Aims and Goals concluded that the firm has been growing too fast. The authors bluntly reported, "Our preoccupation with the geographic expansion and new practice possibilities has caused us to neglect the development of our technical and professional skills." The report concluded that McKinsey had been too willing to accept routine assignments from marginal clients, that the quality of work done was uneven, and that while its consultants were excellent generalist problem solvers, they often lacked the deep industry knowledge or the substantive specialized expertise that clients were demanding.

One of the Commission's central proposals was that the firm had to recommit itself to the continuous development of its members. This meant that growth would have to be slowed and that the MGM-to-associate ratio be reduced from 7 to 1 back to 5 or 6 to 1. It further proposed that emphasis be placed on the development of what it termed "T-Shaped" consultants—those who supplemented a broad generalist perspective with an in-depth industry or functional specialty.

Practice Development Initiative

When Ron Daniel was elected Managing Director in 1976—the fourth to hold the position since Bower had stepped down nine years earlier—McKinsey was still struggling to meet the challenges laid out in the Commission's report. As the head of the New York office since 1970, Daniel had experienced first hand the rising expectations of increasingly sophisticated clients and the aggressive challenges of new competitors like BCG. In contrast to McKinsey's local office-based model of "client relationship" consulting, BCG began competing on the basis of "thought leadership" from a highly concentrated resource base in Boston. Using some simple but powerful tools, such as the experience curve and the growth-share matrix, BCG began to make strong inroads into the strategy-consulting market. As McKinsey began losing both clients and recruits to BCG, Daniel became convinced that his firm could no longer succeed pursuing its generalist model.

One of his first moves was to appoint one of the firm's most respected and productive senior partners as McKinsey's first full-time director of training. As an expanded commitment to developing consultants' skills and expertise became the norm, the executive committee began debating the need to formally updating the firm's long-standing mission to reflect the firm's core commitment not only to serving its clients but also to developing its consultants. (Exhibit 2.)

But Daniel also believed some structural changes were necessary. Building on an initiative he and his colleagues had already implemented in the New York office, he created industry-based Clientele Sectors in consumer products, banking, industrial goods, insurance, and so on, cutting across the geographic offices that remained the primary organizational entity. He also encouraged more formal development of the firm's functional expertise in areas like strategy, organization and operations where knowledge and experience were widely diffused and minimally codified. However, many—including Marvin Bower—expressed concern that any move towards a product-driven approach could damage McKinsey's distinctive advantage of local presence which gave partners strong connections with the business community, allowed teams to work on site with clients and facilitated implementation. It was an approach that they felt contrasted sharply with the "fly in, fly out" model of expert-based consulting.

EXHIBIT 2   McKinsey's Mission and Guiding
Principles (1996)

McKinsey Mission

To help our clients make positive, lasting, and
    substantial improvements in their performance and to
    build a great Firm that is able to attract, develop,
    excite, and retain exceptional people.

Guiding Principles

Serving Clients

Adhere to professional standards

Follow the top management approach

Assist the client in implementation and capability
    building

Perform consulting in a cost-effective manner

Building The Firm

Operate as one Firm

Maintain a meritocracy

Show a genuine concern for our people

Foster an open and nonhierarchical working atmosphere

Manage the Firm's resources responsibly

Being a Member of the Professional Staff

Demonstrate commitment to client service

Strive continuously for superior quality

Advance the state-of-the-art management

Contribute a spirit of partnership through teamwork
    and collaboration

Profit from the freedom and assume the responsibility
    associated with self-governance

Uphold the obligation to dissent

Nonetheless, Daniel pressed ahead, and the industry sectors quickly found a natural client base.
Feeling that functional expertise needed more attention, he assembled working groups to develop
knowledge in two areas that were at the heart of
McKinsey's practice—strategy and organization.
To head up the first group, he named Fred Gluck, a
director in the New York office who had been out-

spoken in urging the firm to modify its traditional
generalist approach. In June 1977, Gluck invited a
"Super Group" of younger partners with strategy
expertise to a three-day meeting to share ideas and
develop an agenda for the strategy practice. One described the meeting:

> We had three days of unmitigated chaos. Someone
> from New York would stand up and present a
> four-box matrix. A partner from London would
> present a nine-box matrix. A German would
> present a 47-box matrix. It was chaos . . .). but at
> the end of the third day some strands of thought
> were coming together.

At the same time, Daniel asked Bob Waterman
who had been working on a Siemens-sponsored
study of "excellent companies" and Jim Bennett, a
respected senior partner to assemble a group that
could articulate the firm's existing knowledge in the
organization arena. One of their first recruits was an
innovative young Ph.D. in organizational theory
named Tom Peters.

Revival and Renewal

By the early 1980s, with growth resuming, a cautious optimism returned to McKinsey for the first
time in almost a decade.

Centers of Competence

Recognizing that the activities of the two practice
development projects could not just be a one-time
effort, in 1980 Daniel asked Gluck to join the central small group that comprised the Firm Office and
focus on the knowledge-building agenda that had
become his passion. Ever since his arrival at the firm
from Bell Labs in 1967, Gluck had wanted to bring
an equally stimulating intellectual environment to
McKinsey. Against some strong internal resistance,
he set out to convert his partners to his strongly held
beliefs—that knowledge development had to be a
central, not a peripheral firm activity; that it needed
to be ongoing and institutionalized, not temporary
and project based; and that it had to be the responsibility of everyone, not just a few.

As one key means of bringing this about, he created 15 Centers of Competence (virtual centers, not

locations) built around existing areas of functional expertise like marketing, change management, and systems. In a 1982 memo to all partners, he described the role of these centers as twofold: to help develop consultants and to ensure the continued renewal of the firm's intellectual resources. For each Center, Gluck identified one or two highly motivated, recognized experts in the particular field and named them practice leaders. The expectation was that these leaders would assemble from around the firm, a core group of partners who were active in the practice area and interested in contributing to its development. (See Exhibit 3 for the 15 Centers and 11 Sectors in 1983.)

To help build a shared body of knowledge, the leadership of each of the 15 centers began to initiate a series of activities primarily involving the core group and less frequently, the members of the practice network. A colleague commented on his commitment to establishing the centers:

> Unlike industry sectors, the centers of competence did not have a natural, stable client base, and Fred had to work hard to get them going. . . . He basically told the practice leaders, "Spend whatever

you can—the cost is almost irrelevant compared to the payoff." There was no attempt to filter or manage the process, and the effect was "to let a thousand flowers bloom."

Gluck also spent a huge amount of time trying to change an internal status hierarchy based largely on the size and importance of one's client base. Arguing that practice development ("snowball making" as it became known internally) was not less "macho" than client development ("snowball throwing"), he tried to convince his colleagues that everyone had to become snowball makers *and* snowball throwers. In endless discussions, he would provoke his colleagues with barbed pronouncements and personal challenges: "Knowing what you're talking about is not necessarily a client service handicap" or "Would you want your brain surgery done by a general practitioner?"

Building a Knowledge Infrastructure

As the firm's new emphasis on individual consultant training took hold and the Clientele Sectors and Centers of Competence began to generate new insights, many began to feel the need to capture and

---

EXHIBIT 3   McKinsey's Emerging Practice Areas: Centers of Competence and Industry Sectors, 1983

Centers of Competence	*Clientele Sectors*
Building institutional skills	Automotive
Business management unit	Banking
Change management	Chemicals
Corporate leadership	Communications and information
Corporate finance	Consumer products
Diagnostic scan	Electronics
International management	Energy
Integrated logistics	Health care
Manufacturing	Industrial goods
Marketing	Insurance
Microeconomics	Steel
Sourcing	
Strategic management	
Systems	
Technology	

leverage the learning. Although big ideas had occasionally been written up as articles for publication in newspapers, magazines, or journals like *Harvard Business Review,* there was still a deep-seated suspicion of anything that smacked of packaging ideas or creating proprietary concepts.

This reluctance to document concepts had long constrained the internal transfer of ideas and the vast majority of internally developed knowledge was never captured.

This began to change with the launching of the McKinsey Staff Paper series in 1978, and by the early 1980s the firm was actively encouraging its consultants to publish their key findings. The initiative got a major boost with the publication in 1982 of two major best-sellers, Peters and Waterman's *In Search of Excellence* and Kenichi Ohmae's *The Mind of the Strategist*. But books, articles, and staff papers required major time investments, and only a small minority of consultants made the effort to write them. Believing that the firm had to lower the barrier to internal knowledge communication, Gluck introduced the idea of Practice Bulletins, two-page summaries of important new ideas that identified the experts who could provide more detail. A partner elaborated:

> The Bulletins were essentially internal advertisements for ideas and the people who had developed them. We tried to convince people that they would help build their personal networks and internal reputations. . . . Fred was not at all concerned that the quality was mixed, and had a strong philosophy of letting the internal market sort out what were the really big ideas.

Believing that the firm's organizational infrastructure needed major overhaul, in 1987 Gluck launched a Knowledge Management Project. After five months of study, the team made three recommendations. First, the firm had to make a major commitment to build a common database of knowledge accumulated from client work and developed in the practice areas. Second, to ensure that the databases were maintained and used, they proposed that each practice area (Clientele Sector and Competence Center) hire a full-time practice coordinator who could act as an "intelligent switch" responsible for monitoring the quality of the data and for helping consultants access the relevant information. And finally, they suggested that the firm expand its hiring practices and promotion policies to create a career path for deep functional specialists whose narrow expertise would not fit the normal profile of a T-shaped consultant.

The task of implementing these recommendations fell to a team led by Bill Matassoni, the firm's director of communications and Brook Manville, a newly recruited Yale Ph.D. with experience with electronic publishing. Focusing first on the Firm Practice Information System (FPIS), a computerized database of client engagements, they installed new systems and procedures to make the data more complete, accurate, and timely so that it could be accessed as a reliable information resource, not just an archival record. More difficult was the task of capturing the knowledge that had accumulated in the practice areas since much of it had not been formalized and none of it had been prioritized or integrated. To create a computer-based Practice Development Network (PDNet), Matassoni and Manville put huge energy into begging, cajoling, and challenging each practice to develop and submit documents that represented their core knowledge. After months of work, they had collected the 2,000 documents that they believed provided the critical mass to launch PDNet.

Matassoni and his team also developed another information resource that had not been part of the study team's recommendations. They assembled a listing of all firm experts and key document titles by practice area and published it in a small book, compact enough to fit in any consultant's briefcase. The Knowledge Resource Directory (KRD) became the McKinsey Yellow Pages and found immediate and widespread use firm-wide. Although the computerized databases were slow to be widely adopted, the KRD found almost immediate enthusiastic acceptance.

Making the new practice coordinator's position effective proved more challenging. Initially, these roles were seen as little more than glorified librarians. It took several years before the new roles were filled by individuals (often ex-consultants) who were sufficiently respected that they could not only act as consultants to those seeking information about their area of expertise, but also were able to impose the discipline necessary to maintain and build the practice's databases.

Perhaps the most difficult task was to legitimize the role of a new class of consultants—the specialist. The basic concept was that a professional could make a career in McKinsey by emphasizing specialized knowledge development rather than the broad-based problem-solving skills and client development orientation that were deeply embedded in the firm's value system. While several consultants with deep technical expertise in specialties like market research, finance, or steel making were recruited, most found it hard to assimilate into the mainstream. The firm seemed uncomfortable about how to evaluate, compensate, or promote these individuals, and many either became isolated or disaffected. Nonetheless, the partnership continued to support the notion of a specialist promotion track and continued to struggle with how to make it work.

Matassoni reflected on the changes:

> The objective of the infrastructure changes was not so much to create a new McKinsey as to keep the old "one firm" concept functioning as we grew . . . Despite all the talk of computerized databases, the knowledge management process still relied heavily on personal networks, old practices like cross-office transfers, and strong "One Firm" norms like helping other consultants when they called. And at promotion time, nobody reviewed your PD documents. They looked at how you used your internal networks to have your ideas make an impact on clients.

Managing Success

By the late 1980s, the firm was expanding rapidly again. In 1988, the same year Fred Gluck was elected managing director, new offices were opened in Rome, Helsinki, São Paulo, and Minneapolis bringing the total to 41. From the partners'

perspective, however, enhancing McKinsey's reputation as a thought leader was at least as important as attracting new business.

Refining Knowledge Management

After being elected MD, Gluck delegated the practice development role he had played since 1980 to a newly constituted Clientele and Professional Development Committee (CPDC). When Ted Hall took over leadership of this committee in late 1991, he felt there was a need to adjust the firm's knowledge development focus. He commented:

> By the early 1990s, too many people were seeing practice development as the creation of experts and the generation of documents in order to build our reputation. But knowledge is only valuable when it is between the ears of consultants and applied to clients' problems. Because it is less effectively developed through the disciplined work of a few than through the spontaneous interaction of many, we had to change the more structured "discover-codify-disseminate" model to a looser and more inclusive "engage-explore-apply-share" approach. In other words, we shifted our focus from developing knowledge to building individual and team capability.

Over the years, Gluck's philosophy "to let 1,000 flowers bloom" had resulted in the original group of 11 sectors and 15 centers expanding to become what Hall called "72 islands of activity," (Sectors, Centers, Working Groups, and Special Projects) many of which were perceived as fiefdoms dominated by one or two established experts. In Hall's view, the garden of 1,000 flowers needed weeding, a task requiring a larger group of mostly different gardeners. The CPDC began integrating the diverse groups into seven sectors and seven functional capability groups (see Exhibit 4). These sectors and groups were led by teams of five to seven partners (typically younger directors and principals) with the objective of replacing the leader-driven knowledge creation and dissemination process with a "stewardship model" of self-governing practices focused on competence building.

EXHIBIT 4   Group Framework for Sectors and Centers

Functional Capability Groups	*Clientele Industry Sectors*
Corporate Governance and Leadership	*Financial Institutions*
Corporate organization	Banking
Corporate management processes	Insurance
Corporate strategy development	Health care payor/provider
Corporate relationship design and management	
Corporate finance	*Consumer*
Post-merger management	Retailing
	Consumer industries
Organization (OPP/MOVE)	Media
Corporate transformation design and leadership	Pharmaceuticals
Energizing approaches	
Organization design and development	
Leadership and teams	*Energy*
Engaging teams	Electrical utilities
	Petroleum
	Natural gas
	Other energy
Information Technology/Systems	
To be determined	
	Basic Materials
Marketing	Steel
Market research	Pulp and paper
Sales force management	Chemicals
Channel management	Other basic materials
Global marketing	
Pricing	*Aerospace, Electronics, and Telecom*
Process and sector support	Telecom
	Electronics
	Aerospace
Operations Effectiveness	
Integrated logistics	*Transportation*
Manufacturing	
Purchasing and supply management	*Automotive, Assembly, and Machinery*
	Automotive
Strategy	Assembly
Strategy	
Microeconomics	
Business dynamics	
Business planning processes	
Cross-Functional Management	
Innovation	
Customer satisfaction	
Product/technology development and commercialization	
Core process redesign	

Source: Internal McKinsey & Company document.

Client Impact

With responsibility for knowledge management delegated to the CPDC, Gluck began to focus on a new theme—client impact. On being elected managing director, he made this a central theme in his early speeches, memos, and his first All Partners Conference. He also created a Client Impact Committee, and asked it to explore the ways in which the firm could ensure that the expertise it was developing created positive measurable results in each client engagement.

One of the most important initiatives of the new committee was to persuade the partners to redefine the firm's key consulting unit from the engagement team (ET) to the client service team (CST). The traditional ET, assembled to deliver a three- or four-month assignment for a client was a highly efficient and flexible unit, but it tended to focus on the immediate task rather than on the client's long-term need. The CST concept was that the firm could add long-term value and increase the effectiveness of individual engagements if it could unite a core of individuals (particularly at the partner level) who were linked across multiple ETs, and commit them to working with the client over an extended period. The impact was to broaden the classic model of a single partner "owning" a client to a group of partners with shared commitment to each client.

Although client impact studies indicated the new structure led to a longer-term focus and deeper understanding of issues, it also raised some concerns. Some felt that the new approach biased resource allocation to the largest clients with the biggest CSTs. Others felt that CSTs tended to be more insular, guarding proprietary concepts and reaching out less often for firm-wide knowledge.

The latter concern in part reflected changes in the locus of knowledge development being advocated by CPDC. In response to concerns within the partnership about a gradual decline in associates' involvement in intellectual capital development, the CPDC began to emphasize the need for CSTs to play a central role in the intellectual life of McKinsey. (See Exhibit 5 for a CPDC conceptualization.) Be-

---

EXHIBIT 5   CPDC Proposed Organizational Relationships

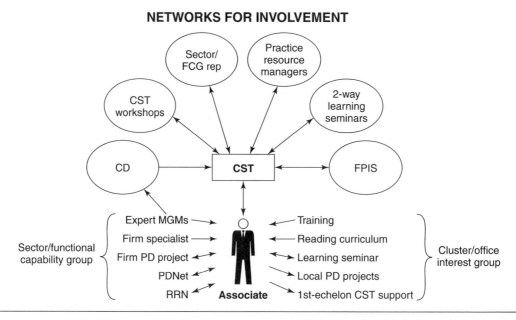

Source: Internal CPDC presentation.

lieving that the CSTs (by 1993 about 200 firm-wide) represented the real learning laboratories, the CPDC sent memos to the new industry sector and capability group leaders advising them that their practices would be evaluated by their coverage of the firm's CSTs. They also wrote to all consultants emphasizing the importance of the firm's intellectual development and their own professional development, for which they had primary responsibility. Finally, they assembled data on the amount of time consultants were spending on practice and professional development by office, distributing the widely divergent results to partners in offices worldwide.

Developing Multiple Career Paths

Despite (or perhaps because of) all these changes, the specialist consultant model continued to struggle. Over the years, the evaluation criteria for the specialist career path had gradually converged with the mainstream generalist promotion criteria. For example, the specialist's old promotion standard of "world-class expertise" in a particular field had given way to a more pragmatic emphasis on client impact; the notion of a legitimate role as a consultant to teams had evolved to a need for specialists to be "engagement director capable"; and the less pressured evaluation standard of "grow or go" was replaced by the normal associate's more demanding "up or out" requirement, albeit within a slightly more flexible timeframe.

Although these changes had reduced the earlier role dissonance—specialists become more T shaped—it also diluted the original objective, and in late 1992 the Professional Personnel Committee decided to create two new career paths for client service support and administrative (CSSA) staff:

- The first reaffirmed a path to partnership for practice-dedicated specialists who built credibility with clients and CSTs through their specialized knowledge and its expert application. Their skills would have them in high demand as consultants to teams (CDs) rather than as engagement directors (EDs).
- The second new option was the practice management track designed to provide a career progression for practice coordinators, who had a key role in transferring knowledge and in helping practice leaders manage increasingly complex networks. Valuable administrators could also be promoted on this track.

Despite the announcement of the new criteria and promotion processes, amongst associates and specialists alike there was still a good deal of skepticism and confusion about the viability of the specialist track to partnership. (See Exhibit 6 for an overview comparison.)

Throughout the period of change, Gluck kept returning to his long-term theme that, "it's all about people." He said:

> There are two ways to look at McKinsey. The most common way is that we are a client service firm whose primary purpose is to serve the companies seeking our help. That is legitimate. But I believe there is an even more powerful way for us to see ourselves. We should begin to view our primary purpose as building a great institution that becomes an engine for producing highly motivated world-class people who in turn will serve our clients extraordinarily well.

Knowledge Management on the Front

To see how McKinsey's evolving knowledge management processes were being felt by those on the firm's front lines, we will follow the activities of three consultants working in three diverse locations and focused on three different agendas.

Jeff Peters and the Sydney Office Assignment

John Stuckey, a director in McKinsey's Sydney office, felt great satisfaction at being invited to bid for a financial services growth strategy study for one of Australia's most respected companies. Yet the opportunity also created some challenges. As in most small or medium sized offices, most consultants in Sydney were generalists. Almost all with financial industry expertise had been "conflicted out" of the project due to work they had done for competing financial institutions in Australia.

Stuckey immediately began using his personal network to find how he might tap into McKinsey's

EXHIBIT 6   Alternative Career Path Focus and Criteria

Career Paths/Roles			
CSS Paths		CSSA Paths	
General Consulting	*Specialized Consulting*	*Practice Expertise*	*Practice Management Administration*
Focus			
Perform general problem solving and lead implementation	Apply in-depth practice knowledge to studies	Leverage practice knowledge across studies	Codify and transfer knowledge
Develop client relationships	Develop client relationships	Create new knowledge	Help administer practice
	Build external reputation		

Source: Internal McKinsey & Company presentation.

worldwide resources for someone who could lead this first engagement for an important new client. After numerous phone calls and some lobbying at a directors' conference he identified Jeff Peters, a Boston-based senior engagement manager and veteran of more than 20 studies for financial institutions. The only problem was that Peters had two ongoing commitments that would make him unavailable for at least the first six weeks of the Australian assignment.

Meanwhile, Stuckey and Ken Gibson, his engagement director on the project, were working with the Sydney office staffing coordinator to identify qualified, available, and nonconflicted associates to complete the team. Balancing assignments of over 80 consultants to 25 ongoing teams was a complex process that involved matching the needs of the engagement and the individual consultants' development requirements. A constant flow of consultants across offices helped buffer constraints, and also contributed to the transfer of knowledge. At any one time 15 to 25 Australian consultants were on short- or long-term assignments abroad, while another 10 to 15 consultants from other offices were working in

Australia. (Firm-wide, nearly 20% of work was performed by consultants on inter-office loans.)

They identified a three-person team to work with Peters. John Peacocke was a New Zealand army engineer with an MBA in finance from Wharton and two years of experience in McKinsey. Although he had served on a four-month study for a retail bank client in Cleveland, since returning to Australia he had worked mostly for oil and gas clients. Patty Akopianz was a one-year associate who had worked in investment banking before earning an MBA at Harvard. Her primary interest and her developing expertise was in consumer marketing. The business analyst was Jonathan Liew, previously an actuary who was embarking on his first McKinsey assignment.

With Peters' help, Stuckey and Gibson also began assembling a group of internal specialists and experts who could act as consulting directors (CDs) to the team. James Gorman, a personal financial services expert in New York agreed to visit Sydney for a week and to be available for weekly conference calls; Majid Arab, an insurance industry specialist committed to a two-week visit and a similar "on-call" availability; Andrew Doman, a London-based financial industry expert also signed on as a CD. Within the Sydney office, Charles Conn, a leader in the firm's growth strategies practice, agreed to lend his expertise, as did Clem Doherty, a firm leader in the impact of technology.

With Gibson acting more as an engagement manager than an engagement director, the team began scanning the Knowledge Resource Directory, the FPIS and the PDNet for leads. (Firm-wide, the use of PDNet documents had boomed in the eight years since its introduction. By early 1996, there were almost 12,000 documents on PDNet, with over 2,000 being requested each month.) In all, they tracked down 179 relevant PD documents and tapped into the advice and experience of over 60 firm members worldwide. A team member explained:

> Ken was acting as EM, but he was not really an expert in financial services, so we were even more reliant than usual on the internal network. Some of the ideas we got off PDNet were helpful, but the trail of contacts was much more valuable . . . Being on a completely different time zone had great advantages. If you hit a wall at the end of the day, you could drop messages in a dozen voicemail boxes in Europe and the United States. Because the firm norm is that you respond to requests by colleagues, by morning you would have seven or eight new suggestions, data sources, or leads.

At the end of the first phase, the team convened an internal workshop designed to keep client management informed, involved, and committed to the emerging conclusions. Out of this meeting, the team was focused on seven core beliefs and four viable options that provided its agenda for the next phase of the project. It was at this point that Peters was able to join the team:

> By the time I arrived, most of the hard analysis had been done and they had been able to narrow the focus from the universe to four core options in just over a month. It was very impressive how they had been able to do that with limited team-based expertise and a demanding client. . . . With things going so well, my main priority was to focus the team on the end product. Once we got a clear logical outline, I

assigned tasks and got out of the way. Most of my time I spent working on the client relationship . . . It was great learning for John and Patty, and both of them were ready to take on a management role in their next engagements.

In November, the team presented its conclusions to the board, and after some tough questioning and challenging, they accepted the recommendations and began an implementation process. The client's managing director reflected on the outcome:

> We're a tough client, but I would rate their work as very good. Their value added was in their access to knowledge, the intellectual rigor they bring, and their ability to build understanding and consensus among a diverse management group . . . If things don't go ahead now, it's our own fault.

John Stuckey had a little different post-engagement view of the result:

> Overall, I think we did pretty good work, but I was a bit disappointed we didn't come up with a radical breakthrough. . . . We leveraged the firm's knowledge base effectively, but I worry that we rely so much on our internal expertise. We have to beware of the trap that many large successful companies have fallen into by becoming too introverted, too satisfied with their own view of the world.

Warwick Bray and European Telecoms

After earning his MBA at Melbourne University, Warwick Bray joined McKinsey's Melbourne office in 1989. A computer science major, he had worked as a systems engineer at Hewlett Packard and wanted to leverage his technological experience. For two of his first three years, he worked on engagements related to the impact of deregulation on the Asia-Pacific telecommunications industry. In early 1992, Bray advised his group development leader (his assigned mentor and adviser) that he would be interested in spending a year in London. After several phone discussions the transfer was arranged, and in March the young Australian found himself on his first European team.

From his experience on the Australian telecom projects, Bray had written a PD document, "Negotiating Interconnect," which he presented at the firm's annual worldwide telecom conference. Recognizing this developing "knowledge spike," Michael Patsalos-Fox, telecom practice leader in London, invited Bray to work with him on a study. Soon he was being called in as a deregulation expert to make presentations to various client executives. "In McKinsey you have to earn that right," said Bray. "For me it was immensely satisfying to be recognized as an expert."

Under the leadership of Patsalos-Fox, the telecom practice had grown rapidly in the United Kingdom. With deregulation spreading across the continent in the 1990s, however, he was becoming overwhelmed by the demands for his help. Beginning in the late 1980s, Patsalos-Fox decided to stop acting as the sole repository for and exporter of European telecom information and expertise, and start developing a more interdependent network. To help in this task, he appointed Sulu Soderstrom, a Stanford MBA with a strong technology background, as full-time practice coordinator. Over the next few years she played a key role in creating the administrative glue that bonded together telecom practice groups in offices throughout Europe. Said Patsalos-Fox:

> She wrote proposals, became the expert on information sources, organized European conferences, helped with cross-office staffing, located expertise and supported and participated in our practice development work. Gradually she helped us move from an "export"-based hub and spokes model of information sharing to a true federalist-based network.

In this growth environment and supported by the stronger infrastructure, the practice exploded during the 1990s. To move the knowledge creation beyond what he described as "incremental synthesis of past experience," Patsalos-Fox launched a series of practice-sponsored studies. Staffed by some of the practice's best consultants, they focused on big topics like "The Industry Structure in 2005," or "The Telephone Company of the Future." But most of the practice's knowledge base was built by the informal initiatives of individual associates who would step back after several engagements and write a paper on

their new insights. For example, Bray wrote several well-received PD documents and was enhancing his internal reputation as an expert in deregulation and multimedia. Increasingly he was invited to consult to or even join teams in other parts of Europe. Said Patsalos-Fox:

> He was flying around making presentations and helping teams. Although the internal audience is the toughest, he was getting invited back. When it came time for him to come up for election, the London office nominated him but the strength of his support came from his colleagues in the European telecom network.

In 1996, Patsalos-Fox felt it was time for a new generation of practice leadership. He asked his young Australian protégé and two other partners—one in Brussels, one in Paris—if they would take on a co-leadership role. Bray reflected on two challenges he and his co-leaders faced. The first was to make telecom a really exciting and interesting practice so it could attract the best associates. That meant taking on the most interesting work, and running our engagements so that people felt they were developing and having fun.

The second key challenge was how to develop the largely informal links among the fast-growing European telecom practices. Despite the excellent job that Soderstrom had done as the practice's repository of knowledge and channel of communication, it was clear that there were limits to her ability to act as the sole "intelligent switch." As a result, the group had initiated a practice-specific intranet link designed to allow members direct access to the practice's knowledge base (PD documents, conference proceedings, CVs, etc.), its members' capabilities (via home pages for each practice member), client base (CST home pages, links to client web sites), and external knowledge resources (MIT's Multimedia Lab, Theseus Institute, etc.). More open yet more focused than existing firm-wide systems like PDNet, the Telecom Intranet was expected to accelerate the "engage-explore-apply-share" knowledge cycle.

There were some, however, who worried that this would be another step away from "one firm" towards compartmentalization, and from focus on building idea-driven personal networks towards creating data-based electronic transactions. In particular, the concern was that functional capability groups would be less able to transfer their knowledge into increasingly strong and self-contained industry-based practices. Warwick Bray recognized the problem, acknowledging that linkages between European telecom and most functional practices "could be better":

> The problem is we rarely feel the need to draw on those groups. For example, I know the firm's pricing practice has world-class expertise in industrial pricing, but we haven't yet learned how to apply it to telecom. We mostly call on the pricing experts within our practice. We probably should reach out more.

Stephen Dull and the Business Marketing Competence Center

After completing his MBA at the University of Michigan in 1983, Stephen Dull spent the next five years in various consumer marketing jobs at Pillsbury. In 1988, he was contacted by an executive search firm that had been retained by McKinsey to recruit potential consultants in consumer marketing. Joining the Atlanta office, Dull soon discovered that there was no structured development program. Like the eight experienced consumer marketing recruits in other offices, he was expected to create his own agenda.

Working on various studies, Dull found his interests shifting from consumer to industrial marketing issues. As he focused on building his own expertise, however, Dull acknowledged that he did not pay enough attention to developing strong client relations. "And around here, serving clients is what really counts," he said. So, in late 1994—a time when he might be discussing his election to principal—he had a long counseling session with his group development leader about his career. The GDL confirmed that he was not well positioned for election, but proposed another option. He suggested that Dull talk to Rob Rosiello, a principal in the New York office who had just launched a business-to-business marketing initiative within the marketing practice. Said Dull:

> Like most new initiatives, "B to B" was struggling to get established without full-time resources, so Rob was pleased to see me. I was enjoying my business marketing work, so the initiative sounded like a great opportunity. . . . Together, we wrote a proposal to make me the firm's first business marketing specialist.

The decision to pursue this strategy was not an easy one for Dull. Like most of his colleagues, he felt that specialists were regarded as second-class citizens—"overhead being supported by real consultants who serve clients," Dull suggested. But his GDL told him that recent directors meetings had reaffirmed the importance of building functional expertise, and some had even suggested that 150%–20% of the firm's partners should be functional experts within the next five to seven years. (As of 1995, over 300 associates were specialists, but only 15 of the 500 partners.) In April 1995, Dull and Rosiello took their proposal to Andrew Parsons and David Court, two leaders of the Marketing practice. The directors suggested a mutual trial of the concept until the end of the year and offered to provide Dull the support to commit full time to developing the B to B initiative.

Dull's first priority was to collect the various concepts, frameworks, and case studies that existed within the firm, consolidating and synthesizing them in several PD documents. In the process, he and Rosiello began assembling a core team of interested contributors. Together, they developed an agenda of half a dozen cutting-edge issues in business marketing—segmentation, multi-buyer decision making and marketing partnerships, for example—and launched a number of study initiatives around them. Beyond an expanded series of PD documents, the outcome was an emerging set of core beliefs, and a new framework for business marketing.

The activity also attracted the interest of Mark Leiter, a specialist in the Marketing Science Center of Competence. This center, which had developed largely around a group of a dozen or so specialists, was in many ways a model of what Dull hoped the B to B initiative could become, and having a second committed specialist certainly helped.

In November, another major step to that goal occurred when the B to B initiative was declared a Center of Competence. At that time, the core group decided they would test their colleagues' interest and their own credibility by arranging an internal conference at which they would present their ideas. When over 50 people showed up including partners and directors from four continents, Dull felt that prospects for the center looked good.

Through the cumulative impact of the PD documents, the conference and word of mouth recommendations, by early 1996 Dull and his colleagues were getting more calls than the small center could handle. They were proud when the March listing of PDNet "Best Sellers" listed B to B documents at numbers 2, 4, and 9 (see Exhibit 7). For Dull, the resulting process was enlightening:

> We decided that when we got calls we would swarm all over them and show our colleagues we could really add value for their clients. . . . This may sound strange—even corny—but I now really understand why this is a profession and not a business. If I help a partner serve his client better, he will call me back. It's all about relationships, forming personal bonds, helping each other.

While Dull was pleased with the way the new center was gaining credibility and having impact, he was still very uncertain about his promotion prospects. As he considered his future, he began to give serious thought to writing a book on business to business marketing to enhance his internal credibility and external visibility.

A New MD, A New Focus

In 1994, after six years of leadership in which firm revenue had doubled to an estimated $1.5 billion annually, Fred Gluck stepped down as MD. His successor was 45-year-old Rajat Gupta, a 20-year McKinsey veteran committed to continuing the emphasis on knowledge development. After listening to the continuing debates about which knowledge development approach was most effective, Gupta came to the conclusion that the discussions were consuming energy that should have been directed towards the activity itself. "The firm did not have to make a choice," he said. "We had to pursue *all* the options." With that conclusion, Gupta launched a four-pronged attack.

He wanted to capitalize on the firm's long-term investment practice development driven by Clientele Industry Sectors and Functional Capability Groups and Supported by the knowledge infrastructure of PDNet and FPIS. But he also wanted to create some new channels, forums, and mechanisms for knowledge development and organizational learning.

Building on an experiment begun by the German office, Gupta embraced a grass-roots knowledge-development approach called Practice Olympics. Two- to six-person teams from offices around the world were encouraged to develop ideas that grew out of recent client engagements and formalize them for presentation at a regional competition with senior partners and clients as judges. The 20 best regional teams then competed at a firm-wide event. Gupta was proud that in its second year, the event had attracted over 150 teams and involved 15% of the associate body.

At a different level, in late 1995 the new MD initiated six special initiatives—multi-year internal assignments led by senior partners that focused on emerging issues that were of importance to CEOs. The initiatives tapped both internal and external expertise to develop "state-of-the-art" formulations of each key issue. For example, one focused on the shape and function of the corporation of the future, another on creating and managing strategic growth, and a third on capturing global opportunities. Gupta saw these initiatives as reasserting the importance of the firm's functional knowledge yet providing a means to do longer term, bigger commitment, cross-functional development.

Finally, he planned to expand on the model of the McKinsey Global Institute, a firm-sponsored research center established in 1991 to study

EXHIBIT 7   PDNet "Best-Sellers": March and Year-to-Date, 1996

Number Requested	*Title, Author(s), Date, PDNet #*	*Functional Capability Group/Sector*
March 1996		
21	**Developing a Distinctive Consumer Marketing Organization** *Nora Aufreiter, Theresa Austerberry, Steve Carlotti, Mike George, Liz Lempres (1/96, #13240)*	Consumer Industries/ Packaged Goods; Marketing
19	**VIP: Value Improvement Program to Enhance Customer Value in Business to Business Marketing** *Dirk Berensmann, Marc Fischer, Heiner Frankemölle, Lutz-Peter Pape, Wolf-Dieter Voss (10/95, #13340)*	Marketing; Steel
16	**Handbook For Sales Force Effectiveness—1991 Edition** *(5/91, #6670)*	Marketing
15	**Understanding and Influencing Customer Purchase Decisions in Business to Business Markets** *Mark Leiter (3/95, #12525)*	Marketing
15	**Channel Management Handbook** *Christine Bucklin, Stephen DeFalco, John DeVincentis, John Levis (1/95, #11876)*	Marketing
15	**Platforms for Growth in Personal Financial Services (PFS201)** *Christopher Leech, Ronald O'Hanley, Eric Lambrecht, Kristin Morse (11/95, #12995)*	Personal Financial Services
14	**Developing Successful Acquisition Programs To Support Long-Term Growth Strategies** *Steve Coley, Dan Goodwin (11/92, #9150)*	Corporate Finance
14	**Understanding Value-Based Segmentation** *John Forsyth, Linda Middleton (11/95, #11730)*	Consumer Industries/ Packaged Goods; Marketing
14	**The Dual Perspective Customer Map for Business to Business Marketing** *(3/95, #12526)*	Marketing
13	**Growth Strategy—Platforms, Staircases and Franchises** *Charles Conn, Rob McLean, David White (8/94, #11400)*	Strategy
Cumulative Index (January–March)		
54	**Introduction to CRM (Continuous Relationship Marketing)—Leveraging CRM to Build PFS Franchise Value (PFS221)** *Margo Geogiadis, Milt Gillespie, Tim Gokey, Mike Sherman, Marc Singer (11/95, #12999)*	Personal Financial Services
45	**Platforms for Growth in Personal Financial Services (PFS201)** *Christopher Leech, Ronald O'Hanley, Eric Lambrecht, Kristin Morse (11/95, #12995)*	Personal Financial Services
40	**Launching a CRM Effort (PFS222)** *Nick Brown, Margo Georgiadis (10/95, #12940)*	Marketing
38	**Building Value Through Continuous Relationship Marketing (CRM)** *Nich Brown, Mike Wright (10/95, #13126)*	Banking and Securities
36	**Combining Art and Science to Optimize Brand Portfolios** *Richard Benson-Armer, David Court, John Forsyth (10/95, #12916)*	Marketing; Consumer Industries/Packaged Goods
35	**Consumer Payments and the Future of Retail Banks (PA202)** *John Stephenson, Peter Sands (11/95, #13008)*	Payments and Operating Products
34	**CRM (Continuous Relationship Marketing) Case Examples Overview** *Howie Hayes, David Putts (9/95, #12931)*	Marketing
32	**Straightforward Approaches to Building Management Talent** *Parke Boneysteele, Bill Meehan, Kristin Morse, Pete Sidebottom (9/95, #12843)*	Organization
32	**Reconfiguring and Reenergizing Personal Selling Channels (PFS213)** *Patrick Wetzel, Amy Zinsser (11/95, #12997)*	Personal Financial Services
31	**From Traditional Home Banking to On-Line PFS (PFS211)** *Gaurang Desai, Brian Johnson, Kai Lahmann, Gottfried Leibbrandt, Paal Weberg (11/95, #12998)*	Personal Financial Services

Source: Month By Month (McKinsey's internal staff magazine).

implications of changes in the global economy on business. The proposal was to create other pools of dedicated resources protected from daily pressures and client demands, and focused on long-term research agendas. A Change Center was established in 1995 and an Operations Center was being planned. Gupta saw these institutes as a way in which McKinsey could recruit more research-oriented people and link more effectively into the academic arena.

Most of these initiatives were new and their impact had not yet been felt within the firm. Yet Gupta was convinced the direction was right:

> We have easily doubled our investment in knowledge over these past couple of years. There are lots more people involved in many more initiatives. If that means we do 5–10% less client work today, we are willing to pay that price to invest in the future. Since Marvin Bower, every leadership group has had a commitment to leave the firm stronger than it found it. It's a fundamental value of McKinsey to invest for the future of the firm.

Future Directions

Against this background, the McKinsey partnership was engaged in spirited debate about the firm's future directions and priorities. The following is a sampling of their opinions:

> I am concerned that our growth may stretch the fabric of the place. We can't keep on disaggregating our units to create niches for everyone because we have exhausted the capability of our integrating mechanisms. I believe our future is in developing

around CSTs and integrating across them around common knowledge agendas.

> Historically, I was a supporter of slower growth, but now I'm convinced we must grow faster. That is the key to creating opportunity and excitement for people, and that generates innovation and drives knowledge development. . . . Technology is vital not only in supporting knowledge transfer, but also in allowing partners to mentor more young associates. We have to be much more aggressive in using it.

> There is a dark side to technology—what I call technopoly. It can drive out communication and people start believing that e-mailing someone is the same thing as talking to them. If teams stop meeting as often or if practice conferences evolve into discussion forums on Lotus Notes, the technology that has supported our growth may begin to erode our culture based on personal networks.

> I worry that we are losing our sense of village as we compartmentalize our activities and divide into specialties. And the power of IT has sometimes led to information overload. The risk is that the more we spend searching out the right PD document, the ideal framework, or the best expert, the less time we spend thinking creatively about the problem. I worry that as we increase the science, we might lose the craft of what we do.

These were among the scores of opinions that Rajat Gupta heard since becoming MD. His job was to sort through them and set a direction that would "leave the firm stronger than he found it."

Reading 6–1

THE KNOWLEDGE-CREATING COMPANY

by Ikujiro Nonaka

In an economy where the only certainty is uncertainty, the one sure source of lasting competitive advantage is knowledge. When markets shift, technologies proliferate, competitors multiply, and products become obsolete almost overnight, successful companies are those that consistently create new knowledge, disseminate it widely throughout the organization, and quickly embody it in new technologies and products. These activities define the "knowledge-creating" company, whose sole business is continuous innovation.

And yet, despite all the talk about "brainpower" and "intellectual capital," few managers grasp the true nature of the knowledge-creating company— let alone know how to manage it. The reason: they misunderstand what knowledge is and what companies must do to exploit it.

Deeply ingrained in the traditions of Western management, from Frederick Taylor to Herbert Simon, is a view of the organization as a machine for "information processing." According to this view, the only useful knowledge is formal and systematic—hard (read: quantifiable) data, codified procedures, universal principles. And the key metrics for measuring the value of new knowledge are similarly hard and quantifiable—increased efficiency, lower costs, improved return on investment.

But there is another way to think about knowledge and its role in business organizations. It is found most commonly at highly successful Japanese

Ikujiro Nonaka is professor of management at the Institute for Business Research of Hitotsubashi University in Tokyo, Japan. His last HBR article, written with Hirotaka Takeuchi, was "The New New Product Development Game" (January–February 1986).

competitors like Honda, Canon, Matsushita, NEC, Sharp, and Kao. These companies have become famous for their ability to respond quickly to customers, create new markets, rapidly develop new products, and dominate emergent technologies. The secret of their success is their unique approach to managing the creation of new knowledge.

To Western managers, the Japanese approach often seems odd or even incomprehensible. Consider the following examples:

- How is the slogan "Theory of Automobile Evolution" a meaningful design concept for a new car? And yet, this phrase led to the creation of the Honda City, Honda's innovative urban car.
- Why is a beer can a useful analogy for a personal copier? Just such an analogy caused a fundamental breakthrough in the design of Canon's revolutionary mini-copier, a product that created the personal copier market and has led to Canon's successful migration from its stagnating camera business to the more lucrative field of office automation.
- What possible concrete sense of direction can a made-up word such as "optoelectronics" provide a company's product-development engineers? Under this rubric, however, Sharp has developed a reputation for creating "first products" that define new technologies and markets, making Sharp a major player in businesses ranging from color televisions to liquid crystal displays to customized integrated circuits.

In each of these cases, cryptic slogans that to a Western manager sound just plain silly—appropriate for an advertising campaign perhaps but certainly not for running a company—are in fact highly effective tools for creating new knowledge. Managers everywhere recognize the serendipitous quality of innovation. Executives at these Japanese companies are *managing* that serendipity to the benefit of the company, its employees, and its customers.

The centerpiece of the Japanese approach is the recognition that creating new knowledge is not simply a matter of "processing" objective information. Rather, it depends on tapping the tacit and often highly subjective insights, intuitions, and hunches of individual employees and making those insights available for testing and use by the company as a whole. The key to this process is personal commitment, the employees' sense of identity with the enterprise and its mission. Mobilizing that commitment and embodying tacit knowledge in actual technologies and products require managers who are as comfortable with images and symbols—slogans such as Theory of Automobile Evolution, analogies like that between a personal copier and a beer can, metaphors such as "optoelectronics"—as they are with hard numbers measuring market share, productivity, or ROI.

The more holistic approach to knowledge at many Japanese companies is also founded on another fundamental insight. A company is not a machine but a living organism. Much like an individual, it can have a collective sense of identity and fundamental purpose. This is the organizational equivalent of self-knowledge—a shared understanding of what the company stands for, where it is going, what kind of world it wants to live in, and, most important, how to make that world a reality.

In this respect, the knowledge-creating company is as much about ideals as it is about ideas. And that fact fuels innovation. The essence of innovation is to re-create the world according to a particular vision or ideal. To create new knowledge means quite literally to re-create the company and everyone in it in a nonstop process of personal and organizational self-renewal. In the knowledge-creating company, inventing new knowledge is not a specialized activity—the province of the R&D department or marketing or strategic planning. It is a way of be-

having, indeed a way of being, in which everyone is a knowledge worker—that is to say, an entrepreneur.

The reasons why Japanese companies seem especially good at this kind of continuous innovation and self-renewal are complicated. But the key lesson for managers is quite simple: much as manufacturers around the world have learned from Japanese manufacturing techniques, any company that wants to compete on knowledge must also learn from Japanese techniques of knowledge creation. The experiences of the Japanese companies discussed below suggest a fresh way to think about managerial roles and responsibilities, organizational design, and business practices in the knowledge-creating company. It is an approach that puts knowledge creation exactly where it belongs: at the very center of a company's human resources strategy.

The Spiral of Knowledge

New knowledge always begins with the individuals. A brilliant researcher has an insight that leads to a new patent. A middle manager's intuitive sense of market trends becomes the catalyst for an important new product concept. A shop-floor worker draws on years of experience to come up with a new process innovation. In each case, an individual's personal knowledge is transformed into organizational knowledge valuable to the company as a whole.

Making personal knowledge available to others is the central activity of the knowledge-creating company. It takes place continuously and at all levels of the organization. And as the following example suggests, sometimes it can take unexpected forms.

In 1985, product developers at the Osaka-based Matsushita Electric Company were hard at work on a new home bread-making machine. But they were having trouble getting the machine to knead dough correctly. Despite their efforts, the crust of the bread was overcooked while the inside was hardly done at all. Employees exhaustively analyzed the problem. They even compared X rays of dough kneaded by the machine and dough kneaded by professional bakers. But they were unable to obtain any meaningful data.

Finally, software developer Ikuko Tanaka proposed a creative solution. The Osaka International Hotel had a reputation for making the best bread in Osaka. Why not use it as a model? Tanaka trained with the hotel's head baker to study his kneading technique. She observed that the baker had a distinctive way of stretching the dough. After a year of trial and error, working closely with the project's engineers, Tanaka came up with product specifications—including the addition of special ribs inside the machine—that successfully reproduced the baker's stretching technique and the quality of the bread she had learned to make at the hotel. The result: Matsushita's unique "twist dough" method and a product that in its first year set a record for sales of a new kitchen appliance.

Ikuko Tanaka's innovation illustrates a movement between two very different types of knowledge. The end point of that movement is "explicit" knowledge: the product specifications for the bread-making machine. Explicit knowledge is formal and systematic. For this reason, it can be easily communicated and shared, in product specifications or a scientific formula or a computer program.

But the starting point of Tanaka's innovation is another kind of knowledge that is not so easily expressible: "tacit" knowledge like that possessed by the chief baker at the Osaka International Hotel. Tacit knowledge is highly personal. It is hard to formalize and, therefore, difficult to communicate to others. Or in the words of the philosopher Michael Polanyi, "We can know more than we can tell." Tacit knowledge is also deeply rooted in action and in an individual's commitment to a specific context—a craft or profession, a particular technology or product market, or the activities of a work group or team.

Tacit knowledge consists partly of technical skills—the kind of informal, hard-to-pin-down skills captured in the term "know-how." A master craftsman after years of experience develops a wealth of expertise "at his fingertips." But he is often unable to articulate the scientific or technical principles behind what he knows.

At the same time, tacit knowledge has an important cognitive dimension. It consists of mental models, beliefs, and perspectives so ingrained that we take them for granted, and therefore cannot easily articulate them. For this very reason, these implicit models profoundly shape how we perceive the world around us.

The distinction between tacit and explicit knowledge suggests four basic patterns for creating knowledge in any organization:

1. *From Tacit to Tacit.* Sometimes, one individual shares tacit knowledge directly with another. For example, when Ikuko Tanaka apprentices herself to the head baker at the Osaka International Hotel, she learns his tacit skills through observation, imitation, and practice. They become part of her own tacit knowledge base. Put another way, she is "socialized" into the craft.

But on its own, socialization is a rather limited form of knowledge creation. True, the apprentice learns the master's skills. But neither the apprentice nor the master gain any systematic insight into their craft knowledge. Because their knowledge never becomes explicit, it cannot easily be leveraged by the organization as a whole.

2. *From Explicit to Explicit.* An individual can also combine discrete pieces of explicit knowledge into a new whole. For example, when a comptroller of a company collects information from throughout the organization and puts it together in a financial report, that report is new knowledge in the sense that it synthesizes information from many different sources. But this combination does not really extend the company's existing knowledge base either.

But when tacit and explicit knowledge interact, as in the Matsushita example, something powerful happens. It is precisely this exchange *between* tacit and explicit knowledge that Japanese companies are especially good at developing.

3. *From Tacit to Explicit.* When Ikuko Tanaka is able to articulate the foundations of her tacit knowledge of bread making, she converts it into explicit knowledge, thus allowing it to be shared with her project-development team. Another example might be the comptroller who, instead of merely compiling a conventional financial plan for his company, develops an innovative new approach to budgetary control based on his own tacit knowledge developed over years in the job.

4. *From Explicit to Tacit.* What's more, as new explicit knowledge is shared throughout an organization, other employees begin to internalize it—that is, they use it to broaden, extend, and reframe their own tacit knowledge. The comptroller's proposal causes a revision of the company's financial control system. Other employees use the innovation and eventually come to take it for granted as part of the background of tools and resources necessary to do their jobs.

In the knowledge-creating company, all four of these patterns exist in dynamic interaction, a kind of spiral of knowledge. Think back to Matsushita's Ikuko Tanaka:

1. First, she learns the tacit secrets of the Osaka International Hotel baker (socialization).

2. Next, she translates these secrets into explicit knowledge that she can communicate to her team members and others at Matsushita (articulation).

3. The team then standardizes this knowledge, putting it together into a manual or workbook and embodying it in a product (combination).

4. Finally, through the experience of creating a new product, Tanaka and her team members enrich their own tacit knowledge base (internalization). In particular, they come to understand in an extremely intuitive way that products like the home bread-making machine can provide genuine quality. That is, the machine must make bread that is as good as that of a professional baker.

This starts the spiral of knowledge all over again, but this time at a higher level. The new tacit insight about genuine quality developed in designing the home bread-making machine is informally conveyed to other Matsushita employees. They use it to formulate equivalent quality standards for other new Matsushita products—whether kitchen appliances, audiovisual equipment, or white goods. In this way, the organization's knowledge base grows ever broader.

Articulation (converting tacit knowledge into explicit knowledge) and internalization (using that explicit knowledge to extend one's own tacit knowledge base) are the critical steps in this spiral of knowledge. The reason is that both require the active involvement of the self—that is, personal commitment. Ikuko Tanaka's decision to apprentice herself to a master baker is one example of this commitment. Similarly, when the comptroller articulates his tacit knowledge and embodies it in a new innovation, his personal identity is directly involved in a way it is not when he merely "crunches" the numbers of a conventional financial plan.

Indeed, because tacit knowledge includes mental models and beliefs in addition to know-how, moving from the tacit to the explicit is really a process of articulating one's vision of the world—what it is and what it ought to be. When employees invent new knowledge, they are also reinventing themselves, the company, and even the world.

When managers grasp this, they realize that the appropriate tools for managing the knowledge-creating company look very different from those found at most Western companies.

From Metaphor to Model

To convert tacit knowledge into explicit knowledge means finding a way to express the inexpressible. Unfortunately, one of the most powerful management tools for doing so is also among the most frequently overlooked: the store of figurative language and symbolism that managers can draw from to articulate their intuitions and insights. At Japanese companies this evocative and sometimes extremely poetic language figures especially prominently in product development.

In 1978, top management at Honda inaugurated the development of a new-concept car with the slogan, "Let's gamble." The phrase expressed senior executives' conviction that Honda's Civic and the Accord models were becoming too familiar. Managers also realized that along with a new postwar generation entering the car market, a new generation of young product designers was coming of age with unconventional ideas about what made a good car.

The business decision that followed from the "Let's gamble" slogan was to form a new-product development team of young engineers and designers (the average age was 27). Top management charged the team with two—and only two—instructions: first, to come up with a product concept fundamentally different from anything the company had ever done before; and second, to make a car that was inexpensive but not cheap.

This mission might sound vague, but in fact it provided the team an extremely clear sense of direction. For instance, in the early days of the project, some team members proposed designing a smaller and cheaper version of the Honda Civic—a safe and technologically feasible option. But the team quickly decided this approach contradicted the entire rationale of its mission. The only alternative was to invent something totally new.

Project team leader Hiroo Watanabe coined another slogan to express his sense of the team's ambitious challenge: Theory of Automobile Evolution. The phrase described an ideal. In effect, it posed the question: if the automobile were an organism, how should it evolve? As team members argued and discussed what Watanabe's slogan might possibly mean, they came up with an answer in the form of yet another slogan: "man-maximum, machine-minimum." This captured the team's belief that the ideal car should somehow transcend the traditional human-machine relationship. But that required challenging what Watanabe called "the reasoning of Detroit," which had sacrificed comfort for appearance.

The "evolutionary" trend the team articulated eventually came to be embodied in the image of a sphere—a car simultaneously "short" (in length) and "tall" (in height). Such a car, they reasoned, would be lighter and cheaper, but also more comfortable and more solid than traditional cars. A sphere provided the most room for the passenger while taking up the least amount of space on the road. What's more, the shape minimized the space taken up by the engine and other mechanical systems. This gave birth to a product concept the team called "Tall Boy," which eventually led to the Honda City, the company's distinctive urban car.

The Tall Boy concept totally contradicted the conventional wisdom about automobile design at the time, which emphasized long, low sedans. But the City's revolutionary styling and engineering were prophetic. The car inaugurated a whole new approach to design in the Japanese auto industry based on the man-maximum, machine-minimum concept, which has led to the new generation of "tall and short" cars now quite prevalent in Japan.

The story of the Honda City suggests how Japanese companies use figurative language at all levels of the company and in all phases of the product development process. It also begins to suggest the different kinds of figurative language and the distinctive role each plays.

One kind of figurative language that is especially important is metaphor. By "metaphor," I don't just mean a grammatical structure or allegorical expression. Rather, metaphor is a distinctive method of perception. It is a way for individuals grounded in different contexts and with different experiences to understand something intuitively through the use of imagination and symbols without the need for analysis or generalization. Through metaphors, people put together what they know in new ways and begin to express what they know but cannot yet say. As such, metaphor is highly effective in fostering direct commitment to the creative process in the early stages of knowledge creation.

Metaphor accomplishes this by merging two different and distant areas of experience into a single, inclusive image or symbol—what linguistic philosopher Max Black has aptly described as "two ideas in one phrase." By establishing a connection between two things that seem only distantly related, metaphors set up a discrepancy or conflict. Often, metaphoric images have multiple meanings, appear logically contradictory or even irrational. But far from being a weakness, this is in fact an enormous strength. For it is the very conflict that metaphors embody that jump-starts the creative process. As employees try to define more clearly the insight that the metaphor expresses, they work to reconcile the conflicting meanings. That is the first step in making the tacit explicit.

Consider the example of Hiroo Watanabe's slogan, Theory of Automobile Evolution. Like any good metaphor, it combines two ideas one wouldn't normally think of together—the automobile, which is a machine, and the theory of evolution, which refers to living organisms. And yet, this discrepancy is a fruitful platform for speculation about the characteristics of the ideal car.

But while metaphor triggers the knowledge-creation process, it alone is not enough to complete it. The next step is analogy. Whereas metaphor is mostly driven by intuition and links images that at first glance seem remote from each other, analogy is a more structured process of reconciling contradictions and making distinctions. Put another way, by clarifying how the two ideas in one phrase actually are alike and not alike, the contradictions incorporated into metaphors are harmonized by analogy. In this respect, analogy is an intermediate step between pure imagination and logical thinking.

Probably the best example of analogy comes from the development of Canon's revolutionary mini-copier. Canon designers knew that for the first personal copier to be successful, it had to be reliable. To ensure reliability, they proposed to make the product's photosensitive copier drum—which is the source of 90% of all maintenance problems—disposable. To be disposable, however, the drum would have to be easy and cheap to make. How to manufacture a throwaway drum?

The breakthrough came one day when task-force leader Hiroshi Tanaka ordered out for some beer. As the team discussed design problems over their drinks, Tanaka held one of the beer cans and wondered aloud, "How much does it cost to manufacture this can?" The question led the team to speculate whether the same process for making an aluminum beer can could be applied to the manufacture of an aluminum copier drum. By exploring how the drum actually is and is not like a beer can, the mini-copier development team was able to come up with the process technology that could manufacture an aluminum copier drum at the appropriate low cost.

Finally, the last step in the knowledge-creation process is to create an actual model. A model is far more immediately conceivable than a metaphor or an analogy. In the model, contradictions get re-solved and concepts become transferable through consistent and systematic logic. The quality standards for the bread at the Osaka International Hotel lead Matsushita to develop the right product specifications for its home bread-making machine. The image of a sphere leads Honda to its Tall Boy product concept.

Of course, terms like "metaphor," "analogy," and "model" are ideal types. In reality, they are often hard to distinguish from each other; the same phrase or image can embody more than one of the three functions. Still, the three terms capture the process by which organizations convert tacit knowledge into explicit knowledge: first, by linking contradictory things and ideas through metaphor; then, by resolving these contradictions through analogy; and, finally, by crystallizing the created concepts and embodying them in a model, which makes the knowledge available to the rest of the company.

From Chaos to Concept: Managing the Knowledge-Creating Company

Understanding knowledge creation as a process of making tacit knowledge explicit—a matter of metaphors, analogies, and models—has direct implications for how a company designs its organization and defines managerial roles and responsibilities within it. This is the "how" of the knowledge-creating company, the structures and practices that translate a company's vision into innovative technologies and products.

The fundamental principle of organizational design at the Japanese companies I have studied is redundancy—the conscious overlapping of company information, business activities, and managerial responsibilities. To Western managers, the term "redundancy," with its connotations of unnecessary duplication and waste, may sound unappealing. And yet, building a redundant organization is the first step in managing the knowledge-creating company.

Redundancy is important because it encourages frequent dialogue and communication. This helps create a "common cognitive ground" among employees and thus facilitates the transfer of tacit knowledge. Since members of the organization share overlapping information, they can sense what others are struggling to articulate. Redundancy also spreads new explicit knowledge through the organization so it can be internalized by employees.

The organizational logic of redundancy helps explain why Japanese companies manage product development as an overlapping process where different functional divisions work together in a shared division of labor. At Canon, redundant product development goes one step further. The company organizes product-development teams according to "the principle of internal competition." A team is divided into competing groups that develop different approaches to the same project and then argue over the advantages and disadvantages of their proposals. This encourages the team to look at a project from a variety of perspectives. Under the guidance of a team leader, the team eventually develops a common understanding of the "best" approach.

In one sense, such internal competition is wasteful. Why have two or more groups of employees pursuing the same product-development project? But when responsibilities are shared, information proliferates, and the organization's ability to create and implement concepts is accelerated.

At Canon, for example, inventing the mini-copier's low-cost disposable drum resulted in new technologies that facilitated miniaturization, weight reduction, and automated assembly. These technologies were then quickly applied to other office automation products such as microfilm readers, laser printers, word processors, and typewriters. This was an important factor in diversifying Canon from cameras to office automation and in securing a competitive edge in the laser printer industry. By 1987—only five years after the mini-copier was introduced—a full 74% of Canon's revenues came from its business machines division.

Another way to build redundancy is through strategic rotation, especially between different areas of technology and between functions such as R&D and marketing. Rotation helps employees understand the business from a multiplicity of perspectives. This makes organizational knowledge more "fluid" and easier to put into practice. At Kao Corpo-

ration, a leading Japanese consumer-products manufacturer, researchers often "retire" from the R&D department by the age of 40 in order to transfer to other departments such as marketing, sales, or production. And all employees are expected to hold at least three different jobs in any given ten-year period.

Free access to company information also helps build redundancy. When information differentials exist, members of an organization can no longer interact on equal terms, which hinders the search for different interpretations of new knowledge. Thus Kao's top management does not allow any discrimination in access to information among employees. All company information (with the exception of personnel data) is stored in a single integrated database, open to any employee regardless of position.

As these examples suggest, no one department or group of experts has the exclusive responsibility for creating new knowledge in the knowledge-creating company. Senior managers, middle managers, and frontline employees all play a part. Indeed, the value of any one person's contribution is determined less by his or her location in the organizational hierarchy than by the importance of the information he or she provides to the entire knowledge-creating system.

But this is not to say that there is no differentiation among roles and responsibilities in the knowledge-creating company. In fact, creating new knowledge is the product of a dynamic interaction among three roles.

Frontline employees are immersed in the day-to-day details of particular technologies, products, or markets. No one is more expert in the realities of a company's business than they are. But while these employees are deluged with highly specific information, they often find it extremely difficult to turn that information into useful knowledge. For one thing, signals from the marketplace can be vague and ambiguous. For another, employees can become so caught up in their own narrow perspective, that they lose sight of the broader context.

What's more, even when employees *do* develop meaningful ideas and insights, it can still be difficult to communicate the import of that information to others. People don't just passively receive new knowledge, they actively interpret it to fit their own situation and perspective. Thus what makes sense in one context can change or even lose its meaning when communicated to people in a different context. As a result, there is a continual shift in meaning as new knowledge is diffused in an organization.

The confusion created by the inevitable discrepancies in meaning that occur in any organization might seem like a problem. In fact, it can be a rich source of new knowledge—*if* a company knows how to manage it. The key to doing so is continuously challenging employees to reexamine what they take for granted. Such reflection is always necessary in the knowledge-creating company, but it is especially essential during times of crisis or breakdown, when a company's traditional categories of knowledge no longer work. At such moments, ambiguity can prove extremely useful as a source of alternative meanings, a fresh way to think about things, a new sense of direction. In this respect, new knowledge is born in chaos.

The main job of managers in the knowledge creating company is to orient this chaos toward purposeful knowledge creation. Managers do this by providing employees with a conceptual framework that helps them make sense of their own experience. This takes place at the senior management level at the top of the company and at the middle management level on company teams.

Senior managers give voice to a company's future by articulating metaphors, symbols, and concepts that orient the knowledge-creating activities of employees. They do this by asking the questions: What are we trying to learn? What do we need to know? Where should we be going? Who are we? If the job of frontline employees is to know "what is," then the job of senior executives is to know "what ought to be." Or in the words of Hiroshi Honma, senior researcher at Honda: "Senior managers are romantics who go in quest of the ideal."

At some of the Japanese companies I have studied, CEOs talk about this role in terms of their responsibility for articulating the company's "conceptual umbrella": the grand concepts that in highly universal and abstract terms identify the common features linking seemingly disparate activities or businesses into a coherent whole. Sharp's dedication to optoelectronics is a good example.

In 1973, Sharp invented the first low-power electronic calculator by combining two key technologies—liquid crystal displays (LCDs) and complementary metal oxide semiconductors (CMOSs). Company technologists coined the term "optoelectronics" to describe this merging of microelectronics with optical technologies. The company's senior managers then took up the word and magnified its impact far beyond the R&D and engineering departments in the company.

Optoelectronics represents an image of the world that Sharp wants to live in. It is one of the key concepts articulating what the company ought to be. As such, it has become an overarching guide for the company's strategic development. Under this rubric, Sharp has moved beyond its original success in calculators to become a market leader in a broad range of products based on LCD and semiconductor technologies, including: the Electronic Organizer pocket notebook, LCD projection systems, as well as customized integrated circuits such as masked ROMs, ASICs, and CCDs (charge-coupled devices, which convert light into electronic signals).

Other Japanese companies have similar umbrella concepts. At NEC, top management has categorized the company's knowledge base in terms of a few key technologies and then developed the metaphor "C&C" (for "computers and communications"). At Kao, the umbrella concept is "surface active science," referring to techniques for coating the surface area of materials. This phrase has guided the company's diversification into products ranging from soap detergents to cosmetics to floppy disks—all natural derivatives of Kao's core knowledge base.

Another way top management provides employees with a sense of direction is by setting the standards for justifying the value of the knowledge that is constantly being developed by the organization's members. Deciding which efforts to support and develop is a highly strategic task.

In most companies, the ultimate test for measuring the value of new knowledge is economic—increased efficiency, lower costs, improved ROI. But in the knowledge-creating company, other more qualitative factors are equally important. Does the idea embody the company's vision? Is it an expression of top management's aspirations and strategic goals? Does it have the potential to build the company's organizational knowledge network?

The decision by Mazda to pursue the development of the rotary engine is a classic example of this more qualitative kind of justification. In 1974, the product-development team working on the engine was facing heavy pressure within the company to abandon the project. The rotary engine was a "gas guzzler," critics complained. It would never succeed in the marketplace.

Kenichi Yamamoto, head of the development team (and currently Mazda's chairman), argued that to stop the project would mean giving up on the company's dream of revolutionizing the combustion engine. "Let's think this way," Yamamoto proposed. "We are making history, and it is our fate to deal with this challenge." The decision to continue led to Mazda's successful rotary-engine sports car, the Savanna RX-7.

Seen from the perspective of traditional management, Yamamoto's argument about the company's "fate" sounds crazy. But in the context of the knowledge-creating company, it makes perfect sense. Yamamoto appealed to the fundamental aspirations of the company—what he termed "dedication to uncompromised value"—and to the strategy of technological leadership that senior executives had articulated. He showed how the rotary-engine project enacted the organization's commitment to its vision. Similarly, continuing the project reinforced the individual commitment of team members to that vision and to the organization.

Umbrella concepts and qualitative criteria for justification are crucial to giving a company's knowledge-creating activities a sense of direction. And yet, it is important to emphasize that a company's vision needs also to be open-ended, susceptible to a variety of different and even conflicting interpretations. At first glance, this may seem contradictory. After all, shouldn't a company's vision be unambiguous, coherent, and clear? If a vision is *too* unambiguous, however, it becomes more akin to an order or an instruction. And orders do not foster the high degree of personal commitment on which effective knowledge creation depends.

A more equivocal vision gives employees and work groups the freedom and autonomy to set their own goals. This is important because while the ideals of senior management are important, on their own they are not enough. The best that top management can do is to clear away any obstacles and prepare the ground for self-organizing groups or teams. Then, it is up to the teams to figure out what the ideals of the top mean in reality. Thus at Honda, a slogan as vague as "Let's gamble" and an extremely broad mission gave the Honda City product-development team a strong sense of its own identity, which led to a revolutionary new product.

Teams play a central role in the knowledge-creating company because they provide a shared context where individuals can interact with each other and engage in the constant dialogue on which effective reflection depends. Team members create new points of view through dialogue and discussion. They pool their information and examine it from various angles. Eventually, they integrate their diverse individual perspectives into a new collective perspective.

This dialogue can—indeed, should—involve considerable conflict and disagreement. It is precisely such conflict that pushes employees to question existing premises and make sense of their experience in a new way. "When people's rhythms are out of sync, quarrels occur and it's hard to bring people together," acknowledges a deputy manager for advanced technology development at Canon. "Yet if a group's rhythms are completely in unison from the beginning, it's also difficult to achieve good results."

As team leaders, middle managers are at the intersection of the vertical and horizontal flows of information in the company. They serve as a bridge between the visionary ideals of the top and the often chaotic market reality of those on the front line of the business. By creating middle-level business and product concepts, middle managers mediate between "what is" and "what should be." They remake reality according to the company's vision.

Thus at Honda, top management's decision to try something completely new took concrete form at the level of Hiroo Watanabe's product-development team in the Tall Boy product concept. At Canon, the company aspiration, "Making an excellent company through transcending the camera business," became a reality when Hiroshi Tanaka's task force developed the "Easy Maintenance" product concept,

which eventually gave birth to the personal copier. And at Matsushita, the company's grand concept, "Human Electronics," came to life through the efforts of Ikuko Tanaka and others who developed the middle-range concept, "Easy Rich," and embodied it in the automatic bread-making machine.

In each of these cases, middle managers synthesized the tacit knowledge of both frontline employees and senior executives, made it explicit, and incorporated it into new technologies and products. In this respect, they are the true "knowledge engineers" of the knowledge-creating company.

Reading 6–2

BUILDING A LEARNING ORGANIZATION

by David A. Garvin

Continuous improvement programs are sprouting up all over as organizations strive to better themselves and gain an edge. The topic list is long and varied, and sometimes it seems as though a program a month is needed just to keep up. Unfortunately, failed programs far outnumber successes, and improvement rates remain distressingly low. Why? Because most companies have failed to grasp a basic truth. Continuous improvement requires a commitment to learning.

How, after all, can an organization improve without first learning something new? Solving a problem, introducing a product, and reengineering a process all require seeing the world in a new light

and acting accordingly. In the absence of learning, companies—and individuals—simply repeat old practices. Change remains cosmetic, and improvements are either fortuitous or short-lived.

A few farsighted executives—Ray Stata of Analog Devices, Gordon Forward of Chaparral Steel, Paul Allaire of Xerox—have recognized the link between learning and continuous improvement and have begun to refocus their companies around it. Scholars too have jumped on the bandwagon, beating the drum for "learning organizations" and "knowledge-creating companies." In rapidly changing businesses like semiconductors and consumer electronics, these ideas are fast taking hold. Yet despite the encouraging signs, the topic in large part remains murky, confused, and difficult to penetrate.

Meaning, Management, and Measurement

Scholars are partly to blame. Their discussions of learning organizations have often been reverential

David A. Garvin is the Robert and Jane Cizik Professor of Business Administration at the Harvard Business School. His current research focuses on the general manager's role and successful change processes. His last HBR article was "How the Baldrige Award Really Works" (November–December 1991).

and utopian, filled with near mystical terminology. Paradise, they would have you believe, is just around the corner. Peter Senge, who popularized learning organizations in his book *The Fifth Discipline,* described them as places "where people continually expand their capacity to create the results they truly desire, where new and expansive patterns of thinking are nurtured, where collective aspiration is set free, and where people are continually learning how to learn together."[1] To achieve these ends, Senge suggested the use of five "component technologies": systems thinking, personal mastery, mental models, shared vision, and team learning. In a similar spirit, Ikujiro Nonaka characterized knowledge-creating companies as places where "inventing new knowledge is not a specialized activity . . . it is a way of behaving, indeed, a way of being, in which everyone is a knowledge worker."[2] Nonaka suggested that companies use metaphors and organizational redundancy to focus thinking, encourage dialogue, and make tacit, instinctively understood ideas explicit.

Sound idyllic? Absolutely. Desirable? Without question. But does it provide a framework for action? Hardly. The recommendations are far too abstract, and too many questions remain unanswered. How, for example, will managers know when their companies have become learning organizations? What concrete changes in behavior are required? What policies and programs must be in place? How do you get from here to there?

Most discussions of learning organizations finesse these issues. Their focus is high philosophy and grand themes, sweeping metaphors rather than the gritty details of practice. Three critical issues are left unresolved; yet each is essential for effective implementation. First is the question of *meaning.* We need a plausible, well-grounded definition of learning organizations; it must be actionable and easy to apply. Second is the question of *management.* We

need clearer guidelines for practice, filled with operational advice rather than high aspirations. And third is the question of *measurement.* We need better tools for assessing an organization's rate and level of learning to ensure that gains have in fact been made.

Once these "three Ms" are addressed, managers will have a firmer foundation for launching learning organizations. Without this groundwork, progress is unlikely, and for the simplest of reasons. For learning to become a meaningful corporate goal, it must first be understood.

What Is a Learning Organization?

Surprisingly, a clear definition of learning has proved to be elusive over the years. Organizational theorists have studied learning for a long time; the accompanying quotations suggest that there is still considerable disagreement (see the insert "Definitions of Organizational Learning"). Most scholars view organizational learning as a process that unfolds over time and link it with knowledge acquisition and improved performance. But they differ on other important matters.

Some, for example, believe that behavioral change is required for learning; others insist that new ways of thinking are enough. Some cite information processing as the mechanism through which learning takes place; others propose shared insights, organizational routines, even memory. And some think that organizational learning is common, while others believe that flawed, self-serving interpretations are the norm.

How can we discern among this cacophony of voices yet build on earlier insights? As a first step, consider the following definition:

> A learning organization is an organization skilled at creating, acquiring, and transferring knowledge, and at modifying its behavior to reflect new knowledge and insights.

This definition begins with a simple truth: new ideas are essential if learning is to take place. Sometimes they are created de novo, through flashes of insight or creativity; at other times they arrive from outside the organization or are communicated by

---

[1]Peter M. Senge, *The Fifth Discipline* (New York: Doubleday, 1990), p. 1.

[2]Ikujiro Nonaka, "The Knowledge-Creating Company," *Harvard Business Review,* November–December 1991, p. 97.

Definitions of Organizational Learning

Scholars have proposed a variety of definitions of organizational learning. Here is a small sample:

Organizational learning means the process of improving actions through better knowledge and understanding. C. Marlene Fiol and Marjorie A. Lyles, "Organizational Learning," *Academy of Management Review,* October 1985.

An entity learns if, through its processing of information, the range of its potential behaviors is changed. George P. Huber, "Organizational Learning: The Contributing Processes and the Literatures," *Organization Science,* February 1991.

Organizations are seen as learning by encoding inferences from history into routines that guide behav-

ior. Barbara Levitt and James G. March, "Organizational Learning," *American Review of Sociology*, Vol. 14, 1988.

Organizational learning is a process of detecting and correcting error. Chris Argyris, "Double Loop Learning in Organizations," *Harvard Business Review,* September-October 1977.

Organizational learning occurs through shared insights, knowledge, and mental models . . . [and] builds on past knowledge and experience—that is, on memory. Ray Stata, "Organizational Learning—The Key to Management Innovation," *Sloan Management Review*, Spring 1989.

---

knowledgeable insiders. Whatever their source, these ideas are the trigger for organizational improvement. But they cannot by themselves create a learning organization. *Without accompanying changes in the way that work gets done, only the potential for improvement exists.*

This is a surprisingly stringent test for it rules out a number of obvious candidates for learning organizations. Many universities fail to qualify, as do many consulting firms. Even General Motors, despite its recent efforts to improve performance, is found wanting. All of these organizations have been effective at creating or acquiring new knowledge but notably less successful in applying that knowledge to their own activities. Total quality management, for example, is now taught at many business schools, yet the number using it to guide their own decision making is very small. Organizational consultants advise clients on social dynamics and small-group behavior but are notorious for their own infighting and factionalism. And GM, with a few exceptions (like Saturn and NUMMI), has had little success in revamping its manufacturing practices, even though its managers are experts on lean manufacturing, JIT production, and the requirements for improved quality of work life.

Organizations that do pass the definitional test—Honda, Corning, and General Electric come quickly to mind—have, by contrast, become adept at translating new knowledge into new ways of behaving. These companies actively manage the learning process to ensure that it occurs by design rather than by chance. Distinctive policies and practices are responsible for their success; they form the building blocks of learning organizations.

Building Blocks
Learning organizations are skilled at five main activities: systematic problem solving, experimentation with new approaches, learning from their own experience and past history, learning from the experiences and best practices of others, and transferring knowledge quickly and efficiently throughout the organization. Each is accompanied by a distinctive mind-set, tool kit, and pattern of behavior. Many companies practice these activities to some degree. But few are consistently successful because they rely largely on happenstance and isolated examples. By creating systems and processes that support these activities and integrate them into the fabric of daily operations, companies can manage their learning more effectively.

1. Systematic problem solving. This first activity rests heavily on the philosophy and methods of the quality movement. Its underlying ideas, now widely accepted, include:

- Relying on the scientific method, rather than guesswork, for diagnosing problems (what Deming calls the "Plan, Do, Check, Act" cycle, and others refer to as "hypothesis-generating, hypothesis-testing" techniques).
- Insisting on data, rather than assumptions, as background for decision making (what quality practitioners call "fact-based management").
- Using simple statistical tools (histograms, Pareto charts, correlations, cause-and-effect diagrams) to organize data and draw inferences.

Most training programs focus primarily on problem-solving techniques, using exercises and practical examples. These tools are relatively straightforward and easily communicated; the necessary mind-set, however, is more difficult to establish. Accuracy and precision are essential for learning. Employees must therefore become more disciplined in their thinking and more attentive to details. They must continually ask, "How do we know that's true?", recognizing that close enough is not good enough if real learning is to take place. They must push beyond obvious symptoms to assess underlying causes, often collecting evidence when conventional wisdom says it is unnecessary. Otherwise, the organization will remain a prisoner of "gut facts" and sloppy reasoning, and learning will be stifled.

Xerox has mastered this approach on a company-wide scale. In 1983, senior managers launched the company's Leadership Through Quality initiative; since then, all employees have been trained in small-group activities and problem-solving techniques. Today a six-step process is used for virtually all decisions (see the insert "Xerox's Problem-Solving Process"). Employees are provided with tools in four areas: generating ideas and collecting information (brainstorming, interviewing, surveying); reaching consensus (list reduction, rating forms, Weighted voting); analyzing and displaying data (cause-and-effect diagrams, force-field analysis);

and planning actions (flow charts, Gantt charts). They then practice these tools during training sessions that last several days. Training is presented in "family groups," members of the same department or business-unit team, and the tools are applied to real problems facing the group. The result of this process has been a common vocabulary and a consistent, companywide approach to problem solving. Once employees have been trained, they are expected to use the techniques at all meetings, and no topic is off-limits. When a high-level group was formed to review Xerox's organizational structure and suggest alternatives, it employed the very same process and tools.[3]

2. Experimentation. This activity involves the systematic searching for and testing of new knowledge. Using the scientific method is essential, and there are obvious parallels to systematic problem solving. But unlike problem solving, experimentation is usually motivated by opportunity and expanding horizons, not by current difficulties. It takes two main forms: ongoing programs and one-of-a-kind demonstration projects.

Ongoing programs normally involve a continuing series of small experiments, designed to produce incremental gains in knowledge. They are the mainstay of most continuous improvement programs and are especially common on the shop floor. Corning, for example, experiments, continually with diverse raw materials and new formulations to increase yields and provide better grades of glass. Allegheny Ludlum, a specialty steelmaker, regularly examines new rolling methods and improved technologies to raise productivity and reduce costs.

Successful ongoing programs share several characteristics. First, they work hard to ensure a steady flow of new ideas, even if they must be imported from outside the organization. Chaparral Steel sends its first-line supervisors on sabbaticals around the globe, where they visit academic and industry

---

[3]Robert Howard, "The CEO as Organizational Architect: An Interview with Xerox's Paul Allaire," *Harvard Business Review*, September-October 1992, p. 106.

Xerox's Problem-Solving Process

Step	Question to Be Answered	Expansion/ Divergence	Contraction/ Convergence	What's Needed to Go to the Next Step
1. Identify and select problem	What do we want to change?	Lots of problems for consideration	One problem statement, one "desired state" agreed upon	Identification of the gap "Desired state" described in observable terms
2. Analyze problem	What's preventing us from reaching the "desired state"?	Lots of potential causes identified	Key cause(s) identified and verified	Key cause(s) documented and ranked
3. Generate potential solutions	How *could* we make the change?	Lots of ideas on how to solve the problem	Potential solutions clarified	Solution list
4. Select and plan the solution	What's the *best* way to do it?	Lots of criteria for evaluating potential solutions Lots of ideas on how to implement and evaluate the selected solution	Criteria to use for evaluating solution agreed upon Implementation and evaluation plans agreed upon	Plan for making and monitoring the change Measurement criteria to evaluate solution effectiveness
5. Implement the solution	Are we following the plan?		Implementation of agreed-on contingency plans (if necessary)	Solution in place
6. Evaluate the solution	How well did it work?		Effectiveness of solution agreed upon Continuing problems (if any) identified	Verification that the problem is solved, or Agreement to address continuing problems

leaders, develop an understanding of new work practices and technologies, then bring what they've learned back to the company and apply it to daily operations. In large part as a result of these initiatives, Chaparral is one of the five lowest cost steel plants in the world. GE's Impact Program originally sent manufacturing managers to Japan to study factory innovations, such as quality circles and kanban cards, and then apply them in their own organizations; today Europe is the destination, and productivity improvement practices the target. The program is one reason GE has recorded productivity gains averaging nearly 5% over the last four years.

Successful ongoing programs also require an incentive system that favors risk taking. Employees must feel that the benefits of experimentation exceed the costs; otherwise, they will not participate. This creates a difficult challenge for managers, who are trapped between two perilous extremes. They must maintain accountability and control over experiments without stifling creativity by unduly penalizing employees for failures. Allegheny Ludlum has perfected this juggling act: it keeps expensive, high-impact experiments off the scorecard used to evaluate managers but requires prior approvals from four senior vice presidents. The result has been a history of productivity improvements annually averaging 7% to 8%.

Finally, ongoing programs need managers and employees who are trained in the skills required to perform and evaluate experiments. These skills are seldom intuitive and must usually be learned. They cover a broad sweep: statistical methods, like design of experiments, that efficiently compare a large number of alternatives; graphical techniques, like process analysis, that are essential for redesigning work flows; and creativity techniques, like storyboarding and role playing, that keep novel ideas flowing. The most effective training programs are tightly focused and feature a small set of techniques tailored to employees' needs. Training in design of experiments, for example, is useful for manufacturing engineers, while creativity techniques are well suited to development groups.

Demonstration projects are usually larger and more complex than ongoing experiments. They involve holistic, systemwide changes, introduced at a single site, and are often undertaken with the goal of developing new organizational capabilities. Because these projects represent a sharp break from the past, they are usually designed from scratch, using a "clean slate" approach. General Foods's Topeka plant, one of the first high-commitment work systems in this country, was a pioneering demonstration project initiated to introduce the idea of self-managing teams and high levels of worker autonomy; a more recent example, designed to re-think small-car development, manufacturing, and sales, is GM's Saturn Division.

Demonstration projects share a number of distinctive characteristics:

- They are usually the first projects to embody principles and approaches that the organization hopes to adopt later on a larger scale. For this reason, they are more transitional efforts than endpoints and involve considerable "learning by doing." Mid-course corrections are common.
- They implicitly establish policy guidelines and decision rules for later projects. Managers must therefore be sensitive to the precedents they are setting and must send strong signals if they expect to establish new norms.
- They often encounter severe tests of commitment from employees who wish to see whether the rules have, in fact, changed.
- They are normally developed by strong multifunctional teams reporting directly to senior management. (For projects targeting employee involvement or quality of work life, teams should be multilevel as well.)
- They tend to have only limited impact on the rest of the organization if they are not accompanied by explicit strategies for transferring learning.

All of these characteristics appeared in a demonstration project launched by Copeland Corporation, a highly successful compressor manufacturer, in the mid-1970s. Matt Diggs, then the new CEO, wanted to transform the company's approach to manufacturing. Previously, Copeland had machined and assembled all products in a single facility. Costs were high, and quality was marginal. The problem, Diggs felt, was too much complexity.

At the outset, Diggs assigned a small, multifunctional team the task of designing a "focused factory" dedicated to a narrow, newly developed product line. The team reported directly to Diggs and took three years to complete its work. Initially, the project budget was $10 million to $12 million; that figure was repeatedly revised as the team found, through experience and with Diggs's prodding, that it could achieve dramatic improvements. The final investment, a total of $30 million, yielded unanticipated breakthroughs in reliability testing, automatic tool adjustment, and programmable control. All were achieved through learning by doing.

The team set additional precedents during the plant's start-up and early operations. To dramatize the importance of quality, for example, the quality manager was appointed second-in-command, a significant move upward. The same reporting relationship was used at all subsequent plants. In addition, Diggs urged the plant manager to ramp up slowly to full production and resist all efforts to proliferate products. These instructions were unusual at Copeland, where the marketing department normally ruled. Both directives were quickly tested; management held firm, and the implications were felt throughout the organization. Manufacturing's stature improved, and the company as a whole recognized its competitive contribution. One observer commented, "Marketing had always run the company, so they couldn't believe it. The change was visible at the highest levels, and it went down hard."

Once the first focused factory was running smoothly—it seized 25% of the market in two years and held its edge in reliability for over a decade—Copeland built four more factories in quick succession. Diggs assigned members of the initial project to each factory's design team to ensure that early learnings were not lost; these people later rotated into operating assignments. Today focused factories remain the cornerstone of Copeland's manufacturing strategy and a continuing source of its cost and quality advantages.

Whether they are demonstration projects like Copeland's or ongoing programs like Allegheny Ludlum's, all forms of experimentation seek the same end: moving from superficial knowledge to deep understanding. At its simplest, the distinction is between knowing how things are done and knowing why they occur. Knowing how is partial knowledge; it is rooted in norms of behavior, standards of practice, and settings of equipment. Knowing why is more fundamental: it captures underlying cause-and-effect relationships and accommodates exceptions, adaptations, and unforeseen events. The ability to control temperatures and pressures to align grains of silicon and form silicon steel is an example of knowing how; understanding the chemical and physical process that produces the alignment is knowing why.

Further distinctions are possible, as the insert "Stages of Knowledge" suggests. Operating knowledge can be arrayed in a hierarchy, moving from limited understanding and the ability to make few

---

Stages of Knowledge

Scholars have suggested that production and operating knowledge can be classified systematically by level or stage of understanding. At the lowest levels of manufacturing knowledge, little is known other than the characteristics of a good product. Production remains an art, and there are few clearly articulated standards or rules. An example would be Stradivarius violins. Experts agree that they produce vastly superior sound, but no one can specify precisely how they were manufactured because skilled artisans were responsible. By contrast, at the highest levels of manufacturing knowledge, all aspects of production are known and understood. All materials and processing variations are articulated and accounted for, with rules and procedures for every contingency. Here an example would be a "lights out," fully automated factory that operates for many hours without any human intervention.

In total, this framework specifies eight stages of knowledge. From lowest to highest, they are:

1. Recognizing prototypes (what is a good product?).
2. Recognizing attributes within prototypes (ability to define some conditions under which process gives good output).
3. Discriminating among attributes (which attributes are important? Experts may differ about relevance of patterns; new operators are often trained through apprenticeships).
4. Measuring attributes (some key attributes are measured; measures may be qualitative and relative).
5. Locally controlling attributes (repeatable performance; process designed by expert, but technicians can perform it).
6. Recognizing and discriminating between contingencies (production process can be mechanized and monitored manually).
7. Controlling contingencies (process can be automated).
8. Understanding procedures and controlling contingencies (process is completely understood).

Source: Adapted from work by Ramchandran Jaikumar and Roger Bohn, "The Development of Intelligent Systems for Industrial Use: A Conceptual Framework," *Research on Technological Innovation, Management and Policy,* Vol. 3 (1986), pp. 182–188.

distinctions to more complete understanding in which all contingencies are anticipated and controlled. In this context, experimentation and problem solving foster learning by pushing organizations up the hierarchy, from lower to higher stages of knowledge.

3. Learning from past experience. Companies must review their successes and failures, assess them systematically, and record the lessons in a form that employees find open and accessible. One expert has called this process the "Santayana Review," citing the famous philosopher George Santayana, who coined the phrase "Those who cannot remember the past are condemned to repeat it." Unfortunately, too many managers today are indifferent, even hostile, to the past, and by failing to reflect on it, they let valuable knowledge escape.

A study of more than 150 new products concluded that "the knowledge gained from failures [is] often instrumental in achieving subsequent successes. . . . In the simplest terms, failure is the ultimate teacher."[4] IBM's 360 computer series, for example, one of the most popular and profitable ever built, was based on the technology of the failed Stretch computer that preceded it. In this case, as in many others, learning occurred by chance rather than by careful planning. A few companies, however, have established processes that require their managers to periodically think about the past and learn from their mistakes.

Boeing did so immediately after its difficulties with the 737 and 747 plane programs. Both planes were introduced with much fanfare and also with serious problems. To ensure that the problems were not repeated, senior managers commissioned a high-level employee group, called Project Homework, to compare the development processes of the 737 and 747 with those of the 707 and 727, two of the company's most profitable planes. The group was asked to develop a set of "lessons learned" that could be used on future projects. After working for three years, they produced hundreds of recommendations and an inch-thick booklet. Several members of the team were then transferred to the 757 and 767 start-ups, and guided by experience, they produced the most successful, error-free launches in Boeing's history.

Other companies have used a similar retrospective approach. Like Boeing, Xerox studied its product development process, examining three troubled products in an effort to understand why the company's new business initiatives failed so often. Arthur D. Little, the consulting company, focused on its past successes. Senior management invited ADL consultants from around the world to a two-day "jamboree," featuring booths and presentations documenting a wide range of the company's most successful practices, publications, and techniques. British Petroleum went even further and established the post-project appraisal unit to review major investment projects, write up case studies, and derive lessons for planners that were then incorporated into revisions of the company's planning guidelines. A five-person unit reported to the board of directors and reviewed six projects annually. The bulk of the time was spent in the field interviewing managers.[5] This type of review is now conducted regularly at the project level.

At the heart of this approach, one expert has observed, "is a mind-set that . . . enables companies to recognize the value of productive failure as contrasted with unproductive success. A productive failure is one that leads to insight, understanding, and thus an addition to the commonly held wisdom of the organization. An unproductive success occurs when something goes well, but nobody knows how or why."[6] IBM's legendary founder, Thomas Watson, Sr., apparently understood the distinction well. Company lore has it that a young manager, after losing $10 million in a risky venture, was called into

---

[4]Modesto A. Maidique and Billie Jo Zirger, "The New Product Learning Cycle," *Research Policy*, Vol. 14, No. 6 (1985), pp. 299, 309.

[5]Frank R. Gulliver, "Post-Project Appraisals Pay," *Harvard Business Review,* March–April 1987, p. 128.

[6]David Nadler, "Even Failures Can Be Productive," *New York Times,* April 23, 1989, Sec. 3, p. 3.

Watson's office. The young man, thoroughly intimidated, began by saying, "I guess you want my resignation." Watson replied, "You can't be serious. We just spent $10 million educating you."

Fortunately, the learning process need not be so expensive. Case studies and post-project reviews like those of Xerox and British Petroleum can be performed with little cost other than managers' time. Companies can also enlist the help of faculty and students at local colleges or universities; they bring fresh perspectives and view internships and case studies as opportunities to gain experience and increase their own learning. A few companies have established computerized data banks to speed up the learning process. At Paul Revere Life Insurance, management requires all problem-solving teams to complete short registration forms describing their proposed projects if they hope to qualify for the company's award program. The company then enters the forms into its computer system and can immediately retrieve a listing of other groups of people who have worked or are working on the topic, along with a contact person. Relevant experience is then just a telephone call away.

4. Learning from others. Of course, not all learning comes from reflection and self-analysis. Sometimes the most powerful insights come from looking outside one's immediate environment to gain a new perspective. Enlightened managers know that even companies in completely different businesses can be fertile sources of ideas and catalysts for creative thinking. At these organizations, enthusiastic borrowing is replacing the "not invented here" syndrome. Milliken calls the process SIS, for "Steal Ideas Shamelessly"; the broader term for it is benchmarking.

According to one expert, "benchmarking is an ongoing investigation and learning experience that ensures that best industry practices are uncovered, analyzed, adopted, and implemented."[7] The greatest benefits come from studying *practices,* the way that work gets done, rather than results, and from

---

[7]Robert C. Camp, *Benchmarking: The Search for Industry Best Practices that Lead to Superior Performance* (Milwaukee: ASQC Quality Press, 1989), p. 12.

involving line managers in the process. Almost anything can be benchmarked. Xerox, the concept's creator, has applied it to billing, warehousing, and automated manufacturing. Milliken has been even more creative: in an inspired moment, it benchmarked Xerox's approach to benchmarking.

Unfortunately, there is still considerable confusion about the requirements for successful benchmarking. Benchmarking is not "industrial tourism," a series of ad hoc visits to companies that have received favorable publicity or won quality awards. Rather, it is a disciplined process that begins with a thorough search to identify best-practice organizations, continues with careful study of one's own practices and performance, progresses through systematic site visits and interviews, and concludes with an analysis of results, development of recommendations, and implementation. While time-consuming, the process need not be terribly expensive. AT&T's Benchmarking Group estimates that a moderate-sized project takes four to six months and incurs out-of-pocket costs of $20,000 (when personnel costs are included, the figure is three to four times higher).

Benchmarking is one way of gaining an outside perspective; another, equally fertile source of ideas is customers. Conversations with customers invariably stimulate learning; they are, after all, experts in what they do. Customers can provide up-to-date product information, competitive comparisons, insights into changing preferences, and immediate feedback about service and patterns of use. And companies need these insights at all levels, from the executive suite to the shop floor. At Motorola, members of the Operating and Policy Committee, including the CEO, meet personally and on a regular basis with customers. At Worthington Steel, all machine operators make periodic, unescorted trips to customers' factories to discuss their needs.

Sometimes customers can't articulate their needs or remember even the most recent problems they have had with a product or service. If that's the case, managers must observe them in action. Xerox employs a number of anthropologists at its Palo Alto Research Center to observe users of new document products in their offices. Digital Equipment has developed an interactive process called "contextual inquiry" that is used by software engineers to observe users of new technologies as they go about their work. Milliken has created "first-delivery teams" that accompany the first shipment of all products; team members follow the product through the customer's production process to see how it is used and then develop ideas for further improvement.

Whatever the source of outside ideas, learning will only occur in a receptive environment. Managers can't be defensive and must be open to criticism or bad news. This is a difficult challenge, but it is essential for success. Companies that approach customers assuming that "we must be right, they have to be wrong" or visit other organizations certain that "they can't teach us anything" seldom learn very much. Learning organizations, by contrast, cultivate the art of open, attentive listening.

5. Transferring knowledge. For learning to be more than a local affair, knowledge must spread quickly and efficiently throughout the organization. Ideas carry maximum impact when they are shared broadly rather than held in a few hands. A variety of mechanisms spur this process, including written, oral, and visual reports, site visits and tours, personnel rotation programs, education and training programs, and standardization programs. Each has distinctive strengths and weaknesses.

Reports and tours are by far the most popular mediums. Reports serve many purposes: they summarize findings, provide checklists of dos and don'ts, and describe important processes and events. They cover a multitude of topics, from benchmarking studies to accounting conventions to newly discovered marketing techniques. Today written reports are often supplemented by videotapes, which offer greater immediacy and fidelity.

Tours are an equally popular means of transferring knowledge, especially for large, multidivisional organizations with multiple sites. The most effective tours are tailored to different audiences and needs. To introduce its managers to the distinctive manufacturing practices of New United Motor Manufacturing Inc. (NUMMI), its joint venture with Toyota, General Motors developed a series of specialized tours. Some were geared to upper and mid-

dle managers, while others were aimed at lower ranks. Each tour described the policies, practices, and systems that were most relevant to that level of management.

Despite their popularity, reports and tours are relatively cumbersome ways of transferring knowledge. The gritty details that lie behind complex management concepts are difficult to communicate secondhand. Absorbing facts by reading them or seeing them demonstrated is one thing; experiencing them personally is quite another. As a leading cognitive scientist has observed, "It is very difficult to become knowledgeable in a passive way. Actively experiencing something is considerably more valuable than having it described."[8] For this reason, personnel rotation programs are one of the most powerful methods of transferring knowledge.

In many organizations, expertise is held locally: in a particularly skilled computer technician, perhaps, a savvy global brand manager, or a division head with a track record of successful joint ventures. Those in daily contact with these experts benefit enormously from their skills, but their field of influence is relatively narrow. Transferring them to different parts of the organization helps share the wealth. Transfers may be from division to division, department to department, or facility to facility; they may involve senior, middle, or first-level managers. A supervisor experienced in just-in-time production, for example, might move to another factory to apply the methods there, or a successful division manager might transfer to a lagging division to invigorate it with already proven ideas. The CEO of Time Life used the latter approach when he shifted the president of the company's music division, who had orchestrated several years of rapid growth and high profits through innovative marketing, to the presidency of the book division, where profits were flat because of continued reliance on traditional marketing concepts.

Line to staff transfers are another option. These are most effective when they allow experienced

---

[8]Roger Schank, with Peter Childers, *The Creative Attitude* (New York: Macmillan, 1988), p. 9.

managers to distill what they have learned and diffuse it across the company in the form of new standards, policies, or training programs. Consider how PPG used just such a transfer to advance its human resource practices around the concept of high-commitment work systems. In 1986, PPG constructed a new float-glass plant in Chehalis, Washington; it employed a radically new technology as well as innovations in human resource management that were developed by the plant manager and his staff. All workers were organized into small, self-managing teams with responsibility for work assignments, scheduling, problem solving and improvement, and peer review. After several years running the factory, the plant manager was promoted to director of human resources for the entire glass group. Drawing on his experiences at Chehalis, he developed a training program geared toward first-level supervisors that taught the behaviors needed to manage employees in a participative, self-managing environment.

As the PPG example suggests, education and training programs are powerful tools for transferring knowledge. But for maximum effectiveness, they must be linked explicitly to implementation. All too often, trainers assume that new knowledge will be applied without taking concrete steps to ensure that trainees actually follow through. Seldom do trainers provide opportunities for practice, and few programs consciously promote the application of their teachings after employees have returned to their jobs.

Xerox and GTE are exceptions. As noted earlier, when Xerox introduced problem-solving techniques to its employees in the 1980s, everyone, from the top to the bottom of the organization, was taught in small departmental or divisional groups led by their immediate superior. After an introduction to concepts and techniques, each group applied what they learned to a real-life work problem. In a similar spirit, GTE's Quality: The Competitive Edge program was offered to teams of business-unit presidents and the managers reporting to them. At the beginning of the three-day course, each team received a request from a company officer to prepare a complete quality plan for their unit, based on

the course concepts, within 60 days. Discussion periods of two to three hours were set aside during the program so that teams could begin working on their plans. After the teams submitted their reports, the company officers studied them, and then the teams implemented them. This GTE program produced dramatic improvements in quality, including a recent semifinalist spot in the Baldrige Awards.

The GTE example suggests another important guideline: knowledge is more likely to be transferred effectively when the right incentives are in place. If employees know that their plans will be evaluated and implemented—in other words, that their learning will be applied—progress is far more likely. At most companies, the status quo is well entrenched; only if managers and employees see new ideas as being in their own best interest will they accept them gracefully. AT&T has developed a creative approach that combines strong incentives with information sharing. Called the Chairman's Quality Award (CQA), it is an internal quality competition modeled on the Baldrige prize but with an important twist: awards are given not only for absolute performance (using the same 1,000-point scoring system as Baldrige) but also for improvements in scoring from the previous year. Gold, silver, and bronze Improvement Awards are given to units that have improved their scores 200, 150, and 100 points, respectively. These awards provide the incentive for change. An accompanying Pockets of Excellence program simplifies knowledge transfer. Every year, it identifies every unit within the company that has scored at least 60% of the possible points in each award category and then publicizes the names of these units using written reports and electronic mail.

Measuring Learning

Managers have long known that "if you can't measure it, you can't manage it." This maxim is as true of learning as it is of any other corporate objective. Traditionally, the solution has been "learning curves" and "manufacturing progress functions." Both concepts date back to the discovery, during the 1920s and 1930s, that the costs of airframe manufacturing fell predictably with increases in cumulative volume. These increases were viewed as proxies for greater manufacturing knowledge, and most early studies examined their impact on the costs of direct labor. Later studies expanded the focus, looking at total manufacturing costs and the impact of experience in other industries, including shipbuilding, oil refining, and consumer electronics. Typically, learning rates were in the 80% to 85% range (meaning that with a doubling of cumulative production, costs fell to 80% to 85% of their previous level), although there was wide variation.

Firms like the Boston Consulting Group raised these ideas to a higher level in the 1970s. Drawing on the logic of learning curves, they argued that industries as a whole faced "experience curves," costs and prices that fell by predictable amounts as industries grew and their total production increased. With this observation, consultants suggested, came an iron law of competition. To enjoy the benefits of experience, companies would have to rapidly increase their production ahead of competitors to lower prices and gain market share.

Both learning and experience curves are still widely used, especially in the aerospace, defense, and electronics industries. Boeing, for instance, has established learning curves for every work station in its assembly plant; they assist in monitoring productivity, determining work flows and staffing levels, and setting prices and profit margins on new airplanes. Experience curves are common in semiconductors and consumer electronics, where they are used to forecast industry costs and prices.

For companies hoping to become learning organizations, however, these measures are incomplete. They focus on only a single measure of output (cost or price) and ignore learning that affects other competitive variables, like quality, delivery, or new product introductions. They suggest only one possible learning driver (total production volumes) and ignore both the possibility of learning in mature industries, where output is flat, and the possibility that learning might be driven by other sources, such as new technology or the challenge posed by competing products. Perhaps most important, they tell

us little about the sources of learning or the levers of change.

Another measure has emerged in response to these concerns. Called the "half-life" curve, it was originally developed by Analog Devices, a leading semiconductor manufacturer, as a way of comparing internal improvement rates. A half-life curve measures the time it takes to achieve a 50% improvement in a specified performance measure. When represented graphically, the performance measure (defect rates, on-time delivery, time to market) is plotted on the vertical axis, using a logarithmic scale, and the time scale (days, months, years) is plotted horizontally. Steeper slopes then represent faster learning (see the insert "The Half-Life Curve" for an illustration).

The logic is straightforward. Companies, divisions, or departments that take less time to improve must be learning faster than their peers. In the long run, their short learning cycles will translate into superior performance. The 50% target is a measure of convenience; it was derived empirically from studies of successful improvement processes at a wide range of companies. Half-life curves are also flexible. Unlike learning and experience curves, they work on any output measure, and they are not confined to costs or prices. In addition, they are easy to operationalize, they provide a simple measuring stick, and they allow for ready comparison among groups.

Yet even half-life curves have an important weakness: they focus solely on results. Some types of knowledge take years to digest, with few visible changes in performance for long periods. Creating a total quality culture, for instance, or developing new approaches to product development are difficult systemic changes. Because of their long gestation periods, half-life curves or any other measures focused solely on results are unlikely to capture any short-run learning that has occurred. A more comprehensive framework is needed to track progress.

Organizational learning can usually be traced through three overlapping stages. The first step is cognitive. Members of the organization are exposed to new ideas, expand their knowledge, and

The Half-Life Curve

Analog Devices has used half-life curves to compare the performance of its divisions. Here monthly data on customer service are graphed for seven divisions. Division C is the clear winner even though it started with a high proportion of late deliveries, its rapid learning rate led eventually to the best absolute performance. Divisions D, E, and G have been far less successful, with little or no improvement in on-time service over the period.

On-Time Service Customer Performance—Monthly Data (August 1987–July 1988)

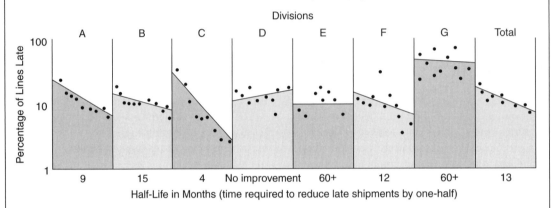

Half-Life in Months (time required to reduce late shipments by one-half)

Source: Ray Stata, "Organizational Learning—The Key to Management Innovation," *Sloan Management Review,* Spring 1989, p. 72.

begin to think differently. The second step is behavioral. Employees begin to internalize new insights and alter their behavior. And the third step is performance improvement, with changes in behavior leading to measurable improvements in results: superior quality, better delivery, increased market share, or other tangible gains. Because cognitive and behavioral changes typically precede improvements in performance, a complete learning audit must include all three.

Surveys, questionnaires, and interviews are useful for this purpose. At the cognitive level, they would focus on attitudes and depth of understanding. Have employees truly understood the meaning of self-direction and teamwork, or are the terms still unclear? At PPG, a team of human resource experts periodically audits every manufacturing plant, including extensive interviews with shop-floor em-

ployees, to ensure that the concepts are well understood. Have new approaches to customer service been fully accepted? At its 1989 Worldwide Marketing Managers' Meeting, Ford presented participants with a series of hypothetical situations in which customer complaints were in conflict with short-term dealer or company profit goals and asked how they would respond. Surveys like these are the first step toward identifying changed attitudes and new ways of thinking.

To assess behavioral changes, surveys and questionnaires must be supplemented by direct observation: Here the proof is in the doing, and there is no substitute for seeing employees in action. Domino's Pizza uses "mystery shoppers" to assess managers' commitment to customer service at its individual stores; L.L. Bean places telephone orders with its own operators to assess service levels. Other companies invite outside consultants to visit, attend meetings, observe employees in action, and then report what they have learned. In many ways, this approach mirrors that of examiners for the Baldrige Award, who make several-day site visits to semifinalists to see whether the companies' deeds match the words on their applications.

Finally, a comprehensive learning audit also measures performance. Half-life curves or other performance measures are essential for ensuring that cognitive and behavioral changes have actually produced results. Without them, companies would lack a rationale for investing in learning and the assurance that learning was serving the organization's ends.

First Steps

Learning organizations are not built overnight. Most successful examples are the products of carefully cultivated attitudes, commitments, and management processes that have accrued slowly and steadily over time. Still, some changes can be made immediately. Any company that wishes to become a learning organization can begin by taking a few simple steps.

The first step is to foster an environment that is conducive to learning. There must be time for reflection and analysis, to think about strategic plans, dissect customer needs, assess current work systems, and invent new products. Learning is difficult when employees are harried or rushed; it tends to be driven out by the pressures of the moment. Only if top management explicitly frees up employees' time for the purpose does learning occur with any frequency. That time will be doubly productive if employees possess the skills to use it wisely. Training in brainstorming, problem solving, evaluating experiments, and other core learning skills is therefore essential.

Another powerful lever is to open up boundaries and stimulate the exchange of ideas. Boundaries inhibit the flow of information; they keep individuals and groups isolated and reinforce preconceptions. Opening up boundaries, with conferences, meet-

ings, and project teams, which either cross organizational levels or link the company and its customers and suppliers, ensures a fresh flow of ideas and the chance to consider competing perspectives. General Electric CEO Jack Welch considers this to be such a powerful stimulant of change that he has made "boundarylessness" a cornerstone of the company's strategy for the 1990s.

Once managers have established a more supportive, open environment, they can create learning forums. These are programs or events designed with explicit learning goals in mind, and they can take a variety of forms: strategic reviews, which examine the changing competitive environment and the company's product portfolio, technology, and market positioning; systems audits, which review the health of large, cross-functional processes and delivery systems; internal benchmarking reports, which identify and compare best-in-class activities within the organization; study missions, which are dispatched to leading organizations around the world to better understand their performance and distinctive skills; and jamborees or symposiums, which bring together customers, suppliers, outside experts, or internal groups to share ideas and learn from one another. Each of these activities fosters learning by requiring employees to wrestle with new knowledge and consider its implications. Each can also be tailored to business needs. A consumer goods company, for example, might sponsor a study mission to Europe to learn more about distribution methods within the newly unified Common Market, while a high-technology company might launch a systems audit to review its new product development process.

Together these efforts help to eliminate barriers that impede learning and begin to move learning higher on the organizational agenda. They also suggest a subtle shift in focus, away from continuous improvement and toward a commitment to learning. Coupled with a better understanding of the "three Ms," the meaning, management, and measurement of learning, this shift provides a solid foundation for building learning organizations.

Chapter 7

Building Transnational Capabilities: The Management Challenge

From the discussions in previous chapters and descriptions in earlier cases, it should be clear that the MNC in the 1990s is markedly different from its ancestor of the pre–World War II era, and even from its immediate predecessor of the 1960s and 1970s. It has been transformed by an environment in which multiple, often conflicting, forces were accelerating simultaneously. The globalization of markets, the acceleration of product and technology life cycles, the renewed assertion of national governments' demands, and, above all, the intensification of global competition made the 1980s a decade of complexity, diversity, and change for most MNCs.

The fast-changing external environment forced most companies to reassess their strategic postures and competitive capabilities. As we have seen, the ability to compete on the basis of a single dominant competitive advantage gave way to a need to develop multiple strategic assets: global-scale efficiency and competitiveness, national responsiveness and flexibility, and a worldwide innovation and learning capability.

In turn, these new strategic-task demands put pressure on existing organization structures and management processes. Traditional hierarchical structures with their emphasis on either-or choices (centralization versus decentralization; product versus geographic divisions) have evolved toward organizational forms we have described as transnational, characterized by integrated networks of assets and resources, multidimensional management perspectives and capabilities, and flexible coordinative processes.

The management implications of all this change are enormous. To succeed in the international operating environment of the present, managers must be able to sense and interpret the complex and dynamic environmental changes; they must be able to develop and integrate the multiple strategic capabilities; and they must be able to build and manage the complicated yet subtle new organizations required to link these sensing and response capabilities, and deliver coordinated action on a worldwide basis. Unless those in key management positions are highly skilled and knowledgeable, companies simply cannot respond to the major new challenges they face.

Yet, surprisingly little attention is devoted to the study of the implications of all these changes on the roles and responsibilities of those who manage today's MNCs. Academics, consultants, and even managers themselves focus an enormous amount of time and energy on analyzing the various international environmental forces, refining the concepts of global strategy, and understanding the characteristics of effective transnational organizations. But without effective managers in place, sophisticated strategies and subtle organizations will fail, and the great risk of the 1990s is that companies are trying to implement third-generation strategies through second-generation organizations with first-generation managers.

In this and the next chapters, we examine the management roles and responsibilities implied by the new challenges facing MNCs—those that take the manager beyond the first-generation assumptions. The tasks differ considerably for those in different parts and in different levels of the organization, so rather than generalizing, we will focus on the core responsibilities of different key management groups. In this chapter, we look laterally, at the roles and tasks of the global business manager, the country manager, and the financial manager in the transnational company. In the next chapter, we explore the relationships across organizational levels and suggest how the roles of front-line, middle, and top-level managers may evolve in the transnationals of the future.

GLOBAL BUSINESS MANAGEMENT

The challenge of developing global efficiency and competitiveness requires management to capture the various scale and scope economies available to the MNC as well as capitalizing on the potential competitive advantages inherent in its worldwide market positioning. This demands a perspective that can see opportunities and risks across national boundaries and functional specialties, and a skill to coordinate and integrate activities across these barriers to capture the potential benefits. This is the fundamental task of the global business manager.

In implementing this important responsibility, the global business manager must initiate or become involved in a variety of diverse activities, whose balance will vary considerably depending on the nature of the business and the company's administrative heritage. Nonetheless, there are three core roles and responsibilities that almost always fall to this key manager: worldwide product or business strategist, architect of worldwide asset and resource configuration, and cross-border coordinator and controller.

Worldwide Business Strategist

Because global competitive interaction increasingly takes place on a global chess board as we discussed in Chapter 3, only a manager with worldwide perspective and responsibility can assess the strategic position and capability in a given business. This requires that companies configure their information, planning, and control systems so that they can be consolidated not only on a country-by-country basis, but also in consistent, integrated global business reports.

This is not to imply that the global business manager alone has the perspective and capability to formulate strategic priorities, or that he or she should undertake that vital task unilaterally. Depending on the nature of the business, there will almost certainly be some need to incorporate the perspectives of geographic and functional managers who will represent strategic interests that may run counter to the business manager's drive to maximize global efficiency. Equally important, the business strategy must fit within the broader corporate strategy that should provide a clear vision of what the company wants to be and explicit values of how it will accomplish its mission.

In the final analysis, however, the responsibility to integrate the different views and reconcile the diverse interests will fall to the global business manager who will need to prepare an integrated strategy of how the company will compete in his or her particular business. In many companies, the manager's ability to do so was often compromised by the fact that the position was created by anointing domestic product division managers with the title of global business manager. Overseas subsidiary managers often felt that these managers not only were insensitive to nondomestic perspectives and interests, but that they biased key strategic decisions like product development and capacity plans towards the domestic organization. In many cases, their concerns were justified.

In the true transnational company, the global business manager need not be located in the home country, and in many cases, great benefits can accrue to relocating several such management groups abroad. Asea Brown Boveri (ABB), the leading electrical engineering company, has deliberately tried to leverage the capabilities of its strong operating companies worldwide and to exploit their location in key strategic markets by locating its worldwide business area management wherever such organizational and strategic dimensions coincide. In its global power transmission business, for example, the business area manager for switchgear is located in Sweden, for power transformers in Germany, for distribution transformers in Norway, and for electric metering in the United States. Even well-established MNCs with a tradition of close control of worldwide business strategy are changing. The head of IBM's $6 billion telecommunications business recently moved her division headquarters to London. She explained that the rationale was not only to move the command center closer to the booming European market for computer networking, but also "[to] give us a different perspective on all our markets."

Architect of Asset and Resource Configuration

Closely tied to the challenge of shaping an integrated business strategy is the global business manager's responsibility for coordinating the distribution of key assets and resources in a configuration that supports the strategic objectives. Again, as in many other key decisions in transnational companies, this does not mean that he or she can make such decisions unilaterally. The input of interested geographic and functional managers must also be weighed. It is the global business manager, however, who is normally best placed to initiate and lead the debate on asset configuration, perhaps through a global strategy committee or a world board with membership drawn from key geographic and functional management groups. Because the allocation of capital is normally a top-management decision, the proposals of such groups will typically be escalated for approval.

In deciding where to locate key plants or develop vital resources, the business manager can never assume a zero base. Indeed, such decisions must be rooted in the company's administrative heritage. In multinational companies like Philips, Unilever, ICI, or Nestlé, many of the key assets and resources that permitted these companies to expand internationally have long been located in national companies operating as part of a decentralized federation. Any business manager trying to shape such companies' future configurations must build on rather than ignore or destroy the important benefits that such assets and resources represent. The challenge to the business manager is to shape the future configuration by leveraging existing resources and capabilities and linking them into a configuration that resembles the integrated network form described in Chapter 5.

Cross-Border Coordinator

This leads directly to the third key role played by most global business managers, that of cross-border coordinator. Although less overtly strategic than the other two responsibilities, it is nonetheless a vital operating function, since it involves deciding on sourcing patterns and managing cross-border transfer policies and mechanisms.

The task of coordinating flows of materials, components, and finished products becomes extremely complex as companies build transnational structures and capabilities. Rather than producing and shipping all products from a fully integrated central plant (the centralized hub model) or allowing local subsidiaries to develop self-sufficient capabilities (the decentralized federation model), transnational companies specialize their operations worldwide, building on the most capable national operations and capitalizing on locations of strategic importance. The resulting worldwide network of specialized operations is highly interdependent, perhaps linking high labor content component plants in Poland and Korea with highly skilled subassembly operations in Germany and Singapore, which in turn supply specialized plants in the United States, England, France, and Japan, each producing particular parts of the company's product line.

The coordination mechanisms available to the global business manager vary from direct central control over quantities shipped and prices charged to the establishment of rules that essentially create an internal market mechanism to coordinate cross-border activities. The former means of control is more likely in situations of product shortage or for products of high strategic importance (e.g., pharmaceutical companies' control over quantities and pricing of shipments of the active ingredients of patented drugs or Coca-Cola's coordination of the supply of Coke syrup worldwide). As products become more commodity-like, however, global product managers may be better advised to ensure that internal transfers reflect the competitive conditions set by the external environment. This led many to develop internal quasi-markets as the principal means of coordination.

One interesting example is provided by the consumer electronics giant, Matsushita. Once the parent company develops prototypes of the following year's models of TV sets, video cameras, CD players, and so on, the product managers host merchandise meetings that are, in effect, huge internal trade fairs to which all Matsushita sales subsidiaries are invited. At these meetings, national sales and marketing directors enter into direct discussions with supply sources, negotiating modifications in product design, price, and delivery schedule to meet their local market needs.

WORLDWIDE FUNCTIONAL MANAGEMENT

The challenge of developing and diffusing innovations on a worldwide basis requires that functional managers evolve from the secondary staff roles they often played and take an active role in transnational management. This vital task is built on knowledge that is highly specialized by function—technological capability, marketing expertise, manufacturing know-how, and so on—and there is a clear need for such functional experts to be linked on a worldwide basis.

The tasks facing functional managers vary widely by specific function (technology transfer may be more intensive than the transfer of marketing expertise, for example), and by business (companies in transnational industries such as telecommunications demand more functional linkages and transfers than do those in industries—retailing, for example—that are more multinational in nature). Nonetheless, we will highlight three basic roles and responsibilities that most worldwide functional managers should play: worldwide scanner of specialized information and intelligence, cross-pollinator of "best practices," and champion of transnational innovation.

Worldwide Intelligence Scanner

Most innovations start with some stimulus driving the company to respond to a perceived opportunity or threat. It may be a revolutionary technological breakthrough, an emerging consumer trend, a new competitive challenge, or a pending government regulation. And it may occur anywhere in the world. Unless a company is able to sense that new stimulus, it will not develop an appropriate response, thereby losing an innovative opportunity to a competitor.

A typical example occurred in the mid-1980s when the radical new Green political party in Germany began achieving important victories in gaining popular support for environmental protection. Companies with good sensory mechanisms in Germany recognized the significance of this development and began adjusting their products, processes, and company policies. Many without such advance warning systems found themselves several years later trying to respond not only to the spreading political and consumer pressures, but also to their more responsive competitors touting their new environment-friendly approaches.

Although strategically important information was often sensed in the foreign subsidiaries of classic multinational or global companies, it was rarely transmitted to those who could act on it, or was ignored when it did get through. The communication problem was due primarily to the fact that the intelligence was usually of a specialist nature that was not always well understood by the generalists who controlled the line organization. To capture and transmit such information across national boundaries required the establishment of specialist information channels that linked local national technologists, marketers, and production specialists with others who understood their needs and shared their perspective.

In transnational companies, functional managers are linked through informal networks that are nurtured and maintained through frequent meetings, visits, and transfers. Through such linkages, these managers develop the contacts and relationships that allow them to transmit information rapidly around the globe. The functional managers at the corporate level become the linchpins in this effort and play a vital role as facilitators of communication and repositories of specialist information.

Cross-Pollinator of "Best Practices"

Overseas subsidiaries can be more than sources of strategic intelligence, however. In a truly transnational company, they can be the source of capabilities, expertise, and innovation that can be transferred to other parts of the organization. Caterpillar's leading-edge flexible manufacturing first emerged in its French and Belgian plants, for example, and much of P&G's liquid detergent technology was developed in its European Technology Center. In both cases, this expertise was transferred to other countries with important global strategic impact.

Such an administrative ability to transfer new ideas and developments requires a considerable amount of management time and attention to break down the not-invented-here (NIH) syndrome that often thrives in international business. In this process, those with worldwide functional responsibilities are ideally placed to play the central cross-pollination role. Not only do they have the specialist knowledge required to identify and evaluate leading-edge practices, they also tend to have a well-developed informal communications network developed with others in their functional area.

The corporate functional managers in particular can play a vital role in this important task. Through informal contacts, formal evaluations, and frequent travel, they can identify where the best practices are being developed and implemented. They are also in a position to arrange cross-unit visits and transfers, host conferences, form task forces, or take other initiatives that will expose others to the new ideas. Legitimizing functional managers' cross-unit linkages and reinforcing their membership in a companywide functional group can do much to break down the NIH syndrome and encourage the transfer of best practices.

Champion of Transnational Innovation

The two previously identified roles ideally position the functional manager to play a key role in developing what we call *transnational innovations.* These are different from the predominantly local activity that dominated the innovation process in multinational companies, or the centrally driven innovation in international and global companies. Transnational innovation requires that traditionally independent or dependent relationships among organizational units worldwide be replaced by an interdependence that encourages some very different innovation processes.

The first (and simplest) form of transnational innovation is what we term *locally leveraged,* and builds on the best-practices discussion above. By scanning their companies' worldwide operations, corporate functional managers can identify local innovations that have applications elsewhere. In Unilever, for example, product and marketing innovation for many of its global brands occurred in national subsidiaries. Snuggle fabric softener was born in Unilever's German company, Timotae herbal shampoo originated in its Scandinavian operations, and Impulse body spray was first introduced by its South African unit. Recognizing the potential that these local innovations had for the wider company, the parent company's marketing and technical groups created the impetus to spread them to other subsidiaries.

The second type of transnational innovation, which we term *globally linked,* requires functional managers to play a more sophisticated role. This type of innovation fully exploits the company's access to worldwide information and expertise by linking and leveraging intelligence sources with internal centers of excellence wherever they may be located. For example, P&G's new global liquid detergent was developed by managing a complex network of relationships among technical and marketing managers worldwide. The product's desired performance responded to the Europeans' need for water-softening capability, the Americans' desire for improved cleaning capability, and the Japanese sensing of an opportunity for a liquid detergent with cold-water effectiveness. The product was developed incorporating technological breakthroughs that had occurred in creating a bleach substitute and enzyme stabilizer from the European Technical Center, an improved surfactant developed in the corporate labs, and new low-temperature performance capabilities contributed by the International Technical Center. By linking and leveraging the company's intelligence and resources worldwide, P&G developed a product that was vastly superior to those being worked on locally and centrally. The new product was successfully introduced as Liquid Tide in the United States, Liquid Ariel in Europe, and Liquid Cheer in Japan.

GEOGRAPHIC SUBSIDIARY MANAGEMENT

In many MNCs, a successful tour as a country subsidiary manager is often thought of as the acid test of general management potential. Indeed, it is often a necessary qualification on the résumé of any candidate for a top-management position. Not only does it provide front-line exposure to the realities of today's international business environment, but it also puts the individual in a position where he or she must deal with enormous strategic complexity from an organizational position that is severely constrained.

We have described the strategic challenge facing the MNC as one of resolving the conflicting demands for global efficiency, multinational responsiveness, and world-wide learning. The country manager is at the center of this strategic tension, since it is at the level of the national subsidiary that the company must defend its market positions against global competitors, satisfy the demands of the host government, respond to the unique needs of local customers, and leverage its local resources and capabilities to strengthen the company's competitive position worldwide.

There are many vital tasks the country manager must play, but we have identified three that capture the complexity of the task and highlight its important linkage role: acting as a bicultural interpreter, becoming the chief advocate and defender of national needs; and the vital front-line responsibility as implementer of the company's strategy.

Bicultural Interpreter

The need for the country manager to become the local expert who understands the needs of the local market, the strategy of competitors, and the demands of the host government is clear. But his or her responsibilities are much broader than this. Because managers at headquarters do not understand the environmental and cultural differences in the MNC's diverse foreign markets, the country manager must be able to analyze the information gathered, interpret its implications, and even predict the range of feasible outcomes implied by the locally gathered intelligence. This role suggests an ability not only to act as an efficient sensor of the national environment, but also to become a cultural interpreter able to communicate the importance of that information to those whose perceptions may be obscured by ethnocentric biases.

There is another aspect to the country's manager's role as information broker that is sometimes ignored. Not only must the individual have a sensitivity to and understanding of the *national* culture, he or she must also be comfortable in the *corporate* culture at the MNC. As the key link between the parent and the often-isolated national organization, the country manager has the responsibility to ensure that the corporation's goals, strategies, and values are clearly understood by a group of employees located thousands of miles from the parent company. Again, the role implies much more than being an information conduit. The manager must interpret the company's broad goals and strategies so they become meaningful objectives and priorities at the local level of operation, and must apply the corporate values and organizational processes in a way that respects local cultural norms.

National Defender and Advocate

As important as the communication role is as a means of educating and informing the organization, it is not sufficient for the country manager to act solely as an intelligent mailbox. It is important that the information and analysis conveyed to corporate headquarters is not only well understood, but is also taken into consideration in the company's important decision-making processes. This is particularly important in MNCs where strong business managers are arguing for a more standardized global approach and corporate functional managers are focusing the attention of their local national counterparts on cross-border linkages. The country manager's role is to counterbalance these centralizing tendencies and ensure that the needs and opportunities that exist in the local environment are well understood and incorporated into the decision-making process.

As the national organization evolves from its early independence to a more mature role as part of an integrated worldwide network of operations, the country manager's normal drive for national self-sufficiency and personal autonomy must be replaced by a less parochial perspective and a more corporate-oriented identity. This does not imply, however, that he or she should stop presenting the local perspective to headquarters management or stop defending the national interests. Indeed, the company's very ability to become a truly transnational company depends on having strong advocates for the need to differentiate its operations locally and to be responsive to national demands and pressures.

Two distinct but related tasks are implied by this important role. The first requires the country manager to ensure that the overall corporate strategies, policies, and organization processes are appropriate from the national organization's perspective. Where the interests of local constituencies are violated or where the subsidiary's position might be compromised by the global strategy, it is the country manager's responsibility to become the *defender* of the national needs and perspectives.

In addition to defending the need for national differentiation and responsiveness, the country manager must also become an *advocate* for his or her national organization's role in the corporation's worldwide integrated system of which it is a part. As MNCs develop more of a transnational strategy, national organizations compete not only for corporate resources, but also for roles in the global operations. To ensure that each unit's full potential is realized, country managers must be able to identify and represent their particular national organization's key assets and capabilities, and the ways in which they could contribute to the MNC as a whole.

Frontline Implementer of Corporate Strategy

While the implementation of corporate strategy may seem the most obvious of tasks for the manager of a front-line operating unit, it is by no means the easiest. The first challenge is provided by the multiplicity and diversity of constituents whose demands and pressures compete for the country manager's attention. Being a subsidiary company of some distant MNC seems to bestow a special status on many national organizations, and subject them to a different and a more intense type of pressure than other local companies. Governments may be suspicious of their motives, unions may distrust their national commitment, and customers may misunderstand their way of operating. Compounding the problem is the fact that corporate management often underestimates the significance of these demands and pressures, especially if their understanding and interpretation are distorted by a cultural bias or a national insensitivity.

Second, the country manager's implementation task is complicated by the corporate expectation that he or she take the broad corporate goals and strategies and translate them into specific actions that are responsive to the needs of the national environment. As we have seen, these global strategies are usually complex and finely balanced, reflecting multiple conflicting demands. Having been developed through subtle internal negotiation, they often leave the country manager very little room for maneuvering.

Pressured from without and constrained from within, the country manager needs a keen administrative sense to plot the negotiating range in which he or she can operate. The action decided upon must be sensitive enough to respect the limits of the diverse local constituencies, pragmatic enough to achieve the expected corporate outcome, and creative enough to balance the diverse internal and external demands and constraints.

As if this were not enough, the task is made even more difficult by the fact that the country manager does not act solely as the implementer of corporate strategy. As we discussed earlier, it is important that he or she also plays a key role in its formulation. Thus, the strategy the country manager is required to implement will inevitably reflect some decisions against which he or she lobbied hard. Once the final decision is taken, however, the country manager must be able to convince his or her national organization to implement it with commitment and enthusiasm.

TOP-LEVEL CORPORATE MANAGEMENT

Nowhere are the challenges facing management more extreme than at the top of an organization that is evolving toward becoming a transnational corporation. Not only do these senior executives have to integrate and provide direction for the diverse management groups we have described, but in doing so, they first have to break with many of the norms and traditions that historically defined their role.

Particularly in the 1960s and 1970s, as increasingly complex hierarchical structures forced them further and further from the front lines of their businesses, top-management's role became bureaucratized in a rising sea of systems and staff reports. As layers of management slowed decision making and the corporate headquarters role of coordination and support evolved to one of control and interference, top-management's attention was distracted from the external demands of customers and competitive pressures and began to focus internally on an increasingly bureaucratic process.

The transnational organization of the 1990s cannot afford to operate this way. Like executives at all levels of the organization, top management must add value, and this means liberating rather than constraining the organization below them. It requires them to remove the bureaucracy that isolated them in the past and get back in touch with the business and the organization.

This is far from a simple task, however. Most businesses are now being forced to compete on the basis of multiple sources of competitive advantage, and the organization required to provide that capability must be both multidimensional and flexible. For those at the top of the transnational, this means more than just creating a diverse set of business, functional, and geographic management groups and assigning them specific roles and responsibilities. It also means maintaining the organizational legitimacy of each group, balancing and integrating their often-divergent influences in the ongoing management process, and maintaining a unifying sense of purpose and direction in the face of often-conflicting needs and priorities.

This constant balancing and integrating role is perhaps the most vital aspect of top-management's job. It is reflected in the constant tension they feel between ensuring long-term viability and achieving short-term results, or between providing a clear overall corporate direction and leaving sufficient room for the experimentation and challenge of conventional wisdom that drive corporate renewal. This tension is reflected in the three core top-management tasks we choose to highlight here. The first, which focuses on the key role of providing long-term direction and purpose, is in some ways counterbalanced by the second, which highlights the need to achieve current results by leveraging performance. The third key task of ensuring continual renewal again focuses on long-term needs, but at the same time may require the organization to challenge its current directions and priorities.

Providing Direction and Purpose

In an organization built around the need for multidimensional strategic capabilities and the legitimacy of different management perspectives, the diversity and internal tension can create an exciting free market of competing ideas and can generate an enormous amount of individual and group motivation. But there is always a risk that these same powerful centrifugal forces could pull the company apart. By creating a common vision of the future and a shared set of values that overarch and subsume managers' more parochial business, functional, or geographic objectives, top management can, in effect, create a corporate lightning rod that captures this otherwise diffuse energy and channels it toward powering a single company engine. At the risk of overwhelming ourselves in metaphors (and worse still mixing them), we have seen how a well-created and carefully articulated vision can become not only a beacon of strategic direction, but also an anchor of organizational stability.

We have identified three characteristics that distinguish an energizing and effective strategic vision from a catchy but ineffective public relations slogan. First, the vision must be clear, and simplicity, relevance, and continuous reinforcement are the key to such clarity. NEC's integration of computers and communications—C&C—is the best single example of how clarity can make a vision more powerful and effective. Top management in NEC has applied the C&C concept so effectively that it describes the company's business focus, defines its distinctive source of competitive advantage over large companies like IBM and AT&T, and summarizes its strategic and organizational initiatives. Throughout the company, the rich interpretations of C&C are understood and believed in.

Continuity is the second key characteristic of a vision that can provide direction and purpose. Despite shifts in leadership and continual adjustments in short-term business priorities, top management must remain committed to the company's core set of strategic objectives and organizational values. Without such continuity, the unifying vision takes on the transitory characteristics of the annual budget or quarterly targets—and engenders about as much organizational enthusiasm.

Finally, in communicating the vision and strategic direction, it is critical to establish consistency across organizational units—in other words, to ensure that the vision is shared by all. The cost of inconsistency can be horrendous. At a minimum, it can result in confusion and inefficiency; in the extreme, it can lead individuals and organizational units to pursue agendas that are mutually debilitating.

Leveraging Corporate Performance

While aligning the company's resources, capabilities, and commitments to achieve common long-term objectives is vital, top management must also achieve results in the short term to remain viable among its competitors and credible with its stakeholders. Top management's role is to provide the controls, support, and coordination to leverage resources and capabilities to their highest level of performance.

In doing so, top managers in transnational companies must abandon old notions of control based primarily on responding to below-budget financial results. Effective top managers rely much more on control mechanisms that are personal and proactive. In discussions with their key management groups, they ensure that their particular responsibilities are understood in relation to the overall goal, and that strategic and operational priorities are clearly identified and agreed upon. They set demanding standards and use frequent informal visits to discuss operations and identify new problems or opportunities quickly.

When such issues are identified, the old model of top-down interference must be replaced by one driven by corporate-level support. Having created an organization staffed by experts and specialists, top management must resist the temptation to send in the headquarters storm troopers to take charge at the first sign of difficulty.

Far more effective is an approach of delegating clear responsibilities, backing them with rewards that align those responsibilities with the corporate goals, then supporting each of the management groups with resources, specialized expertise, and other forms of support available from the top levels of the company.

Perhaps the most challenging task for top management as it tries to leverage the overall performance of the corporation is the need to coordinate the activities of an organization deliberately designed around diverse perspectives and responsibilities. There are three basic cross-organizational flows that must be carefully managed—goods, resources, and information—and each demands a different means of coordination. Because goods flows involve decisions about sourcing, scheduling, and distribution, these are the kinds of issues that normally can be routinized and managed through formal systems and procedures. By contrast, decisions involving the allocation of scarce resources (e.g., capital allocation or key personnel assignments) are usually the ones that top management will want to be involved in directly and personally. But it is the flows of information and knowledge that are often the most vital to the company. Although the more routine information can be managed through formal systems, the key means of vital knowledge generation and diffusion is through personal contact. One of top management's greatest challenges, therefore, is to create and nurture the human interaction that drives these vital flows.

These three flows are the lifeblood of any company, and any organization's ability to make them more efficient and effective depends on top management's ability to develop a rich portfolio of coordinative processes. By balancing the formalization, centralization, and socialization processes, they can exploit the company's synergistic potential and greatly leverage performance.

Ensuring Continual Renewal

Despite their enormous value, either of these first two roles, if pursued to the extreme, can result in a company's long-term demise. A fixation on an outmoded mission can be just as dangerous as a preoccupation with short-term performance. Even together they can lead a company to be doomed by its continuing success. This is especially likely where successful strategies become elevated to the status of unquestioned wisdom and where effective organizational processes become institutionalized as routines. As strategies and processes ossify, management loses its flexibility, and eventually the organization sees its role as protecting its past heritage.

It is top management's role to prevent this from occurring, and there are several important ways in which it can ensure that the organization continues to renew itself rather than just reinventing its past. First, by reducing the internal bureaucracy and constantly orienting the organization to its customers and benchmarking it against its best competitors, top management can ensure an external orientation.

Equally important is its role in constantly questioning, challenging, stirring up, and changing things in a way that forces adaptation and learning. By creating a "dynamic imbalance" among those with different objectives, top management can prevent a myopic strategic posture from developing. (Clearly, this is a delicate process that requires a great deal of top-management time if it is not to degenerate into anarchy or corporate politics.)

Finally, top management can ensure renewal by defining the corporate mission and values statements so that they provide some stretch and maneuverability for management, and also so that they legitimize new initiatives. More than this, those at the top levels must monitor closely the process of dynamic imbalance they create and strongly support some of the more entrepreneurial experimentation or imaginative challenges to the status quo that emerge in such a situation.

Case 7–1   *Kentucky Fried Chicken (Japan) Limited*

In January 1983, Dick Mayer leaned back in his chair and gazed absentmindedly at the Norman Rockwell portrait of Colonel Sanders on his office wall. Mayer, a veteran Kentucky Fried Chicken (KFC) executive, had recently been promoted from vice chairman and head of the company's U.S. operations to chairman and chief executive officer, and for the past few weeks had been focusing his attention on the challenges facing him in Kentucky Fried Chicken–International (KFC–I). As he talked to KFC–I managers about their problems, opportunities and challenges, he was exposed to a wide range of opinion on what was needed to continue KFC's growth and profitability overseas.

At one end of the spectrum was Loy Weston, president of KFC's highly successful joint venture in Japan. Weston's view was that in recent years headquarters staff interference in local national operations was increasingly compromising the spirit of entrepreneurship that had built the overseas business. In Louisville, however, Mayer heard a different story. For example, Gary Burhow, vice president

This case was prepared by Professor Christopher A. Bartlett and Research Assistant U. Srinivasa Rangan. The contributions of Mario Hegewald and Jeff Vincent (MBA, 1984) are gratefully acknowledged.

of strategic planning, felt that the lack of effective planning and control in the early years of KFC–I had led to suboptimal financial performance, inconsistent strategies, and stalled expansion into new markets. He emphasized that the recent efforts by headquarters staff was aimed at supporting the overseas subsidiaries and bringing to them the very considerable resources and experience of the parent company.

The Beginnings

Harland Sanders was born in Henryville, Indiana, in 1890, the son of a farmhand. A sixth-grade dropout, he occasionally worked as a cook. In his late forties, he developed a recipe for chicken based on a pressure cooking method and a secret seasoning mix of eleven herbs and spices. When Sanders' gas station, restaurant, and motel were bypassed by the new interstate highway system in 1956, he decided to try to franchise his chicken recipe. With his white suit, goatee, string tie, and benign charm, he sold some 700 franchises in less than nine years. In allocating franchising rights for KFC, Sanders was generous to his friends and relatives. His management style was to rely on the basic goodness of the people around him and he trusted his franchisees to play fair. There were no management systems or strategic controls.

Industry Growth and Development

Colonel Sanders became a pioneer in one of the fastest-growing industries of the postwar era. Many of the practices he initiated were quickly imitated by others and within a few years, several "rules of the game" came to be accepted in the U.S. fast-food industry.

One of the first norms to be established was expansion through franchising. The high capital cost of opening new stores, together with the need to expand rapidly to stake out the territory, quickly forced companies toward this option. Franchising also allowed companies to capture operating economies, particularly in advertising and raw materials purchasing. As franchises matured, chain managements often became interested in buying them back or opening their own stores. This not only gave them better understanding and control of operations, it also allowed franchising fees to be supplemented by profits.

At the store level, the importance of scale economies was also quickly recognized. Because each restaurant outlet had high fixed costs and small returns on unit sales, traffic volume was crucial. This made location a key success factor, and decisions on which region, town, neighborhood or even side of the street could mean the difference between success and failure.

Within the industry, companies soon learned that effective store management was also a key factor in profitability. Because margins were small, the opportunities for waste, shrinkage, and inefficiency were many, it took a special kind of individual to keep a fast-food outlet operating smoothly and profitably. In addition to ensuring short-term profits, store managers were also responsible for building local public relations, maintaining employee morale, developing customer goodwill, keeping tab on competing chains, and so on. And yet the salaries paid to these entrepreneurial individuals were relatively low for the 60–80 hours a week they devoted to their work. Most were attracted to the company-owned outlets by the prospects for promotion into regional and divisional positions.

As the industry developed, the importance of the chain's overall market image also became increasingly clear. The need for a focused theme or product line was acknowledged to be critical, as was the importance of the consistency and reliability of the product throughout the chain. Successful new product innovations were difficult, and management was always conscious of the risk of confusing the chain's image if it deviated too far from its basic menu and core theme.

Acquisition and Growth: The Late 1960s

By 1964 the 700 KFC outlets were grossing over $37 million a year and the Colonel, now in his mid-70s, had begun to mutter that the "damned business is beginning to run right over me." The time seemed ripe for a change of ownership. When a 29-year-old Kentucky lawyer, John Y. Brown, and a 60-year-old financier, Jack Massey, offered Sanders $2 million, a lifetime salary, and a position in charge of quality control in the business, the Colonel accepted.

Under Brown and Massey, growth exploded. During the next five years, KFC's revenue grew 96 percent a year (from $7 million to $200 million). In 1970, the company was building 1,000 stores a year in the United States. Brown recognized that the key to continued growth was to find, motivate, and retain hard-working and entrepreneurial managers and franchisees. His philosophy was that everyone involved with a KFC operation had a right to expect to become wealthy.

But with the rapid growth, problems soon cropped up. KFC headquarters experienced high turnover in its management ranks, with a number of senior executives leaving in quick succession to become franchisees for KFC's new ventures. If he was to keep these key people, Brown had to find new challenges and promotion opportunities within the company.

About this time, Brown became fascinated with the apparently boundless opportunities for KFC to expand overseas. The rapid economic growth and trend toward two-income families that had fueled the growth of the fast-food industry in the 1950s and 1960s were appearing in the late 1960s in other countries. Despite warnings from some who felt that food tastes differed widely from one country to the next, and that the whole concept of fast food was a cultural phenomenon that could not be transported outside the United States, Brown was convinced there was an opportunity. Besides, he felt he would be able to keep some of his entrepreneurial executives challenged by sending them to start new KFC ventures abroad. One executive later described Brown's international expansion strategy in these terms: "He just threw some mud against the map on the wall and hoped some of it would stick."

The country managers were like Roman governors sent to govern distant provinces with nothing more than an exhortation to maintain Rome's imperial power and reputation. Few had any operating expertise, they were offered little staff support, and the only attention paid to operations was Colonel Sanders' personal efforts to maintain the quality of his original product. Each country manager was on his own to make a success of his venture, and most had to learn the business from scratch.

Changes in the Early 1970s

KFC (Japan): Getting Started

It was against this background that Mitsubishi approached KFC with a proposal to start a joint venture in Japan. The giant Japanese trading company had a large poultry operation and wanted to develop the demand for chicken in its home country. Finding a perfect fit with his priorities, Brown was quick to seize the opportunity. The only problem was, he had nobody in the company equal to such a challenging assignment. But he thought he knew a good candidate—an IBM salesman named Loy Weston.

During the Korean War, Weston had been stationed in Japan and became intrigued with Japanese culture. After the war, he joined IBM's sales department and studied law at night. While at IBM, he

started a dozen entrepreneurial ventures in his spare time, including airplane leasing, coffee machine sales, and sandpaper wholesaling. In the '60s he was based in Lexington, Kentucky, as a member of IBM's new-product sales group. It was then he met John Y. Brown.

After the Mitsubishi contact in 1969, Brown called Weston and asked if he would go to Japan and start a new company. Weston agreed, and soon the two men were discussing how to make the venture work. Brown's directions to Weston were simple. He asked him not to franchise until he had proven the fast-food concept with company-owned stores. Brown's dictum was: "Build a store and make it work; then build another and another." Weston was to receive $200,000 as start-up capital and an annual salary of $40,000. He was promised an expense account after the company had been successfully established. His training consisted of two weeks cooking chicken at a KFC restaurant in Detroit.

Heading east to Japan, Weston decided to stop over in Greece. In Athens, he met the president of Dai Nippon, an Osaka-based printing firm. When the Japanese manager learned that Weston was going to start a new company that would require a lot of printing, he offered to telex to his office and have someone meet Loy. That individual was Shin Ohkawara, a Dai Nippon sales representative.

Weston thought he recognized some real potential in this young salesman and decided to cultivate a friendship with a view to persuading him to join KFC. He asked Ohkawara to take him to different restaurants so he could learn more about the Japanese food industry. This gave Loy an opportunity to scout the market and at the same time to get to know the young Japanese better. Weston used these occasions to impress Ohkawara with the grand plans he had for the new company, playing up the Mitsubishi connection to emphasize KFC's strength and commitment. After about six months, Shin Ohkawara agreed to join KFC.

Despite the fact that no formal joint venture agreement had been signed between Mitsubishi and

KFC in the six months following his arrival in Japan, Weston had gone ahead with the test marketing of KFC products in a local department store, although without a Japanese partner such an operation was strictly illegal. He found that Japanese disliked the mashed potatoes in the KFC standard menu and that the cole slaw was too sweet for local palates. On the spot Weston decided to substitute french fries for the prescribed mashed potatoes, and reduced the cole slaw sugar content from the company-set standard. "These were no-brainers. The idea of getting clearance from the United States didn't even occur to me." The first real KFC store was in the American Park in the EXPO-70 in Osaka. KFC Corp. sent the equipment from Louisville and the store was erected in just two weeks.

The joint venture agreement was finally signed on July 4, 1970. To build on the exposure gained at EXPO-70, two more stores were opened in Osaka. Sites were chosen where land was relatively cheap and where new shopping centers were opening up. In keeping with U.S. practice, stores were large, free-standing structures with 4,400 square feet of floor space. Shin Ohkawara, who managed one of the stores, recalled the early days:

> The stores were exact replicas of the U.S. take-out stores. Although the distinctive architecture was a big plus in the United States, nobody in Japan recognized what we were selling, and sales were very poor. The U.S. manual said that we could not keep the food more than two hours after cooking. So we threw out more chicken than we sold.

The new venture was soon in trouble. Losses mounted and the company had exhausted the $400,000 put up by the joint venture partners. Weston needed to borrow more. Meanwhile he also had to recruit people to run the existing stores. Both he and Ohkawara were putting in 15-hour days and they knew they could not do that indefinitely. The latest threat was the appearance of McDonald's in Tokyo. With all its problems, it appeared KFC–J was heading for an early demise, and Weston wondered how he could turn the operation around.

U.S. Operations: Emerging Problems

By late 1970, KFC faced a changed environment in the United States. The economy went into a recession and the company's revenues and profits began to plateau. Meanwhile, its new diversification ventures, like fish and chips and roast beef, were failing to meet expectations. KFC's stock price fell from a peak of $58 to $18, leading many of those who had hoped to get rich to quit the company. As the management exodus continued, Brown saw an opportunity to install a more professional team to build the systems necessary to gain control.

Competition in fast food in the United States was becoming more intense, and an industry shakeout began. KFC managers started hearing field reports about poor product quality and customer service in their stores. So concerned were they about the emerging economic, competitive, and operating problems in the United States, that they tended to leave the foreign operations to fend for themselves. Amid all this came a rift in the echelons of top management, and in mid-1971, Brown and Massey sold KFC in an exchange of stock valued at more than $275 million to Heublein, Inc., a packaged goods company that had developed strong brand franchises such as Smirnoff Vodka in the United States and many other countries.

To fit into the Heublein organization, which was structured along domestic and international lines, KFC's small international staff was merged with Heublein's international group in Farmington, Connecticut, and a manager from Heublein's international operations was brought in to serve as the vice president of KFC–International. A small staff was assigned exclusively to KFC–I to serve as a link between the overseas subsidiaries and Heublein headquarters. (See Exhibit 1A.)

Despite efforts to establish more control over the subsidiaries, headquarters management found KFC–I's independent-minded subsidiary managers uncooperative. Reports often came too late or with too little information. Sometimes they were not sent at all. Although visits from corporate headquarters to the subsidiaries became more frequent, they were

EXHIBIT 1   KFC International: Organization Structure

A. KFC International: Organization Structure, 1972–73

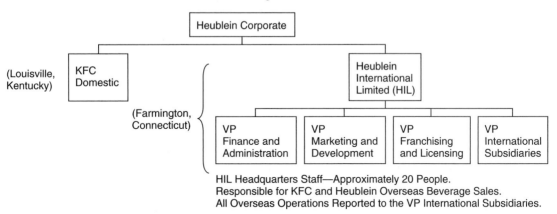

HIL Headquarters Staff—Approximately 20 People.
Responsible for KFC and Heublein Overseas Beverage Sales.
All Overseas Operations Reported to the VP International Subsidiaries.

B. KFC International: Organization Structure, 1975–76

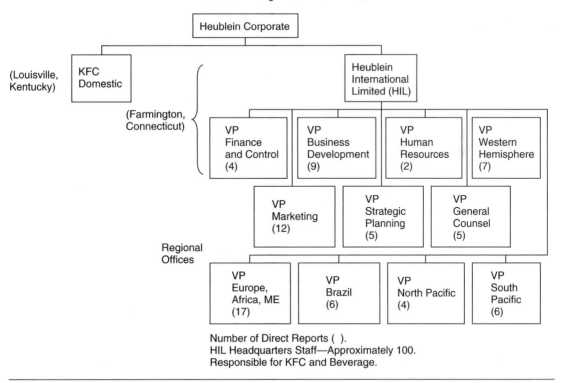

Number of Direct Reports ( ).
HIL Headquarters Staff—Approximately 100.
Responsible for KFC and Beverage.

usually limited to general exchanges of views about the way the subsidiaries were functioning. In the end, each country manager was left with responsibility for expanding within his territory, using funds generated from his existing operations.

Lurching towards the Mid-1970s

KFC (Japan): Shaky Beginnings

In the early 1970s, KFC–J was struggling to get on its feet. After heavy losses in Osaka and a not-so-propitious start in Kobe, the company was operating on a shoestring. In early 1972 Weston went to the United States to make a pitch to the new parent company for additional financing. To his surprise, Heublein agreed to increase their share of KFC–J's equity by $400,000. With matching funds from Mitsubishi, and bank guarantees from both parents, he now received a warmer welcome when he applied for additional debt. Now all he had to do was to make the stores work.

As he continued to wrestle with the start-up challenges, Weston was struck by what he described as a "simple but profound insight." He began thinking of KFC–Japan not as a fast-food company but as a firm in the fashion industry.

> Recognizing that we were selling to young, trendy Japanese who wanted to emulate American habits helped us develop a totally new strategic vision. It also led to lots of changes. First, it meant we had to focus on Tokyo since this was the center of fashion and the source of new trends in Japan. Then we began to focus all marketing efforts on our target group—upscale young couples and children.

These decisions resulted in further changes in product and market strategy. To build volume, stores were located not in suburban shopping centers but near key stations on the commuter lines. High rents and limited space forced them to reduce the standard store size to less than half the area specified in the KFC operations manual. This meant kitchens and equipment had to be totally redesigned. To build volume Loy and his team also decided to add fried fish and smoked chicken products—two favorite

foods of the Japanese—to the menu. They also adjusted prices to compete with a typical take-out Japanese pork dish called *katsudon*. Advertising increasingly deviated from KFC themes, and to accommodate smaller Japanese appetites, "mini-barrels" with 12 rather than the U.S. standard of 21 chicken pieces were introduced. All these decisions, Loy Weston proudly acclaimed, were made locally, without consulting corporate headquarters.

By the end of 1972, the company had opened 14 new stores, most of them in Tokyo. In 1973, 50 more were added. Weston was optimistic that 1974 would be the year KFC–J would turn its first profit. Then the oil crisis hit the Japanese economy, and continuing losses forced a refinancing and a slowdown in store expansion. Loy felt he was starting all over again.

U.S. Operations Facing Difficulties

Meanwhile KFC's domestic operations were in turmoil. Many former franchisees who had become corporate executives under Brown either left on their own or were fired. KFC's sales stagnated. There was widespread discontent among the franchisees, some of whom felt the new owners did not understand the chicken business and were not providing the leadership expected from a franchisor. There was even talk of a class action suit against Heublein among the more disgruntled franchisees. Company stores floundered and began underperforming the franchised operations, further convincing franchisees that the company did not know its own business. Even founder Colonel Sanders was reported to be unhappy, telling a group of journalists that the "chain's gravy was beginning to acquire the look and taste of wallpaper paste." Such disarray was a boon for competitors. The emerging Churches franchise and a number of regional chains began to cut deeply into KFC's dominance of the market.

Not only had growth stopped but by 1976, KFC's sales actually showed a four-year decline of 8 percent. Store-level profits were declining 26 percent annually. As Dick Mayer was to recount later: "Quality, service and cleanliness [in the company-owned stores] were just terrible . . . . Product ratings were inconsistent, standards were almost nonexistent, service time was highly variable, employees were often surly, and the buildings were dirty and run down." In this period, Heublein was not keen on committing funds to what appeared to be a lost cause. Except for sending a few cost-cutting experts to help ease the cash flow problems, management did little to deal with the developing crisis. The prevailing attitude seemed to be that they were in a competitive segment of a saturated industry, and better opportunities lay in diversification.

The Late 1970s: New Direction

KFC–I: Changes in Management

In late 1975, Michael Miles was appointed vice president of international operations for Heublein. At the time, he had had no international experience. Miles had a journalism degree from Northwestern, and before joining KFC in 1971 had spent 10 years with the Leo Burnett Advertising Agency where he had been responsible for the Colonel Sanders account. In 1972, he was named a Heublein vice president and became the head of the Grocery Products Division, which marketed the Grey Poupon, Ortega and A1 Steak Sauce brands. In that capacity, he initiated and completed the first strategic plan for the company. Strategic planning was to become his credo.

As vice president of the international group, Miles was responsible for all of Heublein's international operations, which was primarily its offshore KFC stores and its non–U.S. liquor business. He quickly decided that the collection of largely autonomous KFC subsidiaries would require most of his attention. The performance of many of them left much to be desired. The few operating standards that had been communicated were poorly controlled. Even the basic menu varied widely—South Africa offering hamburgers, Australia serving roast chicken, Japan with its fish, and Brazil with a full-scale wide-choice menu. Some, like KFC–J, had yet to achieve break-even, and other more established operations had begun to show declining profits. Many cited market saturation and more competitive environments as the reason for these poor results.

Miles approached the international operations with a firm conviction that overseas subsidiaries needed more support and control from corporate headquarters, and that a good strategic planning system was the basic starting point. (See Exhibit 1B for organizational impact of changes.)

Recognizing that he was in unfamiliar territory, however, Miles moved with deliberation. He saw planning essentially as an approach to foster a thought process among the country managers. He wanted those individuals who knew how to run the business to make the plans and implement them. Despite immense resistance from the subsidiaries, he persisted in his efforts, and the subsidiaries gradually began adopting his strategic planning approach.

Miles also offered to help the subsidiaries develop new marketing skills. Through periodic seminars he introduced them to market research and new techniques in television advertising that would enhance brand awareness. After about two years, most of the subsidiaries had learned to use these tools and were beginning to apply them routinely.

KFC (Japan): Maturing Operations

In recalling Miles's efforts to introduce planning systems, Loy Weston was blunt:

> One fine morning, he rolled out this nine-page planning document. Headquarters wanted all kinds of data—environment conditions, strengths and weaknesses of our operation, objectives for the next five years, projections, action plans, and so on. It was useless for our needs. It was the same thing with marketing. They said we should be more professional. They asked us to hire a market research company to do a consumer survey. We paid a lot of money for that, and what did it show? That people bought our chicken because it tasted good. Fascinating!

Shin Ohkawara was a little less blunt, but also appeared somewhat skeptical:

> It was ironic. Here we had built our business from scratch with no assistance from the United States and were finally approaching break-even. In contrast to the situation in the States, our stores

were known for their quality, service, and cleanliness, and we had a highly motivated team. Yet the people from the United States were trying to teach us how to manage. They even sent over an American controller so their monthly reports would be filled in correctly.

But we learned to live with it. The strategic planning exercises actually helped us by forcing us to project and to quantify uncertainty for the first time. Of course, we adapted it to Japanese practices. Our Presidents Review is a handwritten document that comes up from all sections and is collated into two three-inch-thick books. We go through this process the first month of the year—not six months ahead as required by the U.S. planning cycle, and obviously not in their prescribed format.

We also learned how to manage our relationships with headquarters better. We learned the rules of the game, like "never show a big jump" and "manage sales and profit to show consistent growth."

In 1976, KFC–J reported its first profit, a modest 14 million yen. Miles offered warm congratulations all around.

The Early 1980s: Reorganization

Headquarters Changes: U.S. Turnaround
During the latter half of the 1970s, KFC's domestic operations continued to slide to the point that the problems could no longer be ignored. In early 1977, Mike Miles was given the company's most challenging assignment: to find out what was wrong with the U.S. business, which accounted for two-thirds of KFC's worldwide sales, and fix it. Miles asked Dick Mayer, who was Heublein's vice president for marketing and planning in the Grocery Products Group, to come to KFC's Louisville headquarters to help with this Herculean task. Mayer worked with Miles and played a major role in developing a turnaround strategy for KFC.

Just as he had done in international, Miles's first act as president of Kentucky Fried Chicken was to introduce a strategic planning process. His analysis identified that the company had lost touch with its customers, and was being outflanked by aggressive new competitors such as Churches. The centerpiece of Miles's turnaround program was what he called a "back-to-basics" program. It stressed quality, service, and cleanliness (QSC) inspections by headquarters-directed mystery shoppers, training programs, strict management control systems, five-year rolling plans, a revamped advertising approach, investments to improve the visual image of stores, and effective franchise relationships.

By 1979, these various programs were beginning to show results. Average sales per store turned around and began increasing at a better than 10 percent per annum rate. Store-level profits rebounded even more dramatically, bringing them close to the levels of the industry leader, McDonald's.

In July 1981, with his reputation greatly enhanced, Mike Miles was named senior vice president responsible for all Heublein's food products in the United States and internationally. Immediately, his attention returned to KFC's foreign subsidiaries where he saw great opportunity to benefit from the techniques just applied so successfully in turning around the U.S. operations.

Soon after taking charge of KFC–I, Miles made three important organizational changes. First, he decided that the international operations could learn more from the U.S. experience if the KFC–I headquarters were moved back to Louisville with the rest of KFC. Second, he hired as the new president of KFC–I, a professional manager with extensive experience in consumer products marketing (with Procter & Gamble) and general management (with the Swift Group of Esmark Corporation). Third, he expanded the staff expertise at KFC–I headquarters to reinforce the planning, service, and control functions he felt were required (Exhibit 2).

Bob Hiatt, the new president of KFC–I outlined his broad objectives:

> When I came here in September 1981, the strategic planning mode was well on its way, but the subsidiaries' independent heritage was still clearly evident. Our objective was to convince them that better strategic plans meant better bottom-line results. In operating terms, you could say our aim was and is to achieve consistency and control worldwide. We want consistency of products and facilities, and we

EXHIBIT 2   KFC–International Organization: 1981

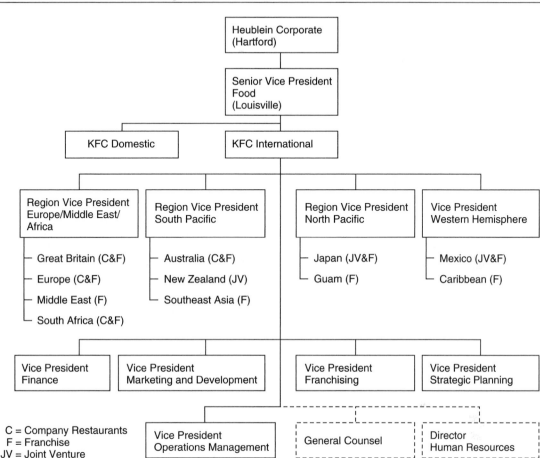

need to control the production and marketing approaches if we are to maintain that consistency.

Gary Buhrow, vice president of strategic planning for KFC–I, discussed the changes in his area of responsibility:

Up to 1981 planning in International had really been a perfunctory exercise. Miles wanted me to make it a more integrated, ongoing activity. To ensure consistency, we developed a standard format to be used by all subsidiaries, we adopted a five-year rolling plan process, and we implemented a more formal staged review procedure (Exhibit 3). As might

be expected, the country managers were not overjoyed.

Donald Lee was the financial vice president at KFC–I. Earlier he had been the international controller and had also served at Heublein headquarters in the finance area. He said:

The number of reports we require has multiplied over the years (Exhibit 4). But we don't apply our requirements rigidly. KFC–Japan is a good example. They baulked when we introduced the new capital expenditure approval procedure for new store openings, and argued that they had traditionally been

EXHIBIT 3   KFC–I Planning Cycle of Calendar

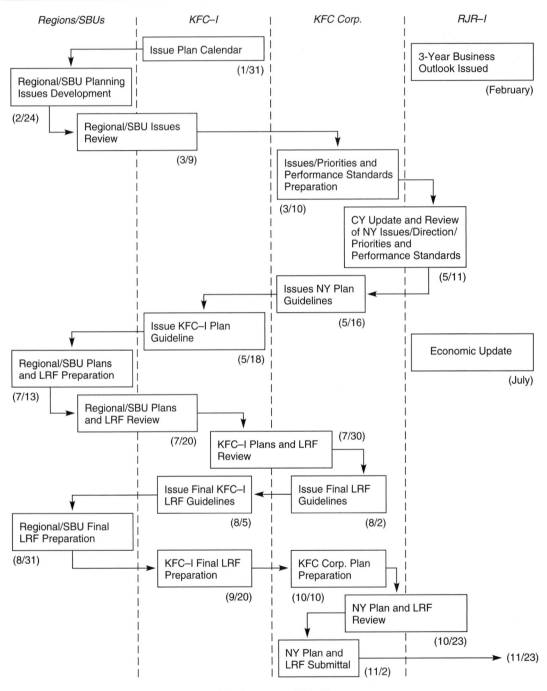

Note: LRF = Long-range forecast, LY = Last year, CY = Current year, NY = Next year.

EXHIBIT 4   List of Reporting Schedules in the
Monthly Financial Package

---

1. Statement of earnings—local currency: current month

1A. Statement of earnings—local currency: year-to-date

2. Statement of earnings—U.S. dollars

3. Full-Year forecast—local currency

4. Current forecast—U.S. dollars: full year

4A. Current forecast—U.S. dollars: quarter by month

5. Balance sheet

6. Balance sheet variance analysis

7. Other earnings data

8. Personnel status report

8A. Equivalent employee analysis

9. Capital expenditure status report

10. Intercompany transactions—statement of earnings

11. Store closing report—reserve reconciliation

11A. Store closing report—explanation

12. Risks and opportunities

13. Receivables management report

14. Intercompany account reconciliation

14A. Intercompany charges/payments

Source: KFC–International.

---

making such investment decisions without headquarters approval. They also said that Mitsubishi did not require prior approval. So we agreed to give them a blanket approval for capital expenditures in the beginning of the year. The problem is that by making such exceptions you weaken the whole system, leaving yourself open for other subsidiaries to demand similar treatment.

In general, we tend to treat the folks in Japan with kid gloves. Loy claims that staff interference will only stifle him. But Loy and Shin cannot take this autonomy business too far. They must realize they are part of a company with lots of opportunities and needs. We need procedures like the capital expenditure approval so we can make sensible choices among competing demands. In Tokyo, they think that we should take a long-term view and

ignore short-term losses. But the reality is we are an American public company and Wall Street will start screaming if the quarterly earnings dip.

In addition to the strategic and financial systems, a new set of controls was introduced at this time. The international operations group was established to transfer to KFC's overseas companies some of the database management systems that had been so helpful in turning around its U.S. business. Gary Masterton, a key manager in the international operations group, explained:

> Our objectives are simple—to increase efficiency and ensure standards on a worldwide basis. The product is sacred, and we must do all we can to ensure its quality and consistency. The sooner we get back to basics—eliminating the ribs in England and the fish in Japan—the sooner we can get control and squeeze out cost savings. And if the U.S. operations were able to use our database system to help drive up per store sales by 60% and to double store level margins in less than six years, we'd be crazy not to try to learn from them in our overseas units.

The new operations control systems asked for store-level information on numbers of chickens, customer traffic, ticket average, menu mix, and speed of service. The availability of comparable data on a worldwide basis, as well as some expert input such as time and motion studies to establish labor efficiencies allowed management to set standards, measure performance, and reward store managers. Efficiency targets, QSC ratings, and performance bonus levels were introduced, and reports on trends at the store level were produced.

The subsidiaries' reaction to the new database operations system varied. For example, New Zealand adopted it with enthusiasm, but in Australia there was a lot of resistance. But there had been a disturbing deterioration in quality, service, and cleanliness in the Australian outlets in recent years, and the Louisville operations group used the resulting decline in sales and profits as the opportunity to step in and implement the back-to-basics program and the supporting database system. Japan also questioned its need to adopt the new systems and programs and challenged headquarters ideas.

Louisville management emphasized it was trying not to be too dogmatic and was willing to adapt the system to their special needs. "We don't ram it down their throats, but we do want the system operating universally," said Masterton. "Those that accept it find it can be a very useful system they can apply locally, and not just data sent back to headquarters for control. We want this to be one of *their* management tools."

KFC (Japan) Reaction

The new management direction and systems of 1981 did not sit well with Loy Weston:

We are slowly being reduced to the role of order-takers. In the first year after Miles came back, we had 22 man-weeks of visitors from the corporate headquarters. Quality control audits, computer people, planners, operations guys, and so on. They questioned everything from our store designs to the smoked chicken, yogurt, and fish on our menu. They gave us hurdle rates for real estate, and operating instructions straight from the American manuals.

They acted as if they had all the answers and we knew nothing. Just because they had introduced crispy chicken in the United States, they thought we should too. I knew it wouldn't work. But I agreed to a test market. It bombed. They didn't like our TV commercials so they made one for us that was so inappropriate we never aired it. Finally, I had to remind them they couldn't do this. We are a joint venture, not a wholly owned subsidiary.

Shin Ohkawara sounded philosophical:

I guess it is all inevitable as we change from a venture-oriented to a professionally managed company. They want us to follow their ideas. Okay, we will give them a try. But we kept thinking there were lots of ways they could also learn from us. For instance, we felt that our 12-piece "mini-barrel" could be a big success elsewhere. And our small store layouts, with their flexible kitchen design, might be very suitable for U.S. shopping malls. We were even experimenting with chicken nuggets in 1981 until we were told to stop.

What worries me, though, is this constant pressure from the United States for improved margins. (Incidentally, Mitsubishi has never asked us for more profit.) People at headquarters want to know why we

have not raised prices for four years now, and only twice in the last 12 years. By pricing our products just 20 percent above supermarket fresh chicken prices, we have expanded demand tremendously. If we use the U.S. pricing formula we will just invite competition.

New Challenges

Just as its new international programs were shaping up, KFC entered an important new chapter in its history. Attracted by Heublein's solid sales growth and strong profit performance, R.J. Reynolds (RJR) acquired the company in October 1982 as part of its continuing strategy of diversifying away from tobacco products (Exhibit 5) shows overall Heublein performance by business). Soon thereafter, Mike Miles was offered the opportunity to become president of Dart and Kraft, and was succeeded as chairman and chief executive of KFC by Richard Mayer.

Mayer, an MBA from Rutgers, had begun his career at General Foods. He joined Heublein in 1973 as director of business development, and subsequently became vice president of strategic planning and marketing at the time Miles was trying to get the company to take a more sophisticated approach to such matters. As the driving force behind KFC's more professional management approach, Mayer held strong convictions about the value of strategic planning:

Strategic planning pervades everything we do at KFC. It has brought great and effective change to our business and the way we market. (But) it clearly reduced marketing's ability to "do its own thing." As more people knew precisely what was going on, there was less tap dancing and more accountability in the marketing function. For example, all menu and pricing proposals required exhaustive marketing analysis. Proposals were reviewed by top management and evaluated by how they would help meet long-term strategic goals, not quarter-to-quarter earnings spikes . . . .

Our best marketing people have become even better after exposure to the planning process. They quickly saw the logic and applied this tool to improve the business . . . . and their careers. Our weaker performers—the "tap dancers" who never saw the light—are now tap dancing on someone else's stage.

EXHIBIT 5   Summary Financial Data of Heublein, Inc.

The Company operated worldwide principally in four business segments: production and marketing of distilled spirits and prepared cocktails (Spirits); production and/or marketing of wines and brandies (Wines); production and sale of specialty food products (Grocery) and operating and franchising principally Kentucky Fried Chicken restaurants (Restaurants). The business segment information for each of the five years ended June 30 is presented below:

(In thousands)	1982	1981	1980	1979	1978
Revenues					
Spirits	$ 877,041	$ 876,546	$ 883,419	$ 819,563	$ 742,575
Wines	387,130	378,497	386,938	368,972	324,794
Grocery	173,545	153,552	131,511	114,193	118,160
Restaurants	699,687	641,526	520,011	466,346	434,583
Consolidated	$2,137,403	$2,050,121	$1,921,879	$1,769,074	$1,620,112
Operating profit					
Spirits	$ 114,696	$ 107,078	$ 93,341	$ 87,599	$ 73,105
Wines	25,965	26,551	32,655	29,422	28,895
Grocery	26,447	21,545	17,904	17,989	17,949
Restaurants	84,087	69,126	51,302	34,966	26,711
Consolidated	251,195	224,300	195,202	169,976	146,660
Interest expense	33,214	28,581	25,361	23,106	25,041
Corporate and miscellaneous—net	20,251	27,683	22,933	15,851	12,319
Income before income taxes	$ 197,730	$ 168,036	$ 146,908	$ 131,019	$ 109,300
Identifiable assets					
Spirits	$ 312,322	$ 318,695	$ 320,379	$ 300,605	$ 272,257
Wines	310,984	318,137	308,445	281,969	221,748
Grocery	58,389	61,601	63,219	66,696	61,170
Restaurants	353,882	316,519	276,682	242,266	227,659
Corporate	140,531	107,900	80,067	80,382	100,412
Consolidated	$1,176,108	$1,122,852	$1,048,792	$ 971,918	$ 883,246

Source: Form 10-K reports.

As he reviewed the international operations, Dick Mayer focused a good deal of time on KFC–Japan. Not only was it one of KFC–I's largest, fastest-growing, and highest-potential units, but in many ways it reflected the challenges that faced the company's entire international operations. Four issues seemed of particular importance in Japan, and indeed for KFC–I.

The most fundamental issue concerned the appropriate level of performance expectations for the overseas units (Exhibit 6 shows KFC–J's growth record). For example, although KFC–Japan ex-pected to open its 400th store by the end of 1983, on a per-capita basis this represented less than one-quarter the level of penetration in the United States. And penetration levels in other countries were even lower. Mayer felt it was important for management to resist the temptation to regard the more established overseas units as mature. KFC–I had to maintain its drive for aggressive growth. But what did he need to do to ensure that such growth would continue?

The second challenge related to the overall issue of headquarters control of international operations.

EXHIBIT 6 KFC–Japan Performance Charts, 1978–1982

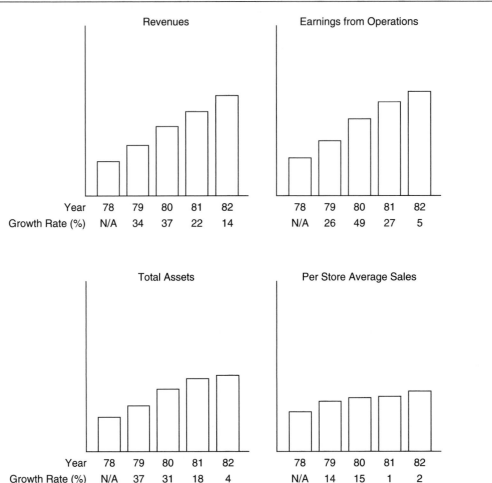

Revenues						Earnings from Operations				
Year	78	79	80	81	82	78	79	80	81	82
Growth Rate (%)	N/A	34	37	22	14	N/A	26	49	27	5

Total Assets						Per Store Average Sales				
Year	78	79	80	81	82	78	79	80	81	82
Growth Rate (%)	N/A	37	31	18	4	N/A	14	15	1	2

Mayer was aware of resistance to the administrative operational controls and systems and considered how hard he should push for their implementation. For example, how could headquarters turn a blind eye to the fact that some overseas units were force-fitting their numbers to meet hurdle rates, submitting approval forms after decisions had been implemented, and writing management reports to appease headquarters rather than provide proper analysis? Should they be willing to accept operational variations like the Japanese company's continued resistance to suggestions that it give up its obsession with menu expansion and devote more attention to improving the basics of its operations? At headquarters, managers claimed there was proven evidence that menu diversity affected the bottom line and hurt quality, but Japan rejected both notions.

A third important issue Mayer identified was the continuing problem of how to expand into new countries. Six countries (Japan, Australia, South Africa, New Zealand, United Kingdom, and Germany) accounted for over 95 percent of overseas earnings, and over the past decade numerous attempts to expand into a variety of new countries had met with very limited success (see Exhibit 7). A diversity of opinion existed on how the company should proceed. Gary Buhrow, vice president–strategic planning, felt the company had to move away from the highly opportunistic and people-dependent approach of the past:

> The world is more complicated than it was 15 years ago. We have to pay more attention to political risks, currency risks, and legal issues. And we need more sophisticated measures of market potential. We have begun to develop a capability at headquarters, a systematic analysis and comparison of new market risks and opportunities. This has helped us prepare a list of priority international market opportunities for KFC. In addition, when managers make market entry proposals and present details of their entry strategy, we have much more data against which to evaluate it and to set financial and operational expectations.

Loy Weston, on the other hand, felt that the string of failures and below-expectation performances in new markets could be tied directly to the deviation from John Y. Brown's mud-on-the-map approach of selecting entrepreneurs, giving them the challenge, and leaving them alone. He explained:

> Expansion into new markets requires a combination of sensitivity and entrepreneurial spark that is found in a different kind of person from your normal breed of corporate officer. When you find the right person—someone with energy, vision, imagination, and above all, willingness to make quick and unorthodox decisions—you have to leave him alone. You can't succeed if there are constant audits, visits, and forms to fill in for headquarters.
>
> Hong Kong is a perfect example of what not to do. They sent an insensitive and patronizing Australian who saw himself as a high-powered corporate executive. He breezed in, hired a secretary, bought a Mercedes and immediately began driving around to inspect potential sites. There was no effort to understand local tastes or customs. He paid exorbitant prices for the sites, entered a joint venture with, of all parties, a U.K.-based conglomerate, and set up standard stores with standard menus. When stores opened, he was not close to the operations and

wasn't even aware that the fish meal–fed chicken he was buying had a strong unpleasant taste. It was a total disaster.

Dick Mayer had an open mind on the issue. But he was concerned that KFC had such limited positions in Korea, Taiwan, Thailand, and Hong Kong—four of the highest-priority countries identified by the new market potential analysis. He learned that these countries were the responsibility of Loy Weston who, four years earlier, had been named vice president for the North Pacific. Shin Ohkawara had succeeded Weston as president and chief executive in Japan leaving Loy free to concentrate entirely on new market entries, but progress was slow. Mayer wondered if he should leave Weston alone, or whether he should authorize more headquarters involvement at this stage?

The question raised the whole issue of the appropriate management skills required to manage the company's overseas operations, and this topic represented the fourth item on Mayer's list of challenges. In considering the matter, he theorized that there were three stages in country management evolution:

> In the entrepreneurial stage there is not much room for managerial orientation. Loy Weston is a real go-getter. But he is an organizational nightmare who gets great joy in pricking the balloons of bureaucracy. At the second stage, we see the development of local baronies as managers use their local knowledge and developing operating skills to build their autonomy. The third stage is marked by the appearance of professional management who respond to planning, measurement, and business development ideas. Only this group can build for the long term.
>
> Unfortunately, there is a widespread belief that professional managers cannot be venturesome or entrepreneurial. But a fast-food operation is inherently an entrepreneurial venture, and the country manager has to deal with the franchisees, who are generally entrepreneurs themselves. If you want to succeed in this business, you can't be a pin-stripe type. So by a kind of natural selection, the right types of managers rise to the top. I believe our professional managers can be the source of the entrepreneurial expansion we are looking for.

EXHIBIT 7 KFC Subsidiaries Abroad in 1983

Europe, Middle East, and Africa

Country	Number of Stores Company	Franchise	Total
South Africa	48	95	143
Great Britain	61	308	369
Germany	3	11	14
Holland	5	2	7
Spain	4	6	10
Denmark	—	3	3
Iceland	—	1	1
Sweden	—	1	1
Switzerland	—	1	1
Kuwait	—	15	15
U.A.E.	—	10	10
Saudi Arabia	—	7	7
Bahrain	—	2	2
Qatar	—	1	1
Lebanon	—	2	2
Yemen	—	2	2
Egypt	—	6	6
	121	473	594

South Pacific

Country	Company	Franchise	Total
Australia	157	69	226
Fiji	—	1	1
Indonesia	—	20	20
Malaysia	—	27	27
New Zealand	42	—	42
Philippines	—	15	15
Singapore	—	23	23
	199	155	354

North Pacific

Country	Number of Stores Company	Franchise	Total
Japan	149	270	419
Quam	—	3	3
Saipan	—	1	1
	149	274	423

Western Hemisphere

Country	Company	Franchise	Total
Argentina	—	1	1
Aruba	—	1	1
Bahamas	—	11	11
Barbados	—	3	3
Bermuda	—	1	1
Cuaracao	—	3	3
Grand Cayman	—	1	1
Haiti	—	3	3
Jamaica	—	10	10
Martinique	—	1	1
St. Maarten	—	1	1
St. Croix	—	3	3
St. Thomas	—	3	3
Trinidad	—	8	8
Costa Rica	—	4	4
Panama	—	7	7
Ecuador	—	5	5
Paraguay	—	1	1
Peru	—	4	4
Venezuela	—	1	1
Puerto Rico	26	—	26
Mexico	38	18	56
	64	90	154
Grand Total	533	992	1,525

Source: KFC International.

Case 7–2   Acer America: Development of the Aspire

In early 1998, Stan Shih, CEO of Taiwan-based personal computer (PC) manufacturer Acer, Inc., was reviewing the first estimates of 1997 year-end results. With revenue of $6.5 billion from own brand and OEM sales, the company was now acknowledged to be the second largest PC manufacturer in the world. Although the performance was respectable in the wake of a dramatic drop in memory chip prices that had plunged the company's semiconductor joint venture into losses, Acer's extraordinary growth period of the mid-1990s was clearly over. (See Exhibit 1.) The ever-restless CEO was wondering how to re-ignite the fire.

Shih was convinced that Acer's mid-1990 successes were due at least in part to the revolutionary "client-server" organizational structure he had introduced in 1992. The concept was inspired by the network computer model, where "client" computers— the strategic business units (SBUs) and regional business units (RBUs) in Acer's organizational metaphor—were capable of complete independence but could also take on the "server" role, adding value for the entire network. To Shih, proof of the client-server structure's potential had come with the 1995 introduction of the Aspire multimedia home PC. Created by Acer America Corporation (AAC), Acer's U.S. marketing subsidiary and one of Acer's five RBUs, this new product confirmed Shih's belief that major initiatives with global potential could be led from any part of the organization without centralized headquarters control.

But Aspire's difficult development experience and its less-than-successful global rollout had also highlighted some of the deficiencies in the client-server model. Business unit independence had re-sulted in problems in communication, project ownership, product proliferation, and transfer pricing— and, in the end, had led to Aspire's $120 million of losses in two years. Shih realized he had to find a way to balance independence with control, but did not want to sacrifice the employee initiative and entrepreneurial spirit he believed the client-server organization had released. Reviewing the lessons from the Aspire, he wondered what changes might be necessary to Acer's radically different strategic and organizational concepts if the company was to grow the Acer brand from its current position as number eight to one of the world's top five PC brands.

Acer's Growth and Expansion[1]

In 1976, with capital of $25,000, Stan Shih, his wife, and three friends established a company they called Multitech to commercialize microprocessor technology in Taiwan. In the mid-1980s, with several successful products in its portfolio, the company (known as Acer after 1987) began expanding internationally, primarily through emerging markets. Typically, the company teamed up with entrepreneurial distributors, eventually creating local joint ventures that not only allowed Acer to reduce its own capital investment and risk, but also obtain committed partners with knowledge of their local market.

In the late 1980s, however, intense competition caused industry prices to drop about 30 percent, and Acer's gross margins fell from about 35 percent in 1988 to about 25 percent a year later. But a public stock offering supported its continued aggressive expansion. Unfortunately, the company made several costly acquisitions in this period and

---

This case was prepared by Professor Christopher A. Bartlett and Research Associate Anthony St. George.

Copyright © 1998 by the President and Fellows of Harvard College. Harvard Business School case 399-011.

---

[1]For a detailed account of Acer's establishment and global expansion, see "Acer, Inc: Taiwan's Rampaging Dragon," HBS. No. 399-010.

EXHIBIT 1 Acer Selected Financials, 1993–1997*

December 16, 1998

| | For the Year | | | | | | | | | |
| | 1993 | | 1994 | | 1995 | | 1996 | | 1997 | |
	Combined	Excluding TI-Acer*	Combined	Excluding TI-Acer*	Combined	Excluding TI-Acer*	Combined	Excluding TI-Acer*	Combined	Excluding TI-Acer*
Total revenue	1,833	1,651	3,220	2,901	5,825	5,262	5,893	5,346	6,509	6,132
Revenue growth (%)	49.4%	38.4%	71.0%	75.7%	80.9%	81.4%	1.2%	1.6%	10.5%	14.7%
Net earnings	86	22	205	103	413	163	188	150	89	262
Net earnings (%)	4.6%	1.3%	6.4%	3.6%	7.1%	3.1%	3.2%	2.8%	1.4%	4.3%
Total equity	497	316	703	420	1,450	939	2,008	1,321	2,065	1,638
Return on equity	18.5%	7.0%	34.2%	28.1%	38.4%	23.9%	10.9%	13.3%	4.4%	17.7%
Total assets	1,584	1,143	2,082	1,520	3,645	2,340	4,192	3,156	4,758	3,608
Return on assets	5.7%	2.0%	11.2%	7.8%	14.4%	8.4%	4.8%	5.5%	2.0%	7.7%
Net investment in property, plant, and equipment	497	181	538	197	963	284	1,347	418	1,470	616
Working capital	173	149	288	280	767	758	996	995	875	974
Number of stockholders	70,000	44,000	70,000	69,000	90,000	89,000	123,000	122,000	155,000	154,000
Number of employees	7,200	6,348	9,700	8,612	15,352	13,942	16,778	15,272	22,948	21,307

*Due to the drastic drop in the market price of DRAM during 1996–97, the Acer Group reported its financial results excluding TI-Acer operations to allow evaluations of non-DRAM Acer Group operations.

soon became overextended. In 1989, Shih decided to hire IBM veteran Leonard Liu to bring discipline to the loose organization and turn the company's fortunes around. Liu gave subsidiaries profit responsibility and restructured the organization into strategic business units (SBUs) responsible for product development and manufacturing, and regional business units (RBUs), responsible for marketing and distribution. (See Exhibits 2a and 2b.) Still the losses continued totaling $26 million on sales of $1 billion in 1991. Liu resigned in April 1992 and Shih resumed the CEO role.

As price wars continued to erode Acer's margins to around 20 percent in 1992, Shih realized that changes had to be made to Acer's business model. Shipping from centralized manufacturing in Taiwan not only delayed new product time-to-market and increased inventory, it also exposed Acer to widespread import duties on hi-tech products. A team of engineers solved the problem by creating "Uniload" assembly system whereby carefully configured palettes of snap-together parts and components were shipped from Taiwan by air or sea depending on weight and price volatility, to assembly centers around the world. Shih labeled this manufacturing system "fast food" manufacturing because of its similarity to McDonald's hamburger assembly approach.

Concurrent with the establishment of dozens of offshore assembly centers, Shih continued to delegate greater decision-making authority. Under an organizational concept he described as the "client-server" model, RBUs were given greater freedom to configure the products to fit their local markets. Coupled with Shih's long-established norm of delegation and Liu's emphasis on holding units profit responsible, this concept operated under the slogan "every man is lord of his castle." The change was not tension-free, however. As RBUs established a greater degree of independence, SBUs felt their role was shifting from product designers and manufacturers to components suppliers.

As the company evolved towards a decentralized federation of independent units close to their markets yet linked by the Acer brand, Shih dubbed the emerging management philosophy "Global brand, local touch." By encouraging business units to enhance "local touch" through local public listing, Shih's hope was to achieve "21 in 21,"—21 locally owned subsidiaries by the twenty-first century. By early 1998, two RBUs and three SBUs were publicly listed companies.

By 1998 Acer had grown to 23,000 employees in 129 companies with 17 manufacturing plants and 30 assembly facilities in 24 countries. Through the client-server system, Acer sales units were located in 44 countries, with particular strength in developing country markets. Although Acer was only the eighth largest brand for PCs in the world overall (more than half its sales were to OEM customers), it was the number one brand in 12 countries in Asia/Pacific, South America, and the Middle East, and in the top five in over 30 countries (see Exhibits 3a and 3b).

AAC and the Birth of the Aspire

Established in 1977 as a sourcing and purchasing agent, Acer America (AAC) was converted into a sales office in 1986. Acquisitions of two network computer manufacturers (Counterpoint and Altos) and a customer service organization (Service Intelligence) plunged the subsidiary into losses beginning in 1988. Losses continued in the early 1990s as industry-wide price cuts severely reduced margins. But through cost controls and the inventory reductions and increased flexibility made possible by the Uniload process, AAC recovered. In 1994, AAC recorded its first profit in six years. (See Exhibit 4.) Hopes for further recovery were pinned to a new multimedia home PC named Aspire.

Local Inspiration: Creating the Concept
In 1993, as the world began to take note of developments in the Internet, the World Wide Web, and new audio, telecom, video, and computing technologies, several companies saw the potential for an advanced multimedia home PC. Among those sensing this opportunity was Michael Culver, AAC's Director of Product Management. With the

EXHIBIT 2a Acer, Inc. Organization Structure, c. 1997

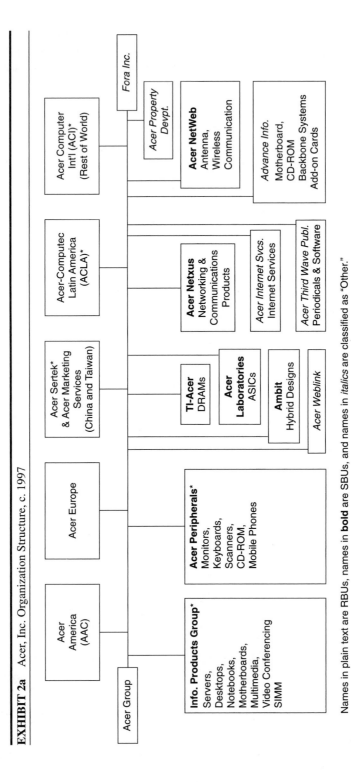

Names in plain text are RBUs, names in **bold** are SBUs, and names in *italics* are classified as "Other."

*Indicates a publicly listed company.

EXHIBIT 2b Acer, Inc. Organization Structure, c. 1997

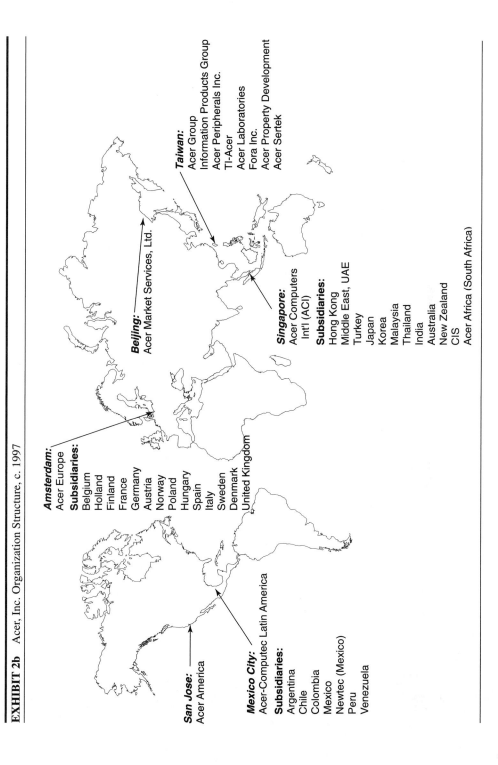

Amsterdam:
Acer Europe
Subsidiaries:
Belgium
Holland
Finland
France
Germany
Austria
Norway
Poland
Hungary
Spain
Italy
Sweden
Denmark
United Kingdom

San Jose:
Acer America

Mexico City:
Acer-Computec Latin America
Subsidiaries:
Argentina
Chile
Colombia
Mexico
Newtec (Mexico)
Peru
Venezuela

Beijing:
Acer Market Services, Ltd.

Taiwan:
Acer Group
Information Products Group
Acer Peripherals Inc.
TI-Acer
Acer Laboratories
Fora Inc.
Acer Property Development
Acer Sertek

Singapore:
Acer Computers
Int'l (ACI)
Subsidiaries:
Hong Kong
Middle East, UAE
Turkey
Japan
Korea
Malaysia
Thailand
India
Australia
New Zealand
CIS
Acer Africa (South Africa)

EXHIBIT 3a   1997 Acer Brand Ranking and Market Share by Product

Product	Worldwide		United States		Latin America		Asia/Pacific		Europe	
	Rank	Market Share	Rank	Market Share	Rank	Market Share	Rank	Market Share	Rank	Market Share
Overall	8	3.6%	9	3.3%	3	9.1%	5	5.8%	10	2.8%
Desktop PCs	8	3.2%	8	3.0%	3	8.6%	6	5.3%	10	2.1%
Portables	6	5.1%	5	5.6%	2	21.5%	3	9.6%	4	7.8%
Servers	6	3.0%	7	2.8%	4	6.8%	4	8.9%	7	3.1%

Source: Company documents.

EXHIBIT 3b   Acer Brand Ranking by Country

Rank	Country
#1	Taiwan, Malaysia, Indonesia, Philippines, Bangladesh, Mexico, Chile, Panama, Uruguay, South Africa, Oman, Morocco,
Top 3	Bolivia, Venezuela, Colombia, Peru, Ecuador, Brazil, Singapore, Thailand, Bahrain, Jordan, Syria, Cyprus, Sri Lanka, United Arab Emirates, Tunisia
Top 5	Honk Kong, Israel, Turkey, Greece, Norway, Finland, Saudi Arabia
Top 10	Australia (6), Holland (7), Italy (7), Germany (7), Austria (9), USA (9), China (9), France (10)

Source: Company documents.

EXHIBIT 4   AAC Simplified Financials: 1990–1997*

(Million US$)	1990	1991	1992	1993	1994	1995	1996	1997
Revenue	161	235	304	434	858	1437	1268	1141
Cost of Sales	133	190	283	399	764	1303	1225	1125
Selling and Marketing	27	61	25	23	55	103	84	72
General Administration	20	16	17	19	20	22	26	29
Research and Development	5	8	6	4	4	4	6	4
Operating Profit/(Loss)	(24)	(40)	(26)	(11)	15	6	(74)	(89)
Non-operating Profit/(Loss)	(1)	(7)	(3)	(5)	(3)	(4)	(7)	3
Profit/(Loss) Before Tax	(25)	(47)	(29)	(16)	12	2	(81)	(86)
Tax	1	(2)	0	0	1	1	0	0
Net Income/(Loss)	(26)	(45)	(29)	(16)	11	1	(81)	(86)
Current Assets	155	153	123	144	242	449	236	304
Fixed Assets (net)	39	43	28	25	25	26	32	33
Other Assets (net)	37	37	31	19	11	9	9	8
TOTAL Assets	231	233	182	188	278	484	276	345
Current Liabilities	155	169	154	136	218	423	243	365
Long-term debt	17	15	18	58	47	10	14	10
Stockholder Equity (including additional capital)	58	50	10	(6)	12	51	19	(30)
Total liabilities	231	233	182	188	278	484	276	345

*Totals may not add due to rounding.

newly granted authority to create local products, the 29-year-old MBA who had joined Acer $2\frac{1}{2}$ years earlier leaped into action with his vision to create "the first Wintel-based PC that could compete with Apple in external design, ease-of-use features, and multimedia capabilities."[2]

To test his ideas, Culver put together a project team which began running focus group studies to examine market needs. One clear outcome of this research was a belief that, in addition to enhanced multimedia capabilities, consumers wanted a home PC that had a different look and feel than the standard putty-colored, boxy PCs that sat in offices throughout the world.

Not having local design capabilities (AAC had a staff of 20 engineers, mainly focused on software design and product testing) and believing that Acer's SBU staff did not have the appropriate skills, Culver and his team looked to external design firms for help. Frog Design, a local Silicon Valley firm that had designed everything from bicycles to consumer electronics, appealed to the Acer team because of its reputation for "thinking outside of the box." At this point, Culver went to Chwang for $200,000 to fund the design phase and approval to go ahead with the project. "The process was incredibly informal," related Culver. "It literally took place in one 20-minute discussion in the hallway in late November."

The Aspire product management team and the designers visited computer retail stores and brainstormed the product's external design. In two months Frog Design developed six foam model prototypes. In January 1995, the AAC team chose the final design: a sleek low-profile shape with rounded edges presented in a choice of colors—charcoal grey or emerald green. (See Exhibit 5.)

Meanwhile, the team had been defining the multimedia capabilities built into the computer. One significant innovation was to be voice-recognition software that would enable users to manipulate programs by voice commands. But the innovations presented significant design challenges. In addition to the microphone and speakers built into the monitor, the PC would also have fax and telephone capabilities with a built-in modem and answering machine.

Global Aspirations: Developing the Product

In the early stages, the design of the product had been top secret, and even Shih viewed it for the first time only in February 1995. His immediate reaction was positive and enthusiastic: "This product will make Acer a household consumer electronics brand." He immediately asked Culver to present the concept at the next meeting of RBU heads. Their response was as immediate as the CEO's, and by May a consensus had emerged to aim for a global launch of Aspire in September.

With RBU heads' support and Shih's commitment to provide significant funds for "global" advertising, Culver and Chwang set out to present Aspire to SBU executives in Taiwan. Although the SBU heads liked the idea, their engineers felt they could be of only limited help at this stage of the development process. As one SBU executive recalled:

> Because the project was owned by AAC, our engineers did not have much influence during the integration phase. Most of the product design was dictated and decided by AAC and Frog Design, so when the SBU engineers came in it was a little too late. This was the first time that the product had been designed from the outside in and the radical housing created many challenges in getting components to fit. When we designed products in Taiwan we worked from the outside in, so we had never run into this kind of problem before.

Because AAC lacked product development experience, four Taiwanese engineers from the Information Products Group (IPG) and Acer Peripherals (API) were sent to the United States in March to aid in the mechanical design. As the project team continued to develop the cosmetic design behind closed doors, the SBU engineers working in parallel on component design realized they had no control over product design. "At first there was a little of the 'not-invented-here' syndrome," Culver recalled, "and we

---

[2]Acer had been in the retail market in the United States since 1990, and in 1992 had introduced the Acer Acros, a slightly reconfigured version of the Acer Power, the company's commercial desktop PC.

EXHIBIT 5 Aspire Design and Characteristics

Acer Aspire -
Key Features

- Sets up in less than five minutes with OOBE

- Multimedia features:
  - CD-ROM drive supports audio and multimedia CDs
  - 16-bit sound card
  - Video playback capability for future MPEG titles

- Voice-activation hardware and software allow for hands-free operation

- 14.4 or 28.8kbps fax modem with telephone answering machine and voice mail capabilities

- High-resolution monitors with integrated microphone & AuraSound™ speakers with 3-D stereo sound

- Stylish ergonomic design and color for any room in the home

- 50 bundled software titles, $1700 value

- Three-year limited warranty with first year on-site service

Easy to Set Up

OOBE (THE OUT-OF-BOX EXPERIENCE)

With Acer's Out-Of-Box Experience (OOBE), Acer Aspire almost sets up by itself.

PULL OUT.

- A step-by-step full-color poster shows you how to unpack and set up!
- Sets up in less than five minutes
- Thoughtfully organized packaging of user's guides, software titles, and accessories

PLUG IN.

Aspire makes it so easy to assemble, you can't go wrong!

- Color-coded cables and connectors
- Simple graphic icons
- Just match the icons and colors

PLAY.

Plug Aspire into your wall outlet or powerstrip and you're ready to go. All in less than five minutes.

Easy to Use

ACE (THE ACER COMPUTER EXPLORER)

ACE, the Acer Computer Explorer gives you the confidence to explore and helps organize, find and launch software. With its simple, clean and intuitive graphics, ACE helps users understand, learn and use their Aspire.

- Clear, photo-real folders aid in identifying key software and information
- Click-free exploration and navigation
- Full-text balloon help for buttons
- Folder and button arrangement with simple "drag 'n drop" mouse moves
- CD-ROM indicator tells you which programs need a CD-ROM disc for use
- ACE software installer makes adding additional titles easy

Source: Company documents.

had to work to make the SBU engineers feel a part of the process." In May, the top-secret development room was finally opened and the design and integration of key components proceeded more easily.

The computer's complex multimedia system was broken down into subassembly systems, each of which was assigned to a manager and a design team. But the greatest challenge came in integrating the components and subassemblies into the final product. Culver explained:

> Different product managers across the globe were responsible for different subassemblies. One might be in charge of the speakers, another in charge of the voice-recognition software. I was in charge of overseeing the entire product development and had to coordinate over 70 different contacts. The biggest problems occurred when we ran into a delay with one of the subassemblies. For example, after we had selected a microphone for the monitor we found that the software didn't recognize the input. We then had to isolate whether it was a problem with the microphone, which would mean resourcing, or the software, which meant redeveloping the application. When a delay threatened to throw off the schedule for the next part of the system we had to make snap decisions and go with them.

Similar problems occurred with many other components. With the answering machine, for example, the unit received the audio input signal but did not play back the message satisfactorily. Engineers had to decide whether the problem was in the software, the microphone input, or the speakers, each of which was the responsibility of a different person. Aspire's innovative design also led to complications. For instance, the unique shape of the computer casing created a problem with the opening and closing of the CD-ROM tray, while the challenge of matching designer colors on components caused additional headaches. In the end, no standard Acer parts were used in Aspire, and Culver estimated that specialized components added 10%–15% to the cost of items such as the CD-ROM units and monitor.

The RBU-SBU coordination challenges were further complicated by the fact that most of Acer's qualified suppliers were in Taiwan. As a result, the Taiwan-based SBU product managers had to source components and send them to AAC for approval and integration into the prototype. One engineer responsible for much of the sourcing described some of the challenges in Taiwan:

> AAC did not have the engineering capabilities that we had in the SBUs, but they didn't trust us to do any of the integration. We would just get components, test them, and send them on to AAC. It didn't matter if we had an opinion on the quality because Acer America insisted on their own review. For example, somebody from the SBU had flagged the CD-ROM tray problem early on, but he wasn't listened to. If AAC encountered a problem with a component, it took almost a week before I heard back from them. Delays like this meant that a couple of times an engineer from Taiwan had to get on a plane and hand-carry components to AAC in order to meet the subassembly deadline.

As a result, production dates kept getting pushed back and costs kept escalating. Projected U.S. demand and constrained supply forced the SBUs in Taiwan to allocate all component units to AAC, abandoning the original plan for a global launch in order to keep the September 1995 U.S. introduction on target to catch the Christmas season. Culver explained.

> The delays in integration caused us to delay manufacturing. Because the monitors were the last to be finalized, we had to ship them by air to get them to the United States in time. This cost almost $70 a monitor instead of the usual $10 by sea and added another $3 million to $5 million to our costs.

Despite the difficulties, the product was designed and manufactured in record time, and shipping began on September 5th—just nine months after concept definition. As Shih commented:

> I believe that if the origins of the Aspire were to have gone through the traditional communications channels—to file reports at headquarters with SBUs and to go through the process of argument, revision, and approval—it would have taken at least one-and-a-half to two years to see the final product. By that time, the daring creativity of the product may have already been diminished.

Planning Implementation:
Creating the Marketing

Parallel to the product development activities, Culver was working on activities with which he was more familiar—a marketing program for the product launch. Having decided to position Aspire for the home environment, the team developed a program to target home users. They assumed that some would be experienced while others would be first-time buyers attracted by the ease-of-use features. To appeal to this broad target group, Aspire would offer its innovative design priced from $1,199 for the basic product to $2,999 for the high-end system with monitor. This put it in the middle of the 15 to 20 percent price gap between the top-tier PC brands like IBM and Compaq and the low-end products like Packard Bell. Distribution would be through specialist computer electronics stores that had previously carried Acer's Acros PC.

Culver was also keen to build Aspire as Acer's flagship brand in the United States, and budgeted $25 million in advertising for four months following the launch. In addition, an intensive public relations program targeted computer trade publications like *PC Magazine,* the general business press like *Business Week,* and even lifestyle magazines like *Architectural Digest.* He also planned to support the launch with extensive merchandising and point of purchase materials. In all, this would be the most ambitious new product launch in AAC's history—and even for the company as a whole.

The Launch

In September 1995, the first month of its introduction, Aspire sold 40,000 units at retail, double AAC's normal monthly sales of the Acer Acros after 3 years on the market. When October sales leaped to 80,000 units, Shih, Chwang, and Culver were ecstatic. Early reviews in the technical magazines were also positive, reinforcing the euphoria in AAC. Caught up in the excitement, Chwang and Culver forecast sales into 1996 at around 100,000 units per month, triggering orders on Taiwan for components and subassemblies to meet this expected demand.

Supernova Burnout?

Then the unexpected happened: sales fell to less than 60,000 units in November and 35,000 in December. The only clue to the reason for the decline came from customer service, where telephone representatives were being swamped, apparently for two main reasons. First, the Aspire still had several minor technical problems that had not been completely resolved before the September deadline—the problem opening and closing the CD-ROM tray was typical. But this was exacerbated by the fact that Aspire had been targeted to first-time computer buyers and many of the calls reflected their inexperience. "Customer service was getting killed," explained Culver. "We couldn't keep up with the calls. Some lasted as long as 30 minutes!"

By the end of December, the AAC team finally acknowledged the need to cut dramatically their forecasts. By that stage, however, the company had already accumulated two to three months of excess inventory of a product that needed design changes. Although Culver and his team paused briefly to celebrate when Aspire was featured in Business Week's annual awards for new product design in 1995, they were more concerned that sales had showed no rebound in early 1996. (See Exhibit 6.)

While other RBU heads had all committed to launch of the Aspire, nobody was clear how this global rollout would be coordinated. Shih was very active behind-the-scenes urging the organization to support Aspire, but also encouraging Culver to take on an informal leadership role—presenting the product plans to top management meetings, hosting visits of other RBU teams to AAC, and updating all RBUs on progress and performance. Despite early tension over the decision that only AAC would be able to launch in September, the other RBU heads mostly deferred to Culver and his team as the product experts. Yet they were looking for advice rather than directives and remained highly protective of their right to adapt the Aspire strategy to local markets—particularly as they watched the problems emerging with the U.S. launch.

By early 1996, Taiwan had developed sufficient production capacity to begin a worldwide phased

EXHIBIT 6 Forecast of Next Month's Sales into Channels vs. Actual Sales into Channels

	1995		1996	
	Forecast	*Actual*	*Forecast*	*Actual*
	(000 units)		*(000 units)*	
January			15	0
February			50	20
March			35	50
April			25	5
May			25	15
June			30	25
July			25	20
August	30	10	50	20
September	50	55	65	45
October	80	70	80	20
November	100	70	80	15
December	40	15	55	5

Source: Company documents.

rollout of Aspire during the spring. However, each RBU argued that the U.S. product would have to be adapted to suit its local markets. Typical was Michael Mak, Managing Director of Acer Hong Kong, who described the process he adopted:

> From the first time I saw Aspire, I knew we had to have this product. I decided we would introduce it in Hong Kong and make a big thing of it. . . . Originally, we brought in the unaltered U.S. product for a "soft-launch." We created interest by taking it on a road show, issuing a press release, and displaying it in a few channels. Although the unadapted product generated some sales, most consumers were concerned by the $3,000 price tag we had to charge. At this stage, we realized we had to make some local modifications. We simplified the user interface and changed the language from English to Chinese, we included a card that allowed the use of a video-CD, we adjusted the phone software for the local telephone system, and we changed the modem. We also created a poster and videotape in Chinese and English showing the user how to get started.

The Hong Kong office had few local technical staff to make these changes. Of 200 people in the Hong Kong organization, only three or four were in product engineering and these individuals coordinated most of the software modifications. The hardware changes were largely handled by ACI, Acer's Asian RBU headquarters in Singapore. ACI negotiated directly with the SBUs, but some components (e.g., the video CD card) were directly sourced locally in Hong Kong.

By the time the Aspire had been launched in more than thirty countries, local adaptations had created over 100 different configurations. As one marketing manager pointed out, "Sometimes even a product of the same model number would have a completely different configuration in another market. For example, what sold in Singapore under one model number was completely different from the same model number sold across the bridge in Malaysia."

While local designs differed, most of the configuration problems—the CD-ROM tray jam, for example—remained the same from region to region. As local sales companies with newly created Uniload lines began assembling components and subassemblies shipped from Taiwan or locally sourced, they experienced many of the same problems AAC had confronted. But because AAC's earlier experience had not been documented or disseminated, each unit would try to find its own solutions. When the RBU contacted Taiwan, the SBUs often were unaware of the problem. Typically, they explained that they had simply supplied components and that the integration expertise was in AAC. The U.S group tried to provide technical support to other SBUs, but often found its resources stretched thin.

Marketing Coordination: A Global Brand?

Similar coordination difficulties hounded the plans to make Aspire the company's first global brand. Acting in his informal global champion role, in September 1995, Culver invited marketing teams from RBUs worldwide to the United States to review their marketing program. "They were all very interested," said Culver, "but when they got back home they pretty much developed their own programs. As a result, Aspire had a very different look and feel from country to country."

The different look began with the cost-driven decision to sell only the emerald green version outside the United States. The local differentiation of product features further emphasized the divergence. But it was in product positioning that the marketing differences were most evident. While Australia largely followed the U.S. positioning of an innovative multimedia PC for home, Taiwan chose to sell it in a stripped down version (e.g., no voice recognition or user interface) as a basic entry-level computer.

Pricing strategies also varied widely. In contrast to AAC's mid-range, value-pricing, Taiwan offered its stripped-down version at a premium price. Meanwhile, the Europeans began by listing Aspire at the top end of the market, then lowered price to build volume. And in Asia, ACI listed Aspire at a $200 premium to mainstream home PCs.

ACI's premium pricing strategy allowed companies in Asia to support a heavy advertising campaign, albeit one very different from Aspire's U.S. approach. Culver explained, "ACI worked with an advertising agency in New Zealand and came up with some pretty interesting ads they ran in Asia. I say 'interesting' because they had a slightly sexual overtone that I don't think would have worked in the States." In contrast, Acer Europe invested comparatively little in advertising, arguing that their PC retail channels (e.g., Dixons in the United Kingdom and Carrefour in France) were still fairly small in relation to Acer's other markets.

Promotions were also very localized. In Hong Kong, for example, Mak and his team developed a special promotion and marketing program for their adapted model. In an unusual move, they teamed with Chase Manhattan Bank to allow the computer to be purchased on a credit card with payments made over 18 months interest free. With the price set around $2,000, the Aspire was finally launched in the fourth quarter of 1996 with locally produced advertisements featuring a popular Hong Kong singer. The credit card–linked program proved to be one of the most successful PC sales campaigns in Hong Kong. Within the first six weeks, the com-

pany received 20,000 orders, making it the number one product in a market of 300,000 units per year.

The success of these various approaches was mixed. While Hong Kong, Singapore, and Australia had considerable success, the Aspire struggled in Europe. Furthermore, the diverse design and marketing approaches created problems for Acer's first globally advertised product. Following his early commitment to fund a global branding campaign, Shih had allocated significant corporate funds to advertising in international periodicals and in-flight magazines, a first for Acer. But because local subsidiaries modified the design and positioned the product to match their market, the global ads were not very effective. For example, a Taiwanese businessman might see an advertisement for a sophisticated prestige product in an international airline's in-flight magazine only to find that the Aspire available in his home country was a stripped down version that did not have the features he sought.

RBU/SBU Negotiations: Growing Tensions

Local independence also presented problems during the internal price negotiation process. After developing its market-tailored configurations, each RBU headquarters generally took tender bids for component parts in their local markets, using that data to negotiate prices with the SBUs in Taiwan. According to client-server organization policies, RBUs were not required to purchase components from an SBU if its quote was more expensive, and SBUs were not required to sell to RBUs if they could obtain better local distribution by selling directly to other customers in that market. In practice, however, the threat of either the RBU or SBU sourcing or selling outside of the company—the "nuclear option" in Acer parlance—was usually enough to keep the two units in line.

Nonetheless, the principle that "every manager was lord of his castle" could lead to unending negotiations. Instead of exercising the nuclear option, price negotiations often ended in stalemates: rather than responding to a renegotiation request, the business units would simply sit on the request for weeks. As Simon Lin, CEO of IPG, pointed out, "In a time-sensitive industry with rapid price fluctuations you can't afford to do this; it delays production and reduces profit margins."

Pricing was not the only area in which negotiations became bogged down. Similar problems surfaced in the area of inventory control. The RBUs bias towards creating unique local configurations made it difficult to redistribute excess inventory to markets where demand was outstripping supply. As a result, there was constant tension between RBUs and SBUs regarding the need for new models that involved only minor changes from an existing model.

Next Generations' Adjustments

From the September 1995 launch on, competition in the United States was intense since other well-known brand companies like Hewlett Packard had also introduced their own multimedia home PCs. At AAC, design teams continued to work on the product idiosyncrasies—component integration, monitor problems, color matching—that continued to plague the manufacturing teams. "After the first generation," remarked one manager, "Mike [Culver] recognized that AAC had limited experience in development and manufacturing, and tried to share more decision-making and coordination with the SBUs. Unfortunately, we were not very successful."

New Product Generations

The design for the second generation, released in February 1996, was reviewed by SBU managers who gave their input, but Frog Design didn't want to compromise the styling to make the product more manufacturable. As a result, technical problems such as the CD tray fit continued. This led to a discussion among the key managers in Taiwan and the United States that concluded with an agreement to make the direct coordination between AAC and the SBUs a priority. They named Arthur Pai, a senior engineering manager from Information Products Group (IPG was the key supplying SBU in Taiwan) the project coordinator with responsibility to gain internal agreement and implementation of their urgent changes.

The third generation, launched in August 1996, sought to resolve continuing technical problems and to capture scale economies by increasing the number of common parts in the product. Under the leadership of IPG's Arthur Pai as project coordinator, the CD-ROM tray problem was fixed, the ambient noise of the machine was dampened, and a quick start-up feature was added. Simultaneously, Culver changed the marketing strategy and segmented the product into three different categories: business, family, and game-enthusiasts. Three differentiated models were sold through different channels—the business version through office superstores, the family version through mass merchants, and the gaming-enthusiast version through consumer electronics superstores. Efforts to reengineer customer service also continued, eventually reducing the 20-minute average wait time to less than two minutes. The customer satisfaction index doubled.

At this time, however, Compaq again cut the prices of its PCs. As Culver recalled:

> Compaq decided to narrow the price gap between top-brand PCs and the secondary brands to about 5%. Basically they priced right on top of us. We didn't create enough perceived value to get a premium like Compaq, but our cost structure for our additional features was too high to match Packard Bell [in the lower tier]. So it took us about 12 months where we lost market share and money, until we got our fifth generation Aspire to market. It was completely redesigned for quality.

For the fifth generation AAC re-engaged Frog Design to design a new housing permitting Aspire to be made entirely of standard rather than custom parts. While keeping the charcoal grey, dealers convinced AAC to change the emerald green version to the industry standard off-white so that they could more easily bundle the Aspire with other peripherals. In August 1997, an entirely revitalized Aspire product line was introduced, including two models priced below the important new $1,000 price point. Simultaneously, the company announced new distribution partnership with Sears and WalMart to capture consumers at the low-level entry point and provide them with an ability to upgrade easily within that line.

Adjusting the Structures and Processes

The product changes were accompanied by parallel organizational changes. In July 1997, Arthur Pai and another engineer from IPG in Taiwan were sent to the United States to coordinate Aspire sourcing and logistics. Pai commented, "AAC didn't understand Taiwan operations very well so we had to send over some individuals who could keep in contact with Taiwan and help with the communication with the component sources." IPG engineers were now tightly integrated into the design process and again felt responsible for the success of the product rather than simply for the supply of component parts.

Subsequently, a more radical structural change was made when AAC was integrated into IPG. As Pai commented, "Acer America learned that it couldn't work without the SBUs, and we learned that Acer America was better off not being totally independent. It was like bringing a runaway teenager back home." With the restructuring, Chwang was made head of a new Acer venture capital company and Max Wu (founder and manager of AAC's components business unit) took over as CEO of AAC. Instead of reporting directly to headquarters, Wu reported to Simon Lin, President of IPG. At the same time, a three-person advisory committee of experienced Taiwan-based managers was assigned to work with AAC top management to develop new strategies and tighten operations. One member was assigned to work on AAC's service programs, a second was to concentrate on manufacturing improvements, while the third was to team up with Culver to strengthen the U.S. consumer business.

Although most AAC managers were aware that for more than a year that Stan Shih, Ronald Chwang, and Simon Lin had been having quarterly meetings about AAC's continuing losses, they were still shocked when the organizational changes were announced. Culver explained:

> We knew Ronald had been under huge pressure and that something had to be done. But after years of independence, it felt like a takeover . . . In the end, we recognized that AAC did not have the scale to succeed in the U.S. market. The changes were designed to help us leverage Acer's global scale more effectively and for IPG to feel more directly accountable for the quality, inventory, sales, and profits in the key market.

By late 1997, Aspire's sales volume had returned to the initial levels reached in the second half of 1995, and AAC's monthly losses had shrunk from $7 million to $3 million. As Culver, now vice president of AAC's consumer products division, put it, "Now we have a second chance." (See Exhibit 7 for Aspire's profit performance.)

Rethinking the Model

While pleased with the turnaround following the mid-year shakeup, Stan Shih was less sanguine about Aspire's long-term prospects. Over the previous two and a half years, the once-promising new product had generated losses of $100 million,

---

EXHIBIT 7   Aspire Profit Performance: Actual vs. Budget, 1995–1997

Millions US$	1995		1996		1997	
	Budget	Actual	Budget	Actual	Budget	Actual
Sales	570	446	1015	454	540	268
Profit	17	(2)	9	(51)	(19)	(38)

Source: Company documents.

plunging AAC back into a loss position. Total sales of the U.S. company in 1997 were running below their 1996 level, and the unit was expected to lose $80 million and sales of about $1 billion for the year. Most of the problems were due to Aspire's difficulties, and Acer's share of the home PC market had fallen from almost 14 percent at its introduction to less than 5 percent by the end of 1997. (See Exhibit 8 for U.S. market share figures.)

Once again, many were urging Shih to give up on his goal of building a global brand, arguing that the company could make much better profits on its component business selling CD-ROM drives, monitors, etc., and on OEM contracts to supply PCs to major players like IBM. (In 1997, the company manufactured 6.2 million computers. It was the number two PC maker in the world, with about half its output being branded and the other half sold under OEM contracts.) But the determined CEO remained firm in his commitment to elevate Acer from its end 1997 ranking as number eight to one of the top five brands in the world. At the same time, however, he felt there

were some important lessons to be learned from the Aspire experience and he began to think through some key strategic and organizational issues.

Strategic Questions

Although the development of the Aspire was exciting because it had emerged in response to opportunities detected in a leading market, its global implementation had been hampered by the subsequent need to adapt the product to different market requirements around the world. A new initiative developed and championed by Stan himself took a different approach and looked for opportunities not yet defined by the market yet believed to have uniform global potential. It focused on what Shih described as low-cost, limited-task devices (he used the term "machines" or "appliances" rather than "computers") that Acer was describing as "XCs." ("X" represented the limitless number of applications these appliances could support; "C" stood for computer.) Costing around $200, these devices would be designed for focused tasks such as to play computer

---

EXHIBIT 8   Acer Market Share

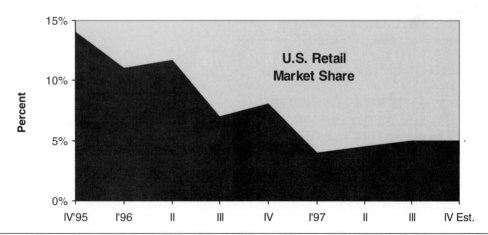

Acer's Home-PC

Source: "A New Attack Plan for Acer America," *Business Week,* December 8, 1997, p. 82.

games, to support home-use applications such as banking or stock tracking, or to surf the Internet.

Shih was excited about the new concept he had invented, which he believed had an annual potential of a billion units by 2010 (ten times the current level of PC sales), of which he hoped Acer would supply 10 percent. Should this become the company's primary thrust in the consumer market? What continuing role, if any, should Aspire have in Acer's product line? And, most important, how should these issues be decided?

Organizational Options

Equally troubling to Shih were the organizational issues raised by the Aspire experience. By making AAC the direct responsibility of IPG, Shih had already signaled that the parent needed to exercise more direct control over its adolescent offspring. Now he wondered if this was enough. Did Acer need a stronger central coordinative capability over its worldwide operations? If so, what form should it take to maintain the independence of the RBUs that had been the foundation of the Client-Server organization model? How could changes be made without sacrificing the "Global Brand, Local Touch" philosophy embodied in the "21 in 21" program that already had spun out several companies? (See Exhibits 9a and 9b for subsidiary ownership information.) How could centralization be enforced with independent publicly listed subsidiaries? Should they be bought out and brought back into the fold? Was it time to modify or even abandon these organizational experiments?

As Shih reflected: "In the mid- and late-1980s, we experienced the difficulties that come with heavily centralized systems and we don't want this to occur again. We have always striven to empower our employees at every level, but it is difficult to strike a balance between our principles in this arena and the need for greater cost efficiency."

EXHIBIT 9a   Acer, Inc. % Stake in Acer Subsidiaries, 1996

Subsidiary	% Stake
Acer America (AAC)	100.0
Acer Europe	100.0
Acer Laboratories	65.7
Acer Computer International	63.4
AMBIT Microsystems	50.0
TI-Acer	48.8
Acer Peripherals	40.9
Acer Sertek	36.2
Information Products Groups (IPG)	100.0
Acer Computec Latino America (ACLA)	23.4

Source: Morgan Stanley Analyst Report, 1996.

EXHIBIT 9b   Estimated Subsidiary Contributions to Acer, 1996–1997

NT$ millions	1996	1997
TI-Acer	229	−217
Acer Sertek	109	134
Acer Peripherals	525	593
Acer America	−1,365	41
Acer Computer International	406	442
Acer Laboratories	22	20
AMBIT	12	16
Acer Europe	−175	17

Source: Morgan Stanley Analyst Report, 1996.

Case 7–3   Walt Disney's Dennis Hightower: Taking Charge

Go out and grow the business. Do something different from what has been done in the past. Develop a strategy and bring it back to us in three months.

This was the challenge Frank Wells, president and COO of the Walt Disney Company, presented to Dennis Hightower, newly hired vice president of Disney Consumer Products for Europe, in June 1987.

The Disney Organization

Founded in 1923 by the Disney brothers, Walt and Roy, with a $500 loan, the Walt Disney Company had grown by 1987 into an entertainment industry giant with sales of nearly $3 billion. The company was involved in film and television production, theme parks, and consumer products (see Exhibit 1).

Disney struck its first consumer product licensing agreement in 1929 with the merchandising of a Mickey Mouse pencil tablet. Subsequently, the Disney Consumer Products (DCP) division was established to manage the licensing of the Walt Disney name and the company's characters, songs, music, and visual and literary properties. By 1987, the division's revenue had reached $167 million, with operating income of $97 million.

The Disney Organization in Europe, 1938–1987

Soon after its inception, DCP became involved with international licensing. In 1934, Walt Disney personally visited Italy to initiate a licensing business with an Italian publisher. After the war, he hired his first country manager for France. Over the

This case was prepared by Professor Ashish Nanda. It contains substantial material from "Dennis Hightower and the Walt Disney Company in Europe" (HBS case 490-010) by Professor T. D. Jick and B. Feinberg.

Copyright © 1994 by the President and Fellows of Harvard College. Harvard Business School case 395-055.

years, the French country manager, who hired all subsequent European country managers and was credited with having essentially built Disney's European business since World War II, came to be regarded as a "living legend."

By 1987, DCP had eight wholly owned European subsidiaries that operated in 20 different markets and together employed 102 people. Each subsidiary reported individually to Barton ("Bo") Boyd, worldwide head of Disney Consumer Products, who was located at Disney's world headquarters in Burbank, California. (Disney's organization chart is presented in Exhibit 2.)

All eight country managers had spent substantial time in their positions (see Exhibit 3). The longer-tenured country managers knew the Disney family personally. Most had known Walt and his brother, Roy Disney, Sr. The Disney children were regularly sent to Europe on vacation, and frequently stayed in the homes of the country managers. Roy Disney, Jr., the company's current vice chairman, had "learned the business" from the French and German country managers when he became active in the company nearly three decades earlier.

Proudly independent and perceived as "senior senators," the country managers for all practical purposes *were* Disney in Europe. They had developed book and magazine publishing and a full range of merchandise licensing of apparel, toys, housewares, and stationery. The business being licensing-driven, management had made little investment in hard assets; it was a very high-margin enterprise.

The country managers operated in very different environments with diverse business compositions. The German market was much larger than the Portuguese market, for example, and whereas German and U.K. operations were historically driven by

EXHIBIT 1 Walt Disney Company Financial Performance and Business Composition

	1940	1950	1960	1970	1980
Financial Performance: 1940–1980					
Sales ($ m)	2.5	7.3	46.4	167	915
Net income ($ m)	(0.1)	0.7	(1.3)	22	135
Return on equity (%)	(1.7)	11.7	(6.2)	10.0	12.6
Business Composition: 1940–1980 (percent of revenue)					
Film/television	77	74	50	41	18
Theme parks/resorts	—	—	39	49	70
Consumer products	23	26	11	10	12

Divisional revenues and operating income: 1981–1987 ($ m)

	1981	1983	1985	1987
Film and Television				
Sales	175	165	320	876
Operating income	35	(33)	34	131
Theme Parks				
Sales	692	1,031	1,258	1,834
Operating income	124	190	255	549
Consumer Products				
Sales	139	111	123	167
Operating income	51	57	56	97

Source: D. J. Collis and E. Holbrook, "The Walt Disney Company (A)," HBS case 388-147.

EXHIBIT 2 Organization Chart of the Walt Disney Company, 1987

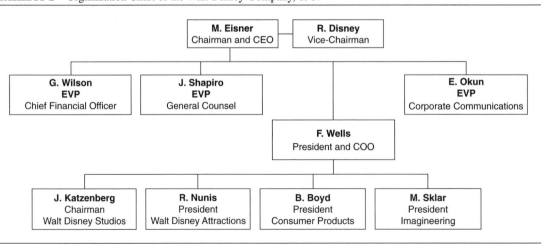

EXHIBIT 3 Disney Consumer Product's European Country Managers, 1987

Country	Age of Country Manager	No. of Years in the Role
France	70	40
Denmark	60	24
Germany	60	30
Belgium	60	35
Italy	60	26
Spain	44	16
Portugal	41	10
United Kingdom	41	15

merchandise licensing, French and Italian operations were driven by book and magazine licensing (see Exhibit 4).

The European Headquarters

Historically, Disney's market penetration in Europe had lagged behind that in the United States. But Disney management foresaw tremendous opportunities opening in Europe during the 1990s. The European Community was moving towards market harmonization and prospects for cooperation across countries were blossoming. Management expected that the 1992 opening of the EuroDisney theme park near Paris would greatly reinforce Disney's presence in Europe.

In order to take full advantage of emerging marketing opportunities, it was decided that a European headquarters for DCP would be established in Paris. Everything concerning the eight country subsidiaries that had previously been managed by Burbank would now be run by Paris. A newly created position, vice president of DCP–Europe, would head the office. The sentiment of the country managers, who had been consulted on this decision, was that the new European head should not be a European; the notion of an American who could "relate" to the studio (as the Burbank headquarters was called) and build credibility locally was much more appealing to them.

Once the decision was made to establish the Paris office, the search firm of Russell Reynolds was hired to recruit candidates for the new European vice president job. Dennis Hightower, head of Russell Reynolds' Los Angeles office, was put in charge of the search.

Recruiting the Recruiter

Boyd and Hightower spent three weeks in Europe meeting with each country manager in an effort to understand the business issues confronting them and get a sense of the kind of person who would win their confidence, respect, and trust. As they interviewed a number of prospective candidates, they became increasingly familiar with one another. "The more I traveled with Hightower," recalled Boyd, "the more I liked him." Hightower recounted the turn of events at that point:

> We were going through a very exhaustive search and had narrowed the list to six final candidates when, one Friday evening, Frank Wells invited me to Burbank for a discussion and sprang a surprise. He said, "While we think we have six good candidates, we have done some checking on you and think that you are the person we want for the job." I was concerned with such a move since the country managers had candidly shared their points of view with me, and it would be uncomfortable for me to now go back as their boss. Frank told me that Boyd had already spoken with the three senior-most country managers from France, Germany, and Italy to share the decision with them and to ask whether they anticipated any problems. The three managers had approved of the choice.

Hightower was appointed vice president of DCP–Europe in June 1987.

Dennis Hightower

Born into a family with a rich military heritage, Dennis Hightower had joined the Army in 1962 "because it offered blacks leadership opportunities that weren't available in industry at that time." Over the next eight years, he served in the Army with distinction. However, upon returning from his

EXHIBIT 4   DCP Europe: Market Size and Performance

The European Market, 1987

	Population (millions)	Per capita GNP (in U.S. $)*	Production (m U.S. $)		
			Merchandise	*Publishing*	*Music*
France	55.5	15,987	155	22	18
Denmark	5.1	19,373	17	2	1
West Germany	61.2	18,183	158	15	37
Italy	57.3	13,129	114	10	6
Spain	38.7	7,499	55	6	3
Portugal	10.2	3,510	11	1	1
United Kingdom	56.8	12,533	114	22	19
Europe	**831.5**	**7,877**			

*1987 exchange rates.

Sources: *European Marketing Data and Statistics,* and *National Accounts OCDE.*

Estimated Composition of DCP–Europe's Revenue and Income in 1987

	Product-line				
$ m	*Merchandise Licensing*	*Publishing*	*Music*	*Others*	*Total*
	Revenue				
France	2.8	5.7	1.5	0.1	10.1
Denmark/Nordic countries	2.5	6.1	0.3	0.1	9.0
West Germany	4.1	4.1	0.4	0.2	8.8
Belgium	1.4	2.0	0.1	0.2	3.7
Italy	3.6	3.6	0.3	0.0	7.5
Spain	1.2	1.0	0.2	0.1	2.5
Portugal	0.4	0.3	0.1	0.0	0.8
United Kingdom	4.2	0.6	0.3	0.1	5.1
Total revenue	**20.2**	**23.4**	**3.2**	**0.8**	**47.6**
Operating income	**15.3**	**17.3**	**2.0**	**0.0**	**34.6**

Source: Disney Consumer Products–Europe.

second tour of duty to the Far East, he was ready for fresh challenges and found new fields of endeavor opening up. Industry, in particular, was becoming more receptive to minorities, so Hightower, in June 1970, resigned from the Army and joined Xerox Corporation. "While working at Xerox," Hightower recalled, "I noticed that people who were doing things, who were moving things, all had MBAs." He applied for and was admitted to Harvard Business School on a fellowship.

Hightower joined McKinsey upon graduating from Harvard. Four years later, in 1978, he left McKinsey for General Electric, where he served in a strategic planning role, and later as a vice president and general manager in Mexico. In 1981, California-based Mattel hired Hightower as vice president of corporate planning. Current considerations rather than any grand plan had motivated Hightower's career moves. He summed up his advancement philosophy thus: "I have always had the confidence that, without my actively seeking them, the right opportunities will find their way to me. Other than follow a generalized desire to associate with the best, I have tried not to overmanage my career."

The next three years proved difficult, as Mattel, facing severe business problems, downsized drastically to about one-third of its 1981 size. Hightower assisted the chairman in restructuring the company, but once the restructuring was completed, the company no longer had an opening at the corporate level and he was out of a job. Family considerations drove his next job choice. "All the good opportunities were on the East Coast," he recalled. "But my family needed geographic stability for some time. They had sacrificed much in support of my career moves. I felt I owed them this one."

Hightower joined Russell Reynolds in 1984 and, two years later, became head of its Los Angeles office.

Accepting the Challenge

As he contemplated his newly created job with Disney: Hightower thought wryly, "If you don't know where you are going, any road will take you there!" His task was to figure out where Disney would be in 1992, and what changes that would entail. He mused:

> These European managers have been running themselves for years. They have been very successful; it is a very profitable business for Disney. It could have been more profitable, but things were fine just the way they were.
>
> So what do I bring to the party? Not only am I an outsider, but I am also a boss they've never had before and probably don't want—no matter how much they may intellectually agree to the need for one.
>
> How am I going to develop a strategy that will unify Europe, grow the business beyond any one individual area, and introduce critical thinking and creative approaches—all in three months? Where do I begin?

Reading 7–1

LOCAL MEMOIRS OF A GLOBAL MANAGER

Gurcharan Das

There was a time when I used to believe with Diogenes the Cynic that "I am a citizen of the world," and I used to strut about feeling that a "blade of grass

is always a blade of grass, whether in one country or another." Now I feel that each blade of grass has its spot on earth from where it draws its life, its strength; and so is man rooted to the land from where he draws his faith, together with his life.

In India, I was privileged to help build one of the largest businesses in the world for Vicks Vaporub, a hundred-year-old brand sold in 147 countries and now owned by Procter & Gamble. In the process, I learned a number of difficult and valuable lessons about business and about myself. The most important lesson was this: to learn to tap into the roots of diversity in a world where global standardization plays an increasingly useful role.

"Think global and act local," goes the saying, but that's only half a truth. International managers must also think local and then apply their local insights on a global scale.

The fact is that truths in this world are unique, individual, and highly parochial. They say all politics is local. So is all business. But this doesn't keep either from being global. In committing to our work we commit to a here and now, to a particular place and time; but what we learn from acting locally is often universal in nature.

This is how globalization takes place. Globalization does not mean imposing homogeneous solutions in a pluralistic world. It means having a global vision and strategy, but it also means cultivating roots and individual identities. It means nourishing local insights, but it also means reemploying communicable ideas in new geographies around the world.

The more human beings belong to their own time and place, the more they belong to *all* times and places. Today's best global managers know this truth. They nourish each "blade of grass."

Managerial basics are the same everywhere, in the West and in the Third World. There is a popular misconception among managers that you need merely to push a powerful brand name with a standard product, package, and advertising in order to conquer global markets, but actually the key to success is a tremendous amount of local passion for the brand and a feeling of local pride and ownership.

I learned these lessons as a manager of international brands in the Third World and as a native of India struggling against the temptation to stay behind the West.

On Going Home

I was four years old when India became free. Before they left, the British divided us into two coun-
tries, India and Pakistan, and on a monsoon day in August 1947 I suddenly became a refugee. I had to flee east for my life because I was a Hindu in predominantly Muslim West Punjab. I survived, but a million others did not, and another 12 million were rendered homeless in one of the great tragedies of our times.

I grew up in a middle-class home in East Punjab as the eldest son of a civil engineer who built canals and dams for the government. Our family budget was always tight: after paying for milk and school fees, there was little left to run the house. My mother told us heroic stories from the *Mahabharata* and encouraged in us the virtues of honesty, thrift, and responsibility to country.

I grew up in the innocence of the Nehru age when we still had strong ideals. We believed in secularism, democracy, socialism, and the U.N.; and we were filled with the excitement of building a nation.

I came to the United States at the age of 12, when the Indian government sent my father to Washington, D.C., on temporary assignment. When my family returned to India a few years later, I won a scholarship to Harvard College and spent four happy years on the banks of the Charles River. My tutor taught me that the sons of Harvard had an obligation to serve, and I knew that I must one day use my education to serve India.

In 1964, in the towering confidence of my 21 years, I returned home. Some of my friends thought I had made a mistake. They said I should have gone on to graduate school and worked for a few years in the West. In fact, I missed the West in the beginning and told myself that I would go back before long; but I soon became absorbed in my new job with Richardson-Vicks in Bombay, and like the man who came to dinner, I stayed on.

From a trainee, I rose to become CEO of the company's Indian subsidiary, with interim assignments at Vicks headquarters in New York and in the Mexican subsidiary. When I became CEO, the Indian company was almost bankrupt, but with the help of a marvelous all-Indian organization, I turned it around in the early 1980s and made it one of the most profitable companies on the Bombay Stock

Exchange. In 1985 we were acquired by Procter & Gamble, and so began another exciting chapter in my life. We successfully incorporated the company into P&G without losing a single employee, and we put ourselves on an aggressive growth path, with an entry first into sanitary napkins and then into one of the largest detergent markets in the world.

At three stages in my life, I was tempted to settle in the West. Each time I could have chosen to lead the cosmopolitan life of an expatriate. Each time I chose to return home. The first after college; the second when I was based in the New York office of Vicks, where I met my Nepali wife with her coveted Green Card (which we allowed to lapse); the third when I was in Mexico running our nutritional foods business, when once again I came home to earn a fraction of what I would have earned abroad.

Apart from a lurking wish to appear considerable in the eyes of those I grew up with, I ask myself why I keep returning to India. I have thrice opted for what appeared to be the less rational course in terms of career and money. The only remotely satisfying answer I have found comes from an enigmatic uncle of mine who once said, "You've come back, dear boy, because as a child you listened to the music of your mother's voice. They all say, 'I'll be back in a few years,' but the few years become many, until it is too late and you are lost in a lonely and homeless crowd."

Yet I think of myself as a global manager within the P&G world. I believe my curious life script has helped to create a mind-set that combines the particular with the universal, a mind-set rooted in the local and yet open and nonparochial, a mind-set I find useful in the global management of P&G brands.

On One-Pointed Success

I first arrived on the island of Bombay on a monsoon day after eight years of high school and college in America. That night, 15-foot waves shattered thunderously against the rocks below my window as the rain advanced from the Arabian sea like the disciplined forward phalanx of an army.

The next morning I reported for duty at Richardson-Vicks' Indian headquarters, which turned out to be a rented hole-in-the-wall with a dozen employees. This was a change after the company's swank New York offices in midtown Manhattan, where I had been interviewed. That evening my cousin invited me for dinner. He worked in a big British company with many factories, thousands of employees, and plush multistoried marble offices. I felt ashamed to talk about my job.

"How many factories do you have?" he wanted to know.

"None," I said.

"How many salesmen do you have?" he asked.

"None," I said.

"How many employees?"

"Twelve."

"How big are your offices?"

"A little smaller than your house."

Years later I realized that what embarrassed me that night turned out to be our strength. All twelve of our employees were focused on building our brands without the distraction of factories, sales forces, industrial relations, finance, and other staff departments. Our products were made under contract by Boots, an English drug company; they were distributed under contract by an outside distribution house with 100 salesmen spread around the country; our external auditors had arranged for someone to do our accounting; and our lawyers took care of our government work. We were lean, nimble, focused, and very profitable.

All my cousin's talk that night revolved around office politics, and all his advice was about how to get around the office bureaucracy. It was not clear to me how his company made decisions. But he was a smart man, and I sensed that with all his pride in working for a giant organization, he had little respect for its bureaucratic style.

If marketing a consumer product is what gives a company its competitive advantage, then it seems to me it should spend all its time building marketing and product muscle and employ outside suppliers to do everything else. It should spin off as many services as someone else is willing to take on and leave everyone inside the company focused on one thing—creating, retaining, and satisfying consumers.

There is a concept in Yoga called one-pointedness (from the Sanskrit *Ekagrata*). All twelve of us were one-pointedly focused on making Vicks a household name in India, as if we were 12 brand managers. I now teach our younger managers the value of a one-pointed focus on consumer satisfaction, which P&G measures every six months for all of its major brands.

Concentrating on one's core competence thus was one of the first lessons I learned. I learned it because I was face-to-face with the consumer, focused on the particular. Somehow I feel it would have taken me longer to learn this lesson in a glass tower in Manhattan.

As so often in life, however, by the time I could apply the lesson I had learned, we had a thousand people, with factories, sales forces, and many departments that were having a lot of fun fighting over turf. I believe that tomorrow's big companies may well consist of hundreds of small decentralized units, each with a sharp focus on its particular customers and markets.

On the Kettle That Wrote My Paycheck

For months I believed that my salary came from the payroll clerk, so I was especially nice to her. (She was also the boss's secretary.) Then one day I discovered the most important truth of my career—I realized who really paid my salary.

Soon after I joined the company, my boss handed me a bag and a train ticket and sent me "up-country." A man of the old school, he believed that you learned marketing only in the bazaar, so I spent 10 of my first 15 months on the road and saw lots of up-country bazaars.

On the road, I typically would meet our trade customers in the mornings and consumers in the evenings. In the afternoons everyone slept. One evening I knocked on the door of a middle-class home in Surat, a busy trading town 200 miles north of Bombay. The lady of the house reluctantly let me in. I asked her, "What do you use for your family's

coughs and colds?" Her eyes lit up, her face became animated. She told me that she had discovered the most wonderful solution. She went into the kitchen and brought back a jar of Vicks Vaporub and a kettle. She then showed me how she poured a spoon of Vaporub into the boiling kettle and inhaled the medicated vapors from the spout.

"If you don't believe me, try it for yourself," she said. "Here, let me boil some water for you."

Before I could reply she had disappeared into the kitchen. Instead of drinking tea that evening we inhaled Vicks Vaporub. As I walked back to my hotel, I felt intoxicated: I had discovered it was she who paid my salary. My job also became clear to me: I must reciprocate her compliment by striving relentlessly to satisfy her needs.

The irony is that all the money a company makes is made *outside* the company (at the point of sale), yet the employees spend their time *inside* the company, usually arguing over turf. Unfortunately, we don't see customers around us when we show up for work in the mornings.

When I became the CEO of the company I made a rule that every employee in every department had to go out every year and meet 20 consumers and 20 retailers or wholesalers in order to qualify for their annual raise. This not only helps to remind us who pays our salaries, we also get a payoff in good ideas to improve our products and services.

The ideal of being close to the customer may be obvious in the commercial societies of the West, but it was not so obvious 20 years ago in the protected, bureaucratic Indian environment. As to the lady in Surat, we quickly put her ideas into our advertising. She was the first consumer to show me a global insight in my own backyard.

Of Chairs, Armchairs, and Monsoons

Two years after I joined, I was promoted. I was given Vicks Vaporub to manage, which made me the first brand manager in the company. I noticed we were building volume strongly in the South but having trouble in the North. I asked myself whether I should try to fix the North or capitalize on the momentum in the South. I chose the latter, and it was the right choice. We later discovered that North Indians don't like to rub things on their bodies, yet the more important lesson was that it is usually better to build on your strength than to try and correct a weakness. Listen to and respect the market. Resist the temptation to impose your will on it.

We were doing well in the South partially because South Indians were accustomed to rubbing on balms for headaches, colds, bodyaches, insect bites, and a host of other minor maladies. We had a big and successful balm competitor, Amrutanjan, who offered relief for all these symptoms. My first impulse was to try to expand the use of Vaporub to other symptoms in order to compete in this larger balm market.

My boss quickly and wisely put a stop to that. In an uncharacteristically loud voice, he explained that Vaporub's unique function was to relieve colds.

"Each object has a function," he said. "A chair's function is to seat a person. A desk is to write on. You don't want to use a chair for writing and a desk for sitting. You never want to mix up functions."

A great part of Vaporub's success in India has been its clear and sharp position in the consumer's mind. It is cold relief in a jar, which a mother rubs tenderly on her child's cold at bedtime. As I thought more about balms, I realized that they were quite the opposite. Adults rub balms on themselves for headaches during the day. Vaporub was succeeding precisely because it was not a balm; it was a rub for colds.

Every brand manager since has had to learn that same lesson. It is of the utmost importance to know who you are and not be led astray by others. Tap into your roots when you are unsure. You cannot be all things to all people.

This did not prevent us from building a successful business with adults, but as my boss used to say, "Adult colds, that is an armchair. But it is still a chair and not a desk."

When I took over the brand we were spending most of our advertising rupees in the winter, a strategy that worked in North America and other countries. However, my monthly volume data stubbornly suggested that we were shipping a lot of Vaporub between July and September, the hot monsoon season.

"People must be catching lots of colds in the monsoon," I told my boss, and I got his agreement to bring forward a good chunk of our media to the warm monsoon months. Sure enough, we were rewarded with an immediate gain in sales.

I followed this up by getting our agency to make a cinema commercial (we had no television at that time) showing a child playing in the rain and catching cold. We coined a new ailment, "wet monsoon colds," and soon the summer monsoon season became as important as the winter in terms of sales.

Another factor in our success was the introduction of a small 5-gram tin, which still costs 10 cents and accounts for 40% of our volume. At first it was not successful, so we had to price it so that it was cheaper to buy four 5-gram tins than a 19-gram jar. The trade thought we were crazy. They said henceforth no one would buy the profitable jar; they would trade down to the tin. But that didn't happen. Why? Because we had positioned the tin for the working class. We were right in believing that middle-class consumers would stay loyal to the middle-class size.

Moves like these made us hugely successful and placed us first in the Indian market share by far. But instead of celebrating, my boss seemed depressed. He called me into his office, and he asked me how much the market was growing.

"Seven percent," I said.

"Is that good?"

"No," I replied, "But *we* are growing twenty percent, and that's why we're now number one in India."

"I don't give a damn that we are number one in a small pond. That pond has to become a lake, and then an ocean. We have to grow the market. Only then will we become number one in the world."

Thus I acquired another important mind-set: when you are number one, you must not grow complacent. Your job is to grow the market. You always must benchmark yourself against the best in the world, not just against the local competition. In the Third World this is an especially valuable idea, because markets there are so much less competitive.

Being receptive to regional variations, tapping the opportunity that the monsoon offered, introducing a size for the rural and urban poor, and learning to resist complacency and grow the market—all are variations on the theme of local thinking, of tapping into the roots of pluralism and diversity.

On Not Reinventing the Wheel

We could not have succeeded in building the Vicks business in India without the support of the native traders who took our products deep into the hinterland, to every nook and corner of a very large country. Many times we faced the temptation to set up an alternative Western-style distribution network. Fortunately, we never gave in to it. Instead, we chose each time to continue relying on the native system.

Following the practice of British companies in India, we appointed the largest wholesaler in each major town to become our exclusive stock point and direct customer. We called this wholesaler our stockist. Once a month our salesman visited the stockist, and together they went from shop to shop redistributing our products to the retailers and wholesalers of the town. The largest stockist in each state also became our Carrying-and-Forwarding Agent (in other words, our depot) for reshipping our goods to stockists in smaller towns. Over time, our stockists expanded their functions. They now work exclusively on P&G business under the supervision of our salesmen; they hire local salesmen who provide interim coverage of the market between the visits of our salesmen; they run vans to cover satellite villages and help us penetrate the interior; they conduct local promotions and advertising campaigns; and they are P&G's ambassadors and lifeline in the local community. The stockists perform all these services for a five percent commission, and our receivables are down to six days outstanding.

In our own backyard, we found and adopted an efficient low-cost distribution system perfected by Indian traders over hundreds of years. Thank God we chose to build on it rather than reinvent the wheel.

On Taking Ancient Medicine

We learned our most important lesson about diversity and tapping into roots shortly after I became head of the company in the early 1980s. We found ourselves against a wall. The chemists and pharmacists had united nationwide and decided to target our company and boycott our products in their fight for higher margins from the entire industry. At the same time, productivity at our plant was falling, while wages kept rising. As a result, our profitability had plummeted to two percent of sales.

Beset by a hostile environment, we turned inward. The answer to our problems came as a flash of insight about our roots, for we suddenly realized that Vicks Vaporub and other Vicks products were all-natural, herbal formulas. All their ingredients were found in thousand-year-old Sanskrit texts. What was more, this ancient *Ayurvedic* system of medicine enjoyed the special patronage of the government. If we could change our government registration from Western medicine to Indian medicine, we could expand our distribution to food shops, general stores, and street kiosks and thus reduce dependence on the pharmacists. By making our products more accessible, we would enhance consumer satisfaction and build competitive advantage. What was more, a new registration would also allow us to set up a new plant for Vicks in a tax-advantaged "backward area," where we could raise productivity dramatically by means of improved technology, better work practices, and lower labor costs.

I first tested the waters with our lawyers, who thought our solution to the problem quite wonderful. We then went to the government in Delhi, which was deeply impressed to discover all the elements of Vaporub's formula in the ancient texts. They advised to check with the local FDA in Bombay. The regulators at the FDA couldn't find a single fault with our case and, to our surprise and delight, promptly gave us a new registration.

Lo and behold, all the obstacles were gone! Our sales force heroically and rapidly expanded the distribution of our products to the nondrug trade, tripling the outlets which carried Vicks to roughly 750,000 stores. Consumers were happy that they could buy our products at every street corner. At the same time we quickly built a new plant near Hyderabad, where productivity was four times what it was in our Bombay plant. Our after-tax profits rose from 2% to 12% of sales, and we became a blue chip on the Bombay Stock Exchange.

Finally, we decided to return the compliment to the Indian system of medicine. We persuaded our headquarters to let us establish an R&D Center to investigate additional all-natural, Ayurvedic therapies for coughs and colds. When I first mooted this idea, my bosses at the head office in the United States practically fell off their chairs. Slowly, however, the idea of all-natural, safe, and effective remedies for a self-limiting ailment sold around the world under the Vicks name grew on them.

We set up labs in Bombay under the leadership of a fine Indian scientist who had studied in the United States. They began by creating a computerized data bank of herbs and formulas from the ancient texts; they invented a "finger-printing" process to standardize herbal raw materials with the help of computers; and they organized clinical trials in Bombay hospitals to confirm the safety and efficacy of the new products. We now have two products being successfully sold in the Indian market—Vicks Vaposyrup, an all-natural cough liquid, and Vicks Hot-sip, a hot drink for coughs and colds. The lab today is part of P&G's global health-care research effort and has 40 scientists and technicians working with state-of-the-art equipment.

Of Local Passions and Golden Ghettos

The story of Vicks in India brings up a mistaken notion about how multinationals build global brands. The popular conception is that you start with a powerful brand name, add standardized product, packaging, and advertising, push a button, and bingo—you are on the way to capturing global markets. Marlboro, Coke, Sony Walkman, and Levis are cited as examples of this strategy.

But if it's all so easy, why have so many powerful brands floundered? Without going into the standardization versus adaptation debate, the Vicks story demonstrates at least one key ingredient for global market success: *the importance of local passion.* If local managers believe a product is theirs, then local consumers will believe it too. Indeed, a survey of

Indian consumers a few years ago showed that 70% believed Vicks was an Indian brand.

What is the universal idea behind Vicks Vaporub's success in India? What is it that made it sell? Was it "rubbing it on the child with tender, loving care?" Could that idea be revived in the United States? Some people argue that the United States has become such a rushed society that mothers no longer have time to use a bedtime rub on their children when they've got a cold. Others feel that Vaporub could make its marketing more meaningful by striking a more contemporary note.

The Vicks story shows that a focus on the particular brings business rewards. But there are also psychic rewards for the manager who invests in the local. Going back to my roots reinvigorated me as a person and brought a certain fullness to my life. Not only was it pleasant to see familiar brown faces on the street, it also was enormously satisfying to be a part of the intense social life of the neighborhood, to experience the joys and sorrows of politics, and to share in the common fate of the nation. But at another level I also began to think of my work as a part of nation building, especially training and developing the next generation of young managers who would run the company and the country. It discharged a debt to my tutor at Harvard and a responsibility that we all have to the future.

Equally, it seems to me, there are powerful though less obvious psychic rewards for an international manager on transfer overseas who chooses to get involved in the local community. When such people approach the new country with an open mind, learn the local language, and make friends with colleagues and neighbors, they gain access to the wealth of a new culture. Not only will they be more effective as managers, they also will live fuller, richer lives.

Unfortunately, my experience in Mexico indicates that many expatriate managers live in "golden ghettos" of ease with little genuine contact with locals other than servants. Is it any surprise that they become isolated and complain of rootlessness and alienation in their new environment? The lesson for global companies is to give each international manager a local "mentor" who will open doors to the community. Ultimately, however, it is the responsibility of individual managers to open their minds, plunge into their local communities, and try to make them their own.

On Global Thinking

It would be wrong to conclude from the Vicks story that managing a global brand is purely a local affair. On the contrary, the winners in the new borderless economy will be the brands and companies that make best use of the richness of experience they get from their geographical diversity. Multinational companies have a natural advantage over local companies because they have talented people solving similar problems for identical brands in different parts of the world, and these brand managers can learn from each other's successes and failures. If a good idea emerges in Egypt, a smart brand manager in Malaysia or Venezuela will at least give it a test.

The Surat lady's teakettle became the basis of a national campaign in India. "One-pointedness" emerged from a hole-in-the-wall in Bombay, but it became the fulcrum on which we built a world-class business over a generation. Advertising for colds during the hot monsoon months seems highly parochial, but it taught us the importance of advertising year round in other places. The stockist system found applicability in Indonesia and China. Even the strange Ayurvedic system of medicine might plausibly be reapplied in the form of efficacious herbal remedies for common ailments in Western countries.

Business truths are invariably local in origin, but they are often expressions of fundamental human needs that are the same worldwide. Local insights with a universal character thus can become quickly global—though only in the hands of flexible, open-minded managers who can translate such ideas into new circumstances with sensitivity and understanding. My admonition to think local is only half the answer. Managers also must remember to think global. The insights we glean from each microcosm are ultimately universal.

Organizational specialists often express a fear that companies will demotivate their local managers by asking them to execute standardized global marketing packages. If they impose these standardized marketing solutions too rigidly, then this fear may be justified. However, this does not happen in successful companies. In fact, the more common disease in a global company is the "not invented here" syndrome, which especially afflicts subsidiaries and managers whose local triumphs have left them arrogant and unwilling to learn from successes in other parts of the world.

We in India were no different. But slowly and painfully we learned that useful lessons can emerge anywhere. For all our efforts to tap into the roots of Indian pluralism, we were dealing with a global brand. The product itself, the positioning, and the packaging were basically the same everywhere. Global brands are not free-for-alls, with each subsidiary doing its own thing. It took us six months, for example, to persuade our marketing people to try a new advertising idea for Vaporub that came from Mexico. It asked the consumer to use Vaporub on three parts of the body to obtain three types of relief. When we finally tried "Three-by-Three" in our advertising, it worked brilliantly.

It is deeply wrong to believe that going global is a one-stop, packaged decision. Local managers can add enormous value as they tap into local roots for insights. But it is equally wrong to neglect the integrity of the brand's core elements. Smart global managers nourish each blade of grass without neglecting the garden as a whole.

On Karma

Although the principles of managing a business in the Third World are the same as in the West, there are still big differences between the two. For me, the greatest of these is the pervasive reality of poverty.

I have lost the towering confidence of my youth, when I believed that socialism could wipe away poverty. The problem of socialism is one of performance, not vision. If it worked, we would all be socialists. Ironically, the legacy of the collectivist bias in Indian thinking has been the perpetuation of poverty. We created an over-regulated private sector and an inefficient public sector. We did not allow the economy to grow and produce the surplus that might have paid for direct poverty programs. We created an exploitative bureaucracy that fed on itself. Today, happily, we are righting the balance by liberalizing the economy, reducing state control, and restoring legitimacy to the market. I am confident that these changes will foster the entrepreneurialism and economic vitality India needs to create prosperity and eliminate the destitution of so many of its people.

Despite the problems, I find managers in India and other poor countries more optimistic than their counterparts in rich nations. The reason is that we believe our children will be better off than our parents were, and this idea is a great source of strength. We see our managerial work as nation building. We are the benign harbingers of technology and modernity. As we learn to manage complex enterprises, we empower people with the confidence they need to become responsible, innovative, and self-reliant.

It seems to come down to commitment. In committing to our work we commit to a here and now, to a particular place and time. The meaning in our lives comes from nourishing a particular blade of grass. It comes from absorbing ourselves so deeply in the microcosm of our work that we forget ourselves, especially our egos. The difference between subject and object disappears. The Sanskrit phrase *nishkama karma* describes this state of utter absorption, in which people act for the sake of the action, not for the sake of the reward from the action. This is also the meaning of happiness.

Reading 7–2

THE MYTH OF THE GENERIC MANAGER: NEW PERSONAL COMPETENCIES FOR NEW MANAGEMENT ROLES

Christopher A. Bartlett
Sumantra Ghoshal

Over the years, the Boston Celtics have won more National Basketball Association championships than any other team in the league. They have achieved that record through the effectiveness of their organization—the exceptional leadership ability of their general managers, as epitomized by the legendary Red Auerbach, the strong team development skills of coaches such as Tom Heinson, and the outstanding on-court talent of players like Larry Bird. But it is clear to everyone in the Celtics organization that the capable general manager, the savvy coach, and the star player all add value in very different ways. While Auerbach's career demonstrates that a good player can occasionally evolve into a great coach, and even go on to become an exceptional general manager, the instances of such a progression are extremely rare. Success in one role is not a good predictor of performance in another. Heinson made the transition from player to coach with ease, yet was not seen to have general management potential; and despite the fact he was one of the game's greatest players ever, few expect Larry Bird to become as successful a coach as Heinson, let alone a general manager of Auerbach's standing.

When it comes to management of companies, both our theory and our practice are very different. In theory, we believe in a generic role called "the manager," who is expected to add value to the company in a generic way, carrying out a generic set of tasks and possessing some generic capabilities. This assumption is manifest in the scores of books and articles on "the manager's job"[1] and in generic distinctions such as those between management and leadership.[2] It is also embedded in the currently burgeoning literature on management competencies.[3] With some important exceptions,[4] our theory of management is that at each organizational level, managers play similar roles and have similar responsibilities, only for a different size and scope of activities. The metaphor is that of the Russian doll: at each level of the hierarchy, the manager is similar but bigger than the manager a level below.

Practice, however, has always been very different from this theory. The Russian doll model of management is firmly rooted in a hierarchical model of organizations. But, in reality, a hierarchy sharply differentiates roles vertically. In hierarchical organizations, top-level managers set direction by formulating strategy and controlling resources; middle-level managers mediate the vertical information processing and resource allocation processes by assuming the role of administrative controllers; and, swamped by direction and control from above, front-line managers find themselves in the role of operational implementers. Despite their differences, however, theory and practice have actually reinforced each other: the theory has made the hierarchy legitimate while the practice has made it operational.

Over the last decade, top-level managers around the world have recognized the limitations of the classic hierarchy. Alarmed by the loss of efficiency, speed, and flexibility, they have delayered and destaffed their organizations, reengineered their operations, and have invested significant amounts of money and management time to spread the message of "empowerment" throughout their companies.[5] However, in most cases all they have bought is a little breathing time. How their companies function has not changed because the behaviors and relationships of their people have not changed.

The reason for this failure is simple. The problems of the hierarchy cannot be overcome without explicitly challenging both the Russian doll theory and the pecking-order practice of management. The reality is that large, diversified companies have and need a CEO or a leadership team, just as much as they have and need managers to run individual units and others to provide intermediate-level coor-

---

[1]Henry Mintzberg's book *The Nature of Managerial Work* (New York, NY: Harper and Row, 1973) is one of the most celebrated pieces of work on this topic. In his analysis, Mintzberg compares the work patterns of managers in very different kinds of managerial jobs in some very different kinds of organizations (such as companies, schools, and public hospitals), treating them as a sample from a population of "managers." The concept of a generic management role is inherent in the study design. The same assumption is also manifest in Peter Drucker's *The Practice of Management* (London: Heinemann, 1955) and John Kotter's *The General Managers* (New York, NY: The Free Press, 1982), although the focus of these authors is clearly on the role of corporate top management. There are some exceptions to this rule, however (see Note 4).

[2]See John Kotter, *A Force of Change: How Leadership Differs from Management* (New York, NY: The Free Press, 1990).

[3]For a recent and comprehensive review of this literature, see Elena P. Antonacopoulou and Louise FitzGerald, "Reframing Competency in Management Development," *Human Resource Management Journal*, 6/1 (1996): 27–48.

[4]Joseph L. Bower's book *Managing the Resource Allocation Process: A Study of Corporate Planning and Investment* (Boston, MA: Division of Research, Graduate School of Business Administration, Harvard University, 1970) is a good example of such exceptions. Based on this study of the resource allocation process, Bower develops a model in which front-line, middle, and top-level managers play clearly differentiated roles. Rosabeth Kanter's article "The Middle Manager as Innovator" [*Harvard Business Review*, 60/4 (1982): 95–105] also highlights such differences in management roles by suggesting the special role that middle managers can play in facilitating innovations.

[5]While these trends are well-known and have been widely documented in the business press, Nitin Nohria's research on the changes in strategy, organization, culture, and governance of the 100 largest U.S.-based companies over the 1978–1994 period provides clear and systematic evidence of these developments. A brief report of this study is available in Nitin Nohria, "From the M-form to the N-form: Taking Stock of Changes in the Large Industrial Corporation," Working Paper no. 16/1996, the Strategic Leadership Research Programme, London Business School, 1996.

dination and integration. Unless their activities and expected contributions are explicitly defined, these managers will tend to slip into the comfortable and familiar role structure of grand strategists, administrative controllers, and operational implementers. The only way to prevent this hierarchical relationship is to define the distinct value added of each of the management groups in terms of the different roles they need to play.

This is a key lesson from our recent research in twenty large European, American, and Asian companies.[6] Based on our analysis of the experiences of these companies, we have developed a model of the roles that front-line, senior, and top-level managers need to play for companies to achieve the organizational capabilities they are seeking.[7] These changes in management roles and personal capabilities are part of a fundamental change in organizational philosophy that is redefining the modern corporation.

---

[6]The twenty companies we studied were: Intel, 3M, AT&T, Corning, Beckton Dickensen, and Andersen Consulting in the United States; Asea Brown Boveri (ABB), Ikea, International Service Systems (ISS), Richardson Sheifield, Cartier, Royal Dutch Shell, Lufthansa, and Philips in Europe: and the LG Group (erstwhile Lucky Goldstar), Canon, Kao Corporation, Komatsu, Toyota, and Reliance Industries in Asia. In each of these companies, we conducted extensive interviews with managers (over 400, in total) at different levels, both in their corporate headquarters and in their different divisions and national subsidiaries. We also collected additional data from a variety of internal and external documents. Except for Toyota, we have written and published detailed case studies on all these companies, which are available either through the Harvard case clearing system or from the International Case Clearing House (ICCH). Our overall findings and conclusions from this study are available in Sumantra Ghoshal and Christopher A. Bartlett, *The Individualized Corporation* (New York, NY: HarperCollins, 1997).

[7]We have described these managerial roles in Christopher A. Bartlett and Sumantra Ghoshal, "Beyond the M-form: Toward a Managerial Theory of the Firm," *Strategic Management Journal,* 14 (Special Issue, Winter 1993): 23–46. In that article, written primarily for our academic colleagues, we have compared and contrasted our descriptions of these roles vis-à-vis those that are implied in some of the key strands of the related literature. In the present article, written primarily for a practitioner audience, we do not refer to this academic literature, but those interested in such references can find them in the 1993 article.

New Organization Model: New Management Roles

To understand the new management roles, one must first recognize the major elements of the emerging organizational framework that is shaping them. Despite the considerable differences in businesses, national origin, and corporate history in companies as diverse as GE, Komatsu, ABB, and Corning, we found that they were converging on a similar post-transformational organization model that represented a major change from their traditional authority-based hierarchies. Other companies we studied—such as 3M, ISS, and Kao—already shared many of these emerging organizational characteristics and therefore had avoided the worst aspects of the classic authority-based hierarchy. In many ways, this latter group provided both the inspiration and the example for other companies undergoing major organizational transformations.

The clearest and most widespread trend we observed was that companies were rethinking their old approach of dividing the organization from the top down into groups, sectors, and divisions. Instead, they were building from the bottom up on a foundation of small front-line operating units. For example, the $35 billion Swiss-based electro-technical giant, ABB, divided its operations into 1,300 local operating companies, each of which operates as a separate legal entity with its own balance sheet and P&L responsibilities. In 3M, the company's $15 billion dollars of sales generated by a portfolio of over 60,000 products are managed by 3,900 profit centers that are at the heart of the company's entrepreneurial process. ISS, the Denmark-based cleaning services organization, attributes its growth into a $2 billion multinational corporation to its policy of forming not one national subsidiary, but four or five small autonomous businesses in each of the 17 countries it has expanded into, allowing each of them to grow by serving a particular client group.

The second common characteristic in the emerging organizational model is the portfolio of cross-unit integrative processes. These processes are designed to break down the insulated vertically oriented relationships that have dominated the classic authority-based hierarchy. In ABB, the tensions embodied in the company's global matrix were resolved through a proliferation of business boards, functional councils, and project teams designed to play a primary role in ABB's management process at every level of the organization. At 3M, the R&D community's carefully developed network of communication channels and decision-making forums became the model for similar relationships to link the company's marketing and manufacturing resources across its portfolio of innovative front-line units. ISS made extensive use both of training and development and of cross-unit meetings and committees to ensure that knowledge and expertise developed in one part of the company were rapidly transferred system-wide.

Finally, in the emerging organization, these changes to the old structure and processes were supported by a strong commitment to genuine empowerment, a philosophy that represented a formidable challenge to the authority-based culture in most classic hierarchies. In ABB, CEO Percy Barnevik based the company's management practice on the twin principles of radically decentralized responsibility and tightly held individual accountability. 3M was known for its core principles that espoused a commitment to entrepreneurship and a belief in the individual. The company had long worked to translate those beliefs into a culture that "stimulates ordinary people to produce extraordinary performance." In his 30 years as the CEO of ISS, Poul Andreassen had developed a set of guiding principles, central to which was a genuine respect for his workers and a delegation of responsibility as close to the individual cleaning contract as possible.

This radically decentralized yet horizontally linked organizational model with a strong culture of empowerment required companies to break with the old hierarchy of nested roles that was implicit in the Russian doll model of management. In these and other companies we studied, operating-level managers had to evolve from their traditional role as front-line implementers to become innovative en-

trepreneurs; senior-level managers had to redefine their primary role from administrative controllers to developmental coaches; and top-level executives were forced to see themselves less as their company's strategic architects and more as their organizational leaders. The implications of such role changes on the distribution of key tasks and responsibilities are profound.

The Operating-Level Entrepreneurial Role

In identifying the new roles and responsibilities of those running business units, national subsidiaries, or other such front-line units, we studied the activities of scores of operating-level managers as they struggled to adjust to the demands of the new corporate model. We focus here on a select group of managers at ABB, 3M, and ISS not as definitive role models, but as illustrations of the framework of management tasks we have developed.

Don Jans headed the relays business unit that was part of Westinghouse's troubled power transmission and distribution business that was sold to ABB in 1989. Westinghouse had long regarded relays as a mature business, and Jans and his team had been encouraged to milk their slowly declining, modestly profitable operation. Yet, when exposed to ABB's decentralized entrepreneurial environment, the same management group turned their mature business into one with the performance profile of a young growth company. Within three years of the ownership change, export sales skyrocketed, new products were introduced, and operating profits doubled. Equally important, the revitalized U.S. relays unit began developing an electronic capability to supplement its traditional electro-mechanical expertise, thus laying the foundation for long-term expansion into a major new growth area.

At 3M, we saw a similar example of front-line entrepreneurship. In 1989, Andy Wong became the leader of a project team that had been struggling for over a decade to commercialize a portfolio of the company's optical technologies that had never found market applications. Over the next four years, Wong redeployed the unit's resources, refocused its energy and attention, protected the operations from several threats to shut them down, and remotivated the discouraged team. By 1994, Wong's unit had become a showcase within 3M by introducing two new products, both of which proved to be highly successful in the marketplace.

At ISS, we observed Theo Buitendijk take over the firm's small Dutch commercial cleaning business and double revenues within two years. He took the company into the specialized higher margin segment of slaughterhouse cleaning, eventually becoming the company's center of expertise in this sector and supporting its expansion throughout Europe. Like Jans, Buitendijk had previously been a traditional line manager in a classic authoritarian hierarchy (in his case, Exxon), but found that the

different organizational context in ISS not only allowed, but encouraged him to redefine his role and change his behavior.

In each of these companies, a similar framework of organizational structure, processes, and culture supported the entrepreneurial activities of front-line managers like Jans, Wong, and Buitendijk as they took the initiative to drive the performance and enhance the capabilities of their units. Among their many tasks and responsibilities, we identified three that were central to their role as entrepreneurs rather than just implementers (see Table 1).

The most striking set of activities and achievements common to the operating-level entrepreneurs we studied were those related to their taking the initiative to create and pursue new business

TABLE 1   Transformation of Management Roles and Tasks

	Operating-Level Managers	*Senior-Level Manager*	*Top-Level Managers*
Changing role	• From operational implementers to aggressive entrepreneurs	• From administrative controllers to supportive coaches	• From resource allocators to institutional leaders
Primary value added	• Driving business performance by focusing on productivity, innovation and growth within front-line units	• Providing the support and coordination to bring large company advantage to the independent front-line units	• Creating and embedding a sense of direction, commitment, and challenge to people throughout the organization
Key activities and tasks	• Creating and pursuing new growth opportunities for the business	• Developing individuals and supporting their activities	• Challenging embedded assumptions while establishing a stretching opportunity horizon and performance standards
	• Attracting and developing resources and competencies	• Linking dispersed knowledge, skills, and best practices across units	• Institutionalizing a set of norms and values to support cooperation and trust
	• Managing continuous performance improvement within the unit	• Managing the tension between short-term performance and long-term ambition	• Creating an overarching corporate purpose and ambition

opportunities. In contrast to the role they played in their previous situations (as implementers of programs and priorities pushed down from above), managers such as Jans and Buitendijk found that they were not only free to initiate new activities, they were expected to do so. Jans rose to the challenge by expanding into export markets in Mexico, Canada, and the Far East and by committing to the development of microprocessor-based relays (despite the substantial up-front investment involved). Buitendijk's move into abattoir cleaning initially caused a sharp drop in his company's profitability but then proved to be a much more attractive segment than the company's highly competitive core business of office cleaning.

Beyond developing new products and markets, these front-line entrepreneurs had all expanded the assets, resources, and capabilities of their operating units. Rather than playing the more traditional passive-dependent role defined by corporate processes such as head count authorization, capital budget allocation, and management development procedures, these individuals saw it as their responsibility to develop the limited resources they had and, as one of them described it, "do more with less." Andy Wong's actions in upgrading his unit's existing technological and manufacturing resources were impressive enough, but his creation of an entirely new marketing capability in a resource-constrained operation was truly entrepreneurial. Through persistent negotiations with senior management, creative internal resource reallocations, and persuasive recruiting within the company, he was able to reinforce his small struggling unit with an experienced marketing manager. He then backed this manager with the distribution support of two other 3M divisions that agreed to help bring his unproven product to market. Don Jans' ability to develop a microprocessor-based product line exhibited the same commitment to build on and leverage existing capabilities. He became recognized as a "giver" rather than a "receiver," as ABB terminology referred to managers who became net developers rather than consumers of the organization's scarce resources.

The third basic responsibility of front-line managers was the one with which they were most familiar: to ensure continuous performance improvement in their operating units. In the new organizational context, however, they were given considerably more freedom, incentive, and support to find ways to do so. Although Don Jans had long been working to maximize operating performance in Westinghouse, within the ABB organization he was able to achieve substantial additional expense cuts, inventory and receivables reductions, and operating efficiency improvements largely because he was given what Barnevik described as "maximum degrees of freedom to execute."

Andy Wong knew that by leveraging his unit's existing assets and resources he could build the credibility and confidence he would need to obtain additional investment and support. It was for this reason that Wong initially invested a large part of his energy in focusing development attention on only two technologies and reducing manufacturing costs by 50%. It was only after gaining organizational confidence in his operating effectiveness that he won both the freedom to engage in the resource development and the time to implement his unit's entrepreneurial new product launch.

These three cases show the untapped potential for performance improvement available to most companies. The dramatically changed management behavior of Jans and Buitendijk along with Wong's rapid transition from engineer to project team leader suggests that inside every hierarchy, even the most authoritarian, there are entrepreneurial hostages waiting to be unleashed. But the new entrepreneurial tasks can only be accomplished after the historical structures, processes, and cultural norms are replaced by a new organizational framework that requires front-line managers to abandon their old implementation role.

The Senior-Level Developmental Role
The risk of redefining the role of operating-level managers as entrepreneurs rather than implementers is that it will fragment the company's resources and capabilities and lead to the kind of undisciplined,

localized expansion that conglomerates experienced in the 1960s. To prevent this, the senior-level managers—those between the front-line units and the corporate-level management—must redefine their role from the historic preoccupation with authority-based control to a focus on support-based management and organization development.

Traditionally, senior managers' power came from their pivotal position in large and complex hierarchies (where they typically were responsible for the organization's divisions, regions, or key functions). They played a vital intermediary role, disaggregating corporate objectives into business unit targets and aggregating business unit plans for corporate review. They were the linchpins in the resource allocation process due to corporate management's reliance on their input in capital budgeting and personnel appointment decisions. They stood at the crossroads of internal communication, interpreting and broadcasting management's priorities, then channeling and translating front-line feedback.

These classic senior management tasks have been challenged by the creation of small independent front-line units, the radical decentralization of assets and resources to support them, and the empowerment of the operating managers in charge. They have been further undermined by the delayering of middle levels of the organization and the impact of new information technologies on internal communication. Left to fulfill their traditional role, senior managers find themselves increasingly frustrated by the irrelevance and powerlessness of their position. Unless there is a radical realignment of their role, this group can become the silent subverters of change whose invisible, yet persistent resistance can derail even the most carefully planned transformation program.

Some companies have successfully redesigned the senior management role by making it a key part of supporting the front-line units, both by coordinating their activities and by coaching their operating-level entrepreneurs. Ulf Gundemark, Don Jan's boss and the head of ABB's worldwide relays business area, played a central role in managing the tension inherent in the company's ambition "to be global and local, big and small, radically decentralized with central reporting and control." Similarly, Paul Guehler, vice president of 3M's Safety and Security Systems Division to which Andy Wong's unit belonged, challenged Wong to define the focus and priorities in his business, while simultaneously helping him build the support and obtain the resources necessary to make it succeed. At ISS, Waldemar Schmidt, head of the European region, supported Theo Buitendijk's new business initiative despite its short-term profit impact, and he led the effort to leverage the expertise his unit developed into a European business capability.

In none of these cases did these managers see their roles in the traditional terms of administrative controllers and information relays. Instead of dominating their front-line managers, usurping their authority, or compromising their sense of responsibility for their operations, this new generation of senior managers added value to that activity through three core tasks. First, they become a vital source of support and guidance for the front-line entrepreneurs; second, they took primary responsibility for linking and leveraging the resources and competencies developed in the front-line units; and third, they played a key role in ensuring resolution of the numerous tensions and conflicts built into the management process (see Table 1).

When a company decides to change its dominant management model from one driven by authority to one built on empowerment, the basic orientation of the senior manager's task is changed from direction and control to development and support. ABB not only reflected this change in its cultural norms, it institutionalized it in the way key senior-level jobs were structured. For example, although Ulf Gundemark was the relays business area head, he had a staff of only four to help him run the $250 million worldwide business. As a result, he routinely asked managers in operating units to take on broader responsibilities, stretching their abilities and developing their contacts and support as they did so. To develop the worldwide relays strategy, he assembled a nine-person team of managers drawn from the front lines of his operating companies. To guide the ongoing business operations, he created a business area board that included his staff members and four key company presidents, including Don Jans. As Jans put it, "I'm a much broader manager today than I was at Westinghouse. . . . We feel we are rediscovering management."

Paul Guehler described his primary job as "to help develop the people to develop the business." He worked intensively with Wong and his team, challenging them to refine their plans, forcing them to commit them to paper, and, most important, encouraging them to communicate and defend them in multiple forums in order to build up their struggling unit's thin support within 3M. At ISS, Waldemar Schmidt had a similar philosophy about his role, stating that "the most important thing I can do is to show an interest, to show that I care about them and their performance." He backed his words with actions, developing a strongly supportive relationship with his front-line managers that manifested itself in frequent telephone calls to say "Well done!" or "How can I help?"

The second element of this role focuses more on the level of organization development, as senior-level managers take on the task of linking the knowledge and expertise developed in their front-line units and embedding them as organizational capabilities to be leveraged company-wide. Gundemark's actions in forcing his front-line relays companies to rationalize and specialize in overlapping structures and responsibilities was a first step in integrating the portfolio of independent relays operations. He then appointed key specialists in each of the companies to functional councils whose primary purpose was to identify best practice and capture other benefits of coordination in R&D, quality, and purchasing. Waldemar Schmidt achieved similar cross-unit linkages through his regular meetings specifically devoted to leveraging the expertise of particular country units. When Theo Buitendijk's unit in Holland was shown to have superior performance in customer retention, for example, Schmidt gave him a day at his next European presidents conference to discuss his approach.

Beyond these important developmental tasks, however, those in senior management positions still must accept responsibility for the performance of the front-line units they supervise. The common bottom-line contribution of the three managers we described is that they all played the pivotal role in ensuring that those reporting to them kept the strategic objectives and operating priorities in balance. In ABB, this task was framed by a global matrix that was designed to legitimize rather than minimize the tensions and paradoxes inherent in most management decisions. To manage the conflict resolution vital to the organization's smooth operation, senior-level managers such as Ulf Gundemark developed and managed a portfolio of supplemental communications' channels and decision forums such as the worldwide business board and the functional councils we described. These and other forums (such as the steering committees that act as local boards for each of the front-line companies) not only serve a development and integration role, but they also become the place where differences are aired and resolution obtained on the conflicting perspectives and interests created by the matrix.

In 3M, this critical balancing role is so ingrained in the culture that senior-level managers such as Paul Guehler have integrated it into their ongoing management approach. For example, in what he terms his "give-and-take management style," Guehler tightened the screws on Wong's operations by requiring them to make the cuts necessary to meet their financial objectives, while behind the scenes he was defending against attempts to close the unit down and was lining up resources and support to back their proposed development initiatives.

Senior-level managers are often the forgotten and forsaken group in the organizational transformation process. Amid rounds of delayering, destaffing, and downsizing, many corporate executives have overlooked the fact that the success of small, empowered front-line units depends on a company's ability to bring large company benefits to those units. Organizations that dismantle their vertical integration mechanisms without simultaneously creating the horizontal coordination processes quickly lose potential scale economies. Even more important, they lose the benefits that come from leveraging each unit's assets, knowledge, and capabilities companywide. At the same time, such intense horizontal flows can also paralyze the organization by distracting or overburdening front-line managers. It is the managers in the middle who can make "inverting the pyramid" operational, not only by developing and supporting the front-line entrepreneurs, but also by absorbing most of the demands of the cross-business, cross-functional, and cross-geographic integration needs. In this way, they can prevent those at the operating level from becoming overwhelmed by the ambiguity, complexity, and potential conflicts that often accompany such horizontal networked organizations and allow them instead to focus on their vital entrepreneurial tasks.

The Top Management Leadership Role

Those at the apex of many of today's large, complex organizations find themselves playing out a role that they have inherited from their corporate forbears: to be the formulators of strategy, the builders of structure, and the controllers of systems. As these three tools became increasingly sophisticated, there was a growing assumption that they could allow organizations to drive purposefully towards their clearly defined goals, largely free from the idiosyncrasies of individual employees and the occasional eccentricities and pathologies of their behavior. To some extent, the objective was achieved. Under the strategy, structure, and systems doctrine of management, most large companies eventually became highly standardized and efficient operations, with individual employees being managed as inputs in the predicable but depersonalized system.

To free these entrepreneurial hostages requires a rollback of this dehumanizing management paradigm and thus a rethinking of top management's role. The role has to change from one grounded in the old doctrine of strategy, structure, and systems to one based on a new philosophy focusing on purpose, process, and people. Those at the top of most

of the entrepreneurial companies in our study had evolved from being the formulators of corporate strategy to becoming the shapers of a broader corporate purpose with which individual employees could identify and feel a sense of personal commitment. Instead of focusing on formal structures that gave them control over the firm's financial resources, they devoted much of their efforts to building processes that added value by having the organization work more effectively together. Rather than becoming overly dependent on the management systems that isolated them from the organization and treated employees as factors of production, they created a challenging organizational context that put them back in touch with people and focused them on affecting individual inputs rather than just monitoring collective outputs.

In this radically redefined view of their role, those at the top first had to create a work environment that fostered entrepreneurial initiative rather than compliant implementation. Poul Andreassen was not someone who readily accepted the status quo. Like many of the CEOs we observed, he was constantly questioning the past and challenging his organization to achieve more. To overcome the constrained potential of continuing to operate ISS as a Danish office cleaning business, Andreassen began to conceive of the company as a more broadly defined professional service organization. His explicit objective was to create a world-class company, "to make ISS and service as synonymous as Xerox and photocopying." By broadening the opportunity horizon, he legitimized the entrepreneurial initiatives of his management team as they expanded into new markets and unexplored business segments. The challenging environment that he developed continued to support the entrepreneurial initiatives of operating-level managers such as Theo Buitendijk (as he developed the abattoirs cleaning business in Holland) and the ISS manager in Germany who saw an opportunity to expand into the former East Germany to start a business in the removal of building rubble.

The second key task common to the top managers we studied was to shape the organizational context necessary to support the radically decentralized structure and the management philosophy of empowerment. To ensure that the organization did not fragment its efforts or dissipate its scarce resources in this more decentralized form, traditional control-based values had to be replaced with norms of trust and support. Over the years, 3M's top managers have created an organization with such values, allowing resources and expertise to move freely across its 3,900 profit centers located in 47 divisions and 57 country operations. From the earliest days, they developed clear integrating norms such as the recognition that while products belong to the division, technologies belong to the company. They reinforced such beliefs by carefully developing a framework for collaboration and support. For example, the strong mutually supportive relationships within 3M's scientific community were formed and reinforced through institutionalized grassroots forums, internal technology fairs, and cross-unit transfer practices. Overarching all of this was a sense of trust embedded in the respect those at the top had for individuals and their ideas. As current CEO Livio "Desi" DeSimone reminds his managers, they must listen carefully to subordinates and continually ask, "What do you see that I am missing?" It was this respectful, supportive, and trusting environment that allowed entrepreneurs like Andy Wong to take risks and that encouraged senior managers like Paul Guehler to back them.

Finally, the top-level managers we observed also played the vital role of providing the organization with a stabilizing and motivating sense of purpose. As chief executive of ABB, Percy Barnevik believed that he had to develop more than just a clear strategy for his newly merged worldwide entity. He felt that he had to create an organizational environment that made people proud to belong and motivated to work for the company. He articulated ABB's overall mission not in terms of its market share, competitive position, or profit objectives, but in terms of the ways in which ABB could contribute to sustainable economic growth and world development. He emphasized a sensitivity to environmental protection and a commitment to improving living

standards worldwide, reflecting those beliefs not only in the company's formal mission statement, but also in the major strategic decisions he took. The company's pioneering investments in Eastern Europe, its transfer of technology to China and India, and its innovations in environmentally sensitive processes gave substance to its articulated purpose. These efforts also made ABB's employees feel that they were contributing to changing the world for the better. As corporate executive VP Goran Lindahl explained, "In the end, managers are loyal not to a particular boss or even to a company, but to a set of values they believe in and find satisfying."

The approach taken by Barnevik and Lindahl (and their counterparts in companies such as 3M and ISS) reflected the simple belief that their job as the top-level leaders was not simply to manage an economic entity whose activities could be directed through strategic plans, resource allocation processes, and management control systems. Equally important was their role as the principal architects of a social institution able to capture the energy, commitment, and creativity of those within it by treating them as valued organizational members, not just contracted company employees. In addition to managing the strategy and structure, they took the time to develop a corporate purpose and shape the integrating organizational processes. Rather than simply monitoring the performance of divisions or subsidiaries through abstract systems, they focused their attention on the people within the organizations—those whose motivations and actions would drive the company's performance.

New Management Roles, New Personal Competencies

Over the past few years, companies as diverse as AT&T, British Airways, BP, Siemens, and The World Bank have invested enormous amounts of management time and effort to define the ideal profile of their future corporate leaders. Siemens, for example, has defined 22 desirable management characteristics under five basic competencies of understanding, drive, trust, social competence, and what they call a "sixth sense." The World Bank's ideal profile identifies 20 attributes and groups them into seven quite different categories of intellectual leadership, team leadership, staff development, work program management, communication, interpersonal impact, and client orientation. Pepsico's desired competency profile for its executives of the future has 18 key dimensions defining how individuals see the world, how they think, and the way they act.

This focus on personal characteristics is understandable given the widespread problems that so many individuals have had adjusting to the transformed organizational environment and performing the redefined management tasks. Indeed, this emerging interest in individual competencies has created a cottage industry among consultants eager to promote their expertise in identifying, measuring, and developing the desired personal capabilities to lead in the new corporate environment. Yet, despite prodigious efforts in designing questionnaires, conducting interviews, and running seminars to define the profile of leadership competencies, few of these programs have won the kind of credibility and support necessary for widespread adoption and application.

One problem is that the profiles that have been generated often include an inventory of personality traits, individual beliefs, acquired skills, and other personal attributes and behaviors assembled on the basis of unclear selection criteria and with little logical linkage to bind them. Furthermore, these profiles are often developed based on surveys of current managers or analysis of the most successful individual performers in the existing context. As such, they risk defining future leadership needs in terms of the historical organizational roles and capabilities that were required to succeed in the old organizational forms.

The most important limitation of these management competency exercises is that they are almost always defined as a single ideal profile. While such an assumption may not have been entirely irrational in the more symmetrical roles typical of the traditional authority-based hierarchy, this extension of the Russian doll model is not viable in the emerging delayered organization with its differentiated set of management roles and tasks.

As part of our research into post-transformation organizations, we studied the adaptation of managers to their redefined responsibilities. Instead of asking managers to describe the personal characteristics they felt were most important, we observed those who had demonstrated their effectiveness in performing the key tasks of the redefined management roles. Rather than trying to develop a list of generic competencies with universal application, we were able to differentiate the profiles of managers who succeeded in adding value in very different ways at each level of the organization.

Despite the fact that we were developing more differentiated profiles based on performance rather than opinion, the notion of individual competencies still seemed too vague and unfocused to be of great practical value. To be more useful to managers, the concept had to be more sharply defined and more clearly applicable to human resource discussions and activities. This led us to develop a simple classification model that helped us allocate the broadly defined competencies into three categories. In the first, we listed deeply embedded personal characteristics like attitudes, traits, and values that were intrinsic parts of the individual's character and personality. The second category included attributes such as knowledge, experience, and understanding that generally could be acquired through training and career path development. The third category was composed of specialized skills and abilities that were directly linked to the job's specific task requirements and were built on the individual's intrinsic capabilities and acquired knowledge (see Table 2).

By categorizing management competencies in this way, we not only gave the concept a sharper definition, but were also able to identify much more clearly how managers could focus attention on different attributes of the profile in various important human resource decisions. In particular, our observations led us to develop some propositions about the role different attributes play in the vital

TABLE 2   Management Competencies for New Roles

Role/Task	Attitude/Traits	Knowledge/Experience	Skills/Abilities
Operating-Level Entrepreneurs	*Results-Oriented Competitor*	*Detailed Operating Knowledge*	*Focuses Energy on Opportunities*
• Creating and pursuing opportunities	• Creative, intuitive	• Knowledge of the business's technical, competitive, and customer characteristics	• Ability to recognize potential and make commitments
• Attracting and utilizing scarce skills and resources	• Persuasive, engaging	• Knowledge of internal and external resources	• Ability to motivate and drive people
• Managing continuous performance improvement	• Competitive, persistent	• Detailed understanding of the business operations	• Ability to sustain organizational energy around demanding objectives
Senior-Management Developers	*People-Oriented Integrator*	*Broad Organizational Experience*	*Develops People and Relationships*
• Reviewing, developing, supporting individuals and their initiates	• Supportive, patient	• Knowledge of people as individuals and understanding how to influence them	• Ability to delegate, develop, empower
• Linking dispersed knowledge, skills, and practices	• Integrative, flexible	• Understanding of the interpersonal dynamics among diverse groups	• Ability to develop relationships and build teams.
• Managing the short-term and long-term pressures	• Perceptive, demanding	• Understanding the means-ends relationships linking short-term priorities and long-term goals	• Ability to reconcile differences while maintaining tension
Top-Level Leaders	*Institution-Minded Visionary*	*Understanding Company in Its Context*	*Balances Alignment and Challenge*
• Challenging embedded assumptions while setting stretching opportunity horizons and performance standards	• Challenging, stretching	• Grounded understanding of the company, its businesses and operations	• Ability to create an exciting, demanding work environment
• Building a context of cooperation and trust	• Open-minded, fair	• Understanding of the organization as a system of structures, processes, and cultures	• Ability to inspire confidence and belief in the institution and its management
• Creating an overarching sense of corporate purpose and ambition	• Insightful, inspiring	• Broad knowledge of different companies, industries and societies	• Ability to combine conceptual insight with motivational challenges

management responsibilities for selecting, developing, and supporting people in their particular job responsibilities.

Selecting for Embedded Traits

There is a high rate of failure among managers attempting to adapt from their historic roles in traditional companies to their newly defined tasks in transformed and reengineered organizations. This underscores the importance of identifying selection criteria that can help product success in radically redefined roles. For example, when ABB was created in 1988 through merger, 300 top and senior management positions were filled. Despite the careful selection of those appointed to these positions, over 40% of them were no longer with the company six years later. As the company's leadership recognized at the time, the central problem was to identify the candidates who had already developed the personal traits that were needed to succeed in the radically different organizational and managerial context that Percy Barnevik had defined for ABB.

When faced with such a situation, most companies we observed tended to select primarily on the basis of an individual's accumulated knowledge and job experience. These were, after all, the most visible and stable qualifications in an otherwise tumultuous situation. Furthermore, selecting on this basis was a decision that could be made by default, simply by requiring existing managers to take on totally redefined job responsibilities.

In such situations, however, past experience did not prove to be a good predictor of future success. The most obvious problem was that much of the acquired organizational expertise was likely to reflect old management models and behavioral norms. Equally problematic were the personal characteristics of those who had succeeded in the old organizational environment. As many companies discovered, the highly task-oriented senior managers who were both comfortable and successful in the well-structured work environment of their traditional company often found great personal difficulty in adjusting to the coaching and integrating roles that became an important part of their redefined responsibilities.

As a result, many companies are coming to believe that it is much more difficult to convince an authoritarian industry expert to adopt a more people-sensitive style than to develop industry expertise in a strong people manager. It is a recognition that is leading them to conclude that innate personal characteristics should dominate acquired experience as the key selection criteria. Equally importantly, they are recognizing that because the management roles and tasks differ widely at each level of the organization, so too will the attitudes, traits, and values of those most likely to succeed in each position. Recruitment and succession planning in such an environment becomes a much more sophisticated exercise of identifying the very different kinds of individuals who can succeed as operating-level entrepreneurs, senior-level developers, and top management leaders.

In ISS, for example, the company had long recognized the vital importance of recruiting individuals who were result-oriented competitors to run their front-line operating units. Although the front-line manager's job at ISS could be regarded as a low-status position managing supervisors in the mature and menial office cleaning business, ISS knew that by structuring the role to give managers status and autonomy, they could attract the kind of energetic, independent, and creative individuals they wanted. Like many of ISS's operating-level entrepreneurs, Theo Buitendijk had spent his early career in a traditional hierarchical company, but he had been frustrated by the constraints, controls, and lack of independence he felt. Status elements like the "managing director" title and the prestige company car signaled the importance ISS attached to this position, but entrepreneurial individuals like Buitendijk were even more attracted by the independence offered by operating their own business behind what ISS managers called "Chinese walls" to prevent unwanted interference. By creating an environment that motivated self-starters would find stimulating, ISS had little difficulty in training them in industry knowledge and helping them develop the specific job skills they required to succeed.

The personal profile required to move to the next level of management was quite different, however, and few of the operating-level entrepreneurs were expected or indeed had an ambition to move up to the divisional management level. One who did was Waldemar Schmidt, an operating-level entrepreneur who had turned around the company's Brazilian business before being appointed head of the European division. Despite his relatively limited knowledge of the European market, Schmidt impressed Poul Andreassen as a people-oriented individual who had a genuine interest in developing and supporting others. Indeed, the company's Five Star training program had originated in Brazil as part of Schmidt's commitment to continually upgrade his employees. Furthermore, he was recognized as being a very balanced individual who tended to operate by influence more than authority, yet was demanding of himself and others. These were qualities that Andreassen regarded as vital in his senior managers and felt they far outweighed Schmidt's more limited European knowledge or experience.

At the top level of the organization, another set of personal qualities was felt to be important. When Poul Andreassen became the president of ISS in 1962, he too was selected primarily on the basis of his personal traits rather than his experience in the company or his proven leadership skills. As a young engineer in his mid-30s, he was frustrated in his job with a traditional large company and was looking for the opportunity to build a very different kind of organization. Despite his lack of industry background of ISS-specific management skills, he was attractive because he was much less interested in running an ongoing company than he was in building a more ambitious organization. His most appealing characteristic was his willingness to question and challenge everything, and even after thirty years in the job, he still felt that his best days were when he could go into the field and confront his division or business unit managers so as to help "stir up new things."

Like Red Auerbach of the Boston Celtics, there will be a few individuals who have the breadth of personal traits and the temperamental range to adapt to the very different roles and tasks demanded of them at different organizational levels. At ISS, Waldemar Schmidt progressed from suc-cessful operating-level entrepreneur to effective senior management developer, and, after Poul Andreassen's retirement, was asked to succeed him as top-level corporate leader. One of management's most important challenges is to identify the personal characteristics that will allow an individual to succeed in a new and often quite different role and, equally important, to recognize when someone who is successful at one level lacks the individual traits to succeed at the next. For those with the perceived potential, however, the next key challenge is to develop the knowledge and expertise that can support and leverage their embedded personal traits.

Developing for Knowledge Acquisition

While training and development activities are rarely very effective in changing the deeply embedded personal traits, attitudes, and values, they are extremely appropriate means of developing the kind of knowledge and experience that allows an individual to build on and apply those embedded individual attributes. For example, as a person who is naturally creative, engaging, and competitive learns more about a particular business, its customers, and technologies, he or she becomes a much more effective and focused operating-level entrepreneur. Poul Andreassen understood this well and made training and development one of the few functions that he controlled directly from ISS's small corporate office. Under the ISS philosophy of ensuring that all employees had the opportunity to use their abilities to the fullest, the Five Star development program defined five levels of training that allowed front-line supervisors with the appropriate profile to gain the knowledge and experience they would need in a broader management job.

Because of its strong promote-from-within culture, 3M also had a long-standing commitment to develop its people to their potential. Soon after a new employee enters the company (within six months for a clerical employee or three years for a laboratory scientist) a formal Early Career Assessment process is initiated both to ensure that the individual is a proper fit with the company and to define a program to prepare them for their next career opportunity. For example, a promising accounting clerk might be set the personal education goal of becoming a Certified Public Accountant within three years, while at the same time being given an internal development assignment to provide experience in preparing financial statements and participating in audits. This process continues (albeit in a somewhat less structured format) throughout an individual's career in 3M, with the company providing internal business courses and technical seminars as well as supporting participation in external education programs.

On-the-job training is still the primary emphasis, and those with the will and the perceived personal potential are given every opportunity to develop that promise. For example, Andy Wong, who turned the struggling Optical Systems (OS) project into a showcase of entrepreneurial success, was carefully prepared for that role over five years. This quiet engineer first caught the eye of Ron Mitsch, a senior R&D executive who was impressed by the young man's tenacious, self-motivated competitiveness— personal qualities that 3M looked for in its front-line entrepreneurs. Wanting to give him the opportunity to prove that potential, the mentor told Wong about an opportunity to lead a small technical development team in the OS unit. While demonstrating his energy and persuasive persistence, Wong began to expand his knowledge about the unit's optical technologies, as he struggled to develop the understanding he needed to focus his team's rather fragmented efforts. After a couple of years in the OS laboratory, Wong was asked to take on the additional responsibility for the unit's inefficient manufacturing operations. Although he had no prior production or logistics experience, his initiatives in rationalizing the complex sourcing arrangements, simplifying the manufacturing process, and consolidating production in a single plant resulted in a 50% cost reduction and simultaneous improvement in product quality. It was through these experiences that Wong was able to broaden his knowledge of the business beyond his focused understanding of the technology and expand his familiarity with the organization's resources beyond his scientific contacts. Through careful career path development, he developed the kind of knowledge and experience he needed to allow him to use his naturally competitive traits effectively as the newly appointed project team leader for optical systems.

While the developmental path for operating-level entrepreneurs focused on enhancing knowledge and expertise in a particular business, market, or function, the track to the next level of management usually required a much richer understanding of the organization and how it operated. Wong's boss Paul Guehler also began his 3M career in the R&D laboratory and was also identified as someone who looked beyond the technologies he was developing to the businesses they represented. It was this budding entrepreneurial attitude that led to his transfer to 3M's New Business Ventures Division. In this position, his natural curiosity and intuitiveness were leveraged by focusing him on the task of exploring market opportunities and business applications for high potential ideas and innovations. After a decade in this division, Guehler was transferred to the Occupational Health and Safety Products Division. In this position, his experience as an R&D manager gave him the opportunity to broaden his understanding of the mainstream organizational processes and how to manage them. A subsequent move to the Disposable Products Division helped him build on that experience, particularly when he was appointed Business Director for disposable products in Europe. This responsibility for a highly competitive product in a fast-changing market greatly expanded his experience in assessing the capabilities and limitations of a diverse group of individuals and organizational units and further expanded his understanding of the organizational dynamics and strategic tensions of having them work together. By the time he was appointed as general manager and later vice president of the Safety and Security Systems Division of which Wong's OS unit was a part, he brought not only hard-headed business knowledge, but some sensitive organizational insights into his new role. As his diagnosis of the OS unit's situation indicates:

> You have to have people in these positions who recognize other people's talents and support their ideals for building a business. My job is to create an environment where people come forward with ideas

and are supported to succeed. . . . So while the OS group probably thought I was being too tough, my objective was to get them to recognize their opportunities, to hold them accountable for their actions, to help them build their credibility, and ultimately to support them so they could succeed. . . . One of my most important roles is not only to develop business, but to develop the people who can develop the business.

At the top level of 3M management, the need for a breadth of knowledge and experience was even greater. In 1991, when the company was planning the transition to a new chief executive, board member and ex-CEO Lou Lehr said that the successful candidate was likely to be a career 3M executive five to ten years from retirement (for no other reason than it usually took 30 to 35 years to accumulate the breadth of experience to be effective in the top job in this diversified company).

Desi DeSimone, the CEO elected in 1991, was described in one news account as "a textbook example of the quintessential 3M CEO." He had moved up through technical, engineering, and manufacturing management positions to assume general management roles as managing director of the Brazilian subsidiary and eventually area vice president of 3M's Latin American operations. He was recognized as a senior manager with top management potential. "There were always people taking an interest in my development," DeSimone said on assuming the CEO job. In classic 3M fashion, he was brought back to corporate headquarters where he could be given experiences that would provide him with the background and knowledge to help him succeed in top-level positions.

Through the 1980s, he was assigned to head up each of 3M's three business sectors in succession, to broaden his knowledge of their markets and technologies as well as to refine the skills necessary to have an impact on their performance. After spending most of his career focused on the company's far-flung units in Canada, Australia, and Latin America, it was important for him to get a better sense of the organization's core structure, processes, and culture. By immersing him in corporate-level activities for more than a decade, 3M's top management and

the board's appraisal committee wanted to ensure that he had the organizational understanding that was vital for any leader. Finally, DeSimone's promotion to the board in 1986 was important not only in bringing his expertise to board-level decisions, but also in broadening him as an executive by exposing him to the perspectives and experiences of top-level executives from other companies in different industries.

In companies like 3M where an understanding of the strongly held organizational values and cultural norms are central to the source of competitive advantage, the importance of a career-long development process must not be underestimated. Sometimes, however, a manager's strong links to the company's existing policies and practices become disadvantageous, particularly when the embedded beliefs have deteriorated into blind assumptions or outmoded conventional wisdom. In such cases, selection of an outsider with the desired personal characteristics can break the pathological cycle of inwardly focused indoctrination. But it does so at the risk of stranding the new leader without the relevant knowledge required to develop the appropriate top management skills for the company. The risks are particularly high were knowledge and experience accumulated in prior work is of limited relevance in the new situation. So while Larry Bossidy was able to make a relatively smooth transition from his top management job at GE to the leadership of Allied, another traditionally structured diversified industrial goods company, John Sculley's move from Pepsico to Apple became problematic due to his lack of computer industry background and his inexperience in managing the more informal network culture of Silicon Valley. Such problems underscore the important linkage between personal traits and acquired knowledge, on the one hand, and the development of the skills and abilities required to perform a job effectively, on the other.

Coaching for Skills Mastery

Of all the elements in the competencies profile, the particular skills and abilities an individual develops are probably the best indicators of job success, since they are the most directly linked to a position's key roles and tasks. Not everyone becomes effective in these highly specific yet critical personal skills, and the challenge for management is to identify those who can succeed and to help them develop these skills. The reason is that most of these skills rely heavily on tacit knowledge and capabilities that often grow out of the interaction between an individual's embedded traits and accumulated experience. So, for example, the critical entrepreneurial ability to recognize potential in people and situations is not an easily trainable skill, but one that often develops naturally in individuals who are curious and intuitive by nature and who have developed a richly textured understanding of their particular business and organizational environment.

Thus while some broader skills can be selected for and other simpler ones can be trained for, most of the critical skills are largely self-developed through on-the-job experience as individuals apply their natural talents and accumulated experience to the particular challenges of the job. In this process, the most effective role management can play is to coach and support those they have selected and prepared for the job by providing the resources, reinforcement, and guidance to encourage the self-development process.

ABB executive vice president Goran Lindahl clearly articulated the notion that an individual's natural characteristics should be the dominant factor in selection: "I will always pick a person with tenacity over one with just experience." Lindahl also spent a substantial amount of his time planning developmental job experiences for the individuals he selected. However, he considered his principal and most difficult management role to be acting as a teacher and a coach to help those in the organization leverage their experiences and fulfill their natural potential. It was this commitment "to help engineers become managers, and managers grow into leaders" that was vital to the development of the skills required to meet the demanding new job requirements.

Don Jans was surprised when he was asked to continue to head the relays company that ABB took over as part of the acquired Westinghouse power transmission and distribution business. "The prevailing view was that we had lost the war," he said, "and that the occupying troops would just move in." Yet Lindahl and Ulf Gundemark (his worldwide relays business manager) were impressed that Jans, like most of the Westinghouse managers, was a very capable individual with long industry experience. They felt that, with proper coaching, his natural energy, persistence, and competitiveness could be channeled towards the new skills he would need to manage in a very different way within ABB.

Jans met their expectations and—with his bosses' encouragement, support, and coaching—was able to develop a whole range of new skills that helped him turn around his relays company. By redefining Jans's company as part of an interdependent global network, ABB's senior-level management was able to refocus his attention on export markets, thereby helping him reignite his latent ability to identify and exploit opportunities. Through their own highly motivating and inspiring management approach, Barnevik, Lindhal, Gundemark, and others provided Jans with role models that encouraged him to tap into his own engaging personality and develop a more motivating approach to drive his people to higher levels of performance. ABB's cultural norm of high interest and involvement in the operations (what Lindahl called the "fingers in the pie" approach) led Jans to expand on his natural results-orientated competitiveness and develop a skill for creating and sustaining energy around the demanding objectives he set for his organization.

Meanwhile, Lindahl was helping support a very different set of new skills in the select few operating-level entrepreneurs that had been identified to take on senior-level business or regional responsibilities. One such individual was Ulf Gundemark, the young manager who was running the Swedish relays company and who had twelve years of experience in various parts of the organization. Lindahl promoted him to worldwide relays manager because he demonstrated the vital personality characteristics that Lindahl described as "generous, flexible, and statesmanlike." Driven by his boss's urging to become a "giver" rather than a "receiver" of management resources and constrained by his lack of division-level staff, Gundemark leveraged his naturally supportive disposition into a sophisticated skill of developing the operating-level managers reporting to him by delegating responsibilities and empowering them to make decisions. Lindahl also encouraged Gundemark to establish formal and informal management forums at all levels of his organization. By applying his flexible and integrative personality to his growing understanding of the organizational dynamics, Gundemark gradually acquired a strong ability to develop interpersonal relationships and team behavior. Finally, largely by following the example of his boss, Gundemark developed the vital senior management skill of maintaining the pressure for both long- and short-term objectives while helping the organization to deal with the conflicts that were implied. Although many were unwilling or unable to manage the very different task requirements of a senior manager's job (indeed, Lindahl estimated that even after careful selection, half the candidates for these positions either stepped aside or were moved out of the role), managers like Gundemark—who were able to develop their people skills and relationship-building skills—usually succeeded in these roles.

At the top levels of management, an even more subtle and sophisticated set of skills and abilities was necessary. More than just driving the company's ongoing operations or developing its resources and capabilities, these individuals had to be able to lead the company to becoming what Lindahl described as "a self-driven, self-renewing organization." The most fundamental skill was one that CEO Percy Barnevik had encouraged in all his top team—to create an exciting and demanding work environment. Harnessing his own innate restlessness, Lindahl focused his naturally striving and questioning personal style on his broad knowledge of the company and its businesses to develop a finely honed ability to challenge managers' assumptions while stretching them to reach for new objectives. His bimonthly business meetings were far from traditional review sessions. Lindahl led his senior managers through scenario exercises that forced them to think beyond straight-line projections and consider how they could respond to new trade barriers, political

realignments, or environmental legislation. He also recognized that it was top management's role to develop the organization's values. "In the end," he said "managers are not really loyal to a particular boss or even to a company, but to the values they represent." One of the most vital was to create an environment of mutual cooperation and trust. By consistently applying his own natural forthright and open personal approach to a sophisticated understanding of the organization, he was able to create a belief in the institution and in the fairness of its management processes that was a prior condition for both entrepreneurial risk taking and shared organizational learning.

Finally, Lindahl's sharp mind and inspiring personal manner were able to articulate messages that provided the organization with conceptual insight about the business while simultaneously providing them with concrete motivational challenges. He routinely demonstrated this ability in his far-sighted views about ABB's role in helping develop the industrial infrastructure in a realigned global political economy. Furthermore, he translated those insights into challenges for his management. As a result of his skills and abilities, the company was able to radically rebalance its own value chain from the developed world to the emerging giants such as China, India, and Eastern Europe.

The reason this set of top management skills is so difficult to develop is that it both reflects and reinforces the conflicts, dilemmas, and paradoxes framed by the post-transformational organization. Unlike the classic top management task that focused on managing "alignment" and ensuring "fit," the role we have described involves at least as much energy being devoted to questioning, challenging and even defying the company's traditional strategic assumptions and embedded organizational practices. The required competencies involve an even greater level of subtlety and sophistication to maintain a balance between challenging embedded beliefs and creating a unifying sense of purpose and ambition. Not surprisingly, only a handful of people have the potential to develop these scarce leadership skills, and perhaps the most critical task of top management is to identify these individuals and provide them with the necessary development opportunities and coaching support to allow them to fulfill that potential.

From Organization Man to Individualized Corporation

The dramatic changes in management roles and the individual competencies required to implement them are part of a broader redefinition of the relationship between the corporation and its employees in the post-transformational organization. In earlier decades, when capital was the scarce resource, top management's primary role was to use its control over investments to determine strategy as well as to create structures and systems to shape employee behavior in ways that would support those capital allocation decisions. The strategy-structure-systems doctrine of management led to the development of what William Whyte termed "the organization man"—the employee whose behavior was molded to suit the needs of the corporation and to support its strategic investments.

As the industrial era evolves into the information age, however, the scarce resource is shifting from capital to knowledge. But because the organization's vital knowledge, expertise, and strategic information exist at the operating levels rather than at the top, the whole authoritarian hierarchy has had to be dismantled and the roles and tasks of each management level radically redefined. Far from wanting to subjugate individual differences by requiring conformity to a standardized organizational model, companies are recognizing that in a knowledge-based environment, diversity of employee perspectives, experience, and capabilities can be an important organizational asset.

This realization implies a fundamental reconceptualization of the underlying management philosophy. Instead of forcing the individual to conform to the company's policies and practices, the overall objective is to capture and leverage the knowledge and expertise that each organizational member brings to the company. Thus the notion of "the organization man" and the Russian Doll model of nested roles that it reflected and supported are giving way to a concept we call "the individualized corporation"—one that capitalizes on the idiosyncrasies and even the eccentricities of exceptional people by recognizing, developing, and applying their unique capabilities.

This change in organizational philosophy has important implications for management practice. One of the most basic needs is to change the multitude of personnel practices aimed at recruiting, developing, and promoting people on the basis of a single corporate model—an approach most recently exemplified by the unrealistic competency lists of personal characteristics, many of which seem to resemble the idealized profile of the Boy Scout Law (trustworthy, loyal, helpful, friendly, and so on). Equally important, however, is the need for employees to accept that their career paths may not lead inexorably up the hierarchy, but will more likely take them where they best fit and therefore where they can add the most value for the organization. Together these changes are exposing the myth of the generic manager and are redefining the basic relationship between companies and their employees in a way that recognizes and capitalizes on diversity rather than trying to minimize and suppress it.

Chapter 8

Preparing for the Future: Evolution of the Transnational

In the seven years since the first edition of this book was published, we have repeatedly been asked both by managers and by our students "what's next?" The model of the transnational company we have described in this book was drawn from the experiences of companies in the mid-1980s. How has leading-edge practice evolved since then? How must the transnational model evolve to respond to the needs of the future?

The question has been given an added urgency by the turmoil experienced by many of the world's largest MNCs over the last decade. Highly publicized problems in companies like IBM, Kodak, and Westinghouse have led many to question the fundamental viability of companies as large, as diversified, and as geographically dispersed as these corporate behemoths. And it is not just in the United States where such problems have been emerging. In Europe, once revered names like Volkswagen, Olivetti, and Philips have been making headlines more as problem cases than as role models. Even much admired Japanese companies such as Mazda, Yamaha, Toshiba, and the Industrial Bank of Japan have lost their lustre as deteriorating performance has led them to contemplate the once unthinkable steps of layoffs and top-management changes.

Some critics have interpreted such turmoil in some of the largest and most visible MNCs as a sign that the era of the large worldwide companies may be over. Though many still survive and even dominate various geographic and business areas, these critics would have us believe that these are the last generation of dinosaurs still roaming the earth completely unaware of their inevitable and impending fate. The meteoric impact of simultaneous market and technological revolutions of the 1990s, they believe, will lead to the extinction of the entire population, to be replaced by more agile small companies or by a completely new genetically engineered species of "virtual corporations."

Based on our own ongoing work in a number of companies, we believe that this news of the MNC's death is exaggerated. Indeed, our own research has indicated that it is precisely because of their experience in the international operating environment that such companies develop the best chance of surviving. Most obviously, this is due to their access to a wider scope of markets and resources and their ability to secure competitive positions and competencies unobtainable by purely domestic companies. But even more important, it is because the management in such companies gains invaluable experience in routinely dealing with the fast-changing, multidimensional demands and opportunities that are part of the global business environment. Through this experience, they develop an organizational capability that is increasingly valuable in today's complex and dynamic operating context.

In many ways, therefore, the transnational organizational and management issues we have described represent perhaps one of the most advanced forms of the modern corporation. The core management challenge in all companies is to embrace rather than to deny or minimize the environmental complexity and uncertainty, and the demanding context of the transnational organization provides the ideal laboratory in which to develop such skills. In short, the challenge of managing across borders is the ideal way to develop the skills required for managing across boundaries of all kinds in the modern corporation.

The case series in this concluding chapter describes the recent history of one company in which this is clearly true. Since its formation through the merger of two second-tier "also-rans" in the electrical equipment business, Asea Brown Boveri (ABB) has emerged as one of the most aggressive competitors in what it describes as the emerging electrotechnical industry. Percy Barnevik, the CEO of this $30 billion company, describes his vision of ABB as an organization that is simultaneously "local and global, big and small, radically decentralized with central reporting and control." This is almost a perfect description of the transnational, and class discussions on the ABB cases will reinforce and highlight many of the environmental, strategic, organizational, operational, and managerial characteristics of the integrated network organization that we have described in the earlier chapters.

At the same time, ABB and several other companies like it are extending the transnational model to what we believe will become an increasingly common form of large MNCs in the future. In this concluding chapter, we describe this emerging management model, which is one possible answer to the "what's next" question. In this process, we also suggest a new way of thinking about large companies. Instead of defining a large company in terms of a formal structure by which the overall company is divided into a series of business, geographic, and functional units, we describe it in terms of three core processes that characterize this new management approach. The *entrepreneurial process* drives the opportunity-seeking, externally focused ability of the organization to open new markets and create new businesses. The *integration process* allows it to link and leverage its dispersed worldwide resources and capabilities to build a successful company.

The *renewal process* maintains its ability to challenge its own beliefs and practices and to continuously revitalize itself so as to develop an enduring institution. Effective management of these three processes also calls for some very different roles and tasks of front-line, middle, and top-level managers. While we illustrate these organizational processes and management roles based on the experiences of different American, European, and Japanese companies, the ABB cases provide an opportunity for reviewing these processes and roles, and their interactions, in the context of a single company.

THE ENTREPRENEURIAL PROCESS: SUPPORTING AND ALIGNING INITIATIVES

The traditional worldwide organization was built in a highly structured manner that allowed those at the top to coordinate and control the multifunctional, multi-business, multinational operations. But this increasingly complex structure looks very different from the top than from the bottom (see Figure 8–1). From the top, the CEO sees order, symmetry, and uniformity—a neat instrument for step-by-step decomposition of the company's tasks and priorities. From the bottom, hapless front-line managers see a cloud of faceless controllers—a formless sponge that soaks up all their energy and time. The result, as described so colorfully by GE's Jack Welch, is an organization that has its face toward the CEO and its backside toward the customer. The key assumption in these companies is that the entrepreneurial tasks would be carried out by the top management, while front-line managers would be primarily responsible for the operational implementation of top-down strategies. Such a management approach had not been a major constraint in the benevolent, high-growth environment that most companies enjoyed in the decades following World War II. Throughout that period of rapid international market expansion, the opportunities for growth were enormous and the key management challenge was to allocate a company's financial resources among competing opportunities.

FIGURE 8–1   Top-Down versus Bottom-Up View of the Organization

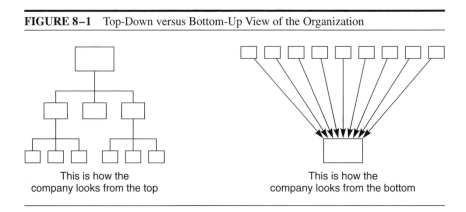

This is how the
company looks from the top

This is how the
company looks from the bottom

But in recent years, not only has market growth slowed, but massive investments have led to severe overcapacity in many industries. Simultaneously, the motivation for companies expanding abroad has increasingly shifted from one focused primarily on securing new markets or low-cost productive inputs, to a worldwide search for vital intelligence or scarce competencies not readily obtainable in the home market. As knowledge and specialized skills have gradually replaced capital as the scarcest and most important source of competitive advantage, managers have become increasingly aware that, unlike money, expertise cannot be accumulated at and allocated from the top. The critical task now is to use the knowledge of widely dispersed front-line managers to identify and exploit fast-moving opportunities. In short, the entrepreneurial function must now be focused not at the top of the hierarchy but at the bottom.

The challenge of rebuilding the initiative, creativity, and drive of those on the front lines of worldwide operations does not, however, mean that a company must now become a society of geographically spread, independent entrepreneurs held together by a top management acting as a combination of a bank and a venture fund. Instead, companies will be required to build an organization in which a well-linked entrepreneurial process will drive the company's opportunity-seeking, externally focused ability to create and exploit avenues for profitable growth wherever they may arise. It is this integrated entrepreneurial process that will bring the worldwide company advantages to the local front-line entrepreneurs and save the entrepreneurial transnational corporation from the myths of internal venturing and "intrapreneurship" that have already proven so flawed in practice. The entrepreneurial transnational corporation will not be a hierarchical organization with a few less layers of management and a few scattered skunk works or genius awards: It will be a company built around a core entrepreneurial process that will drive everybody, and everything the company does.

The entrepreneurial process will require a close interplay among three key management roles. The front-line *entrepreneurs* will be the spearheads of the company, and their responsibility will be to create and pursue new growth opportunities. The *coaches* in senior-management positions will play a pivotal role in reviewing, developing, and supporting the front-line initiatives. Corporate *leaders* at the top of the organization will establish the overall strategic mission of the company that will define the boundary within which the entrepreneurial initiatives must be contained; they will also set the highly demanding performance standards that these initiatives must meet (see Figure 8–2). Just as the structural units of corporate, divisional, and operating-unit management groups were the fundamental building blocks of the hierarchical divisionalized company, the three management roles of entrepreneurs, coaches, and leaders and their interrelationships will be the core building blocks of the new entrepreneurial transnational corporation. The recent reorganization of a large American computer company provides an example of how such a management process can be structured.

Confronted with the challenge of rapidly changing customer demands and the constraints of a traditional matrix organization that impeded the company's ability to marshall its own formidable technological resources to help its customers

FIGURE 8–2   The Entrepreneurial Process: Management Roles and Tasks

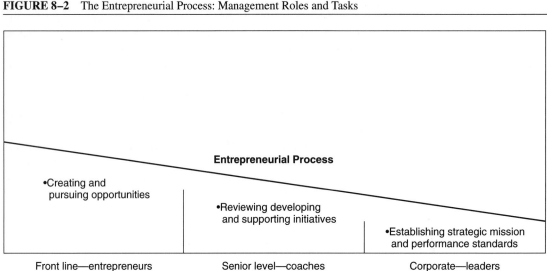

solve ever-more-complex problems, the company decided to restructure itself to create "a network of entrepreneurs in a global corporation." As described by top management, the objective was to create a management approach "which starts with *opportunity* and capitalizes upon the *innovation, creativity,* and *excellence* of people to secure the future of the company." This objective was enshrined in the vision statement: to build "a global IT service company based on people who are enthusiastic about coming to work every day knowing that they are highly valued, encouraged to grow and increase their knowledge and are individually motivated to make a positive difference."

To achieve this vision, the company restructured itself into a large number of relatively small units, each unit being headed by a person formally designated as an entrepreneur. There were different kinds of entrepreneurial units, corresponding to different tasks such as product creation, field sales and support, or industry marketing. All shared a common mandate, however, "to think and act as heads of companies in a networked holding." Pursuit of opportunities was defined as their key challenge. Each entrepreneur was assured significant support and the top management collectively declared that "everyone in the company works for the entrepreneurs." At the same time, it was emphasized that no one could afford to own or control all the expertise, resources, or services necessary for achieving his or her objectives; independent judgment and action had to reflect this pervasive interdependence so as to effectively leverage the network of resources available in a global corporation.

Pursuant to the reorganization, senior regional, divisional, and functional managers were relieved of their normal consolidation and control tasks and were instead regrouped as a pool of coaches. The label of *coach* highlighted that they should not play in the actual game. Yet the metaphor was that of a football coach who bore overall responsibility for the team's success, had the expertise to improve the players' skills, possessed the experience to guide the team's strategy, and had the authority to change players when the need arose.

In operational terms, each entrepreneur has an allotted coach to support him or her, but also a separate "board" that has formal responsibility to "review and question the validity of the entrepreneur's strategy and plan, provide feedback, monitor performance, encourage, stimulate, support, and, via the chairperson, propose rewards or change of the entrepreneur" (see Figure 8–3).

In his or her individual capacity, the coach's main task is to help the entrepreneur succeed both through personal guidance and support on strategic plans and also by acting as a link between the entrepreneur and all others in the company whose resources the entrepreneur might need to succeed. An active role in the entrepreneur's personal development including planning of training inputs and new assignments is defined as an essential part of the coach's role.

The board, of which the assigned coach is often the chairperson, acts in a manner not dissimilar from regular corporate boards. While the chairperson is nominated by the top management, other members are selected by the entrepreneur, in consultation with the chairperson, from the company's pool of coaches. In selecting her board members, the entrepreneur looks for specific technological, industry, or administrative expertise and, if the desired skills are not available within the company, she can appoint outsiders such as customer representatives, professors in technical or management schools, or even one of the employees within her unit.

While the coach, in his personal capacity, is responsible for developing and supporting the entrepreneurial initiatives, the board is the company's key instrument

FIGURE 8–3 The Operational Structure

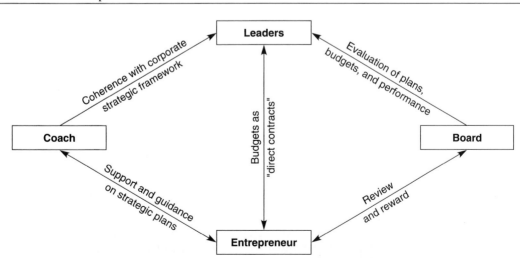

for maintaining rigorous and disciplined financial control. The board's key tasks are to challenge the entrepreneur's plans, review her budget proposals, monitor performance against budgets, and to continuously advise top management on resource allocation decisions. Budgets are seen as sacrosanct both ways: Once the budget is proposed and approved, the entrepreneur must achieve it and must take personal responsibility for initiating any changes in plans that might become necessary because of unforeseen developments. Similarly, no one in the company can tamper with an approved budget except in response to the entrepreneur's demonstrated inability to fulfill to the contract.

Achievement of budgets is the trigger for release of the next set of resources, and managing this multistaged resource allocation process is a key responsibility of the boards. The separation of the development and support responsibilities, which rests with the coach, and the review and reward responsibility, which rests with the board, is designed to prevent both the entrepreneur and the coach from lapsing back into the familiar boss-subordinate role structure and is, therefore, key to protecting the integrity of the system.

While the uniform financial control system provides rigor and discipline to the exercise of bottom-up opportunism, top management of the company also recognized the need for a clear statement of strategic mission to provide direction and coherence to the entrepreneurial process. In contrast to the company's historical focus on proprietary products, the mission statement unambiguously described the need for refocusing on customer service and on providing and integrating multivendor products and services. Further elaboration of the mission highlighted particular industry sectors and specific services for priority attention. The simple yet unambiguous statement was explained and debated throughout the company over a six-month period to ensure not only intellectual understanding but also emotional commitment on the part of all employees.

Just the statement and its elaboration was, however, not enough. The process of discussion and debate revealed the need for establishing some clear performance standards and norms to link the mission with specific projects and plans. In response, top management articulated five key performance parameters—each clearly linked to the mission statement—and set specific overall goals against each parameter. For example, "increase market share faster than competition" or "profit above local competitors" was translated into tangible but differentiated objectives for the different entrepreneurial units, and approval of plans was linked to these objectives.

While this is only one example of how a company can build the entrepreneurial process, it illustrates four key attributes that appear to be common to companies that are able to capture the creative energy of their people to develop new business opportunities.

First, they build their organizations around relatively small units. Matsushita, as we described in the case in Chapter 2, has proliferated the world with its National, Panasonic, Quasar, Technic, and other branded consumer electronic products on the strength of its "one product–one division" concept: As soon as an existing division comes out with a successful new product, it is split up as a separate division. ABB, similarly, is not a $30 billion behemoth: It is a network of 1,300 separate companies, each a legal entity with its own balance sheet and profit and loss statement, with an average of 200 employees per company. One can observe the same practice in companies as diverse as Johnson and Johnson, 3M, and Bertelsmann: To maintain the entrepreneurial spirit each unit must be restricted in size so that every member of the unit can personally know all others.

To build such small units, these companies have abandoned the notion of functionally complete "strategic business units," which own all key resources so as to be in full control over their performance. Instead, they have structured incomplete "performance units" that are interdependent and must use each other's resources to achieve their own goals. The product divisions in Matsushita or Canon do not control the sales units, which are structured as separate companies, as are often the technology units. And, in contrast to the arbitrary and conflict-generating distinctions between cost centers, revenue centers, and profit centers, the performance centers are not differentiated based on their activities. Whether they sell to customers, or produce for internal customers, or work to build new technologies, all performance centers are treated similarly in the planning, budgeting, and control systems.

Second, they create a multistage resource allocation process instead of up-front commitment to a clearly articulated long-term plan. Any employee can propose to start a new business at 3M and "a single coherent sentence can often suffice as starting plan." But, at each stage of developing her proposal, from the initial idea to product development, prototyping, technical and market testing, and commercialization, she must propose a specific budget and clearly quantified mileposts and all approvals are subject to satisfactory performance against the earlier commitments. As 3M managers grudgingly admit, "We spend all our time preparing budgets, but it seems to help."

Third, they tend to adopt a highly structured and rigorously implemented financial control system. At 3M, for example, such financial discipline is maintained through a standardized management reporting system that is applied uniformly to all operating units, who are forbidden by a central directive from creating their own systems. At the level of product families, 3,900 monthly P&L statements are generated centrally, and these are made available on-line to all the units within 10 days of every financial closing. Similarly, at Matsushita, a new division receives start-up capital from the corporate headquarters and loans, when justified under normal commercial conditions; it pays interest on the loans to the corporate "bank" at regular market rates, together with 60 percent of pre-tax profits as dividend. Performance expectations are uniform across all divisions, regardless of the maturity of the market or the company's competitive position. If a division's operating profits fall below 4 percent of sales for two successive years, the divisional manager is replaced.

An essential corollary of such rigorous financial control is the sanctity of the budget of each entrepreneurial unit. In traditional divisionalized companies, budgets are cascaded down across each layer of the hierarchy and managers at each level are expected to achieve the aggregate budget at their level. Such an aggregation process essentially translates into sudden changes of approved budgets for certain units in response to unanticipated problems faced by other units within the administrative control of a common manager. In contrast, in companies with a firm commitment to bottom-up initiative, the budget of the small entrepreneurial units are not changed except in response to variances in the unit's own performance. There is neither a cascading down of budget approvals nor an aggregation up of budget achievements: The budget of each unit is approved separately and its performance is monitored individually right up to the very top of corporate management.

And finally, all these companies have a clearly articulated and widely understood and shared definition of the "opportunity horizon" that provides a lightning rod to direct organizational aspirations and energy into cohesive corporate development. The boundaries of the opportunity horizon tend to be precise enough to clearly rule out activities that do not support the company's strategic mission, and yet broad enough to prevent undue constraints on the creativity and opportunism of front-line managers. Without such a clearly defined strategic mission, front-line managers have no basis for selecting among the diverse opportunities they might confront and bottom-up entrepreneurship soon degenerates into a frustrating guessing game. The actual definition of the boundaries may be stated in very different terms—a strong technology focus in Canon or 3M or specific customer groups in SAS or Cartier, for example—but it provides a basis for strategic choice among different initiatives and serves as a guideline for the entrepreneurs themselves to focus their own creative energy.

THE INTEGRATION PROCESS: LINKING AND LEVERAGING COMPETENCIES

In this world of converging technologies, category management, and global competition, the entrepreneurial process alone is not sufficient. Tomorrow's successful companies will also have a strong integration process to link their diverse assets and resources into corporate competencies, and to leverage these competencies in their pursuit of new opportunities. In the absence of such an integration process, decentralized entrepreneurship may lead to some temporary performance improvement as existing slack is harnessed, but long-term development of new capabilities or businesses will be seriously impeded. Many highly decentralized companies including Matsushita have recently experienced this problem. In describing the transnational organization, we have suggested how worldwide integration can coexist with entrepreneurship at the national level, but the challenge of managing the symbiosis between entrepreneurship and integration extends beyond managing across geographic boundaries to those between the different businesses and functions of a company. The following example will illustrate how such a broader integration process can be built and managed.

Nikkei Business recently ranked Kao as the third in its list of Japan's most creative companies—well ahead of other local superstars including NEC, Toyota, Seibu, and Canon. The company had earned this distinction because of its outstanding record of introducing innovative, high-quality products to beat back not only domestic rivals such as Lion but also its giant global competitors such as Procter & Gamble (P&G) and Unilever. Technological and design innovations in

Merries, Kao's brand of disposable diapers, reduced P&G's market share in Japan from nearly 90 percent to less than 10. Similarly, Attack, Kao's condensed laundry detergent, has seen the company's domestic market share surge from 33 to 48 percent, while that of Lion declined from 31 to 23 percent. In the 1980s, this innovative capability allowed this traditional soap company to expand successfully into personal care products where it established Sofina as the largest selling cosmetics brand in Japan, and into floppy disks in which it has already risen to be the second largest player in North America.

A powerful entrepreneurial process lies at the heart of Kao's innovative ability. It practices all the elements of the entrepreneurial process we have described: small functionally incomplete units driven by aggressive targets, rigorous financial discipline, a structured new product creation process supported by a flexible and multistage resource allocation system, and a clear definition of its strategic mission in terms of utilizing its technological strengths to develop products with superior functionality. However, the wellspring behind this entrepreneurial process has been what Dr. Yoshio Maruta, the chairman of Kao, describes as "biological self-control." As the body reacts to pain by sending help from all quarters, "if anything goes wrong in one part of the company, all other parts should know automatically and help without having to be asked." A companywide integration process has allowed Kao to link and leverage its core competencies in research, manufacturing, and marketing not only to solve problems but also to create and exploit new opportunities. And, this integration process in Kao, like the entrepreneurial process we have described, is built on some well-defined roles, tasks, and value-added on the part of the front-line entrepreneurs, the senior-level coaches, and the corporate leaders (see Figure 8–4).

FIGURE 8–4   The Integration Process: Management Roles and Tasks

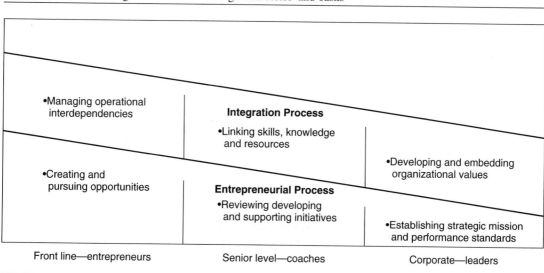

The small and reatively autonomous work units of the entrepreneurial corporation—each responsible for specific customer groups or product lines or functional competencies—create an enormous centrifugal force, which, in the absence of a countervailing centripetal force, can overwhelm the company with inconsistencies, conflicts, and fragmentation. The first task in integration, therefore, is to create a glue to hold the different parts together and to align their initiatives. A set of clear and motivating organizational values provides the basis for such normative integration, and developing, nurturing, and embedding these values become a key task of the management group we have described as corporate leaders.

The organizational processes of Kao are designed to foster the spirit of harmony and social integration based on the principle of absolute equality of human beings, individual initiative, and the rejection of authoritarianism. Free access of everyone to all information "serves as the core value and the guiding principle of what Dr. Maruta describes as Kao's "paperweight organization": a flat structure, with a small handle of a few senior people in the middle, in which all information is shared horizontally and not filtered vertically. "In today's business world, information is the only source of competitive advantage," according to Dr. Maruta. "The company that develops a monopoly on information and has the ability to learn from it continuously is the company that will win, irrespective of its business. This makes it necessary to share all information. If someone has special and crucial information that others don't have, that is against human equality, and will deprive us and the organization of real creativity and learning." These core values of human equality and free sharing of all information are embedded throughout the organization not only through continuous articulation and emphasis by Dr. Maruta and other members of the top-management team but also through their own behaviors and through a set of institutionalized practices.

For example, Dr. Maruta and his top-management colleagues share the tenth floor of Kao's head office building, together with a pool of secretaries. A large part of this floor is open space, with conference tables, overhead projectors, and lounging chairs spread around. This is known as "decision space," where all discussions with and among the top management take place. Anyone passing, including the chairman, can sit down and join in any discussion, on any topic, and they frequently do. The executive vice president in charge of a particular business or a specific territory can, therefore, be engaged in a debate on a topic that he has no formal responsibility for. The same layout and norm are duplicated in the other floors, in the laboratories, and in workshops. Workplaces look like large rooms: There are no partitions, only tables and chairs for spontaneous or planned discussions in which everyone has free access and can contribute as equals.

Every director of the company and most salespeople have a fax machine in their homes to receive results and news. A biweekly Kao newspaper keeps every employee informed about competitors' moves, new product launches, overseas developments, and key meetings. Terminals installed throughout the company ensure that all employees can, if they wish, retrieve data on sales records of any product from any of Kao's numerous outlets, or product development at their own or other branches. The latest findings from each of Kao's research laboratories are available for all to see, as are the details of the previous days' production and inventory at every Kao plant. "They can even," says Dr. Maruta, "check up on the president's expense account." The benefits from this open sharing of data outweigh the risk of leaks, the company believes, and, in an environment of flux, "Leaked information instantly becomes obsolete."

While the corporate leaders carry the principal responsibility for developing and embedding the corporate values that provide the context for integration, it is the front-line entrepreneurs who must integrate the day-to-day activities of the company by managing the operational interdependencies across the different product, functional, and geographic units. This requires certain attitudes and some specific skills, but also some facilitating infrastructures and processes.

In Kao, information technology is a key element of the infrastructure and its own extensive value-added networks (Kao VANs) provide the anchors for operational integration. Fully integrated information systems link the company's marketing, production, and research units. These systems control the flows of materials, products, and ideas from the stage of new product development, to production planning involving over 1,500 types of raw materials, to distribution of over 550 types of final products to about 300,000 retail stores.

Kao's logistics information system (LIS) links the corporate headquarters, all the factories, the independent wholesalers, and the logistics centers through a network that includes a sales planning system, an inventory control system, and an on-line supply system. Using LIS, each salesperson at Kao's 30 wholesalers projects sales plans on the basis of a head office campaign plan, an advertising plan, and past market trends. These are corrected and adjusted at the corporate level and provide the basis for the daily production schedules of each factory. The system designs the optimal machine allocation, personnel schedules for production, the actual quantities to be supplied to each wholesaler based on factory and wholesaler inventories, and the transportation plans for shipping the supplies on the following day. A separate computerized ordering system, built on point-of-sales terminals installed in the retail stores and connected to LIS, allows automatic replenishment of store inventory based on the previous day's sales data.

Kao's marketing intelligence system (MIS) tracks sales by product, region, and market segment. Artificial intelligence tools are used extensively on this system to develop new approaches to advertising and media planning, sales promotion, market research, and statistical analysis. Another sophisticated computerized system, ECHO, codes all telephone queries and complaints about Kao's products online. Linked to MIS, ECHO is an invaluable "window on the customer's mind" that allows the company to fine-tune formulations, labeling, and packaging and also to develop new product ideas.

These extensive IT networks provide the tools for the front-line managers in Kao to carry much of the burden of day-to-day operational coordination and integration, which, in most companies, are the key tasks of middle and senior management. But these IT networks are not seen as a replacement for face-to-face meetings. Indeed the company has one of the most extensive systems of intrafunctional, interfunctional, and interbusiness meetings to facilitate exchange of ideas and joint development of new initiatives and projects. Top management, marketers, and research scientists meet at regular conferences. "Open space" meetings are offered every week by different units, and people from any part of the organization can participate in such meetings. Within the R&D organization, the lifeblood of Kao's innovations, monthly conferences are hosted, in turn, by different laboratories to bring junior researchers together. Researchers can nominate themselves to attend any of these meetings if they feel that the discussions can help their own work, or if they wish to talk separately with someone in the host laboratory. Similarly, any researcher in the host laboratory is free to invite anyone he wishes to meet from any of Kao's several laboratories spread around the world. It is through the collaborative work triggered by such meetings that Kao developed many of its breakthrough innovations, such as a special emulsifier developed jointly by three different laboratories, which later proved to be crucial for Sofina's success. Similar processes are in place in most of the other businesses and functions, and these meetings—perhaps even more than the IT linkages—provide the means for Kao's front-line entrepreneurs to build and leverage their own lateral networks within the company.

But while the leaders create the context of integration and the front-line managers link and align operational activities, it is the group of coaches in senior management who serve as the engine for linking the diverse skills, expertise, and resources in different research, manufacturing, and marketing units to launch the strategic thrusts of Kao and maintain their momentum over time. If the entrepreneurs are the linchpins for the entrepreneurial process, the coaches are the pivots for the integration process.

A companywide total creative revolution project serves as the main vehicle for the senior managers in Kao to constantly pull together teams and task forces from different parts of the company to find creative responses to emerging problems or new opportunities. In the fourth phase in a two-decade-long program that started its life in 1971 as an organizationwide computerization initiative (the CCR movement) and evolved into a total quality control (TQC) program in 1974 and a total cost reduction (TCR) effort in 1986, total creative revolution is aimed at making "innovation through collaborative learning" the centerpiece of Kao's strategic thrust into the 1990s. According to Dr. Maruta, "Kao must be like an educational institution—a company that has learnt how to learn." And senior managers are formally expected to be "the priests"—the teachers who must facilitate this process of shared learning. Thus, when a small and distant foreign subsidiary faced a problem, it is one of these constantly traveling senior managers who helped the local management team identify the appropriate expert in Japan and sponsored a task force to find a creative solution. Similarly, when some factory employees were made redundant following the installation of new equipment, one of these coaches sponsored five of them to form a team to support a factory in the United States to install and commission a plant imported from Japan. Over time, this group became a highly valued flying squad available to help new production units get over their teething troubles.

The success of Sofina was the result of a very similar process, albeit on a much larger scale. Sensing an opportunity to create a high-quality, reasonably priced range of cosmetics that would leverage Kao's technological strengths and emphasize the functionality of "skin care" rather than "image," the top management of Kao presented it as a corporate challenge. To create such a product and to market it successfully, Kao would need to integrate its capabilities both within specific functions, such as diverse technologies in emulsifiers, moisturizers, and skin diagnosis lodged in different laboratories, and across functions including R&D, corporate marketing and sales, production, and market research.

Instead of trying to create one gigantic team involving all the people who would need to contribute to the project, a few senior managers including the head of the Tokyo Research Laboratory, the director of marketing research, and a director of marketing formed themselves into a small team to coordinate the project. They created small task forces, as required, to address specific problems—such as developing a new emulsifier—but kept the lateral coordination tasks among the operating managers at the simplest possible level. When the new emulsifier created some problems of skin irritation, a different group was established to develop a moisturizer and a chemical to reduce irritation. Similarly, when the Sofina foundation cream was found to be sticky on application, they set it up as a challenge for a marketing team, who responded by positioning the product as "the longest lasting foundation that does not disappear with perspiration," converting the stickiness into a strength. This group of senior managers continued to play this integrating and coordinating role for over a decade, as the project evolved from a vision in the early 1970s to a nationwide success in the mid-1980s.

THE RENEWAL PROCESS: MANAGING RATIONALIZATION AND REVITALIZATION

The historical management processes in large MNCs have been premised on the assumption that environmental changes will be relatively linear and incremental. The accounting, budgeting, planning, and control systems have been designed in these companies to provide order and efficiency to an essentially vertical process of managing information. The front-line units provide data. This data is analyzed by middle-level managers to create useful information. Information obtained from several different sources is combined to generate knowledge within the organization. Finally, top management absorbs and institutionalizes this knowledge to build wisdom that becomes a part of the accepted perspectives and norms within the company. In an environment of relative stability, the order and efficiency of such a linear process have allowed these companies to continuously refine their operational processes through incremental accumulation and exploitation of knowledge.

In an environment of often turbulent and unpredictable change, however, incremental operational refinement is not enough; companies now also need the ability to manage strategic renewal. They must establish mechanisms in which internalized wisdoms and established ways of thinking and working are continuously challenged. If the integration process links and leverages existing capabilities to defend and advance current strategies, the renewal process continuously questions those strategies and the assumptions underlying them and inspires the creation of new competencies to prepare the ground for the very different competitive battles the company is likely to confront in the future.

The renewal process is built on two symbiotic components. It consists, on the one hand, of an ongoing pressure for rationalization and restructuring of existing businesses to achieve continuous improvement of operational performance. This rationalization component focuses on resource use—the effectiveness with which existing assets are deployed—and strives for continuous productivity growth. This part of the renewal process aims to refine existing operations incrementally to achieve ever-improving current results. Rigorous benchmarking against best-in-class competitors provides the scorecard on concrete operational measures such as value-added per employee, contributions per unit of fixed and working capital, time to market for new products, and customer satisfaction. This process pinpoints performance gaps and focuses organizational energy on closing those gaps.

The other part of renewal is revitalization—the creation of new competencies and new businesses, the challenging and changing of existing rules of the game, and the leapfrogging of competition through quantum leaps. Driven by dreams and the power of ideas, it focuses on "business not as usual" to create breakthroughs that would take the company to the next stages of its ambition. Revitalization may involve fast-paced, small bets to take the company into new business domains—as Canon is trying in the field of semiconductors—or big "bet the company" moves to transform industries—as AT&T is trying to do in the emerging new field of infocom.

As with entrepreneurship and integration, rationalization and revitalization are also often viewed in mutually exclusive terms. Managers complain of the unsatiable appetite of the stock market for short-term results, which forces them to focus on rationalization rather than revitalization. Some justify poor operating results as the evidence of long-term investments. The renewal process, in contrast, emphasizes the essential symbiosis between the present and the future: There is no long-term success without short-term performance just as short-term results mean little unless they contribute to building the long-term ambition. Rationalization provides the resources needed for revitalization—not just money and people, but also legitimacy and credibility—while revitalization creates the hope and the energy needed for rationalization.

Amid the general bloodbath that has characterized the semiconductor business, Intel has been among the few players who have achieved steady growth together with satisfactory financial returns. While its fortunes have turned with the tide—from spectacular successes in the 1970s when it introduced, in quick succession, the 1130 DRAM, the 1702 EPROM, and the 8086 microprocessor, to heavy losses in the mid-1980s when the company was forced to exit the DRAM and SRAM businesses and cut 30 percent of its workforce, to phenomenal success again with the 80386 32-bit microprocessor in the late 1980s—Intel has so far taken most of the correct turns as it hit the forks in the road, avoiding hitting the dividers, as many of its competitors have done.

In this process, the company has continuously renewed itself, changing its products and strategies and adopting its organization and culture, to respond to the dramatic changes in its business environment. From the "self-evident truth" that Intel was a "jellybean" memory company, it changed itself into a logic devices company—selling boards—and then to a systems house—providing solutions in boxes. From a heritage of manufacturing inefficiency that was almost celebrated as the evidence of creativity in product development, Intel has now become almost cost competitive vis-à-vis its Japanese rivals. Its marketing focus has evolved too, from selling product features to OEM customers in the early 1970s, to benefits-oriented marketing in the late 1970s, to positioning-oriented marketing in the 1980s (emphasizing compatibility with end-user standards), to full-fledged end-user marketing in the 1990s in direct partnership with the final customers of the company's microprocessors. To support these changes, Intel has also transformed its culture. From an organization of and for "bright, talkative, opinionated, rude, arrogant, impatient, and very informal macho men interested only in results and not in niceties," the company has evolved into a better balance between task focus and concern for a friendly work environment in which "people don't have to be Milky the milk biscuit to get their work done, but then, they don't have to be Atilla the Hun either."

Intel's ability to stay one step ahead of competition—which is all that separates the winners from the losers in the semiconductor business—has been built on some demanding roles and contributions of managers at all levels of the company (see Figure 8–5). But, if the front-line entrepreneurs drive the entrepreneurial process and the senior-level coaches anchor the integration process, it is the corporate-level leaders who inspire and energize the renewal process. It is they who create and manage the tensions between short-term performance and long-term ambition, challenging the organization continuously to higher levels of operational and strategic performance.

Till the demise of Noyce in 1990, Intel has been led by the trio of Gordon Moore as chairman, Robert Noyce as vice chairman, and Andy Grove as president, who

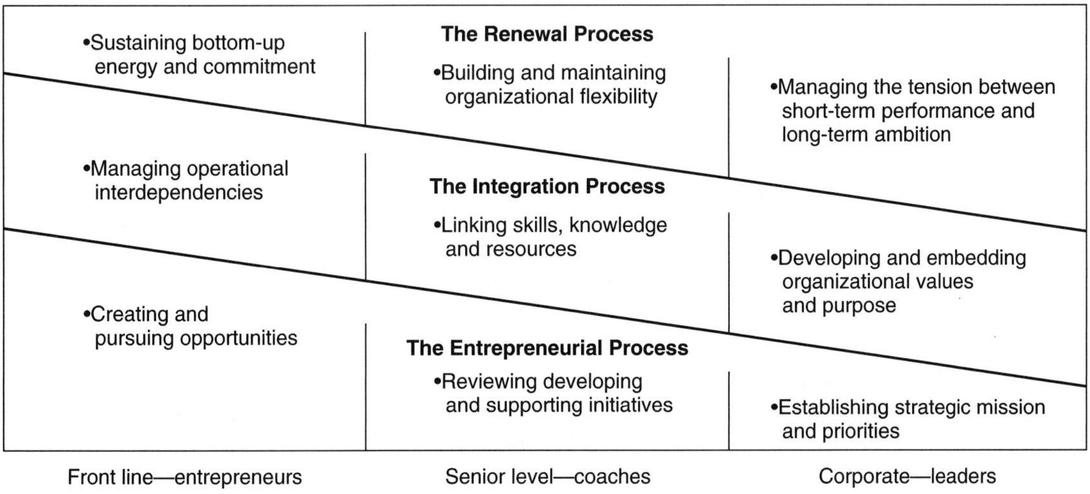

FIGURE 8–5   The Renewal Process: Management Roles and Tasks

collectively formed the company's executive committee. Of these, while Noyce looked after external relations, it was Moore and Grove who guided the company internally: Moore in the role of the technology genius and architect of long-term strategy, and Grove as the detail-oriented resident pragmatist. Moore has been the quiet, long-term–oriented, philosophical champion of revitalization. Grove, on the other hand, has served as the vocal, aggressive, and demanding driver of rationalization. When Motorola's competitive microprocessor gained momentum at the cost of Intel's 16-bit 8086 chip, it was Grove who initiated "operation crush"—an "all out combat" plan, complete with war rooms and SWAT teams, to make 8086 the industry standard. But it was Moore who built the company's long-range planning process and provided the blueprint for technological evolution—what has since come to be known as "Moore's law." In essence, the two have divided the renewal responsibility between them in a way that was originally serendipitous but has since been institutionalized within the company as an unusual management concept: two-in-a-box. It has become normal in Intel for two executives with complementary skills to share the responsibilities of one role.

Whether through a combination of more than one person, as in the case of Andy Grove and Gordon Moore at Intel or Sochiro Honda and Takeo Fujisawa at Honda Motors, or singlehandedly, as Jack Welch is now attempting at GE and Jan Timmer at Philips, creating and managing this tension between the short term and the long term, between current performance and future ambition, between restructuring and revitalization, is a key part of the corporate leader's role in the entrepreneurial corporation. In this role, the leader is the challenger—the one who is constantly upping the ante, and creating the energy and the enthusiasm necessary for the organization to accept the perpetual stretch that such challenging implies.

Personal credibility within and outside the organization is a prerequisite for the corporate leader to play this role, but it is not enough. Charisma sustains momentum for short periods but fatigue ultimately overtakes the organization that depends on individual charisma alone for its energy. To inspire self-renewal, companies must develop an inspiring corporate ambition—a shared dream about the future and the company's role in that future—and must imbed that ambition throughout the organization. Whether the ambition focuses on something as tangible as size, as in Canon's expressed desire to be a company as big as IBM and Matsushita combined, or something less tangible, such as Intel's desire to be the best in the world, what matters is the emotional commitment the leader can build around the dream. Ultimately, it is this emotional commitment that unleashes the human energy required to sustain the organization's ability to continuously renew itself. And developing, marshaling, and leveraging this energy is key to simultaneous rationalization and revitalization, and will perhaps be the single most important challenge for the corporate leaders of the transnational companies of the future.

While the leaders must provide the challenge and the stretch necessary for organizational self-renewal, it is the coaches who must mediate the complex trade-offs that simultaneous restructuring and revitalization imply. It is they who must manage the tension between building new capabilities and stretching existing resources, and the conflict inherent in the high and unrelenting performance demands of the company. This requires enormous flexibility and an environment of mutual trust and tolerance, and creating such processes and attitudes is a key element of the coach's role.

As described by Andy Grove, in the semiconductor business "there are the quick, and there are the dead." In a highly volatile technological and market environment, the company has developed the ability to be very flexible in moving human resources as needs change. Levels change up or down at Intel all the time—people move in every direction, upwards, sideways, or downwards. Careers advance not by moving up the organization but by individuals filling corporate needs. Official rank, decision-making authority, and remuneration—highly correlated in most companies—are treated separately at Intel and this separation among different kinds of rewards lies at the core of Intel's organizational flexibility. But such a system is also susceptible to gaming, and needs a high level of openness and transparency in decision-making processes and mutual trust and tolerance among people to be effective. Flexibility requires not only that the organization act fairly but also that it be seen to be acting fairly; creating and protecting such fairness—necessary in any winning team—is again a key task for the coaches.

Although Intel's action-oriented and direct management style, if somewhat confrontative, has evolved in Grove's mold of aggressive brilliance, it is the senior-management group heading different operating divisions and corporate functions who have embedded the norms of transparency and openness at all levels of the company. Key decisions at Intel are typically made in open meetings, all of which have preannounced agendas and inevitably close with action plans and deadlines. During a meeting, participants are encouraged to debate the pros and cons of a subject aggressively through what is described as "constructive confrontation." But once something has been decided on, Intel has the philosophy of "agree or disagree, but commit." As a result, everyone has the opportunity to influence key decisions relevant to themselves and to openly advocate their perspectives and views and is party to the final decisions, even though the decisions may not always conform to their preferences. The opportunity for such active participation on an equal basis in open and transparent decision processes, coupled with the norm of disciplined and fast implementation once a decision has been taken, creates the environment of trust, which, in turn, is key to the operational and strategic flexibility of the company.

The effectiveness of the renewal process ultimately depends on the ability of front-line managers to generate and maintain the energy and commitment of people within their units. The battles for efficiency and integration, for rationalization and revitalization, are ultimately fought at the level of the salesperson in the field, the operator in the plant, and the individual research scientist or engineer in the laboratory. While the energizing ambition personified by the top management and the open and transparent decision-making processes orchestrated by the senior managers provide the anchors for the grass roots–level commitment at Intel, two other elements of its organizational philosophy and practices also contribute a great deal in maintaining the enthusiasm of its front-line teams.

First, at Intel, there is not only fairness in management processes but there is also fairness in organizational outcomes. In contrast to companies that cut front-line jobs at the first sight of performance problems, Intel adopted the "125 percent solution" to deal with the industrywide recession in the early 1980s: Instead of retrenching people, all salaried workers—including the chairman—were required to work an additional 10 hours per week without additional compensation. When the recession continued in 1982, still unwilling to lay off large numbers of people, the company proposed a 10 percent pay cut on top of the 125 percent solution. As the economy pulled out of the recession, returning the company to profitability, the pay cuts were first restored in June 1983 and, by November 1983, the employees who had accepted pay cuts received special bonuses. Similarly, in 1986, when the memory product bloodbath finally forced the company to reduce its workforce by 30 percent, the cuts were distributed across all levels of the company, instead of being concentrated at the lowest ranks.

Second, at Intel, it is legitimate to own up to one's personal mistakes and to change one's mind. Gordon Moore regretfully but openly acknowledges his personal role in missing the engineering workstation revolution, even though the company was among the pioneers for this opportunity. Andy Grove, the symbol of the company's confrontative, task-oriented culture, had long insisted on not having any recreation facilities in the company. "This is not a country club. You come here to work," he would say to all employees. But as the organization grew, and the need for supplementing the task focus with concern for a friendly work environment became manifest, he gave in and made a celebration of being beaten down. At the dedication of the new facilities, he appeared in his bathing suit and took a shower under a big banner that read, "'There will never be any showers at Intel'—Andy Grove." Such open acknowledgement of errors and good-hearted acceptance of alternatives one has personally opposed creates an environment in which failures are tolerated and changes in strategy do not automatically create winners and losers. It is this overall environment that, in turn, co-opts the front-line managers into the corporate ambition and allows them to sustain energy and commitment at the lowest levels of the organization.

A MODEL FOR THE FUTURE

Over the last decade, many observers of large corporations have highlighted some of the vulnerabilities of the traditional company's strategy and organization described in this chapter. The specific prescriptions of needing to build entrepreneurship, integration, and renewal capabilities are also not new. Academics, consultants, and managers themselves have long recognized these needs to respond to a variety of changing environmental demands. Typically, however, these changing external demands and the consequent need for new internal capabilities have been studied in a piecemeal fashion, triggering ad hoc responses. Facing slowing economic growth and increasingly sophisticated customer demands, companies have attempted to decentralize resources and authority to capture the creative energy and entrepreneurship of front-line managers. But prescriptions of creating and managing chaos have ignored the need for clarity of strategy and the discipline of centralized financial control to channel bottom-up energy into a coherent corporate direction. Companies that have attempted such radical decentralization without a centrally managed strategic framework have soon lost their focus and their ability to leverage resources effectively and have been forced to retreat to the known devil of their old ways.

Observing the ever-increasing pace of globalization of markets and the rising cost, complexity, and convergence of technologies, managers have recognized the need to consolidate and integrate their diverse organizational capabilities. But presented typically with examples of high-tech and highly centralized Japanese companies, they have confused capabilities with technologies, and integration with centralization. Similarly, faced with the rapid enhancement of the skills and resources of once-distant competitors and the changing norms and expectations in the many societies in which they operate, companies have realized the limits of incremental improvements and the need for dramatic change. Yet guided by prescriptions of creating dreamlike, long-term ambitions, they have allowed short-term performance to slip, thereby abandoning the long term too because of increasing resource scarcity.

In contrast to these fragmented and often contradictory prescriptions, we have presented a broad model encompassing the key capabilities we believe companies must develop to respond to the environmental demands of the 1990s. Nothing needs a theory more than practice, and the lack of an integrated theory of the new organization, we believe, has prevented companies from abandoning the old divisional model even though they have long recognized its constraints. The model of the future organization we have presented here is aimed to provide such a theory for practice.

The real challenge in building this new organization lies in the changes in management roles we have described. The metamorphosis of front-line managers, from being operational implementers to becoming aggressive entrepreneurs, will require some very new skills and capabilities. Similarly, the transformation of the middle-management role from that of administrative controller to that of inspiring coach will represent a traumatic change. But the management group that will be most severely challenged in the new organization will be the one currently at the top of the hierarchy. Not only will they have to change their role from that of resource allocator and political arbitrator to that of institutional leader, they will also have to create the infrastructures and the contexts necessary for the others to play the new roles demanded of them. The managers who can build the attitudes and skills appropriate for these new roles and the companies that can develop and retain such managers are likely to emerge as the future winners in the game of global competition.

Case 8–1   Asea Brown Boveri

On August 10, 1987, following six weeks of highly secret negotiations and special directors meetings in Västerås, Sweden, and Zürich, Switzerland, a simultaneous news conference was called in Stockholm and Baden, Switzerland. Within minutes, the stunning details of the largest cross-border merger in European history flashed across newswires throughout the world: the two giants of the European electrical equipment industry—Asea AB of Sweden and BBC Brown Boveri Ltd. of Switzerland—would merge to create Asea Brown Boveri (ABB).

The new ABB would become the world's largest competitor in power generation, transmission, and distribution; in addition, the combined company would be a leading world supplier of process automation systems, robotics, high-speed locomotives, and environmental and pollution control equipment. Asea's 65,000 employees would be combined with BBC's 85,000 employees to create a company comprising 850 separate legal entities operating in 140 countries. In 1988, its first year of combined operations, the new company's pretax income would be US $536 million on sales of US $17.8 billion.

Asea's chief executive officer, Percy Barnevik, (age 46 at the time of the merger) would assume the position of president and chief executive officer of ABB. Thomas Gasser (age 54 at the time of the merger) would become deputy chief executive officer. These men faced the challenge of building a new company on the foundation of two companies that had spent almost a century facing each other as arch rivals.

This case was prepared by Professor Robert Simons and Professor Christopher Bartlett.

Copyright © 1992 by the President and Fellows of Harvard College. Harvard Business School case 192-139.

Creating the New Company

The announcement of the proposed merger was greeted with considerable optimism, with BBC's shares rising 10% in Zurich and Asea's advancing 15% in Stockholm. Asea was seen as contributing superior current profit performance, sophisticated management controls and marketing aggressiveness, while BBC brought a strong order book, $4 billion in cash and marketable securities, and technical expertise. Barnevik's strong leadership also provided analysts with reasons to be bullish. "He's Europe's Jack Welch," said one, repeating an oft-made comparison.

Reshaping the Organization

ABB would start operating as a merged company on January 1, 1988. With only $4\frac{1}{2}$ months to make preparations, Barnevik believed strongly that there could be no honeymoon period, and decided to initiate all the needed changes within the first year. "Sales had to be kept up," he said, "and it was important not to get internally preoccupied. We didn't want people to become paralysed by uncertainty."

The week after the merger announcement, Barnevik selected five key managers from each company to form a ten-person top-level work group. Breaking this group into task forces, he charged them with analyzing how the operations of Asea and BBC could best be fitted together. Within two months, the main features of the new organization had been agreed upon—a new matrix structure that defined 40 business areas, grouped into business segments on one hand and integrated on a national basis through local holding companies on the other hand.

Staffing the New Structure

In late October, Barnevik announced that he wanted the new organization operational by Christmas, and that meant filling hundreds of key management positions. To ensure that this process was perceived as fair, he had the personnel directors from Asea and BBC cross-interview and make recommendations on almost 500 senior-level managers from the two companies. As part of the process, Thomas Gasser and Percy Barnevik personally interviewed over 100 key managers each.

The criteria for those selected for top jobs were demanding: they had to be risk-takers, team players, leaders, and motivators. In Barnevik's words,

> We sought people capable of becoming superstars—
> tough-skinned individuals who were fast on their
> feet, had good technical and commercial
> backgrounds, and had demonstrated the ability to
> lead others. . . . For the merger to work, it is essential
> that we have managers who are open, generous, and
> capable of thinking in group terms.[1]

Communicating Objectives and Priorities

With the new team in place, Barnevik initiated a major program to communicate ABB direction and priorities. In January 1988 he convened a meeting of ABB's top 300 managers in Cannes to explain his management philosophy, operating policies, and to set corporate targets.

Over three days, Barnevik set the agenda for the organization, illustrating concepts and priorities with data contained in 198 overhead transparencies. He also emphasized the importance of the "policy bible"—a 21-page booklet that described the new organizational relationships, the commitment to decentralization and strict accountability, and the company's approach to change. He then asked the 300 managers to translate this message into their local languages and convene similar interactive forums with their own organizations so the message would reach another 30,000 ABB people worldwide within 60 days.

---

[1]Jules Arbose, "ABB: The New Energy Powerhouse," *International Management,* June 1988.

Building Reporting Systems

Barnevik knew that the new organization could not work without a uniform reporting system that could provide managers with accurate and timely information on sales, orders, margins, and other data vital to decision making. When outsiders predicted that such a system could take as long as three years to design and implement in a company as large and complex as ABB, Barnevik and the development team set out to have it in place by August 1988 (in time for the 1989 budget). When the new system (dubbed Abacus) was unveiled on schedule, Barnevik hosted a champagne party for the development team and their spouses.

Rationalizing Operations

The information provided by the new Abacus system was vital to Barnevik's plans to exploit economies in a global enterprise. After analyzing manufacturing costs in all markets, teams of business area managers began discussions on how to increase economies of scale and scope by designating certain plants as specialized production sources for major products around the world. They also introduced other cost savings measures such as component outsourcing, overhead cuts, and inventory reduction. Each business area manager was also responsible for identifying best practices among its participating companies and ensuring the learning was transferred.

Acquiring New Companies

The substantial amount of cash that BBC brought to the merger, supplemented by the resources squeezed from the new organization through rationalization and tighter controls, allowed Barnevik to begin an acquisition program that would restructure the industry. ABB's expansion strategy was rooted in Barnevik's strong belief that the long-term slide in new power generation capacity would reverse itself soon to meet growing demand. Further, because 95% of all past electrical generation contracts in European Community countries had been won by strong national companies, Barnevik believed that new orders would be awarded only to companies that had a strong local presence. These twin beliefs were behind a massive acquisition/joint venture program designed to make ABB "an insider not an invader" in major national markets throughout Europe.

In Germany, Barnevik acquired AEG's steam turbine business and entered a nuclear reactor joint venture with Siemens; in Italy, he signed a joint venture agreement with Finmeccanica; in the UK, he created a partnership to acquire BREL the former British Rail Engineering Limited, and linked up with Rolls Royce. In all, ABB acquired or entered into joint ventures with over 40 companies within 18 months of the announcement of the merger.

By early 1989, Barnevik's attention turned to the huge United States market, and negotiations to acquire Westinghouse's power distribution and transmission business as well as the publicly traded Combustion Engineering group. By 1990, with Westinghouse and Combustion Engineering acquisitions complete, ABB employed 215,000 people in 1,300 wholly owned subsidiaries around the world and generated US $27 billion in revenues (see Exhibit 1). Barnevik reflected on the blistering pace of ABB's acquisitions:

> This is an industry that hasn't changed much in 40 years. I wouldn't say that [ABB's acquisition of all these national companies] is ideal, but you have to move when the industry is moving. . . . If it works it gives us a hell of a competitive edge.

Industry Reaction

This frenetic action in ABB during the late 1980s triggered a major restructuring of the electrical industry throughout Europe. In response to ABB's actions, competitors began reorganizing themselves. Britain's GEC formed a joint venture with Alsthom-Jeumont of France to become Europe's number two power equipment company behind ABB, pushing Germany's Siemens, the long-time industry leader, into third place.

Writing in an internal publication, General Electric's senior vice president of international operations, Paulo Fresco, reflected the feelings of many in the industry:

> The lights are going out all over Europe, and the buccaneers have been turned loose. Among them is Percy Barnevik—this Swede with a beard who swings from country to country like the actor Errol Flynn, cutting deals and forming alliances. . . . A convalescing GE power system may find him the most formidable adversary it has ever faced.

Percy Barnevik: ABB's New Leader

Percy Barnevik was a quiet-spoken, bearded man with strong views and a clear vision of his com-

---

EXHIBIT 1   1990 Revenues by Region (US $ in millions)

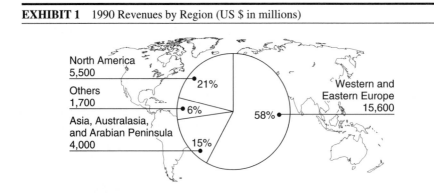

North America
5,500

Others
1,700

Asia, Australasia,
and Arabian Peninsula
4,000

Western and
Eastern Europe
15,600

21%

6%

58%

15%

pany's future. Throughout his youth in Uddevalla, on the rocky Swedish coast, Percy had worked after school and on weekends in his father's print shop, learning the values of hard work and teamwork. After earning his economics degree at the Gothenburg School of Economics, he spent two years as a postgraduate student at Stanford University.

After working in data processing for Sweden's Johnson Group for three years, Barnevik joined the machine tool company Sandvik in 1969, becoming group controller. In 1975 he was given the opportunity to manage Sandvik's U.S. affiliate, and over the next four years his effectiveness in that position caught the eye of Asea's board of directors which hired Barnevik in 1980 to run Asea. His success in rejuvenating the plodding Asea in the early 1980s made him the leading candidate for the top job at ABB.

Even to many of his top managers, Barnevik remained an enigmatic figure. He was clearly European in his origins, yet had been influenced by his American education and management experience, and was truly global in his perspective; he understood technology and was strongly committed to its development, yet remained uncompromisingly marketing oriented; he believed passionately in his long-term vision for ABB and encouraged managers to develop bold strategies to achieve it, yet he insisted that they also achieve their short-term results; and while his personal style was informal and unassuming, he could also be intolerant and blunt. But even those who did not quite understand him, inevitably respected him.

Three characteristics typified Barnevik's personal management style: (1) a strong work ethic, (2) constant communication, and (3) decisiveness. These values were imprinted on the new company he helped to create. Barnevik operated not only at the level of broad strategy, but developed an impressive feel for the details of ABB's ongoing operations. Barnevik believed strongly in setting clear individual targets and providing managers with feedback on their performance. He tracked key current issues and problems and followed up with individual managers who were expected to be able to answer his incisive questions.

Barnevik traveled constantly, and estimated he was on the road 200 days a year. Yet he insisted that while he may often be out of town, he was never out of touch. In his plane or company car, he was frequently on the telephone with key managers worldwide. With his dry sense of humor he pointed out: "I travel a lot, but I'm normally in my office two days a week—Saturday and Sunday."

The intensive travel underscored Barnevik's belief in the importance of constant communication with the organization. "A leader must first be a teacher," he said. Barnevik believed strongly that everyone must understand the corporate philosophy and objectives and the reasons behind them. On virtually all his trips, he took a large briefcase filled with transparencies. His presentations, using two overhead projectors simultaneously and reciting the numbers displayed from memory, were legendary within ABB.

Barnevik believed that ABB managers must expand their jobs and make more decisions. This pressure on managers to decide—and decide quickly—was perhaps the personal characteristic that he had imprinted most indelibly on ABB. His philosophy had been repeated over and over to his team:

> Nothing is worse than procrastination . . . When I look at ten decisions I regret, there will be nine of them where I delayed . . . Better roughly and quickly than carefully and slowly.

He also promoted his "7-3 formula," which reinforced the notion that it was better to make decisions quickly and be right seven out of ten times than to waste time trying to achieve the perfect solution. "Take the initiative and decide—even if it turns out to be the wrong thing. The only thing we cannot accept is people who do nothing." But decisions had to be based on a sound understanding of the business, and on Barnevik's team, sloppy analysis or superficial knowledge were unacceptable. To emphasize that point, he had banned the phrase "I think" at meetings. ("Either you know or you don't," he said.)[2]

Managing the New Company

By early 1989, eighteen months after the merger was announced, Barnevik shifted his focus from putting the new company together to making it work effectively.

The Organizing Principles

The complex new organization was built on twin principles of (1) decentralization of responsibility and (2) individual accountability. Barnevik explained:

> The only way to structure a complex, global organization is to make it as simple and local as possible. ABB is complicated from where I sit. But on the ground, where the real work gets done, all of our operations must function as closely as possible to stand-alone operations. Our managers need well-defined sets of responsibilities, clear accountability, and maximum degrees of freedom to execute.
>
> We are fervent believers in decentralization. When we structure local operations, we always push to create separate legal entities. Separate companies allow you to create real balance sheets with real responsibility for cash flow and dividends. With real balance sheets, managers inherit results from year to year through changes in equity.
>
> ABB is a huge enterprise. But the work of most of our people is organized in small units with P&L responsibility and meaningful autonomy. Our operations are divided into nearly 1,200 companies with an average of 200 employees. These companies are divided into 4,500 profit centers with an average of 50 employees.[3]

The Matrix Organization

Barnevik used the organizing principles of decentralization and accountability as a foundation for his strategic vision of a world-class competitor built on strong national companies. The way he and his management team chose to do this was through the matrix structure that was put in place immediately following the merger. As Barnevik saw it:

> ABB is an organization with three internal contradictions. We want to be global and local, big and small, radically decentralized with centralized reporting and control. If we resolve those contradictions, we create real organizational advantage.
>
> You want to be able to optimize a business globally—to specialize in the production of components, to drive economies of scale as far as you can, to rotate managers and technologists around the world to share expertise and solve problems. But you also want to have deep local roots everywhere you operate—building products in the countries where you sell them, recruiting the best local talent from the universities, working with the local government to increase exports. If you build such an organization, you create a business advantage that's damn difficult to copy.
>
> The matrix is the framework through which we organize our activities. It allows us to optimize our business globally and maximize performance in every country in which we operate.[4]

Exhibit 2 presents a schematic outline of the matrix structure in use at ABB. ABB was organized into 1,300 separate operating companies (listed at the top of each column in Exhibit 2); each company was a legal entity incorporated and domiciled in one of the 140 countries in which ABB operated. Each operating company had a president and management board. These 1,300 operating companies were managed by region. Thus, a company manager would focus his or her efforts on the operations of that business in one country and be responsible for:

- Customer-based regional strategies
- Regional results and profitability
- Day-to-day management of individual profit centers

[2]Jonathan Kapstein and Stanley Reed, "Preaching the Euro-Gospel: ABB Redefines Multinationalism," *Business Week,* July 23, 1990, p. 36.

[3]William Taylor, "The Logic of Global Business: An Interview with ABB's Percy Barnevik," *Harvard Business Review,* March–April 1991, pp. 91–105.

[4]William Taylor, *op. cit.*

EXHIBIT 2   Group Organization Matrix

Business Area	Company			
	Company A	Company B	Company C	Etc.
BA 1	⟶			Worldwide
BA 2				
BA 3				
Etc.		All BAs		

- Human resource development within the regional unit
- Relationships with local governments, communities, labor unions, and the media

Examples of operating companies were ABB Power Generation Inc., North Brunswick, New Jersey, (building power plants) and ABB Fläkt Oy, based in Helsinki, Finland (building environmental protection systems).

Company managers reported in turn to a regional manager who was typically responsible for all the operating companies within a specific country. Gerhard Schulmeyer, for example, one of eleven executive vice presidents, was responsible for 110 ABB operating companies in the United States, including ABB Power Generation Inc. Bert-Olof Svanholm, another executive vice president, was responsible for the 30 ABB companies operating in Finland, including ABB Fläkt Oy.

The other dimension of the matrix (the vertical axis of Exhibit 2) reflected the second clustering of activities of the enterprise into 65 Business Areas (or BAs). Each Business Area represented a distinct worldwide product market. The power transmission activities of ABB, for example, were classified into seven BAs:

- Cables
- Distribution transformers
- High voltage switchgear
- Electric metering

- Network control and protection
- Power systems
- Power transformers

Each Business Area was the responsibility of a BA manager accountable for:

- Worldwide results and profitability
- Development of a worldwide strategy
- R&D and product development
- Worldwide market allocation and sourcing
- Price strategy and price coordination between countries
- Purchasing coordination
- Product and production allocation
- Transfer of know-how in design, production, and quality
- Acquisitions and divestments

Each Business Area manager reported in turn to one of the eleven executive vice presidents responsible for individual business segments (i.e., clusters of related Business Areas).

At the risk of oversimplifying, Business Area managers were responsible for developing worldwide product and technology strategies. Regional managers were responsible for executing these strategies based on the unique needs of local markets. Exhibit 3 illustrates this concept.

The two-dimensional reporting matrix—with regional responsibilities running along one dimension and product responsibilities along the

EXHIBIT 3   The Matrix Organization

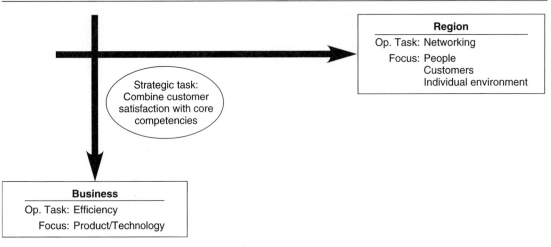

other—required two bosses for each operating manager.

Josef Dürr, president of ABB High Voltage Switchgear Ltd., Zurich, explained:

Our organization seems difficult for an outsider to understand; I will draw you a picture (see Exhibit 4 for Durr's diagram).

My company is part of the power transmission business here in Switzerland. Going up the regional part of the matrix, I report directly to Willy Roos who is responsible for all of the various power transmission businesses based in Switzerland. Willy in turn reports to Ed Somm who is responsible for all ABB businesses—power transmission and others—in Switzerland. Somm is an executive vice president and one of the eleven members of the group executive management.

On the BA dimension, I report directly to Anders Larsson who sits in Sweden. Anders is responsible for businesses like mine—high voltage switchgear—all around the world. Anders Larsson reports to Göran Lindahl, who is the executive vice president in charge of the power transmission segment of the business worldwide.

Thus, I am directly responsible to both Roos and Larsson. I have to coordinate my strategies and targets with each of them, be prepared to answer their

individual concerns, and be accountable to both for my performance.

But each of them also answers to two masters. Roos reports to Somm (regional manager responsible for Switzerland) and to Lindahl (business segment manager responsible for power transmission worldwide).

Larsson, who sits in Sweden and runs the Swedish switchgear company, reports to Anders Narvinger (regional segment manager responsible for all transmission businesses in Sweden) and Lindahl (power transmission segment).

Have I confused you?

The eleven executive vice presidents who formed the group executive management served as the critical integrating link in the matrix structure. Typically each individual assumed responsibility for one or more business segments as well as several regions. Exhibit 5 illustrates the responsibilities of each of the eleven men.

Göran Lindahl, 46, one of the executive vice presidents, explained how it all worked,

Our strategy is to be global with technology and local in our customer orientation. My business does US $5.5 billion in annual sales. The business operates 132 factories in 34 countries. That sounds

EXHIBIT 4   ABB Matrix Relationships: A Representative Example

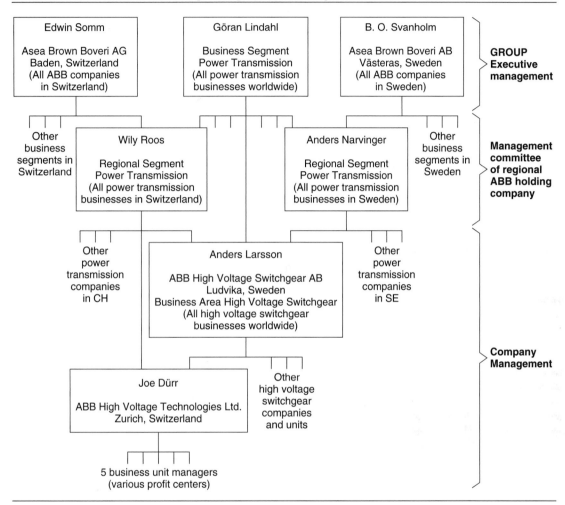

huge doesn't it? But you need to understand that the power transmission business is made up of 750 different profit centers, each with its own P&L. The average profit center generates only $7 million in sales with 45 people.

I have global responsibility for power transmission. That means I am concerned with long-term strategy for the business: product planning, new technologies, acquisitions, and divestments.

If I find overcapacity in a product line, I will suggest closing one or more factories. Do you think

that you will ever find a manager of a local company suggesting we close down a piece of his business?

The local manager is there to be close to the customer, to execute the strategy. If you look at this slide I use in my presentations (Exhibit 6), you will see the concept I am talking about. The Business Areas are concerned primarily with top-down strategy setting as shown by the left arrow. The BAs secondary concern is with actual operations. By the same token, if you look at the right arrow—the bottom-up one—the situation reverses. The regional companies have major responsibility for operations

EXHIBIT 5

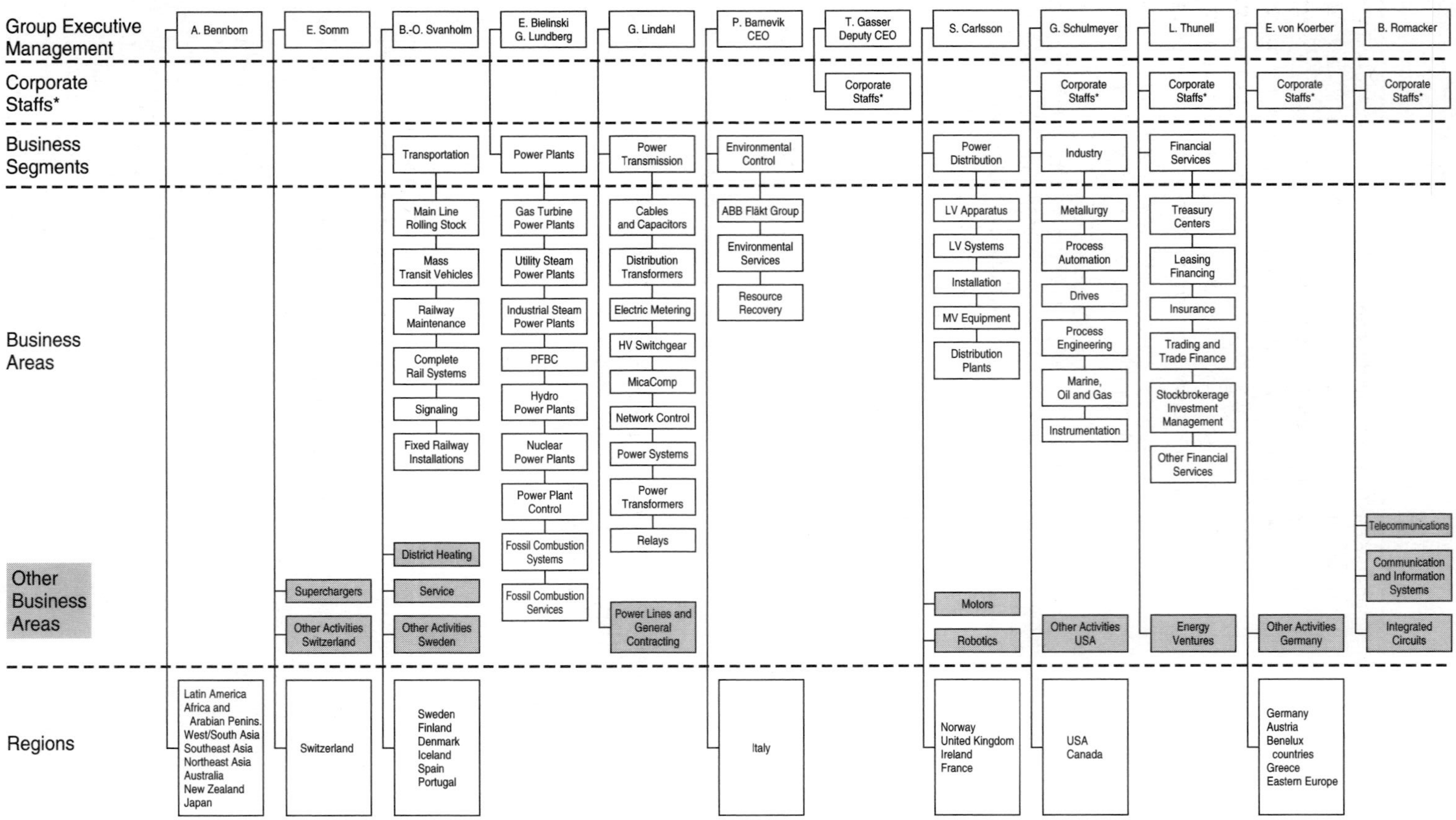

Group Executive Management: A. Bernbom · E. Somm · B.-O. Svanholm · E. Bielinski / G. Lundberg · P. Barnevik CEO · T. Gasser Deputy CEO · S. Carlsson · G. Schulmeyer · L. Thunell · E. von Koerber · B. Romacker

Corporate Staffs*: Corporate Staffs* (repeated)

Business Segments: Transportation · Power Plants · Power Transmission · Environmental Control · Power Distribution · Industry · Financial Services

Business Areas:

- *Transportation:* Main Line Rolling Stock · Mass Transit Vehicles · Railway Maintenance · Complete Rail Systems · Signaling · Fixed Railway Installations
- *Power Plants:* Gas Turbine Power Plants · Utility Steam Power Plants · Industrial Steam Power Plants · PFBC · Hydro Power Plants · Nuclear Power Plants · Power Plant Control · Fossil Combustion Systems · Fossil Combustion Services
- *Power Transmission:* Cables and Capacitors · Distribution Transformers · Electric Metering · HV Switchgear · MicaComp · Network Control · Power Systems · Power Transformers · Relays
- *Environmental Control:* ABB Fläkt Group · Environmental Services · Resource Recovery
- *Power Distribution:* LV Apparatus · LV Systems · Installation · MV Equipment · Distribution Plants
- *Industry:* Metallurgy · Process Automation · Drives · Process Engineering · Marine, Oil and Gas · Instrumentation
- *Financial Services:* Treasury Centers · Leasing Financing · Insurance · Trading and Trade Finance · Stockbrokerage Investment Management · Other Financial Services

Other Business Areas: Superchargers · Other Activities Switzerland · District Heating · Service · Other Activities Sweden · Power Lines and General Contracting · Motors · Robotics · Other Activities USA · Energy Ventures · Other Activities Germany · Telecommunications · Communication and Information Systems · Integrated Circuits

Regions:

- Latin America · Africa and Arabian Penins. · West/South Asia · Southeast Asia · Northeast Asia · Australia · New Zealand · Japan
- Switzerland
- Sweden · Finland · Denmark · Iceland · Spain · Portugal
- Italy
- Norway · United Kingdom · Ireland · France
- USA · Canada
- Germany · Austria · Benelux countries · Greece · Eastern Europe

EXHIBIT 6   The Matrix Organization

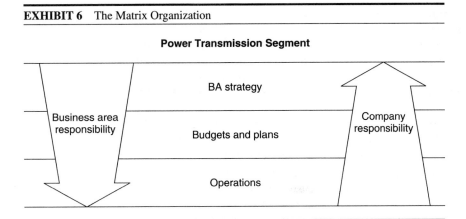

Power Transmission Segment

and secondary involvement in strategy. But the difference is one of degree. The distinction is not black and white.

The center of the chart illustrates that budgets and plans are the key link in this company between strategy and operations.

The ABACUS System

The centrality of budgets and plans in Lindahl's presentation chart underlined the importance that ABB executives attached to their management systems in executing their strategy. A computer-supported reporting system named "ABACUS" provided the ongoing information required for oversight and complex decision making. Barnevik explained:

> We have the glue of transparent, centralized reporting through a management information system called ABACUS. Every month, ABACUS collects performance data on our 4,500 profit centers and compares performance with budget and forecasts. The data are collected in local currencies but translated into U.S. dollars to allow for analysis across borders. The system also allows you to work the data. You can aggregate and disaggregate results by business segments, countries, and companies within countries.
>
> We look for early signs that businesses are becoming more or less healthy. On the tenth of every month, for example, I get a binder with information on about 500 different operations—the 50 Business Areas, all the major countries, and the key companies in key countries. I look at several parameters—new

orders, invoicing, margins, cash flows—around the world and in various business segments. Then I stop to study trends that catch my eye.

> Let's say the industry segment is behind budget. I look to see which of the five Business Areas in the segment are behind. I see that process automation is way off. So I look by country and learn that the problem is in the United States and that it's poor margins, not weak revenues. So the answer is obvious—a price war has broken out. That doesn't mean I start giving orders. But I want to have informed dialogues with the appropriate executives.

Implementation

While many admiring articles had been written about the transformation that Barnevik had begun in ABB, the big question in most observers minds was whether he and his top management team could make the demanding management principles and sophisticated organization structure work effectively. Could Barnevik reconcile the three dilemmas ("we want to be global and local, big and small, radically decentralized with centralized control") that he had built into this organization? Could he achieve the mission that he and his top managers had set out for ABB (see Exhibit 7).

As Barnevik himself acknowledged, "Now comes the crucial test. We have to prove that these new alliances are capable of delivering the advantages that we planned."

EXHIBIT 7 ABB's Mission, Values, and Policies

ABB's Mission

Worldwide economic growth requires dependable and efficient electric power. ABB is committed to help meet this need by promoting energy efficiency, higher productivity, and quality in all its activities. With its advanced technologies and environmental protection techniques ABB's contribution to sustainable growth is environmentally sound and will make economic growth and improved living standards a reality for all nations throughout the world.

Our desire to increase the value of our products is based on continuous technological innovation and on competence and motivation of our employees. Our mission is to be a global leader and to act like one. We will be the most competitive, competent, technologically advanced, and quality-minded electrical engineering company in our fields of activity.

ABB's worldwide leadership position, our presence as a domestic company in key markets, our commitment to research and development, and the motivation of our personnel provide the basis for achieving enhanced customer value and ensuring long-term benefits to our employees and shareholders. As a good corporate citizen, ABB is aware of and fulfills its obligations to society in general, and to our communities in particular.

Everyone in ABB is committed to this mission and the intrinsic values underlying it.

Case 8–2   ABB Deutschland (Abridged)

For 1991 I am aiming for a profit before taxes of DM 500 million. This is a fivefold increase of our 1988 budgeted figure. Thus, we have to close a profit gap of about DM 400 million. As a result, a big challenge lies ahead of us. However, increased profitability is essential to meet our target of a 17% return on equity.

The challenge of a fivefold profit increase in four years was Eberhard von Koerber's message to his colleagues on the Vorstand (executive committee) of ABB's German subsidiary as he chaired his first meeting on January 8, 1988. Although they realized that this would be a tough target to achieve, none of them had any idea of how traumatic the change process would be as they sought to integrate the German operation into the newly merged ABB.

This case combines material from Professor Hugo Uyterhoeven's "ABB Deutschland (A) (Condensed)," case no. 393-051 and "ABB Deutschland (B)," case no. 392-066.

Copyright © 1993 by the President and Fellows of Harvard College. Harvard Business School case 394-019.

The Old Organization; The New Boss

The Baden-Mannheim Relationship

BBC as a multinational company headquartered in Baden, Switzerland, had its largest subsidiary in Mannheim, Germany. This subsidiary was twice as large as the parent's Swiss operation and, until 1986, only 56% owned. BBC cannot be understood without understanding the Baden-Mannheim relationship. From its founding, BBC Germany had conducted its affairs independently in accordance with BBC's local autonomy philosophy. This quickly led to a duplication of activities, which was consistent with the strategy to supply important markets from local factories. Baden and Mannheim, however, found themselves on a collision course when the German operation, confronted with a saturating local market in the 1960s, also wanted to export. The two organizations found themselves face to face in third countries. This rivalry was compounded by the Swiss resentment that the Germans were able to benefit from more generous export insurance and financing help from their government and also from more advantageous bilateral tax treaties. The Germans, on the other hand, resented that they had to get Baden's approval and had to pay the traditional license fee, which they felt put them at a disadvantage vis-a-vis their German competitors. Even though Germany was the largest unit in BBC, it was only a distant second in its home market behind Siemens. Mannheim management felt that Baden interference added an unnecessary handicap in their competitive battles with Siemens.

These conflicts involving export sales were aggravated by a number of other factors. First of all, Mannheim had established an impenetrable Siegfried line by hiding behind German corporate, fiscal, and codetermination law. Corporate law made it impossible for Baden to issue orders given the substantial minority holdings in BBC Deutschland. Tax law made transfers of profits prohibitively expensive. Codetermination law required agreement with the Betriebsrat (works council) which defended the local interests tooth and nail. German executives became experts in the use of these defenses. If they did not use them, they were locally treated as traitors. The Swiss, on the other hand, felt that Mannheim was using these devices shamelessly to thumb their noses at Baden.

There were also many personality conflicts. To paraphrase George Bernard Shaw, Baden and Mannheim were two organizations separated by the same language. The Germans would view the Swiss as provincial, while the Swiss saw the Germans as arrogant. At a meeting involving the KL and the Vorstand, each Vorstand member drove up with a chauffeur in a company Mercedes, while the Swiss KL members drove their own personal cars, which were mostly modest. The Germans were more aggressive and resented when the prudent Swiss slowed them down. The Swiss, in turn, were reluctant to have an already big German subsidiary get

even bigger. The Germans, being bigger, felt more important and resented being dependent on their much smaller Swiss parent. This antagonism led to a long war of attrition as both organizations competed for the same business in third countries, often with different designs. According to many executives, Baden and Mannheim would sometimes compete more fiercely with each other than with their outside competitors. Enormous energy and time went into the solution of internal conflicts. The constant tug of war took a severe toll.

The New Boss

When von Koerber enunciated his five-fold profit improvement target on January 8, 1993, his words fell on an icy silence and were met with visible disbelief by the four old-timers on the Vorstand. Sales and profits had stagnated during the previous five years. Markets were saturated as well as fiercely competitive. Previous profit-improvement programs had failed to produce significant results. Tension and uncertainty in the organization were rampant. The popular head of the Vorstand had been replaced by von Koerber, and two Swedish Asea executives were also appointed to the Vorstand. Even though ABB was a 50-50 merger between equals, Asea's 46-year-old Percy Barnevik had become CEO, and many feared that the Swedes were taking control. Two months earlier, Barnevik had publicly commented that, "It is not too bold or undiplomatic to state that BBC has a large inherent potential to improve its earnings. BBC is today in the situation where Asea was at the beginning of the 1980s."

Also a member of the ABB executive committee, von Koerber, 49, divided his time between Zurich and Mannheim. He had joined the BBC executive committee in September of 1986. Born in Germany and having studied law and economics in his home country and in Switzerland, he had previously worked mostly for BMW, where he joined the Vorstand in 1984 in charge of sales and marketing. He had spent nine years overseas, both in finance and administration, and as country head. He was reluctant to take on the Mannheim assignment since his wife was terminally ill with cancer and there was a nine-year-old daughter at home.

One of his few lucky breaks in inheriting the ABB German operation was the minor overlap between BBC and Asea, given the fact that Asea's beachhead in Germany and the rest of the European Community was very modest indeed. As a result, ABB Deutschland consisted largely of the previously BBC-owned operations. However, the ABB international matrix immediately went into effect. As a result, Vorstand members, who were responsible for business segments (involving a half-dozen related business areas) would report geographically to von Koerber as well as to another member of the ABB executive committee with respect to their business segment. Likewise, the business area heads in Germany would report both to a Vorstand member and to the worldwide ABB business area head.

A Hot Winter in Mannheim

"Koerber raus, Koerber raus" (Koerber get out) shouted a crowd of about 4,500 ABB employees outside the Käfertal head office building in Mannheim. This March 24, 1988, demonstration was part of a two-hour strike to protest a newspaper interview in the local paper by Eberhard von Koerber, Vorstandsvorsitzender of ABB's German subsidiary. The interview was viewed as a provocation by the union leadership. They blamed von Koerber for going public with the results of a confidential meeting which management and the Betriebsrat (works council) had attended two days earlier at the invitation of Lothar Späth, prime minister of the federal state of Baden-Würtenberg, in which Mannheim was located. A member of the Betriebsrat shouted through the megaphone that von Koerber had broken an agreed-upon silence. By doing so, he had poisoned the atmosphere for further talks and had been trying to marshal public opinion against the Betriebsrat and the employees. In several passages of the interview he had "lied," according to the Betriebsrat spokesman. During the joint meeting with Späth, union members had understood that the concept of the Vorstand was still open for modi-

fications. In the interview, however, von Koerber repeated the need to reduce the ABB German workforce of 36,000 by some 3,500–4,000 people. IG Metall,[1] the union representing the blue-collar workers, feared that employment might be reduced by as much as 6,000 people. DAG,[2] the union representing the white-collar employees, blamed von Koerber for not being interested in maintaining Mannheim as ABB's German base. Peter Toussaint, the IG Metall representative in Mannheim and an employee representative on the ABB Deutschland supervisory board, stated: "It is no concept, when von Koerber claims that where we make losses, we have to eliminate the losses. BBC today as in the past is still a healthy company."

The March 24 demonstration was yet one more event in the hot Mannheim winter of 1988. ABB had been founded on January 4, 1988. On January 14, Percy Barnevik presided over ABB's first press conference at which a Mannheim reporter was present. A few days later, a lengthy lead article appeared in the local paper describing how Barnevik had initiated a powerful tempo in order to take advantage of the early merger honeymoon to break the prevailing crusty and immobile structures, especially at BBC. The reporter indicated that to date it had been impossible to overcome the "narrow-mindedness and jealousy in the tense German-Swiss corporate relationship." The article concluded:

> "Restructure first, grow afterwards" is the current ABB formula. But, in times of codetermination, this is easier said than done. Restructuring is a euphemism for job reduction. Barnevik knows full well that only with drastic cuts in employment can he succeed in his ambitious goal to make ABB through cost reductions into one of the world's most profitable electrotechnical companies. How skillful the Swedes will turn out to be will be determined by how successfully they deal with the "social forces," particularly in Germany, Switzerland, and Scandinavia.

---

[1]IG stands for Industriegewerkschaft or industrial union.
[2]DAG stands for Deutsche Angestellten Gewerkschaft.

The author finally suggested that Barnevik's goals were probably too ambitious given the likely organizational and social resistance.

The first shot in the impending battle was fired by Toussaint. In an early February interview he indicated that several hundred jobs were in jeopardy in the Mannheim area. He said: "The catastrophe will be twice as big as we had feared in our wildest dreams. IG Metall recognizes that restructuring measures are necessary, but we did not expect such massive targets." He indicated that the Beherrschungsvertrag[3] of 1986 had become invalid, according to union lawyers, by virtue of the ABB merger and would have to be voted on anew at the June BBC annual meeting. He severely criticized the Swedish managers in ABB and particularly Percy Barnevik. Later, Toussaint commented:

> We were very concerned when we learned about the merger between Asea and BBC. We felt that Asea got the better part of the deal. Admittedly, they were more profitable, but with their restructuring in Scandinavia they had essentially reached the end of the line. Their technology was weaker than that of BBC and they virtually had no beachhead in the European Economic Community. Barnevik, furthermore, with his American-style management approach was a known quantity. BBC had a lot of unrealized substance and Barnevik was obviously going to squeeze everything out until the last drop. We had to get ready to resist this approach. We had to protect jobs, particularly in Mannheim which already had the highest unemployment rate in the state and where BBC was the largest industrial employer. We were not going to surrender without a long hard fight.

The predicted war broke out on February 23. In the early hours of the morning both the mayor of Mannheim and the economics minister of Baden-Würtenberg in Stuttgart were informed that a "reduction of employment of about 10% will have to be accomplished during the next three years." At

8:00 A.M. the Betriebsrat received the news, subsequently IG Metall was informed, and at 11:30 A.M. a press conference was held. Two units in the Käfertal factory complex would be heavily impacted. The Betriebsrat was told that the transformer plant, employing over 500, would have to be closed and 700 out of the 4,000 workers in the power plant unit would lose their jobs. The company also indicated that a complete overhead analysis would be made by McKinsey to prune the administrative apparatus. According to the Betriebsrat, some 20% of the administrative jobs were at risk. With BBC employment standing at 36,000, the local newspaper carried as a headline the next day that 4,000 jobs would be eliminated, of which 1,500 were in Mannheim. The television newscast that evening stated that Mannheim was footing the bill for the elephant marriage between Asea and BBC. Toussaint later commented: "When this announcement came, we decided to engage in a deliberate confrontation with management." It was interesting that the proposed 10% reduction in employment was nothing new to BBC. In the fall of 1986, Fritz Leutwiler as BBC's chairman and chief executive had made such a statement, which was widely reported in the press. At that time, however, Mannheim apparently still felt safe and to be in control. Later, Switzerland's leading newspaper demanded that the German subsidiary contribute its share in cost reductions: "Mannheim to date has "imaginatively and cunningly" escaped from the prescribed personnel reduction of 10% while Switzerland has already on numerous occasions engaged in 'painful bloodletting.'" In 1988, on the other hand, with Barnevik at the helm and von Koerber as the new chief in Mannheim, fears ran deep.

The initial reaction in the local newspaper showed understanding for the Vorstand's position:

> BBC Germany, and particularly its Mannheim location, have been chronically ill for years. With or without merger, major surgery would have been inevitable sooner or later. A reproach clearly is in order. Management should have attempted much earlier, and in smaller steps, to bring about the slow recovery of the sick company units. This applies not

---

[3]The contract required by German law, to be voted on at the shareholder's meeting, to enable a parent company to issue directives to its German subsidiary.

just to the German but to the entire BBC organization. If inaction would have continued a few more years, maybe BBC would have turned into a second AEG.

(AEG, Germany's third-largest electrotechnical concern, had been previously near bankruptcy and had to be rescued by Daimler Benz.) The Käfertal employees felt differently. Spontaneously, about 4,000 people met outside the head office building to be "informed" by the Betriebsrat. This was the prevailing approach in Germany to stop work while still getting paid. Even though five regular Betriebsversammlungen (works assemblies), involving management, the Betriebsrat, and the employees, were scheduled at regular intervals, workers could always request to be informed when events triggering the codetermination law were occurring.

The waves resulting from the February 23 announcement remained not limited to the Käfertal complex. Mannheim's socialist mayor immediately called on the Christian democratic state government for help to alleviate Mannheim's 10% unemployment rate. With state elections scheduled for March 20, he knew that his call would almost certainly yield a response. Observers had been surprised that von Koerber dropped his bomb before the election. Together with Fritz Leutwiler he had visited Helmut Kohl in Bonn in early February and had initially announced that it would take time to work out the restructuring measures and that definite plans would not be submitted until March. The rumor mill and the resulting uncertainty in Käfertal had made it impossible to stick to this initial timetable.

The union response to the February 23 announcement was prompt and strong with the statement that these "plans had nothing to do anymore with restructuring but would lead to the destruction of the German BBC." Several aspects of the Mannheim situation gave the opposition some tactical advantages. They could count on a great amount of sympathy given Mannheim's high unemployment rate and its social-democratic political landscape. In addition, BBC was heavily concentrated in its Käfertal complex, which housed not

only several important product groups but also all administrative activities.[4] A single Betriebsrat, comprising 31 elected members, represented all of Käfertal's 7,700 employees. Four members of the Betriebsrat, while small in number but strong in political influence, belonged to the extreme left of the political spectrum. Finally, under German law, the announced measures, with their personnel and social consequences, required information, consultation, and decision sharing by the Betriebsrat. Compounding the situation was the traditional rivalry between the German and Swiss organizations. Each side traditionally feared that it was taken advantage of at the expense of the other.

Thus, union members were constantly able to exploit numerous occasions to call for work stoppages. One occurred on February 29 with another one following on March 4, each time involving several thousand people. On Tuesday, March 8, almost 6,000 people showed up for the Betriebsversammlung at 9:30 A.M. Von Koerber, flanked by two Vorstand colleagues in charge of power plants and human relations, had to listen to a day of speeches and insults. At the beginning of the meeting some 500 workers from the transformer factory, which was to be closed, walked by the Vorstand's table, each of them depositing a wooden cross on it. The union raised another topic: it alleged that certain activities, which were being transferred to Switzerland, had been financed with German government research grants. Thus, the Swedes and Swiss were portrayed as carrying away technology financed by the German taxpayer. The union also announced counter proposals: for example, the suggestion that Asea robots also be manufactured in Mannheim. The Betriebsversammlung continued for a total of three days (after the first day without von Koerber), thus becoming the longest in German codetermination history.

---

[4]Every German factory above a minimal size had an elected Betriebsrat. Its size varied, depending on the number of workers represented. When several factories and/or offices were involved, the single, large works council was referred to as Gesamtbetriebsrat.

Outside support continued to grow. Union leaders had established contacts with unions in other countries. Sympathy meetings of other BBC Betriebsrate in Germany were held. Church leaders expressed their sympathy and support. Protesters were able to corner Späth at an election campaign meeting, which was also attended by Kohl. Workers refused to work overtime. Two political parties, the SPD and FDP, were planning moves in the Bundestag. Späth promised he would write letters to the two major shareholders in ABB, Peter Wallenberg in Sweden and Stephan Schmidheiny in Switzerland. Finally, on March 22 a three-hour meeting took place involving Späth, the Betriebsrat, and the BBC Vorstand. On the heels of this meeting came the von Koerber interview which led to the "Koerber heraus" demonstration. Interestingly, the title of the interview was "Construction rather than Destruction at BBC" and in it von Koerber promised a real 5% annual growth rate for BBC in the next few years resulting from its changed focus on growth segments. This was in line with a Barnevik comment to a local reporter in January in which he emphasized that the German operation of the new ABB would benefit the most from the merger in the mid-term. ABB wanted to exploit the large German market more fully. However, the union leadership was clearly on a confrontation course and seemed to be unwilling to listen and compromise.

Restructuring the Business

Restructuring in Power Plants

Power plants were the lions of the BBC product line. They also were one of the main battlegrounds of the Swiss-German rivalry. The worldwide recession of the early 1980s, the high real interest rates, and the debt crisis of many developing nations resulted in a severe drop in demand for power plants, creating enormous excess capacities and making export markets fiercely competitive. Not surprisingly, under these conditions, the rivalry between Switzerland and Germany became fiercer as well. At that time, the Swiss Stammhaus was unable to give binding instructions to BBC Mannheim with its large block of minority shareholders. Only in 1986, after acquiring

over 75% of the shares of its German subsidiary, was it possible for the German operation to enter into a Beherrschungsvertrag with its parent so that the Stammhaus could call the shots. Just before the ABB merger, BBC ended five years of unsuccessful efforts to jointly rationalize the Swiss and German power plant operations. It adopted a plan, labeled as Produktionsverbund (manufacturing alliance), under which Switzerland would make all the rotating pieces while Mannheim would limit itself to the stationary pieces and the final assembly. As part of the plan, one of the two Swiss factories would be closed.

The Produktionsverbund itself was not subject to the German codetermination law, but its impact in terms of personnel reductions required involvement of the Betriebsrat. The purpose of the plan was not only to bring about specialization of the hitherto two full-line Swiss and German operations but also to reduce capacity in both countries. Thus, 700 out of the 4,000 workers would lose their jobs in Käfertal. One of the power plant executives commented:

> Up to now both Germany and Switzerland have been making the full product line. In the past, our large home market allowed us to subsidize our exports. But since several years now, the home market has virtually disappeared. We have been accepting export orders at prices which clearly do not cover our costs, simply to keep the factory going. But the factory still is too big even though we are fully integrated by making almost everything in house. In 1987, we incurred DM 130 million[5] in costs which we could have avoided if our capacity had been adjusted to our production volume. Also, we are having difficulty in allocating our indirect costs to specific projects. As a result, we incurred DM 240 million in unallocated costs in 1987.

Another executive talked about the poor pricing of the export orders. He said:

> Here at BBC we are outstanding engineers but poor businessmen. We have been signing orders just to

---

[5]In the first quarter of 1988, DM 1.68 = $1.

keep the factory going. For some time now I have been concerned about this policy, not only because of the red ink but also because we have been exposing ourselves to substantial technical risks in accepting highly sophisticated hitherto unproven projects. Keep in mind that these units have to be installed in developing countries. Fine tuning this equipment at its destination is no easy task.

Immediately after the merger, the KL made it clear that no orders shall normally be accepted below full costs. I have the Cannes statement on my desk, which states: "In a highly fixed-cost, mature, and highly competitive industry we often deal with crazy pricing from competition. It is then necessary to get our own managers away from routine contribution and cash-flow thinking, if we ever shall reach satisfactory profitability. *All costs must be covered.* A loss order is a serious matter and can only be accepted on high management level. We need *more courage to say no* to further worsening of sales conditions or price concessions. That may mean loss of some orders, but it will raise average margin." Time will tell whether this new policy will bring about a change in our behavior. Our previous BBC management for sure was deeply concerned about keeping the factory filled.

In charge of the Mannheim power generation restructuring program was Udo Werlé who had only recently been transferred from a smaller BBC subsidiary, where he had been engaged in an earlier restructuring effort. He said:

Reducing capacity is nothing new to our power plant operation. By the late seventies the factory operated on the basis of 1.4 million manhours. This figure has already been reduced to 0.9 million manhours. However, in spite of these previous manpower reductions, we never reduced capacity enough. We had unused capacity year in, year out. This led to poor motivation of the workforce. We simply cannot continue operating this way. Unless we are competitive, particularly in terms of price, we are placing the entire Käfertal location in jeopardy. Thus, we will be taking measures on three fronts: First, McKinsey will start with us in terms of its overhead analysis. Second, we have the Produktions-verbund with Switzerland. Third, we are planning to drastically reduce capacity not just in terms of manpower but also in terms of machines and factory

space. Of course, the Betriebsrat has the right of codetermination. Unfortunately, at Käfertal we do not have a Betriebsrat just for the power plant factory but one for the entire area. This makes life more difficult, particularly since we have granted too many concessions to them in the past. It is about time that they learn that the good old days of the power plant business have been gone for several years. With Germany having some of the highest wages in the world, we cannot run our factory like a country club if we are going to survive in world competition. The Betriebsrat will have to face these facts of life whether they like it or not.

Restructuring in Transformers

Transformers had been a perennial poor performer at BBC Mannheim. From 1981 through 1987 sales averaged DM 100 million per year, while losses stood on average at DM 20 million per year. The lowest loss year was 1984 with DM 12.5 million, while losses peaked in 1987 at the DM 31.9 million level. The high 1987 loss was in part caused by two very large orders from abroad, accounting for 60% of sales, which were technically unusually demanding. These orders resulted in both penalties and expensive reworkings. To meet these demands, the Käfertal operation borrowed workers from the power plant sector as well as from BBC's Geneva transformer operation.

Transformers were a mature product subject to intensive competition from the industrial and developing world as well as from the Eastern Bloc. In this market BBC pursued a strategy of technological differentiation. However, the traditional organizational separation of R&D and manufacturing led to poor coordination among these functions. As a result, manufacturing was unable to deliver the products on time and with the promised quality and specifications.

BBC was one of five companies producing transformers in Germany. Siemens was the largest producer. BBC and Lepper, which had been acquired by Asea in 1965, were of about equal size. Two other producers were somewhat smaller, with one being controlled by Siemens and the other by a large German utility. The domestic market was small and could have been supplied entirely by one of the five producers. Thus, all producers were forced to compete in the extremely price-sensitive export markets.

Transformers was one of the two German Asea operations which, prior to the merger, overlapped with BBC's activities. During the mid-1980s, the Asea affiliate had been restructured and, at the time of the merger, the Asea mentality was already deeply embedded in this formerly family-owned company. Thus, Lepper, which was located in Bad Honnef near Cologne, produced almost the same volume as BBC with half the people, and its production throughput times took only one-third of the time required at Käfertal. Most importantly, Lepper made a profit.

During the fall of 1987, a working team was appointed to investigate the two parallel German transformer operations and to submit recommendations. Concurrently, the BBC general manager for transformers was relieved of his job and was replaced by Horst Stange, who continued as head of the Bad Honnef operation. Karl-Heinz Barz, who had been transferred in 1986 from the standard products division as controller, was also made responsible for plant management. In early 1988, the technical and marketing directors in Käfertal also left. The responsibility for marketing was transferred to the Bad Honnef organization. Thus, the Mannheim transformer operation was virtually without a top-management team. Käfertal's three-story factory was viewed as out of date and inefficient. Thus, it came as no surprise that the study team recommended that the Käfertal facility be closed. Moreover, in the words of one of the former Asea executives,

> the situation in Käfertal was beyond belief. The technical problems were enormous, deliveries were delayed, and the factory looked like a gigantic traffic jam with stuff standing around everywhere. Also, wages were high since the workforce was covered by the same agreement as the more highly skilled power plant workers. Yet, because of heavy turnover, a good part of the people were new and inexperienced.

The project team indicated that Käfertal had too high a proportion of exports. Thus, the combined capacity of Bad Honnef and Käfertal should be reduced from DM 200 million to about DM 130 million.

The alternative to the closing of Käfertal would be a split of the volume with 55% Bad Honnef, 45% Käfertal and some product specialization, much like the power plant arrangement between Mannheim and Switzerland. This approach, however, would be DM 8 million/year more costly even after reducing manpower in Käfertal by 70% from over 500 to about 150 people and cutting invested capital by one-half. Such drastic cuts, and forgoing loss orders, would be required for Käfertal to reach a break-even level in bad years and profitability in good ones. The project team felt that this second alternative would be difficult to achieve and strongly recommended the first alternative, namely, to close the Käfertal transformer factory and to concentrate all production at the Bad Honnef site. This recommendation, which was communicated to the Betriebsrat, resulted in the 500 wooden crosses ending up on the Vorstand table at the outset of the three-day Betriebsversammlung.

Preparing for the Future

Back to Basics

The Cannes financial targets were translated by von Koerber into a demanding set of performance requirements for ABB's German operations. BBC Mannheim's 1987 performance was not only way below the Cannes targets but also below the current ABB averages. For example, its ROCE stood at 9.9%, and no real growth had occurred during the last several years. Von Koerber saw opportunities for improvements on all fronts. One major effort was to focus on asset reduction, encompassing three elements. The first element involved working capital management. Receivables by 1990 were to be reduced from 17% to 16% and inventory from 44% to 34% of sales. The second element related to a reduction in fixed assets. By reducing excess capacity, floor space could be freed and rented out or sold. The third element consisted of the sale of unneeded property. This was seen as a significant contributor, with gains helping to offset the nonrecurring expenses which the restructuring effort would entail.

A second major effort focused on costs. A hiring stop was ordered; only von Koerber's office was able to grant exemptions. Productivity improvements should be accomplished along several dimensions: reduction of personnel, of floor space, and of throughput times. More subcontracting should be pursued vigorously to replace expensive in-house manufactured parts. A particularly significant opportunity was seen in purchasing. Mannheim's annual purchases amounted to DM 2.4 billion, and it was felt that this large volume would allow it to squeeze at least DM 100 million out of suppliers. Finally, it was felt that the overhead analysis, for which McKinsey had been engaged, would yield substantial cost savings. Von Koerber felt that the added cost of the consultants would be more than offset by the speedy and earlier implementation of the many cost saving actions. He said: "There is no doubt that, in a turnaround, consultants have a very short payback period if they are able to identify quick cost reductions. We did this calculation repeatedly. The millions of Deutschmarks we spent were recovered very quickly. Of course, this is pure cost cutting and has nothing to do with strategy."

A third major effort involved the sales front. More aggressive pricing was suggested, and loss orders became taboo. In addition, McKinsey would be engaged to help Mannheim management search for additional sales opportunities in their existing markets. Von Koerber was convinced that, given the previous lack of market and customer orientation, many such opportunities existed. Thus, after several years of stagnation, Mannheim management was faced with demanding and increasing targets for both orders and sales.

Von Koerber's Remaining Inheritance

Although there were only minor overlaps between the old BBC and Asea businesses in Germany, von Koerber still had to manage them carefully. In addition to the transformer overlap, Asea also had an industry activity in Düsseldorf. This operation was less than one-fifth of BBC's size and furthermore specialized in part in different activities. Thus, it was easily decided to leave only a sales office in

Düsseldorf and bring the rest of the Asea activities to Mannheim to fold them into the BBC operation. The hard nut to crack in industry, which had to be decided by the KL, was the choice of one of three process automation systems. The software development of these systems was extremely expensive. Thus, it was essential for ABB to concentrate either on the Swedish, Swiss, or German system. Finally, von Koerber inherited Asea's robotics activities, with some DM 60 million in sales, which consisted of a sales operation only.

In addition to the power plant and transformer problem areas, von Koerber inherited three other severe cash-drain activities. One was the Lampertheim factory producing large and complex integrated circuits for power plant and transmission use. A plant closing was contemplated, which generated a great deal of Betriebsrat concern and turmoil. The other two problem areas were development activities, one involving the high-temperature nuclear reactor (HTR) and the other the sodium-sulphur high-energy battery for automotive and public transportation use, where BBC had been in the lead without quite reaching an economic breakthrough yet.

In spite of being immersed in restructuring activities, von Koerber was also talking about growth opportunities in the ABB portfolio. Robotics, even though small, was a candidate. So were the environmental controls brought into the marriage. This was particularly important in Germany with its strong Green party and where environmental protection was a political imperative. Von Koerber was also counting on a renaissance of public transportation as roads became congested and environmental concerns increased. He saw standard products as a potential Cinderella, which had lived for too long in the shadow of the large-ticket core businesses. Finally, he hoped that the repair and refurbishing activities could be expanded significantly. To bring this about, he was considering organizing it as an independent activity, which resulted in protests from the core business segments. Von Koerber commented:

> Right now everybody seems to ask me about our growth strategy: Prime Minister Späth, journalists,

church leaders, and employee representatives. All I can do at this point is make headlines without substance. We are at present in a battle for survival and have neither time nor the energy to develop a growth strategy. Yet, everybody wants a description of a bright future although we have no idea what the future holds. When I talk about our growth strategy, I feel as though I am dancing on a tightrope.

Von Koerber was also wondering how he could take advantage of Mannheim's unique position in the ABB group. He saw ABB Deutschland as ABB's platform in the European Community. His unit was the largest in the group. Mannheim accounted for the bulk of ABB's sales in the EC. ABB's position in France was virtually nil given BBC's earlier withdrawal; it was modestly represented in the United Kingdom, and only in Italy, by virtue of BBC's earlier involvement, did it have a position of some significance. Germany had many advantages, such as its export financing and insurance facilities. Also, research support came both from Bonn and Brussels. Human resources for R&D were available in Germany, well trained and highly committed. Cooperative ventures with universities and other research institutes were possible. In sum, German R&D was seen as fully competitive with Japan and the United States.

Others were less sanguine. They pointed out that ABB Deutschland was a relatively small number two in its home market. German wages were among the highest in the world, and productivity improvements needed worker approval under the codetermination law. Also, wouldn't ABB's multidomestic concept with factories all over the world decrease German exports and wouldn't increased subcontracting from low-wage countries result in further reductions in employment? What would be Mannheim's future if ABB carried through its intentions to specialize and optimize on a worldwide basis?

One of von Koerber's major headaches was his concern about management depth in Mannheim. Management development, he felt, had been ignored. How many Mannheim managers would be

able to rise to the challenges resulting from ABB's international matrix? Also, he was not only fighting with the Betriebsrat but also encountering open and underground management resistance to his restructuring plans, even at the highest levels. Barnevik later commented: "The silent resistance from managers was more formidable. In fact, much of the union resistance was fed by management." On how much talent, motivation, and cooperation could von Koerber count? He said:

Our hard-nosed confrontation strategy is subject not only to lots of criticism on the outside but also inside ABB, both in Mannheim and Zurich. Many of my colleagues from the BBC side are urging me to move more gently and slowly. Keep in mind that I am a newcomer here. How do I know what is really going on? Sometimes I feel that I am sitting on top of a huge pudding without knowing what's inside. Middle management normally resists change and rightly so because they are usually the losers, not top management or the workers. This problem is compounded by the fact that these people, given the previous Baden-Mannheim relationship, are trained to resist. Resistance in Mannheim is fine tuned, invisible, and very well organized. As a newcomer, it is difficult for me to know where to act first.

To bring about change, you usually rely on the young people in an organization. But there are very few of them here. Because BBC did not grow and had to cut costs, no people have been hired in recent years. I am now starting to bring in some fresh blood, but the degree and speed at which they can be digested, absorbed, and integrated by the organization is limited. Thus, in addition, I am relying on a few trustworthy colleagues and associates whom I am sure were frustrated in the past and are determined to contribute to a better future. I am using a number of task forces consisting of loyal lieutenants. Also, a dozen McKinsey people are of great help to me. To silence resistance, I am moving some people around and have made a few top-management changes. I know I need to rock the boat, but I don't want to rock it so hard that it capsizes and sinks. I have to watch the point beyond which the boat would capsize. My nightmare is that I will exceed the limit and that we will all sink together.

Case 8–3 ABB's Relays Business: Building and Managing A Global Matrix

It was a casual conversation between the chairmen of Asea and Brown Boveri in 1987 about the dismal state of the utilities equipment market that eventually led to merger talks between these two giant power equipment companies. Within weeks of the announcement in August 1987, Percy Barnevik, the CEO of Asea who was asked to lead the combined operations, had articulated a strategic vision for Asea Brown Boveri (ABB). Convinced that the decade-long decline in new power generation capacity would soon reverse itself, he believed that the new technologies and scale economies required to meet the new demand could only be developed by companies operating on a global scale. At the same time, however, he felt that because of the high level of government ownership or control of power companies, the vast majority of new orders would continue to go to companies with a strong national presence. His strategy was to build a company that could exploit these two major industry trends.

Having articulated his broad vision, Barnevik formed a 10-person top management work group to analyze how the operations of Asea and Brown Boveri could best be linked to achieve it. Because ABB would start operating as a merged company on January 1, 1988, Barnevik wanted quick action. Within two months, the top management team had decided on a matrix structure that would balance the global business focus of an organization built on approximately 60 global business areas (BAs) with the national market focus provided by 1,300 local companies grouped under the umbrella of several country-based holding companies (see Exhibit 1).

This case was prepared by Professor Christopher A. Bartlett.
Copyright © 1993 by the President and Fellows of Harvard College. Harvard Business School case 394-016.

Barnevik then set about selecting the management team that would staff the new organization. To select the 300 key managers who would lead the change process, Barnevik personally interviewed hundreds of Asea and Brown Boveri executives. He was seeking those with good technical and commercial backgrounds who were "tough skinned, fast on their feet, and able to lead" yet also "open, generous, and capable of thinking in group terms."

In January 1988, he assembled this handpicked group of 300 for a three-day meeting in Cannes. In presentations supported with 198 overhead transparencies (an approach that was to become a signature of his communications-intensive management style), Barnevik detailed industry trends, analyzed market opportunities, and profiled ABB's economics and cost structures. But mostly he focused on how the new organization would allow ABB to manage three contradictions—to be global and local, big and small, radically decentralized with central control. (Exhibit 2 presents excerpts from some of his overhead slides.) At the end of the meeting, each manager received a 21-page "policy bible" outlining the major policies and values to be communicated to the next level of the organization.

Barnevik's management model focused on the twin principles of decentralized responsibility and individual accountability. To emphasize the former, he ensured that most of ABB's key resources were controlled directly by the federation of 1,300 front-line companies, whenever possible set up as separate legal entities. To ensure that managers inherited their results from year to year, he gave them control over their balance sheets, including the right to borrow and the ability to retain up to 30% of earnings. Furthermore, he implemented his "30/30/30 rule" in which he decreed that all headquarters

EXHIBIT 1   ABB Matrix Concept

The ABB organization is built on a federation of 1,300 operating companies charged with managing the front-line operations. In each major country or region, these companies are administered through a national holding company, which is responsible for ensuring effective performance of ABB's total market presence. At the same time, each operating company reports to one of 58 Business Areas (BAs) responsible for developing global strategies.

Conceptually, the matrix operates as follows:

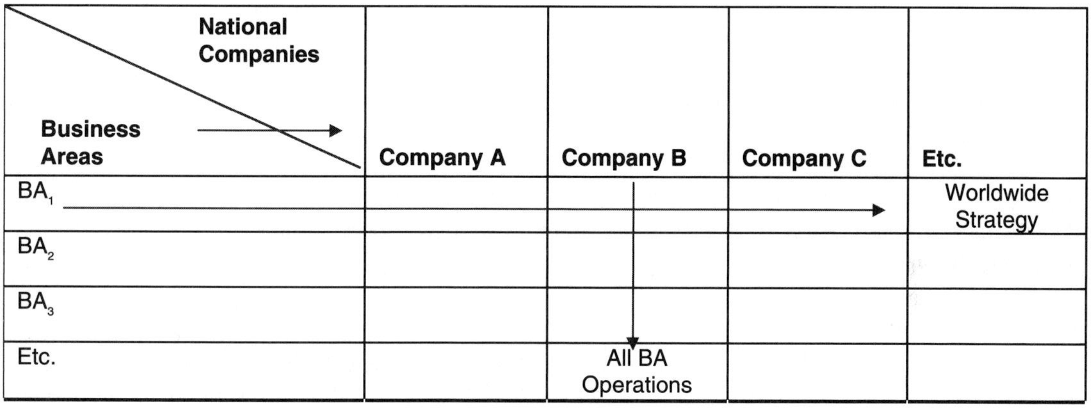

Business Areas / National Companies	Company A	Company B	Company C	Etc.
BA$_1$				Worldwide Strategy
BA$_2$				
BA$_3$				
Etc.		All BA Operations		

Source: Company documents.

organizations—from corporate to business area to regional—should be dramatically downsized by relocating 30% of the headquarters personnel to the front-line companies, by having another 30% provide their value added as outsourced services, and by laying off an additional 30%. To set the example, the staffing level at ABB's combined corporate headquarters was reduced from over 2,000 to only 150.

To ensure accountability, Barnevik assigned a team to develop a new transparent reporting system which aimed at "democratizing information." Dubbed ABACUS, the system was designed to collect uniform dollar-dominated performance data at the level of ABB's 4,500 profit centers. By allowing comparisons against budget and forecast to be aggregated and disaggregated, ABACUS facilitated analysis within and across businesses, countries, and companies or profit centers.

Given control over key resources and provided with current relevant information, managers on the front-lines were expected to act. Barnevik's "7-3 formula" reinforced the notion that it was better to decide quickly and be right seven times out of ten than to delay or to search for the perfect solution. "Better roughly and quickly than carefully and slowly," he said. "The only thing we cannot accept is people who do nothing."

He took these and other aspects of his strongly held beliefs and values out to the field, traveling some 200 days a year, always with his large bag of overhead transparencies. Through continued acquisition and rejuvenated internal growth, within four years ABB grew to become a $29 billion company with over 200,000 employees worldwide—the giant of its industry, dominating previous first-tier players like Siemens, Hitachi, and General Electric (see Exhibit 3). To understand how this rapid growth and

---

EXHIBIT 2   Cannes Top Management Meeting—Excerpts from Barnevik's Slides

---

BA Management Responsibilities
- Worldwide result and profitability
- Establishing a management team—preferably consisting of members from different countries
- Developing a worldwide strategy
- Basic development (typically CAD)
- Coordinating delegated development
- Market allocation scheme and/or tender coordination

Country Management Responsibilities
- Size and complexity of local structure in line with ABB's business presence
- In smaller countries: single company with departments
- In larger countries: holding structure with many subsidiaries and operating units
- Local entities serve their respective markets in line with BA objectives, strategies, and guidelines—they have responsibility for operational results

General Principles of Management Behavior
1. To take action (and stick out one's neck) and do the right things obviously the best behavior
2. To take action and do the wrong things is next best (within reason and a limited number of times)
3. Not to take action (and lost opportunities) is the only unacceptable behavior

Policies for Change
- Identify necessary changes implemented as fast as possible. Small risk that negative changes not considered enough
  - Concentrate on the ones with biggest profit improvements (80-20 rule)
  - 10 times more common to delay than the opposite
- Get over with "negative" changes in a lump sum and avoid prolonging the process and cut it up in pieces. Packages with "positive" and "negative" changes desirable. Important to quickly focus on new opportunities. Means earlier focus on positive changes
- No "fair" reduction in terms of equality between locations-improvements of group profitability counts as main criteria in a broad sense
- Most major changes must be started first year
  - "Honeymoon" of small changes would be detrimental
  - What is not started in the first year will be a lot more difficult later
- The merger creates unique possibilities ("excuses") to undertake long overdue actions which should have been undertaken anyway
- Upcoming merger problems must be resolved fast and on lowest possible level
- Example
  - First cutting capacity, merging and streamlining costs
  - Then with increased competitiveness-growth and new opportunities

  Volume increase is solution to cost problems

EXHIBIT 3 ABB Key Performance Data: 1988–1991

	1988	1989	1990	1991
Revenues	17,832	20,560	26,688	28,883
Operating earnings after depreciation	854	1,257	1,790	609
Net income	386	589	590	609
Acquisition expenditures	544	3,090	677	612
Property, plant, and equipment expenditure	736	783	961	1,035
R&D expenditure	1,255	1,361	1,931	2,342
Operating earnings/revenues	4.8%	6.1%	6.7%	6.6%
Return on equity	12.5	16.8	4.5	13.9
Return on capital employed	13.6	17.0	19.7	17.1
Number of employees	169,459	189,493	215,154	214,399

geographic expansion was managed, this case focuses on the birth and development of one of ABB's almost 60 business areas (BAs) (Exhibit 4).

Building the Relays Organization

In August 1987, Göran Lindahl, Asea's executive vice president responsible for power transmission, found himself on Barnevik's 10-person top management transition team. After presenting a proposal for merging the two power transmission businesses, Lindahl was tapped to head this important segment for ABB as of January 1, 1988.

Creating the Management Team

In the relays business, as in each of the other eight BAs reporting to him, Lindahl's first task was to identify the managers who would drive the integration and capture the synergies that were fundamental to ABB's strategy. He described the process:

> For me, the key qualifications were proven performance in their business, and broad experience in more than one discipline. But, as important as their career background was their personality—their flexibility, integrity, and statesmanship.

He named Anders Fraggstedt, general manager of Asea's relays business based in Västerås, Sweden, to assume the additional role of BA head for ABB's relays business worldwide. To support Fraggstedt in his new role (and also to help minimize the number

of decisions escalated to the corporate level for resolution), Lindahl created a BA board with Fraggstedt as chairman and the relays business managers from Baden, Switzerland, and Vasa, Finland, as the two other members. (The Vasa business had come as part of the acquisition of Stromberg, the Finnish electrical giant.)

At the same time, Lindahl felt that he needed to keep a close personal involvement in the process. But this did not imply that he had an army of staff to monitor operations and control performance against targets. Like others at the group executive level, Lindahl maintained a small staff to help manage his $5 billion global business. Besides himself, it numbered four persons—two controllers, a business development manager, and a secretary.

He saw his key role as providing an environment in which those below him could be most effective. As a first step, he believed he had to create the uncertainty necessary to encourage "unlearning" of old assumptions and behaviors. Through what he referred to as "the framework," Lindahl set challenging goals and objectives for his newly appointed managers—tightly defined at first, but gradually expanding and loosening:

> People are as good as you make them. We have about 8,000 engineers in our 35,000-person segment. They are bright, capable people who make excellent managers. My first task is to provide the frameworks to help them develop as managers; the next challenge

EXHIBIT 4 ABB Organization Structure (1991)

Group Executive Management	A. Benitom	E. Somm	B.-O. Svanholm	E. Bielinski G. Lundberg	G. Lindahl	P. Barnevik CEO	T. Gasser Deputy CEO	S. Carlsson	G. Schulmeyer	L. Thunell	E. von Koerber	B. Romacker
Corporate Staffs*			Corporate Staffs*			Corporate Staffs*	Corporate Staffs*	Corporate Staffs*	Corporate Staffs*	Corporate Staffs*	Corporate Staffs*	Corporate Staffs*

Business Segments

| | | | Transportation | Power Plants | Power Transmission | Environmental Control | | Power Distribution | Industry | Financial Services | | |

Business Areas

Transportation segment:
- Main Line Rolling Stock
- Mass Transit Vehicles
- Railway Maintenance
- Complete Rail Systems
- Signaling
- Fixed Railway Installations

Power Plants segment:
- Gas Turbine Power Plants
- Utility Steam Power Plants
- Industrial Steam Power Plants
- PFBC
- Hydro Power Plants
- Nuclear Power Plants
- Power Plant Control
- Fossil Combustion Systems
- Fossil Combustion Services

Power Transmission segment:
- Cables and Capacitors
- Distribution Transformers
- Electric Metering
- HV Switchgear
- MicaComp
- Network Control
- Power Systems
- Power Transformers
- Relays

Environmental Control segment:
- ABB Fläkt Group
- Environmental Services
- Resource Recovery

Power Distribution segment:
- LV Apparatus
- LV Systems
- Installation
- MV Equipment
- Distribution Plants

Industry segment:
- Metallurgy
- Process Automation
- Drives
- Process Engineering
- Marine, Oil and Gas
- Instrumentation

Financial Services segment:
- Treasury Centers
- Leasing Financing
- Insurance
- Trading and Trade Finance
- Stockbrokerage Investment Management
- Other Financial Services

Other Business Areas

- Superchargers
- Other Activities Switzerland
- District Heating
- Service
- Other Activities Sweden
- Power Lines and General Contracting
- Motors
- Robotics
- Other Activities USA
- Energy Ventures
- Other Activities Germany
- Telecommunications
- Communication and Information Systems
- Integrated Circuits

Regions

| Switzerland | Sweden Finland Denmark Iceland Spain Portugal | | Italy | | Norway United Kingdom Ireland France | USA Canada | Germany Austria Benelux countries Greece Eastern Europe |

Latin America and Arabian Penins., Africa and West/South Asia, Southeast Asia, Northeast Asia, Australia, New Zealand, Japan

824

is to loosen and expand the framework to let them become leaders.

In his definition, leaders were the individuals who had displayed the requisite personal characteristics (which he identified as flexibility, statesmanship and generosity), and who were ready to take responsibility for setting their own objectives and standards. "When I have developed all the managers into leaders," he said, "we will have a self-driven, self-renewing organization."

Communicating the New Philosophy and Values

As he met with his new team, one of the most important items on Lindahl's agenda was to communicate the company's guiding principle of decentralization. He explained:

> The newspapers may describe ABB's power transmission power segment as a $5 billion operation with 35,000 employees, but I think of it as almost two hundred operating companies further divided into 700 profit centers each with about 50 employees and $7 million in revenues. Although the BAs play a vital role in setting strategy, only the local companies can implement the plans and achieve the objectives.

The message was well received by most front-line managers. Don Jans, who had come with Westinghouse's power transmission and distribution business when ABB acquired it in early 1989, reflected the attitude among his colleagues at the time:

> The prevailing view when ABB acquired our business was that we'd lost the war. We were resigned to the fact that the occupying troops would move in and we'd move out. But to our surprise, they not only asked us to stay on, they gave us the opportunity to run the whole relays business—even the Allentown operation that was ABB's own facility in the United States.

To do so, however, required Jans and his colleagues to make major changes in their business assumptions, organizational practices, and management styles. In Westinghouse, Jans had five layers of management between himself and the CEO; in ABB there were only two. In Westinghouse, he had been constantly frustrated by the bureaucracy imposed by

a 3,000-person headquarters; in ABB he had to adjust to the need for self-sufficiency in an organization with only 150 people at corporate. In Westinghouse, decisions had been top-down and shaped by political negotiations; in ABB Jans found many more were delegated and were driven by data and results. He described the first few meetings when he and his colleagues were exposed to the ABB philosophy and values as "an exhilarating experience":

> It was amazing. We were constantly seeing the top guys in meetings and seminars,—Barnevik, Lindahl, Schulmeyer (the North American regional VP). They came with stacks of transparencies and could talk for hours about how the industry was developing, where ABB wanted to be, how it was going to get there, and so on. It was spellbinding; a real education.
>
> Just as important was their willingness to listen to our proposals and invest in the relays business. In Westinghouse, capital allocations had always been tightly managed, but after the mid-1970s, it seemed as if they were even less willing to invest in old core businesses like relays. Not so after 1989. ABB is really committed to this business, and if we can justify an investment, we can usually get the resources.

One of Lindahl's main objectives in his nonstop communications was to instill a clear and strong value system to guide management action. "In the end," he said, "managers are loyal not to a particular boss or even to a company, but to a set of values they believe in and find satisfying." He identified the core values as being an emphasis on quality, not only in products but also in organizational processes and relationships; a commitment to excellence in technology to ensure the business remained at the forefront of the industry; a dedication to productivity and performance not just in the plants but at all levels of the organization; and a belief in people—both customers and employees—as the means to achieving the first three.

Lindahl also used his company visits to emphasize the importance of individual accountability. The company's broad philosophies were translated into specific task requirements for managers at all levels, and Lindahl devoted a substantial amount of

---

EXHIBIT 5   ABB Management

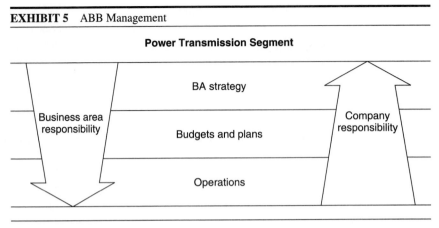

Source: Company documents.

---

time to communicating the appropriate roles, responsibilities, and relationships summarized in a chart that he had discussed with every profit center manager in his segment (see Exhibit 5). While BA management was responsible for setting worldwide strategy and overall operating objectives, local company managers controlled operations and were responsible for profits. The integration of the different interests took place through a rigorous planning and budgeting process; the assurance of appropriate implementation through a sophisticated set of formal and informal controls. Because he believed firmly in the need to control performance against "the framework," one of Lindahl's earliest and most important appointments was "a controller who was sensitive to operations rather than just a number cruncher."

Defining the Agenda

In the early days, Lindahl's "framework" was fairly tight. He wanted his businesses to focus on restructuring themselves rapidly:

> If you want to bring about change, you need to force it, and that means giving the organization a clear vision of your expectations and pushing for results. Eventually, the change process becomes natural and develops its own momentum. I told each BA board that our objective was to conquer the globe in power transmission. At the same time, I kept reminding

them of the need to focus on the customers, watch competitors, and deliver current results. To do that, they would have to deal with the overcapacity we clearly had, and capitalize on the best technology in the combined operations. Which plants were the most efficient? Which technology should become standard? It was a huge undertaking to do all the analysis and negotiate sensitive agreements.

In the early stages of the restructuring process, Lindahl reported getting lots of issues coming up for his review and resolution, but typically he pushed them back down for further discussion. Many such issues involved the painful process of closing plants, reallocating historical market relationships, or cutting traditional product lines. He saw his major job as trying to convert the "winner/loser" mentality into a recognition that the new organization could become "winner/winner."

After a full year of difficult analysis, discussion and negotiation, Anders Fraggstedt and his relays BA board decided on the BA's basic restructuring concept. Vasa, Finland, would assume the leadership role in developing and manufacturing relays for distribution protection of the lower-voltage products that had been Stromberg's specialty and for which it was clearly the technological leader. In high-voltage protection, where both Asea and BBC had strong capabilities, the major overlap in development, manufacturing, and marketing was resolved by giving Västerås, Sweden, primary responsibility for high-voltage products, and Baden, Switzerland, the lead role for project and systems deliveries that engineered multiple products into integrated forms or turnkey installations. Furthermore, to eliminate marketing overlap, Sweden would assume overall responsibility for sales into Europe, North America, and Australia, where bids were mostly for individual relays products, while Switzerland would focus its marketing efforts on Latin America, Africa, and Asia, where project business was more important.

A senior manager of the Swiss relays company reflected on the outcome for his unit:

> Sure, there was concern in Baden. People talked about the Swedes dominating the management, they were concerned that most of our production was being transferred out, and they complained that we lost well-established markets like Germany and France while retaining only the "poor man's countries" in the developing world. But the company was committed to keeping the existing know-how, and Mr. Fraggstedt reassured us that our relays R&D group would be retained. After a long talk with Mr. Lindahl, I was convinced, and I took on the job of persuading the organization to look at the changes more positively.

Restructuring the Business

In December 1988, Göran Lindahl approached Ulf Gundemark, the manager of ABB's Swedish low-voltage switch gear operations, and offered him the opportunity to replace Anders Fraggstedt as the business area head for ABB's $250 million worldwide relays business. It was an attractive opportunity for a 37-year-old engineer who had spent 10 years of his 12-year career with Asea in its relays business.

Like other BA heads, Gundemark would continue to be responsible for his national company's operations, but would also wear a second hat as a worldwide BA manager. To assist him in this new role, he would have a staff of two—a controller and a coordination/business development manager. His first challenge was to integrate the disparate relays oper-

ations of Asea, Brown Boveri, Stromberg, and now Westinghouse.[1] It would be a difficult task to integrate companies that not only had vastly different management cultures, but also had been bitter competitors.

Gundemark saw his first priority being to communicate the broad rationalization principles that had been hammered out in a year-long negotiation process and to implement the major changes. Recognizing that ABB planned to take a one-time restructuring charge against its 1989 results, he initiated the Revaba Project (Restructure Västerås and Baden) to implement the most difficult part of the rationalization plans as quickly as possible. Overall coordination of the project was assigned to a team headed by the R&D manager at Baden and the production manager at Västerås. After allowing the team to set its own goals within the framework defined by the board, Gundemark held all members accountable for achieving their results, reviewing progress every two weeks.

Due to the complexity of Revaba and the acquisition of the Westinghouse operations, the restructuring project took longer than expected. By the end of 1990, however, the new structure of ABB's worldwide relays business was emerging. Production was specialized in four global production centers, development activities in each company were coordinated by a worldwide R&D head, and local manufacturing and engineering activities were defined and legitimized in the 12 non-core relays companies around the world (see Exhibits 6 and 7).

The process linking the worldwide structure was developed and defined by scores of day-to-day decisions that continually confronted Gundemark and his BA board. Soon after the production rationalization had been implemented, for example,

---

[1]In January 1989, ABB acquired a 45% share of Westinghouse's transmission and distribution business with an option to buy the remaining 55%. The joint venture was fully integrated into the ABB. In relays, for example, Don Jans, the ex-Westinghouse relays head, joined the relays BA board now chaired by Gundemark.

EXHIBIT 6 Relays BA Organization

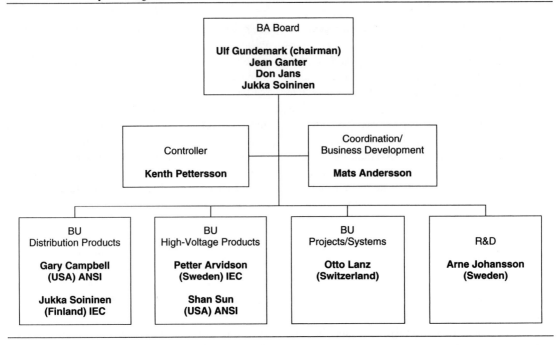

EXHIBIT 7 Relays BA Worldwide Operations

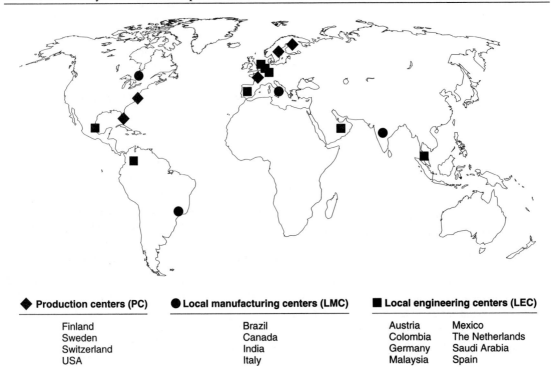

◆ **Production centers (PC)**   ● **Local manufacturing centers (LMC)**   ■ **Local engineering centers (LEC)**

Production centers (PC)	Local manufacturing centers (LMC)	Local engineering centers (LEC)	
Finland	Brazil	Austria	Mexico
Sweden	Canada	Colombia	The Netherlands
Switzerland	India	Germany	Saudi Arabia
USA	Italy	Malaysia	Spain

Gundemark found himself confronting questions about the recently negotiated allocations of export markets. The issue was raised around the Swiss company's responsibility for coordinating sales into Mexico, which earned it a markup on products sourced from other ABB relays operations. Several senior managers felt the company had to shorten the company's lines to its customers and minimize the non-value-added work in the system. Gundemark delegated the issue to a team composed of the marketing managers from the four key supply companies and asked them to develop a proposal. After considerable negotiations, the team reported to the BA board that they could not find a solution. Gundemark pushed the task back to them for further discussion and analysis. Some days later, the team indicated they had reached a majority recommendation supported by three of the four members. Again Gundemark rejected the proposal, demanding a unanimous recommendation. Finally, after three full and exhausting days of negotiation, the marketing managers decided that local companies with strong engineering capabilities should be able to order directly on any production center. Another piece of policy and structure was in place.[2]

New Organizational Structures and Processes

While he was overseeing the restructuring, Gundemark knew there would be significant coordination of operations built on a foundation of specialized yet interdependent operations. In 1989, the only effective integrating mechanism was the BA board Lindahl had established, and Gundemark was concerned that it had become a monthly forum swamped with current operating issues. He wanted to create an organization that would not only relieve this pressure, but also be truer to ABB's decentralization philosophy.

Building on an Asea practice in place for many years, Gundemark established a steering committee for each of the national relays companies. These were, in effect, small local boards with membership drawn from the local relays company, other closely related ABB units, the national holding company, and the corporate relays BA management. Two to four times a year, each steering committee met to discuss its local relays company's operating performance and long-term strategy. At the operating level, such meetings became vital forums for senior-level business and regional managers to review the operations of the local units, and to ensure that the objectives and priorities they were given to those front-line operations were consistent. To the company general managers, they offered an important opportunity to communicate key issues and problems, elicit input and support, and reconcile conflicts.

Although he was relatively new to ABB, U.S. relays general manager Don Jans was quickly becoming accustomed to ABB's collaborative team management style.[3] He found the steering committee to be a "powerful concept." In addition to himself, his relays steering committee, which met quarterly, consisted of Ulf Gundemark as the BA representative, the strategic planning manager, marketing manager, and controller from the U.S. power transmission and distribution (T&D) regional headquarters, and the general manager of the closely related network control company. It was chaired by Joe Baker, the regional ABB Power T&D head, who reported both to Göran Lindahl, his business boss, and to Gerhard Schulmeyer, the president of the U.S. holding company, ABB Inc. (See Exhibit 8 for a representation of the matrix relationships.)

Relays steering committee chairman Baker, a 39-year veteran of Westinghouse, had entered ABB via the acquisition as a self-admitted skeptic of the

---

[2]This process reflected a widespread company philosophy of resolving problems at the lowest levels. As Barnevik often told his managers, "You can escalate a problem to me once, you can escalate it to me twice, but if you escalate it three times, I will probably know it's time to replace you."

[3]As well as serving on Gundemark's relays BA Board, he was also a member of the steering committee for his own relays company, ABB's network control company in the United Sates, and for the relays subsidiaries in Canada and Puerto Rico.

EXHIBIT 8   Partial Matrix Relationships in Relays BA

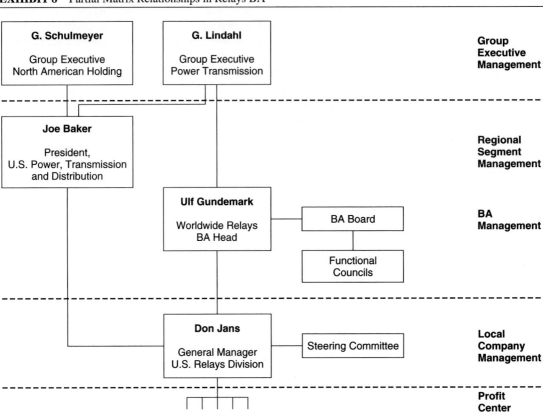

matrix organization. In 1979, Westinghouse had imposed a matrix structure on its international division and the results had been "a complete failure," according to Baker. Eventually, however, he began to acknowledge that the ABB system seemed to be working, and he reflected on the differences:

> In Westinghouse, we recruited first-class people, did an outstanding job of management development, then wasted all that investment by constraining them with a highly authoritarian structure. In ABB, we spent much of our first year thrashing out how we would work together. . . . In the end, it was this culture of delegated responsibility and intensive communication that made this organization work. . . . It was an amazing change; I felt like I'd rediscovered management after 39 years.[4]

In addition to providing local companies with more guidance, Gundemark also wanted to exploit synergies, particularly across the four core compa-

---

[4]After seeing how quickly ABB turned around a business they had struggled for years, senior management at Westinghouse invited Baker to explain how they did it. After he described the change in organization culture and management philosophy that had revitalized the business, a Westinghouse EVP said, "We can't manage with so little direction and so much conflict." Replied Baker, "That's the problem."

nies. To achieve this, he formed functional councils for R&D, total quality, and purchasing and charged each with the task of developing policy guidelines that captured "best practice." Each council was composed of specialists from several operating units, including the four major centers. They met quarterly, usually at a different site not only to expose managers to the various local practices, but also to send a clear signal to the organization. Chairpersons of the councils also rotated on an annual basis, allowing different national units to share the leadership.

All three councils were extremely successful in creating contacts among specialists in diverse geographic locations and providing them with a forum at which to share knowledge. For example, Bill Wallace, manager of total quality in the U.S. relays business, reported enthusiastically on the value created by the council on which he served:

> It's had an enormous impact. There is a lot of cross-fertilization going on. For example, we had been working on time-based management for several years and had delivered impressive reductions in cycle time and inventory levels. In 1990, a team from Finland visited Coral Springs to see what we were doing. Nine months later on a plant tour during a council meeting in Vasa, I was amazed to see how they adapted and successfully implemented our JIT and Kan Ban system.

Larry Vanduzer, Coral Springs purchasing manager, was equally proud of progress on the council on which he served:

> Because material costs can represent 35%–40% of sales value, there is huge potential for economies. Even in our first year when we were focusing mainly on developing the appropriate metrics to evaluate purchasing, we still squeezed out $1 million in cost savings. Now we work mainly on setting goals, certifying and consolidating suppliers, and sharing our learning. Each year we report back to the BA board on progress, and I'd have to say the measurement has created some healthy internal competition. Vasa reduced its lead time to an average 10-day delivery, and we want to challenge them!

New Strategic Process

Having delegated most operating responsibilities to the steering committees, Gundemark wanted to change the role of the BA board to a quarterly forum for discussing strategy, policies, and overall objective-setting. In introducing this longer-term focus, he was determined not to make strategic planning the hollow exercise he had both seen and experienced:

> I wanted to sweep aside a lot of the old assumptions about strategy we inherited from the 1970s and 1980s—that it was defined primarily by top management, that it was communicated through confidential copies kept in locked files, and that it was updated annually, but usually without challenging the underlying assumptions or objectives. I wanted it to become a process that involved all levels of management, was widely communicated, and constantly open to challenge.

In March 1990, he formed a nine-person task force with members drawn from the high-potential middle managers of companies in Brazil, Germany, Finland, the United States, Sweden, and Switzerland, and charged them with the task of creating a clear vision for the relays BA. He set the tone by raising sensitive but important questions that he knew the team would have to confront if they were to develop a worthwhile proposal: How well are each of the companies implementing their new organizational responsibilities? Are we becoming too short-term focused? Is there too much of a Swedish bias in our management? He urged them to be bold, direct, and creative in taking a completely fresh look at the business, and to report back to the BA board in six months.

In September, propelled by a request from Göran Lindahl for a clear global relays strategy by year's end, the BA board heard the group's presentation, which proposed a broad vision focused on seven core elements of the relays business future development (total quality, customer focus, technology, human assets, organization, image, and growth). With further input and refinement by the BA management team, the task force's broad conclusions were developed into a 24-page document titled "Strategy 2000." Once approved, Strategy 2000 was formally unveiled at a worldwide relays management meeting and, within weeks, communicated to the entire organization via specially prepared materials and presentations (see Exhibit 9 for an overview).

Lindahl saw his role in the strategic process as much more than the approver of formal business plans such as the one developed by Gundemark's team. He saw strategy as an ongoing part of management and used his bi-monthly transmission segment management meetings to shape the strategic thinking of his key executives. Here he not only reviewed current performance, but also challenged his nine BA heads (like Gundemark) and 10 major regional managers (like Baker) to stretch their thinking. He would present them with issues such as environmental legislation, trade barriers, or north-south political conflicts and ask them to develop scenarios for how such issues might affect their businesses and how they might deal with the changes. "I try to make such exercises fun," he said, "but you always have to be thinking a little bit ahead."

New Systems and Controls

Throughout this period of orienting and restructuring, Gundemark and other BA managers in the power transmission segment were constantly being reminded by Lindahl not to let the internal changes distract the organization from the marketplace. The historic performance of ABB's various relays units was mixed, with the portfolio of profits and losses about equalizing each other at the time of the merger. After 1989, his big challenge would be to get consistent profitability across all operations, while building an organization that could leverage the restructured business.

With ABACUS in place, budgeting had become a serious and demanding process. In May, Lindahl and his staff prepared a tentative broad gauge budget by BA and by region for the following year. The BA and regional managers in turn allocated their proposed breakdowns to the local company level. By August, a bottom-up response was returned to the corporate office, where it was consolidated and tested. Lindahl would identify gaps or concerns and contact the local manager and the BA head to challenge and negotiate, typically asking what additional support

---

EXHIBIT 9   Relays BA Strategy 2000: Excerpts and Overview

Vision

Our vision is to contribute to a better living standard for the world by producing technically advanced products which are essential to ensure the safe and reliable supply of electric power.

Key Concepts (Excerpts)
- We must communicate our organization, vision, strategy, and results to all employees and tie their activities to the BA goals.
- Employees must feel they have jobs with personal development opportunities and team spirit.
- We will expand . . . through aggressive marketing, refined segmentation . . . and innovative sales concepts.
- Management will communicate a commitment to total quality . . . and we will improve total performance through systematic measurement and analysis of key elements of total quality.
- We will make customer focus plans and follow performance to bring the customer focus culture to all employees.
- We will create a team spirit and make teamwork the method for working together.
- We will push responsibility and authority to the operational level.
- We will have volume growth of 6% per annum and a return on capital employed of 40%.
- We will reduce product development cycle times to one year by 1994.
- Will develop COMSYS as a evolutionary process for creating modular, locally acceptable products using common tools, methods, and design.

Source: Company documents.

they needed to reach the proposed target. It was a communications-intensive process.

Throughout the year, Lindahl tracked the monthly results, and with the help of his controller, tried to identify trends or uncover problems. He had no problem in reaching across levels in the formal organization to check up on emerging problems. Typically, he asked managers "What went wrong? What are you doing about it? What can we do to help?" This ongoing awareness of current business developments and involvement in key decisions throughout the organization was what Lindahl described as "fingers in the pie" management:

> Many companies, particularly in the United States, have evolved towards a kind of abstract management approach with senior executives controlling operations through sophisticated systems. I try to deal directly with the critical issues and the people managing them, and that means I need to put my hands on major changes. Even if I'm wrong, I need to initiate the change, to shake things up, to create an environment of learning. Once that process is initiated, it gains its own momentum.

At the BA level, Gundemark also exploited the new system by supplementing the broad budgeting process with more tailored reporting formats which he selected from the 30 measures tracked by ABACUS. For example, he created a Relays Performance League, which rank-ordered the companies on the basis of their quarterly gross margin, expenses, inventory, and net income percentages. In an effort to motivate managers to seek out best practice, the comparative data was circulated to all relays profit centers, and an award was given for the best overall performance of the year (see Exhibit 10). Those on the bottom of the league table desperately sought out ways to improve their standing, seeking input and support from their higher-ranked colleagues.

But Gundemark emphasized that Göran Lindahl was constantly asking him questions and proposing targets that were not measured by the formal systems. He commented:

> ABACUS is fine, but it can only provide historical financial information. To manage the business properly—and to respond to questions from Göran—

I need to be able to anticipate problems and understand alternative courses of corrective action. And that requires a strong personal management network. We work intensely at that!

Management Challenges

At the end of 1991, Göran Lindahl seemed satisfied with the record that the relays BA had racked up in its first four years. The restructuring of assets and resources had largely been accomplished, and with help of the new operating systems and controls, current performance had been greatly improved. From 1988, when half the relays companies were losing money, within four years all 16 major companies worldwide were contributing to the significantly improved profits. Return on capital employed had almost doubled.

As in most other businesses, ABB's relays management was still trying to fine-tune both its strategy and its organization. In Coral Springs, for example, Don Jans was proud of his unit's achievement since becoming part of ABB: revenues were up 45%, on-time shipments had jumped from 70% to 99%, cycle time had been cut by 70% and inventories had been slashed by 40%. But he was still adjusting to life in a matrix and the conflicts that it created. In particular, he was wrestling with Comsys, a BA-sponsored project to create a common product platform.

Adjusting the New Organization

Although Jans was enthusiastic about the opportunities created by ABB's unique organization structure and management philosophy, he was also becoming increasingly aware of the difficulties of making it work effectively. While acknowledging that ABB's matrix organization brought his relays business much more attention and support than it had received in the old Westinghouse hierarchy, he was becoming aware that the process of obtaining such commitments could often be difficult and frustrating:

> This kind of structure becomes frustrating when your two bosses' priorities don't coincide. For example, we recently got strong support from Gundemark to invest in people to push forward our long-term

---

EXHIBIT 10 Relays BA Performance League: Letter to Local BA Managers

---

February 22, 1991

Dear Friends:

BA Performance League: Actual, 1990

First of all, congratulations on a very successful year. As you know, we exceeded the budget for orders received, revenues, and earnings after financial items (EAFI). This year we reached an important milestone—having all Relays operations contributing with positive earnings.

Congratulations to Attila Magyar and his team in Austria. They have won the 1990 Performance League, outperforming the budget on three of the four measures. . . . The prize, a Minolta camera, will be presented at the next Steering Committee meeting.

- Digging into the year's results, we recognize:
- 67% of the units achieved over-budget gross margins. Good!
- 80% of the units beat their budgets in EAFI. Excellent!
- Only 40% of the units, however, have been able to keep S&A costs below budget.
- And only two countries reached their budgeted inventory and receivable goals.

We are concerned about these developments on the cost and capital side. . . . We suggest that these items be brought up at your next Steering Committee meetings, and that targets and action plans be agreed on so we can together break these negative trends.

Finally, thank you once again for a very positive year. We look forward to a 1991 as successful as 1990.

Yours sincerely,

Ulf Gundemark

Position	Gross Margin (%) (Rank)		S&A/ Revenues (%) (Rank)		Inv. & Rec./ Revenues (%) (Rank)		EAFI/ Revenues (%) (Rank)		Total Points (Ranking)	
1. Austria	35,3	(02)	15,2	(05)	38,5	(06)	20,0	(02)	15	(1)
2. Finland	32,0	(04)	18,9	(06)	41,8	(08)	17,3	(03)	21	(2)
3. Canada	30,9	(05)	19,4	(08)	28,6	(02)	14,4	(07)	22	(3)
4. Allentown	43,3	(01)	29,4	(15)	38,0	(05)	20,1	(01)	22	(4)
5. Spain	29,5	(06)	13,7	(04)	48,6	(09)	17,2	(04)	23	(5)
6. Coral Springs	35,1	(03)	23,3	(14)	31,7	(04)	15,2	(06)	27	(6)
7. Mexico	21,5	(14)	13,0	(03)	12,1	(01)	12,2	(11)	29	(7)
8. Brazil	28,4	(08)	19,4	(08)	56,3	(10)	15,8	(05)	31	(8)
9. Germany	25,1	(11)	19,3	(07)	28,6	(02)	6,9	(13)	33	(9)
10. Saudi Arabia	23,7	(13)	11,2	(02)	87,9	(14)	14,1	(08)	37	(10)
11. Sweden	25,4	(10)	19,9	(11)	41,1	(07)	13,3	(10)	28	(11)
12. Italy	28,7	(07)	20,0	(12)	78,9	(13)	13,6	(09)	41	(12)
13. India	12,1	(15)	8,0	(01)	124,9	(15)	6,9	(13)	44	(13)
14. Netherlands	26,6	(09)	21,1	(13)	68,2	(12)	8,1	(12)	46	(14)
15. Switzerland	25,0	(12)	19,7	(10)	62,2	(11)	5,7	(15)	48	(15)

Note: All figures from ABACUS.

technical development priorities, but Joe Baker says he needs current operating profit and has crunched down on our proposed development funds. I'm not sure where we will end up, but right now it's confusing and frustrating.

Joe Baker agreed that the situation was frustrating, but felt that such negotiations were inevitable:

At Ulf Gundemark's urging, Don asked for approval for $1.5 million for new hires in product development, and at the time I indicated it looked OK. But I live in the matrix too, and when our regional transmission performance started slipping behind budget, I started hearing from Lindahl and Schulmeyer. Don understands that if one business is down, another one has to step up to the plate. I didn't tell him he had to cut R&D, but I did ask him to help with our shortfall.

Well, Don got really mad and wrote me a strong letter. In Westinghouse he probably would have been removed, but here we encourage people to kick back. I didn't like it, but I'm glad he did it. In the end, I talked to Ulf and suggested that if he really wanted the R&D done, maybe he could support it out of Sweden.

The issue arose again at the next Steering Committee Meeting for Jans's U.S. relays company. After further debate, Gundemark agreed to transfer two Swedish technical managers to Coral Springs to initiate Jans's program. In turn, Baker agreed to include the increased development expenditure in the next year's budget.

The Comsys Challenge

Although Jans was very supportive of ABB's philosophy of coordinating key strategy decisions across national boundaries, he had serious concerns about a major BA development project known as the common systems (or Comsys) project. Soon after announcing its formation in 1990, Gundemark challenged the relays R&D council to develop a common platform for future product development across units. As he described the problem:

Despite our coordination and specialization, we are still too compartmentalized. We are captives of our history, and each company tries to position and

protect itself by creating products for its assigned markets. Rather than emphasizing differences in the needs across the European, American, and developing countries markets, we need to develop a common base of hardware and software that can be adapted to local needs and individual customers.

To implement the Comsys project, a cross-country team was formed consisting of two technical experts from each of the four major centers. By early 1992, the nine sub-project teams were still hammering out the details of product design, operating standards, and overall project implementation, and the feeling was that they were years away from having tangible results. Because most local development had been curtailed to focus resources on Comsys, the grumblings of many front-line profit center managers were becoming more audible. Said Gundemark:

It was essential to get middle managers from the various countries involved rather than doing this centrally, even if it does slow things down. But these missionaries are confronting the old views back in their home organizations and are having a hard time selling the new ideas. It may mean we lose some time initially, but we will gain that back multiplied when we get everyone pulling in the same direction.

Don Jans felt that the Comsys problem was not only polluting his team's growing feeling of independent initiative, it was also compromising his unit's current performance by holding up local development projects. Yet he felt conflicted about his response. Should he wear his BA board member's hat and tell his managers to buckle down and make the project work? Or should he put on his company general manager's hat and defend the interests of his Coral Springs profit centers and ask Gundemark for relief from Comsys to focus more local resources back on projects to meet the immediate market needs?

The Future

As Jans prepared for the quarterly BA board meeting in early 1992, he drafted a "balance sheet" of achievements and challenges that would become the basis of a presentation he would make to his colleagues on the relays integration process to date (Exhibit 11). He was pleasantly surprised with the length of the asset side of his balance sheet but realized that most management attention needed to be focused on the "liabilities" side. Jans wondered what the company could do to deal with the kinds of problems he faced. It was a concern that was shared by Ulf Gundemark and Göran Lindahl.

EXHIBIT 11   Evaluation of Relays BA Integration: Excerpts from Don Jan's Presentation to BA Board, February 1992

Success Elements	*Areas for Strengthening*
• Clear vision and expectations from the top	• Tension between BA and country management (long-term vs. short-term)
• Responsibility push down—consensus teams not "top down"	• Internal competition (marketing and technology)
• Good collaborative managers without strong egos—mutual respect	• Profit center concept creates unmet resource needs—psychological impact
• Strong ethic of "what/how/deadline"	• Tension between meeting operating objectives and participating in time-consuming integration processes
• Synergy through integrating devices (Boards, Councils, Centers of Excellence)	• Barriers to technology sharing
• Linking world capability (market access, technology, etc.) to become world class	• Still resistance to lead centers taking leadership in market/business planning
• Best practices-internal benchmarking—internal competition	• Reduce inventories through better support of engineering centers, reduce lead time, and on-time shipments
• Key program as share knowledge, provide focus (TQM, TMB, Supplier Partnering, Customer Focus, etc.)	• Need more people exchanges through benchmarking
• Constant communication	

Case 8–4   Managing Change in the Computer Industry: The Case of Siemens Nixdorf Information Systems

In 1990, when the merger of Nixdorf Computer and the computer division of Siemens was announced, Siemens Nixdorf Information Systems (SNI)—the newly formed German computer giant—raised great hopes. With sales of DM 12 billion and 51,000 employees, SNI fused Siemens' strengths in the mainframe market with Nixdorf's outstanding midrange systems and software solutions; Siemens' customer list of loyal, large corporations with Nixdorf's strong hold on medium and small enterprises; and Siemens' strong organisational discipline with Nixdorf's entrepreneurial spirit and innovative flair. To most observers, it was a marriage made in heaven.

By 1994, however, the marriage had turned into a nightmare. None of the anticipated synergies had materialised, and the difficulties of integrating two very different cultures had combined with a worldwide recession and upheavals in the computer

EXHIBIT 1   Siemens Nixodrf Financial Results for 1991–1996

	1991	1992	1993	1994	1995	1996
Sales (DM millions)						
Germany	7,500	8,400	7,800	7,600	8,300	8,500
International	4,600	4,600	4,100	4,100	4,500	4,100
Worldwide	12,100	13,000	11,900	11,700	12,800	12,600
Capital Expenditure	809	860	493	505	838	749
R&D expenditure	1,700	1,600	1,400	1,200	1,100	900
Net Results	(781)	513	(419)	(350)	23	29
Employees (in thousands)						
Germany	37.6	35.3	31.9	28.7	26.0	24.2
International	14.0	13.1	11.4	10.4	11.2	9.9
Worldwide	51.6	48.4	43.3	39.1	37.2	34.1

industry to produce a constant and growing flow of red ink. SNI had lost money each year, with cumulative losses during the 1990–1994 period reaching a staggering DM 2.1 billion (see Exhibit 1).

It was at this stage that the company hired Gerhard Schulmeyer as its new CEO. A high-tech veteran with stints at companies such as Motorola and Asea Brown Boveri (ABB) behind him, Schulmeyer was viewed as SNI's last great hope of survival. Between 1994 and 1997, he drove through a series of drastic changes, not only in the company's strategy, organisation and work systems, but also in its fundamental managerial philosophy and corporate culture. A stream of actions and initiatives designed to bludgeon a German bureaucracy into an entrepreneurial international company clearly signalled top management's commitment to radical change.

By 1997, these actions had brought about one of Europe's more visible and radical changes in corporate fortunes. The haemorrhage of red ink had been staunched and the company returned to at least modest profitability. The SNI organisation had been fundamentally reshaped and employee satisfaction scores had significantly improved. The business portfolio had been restructured, to place much greater emphasis on the software, solutions and con-

sulting activities. On the negative side, however, the change process was still top-driven and the anticipated bottom-up response had not yet emerged. Young change agents, inspired by Schulmeyer's programs, did not always find the support needed to put their own initiatives into effect. In many quarters resistance to change was still strong.

This case tells the story of SNI's struggle with transformation through the eyes and the experiences of three people. At the top of the organisation, we follow Schulmeyer as he tirelessly stirs up the organisation, creates change initiatives and challenges people to rethink not only the direction, strategy and structure of the company, but also their own behaviour and willingness to change. Just below the CEO, we see the implications and outcomes of Schulmeyer's initiatives through the eyes of Robert Hoog, head of the Middleware division, as he tries to bring about change in his group, leveraging the top-down forces where possible and protecting his organisation from those forces where necessary. Finally, at the frontline, we focus on Klaus Karl, a young software engineer and member of a three-man strategic planning team in the Middleware division as he deals with the various change initiatives and processes, trying to find a way to contribute, yet facing all the uncertainty and swings that such a change effort inevitably creates, especially at the bottom of the pyramid.

We begin, however, with a brief introduction to the information industry, and the challenges to which SNI needed to respond.

The Computer Industry

Between the mid-1980s and the mid-1990s, the computer industry had gone through dramatic changes, which had turned the information highway into a dangerous winding road full of treacherous turns. Several major players teetered on the brink of collapse, IBM and DEC among them, while new participants quickly emerged to play commanding roles. None of the major industry names were immune to the processes of restructuring, downsizing and business refocusing.

The single most important cause of the information industry's transformation was the explosive rise of the personal computer (PC). During the mainframe era, the traditional "centralised" computing model had dominated the corporate workplace. In this model, information was stored in a central database and managed by a single powerful computer. The end-user could access information through "dumb" terminals with limited processing capabilities. Several generations of IBM mainframes epitomized this kind of computing. The personal computer, with its ability not only to store user-specific information but also to perform complicated processing tasks and share information with other network users changed all that. As the industrial worker slowly made room for the knowledge worker, so the "centralized" computing model gave way to the "distributed" version, fuelling new technological demands. As the knowledge content of tasks increased, employees required more flexible and powerful tools which could be quickly tailored to support their needs. Flexibility and customisation were central to the rising population of flat organisations where responsibilities were pushed down the hierarchical ladder. Furthermore, in these new flat organisational models, teamwork and project-based problem-solving were central, mandating shared knowledge, collective decisions, and ultimately a

networked organisation supporting dynamic information links between employees. Connectivity within intra-company networks and Internet access, as well as flexibility at the user level, gained importance rapidly.

Alongside the shift in product demand from mainframe to PC, another powerful trend emerged. With increasing complexity in both technology and the decisions it supported, corporations increasingly looked to buy custom solutions to problems rather than products. In response, computer companies found themselves pushed to become solution providers and ultimately suppliers of professional services and organisational consulting rather than the hardware manufacturers they had been in the past.

The changing patterns of demand had significant implications for the economics of the computer industry. Mainframes had proprietary architectures, were expensive to buy and required constant maintenance. This implied high margins at sales time and a steady cash flow over the maintenance period. On the other hand, the personal computer had a standardised architecture, cost much less, and was easy to make and copy. It was inevitably becoming a commodity.

At the same time the demand for increased processing power and connectivity shifted value from the computer manufacturers to the producers of the underlying microprocessors and the software. In the battle among those producers for the *de facto* PC standard, Intel and Microsoft emerged as the winners.

The growing importance of networks and services gave rise to new opportunities. The development of client/server architectures and the Internet boom opened up new battlefields, where many players fought to establish new industry standards. New types of services blossomed: network installation, network management and network consulting, among others.

Faced with shifts in demand, transformed value chains and reduced margins, computer manufacturers were obliged to revise their strategies. As production shifted from mainframes to higher volumes of medium-power machines—used as servers in networks—and personal computers, cost reduction became crucial. Development of the network and other services also gained importance.

Globalization, too, was critical. On the supply side, companies wanted to reduce labour and supply costs while staying close to innovation centres like the United States. On the demand side, they needed to develop branding, satisfy client demand for global services and increase volumes and market power critical for alliance negotiations.

Alliances became more important as strategic devices. Creation of alliances, with either microprocessor and software producers to bundle together product offerings, or with communication companies to provide more global networking solutions, was vital to market share. In industry thinking, the ability of an IT provider to gain partnership status with big players ranked as a significant source of competitive advantage.

These radical changes in the computer industry served as both midwife to the birth of SNI and source of much of the turmoil the company faced since its inception.

From a Dream to a Nightmare: SNI 1990–1994

When Siemens announced the merger of its Data and Information Systems division with Nixdorf Computer in January 1990, the union brought together the two leading companies in the German and, indeed, European computer industries.

Gracefully old but slow-moving, Siemens was Germany's largest employer, a traditional organisation whose origins went back more than a century. Its computer division was market leader in mainframes in its home market with its proprietary system BS2000. It was also the leader in UNIX-based servers. In 1990 the business was deemed to be a cash cow, having stable revenues of DM 7.7 billion but few prospects for future growth.

Younger and more agile, Nixdorf was an entrepreneurial organisation focused on mid-range systems for medium to small enterprises. Founded in 1952 in a cellar by Heinz Nixdorf, its culture and values seemed closer to a Silicon Valley start-up than a German manufacturer. During its infancy and adolescence it achieved rapid growth and large

profits by developing turnkey hardware and software. However, in the late 1980s, it failed to keep up with key emerging technologies and, stung by a sudden but strong European recession, began posting losses. When these losses swelled to DM 1 billion in 1990, it became clear that the company had no long-term future on its own.

The merger seemed to have all the ingredients for success. Potential benefits included more than just size. On the strategic side, the two companies were entirely complementary, promising a very broad product range as well as increased resources to develop new offerings. Organisationally, SNI would combine the discipline and structure of Siemens with the entrepreneurial spirit and innovation of Nixdorf.

In reality, none of the promises materialised. *The Wall Street Journal* labelled the merger a "management nightmare." The cultures clashed violently. The combined organisational structure proved full of duplications and inconsistencies while the complementary products created conflicts rather than synergies. Indeed, the comprehensive product range seemed to be a weakness as SNI, spreading its efforts across many products, failed to compete effectively with leaner and more focused competitors. The situation was accentuated by a world-wide recession and the radical demand shifts of the computer industry. Sales in 1993 were lower than in 1991 and they fell further in 1994 (Exhibit 1). The company put in place extensive programs to cut costs and improve both efficiency and product quality. Reorganisations were frequent. "Lucky is he who is not reorganised at least once a year," was a slogan common among managers. Headcount was cut steadily each year, from 51,600 employees in 1991 to 39,200 in 1994. All these efforts were in vain however. The company could not achieve profitability, and by 1994 SNI was posting an annual loss of DM 350 million. In October that year, Gerhard Schulmeyer was appointed CEO, with the mission to turn the company around.

In 1994, that was a tall order. SNI's rigid structure made it hard to manoeuvre in fast-paced information markets. At a time when globalization was becoming increasingly important, 65% of SNI's sales still came from Germany, hardly the world's most dynamic IT market. Meanwhile, the trend toward solution businesses, boosted by the increasing complexity of client/server architectures and network design, had caught the company on the hop. The company was still highly focused on products, and the skills and attitudes of people could not easily be adapted to the value chain required by the new type of business.

On the cultural front not much had changed either. In the four years that had passed since the merger of two very different companies, SNI, still divided between ex-Siemens and ex-Nixdorf people, had been unable to develop its own unified culture. Adding to a mountain of problems was low employee morale. In the absence of profits, people were beginning to fall into a "losers" mindset, lacking confidence in themselves and in the future of their firm.

Driving Change from the Top:
Gerhard Schulmeyer

As the new captain, Gerhard Schulmeyer had a mandate to restore the company to profitability and reposition it as a major competitor in the global information industry. During his career, Schulmeyer had had firsthand experience of major corporate transformation efforts, both structural and cultural, not least as a senior manager at Asea Brown Boveri (ABB) and Motorola when each of these companies was in the midst of radical change.

Within the crisis-ridden and bleeding SNI, Schulmeyer could see some key strengths for the future. As a European company with access to a highly skilled work force, SNI was uniquely positioned to develop into the European partner of choice in the information industry. While SNI had ground to make up in shifting its emphasis from manufacturing to providing services, the IT service business was less global in its structure than hardware which meant that its intimate knowledge of the European environment gave it a precious opportunity. In Schulmeyer's words:

There was not much around in the way of European computer manufacturers capable of mounting a long-term serious challenge, so there was a serious opportunity to generate a platform as a leading European competitor. As computers would more and more go to complete solutions, I thought we could develop a unique positioning, in which we could integrate computer sciences with the application of management processes by having an understanding of the local environment, the local industry and the particularities of the European way of doing business, . . .

Between broadly defining the strategy and delivering actual results lay the challenge of putting SNI on its feet. Very few European companies had attempted anything so ambitious. From a regional IT provider SNI aspired to become global, with revenues evenly split between Germany, the rest of Europe and the rest of the world. Its product base would shift from hardware and software to a portfolio of 50% products and 50% services. A traditional German hierarchy would have to transform itself into a lean international entrepreneurial organisation in which responsibility was pushed down to the lowest possible levels.

Initial Actions

As soon as he set foot in SNI's Munich headquarters, Schulmeyer established a highly visible presence within the company. His style exemplified willingness to listen, encouraged frank communication and radiated determination to act. His arrival was quickly regarded by many people as the "last chance the company would have to become profitable." Although some of the ideas that he put forward were not new to employees, they were communicated with a vision, energy, openness and authority that many found to be inspirational. Dressed simply and speaking slowly but precisely, he seemed to have the ability to instill passion and hope, especially in the younger generation. He spent a large part of his early weeks talking to employees and to customers, digging deep into the culture and management style of SNI:

During the first quarter I walked around and talked to people. I met 7,000 people and 50 customers. Understanding how they perceived the company, what they thought the rules of the game were in the company, to understanding what is behaviourally and structurally different to the U.S. high-tech companies I was used to. As I talked to people, I started to get a lot of discussions of the different management styles . . . The Europeans, and specifically Germans, are highly influenced by the value systems of an industrial economy. It is very much a manufacturing, engineering type of culture. For example, in Germany you get told never to give up. In software this is very dangerous. If you know you are wrong, it is better to stop and start something new. It is clear that the current knowledge-based industry has different rules from an industrial-based one, so we had to discuss things and see whether we could change the company's capabilities, to adapt them to the industry we were in.

As this shows, Schulmeyer believed that the evolution from an industrial to a knowledge-based economy had major implications for the computer industry. With markets changing in a matter of days, the ability to quickly reconfigure value chains was a competitive sine qua non. Only a decentralised network organisation could handle such quick changes in competitive posture.

> Not only do markets change fast, but the information content required to complete the transactions is very high. The best way to handle this is a network organisation, because you can generate core competencies and design it so that people know where in the organisation to find the competency required for a particular value chain and can network to bring it together. Designing monolithic organisations to maximise efficiency in single value chains is obsolete. Decentralisation in units is necessary and easy to do, but hardwiring the units to produce value is more difficult.

The Transformation Model

An acclaimed lecturer at MIT, Schulmeyer had his own transformation model to apply (see Exhibit 2). He calculated that SNI's radical change requirements could only be met holistically, addressing structure, systems, behaviour and philosophy. A major cultural shift was needed to support the com-

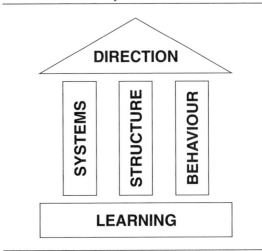

EXHIBIT 2   Schulmeyer's Transformation Model

munications and behavioural requirements of a decentralised structure that left more responsibility to lower managerial levels. Once behaviour had changed and the organisational capabilities improved, it would be possible to establish a dialogue with employees and managers on the direction and purpose of the company. The whole effort had to be underpinned by a continuous learning process for both individuals and the organisation itself. As Schulmeyer explained:

> I had a much firmer opinion when I walked in on how to change organisational capabilities than on what the final direction should be for the company. For the direction and purpose, I wanted to involve the people much more. But to get them involved, I knew I had to change the behavioural and structural capabilities of the company first. Otherwise I would have had no dialogue with them.

The five pillars of Schulmeyer's transformation model were:

Behaviour:

> A 'Culture Change' program in the form of a set of mutually reinforcing initiatives to encourage new behaviours and support the development of new capabilities.

EXHIBIT 3   Change Program Roadmap

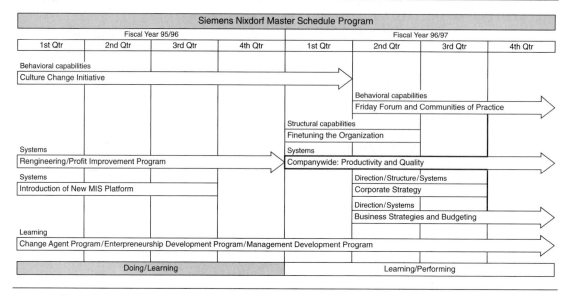

Structure:

To start the long process of transforming SNI into a network organisation, the first step was the definition of a matrix in which the company was broken down into small business units with P&L responsibility and autonomy in the formulation of business strategy.

Systems:

New systems had to provide easy communication and detailed data to support decision making and knowledge sharing within the new structure.

Direction:

A new baselining process would give responsibility for business strategy to the business unit managers. Once clear and sustainable strategies were adopted at the level of the business units, a company vision could be identified, which would be the base for defining the corporate strategy.

Learning:

Substantial resources would be committed to a comprehensive development program for individuals and processes to assist organisational learning, such as scenario planning.

As soon as Schulmeyer had completed his tour of employees and customers he set up a team to design a comprehensive culture-change program. A roadmap (Exhibit 3) was created and published, and execution set in motion immediately in October 1994.

Behaviour: The Culture Change Program

Hanover Events.   The initiative with the most symbolic significance were the four Hanover events, each involving a large number of employees from different parts of the organisation. Hanover I was the first large public event in which employees assembled to discuss the future of SNI and work to change the organisation. Thirty facilitators worked with 400 employees to develop 19 critical renewal topics. The discussions led to the establishment of 60 action teams, with agendas that required tangible results within 90 days.

While Hanover I focused on employees, Hanover II concentrated on customers. Representatives from 50 major customers attended the event, along with 300 employees and 75 senior managers. The customers joined the action teams, which this time addressed problems related to the company's customer orientation. Hanover III brought corporate partners into the action teams. The last event, Hanover IV, took place in October 1996, with a presentation by Schulmeyer on the need to change from a matrix organisation to a network organisation. Again, teams were formed with the aim to improve processes and quality.

The Hanover meetings were designed to help people learn new patterns of behaviour. Instead of the typical hierarchical distinctions, first names were the rule and everyone was free to intervene in the discussions. This atmosphere deeply affected participants, who returned to their day-to-day activities motivated and fired up with a new sense of mission. However, the sceptics and those who didn't attend provided a real barrier to change. In the words of one non-attender:

> People came back from Hanover as if they were brainwashed. They seemed in a kind of trance, full of confidence that now they could change everything. When I met these colleagues later in meetings, I didn't notice any real difference in their behaviour.

In addition, to the many employees who did not participate, the Hanover meetings created a sense of exclusion. Nevertheless, the events provided some very public opportunities for interaction between employees and senior managers. A manager recounted how in one discussion a woman publicly questioned Schulmeyer's sincerity. The CEO invited her to staff his office for three months to see for herself what was really happening at top level. The story served as a vivid demonstration of the CEO's commitment to transparency.

Friday Forums

Whereas the Hanover meetings were large and one-off public events, Friday Forums were an attempt to build a frank and open communication environment within the fabric of the organisation. Any topic could be brought to the meetings, from day-to-day problems to 'hot potatoes' which involved employees from all levels of the company. Information exchanged in the forums were broadcast more widely throughout the organisation via a fortnightly electronic mail. In addition to sharing information, employees were encouraged to form small groups to act on issues raised in the meetings.

Even though this initiative was vigorously sponsored by top management, commitment to Friday Forums among managers varied and some employees were never involved. The effects of the initiative were also limited by the unwillingness of some managers to open up their meetings to employees from other 'areas' of the company, thus hindering information flow.

Structure

"I am a proponent of the concept of globalization by distributing headquarters power which I first tried in Motorola," explained Schulmeyer of his structural ambitions. "I believe in extreme decentralisation. SNI had been a regional organisation, a single huge profit centre, with centralised responsibility and of course risk. It had been built by regions because relationship was everything in selling mainframes. It was a religious decision to choose a service provider, as you were stuck with him for life. Now with open architecture units and low switching costs, the structure had to change to a new architecture, where everything, from R&D to the last salesman, would be run by the lines of business. From a European regional organisation SNI had to become a worldwide line of businesses organisation. We looked at how to build something that would eventually lead to a network organisation and decided on a matrix, which is nothing else but a pre-configured network with only two major communication lines."

In October 1995, building on some earlier work, the company reorganised into a two-dimensional matrix structure. On one axis, as lines of business, the company's products, solutions and services would be managed globally. Each of the 10 lines of business was headed by a single manager, responsible for creating world-wide capabilities and competencies. On the other geographical axis, every region had a regional head. At the intersection points of the

EXHIBIT 4   Graphical Representation of SNI's Matrix Organisation

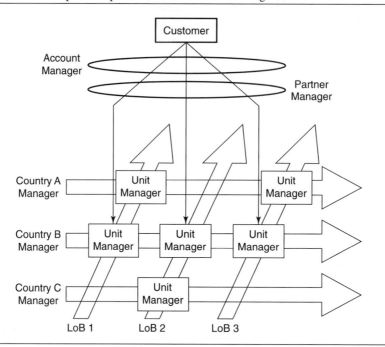

matrix lay 250 business units with full profit-and-loss responsibility (Exhibit 4).

To maintain a single face to the customers, superimposed on each region was a set of account managers, one for each key account. Account managers had no staff support or line authority, but they could draw resources from different parts of the organisation to fulfil special customer requirements.

Systems: Building the "Nervous System"

If the matrix structure constituted the backbone of the organisation, the systems represented its nervous system, serving the vital function of transmitting information across the company. A new state-of-the-art systems architecture mapped the organisation's core processes, such as order processing, materials management and accounting, updating critical data from the 250 business units every month. Managers within the same line of business had access to each other's financial figures. The Ex-

ecutive Board and top management had access to consolidated figures across business lines.

The number of employees connected to the Intranet or e-mail also rose rapidly. By 1997 more than 25,000 employees had access to the service, while data traffic increased exponentially. Schulmeyer himself encouraged people to send him personal mails.

Direction: Baselining as a New Way of Defining and Implementing Business Strategy

Before the transformation, SNI's planning process was based on a standard questionnaire, sent out every year to all Siemens divisions. Planning specialists completed the questionnaires, after which senior management's gentle touch massaged the figures into presentable shape. Business managers were not obliged to commit to deliver the planned results.

As a part of the transformation effort, a new strategic planning process was introduced, called

Business Baselining. In this process, each line of business was responsible for identifying the key value drivers in its business before developing business strategies. Baselining also involved the preparation of a set of financial forecasts to which business managers had to commit and for which they were accountable.

Baselining provoked some scepticism among participating employees, many of them believing that the new procedures were a harbinger of further workforce reductions.

Learning: Developing People

Changing people's behaviour was critical to the success of the transformation. Without new values and behaviours, SNI would probably not have survived. However, equally important was that both individuals and the organisation as a whole possess the skills and processes needed to implement change and assume new responsibilities. Learning thus comprised two elements. The first and most difficult related to the company's culture. People had to learn how to learn and make it a lifelong process. The second element was the challenge of learning specific skills. Development programs were designed to give both a signal of commitment to change and, at the same time, to help individuals develop the skills required by the new company.

Three main initiatives were launched under the banner of the Change Agent Program. Each year 20 promising young managers were selected to join a three-month tailored management-development program at MIT's Sloan School of Management in the United States. Designed as an intensive mini-MBA, the program aimed to give participants the management skills to operate as internal consultants. On graduation, they would act as catalysts for change, working on high-profile projects. To participate in the program, an employee had to define a project and attract both a business and an executive leader as sponsors.

Meanwhile, an Executive Development Program (EDP), carried out in collaboration with several business schools, was aimed at providing middle managers with skills in finance, strategy and other management disciplines to underpin their new P&L responsibilities. Finally, under the Entrepreneurship program, owners of selected promising ideas were vested with resources (both capital and training) to develop them into realities.

Results

After two and a half years of Culture Change, the employee survey in 1996 still showed high resistance to change (Exhibit 5). People remained fearful of the future and for losing their job prospects. Schulmeyer admitted:

> What I underestimated was the resistance to change, and that generated a totally wrong hype. You got tremendous pockets of different belief systems. So you would get enthusiastic people on one side, and on the other side people for whom this was the worst thing that could have happened. One of the lowest improvements was willingness to change—only a 9% change since 1994. On the other hand, we have higher scores for people expressing their opinion. So it's not that there are any secret agendas. It's people who are scared of change. It is difficult to pass on our ideas; communication channels are broken at some points. We now look at feedback mechanisms and managing the organisation as a human organisation rather than a value chain.

Underlying these reactions was an even more fundamental issue: "In Europe now the issue is the belief in the social institutions. Earlier when things turned rough for everyone, losses piled up, people still believed that the institutions could help them. Now they are at a loss and do not know what to do so they turn to the boss for help."

There were positive signs in other aspects, however. "We are considered a major player now," Schulmeyer pointed out. "We manage to recruit good people. In the beginning we had the image of a loser. Now people are excited about what is happening here. Competitors also lure away our staff. This is not such bad news for us. Our experience with change is considered an asset in the market as companies want to know how to deal with it."

EXHIBIT 5 SNI Employee Survey Results

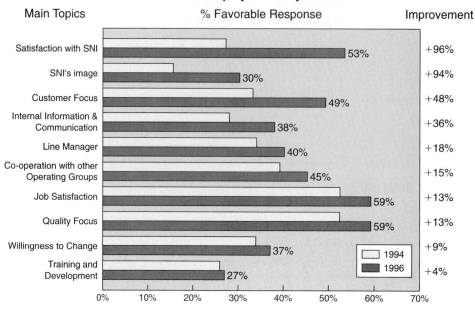

Behavioral Changes
1996 Employee Survey Results

Main Topics	% Favorable Response	Improvement

- Satisfaction with SNI — 53% — +96%
- SNI's image — 30% — +94%
- Customer Focus — 49% — +48%
- Internal Information & Communication — 38% — +36%
- Line Manager — 40% — +18%
- Co-operation with other Operating Groups — 45% — +15%
- Job Satisfaction — 59% — +13%
- Quality Focus — 59% — +13%
- Willingness to Change — 37% — +9%
- Training and Development — 27% — +4%

Legend: 1994, 1996

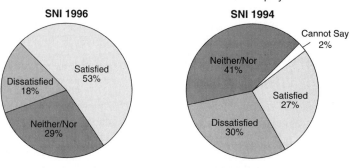

Overall Satisfaction with Siemens Nixdorf as an Employer

SNI 1996
- Satisfied 53%
- Dissatisfied 18%
- Neither/Nor 29%

SNI 1994
- Cannot Say 2%
- Neither/Nor 41%
- Satisfied 27%
- Dissatisfied 30%

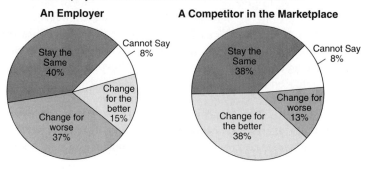

How Employees View Siemens Nixdorf in the Future as . . .

An Employer
- Stay the Same 40%
- Cannot Say 8%
- Change for the better 15%
- Change for worse 37%

A Competitor in the Marketplace
- Stay the Same 38%
- Cannot Say 8%
- Change for worse 13%
- Change for the better 38%

In all, though, the change program was at a critical point. The most significant need now, Schulmeyer recognised, was to win over the sceptics and achieve a critical mass of supporters. Without that, the whole culture change process might lose its impact and become diluted. In turn, that required a rapid improvement in the financial performance. "A situation still close to break-even makes people extremely nervous," he admitted in July 1997. "Costs still have to be reduced if the bottom line is to be improved. Huge productivity gains are required each year to stay afloat. Shifting to services helps, as it absorbs more labour content, but it requires building up, not only the knowledge base but also the ability to sell oneself as opposed to selling a product—the typical German attitude."

At the beginning of the transformation, shaping corporate-level strategy was not Schulmeyer's first priority. He started with a broadly defined vision and went into Baselining, which was the strategy at the business level. In the summer of 1997, Schulmeyer was going to spend a week on an off-site seminar to discuss the next step of developing a corporate strategy. He said:

> At the beginning I said: we need to describe the playing field, which needs the vision. Then we should go deep down in the organisation to get the business strategy . . . 10 lines of business have to develop their own strategy of how to survive in their markets . . .
> Now that we have business strategies and accountability for that, we can start thinking how we can hardwire those strategies in a way that the whole is bigger than the sum of the parts.

> I have to keep on mobilising and energizing, he said, reflecting on the nature and rewards of his job: "There are positive signs when you see people taking the initiative to structure their destinies and reorient themselves to create value. They contribute 50% and we contribute the other 50%; and it makes for a great day whenever you see this. Often, then you get a bad day as you see reluctance and suspicion drowning any positive renewal efforts. And then there are the endless negotiations in this country, especially as my room for manoeuvre is so restricted by labour unions, regulations. It is very stressful.

Managing Change From the Middle: Robert Hoog

Mixed feelings of enthusiasm and anxiety vied for dominance in Robert Hoog as he prepared to present a progress report on the transformation effort in the Middleware division of Open Enterprise Computing (OEC) to Gerhard Schulmeyer. On the one hand his brainchild, the major transformation program he had initiated 15 months ago, seemed to be well on its way to success. The recent employee survey showed high levels of confidence which combined with improved financial performance to form a powerful self-reinforcing engine of change. On the other hand, maintaining the engine's speed and spreading the change momentum to the rest of the organisation were both major anxieties lying ahead.

Hoog vividly recalled the moment he decided to join SNI, terminating a 17-year career with Hewlett Packard that had taken him to several countries and earned him the highest managerial position in HP Germany. When Schulmeyer approached him with a job offer, he agreed to jump ship for two reasons. Firstly, interesting senior positions within HP were mostly in the United States, whereas Robert wanted to remain in Europe. Secondly, the job was a real challenge, with excellent development opportunities; being part of the board of the recently constituted OEC organisation (Exhibit 6), taking charge of the Middleware division and returning it to profit was a difficult task that, if accomplished, could open bright career prospects. "It was the right challenge, at the right place and time. In addition, my previous experience with radical change within HP raised my confidence in succeeding with this one," he explained.

The Middleware division consisted of two departments producing software respectively for the BS2000 and UNIX hardware architectures. The division managed a portfolio of products that generated about DM 200 million in revenues with a staff of more than 600 employees. Its main strengths were its employees' superior technical competence and feature-rich products.

Soon after his arrival at Middleware, Robert Hoog identified several areas of weakness. Firstly, an

EXHIBIT 6   Open Enterprise Computing (OEC) Organizational Chart

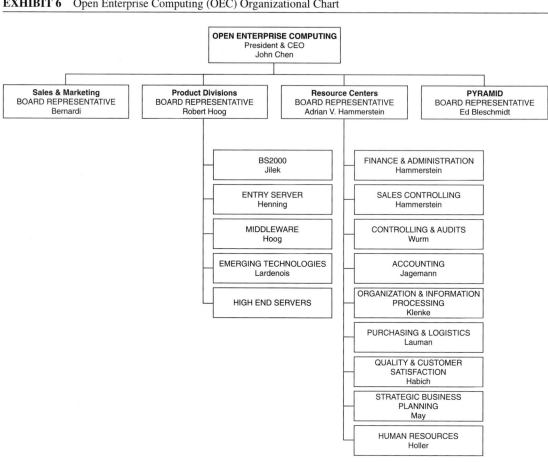

inconsistent structure contained overlapping and often duplicated activities. Each department spoke its own language and used its own processes. Secondly, there was a lack of customer focus. Little importance was paid to marketing activities and channel management. "The problem was not in the product that had the best technology. It was in the marketing space, where we weren't selling the products properly to customers," said Hoog. Thirdly, people were not accustomed to change. "People were used to sitting on the same technologies for many years and expected just to keep going," he explained. As a result, there were few innovative prod-

ucts in the development pipeline and most of the existing ones were related to rapidly declining markets.

To tackle these problems and turn around the division, Hoog quickly engineered a three-phase transformation plan (see Exhibit 7). Phase I addressed the organisational and structural issues; Phase II called for defining mission, values, business strategy and core business processes; Phase III entailed identifying the gaps between present employee skills and required competencies and designing a development plan to fill in these gaps. "In a theoretical model," he said, "I would recommend to start from strategy. However, there was so much dysfunctional activity,

EXHIBIT 7 Transformation Plan for Middleware Division

OEC Middleware Transition Process

Phase I	**Phase II**	**Phase III**
Organisational Restructuring	Team Formation and Development	Skill and Competency Development

• Organisational Assessment	• Relationships	• Key Roles Identified
• Assessment Team Formation	• Values	• Job Descriptions Defined
• Business Model	• Mission	• Position Plans Defined
• Organisational Model	• Goals	• Key Skills Identified
• Impact Assessment	• Responsibilities	• Development Plans Defined
• Organisational Alignment	• Metrics	• Development Tools Identified
• Selection Process Completed	• People Development	• Learning Strategy Implemented
May–Sept 96	Sept–Nov 96	Sept 96–Jan 97

the pain from the structure was so high, that we had to get started from there. I have a fairly simple rule: go where the pain is in the organisation; identify and solve the problem that is causing people the biggest pain; then leverage the success from that to direct remedial action to other areas."

From the beginning, Hoog had a clear conception of the principles driving his management style during the transition phase. Firstly, he would encourage people to take risks. "It is part of your job as a manager to take risks," he reasoned. You have some knowledge, some gut feel and you are willing to take risks. You accept that not everything will succeed—but the important thing is to have the guts to stop early enough. Do not let things drive on trying to cover up the fact that they are not working. You can make mistakes and there is nothing wrong with that, as long as you get enough successful things."

Secondly, he would foster an action orientation, focusing particularly on the process of implementation. "General managers have the tendency to think about a problem and then they always want to come up with a solution which they will sell to or force on somebody else," he reflected. "I stopped people jumping to conclusions too quickly and forced them to think it through, by asking them questions

about the implications of a brilliant idea and the steps required to implement it. I am emphasising the implementation part of a project rather than the expected results. Most people are sloppy about this, immediately assuming the result." Implementation is vital to change management, Hoog believed. "The only way to convince people is by action. Implementing your plan, effectively communicating to people the progress and eventually demonstrating to them that you delivered the promise. This is the real change that we need. But you cannot get it just by lecturing people; instead, having managers who will follow through along these lines, make decisions, accept criticism, act firmly and deliver results; this is what it takes."

Last but not least, Hoog considered a value-driven management style fundamental for success in a company like SNI, facing rapid change and urgently pushing decision responsibility down the hierarchy. He explained: "We know our people are competent to make technical decisions, but what is more difficult is the personal aspect. 'Can I trust the guy?' This is where values come in. Many people nowadays talk about entrepreneurs, new structures, freewheeling and all that stuff. While these are all the right things, I believe you have to accompany them with a strong value system that everybody truly lives on, otherwise it becomes next to impossible to succeed and everything ends up in total chaos."

Phase I

After his appointment, Hoog wasted no time. Within a few days, he had set up a multi-level team co-ordinated by an external consultant to assess the organisational structure and develop restructuring proposals. The method was to identify the mission of each department, understand how it was adding value to the organisation and how this added value could be measured. Then a new structure would be designed to eliminate wasted effort and optimise value-creation activities. Hoog was not directly involved in the team's meetings, but he influenced the outcome through a list of boundary conditions (Exhibit 8) that the new structures had to meet. These encouraged decision making at lower levels by favouring individual ownership of tasks and processes with associated accountability.

The team worked enthusiastically. When the new design was unveiled to an expectant general employee meeting a few weeks later, it was crystal clear to everyone that it represented a complete overhaul of the business. A two-dimensional matrix was proposed. The first dimension of the matrix comprised five support functions, including a new strategic planning function. On the other dimension rested five business lines built around products and customers rather than hardware technologies (see Exhibit 9). Low-value added processes were reduced and duplicate activities along with one layer of management were eliminated. Even though this came at the end of a series of organisational changes, it had strong impact on employees, impressing them not only with the extent of the reform but also with the speed with which it had been put in place. Emotional high noon, however, was yet to come. People gasped when Hoog took the stage to announce the process for filling the new managerial positions: "You have seen the available managerial positions in the new organisational structure. There are no names attached to the positions. Instead there exist job de-

scriptions and key requirements for each position. Any employee who feels he could deliver the requirements can apply for these jobs. This includes people without prior management experience as well as present managers since, effective today, all people presently holding managerial positions lose their job."

Eighteen candidates applied for the nine managerial positions, and Hoog alone interviewed them all. The selection process took longer than planned largely because Hoog had underestimated the importance of holidays in a German company, and when it was over, 40% of the existing managers had lost their jobs. The successful candidates chose their direct reports with a similar process.

Phase II

Once the new organisation was in place, Hoog focused attention on establishing effective alignment in his management team, spending time and effort on identifying values and operating principles that everyone, as people and as managers, could commit to. One of these principles was loyalty to team decisions. Hoog explained, "I made clear that as team members we discuss openly and we may agree or disagree. With luck, most of the time we will reach a consensus. If not, at a certain point a decision must be taken by the leader. Once a decision is taken, I expect that the team will go out and speak with one voice. I do not tolerate people going out and sabotaging a team's decision."

Values and principles were important because not only did they help build trust among the team, but they also provided a common reference for feedback that facilitated behavioural change. "When you present these values and you write down what you mean by them, you can also confront people by saying: 'Look, did we behave according to that value in that meeting? I had the impression that we did not.'" To assess how faithful managers were to their values, Hoog introduced 360-degree performance feedback as part of managers' evaluation measures, which also included a set of agreed key business targets. Management became clearly aware of what

EXHIBIT 8   Boundary Conditions Set by R. Hoog for the Middleware Restructuring

Middleware Boundary Conditions   (Robert Hoog, Issue 1 May 30, 1996)

		Middleware Business Focus (Shared Services)	Product-Line Focus (Development)	
			A B C ...	
			B1 B2	
• Span of control:	Average 10 (5–15)			
• Critical Mass:	Need critical mass to maintain develop core competency over time	**Marketing**		
• Single Performance Measure:	Few well aligned, no compensation	Programs		
• Staff/Service Functions:	High level, high impact but small in size (competence leadership, not "masses"	Messages		
• Staff/Service Functions:	Defined deliverables (–> performance measures), veto right	Ext. Linkages		**GOAL:**
• Product Line Business Resp.:	Orders revenues, investments (expenses), product devt, R&D schedules, quality	...		**Optimize/Maximize The MW Portfolio**
• Balance of Product Line Business vs. MW Business (see chart)		**Business Planning**		*Consistency
• Departments with same similar functions or charter should have similar structure		Technical Framework		*Sharing/Leverage
• Critical interfaces linkages have Identified Owners		Investment Proposals		*Compromize
• Allows/supports temporary project team assignments (weeks, months, years)		Market Research		
• Implement roles/responsibilities of Project Manager		...		(Productivity)
		Technical Support		
		QA and Engineering		
		FA		
		Manufacturing		
		...		
		Goal: Maximize my Product Line Business *Orders/Revenues *Investment (DM, People) *Features, TTM		

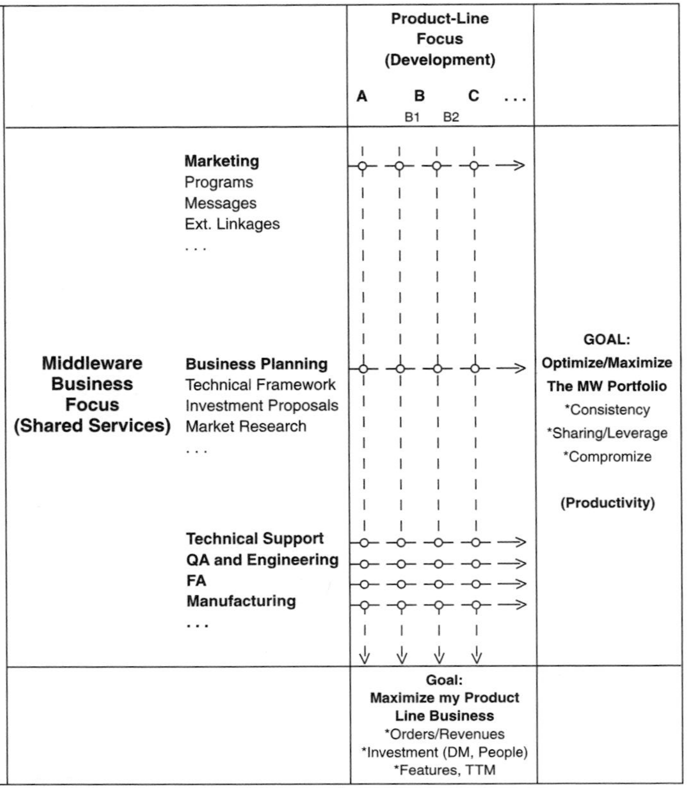

EXHIBIT 9   Organizational Chart of the Middleware Product Division

---

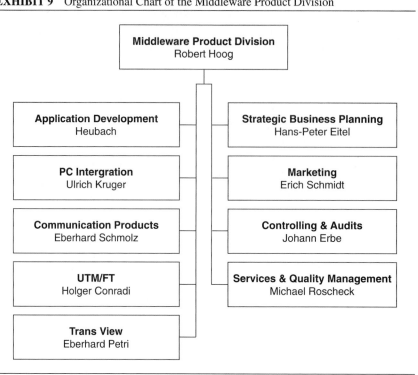

it was held accountable for and how it would be measured.

Once Hoog felt confident that his managers were speaking the same language, he proceeded to examine the business strategy. He felt that strategic and/or managerial decisions needed to be taken and understood at lower levels. That meant changing people's existing mindset and educating them to use more rigorous planning tools. For example, having a single assured customer was no longer enough to justify investing in a new business idea, as in the past. From now on, it would be essential to present research to prove that there was a market big enough to warrant development costs and furthermore that the SNI product could be a market leader.

The next step was to set up a support team to develop a formal strategic business planning process to be used by all product lines. The process was based on analytical frameworks and major emphasis was placed on using market-research data and on teasing out longer-term implications. Training would be provided to enable managers to understand and effectively utilise the process.

For Hoog, the business-planning process combined with the restructuring made a significant contribution to changing managers' and employees' mindsets. Firstly, it helped managers develop a customer focus. The new structure made every manager accountable for specific targets linked to his/her product performance in the marketplace. The planning process provided a way to assess the current and future business potential of products in a directly comparable fashion. Managers now had a transparent way of comparing product potential and related business performance and a simple means of understanding how much customers valued their products.

Secondly, it forced people to consider new products and ideas. The old planning process did not encourage people to think about new opportunities. The new process generated five proposals in the first six months.

Thirdly, in sponsoring new opportunities, managers were forced to evaluate and acknowledge risks. To support their request, they had to provide a business plan that included potential customer and competitor responses. Thus, they became more risk-aware and, as they carried projects through to successful completion, their ability to bear risks was enhanced.

Finally, the process created a "common language" and accelerated decision making by establishing broadly accepted criteria. However, not everything worked faster. Being technical people, they took more time to gather information for developing plans. Hoog commented: "One of the criticisms that we received for the strategic planning approach was: "You want us to get into this planning technique, but we do not know enough to make the right decision—we need more research." "Our response was to point out that by the time you have all the data someone else has a product."

The strategic planning process also helped management assess the global product portfolio. They identified three broad product groups. The first group consisted of support programs which could not become stand-alone business products because they were tightly linked to SNI hardware. The platform-independent programs formed the second group: they had a chance to become free-standing software activities. The last group comprised new business opportunities, products with little revenue but high growth potential. The segmentation proved invaluable to designing the business strategy. In a long meeting with all managers, several important decisions about the product portfolio were reached. As one manager said,

> We could see what we had to do and how to go about getting it done. At last we felt we had a good chance of becoming profitable. But defining a strategy is one thing, delivering it is another. Now

we needed to work at making it happen. We will not be given many chances in the future.

Phase III

While business-line managers started looking at markets and profits again, the divisional management team had a different job to complete. Together, the team members began developing job descriptions and associated competency profiles for all positions in the organisation. Hoog recalled:

> The Middleware organisation was put together from people coming from all over SNI. Consequently, there was no common notion of what, for example, a development engineer was. Different departments had different definitions for the position, making it very difficult for managers to come in and understand what was going on in the organisation. In the past people had used this as a form of protection, because if a manager can't understand what's happening at first glance, he can't easily go in and start making changes.

As they finished the job descriptions and competency profiles, a consulting team was already hard at work designing a skill-development process to make good the deficiencies.

Overcoming Resistance

By June 1997, Hoog's turnaround efforts were producing tangible results which had a pronounced effect on the organisation. The financial recovery, albeit moderate, gave a healthy boost to the workplace morale. Confidence among employees ran high relative to the SNI average, as documented by the employee survey. Nevertheless the transformation effort was far from over. Constant performance improvement was needed to maintain the momentum. Not everybody was on board. There were still many employees who were sceptical about change or who resisted the idea of being held accountable. Hoog admitted:

> Culture change, particularly in large companies, takes longer than you expect. It takes time for people to internalise and support change. SNI is not used to

change and people are scared because they associate change with the loss of job or responsibility.

There was no ready-made recipe for overcoming these difficulties but, for Hoog, there were some things that helped:

Communications are very important: you have to give people the opportunity to talk about it. It doesn't change anything, but letting them vent their fear and frustration is important. In addition, transparent communication is the only way to keep people with you. As the dictum goes: say what you mean and do what you say. At the end of the day, you can only convince them with results, not with words. You can show the slide, and since the slide looks good some will support it, some will be neutral and some will be hostile. As you go ahead and you do a good job, the watchers will become supporters and most of those who resist will eventually come over.

But even after 15 months of productive effort, there were still sceptics among Middleware employees. Hoog recounted:

We were discussing a strategy change when one of the engineers stood up and said we were wrong, because the real issue was not the product, which was fine, but inadequate marketing and sales. I should have gone back and fixed sales, and everything would have been fine. I had to explain to him why I believed the current product would not make it. I said I was glad that someone had raised the issue and given me the opportunity to explain my rationale and the product's life cycle. I probably persuaded some of them, but I knew I wouldn't get everyone's support. When sales start declining, as they will, they will blame me for not investing in marketing. People hold on to the existing product forever. Going after new opportunities and taking risks is something that people still have to learn. It has to do with the embedded culture of avoiding mistakes. I wish it were the reverse; I have a fantasy of people rushing to develop new products so that I would have trouble to find people who wanted to remain to support old products.

While the internal battle was far from over, another front was opening up, this time at the OEC

Business-Line level, as news about the Middleware changes got about. Having a seat on OEC's board, Hoog thought he could grasp the opportunity to leverage the results achieved in his division and instil some change momentum both at group level and ultimately at other divisions within the OEC. Initially, he met hostility. He explained: "Sometimes we hit resistance from managers who thought, 'Who is this new guy?' We had to compromise to get them started. Then, by doing it, people started realising that there was some real value."

As the echoes of what was happening at Middleware spread, other managers began to take notice. Although the value-driven management style remained controversial, soon its strategic planning process, job descriptions and skill development processes were taken up both at the OEC and by some divisions in other groups.

Even more importantly, news of the Middleware initiatives had reached the ear of Schulmeyer himself. Propagating the Middleware message at SNI level would require a different type of power and influence. Could it work where so many other attempts had failed and scepticism was running so high? A middle manager commented: "The change voyage is not a journey that leaders initiate by choosing a destination and buying tickets and maps in a railroad station. It is more like a march in which each individual carries his own as well as other people's burdens as they all traverse through uncharted territory. Survival relies as much on finding the right direction as on taking duties seriously, performing them with the decisiveness, diligence and perseverance demanded by the importance of the task in hand."

In this process, middle managers had to play a critical role, by leveraging what Schulmeyer had built and delivering concrete results. In Hoog's view, "What was missing in the process was people who could translate visions into more operational day-to-day activities." Schulmeyer had developed and articulated a strong vision for the company, and widespread programs such as change agents and communities of practice were implemented, but in the opinion of many managers there was still a problem of follow-through.

Future Challenges

As of July 1997, Hoog was facing challenging new realities. From the strategic viewpoint, his division still lacked a clear focus for its mission: was it in business to profitably develop independent software products? Or did it have to support the sales of SNI proprietary hardware systems at any cost? From the operational viewpoint, a critical mass of people with new skills was required to fill missing competencies. Reaching a balance between re-skilling and replacing staff and evaluating the impact of this decision on people's morale were high on his agenda. Finally, there was the continuing emphasis on culture change to persuade people to take more risks and to learn new skills.

As a member of the OEC board, Hoog had to struggle to provide evidence to support his ideas and sustain the momentum of strong bottom-up change. He admitted: "So far, there are still mixed feelings about, and in some cases strong resistance to, extending the Middleware-type changes to the whole of OEC. We are only at the beginning of the journey."

Managing Change from the Front: Klaus Karl

Klaus Karl joined Siemens in 1988. He had just completed a computer science degree at Munich University and was looking forward to working for the biggest European information company. His first assignment was as a software engineer dealing with large database products.

"We covered a wide range of technical tasks. We did the porting of the software on to our machines and a lot of customer support. It was a difficult job, as we often had to respond to emergency situations at the client's site and got hammered by the client for any product defect. Other than that our life was cool. We had great products, a healthy revenue and what looked like a job for life." After four years on that job Karl was promoted to team leader, heading a group of 10 engineers in the same department. He spent two years in his new assignment, during which the division's financial performance deteriorated. By 1994 it became evident that something would have

to change drastically. "People at my department were for the first time feeling nervous about the company's prospects and our ability to attract customers. It was strange to think like this, because in product-oriented companies like ours the customer was rarely a concern. In my division, except for my group that had built market awareness through regular customer contact, most of the engineers rarely saw one," Karl recalled.

In July of the same year, Karl flew to Paderborn, Germany, to attend a speech by the new CEO, Gerhard Schulmeyer.

"His 30-minute speech on management philosophy was enough for me to adopt his ideas," he recalled. "His points were simple and straightforward . . . . I returned to Munich passionate about telling my colleagues what our 'new hope' looked like. Far from being complex, everything sounded so simple. Sure, transforming SNI would not be easy, but Schulmeyer had broken the change process into separate issues that every single employee could understand and change for himself. There was significant positive resonance when I talked to people in my department. I don't want to claim that everybody walked away thinking exclusively about change. However, people started reflecting, finally, that every single individual might have to change, become more flexible, treat colleagues as friends not foes and be more customer focused."

Looking For a New Job

The next year, 1995, was a year of mobilisation for SNI in general and for the Middleware division in particular. Along with restructuring efforts, significant responsibilities like market research, business plans, pricing, and product planning were delegated to lower levels. The implications of this change were both positive and daunting. As Karl put it: "On one hand, several people were happy to obtain increased responsibilities and freedom to operate creatively. Those guys were the ones who had always shown initiative and diligence in their work. On the other hand, there were those who counted every minute of overtime and only did what they were told to. Seeing what was happening around them, they became really nervous: what will happen to my job; what will I do; I hope it is not me who has to change."

Some people were able to change and weather the turbulence. Others left. Even though Karl himself fully accepted the need for radical transformation, and even though by the end of 1995 much had changed in Middleware in terms of structure and business processes, profits were still elusive. Rumours had it that Karl's business, the relational database, would be outsourced to the main supplier, Fufomix. Klaus wasted no time and started looking around for a new job.

"I was not sure what exactly to do next but I knew that it had to be more business-oriented than technical. Sybase offered me a position as manager for European competency centres. It was the same job as in SNI, but with more responsibilities, better remuneration and good prospects. I always look at good future prospects when taking a step in my life. At the time I thought I had had enough of SNI and was inclined to accept it," confessed Karl.

He was counting the days at SNI. But as he was examining his new hand, fate dealt a different card. One Thursday evening, his boss let him know that if Karl wanted to be part of the change agent program, he would gladly recommend him for a place. Karl had to decide fast, however, as the deadline was the next day.

"On my way home that night, I tried to put my priorities in order," Karl recalled. "Family had always been a priority and after discussing the offer with my wife we decided that even though education was obviously valuable, three months was too long to be away. So the answer was no."

But that wasn't the end of the matter. Next morning, on his way to the office, Karl received new information about the program. It was scheduled in one-month phases and therefore did not require a three-month absence. He had no time to consult his wife. Should he take the opportunity to learn more about business, implement a high-impact project, gain visibility and open up his career, albeit in a troubled company, or move on? Wondering just why he was doing it, Klaus took a deep breath, waved farewell to promotion and enrolled in school instead.

The Change Agent Program

The change agent program took place in Boston. The combined stress of intensive learning and an unfamiliar environment was heavy. On the other hand, the excitement of the learning process was palpable. Designed to provide participants with the capability to understand business and value creation, the capability to lead a change program and to serve as an internal change consultant, the program was attended by Schulmeyer himself, both adding to the stress and impressing on participants the importance of the course.

Each of the chosen change agents had a business project to implement at the end of the course. Conscious that their progress in the company depended closely on the success of their projects, they had started preparing its implementation on day one.

In the fourth week of the program, Karl's project came to an abrupt halt. He learned that his business sponsor had left the company and a week later his executive sponsor retired.

"I was left without support for my project. Things cannot get worse than that for a change agent," said Klaus, appalled. Even when the Middleware and OEC reorganisation brought Robert Hoog and John Chen aboard, both of whom pledged their support, Klaus's stability was short lived.

"After a few conversations with Chen, I got the feeling that my sponsor's agenda was of high nominal but little real support value. It did not seem to be among Chen's priorities. That meant I was back to square one." Karl wrote to Chen diplomatically explaining his concern. The response was frank: "You are right, Klaus. Your project is not on my agenda," said Chen. Karl switched his project, taking heart from an encouraging visit from Schulmeyer who told him that abandoning projects for more interesting opportunities was common practice in the corporate world. Karl's new project entailed developing a new product after concluding some market research for OEC. Chen and Hoog were sponsors.

The Situation at Middleware

Meanwhile, Robert Hoog was working his way through the restructuring of the Middleware division. Hans-Peter Eitel, the strategic planning manager, was handed the key job of implementing the strategic planning process. Looking for people with the skills and the will to move things around in Middleware, Eitel quickly identified a young divisional manager attending the change agent program as a potential candidate. He offered Karl a job with the strategic planning team. Together with Jamie Wilkie, the third member, they would implement the new process in the Middleware division.

Eitel had not only to establish a new strategic planning process but also to introduce customer thinking and other business concepts to the technically minded product-line managers. The team's task would comprise two parts: (1) implement the process, a one-off task involving real change; and (2) provide the strategic planning support function for the Middleware unit on a regular year-round basis.

"I realised that I had graduated in the same class with Hans-Peter when we met," Karl explained. "He made a quick impression on me. After only a few minutes I was convinced he would be a great guy to work with. The job he offered, the implementation of the strategic planning process, seemed challenging and more like a real change agent assignment."

Although an interesting and challenging proposition, Eitel's job offer once more faced Karl with a career decision but this time a starker, riskier one than before. Firstly, the decision was about a functional shift in his career. Although only a tiny step back from the front line, his role would take on a strong internal-consulting element, probably setting a path for the future. Secondly, he might have to abandon the change-agent project for a second time, with the risk of being branded a failure. Last but not least, it was not an easy task to accomplish.

"What Hans-Peter described to me looked like the task of creating our own clients and simultaneously improving the company's processes," reflected Karl. "We were appointed strategic planners but no one would let us plan anything unless we persuaded them that it would be worth something. It would not be easy to persuade technically minded experienced managers to let us show them

how to do things differently. But then again, why shouldn't this be changed? After all, it was for projects like this that I had been trained as a change agent. I also knew that if we did not succeed we would all be touching rock bottom soon. There was, however, an obstacle to me joining his team. The formal requirement of implementing my project was looming in front of me. I frankly expressed both my interest and my reservations about taking the job. I deeply wanted to do it but I couldn't leave my assignment for a second time."

On hearing that Karl was interested in the job, Hoog immediately proposed to split his responsibilities between the change-agent project and the job with Eitel. Karl accepted with alacrity. Looking back at his life over the past year, he was amazed to have experienced such a series of unexpected twists of fortune.

The Action

It was September 1996. Hoog's master plan provided for a product portfolio assessment in December. The assessment was crucial because it would determine resource allocation and staffing among product lines. Being a consensus-driven manager, Hoog wanted things to go smoothly. There were three months left to try to sell the new strategic planning process to managers and, if possible, guide them towards solutions that fitted with Hoog's initial analysis.

The main problem, Karl believed, was that managers had been around too long to accept youngsters telling them how to run their business. They were very technically orientated and some refused to look at things from the business perspective. On the other side, the division's losses created a sense of urgency. The planners decided to make a preliminary reconnaissance study to identify the managers who were open to new ideas and start by holding seminars and workshops for those whose business performance was worst and who would appreciate them most. If successful they would try to get into less welcoming areas too. They decided to be open, let people try out their techniques for themselves, and "walk the talk."

In the first workshop, the aim was to present managers with new techniques for evaluating the product portfolio. On the second day there was near mutiny as the presenters put forward Prof. Michael Porter's five-forces model of competitive strategy. Karl acted quickly. "I rushed to the stage and explained, 'There is no reason to use this particular tool—use any way you judge appropriate to complete the exercise. Now go back to your rooms and finish the exercise.' Five out of five groups used the tools we presented. We realised that it was very important to let people use the techniques before they pass judgement on them. More often than not they will recognise the value it can add to their business." Although the first workshop went well, the team decided that in the future they would let academics run the workshops while they concentrated on facilitating the process.

Persuading people to open their minds proved more difficult to do than the team had thought. The team was young and had everything to prove, while the sense of urgency just raised the voltage in their already electric meetings with managers. At difficult points, Karl had to often step in and save the situation. "More than once I had to appeal to people's emotions and give dramatic speeches before they would even consider spending a minute trying the techniques," he said. He was surprised and gratified to see the positive effect such impromptu, emotional speeches could have.

As time passed the team's techniques improved. "We often used a problem-solving methodology we learned during the Hanover IV event," explained Karl. "It was called FADE, Focus, Analyse, Develop, Execute. On the first day of the workshop I would ask people the simple question: 'Do you know what your problem is?' The answer always was: 'Yes, of course.' " But the reality was that most of the time they didn't know. The only way to make them see their real problem was by walking them through the process of focusing on the problem, analysing and then developing solutions. At the end of the exercise many people were able to see what they couldn't see in the beginning. Only then did they recognise the value of the process. Often we faced extreme reactions. I vividly remember a time when we were explaining some of the techniques to a group of senior people. They just laughed at us. I was standing there unable even to have them consider my proposition. I decided to leave and fight the battle another time. On another occasion a senior manager initially did not even respond to our invitation. It was only after the workshop was over and he had heard positive comments from other people that he finally showed up. I tend to remember the positive examples, but there were many failures."

Nevertheless, after all the battles, the strategic planning process was successfully implemented in Middleware. The portfolio assessment meeting in December went extremely well, and people rapidly reached agreement on the outcome of their analysis and discussions. It was a breakthrough. "It was a really great feeling to have won a small battle in the SNI transformation process, and it was the three of us who did it," exulted Karl. Hoog's support was critical. "I don't know how far we would have got without his support," Karl admitted frankly.

"What next? We do not have profits yet, but there is little doubt that they will follow. The next products out of the development line will find big enough markets to make money," Karl predicted. And even if the numbers did not show it yet, it was enough to look around the place to realise that there was a fresh atmosphere. "People now talk in the corridors about market issues, they leave some doors open and they are more confident of the future. The employee survey confirmed it. Our approval ratings were much higher than the average SNI division." In addition, there were spill-over effects both laterally to other divisions and upwards to the business-line level. People were so impressed with what happened at Middleware that there was a demand to repeat the implementation process at the next level up. This, however, would be a more difficult challenge because of the scope of the project and greater level of resistance. Hoog's absence could be damaging. With him not there, the task would certainly be harder, but now Eitel, Wilkie and Karl at least had the confidence to take it on.

Reading 8–1

THE REINVENTION ROLLER COASTER: RISKING THE PRESENT FOR A POWERFUL FUTURE

Tracy Goss, Richard Pascale, and Anthony Athos

Kodak, IBM, American Express, and General Motors have recently sacked their CEOs. All were capable executives with impressive track records. All had promised turnarounds, and all had spearheaded downsizing, delayering, and reengineering programs in vigorous efforts to deliver those promises. Indeed, most of these efforts lowered costs, increased productivity, and improved profitability—at least for a while. Yet despite this frenzy of activity, the competitive vitality of these companies continued to ebb away until finally their boards felt compelled to act.

What went wrong? The simplistic answer is "leadership." All these boards wound up blaming their CEOs for poor leadership and inadequate strategic vision. But press the members of those boards—or the shaken executives—for a better answer, and you will uncover uncertainty, bafflement, even an occasional muddled insight that the answer

―――――

Tracy Goss is president of Goss/Reid Associates in Austin, Texas, a management consulting firm that works with CEOs and senior executives leading corporate reinvention in major U.S. and international companies. She is a lecturer and author of *Re-Invention: For People Who Want to Change the World,* from Doubleday. *Richard Pascale* is a writer, lecturer, and consultant. He is currently a Perot Fellow and taught for 20 years at Stanford's Graduate School of Business. His March-April 1978 HBR article, "Zen and the Art of Management," won a McKinsey Award. His most recent book, *Managing on the Edge,* was published in 1990 by Simon & Schuster. *Anthony Athos* is a Boston-based consultant who until 1982 was the Jesse Isador Straus Professor at the Harvard Business School. In 1981, he coauthored with Richard Pascale *The Art of Japanese Management* (Simon & Schuster).

lies somewhere deeper than any board or executive is equipped to look.

These experienced businesspeople see the problem as "leadership" because they see the solution as "change." And surely, they tell themselves, any leader deserving of that name can successfully implement change. They are right. With all the practice of the 1980s, every CEO knows how to create cross-functional teams, reduce defects, and redesign business processes in ways that lower costs and improve performance. A CEO who cannot set ambitious new goals and does not know how to try harder to reach them deserves the boot.

But what these CEOs are missing is that such incremental change is not enough for many companies today. Managers groping about for a more fundamental shift in their organizations' capabilities must realize that change programs treat symptoms, not underlying conditions. These companies do not need to improve themselves, they need to reinvent themselves.

Reinvention is not changing what is, but creating what isn't. A butterfly is not more caterpillar or a better or improved caterpillar, a butterfly is a different creature. Leaders of three multinational companies with whom we have worked have grappled with this distinction. When British Airways declared itself the world's favorite airline in the 1980s, it faced the challenge of becoming a different company, not just a better company. The same held true when Europcar decided to become the most user friendly and efficient rental-car company in Europe and not just an omnipresent one. And when Häagen-Dazs chose to make a visit to its European ice-cream shops an exciting event, the company didn't need just to change what it did or how work got done.

When a company reinvents itself, it must alter the underlying assumptions and invisible premises on which its decisions and actions are based. This *context* is the sum of all the conclusions that members of the organization have reached. It is the product of their experience and their interpretations of the past, and it determines the organization's social behavior, or culture. Unspoken and even unacknowledged conclusions about the past dictate what is possible for the future.

To reinvent itself, an organization must first uncover its hidden context. Only when an organization is threatened, losing momentum, or eager to break new ground will it confront its past and begin to understand why it must break with its outmoded present. And only then will a company's employees come to believe in a powerful new future, a future that may seem beyond the organization's reach.

Admittedly, the notion that companies should "stretch" themselves to achieve unprecedented goals is not new. But executives have frequently underestimated the wrenching shift—the internal conflict and soul-searching—that goes hand in hand with a break from the present way of thinking and operating. And because executives have not understood this as they announced their grandiose "strategic intentions," employees have often ignored the call to arms.

Unless managers orchestrate the creation of a new context, all that the organizations are *doing* to improve their competitiveness—whether they are improving service, accelerating product development, or increasing the flexibility of manufacturing—will at worst yield unproductive churnings and at best produce meaningful but episodic change.

But if a company authentically reinvents itself, if it alters its context, it not only has the means to alter its culture and achieve unprecedented results in quality, service ratings, cycle time, market share, and, finally, financial performance, it also will have the ability to sustain these improvements regardless of any changes in the business environment.

One company that nearly succeeded in reinventing itself is the Ford Motor Company. From 1980 through 1982, Ford lost $3 billion. By 1986, its earnings surpassed those of much larger General Motors for the first time since the 1920s. By 1988, Ford's profits reached $5.3 billion, and return on stockholders' equity hit 26.3%. Its market share in the United States had increased five points to 22%. Cycle time for the development of an automobile decreased from eight years to five. Quality, according to J.D. Power surveys, jumped from the bottom 25% to the top 10% of all automobiles that were sold in the United States. And surveys and focus groups of both union and salaried employees recorded dramatic shifts in their perceptions of management, morale, and company loyalty.

The key to these remarkable improvements? Employees consistently reported that Ford had somehow become an entirely different company than it had been five years earlier. Ford had left behind its past as a rigidly hierarchical company driven by financial considerations to pursue a future in which a concern for quality and new products became the overriding priority.

Ford's organizational reinvention proved to be successful. But unfortunately, the company's leaders at the time were not similarly reinvented, as their failure to invest sufficiently in the core business revealed. Sustaining the company's momentum in the 1990s, therefore, has become a challenging task.

Creating a New Context

Most executives who have any inkling of what reinvention entails flinch at the prospect of taking on this 500-pound gorilla. "The journey to reinvent yourself and your company is not as scary as they say it is, it's worse," says Mort Meyerson, chairman of Perot Systems, an information-systems company that is assisting in many corporate reinventions. "You step into the abyss out of the conviction that the only way to compete in the long haul is to be a totally different company. It's a sink-or-swim proposition."

It should come as no surprise, then, that many CEOs end up sinking. After creating a context or being the product of one, they either don't have the courage—or see the need—to throw it away. But in defense of these CEOs, it is easy to look for the root cause of declining competitiveness and not see it.

Consider this analogy. You inherit your grandmother's house. Unknown to you is one peculiarity: all the light fixtures have bulbs that give off blue rather than yellow light. You find that you don't like the feel of the rooms and spend a lot of time and money repainting walls, reupholstering furniture, and replacing carpets. You never seem to get it quite right, but nonetheless, you rationalize that at least it is improving with each thing you do. Then one day you notice the blue lightbulbs and change them. Suddenly, all that you fixed is broken.

Context is like the color of the light, not the objects in the room. Context colors everything in the corporation. More accurately, the context alters what we see, usually without our being aware of it.

Much-abused IBM is an example of a company that has been doing things to the objects in the room without changing the color of the light. IBM was among the vanguard in employing most contemporary business techniques, such as pursuing Six Sigma quality (3.4 defects per one million units), empowerment, delayering, and downsizing. But because IBM failed to alter its context—the "IBM way" of controlling and predicting, every aspect of the business—these change programs did not serve as steps to a powerful future.

The company leaders sought to instill an entrepreneurial spirit that would lead employees to take bold initiatives with new product ideas and with customers. But the context in which they managed made entrepreneurship at IBM an oxymoron. That context—ever-positive and upbeat—demanded that managers demonstrate how a course of action would play out five steps into the future before they could take step one. This left managers unwilling to risk, let alone abandon, what the company had become for what it might be.

At the other end of the spectrum is Motorola, a familiar example of successful reinvention. Over the course of its 65-year history, Motorola has on several occasions decided that a new future was at hand,

first in car radios, then in television, consumer electronics, and semiconductors, and recently in microcomputers, cellular phones, and pagers. Each shift has been marked by fundamentally altering the kind of company that Motorola was in order to compete in entirely different industries. This involved self-imposed upheaval: selling off successful but older businesses and taking big gambles on the new ones.

In facing these challenges, Motorola's leaders realized the importance of context. Motorola was once a collection of fiefdoms dominated by macho engineers who mistakenly thought that they had no serious rivals. But in the late 1970s, CEO Robert Galvin recognized that the inward-looking company was not prepared to face intensifying Japanese competition.

He forced everyone to confront quality problems, divisional limitations, and the Japanese threat. To do so, the company had to become self-questioning, outward looking, and much more humble. A healthy degree of self-criticism replaced the former sense of superiority. In 1989, one year before he stepped down as CEO, Galvin challenged Motorola to become "the world's premier company," a guiding vision that transcended the company's former definition of itself as the best marker of its products.

"The world's premier company" seems too vague to inspire a powerful new future, but as Motorola's employees began to come to terms with the idea, they were spurred by the challenge of being the best in every facet of their business. The vision served as a reminder that the company must constantly challenge its sense of what is possible in order to resist the downward pull of habit and routine.

The Doing Trap

Author Rita Mae Brown defines insanity as doing the same thing again and again but expecting different results. With no awareness of the power of context, we continue to beat our heads against the same wall.

What are we missing? This parallel may help: Scientists at the turn of the century treated time as a constant, a given. But physicists studying light (photons) found increasing experimental evidence that something was amiss. They held fast, however, to the ether-wave theory of light and its central premise that the speed of light was a variable. When Einstein speculated that the speed of light might be a constant, he was drawn to look elsewhere for a variable that could account for the elasticity of the cosmos. Time was the only candidate. Einstein created an intellectual puzzle that forced him to look "outside the box." His consideration of a new possibility launched him on the intellectual odyssey that led to the Special and General Theories of Relativity and revolutionized the world of physics. He created a new context for looking at the universe.

Like time to turn-of-the-century physicists, *doing* is the assumed managerial constant. To manage is to *do* something, managers are selected and promoted based on their ability to get things done. But what if something else is the constant, and doing is the variable?

Like Einstein's thought experiment of riding on a photon of light to see what the world looked like from that perspective, the executive who would master reinvention must journey into a largely unfamiliar and uncomfortable territory, the territory of *being*.[1] Being alters action, context shapes thinking and perception. When you fundamentally alter the context, the foundation on which people construct their understanding of the world, actions are altered accordingly.

Context sets the stage, being pertains to whether the actor lives the part or merely goes through the motions. Organizations and the people in them are being something all the time. On occasion, we describe them as "conservative," or "hard charging," or "resistant to change." Trouble is, aside from such casual generalizations, we concentrate mostly on what we are doing and let being fend for itself.

That may be because we Westerners have few mental hooks or even words for excursions into being. The Japanese chart the journey across life in terms of perfecting one's inner nature, or being. They call it *kokoro*.[2] In contrast, Westerners typically assess their progression through adulthood in terms of personal wealth or levels of accomplishments. To the Japanese, merely *doing* these things is meaningless unless one is able to become deeper and wiser along the way.

Many Western CEOs will undoubtedly say that all this smacks of something philosophical or, far worse, theological and therefore has presumably little relevance for managers. But an organization's being determines its context, its possibilities. Remarkable shifts in context can happen only when there is a shift in being. Since IBM's would-be entrepreneurs continued to act "appropriately" and "conservatively," it is hardly surprising that the context of risk taking that former Chairman and CEO John Akers tried to create never took hold.

Our difficulty in discerning what a business *is* explains why so many efforts at corporate revitalization have failed. Consider all the retail chains throughout the country, including Saks and Macy's, that have tried to counter or capture Nordstrom's magic but with little success. Nordstrom's way of being has enabled it to win in seemingly impossible circumstances. For example, it was able to launch a successful expansion program in the Northeastern United States when that region was gripped by deep recession. That expansion helped Nordstrom become the leading department store chain in the country in terms of sales per square foot. Nordstrom

---

[1]We are indebted to numerous philosophers, scholars, and thinkers who have inquired into the nature of being, especially Werner Erhard, "Transformation and Its Implications for Systems-Oriented Research," unpublished lecture, Massachusetts Institute of Technology, Cambridge, Massachusetts, April 1977, and "The Nature of Tranformation," unpublished lecture, Oxford University Union Society, Oxford, England, September 1981, Martin Heidegger, *What Is Called Thinking* (New York: Harper & Row, 1968), *On the Way to Language* (New York: Harper & Row, 1971), *On Time and Being* (New York: Harper & Row, 1972), and Ludwig Wittgenstein, *Culture and Value* (Oxford: Basil Blackwell, 1980).

[2]See Thomas P. Rohlen, "The Promise of Adulthood In Japanese Spiritualism," *Daedalus.* Journal of the American Academy of Arts and Sciences, Spring 1976, p. 125.

now has 64 stores, annual sales of $2.89 billion, and an annual growth rate of 20%.

While the other chains can copy some of what Nordstrom is doing, they don't seem to realize that Nordstrom is living its motto, "Respond to Unreasonable Customer Requests." This way of being leads employees to relish the challenges that customers toss at them. Usually, meeting these demands entails little more than providing just a bit more service. But occasionally it means hand delivering items purchased by phone to the airport for a customer with a last-minute business trip, changing a customer's flat tire, or paying a customer's parking ticket when in-store gift wrapping has taken longer than expected.

Nordstrom encourages these acts by promoting its best employees, keeping scrapbooks of "heroic" acts, and paying its salespeople entirely on commission, through which they usually earn about twice what they would at a rival's store. For go-getters who really love to sell, Nordstrom is nirvana. But the system weeds out those who can't meet such demanding standards and selects those prepared to be what Nordstrom stands for.

Rivals scrambling to keep up have instituted in-house charm schools and issued vision statements trumpeting the importance of customers and the value of service. They have copied Nordstrom by introducing commissions and incentives. They have loosened their refund policies. Without exception, these actions have failed to close the gap. The problem seems to be an understanding of what it means to respond to unreasonable customer demands. To many salespeople at competing stores, it means that the customer comes first—within reason. Customer demands must be met—unless these demands are ridiculous. But at Nordstrom, each ridiculous customer request is an opportunity for a "heroic" act by an employee, an opportunity to expand on the store's reputation. To compete with Nordstrom, other stores must shift "who they are" in relation to the customer, not just what they do for the customer.

Shifts in being are not merely upbeat intellectual "ah-ha's." "Oh my God" is more likely to be uttered than "Eureka." The acid test of such a shift is whether or not it is intellectually and emotionally jolting. Executives at Europcar, the second largest rental-car company in Europe, understand this phenomenon.

In January 1992, CEO Fredy Dellis surveyed the competitive situation and did not like what he saw. While revenues were rising slowly, profits were plummeting. He estimated that it cost Europcar $13 to process each rental agreement (mostly by hand), compared with $1 at Hertz and Avis. Past attempts at incremental improvement had failed to close this gap. Much of the problem seemed to stem from the company's structure. Europcar had been built through acquisitions and was a loose federation of rental-car companies throughout Europe, each of which was convinced it knew its country best. Worse still, each country fiefdom built and maintained its own operating system, and these incompatible systems could not deal with the increasing number of cross-border travelers. Europcar was a parochial, balkanized organization whose country managers were preoccupied with protecting their national idiosyncrasies and their turf.

Dellis's response was to initiate the Greenway Project, a plan to revamp Europcar's entire operating system—how reservations were made, how rental operations flowed from check-out to check-in, the financially critical activities of fleet purchasing and fleet utilization. But a companywide operating system would drastically change the way the country units did business and would thus threaten their distinct national identities. Bickering between country managers and the design team, whose members themselves were drawn from the separate country operations, threatened the entire project.

But in early 1993, a small miracle happened when the 35 top managers and the design team gathered in Nice, France. The design team had been invited to demonstrate the new system, on which they had made enormous headway with very little input or encouragement from their senior sponsors. But these top managers, finally recognizing the importance of Greenway for lowering Europcar's cost structure to competitors' levels, took on the task of bridging this gulf of distrust and misunderstanding.

As these managers moved through the design team's presentations on the components of the operating system and what it could accomplish in terms of cost reduction and improved service and fleet utilization, the discussion grew animated with much give-and-take. Participants say the disbelief and alienation felt by both designers and senior managers was transformed into growing excitement about the new possibilities for the flow of information throughout the company. Moreover, by uniting all the operations, the whole would become much more formidable than the previous collection of individual parts. The antagonism that had marked relationships between parts of the company began to fade, everyone at the gathering began to behave like part of a team. The shift for Europcar toward becoming a company that could coalesce across geographical borders and through levels of hierarchy to become an innovator in its field was well under way.

Inventing a Powerful Future

Statements of vision from chief executives have bewildered and even amused employees who just don't get why a CEO would describe a future that their experience says can never materialize. The ensuing action plans are built inevitably on company notions about how things *really* work around here and employees' experience of the last change effort. It all adds up to pulling the leaden past toward a future we never seem to reach.[3]

---

[3]Numerous writers have grappled with the relationship of past, present, and future in the workplace, especially Werner Erhard, "Organizational Vision and Vitality: Forward from the Future," unpublished lecture, Academy of Management, San Francisco, California, August 1990, Edward Lindaman and Ronald Lippitt, *Choosing the Future You Prefer* (Washington, D.C.: Development Publications, 1979), Fritz Roethlisberger, *Training for Human Relations* (Boston: Harvard University, Graduate School of Business Administration, Division of Research, 1954), Marvin R. Weisbord, *Productive Workplaces: Organizing and Managing for Dignity, Meaning, and Community* (San Francisco: Jossey-Bass, 1991), pp. 282–85.

As we have said, reinvention entails creating a new possibility for the future, one that past experiences and current predictions would indicate is impossible. Sir Colin Marshall did this by declaring that British Airways would be the "world's favorite airline" when it ranked among the worst. Before its turnaround in the 1980s, the airline's frequent maintenance-related delays, poor food, and Aeroflot-like standards of service had inspired long-suffering customers to say that its initials actually stood for "bloody awful."

A declaration from a leader generates an essential element of reinvention. It creates the possibility of a new future that evokes widespread interest and commitment. When a declaration is well stated, it is always visually imaginable (putting a man on the moon) or exceptionally simple (becoming the world's favorite airline). The declaration becomes the magnetic North, the focal point. By contrast, a vision provides a more elaborate description of the desired state and the criteria against which success will be measured.

A declaration forces you to stand in the new future, undertaking a series of steps not in order to be the world's favorite airline *someday,* but to be that airline *now.* Sir Colin began leading British Airways down that road by going to those who dealt closely with customers and asking them what needed to happen. The answers included everything from making sure that the concourse lights were always on to seeing that meals on short flights were easy to deliver and unwrap. Being the best in customers' eyes also meant putting the airline's operations under the marketing department, so that instead of moving people as if they were packages, all operating decisions would start from a concern for the passenger. Today British Airway's service ranks among the best, and it is one of the most profitable airlines in the world.

But what happens when a company reaches its future? Where does it go from there? This was the situation Häagen-Dazs faced after its stunning success in exporting its "Dedicated to Pleasure" brand identity to the European market in 1989. A team of young, hard-charging recruits from the world's leading food-products companies had thought it would take anywhere from three to five years to gain a presence in a market where competitors ranged from giants like Mars and Nestlé to thousands of home recipe boutiques. Against the odds, this team launched the brand in June 1989, with a daring ad campaign featuring scantily clad couples indulging in the pleasures of ice cream. Within 18 months, Häagen-Dazs was the leading dairy ice cream in Western Europe. The team had pulled off one of the most successful new product launches the packaged food industry had ever seen.

Then an interesting thing began to happen. Once victory was achieved, bureaucracy took over. Paris headquarters began to quarrel with country management teams. Marketing began to flex its muscles at the expense of sales and shops operations. Headquarters in the United States was too worried about Ben & Jerry's encroachments to notice. The young hotshots in Europe began to wonder how to protect their position and, more important, what they could do for an encore.

John Riccitiello, general manager of Häagen-Dazs International, concluded that his organization had already used up its future; incremental improvements, he realized, could not restore momentum. He toyed with embracing the ambitious goal of making Häagen-Dazs Europe's leading premium food brand. But this goal seemed compelling only to top managers, not to everyone in the company.

Riccitiello decided to shift the context of "beating the competition, being the best" and a strategy of selling pleasure to a new context of "celebrating the experience of being alive." He believed that there would be more longevity in a future of selling excitement and pizzazz. A visit to a Häagen-Dazs shop, he determined, would be a memorable event for customers.

This new future generated an important shift in the company's recruitment policy. Interviews with

job candidates are now treated much like theatrical auditions. "We aren't just looking for people to clear tables and dispense ice cream," Riccitiello says. "So when a group of prospects come in, we give them impromptu situations and see what they do. Do they ad-lib? Do they freeze and look to others for the right answer? We ask them to juggle four ice-cream cones. We want our shops to be an event, a place where customers and staff celebrate the experience of something that tastes great and gives you—even if just for a moment—a sense that it's worth being alive. It became our mission to provide that feeling."

To that end, the company created a senior position. This "Director Magic," as the woman given the job has been dubbed, works with shop managers and scoopers to help them generate ideas that make them look forward to their work. When coming to a Häagen-Dazs shop becomes an exciting event for staff and customers, the competition has a hard time measuring up.

Executive Reinvention

During our 35 years of research, writing, teaching, and consulting for U.S., European, and Japanese corporations, we have found, particularly in senior executives, an unwillingness to think rigorously and patiently about themselves or their ideas. We often find senior executives perched like a threatened aristocracy, entitled, aloof, and sensing doom. Flurries of restructuring or downsizing are like the desperate attempts of uncomprehending heirs who try to slow the decline of the family estate. Each successive reaction is misconstrued as bold action to "set things right."

When leading an organization into the future, executives come to a fork in the road. As they come face-to-face with their organizations' needs to reinvent themselves, many executives hope for the best and opt for the prudent path of change. Even when they choose reinvention, their feet get cold. Thrown into the unfamiliar territory of reinvention, where the steps along the path and the outcomes themselves are often unpredictable, the responsible thing to do, many executives think, is to get things back on track. It is not surprising that so many senior executives decline invitations to reinvent themselves and their companies. It is like aging: experts tell us that it is difficult, yet most of us hope to go through it without pain.

There is another choice, but it requires executive reinvention, a serious inquiry into oneself as a leader. This is not a psychological process to fix something that's wrong, but an inquiry that reveals the context from which an executive makes decisions. People have contexts just as organizations do. Our individual context is our hidden strategy for dealing with life, it determines all the choices we make. On the surface, our context is our formula for winning, the source of our success. But on closer examination, this context is the box within which a person operates and determines what is possible and impossible for him or her as a leader and, by extension, for the organization.

A good example is a CEO who wanted to increase the annual revenues of his family-run manufacturing business from $80 million to $200 million within five years. He had been working very hard toward this goal for a number of years and was dissatisfied with the slow progress.

But when people proposed expansion plans, like adding a new product line or entering a new market, all he could see were the incredible problems: the outside executives that would have to be brought on board, the new expertise that existing managers, including complacent family members, would have to acquire, and so on. He refused to endorse such plans, or if he did let a plan go forward, he would halt it whenever contention arose.

If you had asked him how he had spent his day, he would say, "I spent it working on the growth of the company." But when he finally stopped to examine what was going wrong, he realized that he was operating from a context of avoiding conflict, which was inconsistent with a commitment to ambitious growth. He understood that this was why all

the things he was doing to expand the business were not working.

He could then put a clear choice before the family board: either they pursue becoming a $200 million company with their eyes open to the fact that there would be chaos, conflict, and upheaval, or they settle for incremental growth. The board decided on the latter (sales of $100 million). They left achieving the larger future to the next generation.

Managing the Present from the Future

An organization that has a clear grasp of its own assumptions about the past is often motivated to alter the context in which the company is embedded. This in turn requires a shift in the organization's being and a powerful vision of the future. The activities involved in reinventing an organization require persistence and flexibility. Some extend over the entire effort, and others are steps along the way.

1. Assembling a Critical Mass of Key Stakeholders. Leading pilgrims on the journey of reinventing an organization should never be left to the top eight or ten executives. It is deceptively easy to generate consensus among this group, they usually are a tight fraternity, and it is difficult to spark deep self-examination among them. If there are revelations, they may never extend beyond this circle.

As proven by the experiences of such companies as Ford, British Petroleum, Chase Bank, AT&T, Europcar, Thomas Cook, and Häagen-Dazs, this group must encompass a critical mass of stakeholders—the employees "who really make things happen around here." Some hold sway over key resources. Others are central to informal opinion networks. The group may often include critical but seldom-seen people like key technologists and leading process engineers. The goal is a flywheel effect, where enough key players get involved and enrolled that it creates a momentum to carry the process forward.

These key stakeholders first must determine if their company has what it takes to remain competitive and, if not, what to do about it. In the process, such a group will typically put unspoken grievances and suspicions on the table. Its members will learn to work together and to respect nonconforming opinions. All this constitutes a shift in the way participants are being, from a relationship of distrust and resignation toward an authentic, powerful partnership. This is not easy, nor is it enough. But it is a beginning.

Once such a shift has taken place, actions and reactions that previously could not have occurred happen quite naturally, and with surprising results.

Such a watershed event occurred during Ford's transformation in the 1980s. The upper-level managers in charge of the Engineering Division and the Power Train Division, which designed engines and transmissions, were called into one room. Lou Ross, then senior vice president in charge of factories, got right to the point. "Here's the problem," he said, "For 25 years, Power Train and Engineering have been fighting with each other, hurting productivity and quality. Enough is enough. We don't care how long it takes, but we want you to answer one question: Will engineering report to manufacturing, or manufacturing to engineering?"

Now picture a meeting room eight months later, after countless hostile debates. Many of the same people from the Engineering and Power Train divisions were on their hands and knees, discussing the merits of the various organizational charts that covered the floor. There was a lot of give-and-take. Someone asked with an edge of frustration, "Which of these organizational charts is best?" Another person answered, "Maybe *this* is!" A hush fell over the room. He was calling attention to the way they were behaving as colleagues. The important thing was how they were working together, not finding the "perfect" organizational structure. It took another month to put an "organization" together that didn't reorganize at all but simply realigned the flows of communication across the traditional Engineering and Power Train chimneys. The new relationship and all that flowed from it was one of the pillars of Ford's turnaround. This broad-based shift

in being is central to understanding how Ford compressed the time needed to develop a new model from eight years to five and catapulted its product quality from worst to best.

2. Doing an Organizational Audit. The first task of the key stakeholders is to reveal and confront the company's true competitive situation. This process will also reveal the barriers to significant organizational change—the organization's context. A company cannot get from "here" to "there" without first knowing where "here" is any more than it can choose reinvention without knowing where "there" is.

The best approach is through a diagnosis that generates a complete picture of how the organization really works: What assumptions are we making about our strategic position and customer needs that may no longer be valid? Which functional units are most influential, and will they be as important in the future as they were in the past? What are the key systems that drive the business? What are the core competencies or skills of the enterprise? What are the shared values and idiosyncrasies that comprise the organization's being? If explored in-depth, these types of questions generate responses that, taken together, paint a picture of how things really work.

Europcar created small groups to conduct such an audit. Each took on a crucial issue, such as the company's competitive position, the current system for renting automobiles and tracking information, and the consequences of the country structure. What emerged was a picture of a highly fragmented organization that had no idea what it meant to work together as a whole. As a result of the audit, these crucial stakeholders recognized that without the Greenway Project, Europcar would not be able to compete in the Pan-European market.

3. Creating Urgency, Discussing the Undiscussable. There is an unspoken code of silence in most corporations that conceals the full extent of a corporation's competitive weaknesses. But a threat that everyone perceives and no one talks about is far more debilitating to a company than a threat that has been clearly revealed. Companies, like people, tend to be at least as sick as their secrets.

A company must confront its most life-threatening problems in order to summon the courage to break with the past and embrace a new future. *The Book of Five Rings,* a guide for Japanese samurai written four centuries ago, prescribes the practice of visualizing death in battle as vividly as possible before the actual battle. Having experienced "death" beforehand, there is not a lot left to fear, and the warrior fights with complete abandon. Interesting, isn't it, that in confronting the possible, it becomes less probable.

In a sense, managers of companies whose very existence is at stake are lucky, though being honest about the dire situations to which they contributed is painful, it is relatively easy for these managers to convince employees that there is no alternative to a wrenching shift in who and what they are.

4. Harnessing Contention. There is an obscure law of cybernetics—the law of requisite variety—that postulates that any system must encourage and incorporate variety internally if it is to cope with variety externally. This seems innocuous until you consider how variety shows up in organizations. Usually it takes the form of such behavior as siphoning off scarce resources from mainstream activities for back-channel experiments, disagreeing at meetings, and so forth. Almost all significant norm-breaking opinions or behavior in social systems are synonymous with conflict.

Paradoxically, most organizations suppress contention; many managers, among others, cannot stand to be confronted because they assume they should be "in charge." But control kills invention, learning, and commitment.

Conflict jump-starts the creative process.[4] That is why the group process described earlier included a large number of stakeholders. When you extend participation to those really accountable for critical resources, or who hold entrenched positions, or who

have been burned by past change attempts, you guarantee conflicts. But as the group faces and handles difficult issues, there is a shift in how they relate to contention. Participants learn to disagree without being disagreeable.

Emotions often accompany creative tension, and these emotions are not altogether pleasant. At Intel, conflict is blunt, at times brutal. Says one observer: "If you're used to tennis, Intel plays rugby, and you walk away with a lot of bruises. They've created a company that takes direct, hard-hitting disagreement as a sign of fitness. You put it all behind you in the locker room, and it's forgotten by the scrimmage the next day."

On a field trip to Tokyo to assess Intel's competitiveness against Japanese quality and service standards, the top management team of 20 became involved in a fierce argument about the company's approach to the Japanese market. Underlying the finger-pointing were long-smoldering resentments on the part of those representing internal Intel customers who could not get the quality and service they desired from manufacturing. Intel COO Craig Barrett, who then headed manufacturing, was a combative partisan in the melee. As one person who was at the meeting described it: "Four-letter words flew back and forth like ping-pong balls in a Beijing master's tournament."

But two days later, team members sat down, sorted out their differences, and put the actions in motion to help Intel match or surpass its Japanese rivals. Barrett says, "I've got pretty thick skin; it takes a lot to penetrate my strongly held convictions. This kind of hard-hitting session is precisely what we all needed to strip us of our illusions. It made us all realize the games we were playing and how they prevented us from facing Japanese competitive realities."

Contrary to what many Westerners might think about the importance of consensus in Japanese culture, institutionalized conflict is an integral part of Japanese management. At Honda, any employee, however junior, can call for a *waigaya* session. The rules are that people lay their cards on the table and speak directly about problems. Nothing is out of

_____
[4]See Ikujiro Nonaka, "The Knowledge-Cresting Company," HBR November-December 1991, pp. 96–97.

bounds, from supervisory deficiencies on the factory floor to perceived lack of support for a design team. Waigaya legitimizes tension so that learning can take place.

The Japanese have learned to disagree without being disagreeable and to harness conflict in a wide variety of ingenious ways. One of their chief principles of organizational design is redundancy—overlapping charters, business activities, and managerial assignments, duplicative databases, and parallel lines of inquiry.

With our deeply ingrained Western concept of organizations as machines, we are quick to judge such overlaps as inefficient, prime candidates for elimination in the current fervor of business process reengineering. But to the Japanese, redundancy and ambiguity spur tension and encourage frequent dialogue and communication. They also generate internal competition, particularly when parallel paths are pursued in new product development. Honda and Sony often use such techniques, assigning identical tasks to competing teams. Periodic project reviews determine which team gets funded to build the final prototype. Sony's compact disc player was developed in this fashion. The manager in charge handed two teams a block of wood the size of a small paperback book and said, "Build it to fit in this space." He recruited talent from Seiko and Citizen Watch who were familiar with miniaturization and ignorant of the traditional boundaries of audio design. Then he stood back and let them fight it out.

Conflict has its human and organizational costs, but it is also an essential fuel for self-questioning and revitalization. Some Western companies have incorporated conflict into their designs with this trade-off in mind. One is Nordstrom, where there is a built-in tension between providing excellent customer service and taking the idea to such extremes that it threatens economic viability. And since what takes place between staff and customers is the most important piece of Nordstrom's strategy, there are tensions between department heads and buyers, the traditional stars of retailing. Not surprisingly, Nordstrom employees report high tension levels at work. One executive says, "It's wrong to think of Nordstrom as a happy place. But the tensions yield higher performance."

5. Engineering Organizational Breakdowns. It's clear that reinvention is a rocky path and that there will be many breakdowns along the way: systems that threaten to fall apart, deadlines that can't be met, schisms that seem impossible to mend. But just as contention in an organization can be highly productive, these breakdowns make it possible for organizations and individuals to take a hard look themselves and confront the work of reinvention. When an organization sets out to reinvent itself, breakdowns should happen by design rather than by accident.

We might seem to be proposing the willy-nilly seeding of conflict and chaos. Nothing could be further from the truth. Inventing a seemingly impossible future and then managing from that future entails creating concrete tasks that will inevitably lead to breakdowns. These tasks must be carefully selected for the kind of upsets an organization wishes to generate. The executive team must identify the core competencies they wish to build, the soft spots in existing capabilities, and the projects that, if undertaken, will build new muscles.

Nordstrom's practice of providing extraordinary customer service necessarily places a great deal of stress on the system. But revealing the weak spots in a store's ability to respond to customer requests is the first step in strengthening those areas.

Others in Europcar's industry insisted that the company could not achieve its goal in less than two years; it would more likely take three. But Europcar, along with its partner in the project, Perot Systems, decided on an "impossible" 18-month deadline. Managers knew the resulting stress would reveal that Europcar's network of fiercely independent fiefdoms was preventing the company from competing successfully in the Pan-European market. Many country managers claimed that they did not have enough information on what was being designed and could never implement the new approach in time. Many also insisted on high degrees of tailoring to their individual country markets that ultimately would have compromised the new system's efficiency. These deep-seated territorial behaviors had to be exposed and surmounted if a true reinvention were to take place.

The purpose of generating breakdowns is to provide opportunities to enable both the organization and its executives to operate from the new context. Paradoxically, you can fail at the project (as has often happened on the road to scientific discoveries and in the careers of entrepreneurs) and still achieve a shift in being. Winston Churchill claimed that his repeated failures, from the disastrous Gallipoli invasion to defeat in his campaign for a seat in Parliament in the years between World War I and World War II, caused a sufficient shift in who he was to prepare him for the responsibilities of a wartime prime minister.

Those who climb on the reinvention roller coaster are in for a challenging ride. The organization encounters peaks and troughs in morale, as initial euphoria is dampened by conflict and dogged task-force work. Morale rises again as alignment among stakeholders occurs—then recedes in the long and demanding task of enrolling the cynical ranks below. Reinvention is a demanding up and down journey—an adventure, to be sure. And it is destined to be that way.

Index